The SHEET MUSIC

Reference & Price Guide

Second Edition

Marie-Reine A. Pafik
and
Anna Marie Guiheen

COLLECTOR BOOKS
A Division of Schroeder Publishing Co., Inc.

The current values in this book should be used only as a guide. They are not intended to set prices, which vary from one section of the country to another. Auction prices as well as dealer prices vary greatly and are affected by condition as well as demand. Neither the authors nor the publisher assumes responsibility for any losses that might be incurred as a result of consulting this guide.

Searching for a Publisher?

We are always looking for knowledgeable people considered to be experts within their fields. If you feel that there is a real need for a book on your collectible subject and have a large comprehensive collection, contact Collector Books.

Cover Design: Beth Summers
Book Design: Michelle Dowling

COLLECTOR BOOKS
P.O. Box 3009
Paducah, KY 42002-3009

www.collectorbooks.com

DEDICATION

This book is dedicated to Thomas Guiheen, Anna's husband, who allowed a computer to be set up in his living room and to Tim Pafik, Marie's son, who introduced us to and instructed us in the use of the computer.

ACKNOWLEDGMENTS

We wish to thank the following collectors, auction houses, dealers and individuals who have been most helpful in allowing us to use their music and expertise.

Tim Pafik, Laserlight Publishing Inc., Holyoke, MA

The Greniers, A Family Of Photographers, Holyoke, MA

Cynthia O'Connor, South Hadley, MA

Wilfred Ridenour, The Loving Cup Antiques, Belchertown, MA

George Vaughn, Development Analyst, Wakefield, MA

Eileen Nolin, South Hadley, MA

Robert Carrier, Teacher & Sheet Music Collector, South Hadley, MA

Deanne Edwards, Member Ashfield Historical Society, Ashfield, MA

Paul Grenier, Auctioneer, Holyoke, MA

Lee Hall, Antique Dealer, Holyoke, MA

R. Robert Grenier, Professional Photographer, Holyoke, MA

Normand & Claire Grenier, Sheet Music Collectors, Holyoke, MA

Donald Breen, Sheet Music Collector, Holyoke, MA

Mr. William L. Hubbard, Amherst Auction Gallery, Sunderland, MA

Mr. Bruce C. Smebakken, Pioneer Auction Of Amherst, Sunderland, MA

Stephen Whitlock, Antique Center, Northampton, MA

Keith Joseph O'Connor, Public Relations, Holyoke Community College, Holyoke, MA

Fine Arts Center, Music Library, University of Massachusetts, Amherst, MA

Mr. & Mrs. Michael Couture, Computer Experts, South Hadley, MA

Mr. Robert S. Adelson, Antique Dealer, Holyoke, MA

Mrs. Harold Adelson, Antique Dealer and Collector, Holyoke, MA

INTRODUCTION

It has become increasingly obvious for some time that a brief history of sheet music is needed for use by both collector and dealer. A bibliography of sheet music even in condensed form is a lengthy affair that has grown to vast proportions. Sheet music has existed for at least 200 years. Before 1920 it was printed in a large folio, 13½" x 10½". After 1920 it was printed on 9" x 12" paper. You don't have to be able to read music in order to be a collector. Many collectors are not as interested in the music as they are in the art work on the covers. These are most impressive. Some noted artists such as Pfeiffer, Barbelle, Starmer, F. Earl Christy, Rockwell and many others must have made a difference in the sale of sheet music. These artists have long been overlooked for their beautiful and sometimes amusing artistry. Some collectors like to frame sheet music which has a particularly attractive cover. Some prefer to collect those which have photos of stars, musicals, movies or entertainers such as Al Jolson and Eddie Cantor. Others prefer WWI, WWII, pre 1900 or any other categories which might be of interest to them.

We have listed the song titles alphabetically with as much information as was available to us. In parentheses we have inserted the categories in which we specialize.

Example: "Over There" by George M. Cohan, 1917, Norman Rockwell cover appeared on Life Magazine 1918, Signed by Norman Rockwell (Cover Artist, Norman Rockwell, Signed, WWI and George M. Cohan). The title of the song "Over There" is listed alphabetically and then under Norman Rockwell, Signed, WWI and George M. Cohan.

So, if one is collecting George M. Cohan, all his songs are listed in the Alphabetical Listing and also listed under his name.

In most instances the lyricist is listed before the composer of the song.

The prices listed are for copies in MINT condition. If the sheet music has been damaged in any way or cut down in size, then of course the price would be much less.

Good care of sheet music is a must. It should be stored in unsealed plastic bag so it can breathe. The pre 1900 sheets and Sunday supplements should be given extra care, as the paper used at that time was brittle and perishable.

QUOTES AS WRITTEN ON EARLIER SHEET MUSIC

Music Is A Great Requisite of Life. It Is The Sunshine Of Existence.

A Happier World Is Built On Music.

Music Minded People Are The Happiest.

Do Your Bit - Help Win The War.

America's Problem - Ships And Food - To Send The Most Food Possible In Least Shipping Space. Solution: Eat More, Fish, Cheese, Eggs, Poultry & Save Beef, Pork, Mutton For Our Fighters.

Food Will Win The War - Don't Waste It. Save Food - Save Money, Save Lives.

Every War Saving Stamp You Buy Will Help Bring Back Another Soldier Alive.

Try This Over On Your Piano.

Young America We're Strong For You, A Song That Should Be In Every Home.

Sterling on Silver, Berlin on Song.

CONTENTS

CHAPTER 1
ALPHABETICAL LISTING OF SONGS & CURRENT PRICES

A-La-Carte by Abe Holzmann, 1915......................**10.00**

A-Roving I'll Go by Harry Woods, 1931 ....**6.00**

A-Tisket-A-Tasket by Ella Fitzgerald & Al Feldman, 1939, Photo Larry Clinton (Cover Artist, Jorg Harris)......................**10.00**

"A" You're Adorable by Buddy Kaye, Fred Wise & Sidney Lippman, 1948, Photo Buddy Kaye......................**4.00**

"A" You're Adorable by Buddy Kaye, Fred Wise & Sidney Lippman, 1948, Photo Perry Como **5.00**

Aba Daba Honeymoon, The by Arthur Fields & Walter Donovan, 1914, Photo Ruth Roye, Dedicated To Jack Lee & Billy Delaney (Cover Artist, Rose Symbol, Rag, Deco & Dedication)......................**15.00**

Abide With Me by Henry Francis Lyte & S. Liddle, 1896 (Pre 1900)...**6.00**

About A Quarter To Nine by Al Dubin & Harry Warren, 1932, Movie: The Jolson Story, Photo Larry Parks & Evelyn Keyes (Al Jolson) **10.00**

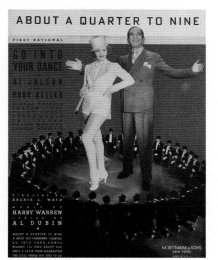

About A Quarter To Nine by Al Dubin & Harry Warren, 1935, Movie: Go Into Your Dance, Photo Al Jolson & Ruby Keeler (Al Jolson) 15.00

Above The Moon by Tardiff & Lessard, 1920 ....**5.00**

Abraham by Andrew B. Sterling & Harry Von Tilzer, 1904......................**10.00**

Abraham by Irving Berlin, 1942 (Irving Berlin) **10.00**

Absence Makes The Heart Grow Fonder by Gillespie & Dillea, 1939 ..**4.00**

Absence Of Malice by Grusin, 1981, Movie: Absence Of Malice, Photo Paul Newman & Sally Field **5.00**

Absent by Catherine Young Glen & John W. Metcalf, 1899 (Pre 1900)....**5.00**

Absent Minded Flo by Sidney Clare, Charles Tobias & J. Fred Coots, 1933 ....**3.00**

Absinthe Frappe by Glen MacDonough & Victor Herbert, 1904 (Victor Herbert)......................**10.00**

Ac-Cent-Tchu-Ate The Positive by Johnny Mercer & Harold Arlen, 1946, Movie: Here Come The Waves, Photo Bing Crosby, Betty Hutton & Sonny Tufts (WWII)......................**18.00**

Accent On Youth by Tot Seymour & Vee Lawnhurst, 1935, Photo Sylvia Sidney & Herbert Marshall......................**8.00**

Accidents Will Happen by Burke & Van Heusen, 1950, Movie: Mr. Music, Photo Bing Crosby, Nancy Olson & Peggy Lee **10.00**

Accordion Joe by Dale Wembrow & "Cornell," 1930 (Cover Artist, Starmer)......................**5.00**

Ace In The Hole by Cole Porter, 1943, Movie: Let's Face It......................**5.00**

Ace Of Diamonds by Losch, 1914 (Cover Artist, Pfeiffer & March) ..**15.00**

Aching Heart by Lent, 1920 ....**5.00**

Across The Alley From The Alamo by Joe Greene, 1947, Photo Stan Kenton **6.00**

Across The Border by Kirby A. Tallmadge, 1917 (WWI & March)....**10.00**

Across The Bridge Of Dreams by Gus Kahn & Joe Burke, 1927 (Cover Artist, Ralph Weir) **5.00**

Across The Continent by Jean Schwartz, 1900 (March) **10.00**

Across The Continent by Johnny Marvin, 1910 (Transportation)......................**8.00**

Across The Rio Grande by Redd, Graff & Ball, 1914......................**6.00**

Across The Wide Missouri by Drake & Shirl, 1951, Movie: Across The Wide Missouri, Photo Clark Gable......................**6.00**

Actions Speak Louder Than Words by Felix McGlennon, 1891 (Pre 1900)......................**12.00**

Acushla! I'm Calling Thee by Josephine Branta Ihmsen, 1914 (Cover Artist, Starmer & Irish)......................**10.00**

Acushla Machree, Return In The Springtime, 1916 (Cover Artist, Pfeiffer & Irish) **16.00**

Adam And Eve Had A Wonderful Time by Seymour Brown & Al Gumble, 1913 (Cover Artist, Starmer) **12.00**

Adelai by George Abbot & J.S. Calleja, 1921......................**5.00**

Adelaide's Lament by Jo Swerling, Abe Burrows & Frank Loesser, 1950, Musical: Guys & Dolls......................**5.00**

Adele by Edward Paulton, Jean Briquet & Adolf Phillipp, 1918 (Cover Artist, Starmer) **10.00**

Adieu Waltz by Rudolph Friml, 1917 ....**4.00**

Adios by Eddie Woods & Enrico Madriguera, 1931......................**5.00**

Adios Muchachos by Carlos Sanders, 1932, Photo Rudy Vallee......................**5.00**

Admiral Dewey's March by E.C. Cary, 1898, Photo And Dedication To Rear Admiral Dewey (Cover Artist, E.S. Fisher, Dedication, Military Personnel, March & Pre 1900) **35.00**

Admiration by Ralph Clifford Jackson, 1916......................**7.00**

Adorable by George Marion Jr. & Richard Whiting, 1933, Movie: Adorable, Photo Janet Gaynor......................**10.00**

Adoration by Maurice Telma, 1903......................**5.00**

Advice by Royden Barrie & Molly Carew, 1935 ....**3.00**

Aeroplane, The (Cover Artist, Pfeiffer)......................**16.00**

Afghanistan by William Wilander & Harry Donnelly, 1920 (Cover Artist, Starmer) **10.00**

Afloat On A Five Dollar Note by J. Fred Helf, 1906 ....**5.00**

Afraid by Fred Rose, 1949, Photo Rex Allen......................**5.00**

Afraid Of The Moon by R. L. Thompson & L. Roberts, 1944......................**5.00**

Afraid To Dream by Mack Gordon & Harry Revel, 1932, Movie: You Can't Have Everything, Photo Alice Faye & Ritz Brothers......................**5.00**

Afraid To Fall In Love by Ralph Blane & Harry Warren, 1947, Movie: Summer Love **4.00**

African Hunter by Edwin F. Kendall, 1909 (Cover Artist, John Frew)**15.00**

African Pas' by Maurice Kerwin, 1902 (Rag)......................**15.00**

After A Million Dreams by Edgar Leslie & Walter Donaldson, 1917......................**5.00**

After A While by Benny Davis & Harry Akst, 1926......................**5.00**

After All by G. H. Kerr & Howard Webster, 1904.................**10.00**

After All by J. Will Callahan & Lee S. Roberts, 1919, Photo Marguerite Sylva **10.00**

After All by James M. Reilly & Arthur Gillespie, 1913, Photo Bessie Wynn (Cover Artist, Starmer) **12.00**

After All by Pitchford & Snow, 1989, Movie: Chances Are, Photo Cybill Shepherd, Robert Downey Jr., Mary Stuart Masterson & Ryan O'Neal **10.00**

After All Is Said And Done by Dave Ringle, 1931 ....**6.00**

After All That I've Been To You by Jack Drislane & Chris Smith, 1912..**5.00**

After All The Good Is Gone by Conway Twitty, 1975, Photo Conway Twitty..**5.00**

After by Mrs. Chas G. Thompson & F. Sudds, 1896 (Pre 1900)..........**10.00**

After Dark by Charles Chancer, 1935 (Cover Artist, Leff) **5.00**

After Dinner Trot by Jos. J. Fecher, 1916.............................**5.00**

After Glow by J.R. Shannon & Harry J. Lincoln, 1915 (Cover Artist, Pfeiffer)..**16.00**

After I'm Gone by Charles Moe & Elsie Thompson, 1924............**5.00**

After I've Called You Sweetheart by Bernie Grossman & Little Jack Little, 1927, Photo Eddie Talbert & Freddie Fisher.............**8.00**

After I've Called You Sweetheart by Bernie Grossman & Little Jack Little, 1927, Photo Lola Fletcher **8.00**

After It's Over Dear by Billy Redford & Fisher Thompson, 1920 (Cover Artist, B.N. & Deco)....................................**10.00**

After Long Absence by Dena Tempest & Wilfrid Sanderson, 1929, Sung by John McCormack...**10.00**

After My Laughter Came Tears by Charles Tobias & Roy Turk, 1928 (Cover Artist, Leff & Deco) **10.00**

After Sundown by Arthur Freed & Nacio Herb Brown, 1933, Movie: Going Hollywood, Photo Bing Crosby & Marion Davies.............**10.00**

After Taps by K. Gannon & F. Weldon, 1918 (WWI) **15.00**

After The Ball by Charles K. Harris, 1892 (Pre 1900) **15.00**

After The Ball by Charles K. Harris, 1920, Movie: The Babe Ruth Story, Photo William Bendix, Claire Trevor & Gertrude Nielsen **15.00**

After The Ball by Charles K. Harris, 1932, Movie: The Jolson Story, Photo Larry Parks & Evelyn Keyes (Al Jolson)...........**12.00**

After The Battle by Paul Dresser, 1905 (Patriotic)..............**15.00**

After The Battle Is Over, Then You Can Come Back To Me by L. Wolfe Gilbert & Anatol Friedland, 1918 (Cover Artist, Starmer & WWI)..**15.00**

After The Cake Walk by Nathaniel Dett, 1900 (Black, Black Face)....**15.00**

After The First Of July by Allen, 1919 (Cover Artist, Pfeiffer & WWI) ..**15.00**

After The Honeymoon by Irving Berlin, 1911 (Cover Artist, Pfeiffer & Irving Berlin) **10.00**

After The Lovin' by Alan Bernstein, Ritchie Adams, 1974, Photo Engelbert Humperdinck **10.00**

After The Rain by Bert Reisfeld, 1939 ....**5.00**

After The Rain by Gus Kahn, Arthur Sizemore & Guy Shrigley, 1922...**10.00**

After The Roses Have Faded Away by Bessie Buchanan & Ernest R. Ball, 1914 ....**10.00**

After The Show We'll Find The Rainbow Again by Harold G. Frost, E. Clinton Keithley & F. Henri Klickmann, 1922, Signed Photo Morette Sisters (Signed)..**10.00**

After The War Is Over by E.J. Pourmon, Andrew B. Sterling & Joseph Woodruff, 1918, Photo Joseph Woodruff (Cover Artist, Starmer & WWI)..**15.00**

After The War Is Over Will There Be Any "Home Sweet Home" by E.J. Pourmon & Joseph Woodruff, 1917, Photo J. Woodruff (Cover Artist, Pfeiffer & WWI)..**15.00**

After They Gather The Hay by Jasper J. Walker, & S.R. Henry, 1906 (Cover Artist, John Frew)..**10.00**

After Twelve O'Clock by Hoagy Carmichael & Johnny Mercer, 1932.**5.00**

After You Get What You Want You Don't Want It by Irving Berlin, 1920 (Irving Berlin)...**10.00**

After You're Gone by Waldron & Duke, 1926 (Transportation) **10.00**

After You've Gone by Henry Creamer & Turner Layton, 1918 (Cover Artist, E.E. Walton & Deco)....................................**10.00**

After You've Had Your Way by Howard, 1916, Photo June Caprice (Cover Artist, Pfeiffer & Deco)....................................**15.00**

Afterglow by Al Stillman, Buck Ram & Phil Levant, 1933, Photo George Duffy, (Cover Artist, Scott).......................................**5.00**

Again by Dorcas Cochran & Lionel Newman, 1948, Movie: Road House, Photo Ida Lupino, Cornel Wilde, Celeste Holm & Richard Widmark..**5.00**

Aggie War Hymn, The by Pinky Wilson & Geo. Fairleigh, 1921.........**5.00**

Agnus Dei by Henry Hadley, 1919......................................**5.00**

Ah, But I've Learned by Roy Turk & J. Fred Coots, 1932, Photo William Hall (Cover Artist, J.M.)..**5.00**

Ah But Is It Love? by E.Y. Harberg & Jay Gorney 1933.................**5.00**

Ah, But It Happens by Dunham & Walter Kent, 1948, (Cover Artist, Barbelle) **5.00**

Ah, So Pure by Von Flotow, 1938, Opera: Martha, Photo Bob Crosby ..**5.00**

Ah! Sweet Mystery Of Life by Rida Johnson Young & Victor Herbert, 1910, Movie: Naughty Marietta, Signed Photo, Victor Herbert (Victor Herbert & Signed) **25.00**

Ah! The Moon Is Here by Irving Kahal & Sammy Fein, 1933, Movie: Footlight Parade, Photo James Cagney, Ruby Keeler, Joan Blondell & Dick Powell (Cover Artist, Jorj Harris).......................**10.00**

Ah-Ha! by Sidney Clare & James V. Monaco, 1925, Photo Ted Lewis (Cover Artist, Politzer) **10.00**

Aimer Et Mourir by Gustave Seynave & Eusebe Champagne, 1916 (Cover Artist, E.S. Fisher)...**10.00**

Ain't Dat A Shame by John Queen & Walter Wilson, 1901 (Black, Black Face) **22.00**

Ain't Dat Scan'lous? by Bob Cole & Billy Johnson, 1901 ....**10.00**

Ain't Got A Dime To My Name by Johnny Burke & Jimmy Van Heusen, 1952, Movie: Road To Morocco, Photo Bing Crosby, Bob Hope & Dorothy Lamour **8.00**

Ain't It A Shame About Mame by Burke & Monaco, 1940, Photo Bing Crosby & Mary Martin **6.00**

Ain't It Kind Of Wonderful by Wilder, 1977, Movie: The World's Greatest Lover, Photo Gene Wilder **5.00**

Ain't Misbehavin' by Razaf, Waller & Brooks, 1929, Movie: Ain't Misbehavin', Photo Rory Calhoun, Piper Laurie, Mamie Van Doren & Jack Carson...**6.00**

Ain't She Sweet? by Jack Yellen & Milton Ager, 1927, Photo Sophie Tucker (Cover Artist, Barbelle & Deco) **22.00**

Ain't That A Grand And Glorious Feeling? by Jack Yellen & Milton Ager, 1927 ....**5.00**

Ain't We Got Fun by Richard A. Whiting, Raymond Egan & Gus Kahn, 1921, Photo Gus Van & Joe Schenck....................**10.00**

Ain't You Ashamed by Simons, 1923 ....**5.00**

Ain't You Coming Back To Dixieland by Raymond Egan & Richard A. Whiting, 1917, Photo Al Jolson (Cover Artist, Barbelle, Al Jolson & Dixie)...**15.00**

Ain't You Coming Back To Old New Hampshire, Molly by Robert Roden & J. Fred Helf, 1906 ....**10.00**

Ain't You Coming Out Malinda? by Andrew B. Sterling, Edw. P. Moran & Harry Von Tilzer, 1921, Photo Gus Van & Joe Schenck (Deco).....**10.00**

Ain't You Got No Time For Love? by L & M Wells, 1942, Movie: She's For Me, Photo Grace McDonald **5.00**

Ain't-Cha' Glad? by Andy Razaf & Thomas Waller, 1933 (Cover Artist, F.S.M.)..**5.00**

Ain'tcha Comin' Out? by Bert Kalmar & Harry Ruby 1939.................**5.00**

Ain'tcha Comin' Out Tonight? by Alec Wilder, 1939, Photo Joe Stafford...**5.00**

Ain'tcha Ever Comin' Back? by Irving Taylor, Axel Stordahl & Paul Weston, 1947, Photo The Merry Marks **4.00**

Ain'tcha Ever Comin' Back? by Irving Taylor, Axel Stordahl & Paul Weston, 1947, Photo Tony Martin **4.00**

Ain'tcha Ever Comin' Back? by Irving Taylor, Axel Stordahl & Paul Weston, 1947, Photo Frank Sinatra **12.00**

Ain'tcha Kinda Sorry Now? by Ned Wever & Milton Ager, 1932 (Cover Artist, Leff) **5.00**

Alabama Cake Walk by George D. Barnard, 1899 (Pre 1900 & Black, Black Face) **15.00**

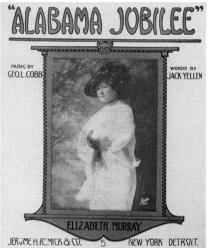

Alabama Jubilee by Jack Yellen & Geo. L. Cobb, 1915, Photo Elizabeth Murray (Dixie)...10.00

Alabama Lullaby by Cal DeVoll, 1919 (Cover Artist, R.S., Deco & Black, Black Face)..**15.00**

Alabama Lullaby by Cal DeVoll, 1919 Small War Edition (Cover Artist, R.S., Deco & Black, Black Face) **15.00**

Alabama Wedding by J. W. Wheeler, 1899 (Pre 1900, March & Black, Black Face)..**20.00**

Alabamy Bound by B. G. DeSylva, Bud Green & Ray Henderson, 1925, Photo Al Jolson (Al Jolson & Black, Black Face) **16.00**

Alabamy Cradle Song by Gus Kahn, Arthur Otis & Egbert Van Alstyne, 1925, Photo Arthur White (Black, Black Face)...........................**16.00**

Aladdin's Genie Dances by Kenneth Kimes, 1951 ....**5.00**

Alamo by DeWitt & Bowers, 1925, Movie: Alamo, Photo Gilda Gray **5.00**

Alamo Rag by Deely & Percy Wenrich, 1910 (Rag)........................**15.00**

Album Lee by B. L. Whelpley, 1898 (Pre 1900)..........................**10.00**

Alcoholic Blues, The by Edward Laska & Albert Von Tilzer, 1919 (Blues) **10.00**

Alexander by Andrew Sterling & Harry Von Tilzer, 1904 ....**10.00**

Alexander Don't You Love Your Baby No More? by Andrew Sterling & Harry Von Tilzer, 1904 (Black, Black Face)........................**15.00**

Alexander's Back From Dixie With His Rag-Time Band by Lew Colwell & Pete Wendling, 1917 (Cover Artist, Standard Photo Engraving, Rag, Dixie & Black, Black Face)..............................**40.00**

Alexander's Bag Pipe Band by Goetz & Sloane, 1912, Musical: Hokey Pokey (Cover Artist, Pfeiffer) **15.00**

Alexander's Band Is Back In Dixieland by Jack Yellen & Albert Gumble, 1919 (Cover Artist, Frederick S. Manning & Dixie)....................**15.00**

Alexander's Ragtime Band by Irving Berlin, 1911 (Cover Artist, Pfeiffer, Irving Berlin & March)............................**25.00**

Alexander's Ragtime Band by Irving Berlin, 1911, Photo Carroll Johnson (Cover Artist, John Frew, Irving Berlin & March)..........**15.00**

Alexander's Ragtime Band by Irving Berlin, 1911, Photo Rose Bery (Cover Artist, John Frew, Irving Berlin & March)....................**15.00**

Alexander's Ragtime Band by Irving Berlin, 1938, Photo Irving Berlin (Cover Artist, John Frew, Irving Berlin & March).......10.00

Alexandria by Arthur A. Penn & Anselm Goetzl, 1919 ....**5.00**

Alfie by Hal David & Burt F. Bacharach, 1966, Movie: Alfie..............**5.00**

Algeria by Victor Herbert, 1908 (Victor Herbert) **10.00**

Alibi Baby by Dorothy Donnelly, Stephen Jones & Arthur Samuels, 1923, Musical: Poppy, Photo Madge Kennedy (Deco)...........................**5.00**

Alice by J. Ascher, 1909 (Cover Artist, J.M.) **5.00**

Alice by Robert E. Harty, 1933 ....**3.00**

Alice Blue Gown by Joseph McCarthy & Harry Tierney, 1919, Musical: Irene (Deco)..**10.00**

Alice I'm In Wonderland Since The Day That I First Met You by T. Morse, 1918 (Cover Artist, Henry Hutt) **10.00**

Alice In Wonderland by Bob Hilliard & Sammy Fain, 1951, Movie: Alice In Wonderland (Disney) **15.00**

Alice In Wonderland by Charles Tobias, Jack Scholl & Murray Mencher, 1933, Photo Teddy Black **5.00**

Alice In Wonderland by Irving Berlin, 1929, Movie: Puttin On The Ritz (Irving Berlin)..**18.00**

Alice Of Old Vincennes by Keithley & Thompson, 1914....................**5.00**

Alice Where Art Thou by Sydney Osborne.............................**4.00**

All Aboard by Oliver Wallace, Frank Churchill & Ned Washington, 1941, Movie: Dumbo (Disney).................................**15.00**

All Aboard For Blanket Bay by Andrew B. Sterling & Harry Von Tilzer, 1910, Dedicated To Little Raymond Sterling (Dedication) **15.00**

All Aboard For Chinatown by Frank Davis & Win Brookhouse, 1915 ....**5.00**

All Aboard For Dixie Land by Jack Yellen & Geo L. Cobb, 1913, Musical: High Jinks, Photo Elizabeth M. Murray (Cover Artist, Starmer & Dixie)..**12.00**

All Aboard For Monkey Town by Drislane & Meyer, 1910 (Cover Artist, Pfeiffer)..**15.00**

All Aboard For Playland by Maurice Solman & Joe Solman, 1920 (Cover, Wilson Art & Deco) **10.00**

All Aboard From Home Sweet Home by Addison Burkhart, Al Piantadosi & Jack Glogau, 1918 ....**5.00**

All Aboard That Ocean Baby by Lou Paley & Herman Paley, 1913, Photo Knowles & White (Transportation)....................**35.00**

All Alone Again Blues by Jerome Kern, 1920 (Blues) **10.00**

All Alone by Irving Berlin, 1924 (Irving Berlin) **10.00**

All Alone by Will Dillon & Harry Von Tilzer, 1910 (Cover Artist, Etherington)...**15.00**

All Alone With You In A Little Rendezvous by Sam Lewis, Joe Young & Ted Snyder, 1924 (Cover Artist, Barbelle).............**10.00**

All America March by J.S. Jamecnik, 1916 (March) **15.00**

All American Girl by Al Lewis, 1932, Photo Ted Fiorito.....**10.00**

All American Swing, The by Mack Gordon & Harry Revel, 1938, Movie: My Lucky Star, Photo Sonja Henie & Richard Greene.................**10.00**

All Ashore by Billy Hill, 1938, Photo Kay Kyser (Cover Artist, Im-Ho)..**5.00**

All Ashore by Billy Hill, 1938, Photo Rudy Vallee (Cover Artist, Im-Ho)..**5.00**

All Ashore by Billy Hill, 1938, Photo Russ Morgan (Cover Artist, Im-Ho)..**5.00**

All Because Of You by Henri Therrien, Sam H. Stept & Bud Green 1928, Photo Henri Therrien (Cover Artist, Pud Lane) **10.00**

All Bound Round With A Woolen String by Charles Seamon, 1898 (Pre 1900)..**15.00**

All By Myself by Irving Berlin, 1921 (Irving Berlin & Deco).............**10.00**

All By Myself by Irving Berlin, 1946, Movie: Blue Skies (Cover Artist, Hal Weinstein, Deco & Irving Berlin)..................**14.00**

All By Myself by West & Jentes, 1920 (Cover Artist, Pfeiffer)...........**15.00**

All By Yourself In The Moonlight by Jay Wallis, 1928 (Deco) **10.00**

All Coons Look Alike To Me by Ernest Hogan, 1896 (Pre 1900 & Black, Black Face)..**25.00**

All Day By Vic Schoen, 1939 ....**5.00**

All Dressed Up by Lorenz Hart & Richard Rodgers, 1939, Movie: Too Many Girls..**5.00**

All Dressed Up With A Broken Heart by Fred Patrick, Claude Reese & Jack Val, 1946, Photo Buddy Clark **4.00**

All Dressed Up With A Broken Heart by Fred Patrick, Claude Reese & Jack Val, 1946, Photo Bob Houston....................**4.00**

All Full Of Talk by Jerome Kern & P.G. Wodehouse, 1916.................**5.00**

All Fussed Up by Richards & Pollack, 1915 ....**5.00**

All God's Chillun Got Rhythm by Kahn, Kaper & Jurmann, 1937, Movie: A Day At The Races, Photo Groucho, Chico & Harpo Marx, Allan Jones & Maureen O'Sullivan **18.00**

All Hands Around by Friedman, 1908 (Cover Artist, Pfeiffer)...........**15.00**

All He Does Is Follow Them Around by Abrahams & Clarke, 1914, Photo Jack Norworth (Cover Artist, Pfeiffer & Deco) **15.00**

All I Can Do Is Just Love You by Grant Clarke, Joe McCarthy & Jimmie V. Monaco, 1915, Photo Dorothy Meuther (Cover Artist, Rose Symbol & Deco) **10.00**

All I Can Do Is Just Love You by Grant Clarke, Joe McCarthy & Jimmie V. Monaco, 1915, Photo Mae Francis (Cover Artist, R.S. & Deco) **10.00**

All I Care About Is You by Little Jack Little, 1931 ....**5.00**

All I Do Is Dream Of You by Arthur Freed & Nacio Herb Brown, 1934, Movie: Sadie McKee, Photo Joan Crawford **10.00**

All I Have Are Sunny Weather Friends by James Kendis & James Brockman, 1920 ....**5.00**

All I Owe Iowa by Richard Rodgers & Oscar Hammerstein II, 1945, Movie: State Fair, Photo Jeanne Crain, Dana Andrews, Dick Haymes & Vivian Blaine..**10.00**

All I Want For Christmas Is My Two Front Teeth by Don Gardner, 1946..**8.00**

All I Want Is A Cottage, Some Roses And You by Charles K. Harris, 1916..**10.00**

All I Want Is Just Your Love by Geo A. Kershaw & Harry Von Tilzer, 1927 (Cover Artist, Malcolm Perret)....................**15.00**

All I Want Is My Black Baby Back by Edwards & Daley, 1914 (Black & Black Face)..**15.00**

All I Want Is One Loving Smile From You-oo-oo by Meyer, 1908 (Cover Artist, Pfeiffer)..**15.00**

All I Want Is Someone by Glenn Leap, 1912, (Cover Artist, Pfeiffer) **15.00**

All I Want Is You by Benny Davis, Harry Akst & Sidney Clare, 1927, Photo Corinne Arbuckle (Cover Artist, Starmer).................**10.00**

All I Want Is You by James, 1915 (Cover Artist, Pfeiffer) **15.00**

All I Want To Do-Do-Do Is Dance by Dubin & Burke, 1929, Movie: Sunny, Photo Marilyn Miller..................................**5.00**

All I've Got To Get Now Is My Man by Cole Porter, 1942, Movie: Panama Hattie..**8.00**

All In A Garden Green by William E. Henley & B. L. Whelpley, 1903...**10.00**

All In A Golden Afternoon by Bob Hilliard & Sammy Fain, 1951, Movie: Alice In Wonderland (Disney) **15.00**

All In, Down And Out by McPherson, Bowman & Smith, 1906.........**10.00**

All Mine, Almost by Charles Newman & Isham Jones, 1933 (Cover Artist, Leff)..**3.00**

All My Life by Sidney Mitchell & Sam Stept, 1936, Photo Phil Regan & Evelyn Knapp (Cover Artist, Sorokin)............................**5.00**

All My Love by Al Jolson, Saul Chaplin & Harry Akst, 1947 (Cover Artist, Jorj & Al Jolson) **5.00**

All My Love by Mitchell Parish & Paul Durand, 1948, Photo Patti Page (Cover Artist, Nick)..**5.00**

All Nuts Don't Grow On Trees by Smaleo & Levine, 1928 (Cover Artist, Pfeiffer)..**15.00**

All O'The World A Home by Elisabeth Johnson, 1926 (Cover Artist, Barbelle)..**10.00**

All Of A Sudden My Heart Sings by Rome, Jamblan & Herpin, 1944, Photo Paul Anka...**5.00**

All Of Me by Seymour Simons & Gerald Marks, 1931, Signed Photo of Russ Columbo (Signed)..**8.00**

All Of My Life by Irving Berlin, 1944 (Irving Berlin).........................**10.00**

All On Account Of A Strawberry Sundae by Mort Dixon & Allie Wrubel, 1934, Movie: Happiness Ahead, Photo Dick Powell (Cover Artist, B. Harris)...**10.00**

All On Account Of Eliza by Stephens & Solomon, 1880 (Pre 1900)...**15.00**

All Or Nothin' by Richard Rodgers & Oscar Hammerstein II, 1943, Musical: Oklahoma...**8.00**

All Or Nothing At All by Jack Lawrence & Arthur Altman, 1940, Photo Jimmy Dorsey & Bob Eberly (Deco)...**5.00**

All Over Nothing At All by J. Keirn Brennan, Paul Cunningham & James Rule 1922 (Deco)...**5.00**

All Over Nothing At All by Peter Tinturin & Jack Lawrence, 1937, Movie: Manhattan Merry-Go-Round...**5.00**

All Over You by Bryan & Kendis, 1914 (Cover Artist, Pfeiffer).........**15.00**

All Right, Louie Drop The Gun by Carter & Johnson, Photo Arthur Godfrey 10.00

All She'd Say Was Umh-Hum by James C. Emery, 1920.....................**5.00**

All That Glitters Is Not Gold by Lee Kuhn, Alice Cornett & Eddie Asherman, 1946, Photo Dee Parker..**3.00**

All That I Ask Of You Is Love by Edgar Selden & Herbert Ingraham, 1910, Photo Frank Morrell (Cover Artist, Starmer).........................**8.00**

All That I Had And All That I Have And All That I Want Is In Ireland by Evans Lloyd, 1917, Photo Earl Holmes (Irish)..............................**10.00**

All That I'm Asking Is Sympathy by Benny Davis & Joe Burke, 1929, Photo Jim & Bud (Cover Artist, Earl & Deco)...............................**5.00**

All That I'm Asking Is Sympathy by Benny Davis & Joe Burke, 1929, Photo Gene Austin (Cover Artist, Earl & Deco).............................**5.00**

All That Love Went To Waste by Barris & Cahn, 1973, Movie: A Touch Of Class, Photo George Segal & Glenda Jackson.........................**3.00**

All The Boys Love Mary by Andrew B. Sterling & Joe Schenck, 1920, Photo Frances White (Cover Artist, Barbelle).............................**10.00**

All The Boys Love Rosie by O'Connor, 1915 (Cover Artist, Pfeiffer)**15.00**

All The Cats Join In by Alec Wilder, Ray Gilbert & Eddie Sauter, 1946, Movie: Make Mine Music (Disney)..**15.00**

All The King's Horses by Sam Coslow, 1935, Movie: A Little White Gardenia, Photo Carl Bresson & Mary Ellis.....................................**5.00**

All The Night Long by Neville Fleeson & Albert Von Tilzer, 1919......**5.00**

All The Quakers Are Shoulder Shakers by Bert Kalmar, Edgar Leslie & Pete Wendling, 1919 (Cover Artist, Barbelle)............................**10.00**

All The Things You Are by Jerome Kern & Oscar Hammerstein II, 1940, Movie: Very Warm For May (Cover Artist, Im-Ho)....................**5.00**

All The Time by Dorothy Fields & Arthur Schwartz, 1939, Movie: Stars In Your Eyes...**5.00**

All The Way by Sammy Cahn & James Van Heusen, 1957, Movie: The Joker Is Wild, Photo Frank Sinatra, Mitzi Gaynor & Jeanne Crain .**5.00**

All The Way Home by Styne & Styne, 1963, Movie: All The Way Home, Photo Jean Simmons & Robert Preston.....................................**4.00**

All The World Will Be Jealous Of Me by Al Dubin & Ernest R. Ball, 1917, Photo Ethel Gray Terry & Robert Armstrong (Cover Artist, White)...**10.00**

All This And Heaven Too by Eddie DeLange & Jimmy Van Heusen, 1939, Photo Ray Noble (Cover Artist, Im-Ho)..............................**3.00**

All This And Heaven Too by Eddie DeLange & Jimmy Van Heusen, 1939, Photo Bobby Byrne..**3.00**

All This And Heaven Too by Eddie DeLange & Jimmy Van Heusen, 1939, Photo Jimmy Dorsey (Cover Artist, Im-Ho).......................**3.00**

All This I Miss by Lawrence G. Morrell & William A. Suter, 1944......**5.00**

All Through The Day by Jerome Kern & Oscar Hammerstein II, 1946, Photo Jean Crain & Cornel Wilde...**5.00**

All Through The Night by Cole Porter, 1934, Movie: Anything Goes ..**6.00**

All Vat's Gold Ain't Glitters by Connolly, 1879 (Pre 1900 & Black, Black Face) **25.00**

All Year Around by Rida Johnson Young, Sigmund Romberg & Victor Herbert, 1924, (Cover Artist, Victor Herbert).............................**5.00**

All's Fair In Love And War by Harry Warren, Al Dubin, Albert Arlen & E.Y. Harburg, 1936..**5.00**

All's Well by Coslow & Whiting, 1935, Movie: Coronado, Photo Eddy Duchin, Johnny Downs, Leon Errol, Jack Haley & Andy Devine...**5.00**

All's Well by Leo Robin & Ralph Rainger, 1939, Movie: Gulliver's Travels...**5.00**

All-Of-A-Twist by Frank E. Hersom, 1920 (Rag)...........................**10.00**

Allah's Holiday by Otto Harbach & Rudolf Friml, 1917, Musical: Katinka...**5.00**

Allegheny Al by Jerome Kern & Oscar Hammerstein II, Movie: High Wide And Handsome, 1937, Photo Irene Dunne & Randolph Scott...........**8.00**

Allegheny Moon by Al Hoffman & Dick Mannery, 1956, Photo Patti Page (Cover Artist, Barbelle)..**6.00**

Alleluia by Anthony Garlick, 1967..**2.00**

Alley Cat Song, The, by Jack Harlen & Frank Bjorn, 1962, Photo David Thorne...**5.00**

Allied Victory March by Harry H. Zickel, 1918 (Cover Artist, Starmer, WWI & March) **25.00**

Alma by Geo V. Hobart & Jean Briquet, 1910, Photo Kitty Gordon (Cover Artist, Keller)..**10.00**

Alma Mia by G. F. Handel, 1941 ....**3.00**

Alma, Where Do You Live? by E. Paulton & Adolf Phillipp, 1910 ......**5.00**

Almost Like Being In Love by Alan Jay Lerner & Frederick Loewe, 1947, Movie: Brigadoon..**5.00**

Aloha Oe by Queen Liliuokalani, 1912 (Cover Artist, Pfeiffer) **15.00**

Aloha Oe by Queen Lydia Liliuokalani 1940 (Cover Artist, NPS).......**8.00**

Alone At Last by Gus Kahn & Ted Fiorito, 1925 (Cover Artist, R.S.)..**5.00**

Alone At Last by Phil Cody & Neil Sedaka, 1977, Photo Neil Sedaka .**6.00**

Alone by Arthur Freed & Nacio Herb Brown, 1935, Movie: A Night At The Opera, Photo Alan Jones, Kitty Carlisle & Groucho, Chico & Harpo Marx..**16.00**

Alone In Lonesome Valley by Maurice Gunsky & Nat. Goldstein, 1932..**5.00**

Alone In Love's Garden by A. W. Linford & Thos. J. Hewitt, 1912 .....**5.00**

Alone, My Lover by Brian Hooker & Rudolf Friml, 1931, Musical: The White Eagle (Cover Artist, Barbelle) **5.00**

Alone Together by Howard Deitz & Arthur Schwartz, 1932 ....**5.00**

Along About Now by Sigman & Ortolani, 1968, Movie: The Biggest Bundle Of Them All, Photo Raquel Welch, Robert Wagner, Edward G. Robinson & Godfrey Cambridge **5.00**

Along Came Ruth by Irving Berlin 1914, Photo Irving Berlin (Cover Artist, John Frew & Irving Berlin) **10.00**

Along The Navajo Trail by Larry Markes, Dick Charles & Eddie DeLange, 1944, Photo, Bing Crosby & Andrews Sisters **10.00**

Along The Road To Singapore by Richard W. Pascoe, Hans Von Holstein & Alma M. Sanders, 1915 ....**5.00**

Along The Rocky Road To Dublin by Joe Young & Bert Grant, 1915, Photo Blanche Ring (Irish) **10.00**

Along The Santa Fe Trail by Dubin, Coolidge & Grosz, 1940, Movie: Along The Santa Fe Trail **8.00**

Along The Trail Where The Blue Grass Grows by Cliff Friend, 1919 **10.00**

Along The Way To Waikiki by Gus Kahn & Richard A. Whiting, 1917 (Cover Artist, Barbelle & Deco) **10.00**

Alouette, New Musical Version by Rudy Vallee, 1945 ....**8.00**

Alpine Hut by Gustav Lange (Cover Artist, John Frew) **10.00**

Alpine Valley by Engelmann & Brehm, 1909 (Cover Artist, Pfeiffer) **15.00**

Alsacian Railroad Gallops by Guignard, 1845 (Pre 1900 & Transportation) **60.00**

Although I Am A Soldier by Ellis, 1903, Photo Edna Wallace Hopper & Cyril (Patriotic) **10.00**

Although I'm Down In Tennessee, My Heart Is Up In Maine by Fields & Scannell, 1914 ....**10.00**

Always by Horwitz & Bowers, 1899 (Pre 1900) **10.00**

Always by Irving Berlin, 1925, Movie: Christmas Holiday, Photo Deanna Durbin (Irving Berlin) **12.00**

Always by Irving Berlin, 1925, Movie: Christmas Holiday, Signed Photo Irving Berlin (Irving Berlin & Signed) **12.00**

Always, Always by Jessie Cavanaugh & P. G. Redi, 1949 ....**5.00**

Always I'm Dreaming Of You by Braman & Denton, 1910 (Cover Artist, Pfeiffer) **15.00**

Always In All Ways by Leo Robin, Richard A. Whiting & Frank Harling, 1930, Movie: Monte Carlo, Photo Jack Buchanan & Jeannette MacDonald (Deco) **14.00**

Always In Love With You by Corum M. Baucom, 1933, Photo Mildred Risley (Cover Artist, J. Wolfe) **3.00**

Always In My Heart by Kim Gannon & Ernesto Lecuona, 1942, Movie: Always In My Heart, Photo Gloria Warren, Kay Francis & Walter Houston **6.00**

Always In The Way by Charles K. Harris, 1916 ....**10.00**

Always Keep A Smile For Mother by Converse, 1884 (Pre 1900) **15.00**

Always Leave Them Laughing When You Say Good-Bye by George M. Cohan (George M. Cohan) 1903 ....**16.00**

Always Me by Chas. K. Harris, 1908 ....**20.00**

Always Take A Girl Named Daisy by Vincent Bryan & Lewis Meyer, 1913 ....**5.00**

Always Take Mother's Advice by Jennie Lindsey, 1884 (Pre 1900) ...**10.00**

Always The Same, Sweet Pal by Weinberg & Stone, 1928, Movie: The Cop, Photo William Boyd & Jacqueline Logan **8.00**

Always Think Of Mother by Haller & Stafford, 1912, Photo Eli Brouilette **5.00**

Always True To You In My Fashion by Cole Porter, 1948, Musical: Kiss Me Kate **8.00**

Am I Blue by Grant Clarke & Harry Akst, 1929, Movie: On With The Show **8.00**

Am I Gonna See You Some More? by Walter Donaldson, 1930 ....**6.00**

Am I That Easy To Forget? by Carl Belew & W.S. Stevenson, 1958 ....**5.00**

Am I The One? by Vallee & West, 1930 ....**5.00**

Am I To Blame by Raymond Klages & Billy Fazioli, 1922 ....**5.00**

Am I Wasting My Time On You by Johnson, 1926 ....**5.00**

Am I Your Once-In-A-While by Abner Silver & Al Hoffman, 1930 ....**5.00**

Amado Mio by Allan Roberts & Doris Fisher, 1946, Movie: Gilda, Photo Rita Hayworth **10.00**

Amapola by Joseph M. Lacalle, 1924, Photo Jimmy Dorsey **5.00**

Amazon March, The by J.S. Zamecnik, 1911 (Lithograph, The Mugler Engraving Co. & March) **15.00**

Amelia Earhart's Last Flight by McEnery, 1939 (Transportation) **50.00**

Amen by Segure, Hardy & Schoen, 1942, Movie: What's Cookin', Photo Woody Herman, Andrews Sisters, Gloria Jean & Jane Frazee **8.00**

A-M-E-R-I-C-A by Mae Greene & Billy Lang, 1917 (Patriotic & WWI) **15.00**

A-M-E-R-I-C-A Means I Love You My Yankee Land by Jack Frost, 1917 (WWI & Patriotic) **15.00**

America by Stephen Sondheim & Leonard Bernstein, 1957, Movie: West Side Story **5.00**

America Calling by Meredith Wilson, 1941 (Patriotic) **5.00**

America First by Howard Kocian, 1916 (Patriotic & WWI) **15.00**

America First by James Brockman, 1916, Picture of Uncle Sam & Miss Liberty (Patriotic & WWI) **25.00**

America First by John Philip Sousa, 1916 (John Philip Sousa, WWI & March) **25.00**

America For Mine by Susie Nelson Furgerson & Courtney Allemong, 1917 (Patriotic & WWI) **10.00**

America Forever! by E. T. Paull, 1917 (Cover Artist, E.T. Paull, Lithograph A.Hoen & March) **35.00**

America, He's For You by Sterling, 1918 (Cover Artist, Pfeiffer & WWI) **15.00**

America Here's My Boy by Andrew B. Sterling & Arthur Lange, 1917 (Cover Artist, Andre DeTakacs, & WWI) 20.00

America I Love You by Edgar Leslie & Archie Gottler, 1915, Photo Alice Moss (Cover Artist, Barbelle & Patriotic) **20.00**

America I Love You by Edgar Leslie & Archie Gottler, 1915, Photo Sophie Tucker (Cover Artist, Barbelle & Patriotic) **25.00**

America I Love You by Edgar Leslie & Archie Gottler, 1915, Signed Photo Eva Tanguay (Cover Artist, Barbelle, Signed & Patriotic) **40.00**

America I Love You & I Hear You Calling Me by Furgerson & Allemong, 1917 (Cover Artist, Pfeiffer & WWI) **15.00**

America It's Up To You by Chas. Ford, 1917 (Cover Artist, Pfeiffer & WWI)..**15.00**

America, Make The World Safe For Democracy by DeVivo & Levy, 1918 (Cover Artist, Pfeiffer & WWI) **15.00**

America! My Home Land by Henry Treleaven & Richard Blaine, 1917 (Patriotic)...**5.00**

America Needs You Like A Mother by Schwartz, 1917 (WWI) **10.00**

America Our Pride by Louis Oesterie, 1917 (WWI) **10.00**

America Prepare by D. S. Day, 1916 (WWI) **15.00**

American Beauty by Alfred Bryan, Edgar Leslie & M. K. Jerome, 1918 (WWI)..**15.00**

American Beauty by Henri J. Van Praag, 1917, Dedicated To Nanette Lehman (Dedication)..**6.00**

American Beauty by Joseph F. Lamb, 1913 (Rag)..............................**15.00**

American Beauty Rose by Hal David, Redd Evans & Arthur Altman, 1950 ....**5.00**

American Born by Eugene Kenney, 1914 (Cover Artist, Pfeiffer).......**15.00**

American Eagles by Irving Berlin, 1942, Movie: This Is The Army, Lt. Ronald Reagan In Cast (WWII, Military Personnel, Irving Berlin & President)..**15.00**

American Girl For Me, The by Flato, 1910 (Cover Artist, Pfeiffer) **15.00**

American Girl March, The by Victor Herbert (Cover Artist, Archie Gunn, March & Victor Herbert)..**20.00**

American Guard by W.A. Pratt, 1897 (Pre 1900 & Patriotic)..............**15.00**

American Guard March, The by Arthur Bergh, 1924 (March)..............**15.00**

American Legion, The by Carl D. Vandersloot, 1920 (Patriotic & March) **20.00**

American Medley by Charles Grobe, 1908 ....**5.00**

American Patrol by Joseph Messina & F. W. Meacham, 1895 (Pre 1900 & March) **15.00**

American Prayer by Albert Stillman, Lawrence Stock & Vincent Rose, 1942 (WWII) **5.00**

American Tango, The by Osborne (Cover Artist, Pfeiffer)..................**10.00**

American Waltz, The by Mitchell Parish & Peter DeRose, 1940 ....**5.00**

Americans Come!, The by Elizabeth A. Wilbur & Fay Foster, 1918, Dedicated To America's Soldiers And Sailors " May The Assurance Of The Love And Grateful Welcome Awaiting Him "Over There" Cheer And Animate The Heart Of Every American Soldier And Sailor." Signed by Fay Foster in New York in May 1918 (WWI, & Signed) **35.00**

Amerikana by John Harris (Patriotic)..**5.00**

Amina by Lincke & MacDonald, 1909 ....**5.00**

Amo by Herbert Ingraham, 1909, Photo Viola Dale (Cover Artist, Starmer).**10.00**

Among My Souvenirs by Leslie & Nicholls, 1927, Movie: The Best Years Of Our Lives, Photo Hoagy Carmichael, Myrna Loy, Dana Andrews & Virginia Mayo **10.00**

Among My Souvenirs by Edgar Leslie & Horatio Nicholls, 1927 (Cover Artist, Helen Van Doorn Morgan)..**10.00**

Among Those Sailing by Nat Simon, Al Stillman & Roy Newell, 1938 (Transportation)...**5.00**

Amor by Sunny Skylar & Gabriel Ruiz, 1942, Movie: Broadway Rhythm, Photo George Murphy & Ginny Simms.......................................**5.00**

Amorita by Robert F. Roden & Herman Paley, 1913...........................**5.00**

Amorous Edith Sawicki by Marino & Jampel, 1945, From Radio Show "Detect & Collect"...**5.00**

An Afterthought by Henneman, 1905...**5.00**

An American In Paris by George Gershwin, 1929 ....**5.00**

An Annapolis Lullaby by Robert Garland & Gustaf Klemm, 1925.......**5.00**

An Apple A Day by Moe Jaffe & Clay Boland, 1936 From The Univ. of Pennsylvania Production "This Mad Whirl" Presented by the Mask & Wig Club...**10.00**

An Apple Blossom Wedding by Jimmy Kennedy & Nat Simon, 1947, Photo Sammy Kaye (Cover Artist, Nick)....................................**5.00**

An Apple For The Teacher by Johnny Burke & James V. Monaco, 1939, Movie: The Star Maker, Photo Bing Crosby & Louise Campbell ...**5.00**

An Echo Of Her Smile by Philander Johnson & Joseph E. Howard, 1919, Photo Joseph Howard (Cover Artist, Starmer)............................**10.00**

An Egyptian Love Dance by Arthur Pryer, 1907 ....**5.00**

An Ev'ning In Caroline by Walter Donaldson, 1931 (Cover Artist, Frederick S. Manning) **5.00**

An Hour Never Passes by Jimmy Kennedy, 1944 (Cover Artist, Geyler)...**4.00**

An Innocent Affair by Walter Kant, Movie: An Innocent Affair, Photo Fred MacMurray & Madeleine Carroll **5.00**

An Irish Song Will Live As Long As Life And Love Shall Last by George A. Kershaw & Walter Scanlan, 1921 (Irish) **10.00**

An Occasional Man by Martin & Blane, 1955, Movie: The Girl Rush, Photo Rosalind Russell & Gloria DeHaven **5.00**

An Old Fashioned Garden In Virginia by Marion Sunshine & Henry I. Marshall, 1915 (Cover Artist, Starmer)......................................**10.00**

An Old Fashioned Home In New Hampshire by Sam M. Lewis & Robert A. King, 1931, Photo Jesse Crawford (Cover Artist, Leff).............3.00

An Old Fashioned Tune Is Always New by Irving Berlin, 1939 (Irving Berlin).**10.00**

An Old Fashioned Wife by Guy Bolton, P.G. Wodehouse & Jerome Kern, 1917, Musical: Oh Boy! **10.00**

An Old Grand Army Man by Harry DeCosta, 1918 (WWI & March).**25.00**

An Old Guitar And An Old Refrain by Gus Kahn, Ben Black & Neil Moret, 1927 (Cover Artist, WRC)...**5.00**

An Old Old Castle In Scotland by Herb Magidson & Ben Oakland (Cover Artist, Im Ho) **3.00**

An Old Sombrero by Lew Brown & Ray Henderson, 1947, Photo Vic Damone (Cover Artist, Nick) **3.00**

An Old Straw Hat by Mack Gordon & Harry Revel, Movie: Rebecca Of Sunnybrook Farm, Photo (Shirley Temple), Randolph Scott, Gloria Stewart, Phyllis Brooks, Jack Haley & Slim Summerville **10.00**

An Old Water Mill by Charlie Tobias Jack Scholl & Murray Mencher, 1934, Photo George Olsen..**3.00**

An Old Water Mill by Charlie Tobias, Jack Scholl & Murray Mencher, 1934, Photo Jack Denny **3.00**

An Operatic Nightmare by Felix Arndt, 1916 ....**5.00**

An Orange Grove In California by Irving Berlin, 1923, Musical: Music Box Review 1923-24 (Irving Berlin)..**15.00**

An Orchid To You by Mack Gordon & Harry Revel, 1933 (Cover Artist, Leff)...**5.00**

An Ordinary Couple by Richard Rodgers & Oscar Hammerstein II, 1959, Movie: The Sound Of Music, Photo Julie Andrews & Christopher Plummer...**10.00**

Anatolian Serenade by Carl Bohm, 1900 ....**5.00**

Anchors Away, Song Of The Navy by Charles A. Zimmermann, 1942 (WWII & Patriotic)..........................**5.00**

And A Little Child Shall Lead Them by Chas. K. Harris, 1906 (Cover Artist, Starmer) **10.00**

And He Blames My Dreamy Eyes by Albert Gumble, 1907, Photo Vesta Victoria..........................**10.00**

And He'd Say "Oo-La-La Wee-Wee" by Harry Ruby & George Jessell, 1919 (Cover Artist, Barbelle, WWI & Deco)..........................**12.00**

And I Am All Alone by Jerome Kern & P.G. Wodehouse, 1916, Musical: Have A Heart..........................**8.00**

And Love Was Born by Oscar Hammerstein II & Jerome Kern, 1932, Movie: Music In The Air..........................**5.00**

And Mimi by Jimmy Kennedy & Nat Simon, 1947, Photo Blue Barron (Cover Artist, Nick)..........................**5.00**

And Mimi by Jimmy Kennedy & Nat Simon, 1947, Photo Harry Cool (Cover Artist, Nick)..........................**5.00**

And Russia Is Her Name by E.Y. Harburg & Jerome Kern, 1943 ....**10.00**

And So, Goodbye by Allie Wrubel, 1938..........................**5.00**

And So To Bed by Mack Gordon & Harry Revel, 1931, Photo Ethel Shutta..**5.00**

And So To Sleep Again by Joe Marsala & Sunny Skylar, 1951, Photo Patti Page **6.00**

And That Ain't All by Bud Green & Sammy Stept, 1919, Signed Photo, Sophie Tucker (Cover Artist, R.S. & Signed) **60.00**

And The Angels Sing by Mercer & Elman, 1939, Movie: The Benny Goodman Story, Photo Steve Allen & Donna Reed..........................**10.00**

And The Band Played On by Palmer & Ward, 1895 (Pre 1900)..........**15.00**

And The Green Grass Grew All Around by William Jerome & Henry Von Tilzer, 1912..........................**5.00**

And Then by Alfred Bryan & Herman Paley, 1920, Photo Bessie Wynn **5.00**

And Then I Remember by Janis Moss Rosenburg, 1956..........................**5.00**

And Then It's Heaven by Eddie Seiler, Sol Marcus & Al Kaufman, 1946, Photo Henry King **3.00**

And Then She'd Knit, Knit, Knit by Moran, 1917 (Cover Artist, Pfeiffer)...**15.00**

And There You Are by Ted Koehler & Sammy Fain, 1945, Movie: Weekend At The Waldorf, Photo Ginger Rogers, Lana Turner, Walter Pidgeon, Van Johnson & Xavier Cugat **12.00**

And They Called It Dixieland by Raymond B. Egan & Richard Whiting, 1916 (Dixie)..........................**10.00**

And They Say He Went To College by Seymour Furth, 1907, Photo Eddie Foy **10.00**

And This Is My Beloved by Robert Wright & Chet Forrest, 1953, Musical: Kismet..........................**6.00**

And To Think I Left My Happy Home For You by Puck & Kalmar, 1914 (Cover Artist, Pfeiffer) **15.00**

Anema E Core by Mann Curtis, Harry Akst, Tito Manlio & Salve d'Esposito, 1944, Photo Eddie Fisher..........................**5.00**

A-N-G-E-L Spells Mary by Fred Wise, Steve Nelson & Al Frisch, 1947..........................**5.00**

Angel Eyes by Alfred Bryan & Herman Paley, 1909..........................**5.00**

Angel Face by Bowers & Saunders, 1961, Movie; The Last Time I Saw Archie, Photo Robert Mitchum, France Nuyen, Jack Webb & Martha Hyer **5.00**

Angel Face by James Brockman & Joseph Nussbaum, 1926..........................**3.00**

Angel Food Rag by Al Marzian, 1911 (Rag)..........................**15.00**

Angel God Sent From Heaven, The by Paul A. Smith, Robert Levenson & Sgt. Frank L. Ventre, 1918, Dedicated To Red Cross Nurse (Cover Artist, Dobinson Engraving, Boston, MA., Red Cross, WWI, Military Personnel & Dedication) **35.00**

Angel In Disguise by Paul Mann & S. Weiss, 1939, Movie: It All Came True, Photo Ann Sheridan & Jeffrey Lynn..........................**5.00**

Angel May Care by Ary Barroso & Erin Drake, 1945, Movie: The Three Caballeros (Disney)..........................**15.00**

Angel Of My Dreams by Cameron & Clarke, 1930 (Cover Artist, Pfeiffer)..........................**10.00**

Angel Of No Man's Land, The by H. MacDonald Barr & Grant Colfax Tullar, 1918 (Cover Artist, Harry Murphy, WWI & Red Cross) ...**25.00**

Angel Voices Ever Near by A. S. Sweet, 1874 (Cover Artist, Walker & Pre 1900)..........................**10.00**

Angel's Dream by Gustav Lange..........................**5.00**

Angel's Prayer by Bevans, 1907..........................**5.00**

Angel's Serenade by G. Braga, Transcription by Sydney Smith, 1924..**3.00**

Angela by Livingston & Evans, 1966, Movie: The Night Of The Grizzly, Photo Clint Walker & Martha Hyer **5.00**

Angela Mia, My Angel by Erno Rapée & Lew Pollack, 1928, Movie: Street Angel, Photo Janet Gaynor & Charles Farrell..........................**20.00**

Angelina by Allan Roberts & Doris Fisher, 1944, Photo Louis Prima...**5.00**

Angels Of Mercy by Irving Berlin, 1941, Written Expressly For And Dedicated To The American Red Cross (Irving Berlin, Red Cross, WWII & Dedicated)..........................**22.00**

Angels Of Night by Harry J. Lincoln, 1909 (Cover Artist, Starmer) ...**15.00**

Angels Of Paradise by Ryder, 1906..........................**5.00**

Angels, We Call Them Mothers Down Here by Bert Kalmar & Harry Ruby, 1921, Photo E. Cantor (Cover Artist, CEM & E. Cantor)..15.00

Angels With Dirty Faces by Fisher & Spitalny, 1936, Movie: Angels With Dirty Faces, Photo James Cagney, Pat O'Brien & Dead End Kids ..**16.00**

Angelus by Eugene Oudin & C. Chaminade **5.00**

Angelus Lullaby, The by Hirsch & Earl, 1921 ....**5.00**

Anglo-Saxon Race, The by Whitfield Hainer, 1913, Respectfully Dedicated To The Cause Of World Peace (Patriotic & Dedication) **20.00**

Angry by Dudley Mecum, Henry & Merritt Brunies & Jules Cassard, 1925 ..**3.00**

Animal Crackers In My Soup by Ted Koehler, Irving Caesar & Ray Henderson, 1935, Movie: Curly Top, Photo Shirley Temple, John Boles & Rochelle Hudson (Shirley Temple) **25.00**

Animal Fair, The by Frederick Johnson, Harry LaForrest & Harley Rosso, 1923 ....**5.00**

Anna Liza's Wedding Day by Irving Berlin, 1913 (Cover Artist, Pfeiffer & Irving Berlin) **15.00**

Anna March by J. S. Fearis, 1906 (March)..........................**10.00**

Annabelle by Lew Brown & Ray Henderson,1923 ....**5.00**

Annapolis (The Midshipman's March) by W. J. Francis Jr., Zoe Elliot & Maurice La Farge, 1933 (March & Patriotic)..........................**15.00**

Annie Doesn't Live Here Anymore by Joe Young, Johnny Burke & Harold Spina, 1933, Photo Guy Lombardo **5.00**

Annie Rooney by Michael Nolan, 1890 (Pre 1900) **15.00**

Annie Rooney's Baby by Paul Jassett, 1890 (Pre 1900) **15.00**

Anniversary March, The by George Rosey, 1895 (Pre 1900 & March)...**20.00**

Anniversary Song by Al Jolson & Saul Chaplin, 1936, Movie: The Jolson Story (Al Jolson)......................**10.00**

Anniversary Waltz, The by Al Dubin & Dave Franklin, 1941 ....**5.00**

Anona by Vivian Grey, 1903 (Indian) **25.00**

Another Kiss by Victor L. Schertzinger, 1928 ....**5.00**

Another Op'nin by Cole Porter, 1948, Musical: Kiss Me Kate.............**5.00**

Another Perfect Day Has Passed Away by Clarence Gaskill, 1933, Photo Ethel Shutta (Cover Artist, Leff) **5.00**

Another Rag by D.A. Esrom & Theodore Morse, 1911, Photo Bermarat Parker Searles (Rag) **15.00**

Another Rose Is Just As Sweet by L.W. Pritzkov, 1898 Boston Herald Sunday Supplement (Cover Artist Bartholemew & Pre 1900)........**8.00**

Answer Go Forth & Find by Alfred G. Robyn, 1919 ....**5.00**

Answer Is Love, The by Charles Newman & Sam H. Stept, 1939, Movie: That's Right You're Wrong......................**5.00**

Answer Mr. Wilson's Call by Billy Gould, 1917 (Cover Artist, Barbelle, President & WWI) **35.00**

Antoinette by Henry Blossom & Victor Herbert, 1914, Musical: The Only Girl (Victor Herbert)......................**10.00**

Anvil Chorus, Arranged by Theo Krausse, 1902 (Cover Artist, John Frew) **5.00**

Anvil Chorus by Verdi, 1910, Opera: Il Trovatore (Cover Artist, Pfeiffer)......................10.00

Anxious by James Kendis & Herman Paley, 1905 (Cover Artist, DeTakacs)......................**15.00**

Any Bonds Today by Irving Berlin, 1941, Theme Song Of The National Defense Savings Program (Irving Berlin & WWII)......................**25.00**

Any Little Girl That's A Nice Little Girl, Is The Right Little Girl For Me by Thomas J. Gray & Fred Fischer, 1910, Photo Violet Macmillan (Cover Artist, Starmer)......................**10.00**

Any Little Melody by Harold Atteridge & Bert Grant, 1920 (Cover Artist, Barbelle) **10.00**

Any Old Place I Can Hang My Hat Is Home Sweet Home To Me by William Jerome & Jean Schwartz, 1901 ....**10.00**

Any Old Place In Yankee Land Is Good Enough For Me by Smith & Cook, 1908 (Cover Artist, Pfeiffer)......................**15.00**

Any Old Place The Gang Goes I'll Be There by Wm. McKennan, 1918 ..**5.00**

Any Old Town Can Be Heaven To You, When There's A Wonderful Girl by H.B. Freeman, 1917 (Cover Artist, Pfeiffer)......................**10.00**

Any Place Is Heaven If You Are Near Me by Edward Lockton & Herman Lohr, 1916 ....**5.00**

Any Place The Old Flag Flies by George M. Cohan (George M. Cohan).**15.00**

Any Rags by Thos. S. Allen, 1902, Photo: Gladys Fisher....................**35.00**

Any Time by Herbert Happy Lawson, 1921, Photo Eddy Arnold & Eddie Fisher **3.00**

Anything Goes by Cole Porter, 1934, Movie: Anything Goes...............**5.00**

Anything Is Nice If It Comes From Dixieland by Grant Clarke, Geo. W. Meyer & Milton Ager, 1919, Small War Edition (Cover Artist, RS & Dixie)......................**15.00**

Anything You Can Do by Irving Berlin, 1946, Movie: Annie Get Your Gun (Irving Berlin)......................**5.00**

Anything You Say by Walter Donaldson, 1928 (Cover Artist, Barbelle & Deco) **10.00**

Anything You Want To Do, Dear by Otto Harbach & Louis A. Hirsch, 1920, From George M. Cohan Musical, Mary (George M. Cohan) **15.00**

Anytime by Lawson, 1921, Photo Eddy Arnold & Eddie Fisher **5.00**

Anytime Is Kissing Time by Frederick Norton, 1916 ....**5.00**

Anytime Is Loving Time by Billy DeVere & Al Herman, 1912 (Cover Artist, Pfeiffer & Deco)......................**15.00**

Anywhere I Wander by Frank Loesser, 1951, Movie: Hans Christian Andersen, Photo Danny Kaye **8.00**

Anywhere In The U.S.A. Is Home To Me by S.E. Clarke, 1910 (Patriotic)..**15.00**

Apalachicola by Johnny Burke & James Van Heusen, 1947, Movie: Road To Rio, Photo Bing Crosby, Bob Hope & Dorothy Lamour...........**5.00**

Appassionata by Clarence Jones, 1916......................**5.00**

Applause by Lee Adams & Charles Strouse, 1970, Musical: Applause.**5.00**

Apple Blossom, Bromo Seltzer Advertising (Advertising).................**20.00**

Apple Blossom Time by Fleeson & Von Tilzer, 1920, Movie: Buck Privates, Photo Andrews Sisters......................**10.00**

Apple Blossoms by H. Engelman, 1905 ....**3.00**

Apple Jack by Charles L. Johnson, 1909 (Rag)......................**20.00**

Apple Sass by Harry Belding, 1914 (Cover Artist, Liesmann & Rag).**15.00**

Apple Song, The by Kim Gannon & Walter Kent, 1948, Movie: Melody Time (Disney)......................**15.00**

Apple Tree & The Bumble Bee by Irving Berlin, 1913 (Cover Artist, Pfeiffer & Irving Berlin)......................**15.00**

Apres La Guerre! (After The War) by B. C. Hilliam, 1919 (WWI).....**10.00**

Apres Un Reve by Romain Bussine & Gabriel Faure, 1923 ....**5.00**

April Blossoms by Otto Harbach, Oscar Hammerstein II, Herbert Stothart & Vincent Youmans, 1923, Musical: The Wildflower **3.00**

April Ecstasy by Madison Cawein & Oley Speaks, 1922 ....**5.00**

April Fool Rag by Jean Schwartz, 1911 (Rag)......................**15.00**

April In My Heart by Helen Meinardi & Hoagy Carmichael, 1938, Movie: Say It In French, Photo Ray Milland & Irene Hervey....................**8.00**

April In Paris by E.Y. Harburg & Vernon Duke, 1932 ....**5.00**

April In Portugal by Jimmy Kennedy & Raul Ferrao, 1953, Photo Vic Damone......................**5.00**

April Love by Paul Francis Webster & Sammy Fain, 1957, Movie: April Love **6.00**

April Played The Fiddle by Johnny Burke & James V. Monaco, 1940, Movie: If I Had My Way, Photo Gloria Jean & Bing Crosby (Cover Artist, HBK) **8.00**

April Showers by B. G. DeSylva & Louis Silvers, 1921, Musical: Bombo, Photo Al Jolson (Al Jolson)......................**14.00**

April Showers by Buddy DeSylva & Louis Silvers, 1932, Movie: The Jolson Story, Photo Larry Parks & Evelyn Keyes (Al Jolson).............**5.00**

April Smiles by Maurice Depret (Cover Artist, Daway) **5.00**

Aquarius by James Rado, Gerome Ragni & Galt MacDermot, 1968, Musical: Hair **5.00**

Arab's Dream, The by Edwin F. Kendall, 1908 ....**5.00**

Arabella, I'll Be Your Fellah by Hotchkiss, 1921 (Black, Black Face)..**12.00**

Arabia, My Land Of Sweet Romance by Hanley, 1915 (Cover Artist, Pfeiffer)..**10.00**

Arabian Moon by Chas. F. Harrison & Fred R. Weaver, 1922 ....**5.00**

Arabian Nights by M. David & Wm. Hewitt, 1918................................**5.00**

Arabian Ooze by Duffy, 1911 (Cover Artist, Pfeiffer)........................**16.00**

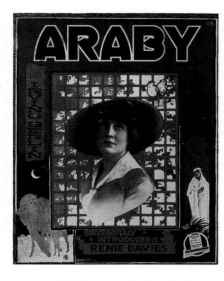

Araby by Irving Berlin, 1915 (Cover Artist, Barbelle & Irving Berlin)..15.00

Arbitration March by Losch, 1915 (Cover Artist, Pfeiffer & March) ..**15.00**

Arcady by Al Jolson & B. G. DeSylva, 1923, Musical: Bombo, Photo Al Jolson (Cover Artist, JVR & Al Jolson)..**10.00**

Are These Really Mine? by Sunny Skylar, David Saxon & Robert Cook, 1945 ....**3.00**

Are We Downhearted? No! by Benny Davis & Archie Gottler, 1928 ...**5.00**

Are You Coming To The Ball by Trix, 1913 (Cover Artist, Pfeiffer)..**10.00**

Are You From Dixie? by Jack Yellen & George L. Cobb, 1915 (Cover Artist, Starmer & Dixie) 25.00**

Are You From Heaven? by L. Wolfe Gilbert & Anatol Friedland, 1917...**8.00**

Are You Going To The Ball This Evening? by Joseph P. Skelly, 1881 (Pre 1900)..**15.00**

Are You Happy? by Jack Yellen & Milton Ager, 1927 ....**5.00**

Are You Livin', Old Man by Redd Evans, Irene Higginbotham & Abner Silver, 1945...**5.00**

Are You Lonesome To-Night? by Roy Turk & Lou Handman, 1926, Photo Blue Barron (Cover Artist, Nick)..**5.00**

Are You Lonesome To-Night? by Roy Turk & Lou Handman, 1927 (Cover Artist, Leff & Deco) **10.00**

Are You Sincere by Alfred Bryan & Albert Gumble, 1908 ....**5.00**

Are You There, Moriarty? by Edward Harrigan & David Braham, 1880 (Pre 1900 & Irish)..**15.00**

Aren't We All by B. G. DeSylva, Lew Brown & Ray Henderson, 1929..**5.00**

Aren't You Glad You're You by Johnny Burke & Jimmy Van Heusen, 1945, Movie: The Bells of St. Mary's, Photo Bing Crosby **14.00**

Argentine Tango Serenade by Weasner, 1925......................................**3.00**

Arizona March by Smith & E.T. Paull (Cover Artist, E.T. Paull & March)..**35.00**

Arizona Waltz by Rex Allen, 1949, Movie: Arizona Cowboy, Photo Rex Allen **3.00**

Arkansas Traveler by Newt Martin, 1941, Photo Patsy Montana **5.00**

Arline by Ernest J. Schuster, 1912...**5.00**

Arm In Arm by Ned Washington, Frances Zinman & Victor Young, 1932, Photo Arthur Tracy The Street Singer.....................................**5.00**

Armorer by Smith & DeKoven, 1890 (Pre 1900)..............................**15.00**

Arms For The Love Of America, by Irving Berlin, 1941 (Irving Berlin & WWII)...**10.00**

Arms Of Love by Alfred Bryan, Francis Wheeler & Pete Wendling, 1928, Photo The Diplomats (Cover Artist, Barbelle & Deco) **10.00**

Arms Of Love by Alfred Bryan, Francis Wheeler & Pete Wendling, 1928, Photo Tina Glenn & Jack Richards (Cover Artist, Barbelle & Deco)..**10.00**

Army Air Corps, The by Capt. Robert Crawford, 1942, Official Song Of United States Army Air Corps (WWII, Patriotic, March & Military Personnel)..**10.00**

Army And Navy by Edmund Braham, 1911 (Cover Artist, T. Ray, Patriotic & March) **25.00**

Army's Made A Man Out Of Me, The by Irving Berlin, 1942, Movie: This Is The Army, Lt. Ronald Reagan In Cast (Irving Berlin, WWII, Military Personnel & President)..**20.00**

Around The Corner by Gus Kahn & Art Kassel, 1930, Photo Art Kassel..**5.00**

Around The World In 80 Days by Harold Adamson & Victor Young, 1956, Movie: Around The World in 80 Days................................**5.00**

Arrah Go On I'm Gonna Go Back To Oregon by Joe Young, Sam Lewis & Bert Grant, 1916, Photo Maggie Cline (Cover Artist, Barbelle & Deco) **15.00**

Arrah Go On, You're Only Fooling by Felix McGlennon, 1895 (Pre 1900)..**15.00**

Art Of Love by Coleman & Raye, 1965, Movie: Art of Love, Photo James Garner, Ethel Merman, Angie Dickinson, Dick Van Dyke & Elke Sommer..**6.00**

Art Song by Victor Herbert, 1917 (Victor Herbert) **5.00**

Arthur Murray Taught Me Dancing In A Hurry by Johnny Mercer & Victor Schertzinger, 1942, Movie: The Fleet's In..............................**5.00**

As Deep As the Deep Blue Sea by Rene Bronner & H.W. Petrie, 1910 (Transportation) **10.00**

As He Rode Her Around In His Wonderful One Horse Shay by Dick Howard & A Fred Phillips, 1914 (Transportation).........................**15.00**

As I Remember You by Beverly & Curly Mahr, 1940...........................**5.00**

As I Remember You by Blane & Martin, 1945, Movie: Abbott And Costello In Hollywood, Photo Abbott & Costello...........................**5.00**

As I Was Saying To The Duchess by Leigh Harline & Ned Washington, 1940, Movie: Pinocchio (Disney)...**25.00**

As If I Didn't Have Enough On My Mind by Charles Henderson, Harry James & Lionel Newman, 1925, Movie: Do You Love Me, Photo Maureen O'Hara, Dick Haymes & Harry James...........................**12.00**

As In Days Of Old by Stauffer & Conley, 1908...................................**5.00**

As Long As I Live by Max Steiner & Charlie Tobias, 1944, Movie: Saratoga Trunk, Photo Ingrid Bergman & Gary Cooper.................**8.00**

As Long As I'm Dreaming by Johnny Burke & James Van Heusen, 1947, Movie: Welcome Stranger Photo Bing Crosby, Joan Caulfield & Barry Fitzgerald..**8.00**

As Long As The Shamrock Grows Green by James Brockman & Nat Osborne, 1913 (Irish)..**10.00**

As Long As The World Goes Round by Andrew B. Sterling & Harry Von Tilzer, 1913 (Deco)..**10.00**

As Long As There Is Love by Eddie McGrath & Harry P. Guy, 1914, Photo Eddie McGrath (Cover Artist, Starmer)..........................**10.00**

As Long As We Still Have Each Other by Blanche Melvin & Carroll Loveday, 1931 ....**5.00**

As Long As We're Together, by Bard & Barton, 1930, Movie: Reno, Photo Ruth Roland **3.00**

As The Lusitania Went Down by Arthur J. Lamb, 1915 (Transportation) .**50.00**

As The Morning Would Seem Without Sunshine, My Life Dear, Would Be Without You by Edgar T. Farren & Meyer Jacobs, 1910 (Cover Artist, Pfeiffer)...**10.00**

As The Petals Fall by Allison & Kellog, 1913 ....**6.00**

As Time Goes By, Movie: Casablanca, Photo Humphrey Bogart & Ingrid Bergman..**16.00**

As We Live & Love We Learn by Robinson & Kortlander, 1920 (Cover Artist, Pfeiffer)...**10.00**

As We Parted At The Gate by E. Austin Keith, 1916......................**8.00**

As We Sat At The Saturday Evening Post by Edgar Leslie, Bert Kalmar & Jean Schwartz, 1915 ....**10.00**

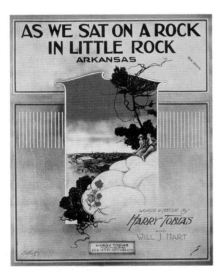

As We Sat On A Rock In Little Rock, Ark. by Harry Tobias & Will J. Hart, 1916, (Cover Artist, Pfeiffer)..15.00

As Years Go By by Charles Tobias & Peter DeRose, 1947, Movie: Song Of Love, Photo Kathryn Hepburn, Paul Henreid & Robert Walker.**8.00**

As You Desire Me by Allie Wrubel, 1932, Photo Morton Downey......**5.00**

As Your Hair Grows Whiter by Harry Dacre, 1897 (Pre 1900) **15.00**

Asia by Goetz & Lindsay, 1912 (Cover Artist, Pfeiffer)....................**10.00**

Asia Minor & You by Cooper & Goetz, 1916 (Cover Artist, Pfeiffer)...**10.00**

Ask Anyone Who Knows by Eddie Seiler, Sol Marcus & Al Kaufman, 1947, Photo Dick Jurgens..**3.00**

Ask Her While The Band Is Playing by Glen MacDonough & Victor Herbert, 1908 (Cover Artist, Starmer & Victor Herbert) **20.00**

Ask The Man In The Moon by Goodwin & Morse, 1891 (Pre 1900) ..**15.00**

Ask The Rose by Jack Yellen & Abe Olman, 1920 (Cover Artist, Helen Van Doorn Morgan) **10.00**

Asleep In The Deep by Arthur J. Lamb & H. W. Petrie, 1898, Musical Supplement Of The New York Journal & Advertiser (Pre 1900) ..**15.00**

Assembly March, The by Hager, 1914 (Cover Artist, Pfeiffer) **10.00**

Asthmore by Bingham & Trotere, 1893 (Pre 1900) **15.00**

At A Cost Of A Woman's Heart by Carter & Braisted, 1907 ....**5.00**

At A Darktown Cake Walk by Charles Hale, 1897 (Pre 1900 & Black) .**25.00**

At A Georgia Camp Meeting by Kerry Mills, 1897 (Pre 1900, Dixie & March) **25.00**

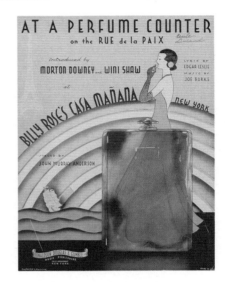

At A Perfume Counter, On The Rue de la Paix by Edgar Leslie & Joe Burke, 1938, Musical: Billy Rose's Casa Manana (Cover Artist, Frederick S. Manning & Deco) 15.00

At Dawning, I Love You by Nelle Richmond Eberhart & Charles Wakefield Cadman, 1906..**5.00**

At Half Past Nine by Sam M. Lewis, Joe Young & Archie Gottler, 1918.**5.00**

At Half Past Two I Will Marry You Tomorrow Afternoon by McDonald & Warner, 1914 (Cover Artist, Pfeiffer) **10.00**

At Last by Mack Gordon & Harry Warren, 1942, Movie: Orchestra Wives, Photo Ray Anthony **5.00**

At Last We're Alone by Martin & Blane, 1955, Movie: The Girl Rush, Photo Rosalind Russell & Gloria DeHaven **6.00**

At Long Last Love by Cole Porter, Movie: You Never Know...............**5.00**

At Night by Alice Meynell & Bryceson-Trehana, 1917......................**5.00**

At Our Little Tango Party by Heath, 1914 (Cover Artist, Pfeiffer)......**10.00**

At Peace With The World by Irving Berlin, 1926 (Irving Berlin)........**10.00**

At Sundown by Geo. D. Wilson, 1903 ....**5.00**

At Sundown by Walter Donaldson, 1927 (Cover Artist, Frederick S. Manning)..**25.00**

At That Bully Wooly Wild West Show by Edgar Leslie, Grant Clarke & Maurice Abrahams, 1913 (Cover Artist, Pfeiffer).........................**15.00**

At The 10 Cent Movie Show by Leo J. Curley & George Christie, 1913 .**10.00**

At The Balalaika by Wright, Forrest & Posford, 1939, Movie: Balalaika, Photo Nelson Eddy **8.00**

At The Ball That's All by J. Leubrie Hill, 1913 From Ziegfield Follies 1913 (Deco) **25.00**

At The Chocolate Bon Bon Ball by Pease & Nelson (Cover Artist, Pfeiffer) **15.00**

At The Codfish Ball by Sidney Mitchell & Lew Pollack, 1936, Movie: Captain January, Photo Shirley Temple (Shirley Temple).............**18.00**

At The Coffee Cooler's Tea by Alex Sullivan & Harry DeCosta, 1918 (Cover Artist, Starmer, Jazz & Black, Black Face).......................**15.00**

At The Court Around The Corner by Irving Berlin, 1921 (Irving Berlin).**10.00**

At The Cross Roads by Ernesto Lecuona, 1929 ....**5.00**

At The Dawning by Brandon, 1917 (Cover Artist, Pfeiffer)...............**10.00**

At The Devil's Ball by Irving Berlin, 1912, Photo Marmion Stone (Cover Artist, Pfeiffer & Irving Berlin)...**15.00**

At The Dixie Military Ball by Ballard MacDonald & Harry Carroll, 1918 (WWI & Dixie)..**20.00**

At The End Of A Beautiful Day by William H. Perrins, 1916 (Cover Artist, Starmer) **10.00**

At The End Of A Weary Day by Henry Wayne Beresford, 1917 ....**5.00**

At The End Of The Road by Ballard MacDonald & James Hanley, 1924 (Cover Artist, Starmer)..**12.00**

At The End Of The Sunset Trail by Ralph Waldo Emerson & Ethwell "Eddie" Hanson, 1926, Photo Eddie Hanson (Cover Artist, A.D. Brown Art)..**8.00**

At The Fall of Babylon by Fred Fisher, 1919, Photo Constance Talmadge & D.W. Griffith (Cover Artist, DeTakacs)..................**10.00**

At The Five And Ten Cent Store by Marvin Lee & Jean Walz, 1915 (Cover Artist, DeTakacs)..**15.00**

At The Flying "W" by Allie Wrubel, 1948, Photo Elliot Lawrence.......**3.00**

At The Gates Of Heaven by Harry Harris, Johnny Keefe & Joe Solman, 1920 (Cover Artist, Wilson Art)....................................**10.00**

At The Midnight Masquerade by Joe Goodwin, A. Seymour Brown & Nat D. Ayer, 1913 ....**5.00**

At The Mississippi Cabaret by A. Seymour Brown & Albert Gumble, 1914 (Cover Artist, Starmer)......................................**15.00**

At The Moving Picture Ball by Joseph H. Santley, 1920.....................**5.00**

At The Old Cross Road by Dennison & Dusenberry, 1914 (Cover Artist, Pfeiffer)..**15.00**

At The Old Town Pump by Harry Von Tilzer, 1917 (Cover Artist, Pfeiffer)..**10.00**

At The Panama Pacific Fair by Sidney Carter & Chas. N. Daniels, 1914.**15.00**

At The Red Rose Cotillion by Frank Loesser, 1948, Movie: Where's Charley, Caricature of Ray Bolger **8.00**

At The Village Smithy by Sockting, 1913.......................................**5.00**

At The Well by Richard Hageman, 1919...**5.00**

At Uncle Tom's Cabin Door by Chas. Bayha & Rubey Cowan, 1912, Photo Weston & Keith (Cover Artist, Hirt & Dixie)....................**10.00**

Atlanta Blues by W.C. Handy, 1924 (Blues).................................**10.00**

Atlanta, Ga. by Sunny Skylar & Artie Shaftel, 1945.........................**5.00**

Atlantic Breakers by Ernest J. Schuster, 1912 (March)......................**15.00**

Atlantic City Pageant, The by John Philip Sousa, 1927 (John Philip Sousa & March) **15.00**

Atop The World, Our Flag by McDonald, 1918 (Cover Artist, Pfeiffer).**10.00**

Au Revoir, But Not Good-bye by Lew Brown & Albert Von Tilzer, 1917 (Cover Artist, E.E. Walton & WWI) 15.00

Au Revoir by Frank Carter & Henry Pellerin, 1933.............................**5.00**

Auf Wiederseh'n, Sweetheart by John Sexton, John Turner & Eberhard Storch, 1951, Photo Vera Lynn **6.00**

Auf Wiedersehen, But Not Goodbye by Louis Weslyn & Fred W. Vanderpool, 1916 (Cover Artist, Barbelle & Deco).........................10.00

Auf Wiedersehen My Dear by Al Hoffman, Al Goodhart, Ed Nelson & Milton Ager, 1932 (Cover Artist, Leff & Deco) **5.00**

Aunt Agar Blues by W. C. Handy, 1920 (Blues)................................**10.00**

Aunt Dinah's Cake Walk by William Needenhammer, 1897 (Pre 1900 & Black, Black Face)..**20.00**

Aunt Mandy's Wedding March, 1899 (Pre 1900, March & Black, Black Face) **22.00**

Auntie Skinner's Chicken Dinner by Fields, Carroll & Morse, 1914 (Black, Black Face) **16.00**

Aupres De Ma Blonde by Richard Manning, 1946 ....**5.00**

Aupres Du Vieux Moulin by A. S. de Pierreville & W.A. Owen, 1913 .**10.00**

Aurora by Mario Lago, Roberto Roberti & Harold Adamson, 1941 Photo Harry Harden **3.00**

Aurora Waltz by Barlow (Cover Artist, Pfeiffer) **10.00**

Auto Race by Percy Wenrich, 1908 (Transportation) **15.00**

Automobile Honeymoon by Norris, 1902 (Transportation) **15.00**

Automobiling by W.C. Parker, 1905 (Transportation).......................**15.00**

Autumn by Julius Vogler, 1900...**2.00**

Autumn by Neil Moret, 1906...**5.00**

Autumn Gold by Gerald Lane, 1906 ....**5.00**

Autumn In New York by Vernon Duke, 1934...................................**2.00**

Autumn In Rome by Cahn, & Weston, 1954, Movie: Indiscretion Of An American Housewife, Photo Jennifer Jones & Montgomery Clift...**6.00**

Autumn Leaves by Jacob Henry Ellis, 1905, Dedicated To Mr. Glenmore N. Snyder, Wilkes-Barre, Pa. (Dedication) **10.00**

Autumn Leaves by Johnny Mercer, Jacques Prevert & Joseph Kosma, 1947...**3.00**

Autumn Leaves by Joseph Kosma, Johhny Mercer & Jacques Prevert, 1950, Photo Roger Williams **3.00**

Autumn Nocturne by Kim Gannon & Josef Myrow, 1941, Photo Shep Fields (Cover Artist, Im Ho)..**3.00**

Autumn Serenade by Sammy Gallop & Peter DeRose, 1945.................**5.00**

Avalon by Al Jolson & Vincent Rose, 1920 (Cover Artist, Frederick S. Manning & Al Jolson) **15.00**

Avalon by Al Jolson & Vincent Rose, 1932, Movie: The Jolson Story, Photo Larry Parks & Evelyn Keyes (Al Jolson)............................**10.00**

Avalon Town by Grant Clarke & Nacio Herb Brown, 1928, Photo Vincent Lopez (Cover Artist, P.M. Griffith & Deco) **5.00**

Ave Maria by A. H. Rosewig, 1926 ....**3.00**

Ave Maria by H. Millard, 1865, Dedicated To Wm. Berge (Pre 1900 & Dedication) **20.00**

Ave Maria by Jerry Castillo & Franz Schubert, 1935 (Cover Artist, L. Kummel)...**6.00**

Ave Maria by Johann Sebastian Bach & Charles Gounod, 1933 ....**3.00**

Ave Maria by Mascagni, 1910, Opera: Cavaleria Rusticana (Cover Artist, Pfeiffer)..**10.00**

Awakening, The by Sarah Shatford & Charles Gilbert Spross, 1904.....**5.00**

Away All Boats by Adelson & Skinner, 1956, Movie: Away All Boats, Photo George Nader & Julie Adams **4.00**

Away Down South In Heaven by Bud Green & Harry Warren, 1927 (Cover Artist, Barbelle) **10.00**

Ay, Ay, Ay by Cecil Cowdrey, 1921..**5.00**

Babbie Waltzes by William Furst, 1897 (Pre 1900)..........................**12.00**

Babes In The Wood by Herbert Reynolds, Schuyler Greene & Jerome Kern, 1915, Musical: Very Good Eddie (Cover Artist, Malcolm Strauss & Deco) **15.00**

Babes On Broadway by Ralph Freed & Burton Lane, 1942, Photo Judy Garland **10.00**

Babies On Our Block, The by Edward Harrigan & David Braham, 1879 (Pre 1900) **15.00**

Baby, Baby, Baby by Jerry Livingston, 1953, Movie: Those Redheads From Seattle, Photo Rhonda Fleming & Teresa Brewer..................**5.00**

Baby, Baby by McClellan & Kerker, 1896 (Pre 1900).......................**15.00**

Baby Blue by Dan J. Sullivan, 1905 ....**10.00**

Baby Blue Eyes by Walter Hirsch, George Jessel & Jesse Grier, 1922, Musical: Troubles of 1922, Photo George Jessel & The Courtney Sisters ..**5.00**

Baby by Gus Kahn & Egbert Van Alstyne, 1919 ....**5.00**

Baby Doll by Armstrong & Clark, 1908..**10.00**

Baby Doll by Hanighen & Hopkins, 1956, Movie: Baby Doll, Photo Carrol Baker **5.00**

Baby Don't Be Mad At Me by Mack David & Ticker Freeman, 1946, Photo Dinah Shore..**3.00**

Baby Don't Get Hooked On Me by Mac Davis, 1972, Photo Mac Davis..**5.00**

Baby Dreams by Robert Levenson, 1919 ....**5.00**

Baby, Everybody Calls Her Baby by Charles Tobias & W.C. Polla, 1921, Sung by Eddie Cantor In Midnight Rounders, Signed Photo Of Eddie Cantor (Signed, Eddie Cantor & Black, Black Face)....................**30.00**

Baby Face by Benny Davis & Harry Akst, 1926 (Deco).......................**5.00**

Baby Feet Go Pitter Patter 'Cross My Floor by Gus Kahn, 1927...........**5.00**

Baby It's Cold Outside by Frank Loesser, 1949, Movie: Neptune's Daughter, Photo Esther Williams & Red Skelton **5.00**

Baby Jim by John B. Archer, 1918..**10.00**

Baby Me by Carroll Carroll & Dick Manning, 1950, Photo Eileen Barton.**3.00**

Baby Mine by J. L. Hatton, 1869 (Cover Artist, Electro Co., Boston & Pre 1900)..**35.00**

Baby Mine by Oliver Wallace, Frank Churchill & Ned Washington, 1941, Movie: Dumbo (Disney)..**15.00**

Baby Mine by Raymond A. Browne & Leo Friedman, 1901 ....**5.00**

Baby Rose by Louis Weslyn & George Christie, 1911, Photo Lee White & Geo Perry (Cover Artist, DeTakacs) **12.00**

Baby Rose by Louis Weslyn & George Christie, 1911, Photo Marie Malatesta (Cover Artist, DeTakacs) **12.00**

Baby Shoes by Joe Goodwin, Ed Rose & Al Piantadosi, 1916 (Cover Artist, Bescardi) **15.00**

Baby Shoes by Joe Goodwin, Ed Rose & Al Piantadosi, 1916 (Cover Artist, Starmer)...**15.00**

Baby Sister Blues by Henry J. Marshall & Marion Sunshine, 1923, Photo Duncan Sisters (Blues) **5.00**

Baby Talk To Me by Lee Adams & Charles Strause, 1960, Movie: Bye Bye Birdie...**5.00**

Baby, Will You Always Love Me True by Billy Johnson & Bob Cole, 1897, Photo Williams & Walker (Pre 1900 & Black, Black Face)**25.00**

Baby, Won't You Say You Love Me by Gordon & Myrow, 1950, Movie: Wabash Avenue, Photo Doris Day, Victor Mature & Phil Harris....**5.00**

Baby Your Mother Like She Babied You by Andrew Donnelly, Dolly Morse & Joe Burke, 1927 (Cover Artist, JVR) **5.00**

Baby's Birthday Party by Ronell, 1930 ....**5.00**

Baby's Laughting In Her Sleep by Gussie L. Davis, 1892 (Pre 1900).**15.00**

Baby's Prayer by Roger L. Halle, 1898 (Pre 1900).............................**10.00**

Baby's Prayer Will Soon Be Answered by Billy Baskette, Gus Van & Joe Schenck, 1919 (WWI) **12.00**

Bachelor Days by Gene Buck & Walter Hirsch, 1916 ....**5.00**

Back At Dear Old Home Sweet Home by Herbert S. Lambert & F. W. Strasser, 1914, Photo Sophie Tucker..**15.00**

Back, Back, Back To Baltimore by Harry Williams & Egbert Van Alstyne, 1904, Photo Inness & Ryan (Cover Artist, Hutaf & Coon)...........**20.00**

Back Home And Broke by Charles K. Harris, 1922, Movie: Back Home And Broke, Photo Thomas Meighan **5.00**

Back Home In Tennessee by Walter Donaldson, 1915, Photo Al Jolson (Al Jolson) **12.00**

Back In The Hills Of Kentucky by Lou Davis, Lou Handman & Billy Heagney (Cover Artist, Frederick S. Manning) **22.00**

Back In The Old Town Tonight by Jeff Branen & Arthur Lange, 1916, Photo Col. Clarence S. Wadsworth, 12th N.G., N.Y. (Cover Artist, DeTakacs, WWI & Military Personnel)......................................**15.00**

Back In Your Own Back Yard by Al Jolson, Billy Rose & D. Dreyer, 1928 (Al Jolson) **10.00**

Back Of Every Cloud There's Sunshine by Charles Daly, Paul Smith & Frank Ventre, 1920 (Cover Artist, W.M. Fisher) **8.00**

Back To Back by Irving Berlin, 1939, Movie: Second Fiddle, Photo Sonja Henie, Tyrone Power & Rudy Vallee (Cover Artist, Im-Ho & Irving Berlin)......................................**14.00**

Back To Childhood's Home & Mother by Dinsmore, 1916 (Cover Artist, Pfeiffer)......................................**15.00**

Back To Dixieland by Jack Yellen, 1914 (Dixie)............**10.00**

Back To God's Country by Paul M. Sarazan & Jack B. Weil, 1919, Dedicated To Nell Shipman (Cover Artist, Frederick S. Manning & Dedication)..**10.00**

Back To Mother by Jack Frost, Paul Biese & F. Henri Klickmann, 1917.**10.00**

Back To My Hometown Gal by Joe Ward & Benjamin Richmond, 1912 (Cover Artist, Rose Symbol) **5.00**

Back To Our Isle Of Dreams by Robert Sperry, 1909 (Cover Artist, Pfeiffer) **15.00**

Back To The Carolina You Love by Grant Clarke & Jean Schwartz, 1914..**5.00**

Back To The Carolina You Love by Grant Clarke & Jean Schwartz, 1914, Photo Manne & Bell (Cover Artist John Frew)......................**5.00**

Back To The Factory, Mary by Clarence Gaskill, 1911 ....**5.00**

Back To The Old Folks by Cook & Lotty, 1934 ....**5.00**

Back Where The School Bell Rang by J. Eugene Johnson & William Nassann, 1911 (Cover Artist, F. Jackson) **10.00**

Back-Water Daughter by McCarron, 1915 (Cover Artist, Pfeiffer & Deco) **15.00**

Backward, Turn Backward by Dave Coleman, 1954 ....**5.00**

Bad And The Beautiful, The by Raskin, 1953, Movie: The Bad And The Beautiful, Photo Kirk Douglas & Lana Turner **6.00**

Bad Humor Man, The by Johnny Mercer & Jimmy McHugh, 1940, Movie: You'll Find Out, Photo Kaye Kyser, Peter Lorre, Boris Karloff, Bela Lugosi & Ginny Simms......................**10.00**

Badge Of Honor, The by M. L. Brean, 1918 (Cover Artist, H.R. Smith & March)......................................**20.00**

Bag Of Rags, A by W. R. MacKanlass, 1912......................**10.00**

Bagdad by Harold Alleridge & Al Jolson, 1918 (Al Jolson)............**10.00**

Bagdad by Jack Yellen & Milton Ager, 1924......................**5.00**

Baggage Coach Ahead, The by Gussie L. Davis, 1906 (Transportation).**20.00**

Bagpipe Dance by Henry S. Sawyer, 1919......................**10.00**

Baia by Ary Barroso & Ray Gilbert, 1945, Movie: The Three Caballeros (Disney) **15.00**

Bake Dat Chicken Pie by Frank Dumont, 1906 (Black, Black Face)...**25.00**

Baldwin Commandery by Harry J. Lincoln, 1906 (March)............**15.00**

Bali Ha'i by Richard Rodgers & Oscar Hammerstein II, 1949, Musical: South Pacific (Cover Artist, BJH) **5.00**

Ballad For Americans by John Latouche & Earl Robinson, 1918 (Patriotic) **10.00**

Ballad Of Bonnie And Clyde by Mitch Murray & Peter Callander, 1967 ....**5.00**

Ballad Of Davy Crockett, The by George Gruns, Photo Fess Parker.....**5.00**

Ballad Of John & Yoko by John Lennon & Paul McCartney, 1969 ....**25.00**

Ballad Of The Green Berets, The by Barry Sadler & Robin Moore, 1966, Photo S.Sgt Barry Sandler (Patriotic & Military Personnel)............**5.00**

Ballerina by Bob Russell & Carl Sigman, 1947, Photo Harry Cool.......**5.00**

Ballin' The Jack by Jim Burris & Chris Smith, 1913, Photo Donald Brian (Cover Artist, DeTakacs)......................**15.00**

Ballin' The Jack by Jim Burris & Chris Smith, 1951, Movie, That's My Boy, Photo Pete Fountain (Cover Artist, Im-Ho)......................**4.00**

Ballin' The Jack by Jim Burris & Chris Smith, 1951, Movie: That's My Boy, Photo Dean Martin & Jerry Lewis......................**6.00**

Ballin' The Jack by Jim Burris & Chris Smith, 1951, Photo Mr. Gene Hodgkins & Miss Irene Hammond (Cover Artist, DeTakacs) **15.00**

Bambalina by Otto Harbach, Oscar Hammerstein II & Vincent Youman, 1923 ....**5.00**

Bambina by Serge Walter, Larry Spier & Al Stillman, 1929 ....**5.00**

Bamboo Bay by Walter Donaldson, Raymond B. Egan & Richard A. Whiting, 1922 ....**5.00**

Banana Boat Song, The by Erik Darling, Bob Carey & Alan Arkin, 1956, Photo The Tarriers......................**3.00**

Bananas by Marvin Hamlisch, 1971, Movie: Bananas, Photo Woody Allen & Louise Lasser......................**6.00**

Band! Band! Band! by S. Brown, 1910......................**3.00**

Band Box Girl, The by A. Wimperis, W. Davidson & Harry Fragson, 1907 (Cover Artist, Starmer)......................**20.00**

Band Of Angels by Sigman & Steiner, 1957, Movie: Band Of Angels, Photo Clark Gable & Yvonne DeCarlo......................**5.00**

Band Played All The Time, The by Buckley, 1915 (Cover Artist, Im-Ho & March) **15.00**

Band Played "Nearer My God To Thee" As The Ship Went Down, The by Mark Beam & Harold Jones, 1912, In Memory Of The Heroes Of The Ill-Fated Titanic (Titanic & Transportation) **75.00**

Band Played On, The by John F. Palmer & Charles B. Ward, 1926, Movie: The Strawberry Blonde, Photo James Cagney & Olivia de Havilland (Cover Artist, Im-Ho) **10.00**

Bandana Days by Noble Sissler & Eubie Blake, 1921 ....**5.00**

Bandana Land by Victor Herbert, 1906 (Victor Herbert)......................**10.00**

Bandanna Babies by Dorothy Fields & Jimmy McHugh, 1928, Musical: Blackbirds of 1928 (Cover Artist, Leff) **10.00**

Bangalore by Earl Burtnett & A.J. Stasny, 1919 ....**10.00**

Bantam Step, 1916 (Cover Artist, Pfeiffer) **10.00**

Barbara by Billy Rose & Abner Silver, 1927 ....**5.00**

Barbara Frietchie by Louis M. Teichman, 1899 (Pre 1900)................**10.00**

Barbara Polka by Sev Kocicky & F. Kovarik, 1940......................**5.00**

Barber's Bear, The by Clarke, 1912 ....**5.00**

Barcarole by M. Louise Baum & Jacques Offenbach, 1909, From Tales of Hoffman (Cover Artist, F.C. Hale)......................**5.00**

Barcarole by Offenbach, 1915 (Cover Artist, Pfeiffer) **10.00**

Barcelona by Gus Kahn & Tolchard Evans, 1926 (Deco)......................**5.00**

Barcelona Tango by Jones, 1914 (Cover Artist, Pfeiffer) **10.00**

Barefoot Trail, The by Marian Phelps & Alvin S. Wiggers, 1920, Sung by John McCormack......................**5.00**

Bargain Day by William Roy, 1949, Signed Photo, Rosemary Clooney (Cover Artist, Im-Ho & Signed)......................**5.00**

Barking Dog, The by Al Stillman, 1954, Photo Crew Cuts................**5.00**

Barnacle Bill The Sailor by C. Robinson & F. Luther, 1920 ....**10.00**

Barney Google by Billy Rose & Con Conrad, 1923, Photo Barney & Sparkplug (Cover Artist, DeBeck) **45.00**

Barnum Had The Right Idea by George M. Cohan (George M. Cohan)..**15.00**

Bartender Bill by McKenna, 1930 (Cover Artist, Pfeiffer) **10.00**

Bas Bleu by Petrie, 1911 (Cover Artist, Pfeiffer).........................**15.00**

Baseball (America's Favorite Game) by Tom Waring, Paul Gibbons & Craig Leitch, 1939, As Sung By The Pennsylvanians As Heard On "Chesterfield Pleasure Time," Photo Paul Douglas & Poley McClintock, Chesterfield Cigarette On Review (Advertising & Sports) ...**65.00**

Basement Blues, The by W.C. Handy, 1924 (Blues)...........................**5.00**

Bashful Baby by Cliff Friend & Abner Silver, 1929, Photo Helen Kane...**5.00**

Bashful Dan And Giggling Ann by Joan Clark, 1928 ....**8.00**

Basin Street Blues by Spencer William, 1933, Photo Phil Harris (Blues) .**5.00**

Basket Of Roses by Fred G. Albers, 1913 (Cover Artist, Jarushek) **10.00**

Batter Up, Uncle Sam Is At The Plate by Tighe, 1918 (Cover Artist, Pfeiffer & WWI) **22.00**

Battle Cry Of Peace, The by Daniel J. Hanifen & Bernard H. Smith, 1915 (Patriotic)..**20.00**

Battle Hymn by Julia Ward Howe & Charles Marshall, 1908 (Patriotic) .**15.00**

Battle In The Sky by J. Luxton, 1915 (Cover Artist, Pfeiffer, WWI & Transportation) **35.00**

Battle Of Gettysburg, The by E.T. Paull, 1917 (Cover Artist, E.T. Paull & Patriotic) **35.00**

Battle Of The Marne by J. Luxton, 1916 (Cover Artist, Barbelle & WWI)..**15.00**

Battle Of The Nations by E.T. Paull, 1915 (Cover Artist, E.T. Paull & WWI) 45.00

Battle Song by Harry Ruby, 1916 (WWI) **15.00**

Battle Song Of Liberty, The by Jack Yellen & George L. Cobb, 1917, Photo Statue Of Liberty & Marching Soldiers (Cover Artist, Starmer, WWI & March) **28.00**

Battle Song Of Prohibition by W.J. Masingham & I.L. Andrews, 1886: Respectfully Dedicated To My Brother, Rev. F. F. Farmilae, Whose Voice, Together With The Voices Of All Who Love To Rescue The Tempted Or Fallen, Is Ever Heard In Defense Of Our Loved Homes And Against Their Great Enemy, The Saloons. May They Not Be Silent Until These Strongholds Of Sin Are Blotted From The Land We Would Leave Our Children. (Dedication & Pre 1900)...................**30.00**

Baubles, Bangles And Beads by Robert Wright & George Forrest, 1953, Musical: Kismet..**5.00**

Bay State, The by Arthur C. Kirkham, 1897 (Pre 1900 & March).......**15.00**

Bayou Lullaby, The by Sammy Cahn & Nicholas Brodsky, 1949, Movie: The Toast Of New Orleans, Photo Kathryn Grayson & Mario Lanza **5.00**

Be A Good Scout by Harold Adamson & Jimmy McHugh, 1938, Movie: That Certain Age, Photo Deanna Durbin......................**10.00**

Be A Little Sweeter To Me by Harry D. Kerr, Earl Burtnett & John Cooper, 1921 (Cover Artist, A.B. Copeland)........................**10.00**

Be Anything by Irving Gordon, 1952, Photo Eddy Howard **6.00**

Be Anything by Irving Gordon, 1952, Photo Helen O'Connell **6.00**

Be Careful, It's My Heart by Irving Berlin, 1942, Movie: Holiday Inn, Photo Bing Crosby, Danny Kaye, Rosemary Clooney & Vera Ellen (Irving Berlin)..**35.00**

Be Careful Little Girl, Be Careful by Mrs. S. N. Ross & Clarke Tate, 1927 ....**5.00**

Be Careful Mary by Dech Howard & Lewis F. Muir, 1915..................**5.00**

Be Good, Be Good, My Father Said by Francis J. Bryant, 1895 (Pre 1900) **15.00**

Be Good, If You Can't Be Good, Be Careful by Harrington & Tate, 1907...**5.00**

Be Good To California, Mr. Wilson, California Was Good To You by Andrew B. Sterling & Robert A. Keiser, 1916, Photo President Woodrow Wilson (Cover Artist, Starmer & Presidents)..........35.00

Be Happy As You Can Be by Carol Vox & Ben Ritchie, 1908 ....**5.00**

Be Happy, Boys To-Night by Henry Blossom & Victor Herbert, 1914, Musical: The Only Girl (Victor Herbert) **10.00**

Be Home When The Clock Strikes Ten by Dodsworth, 1885 (Pre 1900) **15.00**

Be Honest With Me by Gene Autry & Fred Rose, 1941 ....**5.00**

Be My Fireside by Howard Johnson & Lt. Gitz Rice, 1924 (Military Personnel) **12.00**

Be My Life's Companion by Bob Hilliard & Milton DeLugg, 1951 .....**5.00**

Be My Little Baby Bumble Bee by Stanley Murphy & Henry Marshall, 1912 (Cover Artist, Starmer)......................................**12.00**

Be My Love by Sammy Cahn & Nicholas Brodszky, 1949, Movie: The Toast Of New Orleans, Photo Kathryn Grayson & Mario Lanza **5.00**

Be Still, My Heart by Allan Flynn & Jack Egan, 1934 (Cover Artist, Barbelle)..**10.00**

Be Sure He's Irish Then Love Him In That Good Old Irish Way by Jack Glogau, 1912, Photo Emma Carus (Irish) **10.00**

Be Sweet To Me Kid by Joe Howard, Frank Adams & Will Hough, 1947, Movie: I Wonder Who's Kissing Her Now, Photo June Haver **6.00**

Beale St. Blues by W. C. Handy, 1916 (Blues) **10.00**

Beale Street Mama by Roy Turk & J. Russel Robinson, 1923 (Rag)...**10.00**

Bean Song, The by Ray Stanley, 1956, Photo Eileen Barton **5.00**

Beat O' My Heart, The by Johnny Burke & Harold Spina, 1934..........**3.00**

Beatrice Fairfax by Grant Clark, Joseph McCarthy & James V. Monaco, 1915 ....5.00

Beau James by Baker, 1957, Movie: Beau James, Photo Bob Hope & Vera Miles 5.00

Beautiful Annabell Lee by Alfred Bryan, Arne Mettlinger & Geo. W. Meyer, 1920 (Cover Artist, Frederick S. Manning) 20.00

Beautiful, Beautiful World by Sheldon Harnick & Jerry Bock, 1966, Musical: The Apple Tree (Cover Artist, R. Williams) 3.00

Beautiful Bird Of Paradise by Carroll & DeAngelis, 1913 (Cover Artist, Pfeiffer) 15.00

Beautiful Blonde From Bashful Bend, The by George & Newman, 1949, Movie: The Beautiful Blonde From Bashful Bend, Photo Betty Grable, Cesar Romero & Rudy Vallee 12.00

Beautiful Blue Danube, The by Johann Strauss, 1933 ....2.00

Beautiful Briny, The by Sherman & Sherman, 1971, Movie: Bedknobs & Broomsticks, Photo Angela Lansbury & David Tomlinson 3.00

Beautiful by Eddie Leonard & Grace & Jack Stern, 1929, Movie: Melody Lane, Photo Eddie Leonard (Black, Black Face) 16.00

Beautiful by Haven Gillespie & Larry Shay, 1928 (Cover Artist, Ransley Studios & Deco) 10.00

Beautiful Chimes At Sunset by Arthur Lange, 1914 ....5.00

Beautiful Coney Island by Leo Robin & Ralph Rainger, 1943, Movie: Coney Island, Photo Betty Grable, George Montgomery & Cesar Romero 8.00

Beautiful Dark Girl by Gerald McDonald, 1919, Sung By John McCormack (Irish) 10.00

Beautiful Dixie Rose by McKeon & Gutman, 1912 (Dixie) 10.00

Beautiful Dreamer by Stephen C. Foster, 1864 (Stephen C. Foster & Pre 1900) 20.00

Beautiful Eyes by Frankie Adams, Leonard Rosen & Neal Madaglia, 1948, Signed Photo Margaret Whiting (Signed) 10.00

Beautiful Eyes by Geo. Whiting, Carter De Haven & Ted Snyder, 1909, Photo Ila Grannon (Cover Artist, Pfeiffer) 15.00

Beautiful Faces by Irving Berlin, 1920, Movie: Easter Parade, Photo Judy Garland & Fred Astaire (Irving Berlin) 18.00

Beautiful Girls by Freed & Brown, 1933, Movie: Stage Mother, Photo Maureen O'Sullivan & Alice Brady 6.00

Beautiful Hawaii by Mary Earl, 1921 (Cover Artist, Barbelle) 15.00

Beautiful Hawaiian Love by Dorothy Terries & Ethel Bridges, 1920, Small Folio 5.00

Beautiful Isle Of Somewhere by Jessie Brown Pounds & John S. Fearis, 1923, As Sung At Funeral Of Our Martyred President William McKinley (Presidents) 28.00

Beautiful Lady Fair by L. Pauline Maudersley & W. Moffat Devine, 1913, Photo Baby Jeannette 5.00

Beautiful Lady In Blue, A by Sam M. Lewis & J. Fred Coots, 1935 ....5.00

Beautiful Land Of Somewhere by Clyde N. Kramer, Harry Haywood & Fred Heltman, 1918 (Cover Artist, Frank R. Bill & Deco) 10.00

Beautiful Love by Haven Gillespie, Egbert Van Alstyne, Wayne King & Victor Young, 1944, Movie: Sing A Jingle, Photo Allan Jones 5.00

Beautiful Night, Barcarole From Tales of Hoffman, 1916 ....3.00

Beautiful Ohio by Ballard Macdonald & Mary Earl, 1917 (Cover Artist, Barbelle) 12.00

Beautiful Ohio by Ballard Macdonald & Mary Earl, 1918 (Cover Artist, DeTakacs) 16.00

Beautiful Roses by Earl Carroll & Anatol Friedland, Photo Bert Errol, 1914 ....10.00

Beautiful Sahara by Harold Kay, 1919, Movie: Sahara, Photo Louise Glaum 10.00

Beautiful Star Of Heaven by Louis A. Drumheller, 1905 (Cover Artist, Starmer) 15.00

Beautiful Star Of Love by Florence Blackwell, 1918 ....5.00

Beautiful Thoughts Of Love by Jerome Heller, 1910 ....10.00

Beautiful Venice by Jacob Henry Ellis, 1903 ....5.00

Beauty Must Be Loved by Sammy Fain & Irving Kahal, 1934 ....5.00

Bebe by Sam Coslow & Abner Silver, 1923, Photo Bebe Daniels & Respectfully Dedicated To Bebe Daniels (Dedication) 10.00

Bebe by Sam Coslow & Abner Silver, 1923, Photo Eddie Cantor (Eddie Cantor) 10.00

Because by Andrew B. Sterling & Harry Von Tilzer, 1910 ....5.00

Because by Edward Teschemacher & Guy D'Hardelot, 1902 ....3.00

Because by Horwitz & Bowers, 1898 (Pre 1900) 15.00

Because I Love You by Irving Berlin, 1926 (Cover Artist, Leff & Irving Berlin) 10.00

Because I'm Married Now by Herbert Ingraham, 1907, Photo Mabel Hite (Cover Artist, Starmer) 10.00

Because Of You by Al Roberts, 1913, Photo Al Roberts 5.00

Because Of You by Arthur Hammerstein & Dudley Wilkinson, 1940, Movie: I Was An American Spy, Photo Tony Bennett 3.00

Because Of You by Arthur Hammerstein & Dudley Wilkinson, 1940, Photo Ray Barber 5.00

Because Of You by Hammerstein & Wilkinson, 1940, Movie: Beacuse Of You, Photo Loretta Young & Jeff Chandler 8.00

Because Of You by R.N. Doore & Ted Garton, 1918 (Cover Artist, R.E. Kibbe & Deco) 10.00

Because Of You by Walter Hirsch & Ted Fiorito, 1925 ....6.00

Because They All Love You by Tommie Malie & Jack Little, 1924 (Cover Artist, Barbelle & Deco) 10.00

Because You Believe In Me by J. Keirn Brennan & Ernest R. Ball, 1918, Photo Anita Stewart & Earle Williams 5.00

Because You Were An Old Sweetheart Of Mine by Jacobs & Robinson, 1901 ....5.00

Because You're Beautiful by B. G. DeSylva, Lew Brown & Ray Henderson, 1928, Musical: Three Cheers 5.00

Because You're Here by Harold Rabe & Lt. Gitz Rice, 1919 (Military Personnel & WWI) 10.00

Because You're Mine by Harold Rabe & Lt. Gitz Rice, 1919 (Military Personnel & WWI) 10.00

Because You're Mine by Sammy Cahn & Nicholas Brodsky, 1952, Movie: Because You're Mine, Photo Mario Lanza & Doretta Morrow 5.00

Becky Joined A Musical Show by Irving Berlin, 1912 (Cover Artist, Pfeiffer & Irving Berlin) 16.00

Bedelia by William Jerome & Jean Schwartz, 1903, Irish Coon Song Serenade (Cover Artist, Starmer, Irish & Black, Black Face) 22.00

Bee, The by Francois Schubert, 1937 ....**3.00**

Beer Barrel Polka by Lew Brown, Vladimir A. Timm & Jaromir Vejvoda, 1934, Photo Kay Kyser (Cover Artist, Im-Ho) **4.00**

Beer Barrel Polka by Lew Brown, Vladimir A. Timm & Jaromir Vejvoda, 1939, Photo Bill Roberts (Cover Artist, Im-Ho) **4.00**

Beer Barrel Polka by Lew Brown, Vladimir A. Timm & Jaromir Vejvoda, 1939, Photo The Merry Macs (Cover Artist, Im-Ho)....................**4.00**

Bees Knees by Wood, Leslie & Lopez, 1923 ....**5.00**

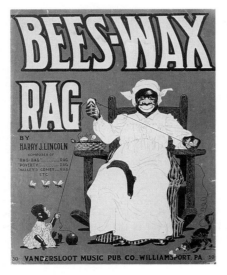

Bees-Wax Rag by Harry J. Lincoln, 1911 (Cover Artist, W.J. Dittmar, Rag & Black, Black Face) 25.00

Beets And Turnips by Cliff Hess & Fred E. Ahlert, 1915....................**8.00**

Before The World Began by Andrew B. Sterling & Alfred Solman, 1917 (Cover Artist, Starmer)....................................**10.00**

Beg Your Pardon by Francis Craig & Beasley Smith, 1947, Photo Eddy Howard **2.00**

Beggar, The by Ted Snyder, 1927, Movie: The Secret Hour, Photo Pola Negri **12.00**

Begging For Love by Irving Berlin, 1930 (Irving Berlin)....................**10.00**

Begin The Beguine by Cole Porter, 1939, Musical: Broadway Melody of 1940, Photo Fred Astaire & Eleanor Powell (Cover Artist, Im-Ho) **3.00**

Begin The Beguine by Cole Porter, 1944, Signed Photo Artie Shaw (Signed) **16.00**

Beginning Of The U.S.A. by Costello & Vanderveer, 1916 (Patriotic)..**10.00**

Behind The Fan by Irving Berlin, 1921 (Irving Berlin)........................**10.00**

Behind The Parlor Door by Joseph P. Skelly, 1882 (Pre 1900) **15.00**

Behold, God Is Mighty by Alfred Wooler, 1912....................................**5.00**

Bei Mir Bist Du Schoen Means That You're Grand by Sammy Cahn, Saul Chaplin, Jacob Jacobs & Sholom Secunda, 1944, Movie: Love Honor And Behave, Photo Priscilla Lane & Wayne Morris (Cover Artist, Merman) **10.00**

Belgian Rose by Geo. Benoit, Robert Levenson & Ted Garton, 1918, Signed Photo Louise Glaum (WWI & Signed) **15.00**

Believe by Tannehill & Rosey, 1899 (Pre 1900)................................**10.00**

Believe In Me by Fred Karlin, 1972, Movie: Believe In Me, Photo Michael Sarrazin & Jacqueline Bisset..............................**6.00**

Believe It, Beloved by George Whiting, Nat Schwartz & J. C. Johnson, 1934 ....**5.00**

Believe It Or Not, It's Always You by Joseph McCarthy & James V. Monaco, 1929 ....**5.00**

Believe Me Beloved by Joseph Herbert & Ephrem Zimbalist, 1920, Musical: Honeydew **5.00**

Believe Me If All Those Endearing Young Charms by Thomas Moore, 1935, Photo Freddy Martin....................................**5.00**

Believe Me If All Those Endearing Young Charms by Thomas Moore,1936, Movie: The Littlest Rebel, Photo Shirley Temple (Shirley Temple)....................................**15.00**

Bell Bottom Trousers by Moe Jaffe, 1944 (Cover Artist, Barbelle, WWII & Patriotic) **10.00**

Bell Hop Rag by Vera Maxwell & A. Braney, 1914 (Rag)................**10.00**

Bella Bella Marie by Don Pelosi, Leo Towers & Gerhard Winkler, 1947.**3.00**

Belle Of Avenue A by Safford Waters, 1895 (Pre 1900) **10.00**

Belle Of Boston, The by P. F. Damm, Boston Herald Sunday Supplement, 1900 (Cover Artist, Goehl)....................................**10.00**

Belle Of Georgia, The by Wm. S. Glynn, 1899 (Cover Artist, E.S. Fisher, Pre 1900 & Black, Black Face) **35.00**

Belle Of Idaho by Rosenberg, 1910 (Cover Artist, Pfeiffer)..............**15.00**

Belle Of Madrid Waltzes by Ben Ritchie, 1910 (Cover Artist, Pfeiffer) .**15.00**

Belle Of The Ball by Chas. K. Harris, 1906 ....**5.00**

Belle Of The Creoles by Harry P. Guy, 1899 (Pre 1900 & Black, Black Face) **10.00**

Belle Of The Yukon, The by Johnny Burke & Jimmy Van Heusen, 1944, Movie: Belle Of The Yukon, Photo Dinah Shore, Randy Scott & Gypsy Rose Lee....................................**6.00**

Belles Of '76 by Chauncey Haines, 1906 (March)..............................**15.00**

Bells Across The Meadows by Albert W. Ketelbey, 1927....................**5.00**

Bells Are Ringing by Comden, Green & Styne, 1956, Movie: Bells Are Ringing, Photo Judy Holliday & Dean Martin..............................**5.00**

Bells by Irving Berlin, 1920 From Ziegfeld Follies of 1920 (Cover Artist, R.S., Irving Berlin & Deco)....................................**20.00**

Bells Of Avalon, The by Mitchell Parish & Joseph Cherney, 1927.......**6.00**

Bells Of St. Mary's, The by Douglas Furber & A. Emmett Adams, 1917, Movie: The Bells Of St. Mary's, Photo Bing Crosby & Ingrid Bergman....................................**10.00**

Bells Of The Sea by Arthur J. Lamb & Alfred Solman, 1922................**5.00**

Bells Of Trinity by Arnold & Brown, 1913 (Cover Artist, E.S. Fisher & Deco) **5.00**

Bells Of Trinity by Arnold & Brown, 1913 (Cover Artist, Pfeiffer)....**10.00**

Bells Of Youth, The by Fiona Macleod & Oley Speaks, 1917..............**3.00**

Bells, The by Lou Klein & Frank Stilwell, 1914, Photo Al Herman (Cover Artist, Starmer)....................................**15.00**

Beloved, Be Faithful by Ervin Drake & Jimmy Shirl, 1950, Signed Photo Russ Morgan (Signed) **5.00**

Beloved by Gus Kahn & Joe Sanders, 1928, Photo Bernard & Ward (Cover Artist, R.S.)....................................**5.00**

Beloved by Gus Kahn & Joe Sanders, 1928, Photo Charlie Crafts (Cover Artist, R.S.)....................................**5.00**

Beloved by Gus Kahn & Joe Sanders, 1928, Photo Parks Sisters (Cover Artist, R.S.)....................................**5.00**

Beloved by Stults, 1910 (Cover Artist, Pfeiffer) **10.00**

Beloved by Victor Schertzinger, 1934, Movie: Beloved, Photo John Boles & Gloria Stuart **5.00**

Beloved by Waggner & Ward, 1945, Movie: Frisco, Photo Susanna Foster....................................**3.00**

Beloved Infidel by Webster & Waxman, 1959, Movie: Beloved Infidel, Photo Gregory Peck & Debrah Kerr....................................**6.00**

Beloved, It Is Morn by Emily Hickey & Florence Aylward, 1896 (Pre 1900)....................................**15.00**

Below The Mason-Dixon Line by Dave Reed, 1910............................**10.00**

Ben Hur Chariot Race March by E. T. Paull, 1894, Respectfully Inscribed To Gen. Lew Wallace (Cover Artist, E.T. Paull, Lithograph, A. Hoen & Co., Pre 1900, March & Military Personel) **55.00**

Bend Low, O Dusky Night by Louise Chandler Moulton & Oley Speaks, 1916 ....**5.00**

Beneath Montana Skies by Neil Knoyle & Bill Nokes, 1929.................**5.00**

Beneath The Moon Of Lombardy by Edward Lockton & Harold Craxton, 1918 ....**5.00**

Beneath The Pines Of Maine by Walter Rolfe, 1901 ....**5.00**

Beneath The Starry Flag by Jerome Hartmann-Koninsky, 1900 (March) **10.00**

Benzine Buggy Man by Alex Kramer, 1908 (Advertising)...................**35.00**

Berlin Echoes by Paul Lincke, 1904..**10.00**

Bernardine by Johnny Mercer, 1957, Movie: Bernardine, Photo Pat Boone & Terry Moore...**5.00**

Besame Mucho by Consuelo Velazquez & Sunny Skylar, 1943 (Deco).**6.00**

Beside A Babbling Brook by Gus Kahn & Walter Donaldson, 1923, Photo Karyl Norman...**5.00**

Beside A Garden Wall by Gus Kahn, Albert Short & Del Delbridge, 1926...**5.00**

Beside A Lazy Stream by Bud Cooper, Nick Lucas & Sam H. Stept, 1928...**5.00**

Beside A Moonlit Stream by Sam Coslow & Frederick Hollander, 1938, Movie: Booloo, Photo Colin Tapley & Jayne Regan **3.00**

Beside An Open Fireplace by Paul Denniker & Will Osborne, 1929 ....**5.00**

Beside That Old Oak Gate by Sam Lewis & Ted S. Barron, 1906........**5.00**

Bess You Is My Woman by DuBose Heyward & Ira & George Gershwin, 1935, Movie: Porgy And Bess, Photo Sidney Poitier, Dorothy Dandridge & Sammy Davis Jr. (Black, Black Face)...........................**12.00**

Bessie And Her Little Brown Bear by Jack Norworth & Albert Von Tilzer, 1906 ....**5.00**

Bessie In A Bustle by Mack Gordon & James V. Monaco, 1944, Movie: Irish Eyes Are Smiling, Photo Monty Wooley, June Haver & Dick Haymes (Cover Artist, Cesareo)...**8.00**

Best In The House Is None Too Good For Reilly by Lawler Blake, 1898 (Pre 1900) **10.00**

Best Man, The by Roy Alfred & Fred Wise, 1946, Photo The Nat King Cole Trio..**5.00**

Best Of My Love, The by Don Henley, Glenn Frey & John David Souther, 1975 ....**6.00**

Best Thing For You, The by Irving Berlin, 1950, Musical: Call Me Madam, Caricature Ethel Merman (Cover Artist, Peter Arno & Irving Berlin)..**10.00**

Best Things Happen While You're Dancing, The by Irving Berlin, 1942, Movie: White Christmas, Photo Bing Crosby, Danny Kaye, Rosemary Clooney & Vera Ellen (Irving Berlin)...**15.00**

Best Things In Life Are Free, The by B.G. DeSylva, Lew Brown & Ray Henderson, 1927, Movie: Good News, Photo June Allyson & Peter Lawford **15.00**

Bethlehem by C. Whitney Coombs, 1889 (Pre 1900) **15.00**

Better Not Roll Those Blue, Blue Eyes by Kay Twomey & Al Goodhart, 1952, Photo Dick Jurgens...**3.00**

Better Than Gold by Charles K. Harris, 1895 (Pre 1900) **15.00**

Betty Co-Ed by Sherman & Lewis, 1930 ....**10.00**

Betty Lou by Walter Rolfe & Henry Proehl, 1942 ....**5.00**

Betty's Music Box by Carrie Jacobs-Bond, 1917................................**10.00**

Between You And Me by Cole Porter, 1939, Movie: Broadway Melody 1940, Photo Fred Astaire & Eleanor Powell (Cover Artist, Im-Ho).**12.00**

Beware by Mort Greene & Harry Revel, 1942, Movie: Call Out The Marines **5.00**

Bewitched by Richard Rodgers & Lorenz Hart, 1941 (Cover Artist, BJH) **5.00**

Beyond Pardon, Beyond Recall by Gussie L. Davis, 1896 (Pre 1900)..**15.00**

Beyond The Blue Horizon by Leo Robin, Richard Whiting & Franke Harling, 1930, Movie: Monte Carlo, Photo Jeannette MacDonald (Deco)..**14.00**

Beyond The Dawn by Fred E. Weatherly & Wilfrid Sanderson, 1911 ..**5.00**

Beyond The Reef by Jack Pitman, 1949, Photo Bing Crosby **3.00**

Beyond The Sea by Jack Lawrence & Charles Trenet, 1945 ....**3.00**

Bianca by Cole Porter, 1948, Musical: Kiss Me Kate **5.00**

Bibbidi-Bobbidi-Boo by Mack David, Al Hoffman & Jerry Livingston, 1949, Movie: Cinderella (Disney)..**15.00**

Bible Tells Me So, The by Dale Evans, 1945, Photo Roy Rogers & Dale Evans **16.00**

Bidin' My Time by George & Ira Gershwin, 1930, Photo Judy Garland, Mickey Rooney & Tommy Dorsey...**5.00**

Big Bad Bill, Is Sweet William Now by Jack Yellen & Milton Ager, 1924...**5.00**

Big Ben by Thomas S. Allen, 1914 ....**5.00**

Big Blonde Baby by Alfred Bryan & Fred Fischer, 1912 (Cover Artist, Starmer) **15.00**

Big Blue Sky Is The Place For Me, The by Mack David & Jerry Livingston, 1952, Movie: Jumping Jacks, Photo Dean Martin & Jerry Lewis **8.00**

Big Boy by Jack Yellen, 1924 ....**5.00**

Big Brown Bear, The by H.A. Heydt & Mana-Zucca, 1919 (Cover Artist, B.F.L.)..**5.00**

Big Chief Cremo by Edgar Leslie & Harry L. Stone, 1907.................**10.00**

Big City Blues by Con Conrad, Sidney D. Mitchell & Archie Gottler, 1929, Movie: Fox Movitone Follies 1929 ....**10.00**

Big Four Two-Step by Bernard, 1897 (Pre 1900 & Transportation)....**15.00**

Big Man by Glen Larson & Bruce Belland, Photo Donny Osmond.......**5.00**

Big Red Motor And The Little Blue Limousine by Richard A. Whiting, 1913 (Transportation)...**15.00**

Big Red Rose Means Love, The by Charles D. Tibbits & Florence M. Hayden, 1915 (Cover Artist, Mac) **10.00**

Big Red Shawl by Bob Cole & Billy Johnson, 1908..........................**10.00**

Big Spender by Cy Coleman & Dorothy Fields, 1969, Movie: Sweet Charity, Photo Shirley MacLaine...**3.00**

Biggest Thing In A Soldier's Life Is The Letter That Comes From Home, The by Robert F. Roden & Edward G. Nelson, 1918, Dedicated To K.C.B. (Cover Artist, E.E. Walton, WWI & Dedication) **15.00**

Bill Bailey, Won't You Please Come Home by Hughie Cannon, 1902, Photo Wilbur Mack (Cover Artist, Dewey & Black & Black Face) 35.00

Bill by Oscar Hammerstein II & Jerome Kern, 1927, Movie: Show Boat **8.00**

Bill Simmons by Geo. A. Spink, 1906 ....**5.00**

Billie Used To Give Her Something Every Night by Hueston, 1913 (Cover Artist, Pfeiffer)..**16.00**

Billiken March by Gideon, 1908 (Cover Artist, Pfeiffer & March) **15.00**

Billy Boy by Lester A. Walton & C. Lucky Roberts, 1917 ....**5.00**

Billy by Joe Goodwin, James Kendis & Herman Paley, 1911, Dedicated To Our Friend Billy "Single" Clifford (Cover Artist, Edgar Keller & Dedications) **15.00**

Billy Co-Ed by J. Paul Fogarty & Rudy Vallee, 1930 ....**5.00**

Billy Dear by Frank Tannehill & Ted S. Barron, 1907, Dedicated To Miss Florence Bindley (Dedication) **10.00**

Billy Green by Lawrence Gifford, 1907, Photo Vesta Victoria **5.00**

Billy "Possums" by H.S. Taylor, 1909 (Cover Artist, Pfeiffer) **15.00**

Billy-Billy Bounce Your Baby-Doll by McCarthy, 1912, Al Jolson's Song Hit (Al Jolson) **16.00**

Bimini Bay by Gus Kahn, Raymond B. Egan & Richard A. Whiting, 1921, Photo Eddie Cantor (Cover Artist, Starmer & Eddie Cantor) **15.00**

Bing! Bang! Bing'em On The Rhine by Mahoney & Flynn, 1918 (WWI).**20.00**

Bird From O'er The Sea, A by White, 1880 (Pre 1900 & Transportation).**15.00**

Bird In A Gilded Cage, A by Arthur Lamb & Harry Von Tilzer, 1900 .**5.00**

Bird Of Love Divine by Kathleen Birch & Haydn Wood, 1912 ....**3.00**

Bird On Nellie's Hat, The by Arthur J. Lamb & Alfred Solman, 1908, Photo May Ward **10.00**

Bird Song by C. S. Courtenay, 1912, Dedicated To Audubon Society Of America (Dedication) **12.00**

Birds And The Bees, The by David & Warren, 1956, Movie; The Birds And The Bees, Photo George Gobel & Mitzi Gaynor **8.00**

Birds And The Brook, The by R.M. Stults, 1893 (Cover Artist, Starmer & Pre 1900) **15.00**

Birds by Moira O'Neill & Carrie Jacobs Bond, 1906 ....**15.00**

Birds Of A Feather by Jack McGowan & Edgar Moran, 1921 (Deco)..**10.00**

Birds, The Bees And The Italians, The by Collins & Rusticelli, 1967, Movie: The Birds, The Bees And The Italians **5.00**

Birth Of A Nation, The by Allen, 1915 (Cover Artist, Pfeiffer & Patriotic) .**15.00**

Birth Of Our Flag, The by Walter V. Ullner, 1898 (Pre 1900 & Patriotic).**20.00**

Birth Of Passion by Otto Hauerbach & Karl Hoschna, 1910, Photo Lina Abarbanell **5.00**

Birth Of The Blues by DeSylva, Brown & Henderson, 1926, Movie: Birth Of The Blues, Photo Bing Crosby, Mary Martin & Brian Donlevy .**10.00**

Bit O'Pink And White, A by Walter Scanlan, 1923 ....**5.00**

Bit Of Blarney by J. Fred Helf & Will A. Heelen, 1904 (Irish) **10.00**

Black And Blue Rag by Hal G. Nichols, 1914 (Rag & Black, Black Face) **24.00**

Black And Tan Fantasy by Edward Kennedy & Duke Ellington, 1927..**10.00**

Black And White Rag by George Botsford, 1908 (Rag) **10.00**

Black Bottom by B. G. DeSylva, Lew Brown & Ray Henderson, 1926.**10.00**

Black Bowl, A by Harry C. Thompson, 1905 ....**10.00**

Black Diamond Express by Alexander, 1897 (Pre 1900 & Transportation) **20.00**

Black Hawk Waltz, The by Mary E. Walsh, 1924 (Cover Artist, Barbelle) **10.00**

Black Jim by J. J. Walker & Herman Avery Wade, 1907 (Black, Black Face) **16.00**

Black Key Polka Mazurka by A. Herzog (Cover Artist, Havelka) **5.00**

Black Swans At Fontainbleu, Palaces In France by James Francis Cooke, 1934 ....**3.00**

Black-Eyed Susan Brown by Herb Magidson, Al Hoffman & Al Goodhart, 1933 ....**6.00**

Blacksmith Blues, The by Jack Holmes, 1952, Photo Ella Mae Morse (Blues) **5.00**

Blacksmith Rag by Rednip, 1920 (Rag) **10.00**

Blackthorn by Joseph J. Sullivan, 1889 (Pre 1900) **15.00**

Blame It On Love by Lanning & Halley, Movie: Blame It On Love, Photo Joan Marsh **3.00**

Blame It On The Blues by Charles L. Cooke, 1914 (Blues) **12.00**

Blame It On The Moon by Phil Baxter, 1930 ....**5.00**

Blame It On The Waltz by Gus Kahn & Alfred Solman, 1926 ....**10.00**

Blarney! by Howson, 1873 (Pre 1900 & Irish) **15.00**

Blarney by Nora Bayes & Jack Norworth, 1909, From Follies of 1909 (Irish) **16.00**

Blaze Away by Abe Holzmann, 1901 (Cover Artist, Carter & March).**20.00**

Blaze Of Glory by Abe Holzmann, 1910 (Cover Artist, Pfeiffer, Patriotic & March) **15.00**

Blaze Of Honor by Harry J. Lincoln, 1915 (Cover Artist, Pfeiffer & March) **15.00**

Bless This House by Helen Taylor & May H. Brahe, 1932 ....**5.00**

Bless You by Douglas Furber & Ivor Novello, 1921 ....**3.00**

Bless Your Heart by Milton Drake, Harry Stride & Duke Enston, 1933, Photo Eddie Duchin (Cover Artist, Leff) **3.00**

Blessed Are The Meek by Anne Campbell Stark & Ward Stephens, 1921 ....**3.00**

Blessed Is He Who Is Loving And Blessed Is She Who Is Loved by Joseph Goodwin & Albert Piantadosi, 1924 (Cover Artist, DeTakacs)......**10.00**

Blessed Is He Who Is Loving And Blessed Is She Who Is Loved by Joseph Goodwin & Albert Piantadosi, 1916 (Cover Artist, Pfeiffer).........**15.00**

Blighty by R. P. Weston & Bert Lee, 1916 (WWI) **10.00**

Blind Mendicant by Bernard Hamblen, 1936 ....**3.00**

Bl-nd and P-g Spells Blind Pig by Junie McCree & Albert Von Tilzer, 1908 (Cover Artist, Hirt) **15.00**

Blind Ploughman, The by Marguerite Radcliffe-Hall & Robert Coningsby Clarke, 1913 ....**5.00**

Blinking Moon by W. C. Powell, 1911 ....**5.00**

Blond Sailor, The by Mitchell Parish, Bell Leib & J. Pfeil, 1945 ....**3.00**

Blondy Let Me Have The Next Dance With You by Geo. W. Meyer, 1907 (Cover Artist, Gene Buck) **10.00**

Bloomer Girl by Harold Arlen & E.Y. Harburg, 1944 ....**5.00**

Blooming Lize by Woodward & Jerome, 1902 ....**10.00**

Blooming Roses by Drumheller, 1910 (Cover Artist, Pfeiffer) **15.00**

Blossom by Chas. Hertzman & Sam Fox, 1907 ....**10.00**

Blossom Fell, A by Howard Barnes, Harold Cornelius & Dominic John, 1905 ....**5.00**

Blossoms Are Falling by Virginia Ferriman, 1927 ....**5.00**

Blossoms On Broadway by Leo Robin & Ralph Rainger, 1937, Movie: Blossoms On Broadway **5.00**

Blow Gabriel Blow by Cole Porter, 1934, Movie: Anything Goes........**6.00**

Bluddle-Uddle-Um-Dum by Larry Morey & Frank Churchill, 1938, Movie: Snow White (Disney) **15.00**

Blue And Sentimental by Count Basie, Jerry Livingston & Mack David, 1947, Photo Count Basie (Cover Artist, Nick)................................**3.00**

Blue And The Grey, The by Paul Dresser, 1900 (Patriotic)................**15.00**

Blue Bell by Edward Madden & Theodore F. Morse, 1904, Photo Marian Littlefield................................**10.00**

Blue Bell by Edward Madden & Theodore F. Morse, 1932, Movie: The Jolson Story, Photo Larry Parks & Evelyn Keyes (Al Jolson).......**10.00**

Blue Bells Of Broadway by Sammy Fain & Paul Francis Webster, 1944, Movie: Lucky Me, Photo Doris Day **5.00**

Blue Bells Of Scotland, The, Variations From Brimley Richards' Album No. 45 (Lithograph, D.R. & Pre 1900)..................**75.00**

Blue Bird Bring Back My Happiness by Geo. Graff Jr. & Bert Grant, 1917 (Cover Artist, Barbelle & WWI)..................**10.00**

Blue Bird by Earl Carroll & Al Piantadosi, 1916 ....**5.00**

Blue Bird Inspiration by M. H. Ryder, 1919 ....**5.00**

Blue Bird Mazurka by Carl Bonner, 1911 ....**3.00**

Blue Bird Of Happiness by Edward Heyman, Harry Par Davies & Sandor Harmati, 1940, Photo Art Mooney (Cover Artist, Harris)................**5.00**

Blue Bird Waltz by Abe Oleman, 1914 ....**10.00**

Blue by Hardman, 1922 ....**5.00**

Blue Champagne by Grady Watts & Frank Ryerson, 1941, Photo Glen Gray & The Casa Loma Orchestra **3.00**

Blue Champagne by Grady Watts & Frank Ryerson, 1941, Photo Jimmy Dorsey..................**4.00**

Blue Chirstmas by Billy Hayes & Jay Johnson, 1948, Photo Russ Morgan .**3.00**

Blue Danube Blues by Anne Caldwell & Jerome Kern, 1921, Musical: Good Morning Dearie (Blues)..................**10.00**

Blue Danube Waltz by Johann Strauss, 1935, Photo Tommy Dorsey (Cover Artist, NPS) **6.00**

Blue Diamonds by Jack Caddigan & Chick Story, 1920, Dedicated To Baby Margaret, Photo Nat Mortan (Dedication)..................**10.00**

Blue English by Jimmy McHugh, 1936..................**5.00**

Blue Evening Blues by Fred Rose, Art Kahn & Vic Burton, 1924 (Cover Artist Jorj Harris)..................**5.00**

Blue Evening by Gordon Jenkins & Joe Bishop, 1939, Photo Shep Fields (Cover Artist, Jorj Harris)..................**4.00**

Blue Evening by Gordon Jenkins & Joe Bishop, 1939, Photo Woody Herman (Cover Artist, Jorj Harris)..................**4.00**

Blue Eyed Violets by Abbie Ford, 1912 (Blues) **5.00**

Blue Eyes Crying In The Rain by Fred Rose, 1948..................**5.00**

Blue Fantasy by Raymond Leveen & Frankie Carle, 1937 ....**5.00**

Blue Feather by Jack Mahoney & Theodore Morse, 1909 (Cover Artist, DeTakacs & Indian)..................**25.00**

Blue Flame by James Noble, Joe Bishop & Les Corday, 1943, Photo Woody Herman..................**3.00**

Blue Gardenia by Bob Russell & Lester Lee, 1943, Movie: The Blue Gardenia, Photo Nat King Cole & Anne Baxter **3.00**

Blue Goose Rag by Raymond Birch, 1916 (Rag)..................**15.00**

Blue Grass by B.G. DeSylva, Lew Brown & Ray Henderson, 1928 (Cover Artist, Pud Lane & Deco)..................**5.00**

Blue Grass Rag, The by Chas. Straight, 1918 (Cover Artist, Rose Symbol & Rag) **10.00**

Blue Gummed Blues by W. C. Handy, 1926 (Blues) **10.00**

Blue Harlem by Edward Kennedy & Duke Ellington, 1935 (Black) ...**10.00**

Blue Hawaii by Irving Caesar, Ira Schuster & Abel Baer, 1929, Photo George Olsen **5.00**

Blue Hawaii by Leo Robin & Ralph Rainger, 1937, Movie: Waikiki Wedding, Photo Bing Crosby & Shirley Ross **6.00**

Blue Hawaii by Robin & Rainger, 1937, Movie: Blue Hawaii, Photo Elvis Presley **8.00**

Blue Is The Night by Fred Fisher, 1930, Movie: Their Own Desire, Photo Norma Shearer **6.00**

Blue Jackets by Haines, 1898, A Song Of The Navy (Pre 1900 & Patriotic)..................**35.00**

Blue Just Blue by Bafunno, 1916 ....**5.00**

Blue Kentucky Moon by Walter Donaldson, 1931, Photo Connie Boswell (Cover Artist, Frederick S. Manning)..................**5.00**

Blue Line Galop by Stephens, 1867 (Pre 1900 & Transportation).......**50.00**

Blue Mirage by Sam Coslow & Lotar Olias, 1954..................**5.00**

Blue Moon by Rodgers & Hart, 1934, Movie: With A Song In My Heart, Photo Susan Hayward & Rory Calhoun **5.00**

Blue Moon by Rodgers & Hart, 1934, Movie: Words And Music, Photo Judy Garland, Lena Horne, Mickey Rooney, Gene Kelly, Ann Southern, June Allyson & Perry Como (Cover Artist, Sorokin) **12.00**

Blue Orchids by Hoagy Carmichael, 1939 ....**8.00**

Blue Pacific Moonlight by Jack Payne & Wallace Herbert, 1930.........**5.00**

Blue Prelude by Gordon Jenkins & Joe Bishop, 1944 (Cover Artist, Barbelle)..................**5.00**

Blue Ridge Mountain Cottage by Al Sherman & Al Lewis, 1929 ....**5.00**

Blue River by Meyer, 1927..................**5.00**

Blue Room, The by Rodgers & Hart, 1934, Movie: Words And Music, Photo Judy Garland, Lena Horne, Mickey Rooney, Gene Kelly, Ann Southern, June Allyson & Perry Como **10.00**

Blue Room, The by Lorenz Hart & Richard Rodgers, 1926 ....**10.00**

Blue Rose by J.R. Shannon & F. K. Logan, 1917 ....**5.00**

Blue September by Mitchell Parish & Peter DeRose, 1940 ....**5.00**

Blue Shadows by Raymond Klages & Louis Alter, 1928, Musical: Earl Carrol Broadway Show, Vanities 7th Edition (Deco)..................**20.00**

Blue Shadows On The Trail by Eliot Daniel & Johnny Lange, 1948, Movie: Melody Time (Disney)..................**15.00**

Blue Skies by Irving Berlin, 1927, Movie: Alexander's Ragtime Band, Photo Tyrone Power, Alice Faye, Don Ameche, Ethel Merman & Jack Haley (Irving Berlin)..................**12.00**

Blue Skies by Irving Berlin, 1927, Movie: Blue Skies (Cover Artist, Leff & Irving Berlin)..................**6.00**

Blue Skies by Irving Berlin, 1927, Movie: Blue Skies (Cover Artist, Hal Weinstein & Irving Berlin)..................**6.00**

Blue Skies Of Normandie by Roy Ingraham, 1921, Photo Edith Clifford..................**8.00**

Blue Skirt Waltz, The by Mitchell Parish & Vaclav Blaha, 1944 ....**5.00**

Blue Sky Avenue by Magidson & Conrad, 1934, Movie: Gift Of Gab, Photo Ruth Etting, Ethel Waters, Wini Shaw, Alice White & Edmund Lowe **8.00**

Blue Star by Edward Heyman & Victor Young, 1955, The Medic Theme, Photo Felicia Sanders **5.00**

Blue Tango by Leroy Anderson, 1951, Photo Leroy Anderson (Cover Artist, Harris)..................**5.00**

Blue True Blue by Harry Holmes, 1907 ....**5.00**

Blue Waters by Ned Washington & Nathaniel Shilkret, 1928, Photo Nathaniel Shilkret (Cover Artist, Barbelle)..................**5.00**

Blueberry Hill by Larry Stock, Al Lewis & Vincent Rose, 1940 (Cover Artist, Im-Ho) **3.00**

Bluebird Of Happiness, by Heyman, Davies & Harmati, 1934, Photo Art Mooney **5.00**

Bluebird Singing In My Heart, A by Sammy Gallop & Michel Emer, 1948 ....**5.00**

Bluebird, The by Clare Kummer, 1918 ....**10.00**

Bluebirds In The Moonlight by Leo Robin & Ralph Rainger, 1937, Movie: Gulliver's Travels..................**10.00**

Bluer Than Blue Over You by Wm. Kernell & Harlan Thompson, 1938, Movie: The Big Party, Photo Sue Carol, Dixie Lee & Jack Smith **6.00**

Blues by L. Rosenthal, 1962, Movie: Requiem For A Heavyweight, Photo Mickey Rooney, Jackie Gleason & Anthony Quinn **10.00**

Blues In The Night by Johnny Mercer & Harold Arlen, 1941, Movie: Blues In The Night, Photo Priscilla Lane & Betty Field (Cover Artist, Im-Ho) **5.00**

Blues My Naughtie Sweetie Gives To Me by Arthur N. Swanstone, Chas. R. McCarron & Carey Morgan, 1919, Photo Herman & Clifton (Cover Artist, Starmer) **6.00**

Blues My Naughtie Sweetie Gives To Me by Arthur N. Swanstone, Chas. R. McCarron & Carey Morgan, 1919, Photo Billie E. Gladstone & Sperrie Matthews (Cover Artist, Starmer)......................**5.00**

Bluff! Bluff! Bluff! by Wm. H. Green & Paul Geary, 1904 (Cover Artist WHG & Black, Black Face) **24.00**

Blushing Roses by Googins, 1918 (Cover Artist, Pfeiffer) **10.00**

Bo-La-Bo by George Fairman, 1919 ....**5.00**

Bo-Peep by Cooke, 1916 ....**5.00**

Bob White What You Gonna Sing Tonight by Johnny Mercer & Bernie Hanighen, 1937 ....**5.00**

Bob's Yer Uncle An' Fanny's Yer Aunt by Tommy Connor & Eddie Lisbona, 1934, Photo Guy Mitchell....................................**5.00**

Bobbin' Up And Down by Esrom & Morse, 1913 (Cover Artist, Pfeiffer & Transportation) **15.00**

Body And Soul by Edward Heyman, Robert Sam & Frank Eyton, 1947, Musical: Three's A Crowd **5.00**

Body And Soul by Green, Heyman, Sour & Eyton, 1947, Movie: Body And Soul, Photo Lilli Palmer, John Garfield & Ann Revere **5.00**

Bogey-Man Is Here, The by Eddie Leonard & Grace & Jack Stern, 1929, Musical: Melody Lane, Photo Eddie Leonard....................**10.00**

Bohemia by Phil Ponce & William C. Polla, 1928 (Cover Artist, Leff)..**8.00**

Boin-N-N-NG by Sam Stept, 1947, Photo Kay Kyser **5.00**

Bojangles Of Harlem by Dorothy Fields & Jerome Kern, 1936, Movie: Swing Time, Photo Fred Astaire & Ginger Rogers......................**10.00**

Bold Dragoons, The by A.G. Crowe **5.00**

Bold Hibernian Boys by Edward Harrigan & David Braham, 1876 (Pre 1900 & Irish) **15.00**

Bold McIntyres by Edward Harrigan & David Braham, 1882 (Pre 1900 & Irish)....................................**15.00**

Bombardier Song, The by Lorenz Hart & Richard Rodgers, 1942, Dedicated To The Bomber Crews Of The U.S. Army Air Forces (Cover Artist, Im-Ho, WWII, Transportation & Dedication)....................**25.00**

Bombay by Jardon, 1907 ....**5.00**

Bombo Shay, The by Henry Creamer, Turner Layton & Henry Lewis, 1915 (Black, Black Face) **15.00**

Bon Bon Buddy, The Chocolate Drop by Alex Rogers & Will Marion Cook, 1907 (Black, Black Face)....................................**30.00**

Bon Soir Cherie by Dorothy Fields & Jimmy McHugh, 1928, Photo Margie Coate (Cover Artist, Starmer) **5.00**

Bon Voyage by W. F. Sudds, 1892 (Pre 1900, March & Transportation) **10.00**

Bonaparte's Retreat by Pee Wee King, 1949, Photo Kaye Starr **3.00**

Bond Street by Burt Bacharach, 1967, Movie: Casino Royale, Photo Burt Bacharach **5.00**

Bone Dry by Sidney Landfield, 1918 ....**5.00**

Bonita Muchacha by Joachim, 1914 (Cover Artist, Pfeiffer) **10.00**

Bonjour Madame by C. Chaplin, 1966, Movie: A Countess From Hong Kong, Photo Charlie Chaplin....................................**12.00**

Bonnie And Clyde by Strouse, 1967, Movie: Bonnie And Clyde, Photo Gene Hackman, Estelle Parsons, Warren Beatty, Faye Dunaway & Michael J. Pollard....................................**16.00**

Bonnie Blue Gal by William Engvick & Jessie Cavanaugh, 1955, Photo Mitch Miller....................................**5.00**

Bonnie Mary by Dave Marion, Musical: Next Week, Photo Dave Marion.**5.00**

Bonnie Sweet Bessie by T. P. Ryder, 1878, Dedicated To Miss Sadie J. Laws (Pre 1900 & Dedication) **10.00**

Boo Hoo by Edward Heyman, Carmen Lombardo & John Jacob Loeb, 1937, Photo Guy Lombardo (Cover Artist, Starmer)......................**3.00**

Boo Hoo by Edward Heyman, Carmen Lombardo & John Jacob Loeb, 1937, Photo Ozzie Nelson (Cover Artist, Starmer)........................**3.00**

Booby by Jack Mahoney & Theodore Morse, 1909............................**10.00**

Boodle by Edward Harrigan & David Braham, 1884 (Pre 1900).........**15.00**

Boogie Blues by Gene Krupa & Ray Biondi, 1946, Photo Gene Krupa...**3.00**

Boogie Man Rag, The by Mort Hyman & Terry Sherman, 1912, Photo Bessie Clifford & Victor Morley (Rag)........................**15.00**

Boogie Rag by Wilber C. Sweatman, 1917 (Cover Artist, Starmer & Rag)....................................**20.00**

Boogie Woogie by Tiny Parham & Clarence "Pine Top" Smith, 1939 (Black, Black Face) **10.00**

Boogie Woogie Maxixe by Sammy Gallop & Bob Crosby, 1953, Photo Ames Brothers (Jazz)....................................**6.00**

Booker T's Are On Parade Today, The by J. Fred Helf, 1908, Photo Lew Dockstader (Cover Artist, Starmer & Black, Black Face) **35.00**

Boola Boo by Otto Hauerbach & Rudolf Friml, 1916, Musical: You're In Love **10.00**

Boom Biddy Boom Boom by Sammy Cahn & Nicholas Brodszky, 1949, Movie: The Toast Of New Orleans, Photo Kathryn Grayson & Mario Lanza **8.00**

Boomp! Pa-Deedle Doddle by Phalen & Todd, 1951, Photo Arthur Murray....................................**5.00**

Boots And Saddles by Glenn W. Ashley, 1910 (March)....................**15.00**

Born At Sea And A Sailor by Graham, 1898 (Pre 1900 & Transportation) **20.00**

Born & Bred In Brooklyn by George M. Cohan, 1923 (George M. Cohan) **15.00**

Born Free by Don Clark & John Barry, 1966, Photo Roger Williams ...**5.00**

Born To Lose by Frankie Brown, 1943 ....**1.00**

Boston Tea Party, The by Frank Ryerson, 1936............................**10.00**

Boston's Fermer Kerl by Bart Tate, Photo Mayor John F. Fitzgerald (Political) **16.00**

Boulevard March by Hussar, 1912 (March) **15.00**

Boulevard Of Broken Dreams, The by Al Dubin & Harry Warren, 1933, Movie: Moulin Rouge, Photo Constance Bennett......................**10.00**

Boulevard Of Memories by Edward Lane & John Jacob Loeb, 1947....**3.00**

Bounce Me Brother With A Solid Four by Don Raye & Hughie Prince, 1941, Movie: Buck Privates, Photo Andrews Sisters & Abbott & Costello....................................**10.00**

Bounding Billows by Elliot, 1827 (Pre 1900) **15.00**

Bouquet Of Roses by Heller (Cover Artist, Pfeiffer) **15.00**

Bouquet Of Roses by Steve Nelson & Bob Hilliard, 1948, Photo Eddy Arnold **3.00**

Bourbon Street Beat by Mack David & Jerry Livingston, TV Series: Bourbon St., Photo Richard Long **10.00**

Bow Down To Uncle Sam by Lester J. Wilson, 1917 (WWI) **10.00**

Bow Wow Blues by Cliff Friend & Will Osborne, 1922 (Blues).........**10.00**

Bower Of Roses by Drumheller, 1910 (Cover Artist, Pfeiffer)............**15.00**

Bowery Buck by Tom Turpin, 1899 (Pre 1900 & Rag) **20.00**

Bowery by Hoyt & Gaunt, 1892 (Pre 1900)......................................**15.00**

Bowery Girls by William Jerome, 1894 (Pre 1900) **20.00**

Bowl of Chop Suey & You-ey, A by Al Goering & Ben Bernie, Movie: Shoot The Works, Photo Ben Bernie & His Merry Lads, 1934 ....**5.00**

Bowl Of Pansies by Jules Reynard, 1914 (Cover Artist, Jaroushek)....**10.00**

Bowl of Roses, Miniatures, A (A Series Of Little Songs) by Robert Coningsby Clarke, 1906...**5.00**

Boy In Khaki–A Girl In Lace, A by Charles Newman & Allie Wrubel, 1942 (Cover Artist, Im-Ho)...**5.00**

Boy Named Lem, A by Lew Brown, Charlie Tobias & Sam H. Stept, 1939, Musical: Yokel Boy...**5.00**

Boy Named Sue, A by Shel Silverstein, 1969, Photo Johnny Cash **5.00**

Boy O'Mine Good Night by Burr & Wilson, 1918 (WWI)..................**15.00**

Boy, Oh Boy! by Frank Loesser & Sammy Timberg, 1941, Movie: Mr. Bug Goes To Town...**5.00**

Boy On A Dolphin by Morakis & Webster, 1957, Movie: Boy On A Dolphin, Photo Alan Ladd, Sophia Loren & Clifton Webb **8.00**

Boy Scouts' Dream, The by V. Paul Jones, 1915 (Cover Artist, Starmer, March & Patriotic)..**25.00**

Boy Scouts Parade by Julius K. Johnson, 1912 (March)....................**20.00**

Boy's Best Friend Is His Mother by Miller & Skelly, 1884 (Pre 1900) .**15.00**

Boys Are Coming Home, The by Edwin L. Taylor, 1919 (WWI) **10.00**

Boys From Yankee Land, The by Franks, 1916 (WWI)......................**15.00**

Boys, Get Ready! by Reginald de Koven, 1918 (WWI & March).......**20.00**

Boys In The Back Room, The by Loesser & Hollander, 1939, Movie: Destry Rides Again, Photo Marlene Dietrich & James Stewart.....**10.00**

Boys In The Trenches Are Calling You, The by Allen, 1918 (WWI)..**20.00**

Boys Of The Blue & Gray, The by Rohacek (Cover Artist, Pfeiffer & Patriotic) **20.00**

Boys Of The U.S.A., The by Al Fields & Arthur G. Franklin, 1917 (Cover Artist, A. Kissel & WWI)...**20.00**

Bramble Bush, The by David & DeVol, 1967, Movie: The Dirty Dozen, Photo Lee Marvin, Telly Savalas, John Cassavetes & Robert Ryan ..**3.00**

Bran' New Little Coon by Rosenfeld, 1891 (Pre 1900 & Black, Black Face) **30.00**

Brannigan's Band by Wellman & Burke, 1876 (Pre 1900) **15.00**

Brass Band Ephraham Jones by Joe Goodwin & Geo. W. Meyer, 1913 (March & Black, Black Face)..**20.00**

Brat, The by Smith & Snyder, 1919, Movie: The Brat, Photo Nazimova ..**6.00**

Brave Jennie Creek by Newkirk, 1895 (Pre 1900 & Transportation)...**25.00**

Bravest Heart Of All by Raymond B. Egan & Richard A. Whiting, 1917 (WWI)..**15.00**

Brazil by Bob Russell, 1939, Movie: Saludos Amigos (Disney) **15.00**

Brazilian Rose by Brennan, 1915 (Cover Artist, Pfeiffer & Deco)......**20.00**

Break The News To Mother by Charles K. Harris, 1916 (Cover Artist, Starmer & WWI) **20.00**

Break The News To Mother Gently by Ed Marks & Joe Stern, 1892 (Pre 1900)...**15.00**

Breakaway by Con Corad, Sidney Mitchell & Archie Gottler, 1929, Movie: Fox Movietone Follies 1929 ....**10.00**

Breakfast At Tiffany's by Henry Mancini, 1961, Movie: Breakfast At Tiffany's, Photo Audrey Hepburn..**8.00**

Breath O'Spring by Grace LeBoy, 1917 (Deco) **5.00**

Breath Of Virginia, A by Jack Mahoney, 1920 (Cover Artist, R.S.)....**5.00**

Breeze And I, The by Al Stillman & Ernesto Lecuona, 1929 (Cover Artist, Scott)..**2.00**

Breeze Blow My Baby Back To Me by Ballard MacDonald, Joe Goodwin & James F. Hanley, 1919, Photo Owsley & O'Day (Cover Artist, Natwick) **10.00**

Breeze Blow My Baby Back To Me by Ballard MacDonald, Joe Goodwin & James F. Hanley, 1919, Photo Kentucky Serenaders (Cover Artist, Natwick) **10.00**

Breeze From Alabama, A by Scott Joplin, 1902 (Scott Joplin)...........**50.00**

Breezin' Along With The Breeze by Richard Whiting, 1926...............**10.00**

Bridal Bouquet Waltzes by Henry S. Sawyer, 1909...........................**5.00**

Bridal Cake Walk by Anthony L. Marish, 1897 (Pre 1900 & Black, Black Face) **28.00**

Bridal Chorus by R. Wagner, 1924, From Opera Lohengrin (Cover Artist, Pfeiffer)..**10.00**

Bridal Dawn by Helen Taylor & Easthope Martin, 1918 ....**5.00**

Bridge Of Sighs by James Thornton, 1900..**5.00**

Bridge, The by Henry W. Longfellow & M. Lindsay, 1927 (Deco) **5.00**

Bridge Too Far, A by Addison, 1977, Movie: A Bridge Too Far, Photo James Crean, Sean Connery, Anthony Hopkins, Lawrence Olivier & Robert Redford **3.00**

Brigadoon by Alan J. Lerner & Frederick K. Loewe, 1947, Movie: Brigadoon **5.00**

Brigand's Love Song, The by H.W. Petrie, 1893 (Pre 1900) **5.00**

Bright Eyes by Harry B. Smith, Otto Motzan & M. K. Jerome, 1920 (Cover Artist, Barbelle & Deco)..5.00

Bright Happy Days by Locke & Walker, 1896 (Pre 1900)..................**15.00**

Bright Little Lantern I Swing, The by Cake, 1893 (Pre 1900 & Transportation)..**25.00**

Bring Along Your Dancing Shoes by Gus Kahn & Grace LeBoy, 1915, Musical: Dancing Around With Al Jolson (Al Jolson) **15.00**

Bring Back, Bring Back, Bring Back The Kaiser To Me by Rowland & Moran, 1917 (Cover Artist, Pfeiffer & WWI)..............................**20.00**

Bring Back My Daddy To Me by William Tracey, Howard Johnson & George W. Meyer, 1917, Photo of Famous Child Star Madge Evans (Cover Artist, Rose & WWI)..**18.00**

Bring Back My Loving Man by Irving Berlin, 1911 (Irving Berlin)....**15.00**

Bring Back My Soldier Boy To Me by Walter Hirsch & Frank Magine, 1918 (Cover Artist, Natwick & WWI) **25.00**

Bring Back The Thrill by Ruth Poll & Peter Rugolo, 1950, Photo Eddie Fisher **5.00**

Bring Back Those Wonderful Days by Darl MacBoyle & Nat Vincent, 1919 (Cover Artist, DeTakacs)...**12.00**

Bring Back Your Love by Atteridge & Schwartz, 1913 (Cover Artist, Pfeiffer & Transportation)...**22.00**

Bring Me A Ring In Spring by Irving Berlin, 1911 (Cover Artist, Pfeiffer & Irving Berlin)...**20.00**

Bring Me A Rose by Charles Shisler, 1918 (Cover Artist, Barbelle)...**10.00**

Bring Me Back My Lovin' Honey Boy by Jack Yellen & Geo. L. Cobb, 1913 ....**10.00**

Bring Out The Flag Boys by John Ford, 1876 (Pre 1900 & Patriotic).**20.00**

Bringing Pretty Blossoms To Strew On Mother's Grave by T. P. Westendorf, 1880 (Pre 1900)...**15.00**

Bringing Up Father In Gay New York by George McManus, 1930 ....**25.00**

Broadway Baby Dolls, by Bryan & Meyer, 1929, Movie: Broadway Babies, Photo Alice White...**6.00**

Broadway Blues by Sherman, 1915 (Blues)...**15.00**

Broadway by Lew Brown & Herman Paley, 1913 (Cover Artist, Pfeiffer)..**15.00**

Broadway Caballero by Lou Forbes & Henry Sullivan, 1941...............**5.00**

Broadway Honeymoon, A by Davis, 1913 (Cover Artist, Pfeiffer) **15.00**

Broadway I'm Longing For You by Reis & Schnabel, 1916 (Cover Artist, Pfeiffer)...**15.00**

Broadway Melody by Arthur Freed & Nacio Herb Brown, 1929, Movie: Broadway Melody, Photo Charles King, Bessie Lowe & Anita Page..**10.00**

Broadway Rhythm by Arthur Freed & Nacio Herb Brown, 1935, Movie: Broadway Melody of 1936...**10.00**

Broadway Rose by Eugene West, Martin Fried & Otis Spencer, 1920 (Cover Artist, Goldbek & Deco) **10.00**

Broken Blossoms by A. Robert King & Ballard MacDonald, 1919, Photo Marion Davies **10.00**

Broken Blossoms by Edgar Long & F. Gottschalk, 1919, Dedicated To D.W. Griffith (Dedication) **10.00**

Broken Doll, A by Clifford Harris & Jas. W. Tate, 1916 ....**5.00**

Broken Hearted Clown by Art Noel & Don Pelosi, 1937....................**5.00**

Broken Hearted Melody by Gus Kahn & Isham Jones, 1922 (Deco).....**5.00**

Broken Home by Will H. Fox, 1891 (Pre 1900)...**15.00**

Broken Melody, A by Phil Stewart & James Blade, 1937....................**5.00**

Broken Promise, A by James Goldsborough, 1957, Movie: Jamboree, Photo The Four Coins...**5.00**

Broken Record, The by Cliff Friend, Chalie Tobias & Boyd Bunch, 1935.**3.00**

Broken-Down Merry-Go-Round by Arthur Herbert & Fred Stryker, 1950, Photo Margaret Whiting & Jimmy Wakely...**3.00**

Broken-Hearted Blues by Dave Ringle, F. Henri Klickmann & Roy Bargy, 1922 (Blues) **10.00**

Broncho Buster by Madden & Jordon, 1907 ....**5.00**

Brooklet, The by J.H. Ripley, 1902 ....**3.00**

Brooklyn Light Quickstep, The by Alla Dopworth, 1839 (Pre 1900) ..**20.00**

Brookside Inn, The by William Jerome & Jean Schwartz, 1921...........**5.00**

Brother Can You Spare A Dime by E. Y. Harburg & Jay Gorney, 1932, Musical: Americana (Cover Artist, Jorj) **3.00**

Brother Sun Sister Moon by Donovan, 1973, Movie: Brother Sun Sister Moon, Photo Graham Faulkner & Judy Bowker...**4.00**

Brotherhood Dance, The by Gimbel, 1968, Movie: The Brotherhood, Photo Kirk Douglas & Alex Cord **5.00**

Brown Eyes, Why Are You Blue by Meryer & Bryan, 1925 ....**5.00**

Brown October Ale by Smith & DeKoven, 1890 (Pre 1900)...............**10.00**

Brown's Jubilee March by Samuel D. Brown, 1881 (Pre 1900 & March).**10.00**

Brownie Rag, The by Frank Wooster & Max Wilkins, 1907, Photo Frank Wooster, Dedicated To Miss Bessie Wood Stewart (Rag & Dedication)...**12.00**

Brunette Polka, The by Wallerstein, 1850 (Pre 1900)...**20.00**

Brush Those Tears From Your Eyes by Oakley Haldeman, Al Trace & Jimmy Lee, 1948, Photo Evelyn Knight...**5.00**

Brush Those Tears From Your Eyes by Oakley Haldeman, Al Trace & Jimmy Lee, 1948, Photo Al Trace & His Silly Symphonists..........**3.00**

Brush Up Your Shakespeare by Cole Porter, 1948, Musical: Kiss Me Kate **5.00**

Bubble, The by Anthony Trimi, 1913...**5.00**

Bubbling Over by John William Kellette, 1919 (Lithograph, Knapp Co. & Deco) **15.00**

"Bubi" Fox Trot by Walter Kollo, 1914 ....**5.00**

Buckle Down, Winsocki by Hugh Martin & Ralph Blane, 1943, Movie: Best Foot Forward, Photo Lucille Ball & Harry James.................**10.00**

Buddha by Ed Rose & Lew Pollack, 1919 ....**5.00**

Buddie Beware by Cole Porter, 1934, Movie: Anything Goes.............**5.00**

Buddy Boy by Esther Van Sciver, Shelby Darnell & Bob Miller, 1942 (WWII) **5.00**

Buddy by Jean Lefavre & W. C. Polla, 1919 (Cover Artist, C. Warde Traver & Lithograph, Knapp)...**15.00**

Buds And Blossoms by A. B. Federe, 1905 ....**3.00**

Budweiser's A Friend Of Mine by Alfred Bryan & Seymour Furth, 1907...**10.00**

Buffalo Flyer, The by Harry B. Lincoln, 1904 (March & Transportation).**15.00**

Buffalo Rag by Tom Turpin, 1904 (Rag) **15.00**

Bugle Blasts by Wayne, 1906 (Patriotic)...**10.00**

Bugle Boy by Engelmann & Brehm, 1909 (Cover Artist, Pfeiffer) **16.00**

Bugle Call Rag by J. Hubert Blake & Carey Morgan, 1916, Photo Cameron Sisters (WWI & Rag)...**20.00**

Bugle Call Rag by J. Hubert Blake & Carey Morgan, 1916, Photo Jean & Jeanette Warner (Cover Artist, Starmer, WWI & Rag) 20.00

Bugle Call Rag by Jack Pettis, Billy Meyers & Elmer Schoebel, 1956, Movie: The Benny Goodman Story, Photo Donna Reed & Steve Allen (Rag) **10.00**

Bugville Parade by Brown, 1901 ....**10.00**

Build A Little Home by Al Dubin & Harry Warren, 1933, Movie: Roman Scandals, Photo Eddie Cantor (Cover Artist, Jorj Harris & Eddie Cantor) **15.00**

Building A Home For You by Santly & Bennet, 1931...**3.00**

Bull Moose March by Brookes C. Peters, 1912 (March) **10.00**

Bull-Frog Patrol, The by Anne Caldwell & Jerome Kern, 1919, Musical: She's A Good Fellow **10.00**

Bully Song by Charles E. Trevathan, 1896 (Pre 1900)...**10.00**

Bum Song, The by McClintock, 1928 ....**10.00**

Bumble Bee by Havez, Donnelly & Blyler, 1911, Ziegfield Follies 1911, Photo Dolly Sisters **10.00**

Bumble Boogie by Jack Pina, 1946..**3.00**

Bumming Around by Pete Graves, 1953...**3.00**

Bump, Bump, Bump In Your Automobile by Harry Von Tilzer, 1912 (Transportation)...**35.00**

Bunch Of Blackberries by Abe Holtzman, 1899 (Pre 1900 & Black)..**20.00**

Bunch Of Noise by Louis Mentel, 1913 (Rag)...................................**10.00**

Bunch Of Roses by Chapi, 1910...**5.00**

Bundle Of Joy by Eugene West & Otis Spencer, 1921 (Cover Artist, Wohlman)...**5.00**

Bundle Of Old Love Letters, A by Arthur Freed & Nacio Herb Brown, 1929, Movie: Lord Byron Of Broadway **5.00**

Bundle Of Southern Sunshine by Sunny Clapp, 1951, Photo Eddy Arnold **3.00**

Bunker Hill by Albert Von Tilzer, 1904 (Patriotic)............................**15.00**

Bunkin Island by G.L. Camden, Boston Sunday Avertiser, Sunday Supplement, November 3, l918 (WWI)......................................**10.00**

Bunny Hop, The by Ray Anthony & Leonard Auletti, 1952.............**2.00**

Burglar Rag, The by Brady & Mahoney & Harry Ferguson, 1912 (Cover Artist, Pfeiffer & Rag)...**15.00**

Burgundy by Tommy Malie, Jimmy Steiger & Harry Richmond, 1925, Photo Albert E. Short (Cover Artist, Barbelle) **10.00**

Burmah Moon by Lieut. Gitz Rice, 1919 (Military Personnel)............**10.00**

Burning Of Rome, The by E.T. Paull, 1903 (Cover Artist, E.T. Paull, Lithograph, A Hoen & March).....................................**35.00**

Burning Sands by Jack Meskill & D. Onivas, 1922 (Cover Artist, Wohlman)...**5.00**

Bury Me Out On The Prairie by Manoloff, 1935 ....**5.00**

Bus Stop Song, The by Darby, 1956, Movie: Bus Stop, Photo Marilyn Monroe & Don Murray...**10.00**

Bushel And A Peck, A by Frank Loesser, 1950, Musical: Guys & Dolls **5.00**

Business Is Business With Me by Chris Smith, 1907 (Black, Black Face)..**25.00**

Busy Little Digits by Carl Demangate, 1928 (Cover Artist, Starmer)....**5.00**

Busybody by Sid Tepper & Roy Brodsky, 1952, Photo Pee Wee King.**3.00**

But Beautiful by Johnny Burke & James Van Heusen, 1947, Movie: Road To Rio, Photo Bing Crosby, Bob Hope, Dorothy Lamour & Andrews Sisters..**5.00**

But I Do–You Know I Do by Gus Kahn & Walter Donaldson, 1926 ....**5.00**

But It Didn't Mean A Thing by Mack David & Jerry Livingston, 1939, Photo Lawrence Welk **3.00**

But Not For Me by George & Ira Gershwin, 1930, Movie: Girl Crazy, Photo, Judy Garland, Mickey Rooney & Tommy Dorsey **8.00**

But Where Are You? by Irving Berlin, 1936, Movie: Follow The Fleet, Photo Fred Astaire & Ginger Rogers (Irving Berlin)....................**10.00**

Butcher Rag by Louis Mentel, 1914 (Rag)..**10.00**

Butterfingers by Irving Berlin, 1934 (Irving Berlin) **10.00**

Butterflies by Steinke, 1911..**5.00**

Butterflies In The Rain by Erell Reaves & Sherman Myers, 1932........**3.00**

Butterfly Ballet by Schulz, 1912 (Cover Artist, Pfeiffer)....................**15.00**

Butterfly by Webster & Wayne, 1934 ....**5.00**

Butterfly Waltz by Freedman, 1919 (Cover Artist, Pfeiffer)...............**15.00**

Button Up Your Overcoat by B.G. DeSylva, Lew Brown & Ray Henderson, 1928, Musical: Follow Thru......................................**5.00**

Buttons And Bows by Jay Livingston & Ray Evans, 1948, Movie: Paleface, Photo Bob Hope & Jane Russell................................**5.00**

Buy A Bond Buy A Bond by W. B. Kernell, 1918 (WWI).................**20.00**

Buy A Liberty Bond For Baby by Morgan, 1917 (Cover Artist, Pfeiffer) & WWI...**15.00**

By A Waterfall by Irving Kahal & Sammy Fain, 1933, Movie: Footlight Parade, Photo James Cagney, Joan Blondell, Ruby Keeler & Dick Powell (Cover Artist, Jorj Harris)...................................**5.00**

By A Wishing Well by Mack Gordon & Harry Revel, 1938, Movie: My Lucky Star, Photo Sonja Henie & Richard Greene **5.00**

By Candle Light by Cole Porter, Movie: You Never Know...................**5.00**

By Heck by S. R. Henry, 1914 ....**10.00**

By Moonshine by Carolus Agghazy, 1913...**10.00**

By The Beautiful Sea by Harold R. Atteridge & Harry Carroll, 1914, Photo Du For Trio (Cover Artist, Pfeiffer & Deco) **15.00**

By The Bend Of The River by Bernhard Haig & Clara Edwards, 1927, Dedicated To Caroline Andrews (Dedication) **5.00**

By The Campfire by Mary Elizabeth Girling & Percy Wenrich, 1919 (WWI)..**15.00**

By The Light Of The Jungle Moon by Powell J. Ford & J. Caldwell Atkinson, 1911...**10.00**

By The Light Of The Silvery Moon by Edward Madden, Gus Edwards & Will D. Cobb, 1932, Movie: The Jolson Story, Photo Larry Parks & Evelyn Keyes (Al Jolson)...**14.00**

By The Light Of The Stars by George A. Little, Arthur Sizemore & Larry Shay, 1925 ....**5.00**

By The Old Cathedral Door by Arthur J. Lamb & Alfred Solman, 1912 .**5.00**

By The Old Mill Where Waterlilies Grow by Morgan, 1912...............**5.00**

By The Old Ohio Shore by Ballard MacDonald & Mary Earl, 1921 (Cover Artist, Starmer)...**5.00**

By The Old Rustic Seat I'll Be Waiting, 1910 (Cover Artist E. S. Fisher) .**5.00**

By The River Of The Roses by Mary Symes & Joe Burke, 1943, Photo Tommy Tucker...**4.00**

By The River Of The Roses by Mary Symes & Joe Burke, 1943, Photo Lawrence Welk..**4.00**

By The Sapphire Sea by Harry B. Smith, Francis Wheeler & Ted Snyder, 1922 ....**5.00**

By The Swanee River by H. W. Myddleton, 1915 ....**5.00**

By The Sycamore Tree by Haven Gillispie & Pete Wendling, 1931 (Cover Artist, Leff)..**5.00**

By The Time I Get To Phoenix by Jim Webb, 1967, Photo Glen Campbell..**3.00**

By The Watermelon Vine Lindy Lou by Thomas S. Allen, 1904 (Cover Artist, Starmer & Black, Black Face).......................................**25.00**

By The Waters Of Babylon by Oley Speaks, 1907 ....**3.00**

By The Waters of Minnetonka by Thurlow Lieurance, 1914, Dedicated To Mr. Alfred Williams (Indians & Dedication) **10.00**

By The Way by Mack Gordon & Josef Myrow, 1948, Movie: When My Baby Smiles At Me, Photo Betty Grable & Dan Dailey **5.00**

Bye And Bye by Lorenz Hart & Richard Rodgers, 1925, Musical: Dearest Enemy...**5.00**

Bye And Bye by Wm. Heagney, 1905..**10.00**

Bye And Bye Sweetheart by Yellen, Valentine & Ford, 1928..............**5.00**

Bye & Bye, You'll See The Sun A-Shining by Moran & Bryan, 1918 (Cover Artist, Pfeiffer & Deco)..**15.00**

Bye Baby Bye by A. L. Powell, 1889 (Pre 1900)...............................**15.00**

Bye Bye Baby by Jule Styne & Leo Robin, 1949, Movie: Gentlemen Prefer Blondes...**5.00**

Bye Bye Baby by Walter Hirsch & Lou Handman, 1936, Photo Pancho (Cover Artist, Barbelle)...**10.00**

Bye Bye Blackbird by Mort Dixon & Ray Henderson, 1926, Photo Gus Edwards (Jazz)..**5.00**

Bye Bye Blues by Fred Hamm, Dave Bennett, Bert Lown & Chauncey Grey, 1930 (Blues) **6.00**

Byebye Land by Chas. E. Roat, 1916...**5.00**

Bye-Bye My Babykins Bye-Bye by Gene Jefferson & Wm. H. Penn, 1899, Supplement Of New York Journal And Advertiser (Pre 1900).......**10.00**

Bye-Bye Pretty Baby by Jack Gardner & Spike Hamilton, 1927..........**5.00**

Bye Lo by Ray Perkins, 1919 (Cover Artist, Barbelle & Black, Black Face)..**16.00**

Bygones by Harry D. Kerr, Irving Abrahamson & Don Warner, 1914..**5.00**

C'est Si Bon by Jerry Seelen & Henri Betti, 1950 ....**2.00**

Cabarabia by Mitchell, Flatow & Gumble, 1927, Movie: Cabaret, Photo Gilda Gray **5.00**

Cabaret by Fred Ebb & John Lander, 1966, Musical: Cabaret..............**3.00**

Cabaret Rag, The by Allen & Daly, 1913 (Cover Artist, Pfeiffer, Deco & Rag) **15.00**

Cabin In The Sky by John Latouche & Vernon Duke, 1940, Movie: Cabin In The Sky **3.00**

Cadet's March by Leota Stilwell, 1932 (Cover Artist, Hauman & March).**5.00**

Caesar And Cleopatra by North, 1963, Movie: Cleopatra, Photo Richard Burton, Liz Taylor & Rex Harrison....................**14.00**

Cairo by Powell, 1916 (Cover Artist, Pfeiffer)...................**10.00**

Caissons Go Rolling Along, The by Brig. Gen. Edmund L. Gruber, 1936, Movie: Ten Gentlemen From West Point, Photo George Montgomery, Maureen O'Hara & John Sutton (March, Patriotic & Military Personnel) **10.00**

Cake Walk In The Sky, The by Ben Harney, 1899 (Pre 1900 & Black, Black Face) **15.00**

Cake Walk Of The Day by Tony Stanford, 1899 (Pre 1900 & Black, Black Face) **15.00**

Calcium Moon, The by Glen MacDonough & A. Baldwin Sloane, 1910, Movie: The Summer Widowers (Cover Artist, Starmer) **15.00**

Calico Rag by Nat Johnson, 1914 (Rag)....................**10.00**

California And You by Ed Leslie & Harry Puck, 1912, Photo Wilson & Bater (Cover Artist, John Frew) **10.00**

California And You by Edgar Leslie & Harry Puck, 1914, Photo Helene Davis....................**10.00**

California by Cliff Freind & Con Conrad, 1922....................**5.00**

California by Jack Lait & Charlie Abot, 1921 ....**5.00**

California Here I Come by Al Jolson, B.G. DeSylva & Joseph Meyer, 1924, Movie: The Jolson Story (Al Jolson)....................**10.00**

California Sunshine by Harry Jentis, 1913 (Rag) **15.00**

California, There's A Garden By The Golden Gate by Harold Freeman, 1914 (Cover Artist, Pfeiffer) **15.00**

Call It A Day by Robert B. Smith & Victor Herbert, 1919, Musical: Angel Face (Victor Herbert)..................**12.00**

Call Me Baby by Young & Williams, 1913 (Cover Artist, Pfeiffer & Deco) **15.00**

Call Me Back Pal O'Mine by Laurence Perricone & Harold Dixon, 1921, Photo H. Dixon **10.00**

Call Me by Tony Hatch, 1945 ....**2.00**

Call Me Darling, Call Me Sweetheart, Call Me Dear, German Text & Music by Bert Reisfeld, Mort Fryberg & Rolf Marbot, English Text by Dorothy Dick, 1931 ....**3.00**

Call Me Mutton Chops by Robert Colby & Jack Wolf, Photo Capri Sisters..................**5.00**

Call Me Up Some Rainy Afternoon by Irving Berlin, 1910, Photo Ashner Sisters (Cover Artist, John Frew & Irving Berlin) **12.00**

Call Me Up Some Rainy Afternoon by Irving Berlin, 1910, Photo Mary Gibson (Cover Artist, John Frew & Irving Berlin) **12.00**

Call Me Up Some Rainy Afternoon by Irving Berlin, 1910, Photo Max Rogers (Cover Artist, John Frew & Irving Berlin)..................**12.00**

Call Of The Canyon by Billy Hill, 1940..................**3.00**

Call Of The Flag, The by L.D. W. & H. Aide, 1917, Dedicated To Our Soldiers–Gift Of Mrs. L. D. Westfield To American Legion Auxiliary (Patriotic & Dedication) **12.00**

Call Of The South, The by Irving Berlin, 1924, Music Box Review, 1925 (Irving Berlin)..................**10.00**

Call Of The Wild by F. H. Losey, 1904 (March) **10.00**

Call Out The Marines by Mort Greene & Harry Revel, 1942, Movie: Call Out The Marines **5.00**

Call, The by Egbert Van Alstyne, 1918, Dedicated To F.W. Kellogg (Cover Artist, Grafton Studios, WWI, March & Dedication) **25.00**

Call To Arms, The by Baker, 1906 (Patriotic).....................**10.00**

Call To Arms, The by Edward Heyman & Arthur Schwartz, 1936, Movie: That Girl From Paris, Photo Lily Pons **10.00**

Calla Lily Rag by Logan Thane, 1907 (Rag).....................**15.00**

Callahan's Gang by Edward Harrigan & David Braham, 1873 (Pre 1900 & Irish).....................**15.00**

Calling Me Back To You by Blanche Ebert Seaver, 1928 ....**5.00**

Calling Me Home To You by Teschenacher & F. Dobel, 1916, Dedicated to Reginald Kelland (Dedication).....................**5.00**

Calling Sweetheart For You by Schafer & Denison, 1918 (Cover Artist, Pfeiffer & Patriotic).....................**15.00**

Calling To Her Boy Just Once Again by Paul Dresser, 1900 (Patriotic)..**15.00**

Calling You Back To Me by Charles Durham, 1921.....................**5.00**

Calm As The Night by Nathan Haskell Dole & Carl Bohm, 1891 (Pre 1900).....................**5.00**

Calypso by John Denver, 1975, Photo John Denver **3.00**

Camouflage by J. Bodewalt Lampe, 1917.....................**10.00**

Camp Meeting Band by L. Wolfe Gilbert & Lewis F. Muir, 1914 (Black, Black Face) **15.00**

Campmeetin' Time by Henry Williams & Egbert Van Alstyne, 1906 (Black, Black Face) **20.00**

Camptown Races by Stephen Foster, 1860 (Pre 1900 & Stephen Foster).....................**25.00**

Campus Rag by Richmond, 1911 (Rag) **10.00**

Can Anyone Explain? by Bennie Benjamin & George Weiss, 1950, Photo Dinah Shore **3.00**

Can Can Dance by J. Offenbach, 1940 (Cover Artist, Im-Ho)..............**5.00**

Can I Forget You by Oscar Hammerstein II & Jerome Kern, 1937, Movie: High Wide And Handsome, Photo Irene Dunne & Randolph Scott.**10.00**

Can You Bring Back The Heart I Gave You by Wm. R. Clay & Chas. J. Johnson, 1924 ....**5.00**

Can You Imagine by Harry Pease, Fred Mayo & Ed. Nelson, 1919 ....**10.00**

Can You Keep A Secret? by Maurice Dunlop, 1916.....................**5.00**

Can You Pay? For A Broken Heart by Charles K. Harris, 1914 ....**10.00**

Can You Tame Wild Wimmen by Andrew Sterling & Harry Von Tilzer, 1918, Photo Jack Norworth (Cover Artist, Pfeiffer)............10.00

Can't Get Indiana Off My Mind by Robert De Leon & Hoagy Carmichael, 1940 ....**5.00**

Can't Get Out Of This Mood by Frank Loesser & Jimmy McHugh, 1942, Movie: 7 Day's Leave, Photo Victor Mature & Ginny Simms........**5.00**

Can't Help Falling In Love by Peretti, Creatore & Weiss, 1961, Movie: Blue Hawaii, Photo Elvis Presley.............**5.00**

Can't Help Lovin' Dat Man by Oscar Hammerstein II & Jerome Kern, 1927, Movie: Show Boat Presented by Florenz Ziegfeld.............**10.00**

Can't Help Singing by Jerome Kern & E. Y. Harburg, 1944, Movie: Can't Help Singing, Photo Deanna Durbin **8.00**

Can't Lose Me, Charlie by Harry S. Miller, 1893 (Pre 1900) **10.00**

Can't Take My Eyes Off You by Bob Crewe & Bob Gaudio, 1967 .....**3.00**

Can't We Be Friends by Howard Dietz & Arthur Schwartz, 1929 ....**5.00**

Can't We Dream A Midsummer Night's Dream by Joe Young & Fred E. Ahlert, 1935.................**5.00**

Can't We Talk It Over by Ned Washington & Victor Young, 1931, Photo Leighton Noble (Cover Artist, Im-Ho).................**5.00**

Can't Yo' Heah Me Callin' Caroline by Wm. H. Gardner & Caro Roma, 1914 (Black, Black Face) **5.00**

Can't You Be Good? by Geo. W. Meyer, 1909 (Cover Artist, Starmer) .**10.00**

Can't You Do A Friend A Favor by Lorenz Hart & Richard Rodgers, 1927, Musical: A Connecticut Yankee.................**5.00**

Can't You Hear Me Calling Geraldine by Mildred Rhadans, 1932, Photo Irma Glen (Cover Artist, Jeanne Wolf) **5.00**

Can't You Hear Your Country Calling by Victor Herbert, 1918 (WWI & Victor Herbert) **15.00**

Can't You Just See Yourself by Sammy Cahn & Jules Styne, 1948, Musical: High Button Shoes.................**7.00**

Can't You Love Me Like You Do In Dreams by Weeks, 1918 ....**5.00**

Can't You See, How I Love You? by Roy Turk & Fred E. Ahlert, 1931 .**5.00**

Can't You See My Heart Beats All For You? by Bert Fitzgibbon & Theodore Morse, 1904.................**10.00**

Can't You Take It Back And Change It For A Boy by Thurland Chattaway, 1911 ....**10.00**

Can't You Understand? by Jack Osterman & Victor Young, 1929 (Cover Artist, Pud & Deco).................**5.00**

Can't Your Friend Get A Friend For Me by Herman Ruby & Lou Handman, 1924 ....**5.00**

Canadian Capers by Gus Chandler, Bert White & Henry Cohen, 1915 (Cover Artist, S.D. & Deco).................**10.00**

Canadian Sunset by Norman Gimbel & Eddie Heywood, 1956.............**2.00**

Candied Cherries by Lucien Denni, 1911 (Rag).................**15.00**

Candle In The Window, A by Mitchell Parish, Charles O'Flynn & Lee David, 1934 ....**5.00**

Candlelight by H. A. Ketchum, 1914 (March) **10.00**

Candy by Mack David, Joan Whitney & Alex Kramer, 1944, Photo Dinning Sisters **3.00**

Candy by Mack David, Joan Whitney & Alex Kramer, 1944, Photo King Sisters.................**2.00**

Candy Dolly by Jessie L. Gaynor, 1959 (Cover Artist, Ivy Bottini) **3.00**

Candy Kisses by George Morgan, 1948, Photo George Morgan **3.00**

Candy Man, The by Bricusse & Newley, 1971, Movie: Willy Wonka & The Chocolate Factory, Photo Gene Wilder & Jack Albertson........**6.00**

Cannibal Rag by Ed. Dangel & Chas. Frank, 1911 (Rag) **10.00**

Cannon Ball by Joseph C. Northup, 1905 ....**5.00**

Canny Sandy by R. Barclay Brown, 1925, Musical Farce: The Jail Birds (Cover Artist, E.S. Fisher).................**3.00**

Capparian March by E.C. Cary, 1895 (Pre 1900 & March) **15.00**

Caprola by Schultz, 1918 (Cover Artist, Pfeiffer) **15.00**

Captain Betty by Lionel Baxter, 1914 (Cover Artist, Carter & March)..**15.00**

Captain Riley Of The U.S.A. by Ella M. Smith, Vernon Strout & Howard I. Smith, 1919 (WWI, Patriotic & Irish).................**10.00**

Captain Swagger by Weinberg & Bibo, 1928, Movie: Captain Swagger, Photo Rod LaRocque & Sue Carol.................**5.00**

Captain, The by Margaret Darrell & James H. Rogers, 1903.............**10.00**

Captains Of The Clouds by J. Mercer & H. Arlen, 1918 (WWI)........**15.00**

Captive Maid, The by George H. Clutsam, 1905 ....**10.00**

Captive, The by David H. Hawthorne, 1909 (March) **15.00**

Cara Mia by Tulio Trapani & Lee Lange, 1954, Photo David Whitfield .**3.00**

Cara Mia by Tulio Trapani & Lee Lange, 1954, Photo Tino Rossi, Small Folio.................**5.00**

Caravan Of Dreams by Fred Ahlert, 1947, Photo Bing Crosby **6.00**

Carbolic Acid Rag by Clarence C. Wiley, 1904 (Cover Artist, DeTakacs & Rag) **20.00**

Careless Hands by Bob Hilliard & Carl Sigman 1949, Photo John Laurenz **3.00**

Careless Rhapsody by Lorenz Hart & Richard Rodgers, 1942, Movie: All's Fair.................**6.00**

Carelessly by Charles & Nick Kenny & Norman Ellis, 1937, Photo Jerry Johnson (Cover Artist, Merman).................**5.00**

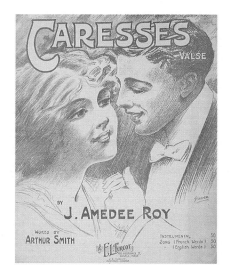

Caresses by Arthur Smith & J. Amedee Roy, 1915 (Cover Artist, Starmer) 10.00

Caresses by James V. Monaco, 1920, Photo Alice Delysia (Cover Artist, Wohlman & Deco).................**10.00**

Carioca by Gus Kahn, Edward Eliscu & Vincent Youmans, 1933, Movie: Flying Down To Rio, Photo Fred Astaire & Dolores Del Rio (Cover Artist, Harris).................**10.00**

Carissima by Arthur A. Penn, 1905 ....**5.00**

Carlo, The by Freed & Brown, 1937, Photo Nelson Eddy **3.00**

Carlotta by Bacher, 1914 (Cover Artist, Pfeiffer).................**10.00**

Carlotta by Cole Porter, 1943, Movie: Can Can **5.00**

Carmen by Georges Bizet **5.00**

Carmen, Carmela by Bobby Worth, Freddy Martin & Ray Austin, 1942.**5.00**

Carmena by Walton & Wilson (Cover Artist, Pfeiffer).................**15.00**

Carnations by Sherwin, 1929, Movie: The Carnation Kid, Photo Douglas Maclean & Frances Lee **5.00**

Carnations March by Tierney, 1911 (Cover Artist, Pfeiffer & March) .**15.00**

Carnival King, The by Ralph K. Elicker & E.T. Paull, 1911 (Cover Artist, E.T. Paull & March) **35.00**

Carnival Of Venice by Barclay Gray & Paganinni, 1940 (Cover Artist, NPS).................**5.00**

Carolina by Lew Brown & Jay Gorney, 1939, Movie: Carolina, Photo Janet Gaynor **5.00**

Carolina Cake Walk, A by Max Dreyfus, 1898 (Pre 1900 & Black, Black Face) **22.00**

Carolina Cake Walk by George D. Mears, 1899 (Pre 1900 & Black, Black Face) **22.00**

Carolina Fox Trot by Will Vodery, 1914 ....**5.00**

Carolina In The Morning by Gus Kahn & Walter Donaldson, 1922, Photo Mildred Patrick **8.00**

Carolina In The Morning by Gus Kahn & Walter Donaldson, 1922, Photo Glad Moffatt **8.00**

Carolina Mammy by Billy James, 1923, Photo Aunt Jemima (Cover Artist, JVR & Black, Black Face) **35.00**

Carolina Mine by Friend & Rosoff, 1926 ....**5.00**

Carolina Moon by Benny Davis & Joe Burke, 1928, Photo Gene Austin (Cover Artist, Leff & Deco) **6.00**

Carolina Moon by Benny Davis & Joe Burke, 1928, Photo Wendell Hall (Cover Artist, Leff & Deco) **6.00**

Carolina Moon by Sam Braverman & Leon Close, 1924 ....**5.00**

Carolina Rolling Stone by Mitchell Parish, Eleanor Young & Harry D. Squires, 1921, Photo Willie & Eugene Howard (Cover Artist, Hoffman) **5.00**

Carolina Sunshine by Walter Hirsch & Erwin R. Schmidt, 1919 (Cover Artist, Barbelle & Black, Black Face) **15.00**

Carolina Sweetheart by Billy James, 1925 ....**5.00**

Carolina's Calling Me by Bob Charles, 1931, Photo Alice Joy, Introduced On Radio by Alice Joy, The Prince Albert Dream Girl (Cover Artist, Leff) **20.00**

Caroline, I'm Coming Back To You by Jack Caddigan & James McHugh, 1916 ....**10.00**

Carry Me Back To Connemara by Brennan & Story, 1915 (Cover Artist, Pfeiffer & Irish) **15.00**

Carry Me Back To Old Virginny by James Bland, 1906 (Black, Black Face & Dixie) **25.00**

Carry On by Stanley Maxted, Gordon V. Thompson & Ernest Dainty, 1939 ....**5.00**

Cascades, The (St. Louis World's Fair) by Scott Joplin, 1904 (Scott Joplin & Rag) **50.00**

Casey Jones, The Brave Engineer by Siebert & Newton, 1909 (Transportation) **25.00**

Casey Jones Went Down On The Robert E. Lee by Lee & Jones, 1912 (Transportation) **20.00**

Casey Social Club by Edward Harrigan & David Braham, 1878 (Pre 1900) **15.00**

Casey, The Pride Of Them All by Ray Gilbert, Ken Darby & Eliot Daniel, 1946, Movie: Make Mine Music (Disney) **10.00**

Casey's Wife by Joe Flynn, 1889 (Pre 1900) **15.00**

Cashmere by Peter DeRose, 1921, Dedicated To Miss Helen Powers (Dedication) **6.00**

Castanets by Christine Rebe, 1929 (Cover Artist, D.G. Hauman) **3.00**

Castle House Rag by James Reese Europe, 1914 (Rag) **15.00**

Castle Of Dreams by Joseph McCarthy & Harry Tierney, 1919, Musical: Irene (Deco) **5.00**

Castle Valse Classique by Ford Dabney, 1914 ....**5.00**

Castles In The Air by Jerome Kern, 1916 ....**5.00**

Cat And The Fiddle, The by Carleton Lee Colby **5.00**

Cat's Whiskers by Fred Tibbot & George Rex, 1923 ....**5.00**

Cat's Whiskers, The by Ed Glastone & Felix Austead, 1923 ....**5.00**

Cataract Rag by Robert Hampton, 1914 (Rag) **15.00**

Catch A Falling Star by Paul Vance & Le Pockriss, 1957, Photo Perry Como **6.00**

Cathedral Chimes by Arnold & Brown, 1913 (Cover Artist, E.S. Fisher) **10.00**

Cathedral Chimes by Arnold & Brown, 1914 (Cover Artist, Pfeiffer) **15.00**

Cathedral Echoes by Caro Roma, 1915 (Cover Artist, Pfeiffer & Deco) **15.00**

Cathedral In The Pines by Charles & Nick Kenny, 1938, Photo Henry Busse (Cover Artist, Merman) **3.00**

Cathedral Morning Chimes by John Martin, 1913 (Deco) **5.00**

Cattle Call, The by Tex Owens, 1943 ....**3.00**

Caucus Race, The by Bob Hilliard & Sammy Fain, 1951, Movie: Alice In Wonderland (Disney) **15.00**

Cauldron Rag, The by Wenrich & Christenson, 1911 (Rag) **15.00**

'Cause I'm In Love by Walter Donaldson, 1928 ....**5.00**

Cause My Baby Says It's So by Al Dubin & Harry Warren, 1937, Movie: The Singing Marines, Photo Dick Powell & Doris Weston (Transportation) **12.00**

Cavalleria Rusticana by Paul Milliet & P. Mascagni **5.00**

Ce Sera Le Pardon by Alcide Giroux, 1917 (Cover Artist, LaForest) **10.00**

Cecile by Frank W. McKee, 1914 ....**10.00**

Cecilia by Herman Ruby & Dave Dreyer, 1925, Photo Dick Jurgens **3.00**

Cecilia by Herman Ruby & Dave Dreyer, 1925, Photo Loomis Orchestra (Deco) **10.00**

Celistia by Bert Grant & Joe Young, 1915 ....**5.00**

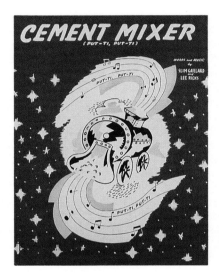

Cement Mixer, Put-Ti, Put-Ti by Slim Gaillard & Lee Ricks, 1946 .5.00

Century Of Progress by John Philip Sousa, 1931 (John Philip Sousa & March) **20.00**

Champagne by Joseph P. Lamb, 1910 (Rag) **15.00**

Champagne Time by George Cates, 1961, Photo Lawrence Welk **5.00**

Champagne Waltz, The by Con Conrad, Ben Oakland & Milton Drake, 1939, Movie: The Champagne Waltz, Photo Gladys Swarthout & Fred McMurray **12.00**

Chances Are by Al Stillman & Robert Allen, 1957, Photo Johnny Mathis .**3.00**

Change Of Heart, A by Harold Adamson & Jule Styne, 1943, Movie: Hit Parade of 1943, Photo John Carroll, Susan Hayward & Many Other Stars **6.00**

Change Partners by Irving Berlin, 1938, Movie: Carefree, Photo Fred Astaire & Ginger Rogers (Cover Artist, Merman & Irving Berlin) ..**10.00**

Changes by Walter Donaldson, 1927 ....**3.00**

Chanson Du Coeur Brise by Maurice Vaucaire, Clarence Lucas & DeMoya, 1914 ....**5.00**

Chant Du 111e Centenaire by R. P. Georges Boileau & Charles Emile Gadbois **5.00**

Chant Of The Jungle by Arthur Freed & Nacio Herb Brown, 1929, Movie: Untamed, Photo Joan Crawford **15.00**

Chante Moi by Mack David, Photo Edith Piaf **5.00**

Chantecleer by Jeanne Delmar, 1910 (Cover Artist, Starmer & March) ..**10.00**

Chapel Bells by Harold Adamson & Jimmy McHugh, 1938, Movie: Mad About Music, Photo Deanna Durbin **8.00**

Chapel By The Sea by M. Greenwald, 1913 ....**5.00**

Chapel Chimes by M. Greenwald, 1916 ....**5.00**

Chapel In The Forest by A. Jungman, 1914 ....**5.00**

Chapel In The Mountains, The by G.D. Wilson, 1887, (Lithograph by Forbes Co. & Pre 1900) **25.00**

Chapel In The Woods by Gustave Lange, 1913 ....**5.00**

Charade by Mancini, 1963, Movie: Charade, Photo Cary Grant & Audrey Hepburn **10.00**

Charanga, The by Hal David & Marco Rizo, Photo Merv Griffin **3.00**

Charcoal, A Study In Black by Gibson Cooke, 1913 (March & Black, Black Face)..................................**15.00**

Charge Of The Light Brigade by E.T. Paull, 1898 (Cover Artist, E.T.Paull, Pre 1900 & March) **35.00**

Charge Of The Uhlans by Bohm, 1908 (Cover Artist, Pfeiffer & Patriotic) **15.00**

Charge, The by Jacob Henry Ellis, 1913 ....**5.00**

Chari Vari by Edwards, 1914 (Cover Artist, Pfeiffer)..................................**15.00**

Charity Begins At Home by Aleen Moss, W. W. Denslow & Maurice Levi, 1915..................................**5.00**

Charlatan March, The by John Philip Sousa, 1888, Photo John Philip Sousa (Pre 1900, March & John Philip Sousa) **30.00**

Charleston Blues by Edward Harrigan & David Braham, 1882 (Blues & Pre 1900)..................................**15.00**

Charleston by Cecil Mack & Jimmy Johnson, 1923, Musical: Runnin' Wild **3.00**

Charleston Rag, The by Eubie Blake, 1899 (Pre 1900 & Rag) **20.00**

Charley My Boy by Gus Kahn & Ted Fiorito, 1924, Dedicated To Charley Foy (Cover Artist, R.S., Deco & Dedication) **10.00**

Charley My Boy by Gus Kahn & Ted Fiorito, 1924, Photo Andrews Sisters, Lisa Kirk, Russ Morgan, Ted Phillips, Tony Pastor & Louis Prima (Cover Artist, Nick) **10.00**

Charlie Chaplin: The Funniest Of Them All by George Boyden, 1915, Photo Charlie Chaplin **20.00**

Charmaine by Erno Rapee & Lew Pollack, 1927, Photo Bernie Cummins (Cover Artist, Barbelle, Patriotic & Deco)..................................**15.00**

Charmaine by Erno Rapee & Lew Pollack, 1927, Photo Jack Housh & Marie Patri (Cover Artist, Barbelle, Patriotic & Deco)..................................**15.00**

Charmina by Yenomah & Rosas, 1925 (Cover Artist, Pfeiffer)..........**10.00**

Charming by Clifford Grey & Herbert Stothart, 1929, Movie: Devil May Care..................................**5.00**

Chase Me I'm Single by Bert Grant, 1913, Photo Florence Tempest ..**10.00**

Chasing Shadows by Benny Davis & Abner Silver, 1935 ....**5.00**

Chateau Three Step by Donaldson, 1916 (Cover Artist, Pfeiffer)........**15.00**

Chattahoochie by Billy Rose, Al Dubin & Sammy Fain, 1924, Photo Billy Glason (Cover Artist, Starmer)..................................**8.00**

Chattanooga Blues by Maceo Pincard, 1916 (Cover Artist, Pfeiffer) ..**15.00**

Chattanooga Choo Choo by Mack Gordon & Harry Warren, 1941, Movie: Sun Valley Serenade, Photo Sonja Henie, John Payne & Glenn Miller......**15.00**

Chattanoogie Shoe Shine Boy by Harry Stone & Jack Stapp, 1950 (Black, Black Face)..................................**4.00**

Chatter-Box by Havez & Silvers, 1920, Movie: Way Down East, Photo Lillian Gish **10.00**

Chatterbox Rag by George Botsford, 1910 (Rag) **10.00**

Chauffeur And The Debutante, The by Vincent Lopez & Hugo Rubens, 1936 ....**5.00**

Chauffeur, The by Cobb, 1906 (Transportation) **15.00**

Che! by Schifrin, 1969, Movie: Che!, Photo Omar Sharif **4.00**

Cheating Muchachita by Marjorie Harper, Alfredo Lepera & Carlos Gardel, 1935, Movie: The Big Broadcast Of 1935..................................**5.00**

Checkers by Edgar Allen & Leo Edwards, 1919, Movie: Checkers, Dedicated To Winnie Sheehan (Dedication & Deco) **12.00**

Checkers Rag by Harry J. Lincoln, 1913 (Rag)..................................**15.00**

Cheek To Cheek by Irving Berlin, 1935, Movie: Top Hat, Photo Fred Astaire & Ginger Rogers (Irving Berlin)..................................**16.00**

Cheer Up Father, Cheer Up Mother by Alfred Bryan & Herman Paley, 1918, Photo Louise Dresser (Cover Artist, E.E. Walton & WWI) **15.00**

Cheer Up Little Darling by Morris Manley, 1917, Photo Of Little Mildred (WWI)..................................**15.00**

Cheer Up Liza by Ray Hubbell, 1917..................................**10.00**

Cheer Up Mary by Alfred Bryan & Herman Paley, 1906 ....**12.00**

Cheerful Blues by Abe Olman, 1917 (Blues) **10.00**

Cherie by Leo Wood & Irving Bibo, 1919 ....**10.00**

Cherie I Love You by Lillian Rosedale Goodman, 1926, Signed Photo Grace Moore (Signed) **10.00**

Cherries, The by Marois & Dartmouth, 1952, Photo Doris Day **3.00**

Cherry Blossoms by Emma I. Hart, 1907 ....**5.00**

Cherry Leaf Rag by Ed Cota, 1909 (Rag)..................................**10.00**

Chestnut Tree, The by Jimmy Kennedy, Tommie Connor & Hamilton Kennedy, 1938, Photo King George VI **8.00**

Chevy Chase by Eubie Blake, 1914 (Rag) **15.00**

Chew, Chew, Chew, Chew Your Bubble Gum by Ella Fitzgerald, Chick Webb & Buck Ram, 1939..................................**5.00**

Chewin' The Rag by Fred Heltman, 1912, Photo Heltman At The Piano (Rag)..................................**10.00**

Cheyenne by Harry Williams & Egbert Van Alstyne, 1906..................**5.00**

Chic, Chic, Chic, Chic, Chicken by Dave Buck & Dave Stamper, 1913.**12.00**

Chicago by Fred Fisher, 1922, Photo Paul Whiteman's Arcadia Orchestra (Cover Artist, Politzer) **8.00**

Chicago by Fred Fisher, 1922, Signed by Fred Fisher (Signed)..........**35.00**

Chicago Express, The by Percy Wenrich, 1905 (Transportation) **15.00**

Chicka Boom by Bob Merrill, 1953 ....**5.00**

Chicken by Bob Cole & Billy Johnson, 1899 (Pre 1900)..................**15.00**

Chicken Chowder by Irene Giblin, 1905 (Rag) **15.00**

Chicken Reel by Joesph M. Daly, 1910..................................**15.00**

Chickery Chick by Sylvia Dee & Sidney Lippman, 1945 (Cover Artist, Barbelle..................................**8.00**

Childhood by Alfred Bryan & Kerry Mills, 1908 ....**15.00**

Childhood Days by Nola Arndt, 1921 ....**10.00**

Childhood Joys by Adelaide K. Mills, 1912..................................**5.00**

Childhood Scenes by Chas. King, 1914 (Cover Artist, Pfeiffer)..........**15.00**

Chili Bean by Lew Brown & Albert Von Tilzer, 1920, Photo Aileen Stanley (Cover Artist, R.S.)..................................**5.00**

Chili Sauce Rag by Max Fischer, 1910 (Rag) **15.00**

Chills And Fever by Theron C. Bennett, 1912 (Rag) **10.00**

Chilly Con Carney, 1907 (Cover Artist, Pfeiffer)..................................**15.00**

Chim Chim Cher-ee by Richard M. Sherman & Robert B. Sherman, 1963, Movie: Mary Poppins, Photo Julie Andrews & Dick Van Dyke (Disney)..................................**10.00**

Chimes At Twilight by Wolff, 1908 (Cover Artist, Pfeiffer) **15.00**

Chimes Of Normandy by Jack Wells, & Alfred Bryan, 1917 (WWI)....**5.00**

Chimes Of Spring by Paul Lincke, 1930 ....**5.00**

Chimes Of Venice by R. G. Grodi, 1912......................**5.00**

Chimes, The by Harry Armstrong, 1912 (Cover Artist, DeTakacs).....**10.00**

Chiming Bells by L. G. Webster, 1914......................**3.00**

Chin-Chin by A. Seymour Brown, 1915, Musical Hip Hip Hooray At N.Y. Hippodrome (Cover Artist, Starmer).....................**15.00**

Chin-Chin Chinaman by Joe Goodwin, Ballard Macdonald & James F. Hanley, 1917 (Cover Artist, J. Hirt) **5.00**

China Dreams by Raymond Egan, Gus Kahn & Edgar Van Alstyne, 1917......................**10.00**

Chinatown My Chinatown by Wm. Jerome & Jean Schwartz, 1910 (Cover Artist, Flo Cooney).....................**10.00**

Chinese Blues by Moore, 1915 (Blues).....................**5.00**

Chinese Firecrackers by Irving Berlin, 1920, Ziegfeld Follies, 1920 (Cover Artist, R.S. & Irving Berlin) **16.00**

Chinese Lullaby by Robert Hood Bowers, 1919, Musical: East Is West, Photo Fay Bainter **6.00**

Ching A Ling's Jazz Bazaar by Howard Johnson & Ethel Bridges, 1920 (Cover Artist, L.S. Reiss & Jazz) **10.00**

Ching Chong by J. Will Callahan & Lee S. Roberts, 1917 (Cover Artist, Standard Photo Engraving).....................**10.00**

Chiquita by L. Wolfe Gilbert & Mabel Wayne, 1928 (Deco) **5.00**

Chitty Chitty Bang Bang by Sherman & Sherman, 1968, Movie: Chitty Chitty Bang Bang, Photo Dick Van Dyke & Sally Ann Howes.......**8.00**

Chlo-e by Gus Kahn & Neil Moret, 1927 Photo Lucille Benstead (Cover Artist, Rangley Studio) **5.00**

Chocolate Choo-Choo, The by Ted Varnick & Wilton Moore, 1947 ....**5.00**

Chocolate Soldier, The by Oscar Straus & Stanislaus Strange, 1909 (Cover Artist, DeTakacs).....................**15.00**

Chong by Harold Weeks, 1919, Small Folio **10.00**

Choo-Choo by Matt Malneck & Frank Trumbauer, 1930, Photo Paul Whiteman (Cover Artist, Barbelle & Transportation).....................**10.00**

Chopin's Polonaise by Harold Potter & Eddie Dorr, 1945, Photo Frederick Chopin **5.00**

Chopsticks by Jack Lawrence & Elliot Daniels, 1939, Photo The Merry Macs (Cover Artist, Im-Ho & Deco).....................**6.00**

Christ Child, The by Dr. Helen Hughes Heilscher & Margaret Zender Beaulieu, 1938 ....**5.00**

Christ Child, The by G.K. Chesterton & Florence Bass, 1942...............**5.00**

Christmas Candle by Kate Louise Brown & Elinor Remick Warren, 1940.....................**2.00**

Christmas Chimes by F. W. Vandersloot, 1915 (Cover Artist, Pfeiffer).....................**15.00**

Christmas Day by Benny Davis & Ted Murry, 1952, Photo Eddie Fisher **3.00**

Christmas In Killarney by John Redmond, James Cavanaugh & Frank Weldon, 1940 (Irish).....................**5.00**

Christmas Song, The by Mel Torme & Robert Wells, 1946 ....**3.00**

Christmas Time Seems Years & Years Away by Irving Berlin (Cover Artist, Pfeiffer & Irving Berlin).....................**15.00**

Christofo Columbo by Speed Langworthy, 1924 ....**5.00**

Christopher Robin Is Saying His Prayers by A. A. Milne & Fraser Simpson, 1941 ....**5.00**

Chrysanthemum Rag, The by Scott Joplin, 1904 (Scott Joplin & Rag) ..**50.00**

Chu-Chi Face by Sherman & Sherman, 1968, Movie: Chitty Chitty Bang Bang, Photo Dick Van Dyke & Sally Ann Howes **8.00**

Church Across The Way by William B. Gray, 1894 (Pre 1900) **15.00**

Church Bells Are Ringing For Mary, The by Elmer Colby, 1927.........**8.00**

Church In The Wildwood, The by Nick Manoloff, 1935 (Cover Artist, LK).....................**5.00**

Cielito Lindo by Jerry Castillo & G. Fernandez, 1935, Photo Eddie Howard **3.00**

Cigarette by John Densmore, 1914.....................**5.00**

Cincinnat-Ti Dancing Pig by Al Lewis & Guy Wood, 1950, Photo Red Foley **3.00**

Cincinnati by Matthew Ott, 1916 (Cover Artist, E.S. Fisher) **5.00**

Cincinnati Enquirer, The by B.F. Kleinbeck, 1901 (March) **10.00**

Cinda Lou by Charles Beetho & Jas. S. Summer, 1919 (Cover Artist, Balcom & Deco) **10.00**

Cinderella by Mack David, Al Hoffman & Jerry Livingston, 1948, Movie: Cinderella (Disney).....................**10.00**

Cinderella by W. C. Powell, 1906 ....**10.00**

Cinderella Sue by Jerome Kern, 1946, Movie: Centennial Summer, Photo Jeanne Crain, Cornel Wilde, Linda Darnell & Wm. Eythe **5.00**

Cindy by Harold Atteridge & Bert Grant, 1920 (Cover Artist, Barbelle)..**10.00**

Cinna Mon Sinner (Selling Lollipop Lies), 1954, Photo Tony Bennett .**6.00**

Circus by Bob Russell & Louis Alter, 1949 ....**4.00**

Circus Days by DeCosta, 1923, Movie: Circus Days, Photo Jackie Coogan.....................**5.00**

Circus Life by Harry J. Lincoln, 1914 (Cover Artist, Pfeiffer) **15.00**

Circus Parade March by E. T. Paull (Cover Artist, E.T. Paull & March)..**35.00**

Circus World by Washington & Tiomkin, 1964, Movie: Circus World, Photo Claudia Cardinale, Rita Hayworth & John Wayne **5.00**

Ciribiribin by A. Pestalozza, 1935, Photo Jan Garber **5.00**

City Of Dreams by Guy Boton, P.G. Wodehouse & Louis A. Hirsch, 1918, Musical: Oh, My Dear **5.00**

Civilization by Victor Schertzinger, 1916, Signed by Artist, Thomas H. Inck (Cover Artist, Rose Symbol, March & Signed) **10.00**

Cla-Wrench, Don't Tweat Me So Wuff by Manuel, 1923 (Transportation & Black, Black Face).....................**20.00**

Clam Bake by Elvis Presley.....................**20.00**

Clancy's Trotter by William B. Glenway, 1890 (Pre 1900)...............**15.00**

Clap Hands For Freedom by Pease, Nelson & Dupre, 1918 (WWI)....**15.00**

Clap Yo' Hands by George & Ira Gershwin, 1930.....................**10.00**

Clap Yo' Hands by Ira & George Gershwin, 1926, Musical: Oh, Kay! .**10.00**

Clap Your Hands If You Want A Little Lovin', 1919 (Cover Artist, Pfeiffer) **16.00**

Clara Jenkins' Tea by Edward Harrigan & David Braham, 1881 (Pre 1900).....................**10.00**

Clavelitos by J. Valverde, 1941, Movie: It Started With Eve, Photo Deanna Durbin.....................**5.00**

Clayton's Grant March by Blake, 1905 (March).....................**15.00**

Clef Club Grand March, The by Europe, 1910 (Cover Artist, Pfeiffer & March).....................**15.00**

Cleopatra by Alfred Bryan & Harry Tierney, 1917, Musical: Sinbad, Photo Al Jolson (Al Jolson).....................**12.00**

Cleopatra Had A Jazz Band by Morgan, 1906 (Jazz).....................**15.00**

Clicquot by Harry F. Reser, 1926, March Featured by Clicquot Club Eskimos, Photo Clicquot Club Eskimos (March & Advertising).........**30.00**

Climax Rag by James Scott, 1914 (Rag) **10.00**

Climb A Tree With Me by Charles K. Harris, 1912 (Cover Artist, Scott & Van Altena).....................**10.00**

Climb Ev'ry Mountain by Richard Rodgers & Oscar Hammerstein II, 1959, Movie: The Sound Of Music, Photo Julie Andrews & Christopher Plummer **5.00**

Climb Ev'ry Mountain by Richard Rodgers & Oscar Hammerstein II, 1959 (Cover Artist, George Martin).....................**5.00**

Climb On Top Of Your Troubles And Smile Just Smile by Frank & Carl Wilson, 1920 (Lithograph by Knapp).....................**10.00**

Climbing Up The Golden Stairs by Monroe Rosenfeld, 1884 (Pre 1900) .**15.00**

Climbing Up The Ladder Of Love by Raymond Klages & Jesse Grier, 1926, Musical: Earl Carroll Vanities, 5th Edition **10.00**

Climbing Up The Scale by Irving Berlin, 1923, Musical: Music Box Revue 1923-24 (Cover Artist, R.S., Irving Berlin & Deco)..........**10.00**

Cling A Little Closer by Mitchell Parish & Erwin Kent, 1947 ....**5.00**

Clinging Vine, The by Harold Levey & Zelda Seal, 1922, Musical: The Clinging Vine **6.00**

Close by Cole Porter, 1937, Movie: Rosalie **6.00**

Close Dem Windows by James Bland, 1880 (Pre 1900 & Black, Black Face) **20.00**

Close To Me by Sam M. Lewis & Peter Derose, 1936, Photo George Hall (Cover Artist, Jorj Harris).....................................**5.00**

Close To My Heart by Andrew B. Sterling & Harry Von Tilzer, 1915 (Cover Artist, Rose Symbol) **10.00**

Close To You by Al Hoffman, Jerry Livingston & Carl G. Lampl, 1943, Photo Frank Sinatra **5.00**

Close Your Eyes by Bernice Petkere, 1933.............................**4.00**

Cloud Kisser by Raymond Birch, 1911 (Rag & Transportation) **25.00**

Clover Blossoms by Jean Herbert & Floyd Thompson, 1932, Photo Snooks **5.00**

Cluck! Cluck! Cluck!, Said The Little Red Hen by Kenny Raught & Curley Mahr, 1941 ....**5.00**

Co-Ed by J.S. Zamecnik, 1914 (March) **10.00**

Coach & Four, A by Jerry Livingston & Ray Evans, 1946 (Transportation)..**5.00**

Coal Black Mammy by Laddie Cliff & Ivy St. Helier, 1921 (Black, Black Face) **15.00**

Coal Smoke by Clarence H. St. Johns, 1904 (Rag) **15.00**

Coaling Up In Colon Town by Ray Egan & Richard A. Whiting, 1916 (Cover Artist, Starmer & Black, Black Face).......................**20.00**

Coax Me by Andrew Sterling & Harry Von Tilzer, 1904, Photo Jesse Mitchell..**10.00**

Coax Me A Little Bit by Charles Tobias & Mat Simon, 1946, Photo Andrews Sisters (Cover Artist, Barbelle).......................**5.00**

Cobbler's Song by Frederick Norton, 1916 ....**5.00**

Cock Eyed Optimist, A by Richard Rodgers & Oscar Hammerstein II, 1949, Musical: South Pacific (Cover Artist, BJH) **5.00**

Cockeyed Mayor Of Kaunakakai, The by Al Stillman & R. Alex Anderson, 1935, Photo Guy Lombardo....................................**5.00**

Cocktails For Two by Arthur Johnston & Sam Coslow, 1934, Movie: Murder At The Vanities (Deco)....................................12.00

Cocoanut Grove by Harry Owens, 1938, Movie: Cocoanut Grove........**6.00**

Coffee Time by Freed & Warren, 1945, Movie: Yolanda And The Thief, Photo Fred Astaire & Lucille Bremer....................................**5.00**

Cohan's Pet Names by George M. Cohan, 1908, Musical: The American Idea (George M. Cohan)..**20.00**

Cohen Owes Me $97 by Irving Berlin, 1915 (Irving Berlin) **15.00**

Col. Stevenson's Quick Step by Rodwitska, To The Mass 24th, Photo Col. Stevenson, VERY RARE (L. Prang & Co., Lithography & Military Personnel) **75.00**

Cold, Cold Heart by Hank Williams, 1951, Photo Tony Bennett **4.00**

Coldest Coon In Town, The by Andrew Sterling & Harry Von Tilzer, 1899 (Pre 1900 & Black, Black Face)..**35.00**

College Life by Jack Drislane & Henry Frantzen, 1905, Dedicated To The College Students Of America (Cover Artist, E.P.C., March & Dedication)..**15.00**

College Rhythm by Mack Gordon & Harry Revel, 1934, Movie: College Rhythm, Photo Joe Penner, Lanny Ross, Jack Oakie & Helen Mack..**5.00**

College Swing by Frank Loesser & Hoagy Carmichael, 1938, Movie: College Swing **6.00**

College Swing by Loesseo & Carmichael, 1938, Movie: College Swing, Photo Betty Grable, Bob Hope, Burns & Allen, Ben Blue, John Payne & Martha Raye **14.00**

College Yell by John F. Barth, 1908 ....**15.00**

College Yell March by J.S. Jamecnik, 1908 (March)..........................**15.00**

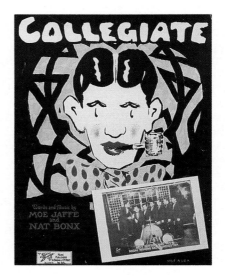

Collegiate by Moe Jaffe & Nat Bonx, 1925, Photo Billy Burton & His Medal Winning Radio Orchestra (Deco)....................................10.00

Colonel Bogey by Alford, 1916, Movie: The Bridge On The River Kwai, Photo Alec Guiness, William Holden & Jack Hawkins.................**12.00**

Colonel Buffalo Bill by Irving Berlin, 1946, Movie: Annie Get Your Gun (Irving Berlin)..**12.00**

Colonial Days by Bob Winter, 1917..**5.00**

Colonial Love by Calvin Grooms, 1913...**5.00**

Colonial Rag by Ernest R. Ball & Julius Lenzberg, 1914 ....**5.00**

Color My World by James Pankow, 1970...**3.00**

Colorado by Hirsch & Dillon, 1924..**5.00**

Colored Four Hundred, The by J.W. Wheeler, 1890 (Pre 1900 & March)..**25.00**

Columbia by Seneca G. Lewis, 1917, Photo Hazel Dawn, Signed by Seneca Lewis & Jerome Remick Co. The Author Has Assigned And The Publisher Contracts To Duplicate To 'The New York Sun's Tobacco Fund' All Royalty Earnings Of The Patriotic March "Columbia" To Provide Smokes For Our Soldiers In France During The War And To Be Used Subsequently For Our War Relief Measures As This Paper May Designate. (WWI, Pariotic, March & Signed)...........**25.00**

Columbia Patrol, The by E.S. Phelps (Patriotic) **15.00**

Columbia The Gem Of The Ocean by David T. Shaw, 1843 (Pre 1900 & Patriotic) **25.00**

Columbus Day March by Peter Tesio, 1909 (Cover Artist, Pfeiffer & March) **15.00**

Come After Breakfast by Chris Smith, 1909 (Black, Black Face) **12.00**

Come Along Boys by Jefford, 1917 (WWI) **16.00**

Come Along by Irving Berlin, 1920, Ziegfeld Follies Of 1920 (Cover Artist, R.S., Irving Berlin & Deco) **10.00**

Come Along Little Girl by Alfred Bryan & J.B. Mullen, 1905 ....**10.00**

Come Along Ma Honey, Down Upon The Swanee by Harold Weeks, 1917 (Black, Black Face) **15.00**

Come Along Sinners by M. H. Rosenfeld, 1881 (Black, Black Face & Pre 1900) **10.00**

Come And Dream With Me In A Persian Garden by Fleta Jan Brown, 1914 (Cover Artist, Starmer) **6.00**

Come And Kiss Your Little Baby by Lew Brown & Albert Von Tilzer, 1912 ....**5.00**

Come Away Little Girl, 1910 (Cover Artist, Pfeiffer) **15.00**

Come Back by Charles K. Harris, 1916 ....**5.00**

Come Back by Evans Lloyd, 1920 (Lithograph, Knapp Co.) **5.00**

Come Back Charleston Blue by Jones, Cleveland & Hathaway, 1972, Movie: Come Back Charleston Blue, Photo Godfrey Cambridge & Raymond St. Jacques **4.00**

Come Back, Dixie by Jack Mahoney & Percy Wenrich, 1915, Photo Dolly Connolly (Dixie & Deco) **10.00**

Come Back, Dixie by Jack Mahoney & Percy Wenrich, 1915, Photo Mae Francis (Dixie & Deco) **10.00**

Come Back, Dixie by Jack Mahoney & Percy Wenrich, 1915, Photo Rooney & Russell (Dixie & Deco) **10.00**

Come Back, Kathleen by Harry B. Norman & Theodore Westman, 1905, Photo Clarice Vance (Cover Atist, E.F.W. & Irish) **10.00**

Come Back Little Girl by Augustus Barratt, 1915, Musical: Girl From Utah (Cover Artist AF) **12.00**

Come Back To Arizona by Alfred Bryan & Herman Paley, 1916 (Cover Artist, Starmer) **10.00**

Come Back To Connemara by M.E. Rourke & Frank H. Grey, 1907, Photo Marie Bordouex (Cover Artist, Starmer & Irish) **15.00**

Come Back To Connemara by M.E. Rourke & Frank H. Grey, 1907, Photo Baby Eddy (Cover Artist, Starmer & Irish) **15.00**

Come Back To Erin by Claribel, 1908 (Cover Artist, Pfeiffer & Irish) ..**15.00**

Come Back To Me My Melody by Irving Berlin, 1912 (Cover Artist, Pfeiffer & Irving Berlin) **15.00**

Come Back To Old Kentucky by Chuck Reisner & Earl Taylor, 1915, Photo Ethel Arnold **5.00**

Come Back To Sorrento by Ernesto de Curtis, 1940 (Cover Artist, NPS) .**5.00**

Come Back To Your Little Grey Home by Freema, 1915 (WWI) **10.00**

Come Back With The Roses In June by Fleta Jan Brown, 1914 (Cover Artist, Pfeiffer) **15.00**

Come Be My Sunshine, Dearie by J.B. Gardner, 1909 (Cover Artist, Pfeiffer) **15.00**

Come Closer To Me by O. Farres, 1945, Movie: Easy To Wed, Photo Van Johnson, Esther Williams & Lucille Ball **12.00**

Come Down, Ma' Evenin' Star by Smith & Stromberg, 1902 ....**10.00**

Come Down, Mrs. Flynn by J. W. Kelley, 1890 (Pre 1900) **15.00**

Come Fly With Me by Cahn & Van Heusen, 1958, Movie: Come Fly With Me, Photo Hugh O'Brien, Frankie Avalon & Pamela Tiffin **12.00**

Come Home by Richard Rodgers & Oscar Hammerstein II, 1951, Musical: Allegro **5.00**

Come Home, Dewey, We Won't Do A Thing To You by Paul Dresser, 1899 (Pre 1900) **15.00**

Come Josephine In My Flying Machine by Alfred Bryan & Fred Fischer, 1910, Photo Blanche Ring (Cover Artist, Starmer & Transportation) .**30.00**

Come, My Lad, And Be A Soldier by Ralph Nairn, 1918 (WWI) **15.00**

Come On Along by Egbert Van Alstyne, 1915 ....**5.00**

Come On And Baby Me by Sam M. Lewis, Joe Young & Geo. W. Meyer, 1916 (Cover Artist, Barbelle) **5.00**

Come On And La-La With Me by Arthur Lange **5.00**

Come On And Whistle by Piantadosi & Bibo, 1943, Photo Marlene Dietrich **5.00**

Come On, Boys by Paul Rubens, 1902 ....**8.00**

Come On Down To Cincinnati Town by Jack Yellen & George L. Cobb, 1916 ....**5.00**

Come On Love Say Hello by Barron, 1910 (Cover Artist, Pfeiffer) **15.00**

Come On Maria by Shields & Murphy, 1910 (Cover Artist, Pfeiffer) .**15.00**

Come On Over by Tommie Malie & Jack Little, 1924 (Deco) **10.00**

Come On Papa by Edgar Leslie & Harry Ruby, 1918, Photo Wellington Cross (Cover Artist, Barbelle, Transportation & WWI) **15.00**

Come On & Play Wiz Me by Bert Kalmar, Edgar Leslie & Harry Ruby, 1919 ....**5.00**

Come On Spark Plug! by Billy Rose & Con Conrad, 1923 (Cover Artist, Debeck) **15.00**

Come On, Take A Dip In The Ocean by Glenn Leap, 1913 (Cover Artist, Pfeiffer) **15.00**

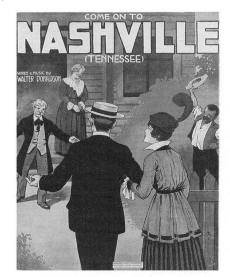

Come On To Nashville, Tennessee by Walter Donaldson, 1916 .....16.00

Come Out, Come Out, Wherever You Are by Jules Styne & Sammy Cahn, 1944, Movie: Step Lively, Photo Frank Sinatra **5.00**

Come Out Of The Kitchen Mary Ann by James Kendis & Chas. Bayha, 1916, Photo Douglas Fairbanks (Cover Artist, Einson) **15.00**

Come Over To Dover by Stanley Murphy & George Botsford, 1914 ..**10.00**

Come Sail Away by Dennis DeYoung, 1977 ....**5.00**

Come Sunny Hours by J. Bud Cushee & J. Montgomery Rogers, 1893 (Pre 1900) **15.00**

Come Take A Jitney With Me by James Thatcher, 1915 ....**8.00**

Come Take A Trip In My Air Ship by Evans & Shields, 1904 (Transportation) **25.00**

Come To Baby, Do! by Inez James & Sidney Miller, 1945, Photo George Auld **3.00**

Come To Me, Bend To Me by Alan J. Lerner & Frederick K. Loewe, 1947, Movie: Brigadoon **5.00**

Come To Me by A. H. Eastman & Fred Heltman, 1918 ....**5.00**

Come To Me by B. G. DeSylva, Lew Brown & Ray Henderson, 1931 .**5.00**

Come To Me Love by Merrill & Dinsmore, 1913 ....**5.00**

Come To Me Now by Edward Storer & Bryceson Trehane, 1917 ....**5.00**

Come To The Fair by Helen Taylor & Easthope Martin, 1917 ....**3.00**

Come To The Land Of Bohemia by Ren Shields & Geo. Evans, 1907 ..**10.00**

Come To The Mardi Gras by Ervin Drake, Jimmy Shirl, Max Bulhoes & Milton de Oliveira, 1947, Photo Denny Miles **3.00**

Come To The Moon by George Gershwin, 1919 ....**10.00**

Come West, Little Girl, Come West by Gus Kahn & Walter Donaldson, 1928, Musical: Ziegfeld Production Whoopee, Photo Eddie Cantor (Cover Artist, Nickel & Eddie Cantor)....................**16.00**

Come Where My Love Lies Dreaming by Stephen Foster, 1855 (Pre 1900 & Stephen Foster)....................**35.00**

Come Where The Lilies Bloom by Will L. Thompson, 1878 (Pre 1900)..**15.00**

Come Ye Lofty, Come Ye Lowly by George Warren, 1897 (Pre 1900).**10.00**

Comes Love by Lew Brown, Charles Tobias & Sam H. Stept, 1939, Musical: Yokel Boy, Photo Jack Pearl, Buddy Ebsen & Judy Canova **5.00**

Comforter, The by Thomas Moore & Charles Fonteyn Manney, 1938..**5.00**

Comic, The by Jusik & Snyder, 1970, Movie: The Comic, Photo Denny Yost & The Classic IV................**3.00**

Comin' In On A Wing And A Prayer by Harold Adamson & Jimmy McHugh, 1943, Photo Eddie Cantor (Cover Artist, Sorokin, Eddie Cantor, WWII & Transportation) **15.00**

Comin' In On A Wing And A Prayer by Harold Adamson & Jimmy McHugh, 1943, Photo Harry James (Cover Artist, Sorokin, WWII & Transportation) **10.00**

Comin' Thro' The Rye by Robert Burns, 1938, Photo Bob Crosby **3.00**

Coming Home by Wilmot & Willeby, 1914 (WWI) **10.00**

Coming Home From Meeting by Edward Harrigan & David Braham, 1884 (Pre 1900) **15.00**

Coming Storm by Benj. O'Donnell, 1904 (March) **5.00**

Commancheros, The by Franks, 1961, Movie: The Commancheros, Photo John Wayne, Ina Balin & Stuart Whitman **4.00**

Comme A Vingt Ans by Emile Barateau & Emile Durand **5.00**

Comme Ci, Comme Ca by Joan Whitney & Alex Kramer, 1947, Photo Frank Sinatra................**5.00**

Committed To The Deep by C.A. White, 1877 (Pre 1900) **15.00**

Commodore Dewey's Victory March by Geo. Maywood, 1898, Dedicated To The American Heroes Of The Battle Of Manila, Photo of Commodore George Dewey (Military Personnel, March, Patriotic, Dedication & Pre 1900) **35.00**

Comrades by Felix McGlennon, 1887 (Pre 1900) **15.00**

Comrades In Arms by F. Clinton Hayes, 1906, Dedicated To Mr. Harold S. Brigham (March & Dedication) **10.00**

Con Amore by Paul Beaumont (Lithograph, Knapp Co.) **10.00**

Concert Valse In E Flat by Alfred Fieldhouse, 1905................**3.00**

Coney Island Baby by Peter Alonzo, 1962................**5.00**

Confess by Bennie Benjamin & George Weiss, 1948, Photo Tony Martin (Cover Artist, Barbelle) **6.00**

Congo Love Song by Bob Cole, J. Rosemond Johnson & Billy Johnson, 1903 ....**10.00**

Congo Nights by Rubey Cowan & Violinsky, 1920 ....**5.00**

Congratulations by Maceo Pinkard, Coleman Goetz, Bud Green & Sam Stept, 1930 (Cover Artist, Pud) **3.00**

Congratulations To Someone by Roy Alfred & Al Frisch, 1953, Photo Tony Bennett **3.00**

Connecticut March, The by William Nassann, 1911 (Cover Artist, Wohlman, Patriotic & March)................**15.00**

Connecticut Yankee In King Arthur's Court, A by Hirsch & King, 1922, Movie: A Connecticut Yankee In King Arthur's Court, Photo Harry Myers **5.00**

Connemara Shore, The by Mary Marriott & Howard Fisher, 1926 (Irish)..**5.00**

Conquerer March, The by E.T. Paull, 1898 (Cover Artist, E.T. Paull, Pre 1900 & March) **35.00**

Consider Yourself by Lionel Bart, 1960, Musical: Oliver (Cover Artist, Irene Haas)................**5.00**

Constantinople by Hanlon, 1917 (Cover Artist, Pfeiffer)....................**15.00**

Constantinople by Harry Carlton, 1928 (Cover Artist, Pud Lane) **10.00**

Constantly by Johnny Burke & Jimmy Van Heusen, 1952, Movie: Road To Morocco, Photo Bob Hope, Bing Crosby & Dorothy Lamour ...**8.00**

Continental, You Kiss While You're Dancing, The by Con Conrad & Herbert Magidson, 1934, Movie: The Gay Divorcee, Photo Fred Astaire & Ginger Rogers................**6.00**

Contrary Mary by Nancy Byrd Turner & Albert Hay Malotte, 1936.....**5.00**

Convent Bells by G. Ludovic, 1903 (Cover Artist, John Frew) **5.00**

Convent Echoes by Carl Bonner, 1911................**3.00**

Convict And The Bird, The by Paul Dresser, 1888 (Pre 1900) **15.00**

Convict And The Rose, The by Betty Chapin, 1925 ....**10.00**

Cooking Breakfast For The One I Love by William Rose & Henry Tobias, 1930, Movie: Be Yourself, Photo Fannie Brice **10.00**

Cool by Stephen Sondheim & Leonard Bernstein, 1957, Movie: West Side Story................**5.00**

Coon, Coon, Coon by Jene Jefferson & Leo Friedman, 1900 (Black, Black Face) **20.00**

Cop Hunters by Julius Lenzberg, 1915................**10.00**

Copper Colored Gal by Benny Davis & J. Fred Coots, 1936, Musical: Cotton Club Parade (Black, Black Face)................**12.00**

Coquette by Irving Berlin, 1928, Movie: Coquette, Photo Mary Pickford (Irving Berlin & Deco) **10.00**

Corn Flower Waltz by Coote, Jr., 1912 ....**10.00**

Corn Huskin' by Corin, 1908 ....**15.00**

Corn Silk by Irving Kahal, Wayne King & Hal Bellis, 1940, Photo Wayne King **5.00**

Cornbelt Symphony by Nev Simons, 1948 ....**5.00**

Cornelius Fitzpatrick McGee by Tom Brown, 1882 (Pre 1900) **15.00**

Corner In My Heart, A by Atteridge, 1910, Musical: The Girl In The Kimona (Cover Artist, Pfeiffer)................**16.00**

Corporal Of The Guard by Losey, 1916 (Cover Artist, Pfeiffer & WWI) **15.00**

Corrugated Rag by E.J. Mellinger, 1911 (Rag) **15.00**

Cosi Cosa by Ned Washington, Bronislaw Kaper & Walter Jurmann, 1935, Movie: A Night At The Opera................**5.00**

Cossack Love Song by George Gershwin, 1926 ....**10.00**

Costa Rica by Lecuona & Ruby, 1946, Movie: Carnival In Costa Rica, Photo Dick Haymes, Vera Ellen, Cesar Romero & Celeste Holm...**5.00**

Cosy Corner by Bratton & Douglas, 1905................**10.00**

Cottage By The Lake, The by J.W. Lloyd & Claude Webber, 1900......**5.00**

Cottage For Sale, A by Larry Conley & William Robison, 1930..........**5.00**

Cottage In God's Garden, A by Carrie Jacobs Bond, 1917 (Cover Artist, Marie Johnson) **15.00**

Cotton Coon's Two Step by C.R. Harrison, 1903 (Black, Black Face).**35.00**

Cotton Fluff by Olive Smith, 1936 (Black, Black Face) **16.00**

Cotton Pickers by Elizabeth Blackburn Martin, 1929 (Cover Artist, D & G. Hauman & Black, Black Face)................**15.00**

Cotton Pickers, The by Chas. Smith Tarbox, 1899 (Pre 1900, March & Black, Black Face)................**50.00**

Cotton Pickin' Time In Alabam by Harold Cool & Arthur J. Daly, 1917.**15.00**

Cotton Pickin' Time In Tennessee by Howard, 1913 (Cover Artist, Pfeiffer & Black, Black Face)................**15.00**

Could Be by Johnny Mercer & Walter Donaldson, 1938, Photo Kay Kyser **5.00**

Could I But Come To You by C. L. Mittell 1913, Photo Billy Argall ...**5.00**

Could It Be You by Cole Porter, 1942, Movie: Something For The Boys.**4.00**

Could The Dreams Of A Dreamer Come True by Jeff Branen & Arthur Lange, 1915 (Cover Artist, DeTakacs)................**10.00**

Could You Be True To Eyes Of Blue by George Cobb & Gus Edwards, 1902 ....**10.00**

Could You Learn To Love Me by Carol Vox & Ben Ritchie, 1909.......**5.00**

Could You Pass In Love by Mack Gordon & Harry Revel, 1938, Movie: My Lucky Star, Photo Sonja Henie & Richard Greene...................**5.00**

Count Every Star by Sammy Gallop & Bruno Coquatrix, 1950, Photo Hugo Winterhalter (Cover Artist, Nick)..........................**3.00**

Count The Days by Tilson & Bason, 1921 ....**5.00**

Count Your Blessings by Cole Porter, 1943, Movie: Mexican Hayride **6.00**

Count Your Blessings Instead Of Sheep by Irving Berlin, 1952, Movie: White Christmas, Photo Bing Crosby, Danny Kaye, Rosemary Clooney & Vera Ellen (Irving Berlin) **5.00**

Country Club Fox Trot by W.T. Pierson, 1914 (Cover Artist, Pfeiffer) .**15.00**

Country Club Rag Time by Scott Joplin, 1909 (Cover Artist, Pfeiffer, Scott Joplin & Rag) **50.00**

Country Style by Johnny Burke & James Van Heusen, 1947, Movie: Welcome Stranger, Photo Bing Crosby, Joan Caulfield & Barry Fitzgerald...**5.00**

Couple Of Swells, A by Irving Berlin, 1947, Movie: Easter Parade, Photo Judy Garland, Fred Astaire, Peter Lawford & Ann Miller (Cover Artist, Hal Weinstein & Irving Berlin)...........................**6.00**

Couple Of Years Ago, A by Larry Stewart & Bert Reisfeld, 1945 ....**5.00**

Cousin Jedediah by H.S. Thompson, 1863 (Pre 1900 & Black, Black Face)...**25.00**

Cover Girl by Ira Gershwin & Jerome Kern, 1944, Movie: Cover Girl.**5.00**

Cover Me Up With The Sunshine Of Virginia by Joe Young, Sam M. Lewis & George W. Meyer, 1923 (Cover Artist, Perret & Deco)....**5.00**

Covered Wagon Days by Will Morrissey & Joe Burrowes, 1923 (Cover Artist, Barbelle) **15.00**

Cow Cow Boogie by Don Raye, Gene DePaul & Benny Carter, 1942 (Cover Artist, Alex Lovy)..15.00

Cowbelles by Sidney D. Mitchell, Lew Klein & Al Piantadosi, 1922 ...**5.00**

Cowboy At Church, The by Mort H. Glickman, 1935, Signed Photo Johnny Marcin (Signed)...**4.00**

Cowboy's Lament, O Bury Me Not On the Lone Prairie, The by John A. Lomax & Oscar J. Fox, 1923......................................**5.00**

Crab Apples by Percy Wenrich, 1908 (Rag & Black, Black Face)......**20.00**

Crack In The World by Douglas, 1965, Movie: Crack In The World, Photo Dana Andrews **3.00**

Cracked Ice Rag by George L. Cobb, 1918 (Rag)..........................**15.00**

Crackerjack by Perrins, 1916 (Cover Artist, Pfeiffer) **10.00**

Cradle Song by Henry J. Sayer & Frank Howard, 1883 (Pre 1900).....**10.00**

Cradle Song (Sweet And Low) by Wm. Vincent Wallace **5.00**

Cradle's Empty-Baby's Gone by Harry Kennedy, 1880 (Pre 1900) **15.00**

Cranky Old Yank by Hoagy Carmichael, 1942 (Transportation)...........**5.00**

Crazy Bone Rag by Charle L. Johnson, 1908 (Cover Artist, Crews Studio & Rag) **20.00**

Crazy Feet by Connelly, Conrad, Mitchell & Cottler, 1930, Movie: Happy Days, Photo Will Rogers, Ann Pennington, Charles Farrell & Janet Gaynor **10.00**

Crazy Heart by Danny Davis & Fred Rose, 1951, Photo Danny Davis **3.00**

Crazy People by Edgar Leslie & James V. Monaco, 1932....................**5.00**

Crazy She Calls Me by Bob Russell & Carl Sigman, 1949...................**5.00**

Crazy Words Crazy Tune Vo-Do-Deo by Jack Yellen & Milton Ager, 1927 (Cover Artist, Barbelle) **5.00**

Creaking Old Mill On The Creek, The by Al Lewis, Larry Stock & Vincent Rose, 1940, Photo Sammy Kaye..............................**5.00**

Creole Belles by J. Bodewalt Lampe, 1900 (March & Black, Black Face)..**15.00**

Creole Rhapsody by Edward Kennedy & Duke Ellington, 1932 (Black, Black Face)...**12.00**

Crescent Beach by Raynolds, 1907 (Transportation) **10.00**

Crescent Schottische by A. Fieldhouse, 1902, Dedicated To Bessie Mackenzie (Dedication) **15.00**

Cricket Polka by Wm. Withers, 1863 (Pre 1900) **35.00**

Crimson Blushes by Ida Lester, 1902......................................**5.00**

Crinoline Days by Irving Berlin, 1922, Musical: Music Box Revue (Irving Berlin)...**10.00**

Crocodile, The by Talbot & Rubens, 1905, Movie: The Blue Moon ...**10.00**

Croon A Little Lullaby by Harry D. Kerr, Chris Schomberg & Clyde Baker 1925, Photo Jack Coakley & His Caribians.......................**5.00**

Crooning by Al Dubin, Herbert W. Weise & William F. Caesar, 1921 (Cover Artist, Hy-Art Studios & Deco)...................................**5.00**

Crooning Water by D. Eardley-Wilmot & Teresa Del Riego, 1913.......**5.00**

Cross My Heart & Hope To Die by Kilgour, 1917 (Cover Artist, Pfeiffer)...**10.00**

Cross My Heart, I Love You by Malia Rosa & Peter DeRosa, 1950 .....**5.00**

'Cross The Great Divide, I'll Wait For You by George W. Meyer & Sam M. Lewis, 1913, Photo Anna Suits..................................**6.00**

'Cross The Great Divide, I'll Wait For You by Lewis & Meyer, 1913 (Cover Artist, Pfeiffer) **10.00**

'Cross The Mason-Dixon Line by Stanley Murphy & Henry Marshall, 1913 (Cover Artist, Starmer & Dixie)..................................**15.00**

Cross Your Heart by Louis Gensler & B. G. DeSylva, 1926 ....**5.00**

Crossing On The Ferry by Newcomb, 1869 (Pre 1900 & Transportation)..**20.00**

Crossing The Bar by H. Lincoln, 1915 (Cover Artist, Pfeiffer) **10.00**

Crossword Mama, You Puzzle Me by Sidney Clare, Willie Raskin & James V. Monaco, 1924 ....**8.00**

Cruel Papa by Will Marion Cooke, 1914 ....**10.00**

Cruising Down The River by Eily Beadell & Nell Tolerton, 1945, Photo Blue Barron...**3.00**

Cry Baby by Young & Norman, 1910 (Cover Artist, Pfeiffer) **10.00**

Cry, Baby, Cry by Remus Harris, Irving Melsher, Jimmy Eaton & Terry Shand, 1938, Photo Kay Kyser (Cover Artist, Merman).................**3.00**

Cry by Churchill Kohlman, Photo Johnnie Ray **5.00**

Cry-Baby Blues by Sam Lewis, Joe Young & Geo. W. Meyer, 1921 (Blues) **10.00**

Cryin' For The Carolines by Sam Lewis, Joe Young & Harry Warren, 1930, Movie: Spring Is Here **10.00**

Cryin' For The Moon by Conley, 1926 ....**6.00**

Crying Because You've Broken My Heart by Geo. L. Wolfson & James White, 1917 ....**5.00**

Crying For You by Ned Miller & Chester Cohn, 1922, Movie: Rice And Old Shoes, Photo Harry J. Conley...............................**5.00**

Crying For You by Ned Miller & Chester Cohn, 1923, Photo Barney Rapp..**3.00**

Cuanto Le Gusta by Ray Gilbert & Gabriel Ruiz, 1948, Movie: A Date With Judy, Photo Wallace Beery, Jane Powell, Elizabeth Taylor, Carmen Miranda, Xavier Cugat & Robert Stack **12.00**

Cuba Hello by Meskill & Wendling, 1929 (Cover Artist, Pfeiffer) **10.00**

Cuban Independence by C. D. Henninger, 1898 (Pre 1900 & March) ..**15.00**

Cuban Love Song, The by Dorothy Fields, Jimmy McHugh & Herbert Stolhart, 1931..**5.00**

Cuban Moon by McKiernan & Spencer, 1920 ....**5.00**

Cuban Pete by Jose Norman, 1946, Photo Desi Arnaz & King Sisters ..**5.00**

Cubanola Glide, The by Vincent Bryan & Harry Von Tilzer, 1909.......**5.00**

Cuckoo Clock, The by Thomas Griselle & Victor Young, 1932............**3.00**

Cuckoo's Call, The by Edgar Selden, 1885, Photo Miss Laura E. Burt (Pre 1900)..**45.00**

Cuddle by Lew Brown & Albert VonTilzer, 1920 ....**5.00**

Cuddle Me Up by Carlo & Sanders, 1924, Musical: Chiffon Girl, Photo Eleanor Paintee **10.00**

Cuddle Up A Little Closer by Otto Harbach & Karl Hoschna, 1932, Movie: Coney Island, Photo Betty Grable, George Montgomery & Cesar Romero **8.00**

Cumberland by Halsey K. Mohr, 1916............................**5.00**

Cup Hunters by Julius Lenzberg, 1915 (Sports)....................**15.00**

Cup Of Coffee, A Sandwich And You, A by Billy Rose, Al Dubin & Joseph Meyer, 1925, Musical: Charlot's Review of 1926 ....**5.00**

Cupboard, The by Walter de la Mare & Dwight Conn, 1928.................**5.00**

Cupid & The Moon by Ward, 1908 (Cover Artist, Pfeiffer) **15.00**

Cupid's Awakening Waltzes by E.T. Paull, 1896 (Cover Artist, E.T. Paull & Pre 1900) **35.00**

Cupid's Dream by Ed Dangel, 1910............................**5.00**

Cupid's Garden by Bert Timoney & Max C. Eugene, 1903..................**5.00**

Cupids I.O.U. by Jack Drislane, Alfred Bryan & Geo. W. Meyer, 1910, Photo Dorothy Golden (Cover Artist, Etherington) **18.00**

Cupids I.O.U. by Jack Drislane, Alfred Bryan & Geo. W. Meyer, 1910, Photo Effie Brooklin (Cover Artist, Etherington) **18.00**

Cupid's Message by Ryder, 1910 (Cover Artist, Starmer)..................**10.00**

Cupid's Patrol by Neil Moret, 1910............................**5.00**

Curfew Bells, The by Alfred Fieldhouse, 1905 ....**3.00**

Curiosity by Joan Whitney, Alex Kramer & Sam Ward, 1947 ....**5.00**

Curious Cures by James Thornton, 1897 (Pre 1900)...........................**15.00**

Curley Head by Sam. M. Lewis & Geo. Meyer, 1913.......................8.00

Curly by Powell, 1909 (Cover Artist, Pfeiffer)..................**15.00**

Curly Head by Wm. McKenna & Albert Gumble, 1910 (Cover Artist, John Frew) **10.00**

Curly Top by Ted Koehler & Ray Henderson, 1935, Movie: Curly Top, Photo Shirley Temple, John Boles & Rochelle Hudson (Shirley Temple)..**10.00**

Curse by Paul Dresser, 1887 (Pre 1900) **15.00**

Curse Of An Aching Heart, The by Henry Fink & Al Piantadosi, 1913, Photo Emma Carus **10.00**

Curse Of The Dreamer, The by Paul Dresser, 1899 (Pre 1900) **15.00**

Custer's Last Charge by John Philip Sousa, 1922 (Cover Artist, E.T. Paull, John Philip Sousa & March)....................................**45.00**

Cute And Cunning Wonderful Baby Doll by Joe Goodwin, Joe McCarthy & Al Piantadosi, 1913, Photo Florence Tempest (Cover Artist, Rose)..**10.00**

Cute Little Things You Do, The by James F. Hanley, 1931, Movie: Young As You Feel, Photo Will Rogers & Fifi Dorsey....................**10.00**

Cutest Little Red-Headed Doll, The by Jack Wolf & Carl Sigman, 1947..**5.00**

Cutey Boy by Williams & Greenberg, 1913 (Cover Artist, Pfeiffer)...**10.00**

Cutey, Tell Me Who Tied Your Tie by Arthur Longbrake & Ed Edwards, 1910 (Cover Artist, Jenkins & Deco)........................15.00

Cutie by Otto Harbach & Rudolf Friml, 1922 ....**5.00**

Cynthia by L. Crockett Davis & F. W. Krafft, 1904 ....**10.00**

Cynthia by Richard Kountz, 1950 ....**2.00**

Cynthia Waltzes by McNair Ilgenfritz, 1905...........................**10.00**

Cynthia's In Love by Jack Owens, Earl Gish & Billy White, 1942, Photo Perry Como (Cover Artist, Barbelle)...........................**5.00**

Daddy by Lemon & Behrend, 1907........................**5.00**

Daddy Found You Down Beside The Garden Wall by Raymond B. Egan, 1917 ....**6.00**

Daddy Has A Sweetheart And Mother Is Her Name by Gene Buck & Dave Stamper, 1912 ....**10.00**

Daddy I Love You More And More Each Day by Sophie Tucker & Fred Strasser, 1914, Photo Sophie Tucker............................**15.00**

Daddy, I Want To Go by Dunn & Stembler, 1915 (Cover Artist, Pfeiffer & WWI)...**20.00**

Daddy Long Legs by Clarence M. Jones, 1914....................**10.00**

Daddy Long Legs by Sam M. Lewis, Joe Young & Harry Ruby, 1919, Photo Mary Pickford, Dedicated to Mary Pickford (Cover Artist, Frederick S. Manning & Dedication)....................................**30.00**

Daddy Wants Someone Too by Rowe, 1909 (Cover Artist, Pfeiffer) ..**15.00**

Daddy Wouldn't Buy Me A Bow-Wow by Joseph Tabrar, 1892 (Pre 1900)..**15.00**

Daddy, You've Been A Mother To Me by Fred Fisher, 1920.............**10.00**
Daddy's Dudeen by George A. Kershaw & Walter Scanlan, 1920........**5.00**
Daddy's Little Girl by Bobby Burke & Horace Gerlach, 1949, Photo Dick Todd (Cover Artist, Frederick S. Manning) **10.00**

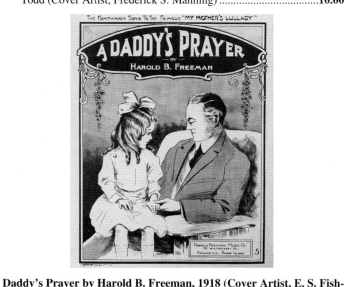

Daddy's Prayer by Harold B. Freeman, 1918 (Cover Artist, E. S. Fisher & WWI) **10.00**
Dafy-Dill, The by Wm. B. Friedlander & Con Conrad, 1923 (Cover Artist, Politzer) **5.00**
Dainty Daffodils by Walter E. Miles, 1915 (Cover Artist, Jaroushek).**10.00**
Dainty Demoiselles by Wm. T. Pierson, 1914 (Cover Artist, Pfeiffer & Deco) **15.00**
Dainty Little Tillie Brown by Karl Lenox, 1905 ....**5.00**
Dainty Miss by Bernard Barnes, 1924....................................**5.00**
Daisies Won't Tell by Anita Owen, 1908 (Cover Artist, Starmer) **10.00**
Daisy Bell (Bicycle Built For Two) by Harry Dacre, 1892 (Pre 1900)....**15.00**
Daisy by C.E. Billings, 1904 (Cover Artist, E.S. Fisher) **10.00**
Dakota Rag by O.H. Andersen, 1899 (Pre 1900 & Rag)......................**15.00**
Dallas Blues by Wand, 1912 (Blues)....................................**10.00**
Daly's Reel by Joeph M. Daly, 1911 (Cover Artist, Pfeiffer & Rag)...**15.00**
Dan-Dan-Danville High by Ralph Blaine & Harry Warren, 1947, Movie: Summer Holiday..**3.00**
Dance Away The Night by Harlan Thompson & Dave Stamper, 1929, Movie: Married In Hollywood **5.00**
Dance Ballerina Dance by Bob Russell & Carl Sigman, 1947, Photo Vaughn Monroe..**5.00**
Dance by Jack Stern & Ed Kamnetz, 1923........................**5.00**
Dance Me Goodbye by Paul Herve, Jean Briquet & Adolph Philipp, 1915, Musical: The Girl Who Smiles....................................**5.00**
Dance My Trouble Away by Stillman & Theodorakis, 1966, Movie: Zorba The Greek, Photo Anthony Quinn....................................**5.00**
Dance Of Dew Drops by William T. "Billy" Mann, 1914 ....**5.00**
Dance Of The Brownies, The 1895 (Cover Artist, Palmer Cox & Pre 1900)..**38.00**
Dance Of The Butterflies by A. J. Stasny, 1920....................**5.00**
Dance Of The Fairy Queen by Drumheller, 1909 (Cover Artist, Pfeiffer) .**15.00**
Dance Of The Fireflies by E. T. Paull & Sentenis (Cover Artist, E.T. Paull) **40.00**
Dance Of The Golden Rods by John J. Fitzpatrick, 1908 ....**10.00**
Dance Of The Honey Bees by Benjamin Richmond, 1902 ....**10.00**
Dance Of The Lunatics by Allen, 1912 ....**10.00**
Dance Of The Moon Birds by A. J. Stasny, 1915....................**12.00**
Dance Of The Sprites by Joseph M. Hopkins, 1945....................**3.00**
Dance Of The Stars by Benjamin Richmond, 1905....................**10.00**

Dance Of The Teenie-Weenies by Alma Sanders, 1916 ....**10.00**
Dance Of The Virgins by Stevenson, 1911 ....**10.00**
Dance Of The Wild Flowers by Percy Wenrich, 1905 ....**5.00**
Dance Tangerine by Howard Johnson & Carlo Sanderson, 1921, Musical: Tangerine..**5.00**
Dance To The Music Of The Ocarina by Irving Berlin, 1950, Musical: Call Me Madam, Caricature, Ethel Merman (Cover Artist, Peter Arno & Irving Berlin) **10.00**
Dance With A Dolly With A Hole In Her Stockin' by Terry Shand, Jimmy Eaton & Mickey Leader, 1944, Photo Will McCune (Cover Artist, Im-Ho) **10.00**
Dance With A Dolly With A Hole In Her Stockin' by Terry Shand, Jimmy Eaton & Mickey Leader, 1944, Photo Evelyn Knight (Cover Artist, Im-Ho) **5.00**
Dance With A Dolly With A Hole In Her Stockin' by Terry Shand, Jimmy Eaton & Mickey Leader, Photo Les Brown (Cover Artist, Im-Ho)..**12.00**
Dance With A Dolly With A Hole In Her Stockin' by Terry Shand, Jimmy Eaton & Mickey Leader, 1946, Photo Dale Belmont (Cover Artist, Im-Ho)..**10.00**
Dance With Me by Irving Berlin, 1939 (Irving Berlin)....................**5.00**
Dancin' Dan by Tracey & Stanley, 1923....................................**5.00**
Dancing By Moonlight by F.H. Losey, 1923 ....**2.00**
Dancing Doll by Ed. Poldini, 1935 (Deco)....................................**3.00**
Dancing Dominoes by Zoe Zimmerman, 1929....................................**5.00**
Dancing Eyes by Griffith J. Jones, 1907 (Cover Artist, Central Engraving Co.) **10.00**
Dancing Fool by Harry B. Smith, Francis Wheeler & Ted Snyder, 1922 (Cover Artist, Frederick S. Manning)....................................**15.00**
Dancing In A Dream by Harris, 1930 (Cover Artist, Pfeiffer) **10.00**
Dancing In the Barn by Tom Turner, 1908....................................**10.00**
Dancing In The Dark by Howard Dietz & Arthur Schwartz, 1931, Musical: The Band Wagon **5.00**
Dancing In The Dark by Wenzlik, 1894 (Pre 1900)....................**10.00**
Dancing Leaves by Walter E. Miles, 1913 ....**3.00**
Dancing 'Neath The Irish Moon by Ballard MacDonald & Harry Puck, 1915, Photo William O'Hare (Irish)....................................**10.00**
Dancing On The Ceiling by Lorenz Hart & Richard Rodgers, 1930, Photo Fred Martin **5.00**
Dancing On The Green by Alelier Beddis, 1915 (Cover Artist, Pfeiffer) .**10.00**
Dancing Shadows by Ernie Golden, 1927 (Cover Artist, Pfeiffer & Deco)..**5.00**
Dancing Starlight by Roden & Glogau, 1910 (Cover Artist, Pfeiffer & Indian)..**20.00**
Dancing Tambourine by W.C. Polla, 1927 (Deco)....................................**5.00**
Dancing The Blues Away by Joseph McCarthy, Charles Johnson & Fred Fisher, 1915 ....**10.00**
Dancing The Jelly Roll by Herman Paley, 1915 (Black, Black Face)..**16.00**
Dancing With My Shadow by Harry Woods, 1934, Musical: Thank You So Much (Cover Artist, Cliff Miska)....................................**5.00**
Dancing With Tears In My Eyes by Al Dubin & Joe Burke, 1930, Photo Rudy Vallee **5.00**
Dangerous Ground by Nelson, Leeds & Nelson, 1947, Photo Roy Rogers **8.00**
Danny Boy by Fred E. Weatherly, 1913 (Irish)....................................**5.00**
Danny By My Side by Edward Harrigan & David Braham, 1891 (Pre 1900)..**15.00**
Danse D'Amour by Brett & Krouse, 1914 (Cover Artist, Pfeiffer)......**10.00**
Dansero by Richard Haymen, Lee Daniels & S. Parker, 1953, Photo Richard Hayman..**2.00**
Danube Waves by J. Ivanovici, 1902 (Cover Artist, John Frew) **5.00**
Dapper Dan by Albert Von Tilzer & Lew Brown, 1921 ....**5.00**

Dar's Somethin' About Yer I Like by John T. Kelly, 1898 (Pre 1900 & Black, Black Face)..**20.00**

Dardanella Blues by Fred Fisher & Johnny Black, 1920 (Cover Artist, Wohlman & Blues)...**10.00**

Dardanella by Fred Fisher, Felix Bernard & Johnny S. Black, 1919 (Cover Artist, DeTakacs).....................................**10.00**

Dark Eyes by Bernice Manoloff, 1935 ....**5.00**

Dark Eyes by Carol Raven, 1929 (Cover Artist, Frederick S. Manning)..**10.00**

Dark Eyes by Manuel Klein, 1913, Vocal & Instrumental Number From The Messrs Shubert's Production "America" 1913-1914 ....**15.00**

Dark Eyes by Max C. Freedman & Harold Potter, 1932 ....**10.00**

Dark Is The Night by Sammy Cahn & Nicholas Brodszky, 1951, Movie: Rich, Young And Pretty, Photo Jane Powell, Danielle Darrieux, Wendell Corey, Fernando Lamas & Vic Damone **5.00**

Dark Star, The by Burns & Sheppard, 1919, Movie: The Dark Star, Photo Marion Davies **12.00**

Darkies' Dream, The by G.L. Lansing, 1891 (Pre 1900 & Black, Black Face) **20.00**

Darkies Ragtime Ball, The by Drislane & Meyer, 1912 (Cover Artist, Pfeiffer & Black, Black Face) **20.00**

Darktown Barbecue by Will M. Cook, 1904, Photo Miss Abbie Mitchell In "The Southerners" (Black, Black Face) **15.00**

Darktown Capers by Starck (Rag) **15.00**

Darktown Dancin' School by Jack Yellen & Albert Gumble, 1920, Musical: Sinbad, Photo Farber Sisters (Cover Artist, Starmer & Deco) **15.00**

Darktown Is Out Tonight by Will Marion Cook, 1898 (Pre 1900) **15.00**

Darktown Strutters' Ball, The by Shelton Brooks, 1917, Photo Elsie White (Cover Artist, Rose Symbol & Black, Black Face).......................**30.00**

Darky Cavalier by David Reed Jr., 1895 (Pre 1900 & Black, Black Face)...**20.00**

Darlin' by Harold G. Frost, 1916.............................**5.00**

Darling, Be Home Soon by Sebastian, 1967, Movie: You're A Big Boy Now, Photo The Lovin' Spoonful **5.00**

Darling, How Could You by David & Livingston, 1951, Movie: Darling How Could You, Photo Joan Fontaine, John Lund, Mona Freeman & Peter Hanson...**5.00**

Darling I by B. C. Hilliam, 1919, Musical: Buddies (WWI)..............**10.00**

Darling, Je Vous Aime Beaucoup by Anna Sosenko, 1936, Photo Hildegarde **5.00**

Darling Lili by Mercer & Mancini, 1970, Movie: Darling Lili, Photo Julie Andrews...**5.00**

Darling Nellie Gray by B. R. Hanby, 1898 (Pre 1900)......................**15.00**

Darling Sue by Sterling, Photo Harry Von Tilzer...............................**3.00**

Darling, What More Can I Do by Autry & Carson, 1945, Photo Gene Autry...**3.00**

Darn That Dream by Eddie DeLange & Jimmy Van Heusen, 1939, Photo Joe Venuti...**3.00**

Darned If The Fellows Can Do Without Girls, Girls, Girls by Billy Gaston, 1910, Photo Ethel Green & Billy Gaston (Cover Artist, Starmer & Deco) **16.00**

Dashing Cavaliers, The by E.T. Paull, 1938 (Cover Artist, E.T. Paull)..**35.00**

Dat Citron Wedding Cake by Edward Harrigan & David Braham, 1880 (Pre 1900 & Black, Black Face)......................**25.00**

Dat Lovin' Rag by Smally & Odar, 1908 (Rag)......................**15.00**

Dat's The Way To Spell Chicken by Sidney Perrin & Bob Slater, 1902 (Black, Black Face) **15.00**

Daughter Of Heaven, The by Ascher, 1913......................**5.00**

Daughter Of Jole Blon, The by Bart Dawson, 1948......................**5.00**

Daughter Of Rosie O'Grady by Brice, Walter Donaldson & Edgar Leslie, 1918 (Irish)......................**10.00**

Daughter Of Rosie O'Grady, The by Cliff Hess & Jos. H. Santly, 1925 (Irish)......................**10.00**

Daughter Of Two Worlds, A by Paul M. Sarazan & M.K. Jerome, 1920, Photo Norma Talmadge (Cover Artist, Frederick S. Manning) **15.00**

Daughters Of Sweet Georgia Brown, The by Ben Bernie, Ken Casey & Ken Sisson, 1939, Photo Ben Bernie (Black, Black Face).............**10.00**

David And Bathsheba by Jenkins, Allen & Roberts, 1951, Movie: David And Bathsheba......................**4.00**

David & Lisa by Lawrence, 1963, Movie: David & Lisa, Photo Keir Dullea & Janet Margolis......................**3.00**

Davy Jones' Locker by H. W. Petrie, 1901 ....**15.00**

Dawn And Dusk by Rex Foster & Henry Ferry, 1916 ....**5.00**

Dawn Brought Me Love And You, The by Lynn Merrick & Richard Kountz, 1928 ....**10.00**

Dawn by Harry H. Williams, 1915 ....**10.00**

Dawn by Mack David & Jerry Livingston, Photo Jaye P. Morgan **5.00**

Dawn Dance by Paul Bliss, 1925 ....**5.00**

Dawn Of Life, The by Mrs. C.F. Alexander & Ellen Wright................**5.00**

Dawn Of The Century March by E. T. Paull, 1900 (Cover Artist, E.T. Paull, Lithograph, A. Hoen & March)......................**40.00**

Dawn Of Tomorrow by Jeanne Gravelle & Joe Green, 1927 (Cover Artist, Barbelle) **5.00**

Day After Day by Richard Himber & Bud Green, 1938, Photo Richard Himber......................**3.00**

Day After Forever, The by Johnny Burke & Jimmy Van Heusen, 1944, Movie: Going My Way, Photo Bing Crosby......................**8.00**

Day And Night by Johnson, 1933......................**5.00**

Day Break by Mabel W. Daniels, 1909 ....**5.00**

Day By Day by Sammy Cahn, Axel Stordahl & Paul Weston, 1945, Photo Bing Crosby......................**5.00**

Day By Day by Sammy Cahn, Axel Stordahl & Paul Weston, 1945, Photo Frank Sinatra......................**5.00**

Day By Day by Stanford, 1900 (Transportation)......................**15.00**

Day Dreams by Maxwell Goldman, 1914 ....**5.00**

Day Dreams Of You by Harold B. Freeman, 1918 (Cover Artist, Pfeiffer).**10.00**

Day Dreams, Visions Of Bliss by Heinrich Reinhardt & Robert B. Smith, 1910, Musical: The Spring Maid, Photo Christie Macdonald & Mizzi Hajos......................**10.00**

Day That's Gone Can Never Come Again by Safford Waters, 1898 (Pre 1900)......................**15.00**

Day We Celebrate by Edward Harrigan & David Braham, 1875 (Pre 1900)......................**15.00**

Day You Came Along, The by Sam Coslow & Arthur Johnston, 1933, Movie: Too Much Harmony, Photo Bing Crosby & Judith Allen .**10.00**

Day You Went Away, The by Louis Phillips & Peter Caporossi, 1915 .**10.00**

Day-Break by Mary Leefe Laurence, 1914 ....**5.00**

Day-Dreaming by Gus Kahn & Jerome Kern, 1941, Photo Bing Crosby (Deco) **5.00**

Daybreak by Harold Adamson & Ferde Grofé, 1942, Photo Tommy Dorsey (Cover Artist, Sorokin) **3.00**

Days Of Wine And Roses by Johnny Mercer & Henry Mancini, 1942, Movie: Days Of Wine And Roses **5.00**

Days When We Were Young, The by Frank W. Howell & Charles B. Weston, 1913 ....**10.00**

De Cake Walk Queen by Harry B. Smith & John Stromberg, 1900 (Black, Black Face) **20.00**

De Darkies Jubilee by Bert Williams & George Walker, 1897 (Pre 1900 & Black, Black Face) **20.00**

De Golden Wedding by James Bland, 1880 (Pre 1900 & Black, Black Face) **20.00**

De Leader Of De Company B by David Reed Jr., 1895 (Pre 1900 & Black, Black Face) **25.00**

De Ol' Ark's A-Moverin' by David W. Guion, 1918 (Black, Black Face) **15.00**

De Ole Time Cake Walk by W. Moody & Lee B. Grabbe, 1898 (Pre 1900 & Black, Black Face) **20.00**

De Stories Uncle Remus Tells, 1899 (Pre 1900 & Black, Black Face) .**35.00**

Dear Eyes That Haunt Me by Harry B. Smith & Emmerich Kalman, 1926, Musical: The Circus Princess **5.00**

Dear Heart by Henry Mancini, Jay Livingston & Ray Evans, 1964, Movie: Dear Heart, Photo Glenn Ford & Geraldine Page **10.00**

Dear Heart by J. Anton Dailey, 1918, Musical: A Knight For A Day, Photo Sallie Fisher (Cover Artist, DeTakacs) **10.00**

Dear Heart by Jean Lefavre, W. C. Polla & Willard Goldsmith, 1919 Knapp Publishing & Deco) **10.00**

Dear Heart, What Might Have Been by Fleta Jan Brown & Herbert Spencer, 1926 ....**10.00**

Dear Hearts And Gentle People by Bob Hilliard & Sammy Fain, 1949, Photo Gordon MacRae **3.00**

Dear Land Of Home by Graham Valmore, 1911....................................**5.00**

Dear Little Boy Of Mine by J. Keirn Brennan & Ernest R. Ball, 1918 (WWI)...**15.00**

Dear Little Buddy Of Mine by Robert Levenson & Edwin Bernard, 1920..**10.00**

Dear Louise by Raymon Moore, 1894 (Pre 1900).............................**15.00**

Dear Love, Remember Me by Harold Harford & Charles Marshall, 1912, Sung by John McCormack **10.00**

Dear Mom by Harris, 1941 (WWII) **10.00**

Dear Old Daddy Long Legs by Neville Fleeson & Albert Von Tilzer, 1919, Photo Mary Pickford (Cover Artist, E.E. Walton) **25.00**

Dear Old Dear by John Hazzard & Benjamin Hapgood Burt, 1908 (Cover Artist, DeTakacs)...**10.00**

Dear Old Dixie by Herbert H. Taylor & Wm. Heagney, 1906 (Dixie)..**15.00**

Dear Old Donegal by Steve Graham, 1942 (Irish) **2.00**

Dear Old Dreamy Honolulu Town by Braner & Lange, 1916 ....**8.00**

Dear Old Eastside by Ed Gardenier & Gus Edwards, 1907 ....**10.00**

Dear Old Fashioned Mother by Friedman, 1920 ....**5.00**

Dear Old Girl by Richard Buck & Theodore Morse, 1913....................**5.00**

Dear Old Glory by McCarthy, 1918 (WWI)....................................**16.00**

Dear Old Grandma's Days by A. B. Sloane, 1904 ....**10.00**

Dear Old Home by Harold Weeks, 1920 ....**3.00**

Dear Old Land Of Mine by Alfred Goodman., 1918 (WWI) **15.00**

Dear Old Ma by Jack Frost & Henry S. Sawyer, 1915 (WWI) **15.00**

Dear Old Moonlight by Harry Creamer, 1909 (Cover Artist, Pfeiffer)...**10.00**

Dear Old Pal Of Mine by Harold Robe & Lt. Gitz Rice, 1918, Signed Photo Of Lt. Gitz Rice (WWI, Military Personnel & Signed) **25.00**

Dear Old Portland Town by Harry L. Stone, 1916....................**5.00**

Dear Old Rose by Jack Drislane & Geo. W. Meyer, 1912 ....**5.00**

Dear Old Songs Of Long Ago by Force, 1913 ....**5.00**

Dear Old Southland by Henry Creamer & Turner Layton, 1921 ....**5.00**

Dear Old Stars And Stripes Good-bye by Harvey Briggs & Harley Wilson, 1902, Photo Werden & Shepard (Cover Artist, Carter & Patriotic) .**20.00**

Dear Old Stars And Stripes, The by Reynolds, 1905 (Patriotic) **15.00**

Dear Old Uncle Sam by Henry I. Marshall, 1918 (WWI) **15.00**

Dear, On A Night Like This by Caesar & Conrad, 1927.....................**5.00**

Dear One by Mark Fisher, Cy Richardson & Joe Burke, 1924 ....**5.00**

Dear Rose Marie by Jean C. Havez & Ted S. Barron, 1913.................**5.00**

Dearest Darling by Dick Robertson, James Cavanaugh & Frank Weldon, 1945, Photo The Three Suns...**3.00**

Dearest Eyes by Teresa Strickland & Lily Strickland, 1916 ....**5.00**

Dearest Girl I Know by Freeman & Allemong, 1919 (Cover Artist, Pfeiffer) **10.00**

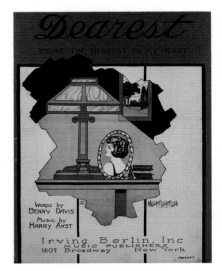

Dearest You're The Nearest To My Heart by Benny Davis & Harry Akst, 1922 (Cover Artist, Perret & Deco) **10.00**

Dearie by Bob Hilliard & Dave Mann, 1950.......................................**3.00**

Dearie by Clare Kummer, 1905 ....**5.00**

Dearie by Courtney Allemong & J. Edwin Allemong, 1917.................**5.00**

Dearie Girl by Margaret Whitney, 1914..**5.00**

Dearly Beloved by Johnny Mercer & Jerome Kern, 1942, Movie: You Were Never Lovelier, Photo Fred Astaire, Rita Hayworth, Adolphe Menjou & Xavier Cugat & His Orchestra **5.00**

Debutante Waltz by Bob Rothberg & Peter Tinturin, 1934, Photo Arthur Murray **5.00**

December And May by Edward B. Marks, 1893 (Pre 1900)...............**15.00**

December Morn by Lincoln, 1915 (Cover Artist, Pfeiffer).................**15.00**

Deck Of Cards, The by T. Texas Tyler, 1952, Photo Wink Martindale (Cover Artist, JoJo)..**10.00**

Dedicated To You by Sammy Cahn, Saul Chaplin & H.H. Zaret, 1936 .**5.00**

Deed I Do by Hirsch & Rose, 1927 ....**5.00**

Deedle-Dee-Dee Detroit by Sidney Holden, Howard Simon & Richard W. Pascoe, 1923 ....**5.00**

Deep Down In My Heart by Frank Tannehill Jr. & Tom Kelley, 1911..**5.00**

Deep Down In Your Heart by Cliff Friend & Dave Franklin, 1947, Photo Russ Carlysle **3.00**

Deep In A Dream by Eddie DeLange & Jimmy Van Heusen, 1938, Photo Henry Busse (Cover Artist, Im-Ho) **5.00**

Deep In A Dream by Eddie DeLange & Jimmy Van Heusen, 1938, Photo Guy, Victor, Carmen & Lebert Lombardo (Cover Artist, Im-Ho) ...**5.00**

Deep In My Heart Dear by Dorothy Donnelly & Sigmund Romberg, 1924, Musical: The Student Prince......**8.00**

Deep In The Arms Of Love by Lou Davis & Roy Ingraham, 1929 (Cover Artist, Frederick S. Manning & Deco) **15.00**

Deep In The Heart Of Texas by Don Swander & June Hershey, 1941, Photo The Three Suns......**5.00**

Deep In The Heart Of Texas by Don Swander & June Hershey, 1941, Photo Bob Allen **5.00**

Deep Purple by Mitchell Parish & Peter DeRose, 1939, Photo & Dedicated to Doris Rhodes (Dedication) **5.00**

Deep River by Harold Potter, 1932......**5.00**

Deep River (Negro Spiritual) Arranged by Jim Smock, 1935 (Black, Black Face) **5.00**

Deep River (Negro Spiritual) by H. T. Burleigh, 1917 (Black, Black Face) **5.00**

Delicado by Jack Lawrence & Waldyr Azevedo, 1952, Photo Percy Faith **3.00**

Delicious by George Gershwin, 1931, Movie: Delicious, Photo Janet Gaynor **12.00**

Delightful Rag by Lester Sell, 1914 (Rag) **15.00**

Della Fox (Little Trooper) March by E. T. Paull, 1898 (Cover Artist, E.T. Paull, March & Pre 1900)......**35.00**

Dengozo by Ernesto Nazareth, 1914, Photo Joan Sawyer & John Jarrott (Cover Artist, Pfeiffer & Deco)......**15.00**

Der Fuehrer's Face by Oliver Wallace, 1942, Movie: Der Fuehrer's Face, Donald Duck On Cover With Fuehrer, V For Victory On Back Cover (WWII & Disney)......**35.00**

Desert Song, The by Otto Harbach, Oscar Hammerstein II, Frank Mandel & Sigmund Romberg, Movie: The Desert Song, 1926 ......**10.00**

Destiny by Bryan & Spencer, 1919, Movie: Destiny, Photo Dorothy Phillips **3.00**

Devoted Hearts by Clark, 1906 (Transportation) **10.00**

Devotion by Fred G. Bowles & G. Marshal Loephe, 1912 ......**5.00**

Devotion by Victor Herbert, 1921 (Victor Herbert) **10.00**

Dew Dew Dewy Day by Charles Tobias, 1927 ......**10.00**

Diamonds Are A Girl's Best Friend by Jule Styne & Leo Robin, 1949, Movie: Gentlemen Prefer Blondes (Cover Artist, Hirsihebo)......**5.00**

Diana by Kummer, 1907......**10.00**

Diane by Erno Rapee & Lew Pollack, 1927, Movie: 7th Heaven (Cover Artist, Barbelle)......16.00

Diane Of The Green Van by J. Will Callahan & F. Henri Klickmann, 1914 ......**8.00**

Dicty-Doo by Carey Morgan, 1914 ......**5.00**

Did Anyone Ever Tell You? by McHugh & Adamson, 1937, Movie: When Love Is Young, Photo Virginia Bruce & Kent Taylor......**5.00**

Did I Make A Mistake In You? by Bob Ellsworth, Dick Howard & Harry Pyke, 1930 ......**5.00**

Did I Remember by Harold Adamson & Walter Donaldson, 1936, Movie: Suzy, Photo Jean Harlow, Cary Grant & Franchot Tone, Dedicated To Jean Harlow (Dedication)......**15.00**

Did You Ever Get Stung? by Lorenz Hart & Richard Rodgers, 1938, Movie: I Married An Angel......**10.00**

Did You Ever Get That Feeling In The Moonlight by James Cavanaugh, Larry Stock & Ira Schuster, 1944, Photo Gene Krupa **5.00**

Did You Ever See A Dream Walking by Mack Gordon & Harry Revel, 1933, Movie: Sitting Pretty, Photo Jack Oakie, Jack Haley & Ginger Rogers......**10.00**

Did You Mean It by Baker, Silver & Lyman, 1927......**5.00**

Did You Mean What You Said Last Night by Joe Young & Bernice Petkere, 1932, Photo Dan Russo (Cover Artist, Leff)......**6.00**

Did Your Mother Come From Ireland by Jimmy Kennedy & Michael Carr, 1936, Photo Kate Smith (Cover Artist, Immy & Irish) **15.00**

Didn't You Believe? by Anne Caldwell & Jerome Kern, 1921 ......**5.00**

Die Greene Kosine (My Cousin From The Old Country) by Hyman Prizart & Abe Schwartz, 1922, Photo Mr. Schwartz Playing Violin & Daughter Playing Piano......**10.00**

Dig Down Deep by Walter Hirsch, Sano Marco & Gerald Marks, 1942, War Bond Song (WWII)......**20.00**

Dig You Later by Harold Adamson & Jimmy McHugh, 1945, Movie: Doll Face, Photo Carmen Miranda, Vivian Blaine, Dennis O'Keefe & Perry Como **10.00**

Digga-Digga Do by Dorothy Fields & Jimmy McHugh, 1928, Musical: Blackbirds Of 1928 (Cover Artist, Leff) **10.00**

Dill Pickles by Charles L. Johnson, 1906 (Rag)......**20.00**

Dime A Dozen by Cindy Walker, 1949, Photo Sammy Kaye......**4.00**

Dime With A Halo by Stein, 1963, Movie: Dime With A Halo, Photo Barbara Luna, Roger Mobley & Rafael Lopez **3.00**

Dinah by Sam Lewis, Joe Young & Harry Akst, 1925, Photo Elizabeth Kennedy (Cover Artist, Barbelle & Deco) **15.00**

Dinah by Sam M. Lewis, Joe Young & Harry Akst, 1925, Photo Francis A. Mangan (Cover Artist, Barbelle & Deco)......**10.00**

Dinah Song by Edgar Smith & John Stromberg, 1898 (Pre 1900)......**15.00**

Ding-Dong! The Witch Is Dead by Hamburg & Arlen, 1939, Movie: The Wizard Of Oz, Photo Judy Garland, Frank Morgan, Bert Lahr, Ray Bolger & Jack Haley......**18.00**

Ding-Toes by Jack "Chick" Caddigan & Oliver E. Story, 1920 ......**5.00**

Dinner At Eight by Dorothy Fields & Jimmy McHugh, 1933, Movie: Dinner At Eight, Photo Jean Harlow, Billie Burke & John Barrymore.**10.00**

Dinner For One Please, James by Michael Carr, 1935, Photo Jackie Heller (Cover Artist, B. Harris) **5.00**

Directorate March by John Philip Sousa, 1898 (John Philip Sousa, Pre 1900 & March) **20.00**

Dirty Hands, Dirty Face by Al Jolson, Edgar Leslie, Grant Clarke & James V. Monaco, 1923, Musical: Bombo, Photo Al Jolson (Al Jolson & Black, Black Face)......**15.00**

Divorce Me C.O.D. by Merle Travis & Cliffie Stone, 1946, Photo Lawrence Welk......**3.00**

Dixiana by Caldwell & Tierney, 1930, Movie: Dixiana, Photo Bebe Daniels & Everett Marshall **6.00**

Dixie by Dorothy Fields & Jimmy McHugh, 1928, Musical: Blackbirds of 1928 (Cover Artist, Leff & Dixie)......**10.00**

Dixie Coon Brigade, The by Walter E. Petry, 1898 (Pre 1900, Dixie, March & Black, Black Face) **35.00**

Dixie Daisy by Halsey K. Mohr, 1911 (Dixie)......**10.00**

Dixie Darlings by Percy Wenrich, 1909 (Dixie) **10.00**

Dixie Dimples by James Scott, 1918 (Cover Artist, Starmer, Rag & Dixie)..**15.00**

Dixie Doodle by Zerkel & McCullough, 1916 (Dixie).......................**10.00**

Dixie Highway by Gus Kahn & Walter Donaldson, 1922 (Cover Artist, Starmer, Dixie & Transportation)...................................**20.00**

Dixie, I Wish I Was In Dixie's Land by Dan Emmett, 1860 (Pre 1900 & Dixie)..**20.00**

Dixie I'm Coming Back To You by E. Di Rocco, 1924 (Cover Artist, Berni, Dixie & Transportation) **20.00**

Dixie Land by Dan D. Emmett, 1906 (Dixie).......................**5.00**

Dixie Land, I Love You by A. S. Hayer & Nat Brown, 1909 (Dixie)..**10.00**

Dixie Lullaby by David Portnoy & Harold Dixon, 1919 (Dixie)..........**6.00**

Dixie Moon by Geo. Buchanan & F. Henri Klickman, 1919 (Dixie)...**10.00**

Dixie Rag, The by Giblin, 1913 (Cover Artist, Pfeiffer).....................**15.00**

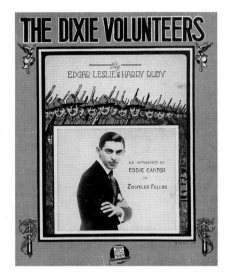

Dixie Volunteers, The by Edgar Leslie & Harry Ruby, 1917, Photo Eddie Cantor (Cover Artist, Barbelle, WWI, Eddie Cantor & Dixie) 20.00

Dixieland Band, The by Johnny Mercer & Bernie Hanighen, 1935, Photo Bing Crosby (Dixie) **5.00**

Dizzy Fingers by Zez Confrey, 1923.....................................**5.00**

Do Do Do by Ira Gershwin & George Gershwin, 1926, Musical: Oh Kay! .**5.00**

Do Do, My Huckleberry Do by Harry & John Dillon, 1893 (Pre 1900).**15.00**

Do I Love You by Cole Porter, 1943, Movie: DuBarry Was A Lady **5.00**

Do I Love You? by Ralph Rainger & Leo Robin, 1934, Movie: Shoot The Works, Photo Ben Bernie & His Merry Lads................................**6.00**

Do I Worry by Stanley Cowan & Bobby Worth, 1940...........................**3.00**

Do It Again by George Gershwin, 1922 ....**5.00**

Do It Again by Irving Berlin, 1912 (Cover Artist, Pfeiffer & Irving Berlin).**15.00**

Do It The Hard Way by Lorenz Hart & Richard Rodgers, 1940, Musical: Pal Joey...**5.00**

Do It While You're Young by Lampert & Loring, 1959, Movie: The Snow Queen..**4.00**

Do It With Me by Harry Armstrong 1914 ....**10.00**

Do Me A Favor, Will Ya? by Beasley Smith & Francis Craig, 1948, Photo Francis Craig..**3.00**

Do Nothin' Till You Hear From Me by Bob Russell & Duke Ellington, 1943, Photo Frank Sinatra (Cover Artist, Sorokin)......................**12.00**

Do Re Mi by Duncan Sisters, Book by Catherine C. Cushing Suggested by Uncle Tom's Cabin by Harriet Beecher Stowe, 1923, Musical: Topsy & Eva, Photo Duncan Sisters (Cover Artist, P.M. Griffith & Black, Black Face)..**22.00**

Do-Re-Mi by Richard Rodgers & Oscar Hammerstein II, 1959, Movie: Sound Of Music, Photo Julie Andrews & Christopher Plummer.....**8.00**

Do Something, 1917, Signed by James Montgomery Flagg (Cover Artist, James Montgomery Flagg, WWI, Patriotic & Signed) **50.00**

Do Something by Bud Green & Sam Stept, 1929, Movie: Nothing But The Truth, Photo Helen Kane **5.00**

Do They Love It by M. Abrahams, 1914 (Cover Artist, Pfeiffer)........**10.00**

Do What You Do by George Gershwin, Ira Gershwin & Gus Kahn, 1929, Ziegfield Show Girl..**5.00**

Do What Your Mother Did, I'll Do The Same As Your Dad by Will Dillon & Albert Von Tilzer, 1916 (Cover Artist, DeTakacs & Deco) 10.00

Do Wuja Starca by C.K. Harris, 1912 ....**3.00**

Do You Believe In Dreams? by Irving Bibo, Don George & Al Piantadosi, 1944, Movie: Pardon My Rhythm....................................**5.00**

Do You Believe In Dreams? by Russell Robinson, Addy Britt & Jack Little 1926 ....**5.00**

Do You Care? by Jack Elliott & Lew Quadling, 1941, Photo Blue Barron **3.00**

Do You, Don't You, Will You, Won't You? by George A. Little, Larry Schaetzlein & Howard Brothers, 1923.......................................**15.00**

Do You Ever Dream Of Me? by Goldye, 1925 ....**5.00**

Do You Ever Think Of Me? by Harry D. Kerr, John Cooper & Earl Burtnett, 1920 (Cover Artist, Delappe & Deco).................................**5.00**

Do You Hear What I Hear by Noel Regney & Gloria Shayne, 1962 .....**5.00**

Do You Know What It Means To Miss New Orleans? by Eddie De Lange & Louis Alter, 1946..**3.00**

Do You Love Me? by Harry Ruby, 1946, Movie: Do You Love Me, Photo Maureen O'Hara, Dick Haymes & Harry James.............................**5.00**

Do You Remember by Carrie Jacobs Bond, 1918 (Cover Artist, Tuniso) **10.00**

Do You Take This Woman For Your Lawful Wife? (I Do, I Do) by Andrew B. Sterling & Harry Von Tilzer, 1913, Photo Harry Von Tilzer **15.00**

Do You Think I Came From Ireland In A Hack? by James Cavanaugh, John Redmond & Frank Weldon, 1947 (Irish)..............................**5.00**

Do You Think You Could Care For A Girl Like Me? by Diditt, 1911 (Cover Artist, Pfeiffer) **12.00**

Doan You Cry, Mah Honey by Albert W. Noll, 1899 (Pre 1900 & Black, Black Face)..**15.00**

Dockstader Rag, The by Les Copeland, 1912 (Rag) **15.00**

Doctor Brown by Fred Irwin, 1914 ....**5.00**

Doctor Doolittle by Bricusse, 1967, Movie: Doctor Doolittle, Photo Rex Harrison **3.00**

Doctor, Lawyer, Indian Chief by Paul Francis Webster & Hoagy Carmichael, 1945, Movie: The Stork Club, Photo Betty Hutton, Don De Fore, Barry Fitzgerald & Andy Russell **12.00**

Dodge Brothers March by Maxwell I. Pitkin & Victor Herbert, 1920, Dedicated by Mr. Herbert to Mr. Horace Dodge In Respectful Appreciation Of His Generous Efforts Towards The Advancement Of American Music (Victor Herbert, March & Dedication) **22.00**

Does It Pay? by Zittel & Sutton, 1907..................................**15.00**

Does The Girl You Left Behind Ever Wish You Back Again? by Robert F. Roden & Theodore Morse, 1910 ....**5.00**

Doin' The New Low Down by Dorothy Fields & Jimmy McHugh, 1928, Musical: Blackbirds Of 1928 (Cover Artist, Leff) **10.00**

Doin' The Racoon by Raymond Klages & J. Fred Coots, 1929..........**10.00**

Doin' The Suzi-Q by Benny Davis & J. Fred Coots, 1936, Musical: Cotton Club Parade..**12.00**

Doin' The Uptown Lowdown by Mack Gordon & Harry Revel, 1933, Movie: Broadway Through A Keyhole......................................**5.00**

Doin' What Comes Natur'lly by Irving Berlin, 1946, Movie: Annie Get Your Gun (Irving Berlin)..**12.00**

Doll Dance, The by Nacio Herb Brown, 1926 (Cover Artist, P.M. Griffith)...**5.00**

Doll House by Wyn, Richman & Davis, 1921 ....**5.00**

Doll's Dream by Theodor Oesten...**5.00**

Dolly Dear by Jack Norworth & Albert Von Tilzer, 1907, Photo Jack Norworth (Transportation)..**10.00**

Dolly O'Dean by Ed. Teschemacher & Landon Ronald, 1903 (Irish) .**10.00**

Dolly On The Street by A. J. Farmer, 1904 ....**10.00**

Dolly's Lullaby by Robert K. Stone, 1932 ....**5.00**

Dolores by Frank Loesser & Louis Alter, 1941, Movie: Las Vegas Nights, Signed Photo Frank Sinatra (Signed) **15.00**

Dominique by Soeur Sourire, O.P., 1963 ....**3.00**

Domino by Don Raye & Louis Farrari, 1940 ....**3.00**

Don Juan by Lee & Axt, 1927, Movie: Don Juan, Photo John Barrymore & Mary Astor...**10.00**

Donkey Serenade, The by Rudolph Friml & Herbert Stothart, 1937, Movie: The Firefly, Photo Jeannette MacDonald & Allan Jones (Cover Artist, Merman) **10.00**

Donkey, The by Gilbert Keith Chesterton & Richard Hageman, 1934..**5.00**

Donna Maria by Claude Debussy & Allie Wrubel, 1941 ....**5.00**

Don't Be A Baby, Baby by Buddy Kaye & Howard Steiner, 1946, Photo Mills Brothers (Cover Artist, A. J. Robinson)..................................**3.00**

Don't Be An Old Maid Molly by Kerry Mills, 1908..........................**10.00**

Don't Be Anybody's Soldier Boy But Mine by Joe Lyons & Frank Magine, 1918 (WWI)...**15.00**

Don't Be Contrary Mary by Felheimer, 1910 (Cover Artist, Pfeiffer).**10.00**

Don't Be Like That by Goetler, Tobias & Pinkard, 1928 (Cover Artist, Pfeiffer)...**10.00**

Don't Be Sad by Anita Owen, 1919 (Cover Artist, Frederick S. Manning) **20.00**

Don't Be What You Ain't by George V. Hobart, E. M. Royle & Silvio Hein, 1905 (Black, Black Face)..**15.00**

Don't Believe Everything You Dream by Harold Adamson & Jimmy McHugh, 1943 ....**5.00**

Don't Bite The Hand That's Feeding You by Hoier & Morgan, 1915...**5.00**

Don't Blame It All On Broadway by Harry Williams, Joe Young & Bert Grant, 1918 ....**5.00**

Don't Blame Me by Dorothy Fields & Jimmy McHugh, 1932 ....**5.00**

Don't Blame Me by Dorothy Fields & Jimmy McHugh, 1932, Movie: Big City, Photo Margaret O'Brien, Robert Preston, Danny Thomas, George Murphy & Betty Garrett **6.00**

Don't Blame Me For What Happens In The Moonlight by Bert Grant & Joe Young, 1914 (Cover Artist, Barbelle)....................................**10.00**

Don't Bring Lulu by Billy Rose, Lew Brown & Ray Henderson, 1925 (Cover Artist, Starmer)..12.00

Don't Cha Go 'Way Mad by Al Stillman & Jimmy Mundy, 1945, Photo Harry James **5.00**

Don't Cross Your Fingers, Cross Your Heart by Al Donahue, Larry Shay & Johnny Marks, 1933 ....**5.00**

Don't Cry Baby by Gus Kahn & Ted Fiorito, 1928, Photo Guy Lombardo (Deco) **5.00**

Don't Cry, Cry Baby by Saul Tepper, Bennie Martini & Clarence Maher, 1949, Photo Eddy Howard (Cover Artist, Barbelle) **3.00**

Don't Cry Frenchy by Sam M. Lewis, Joe Young & Walter Donaldson, 1919 (Cover Artist, Barbelle & WWI) **15.00**

Don't Cry Joe by Joe Marsala, 1940 (Cover Artist, Nick) **3.00**

Don't Cry Little Girl, Don't Cry by Maceo Pinkard, 1919 (Cover Artist, Barbelle, WWI & Deco)..**10.00**

Don't Cry Swanee by Al Jolson, B. G. DeSylva & Con Conrad, 1923, Musical: Bombo, Photo Al Jolson (Al Jolson).............................**12.00**

Don't Drink The Water by Williams & Gordon, 1969, Movie: Don't Drink The Water, Photo Jackie Gleason..**6.00**

Don't Fence Me In by Cole Porter, 1944, Movie: Hollywood Canteen, Photo Andrews Sisters, Jack Benny & Many More Stars (WWII)...**20.00**

Don't Forget Me When You're Gone by West & Redding, 1922 ....**5.00**

Don't Forget The Old Folks At Home by Harry Kennedy, 1882 (Pre 1900)..**15.00**

Don't Forget The Salvation Army (My Doughnut Girl) by Robert Brown, William Frisch, Elmore Leffingwell & James Lucas, 1919, Officially Endorsed & Adopted By The Salvation Army, Photo Doughnut Girl (Cover Artist, E.E. Walton, Salvation Army & WWI)...................**30.00**

Don't Forget To Come Back Home by Gus Kahn & Walter Donaldson, 1923, Photo Tom Kelly (Cover Artist, Wohlman) **10.00**

Don't Forget To Say "No" Baby by Hoagy Carmichael & Johnny Mercer, 1942 ....**5.00**

Don't Forget Tonight's The Night by Richards & Howard, 1915 (Cover Artist, Pfeiffer)..**15.00**

Don't Forget Your Dear Old Home by Wm. Delude, 1913 (Cover Artist, DeTakacs)...**10.00**

Don't Forget Your Dear Old Mother by H.H. Schultz & Courtney & J.J. Allemong, 1918 (WWI)..**15.00**

Don't Forget Your Mother by Herndon Pence, 1934 ....**5.00**

Don't Get Around Much Anymore by Bob Russell & Duke Ellington, 1942, Photo Glen Gray **5.00**

Don't Get Married Any More, Ma by Henry Pether, 1907, Photo Vesta Victoria **10.00**

Don't Give Up The Old Love For The New by James Thornton, 1896 (Pre 1900)...**15.00**

Don't Give Up The Ship by Al Dubin & Harry Warren, 1918 (WWI) .**15.00**

Don't Give Up The Ship by Al Dubin & Harry Warren, 1935, Movie: Shipmates Forever, Photo Dick Powell & Ruby Keeler **15.00**

Don't Go To Sleep by Arthur Freed & Oscar Levant, 1932, Photo John L. Fogarty...**6.00**

Don't Go To The Ball Tonight by J. H. Warner, 1899 (Pre 1900).......**15.00**

Don't Hang Your Dreams On A Rainbow by Irving Kahal & Arnold Johnson, 1929, Review: Earl Carroll's New Annual Review "Sketch Book" **6.00**

Don't Hold Everything by B. G. DeSylva, L. Brown & R. Henderson, 1928, Musical: Hold Everything (Cover Artist, Helen Van Doorn Morgan)..**15.00**

Don't It Mean A Thing To You by Grant Clark & Harry Akst, 1929, Movie: On With The Show **5.00**

Don't Leave Me Daddy by Jos. M. Verges, 1916 (WWI & Deco) **15.00**

Don't Leave Me Mammy by Benny Davis, B. G. DeSylva, Con Conrad & Henry W. Santly, 1922 ....**10.00**

Don't Leave Your Wife Alone by Irving Berlin, 1912 (Cover Artist, Pfeiffer & Irving Berlin)...**15.00**

Don't Let It Happen Again by Al J. Neiburg & Robert Levenson, 1934..**5.00**

Don't Let Me Down by John Lennon & Paul McCartney, 1969, Photo John Lennon & Paul McCartney **30.00**

Don't Let That Moon Get Away by Johnny Burke & James V. Monaco, 1938, Movie: Sing You Sinners, Photo Bing Crosby, Fred MacMurray & Donald O'Connor **6.00**

Don't Let The Stars Get In Your Eyes by Slim Willet, 1952, Photo Perry Como **5.00**

Don't Let This Waltz Mean Good-Bye by Meskill & Von Tilzer, 1934, Movie: Gift Of Gab, Photo Ruth Etting, Ethel Waters, Wini Shaw, Alice White & Edmund Lowe **5.00**

Don't Let Your Foot Slip Hiram by Norma Gregg, 1917 (Cover Artist, Goddard & WWI)...**15.00**

Don't Marry Me by Richard Rodgers & Oscar Hammerstein II, 1961, Movie: Flower Drum Song...**5.00**

Don't Mention Love To Me by Dorothy Fields & Oscar Levant, 1935, Movie: In Person **5.00**

Don't Mention My Name by Edward E. White & Edward Cooper, 1952 .**5.00**

Don't Mind The Rain by Ned Miller & Chester Cohn, 1924 ....**5.00**

Don't Nobody Bring Me No Bad News by Smalls, 1975, Movie: The Wiz, Photo Diana Ross, Nipsey Russell, Ted Ross & Michael Jackson...**6.00**

Don't Save Your Love by Walter Bullock & Harold Spina, 1937, Movie: 52nd Street **6.00**

Don't Say Good Night by Al Dubin & Harry Warren, 1934, Photo Kay Francis, Dick Powell, Dolores Del Rio, Al Jolson & Ricardo Cortez (Cover Artist, Harris & Al Jolson) **10.00**

Don't Say Goodby If You Love Me by Davis & Dodd, 1936................**5.00**

Don't Send Me Back To Petrograd by Irving Berlin, 1924, Music Box Revue 1925 (Irving Berlin)..**10.00**

Don't Send Your Wife To The Country by B. G. DeSylva & Louis Silvers, 1921, Musical: Bombo, Photo Al Jolson (Al Jolson) **15.00**

Don't Sit Under The Apple Tree by Lew Brown, Charlie Tobias & Sam H. Stept, 1942, Photo Kay Kyser (WWII).......................................**5.00**

Don't Slam That Door by Lynot, 1916 (Cover Artist, Pfeiffer) **10.00**

Don't Sweetheart Me by Cliff Friend & Charlie Tobias, 1943, Photo Sammy Kaye (Cover Artist, Im-Ho) **3.00**

Don't Sweetheart Me by Cliff Friend & Charlie Tobias, 1943, Photo Eddie Cantor (Cover Artist, Im-Ho & Eddie Cantor)...............................**8.00**

Don't Take Advantage by Howard E. Rogers & James V. Monaco, 1919, Photo Sophie Tucker, Eddie Cantor, Felix Adler, Milt Francis, Frank Gaby, Rae Samuels, Willie Smith & George Jessel (Transportation)...**10.00**

Don't Take Away Those Blues by Joe McKiernan & Norman Spencer, 1920 (Blues) **10.00**

Don't Take My Darling Boy Away by Will Dillon & Albert Von Tilzer, 1915 (WWI)...**15.00**

Don't Take Your Love From Me by Henry Nemo, 1941 ....**2.00**

Don't Tell A Lie About Me, Dear by James Cavanaugh, John Redmond & Frank Weldon, 1942 ....**5.00**

Don't Tell A Secret To A Rose by Leo Robin & Ralph Rainger, 1937, Movie: Big Broadcast Of 1938, Photo Shirley Ross, Caricature of W.C. Fields, Bob Hope, Martha Raye & Ben Blue.....................**12.00**

Don't Tell Her That You Saw Me by Paul Dresser, 1896 (Pre 1900) **15.00**

Don't Tell The Folks That You Saw Me by Allen & Daly, 1915 (Cover Artist, Pfeiffer & WWI)..**15.00**

Don't Try To Steal The Sweetheart Of A Soldier by Alfred Bryan, Gus Van & Joe Schenck, 1917, Signed Photo Anna Chandler (Signed & WWI)..**25.00**

Don't Wait Too Long by Irving Berlin, 1925 (Irving Berlin) **10.00**

Don't Wake Me Up by L. Wolfe Gilbert & Mabel Wayne, 1925 ....**5.00**

Don't Wake Me Up, I Am Dreaming by Beth S. Whitson & Herb Ingraham, 1910, Photo Bessie Wynn (Deco).......................................**10.00**

Don't Wake Me Up, I Am Dreaming by Beth S. Whitson & Herb Ingraham, 1910, Photo Eva Shirley (Deco) **10.00**

Don't Wake Up My Heart by Sam W. Lewis, Geo W. Meyer & Pete Wendling, 1938 ....**5.00**

Don't Waste Your Tears Over Me by A. J. Stasny, 1923 (Deco)..........**5.00**

Don't Wear Your Heart On Your Sleeve by Ed Marks & Joe Stern, 1901...**10.00**

Don't Worry by Kim Gannon & Jule Styne, 1943, Movie: Salute For Three, Photo, Betty Rhodes, McDonald Carey & Donna Drake (WWII)...**10.00**

Don't Worry 'Bout Me by Ted Koehler & Rube Bloom, 1939, Musical: Cotton Club Parade, World Fair 1939 (Cover Artist, Im-Ho)........**10.00**

Don't Worry 'Bout Me by Ted Koehler & Rube Bloom, 1939, Photo Frank Sinatra...**3.00**

Don't Worry Me by Richard Rodgers & Oscar Hammerstein II, 1961, Movie: Flower Drum Song...**5.00**

Don't You Ever Think About Me Dearie by Cahill, 1911 (Cover Artist, Pfeiffer)...**10.00**

Don't You Go Tommy by C. T. Lockwood, 1867 (Pre 1900)..............**15.00**

Don't You Know I Care? by Duke Ellington & M. David, 1944..........**5.00**

Don't You Love Me Anymore by Mack David, Al Hoffman & Jerry Livingston, 1947, Photo Anita Ellis..**3.00**

Don't You Love Me Anymore? by Mack David, Al Hoffman & Jerry Livingston, 1947, Photo Jack Smith **3.00**

Don't You Love Your Baby No More? by Jack Frost, 1915................**5.00**

Don't You Remember? by Ed. Dangel & Charles Frank, 1911 ....**5.00**

Don't You Remember Me? by Sunny Skylar & Frankie Carle, 1945....**3.00**

Don't You Remember Sally? by Walter Hirsch, Bernie Grossman & Milton Samuels, 1928...**5.00**

Don't You Remember The Day? by Cliff Hess, 1918 (Cover Artist, Barbelle) **10.00**

Don't You Think It's Time To Marry? by Gus Edwards, 1906, Movie: The Blue Moon **6.00**

Don't You Think You'd Better Let Me Try? by J. Will Callahan & Will L. Livernash, 1918, Photo Celeste Brooks (Cover Artist, Pfeiffer & Deco) **15.00**

Don't You Want A Paper Dearie? by Jerome Kern, 1916....................**5.00**

Don't You Want To Take Me? by Anne Caldwell & Jerome Kern, 1920, Musical: The Night Boat **5.00**

Don't You Wish You Were Back Home Again? by Chas. K. Harris, 1913, Minstrel (Cover Artist, White, N.Y. & Black, Black Face) **25.00**

Doo Dah Blues by Billy Rose & Ted Fiorito, 1922 (Blues)................**10.00**

Doodle Oodle Dee Means Won't You Marry Me? by Theodore Morse, 1914 ....**12.00**

Doodle-Doo-Doo by Kassel & Stitzel, 1924 ....**3.00**

Door Of My Dreams by Otto Harbach, Oscar Hammerstein II & Rudolf Friml, 1924, Musical: Rose Marie **5.00**

Dope by W. C. Powell, 1906 (Rag) **10.00**

Dora Dean by Williams & Walker, 1895 (Pre 1900)...........................**10.00**

Dora? Laura? by Denham Harrison & J.A. Bentham, 1905 ....**5.00**

Dorine Of Dublin by Gladys G. Dennis & Harry H. Williams, 1915, Photo Signed by Bonita (Irish & Signed) **10.00**

Dorothy by Seymour Smith, 1907 (Cover Artist, M.E.C.)....................**5.00**

Dorothy Waltzes by John C. Rodenbeck, 1914 (Cover Artist, Pfeiffer).**15.00**

Double Clog Dance by J.L.G., 1864 (Pre 1900)...............................**25.00**

Double Trouble by Leo Robin, Richard Whiting & Ralph Rainger, 1935, Movie: The Big Broadcast of 1936, Photo Lyda Roberti & Jack Oakie **10.00**

Dove Of Peace Waltzes by Loveland, 1915 (Cover Artist, Pfeiffer)....**10.00**

Down Among The Sheltering Palms by James Brockman & Abe Olman, 1915, Photo Pied Pipers.......................................**5.00**

Down Among The Sheltering Palms by James Brockman & Abe Olman, 1915, Photo Al Jolson (Cover Artist, R.S. & Al Jolson)................**15.00**

Down Among The Sleepy Hills Of Ten-Ten-Tennessee by Joe Young, Sam M. Lewis & Geo. W. Meyer, 1923 (Cover Artist, Perret)........**8.00**

Down Among The Sugar Cane by Avery, Hart, Mack & Smith, 1908 (Cover Artist, Pfeiffer) **15.00**

Down Argentina Way by Gordon & Warren, 1940, Movie: Down Argentina Way, Photo Betty Grable, Don Ameche & Carmen Miranda ...**12.00**

Down Around The 'Sip 'Sip 'Sippy Shore by Joe Young, Sam Lewis & Walter Donaldson, 1921 ....**10.00**

Down At Mammy Jinny's Cabin Door by Kempner, 1910 (Cover Artist, Pfeiffer & Black, Black Face) **20.00**

Down At The Huskin' Bee by Halsey K. Mohr, 1917 (Dixie & March) .**10.00**

Down At The Huskin' Bee by S. R. Henry, 1909 (Dixie & March) **15.00**

Down At The Old Swimming Hole by Wilson & Brennan, 1921 ....**10.00**

Down Beside The Cider Mill by Bryan & Gumble, 1920 (Cover Artist, Pfeiffer)..**10.00**

Down By The Erie Canal by Geo M. Cohan (George M. Cohan)........**15.00**

Down By The Meadow Brook by Pete Wendling & Edgar Leslie, 1919 (Cover Artist, Barbelle) **5.00**

Down By The Old Apple Tree by Wilson & J.Kiern Brennan, 1923.....**6.00**

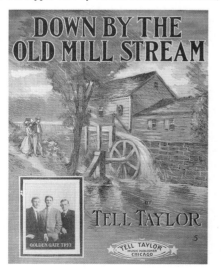

Down By The Old Mill Stream by Tell Taylor, 1910, Photo Golden Gate Trio **10.00**

Down By The Old Rustic Well by Bob Miller, Wayne King & Jack Erickson, 1933, Photo Art Sotherley..............................**5.00**

Down By The Rio Grande by Al M. Herman & Roy H. King, 1911 ....**5.00**

Down By The River by Lorenz Hart & Richard Rodgers, 1935, Movie: Mississippi, Photo Bing Crosby & Joan Bennett **15.00**

Down By The Winegar Woiks by Don Bestor, Roger Lewis & Walter Donovan, 1925..**15.00**

Down De Lover's Lane by Paul Lawrence Dunbar, 1900, Photo Virginia Earle (Black, Black Face)..............................**20.00**

Down Georgia Way by Geo. B. Norton & J. F. Barrie, 1913 (Cover Artist, Starmer & Dixie) **10.00**

Down Home In Tennessee by W. Jerome & Walter Donaldson, 1915 ..**5.00**

Down Home Rag by Wilber C.S. Sweatman, 1911, Photo Maurice & Florence Walton (Cover Artist, Starmer, Rag & Black, Black Face)..**15.00**

Down Honolulu Way by J.E. Dempsey, Earl Burtnett & Jos. A. Burke, 1916 ....**5.00**

Down In Bom Bombay by Ballard MacDonald & Harry Carrol, 1915, Photo Al Jolson (Cover Artist, Dunk & Al Jolson).....................**15.00**

Down In Borneo Isle by Henry Creamer & Turner Layton, 1917.........**5.00**

Down In Chattanooga by Irving Berlin, 1913 (Cover Artist, Pfeiffer & Irving Berlin)..**15.00**

Down In Chinatown by Joe Meyer & Geo. P. Hulten, 1920 ....**5.00**

Down In Dear Old New Orleans by Joe Young, Conrad & Whidden, 1912, Photo Clarice Vance (Cover Artist, Starmer)....................**12.00**

Down In Gossip Row by Edward Harrigan & David Braham, 1882 (Pre 1900)..**10.00**

Down In Honky Tonky Town by Chas. McCarron & Chris Smith, 1916 .**10.00**

Down In Jungle Town by Edward Madden & Theodore Morse, 1908..**10.00**

Down In Maine by Halsey K. Mohr, 1910 (Cover Artist, Pfeiffer)......**15.00**

Down In My Heart My Darling by Jones, 1916 (Cover Artist, Pfeiffer & Deco) **10.00**

Down In Old Havana Bay by Madden & Phillips, 1911 ....**5.00**

Down In Old Nantucket by Ryan, 1913 (Transportation) **5.00**

Down In Pickaninny Alley by Harry DeCosta, Addy Britt & Dick Finch, 1924 (Black, Black Face) **15.00**

Down In Poverty Row by Gussie L. Davis & Arthur Trevelyan, 1895 (Pre 1900)..**10.00**

Down In Shady Lane by Ballard & Kelly, 1910.................................**5.00**

Down In Sunny Honey Town by Jack Mahoney & Theodore Morse, 1910..**5.00**

Down In The Deep, Let Me Sleep When I Die by H.W. Petrie (Transportation)..**10.00**

Down In The Depths by Cole Porter, 1936, Movie: Red, Hot & Blue...**5.00**

Down In The Glen by Harry Gordon & Tommie Connor, 1947 ....**3.00**

Down In The Old Apple Orchard by Ted Garton & Wm. R. Clay, 1917 .**5.00**

Down In The Old Cherry Orchard by Alfred Bryan & S.R. Henry, 1907 ....**10.00**

Down In The Old Meadow Lane by Harry Williams, 1911 ....**5.00**

Down In The Old Neighborhood by George Moriarty & Richard Whiting, 1915 ....**10.00**

Down In The Subway by Jean Schwartz & M. K. Jerome, 1904 ....**10.00**

Down In The Vale Of Shenandoah by Chas. K. Harris, 1906.............**10.00**

Down Kentucky Way by James W. Casey, 1919 ....**5.00**

Down On MacConnachy Square by Alan Jay Lerner & Frederick J. Loewe, 1947, Movie: Brigadoon..............................**5.00**

Down On Melody Farm by Sammy Kahn, Bronislaw Kaper & Walter Jurmann, 1937, Movie: Everybody Sing, Photo Judy Garland **16.00**

Down On The Farm by Billy Dale, Charles, Parrott, Jimmy Adams & Harry Harrison, 1923 (Cover Artist, Politzer)....................**10.00**

Down On The Farm by DuBois, 1890 (Pre 1900) **15.00**

Down On The Florida Shore by Ballard Macdonald & Harry Carroll, 1926 ....**6.00**

Down South by B.G. DeSylva & Louis Silvers, 1921, Musical: Bombo, Photo Al Jolson (Al Jolson)..**12.00**

Down South by Sigmund Spaeth & Wm. H. Myddleton, 1927 (Cover Artist, Rose)..**10.00**

Down T'Uncle Bill's by Hoagy Carmichael & Johnny Mercer, 1934 ...**5.00**

Down The Lane & Home Again by Edgar Leslie, Bert Kalmar & M.K. Jerome, 1919...**5.00**

Down The Old Ox Road by Coslow & Johnston, 1933, Movie: College Humor, Photo Bing Crosby, Burns & Allen, Mary Carlisle, Jack Oakie & Richard Arlen **12.00**

Down The River Of Golden Dreams by John Klenner & Nathaniel Skilkret, 1930...**3.00**

Down The Sunset Trail To Avalon by Jack Frost & E. Clinton Keithley, 1916 ....**5.00**

Down The Trail Of The Old Dirt Road by Richard Howard & Nat Vincent, 1918 (Cover Artist, Barbelle & WWI) **20.00**

Down The Trail To Home Sweet Home by Ernest R. Ball, 1920 ....**5.00**

Down The Trail To Mother Dear by L.W. Lewis, 1918 (WWI) **10.00**

Down The Winding Road Of Dreams by Margaret Cantrell & Ernest R. Ball, 1922...**5.00**

Down To The Folies Bergere by Irving Berlin, 1911 (Cover Artist, Pfeiffer & Irving Berlin)...**15.00**

Down Upon The Old Swanee by William J.McKenna, 1913.................**5.00**

Down Went McGinty Dressed In His Best Suit Of Clothes by Joseph Flynn, 1889 (Pre 1900 & Irish) **15.00**

Down Where The Blue Grass Grows by Roden & Kendis, 1915 (Cover Artist, Pfeiffer)...**10.00**

Down Where The Breezes Blow by Moss, 1903 (Transportation).......**10.00**

Down Where The Cotton Blossoms Grow by Andrew Sterling & Harry VonTilzer, 1901...**15.00**

Down Where The Old Mill Stream Flows by Taylor & Smith, 1914.....**5.00**

Down Where The Silvery Mohawk Flows by Rosenfeld & Heinzmann, 1904 ....**10.00**

Down Where The Sun Goes Down by Isham Jones & Verne Buck, 1928, Photo Verne Buck (Cover Artist, JVR)........................**3.00**

Down Where The Swanee River Flows by Chas. McCaron, Charles S. Alberte & Albert VonTilzer, 1916, Photo Al Jolson (Al Jolson)...**12.00**

Down Where The Sweet Potatoes Grow by Harry Von Tilzer, 1917 (Cover Artist, Pfeiffer)..**10.00**

Down Where The Tennessee Flows by Sherwood & Rule, 1913 (Cover Artist, Pfeiffer, Al Jolson & Black, Black Face)..........**15.00**

Down Where The Werzburger Flows by Raymond Brown & Harry VonTilzer, 1902...**10.00**

Down Yonder by L. Wolfe Gilbert, 1948, Photo Spade Cooley **3.00**

Dream, A by Charles B. Cory & J.C. Bartlett, 1923, Dedicated To Miss Gertrude Edmands (Cover Artist, Haskell Coffin & Dedication) ..**15.00**

Dream A Little Dream Of Me by Gus Kahn, W. Schwandt & F. Andree, 1931, Photo Frankie Laine.....................................**5.00**

Dream A Little Dream Of Me by Gus Kahn, W. Schwandt & F. Andree, 1931, Photo Dinah Shore....................................**5.00**

Dream Awhile by Johnny Mercer & Phil Ohman, 1936, Photo Frank DeVol...**2.00**

Dream by Johnny Mercer, 1944, Photo Frank Sinatra...........................**6.00**

Dream by Johnny Mercer, 1945, Photo Freddie Martin (Cover Artist, Holley)..**3.00**

Dream by Johnny Mercer, 1945, Photo The Pied Pipers **5.00**

Dream Daddy by Louis Herscher & George Keefer, 1923, Photo Jack Chapman & His Orchestra (Cover Artist, Perret & Deco).............**5.00**

Dream Dancing by Cole Porter, 1941, Movie: You'll Never Get Rich..**6.00**

Dream Days by Chas. L. Johnson, 1913...**5.00**

Dream Days by Morrison, 1914 (Cover Artist, Pfeiffer).....................**10.00**

Dream Days, Vision Of Bliss by Reinhardt & Smith, 1909 ....**5.00**

Dream! Dream! by Harry Smith & Victor Jacobi, 1917.......................**5.00**

Dream, Dream, Dream by John Redman & Lou Ricca, 1946 ....**3.00**

Dream Garden Reverie by Vandersloot, 1916 (Cover Artist, Pfeiffer)...**10.00**

Dream House by Lynn Cowan, 1926..**5.00**

Dream I Had Last Night, The by Jack Caddigan, James A. Brennan & O.E. Story, 1915 ....**10.00**

Dream Is A Wish Your Heart Makes, A by Mack David, Al Hoffman & Jerry Livingston, 1949, Movie: Cinderella (Disney)...............**10.00**

Dream Kisses by Jack Yellen & M.K. Jerome, 1927, Photo Anna Chandler (Cover Artist, Barbelle) **5.00**

Dream Kisses by Jack Yellen & M.K. Jerome, 1927, Photo Ginger Rogers (Cover Artist, Barbelle & Deco)...........................**20.00**

Dream Kisses by Jack Yellen & M.K. Jerome, 1927, Photo Melba Caldwell (Cover Artist, Barbelle & Deco)..............................**5.00**

Dream Kisses by Jack Yellen & M.K. Jerome, 1927, Photo Sophie Tucker (Cover Artist, Barbelle & Deco)..............................**22.00**

Dream Kisses by Walter Rolfe, 1911 (Cover Artist, Starmer) **10.00**

Dream Lover by Clifford Grey & Victor Schertzinger, 1929, Movie: The Love Parade **5.00**

Dream Maker In Japan by Sam Lewis, Joe Young & Rudolf Friml, 1924..**5.00**

Dream Melody by Ted Koehler, Frank Magine & C. Nast, 1922, Photo The Misses Dennis: Ruth, Ann & Cherie **5.00**

Dream Mother by Al Lewis, Al Sherman & Joe Burke, 1929, Photo Dick Robertson (Cover Artist, Leff) **3.00**

Dream Of A Soldier Boy, The by Al Dubin & James V. Monaco, 1917 (WWI)..**20.00**

Dream Of Autumn by F.H.Losey, 1909 ....**5.00**

Dream Of Love And You by Glenhall Taylor, 1926, Photo Silver Masked Tenor (Deco)...**5.00**

Dream Of Olwen, The by Winifred May & Charles Williams, 1945.....**5.00**

Dream Of Paradise by Johnston, 1902..**5.00**

Dream Of The Flowers by Chas. Cohen, 1909 ....**5.00**

Dream Of The Rose by Jos. J. Kaiser, 1907 (Cover Artist, Mitchell)..**10.00**

Dream Of The Rose by Will B.Morrison, 1912.......................................**5.00**

Dream Of The South, A by Harry Lincoln, 1909 ....**5.00**

Dream On by E.S. Phelps, 1918 ....**5.00**

Dream On Little Dreamer by Fred B. Burch & Jan Crutchfield, 1965, Photo Perry Como **5.00**

Dream Peddler's Serenade, The by John Rufus Sharp III & Johnny Mercer, 1950 ....**5.00**

Dream River by Billy Hill, 1928 ....**5.00**

Dream Ship, Sail On To Slumberland by J.E. Allemong & Harold B. Freeman, 1919 ....**3.00**

Dream Sweetheart by Bud Green, 1932 (Cover Artist, Barbelle & Deco)..**10.00**

Dream Tango, The by Uriel Davis, 1913..**5.00**

Dream That Gave You Back To Me by Mueller, 1915 (Cover Artist, Pfeiffer) **10.00**

Dream Time by Benny Davis & J. Fred Coots, 1936 ....**3.00**

Dream Train by Charles Newman & Billy Baskette, 1928, Photo Guy Lombardo..**5.00**

Dream Valley by Nick Kenny, Charles Kenny & Joe Burke, 1940, Photo Joey Kearns (Cover Artist, Sorokin) **3.00**

Dream Waltz by F. Henri Klickman, 1914, Photo Mae Murray...........**5.00**

Dream Waltz by W.C. Powell, 1910...**5.00**

Dream Waltzes by McDonald, 1909 (Cover Artist, Pfeiffer)..............**10.00**

Dream Within A Dream, A by Edgar Allen Poe & E.G. Sonneck, 1917.**10.00**

Dreamer by Don Blanding & Albert Hay Malotte, 1928.......................**5.00**

Dreamer Of Dreams by Gus Kahn & Ted Fiorito, 1924, Photo Austin Young (Cover Artist, Frederick S. Manning & Deco) **12.00**

Dreamer, The by Frank Loesser & Arthur Schwartz, 1943, Movie: Thank Your Lucky Stars, Photo Eddie Cantor, Humphrey Bogart & Many Other Stars (Eddie Cantor) **12.00**

Dreamer With A Penny by Allan Roberts & Lester Lee, 1949, Musical: All For Love, Photo Grace & Paul Hartman & Bert Wheeler..........**5.00**

Dreamer's Holiday, A by Kim Gannon & Mabel Wayne, 1949, Photo Perry Como (Cover Artist, Nick) **6.00**

Dreamer's Holiday, A by Kim Gannon & Mabel Wayne, 1949, Photo Vic Damone (Cover Artist, Nick) **5.00**

Dreaming by Earl Carroll & Archibald Joyce, 1911, Photo Kitty Gordon..**5.00**

Dreaming by L.W. Heiser & J. Anton Dailey, 1906.............................**5.00**

Dreaming by Volz, 1917 (Cover Artist, Pfeiffer).............................**10.00**

Dreaming Love Of You by Chas. K. Harris, 1905 (Cover Artist, Starmer)..**15.00**

Dreaming Of Home Sweet Home by Ballard MacDonald & James F. Hanley, 1918 (Cover Artist, Starmer & WWI) **20.00**

Dreaming Of Mother At Twilight by Billy Lang, 1921 (Cover Artist, E.S. Fisher)..**16.00**

Dreaming Of The Same Old Girl by Gus Kahn & Egberg Van Alstyne, 1920 (Cover Artist, Pfeiffer & Deco).....................................**10.00**

Dreaming Of You by Rene Bronner & H.W. Petrie, 1910 ....**5.00**

Dreaming Out Loud by Sam Coslow, 1940, Movie: Dreaming Out Loud, Photo Frances Langford, Lum & Abner, Frank Craven, Phil Harris & Bobs Watson (Cover Artist, HBK)..**4.00**

Dreaming Sweet Dreams Of Mother by Jack Cadigan & Jas. H. Brennan, 1919 ....**10.00**

Dreaming Waltz by Adelaid Aguero, 1911 ....**10.00**

Dreamland Brings Memories Of You by Ernie Erdman & Celia Tomkins, 1919 (Deco)...**15.00**

Dreams by Andrew B. Sterling & Harry Von Tilzer, 1919 (Cover Artist, EEW) **5.00**

Dreams by Denison & Dusenberry, 1911 ....**5.00**

Dreams, Just Dreams by Irving Berlin & Ted Snyder, 1909 (Cover Artist, John Frew & Irving Berlin) **15.00**

Dreams, Just Dreams by R.N. Doore & Richard Howard, 1919, Photo Alice Joyce..**10.00**

Dreams, Nothing More Than Dreams by Jose Valdez & Wilbur Chenoweth, 1929, Photo Rudy Vallee.....................................**5.00**

Dreams Of A Soldier Boy, The by Alfred Dubin & James V. Monaco, 1918 (WWI)..**15.00**

Dreams Of Long Ago by Earl Carroll & Enrico Caruso, 1912, Signed Photo Enrico Caruso, Especially Composed by Enrico Caruso For Henry W. Savage's Production "The Million" (Cover Artist, Mishkin Studio & Signed) **40.00**

Dreams Of Long Ago by Morton David & Horatio Nicholls, 1919.......**5.00**

Dreams Of Love by Harvey & Simon, 1912 (Cover Artist, Pfeiffer & Deco) **15.00**

Dreams Of Mother by Jack Caddigan & Jas. H. Brennan, 1914 ....**5.00**

Dreams Of My Own Land by Douglas Dean, 1895 (Pre 1900)...........**15.00**

Dreams Of Spring by Ventrice Crocker, 1913....................................**5.00**

Dreamy Alabama by Ballard Macdonald & Mary Earl, 1919 (Cover Artist, Frederick S. Manning & Lithograph, Hayes, N.Y.) **15.00**

Dreamy Amazon by L. Wolfe Gilbert, Darl MacBoyle & Nat Vincent, 1919 ....**5.00**

Dreamy Carolina Moon by Erwin R. Schmidt, 1925....................**5.00**

Dreamy Hawaii by Ray Sherwood & F.W.Vandersloot, 1921 ....**5.00**

Dreamy Hawaiian Moon by Harry Owens, 1938, Movie: Cocoanut Grove...**6.00**

Dreamy Melody by Ted Koehler, Frank Magine & C. Naset, 1922, Photo Art Landry And His Call Of The North Orchestra........................**5.00**

Dreamy Melody by Ted Koehler, Frank Magine & C. Naset, 1922, Photo The Misses Dennis: Ruth, Ann & Cherie.................................**5.00**

Dreamy Moon by Sidney Carter & Walter Smith, 1917 (Cover Artist, L.E. Morgan) **5.00**

Dreamy Old New England Moon by Marty Berk, Frank Capano & Max C. Freedman, 1948, Photo Vaughn Monroe....................................**5.00**

Dreamy Oriental Melody by E.T. Paull, 1920 (Cover Artist, E.T. Paull & March) **35.00**

Dreamy South Sea Moon by Hoyt, 1929 (Cover Artist, Pfeiffer)........**10.00**

Dress Up Your Dollars In Khaki by Lister Alwood & Richard Whiting, 1918, Introduced by National War Saving Committee (Cover Artist, Wayne Plates & WWI)...**25.00**

Drifting Along To The Isle Of Love by Wilbur Weeks & M. Alexander, 1920 ....**10.00**

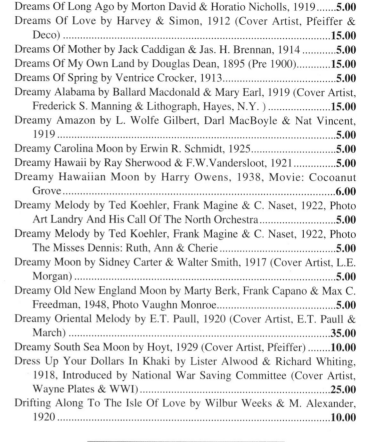

Drifting by Arthur J. Lamb & W.C. Polla, 1920 (Lithograph, Knapp Co. & Deco) **12.00**

Drifting In A Lover's Dream by Herbert Leslie, 1933 ....**3.00**

Drifting On by Howard Johnson & Joseph Santly, 1919 (Deco) **10.00**

Driftwood by Davis, Davis & Lyman, 1928..**5.00**

Driftwood by Gus Kahn & Lew Gold, 1926 (Cover Artist, Perret) **10.00**

Drill, Ye Tarriers, Drill by Thomas Casey, 1888 (Pre 1900) **15.00**

Drink! Drink! Come Brother Drink! by Paul Raasch & Edw. B. Macks Jr., 1930 ....**6.00**

Drink To Me Only With Thine Eyes by Ben Jonson, Arranged by Roger Quilter, 1921 ....**5.00**

Drink Up, Boys by Arthur West, 1890 (Pre 1900) **15.00**

Drinking Song by Dorothy Donnelly & Sigmund Romberg, 1925 ....**3.00**

Drip, Drip, Drip Went The Waterfall by Ballard MacDonald & Harry Carroll, 1915, Photo Mercedes Lorenze & James Duffy **5.00**

Drowsy Head by Irving Berlin & Vaughn DeLeath, 1921 (Irving Berlin) **10.00**

Drowsy Waters by Ailau & Howard, 1917.................................**5.00**

Druid's Prayer by Davson, 1910..**5.00**

Drum Beat by Washington & Young, 1954, Movie: Drum Beat, Photo Alan Ladd & Audrey Dalton **5.00**

Drum Major March by Jacob Henry Ellis, 1921 (March) **10.00**

Drum Major, The by Bert Brown, 1912 (March) **10.00**

Drums In My Heart by Edward Heyman & Vincent Youmans, 1932....**5.00**

Drums In The Night by Frank Loesser & Jimmy McHugh, 1940, Movie: Buck Benny Rides Again, Photo Jack Benny, Phil Harris, Ellen Drew, Dennis Day & Rochester **12.00**

Dry Yo' Eyes by Sigmund Landsberg, 1904 (Black, Black Face) **15.00**

Dubarry, The by Rowland Leigh & Carl Millocker, 1941, Photo Grace Mcore (Cover Artist, Harris) **5.00**

Dublin Rag, The by Harold R. Atterridge & Phil Schwartz, 1910, Musical: Madame Sherry, Photo Elizabeth Murray (Cover Artist, Pfeiffer, Irish & Rag) **16.00**

Duel Of Hearts And Eyes, The by Kerry Mills, 1903 ....**15.00**

Duke Of Ka-Ki-Ak! by Leslie & Donaldson, 1929, Movie: Hot For Paris, Photo Fifi Dorsay, Victor McLaglen, El Brendel & Raoul Walsh..**6.00**

Duna by Marjorie Pickthall & Josephine McGill, 1914 ....**5.00**

Dunk A Doughnut by Raymond Leveen & Frankie Carle, 1939 ....**5.00**

Dusting The Keys by J.Edward Killalea & Edward Claypoole, 1923 (Rag) **10.00**

Dusty Dudes Cake Walk by Jean Schwartz, 1899 (Pre 1900 & Black, Black Face) **20.00**

Dusty Road by Rene & Rene, 1935, Photo Nelson Eddy **5.00**

Dwarfs' Yodel Song, The by Larry Morey & Frank Churchill, 1938, Movie: Snow White (Disney)...**10.00**

Dying Poet, The by Gottschalk, 1907.......................................**10.00**

E-Yip-Yow! Yankee Boys, Welcome Home Again by Bob E. Sear & Al W. Brown, 1918 (WWI) **15.00**

Each Little Feeling by Jas. E. Dempsey & J.C. Schmid, 1912 (Cover Artist, Pfeiffer)...**10.00**

Each Stitch Is A Thought Of You Dear by Al Sweet & Billy Baskette, 1918, Dedicated To That Army Of Noble Women-Mothers-Sisters And Sweethearts Who Are Doing Their Bit For The Boys "Over There" (Cover Artist, Henry Hutt, Dedication & WWI)................**25.00**

Eadie Was A Lady by B.G. DeSylva, Richard A. Whiting & Nacio Herb Brown, 1932, Movie: Take A Chance **5.00**

Early Autumn by Johnny Mercer, Ralph Burns & Woody Herman, 1952, Photo Woody Herman **2.00**

Early Bird by Sidney Mitchell & Lew Pollack, 1936, Movie: Captain January. Photo Shirley Temple (Shirley Temple)..............**12.00**

Easiest Way, The by Arthur E. Behim, 1909.................................**5.00**

East Of St. Louis Blues by W.C. Handy, 1937 (Blues) **5.00**

East Of The Sun & West Of The Moon by Brooks Bowman, 1935, Musical: Stags At Bay **5.00**

East Side Of Heaven by Johnny Burke & James V. Monaco, 1939, Movie: East Side Of Heaven, Photo Bing Crosby, Joan Blondell & Baby Sandy.......**5.00**

East, West, Hames' Best by Bill McDonnell & Alec Finlay, 1952, Signed Photo Alec Finlay, Dedicated To Scots Everywhere (Signed & Dedicated) **12.00**

Eastbound Train, The by Nick Manaloff, 1935, Photo Winnie, Lou & Sally (Cover Artist, Lou Kummel & Transportation) **10.00**

Easter Parade by Irving Berlin, 1947, Movie: Easter Parade, Photo Judy Garland, Fred Astaire, Peter Lawford & Ann Miller (Irving Berlin).......**16.00**

Easter Sunday Parade, The by George M. Cohan, 1927 (George M. Cohan) **15.00**

Eastern Moon by M.E. Rourke & Jerome Kern, 1907, Musical: Morals Of Marcus, Photo Marie Doro (Cover Artist, Gene Buck).................**10.00**

Easy Street by Alan Rankin Jones, 1941 ....**5.00**

Easy Street by William H. Penn, 1905, Photo Toby Claude **10.00**

Easy To Love by Cole Porter, 1936, Movie: Born to Dance, Photo Eleanor Powell **6.00**

Easy Winners by Scott Joplin, 1901 (Scott Joplin & Rag).................**50.00**

Ebb Tide by Carl Sigman & Robert Maxwell, 1953, Photo Frank Chacksfield (Cover Artist, Sorokin)..**3.00**

Ebb Tide by Leo Robin & Ralph Rainger, 1937, Movie: Ebb Tide **5.00**

Ebony Rhapsody by Johnston & Coslow, 1934, Movie: Earl Carroll's Murder At The Vanities..**10.00**

Echoes by Bennie Benjamin & George Weiss, 1949, Photo Sammy Kaye **3.00**

Echoes From The Snowball Club by Harry P. Guy, 1898 (Cover Artist, Levytype Co., Pre 1900 & Rag) **25.00**

Echoes From The Woodland by Walter, 1903................................**5.00**

Echoes Of Love by Jacob Henry Ellis, 1914 ....**5.00**

Echoes Of The Wildwoods by Louis A. Drumheller, 1904, Dedicated To B.G. Mickel (Cover Artist, Gillam & Dedication) **10.00**

Ecstatic by Vernon Eville, 1914 (Deco).............................**12.00**

Eddie Cantor's "Automobile Horn" Song by Clarence Gaskill, 1929 (Eddie Cantor & Transportation)..**20.00**

Eddie, Steady by Eddie Cantor, 1923, Ziegfeld Follies, Photo Eddie Cantor In Black Face (Cover Artist, Politzer, Eddie Cantor & Black, Black Face) **25.00**

Edelweiss by Paul West & Gustave Kerker, 1907, Musical: The White Hen (Cover Artist, Etherington) **15.00**

Edelweiss by Richard Rodgers & Oscar Hammerstein II, 1959, Movie: The Sound Of Music, Photo Julie Andrews & Christopher Plummer......**8.00**

Edelweiss Glide by F.E. Vanderbeck, 1908 ....**10.00**

Educate Your Feet by Jack Yellen, Milton Ager & Henry Sullivan, 1929, Musical Comedy: First Edition Of Murray Anderson's Almanac**10.00**

Eeny Meeny Miney Mo by Johnny Mercer & Matt Malneck, 1935, Movie: To Beat The Band (Cover Artist, Barbelle)....................................**6.00**

Egypt by Clare Kummer, 1903 ....**5.00**

Egyptian Moonlight by Jack Caddigan & A. Fred Phillips, 1919 ....**5.00**

Egyptian Nights by Flynn & Siragusa, 1919 (Cover Artist, Pfeiffer) ..**10.00**

Egyptland by Costello & Casey, 1919 (Cover Artist, Pfeiffer)...........**10.00**

Eight Little Notes by Charlie Tobias, Nelson Cogan & Sammy Fain, 1938 ..**5.00**

Eight Little Songs Without Words by B. Cecil Klein, 1891 (Pre 1900)..**5.00**

Eileen Alanna by Thomas Marble, 1873 (Pre 1900) **10.00**

Eileen by Ernest J. Schuster, 1912, Photo Ernest J. Schuster (Cover Artist, Paul Creasey)....................**10.00**

Eileen by Henry Blossom & Victor Herbert, 1917 (Victor Herbert)....**10.00**

Eileen by Spurr, 1914 (Cover Artist, Pfeiffer)....................**10.00**

Eileen, From Old Killarney by Allen Spurr, 1914, Photo Smith & Fleming (Irish)....................**10.00**

Eily Machree by Stout & Braham, 1878 (Pre 1900)............**10.00**

Eisenhower, 1950 Inauguration, 1953 (President & Political) **15.00**

Either It's Love Or It Isn't by Roberts & Fisher, 1946, Movie: Dead Reckoning, Photo Humphrey Bogart & Lizabeth Scott **12.00**

El Capitan March by John Phillip Sousa, 1898 (John Philip Sousa, March & Pre 1900) **20.00**

El Choclo by Valloldo, 1913 ....**5.00**

El Irrisistible by Egbert Van Alstyne, 1914....................**5.00**

El Paso by Eugene West & Clarence Senna, 1921 ....**5.00**

Elaine, My Moving Picture Queen by Charles Elbert & Howard Wesley, 1915, Signed Photo Of Pearl White, Dedicated To Pearl White (Signed & Dedication)....................**12.00**

Eldorado by Edgar Allen Poe & O.G. Sonneck, 1917....................**10.00**

Eleanor: A Serenade by Jessie L. Deppen, 1914, Dedicated To My Friend Rae Eleanor Ball (Cover Artist, Parmelee & West & Dedication) **15.00**

Elevator Man by Irving Berlin (Cover Artist, Pfeiffer & Irving Berlin).**15.00**

Eleventh Hour Melody by King Palmer & Carl Sigman, 1956, Photo Al Hibbler **3.00**

Eli, Eli by Jacob Koppel Sandler, 1919, Photo Jacob Koppel Sandler...**5.00**

Eli Green's Cake Walk by Sadie Kominsky, 1899 (Pre 1900 & Black, Black Face)....................**20.00**

Eli-Eli by R. A. Zagler, 1909, Photo Sophia Karp **5.00**

Elinore by Harry D. Kerr, 1908 (Cover Artist, Starmer)....................**10.00**

Elite Syncopations by Scott Joplin, 1902 (Scott Joplin & Rag) **50.00**

Eliza by Gus Kahn & Ted Fiorito, 1924 ....**5.00**

Elmer's Tune by Elmer Albrecht & Sammy Gallop, 1941, Photo Dick Jurgens & His Orchestra....................**10.00**

Elsie From Chelsea by Harry Dacre, 1896 (Pre 1900) **15.00**

Elsie Shultz-En-Heim by Cliff Friend & Abner Silver, 1926 (Cover Artist, Leff) **5.00**

Elves At Play by Edw. A. Mueller, 1914....................**5.00**

Emblem Of Peace by G.A. Reeg, Jr., 1914....................**10.00**

Embraceable You by George & Ira Gershwin, 1930, Movie: Rhapsody In Blue....................**2.00**

Embraceable You by George & Ira Gershwin, 1942, Movie: Girl Crazy, Photo Judy Garland & Mickey Rooney....................**12.00**

Emily by Mercer & Mandel, 1964, Movie: The Americanization Of Emily, Photo Julie Andrews & James Garner **4.00**

Emmalina by Bert Potter, 1906....................**5.00**

Emmet's Castle Bells by J.K. Emmet, 1879 (Pre 1900)....................**15.00**

Emmet's Cuckoo Song by J.K. Emmet, 1879 (Pre 1900) **15.00**

Emmet's Love Of The Shamrock by Carlton & Emmet, 1879 (Pre 1900 & Irish)....................**15.00**

Emmet's Lullaby by J.K. Emmet, 1875 (Pre 1900)....................**15.00**

Emmet's Mountain Song by J.K. Emmet, 1878 (Pre 1900) **15.00**

Emmet's Sweet Violets by J. K. Emmet, 1882 (Pre 1900)....................**15.00**

Empty Is The Bottle, Father's Tight by Walter Delaney, 1878 (Pre 1900) **15.00**

Empty Saddles by J. Kiern Brennan & Billy Hill, 1936, Movie: Rhythm On The Range, Photo Bing Crosby **12.00**

En Ballon by D'Orso, 1880 (Pre 1900 & Transportation)....................**20.00**

Enchanted Glade, The by G. Hubi Newcomb & Lois Barker, 1915 ....**10.00**

Enchanted Hour by N. Elm & H.Mouton, 1911 ....**5.00**

Enchanted Sea, The by Frank Metis & Randy Starr, 1959....................**5.00**

Encore, Cherie by J. Fred Coots, 1947, Photo Eddy Howard....................**5.00**

End Of A Perfect Day, The by Carrie Jacobs Bond & J.P. McEvay, 1918, Shows Statue Of Liberty, Special Peace Edition (WWI) **35.00**

End Of The Lonesome Trail, The by Herman Ruby & Ray Perkins, 1929, Movie: The Great Divide....................**10.00**

End Of The Road, The by William Dillon & Harry Lauder, 1924 (Cover Artist, Starmer) **15.00**

Ending With A Kiss by Harlan Thompson & Lewis Gensler, 1934, Movie: Melody In Spring, Photo Lanny Ross & Mary Boland **5.00**

Endless Love by Richie, 1981, Movie: Endless Love, Photo Brooke Shields & Martin Hewitt....................**5.00**

Enduring Love by E.M. Def & Mme Lillian Nordica, 1890 (Pre 1900).**10.00**

Engineer Girls by Private Frank W. Fox & Dorothy R. Godfrey, 1918 (Cover Artist, Billy Williams, WWI & Military Personnel)....................**15.00**

Enid by Mary Earl, 1918....................**5.00**

Entertainer, The by Scott Joplin, 1903 (Scott Joplin & Rag) **50.00**

Entertainer's Rag, The by Jay Roberts, 1912 (Rag & Dixie) **20.00**

Enticement by Eporue Yenbad, 1914 ....**5.00**

Erin Beautiful Erin by Hugo Hamlin, 1916, Photo Hugo Hamlin (Irish).**10.00**

Erin's Faith And Hope by William Turner, Sr., 1920 (Irish) **10.00**

Erin's Isle And You by J.R. Shannon & J.S. Zamecnik, 1914 (Irish)..**10.00**

Erma by S.S. Oakford, 1900 (Lithograph Raphael Fassett) **10.00**

Erotik by M. Greenwald & Edward Grieg, 1920....................**6.00**

Eskimo by Perry & Castello, 1909 ....**5.00**

Espanita by George Rosey, 1895 (Pre 1900)....................**10.00**

Estelle by Frankie Carle, 1930....................**5.00**

Estrellita by Manuel M. Ponce, 1914 (Cover Artist, N.P.S.)....................**5.00**

Eternal Flame, The by J. Keirn Brennan & Ernest R. Ball, 1922, Movie: The Eternal Flame, Photo Norma Talmadge **10.00**

Ethiopa by Joseph F. Lamb, 1909 (Rag) **10.00**

Etoile Du Soir by Alf. De Musset & Amt. Gilis **5.00**

Eugenie by Fraser Simpson, 1906 ....**5.00**

Euphonic Sounds by Scott Joplin, 1909 (Cover Artist, Pfeiffer, Scott Joplin & Rag)....................**50.00**

Ev'ry Day I Love You by J. Styne & S. Cahn, 1948, Movie: Two Guys From Texas, Photo Dennis Morgan, Jack Carson & Dorothy Malone....................**10.00**

Ev'ry Day Of My Life by Jimmie Crane & Al Jacobs, 1953, Photo Bobby Vinton **3.00**

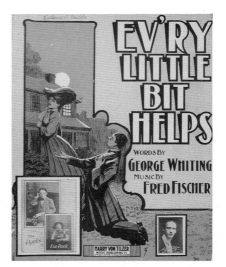

Ev'ry Little Bit Helps by George Whiting & Fred Fischer, 1904, Photo Harry & Eva Puck (Cover Artist, Jenkins & Black, Black Face) ..25.00

Ev'ry Morn I Bring Her Chicken by Harry J. Breen & T. Mayo Geary, 1903 (Black, Black Face) **15.00**

Ev'ry Night About This Time by Ted Koehler & James V. Monaco, 1942 (Cover Artist, Im-Ho)......................................**5.00**

Ev'ry Night I Cry Myself To Sleep Over You by Howard Johnson, Leo Wood & Irving Bibo, 1923......................**5.00**

Ev'ry Step Toward Killarney by Evans, 1925 (Irish)......................**5.00**

Ev'ry Thing I Love by Cole Porter, 1943, Movie: Let's Face It............**5.00**

Ev'ry Time We Say Goodbye by Cole Porter, 1944 ....**5.00**

Ev'ry Time You'd Do It In A Country Town by Moray (Cover Artist, Pfeiffer)......................**15.00**

Ev'ry Time You're Lonely, Don't Forget That I'm Lonely Too by Leslie, 1912 (Cover Artist, Pfeiffer) **16.00**

Ev'ry Where by Larry Kahn & Tolchard Evans, 1955......................**5.00**

Ev'rybody Clap Hands by Al Hoffman, Mann Curtis & Alex M. Kramer, 1950 ....**5.00**

Ev'rybody Loves You by Al Dubin & Little Jack Little, 1928 (Cover Artist, Barbelle) **5.00**

Ev'rybody's Somebody's Fool by Howard Greenfield & Jack Keller, 1960, Photo Connie Francis......................**3.00**

Ev'ryone Says I Love You by Bert Kalmar & Harry Ruby, 1932..........**5.00**

Ev'rything Depends On You by Charles Carpenter, Louis Dunlap & Earl Hines, 1935, Photo Earl Hines......................**5.00**

Ev'rything I've Got by Lorenz Hart & Richard Rodgers, 1942, Movie: All's Fair......................**6.00**

Ev'rythings Been Done Before by Harold Adamson, Edwin Knopf & Jack King, 1935, Photo Art Jarrett & Jean Harlow **10.00**

Evangeline by Al Jolson & Billy Rose, 1929, Movie: Evangeline, Photo Dolores Del Rio (Al Jolson) **12.00**

Eve Wasn't Modest Til She Ate That Apple by Charles R. McCarron, 1917 ....**5.00**

Evelina by Harold Arlen & E.Y. Harburg, 1944 ....**5.00**

Evelyn by Anne Caldwell & Hugo Felix, 1916, Musical: Pom Pom **5.00**

Evelyn by Paul Weston & Sid Robin, 1948, Photo Kay Kyser **5.00**

Even Song by Arthur Charlton, 1916 ....**5.00**

Evening by Egbert Van Alstyne, 1914 ....**6.00**

Evening by Landon Ronald, 1901 ....**6.00**

Evening Bringing Dreams Of You by Abel, 1925......................**6.00**

Evening Brings Love Dreams Of You by Earl Burtnett & Haven Gillespie, 1919 ....**5.00**

Evening Brings Rest And You by Edna Stanton Whaley & F.H. Bishop, 1916 ....**5.00**

Evening Chimes by A.F. Marzian, 1913 (Cover Artist, Dean Cornwell) **10.00**

Evening Chimes by Liebich, 1869 (Pre 1900)......................**15.00**

Evening Glow by McKanlass, 1912 ....**5.00**

Evening Is Come by Colin Stern & Ernest Nichol, 1915 ....**5.00**

Evening Shadows by F.W. Vandersloot, 1916 (Cover Artist, Pfeiffer) ..**10.00**

Evening Thoughts by Kathryn Bayley, 1902......................**10.00**

Evening Whispers by Rudd, 1915 (Cover Artist, Pfeiffer & Deco) **10.00**

Everlasting Day, The by R.M. Wellsbourne & Frederick Bevan, 1895 (Pre 1900)......................**12.00**

Every Chicken Likes Style by Goulart (Cover Artist, Pfeiffer)............**15.00**

Every Darkey Is A King by Dunbar, Moran & Cook, 1902 (Black, Black Face) **15.00**

Every Day by Fred Jackson, Arthur Jackson, William Daly & Paul Lannin, 1920, Musical: For Goodness Sake **5.00**

Every Day by Williams & Brooks, 1918 ....**5.00**

Every Day's A Holiday by Sam Coslow & Barry Trevers, 1937, Movie: Every Day's A Holiday, Caricature Mae West......................**10.00**

Every Little Bit Added To What You've Got Makes Just A Little Bit More by Will & Lawrence Dillon, 1907......................**12.00**

Every Little Dog Must Have His Day by Chauncey Olcott, 1902 (Irish) **10.00**

Every Little Memory Of You by E. Van Every & James Kendis, 1916 ....**5.00**

Every Little Movement Has A Meaning Of It's Own by Otto Harbach & Karl Hoschna, 1932, Movie: The Jolson Story, Photo Larry Parks & Evelyn Keyes (Al Jolson) **12.00**

Every Minute Of The Hour Every Hour Of The Day by Nick & Chas. F. Kenny, 1936, Photo Vincent Lopez......................**3.00**

Every Moment You're Lonesome, I'm Lonesome Too by Richmond, 1911 (Cover Artist, Pfeiffer) **15.00**

Every Mother's Son by Gregg, 1917 (WWI)......................**15.00**

Every Night At Eight by Dorothy Fields & Jimmy McHugh, 1935, Movie: Every Night At Eight, Photo George Raft & Alice Faye **10.00**

Every Night There's A Light by Paul Dresser, 1898 (Pre 1900)..........**15.00**

Every Race Has A Flag But The Coon by Will A. Heelen & J. Fred Helf, 1899 (Pre 1900 & Black, Black Face)......................**20.00**

Every Sunday Morning by Homer Cholvin & Ed Jacobsen, 1932..........**5.00**

Every Tear Is A Smile In An Irishman's Heart by Daniel Sullivan, Alma Sanders & Monte Carlo, 1919 (Irish) **10.00**

Every Time I Meet You by Gordon & Myrow, 1948, Movie: The Beautiful Blonde From Bashful Bend, Photo Betty Grable, Cesar Romero & Rudy Vallee **10.00**

Every Time You Touch Me by Charlie Rich & Billy Sherrill, 1975......**2.00**

Everybody Has A Laughing Place by Allie Wrubel & Ray Gilbert, 1946, Movie: Song Of The South (Disney)......................**10.00**

Everybody Loves A Chicken by Bobby Jones, 1912, Dedicated To Miss Mazie Elliotte (Cover Artist, E.S. Fisher, Dedication & Deco)......................**20.00**

Everybody Loves A Chicken by Bobby Jones, 1912, Photo Minnie Burke, Dedicated To Miss Mazie Elliotte (Cover Artist, Starmer, Dedication & Deco)......................**20.00**

Everybody Loves A Chicken by Bobby Jones, 1912, Photo Warner & Gallagher, Dedicated To Miss Mazie Elliotte (Cover Artist, Starmer, Dedication & Deco) **20.00**

Everybody Loves A College Girl by Kerry Mills, 1911......................**12.00**

Everybody Loves A Soldier by Manuel Klein, 1913, Musical: The Messrs Shuberts' Production "America", 1913-1914 At N.Y. Hippodrome (WWI)......................**16.00**

Everybody Loves An Irish Song by McKenna, 1916 (Cover Artist, Pfeiffer & Irish) **10.00**

Everybody Loves Me But The One I Love by Gus Edwards, 1908 ....**5.00**

Everybody Loves My Girl by Sam Lewis, Joe Young & Abrams, 1927, Photo Cliff Edwards **5.00**

Everybody Loves Rag by Dick Howard & A. Harriman, 1914 (Cover Artist, Pfeiffer, Deco & Rag)......................**15.00**

Everybody Loves Somebody by Irving Taylor & Ken Lane, 1948, Photo Dean Martin......................**5.00**

Everybody Loves Somebody by Irving Taylor & Ken Lane, 1948, Photo Peggy Lee **10.00**

Everybody Rag With Me by Kahn & LeBoy, 1914 (Rag) **15.00**

Everybody Sing by Brown & Freed, 1937, Movie: Broadway Melody 1938, Photo Eleanor Powell, Robert Taylor, Judy Garland, Sophie Tucker & George Murphy **12.00**

Everybody Snap Your Fingers With Me by Kalmar, 1913 (Cover Artist, Pfeiffer)......................**15.00**

Everybody Sometime Must Love Someone by Gene Buck & Dave Stamper, 1913 ....**10.00**

Everybody Step by Irving Berlin, 1921 (Irving Berlin)......................**10.00**

Everybody Tango by Paul Pratt, 1914 ....**5.00**

Everybody Tap by Jack Yellen & Milton Ager, 1929, Movie: Chasing Rainbows **5.00**

Everybody Two Step Rag by Earl C. Jones & Wallie Herzer, 1912, Photo Miss Nellie Beaumont (Cover Artist, Morgan & Rag) **10.00**

Everybody Wants A Key To My Cellar by Ed Rose, Billy Baskette & Lew Pollack, 1919 (Cover Artist, DeTakacs)......................**15.00**

Everybody Works But Father by Jean Havez, 1905, Lew Dockstader & His Great Minstrel Company, Photo Lew Dockstader (Cover Artist, Starmer & Black, Black Face).....................**25.00**

Everybody's Buddy By Bernie Grossman & Billy Frisch, 1920 (Cover Artist, Barbelle) **10.00**

Everybody's Crazy 'Bout The Doggone Blues, But I'm Happy by Henry Creamer & Turner Layton, 1918 (Cover Artist, Walton & Blues).**10.00**

Everybody's Crazy 'Bout The Fox Trot by F. Henri Klickman & E. Will Callahan, 1914......................**5.00**

Everybody's Crazy Over Dixie by Bobby Jones, Ruby Cowan & Will Donaldson, 1919 (Cover Artist, Walton & Dixie)........................**10.00**

Everybody's Doin' It Now by Irving Berlin, 1911, As Sung By Lydia Barry At The Winter Garden, N.Y., Photo Eugenie LeBlanc (Cover Artist, Gene Buck & Irving Berlin) **12.00**

Everybody's Doin' It Now by Irving Berlin, 1911, As Sung By Lydia Barry At The Winter Garden, N.Y., Photo Billie James (Cover Artist, Gene Buck & Irving Berlin) **10.00**

Everybody's Doin' It Now by Irving Berlin, 1911, As Sung By Lydia Barry At The Winter Garden, N.Y., Photo Betty Bond (Cover Artist, Gene Buck & Irving Berlin) **12.00**

Everybody's Doin' It Now by Irving Berlin, 1911, Photo Blanche Baird, The Tailor Made Girl (Cover Artist, Gene Buck & Irving Berlin)..**10.00**

Everybody's Got A Home by Oscar Hammerstein II & Richard Rodgers, 1955, Movie: Pipe Dream......................**10.00**

Everybody's Happy When The Moon Shines by Kerry Mills, 1909....**10.00**

Everybody's Rag by Dan Goldsmith & R. Sharp, 1909 (Rag)............**10.00**

Everybody's Talkin' by Fred Neil, 1968, Movie: Midnight Cowboy, Photo Harry Nilsson......................**3.00**

Everybody's Waiting For Somebody Else by B.C. Hillian, 1919 (WWI) .**10.00**

Everyday Is Ladies' Day With Me by Henry Blossom & Victor Herbert, 1906 (Victor Herbert) **10.00**

Everyone In Town Likes Mary by Schwartz & Ehrlich, 1912 (Cover Artist, Pfeiffer & Deco)......................**10.00**

Everyone Is In Slumberland But You And Me by Youngs & Moore, 1905......................**5.00**

Everyone Is Welcome In The House Of The Lord by Milt Lance & Lucius Leroy, 1951......................**5.00**

Everyone Was Meant For Someone by Bert Kalmar, Harry Ruby, Jan Rubini & Salvatore Santaella, 1919 ....**5.00**

Everything About You Tells Me That You're Irish by Shafer & Ringle, 1920 (Irish) **10.00**

Everything At Reilly's Must Be Done In Irish Style by John & W.W. West, 1899 (Pre 1900 & Irish)......................**15.00**

Everything He Does Just Pleases Me by Smith, 1914 (Cover Artist, Pfeiffer) **10.00**

Everything I Have Is Yours by Harold Adamson & Burton Lane, 1933, Movie: Dancing Lady, Photo Joan Crawford & Clark Gable ..**10.00**

Everything Is K.O. In Kentucky by Raymond Egan & Richard Whiting, 1923 ....**5.00**

Everything Is Peaches Down In Georgia by Grant Clark, Milton Ager & Geo W. Meyer, 1918, Small War Edition **10.00**

Everything Is Peaches Down In Georgia by Milton Ager & George W. Meyer, 1918......................**5.00**

Everything Is Rosie Now For Rosie by Irving Berlin, 1919 (Irving Berlin) **12.00**

Everything Reminds Me Of That Old Sweetheart Of Mine by Tracey & Harriman, 1914 (Cover Artist, Pfeiffer) **10.00**

Everything's Gonna Be All-Right by Benny Davis & Harry Akst, 1926...**5.00**

Everything's In Rhythm With My Heart by Sigler, Goodhart & Hoffman, 1935, Movie: First A Girl, Photo Jessie Matthews......................**5.00**

Everytime We Say Goodbye by Cole Porter, Movie: Seven Lively Arts......................**5.00**

Everywhere You Go by Larry Shay, Joe Goodwin & Mark Fisher, 1927, Photo Guy, Lebert & Carmen Lombardo (Cover Artist, Nick)........**5.00**

Evil Eye, The by Leonard, Sullivan & Mills, 1920, Movie: The Evil Eye, Photo Benny Leonard **3.00**

Exactly Like You by Dorothy Fields & Jimmy McHugh, 1930............**5.00**

Excelsior Rag by Joseph F. Lamb, 1909 (Rag) **15.00**

Exelsior, Medley of Sacred Songs, Arranged by Hamilton J. Hawley, 1909 ....**5.00**

Exodus Song, The by Pat Boone & Ernest Gold, Movie: The Exodus, Otto Preminger Presents, Paul Newman, Eva Marie Saint, Ralph Richardson, Peter Lawford, Lee J. Cobb, Sal Mineo, John Derek, Hugh Griffith, Gregory Ratoff & Jill Haworth (Transportation)......................**8.00**

Experience by Johnny Burke & James Van Heusen,1947, Movie: Road To Rio, Photo Bing Crosby, Bob Hope & Dorothy Lamour **5.00**

Extra, Extra by Irving Berlin, 1949, Musical: Miss Liberty (Irving Berlin) **5.00**

Eyes Of Blue by Stone & Young, 1953, Movie: Shane, Photo Alan Ladd, Jean Arthur & Van Heflin **5.00**

Eyes Of Irish Blue, The by Martha Haskell Clark & Letta Lynn, 1913 (Irish) **10.00**

Eyes Of The Army by Richard A. Whiting, 1918 (WWI)...................**15.00**

Eyes Of The Soul by Williams & Fischer, 1919, Movie: Eyes Of The Soul, Photo Elsie Ferguson......................**6.00**

Eyes Of The World, The by Jeff Branen & Arthur Lange, 1913.........**10.00**

Eyes That Say I Love You by Fred Fisher, 1919 (Cover Artist, DeTakacs)......................**10.00**

Fabulous Mister Crow, The by Buddy Bernier, Carl Sigman & Joseph Meyer, 1942 ....**5.00**

Face To Face With The Girl Of My Dreams by Howard, 1914 (Cover Artist, Pfeiffer)......................**10.00**

Faded Coat Of Blue, The by J.H. McNaughton, 1865 (Pre 1900)........**15.00**

Faded Love Letters Of Mine by Richard W. Pascoe, Luella Lockwood Moore & Will E. Dulmage, 1922 (Cover Artist, Chas. Roat & Deco)......................**5.00**

Faded Rose by Richard W. Pascoe, Luella Lockwood Moore & Will E. Dulmage, 1924......................**5.00**

Faded Summer Love, A by Phil Baxter, 1914, Photo Husk O'Hare **3.00**

Fair Debutante by Jules Reynard, 1922......................**5.00**

Fair Illinois by Bruce & Ted Snyder, 1910 (Cover Artist, Pfeiffer).....**15.00**

Fair Nellita by Joseph Dignam, 1897 (Pre 1900) **15.00**

Fairy Footsteps by Statham, 1892 (Pre 1900)......................**15.00**

Fairy Kisses by Johnson, 1908 ....**5.00**

Fairy Moon by Charles K. Harris, 1911, Photo Grace Edmonds **10.00**

Fairy Pipers, The by Fred E. Weatherly & A. Herbert Brewer, 1912 ....**5.00**

Fairy Queen by Percy Wenrich, 1907......................**6.00**

Fairy Tales by B.C. Hilliam, 1919, Musical: Buddies.........................**10.00**

Fairy Tales March Ballad by Hanlon & Morrissey, 1911, Photo Hanlon & Morrissey (Cover Artist, Pfeiffer & March)......................**15.00**

Fairy Wedding by E. Mack, 1863, Dedicated To Gen. Tom Thumb & Wife (Cover Artist, T. Sinclaire, Pre 1900 & Dedication)............**50.00**

Fairy Wedding by J. W. Turner, 1902 (Cover Artist, John Frew)........**10.00**

Faith Can Move Mountains by Ben Raleigh & Guy Wood, 1952, Photo Johnnie Ray **5.00**

Faithful Forever by Leo Robin & Ralph Rainger, 1939, Movie: Gulliver's Travels **8.00**

Faithfully Yours by James Brockman, Abe Lyman & Ted Snyder, 1931 (Cover Artist, Barbelle)......................**5.00**

Fallen By The Wayside by Charles K. Harris, 1892 (Pre 1900)..........**15.00**

Falling by Will Collins, Ed Cameron & Buddy Fields, 1922, Photo Joseph Lertora **5.00**

Falling In Love Again by Frederick & Hollander, 1930, Movie: The Blue Angel, Photo Marlene Dietrich & Emil Jennings............................**10.00**

Falling In Love With Love by Lorenz Hart & Richard Rodgers, 1938, Musical: The Boys From Syracuse.....................................**5.00**

Falling In Love With You by Johnny Meyer & Benny Davis, 1926......**5.00**

Falling Waters by J.L. Truax, 1933 (Cover Artist, Pfeiffer).................**10.00**

False And Fair by Claribel & Gustave Ferrari, 1917..............................**5.00**

False Faces by Edgar Leslie & Pete Wendling, 1919.............................**5.00**

False Prophet by Reginald V. Darow & John Prindle Scott, 1922.........**3.00**

Family Sing, A Sing Along With Mitch, 1962 (Cover Artist, Norman Rockwell)..**35.00**

Famous Overture For Piano, 1912 (Cover Artist, Pfeiffer) **10.00**

Fancy Fants by Livingston & Evans, 1950, Movie: Fancy Pants, Photo Bob Hope & Lucille Ball.........................**10.00**

Fanny by Rome, 1954, Movie: Fanny, Photo Leslie Caron, Maurice Chevalier & Charles Boyer............................**10.00**

Far Away Places by Joan Whitney & Alex Kramer, 1948, Pan Am. Advertising On Back Cover (Cover Artist, Nick, Advertising & Transportation)..**12.00**

Far From the Madding Crowd by Shaper & Ornade, 1967, Movie: Far From The Madding Crowd, Photo Julie Christie, Peter Finch, Terence Stamp & Alan Bates **3.00**

Fare Thee Well, Molly Darling by W.D. Cobb & Kerry Mills, 1902 ..**10.00**

Farewell by A. H. Eastman & Fred Heltman, 1917 (Deco)....................**5.00**

Farewell by Harry Stoddard & Marcy Klauber, 1930, Movie: Party Girl, Photo Douglas Fairbanks, Jr. & Jeannette Loff............................**10.00**

Farewell Killarney by Gus Edwards, 1908, Photo Julius Marx (Irish).**10.00**

Farewell My Love by Chas. Roth, 1914 (Cover Artist, Pfeiffer).........**10.00**

Farewell My Love by Harry Kogen, Henry Busse & Lou Holzer, 1938, Photo Frankie Masters (Cover Artist, Merman)..............................**3.00**

Farewell, My Loved Ones by Gladys G. Dennis & Harry H. Williams, 1915, Dedicated To Mrs. Wm. G. Dennis (WWI & Dedication)...**15.00**

Farewell To Arms by Allie Wrubel & Abner Silver, 1933, Movie: A Farewell To Arms, Photo Helen Hayes & Gary Cooper **8.00**

Farmer And The Cowman, The by Richard Rodgers & Oscar Hammerstein II, 1943, Musical: Oklahoma **5.00**

Farming by Cole Porter, 1943, Movie: Let's Face It.............................**5.00**

Farmyard Blues by Chris Smith & Henry Tray, 1917 (Blues) **10.00**

Fascinating Devil by Joseph McCarthy & Jimmie Monaco, 1930, Movie: Let's Go Places..**5.00**

Fascination by Dick Manning & F.D. Marchetti, 1945, Photo Dick Jacobs **5.00**

Fascination by Louis Silvers, 1922...**5.00**

Fascination by Powell, 1906...**5.00**

Fashion Rag by Chas. Cohen, 1912 (Cover Artist, Dittmar, Rag & Black, Black Face) **15.00**

Fast Line Galop by Beck, 1853 (Pre 1900 & Transportation)............**100.00**

Fatal Rose Of Red, The by Gardenier & Helf, 1900 (Black, Black Face) ..**10.00**

Fatal Wedding, The by Gussie L. Davis, 1893 (Pre 1900)...................**15.00**

Father Brings Home Something Every Day by Gus Edwards, 1909......**5.00**

Father Of The Land We Love by George M. Cohan, 1931, Photo President & General George Washington (Cover Artist, James Montgomery Flagg, President, Patriotic, George M. Cohan & Military Personnel)..**50.00**

Fatherland, The Motherland, The Land Of My Best Girl by Carrol & McDonald, 1914 (Cover Artist, Pfeiffer & WWI) **20.00**

Faust Waltz by Charles Gounod, 1935 ....**3.00**

Fawn, The by Wm. Schiller, 1912 (Cover Artist, Pfeiffer) **10.00**

Fawneyes by Charles L. Johnson, 1908 (Indian)..................................**25.00**

Feather Your Nest by James Kendis, James Brockman & Howard Johnson, 1920, Signed Photo Elsie White (Cover Artist, Rose Symbol & Signed)..**10.00**

Feather Your Nest by James Kendis, James Brockman & Howard Johnson, 1920, Photo Anna Chandler (Cover Artist, Rose Symbol).....**10.00**

Feather Your Nest by Kendis, Brockman & Howard Johnson, 1920, Photo Etta Hager (Cover Artist R.S.)..**10.00**

Feed The Birds by Sherman & Sherman, 1963, Movie: Mary Poppins, Photo Julie Andrews & Dick Van Dyke.........................**5.00**

Fee-Fi-Fo-Fum by Paul J. Smith & Arthur Quenzer, 1947, Movie: Fun And Fancy Free (Disney) **10.00**

Feeling In My Heart, A by George M. Cohan, 1927 (George M. Cohan) ..**10.00**

Felicity Rag by Scott Joplin & Scott Hayden, 1911 (Scott Joplin & Rag)..**50.00**

Felix The Cat by Alfred Bryan, Max Kortlander & Pete Wendling, 1928..**10.00**

Fella With An Umbrella, A by Irving Berlin, 1947, Movie: Easter Parade, Photo Judy Garland & Fred Astaire (Irving Berlin).....................**10.00**

Fellow Needs A Girl, A by Richard Rodgers & Oscar Hammerstein II, 1951, Musical: Allegro..**5.00**

Fencing Girl, The by Edwin E. Wilson, 1902 (Cover Artist, F.G. Kohl & March) **15.00**

Fernande by Remi Lormes, 1908 (Cover Artist, Pfeiffer)...................**10.00**

Ferry-Boat Serenade by Harold Adamson & E. Di Lazzaro, 1940, Photo Gray Gordon..**5.00**

Ferryboat Polka by Albert Gamse & Frank Wojnarowski, 1948, Photo Frank Wojnarowski (Cover Artist, Frederick S. Manning)..............**5.00**

Fiddle Dee Dee by Sammy Cahn & Jule Styne, 1949, Movie: It's A Great Feeling, Photo Dennis Morgan, Doris Day & Jack Carson..........10.00

Fiddle-Faddle by Leroy Anderson, 1947...**5.00**

Fidelite by Arthur Smith & Philias Champagne, 1914..........................**5.00**

Fido Is A Hot Dog Now by Raymond Walker, 1914 ....**10.00**

Fifi by Sam Coslow & Barry Trivers, 1937, Movie: Every Day's A Holiday, Caricature of Mae West **10.00**

Fifteen Kisses On A Gallon Of Gas by David, 1939 (Transportation).**10.00**

Fifth Ave. by Joseph M. Daly, 1936..**5.00**

Fig Leaf Rag by Scott Joplin, 1908 (Cover Artist, Barbelle, Rag & Scott Joplin) **60.00**

Fight Is On, The by J.F. Shannon & Carl D. Vandersloot, USN, 1918 (Cover Artist, Starmer, WWI, March & Military Personnel).........**20.00**

Fighting Navy Of The Good Old U.S.A., The by Sam Keane & Stanley Henry, 1917 (Cover Artist, Pfeiffer, WWI & Transportation).......**35.00**

Fighting The Flames by Rubens, 1904 (Cover Artist, Pfeiffer) **15.00**

Filibuster, The by Richard H. Barker, 1898 (Pre 1900 & March)........**25.00**

Find Me A Girl by Sam M. Lewis & Geo W. Meyer, 1912 (Cover Artist, Rose Symbol) **10.00**

Find Me A Primitive Man by Cole Porter, 1929, Musical: Fifty Million Frenchmen **5.00**

Finders Keepers, Losers Weepers by Paul Corbell & Merton H. Bories, Movie: Finders Keepers, Photo Laura LaPlante.....................**5.00**

Fine Romance, A by Dorothy Fields & Jerome Kern, 1936, Movie: Swing Time, Photo Fred Astaire & Ginger Rogers **10.00**

Fine Thing by Mercer & Dolan, 1947, Movie: Dear Ruth, Photo William Holden, Joan Caulfield, Billy DeWolfe, Edward Arnold & Mona Freeman **3.00**

Finesse by Bernard Maltin & Ray Doll, 1929 ....**5.00**

Finest Flag That Flies, The by Hughes & Richardson, 1916 (Cover Artist, Pfeiffer & Patriotic)...**15.00**

Finest On Parade, The by Joseph P. Skelly, 1883 (Pre 1900) **15.00**

Finger Of Suspicion, The by Paul Mann & Al Lewis, 1934................**5.00**

Finnegan Gave It To Me by Vaughn & Cunningham, 1912 (Cover Artist, Pfeiffer & Irish) **15.00**

Finnegan, The Umpire by Monroe Rosenfeld, 1890 (Pre 1900 & Sports) **25.00**

Fire And Rain by James Taylor, 1969, Photo James Taylor **5.00**

Fire Drill March by Harry J. Lincoln, 1909 (March)............................**16.00**

Fire Master, The by Harry J. Lincoln, 1904 (March) **16.00**

Fire Worshippers by Harry J. Lincoln, 1904 (March) **16.00**

Fireflies by Paul Lincke, 1910...**5.00**

Fireman's Dream, The by Percy Wenrich, 1907 (March) **10.00**

Fires Of Faith by Sam M. Lewis, Joe Young & M.K. Jerome, 1919 .....**5.00**

First Comes Your Duty To The Flag by Albert Von Tilzer, 1901 (Patriotic)...**15.00**

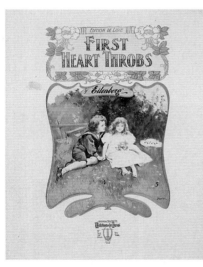

First Heart Throbs by Rich Eilenberg, 1902 (Cover Artist, Starmer)..15.00

First Hungarian Rhapsody by Moissaye Boguslawski, 1936 (Cover Artist, James Axeltod) **3.00**

First Kiss, The by Dubin & Robinson, 1928, Movie: The First Kiss, Photo Gary Cooper & Fay Wray **15.00**

First Rose Of Summer, The by Anne Caldwell & Jerome Kern, 1919, Musical: She's A Good Fellow **15.00**

First Rose, The by Frances Ward & Liza Lehmann, 1913 ....**5.00**

First Time I Saw You, The by Allie Wrubel & Nathaniel Skilkret, 1937, Movie: Toast Of New York, Photo Edward Arnold, Cary Grant, Jack Oakie & Frances Farmer (Cover Artist HBK)..........................**12.00**

First Time I Saw Your Face, The by Ewan MacColl, 1972 ....**3.00**

First You Do The Rag, Then You Bombershay by Andrew B. Sterling & Harry Von Tilzer, 1898 (Pre 1900 & Rag)....................................**20.00**

Fishin' For The Moon by Eddie Seiler, Sol Marcus & Guy Wood, 1950..**5.00**

Fishing For The Moon by D.K.Stevens, 1907, Musical: The Green Bird, Photo Elsa Ryan...**20.00**

Fishing Time by Sweet, 1920 (Cover Artist, Pfeiffer).......................**10.00**

Five Foot Two Eyes Of Blue by Sam Lewis, Joe Young & Ray Henderson, 1949..**3.00**

Five Minutes More by Sammy Cahn & Jule Styne, 1946, Photo Bob Crosby **5.00**

Five Minutes More by Sammy Cahn & Jule Styne, 1946, Photo George Olsen **5.00**

Five Minutes With Mr. Thornhill by Claude Thornhill, 1942................**5.00**

Five Pennies, The by Sylvia Fine, 1959, Movie: The Five Pennies, Photo Danny Kaye & Louie Armstrong **5.00**

Five Semi-Classic Ballads by Stutts, 1910 (Cover Artist, Pfeiffer & Deco)...**10.00**

Five Weeks In A Balloon by Desmond & Thielmann, 1962, Movie: Five Weeks In A Balloon, Photo Fabian, Barbara Eden, Red Buttons & Peter Lorre **5.00**

Five-Six-Seven-Eight, Nine Little Miles From Ten-Ten-Tennessee by Al Sherman, Al Lewis & Con Conrad, 1930...................................**5.00**

Fizz Water by Eubie Blake, 1914 (Rag) **15.00**

Flag At Sundown, The by Maloney, 1910 (Cover Artist, Pfeiffer, Patriotic & Deco) **20.00**

Flag Of My Heart by G. Ferrari, 1918 (WWI) **10.00**

Flag Of My Heart & Home by Aronson, 1917 (Cover Artist, Pfeiffer, Patriotic & WWI) **15.00**

Flag Of Our Country Long May Thou Wave by Snow, 1918 (WWI)..**12.00**

Flag Of The U.S.A., The by J.J. Donahue, 1918 (WWI)....................**15.00**

Flag That Had Never Retreated, The by Hogan, 1918 (WWI)............**15.00**

Flag That Train by Richmond, Rothchild & McPhail, 1925 (Transportation)...**10.00**

Flapper Blues, The by Bob Alterman & Claude Johnson, 1922 (Blues & Deco) **10.00**

Flapperette by Jesse Greer, 1926 ....**5.00**

Flash-Light March, The by E.T. Paull & Ellis, 1919 (Cover Artist, E.T. Paull & March) **40.00**

Flatterer, The by Cecile Chaminade, 1924 ....**3.00**

Flea In Her Ear, A by Cahn & Kaper, 1968, Movie: A Flea In Her Ear, Photo Rex Harrison **6.00**

Fleet's In, The by Johnny Mercer & Victor Schertzinger, 1942, Movie: The Fleet's In...**5.00**

Fleur-De-Lys, Flow'r Of France Bloom Again by Robert Levenson, 1919 (Cover Artist, V.C. Plunkett & WWI)....................................**15.00**

Fleurs Fances by A.B. Caron, M.D. & G.A. Clement, 1916 ....**5.00**

Flight Of The Air Ship, The by H. Zeiler, 1908 (Transportation)........**35.00**

Flight Of The Bumble Bee, The by N. Rimsky Korsakoff, 1935...........**3.00**

Flipity Flop by L.H. Dougherty, 1901 (March) **15.00**

Flirtation Dance by Arthur L. Brown, 1898 (Pre 1900) **5.00**

Flirtation Walk by Mort Dixon & Allie Wrubel, 1934, Movie: Flirtation Walk, Photo Ruby Keeler & Dick Powell....................................**12.00**

Flirting In The Twilight by Kemble & Braham, 1870 (Pre 1900)........**15.00**

Flirting On The Ice by French & Mullaly, 1877 (Pre 1900)...............**15.00**

Flo by Stewart & Monroe, 1904 ....**10.00**

Floatin' Down The Mississippi by Wm. J. McKenna, 1924 ....**10.00**

Floatin' Down To Cotton Town by Jack Frost & F. Henri Klickmann, 1919 (Transportation & Black, Black Face)................................**20.00**

Floating Along by B.C. Harris & Edward Buffington, 1906 (Cover Artist, Tozmire) **10.00**

Floating Down The Mississippi River On My Way To New Orleans by Ballard MacDonald & Albert Von Tilzer, 1915.............................**8.00**

Floating Down The River by Roger Lewis & James White, 1913, Photo Emma Carus (Transportation) **15.00**

Flor de' Brazil by Arthur DeCastro, 1914 ....**5.00**

Floradora by Hall & Stuart, 1903 ....**5.00**

Floreine by Ernest J. Schuster, 1912......................................**5.00**

Florence by Herbert W. Joyce & Emory R. Ruby, 1906 (Cover Artist, J.B. Eddy) **15.00**

Florentine Waltzes by Unger, 1914 (Cover Artist, Pfeiffer) **10.00**

Florian's Song by B. Godard, 1884 (Pre 1900) **5.00**

Florida by Abel Green & Jesse Greer, 1925 ....**5.00**

Florida Glide Waltzes by Will L. Thompson, 1896 (Pre 1900)...........**15.00**

Florida, The Moon And You by Gene Buck & Rudolph Friml, 1926....**5.00**

Flow Along River Tennessee by Alfred Bryan, Albert Gumble & Jack Wells, 1913 (Cover Artist, Starmer).................................**10.00**

Flower Bells, On A Summer Afternoon by Manuel Klein, 1913, Musical: Shuberts' Production At New York Hippodrome "America" 1913-1914 ....**12.00**

Flower From My Angel Mother's Grave by Harry Kennedy, 1878 (Pre 1900)..**15.00**

Flower Garden Ball by Jerome & Schwartz, 1913 (Cover Artist, Pfeiffer) **10.00**

Flower Of Love by Mendoza, Breyer & Ruby, 1928, Movie: White Shadows In The South Seas, Photo Monte Blue & Racquel Torres.........**5.00**

Flower Of The Orient by Benjamin Richmond, 1903 ....**5.00**

Flower Song by Gustave Lang, 1915.......................................**5.00**

Flower Song, The by Gounod, 1910 (Cover Artist, Pfeiffer) **10.00**

Flowerland Waltzes by Powell, 1915 (Cover Artist, Pfeiffer)..............**15.00**

Flowers That Bloom In The Spring, Tra-La, The 1908 (Cover Artist, Pfeiffer) **16.00**

Fly Away Birdie To Heaven by Chas. K. Harris, 1905 ....**10.00**

Fly Me To The Moon by Bart Howard, 1954, Photo Bart Howard.......**5.00**

Flying Down To Rio by Gus Kahn, Edward Eliscu & Vincent Youmans, 1933, Movie: Flying Down To Rio, Photo Fred Astaire & Dolores Del Rio **10.00**

Flying Fancies by Losey, 1914 (Cover Artist, Pfeiffer) **10.00**

Flying Spray by G.M. Adamson, 1903......................................**5.00**

Flying Trapeze Waltz by Richter, 1855 (Pre 1900)............................**15.00**

Foggy Day by George & Ira Gershwin, 1937, Movie: A Damsel In Distress, Photo Fred Astaine, Joan Fontaine & George Burns & Gracie Allen **5.00**

Folies Bergere March by Paul Lincke, 1899 (Pre 1900 & March).......**15.00**

Folks Who Live On The Hill, The by Jerome Kern & Oscar Hammerstein II, 1937, Movie: High, Wide And Handsome, Photo Irene Dunne & Randolph Scott **5.00**

Follow The Crowd by Irving Berlin, 1914 (Irving Berlin)..................**10.00**

Follow The Flag by Raymond Hubbell, 1918 (WWI)..........................**10.00**

Follow The Fold by Jo Swerling, Abe Burrows & Frank Loesser, 1950, Musical: Guys & Dolls...**5.00**

Follow The Swallow by Billy Rose, Mort Dixon & Ray Henderson, 1924, Photo Clark Morrell (Cover Artist, Frederick S. Manning & Deco) **10.00**

Follow Your Heart by Schertzinger, Mitchell & Bullock, 1936, Movie: Follow Your Heart, Photo Marion Talley & Michael Bartlett **3.00**

Follow Your Heart by Sidney Mitchell & Victor Schertzinger, 1936, Movie: Follow Your Heart **6.00**

Following In Father's Footsteps by E.W. Rogers, 1902.....................**10.00**

Following The Sun Around by Harry Tierney & Joseph McCarthy, 1929, Ziegfeld Movie: Rio Rita, Photo Bebe Daniels & John Boles **10.00**

Fool That I Am by Floyd Hunt, 1946 ....**3.00**

Fool There Was, A by Alex Dubin & Gustav Benkhart, 1913 (Cover Artist Ayers) **5.00**

Foolin' by Francis Craig, Jack Clifford & Charles Farrow,1946, Photo Lenny Herman **3.00**

Foolish Heart by Ogden Nash & Kurt Weill, 1943, Movie: One Touch Of Venus **3.00**

Foolishness Rag, 1911 (Rag)..**15.00**

Fools Fall In Love by Irving Berlin, 1939 (Irving Berlin)....................**5.00**

For All Eternity by S.A. Herbert & Angelo Mascheroni, 1906..............**3.00**

For All We Know by Sam Lewis & J. Fred Coots, 1934, Photo Colonel Gene Burchell (Cover Artist, HBK & Military Personnel)..............**5.00**

For Days And Days by Bert Kalmar & Harry Puck, 1913 (Cover Artist, Pfeiffer)..**15.00**

For Dixie And Uncle Sam by J. Keirn Brennan & Ernest R. Ball, 1916 (Cover Artist, Starmer, March, WWI & Dixie)...........................**20.00**

For Ev'ry Lonely Heart by Kahn, Stolhart & Ward, 1939, Movie: Broadway Serenade, Photo Jeannette Macdonald...............................**10.00**

For Every Boy Who's Lonely by Harbach & Hoschna, 1911 ....**10.00**

For Every Boy Who's On The Level, There's A Girl That's On The Square by Pease & Nelson, 1920 (Cover Artist, Pfeiffer)..............**10.00**

For Every Girl Who Is Anyone's Girl, There Is Always Somebody To Blame by Howard, 1916, Photo Pauline Frederick (Cover Artist, Pfeiffer & Deco)..**10.00**

For Every Man There's A Woman by Leo Robin & Harold Arlen, 1948, Movie: Casbah..**5.00**

For Every Tear You've Shed I'll Bring A Million Smiles by Bard & Lawrence, 1919 (Cover Artist, Pfeiffer & Deco) **10.00**

For Freedom And Ireland by Woodward & Mack, 1900 (Irish)...........**10.00**

For His Mother's Sake by Nathan, 1904 (Patriotic) **10.00**

For It Is My Land And Your Land by Joy Mills, 1918 (WWI)............**10.00**

For Johnny And Me by Lew Brown & Albert Von Tilzer, 1919 (Cover Artist, Frederick S. Manning & Deco) **15.00**

For Killarny And You by J. Brandon Walsh & Louise Teasdale, 1910 (Irish)...**5.00**

For Love And Honor by B. Alberts, 1904 (March & Patriotic) **15.00**

For Me And My Gal by Edgar Leslie, E. Ray Goetz & Geo. W. Meyer, 1932, Movie: For Me And My Gal, Photo Judy Garland, Gene Kelly & George Murphy **10.00**

For Me And My Gal by Edgar Leslie, E. Ray Goetz & Geo. W. Meyer, 1917, Photo Fanny Brice & King (Cover Artist, Barbelle)............**10.00**

For Me And My Gal by Edgar Leslie, E. Ray Goetz & Geo. W. Meyer, 1917, Photo Clark & Bergman (Cover Artist, Barbelle)..........10.00

For My Baby by Irving Kahal, Francis Wheeler & Ted Snyder, 1927, Photo Ruth Etting (Cover Artist, Barbelle & Deco)......................**10.00**

For My Mother by Albert Hay Malotte, 1939, Taken From Poem Written by Bobby Sutherland Aged 12..**5.00**

For Old Glory by J. Cheever & William Furst, 1898, New York Journal Sunday Supplement (Pre 1900) **10.00**

For Old Glory, Picture of General George Washington Crossing Delaware (Patriotic, Military Personnel & Presidents)....................................**30.00**

For Old Glory, Uncle Sam, We Are Preparing by Irving, 1917 (Cover Artist, Pfeiffer, Patriotic & WWI)....................................**20.00**

For Old Times Sake by B.G. DeSylva, Lew Brown & Ray Henderson, 1928, (Cover Artist, Pud Lane) **5.00**

For Once In My Life by Ronald Miller & Orlando Murden, 1967, Photo Tony Bennett **5.00**

For Sale A Baby by Charles K. Harris, 1903....................................**10.00**

For Sentimental Reasons by Abner Silver, Al Sherman & Edward Heyman, 1936 (Cover Artist, Henri Lamothe) **3.00**

For Sentimental Reasons by Dick Watson & William Best, 1946, Photo Eddy Howard....................................**3.00**

For Surely I Will Come Back To You by Robert Lloyd, 1919 (WWI) .**10.00**

For The First Time I've Fallen In Love by Charles Tobias & David Kapp, 1943, Photo Sammy Kaye **5.00**

For The First Time, I've Fallen In Love by Charles Tobias & David Kapp, 1943, Photo Dick Haymes....................................**5.00**

For The First Time, I've Fallen In Love by Charles Tobias & David Kapp, 1943, Photo Kay Kyser....................................**5.00**

For The First Time, I've Fallen In Love by Charles Tobias & David Kapp, 1943, Photo Guy Lombardo **5.00**

For The Flag, For The Home, For The Family by George M. Cohan (George M. Cohan & Patriotic) **15.00**

For The Freedom Of The World, Greatest Patriotic Song Ever Written, by Edmund Vance Cooke & J.S. Zemecnik, 1917, Song Of Nations, Dedication: To All The Allies, Each And Every Nation: To The Splendid Soldiers In The Trenches And The Brave Women At Home: To All Who Have Made Their Sacrifice For The Freedom Of The World, Is This Song Dedicated (Dedication & Patriotic)....................................**25.00**

For The Good Times by Kris Kristofferson, 1968....................................**5.00**

For The Honor Of The Flag by Raymond Hubbell, 1918 (WWI)........**15.00**

For The Sake Of A Rose by Addison Burkhardt & Albert Piantadosi, 1916 (Cover Artist, Starmer & Deco) **10.00**

For The Sake Of Auld Lang Syne by George Graff, Jr., Annelu Burns & Ernest R. Ball, 1920, Photo Shirley Mason (Deco)..............12.00

For The Sake Of The Baby At Home by Al Dubin & F. Henri Klickmann, 1924 ....**5.00**

For The Sake Of Wife And Home, Theme Suggested By The Thaw-White Tragedy, by Fred Leopold, 1913, Photo Harry Kendall Thaw.......**25.00**

For The Two Of Us by Edgar Leslie & Harry Ruby, 1918 ....**5.00**

For The Wearing Of The Green by Bert Potter, 1911 (Irish) **10.00**

For You A Rose by Will D. Cobb & Gus Edwards, 1917 (Cover Artist, Pfeiffer)....................................**15.00**

For You A Rose by Will D. Cobb & Gus Edwards, 1917 (Cover Artist, Harrison Fisher)....................................**35.00**

For You Alone by Henry E. Geehl & P.J. O'Reilly, 1911 ....**5.00**

For You Alone by S. Habelow, 1919 (Cover Artist, Starmer & Deco)**10.00**

For You And Me by Thekla Hollingsworth & Jessie L. Deppen, 1926 .**5.00**

For You And The Grand Old Flag by Coleman, 1910 (Patriotic) **15.00**

For You by Al Dubin & Joe Burke, 1930....................................**5.00**

For You by Laurence Montague, 1911 ....**5.00**

For You, For Me, For Evermore by George Gershwin, 1941................**5.00**

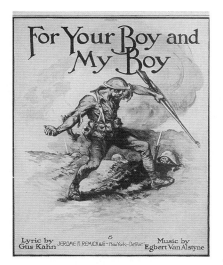

For Your Boy And My Boy by Gus Kahn & Egbert Van Alstyne, 1918 (WWI)....................................15.00

For Your Country And My Country by Irving Berlin, 1917 (WWI & Irving Berlin)....................................**15.00**

For-Get-Me-Not by Schultz, 1915 (Cover Artist, Pfeiffer & Deco).....**10.00**

Ford by Zickel, 1908 (Transportation)....................................**25.00**

Ford March, The, Advertising Ford Motor Co., Model T. On Front And Back (March & Advertising)....................................**45.00**

Forever And A Day by Thomas B. Aldrich & Richard Smythe, 1910...**5.00**

Forever And Ever by Malia Roasa & Franz Winkler, 1947, Photo Perry Como **6.00**

Forever And Ever by Malia Rosa & Franz Winkler, 1948, Photo Dinah Shore (Cover Artist, Sorokin)....................................**6.00**

Forever And Ever by Malia Rosa & Franz Winkler, 1948, Photo Gracie Fields (Cover Artist, Sorokin) **6.00**

Forever And Ever by Malia Rosa & Franz Winkler, 1948, Photo Margaret Whiting (Cover Artist, Sorokin) **6.00**

Forever by Buddy Kellen, 1960, Photo Little Dippers **5.00**

Forever by Leo Robin & Ralph Rainger, 1939, Movie: Gulliver's Travels **5.00**

Forever by Wm. B. Friedlander & Con Conrad, 1923 (Cover Artist, Politzer) **5.00**

Forever Darling by Cahn & Kaper, 1955, Movie: Forever Darling, Photo Lucille Ball, Desi Arnaz & James Mason **8.00**

Forever I Call To Thee by Norma Gray, 1912....................................**5.00**

Forever Is A Long Long Time by Darl MacBoyle & Albert Von Tilzer, 1916 ....**5.00**

Forevermore by Callahan & Smith, 1912....................................**5.00**

Forget by Mack & Aldens, 1905 ....**5.00**

Forget If You Can by Jack Manus, Kay Upham & Len Joy, 1938 (Cover Artist, Scott)....................................**5.00**

Forget Me Not My American Rose by Ray Sherwood, 1918 (WWI) ..**10.00**

Forget-Me-Not, The by Carrie Jacobs Bond, 1925................................**15.00**

Forgive Me by Jack Yellen & Milton Ager, 1927, Photo Grace Hayes (Cover Artist, Barbelle & Deco)..**10.00**

Forgive Me by Jack Yellen & Milton Ager, 1927, Photo Lillian Roth (Cover Artist, Barbelle & Deco)..**10.00**

Forgive Me by Jack Yellen & Milton Ager, 1927, Photo Sophie Tucker (Cover Artist, Barbelle) **22.00**

Forgive Me Lord by Ord Hamilton, 1950..**3.00**

Forgiveness, We'll All Need Forgiveness Someday by Cohern, Harris & Trainer, 1919 (Cover Artist, Pfeiffer & Deco) **10.00**

Forgotten by Coweles & Ditson, 1895 (Pre 1900) **15.00**

Fortune Teller, The by Maurice Arnold, 1902................................**8.00**

Forty Five Minutes From Broadway by George M. Cohan, 1933, Movie: Yankee Doodle Dandy, Photo James Cagney & George M. Cohan (George M. Cohan)..**10.00**

Forty Second Street by Al Dubin & Harry Warren, 1932, Movie: Forty Second Street, Photo Bebe Daniels, George Brent, Ruby Keeler, Warner Baxter, Ginger Rogers, Dick Powell, Una Merkel & Guy Kibbe **12.00**

Forty Second Street by Al Dubin & Harry Warren, 1932, Movie: The Jolson Story, Photo Larry Parks & Evelyn Keyes (Al Jolson) ..10.00

Fountain Fay by Reinhardt & Smith, 1909..**5.00**

Fountain, The by Carl Bohm, 1932 ....**5.00**

Fountain Waltzes by DeMicheles, 1910..**5.00**

Four Brave Sailors by Esther C. Benson, 1922 (Patriotic) **10.00**

Four Jacks March by Losch, 1907 (March)..**10.00**

Four Leaf Clover by Brownell & Higginson, 1897 (Pre 1900 & Irish) .**15.00**

Four Little Blackberries by Lawrence B. O'Connor, 1907 (Cover Artist, Starmer & Black, Black Face)..**50.00**

Four Little Sugarplums by Lawrence B. O'Connor, 1918 (Cover Artist, Starmer & Black Black Face) **50.00**

Four Walls by Al Jolson, Billy Rose & Dave Dreyer, 1927 (Al Jolson)..**10.00**

Four Winds And The Seven Seas, The by Hal David & Don Rodney, 1949 ....**5.00**

Fox Hunter's March, The by William H. Penn, 1900 (March & Sports) ..**20.00**

Fox Tail March by Zamecnik, 1917 (March) **10.00**

Fox Trot by F. Henri Klickman, 1914 ....**5.00**

Foxy Fox Trot by Moray, 1915 (Cover Artist, Pfeiffer & Deco) **10.00**

Fraidy Cat by Elliott, 1909 ....**5.00**

France America by Larrieu, 1917 (Cover Artist, Pfeiffer & Patriotic) .**10.00**

Frankie And Johnny by Boyd Bunch & Bert Leighton, 1942, Photo Guy Lombardo (Cover Artist, Sig Ch)..**3.00**

Frat March by John F. Barth, 1910 (Cover Artist, T. Ray & March) ...**15.00**

Fraternity Blues by Spencer Murphy & Kay Kyser, 1930, Photo Kay Kyser (Cover Artist, Leff & Deco)..**5.00**

Freckles by Cliff Hess, Howard Johnson & Milton Ager, 1919, Small Folio, Signed Photo Nora Bayes (Cover Artist, R.S. & Signed)....**20.00**

Freckles Rag by Larry Buck, 1905 (Rag)..**15.00**

Freddy And His Fiddle by Robert Wright & George Forrest, 1944, Movie: Song Of Norway..**2.00**

Free by Dana Seusse & Edward Heyman, 1933................................**3.00**

Freedom For All Forever by B.C. Hilliam, 1918 (WWI & Patriotic) ..**10.00**

Freedom For All Forever by Edward F. Cogley & Wm. E. Bock, 1918 (WWI & Patriotic) **10.00**

Freedom Ring by James Eaton & Robert Stolz, 1942 ....**5.00**

Freedom Train, The by Irving Berlin, 1933, Photo Spirit Of 1776 Train (Irving Berlin & Transportation) **10.00**

French Pastry Rag by Les Copeland, 1914 (Cover Artist, Starmer & Rag) .**10.00**

Frenchy Come To Yankee Land by Sam Ehrlich & Con Conrad, 1919 (Cover Artist, E.E. Walton & WWI) **10.00**

Frenesi by Ray Charles & S.K. Russell, 1939 ....**5.00**

Friend Of Yours, A by Johnny Burke & Jimmy Van Heusen, 1944, Movie: The Great John L, Photo Linda Darnell, Barbara Britton, Lee Sullivan & Greg McClure **10.00**

Friendless Blues by W.C. Handy, 1926 (Blues) **10.00**

Friendly Mountains by Johnny Burke, 1948, Movie: Emperor Waltz, Photo Bing Crosby & Joan Fontaine **5.00**

Friendly Persuasion by Dimitri Tiomkin, 1956, Movie: Friendly Persuasion..**5.00**

Friendly Tavern Polka by Jerry Bowne & Frank DeVol, 1941, Photo Horace Heidt (Cover Artist, Im-Ho)..**5.00**

Friends by Howard Johnson, Geo. W. Meyer & Jos. H. Santly, 1919, Small Folio, War Edition (Cover Artist, R.S. & WWI) **10.00**

Friends by John & Taupin, 1970, Movie: Friends, Photo Elton John & Bernie Taupin **6.00**

Friends Of Yesterday by Godfrey Pope & Nellie Simpson, 1919..........**5.00**

Friendship by Cole Porter, 1943, Movie: DuBarry Was A Lady **5.00**

Frisky by Mel B. Kaufman, 1919 ....**5.00**

Frobi Of The Brownies by Palmer Cox, 1896 (Pre 1900) **45.00**

Frog Legs Rag by James Scott, 1906 (Rag)..**15.00**

Frolic Of The Crickets by Edwards, 1914 (Cover Artist, Pfeiffer) **15.00**

From A.M. To P.M. by Harry Tobias, Neil Moret & Ted Fiorito, 1932 **5.00**

From Far Peru by Ivan Caryll & Lionel Monckton, 1907 (Cover Artist, Starmer..**15.00**

From Galilee A Mother Came by J. Sheldon Tyler & Geoffrey O'Hara, 1929 ....**5.00**

From Here To Eternity by Fred Karger, 1953, Movie: From Here To Eternity, Photo Burt Lancaster, Montgomery Clift & Frank Sinatra **10.00**

From Here To Shanghai by Irving Berlin, 1917 (Irving Berlin)...........**10.00**

From Now On by Cole Porter, 1938, Movie: Leave It To Me **6.00**

From O'er The Hills Of Old New Hampshire by Ted Garton & Robert Levenson, 1918 (Cover Artist, Pfeiffer)..**15.00**

From One Till Two, I Always Dream Of You by Larry Bard & Joe Hoover, 1926 (Cover Artist, Barbelle & Deco)............................**10.00**

From Russia With Love by Lionel Bart, 1963, Movie: From Russia With Love, Photo Sean Connery As James Bond **25.00**

From Spring To Winter by Merton E. Davis & H.A. Pooley, 1945.......**2.00**

From The Land Of Skye-Blue Water by Nelle Richard Eberhart & Charles Wakefield Cadman, 1937 ....**5.00**

From The Top Of Your Head To The Tip Of Your Toes by Mack Gordon & Harry Revel, 1935, Movie: Two For Tonight, Photo Bing Crosby & Joan Bennett **12.00**

From This Day Forward by Mort Greene & Leigh Harline, 1946, Movie: From This Day Forward, Photo Joan Fontaine..................**5.00**

From This Day On by Alan Jay Lerner & Frederick Loewe, 1947, Musical: Brigadoon..................**5.00**

From This Moment On by Cole Porter, 1950, Musical: Out Of This World..................**3.00**

Frosty The Snow Man by Steve Nelson & Jack Rollins, 1950..............**3.00**

Frou-Frou by Edward Jose, 1915..................**10.00**

Frozen Bill Rag by Arthur Pryor (Rag)..................**15.00**

Fryksdals Polska by Wellners (Cover Artist, L.S.)..................**5.00**

Fu by Georpe P. Howard, 1919..................**5.00**

Fuddy Duddy Watchmaker, The by Frank Loesser & Jimmy McHugh, 1943, Movie: Happy Go Lucky, Photo Mary Martin, Dick Powell, Betty Hutton, Eddie Bracken & Rudy Vallee..................**12.00**

Full Moon And Empty Arms by Buddy Kaye & Ted Mossman, 1946, Photo Eileen Barton..................**5.00**

Full Of Pep by Joseph M. Daly, 1915 (Cover Artist, Pfeiffer & Deco)..**10.00**

Fun And Fancy Free by Bennie Benjamin & George Weiss, 1947, Movie Fun And Fancy Free (Disney)..................**10.00**

Funny by Larry Yoell & Frank Anderson, 1925..................**5.00**

Funny, Dear What Love Can Do by Joe Bennett, Geo Little & Charley Straight, 1929..................**5.00**

Funny Moon by McCarthy, 1910 (Cover Artist, Pfeiffer)..................**15.00**

Funny Old Hills, The by Leo Robin & Ralph Rainger, 1938, Movie: Paris Honeymoon, Photo Bing Crosby & Shirley Ross..................**12.00**

Furlough Waltz, The by Claude Marquis, 1945, Photo Guy Lombardo..**5.00**

Fuss And Feathers by J.C. Halls, 1918 (Cover Artist, H.R. Smith, Rag & Black, Black Face)..................**25.00**

Futurist, The by Burch, 1914 (Cover Artist, Pfeiffer & Deco)..................**20.00**

Fuzzy Wuzzy by Al Hoffman, Milton Drake & Jerry Livingston, 1944..**5.00**

G.I. Jive by Johnny Mercer, 1942 (Cover Artist, Holley & WWII)..................**10.00**

Gabriel's Band by James Bland (Pre 1900 & Black)..................**20.00**

Gaby Glide, The by Harry Pilar & Louis Hirsch, 1911, Photo Gaby Deslys & Harry Pilar (Cover Artist, Starmer & Rag)..................**15.00**

Gadfly, The by H.L. Berger, Boston Herald Sunday Supplement, 1900..**10.00**

Gal In Calico, A by Arthur Schwartz & Leo Robin,. 1946, Movie: The Time, The Place And The Girl, Photo Dennis Morgan, Jack Carson, Martha Vickers, Janis Paige & Carmen Cavallero (Cover Artist, A. Joel Robinson)..................**10.00**

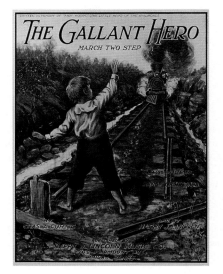

Gallant Hero, The by Chas. A. Curtis, 1920, Written In Memory Of "Andy Moore," The Little Hero Of The Railroad (Transportation & March)..................16.00

Galveston by Webb, 1968, Photo Glen Campbell..................**5.00**

Galway Bay by Dr. Arthur Colahan, 1947, Signed Photo Bing Crosby (Irish & Signed)..................**10.00**

Gangster's Warning, The by Gene Autry, 1932, Photo Curt Poulton....**5.00**

Garden Dance, A by G. Vargas, 1914 (Deco)..................**5.00**

Garden I Love, The by H.S. Reed & Godfrey Nutting, 1908..................**5.00**

Garden In The Rain, A by James Dyrenforth & Carroll Gibbons, 1946, Photo Perry Como (Cover Artist, Cesareo)..................**5.00**

Garden Of Allah, The by Little, Baskett & Flatow, 1917, Movie: the Garden Of Allah..................**5.00**

Garden Of Dreams by Cook & DeKoven, 1903 (Cover Artist, Starmer)..................**10.00**

Garden Of Dreams by Harry J. Lincoln, 1909 (Cover Artist, Starmer & Deco)..................**10.00**

Garden Of Eden by J. Russell Robinson, 1918 (Cover Artist, Starmer)..................**10.00**

Garden Of Flowers by J.R. Shannon & F. W. Vandersloot, 1916 (Cover Artist, Pfeiffer)..................**10.00**

Garden Of Girls, The by Anna Helmund, 1911..................**5.00**

Garden Of Love by Walter Rolfe, 1909..................**5.00**

Garden Of Memories by F.W. Vandersloot, 1916 (Cover Artist, Pfeiffer).**10.00**

Garden Of My Dreams by Gene Buck & Dave Stamper, 1918, Musical: Ziegfeld Follies 1918 (Deco)..................**20.00**

Garden Of Roses, The by J.E. Dempsey & Johann C. Schmid, 1909....**5.00**

Garden Of The Moon by Al Dubin, Harry Warren & Johnny Mercer, 1938, Movie: Garden Of The Moon, Photo Pat O'Brien, John Payne & Margaret Lindsay (Cover Artist, Merman)..................**10.00**

Garden Of Your Heart, The by Ed. Teschemacher & Francis Dorel, 1914..**5.00**

Gardener, The by Hugo Wolf..................**5.00**

Garland Of Old Fashioned Roses by C.H. Musgrove & E. Clinton Keithley, 1911..................**5.00**

Garland Of Roses by Streabbog, 1936..................**5.00**

Gasoline Gus & His Jitney Bus by Gay, 1915 (Transportation)..........**30.00**

Gates Of Gladness, The by J. Keirn Brennan, Paul Cunningham & Bert Rule, 1919, Photo, Jean Page & Denton Vane..................**5.00**

Gateway Of Dreams, The by J. Will Callahan & Granville English, 1928..**5.00**

Gather The Rose by Brian Hooker & Rudolf Friml, 193l, Musical: The White Eagle (Cover Artist, Barbelle)..................**10.00**

Gathering The Myrtle With Mary by William J. Scanlan, 1886 (Pre 1900)..................**15.00**

Gaucho Serenade, The by James Cavanaugh, John Redmond & Nat Simon, 1939, Photo Sammy Kaye (Cover Artist, Im-Ho)..................**5.00**

Gay Chauffeur, The by Valentine, 1907 (Transportation)..................**20.00**

Gee! Ain't It Great To Be Home by Phil Capvell, 1911 (Cover Artist, Starmer)..................**10.00**

Gee! But I Hate To Go Home Alone by Joe Goodwin & James E. Hanley, 1922, Photo White Sisters (Cover Artist, Wohlman)..................**3.00**

Gee! But I Hate To Go Home Alone by Joe Goodwin & James F. Hanley, 1922, Photo Marshall Montgomery (Cover Artist, Wohlman)..................**3.00**

Gee, But I Like Music With My Meals by Seymour Brown & Nat D. Ayer, 1911..................**6.00**

Gee, But I'd Like To Make You Happy by Reggie Montgomery, 1930, Movie: Good News..................**5.00**

Gee! But I'm Crazy For The Summertime by Jas. A. Brennan, 1911, Dedicated To Monponsett & It's Many Charms (Cover Artist, E.S. Fisher, & Dedication)..................**15.00**

Gee But I'm Lonesome by W.A. Lang & May Greene, 1912, Dedicated to Harry C. Husted, Bridgeport, Conn. (Cover Artist, Pfeiffer, Dedication & Deco)..................**10.00**

Gee! But I'm So Awful Lonesome by Chas. K. Harris, 1914..............**10.00**

Gee, But It's Great To Meet A Friend From Your Home Town by Wm. Tracey & Jas. McGavisk, 1910, Photo Sadie Helf..................**10.00**

Gee! But There's Class To A Girl Like You by W.R. Williams, 1908, Photo Marion Murray **10.00**

Gee! But There's Class To A Girl Like You by W. R. Williams, 1908, Photo Maud Lambert **10.00**

Gee! But This Is A Lonesome Town by Billy Gaston, 1906, Photo Eddie Foy **5.00**

Gee Dear I'm Lonesome by Baldwin, 1931 ....**5.00**

Gee, I Wish I Was Back In The Army by Irving Berlin, 1942, Movie: White Christmas, Photo Bing Crosby, Danny Kaye, Rosemary Clooney & Vera Ellen (Irving Berlin) **12.00**

Gee, I'm Scared by Halon & Morrisey, 1911 (Cover Artist, Pfeiffer) .**10.00**

Gee, It Must Be Tough To Be A Rich Man's Kid by Edwards & Cobb, 1912 (Cover Artist, Pfeiffer) **10.00**

Gee, It's Good To Hold You by Allan Roberts & Doris Fisher, 1945, Photo Woody Herman **3.00**

Gee! It's Great To Be Home Again by Ella M. Smith, G. Vernon Strout & Howard I. Smith, 1919 (WWI) **15.00**

Gee, Officer Krupke by Stephen Sondheim & Leonard Bernstein, 1957, Movie: West Side Story **5.00**

Gee! What A Wonderful Time We'll Have When The Boys Come Home by Mary Earl, 1917 (WWI) **15.00**

Gee Whiz by Abe Losch, 1919 ....**5.00**

Genee Waltzes by Maurice Levi, 1918, Ziegfeld's Soul Kiss, Photo Adeline Genee **10.00**

General Delivery by Ellis & Vinton, 1911 (Cover Artist, Pfeiffer & March) **15.00**

General Garfield's Grand March, 1890, Photo President Garfield (President, March, Military Personnel & Pre 1900) **28.00**

General Morgan's Parade March by C.L. Undernes, 1859 (Military Personnel, March & Pre 1900) **35.00**

General Pershing by Carl D. Vandersloot, 1918, Photo General Pershing (Cover Artist, Starmer, WWI, March & Military Personnel) **25.00**

General Sherman & Boys In Blue (Military Personnel, Pre 1900 & Patriotic) ..**35.00**

General Sherman's Funeral March by George Maywood, 1891, Respectfully Dedicated To His Bereaved Family (Pre 1900, Military Personnel, March & Dedication) **35.00**

General U.S. Grant's Grand March Reception by Mack, 1858 (President, March, Military Personnel & Pre 1900) **25.00**

General Von Stueben by Engles, 1925 (Military Personnel & Patriotic) ..**15.00**

General's Fast Asleep, The by Jimmy Kennedy & Michael Carr, 1935 (Patriotic) **15.00**

Genevieve by Will S. Hays, 1921 ....**5.00**

Gentle Annie by Stephen Foster, 1850 (Stephen Foster & Pre 1900) ..**25.00**

Gentle On My Mind by John Hartford, 1967, Photo Glen Campbell.....**5.00**

Gentleman Is A Dope, The by Richard Rodgers & Oscar Hammerstein II, 1951 ....**5.00**

Gentleman Obviously Doesn't Believe, The by Eddie Pola & Michael Carr, 1935, Photo Rudy Vallee...**10.00**

George Washington Bicentennial by John Philip Sousa, 1930 (John Philip Sousa, President, Patriotic & March) **20.00**

Georgette by Lew Brown & Ray Henderson, 1922, Musical: Greenwich Village Follies, Photo Ted Lewis (Cover Artist, Wohlman & Deco) **12.00**

Georgia by Howard Johnson & Walter Donaldson, 1922 ....**5.00**

Georgia Camp Meeting by Kerry Mills, 1897 (Pre 1900) **15.00**

Georgia Giggle, The by Will L. Livernash, 1918, (Rag & Black, Black Face) **15.00**

Georgia Lee by Ruth Fernandez Such, 1915 ....**10.00**

Georgia Lullaby by Charles J. Cordray, 1923 ....**5.00**

Georgia Moon by Jean C. Havez & Ted S. Barron, 1914 (Cover Artist, DeTakacs)...**10.00**

Georgia On My Mind by Stuart Correll & Hoagy Carmichael, 1941, Signed Photo Hoagy Carmichael (Signed)...**12.00**

Georgia On My Mind by Stuart Gorrell & Hoagy Carmichael, 1941, Photo Jimmy Dorsey...**3.00**

Georgia Pines by Jo Trent & Peter DeRose, 1929 (Deco)...**5.00**

Georgia Rag, The by Albert Gumble, 1910 (Cover Artist, Starmer, Rag & Black, Black Face)...**20.00**

Georgia Rose by Alex Sullivan, Jimmy Flynn & Harry Rosenthal, 1921 (Cover Artist, JVR)...**10.00**

Georgiana by Red McKenzie, Frankie Carle & Austen Croom-Johnson, 1937 ....**5.00**

Geraldine by Henry Lodge, 1915 (Cover Artist, Starmer & Deco)......**10.00**

German's Triumphal March by Charles & Jacob Kunkel, 1870 (Pre 1900 & March) **10.00**

Geronimo by Dempsey & Lilly, 1925 (Indian) **25.00**

Get An Automobile by Watts, 1906 (Transportation) **25.00**

Get Away For A Day by Sammy Cahn & Jule Styne, 1948, Musical: High Button Shoes **5.00**

Get Away From That Window by Harry Bennet, 1889 (Pre 1900)......**10.00**

Get 'Em In A Rumble Seat by Marshall, 1927 (Transportation)..........**25.00**

Get Happy by Melville Collins, 1907, Photo Eva Tanguay (Cover Artist, Gene Buck)...**15.00**

Get On The Funny Walk by Joseph J. Sullivan, 1889 (Pre 1900)........**15.00**

Get On The Raft With Taft, 1908, Full Page Photo Of Taft (Presidents & Political)...**35.00**

Get On Your Sneak Shoes Children by Gussie L. Davis, 1898 (Pre 1900) **15.00**

Get One For Me by Brown & Cooper, 1914 (Cover Artist, Pfeiffer)...**10.00**

Get Out And Get Under The Moon by Chas. Tobias, William Jerome & Larry Shay, 1928, Photo Paul Small (Cover Artist, Leff & Deco)...**3.00**

Get Out Of Town by Cole Porter, 1938, Movie: Leave It to Me 10.00

Get Thee Behind Me Satan by Irving Berlin, 1936 (Irving Berlin)........**5.00**

Get This Slow Rag by Blaufuss, 1913 (Cover Artist, Pfeiffer & Rag)...**15.00**

Get Together by Chet Powers, 1963, Photo The Young Bloods **5.00**

Get Up, Jack, John Sit Down by Edward Harrigan & David Braham, 1885 (Pre 1900) **15.00**

Get Up Those Stairs Mademoiselle by Clifford Jackson & Royal Brent, 1947, Signed Photo Tony Pastor (Signed)...**5.00**

Get Up You Sleepyhead by Ella Allen, 1933 ....**3.00**

Get Your Money's Worth by Irving Jones, 1897 (Pre 1900) **10.00**

Getting To Know You by Richard Rodgers & Oscar Hammerstein II, 1951, Movie: The King And I **5.00**

Ghost Melody, The by William & Maxwell (Cover Artist, Pfeiffer) ...**10.00**

Ghost Of A Coon, The by Bert Williams & George Walker, 1900 (Black, Black Face)......................................**25.00**

Ghost Of John James Christopher Benjamin Bings, The, 1887 (Pre 1900) **15.00**

Ghost Of The Ukelele, The by James Brockman, 1916 ....**5.00**

Ghost Of The Violin, The by Kalmer & Snyder, 1912, Photo Courtney Sisters (Cover Artist, Pfeiffer)......................................**10.00**

Ghost Riders In The Sky, 1947, Signed Photo Vaughn Monroe (Signed)..**24.00**

Ghost That Never Walked by M.K. Jerome & Jean Schwartz, 1904 ...**10.00**

Giannina Mia by Otto Harbach & Rudolf Friml, 1912...........................**3.00**

Giant by Webster & Tiomkin, 1956, Movie: Giant, Photo James Dean, Liz Taylor & Rock Hudson.......................................**10.00**

Gibson Girl, The by Richard H. Zinke, 1901 ....**35.00**

Giddap Mule by Leonard W. Ware, 1918 (WWI)......................**15.00**

Giddy Giddap! Go On! Go On! by Jack Frost, 1917 (WWI & Transportation)...**15.00**

Gideon Bible by Steve Allen, 1954, Photo Steve Allen **5.00**

Gidget by Washington & Karger, 1958, Movie: Gidget, Photo Sandra Dee, Cliff Robertson & James Darren **3.00**

Gigi by Alan J. Lerner & Frederick Loewe, 1958, Movie: Gigi **5.00**

Gigolo by Haven Gillespie & Earl Hagen, 1924 ....**5.00**

Gimme A Little Kiss Will "Ya" Huh? by Roy Turk, Jack Smith & Maceo Pinkard, 1954......................................**2.00**

"Gimme" A Little Kiss Will "Ya" Huh? by Roy Turk, Jack Smith & Maceo Pinkard, 1926, Photo Ilene Woods **3.00**

Gin, Gin Ginny Store by Irving Berlin, 1922 (Irving Berlin)..............**10.00**

Ginger Blues by Edward Harrigan & David Braham, 1876 (Pre 1900 & Blues)......................................**15.00**

Gingham Girl, The by Albert Von Tilzer **10.00**

Gipsy Dance by Heinrich Lichner, 1902 (Cover Artist, Havelka) **1500**

Gipsy Trail, 1897 (Pre 1900) **15.00**

Girl, A Girl, A by Bennie Benjamin, George Weiss & Al Bandini 1954, Photo Eddie Fisher......................................**3.00**

Girl At The End Of The Line, The by Burbridge, 1905 ....**10.00**

Girl Behind The Venetian Blind, The by Cliff Friend & Dave Franklin, 1939 ....**5.00**

Girl For Each Month Of The Year, A by Channing Pollack & Louis A. Hirsch, Ziegfeld Follies of 1915 (Cover Artist, DeTakacs) **15.00**

Girl Friend by Lorenz Hart & Richard Rodgers, 1926 ....**5.00**

Girl Friend Of A Boy Friend Of Mine, A by Gus Kahn & Walter Donaldson, 1931, Movie: Whoopee......................................**5.00**

Girl Friend Of The Whirling Dervish, The by Al Dubin, Harry Warren & Johnny Mercer, 1938, Movie: Garden Of The Moon, Photo Pat O'Brien, Margaret Lindsay & John Payne **6.00**

Girl From Ipanema by Vinicius DeMoroes, Norman Gimbel & Antonio Carlos Jobim, 1943......................................**3.00**

Girl From Jones Beach, The by Seiler & Marcus, 1949, Movie: The Girl From Jones Beach, Photo Ronald Reagan, Virginia Mayo & Eddie Bracken (President) **8.00**

Girl From Paree by Paul Herve, Jean Biquet & Adolf Philipp, 1915, Musical: The Girl Who Smiles **10.00**

Girl Has Eye Trouble, The by Gus Kahn & Ted Fiorito, 1926 ....**5.00**

Girl He Left Behind Him Has The Hardest Fight Of All, The by Al Bryan, Edgar Leslie & Harry Ruby, 1918 (Cover Artist, Barbelle & WWI)..**15.00**

Girl I Couldn't Get, The by D.A. Starnes & Harry Jay, 1920, Photo Dottie Ray Greene **8.00**

Girl I Know, A by Loveland & Lincoln, 1914 (Cover Artist, Pfeiffer).**10.00**

Girl I Left Behind Me, The by W.B. Miller, 1866 (Pre 1900).............**15.00**

Girl I Loved In Sunny Tennessee, The by Braisted & Carter, 1899 (Pre 1900)......................................**15.00**

Girl I Loved Out In The Golden West, The by C.H. Scoggins & Charles Avril, 1903......................................**10.00**

Girl I Should Have Married Long Ago, The by Will F. Burke, 1904 ..**10.00**

Girl In The Bonnet Of Blue, The by Ross Parker, 1938 (Cover Artist, Merman)......................................**3.00**

Girl In The Gingham Gown, The by Manuel Klein, 1913, Musical: Schuberts Production America (Patriotic)......................................**20.00**

Girl In The Little Green Hat, The by Jack Scholl, Bradford Browne & Max Rich, 1933, Photo Fran Frey **5.00**

Girl In the Purple Mask, The by Ralph & Barron, 1917, Movie: The Girl In the Purple Mask, Photo Grace Cunard & Francis Ford................**6.00**

Girl Next Door by Martin & Blane, 1954, Photo Jane Powell, Vic Damone, Edmund Purdom & Debbie Reynolds......................................**5.00**

Girl Of Dreams by Sunny Clapp, 1927......................................**5.00**

Girl Of Mine by Harold Freeman, 1917 (Cover Artist, Rolf Armstrong & Lithograph Knapp Co.)......................................**20.00**

Girl Of Mine by John Kemble & Lester W. Keith, 1905 ....**10.00**

Girl Of My Dreams by Charles Tobias, Henry Tobias & W. C. Polla, 1920 (Lithograph Knapp Co.) 16.00

Girl Of My Dreams by Sunny Clapp, 1927, Photo Abe Lyman & His Ambassador Orchestra (Cover Artist, Perret & Deco) **5.00**

Girl Of My Dreams by Sunny Clapp, 1927, Photo Whitey Kaufman's Original Pennsylvania Serenaders (Cover Artist, Perret & Deco) ...**5.00**

Girl Of My Heart by Lillian H. Sarver & Harry J. Lincoln, 1919, Photo Dottie Ray Greene **8.00**

Girl Of My Heart, The by John T. Kelly, 1883 (Pre 1900) **15.00**

Girl On The Automobile by Nathan, 1905 (Transportation)................**15.00**

Girl On The Magazine Cover by Irving Berlin, 1916 (Irving Berlin) ..**12.00**

Girl On The Police Gazette, The by Irving Berlin, 1937, Movie: On The Avenue, Photo Dick Powell & Alice Faye (Irving Berlin).............**15.00**

Girl On The Prow, The by Frank Mandel, Oscar Hammerstein II & Sigmund Romberg, 1928 ....**5.00**

Girl That I Marry, The by Irving Berlin, 1947, Movie: Annie Get Your Gun (Irving Berlin)......................................**12.00**

Girl That You've Forgotten Has Not Forgotten You, The by Edward I. Boyle, 1923......................................**5.00**

Girl Upstairs, The by Alfred Newman, 1955, Movie: The Seven Year Itch, Photo Marilyn Monroe **20.00**

Girl Who Broke My Heart, The by Al Dubin & J. Russell Robinson, 1928......................................**5.00**

Girl Who Came From Peru, The by Charlie Tobias & Carlos Maduro, 1941 ....**3.00**

Girl Who Is Loved By All, The by Tony Stanford, 1897 (Pre 1900) ...**15.00**

Girl Who Threw Me Down by Albert Gumble, 1907...........................**5.00**

Girl Who Wears A Red Cross On Her Sleeve, The by Mahoney & Howley, 1915 (Cover Artist, Pfeiffer, Red Cross & WWI)...................**35.00**

Girl With A Brogue, 1909 (Irish) **10.00**

Girl With The Dreamy Eyes by Michael Carr & Eddie Pola, 1935 ....**5.00**

Girl With The Golden Braids, The by Stanley Kahan & Eddie Snyder, 1947, Photo Perry Como **5.00**

Girl You Dream About, The by Richard Stahl **5.00**

Girlie by Berton Braley & Jerome Kern, 1918, Musical: Toot Toot....**10.00**

Girlie by Courtney & Allemong, 1915 (Cover Artist, Pfeiffer) **10.00**

Girlie Was Just Made To Love, A by Joe Goodwin & George W. Meyer, 1911 (Cover Artist, Pfeiffer) **15.00**

Girlie Was Just Made To Love, A by Joe Goodwin & George W. Meyer, 1911 (Cover Artist, Starmer) **15.00**

Girls by Alfred Bryan & Harry Carroll, 1919 (Cover Artist, Starmer)..**10.00**

Girls by Cole Porter, 1943, Movie: Mexican Hayride..........................**5.00**

Girls Of France by Alfred Bryan, Edgar Leslie & Harry Ruby, 1918 (WWI)..**15.00**

Girls Of My Dreams, The by Irving Berlin, 1920, Musical: Ziegfeld Follies, 1920 (Cover Artist, RS, Deco & Irving Berlin)......................**15.00**

Girls Were Made To Love & Kiss by Franz Lehar & A.P. Herbert, 1925...**3.00**

Git A Horse by Reed, 1902..**20.00**

Give A Little Credit To The Navy by B.G. DeSylva, Gus Kahn & Albert Gumble, 1918, Dedicated To Commander Buel Franklin, USNRF, Photo of Commander Franklin (Cover Artist, Starmer, Dedicated, Military Personnel & WWI)..**25.00**

Give A Little Whistle by Carolyn Leigh & Cy Coleman, 1960, Movie: Wildcat...**5.00**

Give A Little Whistle by Leigh Harline & Ned Washington, 1940, Movie: Pinocchio (Disney) **10.00**

Give Back My Sweetheart To Me by Charles K. Harris, 1911 (Cover Artist, Pfeiffer)..**10.00**

Give Me A Heart To Sing To by Washington & Young, 1934, Movie: Frankie And Johnnie, Photo Helen Morgan **3.00**

Give Me A Honeymoon That's Irish by Dubin, Burke & Welch, 1910 (Cover Artist, Pfeiffer & Irish) **15.00**

Give Me A Hundred Reasons by Ann Jones, 1949 ....**5.00**

Give Me A Kiss By The Numbers by Lieut. Joseph F. Trounstine, USR, 1918 (Cover Artist, Rose Symbol, Military Personnel, March & WWI)..**10.00**

Give Me A Little Bit More Than You Gave by Reilly & Carus, 1917 (WWI)..**15.00**

Give Me A Moment, Please by Leo Robin, Richard A. Whiting & W. Franke Harling, 1930, Photo Rubinoff And His Violin (Deco) **10.00**

Give Me A Moment Please by Leo Robin, Richard A. Whiting & W. Franke Harling, 1930, Movie: Monte Carlo, Photo Jack Buchanan & Jeannette MacDonald **10.00**

Give Me A Spin In Your Mitchell by Bill Gilson, 1909 (Transportation)...**22.00**

Give Me A Ukelele, And A Ukelele Baby by Lew Brown & Gene Williams, 1926 (Cover Artist, Starmer) **10.00**

Give Me All Of You by Earl Carroll & Milton Schwarzwald, 1918......**5.00**

Give Me Liberty Or Give Me Love by Ralph Grainger & Leo Robin, 1933, Movie: Torch Singer, Photo Claudette Colbert.....................**8.00**

Give Me My Mammy by B.G. DeSylva & Louis Silvers, 1921, Musical: Bombo, Photo Al Jolson (Al Jolson) **12.00**

Give Me One Hour by Brian Hooker & Rudolf Friml, 1931, Musical: The White Eagle (Cover Artist, Barbelle) **10.00**

Give Me The Moon Over Brooklyn by Jason Matthews & Terry Shand, 1946 (Cover Artist, Barbelle) **5.00**

Give Me The Moonlight, Give Me The Girl And Leave The Rest To Me by Lew Brown & Albert Von Tilzer, 1917 ....**12.00**

Give Me The Right To Love You by Ben Bard & Abe Glatt, 1917 (Cover Artist, Pfeiffer & Deco) **15.00**

Give Me The Single Life by Ruby & Bloom, 1945, Movie: Wake Up And Dream, Photo June Haver, John Payne & Charlotte Greenwood.....**3.00**

Give Me Your Hand by Dorothy Stewart, 1949 ....**5.00**

Give Me Your Tired & Poor by Irving Berlin, 1949, Musical: Miss Liberty (Irving Berlin)..**15.00**

Give My Love To Dixie by Levenson & Cobb, 1920 (Cover Artist, Pfeiffer) **10.00**

Give My Love To Mother by Gould & Mullen, 1911 (Cover Artist, Pfeiffer) **10.00**

Give My Regards To Broadway by George M. Cohan, 1933, Movie: Yankee Doodle Dandy, Photo James Cagney & George M. Cohan (George M. Cohan)...**18.00**

Glad Rag Doll by Jack Yellen, Milton Ager & Dan Dougherty, 1929, Movie: Glad Rag Doll, Photo Dolores Costello (Cover Artist, Barbelle & Deco) 15.00

Glad Rags by Gould & Williams, 1914 (Rag)....................................**15.00**

Gladiolus Rag by Scott Joplin, 1907 (Scott Joplin & Rag) **50.00**

Gliders-Skating Waltz, The by William Schroeder, 1916 (Sports) **15.00**

Gliding Down The Stream by Edward Harrigan & David Braham, 1875 (Pre 1900) **15.00**

Gliding Thru The Shadows by Neville Warren & Fred M. Stewart, 1919 (Cover Artist, Barbelle & Deco)...**10.00**

Gloomy Sunday by Laszlo Javor, Rezso Seress & Sam M. Lewis, 1933 (Cover Artist, Jorj)...**3.00**

Gloria by Leon Rene, 1948, Photo Ray Anthony **3.00**

Gloria's Romance by Murray, 1916, Movie: Gloria's Romance, Photo Billie Burke **3.00**

Glorianna by Lew Pollack & Sidney Clare, 1928................................**5.00**

Glorious Beer by Leggett & Goodwin, 1895 (Pre 1900)....................**10.00**

Glorious Columbia by James Odea & Alfred Solman, 1898, Boston Herald Sunday Supplement (Pre 1900) **10.00**

Glory Of Jamestown by James W. Casey, 1907 (March & Indian) **25.00**

Glory Of Love by Billy Hill, 1936 ....**5.00**

Glory Of The Moonlight, The by Peter Wenrich, 1915.......................**10.00**

Glory Of Womanhood by Harry J. Lincoln, 1917 (Cover Artist, Starmer)...**10.00**

Glory To God In The Highest! by F. Farington Harker, 1915..............**6.00**

Glowworm And The Moth, The by Max S. Witt & Frederic Rouken, 1902, Photo Marie Cahill..**10.00**

Glow-Worm, The by Paul Lincke, 1902 (Cover Artist, Etherington) ..**20.00**

Go Ahead, Propose by Barratt, 1919 (Cover Artist, Pfeiffer) **10.00**

Go Away Little Girl by Carole King, 1962, Photo Donny Osmond.......**6.00**

Go Down Moses by H.T. Burleigh, 1917 (Black, Black Face) **10.00**

Go Fly A Kite by Johnny Burke & James V. Monaco, 1939, Movie: The Star Maker, Photo Bing Crosby.....................**12.00**

Go Home And Tell Your Mother by Dorothy Fields & Jimmy McHugh, 1930, Movie: Love In The Rough, Photo Robert Montgomery & Dorothy Jordan **6.00**

Go Long Mule by Henry Creamer & Robert King, 1924....................**10.00**

Go The Other Way by Harry J. Lincoln (Cover Artist, Dittmar) **10.00**

Go To Sleep, Curley Head by Oliver, 1908.................................**10.00**

Go To Sleep, Little Baby by Judy & Zeke Canova & Harry & Henry Tobias, 1946 ....**5.00**

Go To Sleep My Baby, That's The Nicest Way To Say Good Night by Harold Robe & Jeff Godfrey, 1916, Dedicated To Ida Robe (Dedication)................**12.00**

Go Way Back And Sit Down by Al Johns, 1901 (Black, Black Face).**20.00**

Goblin's, Grand Galop De Concert by Lincoln, 1915 (Cover Artist, Pfeiffer) **10.00**

God Be With Our Boys To-Night by Fred G. Bowles & Wilfrid Sanderson, 1917 (WWI) **10.00**

God Bless America by Irving Berlin, 1939, First Performance by Kate Smith 1938 (Cover Artist, Im-Ho, Irving Berlin & Patriotic)........**12.00**

God Bless The Child by Arthur Herzog Jr. & Billie Holiday, 1951, Photo Billie Holiday **5.00**

God Bring You Safely To Our Arms Again by Kate Gibson & Vincent Shaw, 1917 (WWI).................**10.00**

God Remembers Everything by Kathleen Egan & Albert Arlen, 1935..**5.00**

God Remembers When The World Forgets by Clifton Bingham & Carrie Jacobs Bond, 1913, Linen Cover.................**15.00**

God Save America by Arthur West, 1918 (WWI)................**15.00**

God Spare Our Boys Over There by William Jerome & J.F. Mahoney, 1918 (WWI).................**15.00**

God's Service Flag Of Love by Storey & Wood, 1919 (Cover Artist, Pfeiffer) **10.00**

Goddess, The by Murray & Richmond, 1915, Photo Anita Stewart (Cover Artist, Pfeiffer).................**10.00**

Goin' Cotin' by Mercer & DePaul, 1954, Movie: Seven Brides For Seven Brothers, Photo Jane Powell & Howard Keel **5.00**

Goin' Out Of My Head by Teddy Randazzo & Bobby Weinstein, 1964..**5.00**

Goin' Steady by Young, 1952 ....**5.00**

Goin' To Heaven On A Mule by Dubin & Warren, 1934, Movie: Wonder Bar, Photo Al Jolson, Kay Francis, Dick Powell, Dolores Del Rio & Ricardo Cortez (Al Jolson) **12.00**

Goin To The County Fair by Lessing & Cook, 1912 ....**5.00**

Going Down by William J. Harry & William L. Baker, 1947, Photo Robert Baker.................**5.00**

Going For A Pardon by James Thornton, 1896 (Pre 1900) **15.00**

Going Home With Nelly After Five by Edward Harrigan & David Braham, 1882 (Pre 1900) **15.00**

Going My Way by Johnny Burke & Jimmy Van Heusen, 1944, Movie: Going My Way, Photo Bing Crosby **5.00**

Gold And Silver Waltz by Franz Lehar, 1910.................**5.00**

Gold Diggers' Song, The by Al Dubin & Harry Warren, 1933, Musical: Gold Diggers Of 1933 ....**10.00**

Gold Dust Twins by Nat Johnson, 1913 (Cover Artist, Crews Studio, Rag & Black) **25.00**

Gold Will Buy 'Most Anything But A True Girl's Heart by Monroe Rosenfeld, 1898 (Pre 1900) **16.00**

Golden Brown Blues by W.C. Handy, 1927 (Blues).................**10.00**

Golden Chords Waltz by F.S. Ogilvie, 1893 (Pre 1900) **15.00**

Golden Dreams by Billy B. Van & Beaumont Sisters, 1911.................**5.00**

Golden Earrings by Jay Livingston, Ray Evans & Victor Young, 1946, Movie: Golden Earrings, Photo Ray Milland & Marlene Dietrich..**15.00**

Golden Flyer March, The, 1910 (Cover Artist, Pfeiffer & March) **15.00**

Golden Gate March & Two Step by Bernard Stern, 1914, Dedicated To The Panama Pacific International Exposition, San Francisco (Dedication & March) **15.00**

Golden Gate Open For Me by James Kendis & James Brockman, 1919 (Cover Artist, R.S. & Deco) **5.00**

Golden Girl, Indian Love Song by Howard, Adams & Hough, 1909 (Indian) **25.00**

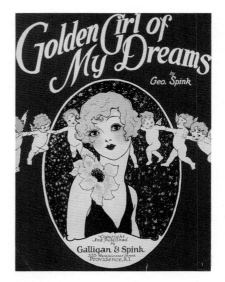

Golden Girl Of My Dreams by Geo Spink, 1927 (Cover Artist, Barbelle & Deco) **10.00**

Golden Glow by Joseph P. Cohen, 1907 ....**5.00**

Golden Key, The by Carrie Jacobs Bond, 1924.................**15.00**

Golden Spider by Chas. L. Johnson, 1910 (March).................**10.00**

Golden Star Waltz by L. Steabbog, 1922 ....**2.00**

Golden Twilight by LaFarge, 1907.................**5.00**

Golden Wedding by James Bland Of Sprague's Georgia Minstrels, 1879 (Pre 1900 & Black, Black Face).................**22.00**

Golden Years, 1953, Movie: Houdini, Photo Tony Curtis & Janet Leigh...**5.00**

Goldenrod Two-Step by Chadwick, 1896 (Pre 1900) **15.00**

Goldfinger by Bricusse, Newley & Barry, 1964, Movie: Goldfinger, Photo Sean Connery & Honor Blackman **8.00**

Golliwog's Cake Walk by Claude Debussy, 1908 (Black, Black Face)....**16.00**

Golly Walk, The by Murray, 1963, Movie: Wives And Lovers, Photo Janet Leigh, Van Johnson, Shelley Winters, Ray Walston & Martha Hyer **5.00**

Gondolier, The by Powell, 1904 (Transportation)...............................**15.00**

Gondoliers by Ethelbert Nevin, 1937 ....**5.00**

Gone Are The Days by Billy Joyce & Rubey Collins, 1920 ....**5.00**

Gone Are The Days by MacDonald & Z, 1914 (Cover Artist, Pfeiffer).**10.00**

Gone Before by Dexter Smith & C.A. White, 1869 (Pre 1900) **15.00**

Gone, Gone, Gone by Hollander, 1904 (Black, Black Face)...............**15.00**

Gone With The Dawn by Billy Rose, Stanley Joseloff & Dana Suesse, 1937 ....**5.00**

Gone With The Wind by Herb Magidson & Allie Wrubel, 1937, Movie: Gone With The Wind **10.00**

Gonna Get A Girl by Al Lewis & Howard Simon, 1947, Photo Tony Pastor..**2.00**

Good As Gold by James Kendis, James Brockman, Al Hoffman & Sherman, 1921 ....**5.00**

Good-Bye by Zelda Sears & Harold Levey, Musical: Lady Billy, 1920..**10.00**

Goodbye Again by Sam M. Lewis, J. Fred Coots & Harold Adamson, 1933 ....**5.00**

Good Bye Alexander, Good Bye Honey Boy by Henry Creamer & Turner Layton, 1918 (Cover Artist, E.E. Walton, WWI & Black, Black Face) **20.00**

Good-bye And Luck Be With You, Laddie Boy by Will D. Cobb & Gus Edwards, 1917 (Cover Artist, Edgar Keller & WWI) **20.00**

Good-By Betty Brown by Jack Mahoney & Theodore Morse, 1910, Photo Dolce Sisters (Cover Artist, Hirt & March) **10.00**

Good-Bye Boys by Andrew B. Sterling, William Jerome & Harry Von Tilzer, 1913, Movie: Honeymoon Express, Photo Al Jolson In Blackface, Dedicated To Edwin A. Starn (Cover Artist, Gene Buck, Al Jolson, Dedication & Black, Black Face) **35.00**

Goodbye Broadway, Hello France by C. Francis Reisner, Benny Davis & Billy Baskette, 1917 (Cover Artist, R.S., WWI & Transportation) ...**25.00**

Goodbye Dear, I'll Be Back In A Year by Mack Kay, 1940, Photo Ronnie Kemper (Cover Artist, Cliff Miska) 12.00

Goodbye Dixie Goodbye by Trace & Mohr, 1920 (Dixie)..................**10.00**

Goodbye Dixie Lee by Robert Levenson & G. Vernon Strout, 1917 (Cover Artist, Starmer & Dixie) **15.00**

Good-Bye, Dolly Gray by Will D. Cobb & Paul Barnes, 1900...........**10.00**

Good Bye Eliza Jane by Andrew B. Sterling & Albert Von Tilzer, 1903 (Black, Black Face) **20.00**

Good-Bye Flo by George M. Cohan (George M. Cohan) **15.00**

Goodbye France by Irving Berlin, 1918 (Cover Artist, Barbelle, WWI & Irving Berlin)..**15.00**

Goodbye Germany by J. Edwin McConnell & Lincoln McConnell, 1918 (WWI)...**20.00**

Good-bye Girlie & Remember Me by Irving Berlin, 1909 (Cover Artist, Pfeiffer & Irving Berlin)..**15.00**

Good-Bye, Good Luck, God Bless You by J. Keirn Brennan & Ernest R. Ball, 1914 ....10.00

Good-Bye Happy Days by Fred DeGresac, Edward Paulton & Silvio Hein, 1917, Musical: John Cort Presents Flo-Flo (Deco) **10.00**

Goodbye Lil' Liza Jane by Hugh McNutt & Karl Johnson, 1918 (WWI & Black, Black Face)..**20.00**

Good-bye, Little Dream, Good-bye by Cole Porter, 1936, Movie: Red Hot And Blue..**10.00**

Good Bye Little Girl Good-Bye by Will D. Cobb & Gus Edwards, 1904, Photo Corinne Griffith & Walter McGrail (Patriotic)...................**15.00**

Good-Bye Little Girl Good-Bye by Will D. Cobb & Gus Edwards, 1904, Photo Flo Adler (Patriotic) **15.00**

Good-bye, Little Girl Of My Dreams by Richard Howard & A. Fred Phillips, 1912 (Cover Artist, Starmer & Deco) **15.00**

Good Bye Little Rosebud by Otto Harbach, Oscar Hammerstein II, Herbert Stothart & Vincent Youmans, 1923, Musical: The Wildflower........**5.00**

Goodbye Ma Honey I'm Gone by Billy B. Johnson & Chris Smith, 1906..**10.00**

Goodbye Maggie Doyle by Jean Schwartz, 1905 (Irish).....................**10.00**

Goodbye Mister Greenback by Thos. S. Allen, 1906..........................**10.00**

Good-Bye, Mollie May by Fitzpatrick, 1917 (WWI)..........................**15.00**

Good-Bye, Mother Machree by J.Keirn Brennan & Ernest Ball, 1918 (Irish) **10.00**

Good-bye My Canada by Lockwood, 1915 (Cover Artist, Pfeiffer & Deco) **15.00**

Goodbye My Honey, I'm Gone by M. H. Rosenfield, 1888 (Pre 1900) ..**15.00**

Good-Bye My Lady Love by Jos. E. Howard, 1904, Photo Ida Emerson **10.00**

Good-bye My Own Dear Heart by Leap, 1913 (Cover Artist, Pfeiffer) .**10.00**

Good-Bye My Soldier Boy by Gregg, 1917 (WWI)............................**15.00**

Good-Bye My Soldier Lad by Thurland Chattaway, 1905 (Patriotic)..**15.00**

Good-Bye My Sweetheart Rose by R. M. Kane & J. L. Chandler, 1912 (Patriotic) **15.00**

Goodbye, Old Girl by Richard Adler & Jerry Ross, 1955, Musical: Damn Yankees **5.00**

Good-Bye Pal by Otto Harbach & Karl Hoschna, 1906.....................**10.00**

Good-bye Paradise, Good-bye by Howard & Jentes, 1915 (Cover Artist, Pfeiffer)..**10.00**

Goodbye Peter Goodbye Paul I'm Going To Take The Marriage Vow by Herb Ingraham, 1910..**10.00**

Good-bye Ragtime by Morgan, 1913 (Cover Artist, Pfeiffer & Rag)..**15.00**

Goodbye Red Man Goodbye by Ted Snyder, 1916 (Indian)...............**25.00**

Good-bye Rose by Addison Burkhardt & Herbert Ingraham, 1910 (Cover Artist, Starmer)..**10.00**

Goodbye Sally Good Luck To You by Sergeant Sam Habelow, 1919, Published by Chief Yeoman Geo.Jeffrey & Sergeant Samuel Habelow, Salvation Army Girl & Soldier On Cover (Cover Artist, Starmer, WWI, Military Personnel & Salvation Army)......................**35.00**

Goodbye Shanghai by Howard Johnson & Joseph Meyer, 1921............**5.00**

Good-Bye Sis by Will D. Cobb & Theodore Morse, 1909, Photo Kenney & Hollis **10.00**

Good-Bye, Slim by Walter Donaldson, 1918 (WWI).........................**15.00**

Goodbye Sue by Rule, Ricca & Loman, 1943, Photo Morton Downey.**3.00**

Good-Bye Summer, So Long Fall, Hello Winter by Percy Wenrich, 1913..**10.00**

Goodbye Sunshine, Hello Moon by Buck & Eckstein, 1919 ....**5.00**

Good Bye, Sweetheart, Good Bye by Arthur Lamb & Albert Von Tilzer, 1915..**10.00**

Goodbye To Rome, Arriverderci, Roma by Carl Sigman & R. Rascel, 1955, Photo Georgia Gibbs **3.00**

Good-bye Uncle Sammy by Hoffman, 1911 (Cover Artist, Pfeiffer & Patriotic) **15.00**

Good-Bye, When I Say Good-Bye To You by Pease & Nelson (Cover Artist, Pfeiffer)..**15.00**

Good-Day Marie by Emile Pessard, 1894 (Pre 1900) **15.00**

Good Enough by Rollin Howard, 1871 (Pre 1900 & Black, Black Face)..**20.00**

Good For Nothin' But Love by Eddie De Lange & Jimmy Van Heusen, 1939, Photo Guy Lombardo & His Brothers, Victor, Carmen & Lebert (Cover Artist, Im-Ho)..**3.00**

Good For Nothin' But Love by William Kernell & Harlan Thompson, 1930, Movie: The Big Party, Photo Sue Carol, & Dixie Lee (Deco) **10.00**

Good, Good, Good, That's You-That's You by Allan Roberts & Doris Fisher, 1944, Photo Joan Brooks.....................................**3.00**

Good Gravy Rag by Harry Belding, 1913, Photo Miss Mike Berkin (Rag)..**15.00**

Good Little Bad Little You by Bud Green & Sam H. Stept, 1928 ....**5.00**

Good Luck Mary by Bryan, Leslie & Piantadosi, 1909 (Cover Artist, Pfeiffer, March & Deco)..**20.00**

Good Luck Sweetheart by Ray Klages & J. Fred Coots, 1933, Photo Phil Regan (Cover Artist, Leff)..**15.00**

Good Man Is Hard To Find, A by Eddie Green, 1918, Photo Jack Norworth..**8.00**

Good Morning by Freed & Brown, 1939, Movie: Babes In Arms, Photo Judy Garland & Mickey Rooney **14.00**

Good Morning Carrie! by McPherson, Smith & Brymm, 1901 (Black, Black Face)..**25.00**

Good Morning Dixieland by Marshall, 1916 (Dixie)..........................**10.00**

Good Morning Glory by Mack Gordon & Harry Revel, 1933, Movie: Sitting Pretty, Photo Jack Oakie, Ginger Rogers & Jack Haley **10.00**

Good Morning Glory by Will J. Harris & Harry I. Robinson, 1917.......**5.00**

Good Morning Mr. Zip, Zip, Zip by Robert Lloyd, 1918 (Cover Artist, Henry Hutt & WWI)...**15.00**

Good Night by Clarence Ousley & Carrie Jacobs Bond, 1915, Dedicated To Mr. Victor Sincere (Dedication) **15.00**

Good Night Angel by Herb Magidson & Allie Wrubel, 1937, Movie: Radio City Revels, Photo Bob Burns, Milton Berle, Ann Miller, Kenny Baker & Many Other Stars **12.00**

Good-Night Beloved, Good-Night by J. Everett Fay & James B. Oliver, 1902 ....**8.00**

Good Night Boat by Anne Caldwell & Jerome Kern, 1920, Musical: The Night Boat...**10.00**

Good-Night, Dear Heart by Frank Bentz & Henry E. Geehl, 1908......**10.00**

Good Night Dearie by Frank W. Warren, S. R. Henry & D. Onivas, 1919 (Lithograph, Knapp) **15.00**

Good Night Germany by Meyer, 1918 (WWI)...................................**15.00**

Good Night-Good Night by Ed Gardiner & Ernest Ball, 1913.............**5.00**

Goodnight, Irene by Huddie Ledbetter & John Lomax, 1950, Photo The Weavers & Gordon Jenkins...**3.00**

Goodnight Ladies by Henry H. Williams & Egbert Van Alstyne, 1911 ....**10.00**

Good Night Little Girl Of My Dreams by Charlie Tobias & Joe Burke, 1933, Photo Paul Whiteman (Cover Artist, Leff)......................**5.00**

Good Night, Little Girl Of My Dreams by Charlie Tobias & Joe Burke, 1933, Photo Norman Cloutier (Cover Artist, Leff) **5.00**

Good Night, Little Girl Of My Dreams by Charlie Tobias & Joe Burke, 1933, Photo Phil Regan (Cover Artist, Cliff Miska & Deco)..........**5.00**

Good Night Lovely Little Lady by Mack Gordon & Harry Revel, 1934, Movie: We're Not Dressing, Photo Bing Crosby & Carole Lombard..**12.00**

Good Night Moon by Walter Donaldson, 1931...................................**5.00**

Good-Night Moonlight by Jack Mahoney & Theodore Morse, 1909 (March) **15.00**

Goodnight Moonlight by Ed Rose & Frank Magine, 1929 ....**15.00**

Good Night Mr. Moon by Eli Dawson & Albert Von Tilzer, 1911, Photo Chas. Nevins & Ada Gordon..**10.00**

Goodnight, My Love by Gus Arnheim, Harry Tobias & Jules Lemare, 1932 ....**10.00**

Goodnight My Love by Mack Gordon & Harry Revel, 1936, Movie: Stowaway, Photo Shirley Temple, Robert Young & Alice Faye (Shirley Temple) 20.00

Goodnight Nurse by Thos. J. Gray & W. E. Walker, 1912, Photo Mae West (Cover Artist, Starmer)...**16.00**

Good Night Roses by Max C. Freedman & Morris Silnutzer, 1919 (Cover Artist, DeTakacs)..**5.00**

Goodnight, Sleep Tight by Sylvia Fine, 1959, Movie: The Five Pennies, Photo Danny Kaye & Louis Armstrong **6.00**

Good Night, Sweet Dreams by Bischoff, 1887 (Pre 1900).................**15.00**

Good-Night Sweet Dreams Good-Night by Leonard Whitcup & Teddy Powell, 1938 ....**5.00**

Good Night Sweetheart by Ray Noble, Jimmy Campbell & Reg Connelly, 1931, Musical: Earl Carroll Vanities, 9th Edition, Photo Eddie Cantor (Eddie Cantor) **10.00**

Good Night Sweetheart (Rudy Vallee's Theme Song) by Ray Noble, Jimmy Campbell & Reg Connelly, 1931 Musical: Earl Carroll Vanities 9th Edition, Favorite Song Of The King & Queen Of England, Photo Rudy Vallee..**12.00**

Good Night Vienna by Holt Marvell & George Posford, 1932.............**5.00**

Good Night Wherever You Are by Dick Robertson, Al Hoffman & Frank Weldon, 1944, Photo Ginny Sims (Cover Artist, Starmer)..............5.00

Good Old U.S.A, The by J. Drislane, 1906 (Patriotic) **10.00**

Good Old Winter Time by Fyfe & Cheney, 1912 ....**5.00**

Good Shepherd, The by Beardsley Van de Water, 1892 (Pre 1900) **5.00**

Good Ship Honeymoon, The by R.H. Burnside & Raymond Hubbel, 1915, Musical: Hip Hip Hooray, At New York Hippodrome **15.00**

Good Ship Mary Ann, The by Gus Kahn & Grace LeBoy (Cover Artist, Starmer & Transportation)...**15.00**

Good Times Are Coming by Stella Pierson, 1933, Photo Bob Forsans (Cover Artist, L.S. Heflay) **5.00**

Good-Will Movement, The by Cole Porter, 1943, Movie: Mexican Hayride **6.00**

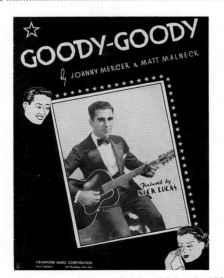

Goody Goody by Johnny Mercer & Matt Malneck, 1936, Photo Nick Lucas (Cover Artist, HBK)...5.00

Goody, Goody, Goody, Goody, Good by Irving Berlin, 1912 (Cover Artist, Pfeiffer & Irving Berlin)...**15.00**

Goofus by Gus Kahn, Wayne King & William Harold, 1932...............**5.00**

Gootmon Is A Hootmon Now by Sam M. Lewis, Joe Young & Bert Grant, 1916 (Cover Artist, Barbelle) **15.00**

Gorgeous by Benny Davis & Harry Akst, 1907, Photo Joe Darcy (Cover Artist, Natwick & Deco)..**15.00**

Got A Gal In Californ-I-A by Leo Robin & John Boles, 1935, Movie: Rose Of The Rancho..**5.00**

Got Me Doin' Things by Mack Gordon, 1935, Movie: Love In Bloom, Photo Dixie Lee & Joe Morrison...**5.00**

Got My Mind On Music by Mack Gordon & Harry Revel, 1937, Movie: Sally, Irene And Mary, Photo Alice Faye, Fred Allen & Many More Stars **10.00**

Got No Time by Gus Kahn & Richard A. Whiting, 1925 (Cover Artist, Leff)...**5.00**

Got Your Habits On by John Queen, 1899 (Pre 1900) **15.00**

Gotta Be This Or That by Sunny Skylar, 1945, Photo Benny Goodman (Cover Artist, Merman) **5.00**

Gotta Be This Or That by Sunny Skylar, 1945, Photo Bill Cooper (Cover Artist, Merman) **5.00**

Gotta Big Date With A Little Girl by Harry Charles & Henry Tobias, 1938 ....**5.00**

Gotta Feelin For You by Joe Trent & Louis Alter, 1929, Movie: Hollywood Review of 1929..**10.00**

Gotta Get Some Shut-Eye by Johnny Mercer & Walter Donaldson, 1939, Photo Leighton Noble..**3.00**

Gotta Go To Town by Mort Dixon, Joe Young & Harry Warren, 1931, Musical: The Laugh Parade (Cover Artist, Gorj)...........................**5.00**

Gotta Travel On by Paul Clayton, 1958 ....**2.00**

Götterdammerung by Richard Wagner, 1913...................................**10.00**

Grace And Beauty by James Scott, 1909 (Rag).................................**20.00**

Grace & Beauty Waltzes by Loveland, 1915 (Cover Artist, Pfeiffer & Deco) **15.00**

Grace Conroy by Michael Nolan, 1892 (Pre 1900) **15.00**

Grace O'Moore by Max S. Witt, 1895 (Pre 1900) **15.00**

Graduation Day by Joe Sherman & Noel Sherman, 1956, Photo The Four Freshman **5.00**

Gramachree, Be True To Me by Frank Fogarty, 1911 (Irish) **10.00**

Granada by Augustin Lara, 1950..**3.00**

Grand Daddy by Louis Breau & Chas. Tobias, 1923 (Cover Artist, Paderewski) **10.00**

Grand Trunk Waltzes by D'Albert, 1854 (Pre 1900 & Transportation)..**15.00**

Grandfather's Clock by Abner Silver, Nick Kenny & Mack David, 1934, Movie: New York Town (Cover Artist, Harris) **8.00**

Grandfather's Clock by Henry C. Work, 1876 (Pre 1900)..................**15.00**

Grandma's Shamrocks by E. A. Suttan & James C. Reckel, Advertising Bromo Seltzer (Advertising) **25.00**

Grange Song by Reynolds, 1904 ....**5.00**

Granny by L. Wolfe Gilbert & Alex Belledna, 1919 (Cover Artist, DeTakacs)...**5.00**

Granny "You're My Mammy's Mammy" by Joe Young, Sam M. Lewis & Harry Akst, 1921 (Cover Artist, R.S. & Black, Black Face)..........**12.00**

Grant Ave. by Richard Rodgers & Oscar Hammerstein II, 1961, Movie: Flower Drum Song **5.00**

Grass Grows Greener, Way Down Home, The by Jack Yellen & Dan Dougherty, 1928 ....**5.00**

Grass Is Always Greener, The by Raymond Egan & Richard Whiting, 1924 ....**8.00**

Grasshopper's Hop, The by Gold, 1916 (Cover Artist, Pfeiffer)..........**10.00**

Grateful, O Lord Am I by Caro Roma & William H. Gardner, 1920.....**5.00**

Gratitude by Ed Teschemacher & Charles Marshall, 1913 ....**5.00**

Gravel Rag, The by Charlotte Blake, 1908 (Cover Artist, DeTakacs & Rag) **15.00**

Gray Rocks And Grayer Sea by C.G.D. Roberts & Kate Vannah, 1899 (Cover Artist, Hauman & Pre 1900)................................**15.00**

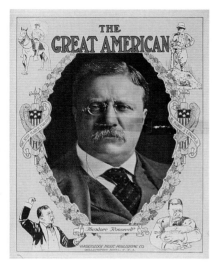

Great American, Theodore Roosevelt, The by Harry J. Lincoln, 1919, Photo Theodore Roosevelt, Dedicated To The American Legion & In Memory Of Theodore Roosevelt (Cover Artist, Harris & Ewing, President & Dedication)......................................40.00

Great Day by William Rose, Edward Eliscu & Vincent Youmans **5.00**

Great Divide, The by Gimbel & Schifrin, 1969, Movie: Bullitt, Photo Steve McQueen & Jacqueline Bisset.................................**5.00**

Great Graphic Balloon Galop, The by Fitch, 1873 (Pre 1900 & Transportation) **25.00**

Great Rock Island Route, The by J.A. Roff, 1882 (Pre 1900 & Transportation)..**30.00**

Great Snakes! by Ernest Reeves, 1911 ....**5.00**

Greatest Day The World Will Ever Know, The by Ed Morton, James Dempsey & Joe Burke, 1918, Photo Ed Morton (Cover Artist, Pfeiffer & WWI))..**10.00**

Greatest Love Of All, The by Leo Wood, 1919, Movie: One Week Of Life, Photo Pauline Frederick (Cover Artist, RS) **10.00**

Greatest Miracle Of All by Marie Wardall & David W. Guion, 1918 (Black, Black Face) **15.00**

Greatest Question, The by Paul M. Sarazan & M.K. Jerome, 1920 (Cover Artist, Frederick S. Manning)...............................**15.00**

Greatest Thing That Came From France, The by Harry Pease & Ed. G. Nelson, 1918 (WWI) **15.00**

Green Beret, The by P.G. Fairbanks & C.W.D. Ken Whitcomb, 1964 (Patriotic)...**5.00**

Green Eyes by Adolfo Utrera, Nilo Menendez, E. Rivera & E. Woods, 1941, Photo Jimmy Dorsey, Helen O'Connell & Bob Eberly **5.00**

Green Hat by Scholl, Browne & Rich, 1933 ....**5.00**

Green I Love The Best, The by E.S. Ufford, 1897 (Pre 1900) **20.00**

Green Leaves Of Summer, The by Webster & Tiomkin, 1960, Movie: The Alamo, Photo John Wayne & Linda Cristal **5.00**

Green River by Eddie Cantor, Gus Van & Joe Schenck, 1920, Photo Eddie Cantor (Eddie Cantor) **10.00**

Green-Eyed Dragon, The by Greatrex Newman & Wolseley Charles, 1926 ....**5.00**

Greenwich Village Sue by A. Swanstrom & Carey Morgan, 1920 ....**5.00**

Greyhound March, The by John Parker, 1912 (Cover Artist, Pfeiffer & March) **15.00**

Grieving by Shields & Conlin, 1911 ....**5.00**

Grieving For You by Joe Gibson, Joe Ribaud & Joe Gold, 1920, Photo Al Jolson (Cover Artist, J.V.R. & Al Jolson)....................**15.00**

Grizzly Bear, The by Irving Berlin & George Botsford, 1910, Photo Maude Raymond (Irving Berlin & Rag)........................**16.00**

Grover Cleveland's Grand March by Louis List, 1892, Photo Grover Cleveland (Presidents, Pre 1900 & March)...................**40.00**

Guardian Angel, The by Charles Gounod..**10.00**

Guess by Roy L. Burtch, 1922 (Transportation).................................**15.00**

Guild Polka Militaire by Fox, 1876 (Pre 1900) **15.00**

Guilty by Gus Kahn, Harry Akst & Richard A. Whiting, 1931, Photo Dinah Shore (Cover Artist, Leff)......................................8.00

Guilty by Gus Kahn, Harry Akst & Richard Whiting, 1931, Photo Morton Downey..**6.00**

Guitar Boogie by Arthur Smith, 1946, Photo Arthur Smith **5.00**

Gum Shoe Fox Trot, by Stark, 1917 ....**10.00**

Gunga Din by Rudyard Kipling & Charles Gilbert Spross, 1925.........**10.00**

Gunner's Mate, The by Brown, 1901 (Transportation) **15.00**

Guy Is A Guy, A by Oscar Brand, 1952, Photo Doris Day **8.00**

Guy Named Joe, A by Jim Carhart & Bus Davis, 1945, Photo Gertrude Lawrence **5.00**

Guys & Dolls by Jo Swerling, Abe Burrows & Frank Loesser, 1950, Musical: Guys & Dolls..**5.00**

Gypsy Blues by Noble Sissle & Eubie Blake, 1921, Musical: Shuffle Along (Blues) **8.00**

Gypsy In Me by Cole Porter, 1934, Movie: Anything Goes **5.00**

Gypsy Jan by Harry B. Smith & Victor Herbert, 1898 (Pre 1900 & Victor Herbert)..**20.00**

Gypsy Joe by Gus Kahn & Walter Donaldson, 1928, Musical: Ziegfeld Production Whoopee, Photo Eddie Cantor (Cover Artist, Nickel & Eddie Cantor)..**16.00**

Gypsy Love Song by Harry B. Smith & Victor Herbert, 1898 (Pre 1900 & Victor Herbert) **10.00**

Gypsy Lover by Kendall Burgess & Harold Raymond, 1936 ....**5.00**

Gypsy Moonbeams by Lieut. Wm. B. Davidson & Lee M. Walker, 1919 (Cover Artist, E.E. Walton & Military Personnel) **15.00**

Gypsy Song by Harry Smith & Victor Jacobi, 1917 ....**5.00**

Gypsy, The by Billy Reid, 1947, Photo Sammy Kaye (Cover Artist, Nick)...**5.00**

Gypsy Told Me, A by Sam Pokrass & Jack Yellen, 1938, Movie: Happy Landing, Photo Sonja Henie, Don Ameche & Ethel Merman........**10.00**

Ha-Cha-Cha by Werner Richard Heymann & Gus Kahn, 1934, Movie: Caravan...**5.00**

Hail, Hail The Gang's All Here by Theodore Morse, Arthur Sullivan, and D.A. Esrom, 1917 (Cover Artist, Rose Symbol)............................**10.00**

Hail To The Redskins by Bert Kalmar & Harry Ruby, 1938 (Indian) .**50.00**

Hair Of Gold Eyes Of Blue by Sunny Skylar, 1948 ....**2.00**

Half A Moon by Eddie Dowling & James F. Hanley, 1926, Musical: Honeymoon Lane, Photo Eddie Dowling..**6.00**

Half And Half by F. Henri Klickman, 1914 ....**3.00**

Half As Much by Curley Williams, 1951, Photo Rosemary Clooney **5.00**

Half Moon On The Hudson by Walter Bullock & Harold Spina, 1937, Movie: Sally, Irene And Mary, Photo Alice Faye, Fred Allen & Many More Stars..**10.00**

Half Way To Heaven by Al Dubin & J. Russell Robinson, 1928, Signed Photo Harry Fox (Cover Artist, Barbelle, Signed & Deco)............**10.00**

Hallelujah by Leo Robin, Clifford Grey & Vincent Youmans, 1927, Musical: Hit The Deck...**10.00**

Hallelujah I'm A Bum by Jack Waite, 1928.......................................**15.00**

Halls Of Ivy, The by Henry Russell & Vick Knight, 1950...................**5.00**

Hallucination Of Love by Howard Johnson & Carlo Sanderson, 1921, Musical: Tangerine **10.00**

Hamlet Was A Melancholy Dane by William Jerome & Jean Schwartz, 1903 ....**10.00**

Hammock Love Song by Herbert & DeKoven, 1909...........................**10.00**

Hand In Hand Again by Raymond B. Egan & Richard Whiting, 1919..**5.00**

Hand Me Down My Walking Cane by James Bland, 1880 (Pre 1900 & Black, Black Face)...**15.00**

Hand Of Friendship by Lincoln, 1915 (Cover Artist, Pfeiffer & Deco)..**15.00**

Hand Of You, The by Carrie Jacobs Bond, 1920 ....**15.00**

Hand That Rocked My Cradle Rules My Heart, The by Irving Berlin, 1919, Signed Photo Irving Berlin (Cover Artist, Barbelle & Irving Berlin)..**20.00**

Handful Of Earth From Mother's Grave by Joseph Murphy, 1883 (Pre 1900)..**15.00**

Handful Of Stars, A by Jack Lawrence & Dan Shapiro, 1940 ....**5.00**

Handle Me With Care by Jerome & Schwartz, 1907 (Cover Artist, Pfeiffer & Deco) **15.00**

Hands Across The Border by Mort Greene & Harry Revel, 1942, Movie: Call Out The Marines **8.00**

Hands Across The Sea by John Philip Sousa, 1899 (John Philip Sousa, Pre 1900 & March) **20.00**

Hands Across The Table by Mitchell Parish & Jean Delettre, 1934, Musical: Continental Varieties, Photo Lucienne Boyer (Cover Artist, Leff)..**5.00**

Hands Up! by Lamb & Helf, 1911 (Cover Artist, Pfeiffer & Deco) **10.00**

Handsome, Brave Life Saver, The by Al Gumble **10.00**

Handsome Harry by F.W. Hager, 1904 (March) **15.00**

Hang Onto A Rainbow by Green & Stept, 1930, Movie: Show Girl In Hollywood, Photo Alice Fay **12.00**

Hang Out The Front Door Key by Benj. H. Burt.................................**5.00**

Hang Your Heart On A Hickory Limb by Johnny Burke & James V. Monaco, 1939, Movie: East Side Of Heaven, Photo Bing Crosby, Joan Blondell & Baby Sandy...**6.00**

Hankerin' By Jule Styne & Sammy Cahn, 1948, Movie: Two Guys From Texas, Photo Dennis Morgan, Jack Carson & Dorothy Malone **5.00**

Hannah Won't You Open Up That Door by Andrew Sterling & Harry Von Tilzer, 1904 (Black, Black Face)..**20.00**

Happiness by Fred Fischer & Joe Jordan, 1908................................**10.00**

Happiness by Geo. W. Meyer, 1921 ....**10.00**

Happiness by H. C. Weasner, 1919 (Cover Artist, Starmer & Deco)...**10.00**

Happiness by Vera Ross & Clara Edwards, 1923................................**10.00**

Happiness Is A Thing Called Joe by E. Y. Harburg & Harold Arlen, 1942, Movie: Cabin In The Sky **5.00**

Happiness, Where Are You? by L. Wolfe Gilbert & Leon Flatow, 1919 ....**5.00**

Happy Birthday Song by Fred Waring, 1950, Fred Waring's Tribute To Jolly Green Giant's 20th Anniversary, Photo Jolly Green Giant On Back Cover (Advertising) 20.00

Happy Birthday To Love by Dave Franklin, 1939, Movie: That's Right You're Wrong...**6.00**

Happy Days And Lonely Nights by Rose & Fisher, 1928....................**5.00**

Happy Days Are Here Again by Jack Yellen & Milton Ager, 1929, Movie: Chasing Rainbows (Deco)..**15.00**

Happy Days by Beck & Foote, 1919 ....**5.00**

Happy Days by Maurice Levi, 1907, Musical: The Soul Kiss (March) **10.00**

Happy Days In Dixie by Kerry Mills, 1898 (Pre 1900, Dixie & March)..**20.00**

Happy Feet by Al Stillman & Roy Ross, 1950, Photo Al Jarvis & Betty White **5.00**

Happy Go Lucky Lane by Sam M. Lewis, Joe Young & Joseph Meyer, 1928 ....**5.00**

Happy Go-Lucky by Frank Loesser & Jimmy McHugh, 1943, Movie: Happy Go Lucky, Photo Mary Martin, Dick Powell, Betty Hutton, Eddie Bracken & Rudy Vallee **5.00**

Happy Holiday by Irving Berlin, 1942 (Irving Berlin)........................**5.00**

Happy Hooligan by Theodore F. Morse, 1907 ....**15.00**

Happy Hours In Coontown by Brown, 1899 (Pre 1900 & Black, Black Face) **20.00**

Happy Humming Bird by Mort Dixon & Harry Woods, 1929.............**10.00**

Happy In Love by Jack Yellen & Sammy Fain, 1941 ....**5.00**

Happy Land by Lawrence Gilbert, 1915...**5.00**

Happy Landin' With Landon, Official Republic Campaign Song by Jack Stern & Sid Caine, Photo Alf Landon **28.00**

Happy Little Country Girl by Irving Berlin, 1913 (Cover Artist, Pfeiffer & Irving Berlin) **15.00**

Happy New Year, Darling by Carmen Lombardo & Johnny Marks, 1949...**5.00**

Happy School Days by Sudds, 1881 (Pre 1900)................................**15.00**

Happy Talk by Richard Rodgers & Oscar Hammerstein II, 1949, Musical: South Pacific (Cover Artist, BJH) **5.00**

Happy Times by Sylvia Fine, 1949, Movie: The Inspector General, Photo Danny Kaye **12.00**

Happy Tom O'Day by Gary, 1915 (Irish) **10.00**

Happy Wanderer, The by Antonia Ridge & Friedr. W. Moller, 1954, Photo Alfred Drake..**5.00**

Happy Wanderer, The by Antonia Ridge & Friedr. W. Moller, 1954, Photo Henri Rene..**5.00**

Happy Wanderer, The by Antonia Ridge & Friedr. W. Moller, 1954, Photo Norman Luboff..**5.00**

Harbor Lights by Jimmy Kennedy & Hugh Williams, 1937 (Transportation)..**5.00**

Harbor Of Dreams by J.R. Shannon, 1917 ....**5.00**

Harbor Of Home, Sweet Home by Lamb & Solman, 1905 ....**10.00**

Harbor Of Love, The by Earl C. Jones & Charlotte Blake, 1911 ....**5.00**

Hard Boiled Rag by Louis Mentel, 1914 (Rag & March) **15.00**

Hard Hearted Hannah by Jack Yellen, Milton Ager, Bob Bigelow & Chas. Bates, 1924 ....**5.00**

Hard Times Come Again No More by Stephen Foster, 1850 (Stephen Foster, Pre 1900 & Black, Black Face) **35.00**

Hard To Get by Jack Segal, 1955, From TV Program, Justice, Signed Photo Giselle MacKenzie (Signed) **12.00**

Harding, You're The Man For Us, Official Republic Campaign Song by Al Jolson, 1920, Photo President Harding & President Coolidge (President)..**30.00**

Harem Scarem Rag, Some Rag! by Lem Trombley, 1912 (Rag) **15.00**

Harlem Nocturne by Earle Hager, 1946 ....**2.00**

Harlem Rag by Tom Turpin, 1897 (Pre 1900 & Rag) **15.00**

Harmonica Henry by Phil Baxter, 1930..................................**5.00**

Harmony Rag by Hal G. Nichols, 1911 (Cover Artist, Art Craft & Rag)...**10.00**

Harnden's Express Line Gallopade & Trio by Firth & Hall, 1841 (Pre 1900 & Transportation) **50.00**

Harp With The Broken String, The by Joseph McCarthy & James F. Hanley, 1930 ....**5.00**

"Harrigan" by George M. Cohan, 1933, Movie: Yankee Doodle Dandy, Photo James Cagney & George M. Cohan (George M. Cohan).....**16.00**

Harry Fox Trot by Lew Pollock, 1918..................................**5.00**

Harvardiana by R. G. Williams, 1909..................................**10.00**

Has Anybody Here Kissed Toodles? by Dan J. Sullivan, 1915 (Cover Artist, E.S. Fisher) **10.00**

Has Anybody Here Seen Kelly? by C. W. Murphy & Will Letters, 1909, Photo Nora Bayes (Cover Artist, Gene Buck & Irish) 15.00

Hat Me Father Wore by Ferguson & McCarthy, 1876 (Pre 1900 & Irish) **15.00**

Hat Me Father Wore On St. Patrick's Day, The by William Jerome & Arthur Schwartz, 1909 (Irish)..**15.00**

Hat's Off Here Comes A Lady by Joe Young & Bernice Petkers, 1932 ..**5.00**

Hats Make The Woman by Victor Herbert, 1905 (Victor Herbert)......**10.00**

Hats Off To Me by Edward Harrigan & David Braham, 1890 (Pre 1900) **15.00**

Hats Off To The Red White And Blue by Ralph F. Beegan, 1918 (WWI) **15.00**

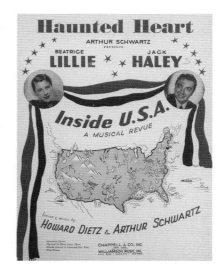

Haunted Heart by Arthur Schwartz & Howard Dietz, 1948, Musical: Inside U.S.A. Photo Beatrice Lillie & Jack Haley (Cover Artist, BJH)..8.00

Haunting Melody by Ben Russell, Larry Spier & Larry Schloss, 1925 .**5.00**

Haunting Memory by E. C. Pierce & Carrie Jacobs Bond, 1912, Linen Cover **15.00**

Haunting Rag, Instructions by Julius Lenzberg, 1911 (Cover Artist, DeTakacs & Rag) **15.00**

Haunting Waltz by M. J. Gunsky & Nat Goldstein, 1921, Musical: Angel Face..**5.00**

Hava Nagila by David Taxe & Daniel Gould, 1960..........................**5.00**

Havana, Back To Havana & You by Charles Adler & Jack London, 1918 (Cover Artist, Barbelle)..**10.00**

Havanola by Hugo Frey, 1916..**5.00**

Have A Heart by Gene Buck & Jerome Kern, 1916, Musical: Ziegfeld Follies 1916..**12.00**

Have A Little Faith In Me by Sam Lewis, Joe Young & Harry Warren, 1930, Movie: Spring Is Here **10.00**

Have A Smile For Everyone You Meet by J. Keirn Brennan, Paul Cunningham & Bert Rule, 1918, Photo Corinne Griffith **5.00**

Have I Stayed Away Too Long by Frank Loesser, 1943 (Cover Artist, WJH)..**5.00**

Have I Told You Lately That I Love You by Scott Wiseman, 1946, Photo Bing Crosby & Andrews Sisters..................................**10.00**

Have Mercy by Buck Ram & Chick Webb, 1939 ....**5.00**

Have You A Little Fairy In Your Home by G.H.E. Hawkins, Arthur Gillespie & Chas. N. Daniels, 1911..**10.00**

Have You Ever Been In Ireland In April? by George Spink, 1927 (Irish)..**10.00**

Have You Ever Been Lonely by George Brown & Peter DeRose, 1933, Photo Bing Crosby (Cover Artist, Barbelle) **6.00**

Have You Ever Been Lonely by George Brown & Peter DeRose, 1933, Photo Johnny Johnson (Cover Artist, Barbelle) **6.00**

Have You Ever Been Lonely by George Brown & Peter DeRose, 1933, Photo Mark Fisher (Cover Artist, Barbelle) **6.00**

Have You Forgotten? by Kerr, Burtnett, Cooper & Stevenson, 1921 ....**5.00**

Have You Forgotten? by Leo Robin & Dana Suesse, 1931 ....**5.00**

Have You Forgotten Marguerite? by C.M. Denison & E. F. Dusenberry, 1912 ....**5.00**

Have You Forgotten So Soon? by Edward Heyman, Sam Coslow & Abner Silver, 1938, Signed Photo Ozzie Nelson (Cover Artist, Im-Ho & Signed)...**5.00**

Have You Got Any Castles, Baby? by Johnny Mercer & Richard Whiting, 1937, Movie: Variety Show, Photo Dick Powell & Priscilla & Rosemary Lane **5.00**

Have You Seen My Henry Brown by Dave Clark & Albert Von Tilzer, 1905 (Black, Black Face) **20.00**

Have You Seen My Little Girl by Williams & Rosemont, 1920 (Cover Artist, Pfeiffer)...**10.00**

Have You Seen My Sweetheart In His Uniform Of Blue? by George L. Cobb & Gus Edwards, 1902 (Patriotic).......................................**15.00**

Haven't Got Time For The Pain by Jacob Brackman, 1974, Photo Carly Simon..**5.00**

Hawaii by David & Bernstein, 1966, Movie: Hawaii, Photo Julie Andrews, Max Von Sydow & Richard Harris..................................**3.00**

Hawaii by E. Clinton Keithley & F. Henri Klickmann, 1922.................**5.00**

Hawaii & You by Robert F. Roden & Robert A. Keiser, 1917 ....**5.00**

Hawaiian Blue by Stanley Murray, 1916......................................**5.00**

Hawaiian Bluebird by Morgan, 1919 ....**5.00**

Hawaiian Blues by Howard Johnson & Carlo Sanderson, 1921, Musical: Tangerine **10.00**

Hawaiian Butterfly by George A. Little, Billy Baskette & Joseph Santly, 1917, Photo Scarpioff (Cover Artist, Rose Symbol & Deco) **10.00**

Hawaiian Butterfly by George A. Little, Billy Baskette & Joseph Santly, 1917, Photo Klein Bros. (Cover Artist, Rose Symbol & Deco).....**10.00**

Hawaiian Butterfly by George A. Little, Billy Baskette & Joseph Santly, 1917, Photo Dorothy Meuther (Cover Artist, Rose Symbol & Deco)...........**10.00**

Hawaiian Dream Boat by Charlie Harrison, Louis O'Connell & Fred Rose, 1927, Photo Chet Frost **5.00**

Hawaiian Dreams by Sidney Carter & Herbert B. Marple, 1916 ....**5.00**

Hawaiian Echoes by James W. Casey, 1917 ....**5.00**

Hawaiian Hospitality by Harry Owens & Ray Kinney, 1937.................**5.00**

Hawaiian Lullaby by Dorothy Terriss & Ethel Bridges, 1919 ....**5.00**

Hawaiian Moonlight by F. Henri Klickmann, 1917 ....**5.00**

Hawaiian Nights by Lee S. Roberts, 1919....................................**5.00**

Hawaiian Paradise by Harry Owens, 1935 ....**3.00**

Hawaiian Rainbow by Jeanne Gravelle & Bob Haring, 1921 (Cover Artist, Hoffman) **5.00**

Hawaiian Rose by Paul B. Armstrong & F. Henri Klickmann, 1918.....**5.00**

Hawaiian Smiles by Ballard MacDonald & Mary Earl, 1919 ....**15.00**

Hawaiian Sunrise by L. Wolfe Gilbert & Carey Morgan, 1917 ....**5.00**

Hawaiian Sunshine by Harry Morgan, 1916......................................**10.00**

Hawaiian Twilight by Herbert B. Marple, 1918 ....**5.00**

Hawaiian Wedding Song, The by Al Hoffman, Dick Manning & Charles E. King, 1948, Photo Andy Williams...**5.00**

Hawaiian Whispers by Prince Moki & Malie Kalani, 1922 ....**5.00**

Ha-Za-Za by Kalman, 1914 ....**5.00**

He by Richard Mullan & Jack Richards, 1954, Photo Maguire Sisters..**2.00**

He Ain't Got Rhythm by Irving Berlin, 1937, Movie: On The Avenue, Photo Dick Powell & Alice Faye (Irving Berlin) **10.00**

He Brought Home Another by Paul Dresser, 1896 (Pre 1900)............**15.00**

He Came From Milwaukee by Edward Madden, Ben M. Jerome & Louis A. Hirsch, 1910 (Cover Artist, Starmer) **5.00**

He Carved His Mother's Name Upon The Tree by Henry V. Neal & Gussie L. Davis, 1899 (Pre 1900)...**15.00**

He Certainly Was Good To Me by Havez & Sloane, 1898 (Pre 1900) .**15.00**

He Didn't Split The Wood by William Jerome, 1892 (Pre 1900) **15.00**

He Fought For The Cause He Thought Was Right by Paul Dresser, 1896 (Pre 1900) **15.00**

He Goes To Church On Sunday, by Vincent Bryan & Albert Goetz, 1907...**10.00**

He Got Right Up On The Wagon by Harry Williams & Egbert Van Alstyne, 1910...**10.00**

He Knows His Groceries by Lou Breau, 1926 ....**5.00**

He Laid Away A Suit Of Gray To Wear The Union Blue by Wickes & Jansen, 1901 (Patriotic) **15.00**

He Loves It by Grant Clarke, Edgar Leslie & Pete Wendling, 1922, Photo Margaret Young (Cover Artist, Barbelle)......................................**5.00**

He May Be Old But He's Got Young Ideas by Howard Johnson, Alex Gerber & Harry Jentes, 1916...**10.00**

He Never Came Back by William Jerome, 1891 (Pre 1900)...............**15.00**

He Never Cares To Wander From His Own Fireside by Felix McGlennon, 1892 (Pre 1900) **15.00**

He Played It On His Fid-Fid-Fiddle-Dee-Dee by Irving Berlin, & Goetz, 1912 (Cover Artist, Pfeiffer & Irving Berlin)..............................**15.00**

He, She & Me by Guy Lombardo & Charles Newman, 1929, Photo "Cookie" & His Gingersnaps **5.00**

He Used To Be A Farmer But He's A Big Town Slicker Now by Andrew Sterling & Harry Von Tilzer, 1919...**10.00**

He Walked Right In, Turned Around, And Walked Right Out Again by Ed Rose & Maxwell Silver, 1906 ....**10.00**

He Wants Someone To Call Him Papa by L. Wolfe Gilbert & Lewis F. Muir, 1913 ....**10.00**

He Was A Perfect Gentleman by Johnny Burke & Jimmy Van Heusen, 1944, Movie: The Great John L., Photo Linda Darnell, Barbara Britton, Lee Sullivan & Greg McClure **5.00**

He Was A Soldier From the U.S.A. by J. Fred Lawton & Howard Kocian, 1917 (WWI)...**15.00**

He Was Always Fooling Around by William Jerome & Abner Greenberg, 1914, Photo Charles E. Evans (Cover Artist, Pfeiffer)...................**10.00**

He Wears A Pair Of Silver Wings by Eric Maschwitz & Michael Carr, 1941, Photo Jerry Wald (Cover Artist, Sig Ch & WWII) **5.00**

He Wears A Pair Of Silver Wings by Eric Maschwitz & Michael Carr, 1941, Photo Kay Kyser (Cover Artist, Sig Chi & WWII) 5.00

He Went In Like A Lion And Came Out Like A Lamb by Andrew B. Sterling, 1920...**10.00**

He Who Loves Me And Runs Away by Kahn & Friml, 1937, Movie: The Firefly, Photo Jeannette Macdonald & Allan Jones **10.00**

He Will Understand by Otto Harbach & Rudolf Friml, 1916, Musical: You're In Love **10.00**

Headin' Home by Ned Washington & Herbert Stothart, 1935, Movie: Here Comes The Band, Photo Ted Lewis, Virginia Bruce & Harry Stockwell **10.00**

Headless Horseman, The by Don Raye & Gene DePaul, 1949, Movie: Adventures Of Ichabod Crane & Mr. Toad (Disney)....................**16.00**

Health, Wealth & Happiness by Frank M. Witmark, 1900 ....**10.00**

Hear Me When I Call by Alfred Wooler, 1926 ....**1.00**

Hear My Song, Violetta by Bernier, Emmerich, Klose & Lubesch, 1937...**3.00**

Heart Ache Memories And You by Dorothy Fields, 1927 ....**5.00**

Heart Aches by Jack Norworth, 1919 (Cover Artist, Barbelle & Deco) ..**10.00**

Heart And A Rose, A by C.M. Denison & A.J. Holmes, 1910 ....**5.00**

Heart And Soul by Frank Loesser & Hoagy Carmichael, 1938, Movie: A Song Is Born, Photo Larry Clinton & His Orchestra.......................**5.00**

Heart And Soul by Frank Loesser & Hoagy Carmichael, 1938, Photo The Four Aces...**2.00**

Heart Beats by Walter E. Miles, 1913 ....**10.00**

Heart Bowed Down, The, Opera Gem Series, 1910 (Cover Artist, Pfeiffer)...**10.00**

Heart by Richard Adler & Jerry Ross, 1955, Musical: Damn Yankees .**6.00**

Heart For Sale, A by Anne Caldwell & Jerome Kern, 1920, Musical: The Night Boat..**10.00**

Heart Full Of Love, A by Eddy Arnold, Steve Nelson & Ray Sohnel, 1948, Photo Eddy Arnold **3.00**

Heart O'Mine by Keiser, 1913 (Cover Artist, Pfeiffer).......................**10.00**

Heart Of Gold by Robert E. Service & Charles Fonteyn Manney, 1920 ..**5.00**

Heart Of Humanity by Roy Turk & Ray Perkins, 1919, Small Folio (Cover Artist, Barbelle & Deco)..**10.00**

Heart Of Mine by Ralph C. Smith, 1917 ....**5.00**

Heart Of My Heart, The by Ben Ryan, 1926, Photo Ron Cornell, Johnny Desmond & Alan Dale..**5.00**

Heart That Loves Thee, A by Charles Gounod, 1891 (Pre 1900)...........**5.00**

Heart That's Free, A by Thomas T. Railey & Alfred G. Robyn, 1915, Movie: Two Weeks With Love, Photo Jane Powell.......................**5.00**

Heart Whispers by Sydney P. Harris, 1905 ....**10.00**

Heart's Haven by Robert L. Remington & Bayley Jordan, 1922 ....**5.00**

Heartaches by John Klenner & Al Hoffman, 1931, Signed Photo Eddy Howard (Signed)..**5.00**

Heartaches by John Klenner & Al Hoffman, 1931, Signed Photo Guy & Carmen Lombardo (Cover Artist, Frederick S. Manning & Signed) ..**5.00**

Heartbreak Hotel by Mae Boren Axton, Tommy Durden & Elvis Presley, 1956, Photo Elvis Presley **38.00**

Heartbreaker by Morty Berk, Frank Capano & Max C. Freedman, 1952..**3.00**

Heartbroken by Springer & Ebb, 1953, Photo Judy Garland **12.00**

Heartbroken, Lonesome And Blue by Daniel F. Cavanaugh, 1927........**5.00**

Hearts Are Never Blue In Blue Kalua by Lani McIntire, Alfred Bryan & George McConnell, 1938, Photo Lani McIntire (Cover Artist, Cliff Miska)...**3.00**

Hearts by Chas. K. Harris, 1905 ....**10.00**

Hearts & Flowers by Theo. M. Tobani, 1899 (Cover Artist, Franklin Co. Engarving & Pre 1900)...**10.00**

Hearts Of Promise Waltzes by Loveland, 1915 (Cover Artist, Pfeiffer & Deco) **10.00**

Hearts Of Stone by Jackson, 1954 ....**5.00**

Heartsease by Alfred Bryan & Neil Moret, 1919, Dedicated To Tom Moore (Dedication) **5.00**

Heat Wave by Irving Berlin, 1933, Musical: Easter Parade (Irving Berlin) **10.00**

Heather On The Hill, The by Alan J. Lerner & Frederick K. Loewe, 1947, Movie: Brigadoon...**5.00**

Heaven Born Banner, The by Vincent Bryan & Gertrude Hoffman, 1905, Dedicated to The School Children Of America, Music Section New York American And Journal, Sunday February 25, 1906 (Cover Artist, Eddy, Patriotic & Dedication) **20.00**

Heaven Can Wait by Eddie DeLance & Jimmy Van Heusen.................**5.00**

Heaven Is A Raft On A River by Robert & Helen Thomas, 1954, Photo Jane Pickens...**5.00**

Heaven Will Protect The Working Girl by Smith & Sloane, 1909 ......**10.00**

Heaven's Artillery by Harry J. Lincoln & J. Dittmar, 1914 (Cover Artist, Dittmar, WWI & March) **30.00**

Heaven's Eternal King by Erik Meyer Helmund, 1888 (Pre 1900)......**15.00**

Heavenly Music by Sam Coslow, 1943, Movie: Heavenly Music, Photo Mary Elliott & Fred Brady **3.00**

He'd Have To Get Under–Get Out And Get Under by Grant Clarke, Edgar Leslie & Maurice Abrahams, 1913, Photo Bobby North (Cover Artist, Pfeiffer & Transportation)..**35.00**

He'd Keep On Saying Good-Night by Bob Harty & Ernest Breuer, 1914, Photo Blanche Ring (Cover Artist, Starmer & Deco) 10.00

He'd Push It Around by Clark & Leslie, 1914 (Cover Artist, Pfeiffer)**10.00**

Hee Haw by P. Wendling & M. Ager, 1915...**5.00**

Heidelberg Stein Song by Pixley & Luders, 1902...............................**10.00**

Heigh-Ho by Larry Morey & Frank Churchill, 1938, Movie: Snow White (Disney) **16.00**

Helen by Jacob Henry Ellis & Al Wilson, 1908 (Cover Artist, Pfeiffer)**15.00**

Helen Polka by Walt Dana, Albert Gamse & Jimmy Carroll, 1947.......**2.00**

Heliotrope Bouquet by Louis Chauvin & Scott Joplin, 1907 (Scott Joplin & Rag) **50.00**

Heliotrope Rag by Braham, 1906 (Rag) **15.00**

He'll Have To Cross The Atlantic by Sammy Cahn & Jule Styne, 1945...**5.00**

Hello, Aloha! by L. Wolfe Gilbert & Abel Baer, 1926 ....**5.00**

Hello Angel Face by White, 1909 ....**5.00**

Hello, Baby by Edward Harrigan & David Braham, 1884 (Pre 1900) ..**15.00**

Hello Baby by Herb Magidson, Ned Washington & Michael H. Cleary, 1929 ....**5.00**

Hello Beautiful by Walter Donaldson, 1931, Photo Maurice Chevalier (Cover Artist, Frederick Manning)..**12.00**

Hello Bluebird by Cliff Friend, 1926 (Cover Artist, Leff) **5.00**

Hello Central, Give Me Heaven by Charles K. Harris, 1916 ....**10.00**

Hello Central! Give Me No Man's Land by Joe Young, Sam M. Lewis & Jean Schwartz, 1918, Photo William Schoen (Cover Artist, Barbelle & WWI)...**15.00**

Hello Central! Give Me No Man's Land by Joe Young, Sam M. Lewis & Jean Schwartz, 1918, Musical: Sinbad, Introduced by Al Jolson, Photo Al Jolson (Cover Artist, Barbelle, WWI & Al Jolson)..................**16.00**

Hello Central! Give Me No Man's Land by Sam M. Lewis, Joe Young & Jean Schwartz, 1918, Photo Harry Cooper (Cover Artist, Barbelle & WWI)...**15.00**

Hello Cutie by Cliff Friend, 1927, Photo Al Foster (Cover Artist, Stocker & Deco) **15.00**

Hello Daddy, I Knew That Was Your Car by Browne, 1896 (Pre 1900 & Transportation) **20.00**

Hello Dolly by Jerry Herman, 1963, Musical: Hello Dolly **10.00**

Hello Everybody by Valmore Gaucher & Marie L. Amelotte-Belisle, 1927, Respectfully Dedicated To Roxy & His Gang (Dedication) ..**5.00**

Hello Frisco by Gene Buck & Louis A. Hirsch, 1915, Musical: Ziegfeld Follies 1915 (Cover Artist, DeTakacs & Deco) **25.00**

Hello! General Pershing, How's My Daddy To-Night? by Lew Porter, 1918, Photo General Pershing (Cover Artist, DeTakacs, WWI & Military Personnel) **35.00**

Hello Hawaii How Are You? by Edgar Leslie, Bert Kalmar & Jean Schwartz, 1914, Photo Willie & Eugene Howard (Cover Artist, Barbelle).........**10.00**

Hello! Hello! Hello!, What A Wonderful Word Hello by Cal DeVoll, 1948 ....**3.00**

Hello, It's Me by Todd Rundgren, 1968..**4.00**

Hello Lindy, Photo of Lindbergh Plane (Lindbergh & Transportation) **35.00**

Hello Ma Baby by Ida Emerson & Joe Howard, 1899 (Cover Artist, Starmer, Pre 1900 & Black, Black Face) **35.00**

Hello Ma! I Done It Again by Leo Robin & Ralph Rainger, 1941, Movie: Tall, Dark And Handsome, Photo Cesar Romero & Milton Berle...**5.00**

Hello Muddah, Hello Fadduh, A Letter From Camp by Allan Sherman & Lou Busch, 1963, Photo Allan Sherman **10.00**

Hello, My Darling Mother by Goldstein, 1918 (Cover Artist, Pfeiffer & WWI) **15.00**

Hello My Dearie by Dave Stamper, 1917, Musical: Ziegfeld Follies 1917 (Cover Artist, Kirchner) **16.00**

Hello My Lulu by Bob Cole & Howard Johnson, 1905, Photo Peter Dailey (Black, Black Face) **20.00**

Hello, My Sweetheart I Love You by Heath & James 1916 ....**5.00**

Hello Stranger by Edgar Leslie & Lewis F. Muir, 1911....................**10.00**

Hello, Swanee, Hello by Sam Coslow & Addy Britt, 1927 (Cover Artist, Barbelle) **10.00**

Hello Virginia by Elliott & Friend, 1920 (Cover Artist, Pfeiffer)........**10.00**

Hello, Wisconsin by Bert Kalmar, Edgar Leslie & Harry Ruby, 1917 ..**5.00**

Hello Young Lovers by Richard Rodgers & Oscar Hammerstein II, 1951, Movie: The King And I **5.00**

Helmaredi Waltz by Downs & Allison, 1914 (Cover Artist, Pfeiffer & Deco) **10.00**

Help Bring Our Stars And Stripes Across The Rhine by Richard H. Unterdorfel, 1918 (WWI & March)..**16.00**

Help by The Beatles..**25.00**

Help! Help! Help! I'm Sinking In A Beautiful Ocean Of Love by Kilgour, 1917 ....**10.00**

Hen Cackle Rag by Chas. L. Johnson, 1913 (Rag)............................**15.00**

Henrietta by Ford & Bratton, 1895 (Pre 1900)....................................**15.00**

Henry Hudson Was A Bold Jack Tar by Ren Shields, 1909 (Transportation)..**15.00**

Henry's Made A Lady Out Of Lizzie by O'Keefe, 1928 (Transportation) **15.00**

Her Beaus Are Only Rainbows by Alfred Bryan & Geo. W. Meyer, 1926..**5.00**

Her Danny by Hale N. Byers & Chris Schonberg, 1919 ....**5.00**

Her Eyes Don't Shine Like Diamonds by Dave Marion, 1894 (Pre 1900) **15.00**

Her Golden Hair Was Hanging Down Her Back by Monroe Rosenfeld, 1884 (Pre 1900) **15.00**

Her Greatest Charm by Carrie Jacobs Bond, 1901, Dedicated to Miss Julia Putnam **15.00**

Her Name Is Jane by E. Clark Reed, 1894, Photo Little Irene Franklin (Pre 1900) **15.00**

Her Name Is Jane by E. Clark Reed, 1894, Photo Vesta Tilley (Pre 1900) **15.00**

Her Own Boy Jack by J.F. Mitchell, 1886 (Pre 1900)........................**16.00**

Her Tears Drifted Out With The Tide by Paul Dresser, 1890 (Pre 1900) **15.00**

Herald of Peace by E.T. Paull, 1914, Cover Dedicated To Mabel Boardman, Chairman National Relief Board American Red Cross (Cover Artist, E.T. Paull, March, Red Cross & Dedication) **50.00**

Here Am I Broken Hearted by B. G. DeSylva, Lew Brown & Ray Henderson, 1927, Photo Johnnie Ray **5.00**

Here Come The British by John Mercer & Bernard Hanighen, 1934 ....**5.00**

Here Comes Heaven Again by Adamson & McHugh, 1945, Movie: Doll Face, Photo Vivian Blaine, Dennis O'Keefe, Perry Como & Carmen Miranda..**5.00**

Here Comes My Daddy Now by L. Wolfe Gilbert & Lewis F. Muir, 1912..**10.00**

Here Comes Santa Claus by Gene Autry & Oakley Haldeman, 1947, Photo Gene Autry **3.00**

Here Comes The Bride by Lew Brown & Albert Von Tilzer, 1912.....**15.00**

Here Comes The Navy by Lew Brown, V.A. Timm & Jaromir Vejvada, 1934 (Cover Artist, Sig Ch. & Transportation) **10.00**

Here Comes The Sandman by Al Dubin & Harry Warren, 1937 ....**5.00**

Here Comes The Show Boat by Billy Rose & Maceo Pinkard, 1927 ....**5.00**

Here Comes The Sun by Arthur Freed & Harry Woods, 1930, Photo Art Kassel..**5.00**

Here Comes The Whippoorwill by J. Brandon Walsh & Terry Sherman, 1913 ....**5.00**

Here I Am Broken Hearted by B.G. DeSylva, Lew Brown & Ray Henderson, 1927..**5.00**

Here I Am by B. G. DeSylva, Lew Brown & Ray Henderson, 1926 .....**5.00**

Here I Am by David & Bacharach, 1965, Movie: What's New Pussycat?, Photo Peter Sellers, Woody Allen, Peter O'Toole, Romy Schneider & Capucine **6.00**

Here I'll Stay by Alan Jay Lerner & Kurt Weill, 1948, Movie: Love Life (Cover Artist BJH)..**5.00**

Here In My Arms by Lorenz Hart & Richard Rodgers, 1925, Musical: Dearest Enemy, Photo Helen Ford (Deco) **8.00**

Here In My Heart by Pat Genaro, Lou Levinson & Bill Borrelli, 1952 .**2.00**

Here Is My Heart by Leo Robin & Ralph Rainger, 1934 ....**5.00**

Here It Is To-Morrow Again by Paul Gibbons & Roy Ringwald, 1938.**5.00**

Here Lies An Actor by Paul Dresser, 1898 (Pre 1900).........................**15.00**

Here Lies Love by Leo Robin & Ralph Rainger, 1932, Movie: Big Broadcast, Photo Bing Crosby, Leila Hyams, Stewart Irvin, Kate Smith, Burns & Allen, Cab Calloway, Vincent Lopez, Mills Brothers & Arthur Tracy .**10.00**

Here, There And Everywhere by John Lennon & Paul McCartney, 1966, Photo Beatles **30.00**

Here You Are by Leo Robin & Ralph Rainger, 1942, Movie: My Gal Sal, Photo Rita Hayworth & Victor Mature **8.00**

Here You Are by Leo Robin & Ralph Rainger, 1943...........................**5.00**

Here's A Hand by Lorenz Hart & Richard Rodgers, 1942, Movie: All's Fair..**5.00**

Here's A Kiss by Lorenz Hart & Richard Rodgers, 1925, Musical: Dearest Enemy (Deco)..**8.00**

Here's A Rose For You by Al Dubin & Geo. B. McConnell, 1914 ....**5.00**

Here's Hoping by Harold Adamson & J. Fred Coots, 1932, Photo Phil Levant (Cover Artist, Leff & Deco) **2.00**

Here's Love In Your Eye by Leo Robin & Ralph Rainger, 1936, Movie: The Big Broadcast of 1937, Photo Jack Benny & Many Stars.......**10.00**

Here's To A Rose by H. Sylvester Krouse, 1899 (Pre 1900) **15.00**

Here's To The Friend In Stormy Weather by George Botsford, 1912 ...**5.00**

Here's To The Land We Love Boys by Henry Blossom & Victor Herbert, 1914, Musical: The Only Girl (Victor Herbert) **10.00**

Here's To Your Boy And My Boy by George Fariman, 1918 (WWI) ..10.00

Hermitage, The by Hussar, 1910 (Cover Artist, Pfeiffer)....................**15.00**

Hernando's Hideaway by Richard Adler & Jerry Ross, 1954, Musical: The Pajama Game..**5.00**

Hero Of The Isthmus by Lampg, 1912 (Patriotic)..............................**10.00**

Hero Till Judgement Day by M. H. Rosenfeld, 1897 (Pre 1900).........**15.00**

He's A College Boy by Mahony & Morse, 1909 ....**10.00**

He's A Cousin Of Mine by McPherson & Chris Smith, 1906 ....**5.00**

He's A Dear Old Pet by Jean Schwartz, 1911 (Cover Artist, Pfeiffer & Deco) **15.00**

He's A Devil In His Own Home Town by Grant Clark & Irving Berlin, 1914, Photo Harry S. LeVan (Cover Artist, John Frew & Irving Berlin)..**10.00**

He's A Devil In His Own Home Town by Grant Clark & Irving Berlin, 1914, Photo Fannie Brice (Cover Artist, John Frew & Irving Berlin)..**15.00**

He's A Good Man To Have Around by Jack Yellen & Milton Ager, 1929, Movie: Honky Tonk **6.00**

He's A Rag Picker by Irving Berlin, 1914, Photo Ray Samuels (Cover Artist, John Frew & Irving Berlin)..**15.00**

He's A Right Guy by Cole Porter, 1942, Movie: Something For The Boys ..**5.00**

He's Coming Back by Kalmar & Schwartz, 1911 (Cover Artist, Pfeiffer).**10.00**

He's Coming Home On The 8 O'Clock Train by Kendall, 1912 (Transportation) **15.00**

He's Doing His Bit, For The Girls by Hanlon & Von Tilzer, 1917 (Cover Artist, Pfeiffer & WWI)..**15.00**

He's Got A Bungalow by Edward Grossmith & Ted D. Ward, 1916, Photo Sophie Tucker (Cover Artist, DeTakacs) **20.00**

He's Got Me Hook, Line And Sinker by Pearl King, 1956, Photo Dorothy Collins..**5.00**

He's Got My Goat by Smith, 1912 (Cover Artist, Pfeiffer) **10.00**

He's Got The Whole World In His Hands by Geoff Love, 1957, Photo Laurie London **2.00**

He's Got Those Big Blue Eyes Like You, Daddy Mine by Lew Wilson & Alfred Dubin, 1918, Photo Mae March (WWI) **15.00**

He's Had No Lovin' For A Long Long Time by Wm. Tracey & Maceo Pinkard, 1919 (Cover Artist, E.E. Walton & WWI)......................**10.00**

He's In Love by Robert Wright & Chet Forrest, 1953, Musical: Kismet...**6.00**

He's Me Pal by Bryan & Edwards, 1905....................................**10.00**

He's My Brudda In Law by Will A. Heelan & Seymour Furth, 1909..**10.00**

He's My Cousin, If She's Your Niece by Alfred Bryan & Chris Smith, 1914, Photo Clarice Vance (Cover Artist, Starmer)......................**10.00**

He's My Friend Philligo by Shay, 1911 (Cover Artist, Pfeiffer)..........**10.00**

He's My Guy by Don Raye & Gene DePaul, 1942, Photo Helen Forrest & Harry James (Cover Artist, Im-Ho)..**3.00**

He's My Uncle by Charles Newman & Lew Pollack, 1940, Introduced by Dick Powell On The Maxwell House Coffee Time With Special Version For School Children (Advertising & Patriotic)......................**20.00**

He's On A Boat That Sailed Last Wednesday, He's Coming Home by Joe Goodwin & Lew Brown, 1913, Photo R.M.S. Mauretania (Transportation) **35.00**

He's One-A In The Army by Redd Evans, 1941 (WWII) **10.00**

He's Our "Al" by Albert Von Tilzer & A. Seymour Brown, 1928, Dedicated To Hon. Alfred E. Smith, Photo Al Smith (Cover Artist, Perret & Dedication) **25.00**

He's So Good To Me by Irving Berlin, 1913 (Cover Artist, Pfeiffer & Irving Berlin)..**15.00**

He's So Unusual by Sherman & Lewis & Abner Silver, 1939, Movie: Sweetie, Photo Helen Kane **6.00**

He's Such A Wonderful Boy by Motzan, 1915 (Cover Artist, Pfeiffer)..**10.00**

He's The Last Word by Gus Kahn & Walter Donaldson, 1927 ....**5.00**

Hesitation Blues by W.C. Handy, 1915 (Blues) **5.00**

Hesitation by Jas. M. Shaw, 1913, Photo Maurice & Florence Walton (Deco) **15.00**

Hesitation Con Amore by W.C. Powell, 1914 (Cover Artist, Natwick & Deco) **15.00**

Hesitation D'Amour by Barrie, 1914 (Cover Artist, Pfeiffer & Deco) **15.00**

Hesitation Waltz by F. Henri Klickmann, 1913 ....**5.00**

Hewitt's Quick Step, 1840, As Performed By The Jefferson Guards Band, Dedicated To Lieut. James L. Hewitt, Officers & Members Of N.Y. Light Guard, Rebhun, Firth Pond Co., N.Y. Publishers, Large Lithograph View Of Soldier On Cover (Pre 1900, Military Personnel, Dedication, March & Lithograph)......................................**30.00**

Hey! Ba-Ba-Re-Bop by Lionel Hampton & Curley Hamner, 1945, Photo Lionel Hampton (Cover Artist Im Ho) **5.00**

Hey, Babe, Hey by Cole Porter, 1936, Movie: Born To Dance, Photo Eleanor Powell..**5.00**

Hey, Good-Lookin' by Cole Porter, 1942, Movie: Something For The Boys..**5.00**

Hey Jude by John Lennon & Paul McCartney, 1968, Photo Beatles ...**25.00**

Hey, Look Me Over by Carolyn Leigh & Cy Coleman, 1960, Movie: Wildcat, Caricature of Lucille Ball.................................**5.00**

Hey Punchinello by Livingstone & Evans, 1954, Movie: Three Ring Circus, Photo Martin & Lewis & Martha Hyer **3.00**

Hey, Rube by Matthews & Bulger, 1891 (Pre 1900)..............**15.00**

Hey There by Richard Adler & Jerry Ross, 1954, Musical: The Pajama Game..**6.00**

Hey, What Did The Blue Jay Say? by Koehler & McHugh, 1936, Movie: Dimples, Photo Shirley Temple (Shirley Temple) **10.00**

Hi, Ho! Let Her Go, Gallagher by William W. Delaney, 1887 (Pre 1900).**15.00**

Hi Ho The Merrio by Lew Brown, Lou Davis & Con Conrad, 1926.....**5.00**

Hi, Neighbor by Jack Owens, 1941, Movie: San Antonio Rose.............**5.00**

Hi Yo Silver (Lone Ranger's Song), Photo Lone Ranger & Tonto........**5.00**

Hi-Diddle-Dee-Dee by Leigh Harline & Ned Washington, 1940, Movie: Pinocchio (Disney) **10.00**

Hi-Ho Lack-A-Day, What Have We Got To Lose by Gus Kahn, Charlotte Kent & Louis Alter, 1933, Photo Helen Morgan (Cover Artist, Leff) ..**5.00**

Hi-Lili-Hi Lo by Bronislau Kaper, 1953, Movie: Lili, Photo Leslie Caron, Mel Ferrer & Jean Pierre Aumont **6.00**

Hiawatha by James O'Dea & Neil Moret, 1903, Photo Amelia Stone (Indian) **8.00**

Hiawatha Waltz by Jimmie McHugh, 1919 (Cover Artist, DeTakacs & Indian)...**20.00**

Hiawatha's Lullaby by Joe Young & Walter Donaldson, 1933, Photo Helene Daniels (Cover Artist, Leff & Indian)................**3.00**

Hiawatha's Melody Of Love by Alfred Bryan, Artie Mehlinger & Geo. W. Meyer, 1920 (Cover Artist, Frederick S. Manning & Indian)........**35.00**

Hickory Dickory Dock by Edward G. Nelson & Fred Rose, 1936.........**5.00**

Hidden Charms by Arthur Lange, 1913 (Cover Artist, DeTakacs) **15.00**

Hidden Pearls by Marshall Roberts & Haydn Wood, 1918 (Deco)........**5.00**

Hifalutin Rag by Henry Lodge, 1918 (Rag & Deco)............**15.00**

Higgledy-Piggledy by Edgar Smith & Maurice Levy, 1904, Photo Anna Held **8.00**

High And The Mighty, The by Washington & Tiomkin, 1954, Movie: The High And The Mighty, Photo John Wayne, Jan Sterling, Claire Trevor, Phil Harris, Laraine Day & Robert Stack **10.00**

High Brow Colored Lady by Duncan Sisters. Book By Catherine C. Cushing Suggested By Uncle Tom's Cabin, By Harriet Beecher Stowe, 1923, Musical: Topsy & Eva, Photo Duncan Sisters (Cover Artist, P.M. Griffith & Black, Black Face)....................................**16.00**

High Cost Of Loving, The by George W. Meyer & Alfred Bryan, 1914, Photo Morine Coffey (Cover Artist, Rose) **5.00**

High Flyer, The by J.C. Heed, 1904 (March) **15.00**

High Hopes by Sammy Cahn & James Van Heusen, 1959, Movie: A Hole In The Head, Photo Frank Sinatra, Ed. G. Robinson, Eleanor Parker, Carolyn Jones & Thelma Ritter......................................**12.00**

High Jinks by Whidden & Conrad, 1910 (Cover Artist, Pfeiffer & Rag)..**15.00**

High On A Windy Hill by Joan Whitney & Alex Kramer, 1940 ....**5.00**

High School Cadets by John Philip Sousa, 1890 (John Philip Sousa & Pre 1900)..**20.00**

High School Two Step, The by E.C. Porter, 1894 (Pre 1900).............**15.00**

High Up On A Hill-Top by Abel Baer, Jimmy Campbell & Richard Whiting, 1928 ....**5.00**

High, Wide And Handsome by Jerome Kern & Oscar Hammerstein II, 1937, Movie: High Wide And Handsome, Photo Irene Dunn & Randolph Scott..**8.00**

High Yellow Cake Walk by F. Henri Klickmann, 1915 (Black, Black Face) **15.00**

High-High-High Up In The Hills by Sam Lewis, Joe Young & Maurice Abrahams, 1927 (Cover Artist, Starmer)......................**10.00**

Highland Grand March by Bailey, 1877 (Pre 1900 & March) **15.00**

Highways Are Happy Ways by Larry Shay, Harry Harris & Tommie Malie, 1926..**10.00**

Hilarity by James Scott, 1910 (Rag) **10.00**

Hill Billy Wedding In June, A by Log Cabin Boys, Freddie Owen & Frankie More, 1933, Photo Benny Meroff **3.00**

Hillbilly Fever by George Vaughn, 1950, Photo Kenny Roberts...........**5.00**

Hindoo Lady by Cliff Friend, 1919 ....**5.00**

Hindu Rose by Weslyn & Moret, 1919 (Cover Artist, Pfeiffer)...........**10.00**

Hindu Slumber Song by Soropini Naidu & Harriet Ware, 1909 ....**10.00**

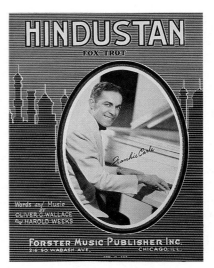

Hindustan by Oliver G. Wallace & Harold Weeks, 1918, Photo Frankie Carle 10.00

Hindustan by Oliver G. Wallace & Harold Weeks, 1918, Photo Rubinoff..**5.00**

Hinkey Dee by Harry Morris, 1902 ....**10.00**

Hinkey-Dinkey Parlez-Vous by Al Dubin, Joy Mills, Jimmy McHugh & Irwin Dash, 1918 (WWI).....................................**15.00**

Hip Hip Hoo-Ray For The Good Old U.S.A. by Fletcher, 1916 (WWI)...**15.00**

Hippity Hop by Sam Lewis, Joe Young & Walter Donaldson, 1919 (Irish)...**5.00**

Hippodrome Tango by Manuel Klein, 1913, Musical: America 1913-14...**15.00**

Hiram Green Good-Bye by Henry Gillespie & Clarence M. Chapel, 1905 (Cover Artist, Henrich)......................................**10.00**

His Buttons Are Marked U.S. by Carrie Jacobs Bond, 1902 (Patriotic).**15.00**

His Last Thoughts Were Of You by Ed Marks & Joe Stern, 1894 (Pre 1900)...**15.00**

His Lullaby by Robert Healy & Carrie Jacobs Bond, 1907, Dedicated To Madame Schumann Heink (Dedication) **15.00**

His Majesty And The Maid by C. D. Henninger, 1904 (March)..........**15.00**

His Majesty, The American by Lew Brown & Albert Von Tilzer, 1919 (WWI)..**10.00**

His Rocking Horse Ran Away by Johnny Burke & Jimmy Van Heusen, 1944, Movie: And The Angels Sing, Photo Dorothy Lamour, Fred MacMurray & Betty Hutton **6.00**

Hit The Grit by Al Wilson, 1911 ....**5.00**

Hit The Road To Dreamland by Johnny Mercer & Harold Arlen. 1942, Movie: Star Spangled Rhythm, Photo Bing Crosby, Bob Hope, Dorothy Lamour & Many Other Stars......................**10.00**

Hitch On De Golden Trolley by Monroe Rosenfeld, 1902 (Black, Black Face) **20.00**

Hitchy Koo by L. Wolfe Gilbert & Lewis F. Muir, 1912, Photo Maude Rockwell (Cover Artist, DeTakacs) **12.00**

Ho Ho Song, The by Red Buttons & Joe Darion, 1953, Photo Red Buttons **5.00**

Ho-Hum! by Edward Heyman & Dana Suesse, 1931...................**5.00**

Hobble Rag, The by Hanlon & Morrissey, 1911, Photo Hanlon & Morrissey (Cover Artist, Pfeiffer & Rag)..............................**15.00**

Hobomoko by Ernest Reeves, 1907 (Indian).............................**25.00**

Hoe Your "Little Bit" In Your Own Back Yard by Cahill & Andino, 1917 (Cover Artist, Pfeiffer) **10.00**

Hoi-Polloi by Wm. B. Friedlander & Con Conrad, 1923 (Cover Artist, Politzer) **10.00**

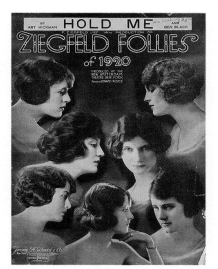

Hold Me by Art Hickman & Ben Black, 1920, Musical: Ziegfeld Follies, 1920 (Deco)...**10.00**

Hold Me by Wm. B. Friedlander, 1923 ....**10.00**

Hold Me Close To Your Heart by Frank A. Wright, 1926...........**5.00**

Hold Me In Your Arms by Ray Heindorf, Charles Henderson & Don Pippin, 1954, Movie: Young At Heart.............................**5.00**

Hold Me In Your Loving Arms by Gene Buck & Louis A. Hirsch, 1915, Musical: Ziegfeld Follies 1915 (Cover Artist, DeTakacs) **15.00**

Hold Me Just A Little Closer by Ben Barnett & Albert Von Tilzer, 1911, Photo Fannie Vedder (Cover Artist, Carter)..................**10.00**

Hold My Hand by Maurice Elwin, Harry Graham & Noel Gay, 1931, Musical: Hold My Hand..**3.00**

Hold My Hand by Ray Henderson, Jack Yellen & Irving Caesar, 1939, Movie: George White's Scandals, Photo Rudy Vallee, Jimmy Durante & Alice Faye..**10.00**

Hold Tight–Hold Tight by Kent Brandow & Robinson Ware Spotswood, 1939 ....**5.00**

Hold Up Rag, The by Van Alstyne & Madden, 1912 (Cover Artist, Pfeiffer & Rag)...**15.00**

Hold Your Man by Arthur Freed & Nacio Herb Brown, 1933, Movie: Hold Your Man, Photo Jean Harlow **10.00**

Holding Hands And You Don't Say Nothing At All by Jack Norwoth & Albert Von Tilzer, 1916...**5.00**

Holiday by Ethel Ponce, 1933 ....**3.00**

Holiday For Strings by David Rose, 1943 ....**5.00**

Holiday In Venice, A by Frank Magine, 1930, Photo LeRoy Maule **5.00**

Holiday Inn by Irving Berlin, 1942 (Irving Berlin) **5.00**

Hollywood At Vine by Lyle Moraine & Jimmie Grier, 1935.................**5.00**

Hollywood Canteen by M. K. Jerome & Ted Koehler, 1944, Movie: Hollywood Canteen, Photo Andrews Sisters, Jack Benny & Many More Stars.......**12.00**

Holy City, The by F.E. Eatherly & Stephen Adams, 1892 (Pre 1900)...**5.00**

Holy Grail, The by Albert Stillman & Georg Frederick Handel, 1945 ..**5.00**

Holy Moses by C. Seymour, 1906 (Rag)...................................**15.00**

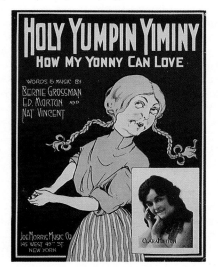

Holy Yumpin Yiminy, How My Yonny Can Love by Bernie Grossman, Ed Morton & Nat Vincent, 1918, Photo Clara Morton...10.00

Home by Peter Van Steeden & Harry & Jeff Clarkson, 1931 (Cover Artist, Hap Hadley)...**5.00**

Home Again Blues by Irving Berlin & Harry Akst, 1921 (Cover Artist, R.S., Irving Berlin, Blues & Deco)................................**10.00**

Home Again by F. W. Vandersloot, 1920 ....**5.00**

Home Again by Weston, 1918 (WWI) **10.00**

Home And You by Ring-Hager, 1919 (Cover Artist, Barbelle & Deco)...**10.00**

Home Coming Week In France by Seneca G. Lewis, 1918 (WWI).....**15.00**

Home Cookin' by Livingston & Evans, 1950, Movie: Fancy Pants, Photo Bob Hope & Lucille Ball..**10.00**

Home For You, A by Brian Hooker & Rudolf Friml, 1931, Musical: The White Eagle (Cover Artist, Barbelle) **10.00**

Home & Harbor Waltz by Koebler, 1908 (Cover Artist, Pfeiffer) **15.00**

Home Is Heaven–Heaven Is Home by Edgar Leslie & Walter Donaldson, 1929 ....**5.00**

Home Is Where The Heart Is by Dave Kapp, Charles Tobias, 1947, Photo Sammy Kaye (Cover Artist, Im-Ho) **5.00**

Home Love And You by Miriam Alvin Roberts, 1922 ....**5.00**

Home On The Range, A by Nick Manoloff, 1935, Photo Jackie Heller..**5.00**

Home On The Range by Andrew Fuller, 1932, Photo Carson J. Robinson (Cover Artist, Sam Cahan) **5.00**

Home Run Polka by Mrs. Bodel, 1867, Printed by J. J. Dosmeyer & Co, Cincinnati, Ohio, Respectfully Dedicated To The National Baseball Club Of Washington, D.C., Full Field Photo On Cover With Baseball Players. Sold At Auction In Wethersfield, Connecticut, 1988, Appeared In Antiques & The Arts Weekly March 11, 1988 (Pre 1900, Sports & Dedication) **1,200.00**

Home Sweet Home by Presser, 1914.....................**3.00**

Home Sweet Home Polka by Arthur Berman & Leni Mason, 1948, Photo Texas Jim Robertson **5.00**

Home To My Blue Hills by Colin Wendell, 1937.....................**5.00**

Home Town by Jimmy Kennedy & Michael Carr, 1937.....................**3.00**

Home Where You'll Always Be Welcome by Sam Keane & Stanley Henry, 1917 ....**5.00**

Home-Made Happiness by Harold Levey & Zelda Sears, 1922.............**3.00**

Homecoming March, The by E.T. Paull, 1908 (Cover Artist, E.T. Paull & March) **35.00**

Homesick by Irving Berlin, 1922 (Irving Berlin) **5.00**

Homestead On The Hill by Porter, 1913 (Cover Artist, Pfeiffer & Deco).....................**15.00**

Homeward Bound by Howard Johnson, Coleman Goetz & Geo. Meyer, 1917 Photo Emma Carus (Cover Artist, Rose, WWI & Transportation).....................**30.00**

Homeward Bound by Howard Johnson, Coleman Goetz & Geo. Meyer, 1917, Photo U.S. Transport Ships & Lewis & Dodye (Cover Artist, Rose Symbol, WWI & Transportation).....................**30.00**

Homeward Bound by Howard Johnson, Coleman Goetz & George Meyer, 1917, Photo U.S. Transport Ships & Harry Cooper (Cover Artist, Rose Symbol, WWI & Transportation).....................**30.00**

Homework by Irving Berlin, 1949, Musical: Miss Liberty (Irving Berlin) **6.00**

Homing by Arthur L. Salmon & Teresa Del Riego, 1917 ....**3.00**

Honest Abe March by Bert Lowe, 1909, Photo Abraham Lincoln (Presidents & March).....................**35.00**

Honest And Truly by Fred Rose, 1924 (Deco).....................**15.00**

Honestly by Charles Newman & Isham Jones, 1933.............**5.00**

Honey by Bobby Russell, 1968, Photo Bobby Goldsboro **3.00**

Honey by Odoms & Raybould, 1913.....................**5.00**

Honey by Seymour Simons, Haven Gillespie & Richard A. Whiting, 1928, Photo Mildred Hunt (Deco).....................**5.00**

Honey by Seymour Simons, Haven Gillespie & Richard A. Whiting, 1928, Movie: Her Highness & The Bellboy, Photo Hedy Lamarr, Robert Walker & June Allyson **10.00**

Honey by Seymour Simons, Haven Gillespie & Richard A. Whiting, 1928, Photo Rudy Vallee (Deco).....................**15.00**

Honey Boy by Albert Von Tilzer & Jack Norworth, 1907, Photo Mildred Hanson **15.00**

Honey Boy by Jack Norworth & Albert Von Tilzer, 1907, Photo Francis Dooley (March) **15.00**

Honey Boy by Albert Wood (Black, Black Face) **20.00**

Honey Boy, My Heart Is Calling For You by Harris (Cover Artist, Pfeiffer) **15.00**

Honey Bun by Richard Rodgers & Oscar Hammerstein II, 1949, Musical: South Pacific (Cover Artist, BJH) **5.00**

Honey-Bun by Zelda Sears & Vincent Youmans, 1923, Musical: Lollipop, Photo Ada May (Deco).....................**5.00**

Honey Bunch by Dan Caslar, 1915, Photo Dolly Sisters & Harry Von Tilzer (Cover Artist, Rose Symbol).....................**10.00**

Honey Bunch by DeCosta, 1919 (Cover Artist, Pfeiffer & Deco) **10.00**

Honey, Dat's All by Egbert Van Alstyne, 1921 (Black, Black Face) ..**15.00**

Honey Dear by Bert Potter, 1912, Photo Sam Shephard (Cover Artist, Starmer) **10.00**

Honey Hula by Fred Fisher, 1921.....................**5.00**

Honey, I'm Waiting by McKenna, 1913 (Cover Artist, Pfeiffer).........**10.00**

Honey If Yo' Only Knew by William H. Gardner & Ernest R. Ball, 1916 (Black, Black Face) **15.00**

Honey Land by Ren Shields, Stanley Murphy & Henriette Blanke-Belcher, 1909 (Cover Artist, DeTakacs).....................**15.00**

Honey Man by McCarthy & Piantadosi, 1911 (Cover Artist, Pfeiffer).**10.00**

Honey Rose by McCarthy, Goodwin & Smith, 1912 (Cover Artist, Pfeiffer) **10.00**

Honey! You're Ma Lady Love by Mann, 1897 (Pre 1900 & Black, Black Face).....................**20.00**

Honey! You'se My Turtle Dove by Edgar Smith & W. T. Francis, 1899 (Pre 1900 & Black, Black Face).....................**20.00**

Honey-Babe by Webster & Steiner, 1954, Movie: Battle Cry, Photo Aldo Ray, Mona Freeman & Nancy Olson **4.00**

Honeychile by Jack Elliot & Harold Spina, 1951, Movie: Honeychile, Photo Judy Garland **10.00**

Honeymoon by Carl Demangate, 1903.....................**5.00**

Honey-Moon by Chas. E. Byrne & Charley Straight, 1919 (Cover Artist, E.E. Walton) **5.00**

Honeymoon by Ray Sherwood & Victor Arden, 1909 (Cover Artist, A.S. Trueman) **5.00**

Honeymoon Bells by Jean Havez & George Botsford, 1915 (Cover Artist, John Frew & Deco).....................**10.00**

Honeymoon Blues by Wm. B. Friedlander & Con Conrad, 1923 (Cover Artist, Politzer) **10.00**

Honeymoon Hotel by Al Dubin & Harry Warren, 1933, Movie: Footlight Parade, Photo James Cagney, Joan Blondell, Dick Powell & Ruby Keeler (Cover Artist, Jorj Harris).....................**10.00**

Honeymoon In May, A by Paul Herve, Jean Biquet & Adolf Philipp, 1915, Musical: The Girl Who Smiles.....................**10.00**

Honeymoon Lane by Billy Moll, Eddie Dowling & Jas. F. Hanley, 1931, Photo Eddie Dowling.....................**5.00**

Honeymoon Lane by Jerome Kern, 1916 ....**5.00**

Honeymoon March, The by George Rosey, 1895 (Pre 1900 & March)...**15.00**

Honeymoon Rag by Allen, 1913 (Cover Artist, Pfeiffer & Rag) **15.00**

Honey-Moon Waltzes, The by I. Furman Mulliner, 1912.................5.00

Honeysuckle And The Bee by Albert H. Fitz & William H. Penn, 1901 ..**10.00**

Honeysuckle Rose by Andy Razaf & Thomas Waller, 1929 (Cover Artist, Barbelle) **5.00**

Hong Kong by Richard W. Pascoe, Hans Von Holstein & Alma N. Sanders, 1916 (Cover Artist, W. David, Transportation & Jazz)...**10.00**

Honky Tonky by Chas. McCarron & Chris Smith, 1916 ....**5.00**

Honolulu America Loves You by Grant Clarke & Jimmie V. Monaco, 1916, Photo Brice & King (Cover Artist, Rose Symbol).................**5.00**

Honolulu Blues by M. J. Gunsky & Nat Goldstein, 1923 ....**5.00**

Honolulu Blues, The by Grant Clarke & Jimmie V. Monaco, 1916 ......**5.00**

Honolulu Eyes by Howard Johnson & Violinsky, 1920, Musical: The Passing Show Of 1919, Photo Avon Comedy Four (Cover Artist, JVR).........**10.00**

Honolulu I Love You by Brown, 1917 (Cover Artist, Pfeiffer) 10.00

Honolulu Moon by Fred Lawrence, 1926, Photo Ray West (Cover Artist, J.V.R. & Deco) 5.00

Honor Today Goes To You by Alfred McDermott, 1940 ....3.00

Honorable Profession Of The Fourth Estate, The by Irving Berlin, 1949, Musical: Miss Liberty (Irving Berlin) 10.00

Honored Dead, The by John Philip Sousa, 1896 (John Philip Sousa, March & Pre 1900) 20.00

Hoo-oo by Herb Ingraham, 1907 (Cover Artist, Starmer)...................5.00

Hoodlum, The by Sam M. Lewis, Joe Young & Harry Ruby, 1919, Photo & Dedicated To Mary Pickford (Dedication)...................15.00

Hoodoo Man, The by Nacio Herb Brown, 1924...................5.00

Hooks & Eyes by Harris, 1914 (Cover Artist, Pfeiffer & Deco)...........15.00

Hooray For Hollywood by Johnny Mercer & Richard A. Whiting, 1938..3.00

Hooray For Love by Leo Robin & Harold Arlen, 1948, Movie: Casbah...5.00

Hop A Jitney With Me by Donovan, 1915 (Transportation)...............20.00

Hop, Hop, Hop by Mackinnon & Powell, 1913 (Cover Artist, Pfeiffer & Deco) 15.00

Hop Scotch Polka by William Whitlock, 1949, Photo Gene Rayburn & Dee Finch...................5.00

Horn, The (Le Cor) by Isabella G. Parker & French Words by A. Flegier, 1898 (Pre 1900) 15.00

Horse That Knows The Way, A by Johnny Burke & Jimmy Van Heusen, 1943, Movie: Dixie, Photo Bing Crosby & Dorothy Lamour...........3.00

Horse Told Me, The by Johnny Burke & James Van Heusen, Movie: Riding High, Photo Bing Crosby & Coleen Gray 3.00

Horse Trot, The by Uriel Davis, 1912 (Cover Artist, Starmer) 10.00

Horses by Byron Gay & Richard A. Whiting, 1926, Photo The Ipana Troubadours (Sports)...................15.00

Hosanna! by Isabella G. Parker & Jules Granier, 1909 ....2.00

Hostess With The Mostes' On the Ball, The by Irving Berlin, 1950, Musical: Call Me Madam, Caricature Of Ethel Merman (Cover Artist, Peter Arno & Irving Berlin)...................10.00

Hot Diggity Dog Ziggity Boom by Al Hoffman & Dick Manning, 1941, Signed Photo Perry Como (Signed)...................15.00

Hot Henry by Ballard Macdonald & Harry Carroll, 1926...................5.00

Hot Lips by Henry Busse, Lou Davis & Henry Lange, 1922 (Cover Artist, JVR, Jazz, Blues & Black, Black Face) 20.00

Hot Potato Mambo by Fred Patrick, Photo Jayne & Audrey Meadows .5.00

Hot Stuff by The Monkees...................5.00

Hot Tamale Alley by George M. Cohan, 1896 (George M. Cohan & Pre 1900)...................15.00

Hot Time In The Old Town, A by Joe Hayden & Theo. A. Metz, 1932 (Black, Black Face) 15.00

Hot Toddy by Hendler & Flanagan, 1953 ....5.00

Hot-House-Rag by Paul Pratt, 1914 (Rag) 10.00

Hottentot Love Song by Cole & Johnson, 1906 ....10.00

Hottest Ever Cake Walk, The by Charles Brown & Joe O'Dea, 1898 (Pre 1900 & Black, Black Face)...................20.00

Hour Of Memory, The by J. Will Callahan & A. Dvorak, 1916 ....5.00

Hours I Spent With Thee, The by Roger Lewis & Ernie Erdman, 1914 5.00

Hours I Spent With You, The by Little Jack Little, Joe Young & Sam Lewis, 1927, Photo Little Jack Little (Cover Artist, RS & Deco)....6.00

House By The Side Of The Road, The by Sam Walter Foss & Mrs. M.H. Gulesian, 1927 ....5.00

House I Live In, The by Lewis Allen & Earl Robinson, 1942, Movie: The House I Live In, Photo Frank Sinatra 5.00

House Is Not A Home, A. by Bacharach & David, 1964, Movie: A House Is Not A Home, Photo Shelley Winters & Robert Taylor...............5.00

House Jack Built For Jill, The by Leo Robin & Frederick Hollander, 1936, Movie: Rhythm On The Range, Photo Bing Crosby & Frances Farmer 12.00

House Of Blue Lights, The by Don Raye & Freddie Slack, 1946, Photo Chuck Miller...................3.00

House Of Singing Bamboo, The by Arthur Freed & Harry Warren, 1950, Movie: Pagan Love Song, Photo Esther Williams & Howard Keel...................5.00

House On The Hillside by Harold Skeath & Gustav Klemm, 1939 ......5.00

How About A Cheer For The Navy by Irving Berlin, 1942, Movie: This Is The Army, Lt. Ronald Reagan In Cast (WWII, Irving Berlin, Military Personnel & Presidents)...................20.00

How About Me by Irving Berlin, 1928 (Irving Berlin) 5.00

How About You? by Freed & Lane, 1941, Movie: Babes On Broadway ..3.00

How Am I To Know by Jack King & Dorothy Parker, 1929, Movie: Dynamite, Photo Conrad Nagel, Kay Johnson & Charles Bickford (Deco) 10.00

How Are Things In Glocca Morra? by E. Y. Harburg & Burton Lane, 1946, Movie: Finian's Rainbow (Cover Artist, BJH & Irish)...........5.00

How Beautiful Upon the Mountains by F. Flaxington Harker, 1910 .....2.00

How Can I Forget When There's So Much To Remember by Irving Berlin, 1917 (Irving Berlin)...................10.00

How Can I Go On Without You by Frank Westphal, 1932, Photo Frank Westphal, Featured In Wrigley's Radio Program Presenting Myrt and Marge in "Hayfield's Pleasures of 1932" Over Columbia Broadcasting System (Cover Artist, Harris)...................16.00

How Can Things Be On The Level When The World Is Round? by Chas. B. Lawlor, 1904 ....10.00

How Can You Blame Me by Green, 1916 (Cover Artist, Pfeiffer & Deco)...................10.00

How Can You Forget by Anita Owens, 1912, Photo Grace Van Studdiford (Cover Artist, Starmer)...................5.00

How Can You Mend A Broken Heart by Barry & Robin Gibb, 1971, Photo Bee Gees...................3.00

How Can You Say "No" by Al Dubin, Irving Kahal & Joe Burke, 1932, Movie: Blessed Event, Photo Dick Powell...................5.00

How Come You Do Me Like You Do Do Do? by Gene Austin & Roy Bergere, 1924, Photo Rudy Vallee (Cover Artist, Starmer)...........10.00

How Could So Many People Be So Wrong by Perry Alexander & Jack Rollins, 1947...................5.00

How Could You Believe Me by Lerner & Lane, 1951, Movie: Royal Wedding, Photo Fred Astaire, Jane Powell, Peter Lawford & Sara Churchill 10.00

How Cute Can You Be? by Bill Carey & Carl Fischer, 1946 ....5.00

How D'ya Like Your Eggs by Sammy Cahn & Nicholas Brodsky, 1951, Movie: Rich, Young & Pretty, Photo, Jane Powell, Vic Damone, Wendell Corey, Fernando Lamas & Danielle Darrieux...................5.00

How Deep Is The Ocean by Irving Berlin, 1932 (Irving Berlin)...........5.00

How Do I Know He Loves Me by Wm. B. Friedlander & Con Conrad, 1923 (Cover Artist, Politzer) 10.00

How Do I Know It's Real by Dan Shapiro & Seelen & Lester Lee, 1936, Photo Tommy Tucker...................5.00

How Do I Love Thee by Elizabeth Barrett Browning & Blevins Davis, 1936 ....10.00

How Do I Rate With You? by Coslow & Whiting, 1935, Movie: Coronado, Photo Eddy Duchin, Johnny Downs, Leon Errol, Jack Haley & Andy Devine...................5.00

How Do You Do? by Phil Fleming, Charlie Harrison & Cal DeVoll, 1924, Photo Larry Vincent (Cover Artist, A.D. Brown Art)...................15.00

How Do You Do? by Robert McGimsey, 1946, Movie: Song Of The South (Disney)...................10.00

How Do You Do It Mabel On Twenty Dollars A Week? by Irving Berlin, 1911, Photo Neil McKinley (Cover Artist, Gene Buck & Irving Berlin)...................12.00

How Do You Get That Way? by Robert B. Smith & Victor Herbert, 1919, Musical: Angel Face (Victor Herbert)...................10.00

How Easy It Is To Remember by Thos. S. Allen & Jos. M. Daly, 1914 (Cover Artist, Pfeiffer) **10.00**

How Great Thou Art by Hine, 1955 ....**5.00**

How High The Moon by Hamilton & Lewis, 1940, Photo Les Paul & Mary Ford **5.00**

How I Love A Summer Day by Chas. E. Roat, 1915 ....**6.00**

How I Love My Lu by John Stromberg, 1898 (Pre 1900)..................**15.00**

How Is Evert'ing By You, All-Right? by Kendis, 1913 (Cover Artist, Pfeiffer)..**10.00**

How Is May? by E. S. Ufford, 1897 (Pre 1900) **15.00**

How Late Can You Stay Out Tonight? by Joe Goodwin & Fred Fischer, 1913 ....**5.00**

How Little We Know by Johnny Mercer & Hoagy Carmichael, 1949, Movie: To Have and Have Not, Photo, Humphrey Bogart & Lauren Bacall..**6.00**

How Long Did I Dream by Johnny Burke & Jimmy Van Heusen, 1941, Movie: Playmates, Photo Kay Kyser, John Barrymore, Lupe Velez & Ginny Simms **5.00**

How Long Will It Last by Meyer & Lief, 1931, Movie: Possessed, Photo Joan Crawford & Clark Gable **10.00**

How Lovely Are Thy Dwellings by S. Liddle, 1908................**5.00**

How Lovely To Be A Woman by Lee Adams & Charles Strouse, 1960, Movie: Bye, Bye Birdie..**5.00**

How Lucky You Are by O'Conner and Maurice, 1946........................**5.00**

How Many Hearts Have You Broken by Marty Symes & Al Kaufman, 1943, Photo Joan Brooks..**3.00**

How Many Hearts Have You Broken? by Marty Symes & Al Kaufman, 1943, Photo Imogen Carpenter..................................**3.00**

How Many Times by Irving Berlin, 1939 (Irving Berlin) **5.00**

How Much Does The Baby Weigh by Will S. Hayes, 1880 (Pre 1900) ..**15.00**

How Much Is That Doggie In The Window? by Bob Merrill, 1952, Photo Patti Page (Cover Artist, Barbelle) **12.00**

How Much Is That Doggie In The Window? by Bob Merrill, 1952, Signed & Framed Photo Of Patti Page (Signed) **10.00**

How Soon? by Jack Owens & Carroll Lucas, 1944, Photo Bing Crosby & Carmen Cavallaro **5.00**

How Soon? by Jack Owens & Carroll Lucas, 1944, Photo Vaughn Monroe (Cover Artist, Nick)..**3.00**

How Sorry You'll Be Wait'll You See by Bert Kalmar & Harry Ruby, 1919 ....**5.00**

How Strange by Gus Kahn, Herbert Stothart & Earl Brent, 1939, Movie: Idiot's Delight, Photo Clark Gable & Norma Shearer..................**5.00**

How Sweet Is Love by Marshall, 1912 (Cover Artist, Pfeiffer)...........**10.00**

How Sweet It Is by Jackie Gleason & Irving Caesar, 1963, Photo Jackie Gleason & Frankie Fontaine..**10.00**

How The Gates Came Ajar by Helen L. Bostwick & Eastburn, 1871 (Pre 1900)..**15.00**

How The Money Rolls In by Jean C. Havez & Ted S. Barron, 1913.....**5.00**

How To Win A Girl by Rowe, 1909 (Cover Artist, Pfeiffer)...............**10.00**

How To Win Friends And Influence People by Lorenz Hart & Richard Rodgers, 1938, Movie: I Married An Angel **5.00**

How Would You Like To Kiss Me In The Moonlight by Adamson & McHugh, 1944, Movie: The Princess And The Pirate, Photo Bob Hope & Virginia Mayo **10.00**

How 'Ya Gonna Keep Them Down On The Farm by Joe Young, Sam M. Lewis & Walter Donaldson, 1919 (Cover Artist, Barbelle, WWI & Transportation) **25.00**

How'd Yer Like Ter Be A Dorg by Dave Reed Jr., 1899 (Pre 1900) ..**15.00**

How'd You Like To Be My Beau, 1910 (Cover Artist, Pfeiffer).........**10.00**

How'd You Like To Be My Wife? by J. E. Dempsey............................**5.00**

How'd You Like To Be The Iceman? by Helf & Moran, 1937, Photo Ken Houchins..**5.00**

How'd You Like To Love Me by McKinley, 1909 (Cover Artist, Pfeiffer)..**10.00**

How'd You Like To Spoon With Me? by Jerome Kern, 1916...............**5.00**

How'dja Like To Love Me? by Frank Loesser & Burton Lane, 1938, Movie: College Swing, Photo George Burns, Martha Raye & Bob Hope..**10.00**

How's Chances by Irving Berlin, 1933, Musical: Easter Parade (Irving Berlin)..**12.00**

How's De Mama by Kalmar, 1913 (Cover Artist, Pfeiffer) **10.00**

How's Every Little Thing In Dixie by Jack Yellen & Albert Gumble, 1916 (Cover Artist, Starmer, Dixie & Transportation) **20.00**

Howdy by Lida Keck-Wiggins & Edna Randolph Worrell, 1923.........**5.00**

Huckleberry Finn by Sam M. Lewis, Joe Young & Cliff Hess, 1917 (Cover Artist, Barbelle) **20.00**

Huckleberry Picnic by Frank Dumont, 1879 (Pre 1900) **15.00**

Huckleberry Pie by Hanlon & Conrad, 1918 (Cover Artist, Pfeiffer)..**10.00**

Huggable, Kissable You by Irving Bibo, 1920...................................**5.00**

Huggin' And Chalkin' by Clancy Hayes & Kermit Goell, 1946, Photo Johnny Mercer..10.00

Hugh McCue by George M. Cohan, 1896 (Pre 1900) **15.00**

Hugo by Glay Williamson, Sam Goold & Abner Silver, 1923, Photo Billy Glason..**10.00**

Huguenot, The by Mary Coleridge & Bruceson Treharne, 1917 ....**5.00**

Huguette Waltz by Brian Hooker & Rudolf Friml, 1926 ....**5.00**

Hukilau Song, The by Jack Owens, 1948..**3.00**

Hula Hula Dream Girl by Gus Kahn & Ted Fiorito, 1924 ....**5.00**

Hulda From Holland by Geo C. Mack & Bob Allan, 1917 ....**5.00**

Hulda's Baby by Tobias Toothpick, 1881 (Black, Black Face & Pre 1900) **25.00**

Hullo Home! by B. C. Hilliams, 1919, Musical: Buddies **5.00**

Humming by Louis Breau & Ray Henderson, 1920..............................**3.00**

Hummingbird by Don Robertson, 1955, Photo Les Paul & Mary Ford (Deco) **6.00**

Humoreske by Anton Dvorak, 1911 (Cover Artist, M.R.) **10.00**

Humoreske by Dvorak; Roth & Orr, 1914 (Cover Artist, Pfeiffer)......**10.00**

Humpty Dumpty by Charles Straight, 1914 (Cover Artist, DeTakacs & Rag) **20.00**

Humpty Dumpty Heart by Johnny Burke & Jimmy Van Heusen, 1941, Movie: Playmates, Photo Kay Kyser, John Barrymore, Lupe Velez & Ginny Simms **10.00**

Humpty Dumpty Kid, The by Hamill & Percy Wenrich, 1908...........**10.00**

Hundred Million Miracles, A by Richard Rodgers & Oscar Hammerstein II, 1961, Movie: Flower Drum Song **8.00**

Hundred Years From Now, A by John Bennett & Carrie Jacobs Bond, 1914 ....**15.00**

Hundred Years From Now by Jack Caddigan, J. Kiern Brennan & Oliver Story, 1914...**5.00**

Hunk-A-Tin by Levy, 1918 (Transportation) **20.00**

Hunt Club, The by Theodore O. Taubert, 1915 (Sports) **15.00**

Hunting Song by Frederika Wadley, 1932 ....**5.00**

Hurrah! For The Liberty Boys, Hurrah by E. T. Paull, 1918 (Cover Artist, Pfeiffer, WWI & March) **40.00**

Hurray For Baffin's Bay by Bryan & Morse, 1903 ....**5.00**

Hurricane March, The by E.T. Paull & Alpert (Cover Artist, E.T. Paull & March) **35.00**

Hurry Home by Joseph Meyer, Buddy Bernier & Bob Emmerich, 1938, Photo Kate Smith (Cover Artist, Merman & Patriotic) **10.00**

Hurry, Little Children, Sunday Morn by Edward Harrigan & David Braham, 1883 (Pre 1900) **15.00**

Hurt by Al Piantadosi & Harold Solomon, 1930 ....**3.00**

Hush! Here Comes The Dream Man by R. P. Weston, F.J. Barnes & Maurice Scot **5.00**

Hush, Little Baby, Don't You Cry by Monroe Rosenfeld, 1884 (Pre 1900 & Black, Black Face) **20.00**

Hush Me To Dreams by Kennedy Russell, 1906 ....**10.00**

Hush My Baby Go To Sleep, 1890, Dedicated by Permission of Mrs. President Harrison To Master Ben Harrison McKee (Pre 1900 & Dedication) **22.00**

Hush, My Darlings, Do Not Weep by G. Operti, 1890 (Pre 1900 & Irish) **15.00**

Hush-A-By by Dayton Wegeforth & Carrie Jacobs Bond, 1911 (Black, Black Face) **15.00**

Hush-A-Bye, Baby Mine by Percy Watson & Charles Bertrand, 1920..**5.00**

Hush-A-Bye, Ma Baby (Missouri Waltz) by J. R. Shannon & John Valentine Eppel, 1943, Photo Bing Crosby (Transportation & Black, Black Face) **10.00**

Hush-A-Bye, Ma Baby (Missouri Waltz) by J. R. Shannon & John Valentine Eppel, 1914 (Cover Artist, Carter, Transportation & Black, Black Face) **15.00**

Hush-A-Bye Time by Mel Brewster & Hymon Cheiffetz, 1929 ....**5.00**

Hushabye Mountain by Sherman & Sherman, 1968, Movie: Chitty Chitty Bang Bang, Photo Dick Van Dyke & Sally Ann Howes.................**8.00**

Hustlin' & Bustlin' For Baby by Harry Woods, 1933 ....**5.00**

Hut-Sut Song, The by Leo V. Killian, Ted McMichel & Jack Owens, 1941, Photo The Merry Macs **5.00**

Hyacinth by George Botsford, 1911 (Rag) **10.00**

Hymn That Mother Sang, The by J.R. Hald, 1902 ....**5.00**

Hymn To The Sun by P. G. Wodehouse & Armand Versey, 1939 ....**5.00**

Hymns Of The Old Church Choir, The by Arthur J. Lamb & A. Solman, 1907 ....**5.00**

Hypnotic Rag by Mahoney, 1912 (Cover Artist, Pfeiffer & Rag)........**15.00**

Hysterics Rag by Paul Beise & F. Henri Klickmann, 1914 (Rag)........**15.00**

I Adore You by Robin & Rainger, 1936, Movie: College Highway, Photo Jack Benny, Burns & Allen, Martha Raye & Mary Boland **8.00**

I Ain't Gonna Be Nobody's Fool by Frank Davis, Geo Bennett & Van & Schenck, 1921, Photo Courtney Sisters (Cover Artist, Frederick S. Manning) **10.00**

I Ain't Got Nobody by David Young & Charles Warfield, 1916 (Blues & Black, Black Face)..**15.00**

I Ain't Got Nothin' But The Blues by Don George & Duke Ellington, 1944, Photo Joan Brooks (Blues) **3.00**

I Ain't Got Weary Yet by Howard Johnson & Percy Wenrich, 1918, Small Folio, Patriotic War Edition (WWI) **25.00**

I Ain't Gwin Ter Work No Mo, 1900 (Jazz & Black, Black Face)......**20.00**

I Ain't Lazy I'm Just Dreamin' by Dave Franklin, 1934 ....**3.00**

I Ain't Nobody's Darling by Robert King & Elmer Hughes, 1921 (Cover Artist, Wohlman)..**5.00**

I Ain't Seen No Messenger Boy by Nathen Bivens, 1899 (Pre 1900)...**15.00**

I Ain't That Kind Of A Baby by Irving Kahal, Addy Britt & Sammy Fain, 1927 ....**3.00**

I Always Knew by Cole Porter, 1943, Movie: Something To Shout About..**8.00**

I Am Always Building Castles In The Air by Ted Garton & A. Fred Phillips, 1919 (Cover Artist, W.M. Fisher) **5.00**

I Am An American by Ira Schuster, Paul Cunningham & Leonard Whitcup, 1940 (Patriotic) **5.00**

I Am Ashamed That Women Are So Simple by Cole Porter, 1948, Musical: Kiss Me Kate **6.00**

I Am Climbing Mountains by James Kendis & James Brockman, 1919 (Cover Artist, Frederick S. Manning)................................**10.00**

I Am In Love With Someone by Bobby Jones & Walter Donovan, 1912...**5.00**

I Am Longing For Someone To Love Me by Tate & Macdonald, 1908..**10.00**

I Am Longing For The Old Days, Marguerite by Lamb & Helf (Cover Artist, Pfeiffer)...**10.00**

I Am Longing For Tomorrow When I Think Of Yesterday by Longbrake & Edwards, 1909 (Cover Artist, Pfeiffer) **15.00**

I Am Longing For You by Florence Hoare & Charles Marshall, 1911..**5.00**

I Am The Candy by Graham & Davis, 1904 ....**10.00**

I Am The Captain by Cole Porter, 1939 Movie: Broadway Melody of 1940, Photo Fred Astaire & Eleanor Powell (Cover Artist, Im-Ho)**8.00**

I Am Thinking Of You Mary by Kelly & Cahill, 1914 (Cover Artist, Pfeiffer) **12.00**

I Am Waiting For To-Morrow To Come by Frank Davis, Franklyn Hawelka & Max Prival, 1919 ....**5.00**

I Am Waiting For You Darling At The Old Red Mill by M. F. Sexton & Ernest S. Williams, 1908 ....**5.00**

I Apologize by Al Hoffman, Al Goodhart & Ed Nelson, 1931, Photo Champ Butler..**2.00**

I Asked Willie And I Know Now by Steve White & Julian Eltinge, 1909, Photo Julian Eltinge **5.00**

I Attempt From Love's Sickness To Fly by H. Purcell **3.00**

I Beg Of You, Elvis Presley, 1957..**20.00**

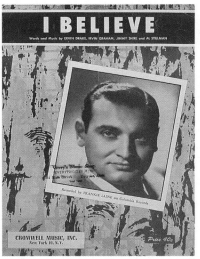

I Believe by Ervin Drake, Irvin Graham & Al Stillman, 1952, Photo Frankie Laine..**6.00**

I Believe In Miracles by Barry Mason & Les Reed, 1976, Photo Engelbert Humperdinck **3.00**

I Believe In Miracles by Lewis, Wendling & Meyer, 1934, Photo Ben Bernie...**5.00**

I Believe In You by Roger Graham & Mary Hill, 1918 ....**5.00**

I Believe It For My Mother Told Me So by Paul Dresser, 1897 (Pre 1900) **15.00**

I Bid You Good-bye Forever by Cohen, 1911 (Cover Artist, Pfeiffer & Deco) **10.00**

I Blush by Lorenz Hart & Richard Rodgers, 1927, Musical: A Connecticut Yankee **10.00**

I Bring You A Song by Frank Churchill & Larry Morey, 1942, Movie: Bambi (Disney)..**10.00**

I Bring You Roses From Loveland by Olive L. Fields, H. W. Willett & H. L. Newman, 1912 ....**5.00**

I Broke My Mother's Heart All Over You by Alfred Bevan & James Kendis, 1916..**5.00**

I Built A Dream One Day by Oscar Hammerstein II & Sigmund Romberg, 1935 (Cover Artist, Jorj)................................**5.00**

I Cain't Say No by Richard Rodgers & Oscar Hammerstein II, 1943, Musical: Oklahoma (Cover Artist, Holley) **6.00**

I Called You My Sweetheart by Howard Johnson, Grant Clarke & Jimmie V. Monaco, 1917, Photo Harry Abrahams (Deco) **5.00**

I Came, I Saw, I Fell by Atteridge, Stanley & Goodman, 1922 ....**5.00**

I Can Dream, Can't I by Irving Kahal & Sammy Fain, 1937, Photo Andrews Sisters & Gordon Jenkins........................**5.00**

I Can Hear The Ukuleles Calling Me by Nat Vincent & Herman Paley, 1916 (Cover Artist, L.P.N.) **5.00**

I Can See You by Sammy Cahn & Nicholas Brodszky, 1951, Movie: Rich, Young And Pretty, Photo Jane Powell, Danielle Darrieux, Wendell Corey, Fernando Lamas & Vic Damone **5.00**

I Can't Afford To Dream by Lew Brown, Charlie Tobias & Sam H. Stept, 1939, Musical: Yokel Boy..**5.00**

I Can't Begin To Tell You by Mack Gordon & James V. Monaco, 1945, Movie: Dolly Sisters, Photo Betty Grable, John Payne & June Haver **12.00**

I Can't Believe It's True by Charles Newman, Ben Bernie & Isham Jones, 1932, Photo Hy C. Geis **2.00**

I Can't Believe That You're In Love With Me by Clarence Gaskill & Jimmy McHugh, 1926 (Deco)................................**5.00**

I Can't Do That Sum by MacDonough & Herbert, 1903 ....**10.00**

I Can't Do Without You by Irving Berlin, 1928, Photo Irving Berlin (Cover Artist, Leff & Irving Berlin)................................**10.00**

I Can't Escape From You by Leo Robin & Richard A. Whiting, 1936, Movie: Rhythm On The Range, Photo Bing Crosby & Frances Farmer **9.00**

I Can't Find A Name Sweet Enough For You by Jack Snyder, 1922 ....**5.00**

I Can't Forget by Howard Dietz, Muriel Pollock & Arthur Schwartz, 1929 ....**5.00**

I Can't Get Started by Ira Gershwin & Vernon Duke, 1935, Musical: Ziegfeld Follies of 1936, Photo Ginny Simms (Cover Artist, Im-Ho) **5.00**

I Can't Get The One I Want by Lou Hardman, Billy Rose & Herman Ruby, 1934 ....**5.00**

I Can't Give You Anything But Love by Dorothy Fields & Jimmy McHugh, 1928, Musical: Blackbirds of 1928, Signed & Inscribed Photo of Jimmy McHugh (Cover Artist, Leff & Signed)...............**10.00**

I Can't Live Without Love by Wm. B. Friedlander, 1923....................**5.00**

I Can't Love You Any More, Any More Than I Do by Herb Magidson & Allie Wrubel, 1940, Photo Glen Carr..............................**5.00**

I Can't Remember by Irving Berlin, 1933, Musical: Easter Parade (Irving Berlin)...**6.00**

I Can't Remember The Words by Jack Yellen, Milton Ager & Henry Sullivan, 1929, Musical: Murray Anderson's Almanac (Deco) **10.00**

I Can't Resist You by Ned Wever & Will Donaldson, 1940, Photo Del Courtney (Cover Artist, Im-Ho) **2.00**

I Can't Stop Loving You Now by Bert Kalmar, Edgar Leslie & Ted Snyder, 1914, Photo Drisdall Sisters (Cover Artist, John Frew)..........**10.00**

I Can't Tell A Lie by Irving Berlin, 1942 (Irving Berlin) **5.00**

I Can't Tell Why I Love You But I Do by Will D. Cobb & Gus Edwards, 1944, Movie: Belle Of The Yukon, Photo Dinah Shore, Gypsy Rose Lee, Randolph Scott & Bob Burns **8.00**

I Can't Think Of Anything Else But You by Eleanor Haley, 1907........**5.00**

I Can't Think Of Nothing Else But You by Harry Dacre, 1896 (Pre 1900) **15.00**

I Cannot Bear To Say Goodbye by Anita Owen, 1918 (Cover Artist, Barbelle & WWI) **10.00**

I Cannot Believe I Lost You by Davis & Prival, 1919 ....**3.00**

I Caught You Making Eyes by Chas. H. Lynch & Richard Tragman, 1904, Photo Miss Vonnie Hoyt, Music Supplement, Hearst's Boston Sunday American Sunday, January 15, 1905 (Cover Artist, J.B. Eddy).....**15.00**

I Certainly Could by Jack Yellen & Milton Ager, 1926........................**5.00**

I Certainly Was Going Some by Creamer, 1913, Photo Bert Williams (Cover Artist, Pfeiffer & Black, Black Face) **15.00**

I Come To Thee by George Graff Jr & Caro Roma, 1916 ....**5.00**

I Concentrate On You by Cole Porter, 1939, Movie: Broadway Melody 1940, Photo Fred Astaire & Eleanor Powell (Cover Artist, Im-Ho)..**10.00**

I Concentrate On You by Cole Porter, 1939, Photo Perry Como **3.00**

I Could Have Danced All Night by Lerner & Lowe, 1956, Movie: My Fair Lady **3.00**

I Could Learn To Love You by John Kemble & Lester W. Keith, 1906 ....**10.00**

I Could Moon Forever Round A Star Like You by Bobby Jones & Mattie Keene, 1909, Dedicated To & Photo of Maude Raymond (Cover Artist, Bryant & Dedication) **10.00**

I Could Say Goodnight To A Thousand Girls by Cobb & Edwards, 1914 (Cover Artist, Pfeiffer & Deco)...**15.00**

I Could Use A Dream by Walter Bullock & Harold Spina, 1937, Movie: Sally, Irene And Mary, Photo Alice Faye, Fred Allen & Many Other Stars **8.00**

I Could Write A Book by Lorenz Hart & Richard Rodgers, 1940, Musical: Pal Joey..**5.00**

I Couldn't Go To Ireland, So Ireland Came To Me by Von Tilzer, 1918 (Cover Artist, Pfeiffer & Irish) **15.00**

I Couldn't Make A Hit With Molly by James Kendis & Herman Paley, 1907 ....**15.00**

I Couldn't Sleep A Wink Last Night by Harold Adamson, Jimmy McHugh, 1943, Movie: Higher & Higher, Photo Frank Sinatra, Michele Morgan & Jack Haley...**5.00**

I Couldn't Stand To See My Baby Lose by Will J. Cobb & Gus Edwards, 1899 (Pre 1900) **15.00**

I Couldn't Stay Away From You by Ben Raleigh & Bernie Wayne, 1948, Photo Frankie Carle..**3.00**

I Cover The Waterfront by Edward Heyman & John W. Green, 1933, Movie: I Cover The Waterfront, Photo Claudette Colbert & Ben Lyon **8.00**

I Cross My Fingers by Kent & Farrar, 1949, Photo Percy Faith **5.00**

I Dare Not Love You by Harry B. Smith & Sigmund Romberg, 1925, Musical: Princess Flavia...**8.00**

I Dare You by Levi, 1914 (Cover Artist, Pfeiffer) **10.00**

I Did It All For You by Sherwood & Rule, 1914 (Cover Artist, Pfeiffer)..**10.00**

I Didn't Know About You by Bob Russell & Duke Ellington, 1944, Photo George Auld (Cover Artist, Sorokin) **3.00**

I Didn't Know What Time It Was by Lorenz Hart & Richard Rodgers, 1939, Movie: Too Many Girls......................................**5.00**

I Didn't Mean A Word I Said by Adamson & McHugh, 1945, Movie: Do You Love Me, Photo Harry James, Maureen O'Hara & Dick Haymes..**5.00**

I Didn't Mean To Make You Cry by Al Piantadosi & Halsey K. Mohr, 1909 (Cover Artist, Pfeiffer) **15.00**

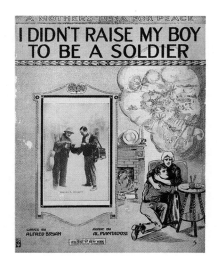

I Didn't Raise My Boy To Be A Soldier, A Mother's Plea For Peace, by Alfred Bryan & Al Piantadosi, 1915, Photo Parillo & Frabito, Dedicated To Every Mother Everywhere (Cover Artist, Rose Symbol, WWI & Dedication) 15.00

I Didn't Raise My Boy To Be A Soldier, A Mother's Plea For Peace, by Alfred Bryan & Al Piantadosi, 1915, Photo Ed Morton, Dedicated To Every Mother Everywhere (Cover Artist, Rose Symbol, WWI & Dedication) **15.00**

I Didn't Raise My Ford To Be A Jitney by Jack Frost, 1915 (Transportation)..**25.00**

I Didn't Think You'd Care by Geo. M. Rosener & Jerry Jarnagin, 1915, Signed Photo Courtney Sisters (Cover Artist, Wohlman, Signed & Deco) **10.00**

I Don't Believe You by Art Conrad, 1923..**15.00**

I Don't Care If It Rains All Night by Sammy Cahn & Jule Styne, 1948, Photo Dorothy Malone, Jack Carson & Dennis Morgan..**6.00**

I Don't Care If The Sun Don't Shine by Mack David, 1949, Photo Tony Martin **5.00**

I Don't Care If You Neber Come Back by Monroe Rosenfeld, 1897 (Pre 1900 & Black, Black Face)..**25.00**

I Don't Care, That's All I Want To Know by Sunny Skylar & Ticker Freeman, 1947, Photo Dinah Shore..**3.00**

I Don't Care What You Used To Be by Al Dubin & Jimmy McHugh, 1924 ....**5.00**

I Don't Care Who Knows It by Harold Adamson & Jimmy McHugh, 1944, Movie: Nob Hill, Photo George Raft, Joan Bennett & Vivian Blaine..**5.00**

I Don't Have To Dream Again by Warren & Dubin, 1936, Movie: Colleen, Photo Dick Powell, Ruby Keeler, Jack Oakie & Joan Blondell **10.00**

I Don't Know Enough About You by Peggy Lee & Dave Barbour, 1946 ..**3.00**

I Don't Know How To Love Him by Tim Rice & Andrew Lloyd Webber, 1970, Musical: Jesus Christ Superstar..**5.00**

I Don't Know Where I'm Going But I'm On My Way by George Fairman, 1917 (Cover Artist, Pfeiffer, Transportation & WWI)..**20.00**

I Don't Know Why by Roy Turk & Fred E. Ahlert, 1931, Movie: Faithful In My Fashion, Photo Donna Reed, Tom Drake & Edward Everett Horton..**5.00**

I Don't Know Why by Roy Turk & Fred E. Ahlert, 1931, Photo Vaughn DeLeath **5.00**

I Don't Like No Cheap Man by Williams & Walker, 1897 (Pre 1900 & Black, Black Face)..**25.00**

I Don't Mind Being All Alone by Clarence Gaskill, Jimmy McHugh & Irving Mills, 1926..**5.00**

I Don't See Me In Your Eyes Anymore by Bennie Benjamin & George Weiss, 1949, Photo Perry Como..**3.00**

I Don't Stand A Ghost Of A Chance With You by Bing Crosby, Ned Washington & Victor Young, 1932, Photo Vaughn Monroe..**4.00**

I Don't Wanna Do It Alone by Bill Hampton & George Duning, 1945 ....**3.00**

I Don't Want The Moon To Shine When I Make Love by Burke, 1912, Photo Mae Burke (Cover Artist, Pfeiffer) **10.00**

I Don't Want The Morning To Come by Arthur J. Lamb & J. Fred Helf, 1908 ....**5.00**

I Don't Want To Be A Little Girlie by Francis B. Manning..**5.00**

I Don't Want To Be Hurt Anymore by McCarthy, 1962, Photo Nat King Cole..**3.00**

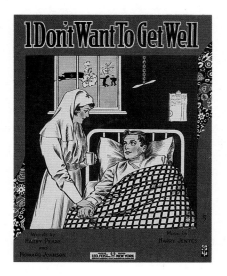

I Don't Want To Get Well by Harry Pease, Howard Johnson & Harry Jentes, 1917 (Cover Artist, Rose Symbol, WWI & Red Cross) 25.00

I Don't Want To Love You by Sgt. Henry Prichard, 1944, Photo Phil Brito (Cover Artist, Merritt & Military Personnel) **5.00**

I Don't Want To Meet Any More People by Stanley Adams & Frankie Carle, 1947, Photo Frankie Carle (Cover Artist, M.S.)..**3.00**

I Don't Want To Play In Your Yard by Philip Wingate & H. W. Petrie, 1894, Photo Cherrie Simpson (Pre 1900)..**15.00**

I Don't Want To Walk Without You by Frank Loesser & Jule Styne, 1941, Movie: Sweater Girl, Photo Eddie Bracken, June Preisser & Betty Jane Rhodes..**5.00**

I Double Dare You by Terry Shand & Jimmy Eaton, 1937, Photo Jerry Freeman (Cover Artist, Starmer)..**5.00**

I Double Dare You by Terry Shand & Jimmy Eaton, 1937, Photo Rudy Vallee (Cover Artist, Starmer)..**5.00**

I Dream Of You by Marjorie Goetschius & Edna Osser, 1944, Photo Tommy Dorsey (Cover Artist, Barbelle)..**3.00**

I Dream Too Much by Dorothy Fields & Jerome Kern, 1935, Movie: I Dream Too Much, Photo Lily Pons (Cover Artist, B. Harris)..**5.00**

I Dreamt by F. Schira, 1872 (Pre 1900)..**3.00**

I Dreamt My Daddy Came Home by Joe Darcey & Lew Porter, 1919 (WWI)..**15.00**

I Dreamt That I Dwelt In Marble Halls, Opera Gems, 1910 (Cover Artist, Pfeiffer)..**10.00**

I Dug A Ditch by Lew Brown, Ralph Freed & Burton Lane, 1943, Movie: Thousands Cheer, Photo Judy Garland & Kathryn Grayson..........**10.00**

I Enjoy Being A Girl by Richard Rodgers & Oscar Hammerstein II, 1961, Movie: Flower Drum Song..**6.00**

I Fall In Love With You Every Day by Frank Loesser & Manning Sherwin, 1938, Movie: College Swing...**5.00**

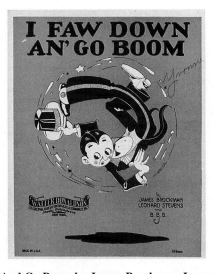

I Faw Down And Go Boom by Jasper Brockman, Leonard Stevens & B.B.B., 1928 (Cover Artist, Pud Lane)..10.00

I Feel A Song Coming On by Dorothy Fields, Jimmy McHugh & George Oppenheimer, 1935, Movie: Every Night At Eight........................**5.00**

I Feel At Home With You by Lorenz Hart & Richard Rodgers, 1927, Musical: A Connecticut Yankee...**5.00**

I Feel Like A Feather In The Breeze by Mack Gordon & Harry Revel, 1935, Movie: Collegiate, Photo Jack Oakie, Joe Penner, Ned Sparks & Frances Langford..**12.00**

I Feel Lonesome Sometimes by McKenna, 1917 (Cover Artist, Pfeiffer)..**15.00**

I Feel Pretty by Stephen Sondheim & Leonard Bernstein, 1957, Movie: West Side Story **8.00**

I Feel The Earth Move by Carole King, 1971, Photo Carole King **3.00**

I Found A Dream by Don Hartman & Jay Gorney, 1935, Movie: Red Heads On Parade, Photo John Boles & Dixie Lee **12.00**

I Found A Four Leaf Clover by Anne Johnston Bailey, 1930, Photo Elizabeth Boatright **6.00**

I Found A Four Leaf Clover by B.G. DeSylva & George Gershwin, 1922, Musical: 4th Annual Production, George White's Scandals **15.00**

I Found A Million Dollar Baby by Rose, Dixon & Warren, 1931, Movie: Million Dollar Baby, Photo, Ron Reagan, Priscilla Lane & Jeffrey Lynn (President) **10.00**

I Found A Million Dollar Baby In The Five And Ten Cent Store by Billy Rose, Mort Dixon & Harry Warren, 1931, Musical: Billy Rose's Crazy Quilt (Cover Artist, Ben Harris) **10.00**

I Found A Rose In The Devil's Garden by Willie Raskin & Fred Fisher, 1921 (Cover Artist, Goldbeck & Deco).......................................**10.00**

I Found The Answer by Johnny Lange, 1957..**4.00**

I Found The End Of The Rainbow by John Mears, Harry Tierney & Joseph McCarthy, 1918 (Cover Artist, DeTakacs)........................**10.00**

I Found You by L. Wolfe Gilbert & Anatol Fried, 1919, Photo Amelia Stone & Armand Kalisz...**5.00**

I Found You Among The Roses by Geo. B. Pitman, 1916 (Cover Artist, Barbelle) **10.00**

I Found You Among The Roses by George W. Pitman, 1914 (Cover Artist Fisher)...**5.00**

I Found You Just In Time by Howard & Harriman, 1914 (Cover Artist, Pfeiffer & Deco) **10.00**

I Gave Her That by B.G. DeSylva, 1919..**6.00**

I Gave My Heart For A Rose by Bayha, Platzman & Barron, 1915 (Cover Artist, Pfeiffer)...**12.00**

I Gave You Up Just Before You Threw Me Down by Bert Kalmar, Harry Ruby & Fred E. Ahlert, 1922 (Cover Artist, Barbelle) **5.00**

I Get A Kick Out Of You by Cole Porter, 1934, Movie: Anything Goes **5.00**

I Get So Lonely by Pat Ballard, 1954...**2.00**

I Get The Blues When It Rains by Marcy Klauber & Harry Stoddard, 1929, Photo Lee Cantor...**5.00**

I Give You All You Ask by Edgar Selden & Melville J. Gideon, 1911, Photo Bessie Wynn (Cover Artist, Starmer) **5.00**

I Give You My Word by Al Kavelin & Merril Lyn, 1940, Signed Photo by Al Kavelin & Photo Bill Darnell (Cover Artist, Im-Ho & Signed)..**6.00**

I Got A "Code" In My "Doze" by Arthur Fields, Fred Hall & Billy Rose, 1929 ....**5.00**

I Got A Feelin' For You: Way Down In My Heart by Edward Madden & Theodore F. Morse, 1904 ....**10.00**

I Got It Bad And That Ain't Good by Edward Kennedy & Duke Ellington, 1941 ....**3.00**

I Got Lost In His Arms by Irving Berlin, 1946, Movie: Annie Get Your Gun (Irving Berlin)...**8.00**

I Got Plenty O' Nuttin by DuBose Heyward & Ira & George Gershwin, 1935, Movie: Porgy And Bess, Photo Sidney Poitier, Dorothy Daindridge & Sammy Davis Jr. (Black, Black Face) 12.00

I Got Rhythm by Ira & George Gershwin, 1930 ....**10.00**

I Got Spurs That Jingle Jangle Jingle by Frank Loesser & Joseph J. Lilley, 1942, Movie: The Forest Ranger, Photo Fred MacMurray & Paulette Goddard **5.00**

I Got You Steve by Ed Morton, 1912 (Cover Artist, Pfeiffer) **15.00**

I Gotta Have My Baby Back by Floyd Tillman, 1949, Photo Red Foley...**6.00**

I Gotta Ride by Frank Loesser & Burton Lane, 1941, Movie: Las Vegas Nights, Photo Frank Sinatra...**8.00**

I Guess I'll Get The Papers And Go Home by Hughie Prince, Dick Rogers & Hal Kanner, 1946...**3.00**

I Guess I'll Have To Change My Plans by Dietz & Schwartz, 1932, Movie: The Band Wagon, Photo Fred Astaire, Cyd Charisse, Nanette Fabray & Jack Buchanan...**10.00**

I Guess I'll Have To Dream The Rest by Mickey Stoner, Martin Block & Harold Green, 1945 (Cover Artist, Im-Ho) **4.00**

I Guess I'll Have To Dream The Rest by Mickey Stoner, Martin Block & Harold Green, 1941, Photo Frank Sinatra **3.00**

I Guess I'll Have To Telegraph My Baby by George M. Cohan, 1898 (George M. Cohan, Pre 1900 & Black, Black Face) **20.00**

I Guess I'll Soon Be Back In Dixieland by Jack Rogers, 1915 (Dixie)..**6.00**

I Guess That Will Hold You For A While by Smart & Williams, 1897 (Pre 1900)...**15.00**

I Had A Little Talk With The Lord by Mann Curtis & Vic Mizzy, 1944 (Cover Artist, Barbelle & WWII).....................................**12.00**

I Had Fifteen Dollars In My Inside Pocket by Harry Kennedy, 1885, (Pre 1900)..**15.00**

I Had The Craziest Dream by Mack Gordon & Harry Warren, 1942, Movie: Springtime In The Rockies, Photo Betty Grable, John Payne, Harry James & Carmen Miranda..................................**12.00**

I Hadn't Anyone Till You by Ray Noble, 1938 ....**3.00**

I Handed It Over To Reilly by Hall & McGlennon, 1892 (Pre 1900)..**15.00**

I Happen To Be In Love by Cole Porter, 1939, Movie: Broadway Melody 1940, Photo Fred Astaire & Eleanor Powell (Cover Artist, Im-Ho)..**12.00**

I Happened To Walk Down First Street by Arthur Schwartz & Leo Robin, 1946, Movie: The Time, The Place And The Girl, Photo Dennis Morgan, Jack Carson, Martha Vickers, Janice Paige & Carmen Cavallero (Cover Artist, A.Joel Robinson) **6.00**

I Hate Men by Cole Porter, 1948, Musical: Kiss Me Kate **6.00**

I Hate Myself by Abner Silver Cornell & Dave Oppenheim, 1930........**5.00**

I Hate Myself For Being So Mean To You by Benny Davis, Joe Young & Milton Ager, 1934, Photo Mary Small (Cover Artist, Leff).............**5.00**

I Hate To Lose You by Grant Clarke & Archie Gottler, 1918 (Cover Artist, Barbelle & Deco)...**10.00**

I Hate To See Those Summer Days Roll By by Happy O'Neil & Bobby Jones, 1912, Photo & Dedicated To Miss Queenie Elliotte (Cover Artist, Starmer & Dedication) **16.00**

I Hate You, Cause I Love You So by Mort Greene & Walter Schumann, 1941 ....**3.00**

I Hate You Darling by Cole Porter, 1943, Movie: Let's Face It **5.00**

I Have A Big Jazz Band by Bowers, 1918 (Jazz) **10.00**

I Have But One Heart by Marty Symes & Johnny Farrow, 1945, Photo Frank Sinatra...**25.00**

I Have Dreamed by Rodgers & Hammerstein, 1951 ....**4.00**

I Have Eyes by Leo Robin & Ralph Rainger, 1938, Movie: Paris Honeymoon, Photo Bing Crosby & Shirley Ross **12.00**

I Have Found A Girl That's Just Like Mother by Jacobs, 1915 (Cover Artist, Pfeiffer)...**10.00**

I Have Lost My Euridice by Harrison Millard & Gluck, Photo Louise Homer & Joanna Gadski, Sunday Supplement, March 6, 1910.....**10.00**

I Have So Little To Give by Bruce Sievier & Pat Thayer, 1935 ....**3.00**

I Have To Have You by Leo Robin & Richard Whiting, 1929 ....**5.00**

I Have You by Charles McCarron & Ed O'Keefe, 1918......................**5.00**

I Haven't Changed A Thing by Henry Nemo, Irving Mills & Mickey Goldsen, 1938..**3.00**

I Haven't Got Time For Anyone Else Till John Gets Home by James V. Monaco, 1918 (WWI)...**12.00**

I Haven't Time To Be A Millionaire by Johnny Burke & James V. Monaco, 1940, Movie: If I Had My Way, Photo Bing Crosby & Gloria Jean..**5.00**

I Hear A Dream by Leo Robin & Ralph Rainger, 1939, Movie: Gulliver's Travels **8.00**

I Hear A Lark At Dawning by Daniel S. Twohig & Christian Kriens, 1928...**3.00**

I Hear A Rhapsody by George Fragos, Jack Baker And Dick Gasparre, 1940 ....**3.00**

I Hear A Rhapsody by George Fragos, Jack Baker & Dick Gasparre, 1940, Movie: Clash By Night, Photo Barbara Stanwyck, Paul Douglas & Frank Sinatra...**8.00**

I Hear The Music Now by Seelen & Fain, 1953, Movie: The Jazz Singer, Photo Danny Thomas & Peggy Lee **8.00**

I Hear You Calling Me by Harold Harford & Charles Marshall, 1908, Movie: Song Of My Heart, Sung By John McCormack (Irish) **10.00**

I Hear You Calling Me, Tennessee by Ford & Russell, 1914 (Cover Artist, Pfeiffer)...**10.00**

I Hear You Knocking by Batholomew & King, 1950, Photo Gale Storm...**3.00**

I Hear Your Voice by Ralph Butler & Tolchard Evans, 1942................**3.00**

I Hear Your Voice In The Shadows by Effie Cutler Coombs & Jacob Henry Ellis, 1918 (Cover Artist, Rose Symbol)........................**12.00**

I Heard A Forest Praying by Sam M. Lewis & Peter DeRose, 1937......**3.00**

I Heard A Robin by Elizabeth Evelyn Moore & Frank H. Grey, 1928 ..**3.00**

I Heard You Cried Last Night by Ted Grouya & Jerrie Kruger, 1943 ...**3.00**

I Heard You Go By by Kathleen Stuart & Daniel Wood, 1922 ....**3.00**

I Hit A New High by Harold Adamson & Jimmy McHugh, 1937, Movie: Hitting A New High, Photo Lily Pons, Jack Oakie, Eric Blore, Edward Everett Horton & John Howard..**5.00**

I Hope I Don't Intrude by Delehanty & Catlin, 1877 (Pre 1900).........**15.00**

I Hope These Few Lines Will Find You Well by Cole & Johnson, 1897 (Pre 1900) **15.00**

I Hope You're Satisfied by Ed Unger Jr., 1934, Signed Photo Ed Unger Jr. (Signed) **5.00**

I Hum A Waltz by Mack Gordon & Harry Revel, 1937, Movie: This Is My Affair, Photo Robert Taylor & Barbara Stanwyck.........................**12.00**

I Just Called To Say I Love You by Stevie Wonder, 1984, Photo Stevie Wonder **5.00**

I Just Came Back From Dear Old Dixie Land by David Stamper, 1912 (Cover Artist, Starmer & Dixie)...**10.00**

I Just Came In To Say Hello by George L. Cobb & Gus Edwards, 1913, Photo J.B. Carson **5.00**

I Just Can't Get Rid Of That Plaster by Chavez, 1912 (Cover Artist, Pfeiffer) **10.00**

I Just Can't Help From Loving That Man by Andrew B. Sterling, Alfred Bryan & Harry Von Tilzer, 1902..**10.00**

I Just Can't Keep From Liking You by Sheppard Camp & Geo A. Norton, 1911, Photo Pauline Moran (Cover Artist, Starmer)......................**5.00**

I Just Can't Make My Eyes Behave by Will Cobb & Gus Edwards, 1906...**10.00**

I Just Kissed Your Picture Goodnight by David & Kent, 1936.............**3.00**

I Just Kissed Your Picture Goodnight by Mack David & Walter Kent, 1936, Photo Phyllis Jeanne **4.00**

I Just Kissed Your Picture Goodnight by Mack David & Walter Kent, 1936, Photo Kay Lorraine **4.00**

I Just Love You by Joe Pasternak & Nicholas Brodsky, 1953, Photo Tony Martin **4.00**

I Just Made Up With That Old Girl Of Mine by George A. Little, Harry Pease & George B. McConnell, 1936, Photo Vincent Lopez............**3.00**

I Just Met The Fellow Who Married The Girl That I Was Going To Get by Al Piantadosi, 1911...**10.00**

I Just Roll Along Havin' My Ups And Downs by Jo Trent & Peter DeRose, 1927 (Cover Artist, R.S.) **5.00**

I Just Wanna Play With You by Mack David & Joe Solman, 1940, Photo Ray Herbeck & Betty Benson **3.00**

I Keep My Wife In The City & Make Love To Her Myself by Bryan & Meyer, 1911 (Cover Artist, Pfeiffer & Deco) **10.00**

I Kiss Your Hand, Madame by Fritz Potter & Ralph Erwin, 1928........**5.00**

I Knew You When by Herb Magidson & J. Fred Coots, 1934.............**3.00**

I Know A Road by J. Kiern Brennan & Albert Von Tilzer, 1919 ....**5.00**

I Know I Got More Than My Share by Grant Clarke & Howard Johnson, 1916 ....**10.00**

I Know, I Know, I Know by Bob Russell & Bronislau Kaper, 1949, Movie: That Midnight Kiss **3.00**

I Know Now by Al Dubin & Harry Warren, 1927, Movie: The Singing Marine, Photo Dick Powell & Doris Weston **10.00**

I Know Some Hearts Were Made To Be Broken by Berg, 1917 (Cover Artist, Pfeiffer)..**10.00**

I Know That You Know by Vincent Youmans, 1930, Movie: Hit The Deck, Photo Jane Powell, Tony Martin, Debbie Reynolds & Walter Pidgeon **8.00**

I Know What It Means To Be Lonesome by James Kendis, James Brockman & Nat Vincent, 1919 (Cover Artist, Henry Hutt) **5.00**

I Know What It Means To Be Lonesome by James Kendis, James Brockman & Nat Vincent, 1918, Signed Photo, June Caprice (Cover Artist, E.E. Walton) **10.00**

I Know You're Somewhere Loving Me by Clarice Manning & Mary Hopkins, 1912...**8.00**

I Learned A Lesson I'll Never Forget by Joe Davis, 1944, Photo Janette **3.00**

I Left My Door Open by Irving Berlin, 1919 (Irving Berlin)................**5.00**

I Left My Heart At The Stage Door Canteen by Irving Berlin, 1942, Movie: This Is The Army, Lt. Ronald Reagan In Cast (Irving Berlin, WWII, Military Personel & President).............................**16.00**

I Left My Heart In San Francisco by George Cory, Signed Photo Tony Bennett (Signed)..**10.00**

I Let A Song Go Out Of My Heart by Irving Mills, Henry Nemo, John Redmond & Duke Ellington, 1943....................................**3.00**

I Like A Girl With A Smile Like You by Jones & Deely, 1912, Photo Jones & Deely (Deco)..**10.00**

I Like Dreamin by Kenny Nolan, 1976, Photo Kenny Nolan..............**3.00**

I Like Everything About You But The Boys by Cobb & Edwards, 1914 (Cover Artist, Pfeiffer) **10.00**

I Like It Better Everyday by Harry Williams, Egbert Van Alstyne & James Brockman, 1912 (Cover Artist, Pfeiffer & Deco))...................**10.00**

I Like It by Bricusse, 1970, Movie: Scrooge, Photo Albert Finney **3.00**

I Like It by Irving Berlin, 1921 (Irving Berlin) **5.00**

I Like Mountain Music by James Cavanaugh & Frank Weldon, 1933, Photo Ethel Shutta **6.00**

I Like My Old Home Town by Harry Lauder, 1923.....................**5.00**

I Like To Call You Sweetheart by Paul Cunningham & Ted Snyder, 1911, Dedicated To Miss Lulu Von Welden (Dedication)...............**10.00**

I Like To Do It by Byron Gay, 1920 (Cover Artist, Millard & Deco) ...**5.00**

I Like To Recognize The Tune by Lorenz Hart & Richard Rogers, 1939, Movie: Too Many Girls..**5.00**

I Like Your Apron And Your Bonnet And Your Little Quaker Gown by John F. Harrington & Alfred J. Lawrence (Cover Artist, Starmer) ..**10.00**

I Like Your Way by Walker & Witt, 1905 ....**5.00**

I Live In Turkey by Irving Berlin, 1920, Musical: Ziegfeld Follies of 1920 (Cover Artist, R.S., Deco & Irving Berlin) **10.00**

I Live The Life I Love by Moe Jaffe & Clay Boland, 1937, From The Mask & Wig Club Of The Univ. Of Pennsylvania Golden Jubilee Production, Fifty-Fifty **6.00**

I Live Uptown by Meyer & Bryan, 1911 (Cover Artist, Pfeiffer)........**10.00**

I Long To Hear The Old Church Choir Again by J. Will Callahan & F. Henri Klickmann, 1914 ....**5.00**

I Long To See My Mother's Face Again by John H. Trayne, 1903, Dedicated To Geo. S. Gates Esq. (Cover Artist, E.S. Fisher & Dedication) **10.00**

I Long To See The Girl I Left Behind by John T. Kelly, 1893 (Pre 1900) **15.00**

I Look At Heaven, When I Look At You by Bobby Worth, Ray Austin & Freddy Martin, 1942, Photo Freddy Martin **3.00**

I Lost A Slice Of Paradise When I Left My Swanee Home by Jack Norworth & Al Piantadosi, 1922 (Black, Black Face) **15.00**

I Lost A Wonderful Pal When I Lost You by Al Dubin, Joe Mittenthal & Irwin Dash, 1924 ....**5.00**

I Lost My Gal From Memphis by Charlie Tobias & Peter DeRose, 1930...**5.00**

I Lost My Heart In A Drive-In Movie by Brooks & Raskin, 1964, Movie: The Patsy, Photo Jerry Lewis, Peter Lorre, Ina Balin & Phil Harris ..**5.00**

I Lost My Heart In Dixieland by Irving Berlin, 1919 (Irving Berlin & Dixie)...**10.00**

I Lost My Heart In Honolulu by Will D. Cobb & Gus Howard, 1916 ...**5.00**

I Lost The Best Pal That I Had by Dick Thomas, 1920 (Cover Artist, Barbelle) **8.00**

I Love A Lassie by Lauder & Grafton, 1906.............................**10.00**

I Love A Little Cottage by Roscoe Gilmore Stott & Geoffrey O'Hara, 1926 (Cover Artist, Ray Parmalee) **10.00**

I Love A Parade by Ted Koehler & Harold Arlen, 1918 (WWI) **15.00**

I Love A Piano by Irving Berlin, 1916 (Irving Berlin).....................**12.00**

I Love But You by Burnette, 1925 ....**3.00**

I Love Her Oh! Oh! Oh! by Joe McCarthy, E. P. Moran & James V. Monaco, 1913, Musical: The Honeymoon Express, Photo Al Jolson (Cover Artist, Rose Symbol & Al Jolson)....................20.00

I Love Her Ooh La La La by Lew Porter, 1919 (WWI) **15.00**

I Love How You Love Me by Barry Mann & Larry Kolber, 1961 ....**2.00**

I Love, I Love, I Love My Wife, But Oh! You Kid! by Jimmy Lucas & Harry Von Tilzer, 1909 (Cover Artist, Gene Buck).....................**15.00**

I Love It by Albert Goetz, 1910.................................**5.00**

I Love Life by Irwin M. Cassel & Mana-Zucca, 1923 ....**5.00**

I Love Louisa by Howard Deitz & Arthur Schwartz, 1931.................**3.00**

I Love Love by Walter O'Keefe, Arthur Swanstrom, Robert Dolan, Albert Sirmay & Arthur Schwartz, 1930, Musical: Princess Charming......**8.00**

I Love My Baby, My Baby Loves Me by Bud Green & Harry Warren, 1956, Photo Jill Corey **3.00**

I Love My Honey Yes I Do by Carleton (Black, Black Face)............**20.00**

I Love My Husband, But Oh, You Henry! by Herbert Ingraham, 1909...**10.00**

I Love My Steady, But I'm Crazy For My "Once-In-A-While" by Irving Hinkley & Allan W.S. Macduff, 1910, Photo Ed Norton (Cover Artist, Starmer) **12.00**

I Love My Wife So Keep Away by Gus Edwards, 1909, Musical: Ziegfeld Follies 1909 ....**12.00**

I Love No One But You by Phil Spitalny, 1927, Photo Jesse Crawford (Cover Artist, Barbelle & Deco)........................**5.00**

I Love Paris by Cole Porter, 1953, Musical: Can Can...................**3.00**

I Love That Lovable Melody by James White, 1917.........................**5.00**

I Love The Girl My Father Loved by Herbert DePierce & Wm. J. O'Gorman, 1911 ....**10.00**

I Love The Ladies by Grant Clark & Jean Schwartz, 1914, Photo Florence Tempest (Cover Artist, Frew).................................**10.00**

I Love The Name Of Mary by Geo. Graff Jr., Chauncy Olcott & Ernest R. Ball, 1910 (Cover Artist, DeTakacs & Irish)...............**12.00**

I Love The Name Of Mother by Connor Lynn & J. W. Gribben, 1912 .**6.00**

I Love The Name Of Mother by Freeman, 1914 (Cover Artist, Pfeiffer)..**10.00**

I Love The U.S.A. by Hardy, 1914 (WWI) **15.00**

I Love The Way You Say Goodnight by Eddie Pola & George Wyle, 1951, Movie: Lullaby Of Broadway, Photo Doris Day & Gene Nelson **10.00**

I Love Them All by Sandy Linzer, 1970, Photo Nancy Sinatra............**3.00**

I Love To Bumpity Bump by Al Sherman, 1928 (Transportation) **15.00**

I Love To Hear An Irish Band Upon St. Patrick's Day by Jerome & Schwartz, 1912 (Cover Artist, Pfeiffer & Irish) **12.00**

I Love To Tango With My Tea by Alfred Bryan & Egbert Van Alstyne, 1915 (Cover Artist, Starmer & Deco) **15.00**

I Love To Whistle by Jimmy McHugh & Harold Adamson, 1938, Movie: Mad About Music, Photo Deanna Durbin.......................**5.00**

I Love You A Thousand Ways by Lefty Frizzell & Jim Beck, 1951, Photo Lefty Frizzell **3.00**

I Love You All The More by Nat Vincent & Darl MacBoyle, 1919 (Cover Artist, E.E. Walton)..............................**10.00**

I Love You, Believe Me, I Love You by Rubey Cowan & Phil Boutelje, 1929, Movie: The Vagabond Lover, Photo Rudy Vallee..............**10.00**

I Love You Best Of All by Tell Taylor, 1915 (Cover Artist, Universal Art) **15.00**

I Love You by Cole Porter, 1943, Movie: Mexican Hayride **5.00**

I Love You by Harlan Thompson & Harry Archer, 1923, Musical: Little Jessie James **10.00**

I Love You California by Frankenstein, 1913 ....**5.00**

I Love You Dear by Al M. Kendall & Rudolf Friml, 1920 (Cover Artist, Raeburn Van Buren)..............................**10.00**

I Love You For Sentimental Reasons by Deek Watson & William Best, 1946, Signed Photo Of Eddy Howard (Signed) **5.00**

I Love You From Coast To Coast by Al Stillman, Alex Hyde & Basil G. Adlam, 1936, Photo Vincent Lopez **5.00**

I Love You, Honey, "Deed I Do" by Carroll Fleming & Geo A. Nichols, 1900 ....**10.00**

I Love You Honolulu by Harry Lauder, 1915, Photo Harry Lauder **10.00**

I Love You–I Hate You by Al Bryan & Geo W. Meyer, 1929, Movie: Careers **8.00**

I Love You, I Love You, I Love You Sweetheart Of All My Dreams by Art Fitch, Kay Fitch & Bert Lowe, 1945, Movie: Thirty Seconds Over Tokyo, Photo Van Johnson, Spencer Tracy & Phyllis Thaxter (WWII) **10.00**

I Love You, I Love You, I Love You, I Love You, Sweetheart Of All My Dreams by Art Fitch, Kay Fitch & Bert Lowe, 1928, Photo William H. Stamm (Deco) **5.00**

I Love You In The Same Old Way by Ford & Bratton, 1896 (Pre 1900)...**15.00**

I Love You Just The Same, Sweet Adeline by Harry Armstrong & Clarence Gaskill, 1919 (March) **10.00**

I Love You Kate In Ireland by Edwin French, 1890 (Pre 1900 & Irish)...**15.00**

I Love You Kid by Diamond & Stone, 1912, Photo May Burke (Cover Artist, Pfeiffer)...........................**10.00**

I Love You Like Lincoln Loved The Old Red, White & Blue by Jerome, Schwartz & Young, 1914 (Cover Artist, Pfeiffer, Patriotic & Presidents) **20.00**

I Love You More Each Day by Fink, 1914 (Cover Artist, Pfeiffer).....**15.00**

I Love You Much Too Much by Don Raye, Alex Olshey & C. Towber, 1940 (Cover Artist, Im-Ho).................................**3.00**

I Love You Much Too Much, Muchacha by Mack Gordon & Harry Revel, 1937, Movie: Wake Up And Live, Photo Walter Winchell, Ben Bernie & Alice Faye.................................**8.00**

I Love You So Much It Hurts by Floyd Tillman, 1948, Photo Perry Como ..**3.00**

I Love You So Much It Hurts by Floyd Tillman, 1948, Photo The Mills Brothers (Cover Artist, James J. Kriegsmann)..............................**5.00**

I Love You Sunday by Charles Byrne & Charlie Straight, 1920...........**3.00**

I Love You–That's One Thing I Know by L. Wolfe Gilbert & Anatol Friedman, 1916.....................................**6.00**

I Love You: The World Is Thine by Frank W. Mead & Burt Shadu, 1907 (Cover Artist, Harrison Fisher)......................................**50.00**

I Love You Truly by Carrie Jacobs Bond, 1920...................................**15.00**

I Loved You The First Time I Met You by Mittendahl, 1912 (Cover Artist, Pfeiffer)................................**10.00**

I Loved You Then As I Love You Now by MacDonald & Mendoza, 1928, Movie: Our Dancing Daughters, Photo Joan Crawford **15.00**

I Loved You Then, I Love You Now, I'll Love You For Evermore by Will R. Garton & Ted Garton, 1915 (Cover Artist, Pfeiffer) **10.00**

I Loved You Wednesday by Silver, Kent & Drake, 1933 ....**3.00**

I Married An Angel by Lorenz Hart & Richard Rodgers, 1938, Movie: I Married An Angel (Cover Artist, Sorokin) **8.00**

I May Be Crazy, But I Ain't No Fool by Rogers & Williams, 1904 ....**10.00**

I May Be Gone For A Long Long Time by Lew Brown & Albert Von Tilzer, 1917, Musical: Kitchy Koo, Photo Grace LaRue (Cover Artist, DeTakacs & WWI) **15.00**

I May Be Wrong by Harry Ruskin & Henry Sullivan, 1929, Movie: Wallflower, Photo Robert Hutton, Joyce Reynolds, Janice Paige & Edward Arnold..**10.00**

I Met You Dear In Dreamland by Berk, 1916 ....**5.00**

I Met You, I Love You, I Want You by Wilson & Lincoln, 1914 (Cover Artist, Pfeiffer)...**10.00**

I Might Be Your Once-In-A While by Robert Smith & Victor Herbert, 1919, Musical: Angel Face, Signed Photo Victor Herbert (Victor Herbert & Signed) **25.00**

I Mind Me In The Mornin' by Waugh & Rosedale, 1910 (Black, Black Face) **16.00**

I Miss A Little Miss by Seymour & Coots, 1930 ....**3.00**

I Miss Daddy's Goodnight Kiss by James Kendis & James Brockman, 1918 (Cover Artist, Rose Symbol & WWI) 20.00

I Miss My Swiss by L. Wolfe Gilbert & Abel Baer, 1925 ....**5.00**

I Miss That Mississippi Miss That Misses Me by Joe Young, Sam M. Lewis & Pete Wendling, 1918 (Cover Artist, Barbelle)................**10.00**

I Miss You by Jessie R. Millar, 1933, Photo Irma Glen (Cover Artist, Fran Hays)..**5.00**

I Miss You Dear by John C. Harris & Herbert Binner, 1913, Photo Flo Adler **10.00**

I Miss You Dear Old Broadway by Ford, 1917 (Cover Artist, Pfeiffer)..**10.00**

I Miss You More Each Day by Nat Vincent & James Kendis, 1916......**5.00**

I Miss You Most Of All by Joe McCarthy & James V. Monaco, 1913..**5.00**

I Miss Your Smile by Edna Shepheard, 1914....................................**12.00**

I Must Be Dreaming by Al Dubin, 1927 ....**5.00**

I Must Be Singing, Singing by Walter & Taubert, 1850 (Pre 1900) **75.00**

I Must Have Been Dreaming by Cole & Johnson, 1900.....................**10.00**

I Must Have One More Kiss Kiss Kiss by Johnny Burke, Al Hoffman, Al Goodhart & Manny Kurtz, 1939...**3.00**

I Must Have That Man by Dorothy Fields & Jimmy McHugh, 1928, Musical: Blackbirds Of 1928 (Cover Artist, Leff) **12.00**

I Must See Annie Tonight by Cliff Friend & Dave Franklin, 1938, Photo Horace Heidt...**5.00**

I Need You Now by Jimmy Crane & Al Jacobs, 1953, Photo Eddie Fisher...**3.00**

I Never Drink Behind The Bar by Edward Harrigan & David Braham, 1883 (Pre 1900) **16.00**

I Never Had A Chance by Irving Berlin, 1934 (Irving Berlin)..............**5.00**

I Never Had A Dream Come True by Allan Roberts & Doris Fisher, 1946, Movie: Talk About A Lady, Photo Jinx Falkenberg, Forrest Tucker, Joe Besser & Stan Kenton **5.00**

I Never Had A Feeling Like I Have For You by Edward A. Denish, 1910..**6.00**

I Never Had A Mammy by Duncan Sisters, Book by Catherine C. Cushing, Suggested by Uncle Tom's Cabin by Harriet Beecher Stowe, 1923, Musical: Topsy & Eva, Photo Duncan Sisters (Cover Artist, P.M. Griffith & Black, Black Face)...............................**15.00**

I Never Knew A Happy Day 'Til I Met You by W. R. Williams, 1911.**5.00**

I Never Knew by Tom Pitts, Ray Egan & Roy K. Marsh, 1920............**6.00**

I Never Knew by Williams, Young & Grant, 1913 (Cover Artist, Pfeiffer)..**10.00**

I Never Knew How Much God Gave To Me by J. Keirn Brennan & Ernest R. Ball, 1923...**5.00**

I Never Knew How Much I Loved You by Dave Ringle, Phoebe Diamond & Burt W. Spear, 1925 (Cover Artist, Politzer & Deco).................**8.00**

I Never Knew How Wonderful You Were by Dorothy Terriss & Joe Burke, 1926 ....**4.00**

I Never Knew How Wonderful You Were by Irving Selzer, Carroll Loveday & Blanche Melvin, 1931...**5.00**

I Never Knew I Could Love Anybody Like I'm Loving You by Tom Pitts, Ray Eagan & Roy K. Marsh, 1920, Musical: Midnight Rounders, Photo Jane Green (Deco)..10.00

I Never Knew I Had A Heart by James Brockman, 1915.....................**5.00**

I Never Knew I Had A Wonderful Wife by Lew Brown & Albert Von Tilzer, 1919..**5.00**

I Never Knew That I Loved You by Frank Fay & Dave Dreyer, 1929, Musical: Oh, What A Girl **10.00**

I Never Knew What Sweetheart Meant Till I Met You by Ted Garton, 1912 ....**5.00**

I Never Knew You Loved Me by Whittaker & Lothian, 1913 (Cover Artist, Pfeiffer)...**10.00**

I Never Liked O'Regan by Joe Flynn, 1890 (Pre 1900 & Irish)..........**15.00**

I Never Mention Your Name by Davis, George & Kent, 1943 ....**3.00**

I Never Met A Beautiful Girl, 'Til I Met You by Jerome & Schwartz, 1912 (Cover Artist, Pfeiffer) **10.00**

I Never See Maggie Alone by Harry Tilsley & Everett Lynton, 1926...**3.00**

I Never Slept A Wink Last Night by Andy Razof & Nat Simon, 1934..**3.00**

I Never Wanted Anything So Good, So Bad by Cobb & Edwards, 1914 (Cover Artist, Pfeiffer) **12.00**

I Never Was Nearer Heaven In My Life by Edgar Leslie, Grant Clarke & Ted Snyder, 1916...**5.00**

I Only Found You For Somebody Else by Charles Newman & Isham Jones, 1932 ....**3.00**

I Only Have Eyes For You by Al Dubin & Harry Warren, 1934 ....**3.00**

I Owe $10.00 To O'Grady by Harry Kennedy, 1887 (Pre 1900 & Irish) ..**15.00**

I Owe You by Hartman & Goodhart, 1930, Movie: Dangerous Dan McGrew, Photo Helen Kane **6.00**

I Paid My Income Tax Today by Irving Berlin, 1942 (Irving Berlin) **5.00**

I Passed By Your Window by Helen Taylor & May H. Brahe, 1921 .....**3.00**

I Poured My Heart Into A Song by Irving Berlin, 1939, Movie: Second Fiddle, Photo Sonja Henie, Tyrone Power & Rudy Vallee (Cover Artist, Im-Ho & Irving Berlin) **8.00**

I Ran All The Way Home by Benny Benjamin & George Weiss, 1951, Photo Eddy Howard **3.00**

I Really Don't Want To Know by Howard Barnes & Don Robertson, 1958 ....**3.00**

I Remember When by Ed Sarche & Percy Haid, 1951, Photo The Song Smiths **6.00**

I Remember You by Johnny Mercer & Victor Schertzinger, 1942, Movie: The Fleet's In, Photo Dorothy Lamour, Jimmy Dorsey & Betty Hutton **5.00**

I Remember You by Vincent Bryan & Harry Von Tilzer, 1908, Photo Louise Dresser (Cover Artist, Gene Buck) **12.00**

I Remember You From Somewhere by Edgar Leslie & Harry Warren, 1930 ....**3.00**

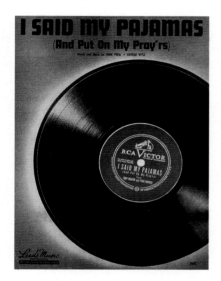

I Said My Pajamas And Put On My Pray'rs by Eddie Pola & George Wyle, 1950 (Cover Artist, Holley) **3.00**

I Said No by Frank Loesser & Jule Styne, 1941, Movie: Sweater Girl, Photo Eddie Bracken, June Preisser & Betty Jane Rhodes **3.00**

I Saw A Star Tonight by Lester O'Keefe & William Stickles, 1939 ......**3.00**

I Saw Her Standing There by John Lennon & Paul McCartney, 1963, Photo The Beatles **30.00**

I Saw Mommy Kissing Santa Claus by Tommie Connor, 1952 ....**5.00**

I Saw Stars by Seigler, Goodhart & Hoffman, 1934 ....**3.00**

I Say It's Spinach by Irving Berlin, 1932, Musical: Face The Music (Cover Artist, Leff & Berlin) **6.00**

I Says To Myself, Says I, Says I–There's The One For Me by Jack Yellen & Harry Akst, 1929, Movie: Bulldog Drummond, Photo Ronald Coleman (Cover Artist, Barbelle) **12.00**

I Scream, You Scream, We All Scream For Ice Cream by Howard Johnson, Billy Moll & Robert King **10.00**

I See A Tree by Michael Hodges, 1936 ....**3.00**

I See The Moon by Meredith Wilson, 1953, Photo The Mariners **3.00**

I See Your Face Before Me by Howard Dietz & Arthur Schwartz, 1937, Musical: Between The Devil **5.00**

I Send You My Heart by Liza Lehmann, 1912 ....**5.00**

I Sent My Wife To The 1,000 Isles by Al Jolson, 1916 (Al Jolson) **10.00**

I Should Care by Sammy Cahn, Axel Stordahl & Paul Weston, 1944, Movie: Thrill Of A Romance, Photo Esther Williams, Van Johnson & Tommy Dorsey (Cover Artist, Barbelle) **5.00**

I Should Have Met You A Long Time Ago by Brown & Paley, 1913 (Cover Artist, Pfeiffer) **10.00**

I Simply Can't Resist You by Hobart & Hoffman, 1906 ....**5.00**

I Sing A Little Tenor by Linton & Gilroy, 1902 ....**5.00**

I Sing All My Love Songs To You by Ingraham & Hoffman, 1930 .....**3.00**

I Sing Of Love by Cole Porter, 1948, Musical: Kiss Me Kate **3.00**

I Still Feel The Same About You by Don Reid & Dick Manning, 1950, Photo Georgia Gibbs **3.00**

I Still Get A Thrill Thinking Of You by Benny Davis & J. Fred Coots, 1930, Photo Francis Craig **3.00**

I Still Get A Thrill Thinking Of You by Benny Davis & J. Fred Coots, 1930, Photo Bert Lown & His Orchestra **5.00**

I Still Get Jealous by Sammy Cahn & Jule Styne, 1948, Musical: High Button Shoes **5.00**

I Still Love To Kiss You Goodnight by Walter Bullock & Harold Spina, 1937, Movie: 52nd Street, Photo Ian Hunter, Pat Paterson, Leo Carrillo, Ella Logan & Many Other Stars **10.00**

I Still Love You by Jack Yellen & Milton Ager, 1928 ....**5.00**

I Surrender Dear by Gordon Clifford & Harry Harris, 1931, Photo Bing Crosby **5.00**

I Talk To The Trees by Alan J. Lerner & Frederick Loewe, 1951 ....**3.00**

I Taut I Taw A Puddy-Tat by Alan Livingston, Billy May & Warren Foster, 1950 ....**6.00**

I Taut I Taw A Puddy-Tat by Livingston, May & Foster, 1950, Photo Sylvester The Cat & Tweety Bird **5.00**

I Think I Like You by Bricusse, 1967, Movie: Doctor Doolittle, Photo Rex Harrison **3.00**

I Think I Oughtn't To Any More by Alfred Bryan, 1907 (Transportation) **10.00**

I Think Of You by Jack Elliot & Don Marcotte, 1941 ....**4.00**

I Think We've Got Another Washington, And Wilson Is His Name by George Fairman, 1917 (WWI & President) **25.00**

I Thought About You by Johnny Mercer & Jimmy Van Heusen, 1939 (Transportation) **5.00**

I Thought I Heard Somebody Calling Me by Irving Jones, 1898 (Pre 1900) **15.00**

I Threw A Kiss Into The Ocean by Irving Berlin, 1942 (Cover Artist, Im-Ho & Irving Berlin) **5.00**

I Told Them All About You by Cliff Friend, 1927, Photo Smalle & Robertson (Cover Artist, Stocker) **5.00**

I Told You So by Lew Brown & Albert Von Tilzer, 1920 (Blues) **5.00**

I Tore Up Your Picture When You Said Good-Bye by Dolly Morse & Andrew Donnelly, 1928 ....**5.00**

I Touched A Star by Allan Roberts, Buddy Bernier & Jerome Brainin, 1940, Movie: Gay New Orleans **6.00**

I Tried To Raise My Boy To Be A Hero by Huston, 1916 (Cover Artist, Pfeiffer & WWI) **15.00**

I Understand by Jim Gannon & Mabel Wayne, 1941, Photo Tommy Dorsey **4.00**

I Understand Just How You Feel by Pat Best, 1953 ....**3.00**

I Used To Be Afraid To Go Home In The Dark by Williams, Van Alstyne & Burt, 1908 (Cover Artist, DeTakacs) **10.00**

I Used To Be Colored Blind by Irving Berlin, 1938, Photo Fred Astaire & Ginger Rogers (Irving Berlin) **16.00**

I Used To Live In Dreamland With Someone Just Like You by Beth Slater Whitson & Jack Glogau, 1913 (Cover Artist, Rose) **10.00**

I Used To Love You But It's All Over Now by Lew Brown & Albert Von Tilzer, 1920 (Cover Artist, Rose Symbol & Blues) **5.00**

I Wake Up Smiling by Edgar Leslie & Fred E. Ahlert, 1933.................**5.00**

I Walk Alone by Herbert W. Wilson, 1943 ....**5.00**

I Walked Back From The Buggy Ride by Adono, Curtsinger & Bibo, 1927...**10.00**

I Wanna Be A Cowboy In The Movies by Sammy Cahn & Jule Styne, 1948, Movie: Two Guys From Texas, Photo Dennis Morgan, Jack Carson & Dorothy Malone **5.00**

I Wanna Be Free by Tommy Boyce & Bobby Hart, 1966, Photo The Monkees **10.00**

I Wanna Be Loved By You by Bert Kalmar, Harry Ruby & Herbert Stothart, 1931, Movie: Three Little Words, Photo Fred Astaire, Red Skelton, Arlene Dahl & Vera Ellen **5.00**

I Wanna Be Loved Like A Baby by Randy Ryan & Sam Wall, 1945....**5.00**

I Wanna Go Home by Jack Joyce & Joe Candullo, 1945, Photo Perry Como (Cover Artist, Nick) **5.00**

I Wanna Go Places And Do Things by Robin & Whiting, 1929, Movie: Close Harmony, Photo Buddy Rogers & Nancy Carroll.................**5.00**

I Wanna Go To The Zoo by Mack Gordon & Harry Revel, 1936, Movie, Stowaway, Photo Shirley Temple (Shirley Temple) **10.00**

I Wanna Go Where You Go, Do What You Do-Then I'll Be Happy by Sidney Clare, Lew Brown & Cliff Friend, 1925, Photo Betty Taylor & Louise Lake (Cover Artist, Leff & Deco) 10.00

I Wanna Sing About You by Cliff Friend & Dave Dreyer **3.00**

I Wanna Wrap You Up, And Take You Home With Me by Remus Harris & Terry Shand, 1939, Photo Blue Barron (Cover Artist, Im-Ho)....**3.00**

I Want A Boy From The U.S.A. by R. H. Unterdorfel, 1911, Photo Larry Dowd & R. H. Unterdorfel (Patriotic & March) **16.00**

I Want A Boy To Love Me by Murphy & Marshall, 1912 (Cover Artist, Pfeiffer & Deco))...**10.00**

I Want A Daddy Who Will Rock Me To Sleep by Philip Bartholomae, John Murray Anderson & A. Baldwin Sloane, 1919, Musical: The Greenwich Village Follies................................**5.00**

I Want A Dixie Sweetheart by Jack Gartland & W. C. Polla, 1919.......**5.00**

I Want A Doll by Ed Moran, Vincent Bryan & Harry Von Tilzer, 1918 (Cover Artist, Pfeiffer) **10.00**

I Want A Girl From Home Sweet Home by Dusenberry & Dennisen, 1914 (Cover Artist, Pfeiffer) **12.00**

I Want A Girl Just Like The Girl That Married Dear Old Dad by Will Dillon & Harry Von Tillzer, 1932, Movie: The Jolson Story, Photo Larry Parks & Evelyn Keyes (Al Jolson) **16.00**

I Want A Girl Just Like The Girl That Married Dear Old Dad by Will Dillon & Harry Von Tilzer, 1909 ....**18.00**

I Want A Little Love From You Dear by Billy Vanderveer & Max Prival, 1916 (Cover Artist, Universal Art Service).......................**5.00**

I Want A Man Like Dad by William Tracey & Gene Cullinan, 1913 (Cover Artist, Callahan) **5.00**

I Want A Military Man by Clement & Stuart, 1900 (Patriotic)............**10.00**

I Want A Postal Card From You by Thomas J. Gray & Fred Fischer, 1908...**5.00**

I Want A Ragtime Bungalow by Bert Kalmar, 1913 (Cover Artist, Pfeiffer & Rag) **10.00**

I Want A Toy Soldier (Cover Artist, Pfeiffer).........................**10.00**

I Want Dem Presents Back by West, 1896 (Pre 1900 & Black, Black Face) **20.00**

I Want My Rib by Dolph Singer & Harry Von Tilzer, 1925 (Cover Artist, Doc Rankin)...**5.00**

I Want My Share Of Love by Chester Cahn & Saul Chaplin, 1939.......**5.00**

I Want Somebody To Cheer Me Up by Gus Kahn & Ted Fiorito, 1935 ..**3.00**

I Want Somebody To Play With by Harry Williams & Egbert Van Alstyne, 1909 (Cover Artist, DeTakacs) **25.00**

I Want Someone To Call Me Dearie by Harry Williams & Egbert Van Alstyne, 1918...**10.00**

I Want Someone To Flirt With Me by Costello & Sterling & Albert Von Tilzer, 1910...**10.00**

I Want Someone Who Hasn't Anyone To Love by Harry McGowan & Sammy Holland, 1912 (Cover Artist, Pfeiffer) **10.00**

I Want The Strolling Good (Cover Artist, Pfeiffer)....................**10.00**

I Want The Twilight And You by Arthur Lamb & Charles H. Maskell, 1920 ....**5.00**

I Want The World To Know I Love You by George M. Cohan, 1907, Musical: The Talk Of New York (George M. Cohan) **15.00**

I Want To Be A Cupid by Holt, 1909 (Cover Artist, Pfeiffer)............**10.00**

I Want To Be A Popular Millionaire by George M. Cohan (George M. Cohan) **15.00**

I Want To Be A Soldier For The U.S.A. by Eva C. Hardy & Adam R. Rocheleau, 1915 (Cover Artist, DeTonnancour, WWI & March) .**15.00**

I Want To Be Good, But They Won't Let Me by Fred Fay & Dreyer (Cover Artist, Pfeiffer & Deco).....................................**12.00**

I Want To Be Happy by Otto Harbach & Irving Caesar & Vincent Youmans, 1924, Musical: No No Nanette.............................**10.00**

I Want To Be In Dixie by Irving Berlin & Ted Snyder, 1912, Photo Kelly & Galvin (Cover Artist, Gene Buck, Irving Berlin & Dixie).........**10.00**

I Want To Be In Dixie by Irving Berlin & Ted Snyder, 1912, Photo McMahon, Diamond & Clemence (Cover Artist, Gene Buck, Irving Berlin & Dixie)...**10.00**

I Want To Be In Georgia When The Roses Bloom Again by Robert Levenson, 1915 (Cover Artist, Pfeiffer) **15.00**

I Want To Be Loved By A Soldier by Fink & Silver, 1918 (Cover Artist, Pfeiffer)..**10.00**

I Want To Be Loved Like A Baby by William Witol, 1922 (Cover Artist, Leff & Deco)..16.00

I Want To Be Loved Like A Leading Lady by Herman Avery Wade, 1908..**5.00**

I Want To Be Miles Away From Ev'ryone, And Just A Little Closer To You by B.G. DeSylva, Lew Brown & Ray Henderson, 1927, Photo The Ipana Troubadours..**5.00**

I Want To Be With You by Bob Rothberg, Adrian Nomis & Ray Block, 1936 ....**3.00**

I Want To Be With You Swan by Fred & Ted Garton, 1916 ....**3.00**

I Want To Dream By The Old Mill Stream by Al Bryan, Jack Meskill & Vincent Rose, 1931...**5.00**

I Want To Go Back To Michigan by Irving Berlin, 1914, Photo McCormack & Irving (Cover Artist, Frew & Irving Berlin).........................**10.00**

I Want To Go To The Land Where The Sweet Daddies Grow by Eddie Moran & Harry Von Tilzer, 1920 (Cover Artist, Barbelle & Deco)..**10.00**

I Want To Go To Tokio by Joe McCarthy & Fred Fisher, 1914, Photo Renie Davies **6.00**

I Want To Go Where You Go by Brown & Friend, Photo Four Jack Roses **8.00**

I Want To Hear A Yankee Doodle Tune by George M. Cohan (George M. Cohan) **15.00**

I Want To Hold Your Hand by The Beatles, 1978 ....**25.00**

I Want To Learn Jazz Dance by Gene Buck & Dave Stamper, 1918, Musical: Ziegfeld Follies, 1918 ....**15.00**

I Want To Learn To Speak Hawaiian by Johnny Noble, 1935 ....**3.00**

I Want To Linger by Stanley Murphy & H. I. Marshall, 1914 (Cover Artist, Starmer & Deco) **12.00**

I Want To Love You While The Music Is Playing by Havez, 1912 (Cover Artist, Pfeiffer) **10.00**

I Want To Marry A Millionaire by Walter Pulitzer **5.00**

I Want To Meander In The Meadow by Harry Woods & Charles Tobias, 1929 ....**3.00**

I Want To See My Tennessee by Jack Yellen & Milton Ager, 1924 .....**5.00**

I Want To Tell Something To Someone by Louis A. LaShier, Photo Louis A. LaShier **6.00**

I Want To Thank Your Folks by Bennie Benjamin & George Weiss, 1947, Photo Perry Como (Cover Artist, Barbelle) **5.00**

I Want What I Want When I Want It by Blossom & Herbert, 1905 ....**5.00**

I Want Yer, Ma Honey by Fay Templeton, 1895 (Pre 1900 & Black, Black Face) **22.00**

I Want You by Brown, 1914 (Cover Artist, Pfeiffer) **10.00**

I Want You by George M. Cohan (George M. Cohan) **15.00**

I Want You Dear Heart To Want Me by Mary M. Hopkins, 1923 ....**5.00**

I Want You For Myself by Irving Berlin, 1931 (Irving Berlin) **8.00**

I Want You, I Need You by Ben Ellison & Harvey Brooks, 1933, Movie: I'm No Angel, Photo Mae West **10.00**

I Want You Mary by Maurice & Joe Solman, 1919 (Cover Artist, W.M. Fisher) **10.00**

I Want You To Meet My Mother by Dubin & Coolidge, 1914 ....**10.00**

I Wants A Man Like Romeo by Robert Adams (Black, Black Face) ...**24.00**

I Wants To Pick A Bone With You by Smith & Bowman, 1904, Sung by Governor Bowen In Vogel's Minstrels, Photo Governor Bowen (Cover Artist, E.S. Fisher & Black, Black Face) **15.00**

I Was A Pilgrim In Loveland by Geo A. Kershaw & Walter Scanlan, 1922 ....**5.00**

I Was Aviating Around by Ren G. May—Pen Name For Irving Berlin (Cover Artist, Pfeiffer & Irving Berlin) **15.00**

I Was Born In Virginia by George M. Cohan, 1933, Movie: Yankee Doodle Dandy, Photo James Cagney & George M. Cohan (George M. Cohan) **15.00**

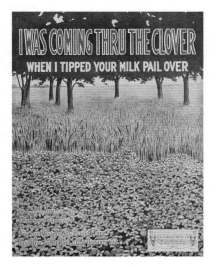

I Was Coming Thru The Clover When I Tipped Your Milk Pail Over by Richard Howard, 1919 ....**8.00**

I Was Doing All Right by Ira & George Gershwin, 1938, Movie: Goldwyn Follies, Photo Adolphe Menjou, Ritz Brothers, Edgar Bergen & Charlie McCarthy **10.00**

I Was Hoping You'd Ask Me by Al Hoffman & Dick Manning, 1958, Photo Janice Harper **5.00**

I Was Lucky by Jack Meskill & Jack Stern, 1935 ....**3.00**

I Was Never Meant For You by Lee Barth & Ruby Lusby, 1912, Big Song Hit From Ed Hutchinson's Stunning Production, A Night On A Roof Garden With Ruby Lusby & Willie Dunlay, Photo Ruby Lusby & Willie Dunlay (Cover Artist, Starmer) **15.00**

I Was Never Nearer Heaven In My Life by Edgar Leslie, Grant Clarke & Ted Snyder, 1916 ....**5.00**

I Was Only A Girl At The Time by Franklin & Green, 1911 (Cover Artist, Pfeiffer) **10.00**

I Was Saying To The Moon by Burke & Johnston, 1936, Movie: Go West Young Man, Photo Mae West **10.00**

I Was So Young by George Gershwin, 1919 ....**5.00**

I Watch The Love Parade by Otto Harbach & Jerome Kern, 1931, Musical: The Cat And The Fiddle **10.00**

I Went Down To Virginia by Sammy Gallop & David Saxon, 1948 .....**3.00**

I Went Home With Michael by Felix McGlennon, 1892 (Pre 1900) ...**15.00**

I Went Out Of My Way by Helen Bliss, 1941 ....**3.00**

I Went To Your Wedding by Jessie Mae Robinson, 1952, Photo Patti Page **8.00**

I Wept, Beloved, As I Dreamed by George Hue, 1911 ....**2.00**

I Whistle A Happy Tune by Richard Rodgers & Oscar Hammerstein II, 1951, Movie: The King And I **8.00**

I Will Always Love You As I Do Today by Herman Kahn & Leo Friedman, 1917 (Cover Artist, Pfeiffer) **12.00**

I Will Love You Always, Just For Auld Lang Syne by Roden, Cuparo & Helf, 1910 (Cover Artist, Pfeiffer) **12.00**

I Will Love You Til The Stars Shall Cease To Shine by L.A. Maxwell & Beatrice A. Bowlby, 1912 ....**4.00**

I Will Love You Till The Old Mill Stream Runs Dry by Jack Frost & James White, 1917 ....**5.00**

I Will Love You When The Silver Threads Are Shining Among The Gold by Roger Lewis & F. Henri Klickmann, 1911 ....**6.00**

I Will Never Change by Cy Coben & Camarata, 1951 ....**4.00**

I Will Wait For Love by Williams & Shaper, 1969, Movie: A Nice Girl Like Me..**3.00**

I Wish by Roberts & Fisher, 1945 ....**5.00**

I Wish I Could Hide Inside This Letter by Charles Tobias & Nat Simon, 1943 ....**5.00**

I Wish I Could Laugh At Love by Mort Dixon, Joe Young & Harry Warren, 1931, Musical: The Laugh Parade (Cover Artist, Gorj)...........**5.00**

I Wish I Didn't Love You So by Frank Loesser, 1947, Movie: Perils Of Pauline, Photo Betty Hutton & John Lund **12.00**

I Wish I Had A Daddy In The White House by Bud Burtson, 1951, Photo Kitty Kallen **8.00**

I Wish I Had A Girl by Gus Kahn & Grace LeBoy, 1907..................**10.00**

I Wish I Had A Sweetheart Like That Old Sweetheart Of Mine by Frank Davis, Sam Braverman & Win Brookhouse, 1941, Photo The Three Suns **3.00**

I Wish I Had My Old Gal Back Again by Jack Yellen, Milton Ager & Lew Pollack, 1926, Photo Sophie Tucker (Cover Artist, Barbelle) **15.00**

I Wish I Had My Old Girl Back Again by Wallace & Macdonald, 1909 ....**6.00**

I Wish I Had Someone To Say Good-bye To by Joe Goodwin, Halsey K. Mohr, 1918 (Cover Artist, DeTakacs & WWI).....................**15.00**

I Wish I Knew by Mack Gordon & Harry Warren, 1945, Movie: Diamond Horseshoe, Photo Betty Grable & Dick Haymes **5.00**

I Wish I Knew by Robert Spencer, Frank Anderson & Harry Bryant, 1922...**5.00**

I Wish I Knew The Name Of The Girl In My Dreams by Allan Roberts & Lester Lee, 1947 Signed Photo Jack Smith (Signed) **4.00**

I Wish I Was In Dixie by C.B. Grobe (Cover Artist, Starmer & Black, Black Face)..**25.00**

I Wish I Was In Heaven Sitting Down by Brown, 1908 (Cover Artist, Pfeiffer & Black, Black Face) **20.00**

I Wish I Were Aladdin by Mack Gordon & Harry Revel, 1935, Movie: Two For Tonight...**5.00**

I Wish I Were Back In Your Arms Tonight by Con Conrad, Sam Lewis & Al Sherman, 1930..**3.00**

I Wish I Were Twins by DeLange, Loesser & Meyer, 1942 ....**5.00**

I Wish You All The Luck In The World by Abe Olman, 1918..............**5.00**

I Wish You Were Jealous Of Me by Earl Haubrick & Glen Rowell, 1926, Photo Marguerite Werner (Cover Artist, Gentle)...........**5.00**

I Wish You Were Jealous Of Me by Earl Haubrick & Glen Rowell, 1926, Photo Grace Aldrich (Cover Artist, Gentle & Deco) **7.00**

I Wish You'd Keep Out Of My Dreams by Grant Clark, Edgar Leslie & Jean Schwartz, 1913 (Cover Artist, Pfeiffer & Deco))...................**10.00**

I Wished On The Moon by Dorothy Parker & Ralph Rainger, 1935, Movie: Big Broadcast 1935, Photo Bing Crosby **8.00**

I Woke Up Too Soon by Dave Franklin, 1934 ....**3.00**

I Won't Be Home Anymore When You Call by Dick Jurgens & Billy Fairman, 1947 ....**4.00**

I Won't Be Home Till August by Alfred Bryan & Albert Gumble, 1910 ....**5.00**

I Won't Believe It Till I Hear It From You by Martin Block, Victor Selsman & J. Russell Robinson, 1938.................................**5.00**

I Won't Dance by Jerome Kern, 1935, Movie: Roberta, Photo Irene Dunne, Ginger Rogers & Fred Astaire **10.00**

I Won't Play Unless You Coax Me by Al Trahern & Lee Orean Smith, 1906, Photo Jessie Mae Hall (Cover Artist, E.F.W.).....................**10.00**

I Won't Say I Will, But I Won't Say I Won't by B.G. De Sylva & George Gershwin, 1923...**10.00**

I Won't Tell A Soul I Love You by Ross Parker & Hughie Charles, 1938, Photo Leighton Noble...**3.00**

I Won't Tell A Soul I Love You by Ross Parker & Hughie Charles, 1938, Photo Barry Wood **3.00**

I Won't Think About Tomorrow by Gorney & Lerner, 1933, Movie: Embarrassing Moments, Photo Chester Morris, Marion Nixon & Walter Woolf...**6.00**

I Wonder As I Wander by John Jacob Niles & Lewis Henry Horton, 1944..**3.00**

I Wonder by Abner Silver, Maceo Pinkard & Benny Davis, 1928 (Cover Artist, R.S. & Deco) **5.00**

I Wonder by Irving Berlin, 1919, Signed Photo Constance Talmadge (Irving Berlin, Deco & Signed)..**15.00**

I Wonder How I Look When I'm Asleep by B. G. DeSylva, Lew Brown & Ray Henderson, 1927 ....**4.00**

I Wonder How The Old Folks Are At Home by Herbert S. Lambert & F. W. Vandersloot, 1909 (Cover Artist, H.J. Dittmar).............10.00

I Wonder, I Wonder, I Wonder by Daryl Hutchins, 1947, Photo Joey Kearns..**3.00**

I Wonder If She's Waiting by Andrew Sterling & Harry Von Tilzer, 1899 (Pre 1900) **15.00**

I Wonder If She's Waiting In Her Old New England Town by Lamb, Reed & Bowers, 1917 (Cover Artist, Pfeiffer & WWI) **15.00**

I Wonder If You Miss Me by Rose & Snyder, 1904 ....**5.00**

I Wonder If You Miss Me Sometimes by Mills & Scott, 1915 (Cover Artist, Pfeiffer)..**10.00**

I Wonder If You Miss Me To-Night by Harry Pease & Ed. G. Nelson, 1928 (Cover Artist, Barbelle) **5.00**

I Wonder If You Still Care For Me by Harry B. Smith, Francis Wheeler & Ted Snyder, 1921 (Cover Artist, Barbelle & Deco)......................**10.00**

I Wonder What He's Doing To-Night by Joe Goodwin & James F. Hanley, 1917 (Cover Artist, Barbelle & WWI) **16.00**

I Wonder What Will William Tell by Allen, 1913 (Cover Artist, Pfeiffer)..**10.00**

I Wonder What's Become Of Joe? by Roy Turk & Maceo Pinkard, 1926, Photo Billy Glason (Deco) **5.00**

I Wonder What's Become Of Sally by Jack Yellen & Milton Ager, 1924, Photo Gus Van & Joe Schenck (Cover Artist, Perret)....................**8.00**

I Wonder What's Become Of Sally by Jack Yellen & Milton Ager, 1924, Photo Al Jolson (Cover Artist, Perret & Al Jolson) **12.00**

I Wonder Where My Baby Is To-Night by Gus Kahn & Walter Donaldson, 1925, Photo Evelyn Hoey (Cover Artist, R.S.)........................**6.00**

I Wonder Where My Easy Rider's Gone by Shelton Brooks, 1913 (Sports) **15.00**

I Wonder Where My Hula Girl Has Gone by Johnny Noble, Treva Bluett & Walter Donaldson, 1938...**5.00**

I Wonder Where My Lovin' Man Has Gone by Earle C. Jones & Richard Whiting, 1914 ....**5.00**

I Wonder Where She Is Tonight by Paul Dresser, 1899 (Pre 1900).....**15.00**

I Wonder Where You Are Tonight by Ritchie, 1911 (Cover Artist, Pfeiffer) **10.00**

I Wonder Who's Dancing With You To-Night by Mort Dixon, Billy Rose & Ray Henderson, 1924 ....**5.00**

I Wonder Who's Kissing Her Now by Hough, Adams & Howard, 1909 ..**5.00**

I Wonder Who's Kissing Her Now by Will M. Hough, Frank R. Adams & Joseph E. Howard, 1947, Movie: I Wonder Whose Kissing Her Now, Photo June Haver **5.00**

I Wonder Who's Next In Your Heart by Chas. K. Harris, 1914 (Cover Artist, Pfeiffer & Deco)..**15.00**

I Wonder Why Bill Bailey Don't Come Home by Fogarty, Woodward & Jerome, 1902 (Black, Black Face)....................................**20.00**

I Wonder Why I Love You by Jack Clifton & Edmund Braham, 1920...**5.00**

I Wonder Why She Kept On Saying Si-Si by Al Jolson, 1918 (Al Jolson)..**10.00**

I Work Eight Hours, I Sleep Eight Hours, That Leaves Eight Hours For Love by Bert Kalmar & Ted Snyder, 1915 ....**5.00**

I Wouldn't Change Dat Gal For No Other by Aubrey Boucicault, 1899 (Pre 1900 & Black, Black Face)..**22.00**

I Wouldn't Change You For The World by Charles Newman & Isham Jones, 1931, Photo Tom Brown...**3.00**

I Wouldn't Do It For Anybody But You by Jack Frost & F. Henri Klickmann, 1919 ....**6.00**

I Wouldn't Steal The Sweetheart Of A Soldier Boy by Herman Paley and Alfred Bryan, 1918 (WWI) **10.00**

I Wrote A Song For You by Dolph Singer & Sam Morrison, 1936, Movie: Summer Wives **8.00**

I Wuv A Wabbit by Milton Berle, Ervin Drake & Paul Martell, 1945 (Cover Artist, Barbelle)..10.00

Ice Palace March by E.T. Paull, 1898 (Cover Artist, E. T. Paull, Pre 1900 & March) **35.00**

Ichabod by Don Raye & Gene DePaul, 1949, Movie: Adventures Of Ichabod Crane & Mr. Toad (Disney) **15.00**

I'd Be A Dreamer by Walter Perkins & Harold Rossiter, 1926 ....**3.00**

I'd Be Lost Without You by Sunny Skylar, 1946, Photo George Paxton ..**4.00**

I'd Be Lost Without You by Sunny Skylar, 1946, Photo Jerry Wald.....**4.00**

I'd Be Lost Without You by Sunny Skylar, 1946, Photo Jimmy Palmer..**4.00**

I'd Be Proud To Be The Mother Of A Soldier, 1918 (WWI)..............**15.00**

I'd Build A World In The Heart Of A Rose by Morton David & Horatio Nichols, 1918...**5.00**

I'd Climb The Highest Mountain If I Knew I'd Find You by Lew Brown & Sidney Clare, 1926 (Cover Artist, Leff)....................**5.00**

I'd Do It All Over Again by Dick Robertson, James Cavanaugh & Frank Weldon, 1945, Photo Frankie Carle **3.00**

I'd Do The Same Thing A Million Times by Sherwood & Rule, 1914 (Cover Artist, Pfeiffer & Deco)....................................**10.00**

I'd Feel At Home If They'd Let Me Join The Army by Albert Gumble, 1918 (WWI)...**10.00**

I'd Give A Million Tomorrows by Milton Berle & Jerry Livingston, 1948, Photo Arthur Godfrey...**6.00**

I'd Give The World To Win The One Who's All The World To Me by Jeff T. Branen & Arthur W. Lange, 1910.....................**12.00**

I'd Know You Anywhere by Johnny Mercer & Jimmy McHugh, 1940, Movie: You'll Find Out, Photo Kay Kyser, Ginny Simms, Peter Lorre, Boris Karloff & Bela Lugosi **10.00**

I'd Leave My Happy Home For You by Will A. Heelan & Harry Von Tilzer, 1899 (Pre 1900 & Black, Black Face) **20.00**

I'd Like To Be In Texas For The Round Up In The Spring by Nick Manoloff, 1932, Photo Happy Chappies Radio Favorites (Cover Artist, L. Kummel) **5.00**

I'd Like To Be Liked By A Nice Little Girl Who'd Like To Be Liked By Me by Costello, Marshall, Baer & Ross, 1912 (Cover Artist, Pfeiffer)...**12.00**

I'd Like To Be On An Island With You by Alfred Bryan, Jack Wells & Albert Gumble, 1914 (Cover Artist, Starmer)....................**10.00**

I'd Like To Be Rip Van Winkle, In Rip Van Winkle Town by Edgar Leslie & Pete Wendling, 1919..**5.00**

I'd Like To Be Your Sweetheart by Jones, 1913 (Cover Artist, Pfeiffer)...**10.00**

I'd Like To Build A Little House For You by McDonald & Walker, 1911 (Cover Artist, Pfeiffer) **10.00**

I'd Like To But I Won't by Wynn & Baron, 1910 (Cover Artist, Pfeiffer & Deco) **12.00**

I'd Like To Find Another Girl Like Mary (Cover Artist, Pfeiffer) **10.00**

I'd Like To Give You Something That You've Never Had Before by Melville Collins, 1913 ....**16.00**

I'd Like To Have A Million In The Bank by Herbert Reynolds, Schuyler Greene & Jerome Kern, 1915, Musical: Very Good Eddie (Cover Artist, Malcolm Straus) **15.00**

I'd Like To Make A Million by Walt, Warner & George Weidler, 1949, Photo Nat King Cole...**5.00**

I'd Like To Meet Your Father by M. E. Rourke & Jerome Kern, 1907.**5.00**

I'd Like To Rock A Cradle by Harry F. Kissell, 1924 ....**6.00**

I'd Like To See A Little More Of You by George L. Cobb & Gus Edwards, 1906 ....**5.00**

I'd Like To See It All, Wouldn't You? by Jeff Godfrey, 1909 ....**5.00**

I'd Like To See Samoa Of Samoa by Walter Bullock & Harold Spina, 1937, Movie: 52nd Street **5.00**

I'd Like To See The Kaiser With A Lily In His Hand by Henry Lewis, Howard Johnson & Billy Frisch, 1918, Musical: Doing Our Bit, Photo Henry Lewis (WWI)..**15.00**

I'd Like To Spend A Honeymoon With You by Nelson, Gideon & Davis, 1915 (Cover Artist, Pfeiffer) **10.00**

I'd Like To Take You Away by Smith & Riesenfeld, 1919 (Cover Artist, Barbelle)...**5.00**

I'd Like To Teach The World To Sing by B. Backer, B. Davis, R. Cook & R. Greenaway, 1971 ....**3.00**

I'd Like To Wander Back Again To Kidland by White & Livernash, 1917 (Cover Artist, Pfeiffer & Deco)....................................**10.00**

I'd Love To Call You My Sweetheart by Joe Goodwin, Larry Shay & Paul Ash, 1926, Photo Wardell & LaCoste (Cover Artist, A. Lekberg & Deco) **6.00**

I'd Love To Call You My Sweetheart by Paul Ash, Joe Goodwin & Larry Shey, 1926, Photo Eddie Cantor (Eddie Cantor).........................**12.00**

I'd Love To Dance An Old Fashioned Waltz by Fairman & Cohen, 1918 (Cover Artist, Pfeiffer) **10.00**

I'd Love To Fall Asleep And Wake Up In My Mammy's Arms by Sam M. Lewis, Joe Young & Fred E. Ahlert, 1920 (Black, Black Face) **10.00**

I'd Love To Live In Loveland With A Girl Like You by W. R. Williams, 1947, Photo Bing Crosby **6.00**

I'd Love To Live In Loveland With A Girl Like You by W. R. Williams, 1910, Photo Maud Lambert................................**12.00**

I'd Love To Live In Loveland With A Girl Like You by W. R. Williams, 1910, Photo Grace Wilson................................**12.00**

I'd Rather Be A Country Girl by Harry Tobias, 1915 (Cover Artist, Pfeiffer) **10.00**

I'd Rather Be A Lobster Than A Wise Guy by Edward Madden & Theodore F. Morse, 1908 ....**10.00**

I'd Rather Be Kissed 'Neath A Mistletoe Bough, Than Spoon Under Any Old Tree by Farran & Osborne, 1913 (Cover Artist, Pfeiffer).......**15.00**

I'd Rather Be Outside A Looking In Than On The Inside Looking Out by Hamill & Snyder, 1906................................**10.00**

I'd Rather Be The Girl In Your Arms by Harlan Thompson & Harry Archer, 1926 (Cover Artist, JVR & Deco)................................**6.00**

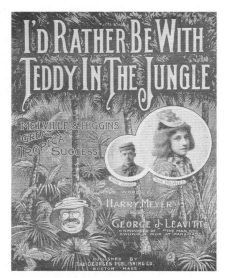

I'd Rather Be With Teddy In The Jungle by Harry Meyer & George J. Leavitt, 1909, Photo Robt. Higgins & Mae Melville.............10.00

I'd Rather Float Through A Dreamy Old Waltz With, You, You, You by Norton, 1908................................**5.00**

I'd Rather Have A Girlie Than An Automobile by Dillon, 1908 (Transportation) **15.00**

I'd Rather Have You by Abner Silver & Alan Walker, 1930................**4.00**

I'd Rather Lead A Band by Irving Berlin, 1936, Movie: Follow The Fleet, Photo Fred Astaire & Ginger Rogers (Irving Berlin)................**15.00**

I'd Rather Listen To Your Eyes by Harry Warren, 1935, Movie: Shipmates Forever, Photo Dick Powell & Ruby Keeler................**10.00**

I'd Rather Two Step Than Waltz, Bill! by Benjamin Hapgood Burt, 1907 (Cover Artist, DeTakacs)................................**12.00**

I'd Rather Write A Song by George M. Cohan (George M. Cohan)....**10.00**

I'd Still Believe You True by Paul Dresser, 1900 ....**10.00**

Ida Belle by Smith & Duke, 1952................................**3.00**

Ida Clare (I Declare) by Karl Lenox, 1907................................**5.00**

Ida I Do by Isham Jones & Gus Kahn, 1925 (Cover Artist, Perret).......**6.00**

Ida, Sweet As Apple Cider by Eddie Leonard & Eddie Munson, 1932, Photo Eddie Leonard & Benny Goodman (Black, Black Face).....**15.00**

Idaho by Jesse Stone, 1942, Photo Alvino Rey **2.00**

Idol Dreams by George Gershwin, 1920 ....**5.00**

Idol Of Erin, The by Maxwell Driscoll, 1923 (Irish)................................**5.00**

If by Robert Hargreaves, Stanley Damerell & Tolchard Evans, 1934, Photo Vic Damone (Cover Artist, Nick)................................**3.00**

If by Robert Hargreaves, Stanley J. Damerell & Tolchard Evans, 1934, Photo Perry Como (Cover Artist, Nick)................................**3.00**

If by Robert Hargreaves, Stanley J. Damerell & Tolchard Evans, 1934, Photo Jo Stafford (Cover Artist, Nick)................................**3.00**

If A Girl Like You Loved A Boy Like Me by Will D. Cobb & Gus Edwards, 1905, Photo Dorothy Russell................................**10.00**

If A Girl Like You Loved A Boy Like Me by Will D. Cobb & Gus Edwards, 1905, Photo Frances Savage................................**10.00**

If A Mother's Prayers Are Answered, Then I Know You'll Come Back To Me by Paul B. Armstrong & F. Henri Klickmann, 1918 (WWI)...**15.00**

If A Rooster Can Love So Many Chickens Can't A Man Love More Than One by Alfred Bryan & Geo. W. Meyer, 1912 (Cover Artist, Rose)...........**20.00**

If A Wish Could Make It So by Otto Harbach, Oscar Hammerstein II & Herbert Stothart, 1920, Musical: Tickle Me................................**3.00**

If All The Stars Were Diamonds by Frank Bentz & Henry E. Geehl, 1908................................**6.00**

If All The Stars Were Pretty Babies by Billy Rose & Fred Fisher, 1927..**6.00**

If Dreams Come True by J. Will Callahan & Will B. Morrisson, 1912 (Cover Artist, Floyd Crew)................................**5.00**

If Dreams Were Only True by Pulford & Dailey, 1912 ....**5.00**

If Ever I Forget You by Frank Tannehill Jr. & Maurice Barron, 1913.**12.00**

If Ever I Would Leave You by Frederick Loewe & Alan Jay Lerner, 1960, Movie: Camelot................................**3.00**

If Every Girl Was A Girl Like You by Will A. Heelan & Seymour Furth, 1909, Photo Dorothy Morton (Cover Artist, Starmer) **10.00**

If Every Girl Were A Beautiful Rose by Heinzman, 1908................................**5.00**

If Every Star Was A Little Pickaninny by Joe McCarthy & Leo Edwards, 1913 (Black, Black Face) **20.00**

If He Can Fight Like He Can Love, Good Night, Germany! by Grant Clarke, Howard E. Rogers & Geo W. Meyer, 1918, Photo Ray Samuels, War Edition (Cover Artist, Rose & WWI) **15.00**

If He Cared by Clifford Grey & Herbert Stothart, 1929, Movie: Devil May Care................................**5.00**

If He Looks Good To Mother Don't Look For Another by Meyer, 1913..**5.00**

If I Can't Have You by Alfred Bryan & Geo. Meyer, 1929, Movie: Footlights And Fools, Photo Colleen Moore (Deco)................................**12.00**

If I Can't Have You by Walter Donaldson, 1927 ....**5.00**

If I Cared A Little Bit Less by Berkeley Graham & Carley Mills, 1942, Photo Four Ink Spots................................**3.00**

If I Cared For Someone Else by Alfred Bryan, Jimmy V. Monaco & Pete Wendling, 1927 ....**6.00**

If I Catch The Guy Who Wrote Poor Butterfly by M.K. Jerome & Arthur Green, 1916 ....**8.00**

If I Catch The Man That Taught Her To Dance by William J. Scanlon, 1882 (Pre 1900) **15.00**

If I Could Be With You One Hour Tonight by Henry Creamer & Jimmy Johnson, 1949, Movie: Flamingo Road, Photo Joan Crawford & Zachary Scott................................**6.00**

If I Could Blot Out The Past by Gussie L. Davis, 1896 (Pre 1900) **15.00**

If I Could Gain The World By Wishing, I Would Only Wish For You by Gardenier & Brockman, 1918 (Cover Artist, Pfeiffer & Deco) **10.00**

If I Could Have You Now by Bryan & Wells, 1913 (Cover Artist, Pfeiffer)................................**12.00**

If I Could Hear Your Voice Again, 1897 (Pre 1900) **15.00**

If I Could Live To Love You by Paul Benedex & Alfred Solman, 1914.**5.00**

If I Could Make You Care by Brown & Kornspan, 1930................................**3.00**

If I Could Peep Thru The Window Tonight by Joe McCarthy, Gus Van & Joe Schenk, 1918 (Cover Artist, DeTakacs & WWI)................................**15.00**

If I Could Tell You by Isabelle Firestone, 1943 ....**4.00**

If I Could Write A Song by Neil Sedaka & Howard Greenfield, 1971 ..**2.00**
If I Didn't Care by Jack Lawrence, 1939.................................**3.00**
If I Don't Get You I'll Get Your Sister by Robert Lewis & Roy Barton, 1911, Photo Lew Roberts **5.00**
If I Ever Love Again by Russ Carlyle & Dick Reynolds, 1949 ....**5.00**
If I Find Spanish Joe From Mexico Oh-o-o-o! Oh o-o-o! by Lew Brown & Lewis F. Muir, 1915 ....**6.00**
If I Find The Girl by Herbert Reynolds, Schuyler Greene & Jerome Kern, 1915, Musical: Very Good Eddie (Cover Artist, Malcolm Strauss) ..**15.00**
If I Forget by Alfred Anderson & DeKoven Thompson, 1911 (Cover Artist, Bescardi Co.) **12.00**
If I Forget You by Irving Caesar, 1933...............................**3.00**
If I Give My Heart To You by Jimmie Crane, Al Jacobs & Jimmy Brewster, 1953, Photo Doris Day..............................**5.00**
If I Give My Heart To You by Jimmy Crane, Al Jacobs & Jimmie Brewster, 1954, Photo Monica Lewis **5.00**
If I Had A Dozen Hearts by Paul Francis Webster & Harry Revel, 1945, Movie: The Stork Club, Photo Betty Hutton, Barry Fitzgerald, Don DeFore & Andy Russell **10.00**
If I Had A Girl Like You by Louis W. McDermott, 1930, Photo Rudy Vallee (Deco)..**12.00**
If I Had A Million Dollars by Johnny Mercer & Matt Melneck, 1934, Movie: Transatlantic Merry Go-Round, Photo Gene Raymond, Jack Benny, Frank Parker & Nancy Carroll **5.00**
If I Had A Son For Each Star In Old Glory by J.E. Dempsey & Joseph A. Burke, 1917, Photo Brice & King (Cover Artist, Rose & WWI)...**15.00**
If I Had A Talking Picture Of You by B.G. DeSylva, Lew Brown & Ray Henderson, 1929, Movie: Sunny Side Up, Photo Janet Gaynor.....**10.00**
If I Had A Thousand Lives To Live by Solman & McGuire, 1908........**5.00**
If I Had A Wishing Ring by Marla Skelton & Louis Alter, 1945, Movie: Breakfast In Hollywood..................................**8.00**
If I Had A Wishing Ring by Shelton & Alter, 1945, Movie: Breakfast In Hollywood, Photo Tom Breneman, Bonita Grandville & Andy Russell **5.00**
If I Had My Choice Of The World's Pretty Girls by Robert F. Roden & J. Fred Helf, 1909 (Cover Artist, Jenkins) **10.00**
If I Had My Life To Live Over by Henry Tobias, Moe Jaffe & Larry Vincent, 1948, Photo Buddy Clark..............................**10.00**
If I Had My Life To Live Over by Henry Tobias, Moe Jaffe & Larry Vincent, 1948, Photo Kate Smith **5.00**
If I Had My Way by Lou Klein & James Kendis, 1913 (Cover Artist, Pfeiffer & Deco) **12.00**
If I Had My Way by Lou Klein & James Kendis, 1913, Photo Bing Crosby (Cover Artist, Barbelle) **12.00**
If I Had My Way by Lou Klein & James Kendis, 1913, Photo Rudy Vallee (Cover Artist, Barbelle) **12.00**
If I Had My Way by Lou Klein & James Kendis, 1913, Photo Woody Herman (Cover Artist, Barbelle) **6.00**
If I Had Never Loved You by Kusik & Becaud, 1972, Movie: The Deadly Trap, Photo Faye Dunaway **4.00**
If I Had Somebody To Love by Billy Hill & Peter DeRose, 1933, Photo The Sizzlers (Cover Artist, Leff).............................**6.00**
If I Had The World To Give You by J. Hayden Clarendon, 1909..........**3.00**
If I Had You by Edward M. Leonard & Harry Silverman, 1914, Photo & Dedicated To Bertha Leigh Leonard (Dedication) **10.00**
If I Had You by Irving Berlin, 1914 (Irving Berlin)...................**10.00**
If I Had You by Ted Shapiro, Jimmy Campbell & Reg. Connelly, 1928, Prince Of Wales's Favorite Fox Trot (Deco) **10.00**
If I Have To Go On Without You by Harry Woods & Al Dubin, Photo Kate Smith..**5.00**
If I Knew Then What I Know Now by Dick Jurgens & Eddy Howard, 1939, Photo Dick Jurgens **3.00**

If I Knew You Were Comin' Id've Baked A Cake by Al Hoffman, Bob Merrill & Clem Watts, 1950, Photo Eileen Barton **6.00**

If I Knock The L-Out Of Kelly, It Would Still Be Kelly To Me by Sam M. Lewis, Joe Young & Bert Grant, 1916 (Cover Artist, Barbelle & Irish) 18.00

If I Loved You by Oscar Hammerstein II & Richard Rodgers, 1945, Movie: Carousel, Photo Gordon Macrae & Shirley Jones (Cover Artist, BJH) 12.00
If I Loved You More by Charles Newman & J. Fred Coots, 1938.........**3.00**
If I Only Had A Brain by Ray Bolger & E.Y. Harburg, 1939, Movie: Wizard Of Oz, Signed by E.Y. Harburg (Signed)................**25.00**
If I Only Had A Home, Sweet Home by Johns & McDermott, 1907.....**5.00**
If I Only Had A Sweetheart Like You by Mittenthal & Christie, 1910 (Cover Artist, Pfeiffer) **10.00**
If I Only Had You by Harry Pease & Ed. G. Nelson, 1919 (Cover Artist, Pfeiffer)..**10.00**
If I Ruled The World by Leslie Bricusse & Cyril Ornadel, 1963, Photo Tony Bennett **6.00**
If I Should Lose You by Leo Robin & Ralph Rainger, 1935, Movie: Rose Of The Rancho, Photo Gladys Swarthout **10.00**
If I Thought You Wouldn't Tell by Irving Berlin, 1909 (Cover Artist, Pfeiffer & Irving Berlin).................................**12.00**

If I Told You by Otto Harbach, Oscar Hammerstein II, Vincent Youmans & Herbert Stothart, 1923, Musical: The Wildflower......................**8.00**

If I Was A Millionaire by Will D. Cobb & Gus Edwards, 1910 ....**5.00**

If I Were A Bell by Jo Swerling, Abe Burrows & Frank Loesser, 1950, Musical: Guys & Dolls......................**5.00**

If I Were A Carpenter by Tim Hardin, 1966, Photo Johnny Cash & June Carter......................**3.00**

If I Were King by E. Magnus Ingleton, Clifford Grey & I.B. Kornblum, 1926, Musical: Patsy......................**5.00**

If I Were The Ocean And You Were The Shore by Alfred Bryan & Jack Wolfe, 1914 (Cover Artist, Pfeiffer) **10.00**

If I Were You by Buddy Bernier & Bob E. Emmerich, 1938, Photo Sammy Kaye......................**3.00**

If I Were You, I'd Fall In Love With Me by Jack Murray & Sammy Fain, 1929 ....**5.00**

If I'm Dreaming by Al Dubin & Joe Burke, 1929, Movie: Sally **8.00**

If I'm Lucky by Edgar DeLange & Josef Myrow, 1946, Movie: If I'm Lucky, Photo Vivian Blaine, Perry Como, Harry James & Carmen Miranda (Cover Artist, A. Joel Robinson) **5.00**

If I'm Not At The Roll Call, Kiss Mother Good-bye For Me by George L. Boyden, 1918 (Cover Artist, Pfeiffer & WWI)......................**16.00**

If I'm Not At The Roll Call, Kiss Mother Good-Bye For Me by George L. Boyden, 1918, Small War Edition (Cover Artist, Pfeiffer & WWI)..**15.00**

If It Rains-Who Cares by Edgar Leslie & Joe Burke, 1938, Photo Al Donahue (Cover Artist, Cliff Miska)......................**5.00**

If It Takes A Thousand Years by J. Kiern Brennan & Ernest Ball, 1915...**5.00**

If It Wasn't For The Irish & The Jews by Jerome & Schwartz, 1912 (Cover Artist, Pfeiffer & Irish)......................**10.00**

If It Wasn't For You I Wouldn't Be Crying Now by Buddy Fields, Gene Rose, Harold Berg & Herb Wiedoft, 1934, Photo Chas Crafts & Jack Sheehan (Cover Artist, JVR & Deco) **5.00**

If It Weren't For You Dear by Charles Newman, 1928 ....**5.00**

If Love Were All by Martha Lois Wells & William Axt, 1922......................**3.00**

If Loving Is Forgetting by Freeman, 1919 (Cover Artist, Pfeiffer)......**10.00**

If Mothers Could Live On Forever by Harry Tobias, Howard Johnson & Henry H. Tobias, 1937, Signed Photo Bobby Breen (Cover Artist, Barbelle) **5.00**

If Sammy Simpson Shot The Shutes by Moran, 1917 (Cover Artist, Pfeiffer & WWI) **10.00**

If She Was What She Was When She Was Sweet 16 by Branen & O'Keefe, 1914 (Cover Artist, Pfeiffer)......................**12.00**

If Somebody Only Would Find Me by Rida Johnson Young & Victor Herbert, 1924, Musical: Dream Girl (Victor Herbert)......................**6.00**

If Someone Had Told Me by Tobias & DeRose, 1952, Movie: About Face, Photo Gordon Macrae, Phyllis Kirk & Eddie Bracken **5.00**

If That's The Way You Want It, Baby by Charles Tobias, Al Lewis & Harry Tobias, 1943, Photo Hal McIntyre......................**3.00**

If That's What You Want Here It Is by Shepart N. Edmonds, 1920 (Cover Artist, Barbelle & Black, Black Face)......................**15.00**

If That's Your Idea Of A Wonderful Time Take Me Home by Irving Berlin, 1914 (Cover Artist, John Frew & Irving Berlin)......................**12.00**

If The Dreams That I Dream Come True by Wells, Photo Esther Walker ..**5.00**

If The Flowers Could Only Speak by Kenney, 1913......................**5.00**

If The Girl Came Home To You by Jack Caddigan & Chick Story, 1913 ..**5.00**

If The Girls In This World Were Fishes by Winifred White & Harry Jay, 1920, Photo Dottie Ray Greene......................**5.00**

If The Man In The Moon Were A Coon by Fred Fisher, 1905 (Black, Black Face)......................**22.00**

If The Moon Turns Green by Paul Cates & Bernard Hanighen, 1935 ...**4.00**

If The Moon Was A Great Banjo by Gene Buck & Dave Stamper, 1913..**6.00**

If The Rest Of The World Don't Want You, Go Back To Mother And Dad by Alex Gerber & Dave Dreyer, 1923......................**6.00**

If The Rose Could Tell It's Story by Pennington & James, 1913, Photo Frank Lane (Cover Artist, Pfeiffer & Deco)......................**10.00**

If The Waters Could Speak As They Flow by Charles Graham, 1887 (Pre 1900)......................**15.00**

If The Wind Had Only Blown The Other Way by Thomas J. Hewitt, 1916......................**5.00**

If The World Should End Tomorrow, I'd Be Tonight With You by Joe McCarthy & Jimmie V. Monaco, 1915......................**6.00**

If There Is Someone Lovelier Than You by Howard Deitz & Arthur Schwarts, 1934......................**5.00**

If They Don't Stop Making Them So Beautiful by Cobb & Edwards, 1913 (Cover Artist, Pfeiffer & Deco)......................**10.00**

If They Ever Had An Income Tax On Love by Ned Washington & James V. Monaco, 1931, Photo Gus Arnheim **15.00**

If They Ever Put A Tax On Love by Sam Ehrlich & Nat Osborne, 1918 (Cover Artist, Pfeiffer) **15.00**

If They'd Only Move Old Ireland Over Here by Jamie Kelly, Lou Klein & Frank Gilley, 1913 (Irish)......................**5.00**

If This Isn't Love by E.Y. Harburg & Burton Lane, 1946, Movie: Finian's Rainbow (Cover Artist, BJH & Irish)......................**5.00**

If This Rose Told You All It Knows by Theodore Morse, 1910...........**5.00**

If War Is What Sherman Said It Was by Andrew B. Sterling & Albert Gumble, 1915 (WWI & Military Personel)......................**16.00**

If Washington Should Come To Life by George M. Cohan (George M. Cohan) **12.00**

If We Can't Be The Same Old Sweethearts, We'll Just Be The Same Old Friends by Joe McCarthy & Jimmie V. Monaco, 1915 (Cover Artist, Rose Symbol) **10.00**

If We Could Always Live In Dreams by Tracy & Walker, 1914 (Cover Artist, Pfeiffer & Deco)......................**10.00**

If We Could Be A-L-O-N-E by Milton Drake, Al Hoffman & Jerry Livingston, 1950, Photo Fred Waring......................**4.00**

If We Never Should Meet Again by Edgar Leslie & Walter Donaldson, 1929 ....**8.00**

If We Were Alone by Smith, 1912 (Cover Artist, Pfeiffer)......................**10.00**

If We'd Meet The Right One First by W.R. Williams, 1911......................**5.00**

If What You Say Is True by Mack Gordon & Henry Nemo, 1939.........**3.00**

If Winter Comes, Summer Will Come Again by Reginald Arkell & H. M. Tennent, 1922 ....**3.00**

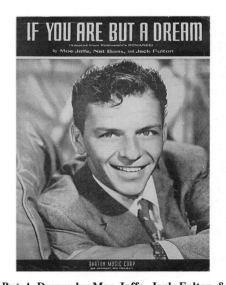

If You Are But A Dream by Moe Jaffe, Jack Fulton & Nat Bonx, 1941, Photo Frank Sinatra......................10.00

If You Are There by F. H. Bishop, 1904 ....**5.00**

If You Believe by Irving Berlin, 1939 (Iriving Berlin) **5.00**

If You Believe In The Fairies by Marion Winton, 1927, Photo Vincent St. John (Cover Artist, M.E. Cramer & Irish).......................................**8.00**

If You Believed In Me by L. Wolfe Gilbert & Abel Baer, 1929 (Cover Artist, Pud)..**5.00**

If You Build A Better Mousetrap by Johnny Mercer & Victor Schertzinger, 1942, Movie: The Fleet's In, Photo Dorothy Lamour & Helen O'Connell...**6.00**

If You Can't Get A Girl In The Summertime, You'll Never Get A Girl At All by Bert Kalmar & Harry Tierney, 1915, Photo Jack Ryan & Harry Tierney (Cover Artist, Barbelle)...**12.00**

If You Can't Have The Girl Of Your Dreams by Young & Warren, 1930...**5.00**

If You Can't Sing It You'll Have to Swing It by Sam Coslow, 1936, Movie: Rhythm On The Range **5.00**

If You Cared For Me As I Care For You by Ed Rose & Ted Snyder, 1908 (Cover Artist, Etherington)..**12.00**

If You Could Care by Arthur Wimperis & Herman Darewski, 1949, Movie: Task Force, Photo Jane Wyatt & Gary Cooper..................**10.00**

If You Don't Think So You're Crazy by Roy Turk & J. Russel Robinson, 1922 (Cover Artist, Frederick S. Manning & Deco).....................**15.00**

If You Don't Want Me by Irving Berlin, 1913, Photo Belle Baker (Cover Artist, Pfeiffer & Irving Berlin)...**10.00**

If You Don't Want Me by Irving Berlin, 1913, Sung by Clark & Bergman in Jesse Laskey's Trained Nurse, Photo Clark & Bergman (Cover Artist, Pfeiffer & Irving Berlin)...**12.00**

If You Ever Get Lonely by Gus Kahn & Henry Marshall, 1916...........**5.00**

If You Forget by F. E. Weatherly & Clara Schleifforth, l899, Music Supplement Of The New York Journal And Advertiser, Sunday, August 18, 1901 (Cover Artist, P. Stanlaws & Pre 1900).....................**10.00**

If You Had All The World And Its Gold by Bartley Costello, Harry Edelheit & Al Piantadosi, 1916 (Cover Artist, Starmer) **10.00**

If You Had All The World And Its Gold by Bartley Costello, Harry Edelheit & Al Piantadosi, 1916, Signed Photo Eva Tanguay (Signed) **25.00**

If You Had All The World And Its Gold by Harry Edelheit, Bartley Costello & Al Piantadosi, 1916, Photo Perry Como (Cover Artist, Nick) **3.00**

If You Knew Susie by B.G. DeSylva & Joseph Meyer, 1944, Movie: The Eddie Cantor Story, Photo Eddie Cantor (Eddie Cantor & Black, Black Face) **20.00**

If You Knew Susie Like I Know Susie by B.G. DeSylva, 1925, Musical: Big Boy, Photo Al Jolson (Al Jolson) **20.00**

If You Look In Her Eyes by Otto Harbach & Louis A. Hirsch, 1917..**10.00**

If You Love Me by Geoffrey Parsons, Edith Piaf & Marguerite Monnot, 1949, Signed Photo Vera Lynn (Signed)....................................**8.00**

If You Only Had My Disposition by Chas. McCarron & Albert Von Tilzer, 1915 (Cover Artist, DeTakacs)..**15.00**

If You Please by Johnny Burke & Jimmy Van Heusen, 1943, Movie: Dixie, Photo Bing Crosby & Dorothy Lamour...........................**10.00**

If You Saw All That I Saw In Arkansas by Will J. Harris & Milton Ager, 1917 ....**6.00**

If You Saw What I Saw You'd Go To Utah by Howard Patrick, 1917..**8.00**

If You See Sally by Gus Kahn, Ray Egan & Walter Donaldson, 1927 (Cover Artist, JVR)...**5.00**

If You Talk In Your Sleep, Don't Mention My Name by A. Seymour Brown & Nat D. Ayer, 1911...**5.00**

If You Want The Rainbow by Ed Rose & Mort Dixon, 1928 ....**5.00**

If You Want To Linger Longer by George Getsey, Roy Ingraham & Olson, 1922..**5.00**

If You Want To Make A Hit With The Ladies, Tell Them They're Beautiful by Edgar Leslie, Bert Kalmar & Harry Ruby, 1919 (Cover Artist, Frederick S. Manning)...**15.00**

If You Were Mine by Al Bryan & Geo W. Meyers, 1929, Movie: Twin Beds **5.00**

If You Were My Girl by O.E. McFarland, 1932, Photo Irma Glen (Deco)...**5.00**

If You Were Only Mine by Charles Newman & Isham Jones, 1932 .....**3.00**

If You Were The Only Girl by Clifford Grey & Nat D. Ayer, 1939, Movie: The Vagabond Lover, Photo Rudy Vallee.......................**10.00**

If You Were The Only Girl by Clifford Grey & Nat D. Ayer, 1939, Photo Perry Como **10.00**

If You Were The Opening Rose by Thomas J. Hewitt, 1916................**5.00**

If You Won't Be Good To Me by Feist & Corin, 1908.......................**5.00**

If You Would Care For A Lonely Heart by Arthur J. Lamb & W. C. Polla, 1920 ....**5.00**

If You'll Be A Soldier, I'll Be A Red Cross Nurse by Harry Tierney, 1918 (WWI & Red Cross)...**25.00**

If You'll Come Back by Eugene West, Otis Spencer & Rubey Cowan, 1920 (Cover Artist, Barbelle) **5.00**

If You'll Say "Yes" Cherie by Ray Noble, 1934................................**3.00**

If You'll Smile by Fahey, 1919 (Cover Artist, Pfeiffer).....................**10.00**

If You're Crazy About The Women You're Not Crazy At All by Edgar Leslie, Albert Bryan & Harry Ruby, 1918 ....**5.00**

If You're In Love You'll Waltz by Harry Tierney & Joseph McCarthy, 1929, Movie: Rio Rita, Photo Bebe Daniels & John Boles...........**10.00**

If You're Irish Come Into The Parlor by Shaun Glenville & Frank Miller, 1946 (Irish) **5.00**

If You're Looking For A Sweetheart, What's The Matter With Me? by Maurice Porcelain, 1909...**10.00**

If You're Only Fooling 'Round Me, Why Don't You Put Me Wise by George J. Bennett, 1920, Photo Mollie King **5.00**

If You've Never Been In Dreamland You've Never Been In Love by Marvin Lee, Roger Graham & May Hill, 1917......................................**6.00**

Ike For Four More Years by Irving Berlin, 1956 (Irving Berlin, President & Political) **25.00**

Ike, Mr. President, Photo of White House, 1953 (Political & President) ..**25.00**

Il Bacio, The Kiss by Luigi Ardite, 1940 ....**5.00**

Il Est Revenu–Mon Soldat by Loic Le Gouriadec, 1916 (Cover Artist, E.S. Fisher)...**10.00**

Il Trovatore Waltz, 1908 (Cover Artist, Pfeiffer)...............................**10.00**

I'll Always Be In Love With You by Herman Ruby, Bud Green & Sammy Stept, 1929, Movie: Syncopation, Photo Morton Downey...........**12.00**

I'll Always Be Mother's Boy by Bud Green & Sammy Stept, 1929, Movie: Mother's Boy, Photo Morton Downey **8.00**

I'll Always Be Waiting For You by Henry Bergman, Jack Curtis & Newton Alexander, 1919 (Lithograph W.F. Powers Co., Inc., N.Y.)....**12.00**

I'll Always Keep A Corner In My Heart For Tennessee by Grant Clarke & Walter Donaldson, 1920 (Cover Artist, Rose Symbol)...................**6.00**

I'll Always Love You by Jerry Livingston & Ray Evans, 1950, Movie: My Friend Irma Goes West, Photo John Lund, Corinne Calvet, Diana Lynn, Dean Martin, Jerry Lewis & Marie Wilson **10.00**

I'll Always Remember September by Al Hoffman, Al Goodhart & Ed Nelson, 1931..**3.00**

I'll Always Remember You by Jack Caddigan & Billy Coty, 1917 (Deco)...**15.00**

I'll Anchor My Ship In Your Harbor Of Love by Hughes & Richardson, 1915 (Cover Artist, Pfeiffer) **12.00**

I'll Await My Love by Howard, 1883 (Pre 1900 & Transportation)....**15.00**

I'll Be A Pal To Your Boy by Alfred Bryan, Al Sherman & Harry Blythe, 1928 ....**5.00**

I'll Be A Santa Claus To You by Gene Buck & Louis A. Hirsch, 1915, Musical: Ziegfeld Follies 1915 (Cover Artist, DeTakacs) **15.00**

I'll Be A Soldier Boy by James Thatcher, 1915 (WWI).....................**12.00**

I'll Be Around by Alec Wilder, 1942, Photo Mills Brothers.................**3.00**

I'll Be Back In Dear Old Dublin, The Day That Ireland's Free by Francis X. Foley & Jerry Maloney, 1920 (Cover Artist, E.S. Fisher & Irish)....**10.00**

I'll Be Blue Just Thinking Of You by Richard Whiting & Pete Wendling, 1930, Photo Jan Garber **6.00**

I'll Be Dreaming Of To-Morrow by H.I. Moore & Irving Gilbert, 1920 (Cover Artist, Pfeiffer) **10.00**

I'll Be Faithful by Ned Washington & Allie Wrubel, 1933, Photo Jack Fulton (Cover Artist, Leff) **3.00**

I'll Be Glad To Get Back by Martin Swauger, R.A. Wilson & W. C. Polla, 1919 (Lithograph, Knapp Co.) **10.00**

I'll Be Happy When The Preacher Makes You Mine by Sam M. Lewis, Joe Young & Walter Donaldson, 1919...**10.00**

I'll Be Hard To Handle by Bernard Dougall & Jerome Kern, 1933, Movie: Roberta (Deco) **10.00**

I'll Be Home For Christmas by Kim Gannon, Walter Kent & Buck Ram, 1956, Photo Bing Crosby **5.00**

I'll Be In My Dixie Home Again To-Morrow by Roy Turk & J. Russell Robinson, 1922 (Cover Artist, Barbelle & Dixie)................12.00

I'll Be In My Dixie Home Again To-Morrow by Roy Turk & J. Russell Robinson, 1922, Musical: Make It Snappy, Photo Eddie Cantor (Eddie Cantor & Dixie)..**10.00**

I'll Be Rich When I Marry You by Joseph McCarthy & Charles Marshall, 1919 ....**5.00**

I'll Be Seeing You by Irving Kahal & Sammy Fain, 1938, Photo Freddy Martin **5.00**

I'll Be Seeing You by Irving Kahal & Sammy Fain, 1938, Photo Hildegarde **5.00**

I'll Be There by Arthur Swanstrom, Albert Sirmay & Arthur Schwartz, 1930, Musical: Princess Charming..**6.00**

I'll Be There, Laddie Boy, I'll Be There by Jack Frost & E. Clinton Keithley, 1918 (WWI)...**15.00**

I'll Be Thinking Of You by Al Hoffman & Dick Manning, Photo Merv Griffin **3.00**

I'll Be True To My Honey Boy by George Evans, 1894 (Pre 1900)....**15.00**

I'll Be Waiting In The Gloaming, Sweet Genevieve by J. Fred Helf, 1905 (Dixie)...**10.00**

I'll Be Walkin' With My Honey by Buddy Kaye & Sam Medoff, 1945 ....**3.00**

I'll Be Welcome In My Home Town by Tracey & Jentens, 1912 (Cover Artist, Pfeiffer)...**10.00**

I'll Be With You In Apple Blossom Time by Neville Fleeson & Albert Von Tilzer, 1920, Dedicated to Mme Emma Trentini (Cover Artist, R.S. & Dedication)..10.00

I'll Be With You In Apple Blossom Time by Neville Fleeson & Albert Von Tilzer, 1920, Movie: Buck Privates, Photo Andrews Sisters...**5.00**

I'll Be With You When The Clouds Roll By by The Three White Kuhns, Robert, Paul & Charles, 1922, Photo Joe Whitaker (Cover Artist, Starmer) **5.00**

I'll Be With You When The Roses Bloom Again by Will D. Cobb & Gus Edwards, 1901 ....**5.00**

I'll Be Your Own by Bush, 1900 (Transportation).............................**10.00**

I'll Be Your Regular Sweetie by Fred Rose, George Little & Peter S. Frost, 1920 (Cover Artist, Knapp Co.) **10.00**

I'll Be Your Valentine by John Murray Anderson, Arthur Swanstrom & A. Baldwin Sloane, 1920, Musical: The Greenwich Village Follies Of 1920 (Deco)..**10.00**

I'll Bring A Rose by Richard Coburn & Vincent Rose, 1920 (Cover Artist, Frederick S. Manning)..**15.00**

I'll Build A Bungalow by Oscar Hammerstein II & Herbert Stothart, 1922, Musical: Daffy Dill...**5.00**

I'll Build A Little Cabin Where The Swanee River Flows by Ballard MacDonald & Harry Plan, 1912 ....**5.00**

I'll Build A Stairway To Paradise by Gershwin, DeSylva & Gershwin, 1922, Movie: An American In Paris, Photo Gene Kelly & Leslie Caron **10.00**

I'll Buy That Dream by Herb Magidson & Allie Wrubel, 1945, Movie: Sing Your Way Home, Photo Marcy McGuire, Glenn Vernon, Jack Haley & Ann Jeffreys **5.00**

I'll Buy The Ring by Ed Rose, Wm. Raskin & Jack Mills, 1919 ....**5.00**

I'll Capture Your Heart Singing by Irving Berlin, 1942, Movie: Holiday Inn, Photo Bing Crosby, Danny Kaye, Rosemary Clooney & Vera Ellen (Irving Berlin) **10.00**

I'll Change Your Shadows To Sunshine by Griffith, 1912 ....**5.00**

I'll Close My Eyes by Buddy Kaye & Billy Reed, 1945, Signed Photo Dinah Shore (Signed) **3.00**

I'll Close My Eyes by Buddy Kaye & Billy Reid, 1945, Signed Photo Sammy Kaye..**3.00**

I'll Close My Eyes To Everyone Else by Nick Kenney, Arthur Terker & Peter Tinturin, 1934, Photo Phil Levant **3.00**

I'll Close My Eyes To The Rest Of The World And Dream Sweet Dreams Of You by Cliff Friend, 1929 ....**5.00**

I'll Come Back To You by F. Berberich, C.P. Goewey & H.L. Earnshaw, 1914 ....**10.00**

I'll Come Back To You When It's All Over by Lew Brown & Kerry Mills, 1917, Photo Dorothy Meuther (WWI) **16.00**

I'll Come Back When The Autumn Leaves Are Falling by Carl O. Peterson, 1908..**5.00**

I'll Dance At Your Wedding by Frank Loesser & Hoagy Carmichael, 1941, Movie: Mr. Bug Goes To Town **5.00**

I'll Dance At Your Wedding by Herb Magidson & Ben Oakland, 1947, Photo Tony Martin..**5.00**

I'll Dance At Your Wedding by Herb Magidson & Ben Oakland, 1947, Photo Lenny Herman..**5.00**

I'll Do It All Over Again by A. Seymour Brown & Albert Gumble, 1914 (Cover Artist, Starmer)..**5.00**

I'll Fly to Hawaii by Davis & Schuster, 1926 ....**5.00**

I'll Follow My Secret Heart by Noel Coward, 1934, Romantic Comedy: Conversation Piece (Cover Artist, Jorj)..**10.00**

I'll Follow You by Melville J. Gideon, 1912, Signed Photo of Rock & Fulton (Signed) **10.00**

I'll Forget You by Annelu Burns & Ernest R. Ball, 1920 ....**6.00**

I'll Get By As Long As I Have You by Roy Turk & Fred E. Ahlert, 1928 (Cover Artist, Leff & Deco) **12.00**

I'll Get You Some Day by Jack Stern, Clarence Marks & Nora Lee Haymond, 1921 ....**5.00**

I'll Give A Penny For Your Thoughts, 1909 (Cover Artist, Pfeiffer) ..**10.00**

I'll Give The Gold In My Heart For The Diamonds In Your Eyes by Lamb & Edwards, 1912 (Cover Artist, Pfeiffer) **12.00**

I'll Give The World For You by Katharine Bainbridge & J.S. Zamecnik, 1925 ....**15.00**

I'll Go Home With Bonnie Jean by Alan J. Lerner & Frederick Loewe, 1947, Movie: Brigadoon..**5.00**

I'll Go On The Route For You by George M. Cohan, 1909 (Cover Artist, Pfeiffer & George M. Cohan)..**20.00**

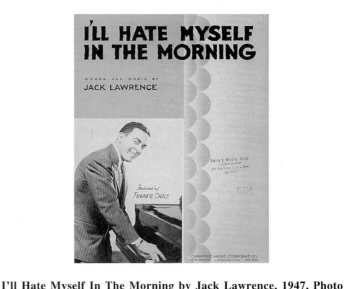

I'll Hate Myself In The Morning by Jack Lawrence, 1947, Photo Frankie Carle **6.00**

I'll Have The Last Waltz With Mother by Harry Tobias, Charles Tobias & Geo J. Bennett, 1934..**4.00**

I'll Have To Telegraph Another Baby by Manley, 1899 (Pre 1900)....**20.00**

I'll Have Vanilla by Redmond Farrar & Arthur Terker, 1934, Photo Eddie Cantor (Eddie Cantor) **10.00**

I'll Hold You In My Heart by Eddy Arnold, Hal Horton & Tommy Dilbeck, 1947, Photo Eddy Arnold..**3.00**

I'll Keep A Warm Spot In My Heart For You by Williams & Walker, 1906 ....**5.00**

I'll Keep On Dreaming by Harry B. Smith & Emmerich Kalman, 1924, Musical: Princess Maritza **6.00**

I'll Keep On Loving You by Richard Coburn & Vincent Rose, 1921 ...**7.00**

I'll Keep The Lovelight Burning by Tobias, Kenny & Levey, 1918, WWI)..**12.00**

I'll Know by Jo Swerling, Abe Burrows & Frank Loesser, 1950, Musical: Guys & Dolls..**5.00**

I'll Love You All Over Again by Harry Pease, H. Edeheit & F. Mayo .**3.00**

I'll Love You Just The Same by Leighton & Leighton & Harry Ellis, 1907, Photo The Quartette..**5.00**

I'll Love You More For Losing You A While by Raymond Egan & Richard Whiting, 1918 (WWI)..**12.00**

I'll Make That Black Gal Mine by D. Reed & C.B. Ward, 1896 (Pre 1900 & Black, Black Face)..**16.00**

I'll Miss You In The Evening by Irving Berlin, 1932 (Irving Berlin)....**5.00**

I'll Never Ask For More by Roy Turk & Fred Ahlert, 1928 ....**3.00**

I'll Never Fall In Love Again by Jimmie Currie, 1962, Photo Tom Jones..**3.00**

I'll Never Have To Dream Again by Charles Newman & Isham Jones, 1932, Photo Mark Fisher **3.00**

I'll Never Hear You Sing Again Old Comin' "Thro" The Rye by Dudley & Wilkins, 1915 (Cover Artist, Pfeiffer)..**10.00**

I'll Never Leave You by Arthur Swanstrom, Albert Sirmay & Arthur Schwartz, 1930, Musical: Princess Charming **5.00**

I'll Never Let A Day Pass By by Victor Schertzinger, 1941, Movie: Kiss The Boys Goodbye, Photo Mary Martin **5.00**

I'll Never Love Again by Al Stewart & Ignacio Fernandez Esperon, 1904, Photo Andy Russell **5.00**

I'll Never Love Again by Al Stewart & Ignacio Fernandez Esperon, 1920, Signed Photo Dennis Day..................................**5.00**

I'll Never Love Another Girl But You by Geo. A. Nichols, 1900 ....**5.00**

I'll Never Say "I Love You" by Allan Roberts & Lester Lee, 1947, Movie: Sign Of The Ram, Photo Susan Peters **6.00**

I'll Never Say Never Again, Again by Harry Woods, 1935..................**3.00**

I'll Never Smile Again by Ruth Lowe, 1941, Movie: Las Vegas Nights, Photo Pied Pipers & Frank Sinatra.....................................**5.00**

I'll Never Stop Loving You by Gus Kahn & Nicholas Brodszky, 1954 ....**3.00**

I'll Only Remember Your Love by Walker & Cookie, 1929 ....**5.00**

I'll Pray For You by Kim Gannon & Arthur Altman, 1942, Photo Freddy Martin **5.00**

I'll Pray For You by Kim Gannon & Arthur Altman, 1942, Photo Teddy Powell **5.00**

I'll Put My Lips Against Yours Anytime by Thos. S. Allen, 1911, (Cover Artist, Pfeiffer)..**15.00**

I'll Remember April by Don Raye, Gene de Paul & Pat Johnston, 1941...**3.00**

I'll Say She Does by Bud DeSylva, Gus Kahn & Al Jolson, 1918, Photo Al Jolson (Al Jolson) **15.00**

I'll See You Again by Noel Coward, 1929, Musical: Bitter Sweet......**16.00**

I'll See You In C-U-B-A by Irving Berlin, 1920, Musical: The Jazz King, Photo Ted Lewis (Cover Artist, R.S. & Irving Berlin)...................**15.00**

I'll See You In My Dreams by Gus Kahn & Isham Jones, 1924, Photo Dave Bernie (Deco) **10.00**

I'll See You In The Sunrise by Marie Calabrese, 1946, Signed by Marie Calabrese (Signed)..**12.00**

I'll See You Thru by Art Kassell & Charles Newman, 1929 ....**5.00**

I'll Settle Down In A Small Country Town, 1914 (Cover Artist, Pfeiffer)..**10.00**

I'll Share All My Play Toys With You by Lindeman & Behrend, 1911 (Cover Artist, Pfeiffer) **10.00**

I'll Share It All With You by Irving Berlin, 1946, Movie: Annie Get Your Gun (Irving Berlin)..**5.00**

I'll Show You A Regular Time by Smith & Krause, 1913 (Cover Artist, Pfeiffer)..**10.00**

I'll Show You Little Girl, I'm Game by Daniel Hanifen & Bernard H. Smith, 1915...**6.00**

I'll Sing You A Thousand Love Songs by Warren & Dubin, 1936, Movie: Cain And Mabel, Photo Clark Gable & Marion Davies..16.00

I'll Sit Right On The Moon by Jimmie V. Monaco, 1912 (Cover Artist, DeTakacs)...**10.00**

I'll Still Belong to You by Brown & Eliscu, 1930, Movie: Whoopee, Photo Eddie Cantor (Eddie Cantor)......................................**8.00**

I'll String Along With You by Al Dubin & Harry Warren, 1934, Movie: Twenty Million Sweethearts, Photo Dick Powell & Ginger Rogers (Cover Artist, Jorg)...**8.00**

I'll Take An Option On You by Leo Robin & Ralph Grainger, 1933....**3.00**

I'll Take Care Of Your Cares by Mort Dixon & James V. Monaco, 1927..**5.00**

I'll Take Romance by Oscar Hammerstein II & Ben Oakland, 1937, Movie: I'll Take Romance, Photo Grace Moore **5.00**

I'll Take You Back To Italy by Irving Berlin, 1917 (Irving Berlin).......**5.00**

I'll Take You Back To Panama by E.J. Meyers & Will Dylmage, 1914 (Cover Artist, Starmer) **5.00**

I'll Take You Home Again Kathleen by Thomas P. Westendorf, 1935, Photo Sammy Kaye (Cover Artist, NPS) **5.00**

I'll Take You Home Again Kathleen by Thomas P. Westendorf, 1944, Photo Mark Fisher (Irish) **5.00**

I'll Take You Home Again Kathleen by Thomas P. Westendorf, 1944 (Cover Artist, Marilyn & Irish) **6.00**

I'll Take You Home Again Pal O'Mine by Harold Dixon & Claude Sacre, 1922, Photo John Steel **5.00**

I'll Teach You How by James Kendis & Herman Paley, 1908, Photo Madge Fox (Cover Artist, DeTakacs) **10.00**

I'll Tell The Man In The Street by Lorenz Hart & Richard Rodgers, 1938, Movie: I Married An Angel **5.00**

I'll Tell The World by Harold B. Freeman, 1919, Photo Mary Pickford (Cover Artist, Leo Sielke, Jr.).......................................**15.00**

I'll Tell Your Mother On You by Collin Coe, 1895 (Pre 1900)...........**15.00**

I'll Wait For Thee by Wm. R. Macaulay & Thos. S. Allen, 1904.........**7.00**

I'll Wait For You In Dreamland by Sigurdson & Baker (Cover Artist, Pfeiffer)..**10.00**

I'll Walk Alone by Sammy Cahn & Jule Styne, 1944, Movie: Follow The Boys, Photo Dinah Shore (WWII).....................................**10.00**

I'll Walk Alone by Sammy Cahn & Jule Styne, 1944, Movie: Follow The Boys, Photo Jimmy Palmer **5.00**

I'll Walk Alone by Sammy Cahn & Jule Styne, 1944, Movie: With A Song In My Heart, Photo Susan Hayward (WWII).......................**5.00**

I'll Walk Beside You by Edward Lockton & Alan Murray, 1941..........**5.00**

I'll Wed The Girl I Left Behind by Will A. Dillon, 1916 (WWI)........**10.00**

I'll Wed You In The Golden Summertime by Alfred Bryan, 1902........**5.00**

Illusion by Bob Russell & S.T. Gallagher, 1946, Photo Xavier Cugat...**4.00**

Illusion by L. Wolfe Gilbert & Carlo Neve, 1914 ....**5.00**

Illusions by Hollander, 1948, Movie: A Foreign Affair, Photo Marlene Dietrich, Jean Arthur & John Lund **8.00**

I'm A Bad Bad Man by Irving Berlin, 1946, Movie: Annie Get Your Gun (Irving Berlin)...**5.00**

I'm A Big Girl Now by Hoffman, Drake & Livingston, 1946, Photo Sammy Kaye...**5.00**

I'm A Bringing Up The Family by Franklin & Green, 1909 (Cover Artist, Pfeiffer)..**12.00**

I'm A Devil With The Ladies by Carl Muller & Vin Plunkett, 1918 (Cover Artist, E.S. Fisher) **10.00**

I'm A Dreamer, Aren't We All by B. G. DeSylva, Lew Brown & Ray Henderson, 1929, Movie: Sunny Side Up, Photo Janet Gaynor.....**10.00**

I'm A Dreamer That's Chasing Bubbles by Frank Magine & Geo. A. Little, 1919 (Cover Artist, Wohlman & Deco) **12.00**

I'm A Dumb-Bell by Irving Berlin, 1921 (Irving Berlin)......................**5.00**

I'm A Fool To Care by Ted Daffon, Photo Les Paul & Mary Ford **5.00**

I'm A Happy Go Lucky Fellow by Leigh Harline & Ned Washington, 1947, Movie: Fun And Fancy Free (Disney)................................**15.00**

I'm A Jazz Man by Rogers & Williams, 1903......................................**10.00**

I'm A Little Teapot by Clarence Kelley & Geo. H. Sanders, 1941, Photo Ronnie Kemper..**3.00**

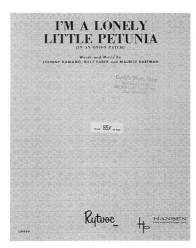

I'm A Lonely Little Petunia In An Onion Patch by Johnny Kamons, Billy Faber & Maurice Hartman, 1946 ....4.00

I'm A Lonesome Melody by Geo W. Meyer & Joe Young, 1915, Photo Jewell Sisters (Cover Artist, Barbelle & Deco).............................**10.00**

I'm A Lonesome Melody by Joe Young & Geo. W. Meyer, 1915, Photo Claire Rochester (Cover Artist, Barbelle & Deco).......................**10.00**

I'm A Long Way From Tipperary by Roger Lewis & Ernie Erdman, 1914, Photo Carl McCulough (Cover Artist, Starmer, WWI & Irish) **10.00**

I'm A Longin' Fo' You by Karl Fuhrmann & Jane Hathaway, 1914, Transportation) **16.00**

I'm A Lover Of Paree by Robin & Rainger, 1933, Movie: The Way To Love, Photo Maurice Chevalier & Ann Dvorak.........................**10.00**

I'm A Member Of The Midnight Crew by Jean Schwartz, 1909 ....**5.00**

I'm A Nurse For Aching Hearts by Gene Buck & Louis A. Hirsch, 1915, Movie: Ziegfeld Follies 1915 (Cover Artist, DeTakacs)................**10.00**

I'm A Sentimental Dreamer by Dailey Paskman & Mel B. Kaufman, 1921 ....**6.00**

I'm A Twelve O'Clock Feller In A Nine O'Clock Town by Whiting & Kalmer, 1917 (Cover Artist, Pfeiffer) **10.00**

I'm A-Comin' A-Courtin' Corabelle by Charles Newman & Allie Wrubel, 1947 ....**4.00**

I'm Afraid Of The Beautiful Girls by George McConnell, 1916 ....**5.00**

I'm Afraid Of You by Al Bryan & Albert Gumble, 1910 (Cover Artist, Starmer) **5.00**

I'm Afraid To Come Home In The Dark by Harry Williams & Egbert Van Alstyne, 1907...**10.00**

I'm Afraid To Love You by Harry Stride, Bert Douglas & Pat McCarthy, 1946, Photo Mills Brothers...**3.00**

I'm All A-Twitter by Robin & Whiting, 1929, Movie: Close Harmony, Photo Nancy Carroll & Buddy Rogers **6.00**

I'm All Alone by Jack Coale & Frank Anderson, 1922 ....**5.00**

I'm All Bound 'Round With The Mason Dixon Line by Sam M. Lewis, Joe Young & Jean Schwartz, 1917, Photo Harry Fox (Cover Artist, Barbelle, Dixie & Deco)..**12.00**

I'm All Dressed Up And No Place To Go by Allen & Daly, 1913 (Cover Artist, Pfeiffer)..**12.00**

I'm All Eyes For Ida by Klein, 1931, Photo Eddie Cantor (Eddie Cantor)..**10.00**

I'm Alone Because I Love You by Joe Young & John Siras, 1930, Photo Kate Smith...**16.00**

I'm Alone Because I Love You by Joe Young & John Siras, 1930, Signed Photo Belle Baker (Signed) **10.00**

I'm Alone by Al Herman, 1915 (Cover Artist, Pfeiffer) **10.00**

I'm Alright by Loggins, 1980, Movie: Caddyshack, Photo Bill Murray, Rodney Dangerfield & Chevy Chase **3.00**

I'm Always Chasing Rainbows by Joseph McCarthy & Harry Carroll, 1918, Movie: The Dolly Sisters, Photo Betty Grable, June Haver & John Payne..**10.00**

I'm Always Home On Sunday by Welch & Burke, 1911 (Cover Artist, Pfeiffer)..**10.00**

I'm Always In Love With Someone by Geo Graff & Ernest Ball, 1921, Movie: Happy Cavalier, Photo Fiske O'Hara **5.00**

I'm Always Watching The Clouds Roll By by Al Piantadosi, 1910 ......**3.00**

I'm An Indian Too by Irving Berlin, 1946, Movie: Annie Get Your Gun (Irving Berlin)..**5.00**

I'm An Old Cowhand by Johnny Mercer, 1936, Movie: Rhythm On The Range, Photo Bing Crosby **5.00**

I'm An Unemployed Sweetheart by Edgar Leslie, Ned Washington & James V. Monaco, 1931 ....**5.00**

I'm At The Mercy Of Love by Benny Davis & J. Fred Coots, 1936, Musical: Cotton Club Parade...**10.00**

I'm At Your Service Girls by Edward Grossmith & Ted D. Ward, 1916, Photo Julian Eltinge (Cover Artist, DeTakacs) **12.00**

I'm Away From The World When I'm Away From You by Sidney Clare & Lew Pollack, 1921 ....**5.00**

I'm Awfully Glad I Met You by Jack Drislane & Geo W. Meyer, 1909 ..**5.00**

I'm Awfully Glad I'm Irish, 1910 (Cover Artist, Pfeiffer & Irish) **10.00**

I'm Awfully Strong For You by George M. Cohan (George M. Cohan) ..**10.00**

I'm Back In Love Again by Cliff Friend, 1927 ....**4.00**

I'm Beginning To See The Light by Harry James, Duke Ellington, Johnny Hodges & Don George, 1944, Photo Eileen Barton........................**6.00**

I'm Beginning To See The Light by Harry James, Duke Ellington, Johnny Hodges & Don George, 1944, Signed Photo Harry James (Signed)..**10.00**

I'm Bringing A Red-Red Rose by Gus Kahn & Walter Donaldson, 1928, Musical: Ziegfeld Production Whoopee, Photo Eddie Cantor (Cover Artist, Nickel & Eddie Cantor)..**16.00**

I'm Bugs About You, 1910 (Cover Artist, Pfeiffer).........................**10.00**

I'm Building A Bridge To Ireland, 1916 (Cover Artist, Pfeiffer & Irish)...**10.00**

I'm Building A Palace In Palestine by Richard Howard, 1916, Photo Clara Kimball Young (Cover Artist, Pfeiffer) **12.00**

I'm Building A Sailboat Of Dreams by Cliff Friend & Dave Franklin, 1939, Photo Guy Lombardo (Cover Artist, Im-Ho) 5.00

I'm Building Up To An Awful Let-Down by Johnny Mercer & Fred Astaire, 1935, Signed Photo Fred Astaire (Signed).......................**10.00**

I'm Certainly Living A Ragtime Life by Gene Jefferson & Robert S. Robert, 1900 (Rag) **15.00**

I'm Climbing Up A Rainbow by Edward G. Nelson & Harry Pease, 1930, Movie: The Big Party, Photo Sue Carol, Dixie Lee & Jack Smith **10.00**

I'm Coming Back To California That's Where I Belong by J. Keirn Brennan & Ernest Ball, 1916 ....**5.00**

I'm Coming Back To Dixie And You by Lyons, Yosco & Mullane (Dixie) **8.00**

I'm Coming Back To You by Chas. K. Harris & Byrd Dougherty, 1913 ..**5.00**

I'm Coming Back To You Maybe by Ted Lewis & Ernest Golden, 1921, Musical: Greenwich Village Follies, Photo Ted Lewis (Cover Artist, Wohlman & Deco)...**10.00**

I'm Coming Home by Tom Post & Frank Magine, 1917 (WWI) **10.00**

I'm Confessin' That I Love You by Neiburg, Dougherty & Reynolds, 1930, Photo Dinah Shore...**8.00**

I'm Counting On You by Milton Drake & Ben Oakland, 1934 (Cover Artist, Jorj)...**6.00**

I'm Crazy About It by Jim Stanford, 1914 (Cover Artist, Pfeiffer & Deco) **10.00**

I'm Crazy 'Bout My Baby by Alexander Hill & Thomas Waller, 1931, Photo Larry Funk (Cover Artist, Barbelle).......................**5.00**

I'm Crazy 'Bout The Turkey Trot by Joe Goodwin, Geo W. Meyer, 1911, Photo Anna Chandler (Cover Artist, Pfeiffer)...............**10.00**

I'm Crying Just For You by Joe McCarthy & James V. Monaco, 1913.**5.00**

I'm Doing What I'm Doing For Love by Jack Yellen & Milton Ager, 1929 ....**5.00**

I'm Done With Rag-Time by Fred Stein & Chas. Robinson, 1900 (Rag) ..**10.00**

I'm Forever Thinking Of You by Lillian Fitzgerald & Clarence Senna, 1919 (Cover Artist, Rolph Armstrong & Lithograph, Knapp).......**20.00**

I'm Getting Corns For My Country by Jean Barry & Dick Charles, 1944, Movie: Hollywood Canteen, Photo Andrews Sisters, Jack Benny & Many More Stars (WWII) **6.00**

I'm Getting Ready For My Mother-In-Law by Jack Norworth, 1906 (Transportation)..**10.00**

I'm Getting Sentimental Over You by Ned Washington & George Bassman, 1940 ....**3.00**

I'm Getting So Now I Don't Care by Dave Ringle, 1923, Photo Rudolph Valentino **50.00**

I'm Getting Tired So I Can Sleep by Irving Berlin, 1942, Movie: This Is The Army, Lt. Ronald Reagan In Cast, Photo Corporal Dave Breger (Irving Berlin, WWII, Military Personnel & President).................**12.00**

I'm Glad For Your Sake by Peter Tinturin & Jack Lawrence, 1938 ......**3.00**

I'm Glad I Can Make You Cry, Gus Hill's Minstrels by Charles R. McCarron & Carey Morgan, 1918, Photo Bessie Hamilton & Gus Hill & Alice Joyce & Evart Overton (Cover Artist, Starmer & WWI).......**10.00**

I'm Glad I Can Make You Cry, Gus Hill's Minstrels by Charles R. McCarron & Carey Morgan, 1918, Photo Alice Joyce & Evart Overton & Fred Freddy (Cover Artist, Starmer & WWI) **10.00**

I'm Glad I Can Make You Cry, Gus Hill's Minstrels, by Charles R. McCarron & Carey Morgan, 1918, Photo Gus Hill, Miss Kraemer of Dealy & Kraemer & Alice Joyce & Evart Overton & Fred Freddy (Cover Artist, Starmer & WWI)...**16.00**

I'm Glad I Waited For You by Sammy Cahn & Jule Styne, 1945, Movie: Tars & Spars, Photo Alfred Drake & Janet Blair (WWII) **10.00**

I'm Glad I'm Married by Albert Von Tilzer, 1908...............................**8.00**

I'm Dreaming Of The Girl I Love by W. A. Lang & May Greene, 1912 (Cover Artist, Pfeiffer) 10.00

I'm Drifting Back To Dreamland by Florence Charlesworth & Charlie Harrison, 1922 ....**4.00**

I'm Falling In Love With Someone by Rida Johnson Young & Victor Herbert, 1910 (Victor Herbert)..**5.00**

I'm Flirting With You by Cliff Friend & Harold Leonard, 1926 ....**3.00**

I'm Following You by Dave Dreyer & Ballard MacDonald, 1929, Movie: It's A Great Life **8.00**

I'm Forever Blowing Bubbles by Jaan Kenbrovin & John William Kellette, 1919, Photo June Caprice **8.00**

I'm Forever Blowing Bubbles by Jaan Kenbrovin & John William Kellette, 1919, Musical: The Passing Show 1918, Colored Painting of Helen Carrington (Cover Artist, Starmer) **16.00**

I'm Glad It Was Only A Dream by Bessie Buchanan & Ernest R. Ball, 1915, Photo Maud Lambert......................................15.00

I'm Glad My Wife's In Europe by Johnson, Goetz & Gottler,1915.......**5.00**

I'm Glad There Is You by Jimmy Dorsey & Paul Madeira, 1942, Photo Jimmy Dorsey...**5.00**

I'm Glad You Are The One You Are by O. E. Story, 1914 ....**5.00**

I'm Glad You're Sorry by Hanlon & Morrissey, 1911 (Cover Artist, Pfeiffer & Deco)..**10.00**

I'm Goin' Back To My Mammy by E. Clinton Keithley, Bonnie Benedict & F. Henri Klickman, 1923 (Black, Black Face & Transportation).....**10.00**

I'm Goin' Shoppin' With You by Al Dubin & Harry Warren, 1935, Movie: Gold Diggers Of 1935...**6.00**

I'm Goin' South by Abner Silver & Harry Woods, 1923, Musical: Bombo, Photo Al Jolson (Al Jolson)...**10.00**

I'm Goin' To Fight My Way Right Back To Carolina by Billy Baskette & Jessie Spiess, 1918 (Cover Artist, DeTakacs & WWI) **15.00**

I'm Goin' To Settle Down Outside Of London Town by Joe McCarthy & James V. Monaco, 1919 ....**7.00**

I'm Going Back To Broadway by Fred E. Mierisch & Chris Smith, 1913, Photo Ulis, Brilant & Ulis (Cover Artist, Pfeiffer & Transportation) ..**22.00**

I'm Going Back To California by J. Keirn Brennan & Ernest R. Ball, 1916..**5.00**

I'm Going Back To Carolina by Billy Downs & Ernie Erdman, 1913, Photo Summers & Morris (Lithograph, Bes Car Di Co., Dixie & Transportation) **15.00**

I'm Going Back To Dixie by Irving Berlin, 1912 (Irving Berlin & Dixie) **15.00**

I'm Going Back To Memphis, Tenn. by Norton & Richards, 1913 (Cover Artist, Pfeiffer).......................................**10.00**

I'm Going Back To My Home Town by Goldie & Harlow, 1916 ....**5.00**

I'm Going Back To My Old Girl by O'Donnell, 1913 ....**5.00**

I'm Going Back To Old Erin by E. Magnus Quist, 1915 (Cover Artist, Pfeiffer & Irish) **15.00**

I'm Going Back To Old Killarney by Harvey & Weasner, 1915 (Cover Artist, Pfeiffer & Irish) **10.00**

I'm Going Back To Old Nebraska by Sherwood & Rule, 1915, Photo Al Jolson (Cover Artist, Pfeiffer & Al Jolson)..................................**15.00**

I'm Going Back To Reno by William Jerome, 1911 ....**5.00**

I'm Going Back To The Farm by Irving Berlin, 1915, Photo Dave Ferguson (Irving Berlin) **12.00**

I'm Going Back To The Girl I Love by Max Clay, 1915 (March).......**10.00**

I'm Going Crazy by Allen, 1910 (Cover Artist, Pfeiffer).....................**12.00**

I'm Going Down To Tennessee by Dorothy Fields & Harry Carroll, 1912 (Cover Artist, Pfeiffer) **10.00**

I'm Going Home To Mobile On The Morgan Line by Leap, 1914 (Cover Artist, Pfeiffer, Deco & Transportation) **20.00**

I'm Going Mad Over You by Gotham Attucks, 1910 (Cover Artist, Pfeiffer) **12.00**

I'm Going Right Back To Chicago by Harry Williams & Egbert Van Alstyne, 1916...**5.00**

I'm Going To Be A Sailor by Wm. Heagney, 1906 (Patriotic)............**10.00**

I'm Going To Bring A Wedding Ring To You In Spring by James White & Jack Frost, 1915, Sung by John McCormack..........................**10.00**

I'm Going To Climb The Blue Ridge Mountains Back To You by Robert Levenson & George B. McConnell, 1919 (Lithograph, W.J. Dobinson Engraving Co.)..**15.00**

I'm Going To Do What I Please by Alfred Bryan & Ted Snyder, 1909 (Cover Artist, Pfeiffer) **10.00**

I'm Going To Follow The Boys by Howard Rogers & James V. Monaco, 1917, Photo Gladys Leslie (WWI) **10.00**

I'm Going To Get Myself A Black Salome by Stanley Murphy & Ed Wynn, 1908 (Cover Artist, Pfeiffer & Black, Black Face) **25.00**

I'm Going To Let The Whole World Know I Love You by Edwards, 1914 (Cover Artist, Pfeiffer) **12.00**

I'm Going To Live Anyhow Till I Die by Shep Edmonds, 1901 ....**10.00**

I'm Going To Pack Myself In Your Arms by Heath, 1926 (Transportation) **6.00**

I'm Going To Stay Right Here In Town by Al Bryan & Al Gumble, 1913 (Cover Artist, Starmer & Transportation) **10.00**

I'm Going To Steal Some Other Fellow's Girl by Lew Brown & Albert Von Tilzer, 1911, Photo Kitty & Fanny Watson (Cover Artist, Hirt) **5.00**

I'm Going To Tell Your Mother by Johnson, 1914 (Cover Artist, Pfeiffer)...**10.00**

I'm Going Way Back Home And Have A Wonderful Time by Wm. Jerome & Jean Schwartz, 1916, Photo Rhoda Bernard (Cover Artist, Barbelle) **10.00**

I'm Gonna Bring A Watermelon To My Girl Tonight by Billy Rose & Con Conrad, 1924, Photo Jan Garber 14.00

I'm Gonna Dance Wit De Guy Dat Brung Me by O'Keefe & Archer, 1927 ....**5.00**

I'm Gonna Knock, Knock, Knock On The Old Front Door by Benny Davis & James F. Hanley, 1922 ....**5.00**

I'm Gonna Let The Bumble Bee Be by Addy Britt & Jack Little, 1926 ....**5.00**

I'm Gonna Live Till I Die by Al Hoffman, Walter Kent & Mann Curtis, 1950, Photo Danny Scholl.......................................**6.00**

I'm Gonna Lock My Heart by Jimmy Eaton & Terry Shand, 1938, Photo Barry Wood (Cover Artist, Merman) **3.00**

I'm Gonna Lock My Heart by Jimmy Eaton & Terry Shand, 1938, Photo Doris Rhodes (Cover Artist, Merman) **3.00**

I'm Gonna Lock My Heart by Jimmy Eaton & Terry Shand, 1938, Photo Kay Kyser (Cover Artist, Merman)...........................**4.00**

I'm Gonna Love That Guy by Frances Ash, 1945, Photo Eddie Stone (Cover Artist, Barbelle & WWII)....................................**5.00**

I'm Gonna Love That Guy by Frances Ash, 1945, Photo Freddy Martin (Cover Artist, Barbelle & WWII)....................................**5.00**

I'm Gonna Make Hay While The Sun Shines In Virginia by Joe Young, Sam Lewis & Archie Gottler, 1916, Photo Lottie Grooper (Cover Artist, Barbelle) **3.00**

I'm Gonna Make Hay While The Sun Shines In Virginia by Joe Young, Sam Lewis & Archie Gottler, 1916, Photo Isabell D'Armond (Cover Artist, Barbelle) **3.00**

I'm Gonna Meet My Sweetie Now by Benny Davis, 1927 ....**3.00**

I'm Gonna Pin A Medal On The Girl I Left Behind by Irving Berlin, 1918 (Irving Berlin)...**10.00**

I'm Gonna Sit Right Down And Write Myself A Letter by Joe Young & Fred E. Ahlert, 1935, Photo Ted Fiorito (Cover Artist, HBK).........**6.00**

I'm Gonna Spend My Honeymoon In Dixie by Howard Rogers & Cecil Arnold, 1919 (Cover Artist, R.S. & Dixie) **5.00**

I'm Gonna Wash That Man Right Outa My Hair by Richard Rodgers & Oscar Hammerstein II, 1949 (Cover Artist, BJH)............................**3.00**

I'm Hans Christian Andersen by Frank Loesser, 1951, Movie: Hans Christian Andersen, Photo Danny Kaye **7.00**

I'm Happy That's All by Jay, 1911, Photo Eva Tanguay (Cover Artist, Pfeiffer)..**16.00**

I'm Happy When I'm By My Baby's Side by Evans & Ward, 1899 (Pre 1900)..**16.00**

I'm Happy When You're Happy by Benny Davis & Abel Baer, 1930..**4.00**

I'm Hatin' This Waitin' Around by Charlie Tobias, Al Lewis & Murray Mencher, 1937, Photo Guy Lombardo & His Royal Canadians **5.00**

I'm Headin' For The Blue Horizon Where The Mountains Meet The Sky by Aston "Deacon" Williams, 1942 (Cover Artist, Barbelle) **3.00**

I'm Hearin' From Erin by L. Wolfe Gilbert & Anatole Friedland, 1917 (Irish) **5.00**

I'm Henry The Eighth I Am by Fred Murray & R. P. Weston, 1965, Photo Herman's Hermits..**3.00**

I'm Hitting The Trail To Normandy, So Kiss Me Goodbye by Charles A. Snyder, 1917 (WWI) **15.00**

I'm Hopelessly In Love With You by Charles Tobias, 1933 ....**6.00**

I'm Hummin' I'm Whistlin' I'm Singin' by Mack Gordon & Harry Revel, 1934, Movie: She Loves Me Not, Photo Bing Crosby....................**8.00**

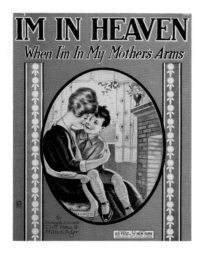

I'm In Heaven When I'm In My Mother's Arms by Howard Johnson, Cliff Hess & Milton Ager, 1920 (Cover Artist, R.S.) 12.00

I'm In Heaven When I'm In Your Arms by Robt. F. Roden, Sam Coslow & Peter Derose, 1919 (Cover Artist, E.E. Walton & Deco)..............**5.00**

I'm In Love Again by Cole Porter, 1925 ....**5.00**

I'm In Love by Sammy Cahn & Jule Styne, 1948, Movie: Romance On The High Seas, Photo Jack Carson, Janis Paige, Don DeFore & Doris Day...**5.00**

I'm In Love With A Girl In Old New Hampshire by Mallory, Cohen & Morrison, 1915, Photo Cole, Russel & Davis (Cover Artist, Pfeiffer).....**10.00**

I'm In Love With Every Girl In The Universe by Herb Sanford, 1965, Photo Miss Universe...**5.00**

I'm In Love With One Of The Stars by George M. Cohan, 1909, Musical: The Man Who Owns Broadway (Cover Artist, Pfeiffer & George M. Cohan))...**20.00**

I'm In Love With Someone by Lew Marcus, 1944 ....**3.00**

I'm In Love With The Rose Of My Dreams by Swan, 1917 (Cover Artist, Pfeiffer)..**10.00**

I'm In Love With You by Paul Titsworth, Lynn Cowan, Donald McNamee & King Zany, 1929, Movie: The Great Garbo.............**15.00**

I'm In The Market For You by Joseph McCarthy & James F. Hanley, 1930, Movie: High Society Blues, Photo Janet Gaynor & Charles Farrell..**12.00**

I'm In The Middle Of A Riddle by E. Ray Goetz & Franz Winkler, 1948, Photo Percy Faith...**4.00**

I'm In The Mood For Love by Dorothy Fields & Jimmy McHugh, 1935, Movie: Every Night At Eight, Photo George Raft, Alice Faye, Frances Langford & Patsy Kelly...**12.00**

I'm Just A Black Sheep by H.H. Dawson, 1929, Photo Jack Jackson (Cover Artist, Pfeiffer) **10.00**

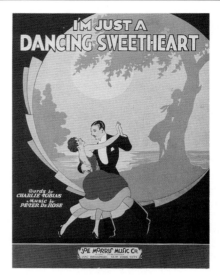

I'm Just A Dancing Sweetheart by Charles Tobias & Peter DeRose, 1931...5.00

I'm Just A Little Blue by Arthur Gillespie & Egbert Van Alstyne, 1922 ..**6.00**

I'm Just A Lonely Little Kid by Jack Norworth & Al Piantadosi, 1922...**5.00**

I'm Just A Sentimental Fool by Frank Mandel, Oscar Hammerstein II & Sigmund Romberg, 1928, Musical: New Moon............................**5.00**

I'm Just A Vagabond Lover by Rudy Vallee & Leon Zimmerman, 1929, Movie: The Vagabond Lover, Photo Rudy Vallee **10.00**

I'm Just Wild About Harry by Sissle & Blake, 1921 ....**5.00**

I'm Keeping Company by Lu Bender, Vee Lawnhurst & Dave Dreyer, 1931..**3.00**

I'm Knee Deep In Daisies by Joe Goodwin, Harold Stanley, Geo. A. Little, Frances Ash & Larry Shay, 1925 ....**6.00**

I'm Knitting A Rosary by Plunkett, 1918 (WWI) **12.00**

I'm Late by Bob Hilliard & Sammy Fain, 1951, Movie: Alice In Wonderland (Disney) **16.00**

I'm Laughing by McNamee & Zany, 1929 ....**3.00**

I'm Learning A Lot From You by Dorothy Fields & Jimmy McHugh, 1930, Movie: Love In The Rough **5.00**

I'm Leaving It All Up To You by Don Harris, 1974, Photo Donny & Marie Osmond **4.00**

I'm Like A Ship Without A Sail by James Kendis & James Brockman, 1919 (Cover Artist, R.S. & Transportation) **5.00**

I'm Livin' Easy by Irving Jones, 1899 (Pre 1900 & Black, Black Face) ..**35.00**

I'm Living A Life Of Shadows by William Witol, 1922.......................**5.00**

I'm Living In The Land Of Dreams by George Fairman, 1921..............**4.00**

I'm Lonesome For My Little Pal by Harold Orlob, 1918 (WWI) ..10.00

I'm Lonesome For You Caroline by Rene Walker & Joe Burke, 1934 (Cover Artist, Cliff Miska & Deco)..**5.00**

I'm Lonesome For You, Dear Old Pal by Ethel & Billie Ritchie, 1922.**5.00**

I'm Longing Always Dear, For You by Caro Roma, 1917 ....**5.00**

I'm Longing For Someone To Love Me by Joseph Howard, 1917 (WWI) **10.00**

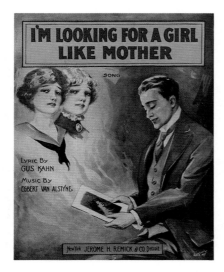

I'm Looking For A Girl Like Mother by Gus Kahn & Egbert Van Alstyne, 1916 (Cover Artist, Einson) 15.00

I'm Looking For A Girl Named Mary by Sammy Stept, 1926..............**6.00**

I'm Looking For A Shady Tree by Greensburg & Jerome, 1914 (Cover Artist, Pfeiffer)..**10.00**

I'm Looking For An Argument by Maurice Porcelain, 1904 (Black, Black Face) **20.00**

I'm Looking Over A Four Leaf Clover by Mort Dixon & Harry Woods, 1927, Photo Art Mooney **5.00**

I'm Looking Over A Four Leaf Clover by Mort Dixon & Harry Woods, 1927, Movie: Jolson Sings Again, Photo Ritz Brothers (Al Jolson)..**15.00**

I'm Loving You (Cover Artist, Pfeiffer)....................................**10.00**

I'm Makin' For Macon In Georgia by Kalmar, 1914 (Cover Artist, Pfeiffer) **12.00**

I'm Makin' Hay In the Moonlight by Seymour & Greer, 1932, Movie: Blessed Event, Photo Dick Powell **5.00**

I'm Making A Bid For Popularity by Harry B. Smith & John Stromberg, 1899 (Pre 1900) **15.00**

I'm Making Believe by Mack Gordon & James V. Monaco, 1944, Movie: Sweet And Low Down, Photo Benny Goodman, Lynn Bari & Jack Oakie..**6.00**

I'm Marching Home To You, Step by Step, Mile By Mile by Abner Silver, Al Sherman & Al Lewis, 1929, Musical: George White's Scandals **10.00**

I'm Mighty Glad I'm Living by George M. Cohan (George M. Cohan)...**10.00**

I'm Missin' Mammy's Kissin' by Sydney Clare & Lew Pollack, 1921 (Black, Black Face) **16.00**

I'm Misunderstood by Compton & Ricca, 1935....................................**3.00**

I'm My Own Grandpaw by Dwight Latham & Moe Jaffe, 1947 ....**3.00**

I'm Needin' You by Young & Little, 1930 ....**3.00**

I'm Nobody's Baby by Benny Davis, Milton Ager & Lester Stanly, 1940, Movie: Andy Hardy Meets Debutante, Photo Judy Garland & Mickey Rooney **25.00**

I'm Not Ashamed Of You Molly, I Want You Just As You Are by Stern, 1914 (Cover Artist, Barbelle & Transportation) **15.00**

I'm Not Jealous by Harry Pease, Ed. G. Nelson & Fred Mayo, 1919, Musical: Good Morning Judge, Photo Molly King **6.00**

I'm Not Jealous by Harry Pease, Ed. G. Nelson & Fred Mayo, 1919, Musical: Sinbad, Photo Farber Sisters (Cover Artist, Barbelle)..............**5.00**

I'm Not Your Steppin' Stone by The Monkees, 1966........................**5.00**

I'm Off For Mexico by J. Will Callahan & F. Henri Klickmann, 1914 (Patriotic) **10.00**

I'm Old Fashioned by Johnny Mercer & Jerome Kern, 1942, Movie: You Were Never Lovelier, Photo Fred Astaire, Rita Hayworth, Adolphe Menjou & Xavier Cugat & His Orchestra **10.00**

I'm On A Long Long Ramble by Sam M. Lewis, Joe Young & Jean Schwartz, 1918, Photo Laura Guerite (WWI) **10.00**

I'm On A See-Saw by Desmond Carter & Vivian Ellis, 1934, Musical: Jack & Jill (Deco)..**3.00**

I'm On Agen With Monaghan And Off Agen With You by R.P. Weston, 1910 ....**5.00**

I'm On My Way by Joe Maxwell (Cover Artist, Pfeiffer & Transportation) **15.00**

I'm On My Way Home by Irving Berlin, 1926 (Cover Artist, Leff & Irving Berlin)..**10.00**

I'm On My Way To Dublin-Bay by Stanley Murphy, 1915, Photo Mary Elizabeth (Cover Artist, Starmer & Irish) **10.00**

I'm On My Way To Mandalay by Al Bryan & Fred Fisher, 1913, Photo Carrie Schenck...**16.00**

I'm On My Way To Reno by William Jerome & Jean Schwartz, 1910 (Cover Artist, Detakacs)...**16.00**

I'm On My Way To Reno by William Jerome & Jean Schwartz, 1910, Photo Mabel Hite (Cover Artist, Starmer)......................................**12.00**

I'm On The Road To Happiness by Sidney Malcolm & Alfred Solman, 1916 ....**5.00**

I'm On The Water Wagon Now by John W. Bratton, 1903, Photo Frank Daniels **5.00**

I'm One Step Ahead Of My Shadow by Sammy Cahn & Saul Chaplin, 1936 ....**5.00**

I'm Only Making Believe by Benny Davis & J. Fred Coots, 1929 (Deco)...**5.00**

I'm Out On The Loose To-Night by Joseph McCarthy & Harry Tierney, Movie: Rio Rita, Photo Bebe Daniels & John Boles.......................**5.00**

I'm Playing With Fire by Irving Berlin, 1932 (Irving Berlin)...............**6.00**

I'm Popeye The Sailor Man by Sammy Lerner, 1934, Movie: Popeye The Sailor, Photo, Popeye, Olive, Wimpy & Bluto...........................**25.00**

I'm Putting All My Eggs In One Basket by Irving Berlin, 1936, Movie: Follow The Fleet, Photo Fred Astaire & Ginger Rogers (Irving Berlin)...**15.00**

I'm Ridin' For A Fall by A. Schwartz, 1943, Movie: Thank Your Lucky Stars, Photo Humphrey Bogart, Errol Flynn & Eddie Cantor (Eddie Cantor)..**15.00**

I'm Ridin' Straight To Heaven by Carroll Loveday & Mac Clifford, 1931 ....**5.00**

I'm Saying Good Bye Tonight by F. H. Branan & M. L. Branan, 1931..**6.00**

I'm Shooting High by Jimmy McHugh, 1963, Photo Lainie Kazan **3.00**

I'm Sittin' High On A Hill Top by Gus Kahn & Arthur Johnston, 1935, Movie: Thanks A Million, Photo Dick Powell..............................**10.00**

I'm Sitting On Top Of The World by Sam M. Lewis, Joe Young & Ray Henderson, 1932, Movie: The Jolson Story, Photo Larry Parks & Evelyn Keyes (Al Jolson) **12.00**

I'm So Glad by Schackman, 1973, Movie: Book Of Numbers, Photo Raymond St. Jacques, Freda Payne & Philip Thomas...........................**3.00**

I'm So Glad Trouble Don't Last Alway by R. Nathaniel Dett, Negro Spiritual, 1919 (Black, Black Face) **5.00**

I'm So Lonesome by Jack Clifton & Edmund Braham, 1920 ....**6.00**

I'm So Melancholy by Ben Ryan & Lou Handman, 1929, Photo Jack Osterman (Cover Artist, Barbelle & Deco)....................................**7.00**

I'm So Sleepy by Harry Kelly, 1905 ....**5.00**

I'm Sorry by Jack Norworth & Albert Von Tilzer, 1906, Musical: About Town, Photo Louise Dresser (Cover Artist, Carter).......**12.00**

I'm Sorry For Myself by Irving Berlin, 1939 (Irving Berlin).......**5.00**

I'm Sorry I Made You Cry by N.J. Clesi, 1918 (Cover Artist, A.H. Keller).......**10.00**

I'm Sorry I Made You Cry by Robert Hood Bowers, 1918.......**6.00**

I'm Sorry Sally by Gus Kahn & Ted Fiorito, 1928 (Cover Artist, JVR & Deco).......**5.00**

I'm Sorry The Day I Laid My Eyes On You by Shelton Brooks, 1915, Signed by E.P. Pfeiffer & Biscardi (Cover Artist, Pfeiffer & Signed).......**22.00**

I'm Stepping Out With A Memory Tonight by Herb Magidson & Allie Wrubel, 1940.......**5.00**

I'm Still Caring by Rudy Vallee & John Klenner, 1929, Signed Photo Rudy Vallee (Cover Artist, Barbelle & Signed).......**16.00**

I'm Sure Of Everything But You by Charles O'Flynn, George Meyer & Pete Wendling, 1923.......**5.00**

I'm Takin' A Shine To You by Herb Magidson & Allie Wrubel, Movie: Radio City Revels, Photo Bob Burns, Milton Berle, Ann Miller, Kenny Baker and Many Other Stars.......**6.00**

I'm Tellin' The Birds–Tellin' The Bees How I Love You by Cliff Friend & Lew Brown, 1926.......**5.00**

I'm The Brother Of Lily Of The Valley by L. Wolfe Gilbert, Anatol Friedland & Henry Lewis, 1918, Musical: Winter Garden Production: Doing Our Bit, Photo & Signed by Henry Lewis (Signed).......**12.00**

I'm The Candy by Harry Graham & Benny Davis, 1904, Music Section New York American And Journal, Sunday, January 14, 1906 (Cover Artist, Eddy).......**10.00**

I'm The Echo by Fields & Kern, 1935, Movie: I Dream Too Much, Photo Lily Pons.......**8.00**

I'm The Good Man That Was So Hard To Find by Bud Green & Al Piantadosi, 1920.......**6.00**

I'm The Greatest Father Of Them All by Jerome, Lilley & Foy, 1955, Movie: The Seven Little Foys, Photo Bob Hope.......**5.00**

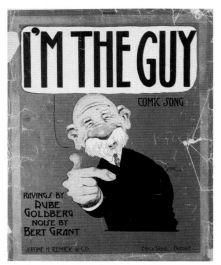

I'm The Guy by Rube Goldberg & Bert Grant, 1912 (Cover Artist, Rube Goldberg).......25.00

I'm The Guy That Paid The Rent For Mrs. Rip Van Winkle by Geo. Fairman, 1914 (Cover Artist, Rose).......**10.00**

I'm The Last One Left On The Corner by Ed Moebus, Fred Whitehouse & Frank Stilwell, 1930.......**3.00**

I'm The Man Who Broke The Bank At Monte Carlo by Fred Gilbert, 1892 (Pre 1900).......**15.00**

I'm Throwing Rice, At The Girl That I Love by Steve Nelson, Ed Nelson Jr. & Eddy Arnold, 1949, Photo Eddy Arnold.......**3.00**

I'm Thru With Love by Gus Kahn, Matt Malneck & Fred Livingston, 1932.......**5.00**

I'm Tickled Pink With A Blue Eyed Baby by Charles O'Flynn & Pete Wendling, 1930, Photo Husk O'Hare (Cover Artist, Leff & Deco)..**3.00**

I'm Tickled To Death That You're Irish by Sam M. Lewis, Joe Young & Walter Donaldson, 1919 (Irish).......**3.00**

I'm Tired by William Jerome & Jean Schwartz, 1901.......**10.00**

I'm Tired Of Being Alone by Bibo, Phillips & Cantor, 1925.......**3.00**

I'm Tired Of Everything But You by Isham Jones, 1925.......**5.00**

I'm Tired Of Making Believe by Kelley, 1928 (Cover Artist, Pfeiffer)..**10.00**

I'm Tying The Leaves So They Won't Come Down by E.S.S. Huntington & J. Fred Helf, 1907, Photo Dave Carter.......**12.00**

I'm Tying The Leaves So They Won't Come Down by E.S.S. Huntington & J. Fred Helf, 1907, Photo Ruth Wright (Cover Artist, Starmer)..**15.00**

I'm Up On A Mountain Talking To The Sky by Abner Silver & Dave Oppenheim, 1930, Photo Rudy Vallee (Cover Artist, Julian Noveno).......**10.00**

I'm Waiting by Elizabeth Dunphy & William J. Short, 1926.......**3.00**

I'm Waiting For Ships That Never Come In by Jack Yellen & Abe Olman, 1919.......**8.00**

I'm Waiting For The Blue Moon To Shine by Williams, 1927.......**6.00**

I'm Waiting For Tomorrow To Come by Frank Davis, Franklin Hawelka & Max Prival, 1919 (Cover Artist, Linder).......**5.00**

I'm Walking Around In A Dream by Ted Lewis, Larry Yoell & Norman Spencer, 1929, Photo Ted Lewis.......**5.00**

I'm Walking Behind You by Billy Reid, 1953 (Cover Artist, Im-Ho)..**3.00**

I'm Wearing My Heart Away For You by Charles K. Harris, 1902, Photo Lillain Lawson (Cover Artist, E. Kornrelch).......**10.00**

I'm Wearing My Heart Away For You by Charles K. Harris, 1902, Photo James A. Doyle (Cover Artist, E.Kornrelch).......**10.00**

I'm Wild About Horns On Automobiles That Go "Ta-Ta-Ta-Ta" by Clarence Gaskill, 1929 (Transportation).......**15.00**

I'm Wingin' Home by Benee Russell & Henry H. Tobias, 1928.......**5.00**

I'm Wishing by Larry Morey & Frank Churchill, 1937, Movie: Snow White (Disney).......**10.00**

I'm With You by Huston, 1918.......**5.00**

I'm With You by Walter Donaldson, 1931.......**5.00**

I'm Yours by Johnny Green & E. Y. Harburg, 1930, Photo Ruth Etting.......**5.00**

I'm Yours by Robert Mellin, 1952.......**3.00**

I'm Yours For The Asking by Bert Kalmar & Harry Ruby, 1937.......**4.00**

Imagination by J. Burke & Jimmy Van Heusen.......**3.00**

Imogene by F. W. Swann & Anita Comfort, 1898, Supplement To The New York World, Sunday, April 29, 1900, Photo Anita Comfort (Cover Artist, Clifton & Pre 1900).......**16.00**

Impecunious Davis by Kerry Mills, 1899 (Pre 1900 & Black, Black Face).......**20.00**

Imperial March And Two Step by Newton B. Heims, 1915 (March)..**10.00**

Imperial Rag by Billie Talbot, 1914 (Rag).......**15.00**

Impossible, Closing Theme Of The Steve Allen-NBC-TV Sunday Night Show by Steve Allen, 1946, Photo Jayne Mansfield, Hal March & Carol Haney.......**5.00**

In A Bamboo Garden by Walter Donaldson, 1928.......**3.00**

In A Boat For Two by Ruby, Lange, Liggy & Klapholz, 1921 (Transportation).......**6.00**

In A Bungalo, Where The Red, Red Roses Grow by Jerome & Schwartz, 1913 (Cover Artist, Pfeiffer).......**10.00**

In A Bungalow by Wm. B. Friedlander & Con Conrad, 1923 (Cover Artist, Politzer).......**10.00**

In A Canoe by J. Paul Fogarty & Jules Kay Stein, 1930 (Transportation)..**5.00**

In A Chinese Temple Garden by Albert W. Ketelbey, 1923 (Cover Artist, Wohlman).......**8.00**

In A Corner Of The World All Our Own by Gus Kahn & Jesse Crawford, 1922 ....**3.00**

In A Cottage On The Mississippi Shore by King, 1915 (Cover Artist, Pfeiffer)...**10.00**

In A Cozy Kitchenette Apartment by Irving Berlin, 1921 (Irving Berlin) ..**5.00**

In A Friendly Little Harbor by Eddie Seiler & Sol Marcus, 1943 (Cover Artist, Im-Ho)...**3.00**

In A Garden Of Roses by Babbitt, 1954, Photo Joni James **3.00**

In A Garden Of Roses With You by Morey Davidson, C.D. Whipple, 1926 ....**35.00**

In A Hupmobile For Two by Brady & Alexander, 1910 (Transportation) **15.00**

In A Kingdom Of My Own by George M. Cohan (George M. Cohan) ..**10.00**

In A Little Book Shop by Kay Twomey, Al Goodhart & George Meyer, 1947, Photo Buddy Weed..**3.00**

In A Little Garden, You Made Paradise by Felice S. Lula & Earl Whitemore, 1926 (Cover Artist, Starmer)..**6.00**

In A Little Gypsy Tea Room by Edgar Leslie & Joe Burke, 1935.........**5.00**

In A Little Hula Heaven by Leo Robin & Ralph Rainger, 1937, Movie: Waikiki Wedding, Photo Bing Crosby & Shirley Ross.................**5.00**

In A Little Italian Garden by Douglas Furber & Westell Gordon, 1929 ...**5.00**

In A Little Spanish Town by Sam Lewis, Joe Young & Mabel Wayne, 1926, Photo Wilton Sisters (Cover Artist, JVR & Deco)................**6.00**

In A Little Spanish Town by Sam Lewis, Joe Young & Mabel Wayne, 1926, Photo Mickey Alpert (Cover Artist, JVR & Deco) **6.00**

In A Little Spanish Town by Sam Lewis, Joe Young & Mabel Wayne, 1926, Photo Roselle & Mack (Cover Artist, JVR & Deco) **6.00**

In A Little Swiss Chalet by Norman Zeno & Will Irwin, 1936 (Cover Artist, Jorj Harris)..**3.00**

In A Little Town Across The Border by Billy Hill & Mabel Wayne, 1932 ....**3.00**

In A Little Town Near By by Amy Ashmore Clark & Florence Turner-Haley, 1922..**3.00**

In A Little While by Gus Kahn, Ray B. Egan & William Ortmann, 1928, Musical: Nobody's Girl **5.00**

In A Love Boat With You by Harold Atteridge, Sigmund Romberg & Jean Schwartz, 1919 ....**6.00**

In A Mist by Bix Beiderbecke, 1928 ....**3.00**

In A Monastery Garden by Albert W. Ketelberg, 1915.........................**8.00**

In A Persian Market by Albert W. Ketelbey, 1920 (Cover Artist, MAC)..**5.00**

In A Persian Palace by Otto Harbach & D. Savino **5.00**

In A Pretty Little Hilly-Billy Town by Al Dubin & Joe Burke, 1931 ....**5.00**

In A Red Rose Garden by Gaston, 1912 (Cover Artist, Pfeiffer & Deco) ..**10.00**

In A Sentimental Mood by Edward Kennedy & Duke Ellington, 1935 .**3.00**

In A Shanty In Old Shanty Town by Joe Young, John Siras & Little Jack Little, 1932, Photo Ozzie Nelson (Cover Artist, Harris)..................**3.00**

In A Shanty In Old Shanty Town by Joe Young, John Siras & Little Jack Little, 1932, Photo Abe Lyman (Cover Artist, Harris)....................**3.00**

In A Shanty In Old Shanty Town by Joe Young, John Siras & Little Jack Little, 1932, (Cover Artist, Barbelle) **3.00**

In A Shanty In Old Shanty Town by Joe Young, John Siras & Little Jack Little, 1932, Photo Alice Joy, Radio's Dream Girl (Cover Artist, Harris)..**3.00**

In A Shelter From A Shower by Whiting, Leveeb & Breuer, 1933 ....**3.00**

In A Shower Of Stars by Gould & Heyman, 1945, Movie: Delightfully Dangerous, Photo Jane Powell, Constance Moore, Ralph Bellamy & Morton Gould **8.00**

In A Spanish Garden by Eisel Holt, 1929...**3.00**

In A World Of My Own by Bob Hilliard & Sammy Fain, 1951, Movie: Alice In Wonderland (Disney) **10.00**

In Acapulco by Mack Gordon & Harry Warren, 1945, Musical: Billy Rose's Diamond Horseshoe..**5.00**

In After Years by Young & Grant, 1912 (Cover Artist, Pfeiffer & Deco)..**10.00**

In All My Dreams, I Dream Of You by McCarthy & Piantadosi, 1910 (Cover Artist, Pfeiffer) **10.00**

In An Auto Car by Sutton, 1908 (Transportation)...............................**16.00**

In An Eighteenth Century Drawing Room by Raymond Scott & Jack Lawrence, 1939 (Cover Artist, Im-Ho) **3.00**

In An Old Dutch Garden by Mack Gordon & Will Grosz, 1939............**5.00**

In Arizona by Freeman, 1917 (Cover Artist, Pfeiffer).........................**10.00**

In Autumn Time by Arthur E. Buckman & Jacob Henry Ellis, 1913.....**3.00**

In Banjo Land by Clarke & Schwartz, 1912 (Cover Artist, Pfeiffer)...**10.00**

In Blinky Winky Chinky Chinatown by Wm. Jerome & Jean Schwartz, 1915 (Cover Artist, Barbelle) **5.00**

In Bye Lo Land by Seymour Furth, 1913 ....**5.00**

In Cherry Blossom Time by Braton & Salzer, 1914 (Cover Artist, Pfeiffer) **10.00**

In China by A.J. Stasney & Otto Motzan, 1919 ....**3.00**

In Cleopatra's Land by Glad Forster, 1919 ....**5.00**

In Dear Old Frisco by Hein & Manning, 1915 (Cover Artist, Pfeiffer)..**10.00**

In Dear Old Georgia by Harry Williams & Egbert Van Alstyne, 1905..**5.00**

In Dear Old Illinois by Paul Dresser, 1902...**8.00**

In Dear Old Ireland by A. Taylor Craig, 1912 (Irish)..........................**5.00**

In Dear Old Ireland by Gladys G. Dennis & Mabel Tilton, 1915 (Irish)..**5.00**

In Dear Old Nebraska by Jack Snyder, 1922.......................................**6.00**

In Dear Old Saskatoon by Swift, 1914 (Cover Artist, Pfeiffer)...........**10.00**

In Dear Old Tennessee by Dorothy Fields & Charles Newman, 1909 (Dixie)...**5.00**

In Dixie Land With Dixie Lou by Jack Drislane & Geo W. Meyer, 1912, Photo Bunny Gray (Cover Artist, Starmer & Dixie)......................**10.00**

In Dreamland Town by Smalley, 1911 (Cover Artist, Pfeiffer) **10.00**

In Dreams Alone I Find Thee True by Will B. Morrison, 1912 ....**5.00**

In Dreamy Panama by Norton, 1914 (Cover Artist, Pfeiffer)..............**10.00**

In Flanders Fields by Lieut. Col. John McCrae & Mark Andrews, 1919 (WWI & Military Personnel)..**15.00**

In Flanders Fields The Poppies Grow by Lieut. Col. John McCrae & John Philip Sousa, 1918 (WWI, John Philip Sousa & Military Personnel)..**20.00**

In Good Old New York Town by Paul Dresser, 1899 (Pre 1900)........**15.00**

In Her Cradle Baby's Sleeping by J. A. Barney, 1871 (Pre 1900) **15.00**

In Holland by Clair Van Lynden, 1915, Respectfully Dedicated by The Composer To Her Royal Majesty Queen Wilhelmina Of Holland (Dedication)..**10.00**

In Honolulu By The Sea by Jack Frost, 1915 ....**3.00**

In Love In Vain by Leo Robin & Jerome Kern, 1946, Movie: Centennial Summer, Photo Jeanne Crain, Cornell Wilde, Linda Darnell & Wm. Eythe...**3.00**

In Love's Garden, Just You And I by Arthur Gillespie & Will Osborne, 1913 (Cover Artist, Pfeiffer) **10.00**

In Maytime by Jack Snyder, 1922 ....**3.00**

In My Arms by Frank Loesser & Ted Grouya, 1943............................**3.00**

In My Beautiful, Beautiful Dreams by Joe Goodwin, 1913 (Cover Artist, Rose Symbol) **6.00**

In My Bouquet Of Memories by Sam Lewis, Joe Young & Harry Akst, 1928 (Deco)..**6.00**

In My Canoe by Isham Jones & O. E. Story, 1913................................**3.00**

In My Castle Of Dreams With You by Larry Walker, 1930 ....**3.00**

In My Dream Of You by K.M. Roberts & V. Dattilo, 1922...................**5.00**

In My Dreams I Picture Mother by John A. Speed & Frank X. Fries, 1922 ....**6.00**

In My Garden by Isabelle Firestone & Ed O'Keefe, 1929 ....**3.00**

In My Garden Of Auld Lang Syne by George Graff & Jessie L. Deppen, 1942 ....**5.00**

In My Garden Of Golden Dreams by Wilfred Harris, 1926.................**3.00**

In My Garden Of Long Ago by Harold Frost & Jeannette Duryea, 1919 ....**5.00**

In My Gondola by Bud Green & Harry Warren, 1926.........................**3.00**

In My Harem by Irving Berlin, 1913, Photo W.Jerome DeClerco (Cover Artist, Gene Buck & Irving Berlin).............................**12.00**

In My Heart, It's You by Charles O'Flynn, Max Rich & Al Hoffman, 1930 ....**4.00**

In My Heart–On My Mind–All Day Long by Bert Kalmar & Harry Ruby, 1921 ....**5.00**

In My Hide-Away by K.L. Binford, 1932 ....**3.00**

In My Home Town by Geo. Fairman, 1913 ....**5.00**

In My Hometown by Browne & Powell, 1916 (Cover Artist, Pfeiffer)..**12.00**

In My Merry Oldsmobile by Vincent Bryan & Gus Edwards, 1905, Photo Anna Fitzhugh (Transportation).......................25.00

In My Old Home Town by Walsh, 1910 (Transportation)...................**10.00**

In My Tippy Canoe by Fred Fisher, 1921 ....**3.00**

In Old California With You by E. Clinton Keithly & F. Henri Klickmann, 1922 ....**4.00**

In Old Kentucky by Al Stewart, 1919 ....**4.00**

In Old Manila by Mary Earl, 1920 (Cover Artist, Wohlman) **5.00**

In Our Hide-Away by Irving Berlin, 1962 (Irving Berlin) **3.00**

In Our Mountain Bower by Howard Johnson & Carlo Sanderson, 1921, Musical: Tangerine...**10.00**

In Our Rendezvous by Grover G. Pace, 1932, Photo Bert Lown **3.00**

In Pekin by William Loraine, 1899 (Pre 1900)...................**15.00**

In Philadelphia by Gus Edwards, 1909 (Transportation)....................**15.00**

In Poppyland by Fred G. Albers, 1914 (Cover Artist (Jaroushek) **12.00**

In Rank And File by Gustave Lange (Cover Artist, Rose Symbol, March & WWI)...**15.00**

In Room 202 by Edgar Leslie, Bert Kalmar & Dave Harris, 1919.........**3.00**

In San Domingo by Ted Snyder, 1917 ....**3.00**

In Secret Service I Won Her Heart by Alfred Bryan & Norman Spencer, 1919 ....**6.00**

In Shadowland by J. Stanley Brothers Jr., 1919 ....**6.00**

In Shadowland by Sam Lewis, Joe Young, Ruth Brooks & Fred E. Ahlert, 1924 ....**8.00**

In Sunny Italy by Fred Fischer, 1908 (Cover Artist, Gene Buck) **5.00**

In Sweet September by Pete Wendling, 1920.......................**3.00**

In That Blue Ridge Vale Of Love by Mohr, 1914 (Cover Artist, Pfeiffer)...**12.00**

In The Arms Of Love by Henry Mancini, Jay Livingston & Roy Evans, 1966, Movie: What Did You Do In The War Daddy? **3.00**

In The Autumn by Duncan Sisters, Book By Catherine C. Cushing, Suggested By Uncle Tom's Cabin by Harriet Beecher Stowe, 1923, Musical: Topsy & Eva, Photo Duncan Sisters (Cover Artist, P.M. Griffith & Black, Black Face)................................**12.00**

In The Baggage Coach, Ahead by Gussie L. Davis, 1896 (Pre 1900 & Transportation) **22.00**

In The Barracks by J.A. Silberberg, 1898 (Pre 1900 & March) **20.00**

In The Beautiful Garden Of Dreamland by Cobb, 1916 (Cover Artist, Pfeiffer)..**10.00**

In The Blue Of Evening by Adair & D'Artega, 1942, Photo Russ Morgan (Cover Artist, Nick)....................................**3.00**

In The Blue Of Evening by Tom Adair & D'Artega, 1942, Photo Frank Sinatra (Cover Artist, Nick)........................**3.00**

In The Bough Of The Banyan Tree by MacDonald & Thompson, 1915 (Cover Artist, Pfeiffer) **10.00**

In The Candle-Light, Fannie Ward & John W. Dean In Madam President by Fleta Jan Brown, 1918, Photo Bessie Wynn (Cover Artist, White)....**5.00**

In The Chapel In The Moonlight by Billy Hill, 1936, Photo Henry King (Cover Artist, Barbelle) **5.00**

In The Chapel In The Moonlight by Billy Hill, 1936, Photo Kitty Kallen...**3.00**

In The Chapel In The Moonlight by Billy Hill, 1936, Photo Mary Small (Cover Artist, Barbelle) **5.00**

In The City Of Sighs And Tears by Andrew Sterling & Kerry Mills, 1902, Photo Josie Flynn **10.00**

In The City Where Nobody Cares by Charles K. Harris, 1910 ....**5.00**

In The Cool, Cool, Cool Of The Evening by Johnny Mercer & Hoagy Carmichael, 1951, Movie: Here Comes The Groom, Photo Bing Crosby & Jane Wyman **5.00**

In The Cozy Winter Time by Max Clay, 1915 (Cover Artist Crowe, SSS)...**10.00**

In The Days Of Auld Lang Syne by Moran & Von Tilzer, 1917 (Cover Artist, Pfeiffer)..**12.00**

In The Days Of Girls And Boys by Blanche Merrill & Leo Edwards, 1911, Photo Helen Vincent...**10.00**

In The Days Of Makebelieve by Harold Stanley & Dan Frederic, 1920 ..**4.00**

In The Days Of Old Black Joe by James Brockman, 1917 (Black, Black Face) **10.00**

In The Depths Of The Coral Caves by Harrington Leigh....................**4.00**

In The Dingle Dongle Dell by Claire Kummer, 1904 ....**6.00**

In The Dusk by Bernard Hamblen & Frank H. Grey, 1919 (Deco)........**4.00**

In The Evening By The Moonlight by Bland, 1908 (Cover Artist, Pfeiffer)..**15.00**

In The Evening By The Moonlight In Dear Old Tennessee by Keithley & Thompson, 1914, Photo King Baggot **5.00**

In The Evening by Walter Donaldson & James F. Hanley, 1924, Photo Harry Fox (Cover Artist, Wohlman) **6.00**

In The Flower Garden by Martin, 1911 (Cover Artist, Pfeiffer) **10.00**

In The Garden Of My Heart by Caro Roma & Ernest R. Ball, 1908......**5.00**

In The Garden Of The Gods by J. Kiernan Brennan & Ernest R. Ball, 1914 ....**5.00**

In The Garden Of To-Morrow by Geo Graffe Jr. & Jessie L. Deppen, 1924 ....**5.00**

In The Gloaming by Annie Fortescue Harrison, 1935, Photo Harry Kogen **3.00**

In The Gloaming I Hear You Calling Me by Joe Lyons & E. Clinton Keithley, 1915 ....**6.00**

In The Gloaming Mother Darling by Fritz Potter & Earl Whitmore, 1918...**6.00**

In The Gloaming Of Wyoming, I'll Come Roaming Back To You by Harold B. Freeman & J. Edwin Allemong, 1919 (Cover Artist, Pfeiffer)...**12.00**

In The Gloaming Was The Song She Sang To Me by Gillespie & Davis, 1911 ....**5.00**

In The Glory Of The Moonlight by Percy Wenrich, 1915 ....**5.00**

In The Glory Of Your Eyes by Earle C. Jones & Chas. N. Daniels, 1913 (Cover Artist, Starmer)..**10.00**

In The Gold Fields Of Nevada by Edgar Leslie & Archie Gottler, 1915..**6.00**

In The Golden Autumn Time, My Sweet Elaine by Richard H. Gerard & S.R. Henry, 1905 ....**12.00**

In The Golden Harvest Time by Robert J. Roden & Geo W. Meyer, 1902 (Cover Artist, Rose Symbol) **5.00**

In The Good Old Fashioned Way by Harris, 1901 ....**5.00**

In The Good Old Summertime by Ren Shields & George Evans, 1958.**4.00**

In The Good Old Wintertime by Mack Gordon & Harry Revel, 1934, Movie: Shoot The Works, Photo Ben Bernie & His Merry Lads.....**5.00**

In The Harbor Of Home Sweet Home by C. M. Denison & A. J. Holmes, 1910 (Cover Artist, MWCC & Transportation) **10.00**

In The Haven Of My Heart by Buckman & Ellis, 1914 (Cover Artist, Pfeiffer)..**12.00**

In The Heart Of A Fool by Max C. Freeman & Harry D. Squires, 1919, Photo Donna Montran (Cover Artist, Starmer & Deco)..................**6.00**

In The Heart Of A Rose by J. W. Walsh & George De Carme, 1912, Photo Lady Sen Mei, Dedicated To Miss Clara Inge (Dedication) **5.00**

In The Heart Of An Irish Rose by E. Clinton Keithley, 1916 (Irish) **5.00**

In The Heart Of Dear Old Italy by Eugene West & Jack Glogau, 1921.**5.00**

In The Heart Of Hawaii by L. W. Lewis & James W. Casey, 1917.......**5.00**

In The Heart Of Old New Hampshire by Harold Freeman, J. Stanley Brothers & J. Edwin Allemong, 1918 ....**5.00**

In The Heart Of The Berkshire Hills by Claude Hager & Walter Goodwin, 1918 ....**6.00**

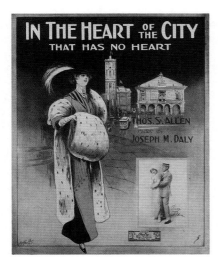

In The Heart Of The City That Has No Heart by Thos. S. Allen & Joseph M. Daly, 1913, Photo Pierce & Alden (Cover Artist, Pfeiffer).......12.00

In The Heart Of The City That Has No Heart by Thos. S. Allen & Joseph M. Daly, 1913, Photo Cooper & Eshell (Cover Artist, Pfeiffer)....**10.00**

In The Heart Of The Hills by Harry D. Kerr & Dorothy Lee, 1926 (Cover Artist, Ray Parmelee) **10.00**

In The Heart Of The Kentucky Hills by L. Wolfe Gilbert & Louis F. Muir, 1913 ....**5.00**

In The Hills Of Old Kentucky, by Johnson & Shannon, 1914 ....**5.00**

In The House Of Hugs And Kisses by Arthur J. Lamb & Wm. H. Penn, 1906 (Cover Artist, Starmer)..**10.00**

In The House Of Too Much Trouble by Will A. Heelan & J. Fred Helf, 1900 ....**5.00**

In The Hush Of The Night by Sammy Lerner & Al Hoffman, 1929......**5.00**

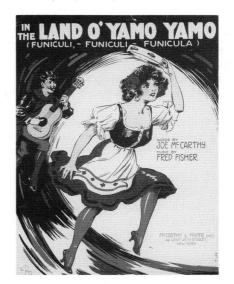

In The Land O' Yamo, Yamo by Joe McCarthy & Fred Fisher, 1917 (Cover Artist, DeTakacs) 10.00

In The Land Of Beginning Again by Grant Clarke & George W. Meyer, 1946, Movie: The Bells Of St. Mary's, Photo Bing Crosby **5.00**

In The Land Of Beginning Again by Grant Clarke & George W. Meyer, 1918, War Edition (Patriotic & WWI) **16.00**

In The Land Of Harmony by Bert Kalmar & Ted Snyder, 1911, Photo Edward Brill (Cover Artist, John Frew) **12.00**

In The Land Of Harmony by Bert Kalmar & Ted Snyder, 1911, Photo Gertrude Fiske (Cover Artist, John Frew) **12.00**

In The Land Of Honeymoon by Spurr, 1912.....................................**5.00**

In The Land Of Let's Pretend by Grant Clarke & Harry Akst, 1929, Movie: On With The Show **8.00**

In The Land Of Let's Suppose by Leo Robin, Chas. Rossoff & Mack Davis, 1928..**3.00**

In The Land Of Love With The Song Birds by F. Wallace Rega, 1915.**5.00**

In The Land Where The Shamrock Grows by W. L. Beardsley & Phil Schwartz, 1919 (Irish) **5.00**

In The Land Where They Don't Say Good-Bye by E. R. Williams, 1925...**3.00**

In The Little Home I Am Building For You by Billy Day, 1917 (Cover Artist, Pfeiffer)...**10.00**

In The Little Old Red Schoolhouse by Wilson & Brennan, 1922 ....**6.00**

In The Lives Of Famous Men by Moran & Furth, 1908 ....**6.00**

In The Meadow by Carrie Jacobs Bond, 1925, Dedicated To Joseph Diskay (Dedication)..**15.00**

In The Mellow Days Of Autumn by Burt Barsooh & Bert Carlson, 1913...**5.00**

In The Middle Of A Dream by Al Stillman, Einar Swain & Tommy Dorsey, 1939, Photo Tommy Dorsey **5.00**

In The Middle Of A Kiss by Sam Coslow, 1935, Movie: College Scandals, Photo Arline Judge **5.00**

In The Middle Of An Island by Nick Aquaviva & Ted Varneck, 1957 .**3.00**

In The Middle Of Nowhere by Harold Adamson & Jimmy McHugh, 1944, Movie: Something For The Boys **5.00**

In The Middle Of The Night by Billy Rose & Walter Donaldson, 1925**5.00**

In The Mission Of St. Augustine by Jack Chiarelli, 1953 ....**3.00**

In The Mood by Andy Razaf & Joe Garland, 1936, Photo Glenn Miller (Cover Artist, Im-Ho)...**10.00**

In The Mood by Andy Razaf & Joe Garland, 1954, Movie: The Glenn Miller Story, Signed Photo Glenn Miller (Signed)....................**120.00**

In The Moon Mist by Jack Lawrence, 1946, Photo Jerry Wald (Cover Artist, Nick)..**4.00**

In The Moon Mist by Jack Lawrence, 1946, Photo Johnny Desmond (Cover Artist, Nick)..**4.00**

In The Moon Mist by Jack Lawrence, 1946, Photo Randy Brooks (Cover Artist, Nick)..**4.00**

In The Moonlight by Bert Kalmar & Harry Ruby, 1932 ....**3.00**

In The Morning By The Bright Light by James Bland, 1870 (Pre 1900 & Black, Black Face)..**15.00**

In The Navy by Howard, 1918 (WWI)..**10.00**

In The Old Town Hall by Harry Pease, Ed. G. Nelson & Howard Johnson, 1921, Musical: Ziegfeld Follies, 1921, Photo Gus Van & Joe Schenck (Deco) **10.00**

In The Palace Of Dreams by Frank Tyler Daniels & Leo Friedman, 1914..**5.00**

In The Parlor, With The Lamp Turned Low by Edward Madden & Dorothy Jardon, 1906 ....**5.00**

In The Philippines He's Sleeping by Nina Grant, 1913 (Cover Artist, Pfeiffer)...**10.00**

In The Purple Twilight by Percy Wenrich, 1924...................................**4.00**

In The Quiet Of An Autumn Night by Pat Ballard & Ray Henderson, 1934 ....**3.00**

In The Shade Of A Sheltering Tree by Irving Berlin, 1924, Musical: Music Box Revue, 1925 (Irving Berlin)...................................**10.00**

In The Shade Of The Cocoanut Tree by Merritt, 1914............................**5.00**

In The Shade Of The Old Apple Tree by Harry Williams & Egbert Van Alstyne, 1905, Photo Anna Fitzhugh...............................**12.00**

In The Shadow Of The Alamo by J. Will Callahan & Neil Moret, 1914 (Cover Artist, Starmer) **10.00**

In The Shadow Of The Dear Old Blarney Stone by Jean C. Havez & Ted S. Barron, 1918 (Irish).......................................**5.00**

In The Shadow Of The Desert Palm by E. J. Myers & Will E. Dulmage, 1918 ....**5.00**

In The Shadow Of The Pines I'll Wait For You by Glenn Leap, 1913 (Cover Artist, Pfeiffer) **10.00**

In The Shadow Of The Sycamore by Leo Bennett, 1914 ....**5.00**

In The Shadows by Herman Finck, 1911 ....**5.00**

In The Sleepy Hills Of Tennessee by Herbert Goodman, Dean Upson & Curt Poulton, 1933..**3.00**

In The Spotlight by Lodge & Nichols, 1917, Photo Rubini **6.00**

In The Spring by Addy Britt & Jack Little, 1926 ....**5.00**

In The Still Of The Night by Cole Porter, 1937, Movie: Rosalie...........**4.00**

In The Sunset's Golden Glow by Concannon & Hoyt, 1909 ....**5.00**

In The Sweet Bye And Bye by Alfred Bryan, Francis Wheeler & Pete Wendling, 1928 (Cover Artist, Barbelle & Transportation)...........**10.00**

In The Sweet Bye & Bye by Ted Garton, 1919....................................**5.00**

In The Sweet Long Ago by Bobby Heath, Alfred Solman & Arthur Lange, 1916 (Cover Artist, DeTakacs)..**10.00**

In The Town Where I Was Born by Dick Howard, Billy Tracey & Al Harriman, 1914 (Cover Artist, Pfeiffer) **12.00**

In The Twilight by Schleifforth, 1892 (Cover Artist, Pfeiffer & Pre 1900) **15.00**

In The Vale Of The Old Berkshire Hill by George Thomas Stoddard, 1905 ....**10.00**

In The Valley Of Roses With You by Arthur J. Lamb & J. Messina, 1919 (Cover Artist, Walton) **5.00**

In The Valley Of The Moon by Charlie Tobias & Joe Burke, 1933, Photo Dick Messner (Cover Artist, Cliff Miska & Deco) **4.00**

In The Valley Of The Moon by Charlie Tobias & Joe Burke, 1933, Photo Frank Lamarr (Cover Artist, Cliff Miska & Deco) **4.00**

In The Valley Of The Moon by Charlie Tobias & Joe Burke, 1933, Photo Joe Candullo (Cover Artist, Cliff Miska & Deco)........................**4.00**

In The Valley Of The Moon by Charlie Tobias & Joe Burke, 1933, Photo The Do-Re-Me-Girls (Cover Artist, Cliff Miska & Deco)..............**4.00**

In The Valley Of The Moon by Jeff Branen, 1913 (Cover Artist, DeTakacs)..**6.00**

In The Valley Where The Bluebirds Sing by Alfred Solman & M. H. Rosenfeld, 1906 ....**6.00**

In The Village By The Sea by Andrew B. Sterling & Stanley Crawford, 1903, Photo John P. Curran (Transportation)................................**10.00**

In The Vine Covered Church Way Back Home by Weldon & Miller, 1933 ....**4.00**

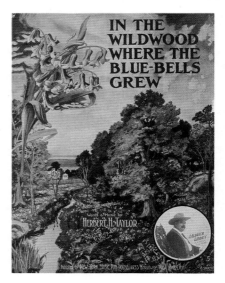

In The Wildwood Where The Blue-Bells Grew by Herbert H. Taylor, 1907, Photo J. Aldrich Libbey (Cover Artist, Starmer)............12.00

In The Winter When The Snow Comes Down by James Thatcher, 1915 ....**5.00**

In Those Good Old Country Days by Bryan & Meyer, 1908 (Cover Artist, Pfeiffer)..**12.00**

In Tyrol by Al H. Wilson, 1900, Photo Al Wilson (Cover Artist, Starmer)..**10.00**

In Vacation Time by Andrew B. Sterling & Harry Von Tilzer, 1905, Photo Sadie Leonard (Cover Artist, Jenkins) **12.00**

In Your Arms As We Waltz by John Dolph & Alex Reilly, 1923 ....**3.00**

In Your Arms by Elmer Floyd & Al Glaser, 1919 (Cover Artist, Barbelle)..**5.00**

In Your Eyes by Robert Levenson & Edwin Bernard, 1920 ....**3.00**

In Your Old Little Way by Charles Newman & J. Fred Coots, 1937.....**3.00**

In Zanzibar-My Little Chimpanzee by Will D. Cobb & Gus Edwards, 1904 ....**5.00**

Inch Worm, The by Frank Loesser, 1951, Movie: Hans Christian Andersen, Photo Danny Kaye **6.00**

Indian Cradle Song by Gus Kahn, 1927 (Indian) **15.00**

Indian Dawn by Charles O. Roos & J. S. Zamecnik, 1929 (Indian).....**15.00**

Indian Love Call by Otto Harbach, Oscar Hammerstein II & Rudolf Friml, 1924, Musical: Rose Marie (Indian)..**12.00**

Indian Lullaby by Glick & Wilson, 1925 (Indian) **15.00**

Indian Rag by Seymour Brown & Nat D. Ayer, 1912 (Indian & Rag)..**15.00**

Indian Slumber Song by Joseph Mendelson & F. Francis Hayden, 1937 (Indian) **5.00**

Indian Summer by Al Dubin & Victor Herbert, 1939, Photo George Olsen (Cover Artist, Im-Ho & Victor Herbert) **5.00**

Indiana by Ballard MacDonald & James F. Hanley, 1917 (Cover Artist, Starmer) **5.00**

Indiana Lullaby by Dorothy Terriss & Don Kendall, 1922...................**5.00**

Indiana Moon by Benny Davis & Isham Jones, 1923 (Cover Artist, Perret)..**5.00**

Indianola by S. R. Henry & D. Onivas, 1917 (Cover Artist, Starmer & Indian)..**10.00**

Indians Along Broadway by Hapgood Burt, 1905 ....**5.00**

Indians And Trees by George M. Cohan (George M. Cohan)..............**10.00**

Infantry-Kings Of the Highway, The by R.J. Burt, Sr., 1942 (Cover Artist, Frederick S. Manning, WWII & March) **10.00**

Inka Dinka Doo by Durante & Ryan, 1933, Movie: Palooka, Photo Jimmy Durante **10.00**

Instant Girl by Crawford, 1965, Photo Bobby Vee, Jackie Deshannon & Eddie Hodges......................**3.00**

Intermission Rag by Charles Wellinger, 1906 (Rag)..........................**15.00**

International Fox Trot, The by Eugene Platzmann, 1916 (Patriotic) ...15.00

International Rag by Irving Berlin, 1913 (Irving Berlin & Rag)..........**15.00**

Into Each Life Some Rain Must Fall by Allan Roberts & Doris Fisher, 1944 ....**5.00**

Into My Heart by Roy Turk & Fred Ahlert, 1930, Movie: In Gay Madrid..................................**5.00**

Into The Dawn With You by Arthur J. Lamb & Dorothy Lee, 1928 .....**5.00**

Into The Night by Clara Edwards, 1939 ....**3.00**

Introduce Me by Mel B. Kaufman, 1916......................**3.00**

Iola by Chas. L. Johnson (Indian)......................**15.00**

Iola by James O'Dea, 1906 (Indian) **15.00**

Ireland Is Calling by George & Minnie Jeffords, 1917 (Irish) **5.00**

Ireland Is Heaven To Me by Griffin, 1923 (Irish) **5.00**

Ireland Is Ireland To Me by Fisk O'Hara, J. Kiern Brennan & Ernest Ball, 1915 (Irish) **5.00**

Ireland Mother Ireland by P. J. O'Reilly & Raymond Loughborough, 1922, Movie: Song Of My Heart, Sung By John McCormack (Irish).......**10.00**

Ireland Must Be Heaven, For My Mother Came From There by Joe McCarthy, Howard Johnson & Fred Fischer, 1916, Photo Neil McKinley (Cover Artist, Rose & Irish) **12.00**

Ireland Must Be Heaven, For My Mother Came From There by Joe McCarthy, Howard Johnson & Fred Fischer, 1916, Photo Marie Russell (Cover Artist, Rose & Irish)......................**10.00**

Ireland Must Be Heaven, For My Mother Came From There by Joe McCarthy, Howard Johnson & Fred Fischer, 1916, Photo Burns & Kissen (Cover Artist, Rose & Irish) **10.00**

Ireland, My Ireland by R.C. Young, 1914 (Cover Artist, Pfeiffer & Irish)..**10.00**

Ireland, We Sympathize With You by Fahey, 1919 (Cover Artist, Pfeiffer & Irish) **10.00**

Ireland Will Go On Forever by Jacob Henry Ellis, 1918 (Irish) **5.00**

Ireland's Loss Was Heaven's Gain by Wm. Tracey, Joe Goodwin & Nat Vincent, 1917 (Irish)......................**5.00**

Irene by Joseph McCarthy & Harry Tierney, 1919, Musical: Irene **5.00**

Iris by Jules Reynard, 1917......................**5.00**

Iris by Kaufman, 1912 (Cover Artist, Pfeiffer)......................**10.00**

Irish Beauties by Percy Wenrich, 1911 (Irish)......................**5.00**

Irish Eyes Of Love by Ernest Ball, 1914 (Irish)......................**5.00**

Irish Fox Trot, The by Paul Biese, 1915 (Irish)......................**5.00**

Irish Have A Great Day To-Night, The by Henry Blossom & Victor Herbert, 1917 (Irish & Victor Herbert) **10.00**

Irish Jubilee by Jim Thornton, 1890 (Pre 1900 & Irish)......................**15.00**

Irish Soldier Boy, The by Bill Lanyon & Pat DeWitt, 1950, Photo Connie Foley (Irish)......................**3.00**

Irish Tango, The by J. Brandon Walsh & Ernest Breuer, 1914 (Irish)...**5.00**

Irish Were Egyptians Long Ago by Bryan & Smith, 1920 (Cover Artist, Pfeiffer & Irish) **10.00**

Irishman's Home Sweet Home by Felix McGlennon, 1880 (Pre 1900 & Irish)......................................**15.00**

Iron Claw, The by Benjamin Richmond, 1916, Photo Pearl White (Cover Artist, Starmer) **10.00**

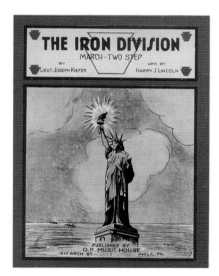

Iron Division, The by Lieut. Joseph Kiefer, 1919, Dedicated To 28th Division (WWI, March, Military Personnel & Dedication)......22.00

Irresistable Rag by Powell, 1910 (Cover Artist, Pfeiffer & Rag).........**10.00**

Is Everybody Happy? by Williams, Hogan & Lemonier, 1905..............**5.00**

Is He The Only Man In The World by Iring Berlin, 1962 (Irving Berlin)...**5.00**

Is It A Sin–My Loving You? by Emma Carus, Vincent Bryan & Walter Leopold, 1928, Photo Emma Carus......................**12.00**

Is It The Girl, Or Is It The Gown by Cole Porter, Movie: Seven Lively Arts **5.00**

Is It True What They Say About Dixie by Irving Caesar, Sammy Lerner & Gerald Marks, 1936 (Dixie)......................**5.00**

Is It Warm Enough for You? by James Kendis, 1906 ....**5.00**

Is Sally Still Waiting For Me by Lou Breese, Jack Faseinato & Tim Gayle, 1943 ....**3.00**

Is She My Girl-Friend? by Jack Yellen & Milton Ager, 1927 ....**5.00**

Is That The Way To Treat A Sweetheart by Charlie Tobias & Nat Simon, 1938, Photo Doris Rhoades (Cover Artist, Merman) **6.00**

Is There Any Better Country Than The U.S.A? by Harry C. Eldridge 1912 ....**5.00**

Is There Still Room For Me Neath The Old Apple Tree by Edgar Leslie, Lew Brown & Maurice Abrahams, 1915 ....**6.00**

Is You Is Or Is You Ain't My Baby by Billy Austin & Louis Jordan, 1944, Movie: Follow The Boys, Photo George Raft, Zorina, Andrews Sisters, Dinah Shore & Louis Jordan **5.00**

Isabella by Barnett & Pflueger, 1896 (Pre 1900)...........................**16.00**

Isabelle by Ford & Bratton, 1896 (Pre 1900) **15.00**

Isadore by Glann, 1912 (Cover Artist, Pfeiffer) **10.00**

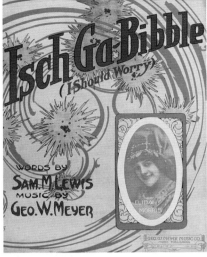

Isch Ga-Bibble, I Should Worry by Sam M. Lewis & Geo. W. Meyer, 1913, Photo Elida Morris **10.00**

I'se A Lady by Kennett & Udall, 1899 (Pre 1900 & Black, Black Face)..**20.00**

I'se A-Waitin For Yer Josie by Fred W. Leigh & Henry E. Pether, Sung by G. H. Elliott (Black, Black Face)..**35.00**

I'se Got Another Nigger On Ma Staff by Andrew B. Sterling & Harry Von Tilzer, 1897 (Pre 1900 & Black, Black Face) **30.00**

Island In the Sun by Belafonte & Burgess, 1956, Movie: Island In The Sun, Photo Harry Belafonte..**3.00**

Island In The West Indies by Ira Gershwin & Vernon Duke, 1935, Ziegfeld Follies 1936..**5.00**

Isle D'Amour by Earl Carroll & Leo Edwards, 1913, Ziegfeld Follies 1913 ....**10.00**

Isle Of Beautiful Dreams by Herbert O. Sontag, 1921 (Deco)..............**5.00**

Isle Of Capri by Jimmy Kennedy & Will Grosz, 1934, Photo Xavier Cugat **5.00**

Isle Of Paradise by Mary Earl & Ted Fiorito, 1921 ....**5.00**

Isn't It A Shame by Abner Silver, Al Sherman & Al Lewis, 1934..**5.00**

Isn't It Great To Be Married by Herbert Reynolds, Schuyler Greene & Jerome Kern, 1915, Musical: Very Good Eddie (Cover Artist, Malcolm Strauss) **16.00**

Isn't It Heavenly by E. Y. Harburg & Geo F. Meyer, 1933 ....**3.00**

Isn't It Kinda Fun by Richard Rodgers & Oscar Hammerstein II, 1945, Movie: State Fair, Photo Jeanne Crain, Dana Andrews, Dick Haymes & Vivian Blaine..**6.00**

Isn't It Romantic? by Lorenz Hart & Richard Rodgers, 1932, Movie: Love Me To-Night, Photo Maurice Chevalier..**10.00**

Isn't She The Busy Little Bee by Kilgour, 1917 (Cover Artist, Pfeiffer)..**10.00**

Isn't That Just Like Love? by J. Burke & Jimmy Van Heusen, 1940 ....**3.00**

Isn't This A Lovely Day by Irving Berlin, 1935, Movie: Top Hat, Photo Fred Astaire & Ginger Rogers (Irving Berlin) **12.00**

It Ain't Gonna Rain No Mo' by Wendell Hall, 1923, Photo Wendell Hall (Black, Black Face) **10.00**

It Ain't Necessarily So by Du Bose Heyward & Ira & George Gershwin, 1935, Movie: Porgy And Bess, Photo Sidney Poitier, Dorothy Dandridge & Sammy Davis, Jr., 1935 (Black, Black Face)..**12.00**

It Ain't No Lie by Moran & Helf, 1897 (Pre 1900)...........................**15.00**

It All Comes Back To Me Now by Hy Zaret, Joan Whitney & Alex M. Kramer, 1940 ....**3.00**

It All Depends On You by B. G. DeSylva, Lew Brown & Ray Henderson, 1926, Photo Paul Forster (Cover Artist, J & S Studio)....................**5.00**

It All Depends On You by B. G. DeSylva, Lew Brown & Ray Henderson, 1926, Musical: Big Boy, Photo The Ipana Troubadours.................**5.00**

It All Depends On You by B. G. DeSylva, Lew Brown & Ray Henderson, 1926, Musical: Big Boy, Photo Al Jolson (Cover Artist, J & S Studio & Al Jolson)..**10.00**

It by Otto Harbach, Oscar Hammerstein II & Sigmund Romberg, 1926, Movie: The Desert Song..**6.00**

It Can't Be The Same Old Farm by Granville & Jackson, 1915 (Cover Artist, Pfeiffer)..**10.00**

It Can't Be Wrong by Kim Gannon & Max Steiner, 1942, Movie: Now Voyager, Photo Bette Davis (Cover Artist, Holley)....................**15.00**

It Couldn't Be True by Sylvia Dee & Sidney Lippman, 1946, Photo Perry Como (Cover Artist, Barbelle) **3.00**

It Couldn't Occur In New York by Ben Warren & Dax Cruger, 1890 (Pre 1900)..**15.00**

It Doesn't Cost Anything To Dream by Dorothy Fields & Sigmund Romberg, 1944 ....**3.00**

It Don't Make Sense by Leo Robin & Ralph Rainger, 1938, Movie: Give Me A Sailor, Photo Martha Raye, Bob Hope, Betty Grable & Jack Whiting..**10.00**

It Don't Mean A Thing If You Ain't Got That Swing by Edward Kenne..**5.00**

It Don't Seem Like The Same Old Smile by James Thornton, 1896 (Pre 1900)..**15.00**

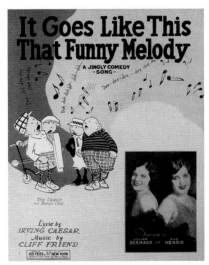

It Goes Like This, That Funny Melody by Irving Caesar & Cliff Friend, 1928, Photo Lillian Bernard & Flo Henrie **10.00**

It Goes Like This, That Funny Melody by Irving Caesar & Cliff Friend, 1928, Photo James DeLuca **10.00**

It Had To Be You by Gus Kahn & Isham Jones, 1924, Photo Elsie Huber..**5.00**

It Had To Be You by Gus Kahn & Isham Jones, 1939, Movie: Show Business: Photo Eddie Cantor & George Murphy (Eddie Cantor)........**10.00**

It Happened In Monterey by Billy Rose & Mabel Wayne, 1930, Movie: King Of Jazz, Photo Paul Whiteman..**12.00**

It Happened In The Starlight by Martin Broones, 1937 ....**3.00**

It Happened When Your Eyes Met Mine by Roy Turk & Harry Akst, 1934..**3.00**

It Happens All The Time by Stillman & Trovajoli, 1969, Movie: Seven Golden Men, Photo Rosanna Podesta..**3.00**

It Is Destiny by Grey & Straus, 1930, Movie: A Lady's Morals, Photo Grace Moore **8.00**

It Is No Secret, What God Can Do by Stuart Hamblen, 1950 (Cover Artist, Holley)..**3.00**

It Is Not Because Your Heart Is Mine by Adelaide Anne Proctor & Herman Lohr, 1910...**5.00**

It Isn't Fair by Richard Himber, Frank Warshauer & Sylvester Sprigato, 1933, Photo Ray Dorey **4.00**

It Isn't Fair by Richard Himber, Frank Warshauer & Sylvester Sprigato, 1933, Photo Benny Goodman...**4.00**

It Isn't Fair by Richard Himber, Frank Warshauer & Sylvester Sprigato, 1933, Photo Sammy Kaye **4.00**

It Isn't Hard To Love A Girl Like You by Martin Swanger & W. C. Powell, 1911 ....**10.00**

It Looks Like A Big Night Tonight by Harry Williams & Egbert Van Alstyne, 1908, Signed Photo Lillian Ashley (Signed)..................**12.00**

It Looks Like Rain In Cherry Blossom Lane by Edgar Leslie & Joe Burke, 1937, Photo Guy Lombardo (Cover Artist, Cliff Miska) **10.00**

It Looks Like Rain In Cherry Blossom Lane by Edgar Leslie & Joe Burke, 1937, Photo Sammy Kaye **10.00**

It Looks Like Susie by Cliff Friend, 1931 ....**3.00**

It Made You Happy When You Made Me Cry by Walter Donaldson, 1926 ....**5.00**

It Makes Me Think Of Home Sweet Home by Frank D. Bryan, 1914 (Cover Artist, Pfeiffer) **10.00**

It Makes No Difference Now by Jimmie Davis & Floyd Tillman, 1939, Photo Wilf Carter...**3.00**

It Makes No Difference Now by Jimmie Davis & Floyd Tillman, 1939, Photo Jimmie Davis..**3.00**

It May Be Far To Tipperary, It's A Longer Way To Tennessee by Arthur Lamb & Alfred Solman, 1914 (WWI)...**16.00**

It Might As Well Be Spring by Richard Rodgers & Oscar Hammerstein II, 1945, Movie: State Fair, Photo Jeanne Crain, Dana Andrews, Dick Haymes & Vivian Blaine...**5.00**

It Might Have Been by Chas. K. Harris, 1908 (Cover Artist, Starmer) **10.00**

It Might Have Been by Cole Porter, 1943, Movie: Something To Shout About **6.00**

It Might Have Been You by Sam Coslow, 1920 (Cover Artist, Pfeiffer & Deco) **10.00**

It Must Be Love by Meyer, 1912 (Cover Artist, Pfeiffer)....................**10.00**

It Must Be Someone Like You by Harold G. Frost, Charley Straight & Roy Bargy, 1921 ....**5.00**

It Must Be True by Harry Barris, Gus Arnheim & Gordon Clifford, 1930..**3.00**

It Must Have Been Some Wonderful Boy by Wm. Tracey & Jack Stern, 1918 (Cover Artist, Barbelle) **5.00**

It Only Happens Once by Frankie Laine & Carl Fischer, 1945..............**3.00**

It Only Happens When I Dance With You by Irving Berlin, 1947, Movie: Easter Parade, Photo Judy Garland, Fred Astaire & Ann Miller (Irving Berlin)..**15.00**

It Pays To Be Ignorant by Tom Howard Jr., 1944....................**3.00**

It Seems Like Old Times by Carmen Lombardo & John Jacob, 1946 ...**3.00**

It Seems To Be Spring by Geo. Marion Jr. & Richard A. Whiting, 1930, Movie: Let's Go Native..**5.00**

It Started All Over Again by Bill Carey & Carl Fischer, 1942 (Cover Artist, Barbelle) **5.00**

It Takes A Girl To Do It Every Time by Matt Woodward, 1891 (Pre 1900)..**15.00**

It Takes A Little Rain With Sunshine To Make The World Go Round by Ballard Macdonald & Harry Carroll, 1913, Photo Anna Driver (Cover Artist, Starmer) **12.00**

It Takes A Long Tall Brown Skin Girl To Make A Preacher Put His Bible Down by Will E. Skidmore, 1917 (Cover Artist, Pfeiffer & Black, Black Face)..**20.00**

It Took Nineteen Hundred And Nineteen Years, To Make A Girl Like You by Frank Tannenhill & Ted Snyder, 1919 (Cover Artist, J.P. Tlikoley) **10.00**

It Used To Be Me by Charles O'Flynn, Howard Phillips & Peter Wendling, 1932 ....**3.00**

It Was A Lover And His Lass by Shakespeare & R. H. Walthew, 1892 (Pre 1900) **16.00**

It Was Christmas In London by Richard W. Pascoe, Will Dulmage & H. O'Reilly Clint, 1947 (Cover Artist, I. Geyler) **3.00**

It Was For Me by Charles B. Blount, 1916 ....**5.00**

It Was Just A Song At Twilight by Granville & Jackson, 1915 (Cover Artist, Pfeiffer)...**10.00**

It Was Only A Sun Shower by Irving Kahal, Francis Wheeler & Ted Snyder, 1927 ....**5.00**

It Was So Beautiful by Arthur Freed & Harry Barris, 1932.................**3.00**

It Was Written In The Stars by Leo Robin & Harold Arlen, 1948, Movie: Casbah **6.00**

It Wasn't My Fault by Herbert Reynolds & Jerome Kern, 1916, Musical: Love O'Mike **10.00**

It Will Be A Long Long Time by Will J. Hardman, 1900 (Cover Artist, H. Habermann & Black, Black Face)...**25.00**

Italian Eyes by Bellucia & Fredericks, 1912 (Cover Artist, Pfeiffer) ..**10.00**

Italian Girl by Joe Goodwin & Geo. W. Meyer, 1911, Photo Anna Chandler (Cover Artist, Pfeiffer) **15.00**

Italian Street Song by Rida Johnson Young & Victor Herbert, 1921, Movie: Naughty Marietta, Photo Jeannette Macdonald & Nelson Eddy (Victor Herbert) **10.00**

Italy by Gus Edwards & Geo. F. Meyer, 1912 ....**5.00**

It'll Come To You by Irving Berlin, 1939 (Irving Berlin) **5.00**

It's A Big Wide Wonderful World by John Rox, 1940.........................**6.00**

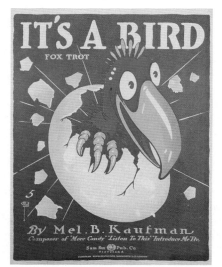

It's A Bird by Mel B. Kaufman, 1917 (Cover Artist, Ray) 8.00

It's A Blue World by Bob Wright & Chet Forrest, 1940, Movie: Music In My Heart, Photo Tony Martin & Rita Hayworth **10.00**

It's A Good Day by Peggy Lee & Dave Barbour, 1946........................**3.00**

It's A Grand Night For Singing by Richard Rodgers & Oscar Hammerstein II, 1945, Movie: State Fair, Photo Jeanne Crain, Dick Haymes & Vivian Blaine..**12.00**

It's A Great Day For The Irish by Roger Edens, 1940 (Irish) **5.00**

It's A Great Life, If You Don't Weaken by Leo Robin, Richard A. Whiting & Newell Chase, 1930...**3.00**

It's A Hap-Hap-Happy Day by Al J. Neiburg, Sammy Timberg & Winston Sharples, 1939, Movie: Gulliver's Travels..**5.00**

It's A Hot Night In Alaska by Robin & Styne, 1951, Movie: Meet Me After The Show, Photo Betty Grable, Macdonald Carey & Eddie Albert..**10.00**

It's A Hundred To One You're From Dixie by L. Wolfe Gilbert & Harry Morgan, 1917 (Dixie)..**5.00**

It's A Hundred To One You're In Love by Lou Klein & Harry Von Tilzer, 1916 (Cover Artist, R.S.)..**6.00**

It's A Lonesome Old Town by Charles Tobias & Charles Kisco, 1930..**5.00**

It's A Long Long Time Since I've Been Home by Josephine E. Vail, 1916 (Cover Artist, Starmer)..**10.00**

It's A Long, Long Way To The U.S.A. & The Girl I Left Behind by Val Trainor & Harry Von Tilzer, 1917 (Cover Artist, Pfeiffer & WWI)..**16.00**

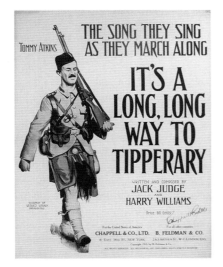

It's A Long, Long Way To Tipperary by Jack Judge & Harry Williams, 1912, Photo Tommy Atkins (Patriotic & WWI).......20.00

It's A Long Time Between Kisses by Gus Kahn, Harry Akst & Richard A. Whiting, 1931 ....**3.00**

It's A Long Way From Here To "Over There" by Lew Payton, 1918 (WWI)..**10.00**

It's A Long Way To Berlin But We'll Get There by Arthur Fields & Leon Flatow, 1917, Photo Maurice Burkhardt, Dedicated To Lt. Joseph E. Barrell & Lieut. Eugene J. Orsenigo, 71st New York (Cover Artist, Rose, Dedication, Military Personnel & WWI) **20.00**

It's A Long Way To Berlin But We'll Get There by Arthur Fields & Leon Flatlow, 1917, Photo Neil McKinley, Dedicated To Lt. Joseph E. Barrell & Lieut. Eugene J. Orsenigo, 71st New York (Cover Artist, Rose, Dedication, Military Personnel & WWI) **20.00**

It's A Lovely Day Today by Irving Berlin, 1950, Musical: Call Me Madam, Caricature Ethel Merman (Cover Artist, Peter Arno & Irving Berlin)..**10.00**

It's A Lovely Day Tomorrow by Irving Berlin, 1939 (Irving Berlin)....**5.00**

It's A Man, Ev'ry Time, It's A Man by Al Dubin, Jimmy McHugh & Irwin Dash, 1923, Photo McGowan & Knox **5.00**

It's A Man, Ev'ry Time, It's A Man by Al Dubin, Jimmy McHugh & Irwin Dash, 1923, Photo Mel Klee..**5.00**

It's A Most Unusual Day by Harold Adamson & Jimmy McHugh, 1948, Movie: A Date With Judy..**5.00**

It's A Rambling Flivver by Byron Gay, 1917 (Transportation)..........**15.00**

It's A Short Way Thro' Mother's Doorway But It's A Long Way Back To Mother's Knee by Andrew B. Sterling, Bernie Grossman & Arthur Lange, 1917, Photo Baby Violet Stroud (Cover Artist, Starmer)....**16.00**

It's A Short Way Through Mother's Doorway But It's A Long Way Back To Mother's Knee by Andrew Sterling, Bernie Grossman & Arthur Lange, 1917, Photo Flo Davis (Cover Artist, Starmer)................**10.00**

It's A Sin by Fred Rose & Zeb Turner, 1948 ....**3.00**

It's A Sin To Tell A Lie by Billy Mayhew, 1936, Photo Connie Gates (Cover Artist, Weldy Baer) **5.00**

It's A Sin To Tell A Lie by Billy Mayhew, 1936, Photo Guy Lombardo (Cover Artist, Weldy Baer) **5.00**

It's A Wonderful World After All by Newton Alexander, 1923..........**3.00**

It's All A Dream by Jack Yellen & George L. Cobb, 1915................**5.00**

It's All In The Game by Carl Sigman & Gen. Charles G. Dawes, 1912, Photo Tommy Edwards **2.00**

It's All In The Game by Dawes & Sigman, 1951..**3.00**

It's All Over Now by F. Williams & The Kreys, 1918 (Cover Artist, Pfeiffer & WWI)..**20.00**

It's All Over Now by George Fairman, 1918 (WWI)..**15.00**

It's All So New To Me by Ted Koehler, Irving Caesar & Ray Henderson, 1935, Movie: Curly Top, Photos Of Shirley Temple (Shirley Temple)..........**10.00**

It's All Yours by Dorothy Fields & Arthur Schwartz, 1939, Movie: Stars In Your Eyes **5.00**

It's Almost Tomorrow by Wade Buff & Gene Adkinson, 1933..............**3.00**

It's Always Fair Weather by Hovey & Bullard, 1902 ....**5.00**

It's Always The Darkest Just Before The Sunrise by Joe McKiernan & Joe Ghirardelli, 1925..**5.00**

It's Always You by Johnny Burke & Jimmy Van Heusen, 1941, Photo Russ Morgan..**3.00**

It's An Old Southern Custom by Jack Yellen & Joseph Meyer, 1935, Movie: George White's 1935 Scandals **5.00**

It's An Old Spanish Custom In The Moonlight by Edgar Leslie & George W. Meyer, 1930 ....**5.00**

It's Anybody's Spring by Johnny Burke & Jimmy Van Heusen, 1945, Movie: Road To Utopia, Photo Bing Crosby, Bob Hope & Dorothy Lamour..**10.00**

It's Been A Long Long Time by Sammy Cahn & Jule Styne, 1945, Photo Eddie Howard..**3.00**

It's Been A Long Long Time by Sammy Cahn & Jule Styne, 1945, Photo Russ David..**5.00**

It's Been A Long Long Time by Sammy Cahn & Jule Styne, 1945, Photo Bing Crosby..**5.00**

It's Been A Long Long Time by Sammy Cahn & Jule Styne, 1945, Photo Danny O'Neil..**5.00**

It's Been A Long Long Time by Sammy Cahn & Jule Styne, 1945, Photo Randy Brooks..**5.00**

It's Been A Long Long Time by Sammy Cahn & Jule Styne, 1945, Photo Harry James..**5.00**

It's Been A Long Long Time by Sammy Cahn & Jule Styne, 1945, Photo Stan Kenton..**5.00**

It's Been So Long by Harold Adamson & Walter Donaldson, 1935, Movie: The Great Ziegfeld..**10.00**

It's D'Lovely by Cole Porter, 1936, Movie: Red Hot And Blue (Cover Artist, Jorj Harris)..**5.00**

It's Dangerous To Love Like This by Tot Seymour & Vee Lawnhurst, 1935 ....**3.00**

It's Dark On Observatory Hill by Johnny Burke & Harold Spina, 1934 (Cover Artist, Leff)..**3.00**

It's Delightful To Be Married by Christine & Scotto, 1906................**5.00**

It's Dreamtime by Jack Brooks & Walter Schuman, 1946, Movie: I'll Be Yours, Photo Deanna Durbin (Cover Artist, Barbelle) **5.00**

It's Easier Said Than Done by Carmen Lombardo & John Jacob Loeb, 1938 (Cover Artist, Sorokin)..**5.00**

It's Easier Said Than Done by Carmen Lombardo & John Jacob Loeb, 1938, Photo Frank Daly (Cover Artist, Leff) **5.00**

It's Easy For You To Remember, But It's So Hard For Me To Forget by Al Piantadosi & Sammy Stept, 1919, Photo Alice Joyce (Cover Artist, R.S.)...**6.00**

It's Easy To Remember by Lorenz Hart & Richard Rodgers, 1935, Movie: Mississippi, Photo Bing Crosby & Joan Bennett **10.00**

It's Forty Miles From Schenectady To Troy by McClellan & Kerker, 1896 (Pre 1900)...**15.00**

It's Good Enough For Me by Clark & Christie, 1909 (Cover Artist, Pfeiffer)..**10.00**

It's Good Enough For Me by Neal Harper & Clarence West, 1905 (Cover Artist, J.B. Eddy)...**15.00**

It's Got To Be Someone I Love by William Dillon & Alfred Doyle, 1910 (Cover Artist, Etherington)...**15.00**

It's Great To Be A Doughboy In The Army by Shep Camp, 1918 (WWI)...**10.00**

It's Great To Be Married by Howard Johnson & Carlo Sanderson, 1921, Musical: Tangerine...**10.00**

It's Hard To Love Somebody by Mack & Smith, 1907 (Cover Artist, Pfeiffer)..**10.00**

It's Home by Jack Yellen & Jay Gorney, 1924, Movie: Home.............**5.00**

It's Impossible by A. Manzanero & Sid Wayne, 1968, Photo Perry Como...**5.00**

It's Just A New Spanish Custom by Mack Gordon & Harry Revel, 1934, Movie: We're Not Dressing, Photo Bing Crosby & Carole Lombard ..**8.00**

It's Just Because It's You by Will J. Harris & Victor Young, 1928.......**5.00**

It's Lonesome Here by Milford, 1916, Photo Billy Murray (Cover Artist, Pfeiffer)...**10.00**

It's Love, Love, Love by Mack David, Joan Whitney & Alex M. Kramer, 1943 (Cover Artist, Barbelle) **5.00**

It's Magic by Sammy Cahn & Jule Styne, 1948, Movie: Romance On The High Seas, Photo Jack Carson, Janis Paige, Don DeFore & Doris Day **10.00**

It's Moonlight All The Time On Broadway by Ren Shields & Percy Wenrich, 1908...**10.00**

It's My Lazy Day by Burnette, 1946, Movie: Bordertown Trails, Photo Smiley Burnette **3.00**

It's Never Too Late To Be Sorry by J.E. Dempsey & Jos. A. Burke, 1918, Photo Marguerite Snow (Cover Artist, L.S.)..................................**5.00**

It's Nobody's Business But My Own by Will E. Skidmore, 1919.........**5.00**

It's Not The First Time You Left Me, But It's The Last Time You'll Come Back by Geo J. Bennett & M.K. Jerome, 1923, Photo Belle Hawley (Cover Artist, Barbelle & Deco)...................................12.00

It's Not What You Were, It's What You Are Today by Dave Marion, 1898 (Pre 1900) **15.00**

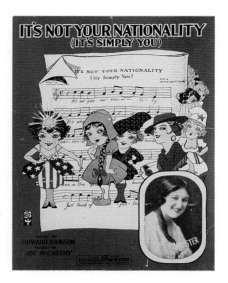

It's Not Your Nationality by Joe McCarthy & Howard Johnson, 1916...6.00

It's On, It's Off by Coslow & Siegel, 1937, Movie: Double Or Nothing, Photo Martha Raye **8.00**

It's Only A Paper Moon by Billy Rose, E. Y. Harburg & Harold Arlen, 1933, Movie: Too Young To Know, Photo Joan Leslie & Robert Hutton ..**10.00**

It's Raining Sunbeams by Sam Coslow & Frederick Hollander, 1937, Movie: 100 Men And A Girl, Photo Deanna Durbin, Leopold Stokowski, Mischa Auer & Adolphe Menjou **10.00**

It's Raining Sundrops by Styne & Cahn, 1950, Movie: The West Point Story, Photo, James Cagney, Doris Day, Gene Nelson, Virginia Mayo & Gordon Macrae...**10.00**

It's So Nice To Have A Man Around The House by Jack Elliott & Harold Spina, 1950, Photo Dinah Shore...**10.00**

It's So Peaceful In The Country by Alec Wilder, 1942, Photo Mildred Bailey **3.00**

It's So Temptin' by Jimmie V. Monaco, 1915 ....**5.00**

It's Sunday Down In Caroline by Marty Symes, Al J. Neiburg & Jerry Levinson, 1933 (Cover Artist, Leff)...**3.00**

It's Swell Of You by Mack Gordon & Harry Revel, 1937, Movie: Wake Up And Live, Photo Walter Winchell, Ben Bernie & Alice Faye..**15.00**

It's The Animal In Me by Mack Gordon & Harry Revel, 1934, Movie: We're Not Dressing, Photo Bing Crosby & Carole Lombard........**10.00**

It's The Dreamer In Me by Jimmy Van Heusen & Jimmy Dorsey, 1938, Photo Jimmy Dorsey **3.00**

It's The Flag by Lottie Simmons, 1918 (Cover Artist, Pfeiffer & Patriotic) .**15.00**

It's The Girl Behind The Man by Stanley Murphy & Harry Von Tilzer, 1912 ....**6.00**

It's The Pretty Things You Say by Al Bryan & Ted Snyder, 1908, Photo Charlotte Cole..**12.00**

It's The Pretty Things You Say by Al Bryan & Ted Snyder, 1908, Photo Little Amy Butler (Cover Artist, DeTakacs).................................**16.00**

It's The Talk Of The Town by Marty Symes, Al J. Neiburg & Jerry Levinson, 1933, Photo Glen Gray (Cover Artist, Leff) **5.00**

It's The Three Leaves Of The Shamrock by Allen & Daley, 1915 (Cover Artist, Pfeiffer & Irish) **10.00**

It's Time For Every Boy To Be A Soldier by Harry Tierney & Alfred Bryan, 1917, Photo Abe Lincoln & Woodrow Wilson (WWI & President)..**38.00**

It's Time To Close Your Drowsy Eyes by Henry Frantzen, 1910 (Black, Black Face) **10.00**

It's Time To Say Aloha by Charlie Tobias & Sammy Fain, 1938, Broadway Show: Hellzapoppin (Cover Artist, Merman) **5.00**

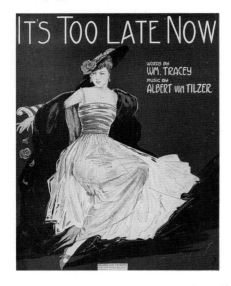

It's Too Late Now by Wm. Tracey & Albert Von Tilzer, 1914 ......10.00

It's Tulip Time In Holland by Dave Radford & Richard Whiting, 1915 ..**6.00**

It's Watcha Do With Whatcha Got by Larry Morey & Eliot Daniel, 1948, Movie: So Dear To My Heart (Disney) **10.00**

It's You by B. G. DeSylva & Louis Silvers, 1921, Musical: Bombo, Photo Al Jolson (Al Jolson) **15.00**

It's You by Benny Davis & Con Conrad, 1921 ....**5.00**

It's You by May Singhi Breen, Milton Charles & Art Kassel, 1926 ......**5.00**

It's You by Silverstein & Zahler, 1929, Movie: College Love, Photo George Lewis & Dorothy Gulliver **8.00**

It's You I Love by Benny Davis, J. Fred Coots & Arthur Swanstrom, 1929, Movie: Sons O'Guns **12.00**

It's You Or No One by Sammy Cahn & Jule Styne, 1948, Movie: Romance On The High Seas, Photo Jack Carson, Janis Paige, Don DeFore & Doris Day **8.00**

It's You Since The World Began by Earl Carroll & Leo Edward, 1916 ...**5.00**

It's Your Carriage That Counts by Howard Johnson & Carlo Sanderson, 1921, Musical: Tangerine **8.00**

I've A Longing In My Heart For You, Louise by Chas. K. Harris, 1900 ..**10.00**

I've A Million Reasons by M. E. Rourke & Jerome D. Kern, 1907 .....**10.00**

I've A Strange New Rhythm In My Heart by Cole Porter, 1937, Movie: Rosalie **5.00**

I've A World Of Love In My Heart For You by Burt, 1910 (Cover Artist, Pfeiffer) **12.00**

I've Always Loved You by Harold Rome & Aaron Goldmark, 1946, Movie: I've Always Loved You, Photo Philip Dorn & Catherine Mcleod **5.00**

I've Been Drafted Now I'm Drafting You by Lyle Moraine & Chuck Foster, 1941, Signed Photo, Dottie Lamour & Bob Hope (Signed) **12.00**

I've Been Floating Down The Old Green River by Bert Kalmar & Joe Cooper, 1915, Photo Florence Moore (Cover Artist, Barbelle & Deco) **10.00**

I've Been Longing A Long Time For You by Hoyt & Gideon, 1909 (Cover Artist, Pfeiffer) **15.00**

I've Been Longing, Longing Dear For You by DeAngelis & Francis, 1911 (Cover Artist, Pfeiffer) **10.00**

I've Been Saving For A Rainy Day by Arthur Swansthrom & Dorothy Clark, 1921 ....**6.00**

I've Been Through The Mill by Lewis F. Muir, 1913 ....**5.00**

I've Been To Gay Paree by McGlennon, Conley & Sayers, 1893 (Pre 1900) **15.00**

I've Been Waiting For You All The Time by Anne Caldwell & Jerome Kern, 1919, Musical: She's A Good Fellow **8.00**

I've Come Here To Stay by Edward Harrigan & David Braham, 1890 (Pre 1900) **15.00**

I've Come To Wive It Wealthily In Padua by Cole Porter, 1948, Musical: Kiss Me Kate **5.00**

I've Fallen In Love With You by Will Tinsley & Robert E. Harty, 1931, Photo The Two Graces (Cover Artist, Heff Ley) **5.00**

I've Found My Loving Man by William Tracy & W. Raymond Walker, 1912 ....**5.00**

I've Found My Sweetheart Sally by Jack Yellen & Leo Pollack, 1925, Photo Charles Purcell (Cover Artist, Barbelle) **3.00**

I've Found Somebody New Instead Of You by Leo Robin & Joseph Meyer, 1931 ....**5.00**

I've Given Many Kisses, But Not The Kind, Sweetheart, I Give To You by Stanford, 1914 (Cover Artist, Pfeiffer) **10.00**

I've Gone Goofy Over Miniature Golf by Leo Diston, Mitchell Parisu & Frank Perkins, 1930 (Sports) **16.00**

I've Got A Date With A Dream by Mack Gordon & Harry Revel, 1938, Movie: My Lucky Star, Photo Sonja Henie, Richard Greene, Joan Davis, Buddy Ebsen & Art Jarrett **10.00**

I've Got A Feelin' You're Foolin' by Arthur Freed & Nacio Herb Brown, 1935, Movie: Broadway Melody of 1936 ....**5.00**

I've Got A Feeling For You by Madden & Moore, 1904 ....**6.00**

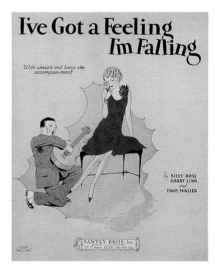

I've Got A Feeling I'm Falling by Billy Rose, Harry Link & Thomas Waller, 1929 (Deco) 10.00

I've Got A Feeling In My Heart For You by Al Herman, 1915 (Cover Artist, Pfeiffer) **10.00**

I've Got A Gal For Every Day In The Week by Pat Rooney & Harry Von Tilzer, 1900 ....**10.00**

I've Got A Gal In Kalamazoo by Mack Gordon & Harry Warren, 1942, Movie: Orchestra Wives, Photo Glenn Miller & Many Stars **10.00**

I've Got A Little Home In The Country by Harry D. Kerr & C. Arthur Fifer, 1919 ....**5.00**

I've Got A Locket In My Pocket by Mack David & Art Kassell, 1945 .**5.00**

I've Got A Lovely Bunch Of Cocoanuts by Fred Heatherton, 1949 (Cover Artist, Nick) **5.00**

I've Got A New Job by D.G. Nelson, 1918 (Cover Artist, Barbelle & WWI) **10.00**

I've Got A New Love Affair by Bickley Reichner, M. Cooper Paul & Harry Link, 1930 (Cover Artist, Leff & Deco) **5.00**

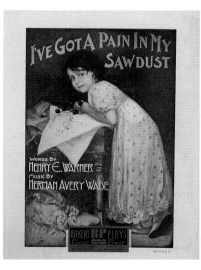

I've Got A Pain In My Sawdust by Henry E. Warner & Herman Avery Wade, 1908...**10.00**

I've Got A Pocket Full Of Sunshine by Arthur Johnston & Gus Kahn, 1935, Movie: Thanks A Million, Photo Dick Powell, Ann Dvorak & Paul Whiteman **8.00**

I've Got A Pocketful Of Dreams by John Burke & James V. Monaco, 1938, Movie: Sing You Sinners, Photo Bing Crosby, Fred MacMurray & Donald O'Connor **15.00**

I've Got A Rainbow Round My Shoulder by Dave Dreyer, 1928..........**5.00**

I've Got A Red Cross Rosie Going Across With Me by Edgar Leslie, Bert Kalmar & Harry Ruby, 1917 (WWI & Red Cross)........................**35.00**

I've Got A Sixpence by Desmond Cox, 1943 ....**3.00**

I've Got A Smile That's Worth A Million Dollars, 1913 (Cover Artist, Pfeiffer)...**10.00**

I've Got A Sweet Tooth Bothering Me by Irving Berlin, 1916 (Irving Berlin)..**12.00**

I've Got A Ten Day Pass For A Honeymoon by Walter Donaldson, Ballard MacDonald & James F. Hanley, 1918, Photo Mollie King (WWI) **15.00**

I've Got An Invitation To A Dance by Marty Symes, Al J. Neiburg & Jerry Levinson, 1934 ....**3.00**

I've Got Beginner's Luck by Ira & George Gershwin, 1937, Movie: Shall We Dance, Photo Fred Astaire & Ginger Rogers..........................**10.00**

I've Got My Captain Working For Me Now by Irving Berlin, 1919 (Irving Berlin & WWI)..**10.00**

I've Got My Eyes On You by Cole Porter, 1939, Movie: Broadway Melody 1940, Photo Fred Astaire & Eleanor Powell (Cover Artist, Im-Ho)...**10.00**

I've Got My Eyes On You by Hager, Ring & Morse, 1902, Photo John Nestor...**6.00**

I've Got My Love To Keep Me Warm by Irving Berlin, 1937, Movie: On The Avenue, Photo Dick Powell & Alice Faye (Irving Berlin) **12.00**

I've Got My Love To Keep Me Warm by Irving Berlin, 1937, Photo Les Brown (Irving Berlin)..**5.00**

I've Got My Washin' To Do by Al Moritz, Photo Janette Davis..........**5.00**

I've Got No Strings by Leigh Harline & Ned Washington, 1940, Movie: Pinocchio (Disney) **10.00**

I've Got Plenty To Be Thankful For by Irving Berlin, 1942 (Irving Berlin)..**12.00**

I've Got Rings On My Fingers by Weston & Barnes & Maurice Scott, 1909, Musical: The Yankee Girl, Photo Blanche Ring.............**10.00**

I've Got The Army Blues by L. Wolfe Gilbert & Carey Morgan, 1916 (WWI)...**15.00**

I've Got The Blue Ridge Blues by Charles A. Mason, Charles S. Cooke & Richard Whiting **5.00**

I've Got The Blues But I'm Too Mean To Cry by Mitchell Parish, Eleanor Young & Harry D. Squires, 1921, Photo Sophie Tucker (Cover Artist, Hoffman) **16.00**

I've Got The Blues For Home Sweet Home by William Jerome, E. Ray Goetz & George W. Meyer, 1916...**10.00**

I've Got The Blues For My Kentucky Home by Clarence Gaskill, 1920, Photo Nelson Cronin, Dedicated To Flo Bert Of Brendel & Bert (Cover Artist, Dunk & Dedication)...**12.00**

I've Got The Finest Man by Creamer & Europe, 1912 (Cover Artist, Pfeiffer) **10.00**

I've Got The Girl by Walter Donaldson, 1926 ....**5.00**

I've Got The Mumps by Franklin & Green, 1909 (Cover Artist, Pfeiffer)..**15.00**

I've Got The Nicest Little Home In Dixie by Walter Donaldson, 1912 (Cover Artist, Dunk & Dixie)..**10.00**

I've Got The Profiteering Blues by Al Wilson & Irving Bibo, 1920 (Blues) **10.00**

I've Got The Right Girl Now by Stanford, 1917 (Cover Artist, Pfeiffer)...**10.00**

I've Got The Right To Sing The Blues by Hoagy Carmichael, 1932 (Blues) **6.00**

I've Got The Sun In The Morning by Irving Berlin, 1946, Movie: Annie Get Your Gun (Irving Berlin)...**10.00**

I've Got The Time, I've Got The Place, But It's Hard To Find The Girl by Ballard Macdonald & S. Henry, 1910, Photo Miss Hetty King **10.00**

I've Got To Sing A Torch Song by Al Dubin & Harry Warren, 1933, Movie: Gold Diggers 1933, Photo Ginger Rogers **10.00**

I've Got To Stop Dreaming Of You by Bert Kalmar, Sid Silvers & Harry Ruby, 1937 ....**3.00**

I've Got You Under My Skin by Cole Porter, 1936, Movie: Born To Dance, Photo Eleanor Powell **10.00**

I've Gotta Be Me by Walter Marks, 1967, Musical: Golden Rainbow, Photo Steve Lawrence & Eydie Gorme..**3.00**

I've Gotta Yen For You by Geo. Marion Jr. & Richard A. Whiting, 1930, Movie: Let's Go Native, Photo Jeannette MacDonald & Jack Oakie..**8.00**

I've Grown So Used To You by Thurland Chattaway, 1901 ....**10.00**

I've Had Many A Sweetheart But None Like You by Harry D. Kerr, 1907..**5.00**

I've Heard That Song Before by Jule Styne & Sammy Cahn, 1942, Movie: Youth on Parade, Photo Harry James.............................**5.00**

I've Just Come Back To Say Goodbye by Charles K. Harris, 1897 (Pre 1900)...**15.00**

I've Lived, I've Loved, I'm Satisfied by Lew Brown, Ben Barnett & Albert Von Tilzer, 1919 (Cover Artist, Walton) **6.00**

I've Lost My Heart But I Don't Care by Howard-Hough & Adams, 1908..**5.00**

I've Lost My Heart by S. R. Henry & Harry Hamilton, 1931 ....**3.00**

I've Lost My Teddy Bear by Christine, 1908 ....**5.00**

I've Lost You, So Why Should I Care by Richard Howard, 1916, Photo Theda Bara (Cover Artist, SSS) 10.00

I've Loved You Since You Were A Baby by Joe McCarthy & Al Piantadosi, 1915...**5.00**

I've Made Up My Mind To Forget You, But I Can't Let You Out Of My Heart by May Tully & Martin Broones, 1923 (Cover Artist, Perret)...**5.00**

I've Never Been In Love Before by Jo Swerling, Abe Burrows & Frank Loesser, 1950, Musical: Guys & Dolls.........................**5.00**

I've Only Been Down To The Club by Skelly & Austin, 1876 (Pre 1900) **15.00**

I've Only Myself To Blame by Holt, 1917 (Cover Artist, Pfeiffer).....**10.00**

I've Only Myself To Blame by Redd Evans & Dave Mann, 1948, Photo Frankie Lane **3.00**

I've Only One Idea About The Girls And That's? by Joe McCarthy, Earl Carroll & Al Piantadosi, 1914 ....**5.00**

I've Sent My Wife To The Seashore by Dubin & Cormack, 1914.........**5.00**

I've Told Every Little Star by Oscar Hammerstein II & Jerome Kern, 1932, Movie: Music In The Air....................................**8.00**

I've Waited A Lifetime For You by Joe Goodwin & Gus Edwards, 1929...**5.00**

I've Waited, Honey, Waited Long For You by Geo. A. Nichols, 1899 (Pre 1900 & Black, Black Face).......................................**15.00**

I've Your Number by Joe Goodwin & Geo W. Meyer, 1911 (Cover Artist, Pfeiffer)..**10.00**

Ivory Kapers by Fahrmeyer, 1929 (Cover Artist, Pfeiffer) **10.00**

Ivory Tower by Jack Fulton & Luis Steele, 1956, Photo Cathy Carr.....**3.00**

Ivy by Hoagy Carmichael, 1947, Movie: Ivy, Photo Joan Fontaine.......**5.00**

Ivy, Cling To Me by Alex Rogers, Isham Jones & Jimmy Johnson, 1922...**5.00**

I'ze Your Nigger If You Wants Me Liza' Jane by Paul Dresser, 1896 (Pre 1900 & Black, Black Face)...**25.00**

Izme by A.S. Scott-Gatty, 1914...**5.00**

J'aime Mon Amour by Ivan Caryll, 1918 ....**5.00**

Jack, How I Envy You by Harry Von Tilzer, 1897 (Pre 1900) **15.00**

Jack In The Box by Zez Confrey, 1927 ....**5.00**

Jack O'Lantern Girl, The by Herbert, 1905.................................**5.00**

Jack Rabbit Rag by Garcia, 1909 (Rag)....................................**10.00**

Ja-Da by Bob Carleton, USNRF, 1918, Photo Ja Da Trio, Small Folio, War Edition, (Cover Artist, DeHaven, WWI & Military Personnel) **25.00**

Jagtime Johnson's Ragtime March by Ryder, 1905 (March & Rag)....**15.00**

Jake, Jake, The Yiddisher Ball Player by Merrill, 1913 (Cover Artist, Pfeiffer & Deco) **15.00**

Jalousie by Vera Bloom & Jacob Gade, 1945 ....**2.00**

Jambalaya by Hank Williams, 1952, Photo Hank Williams..................**3.00**

Jambalaya by Hank Williams, 1952, Photo Jo Stafford **3.00**

Jamboree by Harold Adamson & Jimmy McHugh, 1936, Movie: Top Of The Town..**5.00**

James Dean by Jackson Browne & Glenn Frey, Photo The Eagles......**10.00**

Jane by Halsey K. Mohr, 1915 (Cover Artist, DeTakacs)....................**10.00**

Jane, I Love No One But You by Art Hickman & Ben Black, 1920......**5.00**

Japan's Triumphal March by Caird M. Vandersloot, 1904 (March)....**10.00**

Japanese Love Song by Clayton Thomas, 1900 ....**10.00**

Japanese Moon by Dorothy Terris & Austin Huntley, 1922 (Cover Artist, JVR & Deco) **6.00**

Japanese Night Song by Sauners & Janson, 1930 ....**5.00**

Japanese Sandman, The by Raymond B. Egan & Richard A. Whiting, 1920 (Cover Artist, Frederick S. Manning **15.00**

Japanese Serenade, A by William Loraine, 1899 (Pre 1900) **15.00**

Japansy by John Klenner, 1927 ....**3.00**

Jasmine Door, The by Weather & Scott **5.00**

Jasmine Speaks Of You, Jessie Mine, The by Arthur J. Lamb, 1907...**10.00**

Jasper Jenkins, De Cake-Walking Coon by Henry P. Vogel, 1898 (Pre 1900 & Black, Black Face)...**25.00**

Jasper's Triumphal March by C. M. Vandersloot, 1914 (March) **5.00**

Java by Friday, 1958 ....**3.00**

Java Jive by Ben Oakland, Photo King Sisters (Jazz) **5.00**

Jazz Babies' Ball by Charles Bayha & Maceo Pinkard, 1920 (Jazz) ..10.00

Jazz Baby by Blanche Merrill & M. K. Jerome, 1919 (Cover Artist, Barbelle, Deco & Jazz)...**15.00**

Jazz Band Blues by Walter Hirsch & James White, 1919 (Jazz) **5.00**

Jazz Me Blues by Tom Delaney, 1921 (Blues)................................**5.00**

Jazz Nocturne by Dana Suesse, 1931 (Jazz)..................................**5.00**

Jazzapation by Claypool, 1920 (Cover Artist, Pfeiffer) **10.00**

Jazzin' The Blues Away by Jeff Branen, 1918 (Jazz) **5.00**

Jazzola by Al M. Kendall, J. Russel Robinson & Theodore Morse, 1919 (Cover Artist Lionel S. Reiss & Jazz) **10.00**

Jazzy Jazzy Sound In All Chinatown by Herman Bush, Louis F. Borromeo & Al Hether, 1920, Photo Louis F. Borromeo (Cover Artist, DeHaven & Jazz) **5.00**

Je T'aimerai Toujours by Winefred Goodwin Bocar, Arthur Smith & Louis N. Guilbault, 1915 (Cover Artist, Starmer) 10.00

Jealous by Tommie Malie, Dick Finch & Jack Little, 1929 (Cover Artist, Frederick S. Manning) **20.00**

Jealous Heart by Jenny Lou Carson, 1944, Photo Al Morgan **3.00**

Jealous Of You by Max C. Freeman, Nelson Ingham & Ed Johnson, 1921 ....**5.00**

Jean by Rod McKuen, 1969, Movie: Prime Of Miss Jean Brodie, Photo Oliver **5.00**

Jeanie Morrison by Mothervell & Dempster, 1843 (Pre 1900) **35.00**

Jeanie With The Light Brown Hair by Stephen C. Foster, 1939, Photo Dale Evans (Cover Artist, NPS, Deco & Stephen Foster) **10.00**

Jeannette by Jethro Bithell & Bryceson Treharne, 1917 ....**5.00**

Jeannine, I Dream Of Lilac Time by L. Wolfe Gilbert & Nathaniel Skilkret, 1928, Musical: Lilac Time, Photo Colleen Moore **10.00**

Jeepers Creepers by Johnny Mercer & Harry Warren, 1938, Movie: Going Places, Photo Dick Powell & Anita Louise (Cover Artist, Im-Ho) **5.00**

Jennie by Orville F. Barcus & Harry J. Lincoln, 1921, Musical: Girl Of My Heart, Photo Dottie Ray Greene **10.00**

Jenny Get Your Hoe Cake Done by Sweeney, Frith & Hale (Pre 1900 & Black, Black Face) **75.00**

Jericho by Leo Robin & Richard Myers, 1929 ....**5.00**

Jerry You Warra A Warrior In The War by Dannie O'Neil & Billy Baskette, 1919, Dedicated to Jerry Vogel, War Edition, Small Folio (Cover Artist, R.S., WWI, Irish & Dedication) **20.00**

Jersey Bounce by Robert B. Wright, Bobby Plater, Tiny Bradshaw & Edward Johnson, 1941 (Cover Artist, Henri Lamotte) **3.00**

Jersey Carnival, The by Daniel Lieberfeld, 1904 (March) **10.00**

Jerusalem by Henry Parker, 1933 ....**2.00**

Jerusalem, Jerusalem by Naomi Shemer & Norman Newell, Photo Eddie Fisher **5.00**

Jes' Come Aroun' Wid An Automobile by Baker, 1902 (Transportation & Black, Black Face) **25.00**

Jesse James by Jerry Livingston, 1954, Photo Eileen Barton **5.00**

Jesus Calls Us by C. F. Alexander & F. G. Albert, 1928 ....**5.00**

Jim by Jim Ceasar Petrillo, Edward Ross & Nelson Shawn, 1941, Photo Dinah Shore **5.00**

Jim Crow Polka, Sung by Christy's Minstrel, 1847, Photo Performers In Black Face (Pre 1900 & Black, Black Face) **50.00**

Jim, Jim, Don't Come Back "Till You Win" by Ben Ryan, Bert Hanlon & Harry Von Tilzer, 1918 (Cover Artist, Pfeiffer & WWI) **10.00**

Jim, Jim, I Always Knew You'd Win by Ben Ryan, Bert Hanlon & Harry Von Tilzer, 1918 (Cover Artist, Pfeiffer & WWI) **10.00**

Jiminy Cricket by Leigh Harline & Ned Washington, 1940, Movie: Pinocchio (Disney) **10.00**

Jimmie Boy by Edward I. Boyle, 1918 (Cover Artist, John Shaw, Jr., WWI, March & Patriotic) **15.00**

Jimmies Mean Mama Blues by Jimmy Rodgers, Walter O'Neal & Bob Sawyer, 1931 (Blues) **10.00**

Jimmy Had A Nickel by Maurice Sigler, Al Goodhart & Al Hoffman, 1933, Photo Fred Waring (Cover Artist, Wohlman) **5.00**

Jimmy I Love But You by Harry B. Smith, Francis Wheeler, Al Trebla & Frank Capie, 1922...**5.00**

Jimmy, My Lovin' Jimmy, 1914 (Cover Artist, Pfeiffer).................**12.00**

Jimmy, The Pride Of Newsboy Row by A. Baldwin Sloane, 1900......**10.00**

Jimmy Valentine by Madden & Edwards, 1928 ....**6.00**

Jinga Bula Jing Jing by Sam M. Lewis, Joe Young & M. K. Jerome, 1920 (Cover Artist, Barbelle) **5.00**

Jingle Bell Rock by Joe Beal & Jim Boothe, 1957.................**1.00**

Jingle Bells (Cover Artist, Pfeiffer)...**10.00**

Jitney Bus, The by Lessing & Ingraham, 1915, Movie: A Jitney Bus Elopment, Photo Charlie Chaplin **10.00**

Joan Of Arc by Roden & Kendis, 1916, Movie: Joan Of Arc, Photo Geraldine Farrar **10.00**

Joan Of Arc They Are Calling You by Alfred Bryan, Willie Weston & Jack Wells, 1917, Photo Joan Of Arc On Horseback (Cover Artist, Barbelle & WWI) **12.00**

Jockey Hat & Feather by Julia Brodwig, 1860 (Pre 1900) **50.00**

Jockey On The Carousel, The by Jerome Kern, 1935, Movie: I Dream Too Much, Photo Lily Pons **15.00**

Jogo Blues by W. C. Handy, 1903 (Blues) **12.00**

John Fitzgerald by Jos. M. Daly, 1909 (March) **10.00**

John Henry Blues by W. C. Handy, 1922 (Blues) **10.00**

John Henry, March, 1903 (Transportation, March & Black, Black Face)...**20.00**

John T. Scopes Trial (Convicted For Teaching Evolution) by Vernon Dalhart, 1925, Signed Photo In Metal Frame (Signed).....................**85.00**

Johnny Doughboy Found A Rose In Ireland by Kay Twomey & Al Goodhart, 1942, Photo Kate Smith (Cover Artist, Im-Ho, WWII & Ireland) **10.00**

Johnny Doughboy Found A Rose In Ireland by Kay Twomey & Al Goodhart, 1942, Photo Kenny Baker (WWII & Irish) **5.00**

Johnny Fedora And Alice Blue Bonnet by Allie Wrubel & Ray Gilbert, 1946, Movie: Make Mine Music (Disney) **10.00**

Johnny Get A Girl by Stanley Murphy & Harry Puck, 1916, Photo Moore, Gardner & Rose (Cover Artist, DeTakacs) **12.00**

Johnny Get Your Gun by Monroe Rosenfeld, 1886 (Pre 1900) **15.00**

Johnny Is The Boy For Me by Les Paul, Marcel Stillman & Paddy Roberts, 1953, Photo Les Paul & Mary Ford **5.00**

Johnny One Note by Rodgers & Hart, 1937, Movie: Words And Music, Photo Judy Garland, June Allyson, Lena Horne, Gene Kelly, Mickey Rooney & Ann Southern **12.00**

Johnny Q. Public by George M. Cohan (George M. Cohan)..............**10.00**

Johnny Zero by Mack David & Vee Lawnhurst, 1943 (WWII & Transportation) **10.00**

Johnny's In Town by Jack Yellen, Geo W. Meyer & Abe Olman, 1919, Small War Edition (Cover Artist, R.S. & WWI) **15.00**

Johnson Rag by Jack Lawrence, Guy Hall & Henry Kleinkauf, 1945, Photo Frankie Masters (Rag).................................**3.00**

Jolly Blacksmiths, The by E. Braham & E.T. Paull, 1905 (Cover Artist, E.T. Paull & March) **35.00**

Jolly Boys In Gray, The by Alfred Roth, 1903 (Patriotic & March)....**20.00**

Jolly Cobbler, The by Gay A. Rimert & Frank G. Reimert, 1920 (Cover Artist, Crit & March)....................................**16.00**

Jolly Fellows by Vollsterdt, 1905 ....**5.00**

Jolly Jingles by W.C. Powell, 1907 (Cover Artist, T.Ray & March)...**10.00**

Jolly Peter by Werner & Kernsten, 1922.....................**5.00**

Jolly Pickaninnies by Edna Randolph Worrell & Elizabeth F. Guptill, 1916 (Black, Black Face) **15.00**

Jolly Sailor, A by Harry J. Lincoln, 1908 (March)....................**15.00**

Jones Boy, The by Mann Curtis & Vic Mizzy, 1935 ....**4.00**

Joobalai by Leo Robin & Ralph Rainger, 1938, Movie: Paris Honeymoon, Photo Bing Crosby & Shirley Ross **8.00**

Josephine by Gus Kahn, Wayne King & Burke Bivens, 1937, Photo Johnny Long (Deco)..5.00

Josephine My Jo by J. T. Brymm, 1901 ....**10.00**

Josephine Please No Lean On The Bell by Ed. G. Nelson, Harry Pease & Duke Leonard, 1945, Movie: The Eddie Cantor Story, Photo Eddie Cantor In Black Face (Eddice Cantor & Black, Black Face).........**20.00**

Joshu-Ah by George Arthurs & Bert Lee, 1911 ....**3.00**

Josie by Henry Arthur Blumenthal, 1904, Music Supplement Hearst Boston Sunday American, Sunday, July 2, 1905 ....**10.00**

Josie by Styne & Cahn, 1946, Movie: The Kid From Brooklyn, Photo Danny Kaye & Vera Ellen.................................**5.00**

Josie O'Neill by Richard H. Gerard & Harry W. Armstrong, 1904 (Cover Artist, Hall & Irish) **10.00**

Journey To A Star, A by Leo Robin & Harry Warren, 1943, Movie: The Gang's All Here, Photo Alice Faye, Carmen Miranda, Phil Baker & Benny Goodman & His Orchestra.................................**14.00**

Journey's End by Bert French, Joseph McCarthy, Harry Tierney & Frank Craven, 1922, Musical: Up She Goes.................................**8.00**

Joy Bells by Cliff Friend & Joe Santly, 1927 ....**3.00**

Joys Of The Dance by Sadie Koninsky, 1914 ....**6.00**

Juba by R. Nathaniel Dett, 1913 (Black, Black Face) **10.00**

Jubilee by Stanley Adams & Hoagy Carmichael, 1937, Movie: Every Day's A Holiday, Caricature, Mae West......................**10.00**

Jubilo by Anne Caldwell & Jerome Kern, 1919, Musical: She's A Good Fellow **12.00**

Judy by Hoagy Carmichael & Sammy Lerner, 1934..............**10.00**

Judy, You're The Jewel Of Them All by George A. Kershaw & Walter Scanlan, 1921...**5.00**

Jumping Jack Jubilee by A. B. Woods, 1901 ....**10.00**

Jumping Jupiter by Richard Carle, 1910 ....**6.00**

June Brought The Roses by Ralph Stanley & John Openshaw, 1924 ....**5.00**

June Honeymoon by Ted Snyder, 1911......................**5.00**

June, I Love No One But You by Art Hickman & Ben Black, 1920......**5.00**

June In January by Leo Robin & Ralph Rainger, 1936, Movie: Here Is My Heart, Photo Bing Crosby & Kitty Carlisle.........................**8.00**

June Is Bustin' Out All Over by Richard Rodgers & Oscar Hammerstein II, 1945, Movie: Carousel, (Cover Artist, BJH) **5.00**

June Moon by Joe Lyons, Frank Magine & Charley Straight, 1921 .....**5.00**

June Night by Abel Baer & Cliff Friend, 1924, Photo Morton Downey**5.00**

June Roses by Sadie Koninsky, 1905 ....**5.00**

June Time by Lucy E. Fedelty & Harry LaForest, 1927 ....**3.00**

June Time In Old New Orleans by M. S. Hudson & Ivan G. Martin, 1909, Photo Leo White.................................**5.00**

June Time Is Love Time by Sidney Clare, Charles Tobias & Al Sherman, 1931 ....**3.00**

Jungle Drums by Guy Lombardo, Charles O'Flynn & Ernesto Lecuona, 1933 ....**4.00**

Jungle Jamboree Rag by Chris Smith, 1913 (Rag)...................**10.00**

Jungle Jubilee, The by Grossman & Watson, 1913 (Cover Artist, Pfeiffer)..**10.00**

Jungledrums by George Spink, 1927......................**3.00**

Junk Man Rag, The by Chris Smith, Ferd E. Mierisch & C. Luckyth Roberts, 1913, Photo Maurice & Florence Walton (Rag).........10.00

Jupiter Forbid by Lorenz Hart & Richard Rodgers, 1942, Movie: All's Fair.................................**5.00**

Just A Baby's Prayer At Twilight, For Her Daddy Over There by Sam M. Lewis, Joe Young & M. K. Jerome, 1918 (Cover Artist, Barbelle & WWI).................................**10.00**

Just A Bird'eye View Of My Old Kentucky Home by Gus Kahn & Walter Donaldson, 1926.................................**5.00**

Just A Blue Serge Suit by Irving Berlin, 1945 (Cover Artist, Cesareo & Irving Berlin) **8.00**

Just A Blue-Eyed Blonde by Gus Kahn & Ted Fiorito, 1931 ....**5.00**

Just A Breath Of Hawaii by Costello & Earl, 1921.....................**5.00**

Just A Chain Of Daisies by Anita Owen, 1911, Photo Anita Owen.......**5.00**

Just A Cottage Small, By A Waterfall by B. G. DeSylva & James F. Hanley, 1925, Photo John McCormack **5.00**

Just A Dance Program Of Long Ago by Herscher & Piantadosi, 1928 (Cover Artist, Pfeiffer) **10.00**

Just A Dream At Dawn by Will Callahan & Bob Sherwood, 1912, Photo Golden Gate Trio (Cover Artist, Dennis)...**5.00**

Just A Dream Of You Dear by Milton Weil & J. Henri Klickmann, 1910..**5.00**

Just A Fair Weather Friend by Johnny Mercer & Matt Malneck, 1934 .**5.00**

Just A Gigolo by Leonello Casuci & Irving Caesar, 1929 ....**5.00**

Just A Girl Like You by Freeman & Ruddy, 1914, Musical: Miss Manhattan (Cover Artist, Pfeiffer & Deco)...**15.00**

Just A Girl That Men Forget by Al Dubin, Fred Rath & Joe Garren, 1923, Photo Crafts & Haley...**10.00**

Just A Girl That Men Forget by Al Dubin, Fred Rath & Joe Garren, 1923, Photo Ulis & Lee..**10.00**

Just A Kid Named Joe by Mack David & Jerry Livingston, 1938, Photo Modernaires...**3.00**

Just A Little Angel by Woolfolk & Barron, 1917, Musical: Paradise Valley (Cover Artist, Pfeiffer)..**15.00**

Just A Little Bit O' Driftwood by Benny Davis, Dohl Davis & Abe Lyman, 1928, Photo Abe Lyman..**5.00**

Just A Little Bit South Of North Carolina by Sunny Skylar, Bette Cannon & Arthur Shaftel, 1941 ....**4.00**

Just A Little Closer by Howard Johnson & Joseph Meyer, 1930, Movie: Remote Control...**8.00**

Just A Little Cottage by Al Harriman & Jack Egan, 1917 (Cover Artist, E.E. Walton) **5.00**

Just A Little Cottage In The Country Calling: Come Back Home by Andrew B. Sterling & Alfred Solman, 1917 (Cover Artist, Starmer & WWI)...**10.00**

Just A Little Drink by Byron Gay, 1925...**5.00**

Just A Little Eden Of Our Own by Arnold & Brown, 1913 (Cover Artist, E.S. Fisher) **10.00**

Just A Little Fond Affection by Elton Box, Desmond Cox & Lewis Ilda, 1944, Photo Gene Krupa (Cover Artist, Geyler).........................**4.00**

Just A Little Fond Affection by Elton Box, Desmond Cox & Lewis Ilda, 1944, Photo Kate Smith (Cover Artist, Geyler) **14.00**

Just A Little Home For The Old Folks by Edgar Leslie & Fred E. Ahlert, 1932 ....**3.00**

Just A Little Kiss For Memory by Mary Landis Holden, 1926..............**5.00**

Just A Little Kiss From A Little Miss by Eddie Kuhn, 1927 ....**6.00**

Just A Little Line by Anne Caldwell & Jerome Kern, 1919, Musical: She's A Good Fellow **8.00**

Just A Little Longer by Irving Berlin, 1926 (Cover Artist, Leff & Irving Berlin)...**10.00**

Just A Little Love Song by Joe Young, Sam Lewis & Joe Cooper, 1922 ..**3.00**

Just A Little Rocking Chair & You by Bert Fitzgibbon, Jack Drislane & Theodore Morse, 1905...**10.00**

Just A Little Song At Twilight by Howard & Daly, 1916 (Cover Artist, Pfeiffer)..**10.00**

Just A Little Sunshine by Buckley, 1914...**5.00**

Just A Little Way Away From Home by Sam Lewis, Joe Young & Oscar Levant, 1928..**5.00**

Just A Little While by Irving Berlin, 1930 (Irving Berlin)...................**5.00**

Just A Memory by B. G. DeSylva, Lew Brown & Ray Henderson, 1927 (Cover Artist, Barbelle) **5.00**

Just A Mother's Dream by Grossman & Magini, 1918 (Cover Artist, Pfeiffer) **15.00**

Just A Night For Meditation by Sam Lewis, Joe Young & Lew Pollack, 1928, Photo Ted Claire (Cover Artist, Barbelle)............................**6.00**

Just A Night For Meditation by Sam Lewis, Joe Young & Lew Pollack, 1928, Photo Charles Ray (Cover Artist, Barbelle) **5.00**

Just A Night In Dream Land by Milton Weill & White-Stocking, 1915 .**5.00**

Just A Prayer Away by Charles Tobias & David Kapp, 1944, Photo Bing Crosby...**4.00**

Just A Prayer Away by Charles Tobias & David Kapp, 1944, Photo Frankie Carle **3.00**

Just A Prayer Away by Charles Tobias & David Kapp, 1944, Photo Kate Smith...**6.00**

Just A Prayer Away by Charles Tobias & David Kapp, 1944, Photo Sammy Kaye..**3.00**

Just A Small Town Sweetheart by Max Clay, 1916 (Cover Artist, Union Engraving) **5.00**

Just A Song Of Long Ago by Albert Stillman, Bill Engvik & Ralph Erwin, 1939 ....**3.00**

Just A Sweetheart by Pasternack, 1928 ....**3.00**

Just A Thought Of You by Joe Goodwin & James F. Hanley, 1919......**5.00**

Just A Word Of Sympathy by Gus Kahn & Egbert Van Alstyne, 1916 (Cover Artist, Starmer)..**5.00**

Just A Year Ago To-Night by Billy Rose & Lee David, 1923, Photo Don Bestor...**6.00**

Just A-Wearyin' For You by Frank Stanton & Carrie Jacobs Bond, 1901...**10.00**

Just Across The Bridge Of Gold by Andrew Sterling & Harry Von Tilzer, 1905..**10.00**

Just An Echo In The Valley by Harry Woods, Jimmy Campbell & Reg Connelly, 1932, Signed Photo Bing Crosby (Cover Artist, Roland & Signed)...**30.00**

Just An Hour Of Love by Al Bryan & Eddie Ward, 1929, Movie: Show Of Shows..**10.00**

Just An Ivy Covered Shack by Morey Davidson & Carl Rupp, 1926 ....**5.00**

Just An Old Love Of Mine by Peggy Lee & Dave Barbour, 1947, Photo Peggy Lee & Dave Barbour..**5.00**

Just An Old Sweetheart Of Mine by Harry J. Breen & Mayo Geary, 1903 ..**5.00**

Just Another Day Wasted Away by Charles Tobias & Roy Turk, 1927 ..**3.00**

Just Another Dream Of You by Benny Davis & Joe Burke, 1932 ....**3.00**

Just Another Kiss by Irving Caesar & J. & N. Hilbert, 1919 ....**5.00**

Just Another Night by Silverstein, Conrad & Newman, 1931, Movie: The Age Of Love, Photo Billie Dove & Charles Starrett **6.00**

Just Another Night by Walter Donaldson, 1928.................................**3.00**

Just Another Poor Man Gone Wrong by Sterling & Von Tilzer, 1919 (Cover Artist, Pfeiffer) **10.00**

Just Any O'Hour, Night Or Day by Alberta Roper, 1936, Photo Dick Oglesby (Cover Artist, Heflay) **4.00**

Just Around The Corner by Dolf Singer & Albert Von Tilzer, 1925, Photo Ted Lewis...**3.00**

Just As Long As You Have Me by Neville Fleeson & Albert Von Tilzer, 1922, Musical: The Gingham Girl...**3.00**

Just As The Boat Went Down, The First Titanic Song, Souvenir Edition by Marvin Lee, 1912, Dedicated To The Heroes Who Went Down With The World's Largest Ship, Shows Picture Of Titanic Before & After It Started (Transportation, Dedication & Titanic)................**75.00**

Just As The Sun Went Down by Kennett & Udall, 1898 (Pre 1900) ...**15.00**

Just As Though You Were Here by Edgar DeLange & John Benson Brooks, 1942, Photo Tommy Dorsey (Cover Artist, Barbelle)........**5.00**

Just As Your Mother Was by Andrew B. Sterling & Harry Von Tilzer, 1917, Musical: Turn To The Right, Photo Ruth Chester (Cover Artist, Pfeiffer)..**12.00**

Just Ask Your Heart by Joe Ricci, 1959, Photo Frankie Avalon...........**3.00**

Just At The Turn Of The Tide by Charles Shackford, 1901 ....**5.00**

Just Because by Skelton & Robin, 1937..**3.00**

Just Because I Let You Call Me Baby Lamb by Feist & Corin, 1909, Photo Sophie Tucker (Cover Artist, Pfeiffer & Rag) **15.00**

Just Because It Reminds Me Of You by Parkins & Norton, 1906 ....**5.00**

Just Because It's You by C. M. S. McLellan & Ivan Caryll, 1913, Musical: The Little Cafe, Photo Miss Hazel Dawn....................................**10.00**

Just Because It's You by Klein & Harling, 1938, Movie: The Whip, Photo Dorothy MacKaill & Ralph Forbes **6.00**

Just Because She Comes From A One-Horse Town by Richard Howard, 1916 ....5.00

Just Because She Made Dem Goo Goo Eyes by Cannon & Queen, 1900 ..10.00

Just Because You Won My Heart by J. Will Calahan & Clarence M. Jones, 1916 ....5.00

Just Because You're You by Cliff Friend, 1932.....................................3.00

Just Because You're You–That's Why I Love You by Roy Turk & J. Russel Robinson, 1922 (Cover Artist, Barbelle & Deco)....................10.00

Just Been Wond'ring All Day Long by Irene Akerley Canning, 1922...5.00

Just Before The Battle Mother by George F. Roat, 1860 (Pre 1900 & Patriotic) 20.00

Just Between Friends by Robert Mellin & Gerald Rogers, 1955 ....3.00

Just Close Your Eyes Big Moon by Beth S. Whitson, 1913 ....5.00

Just Dreaming Of You by A. H. Eastman & Fred Heltman, 1915 ....5.00

Just Drifting Along by Roy Newell & Nat Simon, 1936 (Cover Artist, Barbelle) 5.00

Just For A Dear Little Girl by Allen & Daly, 1910 ....5.00

Just For Fun by Livingston & Evans, 1949, Movie: My Friend Irma, Photo Marie Wilson, John Lund & Martin & Lewis 5.00

Just For Me And Mary by Grant Clarke, Howard E. Rogers & Leo Edwards, 1919 (Cover Artist, DeTakacs)....................................10.00

Just For Now by Dick Redmond, 1948, Movie: Whiplash, Photo Dane Clark & Alexis Smith 6.00

Just For Remembrance by Mitchell Parish, Eleanor Young & Harry D. Squires, 1923 (Cover Artist, Hoffman) 10.00

Just For The Key To Your Heart by Harris & Schmid, 1915 (Cover Artist, Pfeiffer)...10.00

Just For The Love Of A Girl by Slater & Vinton, 1911 (Cover Artist, Pfeiffer)...15.00

Just For The Sake Of Our Daughter by Monroe Rosenfeld, 1897 (Pre 1900) 15.00

Just For The Sake Of Your Mother by Lew Schaeffer, 1917 ....10.00

Just For To-Night by Frank O. French, 1902, Photo Joe E. Blamphin (Cover Artist, Edgar Keller) 10.00

Just For You by Oliver G. Wallace & Arthur Freed, 1919 (Cover Artist, D. Dulin) 12.00

Just For You Dear by Sullivan & Pittman, 1917 ....5.00

Just Forget by Billy Smythe & Art Gillham, 1930 ....3.00

Just Friends by Lewis & Klenner, 1931 ....3.00

Just Give Me A Big Brass Drum by Morse, 1908 (Black, Black Face)..22.00

Just Hangin' Round by Fritz Potter, 1906 (Black, Black Face)............22.00

Just In Love With You by Duncan Sisters, Book By Catherine C. Cushing, Suggested By Uncle Tom's Cabin By Harriet Beecher Stowe, 1923, Musical: Topsy & Eva, Photo Duncan Sisters (Cover Artist, P.M. Griffith & Black, Black Face) 12.00

Just In Time by Comden, Green & Styne, 1956, Movie: Bells Are Ringing, Photo Judy Holliday & Dean Martin......................................8.00

Just Keep A Thought For Me by Harry Kerr & Max Fischer, 1921.......5.00

Just Kiss Yourself Good-bye by William Jerome & Jean Schwartz, 1902 (Black, Black Face) 20.00

Just Let Me Call You Sweetheart by Schwartz, 1925 ....5.00

Just Like A Butterfly by Mort Dixon & Harry Woods, 1927 (Cover Artist, Starmer) 5.00

Just Like A Gipsy by Seymour B. Simons & Nora Bayes, 1919 (Cover Artist, Barbelle) 5.00

Just Like A Melody Out Of The Sky by Walter Donaldson, 1928 (Cover Artist, Barbelle) 5.00

Just Like A Rainbow by Mary Earl & Ted Fiorito, 1921 (Cover Artist, Starmer) 10.00

Just Like A Rose by R.H. Burnside & Raymond Hubbell, 1920 ....5.00

Just Like In A Story Book by Joseph McCarthy & James Hanley, 1930, Movie: High Society Blues...5.00

Just Like The Will O'The Wisp by Vernon J. Stevens & J. Stanley Brothers Jr., 1919..5.00

Just Like Two Birds In A Nest by Eddie Kuhns, 1921.........................5.00

Just Like Washington Crossed The Delaware, General Pershing Will Cross The Rhine by Howard Johnson & Geo W. Meyer, 1918, Photo General Pershing (Cover Artist, Rose Symbol, Military Personnel, WWI & President) 35.00

Just Like You by Steinberg, 1906...5.00

Just Lonesome by Harriet Axtell Johnstone & Carrie Jacobs Bond, 1915, Dedicated To Harriet (Dedication) 16.00

Just Lonesome by Wilmac, Dennis & Magine, 1925, Photo Three Dennis Sisters 6.00

Just Love Me (Cover Artist, Pfeiffer)..10.00

Just My Luck by Johnny Burke & James Van Heusen, 1945...............3.00

Just Once Again by Walter Donaldson & Paul Ash, 1927, Photo Paul Ash (Cover Artist, JVR & Deco)..10.00

Just Once Too Often by Joe Young & Charles Tobias, 1934................3.00

Just One Day by Bobby Heath & Arthur Lange, 1916, Photo Bob Hall (Cover Artist, DeTakacs)...10.00

Just One Day by Bobby Heath & Arthur Lange, 1916, Photo Howard, Kibel & Herbert (Cover Artist, DeTakacs) 12.00

Just One Day by Bobby Heath & Arthur Lange, 1916, Photo Kathryn Miley (Cover Artist, DeTakacs) 12.00

Just One Dearie by Longbrake & Grady, 1909 (Cover Artist, Pfeiffer)...10.00

Just One Girl by Karl Kennett & Lyn Udall, 1898, Photo Lottie Gilson (Pre 1900) 20.00

Just One Kind Word by Cunningham, 1919...5.00

Just One More Chance by Sam Coslow & Arthur Johnston, 1931, Photo Ruth Etting...10.00

Just One More Kiss by Harry Owens & Reggie Montgomery, 1926.....5.00

Just One Of Those Things by Cole Porter, 1935 ....6.00

Just One Way To Say I Love You by Irving Berlin, 1949, Musical: Miss Liberty (Irving Berlin) 5.00

Just One Word Of Consolation by Frank B. Williams & Tom Lemonier, 1905 (Cover Artist, Starmer) 5.00

Just Plain Folks by Stonehill, 1901...10.00

Just Plain Lonesome by Johnny Burke & James Van Heusen, 1942, Movie: My Favorite Spy, Photo Kay Kyser 3.00

Just 'Round The Corner From Broadway by Merrill & Edwards, 1914, Photo Gus Edwards & Co. (Cover Artist, Pfeiffer).......................10.00

Just Say I Love Her by Martin Kalmanoff, Sam Ward, Jack Val & Jimmy Dale, 1950...6.00

Just Set A Light by Neal & Davis, 1896 (Pre 1900)...........................16.00

Just Sing A Song For Ireland by Andrew Sterling & Harry Von Tilzer, 1898 (Pre 1900 & Irish)..15.00

Just Some One by Will R. Anderson, 1907, Photo Anna Wilks...........10.00

Just Someone To Love by Clarence Sayles & Sylvester Cross, 1929....3.00

Just Take Me Down To Wonderland by Thomas S. Allen, 1907 (Cover Artist, Starmer & March)..20.00

Just Tell Them That You Saw Me by Paul Dresser, 1895 (Pre 1900)..15.00

Just The Kind Of A Girl You'd Love To Make Your Wife by Lou Klein & Harry Von Tilzer, 1917, Photo Brice & King (Cover Artist, Strauss-Peyton)..10.00

Just The Kind Of Girl You'd Love To Make Your Wife, 1917 (Cover Artist, Pfeiffer)..10.00

Just The Same by Walter Donaldson & Joe Burke, 1927, Caricature Of Paul Whiteman 5.00

Just The Thing For Me (Cover Artist, Pfeiffer)...................................10.00

Just The Way You Are by Billy Joel, 1977 ....3.00

Just The Way You Are by Ralph Freed, 1950.....................................3.00

Just To Mend Mama's Heart by Sam Lewis, Joe Young & Walter Donaldson, 1919...10.00

Just To See You Once Again by Ben Ritchie, 1909 (Cover Artist, Pfeiffer & Deco) **15.00**

Just Try To Picture Me Back Home In Tennessee by Wm. Jerome & Walter Donaldson, 1915, Photo Al Jolson (Cover Artist, Barbelle & Al Jolson)..**16.00**

Just Wait 'Til We Get Home by Daly & Mitzenthal, 1913 (Cover Artist, Pfeiffer)..**10.00**

Just Walking In The Rain by Johnny Bragg & Robert S. Riley, 1953 ...**3.00**

Just You And I by Frank W. Howell & Charles B. Weston, 1913 ....**5.00**

Just You And Me by Charles Tobias, Harry Tobias & Al Sherman, 1928, Photo Benny Meroff (Cover Artist, R.R. & Deco)..........................**5.00**

Just You And Me by James Thatcher, 1915 ....**5.00**

Just You by Con Barth, 1917 (Cover Artist A. Koch)........................**10.00**

Just You by Greene & Matzan, 1914 (Cover Artist, Pfeiffer & Deco) **10.00**

Just You, I And The Moon, Dear? by Grayce L. Hunt, 1914 (Cover Artist, B & W) **5.00**

Just You, Just Me by Raymond Klages & Jesse Greer, 1929, Movie: Marianne, Photo Marion Davies **8.00**

Just You Mother, Just You by Ira Ballou & Arthur Ballou, 1924 ....**6.00**

Jut Another Kiss by Benny Davis & J. Fred Coots, 1929, Photo Veronica Wiggins **5.00**

Jut As Long As You Have Me by Neville Fleeson & Albert Von Tilzer, 1922, Musical: The Gingham Girl...**3.00**

K Of P, The by Ernest S. Williams, 1908 (March)..............................**5.00**

K-A-H-A-L-A by Harry Owens, Harry Tobias & Neil Moret, 1938......**4.00**

K-K-K-Katy by Geoffrey O'Hara, Army Song Leader, 1918 (The Sensational Stammering Song Success Sung By The Soldiers & Sailors) (WWI & Irish) **10.00**

K-K-K-Katy by Geoffrey O'Hara, Army Song Leader, 1918 (The Sensational Stammering Song Success Sung By The Soldiers And Sailors) WAR EDITION (WWI & Irish)..**22.00**

Ka-Lu-A by Anne Caldwell & Jerome Kern, 1921, Musical: Good Morning Dearie **6.00**

Kachina-Hopi Girl's Dance by Albert Van Sand & Arthur Green, 1914 (Indian) **15.00**

Kaddish Of My Ancestry by Edward B. Marks, 1925.........................**3.00**

Kangaroo Hop, The by Melville Morris, 1914 ....**5.00**

Kansas City by Richard Rodgers & Oscar Hammerstein II, 1943 ....**3.00**

Kansas City Kitty by Edgar Leslie & Walter Donaldson, 1929 ....**3.00**

Kansas City Rag by James Scott, 1907 (Rag) **10.00**

Karavan by Abe Olman & Rudy Wiedoeft, 1919................................**5.00**

Kate, Have I Come Too Early, Too Late by Irving Berlin, 1946, Photo Kate Smith (Cover Artist, HAL-W & Irving Berlin) **12.00**

Kathleen by Helene Mora, 1894 (Pre 1900) **15.00**

Kathleen Mine by Edward Heyman & Vincent Youmans.....................**5.00**

Katie by Cole Porter, 1943, Movie: DuBarry Was A Lady.................**10.00**

Katie Cue by Felix McGlennon, 1892 (Pre 1900) **15.00**

Katie O'Conner by Harry Dacre, 1891 (Pre 1900) **15.00**

Katinka by Ben Russell & Henry Tobias, 1926 (Deco).......................**5.00**

Katinkitschka by George Gershwin, 1931 ....**5.00**

Katrina by Don Raye & Gene DePaul, 1949, Movie: Adventures Of Ichabod Crane & Mr. Toad (Disney) **10.00**

Katy-Did, Katy-Didn't by Frank Loesser & Hoagy Carmichael, 1941, Movie: Mr. Bug Goes To Town **5.00**

Katydid Is The Candy Kid by Harold B. Freeman, 1918 (Cover Artist, Pfeiffer)..**14.00**

Keating Wheel March by Bryan, Photo Keating Bicycle (Advertising & March) **20.00**

Keep A Light In The Window For Me by Jos. Mittenthal & Jacob Henry Ellis, 1907...**8.00**

Keep A Little Dream Handy by David & Livingston, 1952, Movie: Jumping Jacks, Photo Martin & Lewis & Mona Freeman.......................**5.00**

Keep Away From Emmeline by Harry Smith & John Stromberg, 1898, Musical: Hurly Burly, Sung by Faye Templeton (Pre 1900 & Black, Black Face)..**20.00**

Keep Away From The Fellow Who Owns An Automobile by Irving Berlin, 1912 (Cover Artist, Pfeiffer, Irving Berlin & Transportation) **22.00**

Keep Cool & Keep Coolidge by Bruce Harper & Ida Cheever Goodwin, 1924, Official Campaign Song Of The Home Town Coolidge Club Of Plymouth, Vermont (President & Political) **75.00**

Keep It A Secret by Jessie Mae Robinson, 1952.................................**3.00**

Keep Moving March by Pond, 1911 (Transportation & March).........**10.00**

Keep On The Sunny Side by Jack Drislane & Theodore Morse, 1906, Photo Joe Brown (Cover Artist, Carter) **10.00**

Keep On Walking by Irving Berlin, 1913 (Cover Artist, Pfeiffer & Irving Berlin)..**15.00**

Keep Smiling by Eli E. Carr, 1930 ....**3.00**

Keep Sweeping The Cobwebs Off The Moon by Sam M. Lewis & Joe Young, 1927 ....**5.00**

Keep The Boys Happy While They're Away by Wm. Henry, 1918 (Cover Artist, Pfeiffer & WWI)..**15.00**

Keep The Home Fires Burning by Lena Guilbert Ford & Ivor Novello, 1915 (WWI)...**14.00**

Keep The Love Lamp Burning by Harry B. Smith & Hugo Riesenfeld, 1919 (Cover Artist, Barbelle & WWI) **15.00**

Keep The Trench Fires Going For The Boys Out There by Eddie Moran & Harry Von Tilzer, 1918 (Cover Artist, Pfeiffer & WWI)..............**20.00**

Keep Thou My Heart by Edward Lockton & May H. Brahe, 1936........**3.00**

Keep Your Eye On The Girlie You Love by Howard Johnson, Alex Gerber & Ira Schuster, 1916, Photo Sophie Tucker (Cover Artist, Rose & Deco) **10.00**

Keep Your Eye On The Girlie You Love by Howard Johnson, Alex Gerber & Ira Schuster, 1916, Photo Eleanor Sherman (Cover Artist, Rose & Deco) **20.00**

Keep Your Eye On Your Heart by Milton Leeds & Henry Manners, 1940...**3.00**

Keep Your Eyes Down Mary, You're A Big Girl Now by Blick, Egan & Whiting, 1920 (Cover Artist, Pfeiffer) **10.00**

Keep Your Face To The Sunshine by Paul B. Armstrong & F. Henri Klickmann, 1918 (WWI)..**10.00**

Keep Your Foot On The Soft Pedal by Will Dillon & Harry Von Tilzer, 1909 ....**10.00**

Keep Your Head Down, Fritzie Boy by Murphy & David, 1916 (WWI)...**10.00**

Keep Your Skirts Down, Maryanne by King, Sterling & Henderson, 1925 ....**5.00**

Keep Your Sunny Side Up by B. G. DeSylva, Lew Brown & Ray Henderson, 1929 ....**10.00**

Keepin' Out Of Mischief Now by Andy Razaf & Thos. Waller, 1932 ..**5.00**

Keepsakes by Egan & Whiting, 1920 (Cover Artist, Pfeiffer) **10.00**

Keiser, Do Yer Want To Buy A Dog by Gus Williams, 1868 (Pre 1900) **15.00**

Kentucky Babe by R. H. Buck & Geibel, 1897 (Pre 1900) **15.00**

Kentucky Blues by Clarence Gaskill, 1921 (Rag) **10.00**

Kentucky Days by Jack Mahoney & Percy Wenrich, 1912 ....**5.00**

Kentucky Dream by Frank H. Warren, S.R. Henry & D. Onivas, 1918 (Cover Artist, E.E. Walton) **5.00**

Kentucky Dream by Frank H. Warren, S. R. Henry & D. Onivas, 1918, Photo Mabel Normand **10.00**

Kentucky Echoes by L. Wolfe Gilbert & Riky Reilly, 1922 ....**5.00**

Kentucky Home by Abe Brashen & Harold Weeks, 1921 ....**5.00**

Kentucky Lullaby by Mill & Cohn, 1926 ....**5.00**

Kentucky Rose by Brooks, 1915 (Cover Artist, Pfeiffer & Deco) **10.00**

Kentucky Waltz by Bill Monroe, 1946, Photo Bill Monroe **3.00**

Kerry Dance, The by James L. Molloy, 1945 (Irish) **5.00**

Kerry Mills New Barn Dance by Kerry Mills, 1908 ....**10.00**

Kerry Mills Palmetto Slide by Kerry Mills, 1910 ....**10.00**

Kerry Mills Turkey Trot by Kerry Mills, 1914 ....**10.00**

Khaki Bill by Harry Watson, 1917 (WWI) **10.00**

Khaki Bill by Harry Watson, 1917 (WWI) **10.00**

Khaki Boys Of U.S.A., The by Ella M. Smith & Howard I. Smith, 1917, Dedicated To 104th Regiment U.S. Infantry (WWI & Dedication) ..**25.00**

Ki-I-Youdleing Dog, The by Irving Berlin (Cover Artist, Pfeiffer & Irving Berlin) **15.00**

Kick In by Kendis & Richmond, 1915 (Cover Artist, Pfeiffer) **10.00**

Kickin' A Hole In The Sky by William Rose, Ballard Macdonald & Jesse Greer, 1930, Movie: Be Yourself, Photo Fannie Brice **10.00**

Kid Days by George M. Cohan (George M. Cohan) **10.00**

Kid Days by Jesse G. M. Glick & Irving M. Wilson, 1919 ....**5.00**

Kid In The Three Corned Pants, The by Al Lewis & John Jacob Loeb, 1937 ....**5.00**

Kid With The Rip In His Pants, The by Jack Owens, 1944 ....**5.00**

Kids by Lee Adams & Charles Strouse, 1960, Movie: Bye Bye Birdie .**8.00**

Killarney My Home O'er The Sea by Frederick Knight Logan, 1911 (Irish) **5.00**

Kimberly Rag by H.H. Hoyt Jr., 1909 (Rag) **15.00**

Kinda Peculiar Brown by J. Burke & Jimmy Van Heusen, 1943 ....**3.00**

King Bee Tango by F.H. Losey, 1915 ....**5.00**

King Chanticleer by Seymour Brown & Nat D. Ayer, 1910 (Cover Artist, Gene Buck & Rag) **15.00**

King Clown, Irish Reel, The by Joseph Kiefer, 1919 (Irish & March) **10.00**

King Cotton March by John Philip Sousa, 1898 (John Philip Sousa, March & Pre 1900) **30.00**

King Cupid by Blake, 1903 ....**5.00**

King For A Day by Sam Lewis, Joe Young & Ted Fiorito, 1928 (Cover Artist, Leff & Deco) **5.00**

King Of Good Fellows March by Yeager, 1906 (March) **10.00**

King Of The Air by Julius K. Johnson, 1910, Dedicated By Permission To Mr. Glenn H. Curtis, The Famous Aviator (Transportation, March & Dedication) **22.00**

King Of The Deep by W. H. Jude **5.00**

King Of The Forest by Abe Losca, 1909 (Cover Artist, Dittmar & March) **15.00**

King's Horses, And The King's Men, The by Noel Gay & Harry Graham, 1930, Musical: Sweet & Low **10.00**

King's New Clothes, The by Frank Loesser, 1951, Movie: Hans Christian Andersen, Photo Danny Kaye **5.00**

Kinkajou, The by Harry Tierney & Joseph McCarthy, 1929, Movie: Rio Rita, Photo Bebe Daniels & John Boles **10.00**

Kinky Kids Parade, The by Gus Kahn & Walter Donaldson, 1925 (Black, Black Face) **25.00**

Kinky-Head by Maud Luise Gardiner & Edward Morris, 1924 (Black, Black Face) **10.00**

Kismet Rag by Scott Hayden & Scott Joplin, 1913 (Scott Joplin & Rag) **50.00**

Kiss A Miss by Maurice Barron, Cal DeVoll & Jack Yellen,1920 (Cover Artist, Van Doorn Morgan) **10.00**

Kiss And Make Up by Ned Miller, Al Bogate & Carl Hoefle, 1927 ......**3.00**

Kiss Before The Dawn, A by Roy Perkins, 1927 ....**3.00**

Kiss by Gillespie & Newman, 1952, Photo Marilyn Monroe & Joseph Cotton **14.00**

Kiss Goodnight, A by Freddie Slack, Floyd Victor & Melvin Herman, 1945 ..**3.00**

Kiss In the Dark, A by B.G. DeSylva & Victor Herbert, 1922 (Victor Herbert) **5.00**

Kiss In Your Eyes, The by Johnny Burke & R. Heuberger, 1947, Movie: The Emperor Waltz, Photo Bing Crosby & Joan Fontaine **10.00**

Kiss Me by Noel Coward, 1939, Movie: Bitter Sweet, Photo Jeannette Macdonald & Nelson Eddy **10.00**

Kiss Me Again by Henry Blossom & Victor Herbert, 1915 (Victor Herbert) **10.00**

Kiss Me Again Sweetheart by Andrew Martin, 1933, Photo Meredith Leckrone (Cover Artist Jeanne Wolff) **5.00**

Kiss Me And I'll Go To Sleep by Dexter Smith & C. A. White, 1870 (Pre 1900) **15.00**

Kiss Me But Don't Say Good-Bye by John T. Rutledge, 1877 (Pre 1900) **15.00**

Kiss Me Dearie by E. Magnus Quist, 1916 (Cover Artist, Pfeiffer & Deco) **10.00**

Kiss Me Good Night Dear Love by Harry Williams, 1904, Photo Eleanor Robson **10.00**

Kiss Me Goodnight by Ben Bernie, Vernon Stevens, Gladys Gillette & Elmer Olson, 1924, Photo Ben Bernie (Deco) **5.00**

Kiss Me Goodnight by Bud Green & Jesse Greer, 1935, Photo Guy Lombardo **5.00**

Kiss Me Goodnight by Gotlier & Nicholls, 1931, Photo Morton Downey **5.00**

Kiss Me Goodnight, Not Goodbye by James F. Hanley,1931, Movie: Merely Mary Ann, Photo Janet Gaynor & Charles Farrell **12.00**

Kiss Me Goodnight, Out The Window You Must Go by Lew Brown & Joe Goodwin, 1913 ....**10.00**

Kiss Me Honey Do by Edgar Smith & John Stromberg, 1889 (Pre 1900) **15.00**

Kiss Me, I've Never Been Kissed Before by Kalmar & Puck, 1913 (Cover Artist, Pfeiffer) **12.00**

Kiss Me Kate by Cole Porter, 1948, Musical: Kiss Me Kate **6.00**

Kiss Me, My Honey, Kiss Me by Irving Berlin & Ted Snyder, 1910, Photo Little Amy Butler (Cover Artist, Frew & Irving Berlin) **15.00**

Kiss Me My Sweetheart by Phil Baxter, 1930 (Cover Artist, Betty Blades & Deco) **5.00**

Kiss Me Sweet by Milton Drake, 1959 ....**3.00**

Kiss Me With Your Eyes by Haven Gillespie & Raymond B. Eldred, 1929 ....**5.00**

Kiss Of Fire by Lester Allen & Robert Hill, 1952, Photo Georgia Gibbs ..**3.00**

Kiss Of Fire by Lester Allen & Robert Hill, 1952, Signed Photo Tony Martin (Signed) **5.00**

Kiss Of Spring by Phil Staats & Walter Rolfe, 1906 (Cover Artist, Starmer) **6.00**

Kiss That Made You Mine, The by J. Will Callahan, Paul Biese & F. Henri Klickmann, 1915 ....**3.00**

Kiss That You've Forgotten, The by Dorothy Dick & Larry Link, 1931...**6.00**

Kiss To Remember Me By, A by Cosmo Hamilton, Edward F. Breier & Edward A. Weinstein, 1920, Photo Francine Larrimore & Charles Cherry **5.00**

Kiss Your Sailor Boy Good-Bye by Irving Berlin, 1913 (Cover Artist, Pfeiffer, Irving Berlin & Patriotic) **22.00**

Kissamee by J. S. Zamecnik, 1914 (Indian) **10.00**

Kisses From You by Sidney Clare & Faye Furbeck, 1925.................**3.00**

Kisses, The Sweetest Kisses Of All by Alex Sullivan & Lynn Cowan, 1918 (Cover Artist, DeTakacs)........................**5.00**

Kitten On The Keys by Zez Confrey, 1921 ....**5.00**

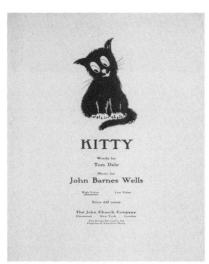

Kitty by Tom Daly & John Barnes Wells, 1919, Dedicated To Mr. James H. Foster, Cleveland, Ohio (Dedication)..........................**6.00**

Kitty by Walter Scanlon, 1923 (Irish)........................**5.00**

Kitty Donohue by Fred Whitehouse & John Ryan, 1922 (Irish)...........**5.00**

Kitty, My Love, Will You Marry Me? by Herbert Hughes, 1918, Movie: Song Of My Heart, Sung by John McCormack..................**10.00**

Klondike Rag by George Botsford, 1928 (Cover Artist, Pfeiffer & Rag)...**10.00**

Knee-Deep In Stardust by Wally Shaw & Chas. J. Gaal, 1941 ....**2.00**

Knock At The Door by Olson, 1924 (Cover Artist, Frederick S. Manning) **15.00**

Knot Of Blue, The by Glen MacDonough & Victor Herbert, 1904 (Victor Herbert)..................................**10.00**

Knowing You by Wood, Eckstein & Henneman, 1948........................**3.00**

Kokomo by Love, Melcher, Phillips & McKenzie, 1988, Movie: Cocktail, Photo Tom Cruise..................................**12.00**

Kokomo, Indiana by Mack Gordon & Josef Myrow, 1947, Movie: Mother Wore Tights, Photo Betty Grable & Dan Dailey..........................**5.00**

L'Amour C'est Comme La Salade by Philias Champagne, 1916 (Cover Artist, F).................................**5.00**

L'Amour Chante by Arthur Smith & Octave Orion, 1914 ....**5.00**

L'Amour Pardonne by Millard G. Thomas & Fred Carbonneau, 1924, Photo Lillian Gish..................................**12.00**

L'Amour Toujours, Tonight For Sure by Sammy Cahn & Nicholas Brodsky, 1951, Movie: Rich, Young & Pretty, Photo Jane Powell, Vic Damone, Wendell Corey, Fernando Lamas & Danielle Darrieux....**5.00**

L'Amour–Toujours–L'Amour by Catherine Chisholm Cushing & Rudolf Friml, 1922 ....**6.00**

L'Inspiration by Kendell Vernon, 1914 (Cover Artist SHW) **3.00**

La Ballerina by Stemberg, 1897 (Pre 1900) **15.00**

La Boheme by G. Puccini, 1898 (Pre 1900).........................**15.00**

La Bomba by Leo Robin & Ralph Rainger, 1936, Movie: The Big Broadcast Of 1937, Photo Jack Benny & Many Stars **8.00**

La Boola Boola by Bob Cole & Billy Johnson, 1907.....................**5.00**

La Brasiliana Tango by Sylvester Belmonte, 1913 (Cover Artist, Starmer)..................................**10.00**

La Camargo by Kurt Schindler, 1918.........................**5.00**

La Cascade by Carl Heins, 1920.........................**3.00**

La Comparsita, The Masked One by Olga Paul & G. H. Matos Rodriguez, 1932, Photo Carlos Molina.........................**6.00**

La Confession by Carey Morgan, 1916.........................**5.00**

La Cucaracha by Carl Field, 1935, Photo Don Pedro....................**5.00**

La Cucaracha by Washington, 1934, Movie: Viva Villa, Photo Wallace Beery & Fay Wray.........................**10.00**

La Detroit by Fraser, 1905.........................**5.00**

La Golandrina, The Swallow by N. Sarradell & Jerry Castillo, 1935, Photo Hunter L. Kahler.........................**4.00**

La Golandrina, The Swallow by N. Sarradell & Jerry Castillo, 1935, Photo Guy Lombardo.........................**4.00**

La Mexicain by Burch & Daly, 1914 (Cover Artist, Pfeiffer & Deco).........................**10.00**

La Pauza by Wilkins, 1914 (Cover Artist, Pfeiffer) **10.00**

La Petite Cafe by May Berger & A. J. Stasny, 1914 (Cover Artist, Pfeiffer)..................................**10.00**

La Petite Coquette by J. S. Zamecnik, 1914.........................**5.00**

La Premiere Neige by Louis J. Paradis & Charles Tanguy, 1911 ....**6.00**

La Rosita by Paul Dupont, 1922.........................**3.00**

La Seduccion by Henri Clique, 1916.........................**3.00**

La Spagnola by Arnstein & Shinker, 1913 (Cover Artist, Pfeiffer) **10.00**

La Valse A Tout Le Monde by Charles Trenet & Charles Jardin, 1936..**4.00**

La Veeda by Nat Vincent & John Alden, 1920 (Cover Artist, Wohlman) ..**5.00**

Ladder Of Roses, The by R.H. Burnside & Raymond Hubbell, 1915, Musical, Hip Hip Hooray **12.00**

Laddie Boy by Will D. Cobb & Gus Edwards, 1907 ....**10.00**

Laddie by J. Fred Lawton & Luella L. Moore, 1914 (Irish).................**6.00**

Laddie In Khaki by Ivor Novello, 1915 (WWI) **10.00**

Ladies Man–Dapper Dan From Dixie Land, The by Lew Brown & Albert Von Tilzer, 1921, Musical: Midnight Rounders, Photo Eddie Cantor (Cover Artist, F.E. Phares, Eddie Cantor & Black, Black Face)....**22.00**

Lady Angeline by Reed & Christie, 1912.........................**5.00**

Lady April Waltz by Fancher, 1896 (Pre 1900) **15.00**

Lady Bird, Cha, Cha, Cha, 1968 (Cover Artist, Norman Rockwell)....**25.00**

Lady Couldn't Be Kissed, The by Al Dubin & Harry Warren, 1937, Movie: The Singing Marines, Photo Dick Powell & Doris Weston **8.00**

Lady Divine by Kountz & Shilkret, 1929, Movie: Divine Lady, Photo Corinne Griffith...**8.00**

Lady Drinks Champagne, The by Meredith Wilson & Alan Jeffreys, 1952, Photo Johnnie Ray...**3.00**

Lady From 29 Palms, The by Allie Wrubel, 1947, Photo Sammy Kaye ..**3.00**

Lady From Fifth Avenue, The by Walter Samuels, Leonard Whitcup & Teddy Powell, 1937, Photo Ben Bernie (Cover Artist, Barbelle) **5.00**

Lady In Red, The by Mort Dixon & Allie Wrubel, 1935, Movie: Caliente, Photo Dolores Del Rio....................................**10.00**

Lady In The Tutti Frutti Hat, The by Leo Robin & Harry Warren, 1943, Movie: The Gang's All Here, Photo Alice Faye, Carmen Miranda, Phil Baker & The King Of Swing, Benny Goodman................................**6.00**

Lady Is A Tramp, The by Rodgers & Hart, 1934, Movie: Words And Music, Photo Judy Garland, Lena Horne, Mickey Rooney, Gene Kelly, Ann Southern, June Allyson & Perry Como **10.00**

Lady Luck by Ray Perkins, 1929, Movie: Show Of Shows **8.00**

Lady Of Dreams by Charles Daniels, 1909 ....**5.00**

Lady Of Liberty by John W. Miller & Paul Wellbaum, 1942 ....**10.00**

Lady Of Love by Alfred Bryan, Pete Wendling & J.S. Zamecnick, 1928...**6.00**

Lady Of Spain by Erell Reaves & Tolchard Evans, 1944, Photo Eddie Fischer **4.00**

Lady Of The Evening by Irving Berlin, 1922, Musical: Music Box Revue (Irving Berlin)...**10.00**

Lady's In Love With You, The by Burton Lane, 1939.........................**4.00**

Lafayette, We Hear You Calling by Mary Earl, 1918 (Cover Artist, Barbelle & WWI) **15.00**

Laff It Off! by Kalmar & Ruby, 1924, Photo Waring Orchestra............**5.00**

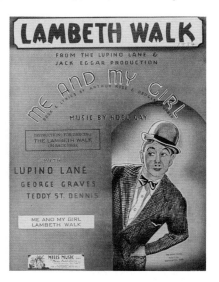

Lambeth Walk by Arthur Rose, Douglas Furber & Noel Gay, 1937, Musical: Me And My Girl, Instructions For Dancing The Lambeth Walk On Back 12.00

Lament To Love by Mel Torme, 1941..**3.00**

Lamp Is Low, The by Mitchell Parish & Peter Shefter, 1939 ....**3.00**

Lamplighter's Serenade, The by Paul Francis Webster & Hoagy Carmichael, 1942, Photo Frank Sinatra...**5.00**

Lamplit Hour, The by Thomas Burke & Arthur A. Penn, 1919 ....**6.00**

Land O'Dreams by O'Keefe, 1920 (Cover Artist, Pfeiffer & Deco)....**10.00**

Land Of Beautiful Dreams by Maurice E. Marks & Charlotte Blake, 1913..**5.00**

Land Of Dreams by Anita Owen, 1919 (Cover Artist, Frederick S. Manning) 15.00

Land Of Golden Dreams, The by C.M. Denison & E.F. Dusenberry, 1912, Photo C.M. Denison & E.F. Dusenberry (Cover Artist, Starmer)..**10.00**

Land Of Hope And Glory by Arthur C. Benson & Edward Elgar, 1902 ..**2.00**

Land Of Long Ago, The by Duncan Sisters, Book By Catherine C. Cushing, Suggested by Uncle Tom's Cabin By Harriet Beecher Stowe, 1923, Musical: Topsy & Eva, Photo Duncan Sisters (Cover Artist, P.M Griffith & Black, Black Face)...**10.00**

Land Of Make Believe, The by Harold B. Freeman, 1919.....................**5.00**

Land Of Might-Have-Been by Edward Moore & Ivor Novello, 1922 ...**3.00**

Land Of My Best Girl, The by Ballard Macdonald & Harry Carroll, 1914 (Cover Artist, Pfeiffer & WWI) **15.00**

Land Of My Sweet Dreams by Wendell Woodhall, 1924.....................**3.00**

Land Of The Long Ago by Charles Knight & Lilian Ray, 1915 ....**5.00**

Land We Love, The by Frank Westfal, 1939..**3.00**

Lane In Spain, A by Al Lewis & Carmen Lombardo, 1926...................**3.00**

Lanky, Yankee Boys In Blue, The by Edward Madden & Theodore F. Morse, 1908 (Patriotic)..**15.00**

Lantern Of Gold by W. Clark Harrington, 1926....................................**3.00**

Lantern Of Love by Raymond W. Peck, Edward Locke & Percy Wenrich, 1924, Musical: Castles In The Air..**8.00**

Lara's Theme by Maurice Jarre, 1965, Movie: Doctor Zhivago, Photo Omar Sharif **5.00**

Lass From County Mayo by Raymond A. Browne, 1897 (Pre 1900 & Irish)..**15.00**

Last Day Of Pompeii, The by Caird M. Vandersloot, 1904 (March) ...**10.00**

Last Farewell, The by J.S. Zamecnik, 1916..**5.00**

Last Long Mile, The by Emil Breitenfeld, 1917 (WWI) **10.00**

Last Mile Home, The by Walter Kent & Walton Farrar, 1949, Signed Photo Sammy Kaye (Signed) **5.00**

Last Night by Halfdan Kjerulp Advertising for Bromo Seltzer (Advertising)..**20.00**

Last Night by Otto Heinzman, 1912...**5.00**

Last Night I Dreamed You Kissed Me by Gus Kahn & Carmen Lombardo, 1928 (Deco) **5.00**

Last Night I Had That Dream Again by Oliver Wallace, 1944 ....**3.00**

Last Night On The Back Porch by Lew Brown & Carl Schraubstader, 1950, Cornell College Song Hit **3.00**

Last Night Was The End Of The World by Andrew B. Sterling & Harry Von Tilzer, 1912 (Cover Artist, Gene Buck) **5.00**

Last Night, When I Dreamed You Had Gone by Richard Howard, 1920..**5.00**

Last Patrol, The by Hugo Riesenfeld & Herbert Stahlberg, 1935 ....**5.00**

Last Rose Of Summer Is The Sweetest Song Of All, The by Arthur Gillespie & Harry Sidney, 1907 ....**10.00**

Last Round Up, Git Along, Little Dogie, Git Along, The by Billy Hill, Musical: Ziegfeld Follies, 1933, Photo Joe Morrison (Cover Artist, Wohlman)..................**10.00**

Last Sweetheart Of Mine, The by Jimmy Monaco & Cliff Friend, 1924...**5.00**

Last Time I Saw Paris, The by Oscar Hammerstein II & Jerome Kern, 1940, Photo Judy Garland **15.00**

Last Trip On The Old Ship, The by John Redmond, Charles J. McCarthy & Lee David, 1939 (Transportation) **10.00**

Last Waltz, The by Less Reed & Barry Mason, 1967, Photo Engelbert Humperdinck **3.00**

Last Week's Kisses by Bernie Wayne, 1949, Photo Harvey Hudson **4.00**

Last Year's Girl by Arthur Swanstrom & Louis Alter, 1933 ....**5.00**

Last Year's Roses by Dempsey & Schmid, 1912 (Cover Artist, Pfeiffer & Deco) **10.00**

Latch String Is Always Hanging Out For You, The by Paul Cohn, 1900, New York Journal & Advertiser Music Supplement..................**10.00**

Later Tonight by Leo Robin & Nacio Herb Brown, 1943, Movie: Wintertime, Photo Sonja Henie, Jack Oakie, Carole Landis, Cesar Romero & Woody Herman..................**10.00**

Latin From Manhattan, A by Al Dubin & Harry Warren, 1932, Movie: The Jolson Story, Photo Larry Parks & Evelyn Keyes (Al Jolson) **10.00**

Latins Know How by Irving Berlin, 1939 (Irving Berlin)..................**5.00**

Laugh And Call It Love by John Burke & James V. Monaco, 1938, Movie: Sing You Sinners, Photo Bing Crosby..................**14.00**

Laugh Clown Laugh by Sam Lewis, Joe Young & Ted Fiorito, 1928, Movie: Laugh Clown Laugh, Photo Lon Chaney..................**12.00**

Laugh & Let The Clouds Roll By by Cobb, Schwartz & Jerome, 1911 (Cover Artist, Pfeiffer) **10.00**

Laugh With A Tear, The by Olcott & Klein, 1908 (Cover Artist, Pfeiffer & Deco) **15.00**

Laughing At Life by Nick & Charles Kenny & Cornell & Bob Todd, 1930..................**3.00**

Laughing Eyes by Powell, 1913 (Cover Artist, Pfeiffer)..................**10.00**

Laughing Irish Eyes by Teepee Mitchell & Sammy Stept, 1936 (Irish) **5.00**

Laughing Love by Christine, 1908 ....**5.00**

Laughing On The Outside, Crying On The Inside by Ben Raleigh & Bernie Wayne, 1946, Photo Dinah Shore, Sammy Kaye, Vincent Lopez & Many Other Stars..................**6.00**

Laughing Water by Frederick W. Hager, 1903 (Cover Artist, Starmer & Indian)..................**20.00**

Laughter Has Come by Ralph Cox, 1925 ....**3.00**

Laura by Johnny Mercer & David Raksin, 1945, Movie: Laura, Photo Dinah Shore..................**5.00**

Laura by Johnny Mercer & David Raksin, 1945, Movie: Laura, Photo Dolly Dawn..................**5.00**

Laura Lee by Meredith Wilson, 1951, Photo Vaughn Monroe **3.00**

Lavender Blue by Larry Morey & Eliot Daniel, 1948, Movie: So Dear To My Heart (Disney) **14.00**

Lawd, You Made The Night Too Long by Sam. M. Lewis & Victor Young, 1932, Photo Guy Lombardo (Cover Artist, Barbelle) **8.00**

Lawrence Of Arabia by Maurice Jarre, 1962, Movie: Lawrence Of Arabia..................**5.00**

Lay Me Down To Sleep In Carolina by Jack Yellen & Milton Ager **5.00**

Lazy by Irving Berlin, 1924 (Irving Berlin) **5.00**

Lazy Countryside by Bobby Worth, 1947, Movie: Fun And Fancy Free (Disney) **10.00**

Lazy Lou'siana Moon by Water Donaldson, 1930 (Cover Artist, Frederick S. Manning) **6.00**

Lazy Luke by George L. Philpot, 1905 (Rag) **15.00**

Lazy Mississippi by Ballard Macdonald & Robert Levenson, 1920 (Cover Artist, Barbelle) **5.00**

Lazy Moon by Bob Cole, J. Rosimond Johnson & Billy Johnson, 1903 (Black, Black Face) **16.00**

Lazy Rhapsody by Mitchell Parish, Ned Washington , Howard Jackson & Harry Sosnick, 1943 ....**3.00**

Lazy River by Carrie Jacobs Bond, 1923 ....**15.00**

Lazy River by Hoagy Carmichael & Sidney Arondin, 1941 ....**3.00**

Lazy Weather by Irving Kahal & Oscar Levant, 1936 ....**3.00**

Lazybones by Johnny Mercer & Hoagy Carmichael, 1933, Photo Guy Lombardo..................**3.00**

Lazybones by Johnny Mercer & Hoagy Carmichael, 1933, Photo Lillian Barnes **4.00**

Le Gigot by S. Romberg, 1913 ....**5.00**

Le Jongleur De Notre-Dame by Maurice Lena & J. Massenet..................**10.00**

Le Naufrage De L'Empress Of Ireland by A. S. de Pierreville & Philias Champagne, 1914 (Irish & Transportation) **35.00**

Le Poeme by Sigmund Romberg, 1913 ....**5.00**

Le Silence by L. De Gramont & Xavier LeRoux, 1898 (Cover Artist, L. Denis, Pre 1900) **18.00**

Le Voyage Aerien by Louis, 1845 (Transportation & Pre 1900) **30.00**

Lead Gently Lord by Harry M. Gilbert & Paul Laurence Dunbar, 1918 ..**3.00**

Lead Kindly Light by Edw. J. Biedermann, 1889 (Pre 1900) **15.00**

Lead Me Into Loveland by Robert Bronson & Herbert Binner, 1913 ....**8.00**

Lead Me To That Beautiful Land by Berlin, Goetz & Snyder, 1912 (Cover Artist, Pfeiffer & Irving Berlin)..................**12.00**

Lead Thou My Soul by Rufus Benton Peery & Rob Roy Peery, 1923 ..**3.00**

Leader Of The German Band, The by Edward Madden & Theodore Morse, 1905 (March)..................**15.00**

Leaf By Leaf The Roses Fall by Whitson & Williams, 1911, Photo Reine Davies **5.00**

Leanin' On The Ole Top Rail by Nick & Charles Kenny, 1939, Photo Leonard Leigh..................**3.00**

Learn To Croon by Sam Coslow & Arthur Johnston, 1933, Movie: College Humor, Photo Bing Crosby..................**10.00**

Learn To Do The Strut by Irving Berlin, 1923, Musical: Music Box Revue (Irving Berlin)..................**10.00**

Learn To Sing A Love Song by Irving Berlin, 1927 (Irving Berlin)....**10.00**

Learning by Marty Symes, Al J. Neiburg & Jerry Levinson, 1934 ....**3.00**

Learning by Sophie Tucker, Jules Buffono & Jimmy Steiger, 1920, Photo Sophie Tucker (Cover Artist, Helen Van Doorn Morgan) **15.00**

Learning McFadden To Waltz by M. F. Carey, 1890 (Pre 1900)..................**15.00**

Learning To Love by Irving A. Hinkley & Allan W. S. MacDuff, 1910 (Cover Artist, E. S. Fisher) **15.00**

Leave It To Love by Lee Berke & Irving Szathmary, 1949, Photo Vaughn Monroe..................**2.00**

Leave Me With A Smile by Earl Burtnett & Chas. Koehler, 1921 (Cover Artist, Barbelle & Deco)..................**10.00**

Leaving On A Jet Plane by John Denver, 1969, Photo Peter, Paul And Mary..................**5.00**

Lee-Ah-Loo by Lehmann & Sinatra, 1952, Movie: Because You're Mine, Photo Mario Lantzman & Doretta Morrow..................**3.00**

Left, A Soldier's Soliloquy by Clarence Gustlin, 1918 (WWI) **15.00**

Left All Alone Again Blues by Ann Caldwell & Jerome Kern, 1920, Musical: The Night Boat (Blues)..................**12.00**

Left Right Out Of Your Heart by Shuman & Garson, 1943, Photo Patti Page **3.00**

Leg Of Mutton by Sigmund Romberg, 1913..................**5.00**

Leg Of Nations, The by Irving Berlin, 1920, Musical: Ziegfeld Follies 1920 (Cover Artist, R.S., Deco & Irving Berlin) **16.00**

Legend Of The Pearls by Irving Berlin, 1921 (Irving Berlin) **10.00**

Legend, The by Zelda Sears & Harold Levey, 1920, Photo Mitzi **5.00**

Legion Of Victory by E. T. Paull, 1921 (Cover Artist, E.T. Paull & March) **35.00**

Lehigh Polka by Dresher, 1875 (Pre 1900 & Transportation).............**30.00**

Lemon Drops by Bernard, 1910 (Cover Artist, Pfeiffer & Rag) **15.00**

Lemon In The Garden Of Love by M. Rourke & Richard Carle, 1906..**5.00**

Lemon Tree by Edward Madden, 1907 ....**5.00**

Lena From Palesteena, 1921, Movie: Midnight Rounder, Photo Eddie Cantor (Eddie Cantor) **15.00**

Lend Me Your Heart & I'll Lend You Mine by Gumble & Mahoney, 1912 (Cover Artist, Pfeiffer & Deco)...**12.00**

Les Ananas by Max Eddy & Fred Pearly, 1923, Photo Maurice Chevalier...**8.00**

Let A Little Pleasure Interfere With Business by Little Jack Little, 1931..**4.00**

Let A Smile Be Your Umbrella by Sammy Fain, Irving Kahal & Francis Wheeler, 1927, Photo Walter Davison (Cover Artist, Barbelle)....**10.00**

Let By-Gones Be By-Gones by Harry Williams, Joe Young & Bert Grant, 1913, Photo Burke & Lorraine (Cover Artist, Pfeiffer) **10.00**

Let 'Er Go by Will Wood, 1907 (March) **15.00**

Let Freedom Ring by Shelley & Mossman, 1940 (Cover Artist, Starmer & Patriotic) **12.00**

Let Him Miss You Just A Little Bit by Charles K. Harris, Gus Van & Joe Schenck, 1917..**12.00**

Let It Rain! Let It Pour! by Cliff Friend & Walter Donaldson, 1925 (Cover Artist, J.R. & Deco)...**6.00**

Let It Snow! by Sammy Cahn & Jule Styne, 1945, Photo Griff Williams ..**4.00**

Let It Snow! by Sammy Cahn & Jule Styne, 1945, Photo Les Brown **4.00**

Let It Snow! by Sammy Cahn & Jule Styne, 1945, Photo Perry Como ..**5.00**

Let Love Awake by Walter E. Grogan & Herbert Oliver, 1911.............**5.00**

Let Lovelight Be Always Shining, For The Loved Ones Away by H. C. Weasner, 1918, Dedicated To John G. Gowans (WWI & Dedication).........**10.00**

Let Me Bring My Clothes Back Home by Irving Jones, 1898 (Pre 1900) **15.00**

Let Me Call You Sweetheart, I'm In Love With You by Beth Slater Whitson & Leo Friedman, 1937 (Cover Artist, Merman).....................**10.00**

Let Me Call You Sweetheart Once Again by Arthur J. Lamb & Chris Smith, 1904...**10.00**

Let Me Dream Again by Sullivan & Stephenson, 1875 (Pre 1900) **15.00**

Let Me Dream by Ray Sherwood & Curtis Gordon, 1919 ....**5.00**

Let Me Entertain You by Stephen Sondheim & Jule Styne, 1959, Movie: Gypsy, Photo Rosalind Russell, Natalie Wood & Karl Malden.......**8.00**

Let Me Go Back by Stoddard, 1904 ....**10.00**

Let Me Go, Lover by Jenny Lou Carson & Al Hill, 1954, Photo Joan Weber..**4.00**

Let Me Have My Dreams by Grant Clarke & Harry Akst, 1929, Movie: On With The Show **8.00**

Let Me In by Bob Merrill, 1951 (Cover Artist, Barbelle) **3.00**

Let Me Kiss The Flag Before I Die by Robert Hood Bowers, 1918, Red Cross Ambulance With Nurse Tending Wounded Soldier (WWI & Red Cross) **35.00**

Let Me Linger Longer In Your Arms by Cliff Friend & Abel Baer, 1924 (Cover Artist JVR & Deco)..**5.00**

Let Me Really Live Tonight by Norton, Burnett & Bennett, 1915 (Cover Artist, Pfeiffer)...**10.00**

Let Me See Your Rainbow Smile by Jean Havez & Ted Barron, 1913 .**5.00**

Let Me Shake The Hand That Shook The Hand Of Sullivan by M. H. Rosenfeld, 1898 (Pre 1900 & Irish)..**20.00**

Let Me Sing And I'm Happy by Irving Berlin, 1932, Movie: The Jolson Story, Photo Larry Parks & Evelyn Keyes (Al Jolson & Irving Berlin) **12.00**

Let Me Sing You To Sleep With A Love Song by Mack Gordon, 1935, Movie: Love In Bloom, Photo Dixie Lee & Joe Morrison...............**5.00**

Let Me Take You Away From Here by M. Pilackey, 1933, Photo Irma Glen (Cover Artist, Heflay)...**6.00**

Let Me Waltz To That Melody by Fred Garton & Ted Garton, 1912 (Cover Artist, Pfeiffer) **10.00**

Let My Home Be Your Home, When You're Down In Dixieland by Al Bernard & Russel Robinson, 1924 (Dixie).................................**10.00**

Let Not Your Heart Be Troubled by Caro Roma & Harris, 1915 (Cover Artist, Pfeiffer & Deco)..**10.00**

Let The Chimes Of Normandy Be Our Wedding Bells by Paul B. Armstrong & F. Henri Klickmann, 1918 (WWI) **16.00**

Let The Flag Fly by L. Wolfe Gilbert, 1917, Photo L. Wolfe Gilbert (WWI)...**15.00**

Let The Rain Pour Down by Foster Carling, 1946, Movie: Song Of The South (Disney)..**10.00**

Let The Rest Of The World Go By by J. Keirn Brennan & Ernest R. Ball, 1919 Dedicated To Julie & Carrie (Dedication).............................**8.00**

Let The Roses Tell by Arthur J. Lamb & Charles H. Maskell, 1924 .....**4.00**

Let Them Alone, They're Married by Carroll, 1914, Photo Marie Dressler (Cover Artist, Pfeiffer) **15.00**

Let There Be Love by Ian Grant & Lionel Rand, 1940.........................**3.00**

Let This Be A Warning To You, Baby by Benny Davis & Lou Handman, 1938, Photo Rose Marie **6.00**

Let This Be Your Mother's Day by Ed Morton, Jas. S. Donahue & Newton B. Heims, 1915, Photo Ed Morton **5.00**

Let Us Dance by Paul Herve, Jean Biquet & Adolf Philipp, 1915, Musical: The Girl Who Smiles......................**10.00**

Let Us Say A Prayer For Daddy by Lew Schaeffer, 1917 (WWI) **10.00**

Let Us Waltz As We Say Goodbye by Beiner, 1925............................**5.00**

Let Your Love Walk In by Joe Greene, 1955, Photo De Castro Sisters.**6.00**

Let Yourself Go by Irving Berlin, 1936, Movie: Follow The Fleet (Irving Berlin)......................................**10.00**

Let's All Be Americans Now by Irving Berlin, Edgar Leslie & Geo. W. Meyer, 1917 (Cover Artist, Barbelle, WWI & Berlin)...................**15.00**

Let's All Be Good Pals Together by Davis & Erfman, 1919 ....**10.00**

Let's All Go 'Round To Mary Ann's by McDonald & Carroll, 1913 (Cover Artist, Pfeiffer) **10.00**

Let's All Go Sleighing Tonight by Alexander Corless & E. Edwin Crerie, 1918 (Cover Artist, E.S. Fisher) **5.00**

Let's All Sing Like The Birdies Sing by Hargreaves, Damerell & Evans, 1923 ....**4.00**

Let's Be Common by Clifford Grey & Victor Schertzinger, 1929, Movie: The Love Parade......................................**5.00**

Let's Be Friendly by Paul Francis Webster & Sammy Fain, 1956, Movie: Hollywood Or Bust, Photo Martin & Lewis & Anita Ekberg..........**5.00**

Let's Begin by Otto Harbach & Jerome Kern, 1933, Movie: Roberta (Deco) **10.00**

Let's Bring New Glory To Old Glory by Harry Warren & Mack Gordon, 1942, Movie: Iceland......................................**6.00**

Let's Bury The Hatchet, In The Kaiser's Head by Addison Burkhardt, 1918 (Cover Artist, J. Domerque & WWI) **20.00**

Let's Call A Heart A Heart by John Burke & Arthur Johnston, 1936, Movie: Pennies From Heaven, Photo Bing Crosby........................**8.00**

Let's Call It A Day by Lew Brown & Ray Henderson, 1932, Musical Revue: Strike Me Pink....................................**8.00**

Let's Call The Whole Thing Off by George Gershwin, 1937 ....**5.00**

Let's Choo Choo Choo To Idaho by Rinker & Huddleston, 1950, Movie: Duchess Of Idaho, Photo Esther Williams, Van Johnson, John Lund & Lena Horne **6.00**

Let's Do It by Cole Porter, 1928...............**5.00**

Let's Drift Away On Dreamer's Bay by Harold Spina & George McConnell, 1931 ....**3.00**

Let's Face The Music And Dance by Irving Berlin, 1936 (Irving Berlin)..**10.00**

Let's Fall In Love by Ted Koehler & Harold Arlen, 1933, Movie: Let's Fall In Love, Photo Ann Southern....................**12.00**

Let's Fill The Old Oaken Bucket With Love by Alfred Bryan, James Kendis & Jack Wells, 1914 (Cover Artist, Starmer) **10.00**

Let's Finish The Job by Watson, 1919 (WWI)...................................**15.00**

Let's Get Friendly by Jack Yellen, Louis Silver & Dougherty, 1931 ....**3.00**

Let's Get Lost by Frank Loesser & Jimmy McHugh, 1943, Movie: Happy Go Lucky, Photo Mary Martin, Dick Powell, Betty Hutton, Eddie Bracken & Rudy Vallee.........................**10.00**

Let's Get The Umpire's Goat by Nora Bayes & Jack Norworth, 1910 (Sports) **25.00**

Let's Get Together by Merchant, 1950..........**3.00**

Let's Give Love Another Chance by Harold Adamson & Jimmy McHugh, 1937, Movie: Hitting A New High, Photo Lily Pons, Jack Oakie, Eric Blore, Edward Everett Horton & John Howard **10.00**

Let's Give Three Cheers For Love by Mack Gordon & Harry Revel, 1934, Movie: College Rhythm, Photo Joe Penner, Lanny Ross, Jack Oakie & Helen Mack.................................**5.00**

Let's Go Back To Dreamy Lotus Land by Jack Frost, Paul Biese & F. Henri Klickmann, 1917 ....**5.00**

Let's Go Bavarian by Harold Adamson & Burton Lane, 1933, Movie: Dancing Lady **10.00**

Let's Go by Berton Braley & Jerome Kern, 1918, Musical: Toot Toot **10.00**

Let's Go by Charles Straight, 1915 ....**5.00**

Let's Go Home by Burt, 1908, Photo Ila Grannon (Cover Artist, Starmer)..................................**10.00**

Let's Go Into A Picture Show by McRee & Von Tilzer, 1908...........**10.00**

Let's Go Native by Geo. Marion Jr. & Richard A. Whiting, 1930, Movie: Let's Go Native **8.00**

Let's Go To Church by Steve Allen, 1950, Photo Jimmy Wakely & Margaret Whiting **5.00**

Let's Go To Cuba by Jack Darrell, 1920, Photo Brock Sisters (Cover Artist, Millard & Deco) **10.00**

Let's Grow Old Together by James Brockman, Will Oakland & Ira Schuster, 1926 ....**5.00**

Let's Grow Old Together, Honey by MacDonald, McKeon & Walker, 1911 (Cover Artist, Pfeiffer) **10.00**

Let's Have Another Cup Of Coffee by Irving Berlin, 1932, Musical: Face The Music (Cover Artist, Leff & Irving Berlin)....................**8.00**

Let's Help The Irish Now by Bennie Grossman & Billy Frisch, 1919, Photo Frank Mullane (Irish & WWI) **15.00**

Let's Join The Army, A Manual Of Arms And Fingers For Boys At The Piano by John Thompson, 1929 (Cover Artist, George Hauman)....**5.00**

Let's Keep The Glow In Old Glory And The Free In Freedom Too by Wilbur D. Nesbit & Robert Speroy, 1918 (WWI)....................**15.00**

Let's Knock Knees by Gordon & Revel, 1934, Movie: Gay Divorcee, Photo Fred Astaire & Ginger Rogers **10.00**

Let's Make Love By The Fireside by J.R. Shannon & James White, 1915 (Cover Artist, Dulin Studio) **5.00**

Let's Make Love While The Moon Shines by Harris & Robinson, 1911 ..**6.00**

Let's Make Memories Tonight by Lew Brown, Charlie Tobias & Sam H. Stept, 1938, Musical: Yokel Boy....................**8.00**

Let's Not Talk About Love by Cole Porter, 1943, Movie: Let's Face It ..**6.00**

Let's Put Out The Lights And Go To Sleep by Herman Hupfeld, 1932, Photo Rudy Vallee (Cover Artist, Jorg Harris) **10.00**

Let's Sail To Dreamland by Harry Kogen, Henry Busse & Lou Holzer, 1938 (Cover Artist, Merman) **3.00**

Let's Say Goodnight To The Ladies by Lew Brown & Bill Gale, 1939 (Cover Artist, Im-Ho & Deco) **5.00**

Let's Sing A Gay Little Spring Song by Frank Churchill & Larry Morey, 1942, Movie: Bambi (Disney)....................**18.00**

Let's Sing A Song About Sue by Gordon & Grosz, 1943 ....**3.00**

Let's Sit And Talk About You by Fields & McHugh, 1931................**6.00**

Let's Start The New Year Right by Irving Berlin, 1942 (Irving Berlin)...**5.00**

Let's Take A Ride On The Jitney Bus by McConnell, 1915 (Transportation)....................................**20.00**

Let's Take An Old Fashioned Walk by Irving Berlin, 1948, Musical: Miss Liberty (Irving Berlin) **10.00**

Let's Take The Long Way Home by Johnny Mercer & Harold Arlen, 1944, Movie: Here Come The Waves **16.00**

Let's Try Again by Charles Newman & Isham Jones, 1932 ....**3.00**

Let's Wait For the Last Train Home by Cunningham & Piani, 1914 (Cover Artist, Pfeiffer & Transportation)....................**10.00**

Let's You And I Just Say Good-bye by George M. Cohan (George M. Cohan) **10.00**

Letter Edged In Black, The by Hattie Nevada, 1897 (Pre 1900).........**15.00**

Letter From Ireland by J. F. Mitchell, 1886 (Pre 1900 & Irish) **15.00**

Letter From No Man's Land, A by Harold B. Freeman, 1918 (Cover Artist, Pfeiffer & World War I)....................**15.00**

Letter Song by Straus & Strange, 1908 ....**5.00**

Letter That Never Came, The by Paul Dresser, 1886 (Pre 1900)........**15.00**

Letter That Never Reached Home, The by Edgar Leslie, Bernie Grossman & Archie Gottler, 1916 (WWI) **10.00**

Letter To Heaven, A by Lizzie Paine, 1888 (Pre 1900)....................**15.00**

Letter To My Mother by Small & Silver, 1933 ....**5.00**

Levee Land by George L. Cobb, 1915 (Cover Artist, Pfeiffer, Dixie & Transportation) **35.00**

Levee Lou by Edward Madden & Gus Edwards, 1912, (Cover Artist, Starmer & Transportation).....................................**20.00**

Liar by Frank Mandel, Oscar Hammerstein II & Sigmund Romberg, 1928, Musical: The New Moon..**10.00**

Liberty Bell, It's Time To Ring Again by Joe Goodwin & Halsey K. Mohr, 1917 (Cover Artist, Barbelle, Patriotic & WWI)................**10.00**

Liberty Bell March, The by John Philip Sousa, 1898 (John Philip Sousa, March & Pre 1900) **35.00**

Liberty by Harry Kennedy, 1884 (Pre 1900).......................**16.00**

Liberty Loan March by John Philip Sousa, 1918 (John Philip Sousa, March & WWI) **25.00**

Liberty Statue Is Looking Right At You by Guy Emprey, 1918 (WWI)...**50.00**

Liberty Waltz by Oscar Duryea & J. Bodewalt Lampe, 1918 (WWI) ...**5.00**

Liebestraum by Jay Arnold & Franz Liszt, 1935, Photo Ray Herbeck (Cover Artist NPS) **6.00**

Lies by George E. Springer & Harry Barris, 1931, Photo Rudy Vallee (Cover Artist, Barbelle) **10.00**

Lies by George E. Springer & Harry Barris, 1931, Photo Russ Columbo (Cover Artist, Barbelle) **10.00**

Life And Love Seem Sweeter After The Storm by Jack Nelson, 1924 (Cover Artist, Barbelle) **6.00**

Life Begins When You're In Love by Brown & Schertzinger, 1936, Movie: The Music Goes Round, Photo Harry Richman & Rochelle Hudson...**10.00**

Life Boat by Felix McGlennon, 1891 (Pre 1900) **15.00**

Life Goes On by Theodorakis, 1966, Movie: Zorba The Greek, Photo Anthony Quinn **5.00**

Life Has Just Begun by Paul Herve, Jean Biquet & Adolf Philipp, 1915, Musical: The Girl Who Smiles.........................**8.00**

Life Is A Dream by Arthur Freed & Oscar Straus **3.00**

Life Is A See-Saw by Smith & Hubbel, 1906........................**5.00**

Life Is A Song by Joe Young & Fred E. Ahlert, 1935, Photo Frank Parker **3.00**

Life Is But A Fading Flower by Hockey, 1911 ....**5.00**

Life Is Just A Bowl Of Cherries by Lew Brown & Ray Henderson, 1931, Musical: George White's Scandals..........................**10.00**

Life Isn't All Roses, Rosie by Al Bryan & Seymour Furth, 1911.........**5.00**

Life Of A Rose, The by B.G. DeSylva & George Gershwin, 1923, Musical: George White's Scandals (Deco).......................**10.00**

Life Would Be Worth Living Again by Jimmie Franklin & Anthony Trini, 1933 ....**5.00**

Life's A Funny Proposition After All by George M. Cohan, 1904 (George M. Cohan).....................................**16.00**

Life's Garden by Fred J. Smith & Carrie Jacobs Bond, 1914 ....**15.00**

Lift Every Voice And Sing by J. W. Johnson & R. Johnson, 1900........**5.00**

Lift The Juleps To Your Two Lips by Grant Clarke & Harry Akst, 1929, Movie: On With The Show **14.00**

Light A Candle In The Chapel by Harry Pease, Ed G. Nelson & Duke Leonard, 1942 (Cover Artist, Im-Ho)......................**3.00**

Light At Evening Time by R. H. Robinson & E. L. Ashford, 1924 ....**3.00**

Light Cavalry by Von Suppe, 1909 (Cover Artist, Pfeiffer)...........**12.00**

Light House By The Sea by Gussie L. Davis, 1886 (Pre 1900) **15.00**

Light In A Lover's Eyes, The by Carlton Russell Foster & Ivy Anderson Foster, 1915 ....**5.00**

Light In The Window by Redd Evans, 1951 ....**3.00**

Light My Fire by The Doors, 1967, Photo The Doors **3.00**

Light Of My Life, The by Mort Greene & Harry Revel, 1942, Movie: Call Out The Marines..................................**6.00**

Lighthouse Bell Is A Wedding Bell, The by Arthur J. Lamb & Alfred Solman, 1925 ....**5.00**

Lighthouse Blues, The by Schuster, Yellman & Piantadosi, 1927 (Cover Artist, Pfeiffer & Blues) **10.00**

Lightning Express by Fitzpatrick, 1905 (Transportation)...................**10.00**

Lightning Rag by Hylands, 1912 (Rag)................................**10.00**

Lights Of My Home Town by C.K. Harris, 1915 (Cover Artist, Pfeiffer)..**10.00**

Lights Out by Billy Hill, 1935, Photo Fred Waring **5.00**

Lights Out by Billy Hill, 1935, Photo Freddy Martin **5.00**

Lights Out by Billy Hill, 1935, Photo Ray Noble **5.00**

Lights Out by Billy Hill, 1935, Photo Rudy Vallee.................**10.00**

Like A Breath Of Spring-Time by Al Dubin & J. Burke, 1929, Movie: Hearts In Exile **8.00**

Like A Diamond From The Sky by Leo Bennett, 1915.......................**5.00**

Like A Rose In My Garden by Ernest W. Chapman & Robert E. Harty, 1930 ....**5.00**

Like A Rose You Have Faded Away by Carl Muller & Jimmie McHugh, 1916 ....**5.00**

Like An Angel You Flew Into Everyone's Heart by Harry A Stone, John McLaughlin, Jimmy McHugh & Irving Mills, 1927, Photo Capt. Chas. A. Lindbergh (Lindbergh, Military Personnel & Transportation)..**40.00**

Like He Loves Me by Anne Caldwell & Vincent Youmans, 1926 ....**5.00**

Like Ships That Pass In The Night by Roden & Petrie, 1916 (Cover Artist, Pfeiffer & Transportation).............................**16.00**

Like Someone In Love by Johnny Burke & Jimmy Van Heusen, 1944, Movie: Belle Of The Yukon, Photo Dinah Shore, Randy Scott & Gypsy Rose Lee.......................................**5.00**

Lil' Black Nigger by Betty Reynolds & Edward Morris, 1924 (Black, Black Face) **15.00**

Lila by Archie Gottler, Charles Tobias & Maceo Pinkard, 1928 (Cover Artist, Helen Van Doorn Morgan & Deco) **16.00**

Lilac Blossoms by Percy Wenrich, 1908, Dedicated To Mrs. E. B. Davis (Cover Artist, Henrich & Dedication) **10.00**

Lilacs In the Rain by Mitchell Parish & Peter DeRose, 1939, Photo Jack Jenney **3.00**

Lilies Of Lorraine by Clifford Grey & Pierre Connor, 1926.................**6.00**

Lillette by Jack Gold, 1948, Photo King Cole Trio **4.00**

Lily Belle by Dave Franklin & Irving Taylor, 1945, Photo Eddie Cantor (Eddie Cantor) **5.00**

Lily Belle by Dave Franklin & Irving Taylor, 1945, Photo Frank Sinatra ..**4.00**

Lily by Ballard MacDonald & Harry Warren, 1927.......................**5.00**

Lily Of France by Weston, Smith & Richmond, 1913 (Cover Artist, Pfeiffer) **12.00**

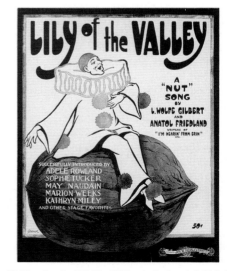

Lily Of The Valley by L. Wolfe Gilbert & Anatol Friedland, 1917 (Cover Artist, Starmer)...**10.00**

Lily Or The Rose, The by Monroe H. Rosenfeld & Alfred Solman, 1907...**10.00**

Limbo Rock by William E. "Billy" Strange & Jon Sheldon, 1962 ....**2.00**

Limehouse Blues by Douglas Furber & Philip Braham, 1924, Musical: Andre Charlot's Revue 1924 (Cover Artist, White Studio) **10.00**

Limerick Girls, The by Chauncey Olcott, 1902 (Irish).........................**10.00**

Limited Express March by Duss, 1894 (Pre 1900, March & Transportation)...**15.00**

Lincoln Centennial Grand March by E. T. Paull, Photo President Lincoln (Cover Artist, E. T. Paull, President & March) **50.00**

Linda by Jack Lawrence, 1945, Photo Charlie Spivak **4.00**

Linda by Jack Lawrence, 1945, Photo Frankie Carle **4.00**

Linda by Jack Lawrence, 1945, Photo Jack Owens.............................**4.00**

Linda by Jack Lawrence, 1945, Photo Patti Clayton **4.00**

Linda by Jack Lawrence, 1946, Photo Buddy Clark **4.00**

Linda Jane by Norworth, Morton & Huston, 1915 (Cover Artist, Pfeiffer)...**10.00**

Lindbergh The Eagle Of The U.S.A. by Howard Johnson & Al Sherman, 1927, Photo Lindbergh Standing Beside Spirit Of St. Louis, Small Photo Of His Mother (Lindbergh & Transportation) **40.00**

Lindy by Frederick H. Martens & Charles Gilbert Spross, 1915 ....**10.00**

Lindy, Lindy! by Eisenbourg, 1927, Map of Flight From USA To France (Lindbergh & Transportation) **50.00**

Linger Awhile by Harry Owens & Vincent Rose, 1923, Photo Jack Shildkret (Cover Artist, JVR & Deco)..**5.00**

Linger Awhile by Harry Owens & Vincent Rose, 1923, Photo Moher & Eldridge (Deco) **10.00**

Linger Awhile by Vincent Rose & Harry Owens, 1923, Photo Ray Miller & Orchestra (Cover Artist, JVR & Deco) **10.00**

Linger Longer, Loo by Younge & Sydney Jones, 1893 (Pre 1900) **15.00**

Lion Hunter's Waltzes, The by Clyde L. Craig, 1901 (Sports) **15.00**

Lion Trainer's March, The by Cesare Forsiello, 1894 (Pre 1900 & March)..**16.00**

Lips by Ott, 1917 ....**3.00**

Lisbon Antigua by Harry Dupree, Raul Portela, J. Galhardo & A. Devale, 1937, Photo Nelson Riddle..**3.00**

List'ning On Some Radio by Gene Buck, Victor Herbert, Louis A. Hirsch & Dave Stamper, 1922, Ziegfeld Follies, 1922 (Victor Herbert & Deco)..**16.00**

Listen, Mary by Constance Wilford & May H. Brahe, 1937................**3.00**

Listen People by Gouldman, 1966, Movie: When The Boys Meet The Girls, Photo, Connie Francis, Harve Presnell, Liberace, Louis Armstrong & Herman's Hermits **12.00**

Listen To Me by Howard Johnson & Carlo Sanderson, 1921, Musical: Tangerine **10.00**

Listen To My Tale Of Woe by Eugene Field, 1884 (Pre 1900) **15.00**

Listen To That Dixie Band by Jack Yellen & George L. Cobb, 1914 (Dixie)..**5.00**

Listen To The German Band by Mack Gordon & Harry Revel, 1932 ...**5.00**

Listen To The Knocking At The Knitting Club by Von Tilzer & Hanlon, 1917, Photo Adele Rowland (Cover Artist, Pfeiffer) **12.00**

Listen To The Mocking Bird by Louis A. Drumheller, 1908 (Cover Artist, Starmer) **10.00**

Listen To The Mocking Bird by Louis A. Drumheller, 1935 (Cover Artist, James Axeltod) **10.00**

Listen To The Silver Trumpets by James Bland (Pre 1900 & Black, Black Face) **16.00**

Listen To This by Mel B. Kaufman, 1916...**5.00**

Listening by Harry Harris, Tony Bell & Joe Jolman, 1921 ....**5.00**

Listening by Irving Berlin, 1924 (Irving Berlin) **5.00**

Little Alabamy Coon by Hattie Starr, 1893 (Pre 1900 & Black, Black Face) **28.00**

Little Angel Told Me So, A by Sam Coslow, 1934, Movie: One Hour Late, Photo Joe Morrison & Helen Twelvetrees (Deco) **8.00**

Little Annie Rooney by Michael Nolan, 1925......................................**5.00**

Little April Shower by Frank Churchill & Larry Morey, 1942, Movie: Bambi (Disney)..**12.00**

Little Arrows by Mike Hazelwood & Albert Hammond, 1968, Photo Leapy Lee **2.00**

Little Birch Canoe And You, A by J. Will Callahan & Lee S. Roberts, 1918 ....**5.00**

Little Bird Told Me, A by Harvey Q. Brooks, 1948, Photo Evelyn Knight...**3.00**

Little Bit Bad, A by Benny Davis, Garry Conley & Al Adridge, 1925..**3.00**

Little Bit Independent, A by Edgar Leslie & Joe Burke, 1935, Photo Ozzie Nelson & Harriet Hilliard (Cover Artist, HBK) **5.00**

Little Bit Independent, A by Edgar Leslie & Joe Burke, 1935, Photo Guy Lombardo (Cover Artist, HBK)...**5.00**

Little Bit Later On, A by Al J. Neiburg & Jerry Levinson, 1936 ....**3.00**

Little Bit O'Honey, A by W.G. Wilson & Carrie Jacobs Bond, 1917, Dedicated to Miss Lucille M. Showalter (Cover Artist, Mrs. Luther D. Derwent, Dedication, & Black, Black Face) **22.00**

Little Bit Of A Fellow by Edward Morris, 1925 ....**5.00**

Little Bit Of Everything, A by Irving Berlin, 1912 (Cover Artist, Pfeiffer & Irving Berlin)..**15.00**

Little Bit Of Heaven Shure They Call It Ireland, A by J. Keirn Brennan & Ernest R. Ball, 1914 (Irish)..**6.00**

Little Bit Of Sunshine From Home, A by Ballard McDonald, Joe Goodwin & James F. Hanley, 1918, Introduced On Vaudeville Stage by Famous Sailor, William J. Reilly (WWI & Military Personnel)................**20.00**

Little Black Me by Thurland Chattaway, 1899 (Pre 1900 & Black, Black Face) **15.00**

Little Blue Bonnet Girl by Fred Fisher, 1918 (Salvation Army & WWI) **35.00**

Little Blue Gate, The by Edward Lynn & Charles Wakefield Cadman, 1930 ....**4.00**

Little Bluebird Of My Heart by Twohig & Grey, 1925.........................**4.00**

Little Bo-Peep Has Lost Her Jeep by Browne, 1942 (Transportation).**10.00**

Little Boy Blue by Ethelbert Nevin, 1891 (Pre 1900) **15.00**

Little Boy Blue by Eugene Field & E. Clare Johnson, 1905 ....**10.00**

Little Boy Blue by H. Engelmann, 1908 (March) **15.00**

Little Boy by Ray Klages & Billy Fazioli **6.00**

Little Boy Called "Tops", A by Edward Madden & Theodore F. Morse, 1904 ....**6.00**

Little Boy That Never Was by Storey, Watson & Cohen, 1918 (Cover Artist, Pfeiffer)...**10.00**

Little Boy's Christmas, A by Claire, Elliott & Hettel, 1959................**5.00**

Little Brook, The by Werner, 1911 (Cover Artist, Pfeiffer)................**10.00**

Little Brown Bird by Helen N. Nightingale & Teresa Del Riego, 1912..**5.00**

Little Brown Gal by Wood, McDiarmid & Noble, 1935 (Black, Black Face) **10.00**

Little Brown Hand by Arthur S. Penn, 1922 ....**5.00**

Little Brown Jug by Eastburn **5.00**

Little Bunch Of Shamrocks, A by Andrew Sterling, Wm. Jerome & Harry Von Tilzer, 1913 (Irish)........................**5.00**

Little Bunch Of Whiskers On His Chin by W. Jerome & A Mack, 1894 (Pre 1900) **15.00**

Little Bungalow, A by Irving Berlin, 1925 (Irving Berlin) **5.00**

Little Butterfly by Irving Berlin, 1923, Musical: Music Box Review 1923-24 (Irving Berlin)............................**12.00**

Little By Little You're Breaking My Heart by Max Clay & Robert Levenson, 1919 (Cover Artist, White, Boston)........................**5.00**

Little Child by Wayne Shanklin, 1953 ....**3.00**

Little Child Came He, A by Claude Warford, 1920 ....**3.00**

Little China Figure, A by Franco Leoni, 1935 ....**5.00**

Little Church Around The Corner, The by Grey & Carroll, 1913 (Cover Artist, Pfeiffer)........................**10.00**

Little Colonel by Paul Francis Webster & Lew Pollack, 1935, Movie: The Little Colonel, Photo Shirley Temple (Shirley Temple) **15.00**

Little Coon's Prayer, A by DeBurgh Darcy & Barbara Hope, 1921 (Black, Black Face) **16.00**

Little Crumbs Of Happiness by J. Brennan & Ernest R. Ball, 1920......**5.00**

Little Curly Hair In A High Chair by Charles Tobias & Nat Simon, 1940, Movie: Forty Little Mothers, Photo Eddie Cantor (Eddie Cantor).**12.00**

Little Curly Head by Bernard Hamblen, 1919........................**5.00**

Little Damozel, The by Fred E. Weatherly & Ivor Novello, 1912.........**4.00**

Little Dancers, The by Lawrence Binton & Richard Hageman, 1935....**5.00**

Little Darling, Dream Of Me by Joseph P. Skelly, 1883 (Pre 1900)....**15.00**

Little Daughter Nell by Edward Harrigan & David Braham, 1883 (Pre 1900)........................**15.00**

Little Did I Know by Nick & Charles Kenny & Abner Silver, 1943, Photo Kate Smith **10.00**

Little Dutch Mill by Ralph Freed & Harry Barris, 1934, Signed Photo Bing Crosby (Signed) **12.00**

Little Em'ly by Dexter Smith & C. A. White, 1870, Repectfully Dedicated To John H. Selwyn, Esq. (Pre 1900 & Dedication)........................**16.00**

Little Empty Stockings by Harry Kennedy, 1883 (Pre 1900)...............**15.00**

Little Fairy March by L. Streabbog, 1935 (March) **5.00**

Little Fighting Soldier Man by Lillian Coffin, 1905, Boston Sunday American Supplement, Photo Lillian Coffin **10.00**

Little Fish In A Big Pond by Irving Berlin, 1949, Musical: Miss Liberty (Irving Berlin)........................**16.00**

Little Flower by Sidney Becket, 1952 ....**3.00**

Little Ford Rambled Right Along, The by Fay Foster & Byron Gay, 1914 (Transportation)........................**25.00**

Little Fraternity Pin by Paul Gibbons & Roy Ringwald, 1937, Movie: Varsity Show **5.00**

Little Fraud by Ned Harrigan, 1871 (Pre 1900)....................**15.00**

Little French Clock, The by Richard Kountz, 1936.....................**5.00**

Little Game Of Love by Lolomon & Osias, 1911 ....**15.00**

Little Genius by Walter G. Samuels, Leonard Whitcup & Teddy Powell, 1937 (Cover Artist, Im-Ho)........................**5.00**

Little Gift Of God by Mary C. Hartnett & Enrico Barraja, 1901 ....**10.00**

Little Girl, A Little Boy, A Little Moon, A by Robert King & Harry Warren, 1927, Photo Four Aristocrats (Cover Artist, Starmer) **12.00**

Little Girl Dressed In Blue, The by F. N. Vinard, 1932, Photo Shelly Jean Davis........................**4.00**

Little Girls We Met Upon The Train by Stauffer, 1896 (Pre 1900 & Transportation) **22.00**

Little Good For Nothing's Good For Something After All, The by L. Klein & H. Von Tilzer, 1918, Photo Laurette Taylor (Cover Artist, Pfeiffer) **12.00**

Little Grey Home In The West, A by D. Eardley-Wilmot & Hermann Lohr, 1911 ....**5.00**

Little Grey Mother by Grossman & DeCosta, 1915 (WWI) **15.00**

Little Grey Mother O'Mine by Evans Lloyd, 1925 ....**5.00**

Little Grey Mother Who Waits All Alone, The by Bernard Grossman & Harry DeCosta, 1915, Photo Mary Maurice, Vitagraph Player (WWI & March) **12.00**

Little Grey Sweetheart Of Mine by Fred Fisher, 1922 ....**5.00**

Little House That Love Built, The by Lam & Blake, 1905 ....**5.00**

Little House Upon The Hill, The by Ballard Macdonald, Joe Goodwin & Harry Puck, 1915, Photo Emma Carus (Cover Artist, Dunk) 10.00

Little House Upon The Hill, The by Ballard Macdonald, Joe Goodwin & Harry Puck, 1915, Photo Bessie Wynn (Cover Artist, Dunk)........**10.00**

Little Irish Rose by Anne Nichols & J. S. Zamecnik, 1928, Movie: Abie's Irish Rose (Irish)........................**12.00**

Little Johnny Dugan by Tom & Andrew Mack, 1893 (Pre 1900)........**15.00**

Little Kinkey Wooley Head by Charles Noel Douglas & Herman Perlet, 1898 (Pre 1900 & Black, Black Face)........................**25.00**

Little Kiss At Twilight, A by Leo Robin & Ralph Rainger, 1938, Movie: Give Me A Sailor, Photo Martha Raye, Bob Hope, Betty Grable & Jack Whiting........................**12.00**

Little Kiss Each Morning, A by Harry Woods, 1930, Movie: The Vagabond Lover, Photo Rudy Vallee........................**10.00**

Little Lady Make Believe by Charlie Tobias & Nat Simon, 1938, Photo Eddie Cantor (Cover Artist, Merman & Eddie Cantor).................**10.00**

Little Lady Make Believe by Charlie Tobias & Nat Simon, 1938, Photo Kate Smith (Cover Artist, Merman)........................**12.00**

Little Lane by Penaloza & Filberto, 1933........................**5.00**

Little Log Cabin Of Dreams by James Hanley & Eddie Dowling, 1927, Respectfully Dedicated To Mary Cook Cowerd (Dedication) **6.00**

Little Lost Child, The by Edward B. Marks & Joseph Stern, 1896 (Pre 1900)........................**35.00**

Little Lost Youth Of Me by Carrie Jacobs Bond, 1923 (Carrie Jacobs Bond) **15.00**

Little Love, A Little Kiss, A by Adrian Ross & Lao Silesu, 1912 (Cover Artist, Frank M. Barton)........................**5.00**

Little Love Will Go A Long, Long Way, A by Carmen Lombardo & John Jacob Loeb, 1938........................**6.00**

Little Man-You've Had A Busy Day by Maurice Sigler, Al Hoffman & Mabel Wayne, 1934 (Cover Artist, Harris) **10.00**

Little Marion Parker by Bill Barrett, 1928..**5.00**

Little Min-Nee-Ha-Ha by Bert Kalmar & Harry Ruby, 1921 (Indian)..**20.00**

Little Miss Okeechobee Oh! Be Mine by Walter Donaldson, 1928.......**5.00**

Little More Pepper, A by Harry J. Lincoln, 1914................................**5.00**

Little Mother by Erno Rapee & Lew Pollack, 1928, Musical: Four Sons, Photo Bob Olsen................................**12.00**

Little Mother Of Mine by Walter H. Brown & H. T. Burleigh, 1917, Sung by John McCormack (WWI)................................**15.00**

Little Nell And I by J. P. Skelly, 1891 (Pre 1900)........................**15.00**

Little Newsboy's Death, The by C. Benjamin & Gus. B. Brighame, 1893 (Pre 1900)................................**20.00**

Little Old Church In England, A by Irving Berlin, 1941 (Irving Berlin)...**12.00**

Little Old Church In The Valley, The by Gus Kahn, Gene Arnold & Egbert Van Alstyne, 1931 (Cover Artist, Ben Harris) **5.00**

Little Old Garden, The by Edward Lockton & Thos. J. Hewitt, 1919 (Cover Artist, Ray) **5.00**

Little Old Lady by Stanley Adams & Hoagy Carmichael, 1936, Musical: The Show Is On, Photo Beatrice Lillie & Bert Lahr **10.00**

Little Old Mill, The by Pelosi, Ilda & Towers, 1947............................**3.00**

Little Old New York by Arthur Schwartz & Howard Dietz, 1929.........**5.00**

Little Old Red Schoolhouse by Wheeler & Durham, 1890 (Pre 1900) 12.00

Little On The Lonely Side, A by Dick Robertson, James Cavanaugh & Frank Weldon, 1944, Photo Guy Lombardo (Cover Artist, Im-Ho) **3.00**

Little On The Lonely Side, A by Dick Robertson, James Cavanaugh & Frank Weldon, 1944, Photo Billy Rogers (Cover Artist, Im-Ho) **3.00**

Little On The Lonely Side, A by Dick Robertson, James Cavanaugh & Frank Weldon, 1944, Photo George Olson & Orchestra (Cover Artist, Im-Ho) **3.00**

Little On The Lonely Side, A by Dick Robertson, James Cavanaugh & Frank Weldon, 1944, Photo Les Baldwin (Cover Artist, Im Ho).....**3.00**

Little One, Good-Bye by E. P. Moran & Silvio Hein, 1906 (Cover Artist, Carter) **10.00**

Little Orphan Annie, 1931, Advertising For Ovaltine (Advertising) ...**42.00**

Little Pal by Buddy DeSylva, Lew Brown & Ray Henderson, 1929, Movie: Say It With Songs, Sung By Al Jolson (Al Jolson) **15.00**

Little Pal by Eddie Dowling & James F. Hanley, 1929, Movie: The Rainbow Man, Photo Eddie Dowling **10.00**

Little Pal Of Mine by J. J. Callahan & G. A. Kurtzeborn, Jr. 1919 (Cover Artist, E. R. Beckham)................................**10.00**

Little Pickaninny Kid by Maria Warfall & David W. Guion, 1919 (Black, Black Face)................................**20.00**

Little Pink Rose, A by Carrie Jacobs Bond, 1912, Dedicated In Memory of Little Bernice (Dedication)................................**16.00**

Little Place That I Call Home by Raymond Rubbell, 1901 ....**10.00**

Little Princess by Lincoln, 1914 (Cover Artist, Pfeiffer & Deco)........**10.00**

Little Puff Of Smoke Good-Night by Ring W. Lardner & G. Harris White, 1910 (Black, Black Face) **15.00**

Little Rag Baby Doll by L. Wolfe Gilbert & Lewis F. Muir, 1913........**5.00**

Little Red Caboose Behind The Train, The by Geo. Diamond, 1912 (Cover Artist, Pfeiffer & Transportation)................................**15.00**

Little Red Fox, The by James Kern, Hy Heath, Johnny Lange & Lew Porter, 1939, Movie: That's Right You're Wrong, Photo Kay Kyser **5.00**

Little Red Monkey by Stephen Gale & Jack Jordan, 1953, Photo Rosemary Clooney **4.00**

Little Red School House, The by Al Wilson & James Brennan, 1922, Photo Bennett Twins **5.00**

Little Rendezvous In Honolulu, A by Edgar Leslie & Joe Burke, 1936 (Cover Artist, Cliff Miska)................................**3.00**

Little Ripple Had Rhythm, The by Leo Robin & Ralph Rainger, 1937, Movie: Big Broadcast Of 1938, Photo Shirley Ross, Caricature, W.C. Fields, Bob Hope, Martha Ray & Ben Blue **12.00**

Little Road by George Graff Jr. & Ernest Ball, 1923 ....**5.00**

Little Road That Leads Back Home, The by Arthur E. Bucknam & Jacob Henry Ellis, 1915 (Cover Artist, Pfeiffer) **10.00**

Little Rover, Don't Forget To Come Back Home by Gus Kahn & Walter Donaldson, 1923................................**5.00**

Little Shawl Of Blue by Thomas J. Hewitt & Edward Teschmacher, 1913................................**6.00**

Little Shepherd's Song, The by William Alexander Percy & Wintter Watts, 1923................................**5.00**

Little Show, The by Howard Dietz & Jean Schwartz, 1929................**7.00**

Little Sir Echo by Adele Girard & Joe Marsala, 1939, Photo Horace Heidt 5.00

Little Skipper by Nick & Charles Kenny, 1939, Photo Charles Barnet Orchestra................................**3.00**

Little Small Town Girl by Jules Loman & Hugo Rubens, 1945 ....**3.00**

Little Soldier by W. C. Powell, 1910 (March)................................**10.00**

Little Something–That's All, A by Thos. S. Allen, 1912, Photo Ed Morton (Cover Artist, Starmer & Deco) **5.00**

Little Stowaway, The by Smith, 1879 (Pre 1900 & Transportation)....**15.00**

Little Street In Heaven That They Call Broadway by A. B. Sloane, 1903................................**12.00**

Little Street Where Old Friends Meet, A by Gus Kahn & Harry Woods, 1932, Photo Will Osborne (Cover Artist, Cliff Miska)...................**5.00**

Little Sweetheart I'm So Lonely by Irene Jefferies, 1913, Dedicated To Miss Ethel Briggs (Dedication) **5.00**

Little Sweetheart Of The Prairie by Brown, 1931 ....**3.00**

Little Tease by Engelman, 1909 (Cover Artist, Pfeiffer)....................**10.00**

Little Things In Life, The by Irving Berlin, 1930 (Irving Berlin) **6.00**

Little Toot by Allie Wrubel, 1948 Movie: Melody Time (Disney)......**10.00**

Little Town In The Ould County Down by Richard W. Pascoe, Monte Carlo & Alma M. Sanders, 1921, Sung by John McCormack (Irish)...........**5.00**

Little Uncle Sam Will Win by Toylan, 1918 (Cover Artist, Pfeiffer & WWI)................................**12.00**

Little White Church In The Niche, The by Rose Estelle Oliver, 1934, Signed Photo Tito Guizar (Cover Artist, Frances Hays & Signed)..**5.00**

Little White Cloud That Cried, The by Johnnie Ray, 1951, Photo Johnnie Ray................................**5.00**

Little White Duck, The by Walt Barrows & Bernard Zaritzky, 1950, Photo Dorothy Olsen................................**3.00**

Little White Gardenia, A by Sam Coslow, 1935, Movie: All The King's Horses, Photo Carl Brisson & Mary Ellis................................**7.00**

Little White Lies by Walter Donaldson, 1930, Photo Dick Haymes......**3.00**

Little White Lies by Walter Donaldson, 1930, Photo Ray O'Hara (Cover Artist, Frederick S. Manning)................................**15.00**

Little White Lies by Walter Donaldson, 1930, Photo Rudy Vallee (Cover Artist, Frederick S. Manning)......................**12.00**

Little White Rose by Wells Hively & Charles Wakefield Cadman, 1937 ....**3.00**

Little Widow Dunn by Edward Harrigan & David Braham, 1882 (Pre 1900)......................**15.00**

Little Willie by Hattie Marshall, 1893 (Pre 1900).............................**16.00**

Little Wooden Head by Leigh Harline & Ned Washington, 1940, Movie: Pinocchio (Disney) **10.00**

Little Wooden Whistle Wouldn't Whistle, The by Billy Curtis & Harry Von Tilzer, 1923, Photo Sophie Tucker (Cover Artist, R. Owles) ..**15.00**

Little Yaller Dog by James M. Gallatly, 1919.......................**10.00**

Little You Know by Joe Young, Milton Ager & Jean Schwartz, 1933..**3.00**

Littler German Band by Gus Williams, 1870 (Pre 1900) **16.00**

Live And Love by Janis & King, 1930, Movie: Madam Satan, Photo Kay Johnson & Reginald Denny **6.00**

Livin' In The Sunlight, Lovin' In the Moonlight by Al Sherman & Al Lewis, 1930, Movie: The Big Pond......................**8.00**

Living A Life Of Dreams by Rubey Cowan, 1930, Signed Photo Rudy Vallee (Cover Artist, BH & Signed) **10.00**

Living The Life I Love by Seelen & Fain, 1953, Movie: The Jazz Singer, Photo Danny Thomas & Peggy Lee **5.00**

Liza by George & Ira Gershwin & Gus Kahn, 1932, Movie: The Jolson Story, Photo Larry Parks & Evelyn Keyes (Al Jolson) **12.00**

Lizzie by R. Barclay Brown, 1925, Musical: The Jail Birds (Cover Artist, E. S. Fisher) **10.00**

Loading Up The Mandy Lee by Stanley Murphy & Henry I. Mashale, 1915 (Cover Artist, Starmer) **10.00**

Loafin' Time by Arthur Altman & Milton Ager, 1935, Photo Joe Sanders (Cover Artist, Pol.) **5.00**

Lobster's Promenade, The by Porter Steele, 1902, Dedicated To My Friend D.L. James (Dedication) **6.00**

Log Cabin Lullaby by Suzanne Byrne, Geoffrey H. Byrne & Ira Schuster, 1936, Photo Guy Lombardo **3.00**

Log Cabin Song by Alexander Kile, 1840 (Pre 1900).......................100.00

Lola, Fairest Daughter Of Panama by Manuel Klein, 1913, Musical: America At N.Y. Hippodrome 1913-14 ....**10.00**

London Paved With Gold by McGlennon, 1892 (Pre 1900) **15.00**

Londonderry Air by Katherine T. Hinkson, 1935, Photo Billy Hills (Irish)........................**5.00**

Lone Grave by Paul Dresser, 1890 (Pre 1900) **15.00**

Lone Star Moon by Cliff Friend & Dave Franklin, 1947, Photo Harry James (Cover Artist, Im-Ho) **3.00**

Loneliness by Lew Pollack & Sidney Clare, 1928 ....**5.00**

Lonely by George Moriarty, Charles Straight & Roy Bargy, 1922........**3.00**

Lonely by Herbert Stothart & Clifford Grey, 1930, Movie: Call Of The Flesh, Photo Ramon Novarro **10.00**

Lonely by Leo Robin & Maurice Yvain, 1922........................**3.00**

Lonely Eyes by Benny Davis & Harry Akst, 1927, Photo Dorothy Daye (Cover Artist, Barbelle) **6.00**

Lonely Goatherd, The by Richard Rodgers & Oscar Hammerstein II, 1959, Movie: The Sound Of Music, Photo Julie Andrews & Christopher Plummer **5.00**

Lonely Heart by Irene Wicker, 1936, As Featured By Eileen Moran In The Popular Radio Program "Today's Children", Photo Wedding Party & Mother Moran. Recipe For Wedding Cake On Back Cover, Sponsored By Pillsbury Flour Mills Co. (Advertising)...................**22.00**

Lonely Heart by Irving Berlin, 1933, Musical: Easter Parade (Irving Berlin)........................**10.00**

Lonely Love by Everett Carter & Ray Sinatra, 1945........................**3.00**

Lonely Street by Kenny Sowder, Carl Belew & W. S. Stevenson, 1956........................**3.00**

Lonely Troubadour by John Klenner, 1929, Dedicated & Photo Rudy Vallee (Dedication)........................**12.00**

Lonesome And Sorry by Benny Davis & Con Conrad, 1926, Photo Taylor & Hawks (Cover Artist, Barbelle & Deco) **10.00**

Lonesome Baby by Joe Goodwin, Seymour Brown & Nat D. Ayer, 1913........................**8.00**

Lonesome Butterfly by Sam Coslow & Peter DeRose, 1921 ....**5.00**

Lonesome by Charles Haendle, 1948, Photo Sammy Kaye **3.00**

Lonesome by Edgar Leslie & George W. Meyer, 1943 ....**3.00**

Lonesome by George W. Meyers, 1909, Photo Irene Romain (Cover Artist, DeTakacs)........................**10.00**

Lonesome Honey Just For You by Kenneth Bisbee & Harry H. Williams, 1912, Signed Photo of Bonita (Signed)........................**5.00**

Lonesome Land by Bernie Foyer & Dave Dreyer, 1920, (Cover Artist, F. Earl Christy & Lithography by Knapp Co.) **50.00**

Lonesome Lover by Al Bryan & Jimmie Monaco, 1933, Photo Guy Lombardo **3.00**

Lonesome Mama Blues by Brown, Nickel & Brown, 1922 (Blues) **5.00**

Lonesome River by Harold B. Freeman & J. Edwin Allemong, 1914 ...**5.00**

Lonesome Road, The by Gene Austin & Nathaniel Shilkret, 1955, Movie: Cha-Cha-Cha Boom!, Photo Perez Prado, Helen Grayco & Luis Ascaraz **5.00**

Lonesome, That's All by Lee S. Robert & Ben J. Bradley, 1918, Signed Photo Rudy Vallee (Signed)........................**15.00**

Lonesomeness by Max Friedman, 1919 (Cover Artist, DeTakacs)......**10.00**

Long After Tonight by Drake, Shirl & Polk, 1947, Movie: Arch Of Triumph, Photo Ingrid Bergman **8.00**

Long Ago And Far Away by Jerome Kern & Ira Gershwin, 1944, Movie: Cover Girl, Photo Rita Hayworth & Gene Kelly........................**5.00**

Long Ago Rose by Gordon Johnstone & Pierre Connor, 1923, Dedicated To W. C. Durant In Memory Of His Mother And Mine (Dedication)...**12.00**

Long Beach By The Sea by Kitchen & Hill, 1918 ....**5.00**

Long Before I Knew You by Styne & Cahn, 1950, Movie: The West Point Story, Photo James Cagney, Doris Day, Gene Nelson, Virginia Mayo & Gordon Macrae........................**12.00**

Long Boy, Good-Bye Ma! Good-Bye Pa! Good-Bye Mule by William Herschell & Barclay Walker, 1917 (Cover Artist, Gaar Williams & WWI)........................20.00

Long Haired Lover From Liverpool by Chris Bowden, 1972, Photo Little Jimmy Osmond........................**3.00**

'Long In Pumpkin Pickin' Time by Mack & Smith, 1909 (Cover Artist, Pfeiffer)........................**15.00**

Long Live America by W. Smith & N. Kenny, 1918 (WWI) **10.00**

Long Live The Night by Otto Harbach, Oscar Hammerstein II, Frank Mandel & Sigmund Romberg, 1926, Movie: The Desert Song **10.00**

Long, Long Letter 'Bout Home Sweet Home by Massell, 1915 (Cover Artist, Pfeiffer)..**12.00**

Long, Long Way From Home, A by Sam M. Lewis & George Meyer, 1914 (WWI)..**15.00**

Long Lost Mama, Daddy Misses You by Harry Woods, 1923 (Cover Artist, Barbelle & Blues)..**5.00**

Long May We Love by Ralph Freed & Roscoe Hillman, 1934 ....**4.00**

Long-Long Ago by Ivan Reid & Gene Platzman, 1919, (Lithograph By Hayes)...**5.00**

Longboat by Ponca, 1909 (Cover Artist, Pfeiffer & Indian) **20.00**

Longing by Matthew Arnold & Noble Cain, 1939.............................**3.00**

Longing Dear For You by John H. Densmore, 1919...........................**5.00**

Longing For Home by Albert Jungmann......................................**5.00**

Longing For You by Bernard Jansen & Walter Dana, 1951...................**3.00**

Look At Me by Brooks & Scharf, 1949, Movie: Yes Sir, That's My Baby, Photo Donald O'Connor, Gloria DeHaven & Charles Coburn **5.00**

Look For The Silver Lining by B. G. DeSylva & Jerome Kern, 1920, Musical: Sally, Photo Marilyn Miller & Leon Errol **10.00**

Look Out For Jimmy Valentine by Gus Edwards, 1910, Photo Gus Edwards **10.00**

Look Out For Mr. Stork by Oliver Wallace, Frank Churchill & Ned Washington, 1941, Movie: Dumbo (Disney) **10.00**

Look Out, Here Comes An American by Harry Von Tilzer, 1908 (Patriotic) **15.00**

Look To The Rainbow by E. Y. Harburg & Burton Lane, 1946, Movie: Finian's Rainbow (Cover Artist, BJH & Irish)..............................**5.00**

Look What My Boy Got In France by William Dillon & Con Conrad, 1918 (WWI)..**15.00**

Look What You've Done, Done by Bert Kalmar & Harry Ruby, 1932 .**3.00**

Look What You've Done To Me by Conrad, Mitchell & Gottler, 1929, Movie: Why Leave Home?, Photo Sue Carol & Nick Stewart **5.00**

Lookie, Lookie, Lookie, Here Comes Cookie by Mack Gordon, 1935, Movie: Love In Bloom, Photo Dixie Lee & Joe Morrison..............**8.00**

Lookin' For Trouble by Myrow, Blane & Wells, 1953, Movie: The French Line, Photo Jane Russell..**4.00**

Lookin' Out My Back Door by John C. Fogerty, 1970, Photo Creedence Clearwater Revival **6.00**

Looking At The World Thru Rose Colored Glasses by Tommie Malie.**5.00**

Looking For A Little Boy by Bolton, Thompson & Ira & George Gershwin, 1925 ....**5.00**

Lookout Mountain by Joe Goodwin & Halsey K. Mohr, 1917, Photo Howard & Hurst (Cover Artist, Dunk)...**10.00**

Lora-Belle-Lee by Sid Miller & Ray Gilbert, 1949, Photo Vaughn Monroe **3.00**

Lord Done Fixed Up My Soul, The by Irving Berlin, 1939 (Irving Berlin) **10.00**

Lord! Have Mercy On A Married Man by Edgar Leslie & J. Fred Helf, 1911, Photos Lew Dockstader (Cover Artist, Pfeiffer & Black, Black Face) **22.00**

Lord Is Good To Me, The by Kim Gannon & Walter Kent, 1948, Movie: Melody Time (Disney) **10.00**

Lord Is My Light, The by Frances Allitsen, 1897 (Pre 1900) **3.00**

Lord Is My Shepherd, The by S. Liddle, 1902 ....**3.00**

Lord's Prayer, The by Dorothy Daczow, 1949..................................**3.00**

Lords Of Creation by Howard Johnson & Carlo Sanderson, 1921, Musical: Tangerine **8.00**

Lorena by Webster, 1857 (Pre 1900)..**15.00**

Lorraine, My Beautiful Alsace Lorraine by Alfred Bryan & Fred Fisher, 1917 (Cover Artist, DeTakacs & WWI)...**15.00**

Lost, A Wonderful Girl by Benny Davis & James F. Hanley, 1922, Photo Margaret Young (Cover Artist, Wohlman) **10.00**

Lost, A Wonderful Girl by Benny Davis & James F. Hanley, 1922, Introduced by Sophie Tucker, Photo Sophie Tucker (Cover Artist, Wohlman)...**16.00**

Lost And Found by Pinky Tomlin & Harry Tobias, 1938....................**3.00**

Lost by Phil Ohman, Johnny Mercer & Macy O. Teetor, 1936, Photo Phil Ohlman & His Orchestra **3.00**

Lost Chord, The by Sir Arthur Sullivan, 1935, Photo Art Jarrett...........**3.00**

Lost In A Fog by Dorothy Fields & Jimmy McHugh, 1934..................**3.00**

Lost In My Dreams by Sidney D. Mitchell & Sam H. Stept, 1936, Movie: Sitting On The Moon, Photo Roger Pryor & Grace Bradley (Cover Artist, Sorokin) **12.00**

Lost In The Shuffle by Buddy Bernier, Larry Spier & Bob Emmerich, 1938 ....**3.00**

Lot Of Livin' To Do, A by Lee Adams & Charles Strouse, 1960, Movie: Bye Bye Birdie **6.00**

Lou'siana Lullaby by Charles Newman, Johnny Burke & Harold Spina, 1933, Photo Ethel Shutta (Cover Artist, Leff)...............................**10.00**

Louise by Leo Robin & Richard A Whiting, 1929, Movie: Innocents Of Paris, Photo Maurice Chevalier..15.00

Louise by Leo Robin & Richard A. Whiting, 1929, Movie: You Can't Ration Love, Photo Betty Rhodes & Johnnie Johnston.................**12.00**

Louisiana by Arthur Freed & Oliver G. Wallace, 1920.........................**5.00**

Louisiana Hayride by Howard Dietz & Arthur Schwartz, 1932, Movie: The Band Wagon, Photo Fred Astaire, Cyd Charisse, Nanette Fabray & Jack Buchanan **6.00**

Louisiana Lize by Bob Cole, 1899 (Pre 1900) **15.00**

Louisiana Lou by Leslie Stuart, 1894 (Pre 1900)..............................**15.00**

Louisiana Purchase by Irving Berlin, 1939 (Irving Berlin) **15.00**

Louisline Polka, The by Chas. D'Albert, 1860 (Pre 1900)...................**45.00**

Lovable And Sweet by Sidney Clare & Oscar Levant, 1939, Movie: The Street Girl **5.00**

Lovable by Gus Kahn & Harry Woods, 1932......................................**3.00**

Love Ain't Likin', Likin' Ain't Love by Earl C. Jones & Charlotte Blake, 1910 ....**6.00**

Love Ain't Nothin' But The Blues by Louis Alter, 1929 (Blues) **5.00**

Love Among The Roses by Delahanty & Coffin, 1869 (Pre 1900)......**15.00**

Love Among The Whispering Pines by Charles B. Weston, 1913.......**10.00**

Love And A Dime by Brooks Bowman, 1935, Musical: Stags At Bay..**8.00**

Love And Devotion by Louis A. Drumheller, 1917 ....**10.00**

Love And Learn by Arthur Schwartz & Edward Heyman, 1936, Movie: That Girl From Paris, Photo Lily Pons...**10.00**

Love And Marriage by Sammy Cahn & James Van Heusen, 1955, Movie: Our Town, Photo Frank Sinatra......................**8.00**

Love And Passion by J. Messina, 1902 ....**5.00**

Love And Passion by Schrader & Moroder, 1980, Movie: American Gigolo, Photo Richard Gere **6.00**

Love Bird by Mary Earl & Ted Fiorito, 1921 (Cover Artist, Wohlman) ...**6.00**

Love Boat by Arthur Freed & Nacio Herb Brown, 1929, Movie: The Broadway Melody, Photo Charles King, Bessie Love & Anita Page..........**8.00**

Love Brought You by George Spink, 1927 ....**5.00**

Love Bug Will Bite You, If You Don't Watch Out, The by Pinky Tomlin, 1937, Photo Pinky Tomlin (Cover Artist, HBK) 5.00

Love by Bert Kaempfert & Milt Gabler, 1964, Photo Nat King Cole....**3.00**

Love by Huenter, 1917 ....**3.00**

Love Came Calling by Catherine Bainbridge & J.S. Zamecnick, 1919 .**5.00**

Love Days by Halsey K. Mohr, 1916 (Cover Artist, Pfeiffer) **10.00**

Love Dreams by George M. Cohan (George M. Cohan)......................**10.00**

Love Dreams by J. J. Crawford & Henriette Blanke-Belcher, 1910 ......**5.00**

Love Dreams by Mort Harris, Raymond Klages, William Axt & David Mendoza, 1928, Movie: Alias Jimmy Valentine......................**10.00**

Love Eyes by Cupero, 1916, Photo Frances X. Bushman (Cover Artist, Pfeiffer)......................**10.00**

Love Eyes by Lee Hazlewood, 1967 Photo Nancy Sinatra **5.00**

Love For Love by Ted Koehler & Eric Wolfgang Korngold, 1947, Movie: Escape Me Never, Photo Errol Flynn, Ida Lupino, Gig Young & Eleanor Parker **5.00**

Love For Sale by Brian Hooker & Rudolf Friml, 1926......................**5.00**

Love For Sale by Cole Porter, 1930, Musical: The New Yorkers..........**8.00**

Love Has A Way by Schertzinger, 1924, Movie: Dorothy Vernon Of Haddon Hall, Photo Mary Pickford......................**10.00**

Love Here Is My Heart by Ross & Silesu, 1915 (Cover Artist, Woolach)......................**5.00**

Love I Adore You by Cooper, 1896 (Pre 1900) **15.00**

Love In A Garden by Goss, 1913 (Cover Artist, Pfeiffer)....................**10.00**

Love In An Automobile by Dixon, 1899 (Pre 1900 & Transportation)..**35.00**

Love In Bloom by Leo Robin & Ralph Rainger, 1934, Movie: She Loves Me Not, Photo Bing Crosby **16.00**

Love In June by George Duffy, Carlyle W. Hall & Tommy Tucker, 1935......................**3.00**

Love Is A Business by Howard Johnson & Carlo Sanderson, 1921, Musical: Tangerine **10.00**

Love Is A Dancing Thing by Howard Deitz & Arthur Schwartz, 1935 .**3.00**

Love Is A Random Thing by George Marion Jr. & Sammy Fain, 1946, Musical: Toplitzky Of Notre Dame (Sports)......................**12.00**

Love Is A Song by Frank Churchill & Larry Morey, 1942, Movie: Bambi (Disney) **18.00**

Love Is A Wonderful Thing by L. Wolfe Gilbert & Anatol Friedland, 1917......................**3.00**

Love Is All by Harry Tobias & Pinky Tomlin, 1940......................**3.00**

Love Is All In All by Ellis & Wilson, 1900......................**5.00**

Love Is All That Matters by Schwartz & Cahn, 1955, Movie: You're Never Too Young, Photo Martin & Lewis......................**8.00**

Love Is Here To Stay by Ira & George Gershwin, 1938, Movie: An American In Paris, Photo Gene Kelly & Leslie Caron......................**4.00**

Love Is Here To Stay by Ira & George Gershwin, 1938, Movie: Goldwyn Follies, Photo Adolphe Menjou, Ritz Brothers, Edgar Bergen & Charlie McCarthy......................**10.00**

Love Is Just A Little Bit Of Heaven by Al Bryan & Abel Baer, 1926 ...**5.00**

Love Is Just A Lottery by Stanley Murphy, Chas McCarron & Albert Von Tilzer, 1916......................**5.00**

Love Is Just Around The Corner by Leo Robin & Lewis E. Gensler, 1934, Movie: Here Is My Heart, Photo Bing Crosby & Kitty Carlisle **10.00**

Love Is Like A Firefly by Harbach, Wright, Forrest & Friml, 1937, Movie: The Firefly, Photo Jeannette Macdonald & Allan Jones..................**8.00**

Love Is Lord Of All by Marie Wardall & David W. Guion, 1919 ....**5.00**

Love Is Love Anywhere by Ted Koehler & Harold Arlen, 1933, Musical: Let's Fall In Love **12.00**

Love Is Mine by Pat Ballard & Chas. Henderson, 1936......................**3.00**

Love Is Only A Dream by Harry D. Kerr & W. C. Lindermann, 1909 ..**5.00**

Love Is So Terrific by Sunny Skylar & Artie Shaftel, 1945..................**3.00**

Love Is The Answer by Webster & Botkin, 1972, Movie: Skyjacked ...**3.00**

Love Is The Sweetest Thing by Ray Noble, 1933 ....**3.00**

Love Is Where You Find It by Earl K. Brent & Nacio Herb Brown, 1948, Movie: The Kissing Bandit......................**5.00**

Love Keeps The World Young by Aronson & Becker, 1910 (Cover Artist, Pfeiffer & Deco) **16.00**

Love Letters by Edward Heyman & Victor Young, 1945, Movie: Love Letters, Photo Jennifer Jones & Joseph Cotten **5.00**

Love Letters In The Sand by Charles & Nick Kenny & J. Fred Coots, 1931, Signed Photo Russ Columbo (Signed) **6.00**

Love Light by Sol Bloom, 1907 ....**5.00**

Love Like This, A by Washington & Young, 1943, Movie: For Whom The Bells Toll, Photo Gary Cooper & Ingrid Bergman **10.00**

Love Locked Out by Max Kester & Ray Noble, 1933 ....**3.00**

Love Look Away by Richard Rodgers & Oscar Hammerstein II, 1961, Movie: Flower Drum Song......................**5.00**

Love Makes The World A Merry Go Round by Harry Lauder, 1923 ....**5.00**

Love Makes The World Go Round by Bob Merrill, 1961, Movie: Carnival......................**8.00**

Love Marches On by Charlie Tobias & John Jacob Loeb, 1936, Photo Bernie Cummins......................**3.00**

Love Me Again by Stults, 1910 (Cover Artist, Pfeiffer) **10.00**

Love Me All The Time by Ed Rose, Ann Dennis & Frank Magine, 1926......................**3.00**

Love Me All The Time by Winthrop Brookhouse, 1907 (Cover Artist, Ray) **10.00**

Love Me, And The World Is Mine by Dave Reed Jr. & Ernest R. Ball, 1906 ....**5.00**

Love Me, As I Love You by Charlie Tobias & Mary Schaeffer, 1937, Photo Rudy Vallee......................**10.00**

Love Me At Twilight by Bert Grant, 1916 ....**3.00**

Love Me Baby Can't You Love Me by Alec Wilder, Photo Johnnie Ray...**4.00**

Love Me by Edward Madden & Albert Gumble, 1911 (Cover Artist, Starmer) **5.00**

Love Me by Sammy Cahn & Jule Styne, 1945, Movie: The Stork Club, Photo Betty Hutton, Don DeFore, Andy Russell & Barry Fitzgerald **12.00**

Love Me Forever by Gus Kahn & Victor Schertzinger, 1935 ....**3.00**

Love Me Forever by Gus Kahn & Victor Schertzinger, 1935, Movie: Love Me Forever, Photo Grace Moore **5.00**

Love Me Forever by Mort Dixon, Joe Young & Harry Warren, 1931, Musical: The Laugh Parade, Photo Ed Wynn (Cover Artist, Gorj) .**8.00**

Love Me Like The Ivy Loves The Old Oak Tree by Geo. J. Moriarty & Richard Whiting, 1914 (Cover Artist, Starmer) **10.00**

Love Me Little, Love Me Long by Frank Fogarty & Jos. E. Howard, 1916 (Cover Artist, Pfeiffer) **10.00**

Love Me Little, Love Me Long by Percy Gaunt, 1893 (Pre 1900) **5.00**

Love Me Longer by Shuman & Farnon, 1966, Movie: Arivederci Baby!, Photo Tony Curtis, Lionel Jeffries & Rosanna Schiaffino..............**3.00**

Love Me Lots And Love Me All The Time by Will A. Boyd & Will T. Pierson, 1909 ....**10.00**

Love Me My Honey Most Any Time At All by Greay, 1915 (Cover Artist, Pfeiffer)..**12.00**

Love Me Or Leave Me by Gus Kahn & Walter Donaldson, 1928, Musical: Ziegfeld Production Whoopee, Photo Eddie Cantor (Cover Artist, Nickel & Eddie Cantor)..**15.00**

Love Me Tender by W. W. Fosdick & George R. Paulton, 1956, Photo Elvis Presley **25.00**

Love Me To-Day by D. Onivas, 1917 ....**5.00**

Love Me To-Night by Brian Hooker & Rudolf Friml, 1926 ....**5.00**

Love Me To-Night by Young, 1932 ....**5.00**

Love Me While The Loving Is Good by Stanley Murphy & Harry Von Tilzer, 1918, Photo Harry Von Tilzer (Cover Artist, DeTakacs) ...**10.00**

Love Me With Your Big Blue Eyes by Kendis & Paley, 1910 (Cover Artist, Edgar Keller) **5.00**

Love, My Heart Is Calling You by Joe Young & Sam M. Lewis, 1923.**3.00**

Love Nest, The by Otto Harbach, Frank Mandell & Louis A Hirsch, 1920, Musical Comedy: Mary, Presented by George M. Cohan (George M. Cohan) **15.00**

Love Never Went To College by Lorenz Hart & Richard Rodgers, 1939, Movie: Too Many Girls..**10.00**

Love Of A Rose by Lieut. Will S. Dillon, E. Elgar & W. C. Polla, 1919, Photo Ethel Clayton (Cover Artist, R.S. & Military Personnel) **10.00**

Love Of My Heart, The by W. Burton Baldry & Godfrey Nutting, 1911 ..**5.00**

Love Of My Life by Cole Porter, 1948, Movie: The Pirate **5.00**

Love Of My Life, The by Allan Jay Lerner & Frederick Loewe, 1947, Musical: Brigadoon **5.00**

Love Or Infatuation by Coslow & Hollander, 1937, Movie: This Way Please, Photo Betty Grable, Charles Buddy Rogers & Mary Livingstone..**10.00**

Love Secrets by J. S. Zamecnik, 1911 ....**5.00**

Love Sends A Little Gift Of Roses by Leslie Cooke & John Openshaw, 1919 ....**5.00**

Love Sings A Song In My Heart by Clarence J. Marks & Joseph Cherniavsky, 1929, Photo Laura LaPlante (Cover Artist Ernest Smythe)..**5.00**

Love Somebody by Joan Whitney & Alex Kramer, 1948, Photo Doris Day & Buddy Clark (Cover Artist, Barbelle) **5.00**

Love Song, A by Zelda Sears & Harold Levey, 1923, Musical: Minnie An Me **10.00**

Love Song From The Buccaneer by David & Bernstein, 1958, Photo Yul Brynner & Charlton Heston..**6.00**

Love Song Of Renaldo by Irving Kahal & Sammy Fain, 1940, Musical: Royal Palm Revue, Photo Abe Lyman, Ruth Terry, The Demarcos, Henry Richmond & Tony Martin **6.00**

Love Song, Opera Gem Series, 1908 (Cover Artist, Pfeiffer)..............**10.00**

Love Song, The by Harry B. Smith & Ed Kunneke, 1925, Musical: The Love Song (Deco)..**10.00**

Love Songs Of The Nile by Arthur Freed & Nacio Herb Brown, 1933, Movie: The Barbarian, Photo Raymond Novarro **10.00**

Love Spark Waltzes by Holtzman, 1909 (Cover Artist, Pfeiffer)........**15.00**

Love Star by Al Lewis, Larry Stock & Vincent Rose, 1945 ....**3.00**

Love Story, A, Intermezzo by Robert Henning & Heinz Provost, 1940, Movie: Intermezzo, Photo Leslie Howard......................................**5.00**

Love Tale Of Alsace Lorraine, A by Lou Davis & J. Fred Coots, 1928 (Patriotic)..**15.00**

Love Tales by Ryan & Rose, 1923 ....**3.00**

Love That Belongs To Me, The by Helen R. Schnapp, 1925 (Cover Artist, Wohlman & Deco)..**5.00**

Love That I Feel For You, The by Brosseau, 1917 (Cover Artist, Pfeiffer)..**10.00**

Love That Lives Forever, The by Geo. P. Wallihan & John Philip Sousa, 1918 (John Philip Sousa)..**20.00**

Love Theme by Sheldon & Goldsmith, 1966, Movie: The Blue Max, Photo James Mason, George Peppard & Ursula Andress **6.00**

Love Thoughts by Ellis & Wilson, 1909 (Cover Artist, Pfeiffer) **15.00**

Love Thy Neighbor by Mack Gordon & Harry Revel, 1934, Movie: We're Not Dressing, Photo Bing Crosby & Carole Lombard...................**15.00**

Love Walked In by Ira & George Gershwin, 1938, Movie: Goldwyn Follies, Photo Adolphe Menjou, Ritz Brothers, Edgar Bergen & Charlie McCarthy..**10.00**

Love Waltz by Jerome Heller, 1911 (Cover Artist, John Frew)............**5.00**

Love Whispers by Jos. M. Daly, 1913 (Cover Artist, Pfeiffer)...........**10.00**

Love Will Find A Way by Al Dubin & Joe Burke, 1929, Movie: In The Headlines **8.00**

Love Will Find The Way by Van Brunt & Von Tilzer, 1917 (Cover Artist, Pfeiffer)..**10.00**

Love Will Make Or Break A Man, Musical: The Man Who Owns Broadway (Cover Artist, Pfeiffer)...**15.00**

Love Won't Let Me Wait by Bobby Eli & Vinnie Barrett, 1975 ....**4.00**

Love You Are Mine Tonight by Barry Winton, Irving Schachtel & Sam Mineo, 1940...**3.00**

Love You Didn't Do Right By Me by Irving Berlin, 1942, Movie: White Christmas, Photo Bing Crosby, Danny Kaye, Rosemary Clooney & Vera Ellen (Irving Berlin)..**15.00**

Love, You Funny Thing! by Roy Turk & Fred E. Ahlert, 1932, Photo Kate Smith...**16.00**

Love, Your Spell Is Everywhere by Elsie Janis & Edmund Goulding, 1929 ....**5.00**

Love's Canoe by Harold Weeks, 1922 ....**5.00**

Love's Dreamy Strain by Brown & Ayer, 1912 (Cover Artist, Pfeiffer) ..**10.00**

Love's Enchantment by Vardley, 1919 ....**3.00**

Love's First Kiss by Edward Lockton & Dorothy Forster, 1923 ....**3.00**

Love's First Kiss by Klages, Axt & Mendoza, 1929, Movie: A Woman Of Affairs, Photo Greta Garbo & John Gilbert................................**12.00**

Love's Garden by Phil Schwartz, 1915 ....**3.00**

Love's Garden Of Roses by Ruth Rutherford & Haydn Wood, 1912....**5.00**

Love's Golden Dream by Henry S. Sawyer, 1907...............................**5.00**

Love's Golden Dream by Lindsay Lennox, 1907, Advertising For Bromo Seltzer (Advertising)..**15.00**

Love's Golden Memories, Chas. H. Maskell, 1926...............................**3.00**

Love's Golden Star by Lewis A. Drumheller, 1907, Dedicated To Miss Marguerite Britton Rudy (Dedication) **10.00**

Love's Little Mary by Lew Brown, Benny Davis & Jesse Greer, 1931.**3.00**

Love's Lullaby by Danidirff, 1913 ....**5.00**

Love's Madrigal by Teschemacher & Rae, 1903 ....**5.00**

Love's Melody by Carolyn Merrill & P. I. Tschaikowsky, 1941, Photo Art Kassell **3.00**

Love's Melody Song by J. R. Shannon, 1918 ....**5.00**

Love's Old Sweet Song by J. L. Molloy, 1935, Photo Jack Owens (Cover Artist L.K.) **6.00**

Love's Reverie by John Martin, 1910 (Cover Artist, Starmer) **10.00**

Love's Rosary by Geo. Buxton & Jennie Innella, 1919 (Cover Artist, Starmer) **5.00**

Love's Roundelay by Oscar Straus, 1908.............................**5.00**

Love's Ship by Alice & Nellie Morrison, 1920 (Cover Artist, Helen Van Doorn Morgan)...**10.00**

Love's Springtime by Ryder, 1901 ....**7.00**

Love's Sweet Dream by Drumheller, 1912 (Cover Artist, Pfeiffer).....**10.00**

Love's Torment by L. E. Berman, Richard Barthelemy & Enrico Caruso, 1909 ....**10.00**

Love's Trials by John A. Seidt, 1913 (Cover Artist, Sickels) **10.00**

Love's Whispering by Gould, 1911 ....**3.00**

Love's Wooing by Fink, 1904 ....**5.00**

Love's Young Dream by Paul Francis Webster & Lew Pollack, 1935, Movie: Little Colonel, Photo & Dedicated To Shirley Temple (Shirley Temple & Dedication) **12.00**

Love-Land by Abe Holzmann, 1905 (Cover Artist, Carter)................**10.00**

Love-Land by Otto Harbach & Rudolf Friml, 1916, Musical: You're In Love **10.00**

Love-Ship, The by Al Herman & Bert Grant, 1915 ....**10.00**

Loveland by Harry I. Robinson & Phil Fleming, 1910 ....**5.00**

Lovelier Than Ever by Frank Loesser, 1948, Musical: Where's Charley, Caricature of Ray Bolger....................................**5.00**

Loveliest Night Of the Year, The by Paul Francis Webster, Juventino Rosas & Irving Aaronson, 1950, Movie: The Great Caruso, Photo Mario Lanza, Ann Blyth & Dorothy Kirstan................**10.00**

Lovelight Bay by Harry Edeilheit & Charlie Pierce, 1919 (Cover Artist, R.S.) **5.00**

Lovelight by Theron C. Bennett, 1919 (Cover Artist, Meserow & Indian)..**25.00**

Lovelight In The Starlight by Ralph Freed & Frederick Hollander, 1937, Movie: Her Jungle Love, Photo Dorothy Lamour & Ray Milland..**10.00**

Lovelight In Your Eyes, The by Jack Yellen & Geo B. McConnell, 1917 (Cover Artist, Starmer)..**15.00**

Lovely Day by Donovan, 1973, Movie: Brother Sun, Sister Moon, Photo Graham Faulkner & Judy Bowker....................................**4.00**

Lovely Is She by Newell & Addison, 1965, Movie: The Amorous Adventures Of Moll Flanders, Photo Kim Novak, Angela Lansbury, Lili Palmer & George Sanders **4.00**

Lovely Lady by Jimmy McHugh & Ted Koehler, 1936, Movie: King Of Burlesque, Photo Alice Faye, William Baxter & Jack Oakie...........**6.00**

Lovely Love Blues by W. C. Handy, 1921 (Blues).............................**5.00**

Lovely Lucerne by Fred W. Leigh & Felix Godin, 1922 ....**3.00**

Lovely Mary by James Thatcher, 1915, Photo James Thatcher **10.00**

Lovely Mary Donnelly by William Allingham & John Philip Sousa, 1918 (John Philip Sousa & Irish) **20.00**

Lovely Springtime by Will Wood, 1911 ....**5.00**

Lovely To Look At by Dorothy Fields, Jimmy McHugh & Jerome Kern, 1935, Movie: Lovely To Look At, Photo Kathryn Grayson, Red Skelton & Howard Keel...**8.00**

Lovely To Look At by Dorothy Fields, Jimmy McHugh & Jerome Kern, 1935, Movie: Roberta, Photo Fred Astaire, Ginger Rogers & Irene Dunne (Cover Artist, Harris)....................................**5.00**

Lover by Richard Rogers & Lorenz Hart, 1933, Movie: Because Of Him, Photo Deanna Durbin **6.00**

Lover Come Back To Me by Frank Mandel, Oscar Hammerstein II & Sigmund Romberg, 1942, Movie: Deep In My Heart, Based On Life Of Sigmund Romberg...**5.00**

Lover Come Back To Me by Frank Mandel, Oscar Hammerstein II & Sigmund Romberg, 1928, Musical: The New Moon **10.00**

Lover, The by Albert Hay Malotte, 1938 ....**3.00**

Lover's Roulette by Charyl Edmonds, Jonah Thompson & Paul Raoul Arenas, 1966, Photo Mel Torme **6.00**

Lover's Waltz by Jack Yellen, Max Kortlander & Henri DeMartini, 1924..**3.00**

Loves Of By-Gone Days by Wilson & Douglas, 1912 (Cover Artist, Pfeiffer)...**10.00**

Lovey Came Back by Joe Young, Sam M. Lewis & Lou Handman, 1923..**4.00**

Lovin' Sam, The Sheik Of Alabam by Jack Yellen & Milton Ager, 1922, Photo Sophie Tucker (Cover Artist, Wohlman) **10.00**

Loving by Manuel Klein, 1910, Musical: The International Cup (Cover Artist, DeTakacs)..**15.00**

Loving Lize by Roger A. Graham & Frederick Pearsall, 1911 ....**6.00**

Lovingless Day by Jack Frost, 1918.....................................**7.00**

Loyal Knights by F. H. Losey, 1907 (March)..............................**10.00**

Loyalty Is The Word Today by Cahill & Andino, 1917 (Cover Artist, Pfeiffer)..**10.00**

Luana by Hiller, 1916 ....**5.00**

Lucille! by Walter Donaldson, 1931......................................**3.00**

Lucinda Cinda Jane by Joseph Hart, 1901, Compliments of Schubert Piano Co. (Lithograph: American Lithograph Co. & Black, Black Face)..**35.00**

Luck Be A Lady by Jo Swerling, Abe Burrows & Frank Loesser, 1950, Musical: Guys & Dolls **5.00**

Lucky Jim by Horowitz & Bowers, 1896 (Pre 1900) **10.00**

Lucky Lindy by L. Wolfe Gilbert & Abel Baer, 1927, Photo Spirit Of St. Louis (Lindbergh & Transportation) **35.00**

Lucky Lips by Leiber & Stoller, Photo Gale Storm **3.00**

Lucky, Lucky, Lucky Me by Milton Berle & Buddy Arnold, 1950, Photo Milton Berle (Cover Artist, Barbelle)................................**3.00**

Lucky Me–Loveable You by Jack Yellen & Milton Ager, 1929, Movie: Chasing Rainbows **6.00**

Lucky Moon by Geo Stevens, 1909 (Cover Artist, Rose)....................**5.00**

Lucy Dale by Harry Linton, 1899 (Pre 1900)................................**10.00**

Lucy Lee by William R. Clay & Charles L. Johnson, 1911 ....**5.00**

Lucy Linda Lady by Reed, 1904 (Black, Black Face)......................**15.00**

Lucy-Anna-Lou by Edward Madden & Gus Edwards, 1910 ....**10.00**

Luella Lee by Esrom, 1912 ....**5.00**

Lull Me To Sleep by Maurice Barron & Harry Kerr, 1914..................**3.00**

Lullaby Blues by Al M. Kendall, J. Russell Robinson & Theodore Morse, 1919 ....**6.00**

Lullaby by Ed Jakolowski, Advertising Bromo Seltzer (Advertising) .**16.00**

Lullaby In Doll Land by John W. Schaum, 1956 ....**3.00**

Lullaby Land by Frank Davis & Max Prival, 1919 (Lithograph Knapp Co.) **5.00**

Lullaby Of Birdland by George Shearing, 1952............................**3.00**

Lullaby Of Broadway by Al Dubin & Harry Warren, 1932, Movie: The Jolson Story, Photo Larry Parks & Evelyn Keyes (Al Jolson).......**16.00**

Lullaby Of The Bells by George Wagner & Edward Ward, 1943.........**3.00**

Lullaby Of The Leaves by Joe Young & Bernice Petkere, 1932 (Cover Artist, Leff)...**5.00**

Lullaby Time by Harold B. Freeman, 1919, Photo Mabel Normand (Cover Artist, L. Sielke, Jr.) **10.00**

Lullabye In Ragtime by Sylvia Fine, 1959, Movie: The Five Pennies, Photo Danny Kaye & Louis Armstrong **5.00**

Luna by Friedman, 1914...**5.00**

Lunch Time Follies by Lorenz Hart & Richard Rodgers, 1927, Musical: A Connecticut Yankee...**5.00**

Lustspiel Overture by Keler Bela, 1909 ....**5.00**

Lyda, Won't You Stop Your Foolin' by Bert Potter, 1905 ....**5.00**

Lydia by Miklos Rozsa, 1941, Movie: Lydia, Dedicated To Merle Oberon (Dedication) **8.00**

M'self by Geo. A. Kershaw & Walter Scanlon, 1922 ....**5.00**

Ma Blushin' Rosie by Edgar Smith & John Stromberg, 1932, Movie: The Jolson Story, Photo Larry Parks & Evelyn Keyes (Al Jolson).......**10.00**

Ma Blushin' Rosie by Edgar Smith & John Stromberg, 1940, Movie: Lillian Russell, Photo Alice Faye......................**8.00**

Ma by Sidney Clare & Con Conrad, 1921, Movie: Eddie Cantor Story, Photo Eddie Cantor in Black Face (Eddie Cantor & Black, Black Face) **20.00**

Ma by Sidney Clare & Con Conrad, 1921, Movie: Ma He's Making Eyes At Me, Photo Constance Moore & Tom Brown (Cover Artist, Im-Ho)......................**10.00**

Ma!, Eddie Cantor's Sensational Hit In The Midnight Rounders, by Sidney Clare & Con Conrad, 1921, Musical: The Midnight Rounders, Photo Of Eddie Cantor (Cover Artist, Wohlman, Eddie Cantor & Black, Black Face)......................**25.00**

Ma Cherie, My Dear by Kendall & Franklin, 1913 (Cover Artist, Pfeiffer) **12.00**

Ma Ebony Belle by Maurice Levi, 1901 (Black, Black Face)......................**15.00**

Ma Honey Gal by Frank Lepine & Charles J. W. Jerreld, 1912 (Black Black Face)......................**15.00**

Ma, I Miss Your Apple Pie by Carmen Lombardo & John Jacob Loeb, 1942 (WWII) **5.00**

Ma Jet Black Lady by Maud Raymond, 1897, Dedicated To Miss Leonore Dunn, Photo Maud Raymond (Pre 1900, Dedication & Black, Black Face) **35.00**

Ma Lady Lu by Brill, 1899 (Pre 1900 & Black, Black Face)......................**22.00**

Ma' Little Sunflower Good Night by Louis Weslyn & Frederick W. Vanderpool, 1918 (Black, Black Face) **5.00**

Ma Mississippi Babe by Dave Harris, 1920 (Black, Black Face) **10.00**

Ma Says I Can't Go For A Ride by Howe, 1895 (Pre 1900 & Transportation)......................**15.00**

Ma' Tiger Lily by H. B. Sloane, 1900 (Black, Black Face) **15.00**

Macaroni Joe by Stanley Smith & Percy Wenrich, 1910 ....**15.00**

Mack The Knife by Marc Blitzstein & Kurt Weill, 1928, Photo Bobby Darin **3.00**

Macnamara's Band by John J. Stamford & Shamus O'Connor, 1940 (March & Irish)......................**5.00**

Macushla by Josephine V. Rowe & Dermot Macmurrough, 1910, Sung by John McCormack (Irish)......................**5.00**

Mad About Him, Sad Without Him, How Can I Be Glad Without Him Blues by Larry Markes & Dick Charles, 1944 (Blues) **5.00**

Mad House Rag, The by Edgar Leslie & Freddy Watson, 1911 (Cover Artist, DeTakacs & Rag) **15.00**

Made For Each Other by Ervin Drake & Jimmy Shirl, 1947, Photo Dick Farney (Cover Artist, James Klugman)......................**3.00**

Made For Each Other by Ervin Drake & Jimmy Shirl, 1947, Photo Joey Kearns (Cover Artist, Brumo) **3.00**

Made In America by Leap, 1914 (Cover Artist, Pfeiffer & Patriotic)..**15.00**

Madelaine by Phil Spitalny & Joe Capwell, 1941, Photo Phil Spitalny & All Girl Orchestra **6.00**

Madelon, I'll Be True To The Whole Regiment by Louis Bousquet & Camille Robert, English Version by Alfred Bryan, 1918 (WWI)..**15.00**

Mademoiselle De Paree by Eric Maschvitz, Henri Conlit & Paul Durand, 1931 ....**5.00**

Mademoiselle From Armentieres by Sergeant Red Rowley & Lt. Gitz Rice, 1915 (WWI & Military Personnel) **20.00**

Madrigal Of May by Maurice Nitke, 1919 ....**5.00**

Maggie Murphy's Home by Edward Harrigan & David Braham, 1890 (Pre 1900 & Irish) **15.00**

Maggie! Yes! Ma'am by Leslie Moore & Johnny Tucker, 1923 ....**6.00**

Magic Is The Moonlight by Charles Pasquale & Maria Grever, 1944, Movie: Bathing Beauty, Photo Red Skelton & Esther Williams......................**5.00**

Magic Melody by Jerome Kern, 1916 ....**5.00**

Magic Mountain, The by Allen & George, 1964, Movie: The Magic Mountain......................**3.00**

Magic Of Your Eyes, The by Arthur A. Penn, 1915 . ...**6.00**

Magic Of Your Love, The by Kahn, Grey & Lehar, 1939, Movie: Balalaika, Photo Nelson Eddy & Ilona Massey......................**8.00**

Magna Carta by John Philip Sousa, 1927 (March & John Philip Sousa) ..**20.00**

Magnificent Matador by Edward L. Alperson, Movie: Magnificent Matador, Photo Maureen O'Hara & Anthony Quinn **5.00**

Magnolia by B. G. DeSylva, Lew Brown & Ray Henderson, 1927 (Cover Artist, Politzer & Deco)......................**10.00**

Magnolias In The Moonlight by Walt Bullock & Victor Schertzinger, 1936, Movie: Follow Your Heart, Photo Marion Talley & Michael Bartlett......................**8.00**

Maguires by Edward Harrigan & David Braham, 1881 (Pre 1900) **10.00**

Mahzel, Means Good Luck by Jack Beckman, Photo The Modernaires ..**3.00**

Maid Of The Mill, The by Hamilton Aide & Stephen Adams **5.00**

Maid Of The Mist by Sadie Koninsky, 1914......................**5.00**

Maid Of The West by Stott & Smith, 1923 ....**5.00**

Maid Of Timbuctoo by Bob Cole & Billy Johnson, 1903......................**5.00**

Maiden With The Dreamy Eyes by Bob Cole, J. Rosemond Johnson & Billy Johnson, 1901 ....**7.00**

Maiden's Bower, The by C.E. Vandersloot, 1908 (Cover Artist, Wenrich)......................**10.00**

Maiden's Prayer, The by Badarzewska, 1914 ....**10.00**

Mairzy Doats by Milton Drake, Al Hoffman & Jerry Livingston, 1943, Photo Vincent Lopez **5.00**

Mairzy Doats by Milton Drake, Al Hoffman & Jerry Livingston, 1943, Photo Kay Kyser......................**5.00**

Majestic Rag by Ben Rawls & Royal Neel, 1914 (Rag)......................**10.00**

Major And The Minor, The by Redd Evans & Earl Bostic, 1942, Movie: The Major And The Minor, Photo Ginger Rogers & Ray Milland **5.00**

Major Gilfeather by Edward Harrigan & David Braham, 1881 (Pre 1900) **15.00**

Make A Fuss Over Me by Edward Madden & Theodore Morse, 1904..**5.00**

Make A Miracle by Frank Loesser, 1948, Musical: Where's Charley, Caricature of Ray Bolger......................**5.00**

Make A Name For Yourself by Heath, Black & Richmond, 1914 (Cover Artist Pfeiffer & Deco)......................**10.00**

Make A Noise Take A Hoop And Roll Away by J. Fred Helf, 1908 .....**5.00**

Make A Wish by Alter, Webster & Straus, 1937 ....**5.00**

Make Believe by Benny Davis & Jack Skilkret, 1927 (Cover Artist, Ben Jorj Harris)......................**10.00**

Make Believe by Oscar Hammerstein II & Jerome Kern, 1927, Movie: Show Boat Presented by Florenz Ziegfeld (Cover Artist, Ben Jorj Harris)......................**10.00**

Make Believe Island by Nick Kenny, Charles Kenny & Will Grosz, 1940, Photo Glenn Miller **6.00**

Make It Another Old Fashioned by Cole Porter, 1942, Movie: Panama Hattie **6.00**

Make It With You by David Gates, 1970 ....**3.00**

Make Love To Me by Bill Norvas, Allan Copeland, Leon Roppolo, Paul Mares, Benny Pollack, George Brunies, Mel Stitzel & Walter Melrose, 1953, Signed Photo Jo Stafford (Signed) **8.00**

Make Love With A Guitar by Raymond Leveen & Maria Grever, 1940, Photo Horace Heidt (Cover Artist, Frederick S. Manning)......................**10.00**

Make Me Love You by Geo W. Meyer & Jack Drislane, 1913, Photo Mabel Williams & Elsie Wales, Two Singing Girls With Eva Tanguay's Vaudeville Co. (Cover Artist, Pfeiffer)...... ....**22.00**

Make Room For The Joy by Hal David & Burt Bacharach, 1958, Movie: Juke Box Rhythm, Photo Jo Morrow, Jack Jones, Brian Donlevy & George Jessel **14.00**

Make That Engine Stop At Louisville by Lewis, Meyer & Richmond, 1914 (Cover Artist, Pfeiffer & Transportation)......................**20.00**

Make The Man Love Me by Dorothy Fields & Arthur Schwartz, 1951, Movie: A Tree Grows In Brooklyn **3.00**

Make Uncle Sam Your Banker, Photo Children Lining Up To Buy War Stamps From Uncle Sam, 1942 (Patriotic & WWII)................**22.00**

Make Up Your Mind Carolina by W. V. McKenney & Fred Phillips, 1922................**5.00**

Make Way For Tomorrow by Jerome Kern & Ira Gershwin & E.Y. Harburg, 1944, Movie: Cover Girl, Photo Rita Hayworth **8.00**

Makin' Faces At The Man In The Moon by Max Rich, Kate Smith, Al Hoffman & Ned Washington, 1931, Photo Neil Golden (Cover Artist, Hap Hadley Studio) **4.00**

Makin Whoopee! by Walter Donaldson & Gus Kahn, 1928, Musical: Ziegfeld Production, Whoopee, Photo Eddie Cantor (Cover Artist, Nickel & Eddie Cantor)................**16.00**

Makin's Of The U.S.A., The by Von Tilzer & Bryan, 1918, Advertising Bull Durham Tobacco (Cover Artist, Pfeiffer, WWI & Advertising) **35.00**

Making Memories by Larry Kusick & Eddie Snyder, 1967, Photo Frankie Lane **3.00**

Malaguena by Marian Banks & Ernesto LeCuona, 1954, Photo Connie Francis 8.00

Malone At The Back Of The Bar by Edward Harrigan & David Braham, 1875 (Pre 1900 & Irish)................**20.00**

Maloney The Rolling Mailman by J. W. Kelly, 1890 (Pre 1900 & Irish) .**20.00**

Mam'selle by Mack Gordon & Edmund Goulding, 1947, Movie: The Razor's Edge, Photo, Tyrone Power, Gene Tierney, John Payne, Anne Baxter, Clifton Webb & Herbert Marshall **10.00**

Mama Don't Scold Me by Rogers & Ted Snyder, 1909 (Cover Artist, Pfeiffer)................**15.00**

Mama Guitar by Glazer & Schulberg, 1957, Movie: A Face In The Crowd, Photo Andy Griffith, Patricia Neal & Lee Remick **6.00**

Mama Inez by Grenet, 1931, Photo Maurice Chevalier **7.00**

Mama's Captain Curly Head by Moran & Von Tilzer, 1918 (Cover Artist, Pfeiffer)................**10.00**

Mama's Melody (Cover Artist, Pfeiffer) **10.00**

Mambo Jambo by Raymond Karl, Charlie Towne & Perez Prado, 1950, Photo Freddy Martin................**4.00**

Mamie Come Kiss Your Honey Boy by May Irwin, 1893 (Pre 1900) .**10.00**

Mamie, Don't Feel Ashamee by William D. Cobb & Gus Edwards, 1901 (Black, Black Face) **10.00**

Mamie Reilly by Maude Nugent, 1897 (Pre 1900)................**12.00**

Mamma Don't Want No Peas An Rice An Cocoanut Oil by Charles, 1931................**6.00**

Mamma Loves Papa, Papa Loves Mamma by Cliff Friend & Abel Baer, 1923, Photo Bernard & Townes (Deco)................**10.00**

Mamma Mia by Bert Davis, 1950 ....**3.00**

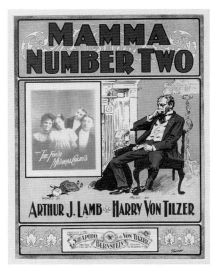

Mamma Number Two by Arthur Lamb & Harry Von Tilzer, 1901, Photo The Four Musical Colbys (Cover Artist, Starmer) 15.00

Mamma That Moon Is Here Again by Leo Robin & Ralph Rainger, 1937, Movie: Big Broadcast 1938, Photo Shirley Ross, Caricature, W.C. Fields, Ben Blue, Martha Raye & Bob Hope **12.00**

Mamma's Boy by Harry Sinclair & J. Fred Helf, 1905, Photo Johnny Carroll (Cover Artist, Jenkins, Patriotic & March)................**25.00**

Mammy Blossom's Possum Party by Arthur Fields & Theodore Morse, 1917 (Black, Black Face) **10.00**

Mammy Dear by C. S. Montayne & Frank H. Grey, 1919................**5.00**

Mammy Jinny's Hall Of Fame by Stanley Murphy & Harry Tierney, 1917 (Black, Black Face) **10.00**

Mammy Jinny's Jubilee by L. Wolfe Gilbert & Lewis F. Muir, 1913 (Cover Artist, DeTakacs & Black, Black Face) **35.00**

Mammy Land by Nomis & Dixon, 1921 (Dixie) **8.00**

Mammy O'Mine by Wm. Tracey & Maceo Pincard, 1919 (Cover Artist, Natwick & Dixie) **10.00**

Mammy O'Mine by Wm. Tracey & Maceo Pinkard, 1919, Photo Stone & Boyle (Cover Artist, DeTakacs & Dixie) **10.00**

Mammy's Chocolate Soldier by Sidney Mitchell & Archie Gottler, 1918 (WWI & Black, Black Face) **15.00**

Mammy's Growing Ole by Geo. Noyes Rockwell, 1914 (Black, Black Face) **6.00**

Mammy's Kinky Headed Coon by Harry Von Tilzer, 1899 (Pre 1900 & Black, Black Face)................**25.00**

Mammy's Lasses Candy Child by Mack & Cook, 1909 (Black, Black Face) **16.00**

Mammy's Little Coal Black Rose by Raymond Egan & Richard A. Whiting, 1916, Photo Adele Rowland (Cover Artist, Starmer & Black, Black Face) **16.00**

Mammy's Little Coal Black Rose by Raymond Egan & Richard A. Whiting, 1916, Photo Al Jolson (Cover Artist, Starmer, Al Jolson & Black, Black Face) **25.00**

Mammy's Little Kinky Headed Boy by Joseph M. White & George J. Trinkaus, 1926 (Black, Black Face) **15.00**

Mammy's Little Pansy by Geo Graff Jr. & Bert Grant, 1918 (Black, Black Face) **20.00**

Mammy's Little Pickaninny Boy by Williams & Walker, 1896 (Pre 1900 & Black, Black Face)................**25.00**

Mammy's Little Pumpkin Colored Coons by Hillman & Sidney Perrin, 1897 (Pre 1900 & Black, Black Face)............................**25.00**

Mammy's Little Sugar Plum (Cover Artist, Pfeiffer)........................**15.00**

Mammy's Lullaby by J. Will Callahan & Lee S. Roberts, 1918 (Cover Artist, L.A. Brunner, Transportation & Black, Black Face) **10.00**

Mammy's Shufflin' Dance by L. Wolfe Gilbert & Melville J. Gideon, 1911, Photo Courtney Sisters (Black, Black Face) **15.00**

Man, A Maid, A Moon, A Boat, A by Charles K. Harris, 1908 (Cover Artist, Scott & Van Altena)......................................**10.00**

Man and A Woman, A by Pierre Barouh, Jerry Keller & Francis Lai, 1946, Movie: A Man and A Woman **5.00**

Man And His Dream, A by Johnny Burke & James V. Monaco, 1940, Movie: Star Maker, Photo Bing Crosby **6.00**

Man Behind The Hammer And The Plow, The by Harry Von Tilzer, 1917 (Cover Artist, Pfeiffer & WWI) **15.00**

Man Doesn't Know, A by Richard Adler & Jerry Ross, 1955, Musical: Damn Yankees......................**3.00**

Man From Laramie, The by Washington & Lee, 1955, Movie: The Man From Laramie, Photo James Stewart & Cathy O'Donnell **6.00**

Man I Love, The by Ira & George Gershwin, 1945, Movie: Rhapsody In Blue......................**10.00**

Man I Love, The by Ira & George Gershwin, 1945, Movie: Strike Up The Band......................**10.00**

Man In The Moon by Harry B. Smith & Edward Kunneke, 1923, Musical: Play Caroline **10.00**

Man On The Flying Trapeze, The by Nick Manoloff, 1935, Photo The Kidoodlers **5.00**

Man On The Flying Trapeze, The by Walter O'Keefe, 1934 (Cover Artist, E.T. Paull) **35.00**

Man That Got Away, The by Arlen & Gershwin, 1954, Movie: A Star Is Born, Photo Judy Garland **12.00**

Man That Wears A Shield (Cover Artist, Pfeiffer)......................**10.00**

Man, The Maid and Cupid, The 1911 (Cover Artist, Pfeiffer)............**10.00**

Man Upstairs, The by Dorinda Morgan, Harold Stanley & Gerry Manner, 1954, Signed Photo Kay Starr (Signed)......................**10.00**

Man Who Owns Broadway, The by George M. Cohan, 1909 (Cover Artist, Pfeiffer & George M. Cohan)......................**25.00**

Man Who Paints The Rainbow, The by Cy Coben, Irving Melsher & Larry Stock, 1947 ....**4.00**

Man With The Banjo, The by Rovert Mellin & Fritz Schulz Reichel, 1954 ....**3.00**

Man With The Golden Arm, The by Cahn & Van Heusen, 1955, Movie: The Man With The Golden Arm, Photo Kim Novak, Frank Sinatra & Eleanor Parker **5.00**

Man With The Horn, The by Eddie de Lange, Jack Jennie & Bonnie Lake, 1946 ....**2.00**

Man With The Ladder And The Hose by Breen & Geary, 1904............**6.00**

Man With The Mandolin, The by James Cavanaugh, John Redmond & Frank Weldon, 1939, Photo Horace Heidt (Cover Artist, Im-Ho) ...**5.00**

Man Wrote A Song, A by Dave Franklin, 1949 ....**3.00**

Man's Song, A by James Thomson, 1904 ....**3.00**

Managua Nicaragua by Albert Gamse & Irving Fields, 1946, Photo Guy Lombardo......................**4.00**

Managua Nicaragua by Albert Gamse & Irving Fields, 1946, Photo Kay Kyser & Orchestra **4.00**

Manana by Peggy Lee & Dave Barbour, 1948, Photo Peggy Lee & Dave Barbour **3.00**

Mandalay by Earl Burtnett, Abe Lyman & Gus Arnheim, 1924, Signed Photo C. Chaplin, Note States: "To Abe Lyman: My Favorite Is Mandalay" (Signed)......................**10.00**

Mandalay by Rudyard Kipling & Harold Dixon, 1927 ....**6.00**

Mandy And Me by McKenna & Guble, 1918 (Black, Black Face) **15.00**

Mandy And The Spiders by Lorraine Tombo, 1927............................**3.00**

Mandy And The Spiders by Tombo, 1927 ....**5.00**

Mandy by Irving Berlin, 1919, Musical: Ziegfeld Follies, 1919 (Irving Berlin)......................**10.00**

Mandy by Irving Berlin, 1942, Movie: White Christmas, Photo Bing Crosby, Danny Kaye, Rosemary Clooney & Vera Ellen (Irving Berlin) **12.00**

Mandy Come Out In The Pale Moonlight by Leonard, Marx & C. Davis, 1912 (Cover Artist, Pfeiffer) **10.00**

Mandy Lane by Wm. J. McKenna, 1918, Photo Lew Dockstader (Black, Black Face)......................**15.00**

Mandy Lee by Thurland Chattaway, 1899 (Pre 1900 & Black, Black Face)......................**15.00**

Mandy Lou by Paul Laurence Dunbar & Frederick Hall, 1926 (Black, Black Face)......................**3.00**

Mandy 'N' Me by Bert Kalmar, Con Conrad & Otto Motzan, 1921 (Cover Artist, Wohlman & Dixie)......................**10.00**

Mandy Won't You Let Me Be Your Beau by Eddie Leonard, 1902 (Black, Black Face)......................**15.00**

Manhattan Beach March by John Philip Sousa, 1898 (John Philip Sousa, Pre 1900 & March)......................**25.00**

Manhattan by Lorenz Hart & Richard Rodgers, 1925 ....**5.00**

Manhattan by Rodgers & Hart, 1934, Movie: Words And Music, Photo Judy Garland, Lena Horne, Mickey Rooney, Gene Kelly, Ann Sothern, June Allyson & Perry Como......................**12.00**

Manhattan Greenery by Rodgers & Hart, 1934, Movie: Words And Music, Photo July Garland, Lena Horne, Mickey Rooney, Gene Kelly, Ann Sothern, June Allyson & Perry Como **12.00**

Manhattan Madness by Irving Berlin, 1932, Musical: Face The Music (Cover Artist, Leff & Irving Berlin)......................**5.00**

Manhattan Masquerade by Louis Alter, 1930......................**3.00**

Manhattan Moonlight by Louis Alter, 1930 ....**3.00**

Manhattan Serenade by Harold Adamson & Louis Alter, 1942.............**5.00**

Mansion Of Aching Hearts, The by Arthur Lamb & Harry Von Tilzer, 1902 ....**5.00**

Many A New Day by Richard Rodgers & Oscar Hammerstein II, 1943, Musical: Oklahoma (Cover Artist, Holley) **5.00**

Many Happy Returns Of The Day by Al Dubin & Joe Burke, 1931, Photo Al Pearce......................**6.00**

Many Happy Returns Of The Day by Al Dubin & Joe Burke, 1931, Photo Ann Leaf **6.00**

Many Tears Ago by Jenny Lou Carson, 1945 ....**3.00**

Many Times by B. G. DeSylva & Vincent Rose, 1924 ....**3.00**

Many Times by Jessie Barnes & Felix Stahl, 1953 ....**3.00**

Many Years by John Anderson & Joe Hearst, 1922......................**3.00**

Manzanillo by A. G. Robyn, 1909......................**10.00**

Maori by Wm. Tyers, 1909 (Cover Artist, Pfeiffer) **10.00**

Maple Leaf Rag by Scott Joplin, 1899, Revised by Bob Russell & Jule Styne (Scott Joplin, Pre 1900 & Rag)......................**35.00**

Maracaibo by Pascall & Almeida, 1958, Movie: Maracaibo, Photo Cornell Wilde & Jean Wallace **5.00**

March Militaire by Franz Schubert, 1936 (March)......................**5.00**

March Of Progress by Williams, 1935 (March) **10.00**

March Of The Cardinals by George M. Cohan (George M. Cohan) **15.00**

March Of The Cards by Bob Hilliard & Sammy Fain, 1951, Movie: Alice In Wonderland (Disney)......................**12.00**

March Of The Flit Soldiers, The by Phil Cook & Harry Reser, 1929, Advertising On Radio Show For Flit, Flit Soldiers On Reverse Side (Advertising & March)......................**35.00**

March Of The Flower Girls by Paul Wachs, 1918 (March) **5.00**

March Of The Iron Horse by Erno Rapee, 1924 (Transportation) **15.00**

March Of The Mannikins by D. Onivas & Walter Hirsch, 1923 (Cover Artist, Wohlman & March) **12.00**

March Of The Nations by Pond, 1910 (March).....................**10.00**

March Of The Old Guard by Clifford Grey & Herbert Stothart, 1929, Movie: Devil May Care (March).....................**7.00**

March Of The Teddy Bear by J. S. Fearis, 1907 (March) **15.00**

March Of The Toys, The by Victor Herbert, 1903 (March & Victor Herbert).....................**15.00**

March Of The Vagabonds by Hooker & Friml, 1925 (March).............**10.00**

March To The White House by Dave Harris, 1924 (Patriotic & March)..**5.00**

March Victorious by E. Black & E. T. Paull, 1923 (Cover Artist, E. T. Paull & March) **35.00**

Marche Heroique by E.E. Guilford, 1905 (Cover Artist, Jenkins & March) **5.00**

Marcheta by Victor Schertzinger, 1914 ....**3.00**

Marching Along Together by Edward Pola, Franz Steininger & Mort Dixon, 1933, Photo Kate Smith (March).....................16.00

Marching Through Georgia by Henry C. Work, 1865 (March, Pre 1900)..**20.00**

Marching Through Germany by Thomas W. Tresidder, 1917 (WWI & March) **20.00**

Marching Thru Georgia by Meacham, 1908 (Cover Artist, Pfeiffer, Patriotic & March) **20.00**

Marching To The Music Of The Band by Wm. Richard Goodall & Harry Von Tilzer, 1900 (March).....................**10.00**

Mardi Gras by Fred Grofe, 1926.....................**5.00**

Mardi Gras Rag by Lyons & Yosco, 1914 (Cover Artist, Pfeiffer & Rag).....................**18.00**

Maree by Fleming, 1919 (Cover Artist, Pfeiffer) **10.00**

Margery by Chas, N. Daniels, 1898 (Pre 1900 & March) **20.00**

Margie by Benny Davis, Con Conrad & J. Russell Robinson, 1920, Movie: The Eddie Cantor Story, Photo Eddie Cantor In Black Face (Eddie Cantor & Black, Black Face) **10.00**

Margie by Benny Davis, Con Conrad & J. Russell Robinson, 1920 (Cover Artist, Barbelle & Deco).....................**12.00**

Marguerite by C. A. White, 1883 (Pre 1900) **15.00**

Maria by Harry Williams & Mose Gumble, 1904, Photo Miss Clarice Vance.....................**10.00**

Maria by Richard Rodgers & Oscar Hammerstein II, 1959, Movie: The Sound Of Music, Photo Julie Andrews & Christopher Plummer...**10.00**

Maria by Stephen Sondheim & Leonard Bernstein, 1957, Movie: West Side Story **12.00**

Maria Elena by Lorenzo Barcelata & S. K. Russell, 1933, Photo Jimmy Dorsey.....................**5.00**

Maria Elena (In French & Spanish) by Lorenzo Barcelata, 1939, Photo Albert Viau, French Canadian Baritone **6.00**

Marianette by Elmer Naylor, Perry Alexander & Lou Herscher, 1927..**3.00**

Marianne by Frank Mandel, Oscar Hammerstein II & Sigmund Romberg, 1928, Musical: The New Moon.....................**5.00**

Marianne by Roy Turk & Fred E. Ahlert, 1955, Movie: Marianne, Photo Marion Davies **5.00**

Marianne by Terry Gilkyson, 1955, Photo Easy Riders **5.00**

Marie by Irving Berlin, 1928, Photo Vilma Banky (Cover Artist, R.S. & Irving Berlin) **10.00**

Marie by Walter Hirsch, Otto Motzan & Henry Santly, 1921.............**3.00**

Marietta by Sterny & Courquin, 1911 ....**5.00**

Marine Fox Trot by Robert Marine, 1915 ....**5.00**

Marine Review, The by Charles D. Tuttle, 1896, Dedicated To The Renowned Leaders Of The U.S. Marine Band (Photo Chromotype Engraving, Philadelphia, Pa., Transportation, Pre 1900, March & Dedication).....................**20.00**

Marines' Hymn, The by L.Z. Phillips, 1919, Printed For Complimentary Distribution By U.S. Marine Corps, Publicity Bureau, 1100 South Broad St., Philadelphia, Pa. (March, WWI & Patriotic) **20.00**

Marines' Hymn, The by L.Z. Phillips, 1932, Movie: To The Shores Of Tripoli, Photo John Payne, Maureen O'Hara & Randolph Scott (Patriotic & March) **15.00**

Marionette by Felix Arndt, 1917 ....**4.00**

Marionettes by Harry B. Smith & Sigmund Romberg, 1925, Musical: Princess Flavia.....................**5.00**

Market On Saturday Night by Edward Harrigan & David Braham, 1882 (Pre 1900) **10.00**

Marnie by Herman, Jason & Shayne, 1964, Movie: Marnie, Photo Sean Connery & Tippi Hedren.....................**3.00**

Maron Of The Siamese by Paul Lincke, 1923.....................**3.00**

Marriage Game, The by Stoddard, DeAngelis & Cort, 1914, Photo Alexander Carlisle (Cover Artist, Pfeiffer) **10.00**

Marry 'Em Young, Treat 'Em Rough, Tell 'Em Nothing! by Phil Ponce, 1922 ....**5.00**

Marry The Man Today by Jo Swerling, Abe Burrows & Frank Loesser, 1950, Musical: Guys & Dolls.....................**5.00**

Marrying For Love by Irving Berlin, 1950, Musical: Call Me Madam, Caricature of Ethel Merman (Cover Artist, Peter Arno & Irving Berlin)......**10.00**

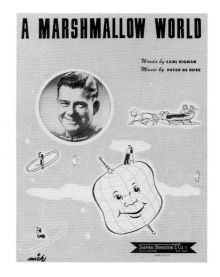

Marshmallow World, A by Carl Sigman & Peter DeRose, 1949, Photo Arthur Godfrey (Cover Artist, Nick).....................5.00

Marshmallow World, A by Carl Sigman & Peter DeRose, 1949, Photo Vaughn Monroe (Cover Artist, Nick).....................**5.00**

Marta by Moise Simons, 1931 ....**3.00**

Marta, Rambling Rose Of the Wildwood by Wolfe Gilbert & Moises Simons, 1931, Movie: The Street Singer, Photo Arthur Tracy (Cover Artist, Frederick Manning)................................**8.00**

Martha by Dorn (Cover Artist, Pfeiffer)................................**10.00**

Martyrs Of The Maine by Gebest, 1898 (Pre 1900) **20.00**

Mary Ann by Benny Davis & Abner Silver, 1927, Photo Rosa Rosalie (Deco)...**5.00**

Mary Ann Callahan by J. Rodan, 1890 (Pre 1900).........................**10.00**

Mary by Otto Harbach & Louis A. Hirsch, 1920, Musical: Mary (George M. Cohan)...**10.00**

Mary by T. Richardson, 1912 ....**5.00**

Mary Dear, Some Day We Will Meet Again by Harry De Costa & M. K. Jerome, 1922...**5.00**

Mary From Maryland by Art Hickman & Ben Black, 1921 (Cover Artist, Barbelle & Deco)..**10.00**

Mary Goes Round by Olsen & Johnson, Jay Levison & Ray Evans, 1940, Movie: Hellzapoppin of 1941 (Cover Artist, Im-Ho).....................**5.00**

Mary Had A Little Lamb by Symes & Maine, 1936 ....**5.00**

Mary I Love You So by Harry J. Lincoln & H. A. Tilton, 1920 ....**10.00**

Mary I'm In Love With You by J. Fred Coots & Ozzie Nelson, 1931, Photo Dave Abrams (Deco)...**5.00**

Mary Kelly's Beau by Edward Harrigan & David Braham, 1880 (Pre 1900)...**18.00**

Mary Lee by Harold Robe & Lieutenant Gitz Rice, 1918 (WWI & Military Personnel)...**20.00**

Mary Lou by Abe Lyman, George Waggner & J. Russell Robinson, 1926, Photo Art Fowler (Cover Artist, Barbelle & Deco)..........................**6.00**

Mary Lou by Abe Lyman, George Waggner & J. Russell Robinson, 1926, Photo Elmer Grasso (Cover Artist, Barbelle & Deco) **6.00**

Mary Lou by Abe Lyman, George Waggner & J. Russell Robinson, 1926, Photo Doris Gutow (Cover Artist, Barbelle & Deco) **6.00**

Mary Malone by Carter, 1908 (Irish).....................................**5.00**

Mary, Mary, Quite Contrary by Frank Loesser & Burton Lane, 1941, Movie: Las Vegas Night, Photo Frank Sinatra.............................**5.00**

Mary McGee by M. E. Rourke & Jerome D. Kern, 1907....................**10.00**

Mary Pickford, The Darling Of Them All by Dave Radford, Daisy Sullivan & Richard Whiting, 1914, Signed Photo Mary Pickford (Signed)...**30.00**

Mary Reagan by Anita Stewart, 1919......................................**5.00**

Mary You Must Marry Me by Anita Owen, 1919 (Cover Artist, Haskell Coffin) **10.00**

Mary You're A Big Girl Now by Bobby Heath & Gus A. Benkhart, 1909...**5.00**

Mary You're A Little Bit Old Fashioned by Brown & Marshall, 1914 .**5.00**

Mary's A Grand Old Name by George M. Cohan, 1933, Movie: Yankee Doodle Dandy, Photo James Cagney & George M. Cohan (George M. Cohan) **10.00**

Mary's Lullaby by Rev. F. J. West, S.J. & Achille P. Bragers, 1943.....**4.00**

Mary's Pet Waltz by E. Mack, 1909.......................................**3.00**

Maryland! My Maryland! by James R. Randall, Advertising For Bromo Seltzer (Advertising)..**30.00**

Masquerade by Paul Francis Webster & John Jacob Loeb, 1932 (Deco)...**5.00**

Masquerade Is Over, The by Herb Magidson & Allie Wrubel, 1938 (Cover Artist, Im-Ho) **3.00**

Masquerade Is Over, The by Herb Magidson & Allie Wrubel, 1938, Photo Bob Craig (Cover Artist, Barbelle)..**3.00**

Masquerade March And Two Step, The by E.T. Paull & Krell (Cover Artist, E.T. Paull & March) **35.00**

Massa's In The Cold Cold Ground by Stephen Foster, 1852 (Stephen Foster, & Pre 1900) **50.00**

Matin De Septembre, September Morn by Henri I. Marshall, 1913.......**5.00**

Matinee by Bob Russell & Carl Sigman, 1948, Photo Gordon MacRae ..**4.00**

Matrimony Rag by Edgar Leslie & Lewis F. Muir, 1911 (Rag)..........**10.00**

Mattinata by Ed Teschemacher & Ruggiero Leoncavallo, 1904...........**3.00**

Maud by Harry B. Smith & John Stromberg, 1899 (Pre 1900) **10.00**

Mavis by L. A. Lefevre & Harold Craxton, 1914........................**3.00**

Mavourneen by John T. McDonough & Walter Scanlan, 1921 (Irish)..**10.00**

Mavourneen, Mavourneen From Dear Old Killarney by Leap, 1915 (Cover Artist, Pfeiffer, Irish & Deco)....................................**22.00**

May Bells by Losey, 1916 (Cover Artist, Pfeiffer) **10.00**

May I? by James O'Dea & Anna Caldwell, 1906, Photo Marie Glazier (Cover Artist, Gene Buck)..**10.00**

May I? by Mack Gordon & Harry Revel, 1934, Movie: We're Not Dressing, Photo Bing Crosby & Carole Lombard..................................**6.00**

May I Have The Next Romance With You? by Mack Gordon & Harry Revel, 1936, Movie: Head Over Heels In Love, Photo Jessie Matthews **5.00**

May I Have This Waltz With You Madame? by George Brown & Enrico Madriguera, 1932...**5.00**

May I Never Love Again by Sano Marco & Jack Erickson, 1940 ....**5.00**

May Morning, A by Frederic E. Weatherly & L. Denza, 1894 (Pre 1900) **5.00**

May The Good Lord Bless And Keep You by Meredith Wilson, 1950 .**3.00**

May Time by B. G. DeSylva & Ed Rose, 1924............................**5.00**

May You Always by Larry Markes & Dick Charles, 1958, Photo Maguire Sisters...**5.00**

Maybe by Allan Flynn & Frank Madden, 1935, Photo Del Casino (Cover Artist, Leff)..**6.00**

Maybe by Allan Flynn & Frank Madden, 1935, Photo Harry James (Cover Artist, Leff)..**6.00**

Maybe by Carmen Lombardo, John Jacob Loeb & Harry Kogen, 1937, Photo The Lombardos, Victor, Carmen & Lebert (Cover Artist, HBK)...**4.00**

Maybe by Carmen Lombardo, John Jacob Loeb & Harry Kogen, 1937, Photo Henry Busse (Cover Artist, HBK) **4.00**

Maybe I Love You Too Much by Irving Berlin, 1933 (Irving Berlin).**10.00**

Maybe I'll Cry Over You by Elton Britt, 1949, Photo Elton Britt **3.00**

Maybe It's All For The Best by Paul Biese, Jack Rose & Jimmy Steiger, 1921 (Cover Artist, Barbelle) **3.00**

Maybe It's Because by Harry Ruby & Johnnie Scott, 1949, Musical: Along Fifth Avenue, Photo Andy & Della Russell (Cover Artist, Nick)...**5.00**

Maybe It's Love by Sidney Mitchell, Archie Gottler & George Meyer, 1930 ....**5.00**

Maybe It's The Moon by Richard A. Whiting, 1931.....................**5.00**

Maybe She Will Someday by Wells & Bryan, 1913 (Cover Artist, Pfeiffer) **10.00**

Maybe, She'll Write Me, She'll Phone Me by Roy Turk, Ted Snyder & Fred E. Ahlert, 1924 (Cover Artist, Barbelle) **6.00**

Maybe Some Day You'll Remember by Arthur J. Lamb & Edward T. Johnson, 1918 ....**5.00**

Maybe This Is Love by B. G. DeSylva, Lew Brown & Ray Henderson, 1928, Musical: Three Cheers...**10.00**

Maybe This Time by Ebb & Kander, 1972, Movie: Cabaret, Photo Liza Minelli **5.00**

Maybe–Who Knows? by Johnny Tucker, Joe Schuster & Ruth Etting, 1929 ....**5.00**

Maybe You Were Made For Me by Al Bryan & Maxwell Silver, 1910 **5.00**

Maybe You Would If You Could by Bryan & Cooper, 1918 (Cover Artist, Pfeiffer)..**10.00**

Maybe You'll Be There by Sammy Gallop & Rube Bloom, 1947, Photo Gordon Jenkins (Cover Artist, Nick).......................................**6.00**

Maybe You'll Change Your Mind by Wm. Tracey & W. Raymond Walker, 1912 ....**6.00**

Maybe You're Not The Only One Who Loves Me by Alfred Bryan & Geo Botsford, 1910 (Cover Artist, Starmer)..**5.00**

Mazie by Sid Caine, Eli Dawson & Lew Gold, 1921............................**3.00**

Mazie, My Dusky Daizy by Will A. Heelen & J. Fred Helf, 1901 (Black, Black Face)..**15.00**

Mazurka Caprice by H. Sylvester Krause, 1899 (Pre 1900)................**10.00**

McCarthy In Piccardy by Massa & Huntington, 1918 (Cover Artist, Pfeiffer & Irish)..**15.00**

McKinley Presidential March (President, Political & March)..............**35.00**

McKinley's Funeral March, 1901, Photo President McKinley (President, Political & March)..**40.00**

McNally's Row Of Flats by Edward Harrigan & David Braham, 1882 (Pre 1900)..**10.00**

Me And My Melinda by Irving Berlin, 1942 (Irving Berlin)..............**10.00**

Me And My Shadow by Billy Rose, Al Jolson & Dave Dreyer, 1927 (Al Jolson)..**5.00**

Me And My Teddy Bear by Jack Winters & J. Fred Coots, 1950, Photo Rosemary Clooney **10.00**

Me And The Boy Friend by Jimmie Monaco & Sidney Clare, 1924, Photo Miss Elizabeth Brice (Cover Artist, Frederick S. Manning & Transportation) **22.00**

Me And The Clock by Jack Meskill, Billy Mann & Pete Wendling, 1929 (Cover Artist, Barbelle) **5.00**

Me And The Man In The Moon by Jimmy Monaco & Edgar Leslie, 1928 (Cover Artist, Pud Lane & Deco)..**5.00**

Me And The Minstrel Band by Alex Rogers, 1904............................**10.00**

Me And The Moon by Walter Hirsch & Lou Handman, 1936, Photo Dick Stabile (Cover Artist, HBK) **4.00**

Me by Irving Berlin, 1931 (Irving Berlin)......................................**10.00**

Me Minus You by Paul Francis Webster, Abel Baer & John Jacob Loeb, 1932 ....**3.00**

Me, Myself And I by Irving Gordon, Allen Roberts & Alvin Kaufman, 1937, Photo Guy Lombardo (Cover Artist, Henri Lamothe & Deco)............**6.00**

Me Too-Ho-Ho! Ha-Ha! by Harry Woods, Charles Tobias & Al Sherman, 1926, Photo Carrie Lillie (Cover Artist, Politzer, Deco & Transportation)..**12.00**

Meadow Brook Fox Trot by Arthur M. Kraus, 1914, Photo Sonia Baraban & Charles Grohs (Cover Artist, Starmer)..........................**5.00**

Meadowlands by V. Gussev, Russian Text by L. Knipper, English Lyric by Olga Paul, 1942, Featured in "Mission To Moscow" Favorite Song Of The Red Army, Story of Former Ambassador Jos. E. Davis (WWII) **12.00**

Meadows–Route 9 On The Turnpike, The by Jack Edwards & Johnny Watson, 1946, Photo Vaughn Monroe On Back Cover **5.00**

Mean To Me by Roy Turk & Fred E. Ahlert, 1929 (Deco)..................**5.00**

Meaning Of U.S.A. by Raymond Browne, 1902 (Patriotic)................**10.00**

Medic Rag by Mary Hale Woolsey, 1910 (Rag) **10.00**

Medicine Man by Williams & Walker, 1899 (Pre 1900)....................**10.00**

Meditation by Lee Sims, 1927 ....**6.00**

Meditation by Louis A. Drumheller, 1909 ....**5.00**

Meet Me At The Station Dear by Sam M. Lewis, Joe Young & Ted Snyder, 1917, Photo Beatrice Lambert (Cover Artist, Barbelle & Transportation) **18.00**

Meet Me At Twilight by Sydney P. Harris, 1914................................**10.00**

Meet Me In Blossom Time by Geo. Moriarty & James R. Shannon, 1914 (Cover Artist, Dorothy Dulin) **10.00**

Meet Me In Bubble Land by Caspar Nathan & Joe Manne & Isham Jones, 1919 ....**6.00**

Meet Me In Frisco And We'll Go Out To The Fair by Will A. Fentress..**6.00**

Meet Me In Rose Time Rosie by Wm. Jerome & Jean Schwartz, 1908, Photo Fannie Ward (March)..**10.00**

Meet Me In Seattle Suzie by Lassers, 1962..**5.00**

Meet Me In St. Louis, Louis by Andrew B. Sterling & Kerry Mills, 1935, Movie: Meet Me In St. Louis, Photo Judy Garland........................**20.00**

Meet Me Josie At the Gate by Geo. M. Clark **5.00**

Meet Me Neath The Persian Moon by Woolf & Fridland, 1914 (Cover Artist, Pfeiffer)..**10.00**

Meet Me Tonight In Dreamland by Beth Slater Whitson & Leo Friedman, 1909, Photo Reine Davies **12.00**

Meet Me Tonight In Dreamland by Beth Slater Whitson & Leo Friedman, 1909, Movie: In The Good Old Summer Time, Photo Judy Garland & Van Johnson **12.00**

Meet Me Tonight Old Pal Of Mine by Martha Boswell, 1932..............**5.00**

Meet Mr. Callaghan by Eric Spear, 1952, Photo Les Paul & Mary Ford (Irish) **5.00**

Meet The Sun Half-Way by Johnny Burke & James V. Monaco, 1940, Movie: If I Had My Way, Photo Bing Crosby & Gloria Jean (Cover Artist, HBK) **12.00**

Melancholy by Ben Ryan & Lou Handman, 1929 ....**3.00**

Melancholy by Norton & Barnett, 1911 ....**5.00**

Melancholy Moon by Harold Weeks & Albert Mallotte, 1921 ....**3.00**

Melancholy Serenade by Jackie Gleason, Photo Jackie Gleason **5.00**

Melba Waltz, The by Norman Newell & Mischa Spoliansky, 1953, Musical: Melba, Photo Patrice Munsell......................................**3.00**

Melinda's Wedding Day Rag by Joe McCarthy, Joe Goodwin & Al Piantadosi, 1913, Photo Geo Leonard & Margaret Meredith (Rag)..........**10.00**

Mello Cello by Harry Williams & Neil Moret, 1921, Photo Dorothy Dixon & Carl Hyson (Cover Artist, C. E. Millard & Deco)....................**15.00**

Mellow Southern Moon by Cecil Teague & Frank Trevor, 1922..........**3.00**

Melody by Hugh Charles & Sonny Miller, 1946................................**3.00**

Melody Divine by Ruby & Spencer, 1929, Movie: The Careless Age, Photo Carmel Myers & Douglas Fairbanks, Jr.....................**8.00**

Melody Farm by Gus Kahn, Bronislaw Kaper & Walter Jurmann, 1937, Movie: Everybody Sing, Photo Allan Jones & Judy Garland........**10.00**

Melody From The Sky, A by Sidney D. Mitchell & Louis Alter, 1936, Movie: The Trail Of The Lonesome Pine, Photo Sylvia Sidney & Fred MacMurray **10.00**

Melody Lane by B. G. DeSylva, Larry Spier & Con Conrad, 1924......**5.00**

Melody Maids by W. Leon Ames, 1914..**5.00**

Melody Of Love by H. Engelmann, 1903..**10.00**

Melody Of Love by Tom Glazer & H. Engelmann, 1954, Photo Four Aces..**5.00**

Melody Of Love, The by Harry B. Smith, Robert B. Smith & Franz Lehar, 1911, Photo Marguerite Sylva..**10.00**

Melody Rag by Raymond Birch, 1911 (Rag) **10.00**

Melody That Made You Mine, The by Cliff Friend & W.C. Polla, 1925 ..**5.00**

Melody Time by George Weiss & Bennie Benjamin, 1948, Movie: Melody Time (Disney) **10.00**

Melon Time In Dixieland by Dave Ringle, 1931 (Cover Artist, H. H. Warner, & Dixie)..**10.00**

Mem'ries by Henry M. Neely & Harold Sanford, 1928 ....**6.00**

Memorie Of Mother And Home by Simpson & Maxwell (Cover Artist, Pfeiffer)..**10.00**

Mem-O-Ries by Morgan Brown & Harry Williams, 1915 (Cover Artist, Premier Engraving Co.)..**5.00**

Memories Are Made Of This by Terry Gilkysan, Rich Dehr & Frank Miller, 1955, Photo Dean Martin (Cover Artist, Barbelle) **3.00**

Memories by Gustave Kahn & Egbert Van Alstyne, 1915 (Deco).......**10.00**

Memories Of France by Al Dubin & J. Russel Robinson, 1928, Dedicated: To Our Pals In The American Legion, We Dedicate This Refrain. If It Makes But One Of You Happy It Was Not Written In Vain, Signed by Al Dubin, 305th F A 7th Division (Cover Artist, Barbelle, Patriotic & Dedication) **15.00**

Memories Of Mother by Edward I. Boyle, 1925 ....**12.00**

Memories Of Spain by J. A. Silberbern, 1897 (Pre 1900)...................**10.00**

Memories Of The South by Rudolph Thaler, 1908 (Black, Black Face)...**15.00**

Memories Of You by Andy Razaf & Eubie Blake, 1944, Photo Steve Allen & Donna Reed **10.00**

Memories, Signed by Barbra Streisand (Signed)...............................**10.00**

Memory Lane by B. G. DeSylva, Larry Spier & Con Conrad, 1924......**5.00**

Memory Lane by Jess Williams & Lester Palmer, 1936 ....**3.00**

Memory Of A Song, The by Worton David & Horatio Nichols, 1922 ..**2.00**

Memory Waltz, The by Benny Davis & Joe Burke, 1933 ....**5.00**

Memphis Blues, The by W.C. Handy, 1913 (Blues) **10.00**

Memphis In June by Paul Francis Webster & Hoagy Carmichael, 1945 ..**3.00**

Mending A Heart by L. Wolfe Gilbert & Joseph Cooper, 1919.............**5.00**

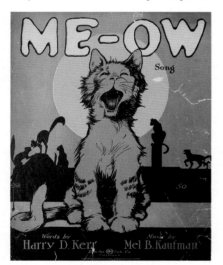

Me-Ow by Harry D. Kerr & Mel B. Kaufman, 1919 (Cover Artist, Ray) ** 10.00**

Mercedes by Geo J. Trinkaus, 1899 (Pre 1900)..................................**10.00**

Merrily On Our Way by Frank Churchill, Charles Wolcott, Larry Morey & Ray Gilbert, 1949, Movie: Adventures Of Ichabod Crane And Mr. Toad (Disney)...**12.00**

Merrily We'll Float Along by Jimmy Kennedy, 1910 (Transportation) ..**15.00**

Merrily We'll Roll Along by Andrew Sterling & Abner Silver, 1918, Photo Al Herman (Cover Artist, DeTakacs) **10.00**

Merry Bells by Julius Vogler, 1902...**10.00**

Merry Christmas Polka, The by Paul Francis Webster & Sonny Burke, 1949 ....**5.00**

Merry Dance, A by Helen Macgregor, 1932 ....**3.00**

Merry Go Round Broke Down, The by Cliff Friend & Dave Franklin, 1937, Photo Russ Morgan (Cover Artist, Merman) **3.00**

Merry Go Round, The by Paul Van Dyke, 1923 (Cover Artist, Carvon)..**5.00**

Merry-Go-Round, The by Ronell, 1936, Movie: Champagne Waltz, Photo Fred Macmurray & Gladys Swarthout **8.00**

Merry-Go-Round Waltz by Jimmy Kennedy & Arthur Finn, 1949, Photo Sammy Kaye (Cover Artist, Nick) **3.00**

Merry Madcap by Bell, 1908 ....**8.00**

Merry Madness by Thomas S. Allen, 1914 (Cover Artist, Starmer) **15.00**

Merry Wedding Bells, 1912 (Cover Artist, Pfeiffer)...........................**10.00**

Merry Widow, The by Franz Lehar, Arranged by Alfred J. Doyle, 1908 (Cover Artist, Gene Buck)...**15.00**

Merry Widow Waltz by Carl Field & Franz Lehar, 1935, Movie: The Merry Widow, Photo Maurice Chevalier & Jeannette MacDonald...**6.00**

Merry Widow Waltz by Carl Field & Franz Lehar, 1935, Photo Glenn Lee **5.00**

Merry Widow Waltz by Carl Field & Franz Lehar, 1935, Photo Paul Whiteman (Cover Artist, NPS & Deco) **5.00**

Message From The Man In The Moon, A by Kahn, Kaper & Jurmans, 1937, Movie: A Day At The Races, Photo Harpo, Groucho & Chico Marx, Allan Jones & Maureen O'Sullivan **8.00**

Message Of Peace by H. Engelmann, 1905 (Cover Artist, Hoffman)....**5.00**

Message Of The Violet by Pixley & Luders, 1902................................**5.00**

Message On The Train by Grimm, 1897 (Pre 1900 & Transportation) ..**15.00**

Meteor Rag by Arthur C. Morse, 1920 (Rag)....................................**10.00**

Metro Polka by Willie Evans & George Vaughn, 1951, Photo Frankie Laine **3.00**

Metropolitan by Frederick Millette, 1911 (March)..............................**8.00**

Mexicali Rose by Helen Stone & Jack B. Tenney, 1935, Signed Photo Bing Crosby (Cover Artist, James Axeltod & Signed) **15.00**

Mexican Moonlight by Jacinto S. Fernandez, 1934 (Cover Artist, Heflay) **3.00**

Mexico by Charles Wolcott & Ray Gilbert, 1945, Movie: The Three Caballeros (Disney) **15.00**

Mexico by Cole, Johnson & Cole, 1904..**5.00**

Meyer by Willie Raskin & Jack Glogau, 1922, Photo Billy Glason **5.00**

Mia Cara by Irving Kahal, Sammy Pierre Fain & Norman, 1930, Movie: The Big Pond, Photo Maurice Chevalier & Claudette Colbert **10.00**

Miami Shore by Victor Jacobi, 1919 ....**6.00**

Michelle by John Lennon & Paul McCartney, 1965, Photo Paul McCartney & The Beatles **15.00**

Mick That Threw The Brick by Davis & Lawler, 1899 (Pre 1900 & Irish) **10.00**

Mickey by Harry Williams & Neil Moret, 1918 (Cover Artist, Pfeiffer) ..**10.00**

Mickey by Harry Williams & Neil Moret, 1918, From Mack Sennett's Movie: Mickey, Dedicated To Mabel Normand, Photo Mabel Normand (Cover Artist, Barbelle, Irish & Dedication) **15.00**

Mid The Blue Grass Of Kentucky by Harris, 1909 ....**10.00**

Mid The Green Fields Of Virginia by Charles K. Harris, 1898, Photo Maude Amber (Pre 1900) **10.00**

Mid The Hush Of The Corn by Gordon Temple **6.00**

Mid The Light Ripples by Franz Schubert, 1857 (Pre 1900 & Transportation)..**20.00**

Mid The Orange Trees And Blossoms She Is Waiting by Robert Skilling, 1901 ....**10.00**

Midnight Fire Alarm, The by Harry J. Lincoln & E.T. Paull, 1900 (Cover Artist, E.T.Paull, Lithograph, A Hoen & March)..........................**35.00**

Midnight Flyer, The by E.T. Paull, 1903 (Cover Artist, E.T. Paull & Transportation) **35.00**

Midnight Kiss by Francis Ellison, Robert E. Harty & Henry Ellison, 1933..**3.00**

Midnight Masquerade by Bernard Bierman, Arthur Berman & Jack Manus, 1946, Photo Blue Barron (Cover Artist, Nick) **4.00**

Midnight Moon by Edward Buffington, 1905 ....**5.00**

Midnight Romance, A by Anita Stewart, 1919, Photo Anita Stewart (Cover Artist, Barbelle) **10.00**

Midnight Rose by Sidney Mitchell & Lew Pollack, 1923, Photo Karyl Norman **8.00**

Midnight Sons, The by McDonough, 1909 (Transportation) **15.00**

Midnight Special by Harry Lincoln, 1910 (Transportation) **25.00**

Midnight Waltz, The by Gus Kahn & Walter Donaldson, 1925, Photo Dan Gregory & His Orchestra (Cover Artist, JVR & Deco) **5.00**

Midnight Whirl, The by Sylvio Hein, 1914 (Cover Artist, DeTakacs & Rag) **20.00**

Midshipmite by Weatherly & Adams, 1870 (Pre 1900) **15.00**

Mighty Lak' A Rose by Frank L. Stanton & Ethelbert Nevin, 1901 (Irish) **5.00**

Mignonette by Heinrich Lichner, 1917 (Cover Artist, Jenkins) **10.00**

Mignonette by Ned Cole, 1898 (Pre 1900) **10.00**

Mikado by Gilbert & Sullivan (Cover Artist, Pfeiffer) **10.00**

Milady by J. S. Zanecnik, 1916 ....**5.00**

Mile A Minute, A by James L. Harlin & Harry J. Lincoln, 1917 (Transportation & March) **25.00**

Milena by James A. Miles, 1910 Advertising Sterling Piano Co., Derby, Conn. (Cover Artist, A. Byrns & Advertising) **20.00**

Miles Apart by Walt Brevig, Charles Dornberger & Joe Davis, 1937, Photo Many Stars (Cover Artist, Frederick S. Manning) **10.00**

Military Parade by Chapman, 1905 (Patriotic) **10.00**

Military Waltz by Frederic Knight Logan, 1917 ....**5.00**

Milkman, Keep Those Bottles Quiet by Don Raye & Gene DePaul, 1944, Movie: Broadway Rhythm, Photo Ginny Simms & Tommy Dorsey ..**5.00**

Million Dreams Ago, A by Lew Quadling, Eddy Howard & Dick Jurgens, 1940, Photo Glenn Miller **5.00**

Million Dreams Ago, A by Lew Quadling, Eddy Howard & Dick Jurgens, 1940, Photo Morgan Baer **5.00**

Million Hearts Are Calling, A by Baskette & Luz, 1922, Movie: Forget-Me-Not, Photo Irene Hunt & William Machin **5.00**

Mimi by Ballard Macdonald & Con Conrad, 1921 (Cover Artist, Wohlman & Deco) **10.00**

Mimi by Lorenz Hart & Richard Rodgers, 1932, Movie: Love Me Tonight, Photo Maurice Chevalier **8.00**

Mind Yo Own Business, 1910 (Cover Artist, Pfeiffer) **10.00**

Mine by B. G. DeSylva & James F. Hanley, 1927 ....**3.00**

Mine by Chapine & Hinshaw, 1912 ....**5.00**

Mine by George Gershwin, 1933 ....**5.00**

Mine by James W. McGee, Paul Benedek & Alfred Solmon, 1911 Dedicated To Mr. William Wade Hinshaw (Cover Artist, E.K & Dedication) **5.00**

Miner's Dream Of Home by Goodwin & Dryden, 1891 (Pre 1900) **15.00**

Minita by Platzman, 1916 (Cover Artist, Pfeiffer) **10.00**

Mink Lament, The by Gordon & Warren 1945, Movie: Diamond Horseshoe, Photo Betty Grable, Dick Haymes, Carmen Cavallaro, William Gaxton & Beatrice Kay **8.00**

Minnie, Shimmy For Me by Jimmy Lucas & Billy Frisch, 1918 ....**5.00**

Minnie The Moocher by Cab Calloway & Irving Mills, 1931 (Cover Artist, Leff) **5.00**

Minnie's In The Money by Leo Robin & Harry Warren, 1943, Movie: The Gang's All Here, Photo Alice Faye, Carmen Miranda, Phil Baker & The King Of Swing, Benny Goodman **5.00**

Minute Waltz by Frederick Chopin, 1945, Photo Diana Lynn **3.00**

Miracle Man, The by Jacques Grandei & Harry B. Smith, 1919 ....**5.00**

Miranda When We Are Made One by Edward Harrigan & David Braham, 1881 (Pre 1900) **15.00**

Misfits, The by North, 1960, Movie: The Misfits, Photo Marilyn Monroe, Clark Gable & Montgomery Clift **10.00**

Miss America by Bernie Wayne, 1940, Photo Bert Parks **5.00**

Miss Brown To You by Leo Robin, Richard Whiting & Ralph Rainger, 1935, Movie: The Big Broadcast of 1935 ....**5.00**

Miss Brown's Cake Walk by Bert Williams, 1896 (Pre 1900 & Black, Black Face) **20.00**

Miss Caroline by O.E. Story, 1914 ....**5.00**

Miss Columbia March by Osborne, 1908 (March) **10.00**

Miss Coquette Waltzes by Charlotte Blake, 1910 ....**5.00**

Miss Julie July by Livingston & Evans, 1948, Movie: Isn't It Romantic, Photo Veronica Lake, Mona Freeman & Billy DeWolfe **5.00**

Miss Liberty by Andrew B. Sterling & Harry Von Tilzer, 1897 (Pre 1900, March & Patriotic) **15.00**

Miss Liberty by Irving Berlin, 1949, Musical: Miss Liberty (Irving Berlin & Patriotic) **10.00**

Miss Liza Jane by Gladys G. Dennis & Harry H. Williams, 1915, Photo Billy Beard (Cover Artist, Acme Engraving Co., & Black, Black Face) **15.00**

Miss Lonely Hearts by Williams & Barry, 1975, Movie: The Day Of The Locusts, Photo Karen Black **3.00**

Miss You by Charles, Harry & Henry Tobias, 1929 ....**3.00**

Mission Chimes by W. Francis, 1911 ....**5.00**

Mississippi Boat Song by Frank Dumont, 1891 (Pre 1900) **15.00**

Mississippi Dream Boat by Lew Brown, Ralph Freed & Sammy Fain, 1943 ....**5.00**

Mississippi Flood Song by Hoover, 1927 ....**4.00**

Mississippi Mammy by Erwin R. Schmidt, Marty Bloom & Casper Nathan, 1924 (Black, Black Face) **10.00**

Mississippi Moon by M.J. Gunsky & Nat Goldstein, 1922, Musical: Passing Show 1922 (Cover Artist, Griffith) **5.00**

Mississippi Moonlight by J. Will Callahan & Lee S. Roberts, 1919 ......**5.00**

Mississippi Mud by Harry Barris, 1927 ....**5.00**

Mississippi River by William Krell, 1897 (Pre 1900 & Rag) **20.00**

Mississippi Shore by Arthur Sizemore & Egbert Van Alstyne, 1919 ....**3.00**

Mississippi Side Step by Leo E. Berliner, 1899 (Pre 1900 & Black, Black Face) **20.00**

Mississippi Steamboat by Helen Walker, 1922 (Dixie) **8.00**

Mississippi Valley Blues, The by Gene Autry & Jimmy Long, 1932, Photo Loretta Kusic **3.00**

Missouri Moon by Mitchell Parish & Henry Lodge, 1929 ....**5.00**

Missouri Waltz by Logan, 1914 (Cover Artist, Pfeiffer) **10.00**

Mistakes by Edgar Leslie & Horatio Nicholls, 1928, Photo Grace & Marie Eline (Deco)..**4.00**

Mister Aeroplane Man Take Me Up To Heaven by Con Conrad & Al Sherman, 1927 (Transportation)......................................**20.00**

Mister And Mississippi by Irving Gordon, 1951, Photo Patti Page (Cover Artist, Nick)..**3.00**

Mister Butterfly by Ballard Macdonald & Leo Edward, 1917 (Cover Artist, Dunk)..**5.00**

Mister Chairman by Martin Hennessey, 1890 (Pre 1900) **10.00**

Mr. Captain Stop The Ship by Felix McGlennon, 1894 (Pre 1900 & Transportation) **25.00**

Mister Dooley by William Jerome & Jean Schwartz, 1902.................**12.00**

Mister Five By Five by Don Raye & Gene DePaul, 1942, Movie: Behind The 8 Ball (Cover Artist, Holley)......................................**5.00**

Mister Gallagher And Mister Shean by Al Shean & Ed Gallagher, 1922, Ziegfield's Follies Of 1922, Photo Al Shean & Ed Gallagher (Cover Artist, Dick Frey & Irish) **10.00**

Mr. Ghost Goes To Town by Will Hudson, Irving Mills & Mitchell Parish, 1936 (Cover Artist, Immy) **4.00**

Mr. Jazz Himself by Irving Berlin, 1917, Photo Watson Sisters (Cover Artist, Barbelle & Irving Berlin)..10.00

Mr. Johnson, Turn Me Loose by Ben Harney, 1896 (Pre 1900 & Black, Black Face)..**20.00**

Mr. Meadowlark by Johnny Mercer & Walter Donaldson, 1940...........**3.00**

Mr. Monotany by Irving Berlin, 1949, Musical: Miss Liberty (Irving Berlin)..**10.00**

Mister Moon Kindly Come Out And Shine by Smith & Bowman, 1903 (Black, Black Face) **35.00**

Mister Moving Picture Man by Geo J. Moriarty & J. R. Shannon, 1912..**5.00**

Mr. Mulligan And Mr. Garrity by Percy Wenrich, 1925, Musical: The Gorilla, Photo Mulligan & Garrity (Cover Artist, Leff & Irish) **10.00**

Mister Pollyanna by Johnny Mercer & Hoagy Carmichael, 1943, Movie: True To Life..**8.00**

Mister Radio Man, Tell My Mammy To Come Back Home by Ira Schuster, Johnny White & Cliff Friend, 1924, Photo Jack & Irving Kaufman (Cover Artist, JVR)..**10.00**

Mister Sandman by Pat Ballard, 1954, Photo Chordettes.....................**3.00**

Mister Snow by Rodgers & Hammerstein, 1945, Movie: Carousel, Photo Gordon Macrae, Shirley Jones & Cameron Mitchell **5.00**

Mister Tap Toe by Terry Gilkyson, Richard Dehr & Frank Miller, 1952, Photo Doris Day **5.00**

Mr. Volunteer, You Don't Belong To The Regulars by Paul Dresser, 1901 (Patriotic)..**15.00**

Mister Whitney's Little Jitney Bus by Clarence Gaskill, 1915 (Transportation)..**20.00**

Mr. Wonderful by Jerry Bock, Larry Holofcener, & Geo. Weiss, 1956..**3.00**

Mr. Yankee Doodle, Are We Prepared? by Joseph J. Barry, & George H. Taylor, Assisted by George H. Malmgren, 1916, Photo George Washington & Admiral Dewey Jackson (Cover Artist, Starmer, President, WWI & Military Personnel)..**38.00**

Mr. Yankee Doodle by Clarke, Leslie & Schwartz, 1912 (Cover Artist, Pfeiffer)..**10.00**

Mister Yoddlin Man by Chris Smith & Ted Snyder, 1911 (Cover Artist, Pfeiffer & Deco)..**15.00**

Misty by Johnny Burke & Erroll Garner, 1955 ....**3.00**

Misty Islands Of The Highlands by Jimmy Kennedy & Michael Carr, 1935 ....**3.00**

Mixed Emotions by Stuart F. Loucheim, 1951, Photo Rosemary Clooney **5.00**

Moanin' Low by Howard Dietz & Ralph Rainger, 1929, Musical: The Little Show **10.00**

Mobile by Bob Wells & David Holt, 1954, Photo Julius LaRosa.........**3.00**

Mockin' Bird Hill by Vaughn Horton, 1949, Photo Les Paul & Mary Ford **3.00**

Mocking Bird by Frederic Lewis, 1903..**5.00**

Mocking Bird Rag by Walsh, 1912 (Rag) **10.00**

Modulations by Clarence M. Jones, 1923..**5.00**

Mohammed by Ballard Macdonald & Mary Earl, 1914......................**5.00**

Mohawk Trail, The by J. Henry Ellis, 1917 (Cover Artist, Rose, Indian & March) **25.00**

Mollie Darling by William S. Hays, 1871 (Pre 1900) **15.00**

Molly And I And The Baby by Harry Kennedy, 1892 (Pre 1900) **10.00**

Molly Brannigan by C. Villiers Stanford, 1903 (Irish)......................**10.00**

Molly by Edmund Goulding & Dan Dougherty, 1929, Musical: The Grand Parade **5.00**

Molly Dear, It's You I'm After by Frank Wood & Henry E. Pether, 1915, Photo Blanche Ring (Cover Artist, Starmer & Irish) **12.00**

Molly, I'm Coming Home Again by Alexander & Pierson, 1915 (Cover Artist, Pfeiffer)..**10.00**

Molly Lee by Jack Mahoney & Theodore Morse, 1909......................**5.00**

Molly-O by Art Hickman & Ben Black, 1921, Photo Mabel Normand (Cover Artist, Barbelle) **12.00**

Molly-O by William Scanlan, 1891 (Pre 1900 & Irish) **15.00**

Molly-O, I Love You by James C. Emery & Norman McNeil, 1921 (Irish)..**10.00**

Moment I Looked In Your Eyes, The by Dorothy Dick & Gene Gifford, 1933 ....**5.00**

Moment I Saw You, The by Howard Dietz & Arthur Schwartz, 1930, Movie: Three's A Crowd..**5.00**

Moment To Moment by Johnny Mercer & Henry Mancini, 1965 ....**1.00**

Moment's Hesitation, A by James V. Monaco, 1914, Photo Joan Sawyer & Jack Jarrot (Deco)..**12.00**

Moments Like This by Frank Loesser & Burton Lane, 1938, Movie: College Swing, Photo, Betty Grable, Bob Hope, Burns & Allen, Ben Blue, John Payne & Martha Raye **8.00**

Moments Or Jewels Of Memory by Chas. Kuhn, Jeff Branen & Robert Kuhn, 1919, Photo Wanda Hawley (Cover Artist, Starmer)...........**5.00**

Moments To Remember by Al Stillman & Robert Allen, 1935, Photo Four Lads **6.00**

Mon Desir by Anne Caldwell & Hugo Felix, 1916, Comic Opera: Pom Pom, Photo Mizzi Hajos..**15.00**

Mon Homme, My Man by A. Willemetz, Jacques Charles & Maurice Yvain, 1920 (Cover Artist, JVR & Deco) **10.00**

Mona by Sanders, 1909 (Cover Artist, Pfeiffer)..**10.00**

Mona by Seymour Rici & E. Harry Kelly, 1938, Photo Bob Hope.......**6.00**

Monastery Chimes by Martin, 1914 (Cover Artist, Pfeiffer)...............**10.00**

Money Isn't Everything by Richard Rodgers & Oscar Hammerstein II, 1951, Musical: Allegro.....................**5.00**

Money Won't Buy Love (Cover Artist, Pfeiffer) **12.00**

Monkey Doodle Dandy by Jack Drislane & Henry Frantzen, 1909.....**12.00**

Monkey Doodle Doo by Irving Berlin, 1913 (Cover Artist, Pfeiffer & Irving Berlin)...............**15.00**

Monkey Lane by Jack Drislane, 1907......................**5.00**

Monkey Rag by Chris Smith, 1911 (Rag) **10.00**

Monsieur Baby by Hornez, 1933, Movie: A Bedtime Story, Photo Maurice Chevalier.....................**10.00**

Montana by Ruth Byrd & Harold Weeks, 1921 (Cover Artist, Fung)....**5.00**

Montana Call by Clifford Grey & Herbert Stothart, 1930, Movie: Montana Moon.....................**5.00**

Montmarte Rose by Tommy Lyman, 1925......................**6.00**

Moo-Cow-Moo, First Prize Dairy Song In Big National Contest Of Chicago Dairy Produce, by Mrs. J. W. Wainwright, 1921 ....**12.00**

Mood Indigo by Irving Mills, Albany Bogard & Duke Ellington, 1931 ....**5.00**

Mood Pensive by Eva Applefield, 1919 (Cover Artist, Ray Parmelee)..**10.00**

Moon by Michael Caleo & Jack Miles, 1932, Photo Lloyd Huntley (Cover Artist, Barbelle) **3.00**

Moon Am Shinin' by Duncan Sisters, Book By Catherine C. Cushing, Suggested By Uncle Tom's Cabin By Harriet Beecher Stowe, 1923, Musical: Topsy & Eva, Photo Duncan Sisters (Cover Artist, P.M. Griffith & Black, Black Face) **10.00**

Moon At Sea by Harry Pease, Vincent Rose & Larry Stock, 1937, Photo Carol Weyman......................**3.00**

Moon Baby by Miller, 1904 ....**5.00**

Moon Country, Is Home To Me by Hoagy Carmichael & Johnny Mercer, 1941 ....**3.00**

Moon Dance by Ernest J. Schuster, 1911 ....**6.00**

Moon Dear by Raymond B. Egan, Richard Whiting & Neil Moret, 1905 (Indian) **20.00**

Moon Dream Shore by Gretchen Dick & Eugene Lockhart, 1924.........**5.00**

Moon Dreams by J. H. Shannon, 1913 ....**5.00**

Moon Face by Edward Heyman & Arthur Schwartz, 1936, Movie: That Girl From Paris, Photo Lily Pons **5.00**

Moon Got In My Eyes, The by John Burke & Arthur Johnston, 1937, Movie: Double Or Nothing, Photo Bing Crosby & Mary Carlisle...**5.00**

Moon Has Its Eyes On You, The by Billy Johnson & Albert Von Tilzer, 1905 ....**5.00**

Moon Is A Silver Dollar, The by Mitchell Parish & Sammy Fain, 1939, Photo Del Courtney **3.00**

Moon Is Always Bigger On Saturday Night, The by Gene Tiller & Ruth Roberts, 1938......................**6.00**

Moon Is Blue, The by Fine & Gilbert, 1953, Movie: The Moon Is Blue, Photo William Holden & Maggie McNamara......................**5.00**

Moon Is In Tears Tonight, The by Scholl & Jerome, 1937 ....**5.00**

Moon Is Low, The by Arthur Freed & Nacio Herb Brown, 1930, Movie: Montana Moon, Photo Joan Crawford **5.00**

Moon Kisses by Benj. Richmond, 1912 ....**5.00**

Moon Love by Mack David, Mack Davis & Andre Kostelanetz, 1939 (Cover Artist, HBK) **5.00**

Moon Maid by Harry Japan, 1915 (Cover Artist, Pfeiffer) **10.00**

Moon Moths by Jacob Henry Ellis, 1903, Dedicated To Mr. Louis W. Fickett (Dedication)......................**8.00**

Moon Of Manakoora, The by Alfred Newman, 1937, Movie: The Hurricane, Photo Dorothy Lamour & Jon Hall **5.00**

Moon Over Miami by Edgar Leslie & Joe Burke, 1935 (Cover Artist, Barbelle) **5.00**

Moon River by Benton Ley & Lee David, 1949 ....**4.00**

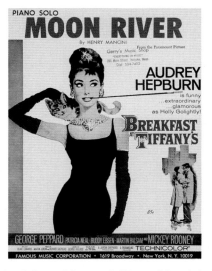

Moon River by Johnny Mercer & Henry Mancini, 1961, Movie: Breakfast At Tiffany's, Photo Audrey Hepburn **8.00**

Moon River by Johnny Mercer & Henry Mancini, 1961, Signed by Henry Mancini (Signed) **15.00**

Moon Shines On The Moonshine, The by Francis DeWitt & Robert Hood Bowers, 1921, Musical: Ziegfeld Follies, Photo Bert Williams (Black, Black Face) **20.00**

Moon Song That Wasn't For Me by Sam Coslow & Arthur Johnston, 1932, Movie: Hello Everybody, Photo Kate Smith......................**15.00**

Moon Winks by Geo. Stevens, 1904 ....**5.00**

Moon Won't Tell On You, The by Jos. C. Barton & Frank Klickmann, 1908, Photo Jeannette Lee **5.00**

Moonbeams On The Lake by John J. Fitzpatrick, 1904 (Cover Artist, Charles Lussier)......................**5.00**

Moonglow by Will Hudson, Eddie DeLange & Iving Mills, 1934 ....**2.00**

Moonlight by Con Conrad, 1921 ....**5.00**

Moonlight by Crane Wilbur & Paul Rubens, 1910, Musical: The Queen Of Bohemia (Cover Artist, Starmer)......................**12.00**

Moonlight by James O'Dea & Neil Moret, 1905, Photo J. A. Driscoll (Cover Artist, Starmer)......................**10.00**

Moonlight And Honeysuckle by Al D. Camdon & Hal Nye, 1921........**3.00**

Moonlight And Roses by Edwin H. Lemare, Ben Black & Neil Moret, 1925, Photo Verne Buck......................**5.00**

Moonlight And Roses Reverie by Bayley & Konsinsky, 1915 (Cover Artist, Pfeiffer)......................**10.00**

Moonlight And Shadows by Leo Robin & Frederick Hollander, 1936, Movie: Jungle Princess, Photo Dorothy Lamour & Ray Milland ..**10.00**

Moonlight At Killarney by William J. Scanlon, 1881 (Pre 1900 & Irish)..**15.00**

Moonlight Ballet by Walter E. Miles, 1937......................**3.00**

Moonlight Bay by Edward Madden & Percy Wenrich, 1912 (Cover Artist, Starmer) **10.00**

Moonlight Becomes You by Frank Butler & Don Hartman, 1952, Movie: Road To Morocco, Photo Bob Hope, Bing Crosby & Dorothy Lamour......................**12.00**

Moonlight Blue Waltz by Homer Deane, 1916 ....**5.00**

Moonlight Dear by Murchison & Hodge, 1909 (Cover Artist, Starmer & Indian)......................**25.00**

Moonlight Down In Dixie by Symon Winkle & Jack Kalin, 1919 (Dixie) **10.00**

Moonlight In Dixie by Fred W. Clement, 1905 (Cover Artist, E.S. Fisher & Dixie) **15.00**

Moonlight In Maryland by Aiken & Whiting, 1920 (Cover Artist, Pfeiffer) **10.00**

Moonlight In Vermont by John Blackburn & Karl Suessdorf, 1945......**5.00**

Moonlight Land by Harold G. Frost, Homer Deane & F. Henri Klickmann, 1921 ....**5.00**

Moonlight Madness, Then You Were Gone by Lou Davis & J. Fred Coots, 1927 ....**5.00**

Moonlight Makes Me Lonesome by Yellen & Cobb, 1915 (Cover Artist, Pfeiffer)..**10.00**

Moonlight Meander, A by S.M. Roberts, 1900 (Black, Black Face) ...**15.00**

Moonlight Mood by Harold Adamson & Peter DeRose, 1942..............**3.00**

Moonlight Mood by Harold Adamson & Peter DeRose, 1942, Photo The King Sisters..**4.00**

Moonlight On The Colorado by Billy Moll & Robert A. King, 1930 (Cover Artist, Barbelle) **5.00**

Moonlight On The Connecticut by W. Sinclair Duncan, 1922 (Cover Artist, M. Bodah)..**5.00**

Moonlight On The Danube by Byron Gay, 1925, Movie: The Blue Danube, Photo Leatrice Joy (Cover Artist, W. R. Cameron) **12.00**

Moonlight On The Hudson by G. D. Wilson, 1894 (Pre 1900).............**20.00**

Moonlight On The Lake by John S. Fearis, 1905.................................**5.00**

Moonlight On The Lake by White, 1873 (Pre 1900 & Transportation)..**20.00**

Moonlight On The Ocean by John Martin, 1904..................................**5.00**

Moonlight On The River by Glenn W. Ashleigh, 1908.........................**5.00**

Moonlight On The Water by Andrew Seidt, 1906................................**10.00**

Moonlight On The Waves by Verner, 1891 (Pre 1900)........................**10.00**

Moonlight Propaganda by Magidson & Malneck, 1945, Movie: Do You Love Me, Photo Harry James, Maureen O'Hara & Dick Haymes ...**8.00**

Moonlight Ripples by Merle Von Hagen, 1917 (Cover Artist, Barbelle & Deco) **10.00**

Moonlight Serenade by Parish & Miller, 1939, Movie: The Glenn Miller Story, Photo James Stewart & June Allyson **10.00**

Moonlight Serenade by Warren B. Smith & John Stromberg, 1898 (Pre 1900)..**10.00**

Moonlight Shadows by John J. Fitzpatrick, 1916 (Cover Artist, Hoffman)..**3.00**

Moonlight Tango by Sidney Prosen & Raymond Carrol, 1953 ....**3.00**

Moonlight, The Rose And You, The by Chas. E. Baer & Johann C. Schmidt, 1910 (Cover Artist, Starmer)..**6.00**

Moonlight Waltz by Victor LaSalle, 1912 (Indian)............................**20.00**

Moonlight Waltz by Frederick Knight Logan, 1914 ....**5.00**

Moonlight Whispers by Al J. Neiburg & Frankie Carle, 1944, Photo Jimmie Dorsey..**3.00**

Moonlight Whispers by Frankie Carle & Al J. Neiburg, 1944, Photo Frankie Carle **3.00**

Moonlight Wooing by Bernise G. Clements & W. Jacobs, 1916 (Cover Artist, Pfeiffer)..**10.00**

Moonlit Waters by Cliff Friend & Nacio Herb Brown, 1927................**4.00**

Moonshine Lullaby by Irving Berlin, 1946, Movie: Annie Get Your Gun (Irving Berlin)..**12.00**

Moonshine Of Kentucky by Atteridge & Carroll, 1920 (Cover Artist, Pfeiffer)..**10.00**

Moonshine Sally by Joe Santly, Joe McCarthy & Howard Johnson, 1916.**10.00**

Moonstruck by Coslow & Johnston, 1933, Movie: College Humor, Photo Bing Crosby & Mary Carlisle..**8.00**

Moontime by G. A. Spink, 1909...**5.00**

Moose Rag by Ted Johnson, 1910, Dedicated To Loyal Order Of Moose (Cover Artist, Pfeiffer, Rag & Dedication) **20.00**

Mop Rag by Remick & Eaton, 1909 (Rag) **10.00**

More And More by Jerome Kern & E. Y. Harburg, 1944, Movie: Can't Help Singing, Photo Deanna Durbin **7.00**

More by Norman Newell, R. Ortolani & N. Oliviero, 1963, Movie: Mondo Cane **3.00**

More by Tom Glazer & Alex Alstone, 1956, Photo Perry Como..........**6.00**

More I Cannot Wish You by Jo Swerling, Abe Burrows & Frank Loesser, 1950, Musical: Guys & Dolls..**3.00**

More I See Of Others, Dear The Better I Like You, The by Henry Blossom & Victor Herbert, 1914, Musical: The Only Girl (Victor Herbert) ..**15.00**

More I See You, The by Mack Gordon & Harry Warren, 1945, Movie: Diamond Horseshoe, Photo Betty Grable & Dick Haymes...........**10.00**

More Than You Know by William Rose, Edward Eliscu & Vincent Youmans, 1929, Photo Margaret Whiting................................**5.00**

More Than You Know by William Rose, Edward Eliscu & Vincent Youmans, 1929, Photo Jane Froman **5.00**

More Work For The Undertakers by Burton, Brooks & Leigh, 1900 ..**15.00**

More You Hurt Me, The by Mort Dixon, Joe Young & Harry Warren, 1931, Musical: The Laugh Parade (Cover Artist, Gorj)..................**6.00**

Morning by Edward Teschemacher & Landon Ronald, 1901 ....**5.00**

Morning Cy! by Harold Atteridge, 1907, Photo Walter Bellrose (Cover Artist, Grover) **8.00**

Morning Will Come by Al Jolson, B. G. DeSylva & Con Conrad, 1923, Musical: Bombo, Photo Al Jolson (Al Jolson) **10.00**

Moses Andrew Jackson, Good-bye by Ren Shields & Ted Snyder, 1906 (Black, Black Face) **22.00**

Mosquitoes' Parade by Howard Whitney, 1900 ....**10.00**

Most Everyone I Know Loves You by Gwen Meredith & Lucien Denni, 1915 ....**5.00**

Most Expensive Statue In The World, The by Irving Berlin, 1949, Musical: Miss Liberty (Irving Berlin) **12.00**

Most Gentlemen Don't Like Love by Cole Porter, 1938, Movie: Leave It To Me **5.00**

Most Wonderful Of All by Lao Silesu, 1919.......................................**5.00**

Moth And The Flame, The by George Taggart & Max S. Witt, 1898 (Pre 1900)..**12.00**

Mother by Dorothy Donnelly & Sigmund Romberg, 1925, Musical: My Maryland..**5.00**

Mother by James Thatcher, 1915...**5.00**

M-O-T-H-E-R, A Word That Means The World To Me by Howard Johnson & Theodore Morse, 1915, Eva Tanguay's Great Mother Song, Signed Photo Of Eva Tanguay (Cover Artist, Rose Symbol & Signed).......**35.00**

Mother Americans, 1917 (Cover Artist, Pfeiffer)............................**12.00**

Mother At Your Feet Is Kneeling by Sister S.C., 1948 ....**3.00**

Mother Dear, God Cares by Mary A. Simpson, 1928 ....**3.00**

Mother Dixie And You by Howard Johnson & Jos. H. Santly, 1927, Photo Harry Cooper (Cover Artist, Rose Symbol, Deco & Dixie)...........**10.00**

Mother Earth by P. J. O'Reilly & Wilfrid Sanderson, 1917.................**5.00**

Mother, I Love You by Howard Smith & Lieut. Gitz Rice, 1918 (WWI & Military Personnel) **16.00**

Mother Is The Best Friend After All by Joseph P. Skelly, 1883 (Pre 1900) **15.00**

Mother Is Waiting For You by Charles O. Tibbits & Anna B. Harmon, 1913 (Cover Artist, McCurdy & WWI) **10.00**

Mother Is Your Best Friend by H. A. Russotto & M. Zavodnick, 1914.**5.00**

Mother Love by Eugene West & Joe Gold, 1919...............................**10.00**

Mother Machree by Rida Johnson Young, Chauncy Olcott & Ernest R. Ball, 1910 (Irish)...**3.00**

Mother Mine She's Just Like You by Comfort, 1918 (Cover Artist, Pfeiffer) **10.00**

Mother My Own by Joe Solman, Ted Garton & George Benoit, 1920 (Cover Artist, W.M. Fisher & Deco)..**3.00**

Mother O'Mine, 1918 (Cover Artist, Pfeiffer) **10.00**

Mother O'Mine by Kipling & Caro Roma (Irish) **10.00**

Mother Of Pearl by Justin E. McCarthy, George Graff & Ernest Ball, 1920 ....**5.00**

Mother Of The Girl I Love by William B. Gray, 1897 (Pre 1900).......**10.00**

Mother Pin A Rose On Me by Lewis, Schlinder & Adams, 1905.........**5.00**

Mother Was A Lady by Edward B. Marks & Joseph Stern, 1896 (Pre 1900)..**10.00**

Mother Was My Best Friend by Herbert H. Powers & Ben Chadwick, 1900, Dedicated to Mrs. Lettia Power (Dedication).......................**5.00**

Mother You're Sunshine To Me by Bernard, 1919 (Cover Artist, Pfeiffer & WWI)..**15.00**

Mother's Appeal To Her Boy by J. Holmes & H. F. Smith, 1889 (Pre 1900)..**15.00**

Mother's Last Letter To Me by C.H. Hughes, 1883 (Pre 1900)..........**16.00**

Mother's Lullaby by Milton Weil, 1920 (Cover Artist, R.S.) **5.00**

Mother's Paisley Shawl by Geo. A. Kershaw & Walter Scanlan, 1922.**5.00**

Mother's Prayer by Arnstein & Gilbert, 1932 ....**5.00**

Mother's Prayer For Her Boy Out There, A by Andrew B. Sterling & Arthur Lange, 1918 (Cover Artist, Starmer & WWI) **15.00**

Mother's Rosary Of Love by Leo Wood & Eddie Dorr, 1929 (Cover Artist, Pfeiffer)..**10.00**

Mothers Of America You Have Done Your Share by Jacob Henry Ellis, 1918, Photo Eva Tanguay (WWI) **22.00**

Mothers Of France by Woods, 1918, Photo Joan Of Arc Statue (Cover Artist, Pfeiffer & WWI)...**15.00**

Motor Girl by Gus Edwards, 1909 (Transportation) **20.00**

Motor King March by Frantzen & Drislane, 1910 (Cover Artist, Pfeiffer, March & Transportation)..**20.00**

Motor March, The by Geo Rosey, 1906 (March & Transportation) **30.00**

Motorcycle Race March by Brower, 1915 (Cover Artist, Pfeiffer & March) **16.00**

Mottoes That Are Framed Upon The Walls by Devere & Mullaly, 1889 (Pre 1900) **15.00**

Mountain Belle by Kinkel, 1902...**5.00**

Mountain Greenery by Lorenz Hart & Richard Rodgers, 1926............**7.00**

Mountains In The Moonlight by Johnnie Ray, 1952, Photo Johnnie Ray..**3.00**

Mounted Police by Harry J. Lincoln, 1921, Photo Robert N. Keck (March) **10.00**

Mousie In The Piano by Kedan & Piantadosi, 1928 (cover Artist, Pfeiffer)..**12.00**

Movie Rag by J. S. Zamecnik, 1913 (Rag).......................................**12.00**

Movin' Man Don't Take My Baby Grand by Kalmar & Snyder, 1911, Photo Jack Manion (Cover Artist, Pfeiffer)...................................**15.00**

Moving Day by Andrew Sterling & Harry Von Tilzer, 1906..............**10.00**

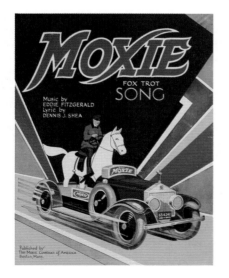

Moxie Fox Trot Song by Dennis J. Shea & Eddie Fitzgerald, 1930, Advertising Moxie (Advertising)..55.00

Mrs. Brady's Daughter by Harry Kennedy, 1882 (Pre 1900)..............**15.00**

Mrs. Casey Jones, The Brave Engineer's Widow by Eddie Newton & T. Lawrence Seibert, 1915 (Transportation)......................................**40.00**

Mrs. Maximum by Lincoln, 1915 (Cover Artist, Pfeiffer) **10.00**

Muddy Water by Jo Trent, Peter DeRose & Harry Richman, 1926 ....**5.00**

Mulberry Moon by C.M. Denison & Fred W. Hager, 1916, Photo Red Feather (Cover Artist, DeTakacs & Indian) **20.00**

Muldoon The Solid Man by Edward Harrigan, 1874 (Pre 1900 & Irish) ..**20.00**

Mule Train by Johnny Lange, Hy Heath & Fred Glickman, 1949 ..6.00

Mulligan Guard by Edward Harrigan & David Braham, 1873, Photo Harrigan & Hart, Dedicated To Mr. Josh Hart (Pre 1900, March & Dedication)..**25.00**

Multiplied By Eight by Howard Johnson & Carlo Sanderson, 1921, Musical: Tangerine **10.00**

Mummies Ball, The by Gunsky & Goldstein, 1921 ....**10.00**

Murder, He Says by Frank Loesser & Jimmy McHugh, 1943, Movie: Happy Go Lucky, Photo Mary Martin, Dick Powell, Betty Hutton, Eddie Bracken & Rudy Vallee **8.00**

Muriel Waltz, by Daly, 1915 (Cover Artist, Pfeiffer)........................**10.00**

Murmuring Zephyr, Perfumed Air by E.S. Wilcox & Adolf Jensen, 1878 (Pre 1900) **10.00**

Murray Walk, The by Paul Biese & F. Henri Klickmann, 1914, Photo Mae Murray **5.00**

Music Box Rag by C. Luckyth Roberts, 1914 (Rag)...........................**10.00**

Music Caressing Of Violins by Harry B. Lincoln & Leo Fall, 1911, Photo Donald Brian..**6.00**

Music From Across The Way by Carl Sigman & James Last, 1970, Photo Andy Williams..**3.00**

Music Goes Round & Around, The by Red Hodgson, Edward Farley & Michael Riley, 1935 (Cover Artist, HBK) **10.00**

Music Is Wonderful When You Are Lonesome by MacFarlane, Williams & Lowe, 1921, Photo Grace Nelson (Cover Artist, Starmer)..........**5.00**

Music Maestro Please! by Herb Magidson & Allie Wrubel, 1938 (Cover Artist, Merman) **5.00**

Music Makes Me by Gus Kahn, Edward Eliscu & Vincent Youmans, 1933, Movie: Flying Down To Rio, Photo Fred Astaire & Dolores Del Rio **6.00**

Music Makes Me Sentimental by Alfred Bryan & Maxwell Silver, 1908, Photo Saide O'Neil (Cover Artist, Hirt).......................................**10.00**

Music Man, The by Robert J. Adams, 1901 ....**10.00**

Music, Music Everywhere by Ted Koehler & Harold Arlen, 1932........**5.00**

Music! Music! Music! by Stephan Weiss & Bernie Baum, 1950, Photo Gene Rayburn & Dee Finch **4.00**

Music Of Wedding Chimes, The by Edgar Leslie & Pete Wendling, 1919 (Cover Artist, Barbelle) **6.00**

Music Stopped, The by Harold Adamson & Jimmy McHugh, 1943, Movie: Higher And Higher, Photo Frank Sinatra..........................**8.00**

Music Vots Music Must Come From Berlin by Kahn & LeBoy, 1911, Photo Eliz. Murray (Cover Artist, Pfeiffer & Deco) **15.00**

Musical Rag Sal by Swauger, 1911 (Cover Artist, Pfeiffer & Rag).....**15.00**

Musical Typist by Ronnie Munro, 1944 ....**3.00**

Muskrat Ramble by Ray Gilbert & Edward Kid Ory, 1950, Photo Dennis Day (Dixie)..**5.00**

Mutual Admiration Society by Matt Dubey & Harold Karr, 1956, Musical: Happy Hunting, Photo Ethel Merman **7.00**

My Adobe Hacienda by Louise Massey & Lee Penny, 1941, Photo Blue Barron **3.00**

My Aeroplane Jane by Lem Trombley, 1912 (Transportation)............**20.00**

My American Beauty Rose, 1915 (Cover Artist, Pfeiffer) **10.00**

My Angel by Erno Rapee & Lew Pollack, 1928, Movie: Street Angel, Photo Janet Gaynor & Charles Farrell..................................**10.00**

My Angel Man by Beam, 1912 (Cover Artist, Pfeiffer)......................**10.00**

My Angeline by L. Wolfe Gilbert & Mabel Wayne, 1929, Inspired By Longfellow's Evangeline..**10.00**

My Auto Lady by Atkins, 1901 (Transportation)...............................**15.00**

My Automobile Girl by Morris, 1900 (Transportation) **15.00**

My Automobile Girl From New Orleans by Davis, 1900 (Transportation)..**15.00**

My Baby Just Cares For Me by Gus Kahn & Walter Donaldson, 1931, Movie: Whoopee **6.00**

My Baby's Arms by Joseph McCarthy & Harry Tierney, 1919, Musical: Ziegfeld Follies 1919..**18.00**

My Bambazoo by Stadiger, 1909 (Cover Artist, Pfeiffer)...................**15.00**

My Bark by Dr. Th. Baker & A Goring Thomas, 1904.........................**5.00**

My Barney Lies Over The Ocean by Joe Young, Sam M. Lewis & Bert Grant, 1919 (Cover Artist, Barbelle & WWI) **10.00**

My Beautiful Castle In Spain by Freeman & Pettine, 1919 (Cover Artist, Pfeiffer)..**10.00**

My Beautiful Chateau Of Love by Paul Cunningham & Alfred J. Doyle, 1915 ....**5.00**

My Beautiful Lady by C.M.S. McLellan & Ivan Caryll, 1911..............**5.00**

My Beautiful Rose by Whitt & Smith, 1912 (Cover Artist, Pfeiffer)...**10.00**

My Belgian Rose by Geo. Benoit, Robert Levenson & Ted Garton, 1918, War Edition, Small Folio (WWI) **15.00**

My Beloved Is Rugged by Jacob Henry Ellis, 1942 (Transportation)....**5.00**

My Beloved Waltzes by C. Baker, 1915 (Cover Artist, Pfeiffer & Deco)..**15.00**

My Best Girl's A Corker by John Stromberg, 1895, Photo Washburn Sisters (Pre 1900) **15.00**

My Best To You by Gene Willadsen & Isham Jones, 1942 ....**4.00**

My Bill From Louisville by Bernard, Weston & Snyder, 1911 (Cover Artist, Pfeiffer)..**10.00**

My Bird Of Paradise by Irving Berlin, 1915, Introduced by Blossom Seeley At The Winter Garden (Cover Artist, Barbelle & Irving Berlin) **15.00**

My Black Baby Mine by Thomas LeMack, 1896 (Pre 1900 & Black, Black Face)..**25.00**

My Black Venus by Barney Fagan, 1897 (Cover Artist, W.S. Cunningham, Pre 1900 & Black, Black Face) **42.00**

My Blackbirds Are Bluebirds by Irving Caesar & Cliff Friend, 1928, Photo Billy Hays..**5.00**

My Blue Heaven by George Whiting & Walter Donaldson, 1927, Photo Mark Fisher (Cover Artist, JVR)..**5.00**

My Blue Heaven by George Whiting & Walter Donaldson, 1927, Photo Walter Donaldson (Cover Artist, JVR) **5.00**

My Blue Ridge Mountain Home by Robison, 1927 ....**5.00**

My Blushing Rose by Alexander & Friedland, 1914 (Cover Artist, Pfeiffer)..**10.00**

My Bonnie by Nick Manoloff, 1936 ....**4.00**

My Boy by Lee & Brewer, 1913 (Cover Artist, Pfeiffer)....................**10.00**

My Boy by Tinker & Ryde, 1922, Movie: My Boy, Photo Jackie Coogan **5.00**

My Brooklyn Love Song by Tibbles & Idress, 1947, Movie: If You Knew Susie, Photo Eddie Cantor (Eddie Cantor) **8.00**

My Brown Eyed Lou by Johnson, 1910 (Cover Artist, Pfeiffer)..........**10.00**

My Brudda Sylvest' by Fred Fisher, 1908...**15.00**

My Buddy by Gus Kahn & Walter Donaldson, 1922, Photo Al Jolson (Al Jolson)..**12.00**

My Buddy by Gus Kahn & Walter Donaldson, 1922, Photo Edward Miller, Dedicated To Irene Hart (Cover Artist, Frederick S. Manning & Dedication) **10.00**

My Buddy by Gus Kahn & Walter Donaldson, 1922, Photo Mary Katherine Campbell (Cover Artist, Frederick S. Manning) **12.00**

My Buddy's Girl by Herb Newman & Murray Schwimmer, 1956........**4.00**

My Cabin Of Dreams by Nick Kenny, Al Frazzini & Nat Madison, 1937, Photo Benny Goodman (Cover Artist, Merman)...........................**10.00**

My Caramel Gal by Cohan & Harris Minstrels, 1909 (Cover Artist, Pfeiffer & Black, Black Face) **20.00**

My Caravan by Ann Caldwell & Hugo Felix, 1920, Musical: The Sweetheart Shop..**6.00**

My Castle On The Nile by Bob Cole, J. Rosimond Johnson & Billy Johnson, 1901 (Black, Black Face)..**15.00**

My Castles In The Air Are Tumbling Down by Arthur J. Lamb & W. C. Polla, 1919 (Lithograph, The Knapp Co.).....................................**10.00**

My Cavalier by Felix F. Feist & Jos. S. Nathan, 1910 ....**8.00**

My Cavalier Waltz by Nathan, 1911 (Cover Artist, Pfeiffer)..............**10.00**

My Chain Of Memories by Mrs. H. Ingraham, 1913 (Cover Artist, Pfeiffer & Deco) **15.00**

My Chocolate Soldier Sammy Boy by Egbert Van Alstyne, 1919 (WWI & Black, Black Face)..**20.00**

My Coal Black Lady by W.T. Jefferson, 1896 (Pre 1900 & Black, Black Face) **25.00**

My Coca Cola Bells (Cover Artist, Pfeiffer) **12.00**

My Cottage In Sunshine Lane by Clifford Gray & Werner Janssen, 1923, Musical: La Butterfly..**6.00**

My Country Has First Call by Mack Gordon, 1910 (Patriotic)............**10.00**

My Country I Hear You Calling Me by Bernie Grossman & Dave Dreyer, 1916 (Patriotic)..**12.00**

My Country 'Tis Of Thee by Jack Stern, 1917 (Patriotic) **10.00**

My Cousin Caruso by Edward Madden & Gus Edwards, 1909, Musical: Ziegfeld Production "Miss Innocence", Drawing, Signed by Enrico Caruso, (Signed) **40.00**

My Cowboy Love Song by David Guion, 1937 ....**3.00**

My Creole Sue by Gussie L. Davis, 1898 (Pre 1900 & Black, Black Face) **22.00**

My Croony Melody by Joe Goodwin & Ray Goetz, 1914, Photo Ethel Kirk (Cover Artist, John Frew & Deco) **10.00**

My Croony Melody by Joe Goodwin & Ray Goetz, 1914, Photo Fred & Adele Astaire (Cover Artist, John Frew & Deco) **10.00**

My Cross Eyed Girl by Long & Autry, 1935 ....**5.00**

My Cup Runneth Over by Tom Jones & Harvey Schmidt, 1966, Musical: I Do! I Do! **5.00**

My Cutie Doll by R.H. Burnside & Raymond Hubbell, 1915, Musical: Hip Hip Hooray at N.Y. Hippodrome **12.00**

My Dad's Dinner Pail by Edward Harrigan & David Braham, 1883 (Pre 1900) **15.00**

My Dad's The Engineer by Harry Graham, 1895 (Pre 1900 & Transportation) **25.00**

My Daddy's Coming Home by David W. Cooper, 1918 (Cover Artist, White Photo, Boston, & WWI) **20.00**

My Daddy's Star by Ivan Reid & Peter DeRose, 1918 (Cover Artist, E.E. Walton & WWI) **22.00**

My Dancing Lady by Dorothy Fields & Jimmy McHugh, 1933, Movie: Dancing Lady **5.00**

My Darling by Edward Heyman & Richard Myers, 1932, Musical: Earl Carroll Vanities 10th Edition (Cover Artist, Harris & Deco) **10.00**

My Darling, My Darling by Frank Loesser, 1948, Musical: Where's Charley? Caricature of Ray Bolger **5.00**

My Dear by Jan Garber & Freddie Large, 1934, Photo Jan Garber **3.00**

My Dear Old Rose by Harold Robe & Jesse Winne, 1920 ....**5.00**

My Dearest Prayer by H.J. Tandler, 1921 ....**6.00**

My Dearest Uncle Sam by Joan Whitney & Alex C. Kramer, 1946, Photo Andrews Sisters (Cover Artist, Im-Ho) **5.00**

My Defenses Are Down by Irving Berlin, 1946, Movie: Annie Get Your Gun (Irving Berlin) **17.00**

My Desert Caravan by Joseph Mendelson & F. Francis Hayden, 1937.**4.00**

My Desire by Nelle Richmond Eberhart & Charles Wakefield Cadman, 1920 ....**4.00**

My Destiny by Mack David & Jerry Livingston, 1950 ....**4.00**

My Devotion by Roc Hillman & Johnny Napton, 1942 ....**3.00**

My Dixie Rosary by Joe Goodwin & William Tracey, 1921 (Dixie)...**10.00**

My Dog Loves Your Dog by Ray Henderson, Jack Yellen & Irving Caesar, 1934, Movie: George White Scandals, Photo Alice Faye **6.00**

My Dream Girl by Rida Johnson Young & Victor Herbert, 1925, Musical: The Dream Girl (Victor Herbert) **10.00**

My Dream House On Air Castle Road by Florence Woods & Henry I. Marshall, 1931 ....**6.00**

My Dream Is Yours by Harry Warren & Ralph Blane, 1949, Movie: My Dream Is Yours, Photo Doris Day **5.00**

My Dream Memory by Sidney Clare & Oscar Levant, 1929, Movie: The Street Girl **5.00**

My Dream O'Dreams by Charles O'Flynn & Henry Welling, 1920 (Cover Artist, Wohlman) **10.00**

My Dream Of Love by Schleifforth, 1899 (Pre 1900) **10.00**

My Dream Of The U.S.A. by Chick, Roth & Snyder, 1908 (Patriotic) .**10.00**

My Dream Of Tomorrow by Nat Burton, Vic Mizzy & Irving Taylor, 1943 (Cover Artist, Holley) **7.00**

My Dream Train (Cover Artist, Pfeiffer)..**10.00**

My Dreamland Girl by C.M. Denison & E.F. Dusenberry, 1913 (Cover Artist, H.J. Dittmar) **10.00**

My Dreams Are Getting Better All The Time by Mann Curtis & Vic Mizzy, 1944, Photo Marion Hutton (Cover Artist, Barbelle)...........**6.00**

My Dreams Are Getting Better All The Time by Mann Curtis & Vic Mizzy, 1944, Movie: In Society, Photo Bud Abbott, Lou Costello & Marion Hutton **8.00**

My Dreams by Fred G. Bowles & Dorothy Lee, 1916, Linen Cover...**10.00**

My Dreamy China Lady by Gus Kahn & Egbert Van Alstyne, 1916 (Cover Artist, Starmer)...**10.00**

My Dreamy Little Lotus Flower by Jessie G.M. Glick & Abe Olman, 1918 ....**5.00**

My Dusky Rose by Thos. S. Allen, 1905 ....**5.00**

My Electric Girl by Harry B. Smith, Francis Wheeler & S.R. Henry, 1923 ....**5.00**

My Evening Star by Virginia K. Logan & Fred Knight, 1919 ....**5.00**

My Fair Lady by Bob Hilliard & Carl Sigman, 1948, Photo Bob Carroll (Cover Artist, Chelson)...**3.00**

My Faith In You by Joe Seitman & David Hutton, 1931 ....**5.00**

My Fate Is In Your Hands by Andy Razaf & Thomas Waller, 1929 .....**5.00**

My Favorite Dream by William Walsh & Ray Noble, 1947, Movie: Fun And Fancy Free (Disney) **10.00**

My Favorite Song by Jack Gold & Moose Charlap, 1952....................**3.00**

My Favorite Things by Richard Rodgers & Oscar Hammerstein II, 1959, Movie: The Sound Of Music, Photo Julie Andrews & Christopher Plummer..**5.00**

My Fine Feathered Friend by Harold Adamson & Jimmy McHugh, 1937, Movie: You're A Sweetheart, Photo Alice Faye, George Murphy, Ken Murray, Oswald, Andy Devine, Charles Winninger & Frances Hunt...**6.00**

My First Love To Last by George Marion & Richard Whiting, 1933....**5.00**

My First Sweetheart by Goodwin & Moquin, 1925 (Cover Artist, Pfeiffer)..**12.00**

My Fox-Trot Girl by Jack Frost, Paul Biese & F. Henri Klickmann, 1917...**5.00**

My Friend by Ervin Drake & Jimmy Shirl, 1954, Photo Eddie Fisher, Featured by Eddie On Coke Time..**10.00**

My Funny, Sunny, Honey Bunny by Irvin Wagner, 1951, Photo Dick Collier...**5.00**

My Funny Valentine by Lorenz Hart & Richard Rodgers, 1937, Movie: Gentlemen Marry Brunettes, Photo Jane Russell & Jeanne Crain .**12.00**

My Future Just Passed by Geo. Marion Jr. & Richard Whiting, 1930 ...**5.00**

My Gal Irene by Benjamin Hapgood Burt, 1908................................**5.00**

My Gal Is A High Born Lady by Barny Fagan, 1896 (Pre 1900 & Black, Black Face) **50.00**

My Gal Sal by Paul Dresser, 1932, Movie: My Gal Sal, Photo Rita Hayworth & Victor Mature **10.00**

My Gal, She Has Some Wonderful Ways by Ed Nelson & Bud Cooper, 1919, (Cover Artist, R.S. Symbol & Deco) **15.00**

My Gal, She Has Some Wonderful Ways by Ed Nelson & Bud Cooper, 1919, (Cover Artist, Gustav Michelson, Lithograph, Knapp Co. & Deco) 20.00

My Galway Rose by George A. Kershaw & Walter Scanlan, 1921 (Irish) **12.00**

My Garden Of Allah For Two by Stanley Murphy & Henry I. Marshall, 1912, Photo Sophie Bernard (Cover Artist, Lampe) **5.00**

My Garden Of Love by Ella M. Smith & W.C. Polla, 1919 (Cover Artist, Armstrong) **35.00**

My Georgia Lady-Love by Andrew B. Sterling & Howard Emerson, 1899 (Pre 1900 & Black, Black Face) **20.00**

My Georgiana Lou by Thos. S. Allen, 1912 (Cover Artist, Pfeiffer) ...**10.00**

My Gift For You by Charles Wakefield Cadman, 1926 (Cover Artist, Adelaide Palmer) **6.00**

My Girl Back Home by Richard Rodgers & Oscar Hammerstein II, 1949, Musical: South Pacific (Cover Artist, BJH) **5.00**

My Girl by Charles Freed, 1952 ....**3.00**

My Greenwich Village Sue by Swanstrom & Morgan, 1920 ....**5.00**

My Guiding Star by Robert Jarvis & James Moorehouse, 1934 ....**5.00**

My Gypsy Rhapsody by Jack Lawrence, Emery Deutsch & Arthur Altman, 1919 (Cover Artist, Scott) **5.00**

My Hannah Lady, Whose Black Boy Is You? by David Reed Jr., 1899 (Pre 1900 & Black, Black Face) **30.00**

My Happiness by Betty Peterson & Borney Bergantine, 1933, Photo John & Sondra Steele **3.00**

My Happy Southern Home by J. R. Homer, 1904 (Cover Artist Jas. K. Bonner) **6.00**

My Harbor Of Sunshine And Smiles by Alfred Hall, Maxwell Klein & James S. Rule, 1923 ....**3.00**

My Havannah Rose by Roberts & Whittaker, 1915 (Cover Artist, Pfeiffer) **10.00**

My Hawaii, You're Calling Me by L. W. Lewis, 1917 ....**3.00**

My Hawaiian Melody by Dave Ringle & J. Fred Coots, 1921 ....**3.00**

My Hawaiian Sunshine by L. Wolfe Gilbert & Carey Morgan, 1916, Photo Marie Russell (Cover Artist, Starmer) **8.00**

My Heart Belongs To Daddy by Cole Porter, 1938, Movie: Leave It To Me **12.00**

My Heart Belongs To Only You by Frank Daniels & Dorothy Daniels, 1952 ....**4.00**

My Heart Cries For You by Carl Sigman & Percy Faith, 1950, Photo Evelyn Knight **5.00**

My Heart Cries For You by Carl Sigman & Percy Faith, 1950, Photo Guy Mitchell **5.00**

My Heart Cries For You by Carl Sigman & Percy Faith, 1950, Photo Dinah Shore **5.00**

My Heart Has Learned To Love You by Dave Reed & Ernest Ball, 1910 (Cover Artist, DeTakacs) **10.00**

My Heart Is A Hobo by Johnny Burke & James Van Heusen, 1947, Movie: Welcome Stranger, Photo Bing Crosby, Joan Caulfield & Barry Fitzgerald **12.00**

My Heart Is A Silent Violin by Eric Von Der Goltz & Oscar J. Fox, 1933 ....**3.00**

My Heart Is An Open Book by Mack Gordon, 1935, Movie: Love In Bloom, Photo Joe Morrison & Dixie Lee **10.00**

My Heart Is Bluer Than Your Eyes by Bryan & Wilhite, 1929, Movie: A Man's Man, Photo William Hoines & Josephine Dunn **5.00**

My Heart Is In The Heart Of Caroline by Morton Downey & Lee David, 1931 ....**5.00**

My Heart Is In The Violet by Gardner, 1905 (Black, Black Face) **10.00**

My Heart Is Taking Lessons by Burke & Monaco, 1938, Movie: Doctor Rhythm, Photo Bing Crosby & Mary Carlisle **5.00**

My Heart Is Unemployed by Harold J. Rome, 1938, Musical: Sing Out The News **5.00**

My Heart Stood Still by Lorenz Hart & Richard Rodgers, 1927, Musical: A Connecticut Yankee **2.00**

My Heart Tells Me by Mack Gordon & Harry Warren, 1943, Movie: Sweet Rosie O'Grady, Photo Betty Grable, Robert Young & Adolphe Menjou **10.00**

My Heart's At Ease by Joe Young & Thomas Waller, 1932 ....**5.00**

My Heart's Tonight In Old New Hampshire by Andrew B. Sterling & Arthur Lange, 1917 ....**5.00**

My Heart's Tonight In Texas by Roden & Witt, 1900 ....**20.00**

My Heart's Way Out In California by Deely, 1914 (Cover Artist, Pfeiffer) **10.00**

My Heaven Is Home by Harry D. Kerr & Errol Collins, 1928 ....**5.00**

My Hero by Rida Johnson Young & Victor Herbert, 1924, Musical: The Dream Girl (Victor Herbert) **5.00**

My Hero by Stanislaus Stange & Oscar Strauss, 1909, Musical: The Chocolate Soldier (Cover Artist, DeTakacs) **15.00**

My Hero-ette by John McNab & Charles Gilbert Spross, 1904 ....**10.00**

My Hidden Treasure by Kalmar, 1913 (Cover Artist, Pfeiffer) **10.00**

My Hindoo Man by Harry H. Williams & Egbert Van Alstyne, 1905, Photo Marie Laurent (Cover Artist, Starmer) **10.00**

My Hindoo Queen by Frederick Seymour & Fred Pike, 1925 ....**6.00**

My Home Town by Gladys G. Dennis & Harry H. Williams, 1915 ......**6.00**

My Homeland by Dana Burnet & Oley Speaks, 1916, Dedicated To My Friend Clarence Whitehill (Dedication) **10.00**

My Homeland by Ruth Wilson Hurley, 1932 ....**3.00**

My Honey Lou by Thurland Chattaway, 1904 (Black, Black Face) **25.00**

My Honey Lu by Jack Frost, Paul Biese & F. Henri Klickmann, 1916 .**5.00**

My Honey Rose by Allen, 1915 (Cover Artist, Pfeiffer) **10.00**

My Honeymoon Man by Sanford & Williams, 1913 ....**5.00**

My Honolulu Bride by Harold Weeks, 1915 (Cover Artist, Dember) **5.00**

My Honolulu Lady by Lee Johnson, 1898 (Pre 1900) **10.00**

My Honolulu Tomboy by Sonny Cunha, 1908 ....**5.00**

My Hour by Gordon Johnstone & Ernest R. Ball, 1925 ....**5.00**

My Hula-Hula Love by Edward Madden & Percy Wenrich, 1911 ....**5.00**

My Idea Of A Good Little Girl Is A Girl Who Is Good To Me by Billy Day, 1917 (Cover Artist, Pfeiffer & Deco) **15.00**

My Ideal by Leo Robin, Richard A. Whiting & Newell Chase, 1930, Photo Barry Wood **5.00**

My Ideal by Leo Robin, Richard A. Whiting & Newell Chase, 1930, Signed Photo Frank Sinatra 5.00

My Indian Maiden by Harry Wilson & Ed J. Coleman, 1904, Photo Genevieve Day, Music Supplement Hearst's Boston Sunday American, Sunday, September 18, 1904 (Cover Artist, J.B. Eddy & Indian)..22.00

My Inspiration Is You by Edgar Leslie & Horatio Nicholls, 1928.........3.00

My Irish American Rose by Sterling, Lange & Browne, 1918, Photo Cotton Pickers (Cover Artist, Pfeiffer, Irish & Black, Black Face).....20.00

My Irish Molly O by Wm. Jerome & Jean Schwartz, 1905, Photo Lillian Ashley (Irish) 10.00

My Isle Of Golden Dreams by Gus Kahn & Walter Blaufuss, 1919, Musical: The Passing Show Of 1919, Photo Dick & George Roth (Cover Artist, Starmer) 12.00

My Japanee, You Darling Of The Gods by Donald Smedt & S. Gibson Cooke, 1904...12.00

My Jersey Lily by Arthur Trevelyan & Harry Von Tilzer, 1900.........10.00

My Josephine by Harry B. Smith & John Stromberg, 1899 (Pre 1900 & Black, Black Face)...20.00

My Keepsake Is A Heartache by Arthur J. Lamb & Clarence M. Jones, 1915 ....5.00

My "Kewpie" Doll by Maurice Gunsky & Nat Goldstein, 1914 (Cover Artist, Morgan) 15.00

My Kid by Al Dubin, Jimmy McHugh & Irwin Dash, 1924, Photo Al Wohlman (Cover Artist, Starmer) 10.00

My Killarney Rose by Jack Snyder, 1923 (Irish) 10.00

My Kind Of Country by Frank Loesser & Jimmy McHugh, 1940, Movie: Buck Benny Rides Again, Photo Jack Benny, Phil Harris, Ellen Drew, Dennis Day & Rochester 6.00

My Kingdom For A Kiss by Harry Warren & Al Dubin, 1936, Movie: Hearts Divided, Photo Marion Davies...10.00

My Lady Chlo by Myron V. Freese, 1901 ....10.00

My Lady Lu by Doty & Brill, 1899 (Pre 1900 & Black) 15.00

My Lady Of The Lamp by Harold Atteridge & Lew Pollack, 1921, Musical: The Passing Show Of 1921...10.00

My Lady Walks In Loveliness by Ernest Charles, 1932 (Deco) 5.00

My Land And Your Land by Cliff Friend & D. Franklin, 1918 (WWI).15.00

My Land, My Flag by R.H. Burnside & Raymond Hubbell, 1915, Musical: Hip Hip Hooray At The New York Hippodrome...10.00

My Land, My Flag by Zoel J. Parenteau, 1918 (WWI)...10.00

My Land Of Romance Arabia by Roden, Polla & Richmond, 1919 (Cover Artist, Pfeiffer)...12.00

My Landlady by Mieristh & Brymm, 1912...5.00

My Last Affair by Haven Johnson, 1936...5.00

My Last Goodbye by Eddy Howard, 1939 ....4.00

My Little Angel by Dazz Jordan & Gordon Charles, 1956, Photo The Four Lads 3.00

My Little Baby Rose by Mannie Lowenstein & Neil Moret, 1915 ....5.00

My Little Bimbo by Grant Clarke & Walter Donaldson, 1920, Photo Aileen Stanley (Cover Artist, R.S.) 5.00

My Little Blue Eyed Girl by Ketchum, 1912 (Patriotic) 10.00

My Little Book Of Poetry by Irving Berlin, 1921 (Irving Berlin)...10.00

My Little Brown Nest By The Sea by Thekla Hollingsworth & Clara Edwards, 1923 ....5.00

My Little Brown Shack And You by W. Clark Harrington, 1926...3.00

My Little Butterfly by Harold Freeman, 1919 (Cover Artist, Fisher) 5.00

My Little China Doll by Gus Van, Joe Schenck & Jack Yellen, 1917 (Cover Artist, Starmer)...12.00

My Little Climbing Rose by Winslow & Wilson, 1913 (Cover Artist, Pfeiffer)...10.00

My Little Coney Isle by Andrew Sterling, 1903...8.00

My Little Congo Maid by Mack Gordon & Halsey K. Mohr (Black, Black Face) 12.00

My Little Cottage Of Dreams by George & Mary Barry, 1941.............6.00

My Little Dream Girl by L. Wolfe Gilbert & Anatol Friedland, 1915 (Cover Artist, Starmer)...10.00

My Little Dutch Colleen by Leo Curley & J.B. Mullen, 1906 (Cover Artist, Starmer & Irish)...12.00

My Little Georgia Rose by Roden & Witt, 1899 (Pre 1900).............10.00

My Little Girl by Sam M. Lewis, Will Dillon & Albert Von Tilzer, 1915 (Cover Artist, DeTakacs) 12.00

My Little Grass Shack In Kialekahua Hawaii by Bill Cogswell, Tommy Harrison & Johnny Noble, 1933, Photo Ben Bernie 3.00

My Little Gypsy Wanda, Won't You Wander Back To Me by Robert Levenson & Ted Garton, 1917 (Cover Artist, Pfeiffer)...10.00

My Little Havana Made by Friedland, 1910 (Cover Artist, Pfeiffer)...10.00

My Little Home On The Hill by Al Sweet, 1922 ....5.00

My Little Home Sweet Home by Edward I. Boyle, 1925...3.00

My Little Lovin' Sugar Babe by Stanley Murphy & Henry I. Marshall, 1912 (Cover Artist, Starmer)...10.00

My Little Moonlight Queen by Ed Dangel & Charles Frank, 1911 ....5.00

My Little Nest Of Heavenly Blue by Franz Lehar, 1926 ....5.00

My Little Persian Rose by Edgar Allan Woolf & Anatol Friedland, 1912, Musical: A Persian Garden (Cover Artist, Starmer)...10.00

My Little Rambling Rose by Harold Freeman, 1916 (Cover Artist, E.S. Fisher) 12.00

My Little Rambling Rose by Harold Freeman, 1918, Photo Gus Van & Joe Schenck (Cover Artist, Starmer) **6.00**

My Little Rose Of Romany by Robert Levenson & Jack Mendelsohn, 1919 (WWI)..**12.00**

My Little Sister Mary by Edgar Leslie & Pete Wendling, 1921 ....**4.00**

My Little Tango Girl by Williams & Mack, 1914 (Cover Artist, Pfeiffer) ..**10.00**

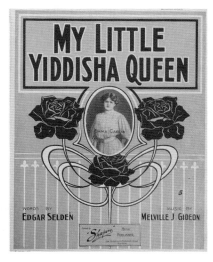

My Little Yiddisha Queen by Edgar Selden & Melville J. Gideon, 1909, Photo Emma Carus (Cover Artist, Pfeiffer) 15.00

My Little Zambezi by Golden, 1905 ....**6.00**

My Lonely Fleur-De-Lis by Bobby Crawford & Frank Magine, 1918 (Cover Artist, Rose Symbol)........................10.00

My Lonely Heart by William Kernell & Charles Wakefield Cadman, 1930...**5.00**

My Long Island Home by Ed Livingston Greenwood, 1928................**3.00**

My Long Lost Love by Sissle, Guthrie & Shewood, 1915 (Cover Artist, Pfeiffer & Deco) **18.00**

My Louisiana Babe by C.C. Clark, 1890 (Pre 1900)..........................**15.00**

My Love Am' Abel by Miss Rae Kopelman & C. Trusiano, 1905......**12.00**

My Love Dreams by Lucille Pyper, 1936................................**5.00**

My Love Parade by Clifford Grey & Victor Schertzinger, 1929, Movie: The Love Parade..............................**5.00**

My Love Song Is A Lullaby by John W. Bratton & Harold Levey, 1941..**3.00**

My Love Song, My Roses And You by Richard Howard, 1919, (Lithograph by Hayes)..............................**15.00**

My Love Song To You by Roy Alfred & Al Frisch, 1954, Signed Photo Of Jackie Gleason (Signed) **15.00**

My Love, The Night And You by Herendeen & Horan, 1935, Movie: A Royal Exchange, Photo Ramon Novarro & Doris Kenyon **4.00**

My Love's All For You by Alice Nadine Morrison, 1920 ....**5.00**

My Lovin' Lou by Garfield Kilgour & Nat Vincnet, 1916 ....**8.00**

My Lovin' Melody Man by Ward, 1913 ....**5.00**

My Lucky Star by B.G.DeSylva, Lew Brown & Ray Henderson, 1928, Musical: Follow Thru **6.00**

My Mad Moment by Geo. Marion Jr. & Richard A. Whiting, 1930, Movie: Let's Go Native...........................**5.00**

My Maggie by William J. Scanlon, 1888 (Pre 1900) **10.00**

My Magnolia Maid by Robert B. Smith & H.T. MacConnell, 1901, Music Supplement Of The New York Journal And Advertiser, Sunday, July 18,1901 (Cover Artist, P. Stanlows)........................**10.00**

My Mama Lives Up In The Sky by Charles K. Harris, 1915 (Cover Artist, Pfeiffer)..**10.00**

My Mama's With The Angels by Little & Little, 1905 ....**15.00**

My Mamie Rose by E. Ray Goetz & Melville J. Gidion, Photo Lydia Barry, 1910..**5.00**

My Mammy by Sam Lewis, Joe Young & Walter Donaldson, 1929, Movie: The Jolson Story, Photo Larry Parks & Evelyn Keyes (Cover Artist, R.S., Al Jolson, Dixie & Black, Black Face) **20.00**

My Mammy by Sam M. Lewis, Joe Young & Walter Donaldson, 1921, Movie: Sinbad, Photo Al Jolson (Cover Artist, RS & Al Jolson) **18.00**

My Mammy by Sam M. Lewis, Joe Young & Walter Donaldson, 1932, Signed Photo, Framed Of Al Jolson (Al Jolson, Signed & Black, Black Face) **150.00**

My Mammy Knows by Harry DeCasta, 1921 (Transportation & Black, Black Face)..**10.00**

My Man by Channing Pollock & Maurice Yvain, 1920........................**6.00**

My Man by Young, Conrad & Whidden, 1912 (Cover Artist, Pfeiffer)..**10.00**

My Man From Caroline by Walter Donaldson, 1930 (Dixie) **5.00**

My Mariuccia, Take A Steamboat by Geo. Ronklyn & Al Piantadosi, 1906, Photo Fred Watson & Morrissey Sisters (Transportation) ...**15.00**

My Mary's Eyes by Wood & Denison, 1918 (Cover Artist, Pfeiffer)..**10.00**

My Massachusetts Home by Edward F. Whitman, 1909 (Cover Artist, H. Clark)..**10.00**

My Melancholy Baby by Norton, Watson & Burnett, 1939, Movie: Birth Of The Blues, Photo Bing Crosby........................**5.00**

My Melody Of Love by Henry Mayer & George Buschor, 1973, Photo Bobby Vinton **2.00**

My Mind's Made Up To Marry Carolina by Lew Brown & Rubey Cowan, 1917 (Cover Artist, E.E. Walton)........................**10.00**

My Mind's On You by Ullman & Simon, 1940 ....**3.00**

My Mississippi Belle by Bob Cole & Billy Johnson, 1903...................**5.00**

My Missouri Home by Little Jack Little, 1930 ....**3.00**

My Mobile Gal by MacConnell, 1900 (Transportation)......................**15.00**

My Mom by Walter Donaldson, 1932......................................**5.00**

My Money Never Gives Out by Irving Jones, 1900...........................**5.00**

My Moonlight Madonna by Paul Webster & Fibich, 1933 ....**3.00**

My Mother Dear by Morton Ellery Setchell & Allenson Robert Fleming, 1927 ....**3.00**

My Mother, My Dad And My Girl by Al Dubin & George McConnell, 1916 ....**6.00**

My Mother Would Love You by Cole Porter, 1942, Movie: Panama Hattie **5.00**

My Mother's Evening Prayer by Bud Green, Charles Pierce & Al Dubin, 1920 ....5.00

My Mother's Eyes by L. Wolfe Gilbert & Abel Baer, 1928, Movie: Lucky Boy, Photo George Jessel 8.00

My Mother's Lullaby by Charles Louis Ruddy & Harold Brown Freeman, 1917 (Cover Artist, Pfeiffer) 10.00

My Mother's Rosary by Sam M. Lewis & Geo. W. Meyer, 1915 (Cover Artist, Barbelle & WWI) 5.00

My Mother's Voice by Wm. E. Cornwell, 1907.....................................5.00

My Mother's Waltz by Dave Franklin, 1945, Photo Bing Crosby 5.00

My! My! by Frank Loesser & Jimmy McHugh, 1940, Movie: Buck Benny Rides Again, Photo, Jack Benny, Phil Harris, Ellen Drew, Dennis Day & Rochester 6.00

My! My! Ain't That Somethin' by Tobias & Tomlin, 1943, Movie: Stormy Weather, Photo Fats Waller, Lena Horne & Cab Calloway 3.00

My Nanky Panky Poo by Sam M. Lewis, Joe Young & Walter Donaldson, 1919 ....5.00

My Nellie's Blue Eyes by William J. Scanlon, 1883 (Pre 1900 & Irish) ..15.00

My Next Romance by Ralph Freed & Ruth Lowe, 1940 ....3.00

My Ohio Home by Gus Kahn & Walter Donaldson, 1927....................3.00

My Old Fashioned Sweetheart Sue by Gladys G. Dennis & Harry H. Williams, 1915..5.00

My Old Kentucky Home by Stephen Foster, 1898, Advertising for Bromo Seltzer (Cover Artist, Starmer, Pre 1900, Stephen Foster & Advertising) 35.00

My Old Kentucky Home Goodnight by Stephen Foster with Variations by Charles Grobe, 1895 (Cover Artist, Wakelan, Stephen Foster & Pre 1900) 12.00

My Old Man by Mort Dixon & Harry Woods, 1929............................5.00

My Old New Hampshire Home by Andrew Sterling & Harry Von Tilzer, 1898 (Cover Artist, FJF & Pre 1900) 15.00

My Old Rose by Leo Wood, Geo MacFarlane & Theodore Morse, 1916, Photo Geo. MacFarlane (Cover Artist, Rose).................................5.00

My Old Sweetheart by Brandon, 1916 (Cover Artist, Pfeiffer)............10.00

My Old Sweetheart Is Coming Back by Henry Fink & Abner Silver, 1918 (WWI)..5.00

My Old Town by Manuel Klein, 1911 ....5.00

My One And Only by George & Ira Gershwin, 1927, Musical: Funny Face, Photo Fred & Adele Astaire..5.00

My One And Only Highland Fling by Ira Gershwin & Harry Warren, 1948, Movie: The Barkleys Of Broadway, Photo Fred Astaire & Ginger Rogers...8.00

My One And Only Love by Robert Mellin & Guy Wood, 1953............3.00

My Oriental Dream by LeRoy J. Robertson & J. Leonard Ivory, 1922 .3.00

My Own by Harold Adamson & Jimmy McHugh, 1938, Movie: That Certain Age, Photo Deanna Durbin...10.00

My Own by Lee Johnson, 1905, Photo Edith Mason 10.00

My Own Home Town In Ireland by Bartley Costello & Alfred Solman, 1915 (Cover Artist, Starmer & Irish)..15.00

My Own Iona by L. Wolfe Gilbert, Anatol Friedland & Carey Morgan, 1916, Photo Brice & King...10.00

My Own Laddie by Arthur Hewitt & David W. Guion, 1919 (WWI) .10.00

My Own, My Gipsy Bride by Hall, 1903 ....8.00

My Own, My Only, My All by Livingston & Evans, 1949, Movie: My Friend Irma, Photo Marie Wilson, John Lund & Martin & Lewis ...3.00

My Own Sweet Nellie Bawn by Banks Winter, 1886 (Pre 1900) 10.00

My Own Sweetheart by Scofield & Smith, 1910 ....8.00

My Own True Love by Mack David & Max Steiner, 1939, Movie: Gone With The Wind, Photo Clark Gable & Vivian Leigh.....................10.00

My Own United States by Stanislaus Stange & Julian Edwards, 1918 (WWI)..10.00

My Parcel Post Man by Kalmar, 1913 (Cover Artist, Pfeiffer)............15.00

My Pauline by Paul Herve, Jean Briquet & Adolph Philipp, 1915, Musical: The Girl Who Smiles..6.00

My Pavo Real Girl by Ben Black, 1918 ....5.00

My Pearl's A Bowery Girl by Jerome & Mack, 1892 (Pre 1900)........10.00

My Poem by Vic Schoen, 1939 ....5.00

My Pony Boy by Bobby Heath & Charlie O'Donnell, 1909 (Cover Artist, DeTakacs)..15.00

My Prayer by Jimmy Kennedy & Georges Boulanger, 1939, Photo Ray Anthony 3.00

My Prayer by Jimmy Kennedy & Georges Boulanger, 1939, Photo Sammy Kaye...4.00

My Pretty Firefly by Stanley Murphy, Jack Glogau & Al Piantadosi, 1915 (Indian) 15.00

My Pretty Indian Maid by R.M. Kane & J.L. Chandler, 1912 (Cover Artist, E.S. Fisher & Indian)..10.00

My Pretty Oriental Maid by Glenn C. Leap, 1915 (Cover Artist, Pfeiffer)..10.00

My Pretty Poppy by Robert Levenson & Jack Mendelsohn, 1918.........6.00

My Pretty Red Rose by Joseph P. Skelly, 1877 (Pre 1900).................15.00

My Raggyadore by Atteridge, 1913 (Cover Artist, Pfeiffer & Transportation)...15.00

My Ragtime Fireman by J. Brandon Walsh, 1912, Photo Rose Beaumont (Cover Artist, DeTakacs & Rag)..15.00

My Red Cross Girl Farewell by McGinnis & Manley (Cover Artist, Pfeiffer & Red Cross)..25.00

My Red Cross Girlie by Harry Bewlay & Theodore Morse, 1917 (Red Cross & WWI)...35.00

My Regular Gal by Bud Green & Harry Warren, 1927........................4.00

My River Home by Joe Young & Bernice Petkere, 1932, Signed Photo Paul Whiteman (Cover Artist, Leff) 5.00

My River Of Dreams by Mel Brewster, H.C. Weasner & John W. Newton, 1939 ....4.00

My Romance by Lorenz Hart & Richard Rodgers, 1935 (Cover Artist, RPB) 5.00

My Rosary For You by Amy Ashmore Clark & Ernest R. Ball, 1916 ...3.00

My Rosary Of Dreams by E.F. Dusenberry & C.M. Dennison, 1919 (Cover Artist, Starmer)..10.00

My Rosary Of Love For You by Brewster & Weasner, 1921 ....3.00

My Rose From The Garden Of Girls by Beth Slater Whitson & W.R. Williams, 1911...5.00

My Rose Is Only You by Harry Jay & George A. Beiderwelle, 1922, Photo Metropolitan Four 5.00

My Rose Of Honolulu by Tom Armstrong, 1911.................................5.00

My Rose Of Tipperary by Hanley, 1915 (Cover Artist, Pfeiffer & Irish)...15.00

My Rose Of Waikiki by Raymond B. Egan & Richard A. Whiting, 1925..5.00

My Rosie Rambler by Harry Williams & Egbert Van Alstyne, 1908 (Cover Artist, DeTakacs)..10.00

My Sahara Rose by Grant Clarke & Walter Donaldson, 1920..............6.00

My Sailor Laddie, Is Coming Back To Me by W.E. Burchell, 1918, Photo Mme Cincotta Gilberti (Cover Artist, E.S. Fisher & WWI)..........15.00

My San Francisco by R.E. Hausrath & Walter Smith 5.00

My Scandinavian Girl by Charles Tobias, Harry Tobias & Al Sherman, 1928 ....8.00

My Schoolday Sweetheart by Jack Yellen & H.C. Weasner, 1917........5.00

My Sergeant And I Are Buddies by Irving Berlin, 1942, Movie: This Is The Army, Lieut. Ronald Reagan In Cast (Irving Berlin, WWII, Military Personnel & President)..15.00

My Shining Hour by Johnny Mercer & Harold Arlen, 1943, Movie: The Sky's The Limit, Photo Joan Leslie & Fred Astaire.....................10.00

My Shining Star Of The Night by Bernard, 1919 (Cover Artist, Pfeiffer)..10.00

My Ship by Kurt Weill & Ira Gershwin, 1941, Movie: Lady In The Dark, Photo Gertrude Lawrence **3.00**

My Silent Love by Edward Heyman & Dana Suesse, 1932 (Cover Artist, Harris) **3.00**

My Sin by B.G. DeSylva, Lew Brown & Ray Henderson, 1929 ....**3.00**

My Singing Sammy by Billy Smythe, 1913 (Cover Artist, Patrick Smith & Black, Black Face) **25.00**

My Sister And I by Hy Zaret, Joan Whitney & Alex Kramer, 1941 (Cover Artist, Im-Ho) **5.00**

My Skylark Love by Fred G. Bowles & Lucien Denni, 1913 (Transportation) **15.00**

My Soldier Boy by Hollenbeck, 1918 (WWI) **10.00**

My Son, My Son by L. Wolfe Gilbert & Lew Pollack, 1939, Movie: My Son, My Son, Photo Madeleine Carroll & Brian Aherne **10.00**

My Song by Lew Brown & Ray Henderson, 1931, Musical: George White's Scandals **10.00**

My Song Of The Nile by Al Bryan & Geo. W. Meyer, 1929, Movie: Drag, Photo Richard Barthelmess **12.00**

My Soul by Carrie Jacobs Bond, 1910 ....**15.00**

My Soul To God, My Heart To Thee! by Hugo Frey, 1870 (Pre 1900)...**15.00**

My South Sea Island Queen by Frank Wooster, 1906 (March)............**10.00**

My Southern Rose by Earle Taylor, 1909 (Cover Artist, Etherington)...**15.00**

My Star by Elsa Maxwell, 1918, Photo Mrs. Oliver Harriman & Miss Anna Fitziu, Dedicated To My Friend Grace Harriman, The Profits Of This Song Are Donated By The Composer To The Armenian And Syrian Relief (Cover Artist, Rose, WWI & Dedication) **20.00**

My Sugar Coated Chocolate Boy by J.F. Mahoney & E. & W. Loos, 1919 (Cover Artist, E. E. Walton & Black, Black Face)........................**25.00**

My Sugar Is So Refined by Sylvia Dee & Sidney Lippman, 1946........**4.00**

My Summer Girl by Paxson, 1912 ....**5.00**

My Sumurun Girl by Jolson & Hirsch, 1912, Photo Al Jolson & Stella Mayhew (Al Jolson) **10.00**

My Sunday Girl by Harry Ruby, Bud Cooper & Sam H. Stept, 1927....**5.00**

My Sunny Sue by Andrew Sterling & Harry Hamilton, 1902.............**12.00**

My Sunny Tennessee by Bert Kalmar, Harry Ruby & Herman Ruby, 1921, Movie: The Midnight Rounders, Photo Eddie Cantor (Cover Artist, Barbelle, Eddie Cantor & Deco)..**10.00**

My Swanee Home by Harry Hamilton, 1919 (Black, Black Face) **10.00**

My Swanee Paradise by Charles Dover & Edwin Harbinson, 1921, Photo Dover & Harbinson **5.00**

My Sweet Adair by L. Wolfe Gilbert & Anatol Friedland, 1915 (Cover Artist, Starmer) **12.00**

My Sweet Cordelia by Edmonds, 1910 (Cover Artist, Pfeiffer)...........**10.00**

My Sweet Egyptian Rose by Edgar Allan Woolf & Anatol Friedland, 1917, Operetta: Bride Of The Nile (Cover Artist, Starmer) **10.00**

My Sweet Hawaiian Doll by Livernash & Rose, 1917 (Cover Artist, Pfeiffer) **10.00**

My Sweet Italian Man by Irving Berlin, 1911 (Cover Artist, Pfeiffer & Irving Berlin) **18.00**

My Sweet Love Call by Charles O. Roos & Homer Grunn, 1913 (Indian) **20.00**

My Sweeter Than Sweet by George Marion Jr. & Richard A. Whiting, 1929, Movie: Sweetie, Photo Jack Oakie, Helen Kane & Nancy Carroll **10.00**

My Sweetest Dreams Are Dreams Of You by E. Miles Sumner & Ed. Dangel, 1911 (Cover Artist, E.S. Fisher) **6.00**

My Sweetheart And I by Mrs. H.H.A. Brach, 1893 (Pre 1900) **10.00**

My Sweetheart by Gus Kahn, Garry Conley & Gene Rodemick, 1924 .**3.00**

My Sweetheart From Old Donegal by George Boyden, 1916, (Lithograph by Union Engraving & Irish)..**12.00**

My Sweetheart Is Somewhere In France by Mary Earl, 1917 (Cover Artist, Starmer & WWI) **15.00**

My Sweetheart, My Mother And Home by Ambrose Wyrick & Geoffrey O'Hara, 1926 ....**5.00**

My Sweetheart Of Long Ago by Paul Dresser, 1891 (Pre 1900) **15.00**

My Sweetheart Of Paradise by John Steel & Charles Wakefield Cadman, 1922 ....**5.00**

My Sweetheart Went Down With The Ship by Roger Lewis & F. Henri Klickmann, Photo Of The Titanic Sinking (Titanic) **75.00**

My Sweetheart's The Man In The Moon by James Thornton, 1892 (Pre 1900) **10.00**

My Sweetie by Irving Berlin, 1917 (Irving Berlin) **10.00**

My Sweetie Went Away by Roy Turk & Lou Handman, 1923 (Cover Artist, Barbelle) **6.00**

My Syncopated Melody Man by Merrill & Cox, 1918 (Cover Artist, Pfeiffer) **10.00**

My Task by Maude Louise Ray, Rev. S.H. Pickup & E.L. Ashford, 1903 ....**5.00**

My Ten Ton Baby And Me by Wilson, 1942 (Transportation).............**5.00**

My Time Of Day by Jo Swerling, Abe Burrows & Frank Loesser, 1950, Musical: Guys & Dolls **5.00**

My Tom Tom Man by Gus Kahn & Robert Van Alston, 1915 (Al Jolson) **10.00**

My Tonio by B.G. DeSylva, Lew Brown & Ray Henderson, 1928, Musical: In Old Arizona **5.00**

My True Love, Loves Me Still by J. Fassett & Edward Morris, 1924 ...**3.00**

My Truly Truly Fair by Bob Merrill, 1941, Photo Guy Mitchell..........**3.00**

My Trundle Bed by Lizzie Hutchinson & John C. Baker, 1860, (Lithograph by Ehrgott & Krebs & Pre 1900)..**75.00**

My Trust In You by Dean & Houghton, 1919..**6.00**

My Uncle Sammy Gals by Jack Frost & F. Henri Klickmann, 1918 (WWI) **10.00**

My Very Own by Claire Kummer, 1906 ....**5.00**

My Virginia Rose by E. Clinton Keithley & F. Henri Klickmann, 1922..**5.00**

My Virginian by Charles K. Harris, 1914, Photo Dustin Farnum (Cover Artist, Pfeiffer & Deco)..**15.00**

My Walking Stick by Irving Berlin, 1938, Movie: Alexander's Ragtime Band, Photo Tyrone Power, Alice Faye, Don Ameche, Ethel Merman & Jack Haley (Irving Berlin) **10.00**

My Way Back Home by Annelu Burns & Geoffrey O'Hara, 1937........**3.00**

My Way, Signed Photo by Frank Sinatra & Paul Anka (Signed).........**50.00**

My Wee Little Hut On The Hill by Horace Gleeson, 1931, Sung by John McCormack **12.00**

My Western Queen by Webber & Johnstone, 1914 (Cover Artist, Pfeiffer)..**10.00**

My Whole Day Is Spoiled by Charles Newman & Jimmy V. Monaco, 1934 ....**5.00**

My Wife's Gone To The Country, Hurrah! Hurrah! by Geo.W Whiting, Irving Berlin & Ted Snyder, 1909, Photo Mary Shirk (Cover Artist, John Frew, Irving Berlin & Transportation)..**15.00**

My Wife's Gone To The Country, Hurrah! Hurrah! by Geo. W. Whiting, Irving Berlin & Ted Snyder, 1909, Photo Maude Emery (Cover Artist, John Frew, Irving Berlin & Transportation)..**15.00**

My Wife's Up In An Airship by Gus Edwards, 1911 (Transportation)..**25.00**

My Wild Irish Rose by Chauncey Olcott, 1898 (Pre 1900 & Irish) **15.00**

My Wild Party Girl by Robin & Whiting, 1929, Movie: World Party, Photo Clara Bow..**10.00**

My Wishing Song by Irving Kahal & Joe Burke, 1932.........................**3.00**

My Wonderful Dream Of You by Nick Campbell & Will L. Livernash, 1918 (Cover Artist, Pfeiffer, Deco & WWI) **22.00**

My Wubba Dolly by Kay & Sue Werner, 1939..**5.00**

My Yankee Doodle Girl by Golden & Blosom, 1910, Photo Elsie Janis (Patriotic)..**10.00**

My Yankee-Irish Girl by Jack Drislane & Theodore Morse, 1908 (Irish)..**10.00**

My Yellow Jacket Girl by Harold Atteridge & Jean Schwartz, 1913, Photo Al Jolson In Front Of Train (Cover Artist, Pfeiffer, Al Jolson & Transportation) **20.00**

My Yukon Rose by Harry D. Kerr & William D. Alexander, 1920, (Cover Artist, C. D. William & Lithograph, Knapp Co.)..........................**10.00**

Myopia Club, The by James A. Battis, 1895 (Pre 1900 & March).......**20.00**

Myopia Fox Trot by Brennan, 1915, Photo Maurice & Florence Walton (Cover Artist, Pfeiffer & Deco)......................................**15.00**

Mysterious Ways by Snow & Pitchford, 1991, Movie: The Butcher's Wife, Photo Demi Moore **4.00**

Mystery In Your Eyes by Charles Boxton, 1937...................................**3.00**

Mystic Dreams Waltzes by Chas. R. Stickney, 1913 ....**5.00**

'N' Everything by Bud DeSylva, Gus Kahn & Al Jolson, 1918 (Al Jolson) **10.00**

Nagasaki by Mort Dixon & Harry Warren, 1928 ....**4.00**

Najo O'Neil by Wiedolft & Holliday, 1921 ....**8.00**

Nan! Nan! Nan! by Edward Madden & Theodore Morse, 1904 ....**5.00**

Nancy Brown by Clifton Crawford, 1901...**5.00**

Nancy by Phil Silvers & Jimmy Van Heusen, 1944..............................**3.00**

Naomi by E. J. Myers & Will E. Dulmage, 1918 ....**5.00**

Napoleon's Last Charge by Edw. Ellis, 1910 (Cover Artist, E.T. Paull, Lithograph, A. Hoen & March)......................................**38.00**

Narcissa by Wendel-Fisher, 1899 (Pre 1900)....................................**10.00**

Narcissus by Ethelbert Nevin, 1899 (Pre 1900)...................................**3.00**

Nasty Man by Jack Yellen, Irving Caesar & Ray Henderson, 1934, Movie: George White's Scandals, Photo Rudy Vallee, Alice Faye & Jimmy Durante **12.00**

National Army Man, The by Clifton Crawford, 1918 (WWI)..............**10.00**

National Awakening, The by Lucien Denni, 1918 (WWI)...................**10.00**

National Defense Military March by J. Bodewalt Lampe, 1916 (March)...**15.00**

National Emblem March by E. E. Bagley, 1911 (Patriotic & March)..16.00

National Songs Of Our Allies, The, Boston Sunday Advertiser, Sunday Supplement, October 27, 1918 (WWI)...........................**10.00**

Naturally by Clarke & Kroger, 1934 ....**3.00**

Nature Boy by Eden Ahberz, 1948 ....**3.00**

Naughty Angeline by Allan Roberts & Lester Lee, 1947, Photo Lawrence Welk...................................**3.00**

Naughty But Nice by Mercer & Warren, 1952, Movie: The Belle Of New York, Photo Fred Astaire & Vera Ellen **6.00**

Naughty Eyes by Cliff Friend & Harry Reichman, 1920, Musical: Cinderella On Broadway (Cover Artist, Barbelle).........................**10.00**

Naughty Lady Of Shady Lane, The by Sid Tepper & Roy C. Bennett, 1954, Photo Ames Bros....................................**3.00**

Naughty Moon by E. Magnus Quist, 1914 ....**5.00**

Navajo by Harry Williams & Egbert Van Alstyne, 1903 (Indian).......**25.00**

Navy Blue by Zimmerman, 1902 (Transportation) **15.00**

Navy Goat, The by Byron Gay, 1921 (Transportation).......................**10.00**

Navy Took Them Over, And The Navy Will Bring them Back, The by Yeoman Howard Johnson, U.S.N. & Ira Schuster, 1918, Small War Folio (Cover Artist, Rose Symbol, WWI & Military Personnel)...**10.00**

Navy's Here, The by Ross Parker & Hughie Charles, 1939...................**5.00**

Nay, Nay Pauline by Jennings I. Cox Jr. & Emerson Foote, Jr., 1898 (Pre 1900 & Black, Black Face)....................................**20.00**

NC-4 March by F. E. Bigelow, 1919, Dedicated To Commander A.C. Read, U.S. Navy (March, Dedication, Miltary Personnel & Transportation) **35.00**

Neapolitan Nights by Harry D. Kerr & J. S. Zamecnik, 1926, Movie: Fazil, Photo Charles Farrell & Greta Nissen **12.00**

Neapolitan Nights by Harry D. Kerr & J. S. Zamecnik, 1926, Photo Charles F. Hughes....................................**10.00**

Near To You by Richard Adler & Jerry Ross, 1955, Movie: Damn Yankees **6.00**

Near You by Kermit Goell & Francis Craig, 1947, Photo Andrews Sisters **6.00**

Near You by Kermit Goell & Francis Craig, 1947, Photo Francis Craig .**3.00**

Near You by Kermit Goell & Francis Craig, 1947, Photo Roger Williams **3.00**

Nearer And Dearer by Haven Gillespie & Egbert Van Alstyne, 1923 ...**5.00**

Nearness Of You, The by Ned Washington & Hoagy Carmichael, 1940 .**5.00**

'Neath Georgia's Nodding Pines by Lincoln G. Scheetz, 1919, Photo James L. Dempsey & Lincoln G. Scheets **5.00**

'Neath The Hawaiian Moon by Vala LaLucia, 1916 (Cover Artist, Pfeiffer) **10.00**

'Neath The Mississippi Moon by Robert F. Rodin & Geo. W. Meyer, 1912..................................**5.00**

'Neath The Old Cherry Tree Sweet Marie by Harry Williams & Egbert Van Alstyne, 1907, Photo Harry Ernest **10.00**

'Neath The Silv'ry Moon by Cliff Friend, 1932, Radio Theme Song Introduced by Arthur Jarrett, Photo Arthur Jarrett **6.00**

'Neath The Stars And Stripes by R. S. Morrison, 1943 (Patriotic) **5.00**

'Neath The Trail Of The Milky Way by Freeman, 1918 (Cover Artist, Pfeiffer)....................................**10.00**

Necessity by E.Y. Harburg & Burton Lane, 1946, Musical: Finian's Rainbow (Cover Artist, BJH & Irish) **5.00**

Nedra Waltzes by Florence McPherran, 1913 ....12.00

Need You by Johnny Blackburn, Teepee Mitchell & Lew Porter, 1949, Photo Gordon MacRae 3.00

Need You by Johnny Blackburn, Teepee Mitchell & Lew Porter, 1949, Photo Jo Stafford 4.00

Negra Consentida, My Pet Brunette by Marjorie Harper & Joaquin Pardave, 1945, Photo Andy Russell (Cover Artist, Merritt) 3.00

Nellie Kelly I Love You by George M. Cohan, 1922, Movie: George M! (George M. Cohan) 12.00

Nellie Kelly, I Love You by George M. Cohan, 1922, Movie: Little Nellie Kelly, Photo Judy Garland & George Murphy 10.00

Nelly Bly by Stephen C. Foster, 1849, First Edition (Stephen C. Foster & Pre 1900) 50.00

Nelly Daily's Dad by Frank Dumont, 1893 (Pre 1900) 10.00

Nelly Was A Lady by Stephen C. Foster, 1849 (Stephen C. Foster & Pre 1900) 50.00

Nephews Of Uncle Sam by George Graff Jr. & Bert Grant, 1917 (WWI) .22.00

Neptune by Zimmermann, 1904 (Transportation) 10.00

Nesting Time by Mort Dixon & James V. Monaco, 1927 ....5.00

Nesting Time by Walter Hirsch & James F. Hanley, 1921 ....5.00

Nestle In Your Daddy's Arms by Lou Herscher & Joe Burke, 1921, Signed by Lillian Price (Cover Artist, JVR, Deco & Signed) 10.00

Neutral by Lincoln, 1915 (Cover Artist, Pfeiffer & Deco) 15.00

Neutrality March, The by Mike Bernard, 1915 (Cover Artist, Pfeiffer & March) 15.00

Never A Day Goes By by Walter Donaldson, Peter DeRose & Mitchell Parish, 1943, Photo Guy Lombardo 3.00

Never Again by Gus Kahn & Isham Jones, 1924 ....5.00

Never Ending Song Of Love by Delaney Bramlett, 1971 ....3.00

Never Forget Your Dear Mother & Her Prayers by Mary Parker Jones, 1912 (Cover Artist, Pfeiffer) 10.00

Never Gonna Dance by Dorothy Fields & Jerome Kern, 1936, Movie: Swing Time, Photo Fred Astaire & Ginger Rogers 5.00

Never Gonna Let You Go by Cynthia Weil & Barry Mann, 1981 ....3.00

Never In A Million Years by Mack Gordon & Harry Revel, 1937, Movie: Wake Up And Live, Photo Walter Winchell, Ben Bernie & Alice Faye .5.00

Never Let Yourself Forget—You Are Irish by J. Keirn Brennan & Ernest R. Ball, 1915 (Irish) 12.00

Never Marry A Girl With Cold Feet! by M.E. Rourke & Jerome Kern, 1907 ....10.00

Never So Beautiful by Jay Livingston & Ray Evans, 1953, Movie: Here Come The Girls 5.00

Never Take No For An Answer by J.F. Mitchell, 1886 (Pre 1900) 10.00

Never Take The Horseshoe From The Door by Edward Harrigan & David Braham, 1880 (Pre 1900) 10.00

Never To Part Again by Ben Baer, Benj. Richmond & Jacob Henry Ellis, 1919 (Cover Artist, Barbelle) 10.00

Never Turn Back by Herb Miller & Irving Berger, 1956 ....5.00

Nevertheless I'm In Love With You by Bert Kalmar & Harry Ruby, 1931, Movie: Three Little Words, Photo Fred Astaire, Red Skelton, Vera Ellen & Arlene Dahl 10.00

New Coon In Town by Paul Allen, 1883 (Pre 1900 & Black, Black Face) 30.00

New Deal Rhythm by E.Y. Harbug & Roger Edens, 1933, Movie: Take A Chance, Photo June Knight & Buddy Rogers 5.00

New Ebbitt, The by John Zemmuman, 1911 (Cover Artist, Pfeiffer) ..10.00

New Express Galop by Evans, 1869 (Pre 1900 & Transportation) 60.00

New Hampshire by Sam M. Lewis & Robert A. King, 1931 (Cover Artist, Leff) 6.00

New Kind Of Man, A by Sidney Clare & Leon Flatow, 1924 (Cover Artist, Frederick S. Manning) 25.00

New Liberty, The by Harry J. Lincoln, 1917, Dedicated To Miss Jessie Thorburn Gowan, Saskatchewan, Canada (March & Dedication) .10.00

New Moon And An Old Serenade, A by Abner Silver, Martin Block & Sam Coslow, 1939, Photo Tommy Dorsey 3.00

New Moon Is Over My Shoulder, A by Arthur Freed & Nacio Herb Brown, 1934, Movie: Student Tour 6.00

New Moon, The by Irving Berlin, 1919, Movie: The New Moon, Photo Norma Talmadge (Irving Berlin) 15.00

New Mown Hay by Jason V. Mathews, 1902 ....10.00

New O'Leans by Gus Kahn & Arthur Johnston, 1935, Movie: Thanks A Million 5.00

New Orleans by DeLange & Alter, 1946, Movie: New Orleans, Photo Arturo De Cordova, Dorothy Patrick, Woody Herman & Band, & Louis Armstrong & Band 6.00

New Orleans by Hoagy Carmichael & Johnny Mercer, 1932 ....5.00

New Recruit, The by James H. Wakelin, 1917 (WWI, March & Patriotic) 15.00

New Sun In The Sky by Howard Deitz & Arthur Schwartz, 1931 ....3.00

New Thought, The by J.C. Heed, 1904 (March) 10.00

New York And Coney Island Bicycle March, by E.T. Paull, 1898 (Cover Artist, E. T. Paull & March) 35.00

New York Rag by George C. Durgan, 1910 (Cover Artist, E.S. Fisher & Rag) 20.00

Newlyweds And Their Baby, The by Al Hoffman, 1918 ....10.00

Newport Belles by Ascher, 1901 ....10.00

Next Sunday At Nine by Evans Lloyd, 1912, Photo Lightner & Jordan (Cover Artist, Starmer) 15.00

Next Time I Say Goodbye I'm Leavin' by Kusik & Snyder, 1968, Movie: A Time To Sing, Photo Hank Williams Jr., Shelley Fabares & Ed Begley 4.00

Next To Your Mother Who Do You Love? by Irving Berlin, 1909 (Cover Artist, Pfeiffer & Irving Berlin) 15.00

Nice To Be Around by Williams & Williams, 1973, Movie: Cinderella Liberty, Photo James Caan & Marsha Mason 4.00

Nice Work If You Can Get It by George & Ira Gershwin, 1937, Movie: Damsel In Distress, Photo Fred Astaire, George Burns & Gracie Allen 5.00

Nickel For A Memory, A by Perry Alexander, Bob Hilliard & Ann Beardsley, 1941 ....3.00

Nigger Toe Rag by H. A. Fischler, 1910 (Cover Artist, Dittmar, Rag & Black, Black Face) 35.00

Night, A Girl, A Moon, A by Davis & Gillespie & Charlotte Blake, 1908 ....7.00

Night After Night Day After Day by Harold G. Frost & F. Henri Klickmann, 1919 ....5.00

Night And Day by Cole Porter, 1932, Movie: Gay Divorce, Photo Frank Sinatra 10.00

Night And Day by Cole Porter, 1944, Movie: Night And Day, Photo Cary Grant & Alexis Smith (Cover Artist, Merritt) 3.00

Night Has A Thousand Eyes, The by Buddy Bernier & Jerry Braimin, 1948, Movie: The Night Has A Thousand Eyes, Photo Gail Russell & John Lund 10.00

Night Has Begun, The by Les Bagley & Maurice Crance, 1939 ....5.00

Night In Manhattan by Leo Robin & Ralph Rainger, 1936, Movie: The Big Broadcast Of 1937, Photo Jack Benny & Many Stars 5.00

Night Is Beginning, The by Gus Kahn & John W. Green 6.00

Night Is Filled With Music, The by Irving Berlin, 1938, Movie: Carefree, Photo Fred Astaire & Ginger Rogers (Irving Berlin) 10.00

Night Is Young And You're So Beautiful, The by Billy Rose, Irving Kahal & Dana Suesse, 1950, Photo Bill Snyder 3.00

Night Is Young And You're So Beautiful, The by Billy Rose, Irving Kahal & Dana Suesse, 1936, Musical: Casa Manana 5.00

Night Is Young, The by Oscar Hammerstein II & Sigmund Romberg, 1935 ....6.00

Night Maloney Landed In New York by Joe Flynn, 1888 (Pre 1900 &
    Irish)..**15.00**
Night Of Kisses, A by Max Prival, 1919......................................**6.00**
Night Of Love, A by B.G. DeSylva & Larry Spier, 1925 ....**5.00**
Night Of My Nights by Robert Wright & Chet Forest, 1953, Musical:
    Kismet...**6.00**
Night Of Nights by Beardsley Van de Water, 1922 ....**5.00**
Night Of Peace by William J. Marsh, 1939....................................**3.00**
Night Over Shanghai by Johnny Mercer & Harry Warren, 1937, Movie:
    The Singing Marines, Photo Dick Powell & Doris Weston **5.00**
Night Owl by Herman Hupfeld, 1933, Movie: Take A Chance, Photo June
    Knight & Buddy Rogers (Cover Artist, Harris) **12.00**
Night Shall Be Filled With Music, The by Will Collins, Buddy Fields &
    Gerald Marks, 1932...**5.00**
Night Time Brings Dreams & Dreams Bring You by Heinzman, 1912
    (Cover Artist, Pfeiffer) **10.00**

**Night Time In Little Italy by Joe McCarthy & Fred Fisher, 1917
    (Cover Artist, DeTakacs) 10.00**
Night Train by Oscar Washington, Lewis C. Simpkins & Jimmy Forrest,
    1952 (Transportation)...**3.00**
Night Train To Memphis by Beasley Smith, Marion Hughes & Owen
    Bradley, 1942..**3.00**
Night Was Made For Love, The by Otto Harbach & Jerome Kern, 1931,
    Musical: The Cat And The Fiddle **6.00**
Night We Called It A Day, The by Tom Adair & Matt Dennis, 1941
    (Cover Artist, Barbelle) **3.00**
Night When Love Was Born, The by Joe Young, Dave Oppenheim &
    Abel Baer, 1932...**6.00**
Night Wind by Bob Rothberg & Dave Pollock, 1934, Photo Guy Lombar-
    do **3.00**
Night Wind, The by Eugene Field & Roland Farley, 1918 ....**3.00**
Night Wind, The by J. Keirn Brennan & Ernest Ball, 1910 ....**5.00**
Night You Gave To Me, The by Walter Logan, 1937 ....**4.00**
Nightime Is The Right Time To Spoon With The Girl You Love by Goodwin
    & Meyer, 1911, Musical: Let George Do It (Cover Artist, Pfeiffer).....**10.00**
Nightingale by Coburn, 1920 (Cover Artist, Frederick S. Manning) ...**15.00**
Nightingale–A Love Song by Drislane & Meyer, 1910 (Cover Artist,
    Pfeiffer)..**16.00**
Nightingale Has A Lyre Of Gold, The by Benjamin Whelpley, 1903 .**10.00**
Nightingale Rag by Will B. Morrison, 1912 (Rag) **10.00**
Nightingale Song, The by Jack Yellen, Milton Ager & Henry Sullivan,
    1929, Musical: First Edition Of Murray Anderson's Almanac **16.00**

Nightingale, The by Randall & Raegge (Cover Artist, Pfeiffer)..........**10.00**
Nightingale's Song by Carl Zeller, 1891 (Pre 1900)..........................**10.00**
Nightingale's Trill, The by J. Arthur Fisher, 1905 ....**5.00**
Nightingale-Intermezzo, 1911 (Cover Artist, Pfeiffer)......................**10.00**
Nightingales Of Lincoln's Inn, The by Herbert Oliver (President)......**10.00**
Nights Of Gladness by Charles Ancliffe, 1913 ....**5.00**
Nights Of Splendor by Harry D. Kerr & J. S. Zamecnik, 1925 ....**10.00**
Nighty Night by Joe Davis, 1941, Photo Hal Morgan......................**3.00**
Nighty-Night by Leslie Beacon, 1941, Photo Alvino Rey & King Sis-
    ters...**3.00**
Nine O'Clock Sal by Jack Leroy, Billy Hayes, Jim Leary & Nelson Ing-
    ham, 1923, Photo Unique Orchestra, Signed by L.R. Clippinger
    (Cover Artist, Perret, Deco & Signed) **10.00**
Ninette by Christine, 1909 ....**5.00**
Ninety And Nine by Elizabeth G. Clephane & Geoffrey O'Hara, 1909 **5.00**
Ninna-Nanna by Wm. A. Reilly, 1944 ....**5.00**
Ninon by E. Paolo Tosti, 1887 (Pre 1900)..................................**5.00**
No Blossoms by Abbie A. Ford, 1905......................................**5.00**
No Can Do by Charles Tobias & Nat Simon, 1945, Musical Copaca-
    bana **10.00**
No Candle Was There And No Fire by Francis M. Costling & Liza
    Lehmann, 1909 ....**4.00**
No Foe Shall Invade Our Land by Alfred Hallam, 1918 (WWI) **15.00**
No Girl Can Take My Old Girls Place by Ford & Atkinson, 1912 (Cover
    Artist, Pfeiffer)...**10.00**
No Greater Love by Molly Picon & Sheldon & Sholom Secunda, 1928 ..**5.00**
No Letter Today by Frankie Brown, 1943, Photo Gene Autry.............**3.00**
No Limit by Godfrey Montagne Lebhar & Bainbridge Crist, 1915 ....**5.00**
No Love, No Nothin' by Leo Robin & Harry Warren, 1943, Movie: The
    Gang's All Here, Photo Alice Faye, Carmen Miranda, Phil Baker &
    King Of Swing Benny Goodman & His Orchestra **10.00**
No Man Of My Own by Isham Jones, 1944 ....**4.00**
No Man's Mamma by Jack Yellen & Lew Pollack, 1925 ....**5.00**
No Moon At All by Redd Evans & Dave Mann, 1948.....................**3.00**
No More Love by Cliff Friend & Carmen Lombardo, 1932 ....**4.00**
No More, No Less by Charles Newman & Isham Jones, 1933 ....**3.00**
No! No! A Thousand Times No! by Al Sherman, Al Lewis & Abner Sil-
    ver, 1934...**5.00**
No No Nora by Gus Kahn, Ted Fiorito & Ernie Erdman, 1921, Photo Ruth
    Etting (Cover Artist, JVR & Deco) **6.00**
No! No! Nora! by Gus Kahn, Ted Fiorito & Ernie Erdman, 1923, Photo
    The Carolinians..**3.00**
No One Believes I Love You by Downs & Silvers, 1915 (Cover Artist,
    Pfeiffer)...**10.00**
No One But You by Lawrence & Brodszky, 1954, Movie: Flame And The
    Flesh, Photo Lana Turner, Pier Angeli & Carlos Thompson **4.00**
No One But You by Lew Brown & Albert Von Tilzer, 1920................**5.00**
No One But You by Robert Mellin & Otto Riedlmayer, 1950..............**3.00**
No One But You Dear Old Dad by Stanley Murphy & Henry I. Marshall,
    1914, Photo Bessie Lyn..**10.00**
No One Can Take Your Place by Wm. H. Gardner & J. Fred Helf, 1904 ..**10.00**
No One Cares For Me by Tell-Taylor, 1902....................................**10.00**
No One Could Do It Like My Father by Irving Berlin & Snyder, 1909
    (Cover Artist, Pfeiffer, Irving Berlin & Deco) **20.00**
No One Else Can Take Your Place by Chas. K. Harris, 1913 (Cover Artist,
    Pfeiffer)..**12.00**
No One Ever Loved You More Than I by Edward B. Marks & Joseph
    Stern, 1896 (Pre 1900)...**10.00**
No One Knows, But The Rose by Sidney D. Mitchell & Westell Gordon,
    1926 ....**5.00**
No One Knows by Francis Mack, 1908, Photo Walter S. Sherwood of Al
    Fields Minstrels **12.00**

No One Said Good-bye To Me by Arthur & Edwards, 1914 (Cover Artist, Pfeiffer & WWI)..**15.00**

No One's Fool by Phil Furman & Fred Rose, 1921 ....**4.00**

No Other Love by Bob Russell & Paul Weston, 1950, Photo Jo Stafford...**3.00**

No Other Love by Rogers & Hammerstein, 1953, Movie: Me & Juliet.**5.00**

No Other Love Is Like A Mother's Love by McCoy & Colburn, 1916 (Cover Artist, Pfeiffer) **10.00**

No Other One by Tot Seymour & Vee Lawnhurst, 1935 ....**3.00**

No Regrets by Harry Tobias & Roy Ingraham, 1936, Photo Joseph Rogers...**3.00**

No Ring On Her Finger by Loesser & Sherwin, 1937, Movie: Blossoms On Broadway...**3.00**

No Show Tonight by Frank Leo, 1899 (Pre 1900) **10.00**

No Star Is Lost by Fred Fisher, 1939, Photo Sammy Kaye..........**6.00**

No Stone Unturned by Lester M. Cox & Melvin Herman, 1953............**4.00**

No Strings by Irving Berlin, 1935, Movie: Top Hat, Photo Fred Astaire & Ginger Rogers (Irving Berlin) **10.00**

No Two People by Frank Loesser, 1951, Movie: Hans Christian Andersen, Photo Danny Kaye..............................**10.00**

No Use Pretending by Otto Harbach & Sigmund Romberg, 1936.........**4.00**

No Wedding Bells For Me by E. P. Moran, Will A. Heelan & Seymour Furth, 1906, Photo Trixie Friganza (Cover Artist, Carter)......16.00

No Wonder by Benny Davis & Joe Burke, 1924 (Cover Artist, JVR & Deco) **10.00**

No Wonder by Buddy Bernier & Bob Emmerich, 1938.............**5.00**

No Wonder I'm Blue by Sam M. Lewis, Joe Young & Fred E. Ahlert, 1920 ....**10.00**

No, You Can't Have My Heart by Cole Porter, Movie: You Never Know **6.00**

Noah Found Grace In The Eyes Of The Lord by Robert Schmertz, 1951...**7.00**

Nobles Of The Mystic Shrine March by John Philip Sousa, 1923 (John Philip Sousa & March) **20.00**

Nobody But You by George Gershwin, 1919.....................**10.00**

Nobody by Alex Rogers, Bert Williams & George Walker, 1905 (Black, Black Face)...**15.00**

Nobody by Rogers & Williams, 1933, Movie: The Seven Little Foys, Photo Bob Hope..**8.00**

Nobody Cares If I'm Blue, Movie: Bright Lights, 1929, Photo Frank Fay, Dorothy Mackaill & Noah Beery **10.00**

Nobody Does It Like You Do by Harris, Cobb & Edwards, 1914 (Cover Artist, Pfeiffer)...................................**10.00**

Nobody Else Can Love Me Like My Old Tomato Can by Downs & Baskette, 1923 ....**10.00**

Nobody Ever Brings Presents To Me by Charles Miller, 1900............**12.00**

Nobody Ever by Irving Caesar & Hugo Frey, 1919 (Cover Artist, Ray Frey)..**10.00**

Nobody Home by Allen & Daly, 1913 (Cover Artist, Pfeiffer) **10.00**

Nobody Home by Williams & Grant, 1914 (Cover Artist, Pfeiffer) **10.00**

Nobody Knows, And Nobody Seems To Care by Irving Berlin, 1919 (Cover Artist, R.S. & Irving Berlin)..........................**10.00**

Nobody Knows But Rosie by James Hanley & Joseph McCarthy, 1930, Movie: The Big Party, Photo Sue Carol, Dixie Lee & Jack Smith ..**5.00**

Nobody Knows But The Lord by Bert Kalmar & Harry Ruby, 1930, Movie: Check And Double Check, Photo Amos N Andy (Amos N Andy & Black, Black Face)..**60.00**

Nobody Knows How I Miss You Dear Old Pals by Eddie Dorr & Lew Porter, 1919, From "Friendly Enemies," Endorsed by President Wilson (Cover Artist, White, Presidents & WWI)........................**35.00**

Nobody Knows The Trouble I've Seen by Jim Smock, 1935, Photo The Cadets (Black, Black Face) **5.00**

Nobody Knows Where Rosie Goes by Walker, 1917 (Transportation)..**15.00**

Nobody Lied by Karyl Norman, Hyatt Berry & Edwin J. Weber, 1922, Photo Karyl Norman (Deco)......................................**10.00**

Nobody Loves A Comic Valentine by Frederick G. Johnson, 1928 ......**4.00**

Nobody Loves Me, 1912 (Cover Artist, Pfeiffer)...................**10.00**

Nobody Seems To Love Me Now by Joe Maxwell, 1904...................**10.00**

Nobody's Heart by Lorenz Hart & Richard Rodgers, 1942, Movie: All's Fair **5.00**

Nobody's Little Girl by Jack Drislane & Theodore Morse, 1907 ....**10.00**

Nobody's Lookin' But The Owl And The Moon by Bob Cole, J. Rosimond Johnson & Billy Johnson, 1901.............................**10.00**

Nobody's Sweetheart by Gus Kahn, Ernie Erdman, Billy Meyers & Elmer Schoebel, 1924...**5.00**

Nocturne by Francis Ledwedge & Michael Head, 1919.....................**3.00**

Nodding Roses by Schuyler Greene, Herbert Reynolds & Jerome Greene, 1915, Musical: Very Good Eddie (Cover Artist, Malcolm Strauss) ..**15.00**

Nola by Felix Arndt, 1926 ....**5.00**

Non E Ver, (Tis Not True) by Frank H. Evans & Titto Mattel, Advertising Bromo Seltzer (Advertising) **30.00**

Nona by F. W. Vandersloot, 1918 (Cover Artist, Henry Hutt).............**10.00**

None But You by Harry J. Lincoln & Reba Vandersloot, 1904...........**10.00**

Noon At Midnight by Lou Holzer & Harry Kogen, 1935 ....**5.00**

Nora, My Irish Queen by Mittenthol, 1911 (Irish) **5.00**

Nora O'Neal by Will S. Hayes, 1922 (Irish) **10.00**

Noreen Mavourneen by Chauncey Olcott, 1902 (Irish)......................**10.00**

Normandy Chimes by W. C. Powell, 1913 (Cover Artist, Pfeiffer).....**10.00**

North Western Railway Polka by Ward, 1859 (Pre 1900 & Transportation) **75.00**

Northern Route March by Smith, 1876 (Pre 1900, March & Transportation)..**50.00**

Norway by Joe McCarthy & Fred Fischer, 1915, Photo Kitty Gordon (Cover Artist, Rose Symbol) **10.00**

Not Because Your Hair Is Curly by Bob Adams, 1906......................**12.00**

Not For A While But Always by Edgar T. Farran & Bob Nolan, 1911 (Cover Artist, DeTakacs).......................................**15.00**

Not For All The Rice In China by Irving Berlin, 1933, Musical: Easter Parade (Irving Berlin)..**10.00**

Not Here, Not There by Mort Dixon & Ernest Breuer, 1923, Photo Vivian Oakland...**6.00**

Not Me by Gray & Piantadosi, 1909 (Cover Artist, Pfeiffer).............**15.00**

Not Mine by Johnny Mercer & Victor Schertzinger, 1942, Movie: The Fleet's In, Photo Dorothy Lamour, Jimmy Dorsey & Betty Hutton **8.00**

Not 'Till Then by Chas. K. Harris, 1912 (Cover Artist, Pfeiffer).........**10.00**

Nothin' But Love by Alsop & Carrie Jacobs Bond, 1912 ....**15.00**

Nothing Can Stop Me Now by Walter Bullock & Harold Spina, 1937, Movie: 52nd St. **5.00**

Nothing Less Than Beautiful by Allie Wrubel, 1933 ....**5.00**

Nothing Lives Longer Than Love by Sam. M. Lewis & Pete Wendling, 1935, Photo Wayne King..**3.00**

Nothing New Beneath The Sun by George M. Cohan (George M. Cohan)..**10.00**

Nothing Seems The Same by Benny Davis & Jessie Greer, 1926........**5.00**

Nothing To Do But Love (Cover Artist, Pfeiffer) **10.00**

Nothing's Too Good For The Irish by Goodwin, 1891 (Pre 1900 & Irish)..**15.00**

November Rose by Jack Snyder, 1922 ....**5.00**

Now And Forever by Al Stillman & Jan Savitt, 1941, Movie: The Outlaw, Photo Jane Russell **10.00**

Now And Then by Joe McKiernan & Norman Spencer, 1920 ....**5.00**

Now And Then, There's A Fool Such As I by Trader, 1952, Photo Harry Snow **5.00**

Now I Know by S.R. Henry, D. Onivas & Frank H. Warren **5.00**

Now I Lay Me Down To Sleep by C. Arthur Pfeiffer, 1918 (Cover Artist, Pfeiffer & WWI)..**20.00**

Now I Lay Me Down To Sleep by Sidney Mitchell & Geo. W. Meyer, 1921, Musical: Midnight Rounders of 1921, Photo Eddie Cantor (Eddie Cantor) **10.00**

Now I'm In Love by Jack Yellen & Ted Shapiro, 1929 ....**4.00**

Now Is Forever by Cahn & Barrie, 1978, Movie: Fingers, Photo Harvey Keitel & Tisa Farrow..**2.00**

Now Is The Hour by Maewa Kaihan, Clement Scott & Dorothy Stewart, 1913, Signed Photo Eddy Howard (Signed)....................**15.00**

Now Is The Hour by Maewa Kaihan, Clement Scott & Dorothy Stewart, 1913, Signed Photo Bing Crosby (Signed)....................**15.00**

Now Is The Hour by Maewa Kaihan, Clement Scott & Dorothy Stewart, 1913, Signed Photo Gracie Fields (Signed)....................**15.00**

Now It Can Be Told by Irving Berlin, 1938, Movie: Alexander's Ragtime Band, Photo Tyrone Power, Alice Faye, Don Ameche, Ethel Merman & Jack Haley (Irving Berlin) **10.00**

Now She Is Wholly Mine by M. Barnett & J. Massenet, 1888 (Pre 1900) **6.00**

Now That I Need You by Frank Loesser, 1949, Movie: Red, Hot And Blue, Photo Bette Hutton & Victor Mature.......................**5.00**

Now That You've Got Me What Are You Going To Do by Williams & Grant, 1913 (Cover Artist, Pfeiffer) **10.00**

Now's The Time To Fall In Love by Al Sherman & Al Lewis, 1931....**3.00**

Number Ten Lullaby Lane by Bob Carlton & Bob Warren, 1940 ....**3.00**

Nutin by Libbie Carpenter, 1915 ....**5.00**

Nutsey Fagan by Rose & Brewer, 1923 ....**12.00**

Nuttin' For Christmas by Sid Tepper & Roy C. Bennett, 1955, Photo Stan Freberg..**3.00**

O Haunting Memory by E. C. Pierce & Carrie Jacobs Bond, 1912 .....**15.00**

O, Katharina by L. Wolfe Gilbert & Richard Fall, 1924 (Cover Artist, A. Hardiakoff) **10.00**

O Land Of Hope And Freedom by Wm. H. Gardner & George Lowell Tracy, 1918 (WWI) **4.00**

O Mary Dear by John McCormack & Edwin Schneider, 1930 ....**4.00**

O Mistress Mine by Roger Quilter, 1906 ....**2.00**

O Sole Mio! by Lulu M. Hauck & E. Di. Capua, 1923 ....**3.00**

O Thou Sublime Sweet Evening Star by Wagner (Cover Artist, Pfeiffer)..**10.00**

O Time Take Me Back by Carrie Jacobs Bond, 1916 ....**15.00**

O'Brannigan Fusilters by Joe Flynn, 1889 (Irish & Pre 1900)............**16.00**

O'Brien Is Tryin To Learn To Talk Hawaiian by Al Dubin & Rennie Cormack, 1916 (Cover Artist, Dunk & Irish)....................**10.00**

Oahu by Carmen Lombardo, 1947 ....**8.00**

Oasis by Harold G. Frost & F. Henri Klickmann, 1919 ....**5.00**

Object Of My Affection, The by Pinky Tomlin, Coy Poe & Jimmie Grier, 1934, Photo Jimmie Grier (Cover Artist, Leff) **5.00**

Ocarina, The by Irving Berlin, 1950, Movie: Call Me Madam, Photo Ethel Merman, Donald O'Connor, George Sanders & Vera Ellen (Irving Berlin)...**8.00**

Ocean Between Us, The by Cawthorn, 1892 (Pre 1900 & Transportation) **10.00**

Ocean Must Be Free by Kohn & Flint, 1917 (WWI) **10.00**

Oceana Roll, The by Roger Lewis & Lucien Denni, 1911 (Patriotic, Rag & Transportation) **20.00**

Of All Things by Al Rinker & Floyd Huddleston, 1950, Movie: Duchess Of Idaho, Photo Esther Williams......................................**8.00**

Of Thee I Sing by Ira & George Gershwin, 1931 ....**10.00**

Of This I'm Sure by Bennie Benjamin & Sol Marcus, 1955, Photo Four Aces **4.00**

Off Shore by Steve Graham & Leo Diamond, 1953, Signed Photo Russ Morgan (Signed)..**3.00**

Off To The Front by Wieghorst & Lace, 1914 (Cover Artist, Pfeiffer, WWI & March) **20.00**

Off To The Wars Of Mexico by Beatty & Johnstone, 1914 (Cover Artist, Pfeiffer & Patriotic)..**15.00**

Off With The Old Love, On With The New by Ballard Macdonald & Harry Carroll, 1914 (Cover Artist, Pfeiffer)..........................**10.00**

Official West Point March, The by Alfred H. Parkam & Philip Egner, 1928 (March) **15.00**

Oh! by Byron Gay, 1919..**8.00**

Oh Babe! by Louis Prima & Milton Kabak, 1950 ....**3.00**

Oh, Baby by Bud G. DeSylva & Walter Donaldson, 1924 (Cover Artist, Perret & Deco)..**5.00**

Oh! Boy What A Girl by Bud Green & Wright & Pessinger, 1925, Musical: Gay Paree, Photo Winnie Lightner (Cover Artist, Wohlman)..**12.00**

"Oh! Brother" Sang The Thrush by Marguerite Radelyffe-Hall & Liza Lehmann, 1913 ....**5.00**

Oh But I Do by Arthur Schwartz & Leo Robin, 1946, Movie: The Time, The Place & The Girl, Photo Dennis Morgan, Jack Carson, Martha Vickers, Janis Paige & Carmen Cavallaro (Cover Artist, A. Joel Robinson)..**8.00**

Oh By Jingo by Lew Brown & Albert Von Tilzer, 1919, Movie: Linger Longer Letty, Photo Charlotte Greenwood (Cover Artist, Pfeiffer) ..**15.00**

Oh Cecilia by Edward Paulton, Glen MacDonough & Jean Gilbert, 1913, Movie: Queen Of The Movies......................................**10.00**

Oh Danny, Love Your Annie by Spencer & Reinherz, 1919 (Cover Artist, Pfeiffer)..**10.00**

Oh Dear Marie by Paul Herve, Jean Briquet & Adolph Philipp, 1915, Musical: The Girl Who Smiles....................**5.00**

Oh Death Where Is Thy Sting by Clarence A. Stout, 1918 (Black, Black Face) **10.00**

Oh, Dem Golden Slippers by James Bland Of Sprague's Georgia Minstrel, 1879, (Pre 1900 & Black, Black Face)....................**35.00**

Oh! Didn't He Ramble by Bob Cole, J. Rosimond Johnson & Billy Johnson, 1902.......................................**12.00**

Oh, Didn't It Rain, Negro Spiritual by H.T. Burleigh, 1919 (Black, Black Face) **4.00**

Oh! Doctor by Rubey Cowan & Billy Joyce, 1920 ....**10.00**

Oh, Donna Clara by Irving Caesar & Robert Katscher, 1930, Movie: The Wonder Bar, Photo Al Jolson (Al Jolson) **15.00**

Oh! Frenchy by Sam Ehrlich & Con Conrad, 1918 (Cover Artist, E.E. Walton & WWI) **10.00**

Oh Gee! Oh Joy! by P.G. Wodehouse & George & Ira Gershwin, 1949..**5.00**

Oh Girls! What A Boy by Garfield Kilgour & Roy Ingraham, 1920 .....**5.00**

Oh, Girly, Girly by Edward Harrigan & David Braham, 1879 (Pre 1900)...**15.00**

Oh! God! Let My Dream Come True by Blanche Merrill & Al Piantadosi, 1916 ....**8.00**

Oh! Harold by Lee S. Roberts, 1922 ....**6.00**

Oh! Harry! Harry! by Nat Vincent & Lew Pollack, 1918, Sung By Sophie Tucker **10.00**

Oh Helen! by Chas. R. McCarron & Carey Morgan, U.S.N., 1918, Photo Henry Lewis (Military Personnel)....................**10.00**

Oh Helen! by Chas. R. McCarron & Carey Morgan, U.S.N., 1918, Photo Sophie Tucker (Military Personnel) **10.00**

Oh! How I Adore You by Harry Stoddard & Marcy Klauber, 1930, Movie: Party Girl, Photo Douglas Fairbanks Jr. & Jeanette Loff................**6.00**

Oh! How I Hate To Get Up In The Morning by Irving Berlin, 1918, Photo Bob Hall, Dedicated To My Friend Private Howard Friend Who Occupies The Cot Next To Mine And Feels As I Do About The Bugler (Cover Artist, Barbelle, Irving Berlin, WWI & Dedicated) **35.00**

Oh How I Laugh When I Think How I Cried About You by Roy Turk, George Jessel & Willy White, 1919 (Cover Artist, Barbelle).....12.00

Oh, How I Love My Darling by Edgar Leslie & Harry Woods, 1924 ...**5.00**

Oh How I Miss You Tonight by Benny Davis, Mark Fisher & Joe Burke, 1924, Photo Loomis Sisters (Cover Artist, Leff & Deco)..............**6.00**

Oh How I Miss You Tonight by Benny Davis, Mark Fisher & Joe Burke, 1924, Photo Eva Clark (Cover Artist, Leff & Deco).......................**6.00**

Oh How I Miss You Tonight by Benny Davis, Mark Fisher & Joe Burke, 1924, Photo Harold Wallace (Cover Artist, Leff & Deco)..............**6.00**

Oh, How I Want You by Arthur J. Lamb & Clarence M. Jones, 1916...**5.00**

Oh How I Wish I Could Sleep 'Till My Daddy Comes Home by Sam Lewis, Joe Young & Pete Wendling, 1918, Photo Al Jolson (Cover Artist, Barbelle, WWI & Al Jolson)..**20.00**

Oh, How She Could Yacki Hacki Wicki Wacki Woo by Stanley Murphy, Chas. McCarron & Albert Von Tilzer, 1916 (Cover Artist, DeTakacs)..**10.00**

Oh, How She Lied by White & Donaldson, 1923 ....**5.00**

Oh I Must Go Home Tonight by William Hargreaves, 1909 (Cover Artist, Gene Buck)..**10.00**

Oh, Joe, Waltz Me Slow by Baer & Roos, 1912 (Cover Artist, Pfeiffer)..**10.00**

Oh, Johnny! Oh, Johnny! Oh! by Ed Rose & Abe Olman, 1917, Photo Nora Bayes (Cover Artist, White).............................**12.00**

Oh, Johnny! Oh, Johnny! Oh! by Ed Rose & Abe Olman, 1917, Signed Photo Henry Lewis (Signed) **10.00**

Oh Joseph by Clare Kummer & Leo Fall, 1922, Musical: Madame Pompadour **5.00**

Oh, Judge, She Was So Nice by Jim Stanford, 1914 (Cover Artist, Pfeiffer) **10.00**

Oh Katerina by L. Wolfe Gilbert, 1924 ....**5.00**

Oh, Lady Be Good by Ira & George Gershwin, 1924, Movie: Lady Be Good **5.00**

Oh! Ma-Ma!, The Butcher Boy, by Lew Brown, Rudy Vallee & Paoli Citorello, 1938 (Cover Artist, CA)...........................**5.00**

Oh, Mamma, Buy Me That by Al Hilman, 1890 (Pre 1900) **10.00**

Oh Marie by Howard Johnson & E. Di Capua, 1932 ....**5.00**

Oh! Min by Ole Olsen & Isham Jones, 1918, Dedicated to Mrs. Sidney Smith (Dedication) **10.00**

Oh Miss Hannah by Thekla Hollingsworth & Jessie L. Deppen, 1924..**5.00**

Oh! Mister Railroad Man Won't You Take Me Back To Alabam by Stanley Murphy & Henry I. Marshall, 1916 (Transportation)...............**10.00**

Oh, Moon Of The Summer Night by Allan J. Flynn, 1918 (Cover Artist, Starmer & WWI) **18.00**

Oh! Mother I'm Wild by Howard Johnson, Harry Pease & Eddie Nelson, 1920 (Cover Artist, L.S. Reiss & Deco)....................**10.00**

Oh Mr. Dream Man by Jimmie V. Monaco, 1911................................**10.00**

Oh, My Love by Joe McCarthy & James V. Monaco, 1914 (Cover Artist, DeTakacs)..**10.00**

Oh! My Pa-Pa by John Turner, Geoffrey Parsons & Paul Burkhard, 1953..**3.00**

Oh! Oh! Miss Phoebe by Harry Von Tilzer, 1900 (Black, Black Face)...**20.00**

Oh, Oh, Oh, A Hypochondriac Rag, 1910 (Cover Artist, Pfeiffer & Rag)...**16.00**

Oh Papa, Oh Daddy by Arthur Robsham, 1920, Musical: Hoyt's Review (Cover Artist, Strand) **5.00**

Oh! Papa, Won't You Be A Pretty Papa To Me by Nat Vincent & James F. Hanley, 1917 (Rag) **10.00**

Oh Promise Me by Clement Scott & Reginald DeKoven, 1917............**3.00**

Oh Say! Can I See You Tonight by Henry Creamer, 1925 (Transportation) **6.00**

Oh! Susanna by Stephen Foster, 1848 (Pre 1900, Stephen Foster & Black, Black Face)..**35.00**

Oh Susie Behave by Rose, 1918...**5.00**

Oh! Sweet Flower Pure And Rare by H. Engelmann & Richard Dillmore, 1902, Opera: Martha (Cover Artist, Starmer)................................**10.00**

Oh! That Cello by Charlie Chaplin, 1916...................................**18.00**

Oh That Kissing Rag by Heath & O'Donnell, 1910 (Cover Artist, Pfeiffer & Rag) **15.00**

Oh! That Moonlight Glide by Junie McCree & Albert VonTilzer, 1910, Photo Tempest & Sunshine (Transportation) **12.00**

Oh That Navajo Rag by Harry William & Egbert Van Alstyne, 1911 (Indian & Rag)..**25.00**

Oh That Teasing Man by Goodwin & Meyer (Cover Artist, Pfeiffer).**10.00**

Oh! That Yankiana Rag by E. Ray Goetz & Melville Gideon, 1908, Photo Anna Held Appearing In Miss Innocence (Cover Artist, Starmer & Rag)..**15.00**

Oh The Pity Of It All by Ralph Rainger & Leo Robin, 1942, Movie: My Gal Sal, Photo Rita Hayworth & Victor Mature **6.00**

Oh! The Woman In Room 13 by Sam M. Lewis, Joe Young & Walter Donaldson, 1919 ....**5.00**

Oh, There Ain't No Flies On Us! by Arthur Leroy Kaser & Joan Clark, 1928 ....**4.00**

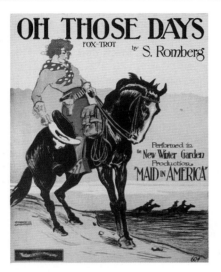

Oh Those Days by Sigmund Romberg, 1915, Musical: Maid In America (Cover Artist, Richard A. Loederer).....................................10.00

Oh, Uncle John by Felix McGlennon, 1895 (Pre 1900) **10.00**

Oh! Virgin Rose by Josephine Victoria Rowe & Charles Marshall, 1916, Sung by John McCormack **10.00**

Oh! What A Beautiful Baby by A. Seymour, 1915 (Cover Artist, Floyd)..**10.00**

Oh What A Beautiful Mornin' by Richard Rodgers & Oscar Hammerstein II, 1943, Musical: Oklahoma (Cover Artist, Holley) **6.00**

Oh What A Beautiful Ocean by William B. Gray, 1897 (Pre 1900 & Transportation) **15.00**

Oh What A Difference In The Morning by Felix McGlennon, 1891 (Pre 1900)..**10.00**

Oh, What A Girl by Frank Fay & Dave Dreyer, 1919..........................**5.00**

Oh What A Night by L. Wolfe Gilbert, Lewis F. Muir & Maurice Abrahams, 1912...**10.00**

Oh! What A Pal Was Mary by Edgar Leslie, Bert Kalmar & Pete Wendling, 1919 (Cover Artist, Barbelle) **10.00**

Oh! What A Time For The Girlies When The Boys Come Marching Home by Sam M. Lewis, Joe Young & Harry Ruby, 1918 (Cover Artist, Barbelle & WWI) **10.00**

Oh What A Wonderful Summer by Harry Pease, Harry Edelheit & Fred Mayo, 1919 (Cover Artist, Barbelle)...**6.00**

Oh, What I'd Do For A Girl Like You by George Whiting & Ted Snyder, 1909 (Cover Artist, Starmer)...**10.00**

Oh! What It Seemed To Be by Bennie Benjamin, George Weiss & Frankie Carle, 1945, Photo Frankie Carle **4.00**

Oh, What's The Use Of Working by Skinner & Godfrey, 1910 (Cover Artist, Pfeiffer)..**15.00**

Oh! Ya! Ya! by Frisch, Osborne & McConnell, 1927 (Cover Artist, Pfeiffer) **10.00**

Oh You Bashful Little Girl by Walsh & Snyder, 1912 (Cover Artist, Pfeiffer) **10.00**

Oh, You Beautiful Doll by Seymour Brown & Nat D. Ayer, 1911 (Cover Artist, Starmer)..**10.00**

Oh! You Beautiful Girl With Those Beautiful Baby Blue Eyes by Howard, Allen & Daly, 1913 (Cover Artist, Pfeiffer)..................................**10.00**

Oh! You Beautiful Person by Anne Caldwell & Jerome Kern, 1919, Musical: She's A Good Fellow..**10.00**

Oh! You Circus Day by Lessing, 1912....................................**6.00**

Oh! You Crazy Moon by Johnny Burke & Jimmy Van Heusen, 1939, Photo Glen Gray (Cover Artist, Im-Ho).......................................**3.00**

Oh! You Crazy Moon by Johnny Burke & Jimmy Van Heusen, 1939, Photo Bob Chester (Cover Artist, Im-Ho)...................................**3.00**

Oh, You Funny Mr. Moon by Moore & Leap, 1912 (Cover Artist, Pfeiffer) **12.00**

Oh! You Georgia Rose by Cole, 1912....................................**8.00**

Oh, You Kid! by Edgar Selden & Melville J. Gideon, 1908, Photo Ida Emerson (Cover Artist, Starmer)..**15.00**

Oh You La La, I Love You by Lew Brown, Ed Moran & Harry Tush, 1918 (WWI)..**6.00**

Oh, You Little Rascal by Leslie & Meyer, 1912 (Cover Artist, Pfeiffer)..**10.00**

Oh You Little Sun-uv-er-gun by Richard Howard & Joseph Solman, 1923 ....**3.00**

Oh! You Million Dollar Doll by Grant Clarke, Edgar Leslie & Maurice Abrahams, 1913, Photo Elizabeth Knowles (Cover Artist, Pfeiffer) **10.00**

Oh You Mr. Moon by Dubin & Burke, 1910 (Cover Artist, Pfeiffer & Deco) **15.00**

Oh You Rag by Dowling & Towle, 1910 (Cover Artist, J. Wilson & Rag)...15.00

Oh, You Silv'ry Bells by Jean C. Havez & Geo. Botsford, 1912 (Cover Artist, Starmer) **8.00**

Oh! You Sweet Little Lady by Mac Stick & Lew Weissman, 1917, Photo Al Lentz (Cover Artist M. Brisman) **12.00**

Oh You Sweet One by Dick Hardt & Moe Jaffe, 1949, Photo Andrews Sisters & Russ Morgan (Cover Artist, George Martin)...................**4.00**

Oh, You Women by Bud Green & Sammy Stept, 1919 ....**10.00**

Oh, You Wonderful Girl by George M. Cohan, 1911 (George M. Cohan)..**10.00**

Oh, You Wonderful Girls! by Wm. B. Friedlander, 1917 ....**10.00**

Ohio by Harry Lauder, 1921..**5.00**

Ois-Ge-Shpielt, All Played Out by David Meyerowitz, 1924, Photo Nina Sheikowitz, Jacob Sheikowitz & David Meyerowitz, 1924.............**5.00**

Ok' L Baby Dok' L by Sidney Miller & Inez James, 1947, Movie: Big City **3.00**

Okalehau by Leo Robin & Ralph Rainger, 1937, Movie: Waikiki Wedding, Photo Bing Crosby & Shirley Ross **5.00**

Oklahoma by Richard Rodgers & Oscar Hammerstein II, 1943, Musical: Oklahoma (Cover Artist, Holley) **5.00**

Oklahoma Hills by Jack & Woody Guthrie, Photo Jack Guthrie **10.00**

Oklahoma I Love You by Opal Harrison Williford, 1938, Signed by Opal Harrison Williford (Cover Artist, Blue Eagle, Indian & Signed)...**10.00**

Ol' Man Mose by Louis Armstrong & Zilmer Trenton Randolph, 1942 (Cover Artist, Barbelle & Black, Black Face)...............................**10.00**

Ol' Man River by Oscar Hammerstein II & Jerome Kern, 1927, Musical: Ziegfeld's Show Boat **12.00**

Ol' Pappy by Al J. Neiburg, Marty Symes & Jerry Levinson, 1934, Photo Glen Gray **4.00**

Ol' Pappy by Al J. Neiburg, Marty Symes & Jerry Levinson, 1934, Photo Ted Black (Cover Artist, Leff) **5.00**

Olcott's Lullaby by Chauncy Olcott, 1899 (Pre 1900) **10.00**

Old Acquaintance by Kim Gannon & Franz Waxman, 1943, Movie: Old Acquaintance, Photo Bette Davis & Miriam Hopkins.......10.00

Old Apple Tree, The by M.K. Jerome & Jack Scholl, 1938, Movie: Swing Your Lady, Photo Humphrey Bogart, Frank McHugh & Many More Stars **10.00**

Old Bachelor, The by Thos. H. Beyly, 1850 (Pre 1900) **35.00**

Old Barn Dance, The by Feist & Corin, 1909 (Cover Artist, Pfeiffer).**15.00**

Old Before My Time by Karliski, 1968, Movie: A Time To Sing, Photo Hank Williams Jr., Shelley Fabares & Ed Begley **3.00**

Old Bell Ringer, The by Wm. H. Gardner & Louis F. Gottschalk, 1902 ..**10.00**

Old Bill Baker by Schuyler Green, Herbert Reynolds & Jerome Kern, 1915, Musical: Very Good Eddie (Cover Artist, Malcolm Strauss)...........**15.00**

Old Black Joe by Stephen Foster, 1877 (Stephen Foster, Pre 1900 & Black, Black Face)...............................**25.00**

Old Black Joe by Stephen Foster, 1940, Photo Dinning Sisters (Cover Artist, N.P.S., Stephen Foster & Black, Black Face) **4.00**

Old Boy Neutral by Schuyler Greene, Herbert Reynolds & Jerome Kern, 1915, Musical: Very Good Eddie (Cover Artist, Malcolm Strauss) ..**15.00**

Old Calico Of Blue by Carroll Loveday, 1922 (Cover Artist, D. Chiary) **5.00**

Old Chaperone, The by Ramey Idriss & George Tibbles, 1947...............................**5.00**

Old Chisum Trail by Tex Ritter...............................**5.00**

Old Clothes-I Buy by Nat Simon & Roy Newell, 1937 (Cover Artist, Barbelle) **5.00**

Old Covered Bridge, The by Billy Hill, 1934, Photo Fred Waring (Cover Artist, Wohlman)...............................**3.00**

Old Covered Bridge, The by Billy Hill, 1934, Photo Jack Fulton (Cover Artist, Wohlman)...............................**3.00**

Old Dog Tray by Stephen Foster, 1853 (Stephen Foster & Pre 1900) **50.00**

Old Fall River Line by Harry Von Tilzer, 1913 (Transportation)........**15.00**

Old Fashioned Garden by Cole Porter, 1919...............................**6.00**

Old Fashioned Girl by Al Jolson, 1922 (Al Jolson) **10.00**

Old Fashioned Mother by Bertrand Brown, 1927 ....**5.00**

Old Fashioned Mother by Chauncey Olcott, 1897 (Pre 1900) **20.00**

Old Fashioned Roses by E. Clinton Keithley, 1914 (Deco) **10.00**

Old Fireplace by Benny Davis & J. Fred Coots, 1936 ....**5.00**

Old Flag Never Touched The Ground, The by J.W. Johnson, Bob Cole & Rosamond Johnson, 1901 (Patriotic)...............................**25.00**

Old Folks Are Sad & Lonely, The by Goodier, Andino & Hall, 1915 (Cover Artist, Pfeiffer) **10.00**

Old Folks At Home Variations by Joseph W. Lerman, 1902 (Cover Artist, John Frew) **5.00**

Old Folks by Dedette Lee Hill & Willard Robinson, 1938 ....**3.00**

Old Folks Rag by Joseph McCarthy & Joe Goodwin, 1913 (Rag).......**10.00**

Old Glory by Hathaway, 1917 (Cover Artist, Pfeiffer, WWI & Transportation)...............................**25.00**

Old Glory by Johnny Mercer & Harold Arlen, 1942, Movie: Star Spangled Rhythm, Photo Bing Crosby, Bob Hope, Dorothy Lamour & Many More Stars (Patriotic) **12.00**

Old Glory by Thomas J. Duggan & Homer N. Bartlett, 1917 (WWI & Patriotic) **15.00**

Old Glory Goes Marching On by Paul R. Armstrong & F. Henri Klickmann, 1918 (WWI & March) **15.00**

Old Glory I Salute You by Vaughn DeLeath, 1929, Special: The Voice Of Firestone Edition. Compliments Of The Firestone Tire Dealer In Your Community, Signed by Vaughn DeLeath (Signed, Patriotic & Advertising)...............................**25.00**

Old Gypsy by Kondor, 1929...............................**5.00**

Old Hickory by Harry J. Lincoln, 1913 (March)...............................**15.00**

Old Home Guard by Sherman & Sherman, 1971, Movie: Bedknobs & Broomsticks, Photo Angela Lansbury & David Tomlinson...............................**3.00**

Old Homestead Fox Trot by Athur S. Penn, 1914...............................**5.00**

Old Homestead, The by James Thatcher, 1915, Photo Denman Thompson & James Thatcher...............................**5.00**

Old Homestead, The by Milt Hagen, 1922...............................**5.00**

Old Homeweek In Alabam' by Jerome & Schwartz, 1913 (Cover Artist, Pfeiffer)...............................**10.00**

Old Jim's Christmas Hymn by William B. Gray, 1896 (Pre 1900)......**10.00**

Old Joe Blues by L. Wolfe Gilbert & Joe Samuels, 1919 (Black, Black Face) **20.00**

Old Lamp-Lighter, The by Charles Tobias & Nat Simon, 1941, Photo Sammy Kaye (Cover Artist, CA) **4.00**

Old Lamp-Lighter, The by Charles Tobias & Nat Simon, 1941, Photo Perry Como (Cover Artist, CA)...............................**4.00**

Old Log Cabin In The Dell, The by C.A. White, 1875 (Lithograph, White Smith & Co., Pre 1900 & Black, Black Face)...............................**75.00**

Old MacDonald Had A Farm by Nick Manoloff & Mort H. Glickman, 1935, Photo Bonnie Blue Eyes & Randall Atcher...............................**5.00**

Old Maid's Ball, The by Irving Berlin, 1913 (Cover Artist, Pfeiffer & Irving Berlin)...............................**16.00**

Old Man Blues by Bert Kalmar & Harry Ruby, 1930, Movie: Check & Double Check, Featuring Amos & Andy (Amos & Andy & Black, Black Face)...............................**60.00**

Old Man Harlem by Hoagy Carmichael & Johnny Mercer, 1933.........**5.00**

Old Man In The Moon by Wm. B. Friedlander, 1923 ....**3.00**

Old Man Jazz by Gene Quaw, 1920 (Cover Artist, Hasen & Jazz) ..10.00

Old Man Shay by Burt, 1905 (Transportation).....................................15.00

Old Man, The by Irving Berlin, 1942, Movie: White Christmas, Photo Bing Crosby, Danny Kaye, Rosemary Clooney & Vera Ellen (Irving Berlin)..12.00

Old Master Painter, The by Haven Gillespie & Beasley Smith, 1949, Photo Gordon MacRae 5.00

Old Mr. Moon, You Did Not Hear The Answer by Chas. D. Tibbits & Anna B. Harmon, 1913, Photo Tucker & Anderson 10.00

Old Music Master, The by Johnny Mercer & Hoagy Carmichael, 1943, Movie: True To Life..5.00

Old Neighborhood by Edward Harrigan & David Braham, 1891 (Pre 1900)..10.00

Old New England Moon by Dave Vance & George P. Howard, 1930, Signed Photo Rudy Vallee With The Following: "To Mem'ries Of Boyhood Days, That Ended All Too Soon, The Home That I Call Heaven, And An Old New...16.00

Old Oaken Bucket by Durkee, 1882 (Pre 1900)....................................15.00

Old Pal, Why Don't You Answer Me? by Sam M. Lewis, Joe Young & M.K. Jerome, 1920 (Cover Artist, Barbelle & Deco).....................5.00

Old Piano Roll Blues, The by Cy Coben, 1949 (Blues) 5.00

Old Postmaster, The by Ed Marks & Joe Stern, 1900 ....15.00

Old Prairie Wagon by White, O'Bryne & Henninger, 1946, Photo Roy Rogers...5.00

Old Road, The by John Prindle Scott, 1920 ....6.00

Old Rustic Bridge O'er The Rill, The by Leroy Durkee & Arthur Tallman, 1908 ....10.00

Old Soft Shoe, The by Roy Jordan & Sid Bass, 1951, Photo Tony Martin & Dinah Shore..5.00

Old South by J.W. Turner, 1876 (Pre 1900)..15.00

Old Spinning Wheel, The by Billy Hill, 1933, Photo Baby Rose Marie (Cover Artist, Wohlman & Deco) 6.00

Old Spinning Wheel, The by Billy Hill, 1933, Photo Fred Waring (Cover Artist, Wohlman & Deco) 6.00

Old Spinning Wheel, The by Billy Hill, 1933, Photo Sam Robbins (Cover Artist, Wohlman & Deco) 6.00

Old Town Is Looking Mighty Good Tonight by Kerry Mills, 1911.....10.00

Old Turnkey by C.A. White, 1882 (Pre 1900)....................................15.00

Old Virginia Rag by Clyde Douglass, 1907 (Rag) 10.00

Old Yeller Dog Of Mine by Edgar Leslie, Grant Clarke & Pete Wendling, 1923 (Cover Artist, Barbelle) 12.00

Olden Golden Days by Dave M. Allan & Bob Allan, 1917 ....10.00

Ole Bossy Cow by Hattie Starr..10.00

Ole Buttermilk Sky by Hoagy Carmichael & Jack Brooks, 1946, Movie: Canyon Passage, Photo Hoagy Carmichael......................................5.00

Ole Buttermilk Sky by Hoagy Carmichael & Jack Brooks, 1946, Movie: Canyon Passage, Photo, Dana Andrews, Brian Donlevy, Susan Hayward & Hoagy Carmichael 5.00

Ole Faithful by Michael Carr & Hamilton Kennedy, 1934, Photo The Ranch Boys (Cover Artist, Wohlman) 5.00

Ole Virginny by J. S. Zamecnik, 1916 ....10.00

Olympic Trail, The by Ray Walker & Art Smith, 1934 ....5.00

Omar by William Lorraine, 1900..10.00

On A Beautiful Night With A Beautiful Girl by Will D. Cobb & Gus Edwards, 1912, Photo Arthur Deacon (Cover Artist, R.S.).............5.00

On A Chinese Honeymoon by W.L. Shockley & C.J. Hausman, 1933 (Cover Artist, Holley)...3.00

On A Coconut Island by R. Alex Anderson, 1936, Photo Larry Kent (Cover Artist, HBK) 3.00

On A Desert Island With You by Lorenz Hart & Richard Rodgers, 1927, Musical: A Conn.Yankee 6.00

On A Dreamy Summer's Night by Cassey, Rosenfeld & Murray, 1916 (Cover Artist, Pfeiffer) 10.00

On A Joy Ride by Kenna, 1909 (Transportation)................................15.00

On A Little Bamboo Bridge by Archie Fletcher & Al Sherman, 1937 (Cover Artist, Cliff Miska & Deco)...5.00

On A Little Dream Ranch by Billy Hill, 1937, Photo Guy Lombardo (Cover Artist, Barbelle) 3.00

On A Monkey Honeymoon by Jack Mahoney & Theodore Morse, Photo Jack Mahoney & Theodore Morse. 1909 (Cover Artist, Hirt) 10.00

On A Moonlight Night by L. Wolfe Gilbert, 1922 (Cover Artist, Wohlman)..3.00

On A Mountain Trail In Old Virginia by George Mack & Bob Allan, 1917 ....3.00

On A Saturday Night by Bratton, 1922 (Transportation) 10.00

On A Slow Boat To China by Frank Loesser, 1948 (Transportation)....5.00

On A Summer Night by Cobb, 1914 ....5.00

On A Summery Night by Chas. Tobias, Al Lewis & Al Sherman, 1929 (Deco) 5.00

On A Sunday Afternoon by Andrew B. Sterling & Harry Von Tilzer, 1929, Movie: Atlantic City, Photo Constance Moore, Brad Taylor & Jerry Colonna..10.00

On A Sunday Afternoon by Arthur Freed & Nacio Herb Brown, 1935, Movie: Broadway Melody Of 1936, Photo Robert Taylor, Jack Benny, Buddy Ebsen & Many More Strars 15.00

On Account-A I Love You by Green & Stept, 1934, Movie: Baby Take A Bow, Photo Shirley Temple, James Dunn & Claire Trevor (Shirley Temple)...10.00

On An Automobile Honeymoon by Jean Schwartz, 1905 (Transportation) 16.00

On Emancipation Day by Dunbar & Cook, 1902................................5.00

On Erin's Green Isle by Kalten Hauser & Reeg, 1916 (Cover Artist, Pfeiffer & Irish)...15.00

On Frisco Bay by Carl Muller & A. Fred Phillips, 1919 (Cover Artist, William Fisher)..5.00

On Guard America by Lanny Ross, 1918 (WWI) 10.00

On Her Veranda by Ponce & Ponce, 1913 ....5.00

On Jersey Shore by Arthur Pryor, 1904 (March)................................8.00

On Lake Champlain by Alfred Bryan & Albert Gumble, 1916.............5.00

On Miami Shore by Wm. LeBaron & Victor Jacobie, 1919 ....6.00

On, Minnesota by Carl Beck & W.T. Purdy, 1909 (March)................10.00

On Mobile Bay by Earle C. Jones & Chas. Daniels, 1910, Photo Abia Latta 5.00

On My Way by Steiner, Livingston & Evans, 1964, Movie: Young Blood Hawk, Photo James Franciscus & Suzanne Pleshette 3.00

On Our Honeymoon by Harris, 1907 (Cover Artist, Starmer) **10.00**

On Ranch 101 by MacDonald & Puck, 1914 (Cover Artist, Pfeiffer)..**10.00**

On Riverside Drive by Al Dubin & Joe Burke, 1929, Photo Gene Austin (Cover Artist, Barbelle) **5.00**

On San Francisco Bay by Vincent Bryan & Gertrude Hoffman, 1906 ..**5.00**

On Such A Night by Wm. B. Friedlander & Con Conrad, 1923 (Cover Artist, Politzer) **1.00**

On The 5:15 by Stanley Murphy & Henry I. Marshall, 1914, Photo Elizabeth Murray (Transportation) **15.00**

On The 7:28 by Marchall, 1915 (Transportation)....................**15.00**

On The Arizona Trail by Dave Oppenheim & Al Piantadosi, 1930 (Cover Artist, Barbelle) **5.00**

On The Atchison, Topeka And The Santa Fe by J. Mercer & H. Warren, 1934, Movie: The Harvey Girls, Photo J. Garland..**16.00**

On The Avenue by Harold Rome & Fred Freed, 1947....................**3.00**

On The Avenue by Will T. Pierson, 1909, The Inaugural March For 1909 (March & Political)....................**30.00**

On The Banks Of Honolulu Bay by McKeon & Weasoner, 1916 (Cover Artist, Pfeiffer)....................**10.00**

On The Banks Of Killarney by Bohannon, 1913 (Cover Artist, Pfeiffer & Irish)....................**15.00**

On The Banks Of Lovelight Bay by W. R. Williams, 1913, Photo Maud Lambert....................**5.00**

On The Banks Of Old Green River by LaShier & Streeter, 1908 (Cover Artist, Pfeiffer)....................**10.00**

On The Banks Of The Brandywine by Oppenheim & Friedland, 1914 (Cover Artist, Pfeiffer) **10.00**

On The Banks Of The Wabash by Paul Dresser, 1897 (Pre 1900)......**10.00**

On The Battle Field by Alcan Moss & Maurice Levi, 1914 (Cover Artist, Denslow, Red Cross & WWI) **36.00**

On The Bay Of Biscay by Harold Robe, 1919 ....**3.00**

On The Beach At Bali-Bali by Al Sherman, Jack Meskill & Abner Silver, 1936 (Cover Artist, Cliff Miska) **5.00**

On The Beach At Waikiki by G.H. Stover & Henry Kailimai, 1916 .....**5.00**

On The Benches In The Park by James Thornton, 1896 (Pre 1900) **10.00**

On The Bombiloo Islands by Tobias, 1915 ....**5.00**

On The Bright Golden Shore by Mary E. Kail & C.A. White, 1873, Dedicated To Miss Nella S. Phillips, Springfield, Mass. (Pre 1900 & Dedication) **16.00**

On The Bumpy Road To Love by Hoffman, Lewis & Menchr, 1938, Movie: Listen Darling, Photo Judy Garland & Freddie Bartholomew..........**10.00**

On The 'Gin' Ginny Shore by Edgar Leslie & Walter Donaldson, 1922, Photo Adele Rowland (Transportation)....................**12.00**

On The Good Ship Lollipop by Sydney Clare & Richard Whiting, 1934, Movie: Bright Eyes, Photo Shirley Temple (Shirley Temple).......**14.00**

On The Green by Rube Bloom, 1934 ....**5.00**

On The Gridiron by Jacob H. Ellis, 1911 (March & Sports)...............**15.00**

On The Hoko Moko Isle by Lou Klein & Harry Von Tilzer, 1916, Photo Sophie Tucker & Harry Von Tilzer (Cover Artist, Rose) **15.00**

On The Honeymoon Express by Lou Klein, James Kendis & Frank Stilwell, 1913 (Cover Artist, Pfeiffer & Transportation)....................**15.00**

On The Island Of Pines by Bryan & Carroll, 1914 (Cover Artist, Pfeiffer)....................**10.00**

On The Isle Of May by Mack David & Andre Kostelanetz, 1940 ....**3.00**

On The Loose by Harry Brooks, 1936....................**3.00**

On The Mississippi by Ballard Macdonald, Harry Carroll & Fields, 1912, Photo Mitchell Girls (Cover Artist, Starmer & Rag)....................**12.00**

On The New York, New Haven & Hartford by Frank J. Conroy & Albert Von Tilzer, 1911 (Transportation)....................**20.00**

On The Old Back Seat Of The Henry Ford by Dillon, 1916 (Transportation)....................**25.00**

On The Old Fall River Line by Andrew Sterling, William Jerome & Harry Von Tilzer, 1913, Photo Harry Von Tilzer (Cover Artist, DeTakacs & Transportation) **15.00**

On The Old Front Porch by Heath & Lang, 1913....................**5.00**

On The Old Lake Trail by Joseph McCarthy & Harry Tierney, 1918, Musical: Kid Boots....................**12.00**

On The Old See Saw by Ed Gardenier & Gus Edwards, 1906............**10.00**

On The Old Virginia Shore by Browning, 1905....................**5.00**

On The Oregon Trail by Billy Hill & Peter DeRose **5.00**

On The Proper Side Of Broadway On A Saturday Night by Will J. Cobb & Gus Edwards, 1902....................**10.00**

On The Riviera by L. Wolfe Gilbert, Van Loan & Vernon Rich, 1926 .**5.00**

On The Road That Leads Back Home by Lt. Gitz Rice, 1918 (Military Personnel & WWI) **15.00**

On The Road To Home Sweet Home by Gus Kahn & Egbert Van Alstyne, 1917 (WWI)....................**5.00**

On The Road To Mandalay by Rudyard Kipling & Oley Speaks, 1907 ..**10.00**

On The Road To Paradise by J. Keirn Brennan & Ernest E. Ball, 1917 ....**5.00**

On The Same Old Road by John H. Flynn, Allan J. Flynn & Albert Piantadosi, 1916 (Cover Artist, Starmer) **6.00**

On The Sandwich Isles by Kilgour & Von Tilzer, 1917 (Cover Artist, Pfeiffer)....................**10.00**

On The Sentimental Side by John Burke & James V. Monaco, 1938, Movie: Doctor Rhythm, Photo Bing Crosby & Mary Carlisle.......**10.00**

On The Shore At Le Lei Wi by Schuyler Greene, Herbert Reynolds & Jerome Kern, 1915, Musical: Very Good Eddie (Cover Artist, Malcolm Strauss) **15.00**

On The Shores Of Italy by Al Piantadosi & Jack Glogau, 1914, Photo Gus Van & Joe Schenck....................**6.00**

On The Shores Of Italy by Al Piantadosi & Jack Glogau, 1914, Photo Mollie King (Cover Artist, Rose Symbol)....................**10.00**

On The Sidewalks Of Berlin by E. Clinton Keithley, 1918 (WWI).....**10.00**

On The South Sea Isle by Harry Von Tilzer, 1916, Photo Harry Von Tilzer & Irene Bordoni (Cover Artist, Pfeiffer)....................**12.00**

On The South Sea Isle by Harry Von Tilzer, 1916, Photo Irene Bordoni (Cover Artist, Pfeiffer) **15.00**

On The Steps Of The Great White Capitol, Stood Martha And George by Grant Clarke, Edgar Leslie & Maurice Abrahams, 1914 (Cover Artist, Pfeiffer, President, Military Personnel & Patriotic) **50.00**

On The Street Of Regret by John Klenner & Pete Wendling, 1942 (Cover Artist, Im-Ho) **4.00**

On The Street Where You Live by Lerner & Lowe, 1956, Movie: My Fair Lady **5.00**

On The Sunny Side Of The Rockies by Roy Ingraham & Harry Tobias, 1937, Movie: Roll Along, Cowboy, Photo Smith Ballew **5.00**

On The Sunny Side Of The Street by Dorothy Fields & Jimmy McHugh, 1930, Movie: Sunny Side Of The Street, Photo Tommy Dorsey **5.00**

On The Sunset Trail by E.C. Vose & A. Fred Phillips, 1915 ....**5.00**

On The Swing Shift by Johnny Mercer & Harold Arlen, 1942, Movie: Star Spangled Rhythm, Photo Bing Crosby, Bob Hope, Dorothy Lamour & Many More Stars **5.00**

On The Trail by Ferde Grofe, 1932 ....**5.00**

On The Way To Home Sweet Home by Sam M. Lewis & Geo W. Meyer, 1915 ....**5.00**

On This Day, O Beautiful Mother, by Louis Lambillotte, 1947............**3.00**

On To Frisco by Leslie & Mohr (Cover Artist, Pfeiffer & Transportation) **15.00**

On To Plattsburg by Bert Lowe, 1916 (WWI) **10.00**

On Top Of Old Smoky by Peter Seeger, 1951....................**4.00**

On Treasure Island by Edgar Leslie & Joe Burke, 1935 (Cover Artist, Cliff Miska & Transportation) **5.00**

On Treasure Island by Leslie & Burke, 1935, Photo Gale Storm...........**3.00**

On Wings Of Memory by Thekla Hollingsworth & Jessie L. Deppen, 1939 ....**5.00**

On Wisconsin by Carl Beck & W.T. Purdy, 1909 (March)..................**15.00**

On Your Wedding Day by Gaston & Holliday, 1917 (Cover Artist, Pfeiffer) **12.00**

Once Aboard The Lugger by David D. Slater (Transportation) **10.00**

Once Again by Howard Kornblum & Myers, 1919................**8.00**

Once In A Blue Moon by Mack Gordon & Harry Revel, 1934, Movie: We're Not Dressing, Photo Bing Crosby & Carole Lombard **8.00**

Once In A Lifetime by Raymond Klages & Jesse Greer, 1928, Musical: Earl Carroll Vanities, 7th Edition (Deco)......................**10.00**

Once In A While by Bud Green & Michael Edwards, 1937, Photo Tommy Dorsey....................**5.00**

Once In Love With Amy by Frank Loesser, 1948, Musical: Where's Charley, Caricature Ray Bolger....................**10.00**

Once More Upon The Sea by Buckley (Transportation)....................**15.00**

One Alone by Otto Harbach, Oscar Hammerstein II, Frank Mandel & Sigmund Romberg, 1926, Movie: The Desert Song..........**10.00**

One And Only For Me, The by Bud Green, James V. Monaco & Harry Warren, 1914 ....**5.00**

One And Only, The by Rida J. Young & Paul Rubens, 1904, Photo Miss Doris Mitchell....................**12.00**

One Boy by Lee Adams & Charles Strouse, 1960, Movie: Bye Bye Birdie....................**5.00**

One Day In June by Joe Goodwin & James F. Hanley, 1917 (Cover Artist, Barbelle) **8.00**

One Day In May by Sam M. Lewis & Robert A. King, 1932 ....**3.00**

One Day We Dance by Carolyn Leigh & Cy Coleman, 1960, Movie: Wildcat....................**5.00**

One Day When We Were Young by Oscar Hammerstein II & Johann Strauss II, 1938, Movie: The Great Waltz, Photo Louise Rainer, Fernand Gravet & Meliza Korjus **12.00**

One Dozen Roses by Dick Jurgens, Country Washburn, Roger Lewis & Walter Donovan, 1942....................**3.00**

One Eyed Jacks by Hugo W. Friedhofer, 1961, Movie: One Eyed Jacks, Photo Marlon Brando **3.00**

One Finger Melody, The by Al Hoffman, Kermit Goell & Fred Spielman, 1950, Photo Frank Sinatra (Cover Artist, Barbelle) **3.00**

One Fleeting Hour by Karl Fuhrmann & Dorothy Lee, 1919 (Cover Artist, Jaroushek)....................**5.00**

One Flower Grows Alone In Your Garden by Otto Harback, Oscar Hammerstein II, Frank Mandel & Sigmund Romberg, 1926, Movie: The Desert Song....................**6.00**

One For All–All For One by Mann Curtis & Maxwell Rick, 1941........**3.00**

One Girl by Irving Berlin, 1923, Musical: Music Box Revue 1923-24 (Cover Artist, R.S., Irving Berlin & Deco) **12.00**

One Hand, One Heart by Stephen Sondheim & Leonard Bernstein, 1957, Movie: West Side Story....................**5.00**

One Has My Name, The Other Has My Heart by Eddie Dean, Dearest Dean & Hal Blair, 1948, Photo Paul Dixon **2.00**

One Hell Of A Woman by Mac Davis, Photo Mac Davis....................**5.00**

One Hour With You by Leo Robin & Richard A. Whiting, 1932, Movie: One Hour With You, Photo Maurice Chevalier (Cover Artist, Harris) **12.00**

One Hour With You by Leo Robin & Richard A. Whiting, 1932, Movie: One Hour With You, Eddie Cantor's Theme Song (Eddie Cantor)..**10.00**

101st Regiment, U.S.A. by Bert Potter, 1917 (Cover Artist, E.A.S, March & WWI)....................**20.00**

One I Love Belongs To Somebody Else, The by Gus Kahn & Isham Jones, 1924 ....**6.00**

One I Love Just Can't Be Bothered With Me, The by Gus Kahn & Seymour Simons, 1929....................**5.00**

One I Love Just Said Good-Bye, The by Cal DeVoll, 1931....................**5.00**

One I Love, The by Gus Kahn & Bronislau Kaper, 1938, Movie: Everybody Sing, Photo Judy Garland **15.00**

One I'm Looking For, The by Harry B. Smith & Emmerich Kalman, 1924, Musical: Countess Maritza **10.00**

One In A Million by Sidney Mitchell & Lew Pollack, 1936, Movie: One In A Million, Photo Sonja Henie....................**5.00**

One In The World, The by Eric Little & Roger Eckersley, 1928...........**5.00**

One Kiss by Frank Mandel, Oscar Hammerstein II & Sigmund Romberg, 1928, Musical: The New Moon....................**3.00**

One Kiss by Leo Wood, Earl Burtnett & Gus Arnheim, 1921 (Cover Artist, JVR)....................**5.00**

One Kiss, One Smile, One Tear by Walter Rafael & John McLaughlin, 1931 (Cover Artist, Borj)....................**5.00**

One Last Kiss by Lee Adams & Charles Strause, 1960, Movie: Bye Bye Birdie **3.00**

One Little Candle by J. Maloy Rosch & George Mysels, 1951, Signed Photo Perry Como (Signed)....................**10.00**

One Little Dream Of Love by Harold Simpson & Westell Gordon, 1926 ..**3.00**

One Little Raindrop by Harry Richman, Jack Meskill & Jean Schwartz, 1930, Photo Eddie Lane....................**4.00**

One Look At You by Wright, Forrest, Stothart & Ward, 1939, Movie: Broadway Serenade, Photo Jeannette Macdonald....................**8.00**

One Look, One Word by Harry B. Smith & Victor Jacobi, 1917...........**5.00**

One Love For Ever by James Dyrenforth & Kenneth Leslie Smith, 1942 ..**3.00**

One Moment Alone by Otto Harbach & Jerome Kern, 1931, Musical: The Cat And The Fiddle **6.00**

One More Dance by Oscar Hammerstein II & Jerome Kern, 1932, Movie: Music In The Air **6.00**

One More Day by J. Keirn Brennan & Ernest R. Ball, 1910................**5.00**

One More Dream by Buddy Kaye & Dick Manning, 1945, Photo Jack Smith....................**5.00**

One More Hour Of Love by Clifford Grey & Oscar Straus, 1931, Movie: Smiling Lieutenant, Featuring Maurice Chevalier **5.00**

One More Night by Billy Rose & Joe Burke, 1927....................**5.00**

One More Time by DeSylva, Brown & Henderson, 1926, Movie: The Best Things In Life Are Free, Photo Gordon McRae, Dan Dailey, Ernest Borgnine & Sheree North **10.00**

One More Tomorrow by Ernesto Lecuone, Eddie DeLange & Josef Myrow, 1945, Movie: One More Tomorrow, Photo Ann Sheridan, Dennis Morgan, Jack Carson & Alexis Smith....................**6.00**

One More Waltz by Dorothy Fields & Jimmy McHugh, 1930, Movie: Love In The Rough, Photo Robert Montgomery & Dorothy Jordan..........**6.00**

One Morning In May by Mitchell Parish & Hoagy Carmichael, 1933 ..**5.00**

One Never Knows, Does One? by Mack Gordon & Harry Revel, 1936, Movie: Stowaway, Photo Shirley Temple (Shirley Temple) **10.00**

One Night In Monte Carlo by Abner Silver, Al Sherman & Al Lewis, 1935, Photo Connie Boswell (Cover Artist, HBK) **5.00**

One Night Of Love by Gus Kahn & Victor Schertzinger, 1934, Movie: One Night Of Love, Photo Grace Moore **10.00**

One O'clock Baby by Lew Brown & Al Jolson, 1927, Photo Al Jolson (Al Jolson).........**16.00**

One Of His Legs Is Longer Than It Really Ought To Be by Lew Dockstader, 1893, Photo Lew Dockstader (Pre 1900 & Black, Black Face).........**32.00**

One Of Us Was Wrong by Gus Kahn & Al Goering, 1931.........**5.00**

One Rose That's Left In My Heart, The by Del Lyon & Lani McIntire, 1936, Photo Kate Smith (Cover Artist, Starmer).........**15.00**

One Rose That's Left In My Heart, The by Del Lyon & Lani McIntire, 1936, Photo Rudy Vallee (Cover Artist, Starmer).........**15.00**

One Song by Larry Morey & Frank Churchill, 1937, Movie: Snow White (Disney) **10.00**

One Summer Night by Sam Coslow & Larry Spier, 1937 ....**3.00**

One Sunday Afternoon by Ralph Blane, 1948, Movie: One Sunday Afternoon, Photo Dennis Morgan, Janice Paige, Don DeFore & Dorothy Malone **4.00**

One Sweetheart Is Enough For Me by Beth Slater Whitson & W.R. Williams, 1913, Photo Lee White & George Perry.........**10.00**

One Touch Of Nature Makes The Whole World Kin by Felix McGlennon, 1897 (Pre 1900) **10.00**

One, Two, Button Your Shoe by John Burke & Arthur Johnston, 1936, Movie: Pennies From Heaven, Photo Bing Crosby.........**5.00**

One, Two, Three Little Hours by John Jacob Loeb, 1936.........**3.00**

One Wonderful Night by E. Clinton Keithley, Joe Lyons & Clarence M. Jones, 1914, Photo Francis X. Bushman **10.00**

One-A-Strike by Arthur Longbrake, 1908 (Sports).........**15.00**

Only A Bowery Boy by Ward & Davis, 1895 (Pre 1900).........**10.00**

Only A Bunch Of Violets by Owen, 1912 (Cover Artist, Pfeiffer).........**10.00**

Only A Butterfly by Clyde Hager & Jerry Sullivan, 1923 ....**5.00**

Only A Chain Of Daisies by Barnes & White, 1910 (Cover Artist, Pfeiffer) **10.00**

Only A Dad–But The Best Of Men by Perrins, 1916 (Cover Artist, Pfeiffer) **12.00**

Only A Faded Rose Bud by William Clay & Chas. L. Johnson, 1913...**5.00**

Only A Kiss by Schwartz & Atteridge, 1910 (Cover Artist, Pfeiffer)....**5.00**

Only A Midnight Adventure by Edgar Leslie & Seymour Simons, 1930..**5.00**

Only A Pansy Blossom by Eben Rexford & Frank Howard, 1883 (Pre 1900).........**10.00**

Only A Rose by Brian Hooker & Rudolf Friml, 1925, Movie: The Vagabond King, Photo Jeannette MacDonald.........**10.00**

Only A Rose by Brian Hooker & Rudolf Friml, 1925, Musical: Vagabond King, Photo Carolyn Thomson.........**8.00**

Only A Rose To Remind You by Happy O'Neil, Harry Jentes & Oliver E. Story, 1912.........**12.00**

Only A Rosebud by Caro Roma, 1895 (Pre 1900) **10.00**

Only A Rosebud by Harold B. Freeman & J. Edwin Allemong, 1919...**3.00**

Only A Year Ago by Fred Bowles & Fred Albers, 1915.........**5.00**

Only Another Boy & Girl by Cole Porter, Movie: Seven Lively Arts ...**5.00**

Only by Irving Caesar & Harry L. Akst, 1919 ....**5.00**

Only For Americans by Irving Berlin, 1949, Musical: Miss Liberty (Irving Berlin & Patriotic) **12.00**

Only For You by Josiah Zuro, Francis Cromon & Chas. Weinburg, 1929, Movie: The Leatherneck, Photo Wm. Boyd.........**5.00**

Only Forever by Johnny Burke & James V. Monaco, 1940, Movie: Rhythm On The River, Photo Bing Crosby & Mary Martin.........**5.00**

Only Friends by Fannie Stearns Davis & Charles Willeby, 1913 ....**5.00**

Only Heart Broken Was Mine, The by E. Clinton Keithly & Thompson, 1914 ....**5.00**

Only Lonely Little Me by Ellwood & Snyder (Cover Artist, Pfeiffer) **10.00**

Only Love Is Real by Arthur Freed & Nacio Herb Brown, 1929, Movie: Lord Byron On Broadway **5.00**

Only Me by Ford & Bratton, 1894 (Pre 1900) **10.00**

Only One by Harry B. Smith & Sigmund Romberg, 1925, Musical: Princess Flavia.........**5.00**

Only One Face In Dreamland by L.Z. Phillips, 1909 ....**5.00**

Only One Girl In The World For Me by Dave Marion, 1895 (Pre 1900)..**10.00**

Only One, The by Anne Croswell & Lee Pochriss, 1963, Musical: Tovarich.........**3.00**

Only, Only One For Me, The by Bud Green, James V. Monaco & Harry Warren, 1914, Photo Rebecca At The Well.........10.00

Only Pal I Ever Had Came From Frisco Town, The by Earle C. Jones & Charles Daniels, 1911.........**10.00**

Only Song I Know, The by J. Keirn Brennan & Ray Perkins, 1929, Movie: Show Of Shows **10.00**

Only You by A.H. Eastman & Fred Heltman, 1919.........**5.00**

Only You by Arthur J. Lamb & Clarence M. Jones, 1915 ....**5.00**

Only You by Frank Keesee & Charles Zimmerman, 1906.........**5.00**

Only You by Harry J. Lincoln & Rena Vandersloot, 1904 ....**5.00**

Oo Lee Long by George Evans, 1899, Photo Etta Stetson (Cover Artist, Carter & Pre 1900) **10.00**

Oo-La-La-Wee-Wee by Harry Ruby, 1919 (WWI).........**10.00**

Ooh That Kiss by Mort, Dixon, Joe Young & Harry Warren, 1931, Musical: The Laugh Parade, Starring Ed Wynn (Cover Artist, Gorj).........**6.00**

Ooh! You Miser You! by Sam Lewis & Pete Wendling, 1934 ....**5.00**

Oooh! Look-A There, Ain't She Pretty? by Clarence Todd & Carmen Lombardo, 1933, Photo Guy Lombardo.........**4.00**

Oop Shoop by Shirley Gunter & The Queens, 1954, Photo The Crew Cuts **3.00**

Oops! by Mercer & Warren, 1952, Movie: The Belle Of New York, Photo Fred Astaire & Vera Ellen.........**10.00**

Op In Me Ansom by George M. Cohan (George M. Cohan) **10.00**

Open The Door, Richard by John Mason, Dusty Fletcher, Dan Howell & Jack McVea, 1947 (Cover Artist, Holley).........**5.00**

Open The Gate To Your Heart by Frederick Owen & Constance White, 1923 ....**6.00**

Open Thy Lattice, Love by George P. Morris & Stephen Foster, 1844, First Song Written by Stephen Foster (Stephen Foster & Pre 1900) **50.00**

Open Up The Golden Gates To Dixieland by Jack Yellen, Gus Van & Jos. Schenck, 1919 (Cover Artist, Barbelle & Dixie)............................**5.00**

Open Up Your Heart by L. Wolfe Gilbert & Dave Lee, 1915..............**5.00**

Open Up Your Heart by Stuart Hamblen, 1953, Photo McGuire Sisters..**4.00**

Open Your Arms My Alabamy by Sam M. Lewis, Joe Young & Geo W. Meyer, 1922 (Cover Artist, R.S.) **5.00**

Opening Of The Season by John Stromberg, 1898 (March & Pre 1900) ..**10.00**

Operatic Rag by Julius Lenzberg, 1914, Dedicated To Arthur Anderson, N.Y. (Dedication & Rag).....................**10.00**

Ophelia Rag by James Scott (Rag) **15.00**

Opportunity by Walter Malone & W.C. Hanley, 1934.........................**6.00**

Orange Blossom Time by Joe Goodwin & Gus Edwards, 1929, From Hollywood Review, 1929, Photo Many Stars **5.00**

Orange Colored Sky by Milton Delugg & Willie Stein, 1950.............**3.00**

Orchids In The Moonlight by Edward Eliscu & Gus Kahn, 1933, Movie: Flying Down To Rio, Photo Fred Astaire & Dolores DelRio **5.00**

Oregon Trail by Peter DeRose, 1935.......................................**4.00**

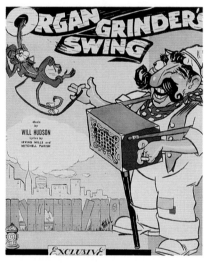

Organ Grinder's Swing by Irving Mills, Mitchell Parish & Will Hudson, 1936 (Cover Artist, Hall) **10.00**

Oriental Echoes by Geo Rosey, 1895 (Pre 1900) **10.00**

Oriental Guard by John Stromberg, 1899 (March & Pre 1900) **15.00**

Oriental Song by Lax & Michelet, 1948, Movie: Atlantis, Photo Maria Montez..................................**3.00**

Oriental Stars by James V. Monaco, 1921......................................**5.00**

Original Dixieland One-Step by Robinson, Crandall & LaRocca, 1939, Movie: The Benny Goodman Story, Photo Steve Allen & Donna Reed......................................**12.00**

Original Rags by Scott Joplin, 1899 (Scott Joplin, Rag & Pre 1900)...**50.00**

Otoyo by Edmund Dana Palmer, 1905 (Cover Artist, E.S. Fisher)........**5.00**

Otto, You Ought To Take Me In Your Auto by Speck, 1905 (Transportation)......................................**15.00**

Otty The Otter by Shaindling & Pattarini, 1955, Movie: The Great Adventure **3.00**

Oui, Oui, Marie by Alfred Bryan, Joe McCarthy & Fred Fisher, 1918 (Cover Artist, DeTakacs & WWI).......................**15.00**

Our Anniversary Waltz by Mary Schaeffer & Larry Stock, 1937..........**5.00**

Our Band by Chas. C. Sweeley, 1910 (Cover Artist, Dittmar & March) ..**10.00**

Our Big Love Scene by Arthur Freed & Nacio Herb Brown, 1933, Movie: Going Hollywood, Photo Bing Crosby & Marion Davies...............**6.00**

Our Boys And Girls by Kaiser, 1903 (Patriotic)..................................**10.00**

Our Bungalow Of Dreams by Tommie Malie, Charlie Newman & Joe Verges, 1927, Photo Harry Lange's Orchestra...............................**5.00**

Our Christmas Waltz by Ed Nelson Jr. & Steve Nelson, 1949..............**3.00**

Our Country's Heros by Barrett, 1910 (Patriotic) **10.00**

Our Country's In It Now!, We've Got To Win It Now by Guy Empey, 1918 (WWI)..................................**50.00**

Our Daring Commodore by Drumond Staley, 1898 (Pre 1900 & March) ..**15.00**

Our Director by F. E. Bigelow, 1924 (Cover Artist, E. S. Fisher & March) **15.00**

Our Flag by Clark, 1859 (Pre 1900 & Transportation)........................**25.00**

Our Gallant 91st Wild West Division by Thomas Bruce, 1919 (WWI)...**25.00**

Our Gallant Hero, Admiral Dewey-Photos Of Dewey With Flags & Eagles (Military Personnel & Political) **35.00**

Our Lady Of Fatima by Gladys Gollahan, 1950.............................**5.00**

Our Lanky Yankee Boys In Brown by Edward Madden, Robert F. Roden & Theodore Morse, 1917 (WWI)......................**10.00**

Our Little Cabaret At Home (Cover Artist, Pfeiffer)........................**10.00**

Our Little Country Home by Harry Franks, 1921 (Cover Artist, Pfeiffer)......................................**10.00**

Our Little Girl by Paul Francis Webster & Lew Pollack, 1935, Movie: Our Little Girl, Photo Shirley Temple (Shirley Temple).....................**12.00**

Our Little Home by L. Wolfe Gilbert, 1923 ....**5.00**

Our Little Home On The Highway by Sam Coslow, 1937 (Transportation) **5.00**

Our Love Affair by A. Freed & Roger Edens, 1940, Movie: Strike Up The Band, Photo Judy Garland & Mickey Rooney **10.00**

Our Love (Based On Tschaikowsky's Romeo & Juliet) by Larry Clinton, Buddy Bernier & Bob Emmerich, 1939 ....**3.00**

Our Penthouse On Third Avenue by Sammy Fain & Lew Brown, 1937, Movie: New Faces Of 1937..................**5.00**

Our Protectors March by A.G. Dolan, 1903, Dedicated To W.T. Cheswell (March & Dedication) **5.00**

Our Quarrels Dear by L. Wolfe Gilbert & Joseph Cooper, 1929 ....**5.00**

Our Sammies by J.R. Shannon & Carl D. Vandersloot, U.S.N., 1918 (WWI & Military Personnel)......................**20.00**

Our Sammy Boys by Guy Call, 1917 (Cover Artist, Pfeiffer, WWI & Transportation) **16.00**

Our "V" For Victory by Francis Wheeler, 1942 (WWII & Patriotic) ..**10.00**

Our Washington by Lottie M. Hull & Jean Buckley. 1914 (Patriotic) .**10.00**

Our Yesterdays by Francis Lake & Herbert Leslie, 1922....................**5.00**

Ours by Cole Porter, 1936, Movie: Red Hot & Blue............................**5.00**

Out In An Automobile by Evans, 1905 (Transportation) **20.00**

Out In The Cold Again by Ted Koehler & Rube Bloom, 1934, Photo Jane Froman...................................**3.00**

Out In The Cold Again by Ted Koehler & Rube Bloom, 1934, Photo Mindy Carson **3.00**

Out In The Great Open Spaces by Sam Coslow & Arthur Johnston, 1932, Photo Kate Smith.....................**5.00**

Out Of A Clear Sky by Sam Lewis, Joe Young, Jan Rubini & Salvatore Santaella, 1919...................................**5.00**

Out Of My Dreams by Richard Rodgers & Oscar Hammerstein II, 1943, Musical: Oklahoma (Cover Artist, Holley) **6.00**

Out Of Nowhere by Johnny Green, 1931 ....**5.00**

Out Of Sight Out Of Mind by Dorothy Fields & Oscar Levant, 1935 ...**5.00**

Out Of Space by Winky Tharp, Eugene Gifford & Joe Bishop, 1924....**5.00**

Out Of The Cradle, Into My Heart by L. Wolfe Gilbert & Anatol Friedland, 1916 ....**5.00**

Out Of The Dawn by Walter Donaldson, 1928 ....**3.00**

Out Of The Dusk To You by Arthur J. Lamb & Dorothy Lee, 1922 .....**3.00**

Out Of The East by Jean C. Havez & Joe Rosey, 1918........................**5.00**

Out Of The Tempest by Edward Grossman & Ted Ward, 1928, Dedicated To John Barrymore (Cover Artist, CE/M & Dedication)...............**16.00**

Out On The Bounding Deep by Irene Jeffries, 1913, Respectfully Dedicated To The Darlings, A Family Of Fishers And Childhood Friends Of The Composer (Cover Artist, C.J.M., Transportation & Dedication)......**25.00**

Out On The Bounding Ocean Deep by Gardinier & Speck, 1909 (Cover Artist, Pfeiffer & Transportation)......**15.00**

Out On The Deep by Hermann Lohr, 1900 (Transportation)......**10.00**

Out Where The Billows Roll High by Petri and Brannen, 1901 (Transportation)......**10.00**

Out Where The Blue Begins by Geo. Graffe Jr., James Francis McHugh & F. Bernard Grant, 1923......**5.00**

Out Where The Breakers Roar by H.W. Petrie, 1903......**10.00**

Out Where The West Begins by Arthur Chapman & Estelle Philleo, 1921......**5.00**

Outcast Unknown,The by Paul Dresser, 1887 (Pre 1900)......**15.00**

Outside by Frank Flynn, 1929......**5.00**

Outside Of That I Love You by Irving Berlin, 1939 (Irving Berlin)....**12.00**

Outside Of You by Warren Duff-Sig Herzig, E.Y. Harburg & Hans Kraly, 1935, Movie: Broadway Gondolier......**5.00**

Over And Over by Crawford, 1965, Movie: C'mon Let's Live A Little, Photo Bobby Vee, Jackie Deshannon & Eddie Hodges......**4.00**

Over In Hero Land by Freed & Silvers, 1918 (Cover Artist, Pfeiffer & WWI)......**15.00**

Over On The Jersey Side by Jack Norworth,1918, Photo Jack Norworth ..**10.00**

Over Pine Mountain Trails by Sherwood & Ganz, 1941, Movie: Over Pine Mountain Trails......**3.00**

Over The Alpine Mountains by Alfred Bryan & Fred Fisher, 1916......**5.00**

Over The Garden Wall by Fox & Hunter, 1879 (Pre 1900)......**15.00**

Over The Hill by Lou Klein, Edgar Allen & Maurice Rubens, 1921 (Cover Artist, Wohlman)......**6.00**

Over The Hills, And Thru The Woods by Hal David, Kahn Keene, Carl Bean & Frankie Masters, 1940......**5.00**

Over The Hills by Frederick Knight Logan, 1923......**5.00**

Over The Hills To Mary by Alfred Bryan & Jack Wells, 1915 (Cover Artist, Starmer)......**10.00**

Over The Mountain by William J. Scanlon, 1881 (Pre 1900)......**10.00**

Over The Phone by Abe Olman, 1917......**5.00**

Over The Rainbow by E.Y. Harburg & Harold Arlen, 1939, Movie: The Wizard Of Oz, Photo Judy Garland......**40.00**

Over The Rainbow by E.Y. Harburg & Harold Arlen, 1939, Movie: The Wizard Of Oz, Signed Photo Judy Garland (Signed)......**425.00**

Over The Rainbow by Harburg & Arlen, 1939, Movie: The Wizard Of Oz, Photo Judy Garland, Ray Bolger, Frank Morgan, Bert Lahr & Jack Haley......**25.00**

Over The Sea To Skye by Robert Lewis Stevenson, 1912......**10.00**

Over The Top by Geoffrey O'Hara, 1917 (WWI & March)......**20.00**

Over The Top With The Best Of Luck by Wensley & Carroll, 1918 (Cover Artist, Pfeiffer & WWI)......**15.00**

Over The Waves by Juventino Rosas, 1924......**5.00**

Over There by George M. Cohan, 1917, Norman Rockwell Cover Appeared On Life Magazine In 1918, Signed By Norman Rockwell (Cover Artist, Norman Rockwell, Signed, WWI & George M. Cohan)......**75.00**

Over There by George M. Cohan, 1917, Photo Nora Bayes (Cover Artist, Barbelle, WWI & George M. Cohan)......**15.00**

Over There by George M. Cohan, 1917, Photo Wm. J. Reilly, U.S.N. (George M. Cohan, Military Personnel & WWI)......**35.00**

Over There by George M. Cohan, 1917, Signed by Norman Rockwell, Matted & Framed (Cover Artist, Norman Rockwell, Signed, WWI & George M. Cohan)......**125.00**

Over Yonder Where The Lilies Grow by Geoffrey O'Hara, 1918 (Cover Artist, Norman Rockwell & WWI)......**30.00**

Overnight by Billy Rose, Charlotte Kent & Louis Alter, 1930, Musical: Sweet And Low......**5.00**

Overture Of Irish Melodies by Richard L. Weaver, 1909 (Cover Artist, Etherington & Irish)......**12.00**

Owl In The Old Oak Tree by Murphy & Burt, 1911 (Cover Artist, Pfeiffer)......**10.00**

Oyster, A Cloister And You by Richard Connels, 1925......**10.00**

Pa Paya Mama by George Sandler, Larry Coleman & Norman Gimbel, 1953......**3.00**

Pack Of Cards, A by Henry Reilly, 1892 (Pre 1900)......**15.00**

Pack Up Your Sins And Go To The Devil by Irving Berlin, 1922 (Irving Berlin)......**10.00**

Pack Up Your Troubles In Your Old Kit Bag And Smile, Smile, Smile by Goerge Asaf & Felix Powell, 1915 (WWI)......**10.00**

Package Of Old Love Letters by White & Goulland, 1870 (Pre 1900) ..**15.00**

Packard And The Ford by Carroll, 1915 (Transportation)......**25.00**

Paddle Addle In Your Little Canoe by Ted Snyder, 1917......**5.00**

Paddle Your Own Canoe by Edward Madden & Theodore Morse, 1905 ..**5.00**

Paddlin' Madelin Home by Harry Woods, 1925, Musical: Sunny, Photo Cliff Edwards......**6.00**

Paddy Duffy's Cart by Edward Harrigan & David Braham, 1881 (Pre 1900)......**15.00**

Paducah by Leo Robin & Harry Warren, 1943, Movie: The Gang's All Here, Photo Alice Faye, Carmen Miranda, Phil Baker & The King Of Swing, Benny Goodman......**6.00**

Pagan Love Song by Arthur Freed & Nacio Herb Brown, 1929, Movie: The Pagan, Photo Esther Williams & Howard Keel......**10.00**

Pagan Love Song by Arthur Freed & Nacio Herb Brown, 1929, Photo Raymond Novaro......**10.00**

Page Miss Glory by Harry Warren, Movie: Page Miss Glory, Photo Marion Davies......**5.00**

Pahjamah by S.R. Henry & D. Onivas, 1919......**5.00**

Painting A Picture Of You by Richard Howard, 1917 (Cover Artist, Starmer)......10.00

Painting That Mother Of Mine by Frank Sturgis & L. Wolfe Gilbert, 1915 (Cover Artist, Starmer)......**10.00**

Painting The Clouds With Sunshine by Al Dubin & Joe Burke, 1929, Movie: Gold Diggers Of Broadway, Photo Many Stars......**6.00**

Painting The Roses Red by Bob Hilliard & Sammy Fain, 1951, Movie: Alice In Wonderland (Disney)......**20.00**

Pair Of Blue Eyes, A by William Kernell, 1940, Movie: Song O'My Heart, Photo John McCormack......**5.00**

Pal Of Mine by Bartley C. Costello & J.S. Nathan, 1905......**8.00**

Pal Of My Cradle Days by Marshall Montgomery & Al Piantadosi, 1925, Photo Henry Murtagh (Deco)......**6.00**

Pal Of My Cradle Days by Marshall Montgomery & Al Piantadosi, 1925, Photo Charles R. Hector (Deco)......**6.00**

Pal Of My Cradle Days by Marshall Montgomery & Al Piantadosi, 1925, Photo Alice Morley (Deco)......**6.00**

Pal Of My Dreams by Rube Benner & George A. Little, 1929.............**5.00**

Pal That I Loved Stole The Gal That I Loved, by Sylvester L. Cross, 1924...**5.00**

Pal That I Loved Stole The Gal That I Loved, The by Harry Pease & Ed Nelson, 1924, Photo Welder Sisters........................**6.00**

Palace Of Peace by C.M. Vandersloot, 1914 (Cover Artist, Dulin & March) **10.00**

Pale Hands (Kashmiri Song) by Lawrence Hope & Amy Woodforde Finden, 1953, Movie: Hers To Hold, Photo Deanna Durbin.................**10.00**

Pale Moon, An Indian Love Song by Jesse G.M. Glick & Frederic Knight Logan, 1920, Dedicated To Miss Rosa Raisa (Cover Artist, Van Doorn Morgan, Indian & Dedication) **10.00**

Pale Venetian Moon, The by Anne Caldwell & Jerome Kern, 1922, Musical: The Bunch And Judy **6.00**

Palesteena by Con Conrad & J. Russel Robinson, 1920, Musical: Broadway..**5.00**

Palm Beach by C.Luckyth Roberts, 1914.....................................**5.00**

Palm Limited, The by Harry J. Lincoln, 1905 (March).......................**18.00**

Palms by B.J. Fause...**5.00**

Pals by Gilbert Wells & Lynn Cowan, 1929 ....**5.00**

Pals Of The Little Red School by Ernie Erdman & Cal DeVoll, 1931 ..**5.00**

Panama Canal, The by Will Wood, 1911 (March) **10.00**

Panama Love Song by Frank Flynn, 1918.......................................**6.00**

Panama Twilight by Wilber D'Lea & Fisher Thompson, 1922 (Cover Artist, Modern Art Service)..**3.00**

Panorama Years by Grant Clarke & James V. Monaco, 1922...............**5.00**

Pansy The Moon Am Shining by Ed Rogers, 1909 ....**12.00**

Papa, Won't You Dance With Me by Sammy Cahn & Jule Styne, 1942, Musical: High Button Shoes..**10.00**

Paper Doll by Johnny S. Black, 1943, Photo Bing Crosby **6.00**

Paper Doll by Johnny S. Black, 1943, Photo Guy Lombardo **6.00**

Paper Doll by Johnny S. Black, 1943, Photo Mills Brothers 5.00

Paper Roses by Janice Torre & Fred Spielman, 1962, Photo Marie Osmond..**8.00**

Parade Of The Wooden Soldiers by Ballard MacDonald & Leon Jessel, 1922 (Cover Artist, A. Joel Robinson)...**3.00**

Paradise Blues by Walter Hirsch & Spencer Williams, 1917 (Blues)....**5.00**

Paradise by Brown & Clifford, 1931, Photo Pola Negri.......................**5.00**

Paradise For Two by Jean Havez & Ted S. Barron, 1912 (Cover Artist, Pfeiffer)...**10.00**

Paradise Island by Mack David, Bert Bacharach & Lionel Hampton, Photo Four Aces...**6.00**

Paradise Isle by Ray Klages, Al Goering & Jack Petis, 1927...............**3.00**

Paradise Lane by Charles O'Flynn & Mickey Addy, 1933...................**5.00**

Paradise Rag, The by Goodwin & Meyer, 1911, Photo Anna Chandler (Cover Artist, Pfeiffer & Rag)...**16.00**

Paradise Street by C. Fox Smith & Alec Rowley, 1933 ....**5.00**

Paragon Rag by Scott Joplin (Cover Artist, Pfeiffer, Scott Joplin & Rag)..**55.00**

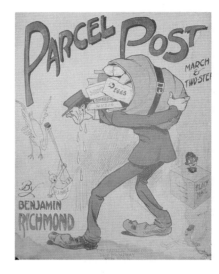

Parcel Post by Benjamin Richmond, 1913 (March) 16.00

Pardon Me Pretty Baby by Roy Klages, Jack Meskill & Vincent Ro, 1931...**5.00**

Pardon Me, While I Laugh by Jules Von Tilzer, Arthur Terker & Bill Heagney, 1925 (Cover Artist, Barbelle)...................................**10.00**

Pardon My Southern Accent by Johnny Mercer & Matt Malneck, 1934, Photo Borrah Minevitch **5.00**

Pardon That Came Too Late, The by Paul Dresser, 1891 (Pre 1900) ..**20.00**

Paris by Sammy Cahn & Nicholas Brodsky, 1951, Movie: Rich, Young & Pretty, Photo Jane Powell, Vic Damone, Fernando Lamas, Wendell Corey & Danielle Darrieux...**5.00**

Paris In The Spring by Mack Gordon & Harry Revel, 1935, Movie: Paris In The Spring, Photo Mary Ellis & Julio Carminati.........................**5.00**

Paris Lullaby by Webster & Fain, 1966, Movie: Made In Paris, Photo Ann Margaret & Louis Jourdain..**3.00**

Paris, Stay The Same by Clifford Grey & Victor Schertzinger, 1929, Movie: The Love Parade **5.00**

Paris Wakes Up And Smiles by Irving Berlin, 1949, Musical: Miss Liberty (Irving Berlin)..**10.00**

Parisian Ball, The by Lew Brown & Herman Paley, 1913...................**5.00**

Parisian Maxine by Nazareth, 1914..**6.00**

Parisian Moonlight by Joe Young & Grace Dalton, 1930.....................**5.00**

Parisienne by Lew Brown & Albert Von Tilzer, 1912, Photo Dave Kindler...**10.00**

Parkin' In The Moonlight by Charles Tobias, Charlie O'Flynn & Peter DeRose, 1931, Photo Larry Funk (Cover Artist, Cliff Miska).........**5.00**

Parkin' In The Park With You by Denniker, 1932 (Transportation)....**12.00**

Parted At The Altar by Gussie L. Davis, 1895 (Pre 1900) **15.00**

Parting by Francis C. Chantereau & Bernardo Fazioli, 1924 (Cover Artist, E.S. Fisher) **10.00**

Party Down by Shelly & Brackett, 1985, Movie: Witness, Photo Harrison Ford...**5.00**

Party's Over, The by Betty Comden, Adolph Green & Jule Styne, 1956, Movie: Bells Are Ringing, Photo Judy Holliday & Dean Martin **5.00**

Pass Me By by Coleman & Leigh, 1964, Movie: Father Goose, Photo Cary Grant & Leslie Caron...**8.00**

Pass That Peace Pipe by Roger Edens, Hugh Martin & Ralph Blane, 1947, Movie: Good News, Photo June Allyson & Peter Lawford **5.00**

Pass The Pickles by Grace LeBoy, 1913 ....**12.00**

Passage-Birds' Farewell by Eugen Hildach, 1926.....................**5.00**

Passing By by John Hess & Paul Misraki, Photo Jean Sablon **5.00**

Passion Flower by Irving Berlin, 1921 (Irving Berlin).........................**10.00**

Pat For Your Baby by Aubrey Boucicault, 1898 (Pre 1900).................**12.00**

Patches by J. Will Callahan & Lee S. Roberts, 1919 (Cover Artist, R. Van Buren) **10.00**

Path Of Flowers by John Dyson, 1887, Dedicated To The Rev. John B. Gough Pidge (Pre 1900, March & Dedication) **10.00**

Path That Leads To You, The by Arthur E. Buckman & Jacob Henry Ellis, 1913 (Cover Artist, Pfeiffer) **10.00**

Patria by Geo. Graff Jr. & Mrs. Vernon Castle, 1917, Inspired By Mrs. Vernon Castle In International Photo Play Patria (Patriotic)...15.00

Paul Revere's Ride by E.T. Paull, 1905 (Cover Artist, E.T. Paull & March) **35.00**

Pauline Waltz by Clarence M. Jones, 1914 ....**5.00**

Pauvre Rose Fanee by Arthur Smith & E.L. Turcot, 1916 (Cover Artist, RS)...........................**5.00**

Pavanne by Gladys Shelley & Morton Gould, 1938 ....**3.00**

Paxinosce by Ella Dinslow Jones, 1905 ....**10.00**

Peace Conference by Harry J. Lincoln, 1915 (March) **10.00**

Peace Of Mind by James Dyrenforth & Carroll Gibbons, 1929.............**5.00**

Peace Patrol, The by Charlie Chaplin, 1916, Photo Charlie Chaplin (Patriotic)....................................**24.00**

Peace, Peace, Reechoed Cheer by Schmidt & Cabello, 1915 (Cover Artist, Pfeiffer & WWI)....................................**15.00**

Peaceful Henry by Harry Kelly, 1901 (Rag) **10.00**

Peach Of A Pair, A by George Marion Jr. & Richard A. Whiting, 1930, Movie: Follow Thru, Photo Charles Rogers, Nancy Carroll, Zelma O'Neal & Jack Haley (Deco)....................................**10.00**

Peacherine by Scott Joplin, 1901 (Scott Joplin & Rag).........................**50.00**

Peaches by Bert Kalmar, Harry Ruby & Con Conrad, 1921 (Cover Artist, Barbelle) **5.00**

Peanut Vendor, The by L. Wolfe Gilbert, Albert Gamse, Moises Simons, 1931 ....**3.00**

Pearly Shells by Webley Edward & Leon Pober, 1964, Photo Billy Vaughn.........................**6.00**

Pecos Bill by Eliot Daniel & Johnny Lange, 1948, Movie: Melody Time (Disney) **10.00**

Peddler Man by Lawrence & Brodszky, 1954, Movie: Flame And The Flesh, Photo Lana Turner, Pier Angeli & Carlos Thompson **6.00**

Peek-A-Boo by Kessler, 1909 (Cover Artist, Pfeiffer).........................**15.00**

Peek-A-Boo by William J. Scanlon, 1881 (Pre 1900).........................**15.00**

Peek-A-Boo Moon by Bob Taylor, 1911 (Cover Artist, John Frew) ...**10.00**

Peg Away by Alfred Bevan, 1904 ....**5.00**

Peg O' My Heart by Alfred Bryan & Fred Fisher, 1913, Signed Photo Laurette Taylor, Dedicated To Laurette Taylor (Dedication, Irish & Signed)....................................**16.00**

Peg O' My Heart by Alfred Bryan & Fred Fisher, 1947, Photo Clark Dennis (Irish)....................................**3.00**

Peggy by Harry Williams & Neil Moret, 1919 (Cover Artist, Frederick S. Manning) **20.00**

Peggy O'Moore by William Scanlon, 1885 (Pre 1900 & Irish) **20.00**

Peggy O'Neil by Harry Pease, Ed. G. Nelson & Gilbert Dodge, 1921 (Cover Artist, Hamilton King & Irish) **35.00**

Peggy O'Neil by Harry Pease, Ed. G. Nelson & Gilbert Dodge, 1921, Photo Mildred Feeley (Cover Artist, JVR & Irish) **10.00**

Peggy O'Neil by Harry Pease, Ed G. Nelson & Gilbert Dodge, 1921, Photo Clara Morton (Cover Artist, JVR)....................................**10.00**

Pekin Peeks by Wade, 1916 (Cover Artist, Pfeiffer).........................**10.00**

Penguin At The Waldorf by Jimmy Eaton, Larry Wagner & Frank Shuman, 1947 ....**5.00**

Penitent, The by Beardsley Van de Water, 1892 (Pre 1900) **10.00**

Pennies From Heaven by John Burke & Arthur Johnston, 1936, Movie: Pennies From Heaven, Photo Bing Crosby **8.00**

Pennsylvania 6-500 by Sigman & Gray, 1940, Movie: The Glenn Miller Story, Photo James Stewart & June Allyson **6.00**

Pennsylvania Polka by Lester Lee & Zeke Manners, 1942, Movie: Give Out Sister, Photo Andrews Sisters (Cover Artist, Sig Chi).............**5.00**

Penny A Kiss–A Penny A Hug, A by Buddy Kaye & Ralph Care, 1940 ....**5.00**

Penny Serenade by Hal Hallifax & Melle Weersma, 1938 ....**3.00**

Penthouse Serenade by Will Jason & Val Burton, 1931 ....**3.00**

Peony Bush, The by Meredith Wilson, 1949.........................**3.00**

People Like You And Me by Mack Gordon & Harry Warren, 1942, Movie: Orchestra Wives: Photo Glenn Miller & Many Stars **8.00**

People Will Say We're In Love by Richard Rodgers & Oscar Hammerstein II, 1943, Musical: Oklahoma (Cover Artist, Holley)..............**8.00**

Pepeeta by R.E. Hildreth, 1903 (Cover Artist, H.C. Whorf) **5.00**

Pepper Pot by Harold Ivers, 1913 (Cover Artist, DeTakacs) **15.00**

Pepper-Up by Harry J. Lincoln, 1920, Photo Harris Bros. Famous Jazz Orchestra (March)........................**10.00**

Peppermint Twist by Joey Dee & Henry Glover, 1961 ....**3.00**

Perfect Day, A by Carrie Jacobs Bond, 1910, Linen Cover **15.00**

Perfect Song, The by Clarence Lucas & Joseph Carl Brill, 1929, Musical Theme Of The Pepsodent Hour, Advertising For Pepsodent Toothpaste, Photo Of Amos & Andy (Advertising & Black, Black Face) **75.00**

Perfectly Terrible by James O'Dea & Anna Caldwell, 1908, Musical: The Top O'The World, Photo Emma Janvier.....................................**12.00**

Perhaps by L.M. French, 1898, Photo Elgie Bowen, Music Supplement Of The New York Journal And Advertiser, Sunday, September 19,1901 (Cover Artist, K.E.R.R. & Pre 1900).....................................**15.00**

Perhaps She's On The Railroad by F. Blume, 1870 (Pre 1900) **35.00**

Pernambuco by Frank Loesser, 1948, Movie: Where's Charley, Caricature Ray Bolger........................**6.00**

Perry's Victory March by Martin, 1913 (Cover Artist, Pfeiffer, March & Military Personnel) **20.00**

Pershing's Crusaders by E.T. Paull, 1918 (Cover Artist, E.T.Paull, March & WW1) **35.00**

Persian Lamb Rag by Percy Wenrich, 1913 (Rag)............................**10.00**

Persian Moon by Cliff Hess & M. B. Kaufman, 1919.........................**5.00**

Persian Pearl by Dave Allan & Bob Allan, 1917..............................**5.00**

Persian Rug by Gus Kahn & Neil Moret, 1927 ....**6.00**

Personality by Henry Blossom & Victor Herbert, 1914, Musical: The Only Girl (Victor Herbert)..**10.00**

Personality by Johnny Burke & James Van Heusen, 1945, Movie: The Road To Utopia, Photo Bing Crosby, Bob Hope & Dorothy Lamour.......**10.00**

Pet Of The Ranch by Kaiser, 1906 ....**5.00**

Peter Cottontail by Steve Nelson & Jack Rollins, 1950 ....**3.00**

Peter Gink from "Peer Gynt" Suite by Geo L. Cobb, 1918 (Cover Artist, Starmer) **5.00**

Peter Gunn by Henry Mancini, 1958, T.V. Theme Music.....................**5.00**

Peter Pan I Love You by Robert King & Ray Henderson, 1924, Movie: Peter Pan, Photo Miss Marilyn Miller, Dedicated To Marilyn Miller (Dedication) **18.00**

Petite Tarantella by Stephen Heller, 1924 ....**2.00**

Petite Waltz, The by E.A. Ellington, Phyllis Claire & Joe Heyne, 1950, Signed Photo Anne Shelton (Signed) **10.00**

Petite Waltz, The by E.A. Ellington, Phyllis Claire & Joe Heyne, 1950, Signed Photo Guy Lombardo (Signed) **10.00**

Petticoats Of Portugal by Michael Durso, Mel Mitchell & Murl Kahn, 1956, Photo Dick Jacobs **5.00**

Phantom Isle by Mamie E. Williams, 1913, Dedicated To Miss Corinne Miller (Dedication) **10.00**

Phil The Fluter's Ball by W.P. French, 1937...**5.00**

Phoebe Jane by Richard Henry Buck & Theodore Morse, 1910...........**5.00**

Phone Bell Rang, The by Mack & Orth, 1910 (Cover Artist, Pfeiffer)**10.00**

Phrenologist Coon, The by Hogan & Accooe, 1901 (Black, Black Face)..**20.00**

Pianissimo by Bernie Benjamin & George Weiss, 1947, Photo Perry Como **5.00**

Piano Concerto In Bb Minor by Peter I. Tschaikowsky, 1941 ....**2.00**

Piano Man by Irving Berlin, 1910 (Irving Berlin).................................**12.00**

Piccalilli Rag by Reeg & Daly, 1912 (Cover Artist, Pfeiffer & Rag) ..**15.00**

Piccolino, The by Irving Berlin, 1935, Movie: Top Hat, Photo Fred Astaire & Ginger Rogers (Irving Berlin)..**16.00**

Piccolo by Van Alstyne, 1912 (Cover Artist, Pfeiffer).........................**10.00**

Piccolo Pete by Phil Baxter, 1930 ....**5.00**

Piccolo, The by Irving Berlin, 1935, Movie: Top Hat, Photo Fred Astaire & Ginger Rogers (Irving Berlin) **16.00**

Pick A Chicken by Mel B. Kaufman, 1914 ....**10.00**

Pick A Little Four Leaf Clover, And Send It Over To Me by C. Francis Reisner, Ed Rose & Abe Olman, 1918 (Cover Artist, A. Brunne, Irish & WWI)..**10.00**

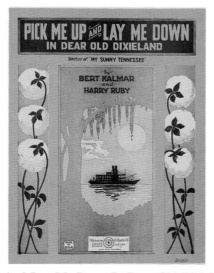

Pick Me Up And Lay Me Down In Dear Old Dixieland by Bert Kalmar & Harry Ruby, 1922 (Cover Artist, Barbelle, Dixie & Transportation)...12.00

Pick, Pick, Pick, Pick On The Mandolin by Irving Berlin, 1912 (Cover Artist, Pfeiffer & Irving Berlin)...**15.00**

Pick Yourself Up by Dorothy Fields & Jerome Kern, 1936, Movie: Swing Time, Photo Fred Astaire & Ginger Rogers **5.00**

Pickaninnies' Heaven by Sam Coslow & Arthur Johnston, 1932, Movie: Hello Everybody, Photo Kate Smith (Black, Black Face) **15.00**

Pickaninny Blues by Harold G. Frost & F. Henri Klickmann, 1919 (Blues & Black, Black Face **20.00**

Pickaninny Blues by McKiernan, 1924 (Blues & Black, Black Face).**15.00**

Pickaninny Waltz Lullaby Blues by Harold Frost & F. Henri Klickmann, 1919 (Blues & Black, Black Face) **20.00**

Pickaninny's Lullaby by Con Conrad, 1920 (Black, Black Face)........**10.00**

Pickaninny's Paradise, The by Sam Ehrlich & Nat Osborne, 1918 (Cover Artist, Pfeiffer & Black, Black Face) **15.00**

Pickanning Christening, A by Winthrop Wiley, 1902 (Black, Black Face)..**12.00**

Pickin' On De Ole Banjo by Widmer, 1915 (Cover Artist, Pfeiffer) ...**10.00**

Pickle In The Middle And The Mustard On Top by Carl Sigman, 1946, Photo Jack Benny **5.00**

Pickles & Peppers by Adaline Sheperd, 1907 (Rag) **20.00**

Picnic For Two, A by Arthur J. Lamb & Albert Von Tilzer, 1905, Photo Adele Ritchie **5.00**

Picture 84 by Charles B. Ward & Gussie L. Davis, 1894 (Pre 1900)...**15.00**

Picture No Artist Can Paint by Moran & Helf, 1899 (Pre 1900)..........**10.00**

Picture Of Dear Old Ireland, A by Costello, 1916 (Irish).....................**8.00**

Picture That Is Turned Toward The Wall by Charles Graham, 1891 (Pre 1900)..**10.00**

Picture The World Loves Best, The by Whitson, Livernash & Ballin, 1916 (Cover Artist, Pfeiffer) **10.00**

Pierrot, Pierette by L. Wolfe Gilbert & Leo Edwards, 1916 ....**5.00**

Pigeon Walk by James V. Monaco, 1914 (Cover Artist, DeTakacs) ...**10.00**

Pilgrim's Chorus, Opera Gems, 1910 (Cover Artist, Pfeiffer) **10.00**

Pine Apple Rag by Scott Joplin, 1908 (Scott Joplin & Rag)...............**50.00**

Piney Ridge by Ballard Macdonald & Halsey K. Mohr, 1915 (Cover Artist, DeTakacs)..**10.00**

Pining Just For You by Bernard & Freeman, 1916 (Cover Artist, Pfeiffer)...**10.00**

Pink Elephants by Mort Dixon & Harry Woods, 1932.........................**3.00**

Pink Elephants On Parade by Oliver Wallace, Frank Churchill & Ned Washington, 1941, Movie: Dumbo (Disney) **10.00**

Pink Panther by Henry Mancini, Signed by Henry Mancini (Signed) .**20.00**

Pink Poodle by Charles L. Johnson, 1914 ....**3.00**

Pinocchio by Leigh Harline & Ned Washington, 1940, Movie: Pinocchio (Disney) **15.00**

Pioneer by Lincoln, 1915 (Cover Artist, Pfeiffer, March & Deco)......**20.00**

Pioneer Limited by Harry Lincoln, 1910 (Transportation)...................**20.00**

Pioneer Song, The by Kim Gannon & Walter Kent, 1948, Movie: Melody Time (Disney)..**10.00**

Pious Peter Cakewalk by Egbert Van Alstyne, 1898 (Pre 1900 & Black, Black Face)..**20.00**

Pipe Dreaming by Cole Porter, Movie: Around The World...................**5.00**

Pipe Of Peace, The by Havez & Hitland, 1907 (Cover Artist, Pfeiffer & Indian)...**25.00**

Pipe Organ Rag , The by S.G. Rhodes, 1912 (Rag)............................**10.00**

Pirate Bold, A by C.F.D. & Emil Fisher, 1927....................................**10.00**

Pirate Dreams by Charles Huerter, 1917 ....**5.00**

Pistol Packin' Mama by Al Dexter, 1943 ....**10.00**

Pitcher Of Beer by Edward Harrigan & David Braham, 1880 (Pre 1900)..**15.00**

Pitter Patter Rag by Jos. M. Daly, 1910 (Rag)....................................**10.00**

Pizzicato Polka by Richard Drigo, 1920..**4.00**

Place For Lovers, A, by Gimbel & DeSica, 1969, Movie: A Place For Lovers, Photo Faye Dunaway & Marcello Mastroianni..................**3.00**

Place For Me Am Home, The (Cover Artist, Pfeiffer) **10.00**

Plaisir D'Amour by Florian & Henry Fevrier, 1904............................**10.00**

Planning, "Pretty's" The Picture I'm Planning by Will D. Cobb & Gus Edwards, 1910 ....**6.00**

Plant A Little Garden In Your Own Back Yard by Fred Leopold, 1917 (WWI)..............................**10.00**

Plant A Watermelon On My Grave & Let The Juice Soak Through by Dumont & Lilly, 1910 (Cover Artist, Pfeiffer) **15.00**

Plant You Now, Dig You Later by Lorenz Hart & Richard Rodgers, 1940, Musical: Pal Joey..............................**5.00**

Plantation Lullaby by Vernon Stevens, Gladys Gillette & Albert Holmes, 1921 (Cover Artist, F. Earl Christy, Deco & Black, Black Face)..............................**25.00**

Plantation Tunes by N. Louise Wright, 1928 (Cover Artist, Lyle Justus & Black, Black Face)..............................**10.00**

Play A Simple Melody by Irving Berlin, 1914 (Irving Berlin).............**10.00**

Play Days by Mort Nathan & John Cooper, 1920 (Cover Artist, Starmer)..............................**5.00**

Play, Fiddle Play by Jack Lawrence, Emery Deutsch & Arthur Altman, 1932, Photo Emery Deutsch (Cover Artist, Frederick S. Manning)..**6.00**

Play Fiddle, Play by Jack Lawrence, Emery Deutsch & Arthur Altman, 1932, Photo Mark Fisher (Cover Artist, Frederick S. Manning)....**20.00**

Play Gypsies–Dance Gypsies by Emerich Kalman & Harry B. Smith, 1924, Musical: Countess Maritza **6.00**

Play Me A Dixie Melody by Harold G. Frost & F. Henri Klickmann, 1920 (Dixie)..............................**10.00**

Play Me A Good Old Fashioned Melody by Grant & Morrisset, 1912 (Cover Artist, Pfeiffer) **10.00**

Play Me A Hurtin' Tune by Sylvia Dee & Sid Lippman, 1952, Photo Andrews Sisters & Guy Lombardo **4.00**

Play Me Hearts & Flowers by Mann Curtis & Sanford Green, 1945, Photo Johnny Desmond **3.00**

Play Me That Sweet Melody by Jack Snyder, 1922 ....**5.00**

Play That Barber Shop Chord by Tracey & Muir, 1910........................**5.00**

Play That Song Of India Again by Leo Wood & Erving Bibo, 1921 (Cover Artist, Lionel S. Reiss & Deco)..............................**12.00**

Play To Me Gypsy by Jimmy Kennedy & Karel Vacek, 1932...............**5.00**

Playing Soldiers by Leon Jessel, 1927..............................**5.00**

Playmates by Fred Fisher, 1922..............................**5.00**

Playmates by Harry Dacre, 1889 (Pre 1900) **10.00**

Playmates by Johnny Burke & James V. Monaco, 1940.......................**5.00**

Playmates by Saxie Dowell, 1940 (Cover Artist HBK) **5.00**

Pleasant Dreams by Mary Earl, 1919 ....**10.00**

Pleasant Dreams by Pete Wendling & Max Kortlander, 1922, Photo Mort Kortlander (Deco) **10.00**

Pleasant Moments Ragtime Waltz by Scott Joplin (Scott Joplin & Rag)..**50.00**

Please Be Kind by Sammy Cahn & Saul Chaplin, 1938, Photo Barry McKinley (Cover Artist, Merman)..............................**4.00**

Please Believe Me by Larry Yoell & Al Jacobs, 1935 ....**3.00**

Please by Leo Robin & Ralph Rainger, 1932, Movie: The Big Broadcast, Photo Bing Crosby, Kate Smith & Many Other Stars...................**15.00**

Please by Sam M. Lewis, Joe Young & Joe Cooper, 1924 ....**3.00**

Please Come Out Of Your Dream by Carl Sigman, 1938 ....**3.00**

Please Do My Family A Favor & Love Me by Clarke & Abrahams, 1914 (Cover Artist, Pfeiffer) **10.00**

Please Don't Love Anybody Else But Me by Smith, 1913 ....**5.00**

Please Don't Monkey With Broadway by Cole Porter, 1939, Movie: Broadway Melody Of 1940, Photo Fred Astaire & Eleanor Powell (Cover Artist, Im-Ho)..............................**8.00**

Please Don't Say "No" by Ralph Freed & Sammy Fain, 1944, Movie: Thrill Of A Romance, Photo Lauritz Melchior, Van Johnson, Esther Williams & Tommy Dorsey **6.00**

Please Don't Take My Lovin' Man Away by Lew Brown & Albert Von Tilzer, 1912, Photo Watson Sisters **10.00**

Please Don't Talk About Me When I'm Gone by Sammy Stept & Sidney Clare, 1930, Movie: Lullaby Of Broadway..............................**5.00**

Please Keep Me In Your Dreams by Tot Seymour & Vee Lawnhurst, 1936..............................**4.00**

Please Learn To Love by B.C. Hilliam, 1919, Musical: Buddies.........**10.00**

Please Let Me Sleep by McPherson & Brymm, 1902 ....**10.00**

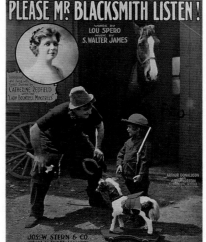

Please Mr. Blacksmith Listen! by Lou Spero & S. Walter James, 1918, From Minstrel "Lady Bountiful Minstrels," Photo Catherine Redfield **15.00**

Please Mr. Conductor Take Me On Your Car by Learned, 1911 (Transportation) **15.00**

Please Mr. Sun by Sid Frank & Ray Geton, 1951. Signed Photo Johnnie Ray (Signed)..............................**5.00**

Please Oh Please by Hanlon & Morrissey, 1912 (Cover Artist, Pfeiffer)..**10.00**

Please, Please Me by Beatles..............................**20.00**

Please, Please, Pretty Please by Jones & Randall, 1909 (Cover Artist, Pfeiffer & Deco) **15.00**

Please Remember by Bobby Troup & Walter Gross, 1953, Photo The Four Freshmen **3.00**

Please Take Me Back Again by James A. Brennan, 1919...................**10.00**

Please Think Of Me by Benny Davis, Russ Morgan & Ted Murry, 1942, Photo Vincent Lopez **3.00**

Please Think Of Me by Benny Davis, Russ Morgan & Ted Murry, 1942, Photo Freddy Martin..............................**3.00**

Plenty Hawk (Cover Artist, Pfeiffer & Indian)..............................**20.00**

Plenty Of Sunshine by B.G. DeSylva, Lew Brown & Ray Henderson, 1927 ....**5.00**

Pliney, Come Kiss Your Baby by David Reed Jr. 1899 (Pre 1900 & Black, Black Face)..............................**25.00**

Plum Pudding by Edward Harrigan & David Braham, 1884 (Pre 1900)...**15.00**

Poeme by Romberg, 1913..............................**10.00**

Poet's Dream by Alfred Solman, 1899, Boston Herald Sunday Supplement (Pre 1900) **10.00**

Poinciana by Buddy Bernier & Nat Simon, 1936..............................**3.00**

Poinsettia by C.Edward Storer, 1911..............................**5.00**

Polar Bear Polka by Albert Berg, 1865 (Pre 1900) **55.00**

Policemen's Ball, The by Irving Berlin, 1949, Musical: Miss Liberty (Irving Berlin)..............................**12.00**

Polka Dot Polka, The by Leo Robin & Harry Warren, 1943, Movie: The Gang's All Here, Photo Alice Faye, Carmen Miranda, Phil Baker & The King Of Swing, Benny Goodman **12.00**

Pollie, Do You Love Me? by John Kemble & Lester W. Keith, 1906 ..**10.00**

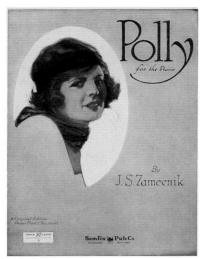

Polly by J. S. Zamecnick, 1926 ....**5.00**

Polly Put The Kettle On by Joseph McCarthy & Harry Tierney, 1918, Musical: Kid Boots...**5.00**

Polly's A Peach by George M. Cohan, 1896 (George M. Cohan & Pre 1900) **15.00**

Polly-Wolly Doodle by Sidney Clare & B.G. DeSylva, 1935, Movie: The Littlest Rebel, Photo Shirley Temple (Shirley Temple) **12.00**

Pompanola by Anne Caldwell, Raymond Hubbell, B.G. DeSylva, Lew Brown & Ray Henderson, 1928, Musical: Three Cheers **5.00**

Pond-Lily Time by Harold G. Frost & F. Henri Klickmann, 1920 ....**5.00**

Poor Bird Of Paradise by Frank Williams & Geo Krause, 1922 ....**5.00**

Poor Butterfly by John Golden & Ray Hubbell, 1916 ....**10.00**

Poor Irish Minstrel by Willie Scanlon, 1882 (Pre 1900 & Irish).........**20.00**

Poor John by Leigh & Pether, 1906..**8.00**

Poor Jud by Richard Rodgers & Oscar Hammerstein II, 1943, Musical: Oklahoma...**5.00**

Poor Little Butterfly Is A Fly Girl Now by Sam Lewis, Joe Young & M. K. Jerome, 1919 (Cover Artist, Frederick S. Manning & WWI) ...**20.00**

Poor Little Heart Broken Doll by Harry Pease, Ed. G. Nelson & Fred Mayo, 1919 (Cover Artist, Dunk)..............................**6.00**

Poor Little Puritan Maiden by Billy Day, 1917 (Cover Artist, Pfeiffer) ..**10.00**

Poor Little Rhode Island by Sammy Cahn & Jule Styne, 1944..............**5.00**

Poor Little Rich Girl, 1913 (Cover Artist, Pfeiffer)............................**12.00**

Poor Little Rich Girl by Jack Caddigan & James A. Brennan, 1914......**6.00**

Poor Little Rich Girl, The by Lew Brown & Herman Paley, 1913, Dedicated To Miss Viola Dana (Dedication) **12.00**

Poor Lizzie by Louis Silver, 1928 (Transportation) **15.00**

Poor Marionette by Gus Kahn & Ted Fiorito, 1931 ....**5.00**

Poor Me by Olin Finney & Bert Adams, 1921 (Cover Artist, James Montgomery Flagg) **40.00**

Poor Papa, He's Got Nothing At All by Billy Rose & Harry Woods, 1926, Photo Bob Cause & His Collegians...**5.00**

Poor Pauline by Chas. McCarron & Raymond Walker, Photo Pearl White **10.00**

Poor People Of Paris, The by Jack Lawrence & Marguerite Monnot, 1956...**3.00**

Pop Corn Man by Will Hudson, Lou Klein & Bill Livingston, 1937.....**3.00**

Pop Goes The Bubble And Soap Gets In My Eyes by Ted Koehler & Burton Lane, 1937, Movie: Artists And Models, Photo Jack Benny **5.00**

Pop Goes Your Heart by Mort Dixon & Allie Wrubel, 1934, Movie: Happiness Ahead, Photo Dick Powell & Josephine Hutchinson **5.00**

Popocatepetl by Bill Hampton & George Dunning, 1941 ....**5.00**

Poppa, Don't Preach To Me by Frank Loesser, 1947, Movie: The Perils Of Pauline, Photo Betty Hutton & John Lund **5.00**

Poppies by Neil Moret, 1904 (Cover Artist, Gene Buck)....................**10.00**

Poppy The Puppy by Johnston, 1951, Photo Gene Autry **3.00**

Poppy Time In Old Japan by E. J. Meyers & Will E. Dulmage, 1915 (Cover Artist, Dulin Studios)...**10.00**

Poppyland by John Henry Mears, Bud DeSylva & George Gershwin, 1920 (Deco) **10.00**

Popsy by Marvin Lee & Al Copeland, 1921 ....**5.00**

Popularity by George M. Cohan, 1906, Photo George M. Cohan (Cover Artist, Rose, George M. Cohan & March) **16.00**

Porcelain Maid by Irving Berlin, 1922, Musical: Music Box Review (Cover Artist, R.S. & Irving Berlin)...**12.00**

Porgy by Dorothy Fields & Jimmy McHugh, 1928, Musical: Blackbirds Of 1928 (Cover Artist, Leff)..**5.00**

Pork And Beans by C. Luckyth Roberts, 1913 (Cover Artist, DeTakacs & Deco) **40.00**

Port Of God Knows Where, The by Wood & DeCosta, 1916 (Cover Artist, Pfeiffer)...**10.00**

Port Of Missing Ships, The by Robert F. Roden & H.W. Petrie, 1910 (Transportation) **15.00**

Portobello Road by Sherman & Sherman, 1971, Movie: Bedknobs & Broomsticks, Photo Angela Lansbury & David Tomlinson............**8.00**

Portrait Of Jennie by Gordon Burge & J. Russel Robinson, 1948, Dedicated To Jennifer Jones, Movie, Portrait Of Jennie, Photo Jennifer Jones (Dedication)..**6.00**

Portrait Of My Love by David West & Cyril Ornadel, 1961, Photo Steve Lawrence **3.00**

Portrait, Photo Of President Taft & Crossed American Flags (Presidents, March & Patriotic)..**40.00**

Possum Song by Dunham & Terry Shand, 1947, Photo Vaughn Monroe...**3.00**

Postage Due by Pee Wee King, Redd Stewart & John Marshal, 1952...**3.00**

Pots And Pans by Charley Grapewin & Jean Schwartz, 1911 (Cover Artist, Starmer)...**12.00**

Pourquoi Les P'tits Cochons! by Raymond Vincy, Ph. Loriol & Ch. Borel-Clerc, 1939, Photo Rolland Bedard **5.00**

Poverty Rag by Harry J. Lincoln, 1909 (Rag) **15.00**

Poverty's Tears Ebb And Flow by Edward Harrigan & David Braham, 1885 (Pre 1900) **15.00**

Powder Blue by Gladys Shelley, Paul McGrane & Harry Moss, 1944 ..**3.00**

Powder Rag by Raymond Birch, 1908 (Cover Artist, Sweeny & Rag) ..**10.00**

Powder Your Face With Sunshine by Carmen Lombardo & Stanley Rochinski, 1948, Photo Lebert, Carmen & Guy Lombardo (Cover Artist, Nick) **5.00**

Power Of Love, The by Colla, Hayes & Lewis, 1985, Movie: Back To The Future, Photo Huey Lewis & The News..**3.00**

Practice Makes Perfect by Don Roberts & Ernest Gold, 1940 (Cover Artist, Im-Ho & Deco)...**5.00**

Practising Up On You by Howard Dietz & Phil Craig, 1930, Movie: Three's A Crowd **5.00**

Prairie Lullaby by Billy Hill, 1934 ....**3.00**

Prairie Rose by Jess Williams & Walter Dill, 1923................................**5.00**

Praise The Lord And Pass The Ammunition! by Frank Loesser, 1942 (WWII) **10.00**

Prancing Pickaninnies by Andrew Sterling & Max Dreyfus, 1899 (Pre 1900 & Black, Black Face)...**20.00**

Pray For The Lights To Go Out by Will E. Skidmore, 1916...............**10.00**

Prayer by June Weybright, 1960...**3.00**

Preacher & The Bear, The by Joe Arzonia, 1938 ....**3.00**

Precious by Raymond Egan, Stephen Pasterbacki & Richard Whiting, 1926 (Cover Artist, JVR & Deco) **8.00**

Precious Little One by Walter G. Samuels, Leonard Whitcup & Teddy Powell, 1935 ....**5.00**

Precious Little Thing Called Love, A by Lou Davis & J. Fred Coots, 1928, Movie: The Shopworn Angel, Photo Gary Cooper & Nancy Carroll (Cover Artist, Leff & Deco) **10.00**

Prelude In C Sharp Minor by Rachmaninoff, 1936 (Deco) **10.00**

Prelude To A Kiss by Irving Gordon, Irving Mills & Duke Ellington, 1938 ....**6.00**

President Garfield Funeral March (President, March & Political) **45.00**

President's Birthday Ball, The by Irving Berlin, 1942 (Irving Berlin).**10.00**

Pretend by Lew Douglas, Cliff Parman & Frank Lavere, 1952, Photo Ralph Marterie..**2.00**

Pretending by Marty Symes & Al Sherman, 1946, Photo Bing Crosby.**5.00**

Pretty As A Picture by Cooper & Bishop, 1872 (Pre 1900) **15.00**

Pretty As A Picture by John E. Barth, 1903 ....**10.00**

Pretty Baby by Kahn, Jackson & Van Alstyne, 1906, Photo Dolly Hackett ..**5.00**

Pretty Cinderella by Will J. Harris, 1926..**4.00**

Pretty Doll by Black & LeGrand, 1968, Movie: A Matter Of Innocence, Photo Hayley Mills..**4.00**

Pretty Face by F. Goulart, 1911 ....**10.00**

Pretty Girl, A Summer's Night by Goodwin & W. Morse, 1891 (Pre 1900)...**10.00**

Pretty Girl Is Like A Melody, A by Irving Berlin, 1919, Movie: Ziegfeld Follies 1919 (Irving Berlin)..**16.00**

Pretty Girl Milking The Cow, The by Frank Furlett, 1940, Photo Art Kassel (Cover Artist, NPS & Irish) **5.00**

Pretty Jennie Slattery by Lawlor & Blake, 1896 (Pre 1900) **10.00**

Pretty Kitty Blue Eyes by Mann Curtis & Vic Mizzy, 1944 ....**3.00**

Pretty Kitty Kelly by Harry Pease & Ed Nelson, 1920, (Lithograph Knapp & Irish) **10.00**

Pretty Little Baby by Sid Silvers & Ben Bernie, 1925 ....**3.00**

Pretty Little Carolina Rose by James Bland (Pre 1900 & Black, Black Face) **20.00**

Pretty Little Dinah Jones by J. S. Mullen, 1902 (Black, Black Face) ..**20.00**

Pretty Little Rainbow, An Indian Love Song by Robert Levenson & Vincent Plunkett, 1919 (Indian) **20.00**

Pretty Little Thing by Tommy Malie & Little Jack Little, 1929 ....**3.00**

Pretty Little Tonkin Girl by Christine, 1907..**5.00**

Pretty Little You by Ben Ryan & Violinsky, 1929..................................**5.00**

Pretty Mamie Clancy by Charles Shackford, 1904................................**8.00**

Pretty Mollie Shannon by Ryan & Wolff, 1901 ....**10.00**

Pretty Peggy by Earl Carroll, 1923, Musical: Earl Carroll Vanities Of 1923 ....**6.00**

Pretzel Pete by Hampton Durand, 1906..**8.00**

Pride Of My Heart And Home by Franklin E. Parker & Claude Weber, 1903 ....**10.00**

Pride Of The Century by Harry J. Lincoln, 1917 ....**5.00**

Pride Of The Prairie by Harry J. Breen & George Botsfors, 1907, Photo Howard & Lewis **8.00**

Prince Imperial Galop by Coote, 1908 (Cover Artist, Pfeiffer)...........**10.00**

Prince Of Pyramid Island by Gladys G. Dennis & Harry H. Williams, 1915 (Cover Artist, Acme Engraving Co.)......................................**10.00**

Princess Beloved by J. W. Cowan & Ry Hibbeler, 1929 ....**3.00**

Princess Rag by James Scott, 1913 (Rag)..**10.00**

Prisoner Of Love by Leo Robin & Russ Columbo, 1931, Photo Perry Como **5.00**

Prisoner's Song, The by Guy Massey, 1924..**5.00**

Private Tommy Atkins by Hamilton & Potter, 1893 (Military Personnel & Pre 1900)...**20.00**

Prize Cake Walk Of The Blackville Swells by Walter V. Uliner, 1899 (Pre 1900 & Black, Black Face)..**22.00**

Prodigal Son by Bill Nye, 1891 (Pre 1900) **10.00**

Prohibition Blues by Ring Lardner & Nora Bayes, 1919 (Blues) **10.00**

Prohibition You Have Lost Your Sting by J. Russel Robinson, Al Siegel & Billy Curtis, Photo Sophie Tucker...**10.00**

Promise by Maurice Gunsky & Eddie Willis, 1926 ....**3.00**

Promise Me Everything, Never Get Anything Blues by Harry Pease & Al Nelson, 1924 (Blues) **10.00**

Promises by Al Hoffman, Milton Drake & Jerry Livingston, 1945, Photo Guy Lombardo (Cover Artist, J. Geyler)..**3.00**

Promises by Al Sherman & Al Lewis, 1930, Photo Byron Holiday (Cover Artist, Leff & Deco) **6.00**

Proud Of A Baby Like You by Schonberg, Stevens & Helnick, 1926...**3.00**

Prove It By The Things You Do by Allan Roberts & Doris Fisher, 1945.**3.00**

Prunella by Atteridge & Carroll, 1914 (Cover Artist, Pfeiffer & Deco) ..**10.00**

Public Melody Number One by Ted Koehler & Harold Arlen, 1937, Movie: Artists & Models, Photo Jack Benny **6.00**

Publican, The by Beardsley Van de Water, 1920 ....**4.00**

Pucker Up And Whistle by Blanche Franklyn & Nat Vincent, 1921, Photo Yvette Rugel (Cover Artist, Barbelle) **10.00**

Puddin' Head Jones by Alfred Bryan & Lou Handman, 1933, Photo Ozzie Nelson..**6.00**

Pulaski Quick Step by James Hooton, Dedicated To General J.L.S. Amee, 1836 (Cover Artist, Thomas Moore, March, Pre 1900 & Dedication) **35.00**

Pullman Porter Blues by Clifford Ulrich & Burton Hamilton, 1921 (Transportation) **20.00**

Pullman Porters On Parade by Irving Berlin, 1913 (Irving Berlin & Transportation) **20.00**

Pullman Porters Parade, The by Ren G. May & Maurice Abrahams, 1913, Photo Murray J. Simons, Photo Train With Porters Marching, New York Central (Cover Artist, Pfeiffer, March & Transportation) **20.00**

Purple Road by Effa Preston & James Beam, 1928.................................**5.00**

Purple Roses by Belle Fenstock, 1942, Dedicated To Glenn Miller (Dedication) **15.00**

Push Dem Clouds Away by Percy Gaunt, 1892 (Pre 1900) **10.00**

Pussy Cat Rag, The by Allen & Daly, 1913 (Cover Artist, Pfeiffer & Rag) **15.00**

Pussy Cat Song, The by Dick Manning, 1948, Photo Bob Crosby & Patty Andrews **6.00**

Pussy Foot by Slap White, 1916...**5.00**

Put A Little Salt On The Bluebird's Tail by Dowling, Hanley & Brockman, 1930, Movie: Blaze Of Glory, Photo Eddie Dowling **6.00**

Put Away A Little Ray Of Golden Sunshine by Sam M. Lewis & Joe Young, 1924, Photo Freeman Sisters (Deco) **5.00**

Put Away A Little Ray Of Golden Sunshine by Sam M. Lewis & Joe Young, 1924, Photo Louise & Mitchell (Deco) **5.00**

Put Away A Little Ray Of Golden Sunshine by Sam M. Lewis & Joe Young, 1924, Photo Lorraine & Minto (Deco) **5.00**

Put Away A Little Ray Of Golden Sunshine by Sam M. Lewis, Joe Young & Fred E. Allert, 1924, Photo Florence King.................................**5.00**

Put 'Em In A Box by Sammy Cahn & Jule Styne, 1948, Movie: Romance On The High Seas, Photo Jack Carson, Janis Paige, Don DeFore & Doris Day...**6.00**

Put It There Pal by Johnny Burke & James Van Heusen, 1945, Movie: Road To Utopia, Photo Bing Crosby, Bob Hope & Dorothy Lamour...**6.00**

Put Me Off At Buffalo by Harry & John Dillon, 1895 (Pre 1900 & Transportation) **20.00**

Put Me To Sleep In Your Heart Dear by Sam Lewis, Joe Young & Bert Grant, 1919 (Cover Artist, Haven & Lithograph by Knapp)....20.00

Put Me To Sleep With An Old Fashioned Melody, Wake Me Up With A Rag by Sam M. Lewis, Dick Howard & Harry Jentes, 1915 (Cover Artist, DeTakacs & Rag) **15.00**

Put Me To The Test by Ira Gershwin & Jerome Kern, 1944, Movie: Cover Girl..**4.00**

Put My Little Shoes Away by Mitchell & Pratt, 1873 (Pre 1900)........**15.00**

Put On A Happy Face by Lee Adams & Charles Strouse, 1960, Movie: Bye Bye Birdie **6.00**

Put On De Golden Shoe by Dan Lewis, 1881 (Black, Black Face & Pre 1900)...**15.00**

Put On Your Old Grey Bonnet by Stanley Murphy & Percy Wenrich, 1909 (Cover Artist, DeTakacs)..**15.00**

Put That Ring On My Finger by Sunny Skylar & Randy Ryan, 1945 ...**3.00**

Put The Blame On Mame by Roberts & Fisher, 1946, Movie: Gilda, Photo Rita Hayworth...**8.00**

Put Your Arms Around Me, Honey by Junie McCree & Albert Von Tilzer, 1910, Musical: Madame Sherry, Photo Alta Virginia Houston **15.00**

Put Your Arms Around Me, Honey by Junie McCree & Albert Von Tilzer, 1910, Photo Elizabeth Murray..**15.00**

Put Your Arms Around Me, Honey by Junie McCree & Albert Von Tilzer, 1910, Musical: Madame Sherry, Photo Anna Boyd....................**15.00**

Put Your Arms Around Me, Honey by Junie McCree & Albert Von Tilzer, 1937, Movie: Coney Island, Photo Betty Grable, George Montgomery & Cesar Romero (Cover Artist, Manning) **16.00**

Put Your Arms Where They Belong by Davis, Santly & Ackman, 1926 ..**3.00**

Put Your Dreams Away by Ruth Lowe, Paul Mann & Stephan Weiss, 1942 ....**3.00**

Put Your Head On My Shoulder by Paul Anka, 1958 ....**5.00**

Put Your Heart In A Song by Churchill & Webster, 1938, Movie: Breaking The Ice, Photo Bobby Breen & Irene Dare **5.00**

Put-Put-Put Your Arms Around Me by Al Hoffman, Mann Curtis & Jerry Livingston, 1942, Photo Tommy Tucker.......................................**4.00**

Put-Put-Put Your Arms Around Me by Al Hoffman, Mann Curtis & Jerry Livingston, 1942, Photo Jack Coffey **4.00**

Puttin On The Ritz by Irving Berlin, 1927, Movie: Blue Skies, Photo Bing Crosby, Fred Astaire & Joan Caulfield (Irving Berlin).................**15.00**

Puzzled Little Cooks by Lytton Cox & Henry S. Sawyer, 1926 ....**3.00**

Q Galop by Leggett, 1884 (Pre 1900 & Transportation) **20.00**

Quality Rag by James Scott, 1911 (Rag)..**10.00**

Que Sera, Sera, Whatever Will Be, Will Be by Jay Livingston & Ray Evans, 1955, Photo Mary Hopkins...**3.00**

Queen Of Hearts, The by J.W. Bratton, 1898 (Pre 1900 & March) **15.00**

Queen Of The Carnival by Walter V. Ullner, 1898 (Pre 1900)............**10.00**

Queen Of The Carnival March by Warner, 1923 (March) **5.00**

Queen Of The Garden by Martin, 1912 (Cover Artist, Pfeiffer) **10.00**

Quentin's Theme by Robert Cobert, 1969...**2.00**

Querida by Edward G. Simon & Jose Valdez, 1929.............................**3.00**

Quest, The by Smith, 1885 (Pre 1900) **10.00**

Quicksilver by Irving Taylor, George Wyle & Eddie Pola, 1949, Photo Bing Crosby..**4.00**

Quiet by Dorothy Dickinson & Wilfrid Sanderson, 1929 ....**3.00**

Quiet Cathedral, The by Iris Mason & Hal Saunders, 1945 ....**3.00**

Quiet Nights Of Quiet Stars by Antonio Carlos Jobin & Gene Lees, 1944...**3.00**

Quit Cryin' The Blues by Felix Lewis, 1931 (Cover Artist, Hap Hadley Studio, Blues & Black, Black Face)...**15.00**

Race Course March, The by E.T. Paull & Glogau (Cover Artist, E.T. Paull & March) **35.00**

Racing Down The Rapids by Lawrence, 1888 (Pre 1900 & Transportation) **25.00**

Rackety Coo! by Otto Hauerback & Rudolf Friml, 1915, Musical: Katinka **6.00**

Radiance In Your Eyes, The by Lieut Ivor Novello, Royal Flying Corps, England, 1918 (Military Personnel) **15.00**

Radio Lady O'Mine by Sam Coslow, Bernard Grossman & Wright & Bessinger, 1924 ....**10.00**

Raffle For The Stove by J.E. Murphy, 1879 (Pre 1900).....................**15.00**

Rag Baby Rag by F. H. Losey, 1909 (Cover Artist, Dittmar, Rag & Black, Black Face)..**20.00**

Rag Classique by Harvy E. Van Dyke, 1915 (Rag).............................**10.00**

Rag Doll by Nacio Herb Brown, 1928 ....**5.00**

Rag Of Rags Syncoper, The by William E. Macquinn, 1915 (Rag).....**10.00**

Rag Picker by Raymond Leveen, George Hayes & Frankie Carle, 1939 .**5.00**

Rag, Rag, Rag by Heat & Flanagan, 1912 (Cover Artist, Pfeiffer & Rag)...**15.00**

Rag Time Drafted Man by Private Arthur E. Williams, 1918 (Cover Artist, Starmer,WWI, Military Personnel, Rag & Black, Black Face)......**32.00**

Rag Time Eating Place by Trombley & Manley, 1912 (Rag) **10.00**

Rag-A-Tag-Rag by Al. W. Brown, 1909 (Rag)........................**10.00**

Rag-Bag by Harry J. Lincoln, 1909 (Rag)..........................**15.00**

Ragamuffin by Jesse Greer, 1929 ....**10.00**

Ragged Edges Rag by Otto Frey, 1910 (Rag).......................**10.00**

Ragged Vagabond, The by Percy Edgar & Eric Randolph, 1919...........**6.00**

Raggedy Man by Riley & Krull, 1908..............................**8.00**

Ragging The Nursery Rhymes by Harold R. Atteridge & Al W. Brown, 1913, Musical: The Passing Show, 1913, Photo Lillian Gonne (Cover Artist, Starmer) **12.00**

Ragging The Scale by Ed B. Claypoole, 1915 (Cover Artist, DeTakacs & Rag)..**15.00**

Raggity Rag by J. B. Lafreniere, 1907 (March & Rag)...............**15.00**

Raggy Fox Trot, The by Goffin, 1915 (Cover Artist, Starmer & Rag) **10.00**

Raggy Military Tune by Sam Lewis, Billy Baskett & Lee S. Roberts, 1912 (Patriotic)..**35.00**

Rags by Louis Silver, Sammy Fain & Harry Richman, 1926.............**5.00**

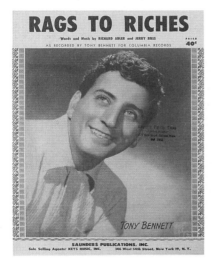

Rags To Riches by Richard Adler & Jerry Ross, 1953, Photo Tony Bennett..**12.00**

Ragtime Annie Lee by Redd Stewart & Pee Wee King, 1952 (Rag) **5.00**

Ragtime Automobile by Greensfelder, 1914 (Transportation)............**15.00**

Ragtime Betty by James Scott, 1909 (Rag) **10.00**

Ragtime Cowboy Joe by Murry Abrams, Louis Muir & Grant Clarke, 1940 (Rag)..**3.00**

Ragtime Dance, The by Scott Joplin, 1906 (Scott Joplin & Rag) **50.00**

Ragtime Dream, The by Joe Goodwin, 1913 (Rag)...................**10.00**

Ragtime Express, The by Atteridge & Jean Schwartz, 1913 (Cover Artist, Pfeiffer & Rag) **15.00**

Ragtime Eyes by Schwartz, Clarke & Leslie, 1912 (Cover Artist, Pfeiffer & Rag) **15.00**

Ragtime Goblin Man, The by Andrew B. Sterling & Harry Von Tilzer, 1911 (Cover Artist, DeTakacs & Rag) **15.00**

Ragtime In The Air by Manuel Klein, 1913, Musical: America 1913-1914 (Rag)...**15.00**

Ragtime Jockey Man, The by Irving Berlin, 1912 (Cover Artist, Pfeiffer, Irving Berlin & Sports)..**25.00**

Ragtime Mephisto, 1913 (Cover Artist, Pfeiffer & Rag)...............**15.00**

Ragtime Nightmare, A by Tom Turpin, 1900 (Rag) **15.00**

Ragtime Organ Morgan by Clarence Gaskill, 1912 (Rag) **10.00**

Ragtime Piano Playing by Syms, 1912 (Cover Artist, Pfeiffer & Rag)..**15.00**

Ragtime Soldier Man, The by Irving Berlin, 1912 (Cover Artist, Pfeiffer, WWI, Rag & Irving Berlin)....................................**25.00**

Ragtime Soldier Man, The by Irving Berlin, 1912 (Cover Artist, Starmer, WWI, Rag & Irving Berlin)....................................**25.00**

Ragtime Violin, The by Irving Berlin, 1911, Photo Fred Stone (Cover Artist, Pfeiffer, Irving Berlin & Rag) **20.00**

Ragtime Violin, The by Irving Berlin, 1911, Photo Poli Carpio (Cover Artist, Pfeiffer, Irving Berlin & Rag) **20.00**

Ragtime Volunteers Are Off To War, The by Ballard MacDonald, 1917 (WWI & Rag)..**15.00**

Ragtime Wedding Bells by George W. Meyer, 1913 (Rag)..............**12.00**

Rah-Rah Boy, The by Wallie Herzer, 1908.........................**10.00**

Rail-Road by Meineke, 1828 (Pre 1900 & Transportation) **100.00**

Railroad Galop by Miller, 1896 (Pre 1900 & Transportation) **30.00**

Railroad Galop by Treloar, 1893 (Pre 1900 & Transportation)...........**30.00**

Railroad Rag by Bimberg, 1911 (Rag & Transportation)................**25.00**

Rain by Billy Hill & Peter DeRose, 1934, Photo Hal Kemp (Cover Artist, Barbelle) **5.00**

Rain by Billy Hill & Peter DeRose, 1934, Photo Loretta Lee (Cover Artist, Barbelle) **5.00**

Rain by Billy Hill & Peter DeRose, 1934, Photo Tony Sacco (Cover Artist, Barbelle) **5.00**

Rain by Eugene Ford, 1927, Photo Brook Johns **5.00**

Rain by Eugene Ford, 1927, Photo Mark Fisher **5.00**

Rain by Pearl G. Curran, 1920....................................**5.00**

Rain by Robert Lewis Shayon & Leah Russell, 1936 ....**5.00**

Rain Drops by Paul De Frank & Gene Hoyt, 1929...................**5.00**

Rain Or Shine by Ross MacLean & Beverly Birks, 1947, Photo Guy Lombardo (Cover Artist, Nick)....................................**4.00**

Rainbow At Midnight by Lost John Miller, 1946, Photo Lost John Miller...**3.00**

Rainbow by Alfred Bryan & Percy Wenrich, 1908 (Cover Artist, DeTakacs & Indian)..**35.00**

Rainbow by Russ Hamilton, 1957 ....**5.00**

Rainbow Isle by Betty Bently & James W. Casey, 1920..............**10.00**

Rainbow Isle by Edward Madden & Lee S. Roberts, 1913 (Cover Artist, Starmer) **5.00**

Rainbow Man by Eddie Dowling & James F. Hanley, 1929, Movie: The Rainbow Man, Photo Eddie Dowling................................**6.00**

Rainbow Military March, The, 1918 (WWI & March) **15.00**

Rainbow Of Love, The by William F. Kirk & Gustave Ferrari, 1917....**5.00**

Rainbow On The River by Paul Francis Webster & Louis Alter, 1936, Movie: Rainbow On The River, Photo Bobby Breen.....................**5.00**

Raindrops Keep Falling On My Head by Hal David & Burt Bacharach, 1969, Movie: Butch Cassidy & The Sundance Kid, Photo Paul Newman, Robert Redford & Katherine Ross.........................**5.00**

Rainy Night In Rio, A by Arthur Schwartz & Leo Robin, 1946, Movie: The Time, The Place And The Girl, Photo, Dennis Morgan, Jack Carson, Martha Vickers, Janis Paige & Carmen Cavallaro (Cover Artist, A. Joel Robinson) **5.00**

Rambler Rose by Harry B. Smith & Victor Jacobi, 1917.............**5.00**

Ramblin' Rose by Noel Sherman & Joe Sherman, 1962, Photo Nat King Cole..**4.00**

Rambling Rose by Joseph McCarthy Jr. & Joe Burke, 1948, Photo Perry Como **4.00**

Rambling Rose by Joseph McCarthy Jr. & Joe Burke, 1948, Photo Tony Pastor (Cover Artist, Nick)......................................**4.00**

Ramona by L. Wolfe Gilbert & Mabel Wayne, 1927, Movie: Ramona, Photo & Dedicated To Dolores Del Rio (Dedication)................**5.00**

Ramshackle Rag by Ted Snyder, 1911 (Rag).......................**10.00**

Rangers Song, The by Harry Tierney & Joseph McCarthy, 1929, Movie: Ziegfeld's Rio Rita, Photo Bebe Daniels & John Boles................**10.00**

Rap Tap On Wood by Cole Porter, 1936, Movie: Born To Dance, Photo Eleanor Powell...**5.00**

Rapid Fire by F. Henri Klickmann, 1912 (March).....................10.00

Raquel by George Whiting & Joe Burke, 1928, Musical: Earl Carroll Vanities, 7th Edition (Deco)...**10.00**

Rastus On Parade by Kerry Mills, 1895 (Pre 1900 & Black, Black Face)..**35.00**

Raus Mit Der Kaiser, He's In Dutch by Andrew B. Sterling, Bartley Costello & Arthur Lange, 1917 (Cover Artist, Starmer & WWI)..**20.00**

Ray Of Sunshine by Leo Wood, Irving Bibo & Werner Janssen, 1921, Musical: Letty Pepper, Photo Charlotte Greenwood.......................**5.00**

Razz-Berries by Frank Banta, 1918 (Cover Artist, Barbelle & Jazz)...**10.00**

Razzle Dazzle by Thompson, 1888 (Pre 1900) **10.00**

Reaching For The Moon by Benny Davis & Jessie Green, 1929 ....**5.00**

Reaching For The Moon by Irving Berlin, 1930 (Irving Berlin).........**12.00**

Ready For The River by Gus Kahn & Neil Moret, 1928.....................**3.00**

Ready To Go Steady by Alec Wilder & Edwin Finckel, 1956, Photo Buddy Rich...**5.00**

Ready To Take A Chance Again by Gimbel & Fox, 1978, Movie: Foul Play, Photo Chevy Chase & Goldie Hawn....................................**5.00**

Ready, Willing And Able by Al Rinker, Floyd Huddleston & Dick Gleason, 1954, Movie: Young At Heart **5.00**

Real Nice Clambake, A by Richard Rodgers & Oscar Hammerstein II, 1945 (Cover Artist, BJM)..**6.00**

Real Slow Rag, A by Scott Joplin, 1903 (Scott Joplin & Rag) **50.00**

Reason, The by Ella Wheeler Wilcox & Teresa Del Riego, 1912.........**5.00**

Rebecca Came Back From Mecca by Bert Kalmar & Harry Ruby, 1921, Musical: The Midnight Rounders, Photo Eddie Cantor (Cover Artist, Laing & Eddie Cantor) **15.00**

Rebecca Of Sunnybrook Farm by Seymour Brown & Albert Gumble, 1914, Photo Valmore & Collins (Cover Artist, Starmer)..............**10.00**

Recess March by Lincoln, 1916 (Cover Artist, Pfeiffer & March) **15.00**

Recessional by Rudyard Kipling & Reginald DeKoven, 1898 (Pre 1900) **6.00**

Reciprocity by Sally Benson, Walter Kent & Kim Gannon, 1951, Movie: Seventeen...**5.00**

Reckless Night On Board An Ocean Liner by Raymond Scott, 1938 (Transportation)..**15.00**

Red As The Rose Of Maytime by Victor Leon, Leo Stein & Franz Lehar, 1958, Musical: From The Merry Widow.......................**6.00**

Red Cross Needs You Now, The by Gus Edwards, 1918 (WWI & Red Cross)..**35.00**

Red Fox Trot by Albert Gumble, 1917...**5.00**

Red Hot Mamma by Gilbert Wells, Bud Cooper & Fred Rose, 1924, Photo Sam J. Heiman & His Orchestra (Cover Artist, Perrett) **8.00**

Red Kiss On A Blue Letter, A by Redd Evans, George Lang & Roger Genger, 1945 ....**5.00**

Red Lips Kiss My Blues Away by Alfred Bryan, James V. Monaco & Pete Wendling, 1927, Photo Cogert & Motto (Cover Artist, Barbelle & Deco)..**6.00**

Red Lips Kiss My Blues Away by Alfred Bryan, James V. Monaco & Pete Wendling, 1927, Photo Kramer Twins, Harblean & Wadell (Cover Artist, Barbelle & Deco)...**5.00**

Red Man by Henry Longboat, 1916 (Indian)...............................**30.00**

Red Moon by Lew Brown, John Traver, Henri de Martini & Max Kortlander, 1922, Dedicated To Marie Traver (Cover Artist, Starmer & Dedication) **5.00**

Red Moon by Lew Brown, John Traver, Henri de Martini & Max Kortlander, 1922, Photo Genevieve Tobin (Deco) **5.00**

Red Nose Pete by Leo Freedman & Harry Link, 1924....................**5.00**

Red Pepper A Spicy Rag by Henry Lodge, 1910 (Rag) **10.00**

Red Peppers by Giles, 1907..**10.00**

Red Raven Rag by Charley Straight, 1915 (Rag)..............................**10.00**

Red, Red, Rose by Rogers & Cook, 1908 (Cover Artist, Pfeiffer).......**10.00**

Red River Valley by Harold Potter, 1935, Movie: Red River Valley, Photo Gene Autry **6.00**

Red Rose Of Love Bloom Again by William F. Kirk & J. Stanton Gladwin, 1920, Dedicated To Rosalind (Dedication & Deco)..............**15.00**

Red Rose Rag, The by Edward Madden & Percy Wenrich, 1911 (Cover Artist, Starmer & Rag)..**15.00**

Red Roses For A Blue Lady by Sid Tepper & Roy Brodsky, 1948, Photo Perry Como...**5.00**

Red Sails In The Sunset by Jimmy Kennedy & Hugh Williams, 1935, Musical: Provincetown Follies, Photo Ray Noble (Cover Artist, Barbelle & Transportation) **10.00**

Red Silk Stockings And Green Perfume by Dick Sanford, Sammy Mysels & Bob Hilliard, 1947 ....**3.00**

Red We Want Is The Red We've Got, The by Jimmy Kennedy & Bickley Reichner, 1950 (Patriotic)...**10.00**

Red Wing by Kerry Mills & Thurland Chattaway, 1907 (Cover Artist, Hirt & Indian)..**40.00**

Reddy Fox Goes Walking by Mildred Hofstad, 1940 (Cover Artist, Hauman) **4.00**

Redhead by Irene Franklin & Burt Green, 1908, Photo Irene Franklin**10.00**

Reduced To $1.99 by Harry C. Eldridge, 1912 ....**5.00**

Redwoods, The by Joseph B. Strauss & Oscar Rasbach, 1937 ....**5.00**

Reflections by Jerome Heller, 1913...**5.00**

Reflections In The Water by Paul Francis Webster & John Jacob Loeb, 1933, Photo Donald Novis...**3.00**

Regatta, The by Moses Gumble, 1900, Boston Herald Sunday Supplement (Cover Artist Arthur G. Hoel) **10.00**

Regimental Song by Brian Hooker & Rudolf Friml, 1931, Musical: The White Eagle (Cover Artist, Barbelle) **10.00**

Regrets by Gustave Seynave & Eusebe Champagne, 1914.................**3.00**

Regular Army O by Edward Harrigan & David Braham, 1875 (Pre 1900) **16.00**

Regular Girl, A by Janis, Kalmar & Ruby, 1919, Movie: A Regular Girl, Photo Elsie Janis...**5.00**

Relax by Johnson, O'Tools & Gill, 1984, Movie: Body Double, Photo Melanie Griffith...**3.00**

Rememb'ring by Duncan Sisters, Book By Catherine C. Cushing, Suggested By Uncle Tom's Cabin By Harriet Beecher Stowe, 1923, Musical: Topsy & Eva, Photo Duncan Sisters (Cover Artist, P.M. Griffith & Black, Black Face)..**12.00**

Remember, Boy, You're Irish by William J. Scanlon, 1886 (Pre 1900 & Irish)..**20.00**

Remember by Earl, Sizemore & Magine, 1921 ....**5.00**

Remember by Irving Berlin, 1925, Photo Irving Berlin (Irving Berlin)...**10.00**

Remember I'm Your Friend by Ed Lockton & Fred Boyle, 1917 (WWI)..**10.00**

Remember Me by Gus Kahn & Jack O'Brien, 1932 ....**5.00**

Remember Me? by Harry Warren & Al Dubin, Movie: Mr. Dodd Takes The Air..**6.00**

Remember Me For Old Times Sake by Carl H. Ossefort, 1914 ....**5.00**

Remember Me I'm The One Who Loves You by Stuart Hamblen, 1950 ..**3.00**

Remember Me To My Old Gal by Moriarty & Brown....................**5.00**

Remember My Forgotten Man by Al Dubin & Harry Warren, 1933, Movie: Gold Diggers Of 1933, Photo Joan Blondell **10.00**

Remember Pearl Harbor by Don Reid & Sammy Kaye, 1942 (WWII)..**12.00**

Remember Poor Mother At Home by W.A. Evans, 1883 (Pre 1900) ..**15.00**

Remember The Rose by Sidney D. Mitchell & Seymour Simons, 1921 (Cover Artist, A.B. Copeland & Deco) **10.00**

Remember When by Buck Ram & Mickey Addy, 1945 ....**2.00**

Remembrance Of Scotland by H.A. Rimmer, 1952 ....**5.00**

Reminiscing by Edgar Leslie & Harry Warren, 1930, Photo Guy Lombardo..**5.00**

Rendezvous With A Dream, A by Leo Robin & Ralph Rainger, 1936, Movie: Poppy, Photo Rochelle Hudson, Richard Cromwell & Caricature of W.C. Fields **12.00**

Repasz Band March by Chas. C. Sweeley, 1901 (March)..................**10.00**

Repent Ye by J.P. Scott, 1917 ....**5.00**

Resignation by Caro Roma, 1908 ....**10.00**

Retreat by Nancy Farnsworth, Tommy Furtado & Anita Boyer, 1952 ..**3.00**

Return To Peyton Place by Webster & Waxman, 1958, Movie: Return To Peyton Place, Photo Carol Lynley & Jeff Chandler **4.00**

Reuben And Cynthia by Percy Gaunt, 1892 (Pre 1900) **10.00**

Reuben Fox Trot by Ed Claypoole, 1914 ....**5.00**

Revelry by Walter V. Ullner, 1898 (Pre 1900)....................**10.00**

Revenge by Sam Lewis, Joe Young & Harry Akst, 1928, Photo Dolores Del Rio, Dedicated To Dolores Del Rio (Cover Artist, C.E. Millard & Dedication) **10.00**

Reverie Waltz by Cyrille Lamar, 1915 ....**5.00**

Revolutionary Rhythm by Davis, Coots & Spier, 1929, Movie: Illusion, Photo Buddy Rogers & Nancy Carroll **5.00**

Rhapsody In Blue by George Gershwin, 1939 ....**3.00**

Rhapsody Rag by Budd L. Cross, 1911 (Cover Artist, Ray & Rag) **15.00**

Rhythm In My Nursery Rhymes by Sammy Cahn, Don Raye, Jimmie Lunceford & Saul I. Chaplin, 1935 ....**5.00**

Rhythm Of The Day by Donald Lindley, 1926 ....**5.00**

Rhythm Of The Islands by Leon Belasco, Jacques Press & Eddie Cherkose, 1940, Movie: It's A Date, Photo Deanna Durbin..........**12.00**

Rickety Rickshaw Man, The by Ervin Drake, 1943 (Transportation)....**5.00**

Ricochet by Larry Coleman, Norman Gimbel & Joe Darion, 1953, Photo Theresa Brewer..**3.00**

Ride A Cock-Horse To Banbury Cross by John Rochette, 1936, Movie: Poor Little Rich Girl, Photo Shirley Temple (Shirley Temple) **10.00**

Ride In A Jitney For Mine, A by Edward I. Boyle, 1915 (Transportation)..**10.00**

Ride Me In A Big Balloon by Harry D. Kerr, 1910 (Transportation) ..**15.00**

Riders In The Sky by Stan Jones, 1949, Photo Burl Ives **3.00**

Ridin' Around In The Rain by Gene Austin & Carmen Lombardo, 1934 ....**3.00**

Ridin' High by Cole Porter, 1936, Movie: Red Hot & Blue (Cover Artist, Jorj Harris)..**6.00**

Riding On A Camel In The Desert by Ralph Butler, Julian Wright & Howard Flynn, 1929 ....**10.00**

Riding On A Rainbow by Berkeley Graham & Carley Mills, 1951 ....**3.00**

Riding On The Elevated Railroad by Sam Devere, 1890 (Pre 1900 & Transportation) **15.00**

Riding Up The River Road by Harry Woods, 1935 (Transportation) ..**10.00**

Riff Song by Otto Harbach, Oscar Hammerstein II, Frank Mandel & Sigmund Romberg, 1926, Movie: The Desert Song..........................**6.00**

Rifle Range, The by Harry J. Lincoln, 1907 (March)........................**10.00**

Right From My Heart by Allen, 1912 (Cover Artist, Pfeiffer)............**10.00**

Right Into Your Arms by Charles Lynes, 1945 ....**3.00**

Right Kind Of Love, The by Mabel Wayne & Kermit Goell, 1943 ....**3.00**

Right Somebody To Love, The by Jack Yellen & Lew Pollack, 1936, Movie: Captain January, Photo Shirley Temple (Shirley Temple)...**10.00**

Right To Happiness, The by Alfred Bryan & Abbey Green, 1919, Movie: The Right To Happiness, Photo Dorothy Phillips (Cover Artist, Starmer) **10.00**

Ring Dem Bells by Bert Kalmar & Harry Ruby, 1930, Movie: Check And Double Check, Photo Amos N Andy (Amos N Andy & Black, Black Face) **60.00**

Ring On Sweet Angelus by Harold Freeman & J. Edwin Allemong......**3.00**

Ring Out, Sweet Bells Of Peace by Wm. H. Gardner & Caro Roma, 1918 (WWI)..**10.00**

Ring Out Wild Bells by E.T. Paull, 1912 (Cover Artist, E.T. Paull)....**35.00**

Ring-Ting-A-Ling by Jerome & Clarke, 1911 (Cover Artist, Pfeiffer)**10.00**

Rings by Alex Sullivan & Lou Handman, 1919................................**3.00**

Rio Nights by Elmer Vincent & Fisher Thompson, 1920 ....**3.00**

Rio Rita by Harry Tierney & Joseph McCarthy, 1929, Movie: Rio Rita, Photo Bebe Daniels & John Boles..**10.00**

Rip Van Winkle Slept With One Eye Open by Alfred Bryan & Fred Fisher, 1918 ....**5.00**

Rip Van Winkle Was A Lucky Man by William Jerome & Jean Schwartz, 1901 ....**8.00**

Ripples Of the Allegheny by Harry J. Lincoln, 1912 (Cover Artist, W.J. Dittmar) **7.00**

Rippling Waters by Wm. T. Pierson, 1908 (Cover Artist, Pfeiffer) **10.00**

Rivals by E.W. Rogers, 1895 (Pre 1900)..........................**5.00**

River Kwai March, The by Arnold, 1957, Movie: The Bridge On The River Kwai, Photo Alec Guiness, William Holden & Jack Hawkins..........**6.00**

River Shannon by Costello & Russell, 1906 (Irish) **5.00**

River Shannon Moon by Walter Wallace Smith, 1923 (Irish)..............**5.00**

River Stay 'Way From My Door by Mort Dixon & Harry Woods, 1931, Photo Kate Smith (Black, Black Face)..................................**16.00**

River Stay 'Way From My Door by Mort Dixon & Harry Woods, 1931, Signed Photo Vincent Lopez (Signed & Black, Black Face).........**20.00**

Riverside by Ella M. Smith & Howard I. Smith, 1913..........................**5.00**

Riverside March, The by Walter V. Ullman, 1898 (Pre 1900 & March).**15.00**

Riviera Rose by Jean Frederick & Horatio Nicholls, 1924 ....**10.00**

Ro-Ro-Rollin' Along by Moll, Richman & Merscher, 1929..................**5.00**

Road For You And Me, The by George Lyons & Bob Yosco, 1918 (Cover Artist, White)..**5.00**

Road Is Open Again, The, NRA Short With Dick Powell by Irving Kahal & Sammy Fain, 1933, Photo Franklin D. Roosevelt & Dick Powell (President)..**35.00**

Road That Leads To Love by Irving Berlin, 1917 (Irving Berlin) **10.00**

Road To Loveland, The by Jone & Blake, 1913 (Cover Artist, Pfeiffer) ..**10.00**

Road To Morocco, The by Johnny Burke & Jimmy Van Heusen, 1952, Movie: Road To Morocco, Photo Bob Hope, Bing Crosby & Dorothy Lamour..**6.00**

Road To The Isles, Song Of The Hebrides, The by Kenneth MacLeod, 1917 ....**10.00**

Roam On My Little Gypsy Sweetheart by Francis Wheeler, Iving Kahal & Ted Snyder, 1927..**5.00**

Roamin' In The Gloamin' by Harry Lauder, 1911 ....**10.00**

Roamin' Thru The Roses by Charles O'Flynn & Peter DeRose, 1930, Photo Pauline Haggard (Cover Artist, Leff)......................5.00

Roaring Volcano by E.T. Paull, 1912 (Cover Artist, E.T. Paull & March) 35.00

Robber's March by Frederick Norton, 1916 (March)..........................10.00

Robin Hood March by Victor L. Schertzinger, 1922, Movie: Robin Hood, Photo Douglas Fairbanks (March)...............................10.00

Robin, Robin, Sing Me A Song by Alfred T. Grubb & Charles Gilbert Spross, 1918...6.00

Robin's Lullaby, The by C.W. Krogman, 1926....................................3.00

Robin's Return, The by Leander Fisher, 1912....................................5.00

Robins And Roses by Edgar Leslie & Joe Burke, 1936, Photo Ray Pearl 3.00

Robinson Crusoe's Isle by O.E. Story, 1913 ....5.00

Rock Around The Island by Darby, 1955, Movie: The Lieutenant Wore Skirts, Photo Sheree North 4.00

Rock Beside The Sea, The by Charlie C. Converse, 1857 (Pre 1900) .25.00

Rock Me In My Swanee Cradle by Mitchell Parish, Eleanor Young & Harry D. Squires, 1921 (Cover Artist, Hoffman) 6.00

Rock Me To Sleep In Your Arms by Polly & Anna & Cal DeVoll, 1929, Photo Ford & Glenn 5.00

Rock Of Ages by Charles E. Cole, 1896 (Pre 1900) 10.00

Rock Of Ages by Thomas Hastings, 1927...3.00

Rock, Rock, Rock, Keep A Rocking by Clarke, Leslie & Schwartz, 1913 (Cover Artist, Pfeiffer) 10.00

Rock-A-Bye Land by Gus Kahn & Egbert Van Alstyne, 1917..............5.00

Rock-A-Bye Land by H.C. Weasner, 1921...5.00

Rock-A-Bye Lullabye Mammy by Grant Clarke & Walter Donaldson, 1920 (Black, Black Face) 10.00

Rock-A-Bye Moon by Howard Johnson, Fred Steele & Morton Lang, 1932, Photo Ethel Shutta (Deco) 10.00

Rock-A-Bye My Baby Blues by Billy Hill & Larry Yoell, 1921, Photo Kelly Sisters (Cover Artist, P.M. Griffith & Blues) 6.00

Rock-A-Bye To Sleep In Dixie by Sylvester Cross, 1929 (Dixie).........5.00

Rock-A-Bye Your Baby With A Dixie Melody by Joe Young, Sam M. Lewis & Jean Schwartz, 1946, Photo Jerry Lewis (Dixie)...............5.00

Rock-A-Bye Your Baby With A Dixie Melody by Joe Young, Sam M. Lewis & Jean Schwartz, 1918, Photo Al Jolson (Cover Artist, Barbelle, Dixie & Al Jolson) 15.00

Rock-A-Bye Your Baby With A Dixie Melody by Joe Young, Sam M. Lewis & Jean Schwartz, 1918, Movie: The Jolson Story, Photo Larry Parks & Evelyn Keyes (Dixie & Al Jolson) 15.00

Rockaby Baby by Effie I. Canning, 1885 (Pre 1900) 10.00

Rockabye Baby by Irving Berlin, 1924, Music Box Revue 1925 (Irving Berlin)..10.00

Rocked In The Cradle Of Liberty by Gus Howard, 1916 (WWI) 10.00

Rocked In The Cradle Of The Deep by J.P. Knight, 1935, Photo Phil Baker (Transportation) 12.00

Rockin' Around The Christmas Tree by Johnny Marks, 1958, Photo Brenda Lee 3.00

Rockin' Chair by Hoagy Carmichael, 1941.......................................4.00

Rockin' Chair Swing by Mary Schaefer & Vincent Lopez, 1937 ....3.00

Rockin' The Boat by Hugo Frey, 1918..10.00

Rocking Horse Parade, The by Emma P. LaFreniere, 1934, Photo Phil Lynch 3.00

Rocky Mountain Moon by Raymond B. Egan, Henry Marshall & Richard A. Whiting, 1923 ....4.00

Rocky Road To Dublin, The by Sam M. Lewis, Joe Young & Dick Finch, 1925 (Cover Artist, Frederick S. Manning & Irish) 15.00

Rogue River Valley by Hoagy Carmichael, 1946 ....4.00

Rogue Song, The by Clifford Grey & Herbert Stothart, 1929...............5.00

Roll Along, Harvest Moon by J. Will Callahan & R.G. Gradi, 1915.....8.00

Roll Along, Kentucky Moon by Bill Halley, 1932...............................3.00

Roll Along Missouri by Bert Kalmar, Harry Ruby & M.K. Jerome, 1923 (Cover Artist, Im-Ho)...5.00

Roll Along Prairie Moon by Ted Fiorito, Harry MacPherson & Albert Von Tilzer, 1935, Movie: Here Comes The Band, Photo Virginia Bruce & Harry Stockwell..12.00

Roll Dem Roly Boly Eyes by Eddie Leonard, 1912 (Black, Black Face)...20.00

Roll 'Em Girls, Roll Your Own by Micky Marr, Bobby Heath & Archie Fletcher, 1925 (Cover Artist, Colegrove Studio) 12.00

Roll 'Em Girls, Roll Your Own by Micky Marr, Bobby Heath & Archie Fletcher, 1925, Photo Billy Glason 6.00

Roll, Mighty Ocean! by J. Astor Broad, 1907 ....10.00

Roll On, Mississippi Roll On by Eugene West, James McCaffrey & Dave Ringle, 1931...3.00

Roll Out Of Bed With A Smile by Joe Young & Milton Ager, 1933 ....3.00

Roll Them Cotton Bales by J.W. Johnson & J. Rosamond Johnson, 1914 (Black, Black Face) 20.00

Rollin' Plains by Leonard Whitcup & Teddy Powell, 1937.................5.00

Rollin' Stone by Mack Gordon, 1951, Photo Perry Como 3.00

Rolling Home by Cole Porter, 1936, Movie: Born To Dance, Photo Eleanor Powell..6.00

Rolling Home by Peter DeRose, 1934 (Transportation).......................5.00

Rolling In His Little Rolling Chair by Joe Goodwin, Ballard MacDonald & Halsey K. Mohr, 1909 ....15.00

Rolling Stones by Edgar Leslie & Archie Gottler, 1916, Photo Anna Chandler (Cover Artist, Barbelle) 10.00

Rolling The Moon by Donald Hutton, Rolin Cooley & Vernon Suckov, 1920 ....3.00

Roman Races March by Harry J. Lincoln, 1914 (March).................10.00

Romance by Edgar Leslie & Walter Donaldson, 1929.........................5.00

Romance by Leslie & Donaldson, Movie: When Johnny Comes Marching Home, Photo Phil Spitalny, Allan Jones, Jane Frazee, Donald O'Connor & Gloria Jean (Patriotic) 10.00

Romance by Otto Harbach, Oscar Hammerstein II, Frank Mandel & Sigmund Romberg, 1926, Movie: The Student Prince 8.00

Romance by Otto Harbach, Oscar Hammerstein II, Frank Mandel & Sigmund Romberg, 1926, Movie: The Desert Song.........................10.00

Romance by Will D. Cobb & Gus Edwards, 1917 ....5.00

Romance Of A Rose by O'Connor, 1908 ....5.00

Romance Of Gold by Barbara Young & Robert Huntington Terry, 1928...3.00

Romance Of Our People by Abner Silver, 1933.................................3.00

Romance Runs In The Family by Al Hoffman, Al Goodhart & Manny Kurtz, 1939, Photo Francis Craig (Cover Artist, Merman).............3.00

Romantic Ruth by Burns & Sheppard, 1920, Movie: The Adventures Of Ruth, Photo Ruth Roland 6.00

Romany Love by Arthur J. Lamb & J.S. Zamecnik, 1922 ....5.00

Romany Rye, The by E.T. Paull, 1909 (Cover Artist, E.T. Paull & Lithograph, A. Hoen & Co.) 35.00

Romany Waltz by Robert A. Keiser, 1918 (WWI)..............................10.00

Romeo Smith And Juliet Jones by Johnny Burke & Jimmy Van Heusen, 1941, Movie: Playmates, Photo Kay Kyser, John Barrymore, Lupe Velez & Ginny Simms..6.00

Rondino by Kreisler, 1915...5.00

Room Full Of Roses by Tim Spencer, 1949......................................3.00

Room Without Windows, A by Ervin Drake, 1948..............................3.00

Roosevelt N.R.A. March Song, 1933 (March, Presidents & Political)..35.00

Rosa Lee by Claude Weber, 1901...5.00

Rosalie by Cole Porter, 1937, Movie: Rosalie, Photo Nelson Eddy & Eleanor Powell..12.00

Rosalie by Daniel James & James R. Homer, 1904 (Cover Artist, Jas. K. Bonnar) 5.00

Rosalita by Al Dexter, 1942 ....**2.00**

Rosary, by Robert Cameron Rogers & Alfred Adams Spencer, 1911....**8.00**

Rosary, The by Ethelbert Nevin & Robert Cameron Rogers, 1911 (Cover Artist, E.B. Bird)..**3.00**

Rose by Arthur Sizemore, Frank Magine & Paul Biese, 1920 ....**5.00**

Rose by George M. Cohan, 1923, Movie: George M! (George M. Cohan)..**10.00**

Rose And A Prayer, A by Remus Harris, Dan Woodward & Chester Conn, 1941, Photo Jimmy Dorsey & Bob Eberly **3.00**

Rose Ann Of Charing Cross by Kermit Goell & Mabel Wayne, 1942, Photo Blue Barron (Cover Artist, Nick, WWII & Red Cross)......**16.00**

Rose Ann Of Charing Cross by Kermit Goell & Mabel Wayne, 1942, Photo Gene Krupa (Cover Artist, Nick, WWII & Red Cross) **16.00**

Rose Atherton, 1820, (Lithograph P.S. Duval, Stone Engraving & Pre 1900)..**100.00**

Rose Dreams by J.R. Shannon & A.J. Stasny, 1916 (Cover Artist, ARK)..**10.00**

Rose For Every Heart, A by Nellie R. Eberhart & Chas. Wakefield Cadman, 1928 ....**5.00**

Rose In Her Hair, The by Harry Warren & Al Dubin, 1935, Movie: Broadway Gondolier, Photo Dick Powell **8.00**

Rose In My Garden Of Dreams, The by Livernash, 1914 (Cover Artist, Pfeiffer)..**10.00**

Rose In The Bud by Barow & Forster, 1907, Movie: The Battle Of The Sexes, Photo Phyllis Haver..**6.00**

Rose Marie by Ed Gardenier & Ed DiCapua, 1908 (Cover Artist, Etherington) 10.00

Rose Marie by Otto Harbach, Oscar Hammerstein II & Rudolf Friml, 1924, Movie: Rose Marie, Photo Jeannette Macdonald & Nelson Eddy..**12.00**

Rose Mary by Bernard E. Fay, 1915, Dedicated To Rose May (Dedication)..**10.00**

Rose O'Day by Charlie Tobias & Al Lewis, 1941 (Irish) **3.00**

Rose O'Mine by Walter Hirsch & Julian Fuhs, 1922, Signed Photo Frances Alda (Signed) **5.00**

Rose Of California, The by Jacob Henry Ellis, 1907, Dedicated To Mr. Victor Eckland, Reading, Pa. (Dedication) **10.00**

Rose Of Heaven by Harry Lincoln, 1919 ....**5.00**

Rose Of Memory Lane, The by Michael Murray & Westell Gordon, 1927..**4.00**

Rose Of Mine by Will R. Garton & Cedric H. Garton, 1913 ....**5.00**

Rose Of My Dreams by Fred Swan, 1919, Photo Mrs. Charlie Chaplin (Cover Artist, V.C. Plunkett)..**16.00**

Rose Of My Heart by Weston Wilson & Neil Moret, 1920, Musical: Ziegfeld's Midnight Frolic, Photo John Steel **10.00**

Rose Of No Man's Land, The by Jack Caddigan & James A. Brennan, 1918, Patriotic War Edition (WWI & Red Cross)................**20.00**

Rose Of No Man's Land, The by Jack Caddigan & James A. Brennan, 1918, Dedicated To The Red Cross Nurse (WWI, Red Cross & Dedication) **20.00**

Rose Of Sunny Italy by Cal DeVoll, Jimmie Altiere & Joseph Chapman, 1922..**6.00**

Rose Of The Moonlight by Freeman, 1914 (Cover Artist, Pfeiffer) **10.00**

Rose Of The Morning by Cyrus Wood & Sigmund Romberg, 1923, Musical: The Passing Show 1923..**10.00**

Rose Of The Mountain Trail, The by Jack Caddigan & James Brennan, 1914, Photo D'Armana & Carter (Cover Artist, Starmer) **10.00**

Rose Of The Prairie Land by Arthur E. Buckman & Jacob Henry Ellis, 1903 (Cover Artist, Pfeiffer) **15.00**

Rose Of The Rancho by Leo Robin & Ralph Rainger, 1935, Movie: Rose Of The Rancho..**5.00**

Rose Of The Rio Grande by Edgar Leslie, Harry Warren & Ross Gorman, 1923 ....**4.00**

Rose Of Tralee by Charles W. Glover & C. Mourdant Spencer, 1935, Photo Cyril Pitts (Irish)..**4.00**

Rose Of Tralee, The by C. Mordaunt Spencer & Charles W. Glover, 1931, Sung by John McCormack (Irish) **6.00**

Rose Of Virginia by Jack Caddigan & Chick Storey, 1920 (Cover Artist, Wohlman)..10.00

Rose Of Washington Square by Ballard Macdonald & James F. Hanley, 1920, As Introduced By Fanny Brice In New Ziegfeld Midnight Frolic, Photo Fanny Brice **20.00**

Rose Of Yesterday, The by Rev. Walter E. Isenhour & Paul Shannon, 1915 ....**5.00**

Rose Petals by Wm. T. Pierson, 1910 (Cover Artist, Pfeiffer)............**10.00**

Rose Queen by Edward Braham, 1912..**5.00**

Rose Room Fox Trot by Art Hickman, 1917..**6.00**

Rose Song by William Scanlon, 1883 (Pre 1900) **15.00**

Rose That Grows In Dreamland Just For You, The by Edith A. Middleton & Billy Smythe, 1913..**5.00**

Rose That Made Me Happy, The by Pace, 1915 ....**5.00**

Rose That Never Fades, The by Brown & Powell, 1916 (Cover Artist, Pfeiffer)..**10.00**

Rose Waltz by W.C. Powell, 1913 ....**4.00**

Rose With A Broken Stem, A by Tolchard Evans, 1937......................**4.00**

Rose-Marie by Anne Caldwell & Jerome Kern, 1921 ....**10.00**

Rosemary by Anne Nichols & J.S. Zamecnik, 1928, Movie: Abie's Irish Rose **8.00**

Rosemary by Roy Mack, 1933 (Cover Artist, Fran Hays) **5.00**

Rosenkes Mit Mandlen, (English-Raisins And Almonds) by J. M. Rumshisky, 1908 ....**10.00**

Roses And Daffodils by Mary C. Call & Paul Shannon, 1915..............**5.00**

Roses And Lilacs by Harris, 1904 (Cover Artist, Starmer) **8.00**

Roses And Memories by Monroe H. Rosenfeld & Ted Snyder, 1909 ...**5.00**

Roses And Thorns by H.H. Schultz & J. Edwin Allemong, 1916 (Cover Artist, DeTakacs)...**10.00**

Roses And Violets by Joseph M. Daly, 1911 (Cover Artist, Starmer).**10.00**

Roses Are Forget-Me-Nots by Al Hoffman, Charles O'Flynn & Will Osborne, 1930...**5.00**

Roses At Twilight by Ben Black & Herbert Marple, 1918...................**5.00**

Roses Bloom For Lovers by Granichstaedten, 1912 ....**5.00**

Roses Bring Dreams Of You by Herbert Ingraham, 1908, Photo Miss Elodia Hunter (Cover Artist, Starmer) **10.00**

Roses Bring Memories Of You by Fred C. Swan, 1919......................**6.00**

Roses by George Marion, 1903 (Cover Artist, Starmer) **5.00**

Roses by Tim Spencer & Glenn Spencer, 1950...................................**3.00**

Roses Have Nothing On You, The by Ernest Orne, 1916 (Cover Artist, Pfeiffer)...**12.00**

Roses In December by Herb Magidson, Ben Oakland & George Jessel, 1937, Movie: The Life Of The Party, Photo Harriet Hilliard, Gene Raymond, Parkarkarkis, Eric Blore, Victor Moore, Helen Broderick & Joe Penner...**5.00**

Roses In The Rain by Al Frisch, Fred Wise & Frankie Carle, 1947, Photo Frank Sinatra...**3.00**

Roses Know, The by Fred H. Martens & Harriet Rush, 1916 ....**5.00**

Roses Of Arcadie by Rachel Storey & Otto Motzan, 1919 (WWI)......**10.00**

Roses Of Beautiful Memories by George B. Pitman & Frederic G. Chiswell, 1916...**5.00**

Roses Of Lorraine by Sidney Carter & Walter Smith, 1918 (WWI)....**10.00**

Roses Of Picardy by Fred E. Weatherly & Hayden Wood, 1916 (Irish)**5.00**

Roses Of Yesterday by Irving Berlin, 1928 (Irving Berlin) **5.00**

Roses Remind Me Of Someone by Schmidd & Dempsey, 1914 (Cover Artist, Pfeiffer)...**10.00**

Rosetime by Vandersloot, 1916 (Cover Artist, Pfeiffer) **10.00**

Rosette by Charles Newman & Carmen Lombardo, 1928 ....**3.00**

Rosewood Spinet, A by Charles Tobias & Nat Simon, 1948, Photo Eddy Howard (Cover Artist, Nick) **4.00**

Rosewood Spinet, The by Charles Tobias & Nat Simon, 1948.............**3.00**

Rosey, Rosey Just Supposey by Andrew B. Sterling & Max Dreyfus, 1899, Boston Herald Sunday Supplement (Cover Artist, Robert C. Dobson & Pre 1900)...**10.00**

Rosie by Lee Adams & Charles Strouse, 1960, Movie: Bye Bye Birdie .**3.00**

Rosie, Make It Rosie For Me by Grant Clarke & J.L. Merkur, 1920.....**4.00**

Rosie, Sweet Rosabel by M.K. Jerome & James V. Monaco, 1912.......**5.00**

Rosy Cheeks by Mitchell Parish, Eleanor Young & Harry D. Squires, 1921 (Cover Artist, Hoffman) **12.00**

'Round Evening by George Whiting, Herbert Steiner & J. Fred Coots, 1928 (Cover Artist, Leff)...**5.00**

'Round Her Neck She Wears A Yellow Ribbon by Norton, 1917 (Cover Artist, Pfeiffer)...**10.00**

'Round My Heart by Mursch, Smith & Brym, 1912 (Cover Artist, Pfeiffer) **10.00**

Round We Go by Henry Parker, 1912 ....**5.00**

Route 66 by Bob Troup, 1946, Photo Nat King Cole **3.00**

Roving Kind, The by Jessie Cavanaugh & Arnold Stanton, 1950, Photo Guy Mitchell...**3.00**

Row Gentle Here, My Gondolier by Heinrich, 1913............................**5.00**

Row, Row, Row by M.K. Jerome & Jimmy V. Monaco, 1912.............**5.00**

Rowdy Dowdy Boys by Conie & McGlennon, 1893 (Pre 1900) **10.00**

Royal Blue by Peter DeRose, 1937 ....**4.00**

Royal Gewgaw, The by E.E. Guilford, 1907 (Cover Artist, Starmer)..**16.00**

Rubber Duckie by Jeffrey Moss, 1970 ....**2.00**

Rubber Neck Jim by John W. Barton, 1889, (Pre 1900 & Black, Black Face) **35.00**

Rubberneckin' by Jones & Warren, 1969, Movie: Change Of Habit, Photo Elvis Presley **5.00**

Ruby by Benny Davis & J. Russell Robinson, 1921 ....**8.00**

Ruby by Mitchell Parish & Heinz Roemheld, 1953, Movie: Ruby Gentry, Photo Jennifer Jones **5.00**

Ruby Tuesday by Mick Jagger & Keith Richards, 1967, Photo Rolling Stones...**5.00**

Rudolph The Red-Nosed Reindeer by Johnny Marks, 1949 ....**5.00**

Rudy, Your Love Songs Reach My Heart by May W. Breen, 1929, Photo Rudy Vallee **10.00**

Ruff Johnson's Harmony Band by Shelton Brooks & Maurice Abrahams, 1914 (March) **10.00**

Rufus, Rastus, Johnson, Brown, What You Gonna Do When De Rent Comes Round? by Andrew Sterling & Harry Von Tilzer, 1905 (Black, Black Face) **35.00**

Rum & Coca-Cola by Morey Amsterdam, Jeri Sullivan & Paul Baron, 1944, Photo Andrews Sisters (WWII)...**12.00**

Rum Tum Tiddle by Edward Madden & Jean Schwartz, 1912 (Cover Artist, Starmer) **10.00**

Rum Tum Tiddle Dance by Schwartz, 1911, Photo Jean Schwartz (Cover Artist, Pfeiffer)...**10.00**

Rumble, Rumble, Rumble by Frank Loesser, 1947, Movie: The Perils Of Pauline, Photo Betty Hutton & John Lund **5.00**

Rumble Seat by Carey Morgan, 1929 (Transportation).......................**15.00**

Rumors Are Flying by Bennie Benjamin & George Weiss, 1946, Photo Perry Como (Cover Artist, Barbelle)...**6.00**

Rumpel-Stilts-Kin by Charles Tobias & Al Lewis, 1939 ....**5.00**

Run Bruder Rabbit, Run by Cole & Johnson, 1906.............................**10.00**

Run Home And Tell Your Mother by Irving Berlin, 1911 (Irving Berlin) **12.00**

Runaway June by Harold Freeman, 1915, Movie: Runaway June, Photo Norma Phillips...**5.00**

Runnin' Wild by Joe Grey, Leo Wood & A. Harrington Gibbs, 1922...**5.00**

Running Between The Raindrops by James Dysenforth & Carroll Gibbons, 1931...**4.00**

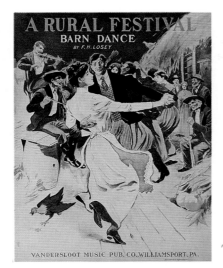

Rural Festival, A by F.H. Losey, 1918 (Cover Artist, Dittmar & Furman) **15.00**

Ruspana by Thomas Field & Mary Earl, 1919 ....**5.00**

Russian Lullaby by Irving Berlin, 1927 (Irving Berlin & Deco)..........**10.00**

Russian March by Mack, 1861 (Pre 1900 & March)...........................**20.00**

Russian Pony Rag by Ramsay, 1910 (Rag) **10.00**

Russian Rag by Cobb, 1918 (Rag).......................................**10.00**

Russian Rose by Sonny Miller & Hugh Charles, 1940 ....**3.00**

Russian Sherr by Abe Schwartz, 1921, Photo Mr. Schwartz & His Daughter..**5.00**

Rustic Divertisement, A by Atelier & Bedois, 1915 (Cover Artist, Pfeiffer) **10.00**

Rustling Leaves by G. Lange (Cover Artist, Pfeiffer) **10.00**

Rusty Can-O Rag by Piantadosi, 1910 (Cover Artist, Pfeiffer & Rag) **15.00**

Rye Waltzes, The by MacLaughlin, 1909 (Cover Artist, Pfeiffer).......**15.00**

'S Wonderful by Ira & George Gershwin, 1927....................................**3.00**

S'posin by Andy Razaf & Paul Denniker, 1929, Photo Charles W. Hamp (Cover Artist, Barbelle) **3.00**

S'posin by Andy Razaf & Paul Denniker, 1929, Photo Johnny Johnson (Cover Artist, Barbelle) **3.00**

Sabbath Chimes by F.Henri Klickmann, 1918 ....**10.00**

Sabel's Sparkling Champagne Song by Josie Sabel, 1894 (Pre 1900) .**10.00**

Sack Waltz, The by John A. Metcalf (Cover Artist, Starmer)................**5.00**

Sacrament by Elizabeth Jacobi & Jas. G. MacDermid, 1913 (Cover Artist, Dorothy Dulin) **6.00**

Sacred Flame, The by Grant Clarke & Harry Akst, 1929, Photo Conrad Nagel..**5.00**

Sad Hawaiian Sea by Lee S. Roberts, 1923..**3.00**

Saddle Your Blues To A Wild Mustang by George Whiting, Buddy Bernier & Billy Haid, 1936 ....**5.00**

Saddle-De-Mooch by Chris Smith, 1915..**8.00**

Sadie Salome Go Home by Irving Berlin, 1909 (Cover Artist, Pfeiffer & Irving Berlin) **15.00**

Sadie Won't You Be My Little Lady? by Gus Edwards, 1905 ....**6.00**

Saftest O' The Family by Harry Lauder & Beaton, 1904......................**8.00**

Sagamore by Eva Williams & Joe Maxwell, 1920 (Cover Artist, Pfeiffer & Indian)..**20.00**

Sahara We'll Soon Be Dry Like You by Bryan & Schwartz, 1919 (Cover Artist, Pfeiffer)..**10.00**

Said The Hornet To The Bee by John Sylvester, 1906..........................**6.00**

Sail Along, Sil'vry Moon by Harry Tobias & Percy Wenrich, 1937, Photo Bing Crosby..**5.00**

Sail On Silvery Moon by Downs & Erdman, 1912 ....**4.00**

Sail On To Ceylon by Edward Madden & Herman Paley, 1916, Photo Joe Niemeyer & Nina Payne (Cover Artist, Starmer)...........................**5.00**

Sailboat In the Moonlight, A by Carmen Lombardo & John Jacob Loeb, 1937, Photo Shep Fields (Cover Artist, Merman & Transportation)...**5.00**

Sailboat In the Moonlight, A by Carmen Lombardo & John Jacob Loeb, 1937, Photo Guy Lombardo (Cover Artist, Merman & Transportation) **6.00**

Sailin' Away On The Henry Clay by Gus Kahn & Egbert Van Alstyne, 1917, Photo Elizabeth Murray..**5.00**

Sailin' On by Gus Kahn, Nathanson Borgel & Anton Dvorak, 1927.....**5.00**

Sailing by Godfrey Marks, 1936, Photo Lawrence Welk & Orchestra (Transportation) **5.00**

Sailing Down The Chesapeake Bay by Jean C. Havez & George Botsford, 1918 (Cover Artist, Starmer & Transportation) **10.00**

Sailing Down The River In The Moonlight Mandy And I by Jack Caddigan & Jas. A. Brennan, 1907 (Cover Artist, Starmer & Transportation) **12.00**

Sailing Home by Walter G. Samuels, Leonard Whitcup & Teddy Powell, 1937 (Cover Artist, Merman & Transportation) **3.00**

Sailing In My Balloon by Scott, 1907 (Transportation) **15.00**

Sailor Boys Have Talk To Me In English by Bob Hilliard & Milton De Lugg, 1955...**5.00**

Sailor's Dream, The by Wheeler, 1880 (Pre 1900) **12.00**

Saint Louis Blues by W.C. Handy, 1914, Photo Rudy Vallee (Cover Artist, Barbelle)..**6.00**

Saint Vitus Rag, The by Hill & Johnson, 1912 (Cover Artist, Pfeiffer & Rag) **15.00**

Sally In Our Alley by Henry Carey, 1902, Musical: Sally In Our Alley (Cover Artist, Starmer)..**15.00**

Sally Of My Dreams by William Kernell, 1928, Movie: Mother Knows Best, Photo Madge Bellamy **10.00**

Sally–Don't Dally by Charles Graham, 1896 (Pre 1900) **10.00**

Salome by William Loraine, 1899 (Pre 1900).....................................**10.00**

Salt Of The Sea For Me, The by Arthur Penn, 1903 (Transportation) .**10.00**

Salt Water Cowboy by Redd Evans, 1944...**4.00**

Salt Your Sugar by Simons, 1923...**5.00**

Salted Peanuts Rag by Chapman & Koninsky, 1911 (Cover Artist, Pfeiffer, Rag & Deco) **20.00**

Salty Sam, The Sailor by C. Franz Koehler, 1937 (Cover Artist, D. & G. Hauman) **5.00**

Salut A Pesth by Henri Kowalski, 1902 (Cover Artist, C.F. Ferraioli & March) **10.00**

Salute The Flag by Victor Bartlett, 1914 (Cover Artist, Pfeiffer & Transportation) **15.00**

Salute To America by Harry J. Lincoln, 1904 (March).......................**10.00**

Salute To Sam Johnson by O.E. Sutton, 1899 (Pre 1900 & Black, Black Face) **15.00**

Salute To Williamsburg by C.E. Duble, 1906 (March)......................**10.00**

Salvation Army, Oh by Edward Harrigan & David Braham, 1885 (Pre 1900 & Salvation Army) **30.00**

Salvation Lassie Of Mine by Jack Caddigan & Chick Story, 1919 (WWI & Salvation Army) **30.00**

Salvation Nell by George Clarke, Edgar Leslie & Theodore Morse, 1913 (Cover Artist, Pfeiffer, WWI & Salvation Army) **30.00**

Sam Fox Trot by George P. Howard, 1915 ....**6.00**

Sam Johnson's Colored Cake Walk by Edward Harrigan & David Braham, 1883 (Pre 1900 & Black, Black Face)...................................**20.00**

Sam, Sam, The Parcel Post Man by Allen & Williams (Cover Artist, Pfeiffer) **12.00**

Sam, The Old Accordion Man by Walter Donaldson, 1927, Photo Williams Sisters (Cover Artist, JVR & Black, Black Face)..........**10.00**

Sam, You Made The Pants Too Long by Fred Whitehouse, Milton Berle, Sam M. Lewis & Joe Young, 1966, Photo Barbara Striesand..........**3.00**

Sam's Song by Jack Elliott & Lew Quadling, 1950, Photo Bing Crosby ..**3.00**

Sambo Outa Work Cake Walk by J.A. Silberberg, 1899 (Pre 1900 & Black, Black Face).....................**15.00**

Same Old Crowd, The by Fred C. Farrell, Joseph C. Farrell & Theodore F. Morse, 1903, Photo Blanche Ring (Cover Artist, Starmer)............**10.00**

Same Old Moon by Jack Yellen, Milton Ager & Henry Sullivan, 1929, Musical: First Edition Of Murray Anderson's Almanac.................**5.00**

Same Old Moon Same Old Sky by Ed Rose & Billy Baskette, 1932, Photo Rudy Vallee.....................**5.00**

Same Old Story, The by Michael Field & Newt Oliphant, 1940 (Cover Artist, Im-Ho).....................**4.00**

Same Old Way, The by Joseph McCarthy & Harry Tierney, 1918, Musical: Ziegfeld's Kid Boots.....................**10.00**

Same Sort Of Girl by Jerome Kern, 1916.....................**5.00**

Sammy by O'Dea & Hutchinson, 1904 ....**5.00**

San Antonio by Harry Williams & Egbert Van Alstyne, 1907 (Cover Artist, Starmer).....................**10.00**

San Antonio Rose by Bob Wills, 1940, Photo Bob Wills (Cover Artist, Im-Ho) **4.00**

San by Lindsay McPhail & Walter Michels, 1920, Musical: Ziegfeld Follies, 1924, Photo George Olsen (Cover Artist, Jay Roland)...........**10.00**

San Fernando Valley by Gordon Jenkins, 1943, Photo Bing Crosby.....**4.00**

San Francisco by Andy Graves & Eddie Jewell, 1915 ....**10.00**

San Francisco by Gus Kahn, Bronislau Kaper & Walter Jurman, 1936 ....**5.00**

San Francisco Bound by Irving Berlin, 1913 (Cover Artist, Pfeiffer & Irving Berlin).....................**15.00**

San Francisco Glide by McCarthy & Piantadosi, 1910 (Cover Artist, Pfeiffer & Deco).....................**15.00**

San Francisco, The Paris Of The U.S.A. by Hirshel Hendler, 1912.....**10.00**

San Jose, 1915 (Cover Artist, Pfeiffer).....................**10.00**

San Salvador by Haven Gillespie, Erwin Schmidt & Jesse Crawford, 1925 ....**3.00**

Sancta Maria, In Dreams I Saw The Angels by Willis Wager & Carl Deis, 1941 ....**3.00**

Sand Dunes by Byron Gay, 1919.....................**5.00**

Sandman by Ralph Freed & Bonnie Lake, 1934 ....**3.00**

Sandman, The by Mary White Slater & Carrie Jacobs Bond, 1912, Dedicated To Marie White Longman (Dedication) **15.00**

Sands Of Time, The by Robert Wright & Chet Forrest, 1953, Musical: Kismet.....................**4.00**

Sandy-Haired Mary In Our Area by Edward Harrigan & David Braham, 1880 (Pre 1900) **15.00**

Sans Toi Without Thee by Anita Owens, 1917 (Deco) **10.00**

Santa Claus Express, The by Abner Silver, Al Sherman & Al Lewis, 1935, Photo Uncle Don (Cover Artist, HBK) **5.00**

Santa Claus For President by Peter Tinturin, 1947.....................**3.00**

Santa Claus Is Comin' To Town by Haven Gillespie & J. Fred Coots, 1934 ....**3.00**

Santa Fe by Williams & Van Alstyne.....................**5.00**

Santa Rosa Rose by Jeff Branen & Lyons & Yosco, 1918 (Cover Artist, Keller) **5.00**

Santa's On His Way by John W. Schaum, 1970 (Cover Artist, J. Hejnal)..**2.00**

Saratoga Glide, The by Harry L. Newman, 1909, Photo Roy S. Sebree (Rag) **10.00**

Sari Waltz by Kalman, 1914.....................**5.00**

Sas'parilla Women And Song by Alfred Bryan & Jean Schwartz, 1919, Musical: Oh, My Dear **5.00**

Sasha, The Passion Of The Pasha by William Rose, Ballard Macdonald & Jesse Greer, 1930, Movie: Be Yourself, Photo Fannie Brice.........**15.00**

Saskatoon Rag by Phil Goldberg, 1915 (Rag).....................**10.00**

Satisfied by Irving Caesar & Cliff Friend, 1929, Photo Rudy Vallee **5.00**

Satisfied With You by Harold Dixon & Sam K. Stept, 1926 ....**4.00**

Saturday by Sidney D. Mitchell & Harry Brooks, 1921, Musical: Snap Shots Of 1921, Photo Nora Bayes.....................**10.00**

Saturday Date by Jack Brooks, 1948 ....**5.00**

Saturday Night by Elton L. Hill & Edward Raggs Johnson, Photo Alvino Rey & Four King Sisters **5.00**

Saturday Night by P.G. Wodehouse & Jerome Kern, 1916.....................**6.00**

Saturday Night by Sammy Cahn & Jule Styne, 1944, Photo Eileen Barton.....................**2.00**

Saturday Night Is The Loneliest Night Of The Week by Sammy Cahn & Jule Styne, 1944, Photo Frank Sinatra (Cover Artist, Barbelle).......**3.00**

Save Dis Little Nigger From De Rain And De Frost by Pauline Story, 1915 (Cover Artist, Pfeiffer & Black, Black Face) **20.00**

Save The Last Dance For Me by Walter Hirsch, Frank Magine & Phil Spitalny, 1931, Photo Morton Downey **4.00**

Save Your Sorrow by B.G.DeSylva & Al Sherman, 1925 ....**3.00**

Savin' Myself For Bill by V. Knight, 1942 (WWII) **3.00**

Saw Mill River Road by Joseph McCarthy & Harry Tierney, 1921, Photo Marshall Montgomery (Cover Artist, JVR) **6.00**

Sawing A Woman In Half by Jack Rock, 1938, Movie: The Big Broadcast Of 1938, Photo Shirley Ross, Carricature, W.C. Fields, Ben Blue, Bob Hope & Martha Raye.....................**5.00**

Say A Little Prayer by Gerry Mason, 1941 ....**3.00**

Say A Little Prayer For Me by Joseph George Gilbert & Horatio Nicholls, 1930, Photo Ruth Etting **10.00**

Say A Prayer For The Boys "Out There" by Bernie Grossman & Alex Marr, 1917, Photo Polly Russell (Cover Artist, Starmer, WWI & Patriotic).....................**20.00**

Say A Prayer For The Boys "Out There" by Bernie Grossman & Alex Marr, 1917, Photo Betty Price (Cover Artist, Starmer, WWI & Patriotic).....................**22.00**

Say A Prayer For The Boys Over There by Herb Magidson & Jimmy McHugh, 1943, Movie: Hers To Hold, Photo Deanna Durbin & Joseph Cotten (WWII).....................**8.00**

Say Au Revoir But Not Goodbye by Harry Kennedy, 1893 (Pre 1900) ..**10.00**

Say Au Revoir But Not Goodbye by Kennedy & E. T. Paull, 1918 (Cover Artist, Pfeiffer, E. T. Paull & WWI) **35.00**

Say Boys–I've Found A Girl by Gus Kahn, 1909 ....**5.00**

Say "Hello" To The Folks Back Home by Benny Davis & Carmen Lombardo, 1931 ....**6.00**

Say It by Frank Loesser & Jimmy McHugh, 1940, Movie: Buck Benny Rides Again, Photo Jack Benny, Phil Harris, Ellen Drew, Dennis Day & Rochester **6.00**

Say It Again by Wm. B. Friedlander & Con Conrad, 1923, Musical: Moonlight (Cover Artist, Politzer) **5.00**

Say It Isn't So by Irving Berlin, 1932 (Irving Berlin) **10.00**

Say It While Dancing by Benny Davis & Abner Silver, 1922 ....**4.00**

Say It With A Slap by Eliot Daniel & Buddy Kaye, 1947, Movie: Fun And Fancy Free (Disney) **16.00**

Say It With Firecrackers by Irving Berlin, 1942 (Irving Berlin) **10.00**

Say It With Flowers by Neville Fleeson & Albert Von Tilzer, 1919 .....**5.00**

Say It With Music by Irving Berlin, 1921, Musical: Music Box Revue (Irving Berlin).....................**10.00**

Say It With Your Heart by Steve Nelson & Norman Kaye, 1952.....................**3.00**

Say Me by Val Burton & Henry Busse, 1929.....................**4.00**

Say Mister Have You Met Rosie's Sister by Charlie Harrison & Fred Rose, 1926 ....**5.00**

Say No, That's All by Frank J. Conroy & Ted Snyder, 1908 (Cover Artist, John Frew) **5.00**

Say Something, Silas by Joan Clark, 1928 ....**3.00**

Say Something Sweet To Your Sweetheart by Sid Tepper & Roy Brodsky, 1948, Photo Eve Young (Cover Artist, BJH & Deco).....................**6.00**

Say, Suz! How 'Bout You? by Thatcher, 1899 (Pre 1900) **10.00**

Say When by Jimmie Mercer, 1950, Signed Photo Richard Hayes........**3.00**

Say When by Kahn Keene, Carl Bean & Frankie Masters, 1940...........**4.00**

Say Yes by Erik Satie, 1953 ....**3.00**

Say Yes Sweetheart Say Yes by Harry B. Smith & Emmerich Kalman, 1924, Musical: Countess Maritza **10.00**

Say You Love Me by Arthur Kassin & Angelo Rose, 1952..................**3.00**

Say You'll Be Mine by Alice Nadine Morrison, 1921 ....**4.00**

Say You'll Be My Lady by Dinad, 1906...**3.00**

Say You're Mine Again by Charles Nathan & Dave Heisler, 1953 ....**3.00**

Says I To Myself, Says I by Ed Moran & Harry Von Tilzer, 1917 (Cover Artist, Pfeiffer & Irish) **15.00**

Says My Heart by Frank Loesser & Burton Lane, 1938, Movie: Cocoanut Grove, Photo Fred McMurray, Harriet Hilliard, Ben Blue & The Yacht Club Boys **5.00**

Scaddle-De-Mooch by Chris Smith, 1915...**5.00**

Scamp Of The Campus, The by Greer & Klages, 1930, Movie: Cheer Up And Smile, Photo Arthur Lake & Dixie Lee **3.00**

Scandal Of Little Lizzie Ford by VonTilzer, 1921 (Transportation)....**15.00**

Scandinavia, Sing Dose Song And Make Dose Music by Ray Perkins, 1921, Musical: Midnight Rounders, Photo Eddie Cantor (Cover Artist, Barbelle & Eddie Cantor) **15.00**

Scaramouche by R.S. Stoughton, 1934 (Deco) 10.00

Scarborough Fair by Paul Simon & Art Garfunkel, Movie: The Graduate **3.00**

Scarecrow Rag by Will B. Morrison, 1912 (Rag) **10.00**

Scarf Dance by Carl Richter, 1944 ....**3.00**

Scarlet Ribbons, For Her Hair by Jack Segal & Evelyn Danzig, 1949, Photo Dinah Shore...**5.00**

Scat Song Skat N Skeet N Hi De Hi by Parish, Perkins & Cab Calloway, 1932 (Cover Artist, Pfeiffer) **10.00**

Scatterbrain by Johnny Burke, Keene Bean & Frankie Masters, 1939...**3.00**

Scented Roses by Joseph Daly, 1909..**5.00**

Schoene Madel by Paul David & Don Rodney, 1948 ....**3.00**

School Bell by Leach & Specht, 1919 (Cover Artist, Pfeiffer) **10.00**

School Bells by Harris (Cover Artist, Pfeiffer) **10.00**

School Day Sweethearts by Glen Edwards, 1923.................................**5.00**

School Days by Burns, Dorr & Shephard, 1919 (Cover Artist, Pfeiffer) ..**10.00**

School Days by Will D. Cobb & Gus Edwards, 1906..........................**10.00**

School Days by Will D. Cobb & Gus Edwards, 1933, Photo Will D. Cobb (Cover Artist, Milas)...**5.00**

School Days by Will D. Cobb & Gus Edwards, 1936, Movie: The Star Maker, Photo Bing Crosby (Cover Artist, Im-Ho)........................**12.00**

School Life by Chas. L. Johnson, 1912, Respectfully Dedicated To All Schools (March & Dedication)...**15.00**

School Of Ragtime by Scott Joplin, 1908 (Scott Joplin & Rag) **50.00**

School Where Lincoln Went by Will Hardy, 1910 (Presidents)..........**10.00**

Schoolhouse Blues, The by Irving Berlin, 1921 (Blues & Irving Berlin)..**10.00**

Schubert's Serenade by Fr. Schubert (Cover Artist, Starmer)..............**5.00**

Scissors And Knives To Grind by Ira Schuster, Paul Cunningham & Harry Jentes, 1939 ....**5.00**

Scissors To Grind by Thos. S. Allen, 1904 ....**3.00**

Scorcher, The by George Rosey, 1897 (Pre 1900 & March)..............**25.00**

Scotch Lassie Jean by Harry Miller, 1873, Sung In "The Tourists In A Pullman Car" (Lithograph, J.H. Bufford, Boston, MA., Pre 1900 & Transportation) **50.00**

Scott Joplin's New Rag by Scott Joplin, 1912 (Scott Joplin & Rag) ...**50.00**

Scottish Medley by S. G. Cook, 1906..**3.00**

Scrambled Eggs by James A. Brennan, 1914 ....**5.00**

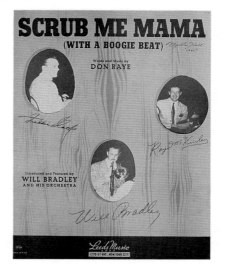

Scrub Me Mama, With A Boogie Beat by Don Raye, 1940, Signed Photos of Freddie Slack, Ray McKinley & Will Bradley (Cover Artist, Im-Ho)..8.00

'Scuse Me Today by Charles K. Harris, 1909 ....**5.00**

Sea Of The Moon, The by Arthur Freed & Harry Warren, 1950, Movie: Pagan Love Song, Photo Esther Williams & Howard Keel...........**10.00**

Sea Shell by Baer & Shisler, 1910...**5.00**

Seal It With A Kiss by Charles Moe, Elsie Thompson & Frank Magean, 1924 ....**5.00**

Seal It With A Kiss by Edward Heyman & Arthur Schwartz, 1936, Movie: That Girl From Paris, Photo Lily Pons...**5.00**

Sealed With A Kiss by Peter Udell & Gary Geld, 1960, Photo Bobby Vinton **2.00**

Searching For Words by Wayne Wood & Kenny Schooler, 1933 ....**3.00**

Seattle by Walter Augustyne, 1909 (Indian).....................................**25.00**

Seattle Town by Harold Weeks, 1923 ....**3.00**

Seben Come Eleben by W. J. Bay, 1899 (Pre 1900 & Rag)...............**20.00**

Second Degree, Full Moon by Edward Harrigan & David Braham, 1880 (Pre 1900) **16.00**

Second Hand Rose by Grant Clarke & James F. Hanley, 1965, Photo Barbara Streisand **4.00**

Second Regiment, Conn. National Guard March, 1898 (Pre 1900 & March) **15.00**

Second Time Around, The by Jimmy Van Heusen & Sammy Cahn, 1961, Movie: High Time, Photo Bing Crosby, Fabian & Tuesday Weld ..**6.00**

Secret Love by Paul Francis Webster & Sammy Fain, 1953, Movie: Calamity Jane, Photo Doris Day & Howard Keel............................**5.00**

Secret Love by Paul Francis Webster & Sammy Fain, 1953, Movie: Calamity Jane, Signed Photo Doris Day (Signed)..........................**30.00**

Secret Of Mine by Fred G. Bowles & John S. Fearis, 1924....................**3.00**

Secretly by Marty Symes & Al Kaufman, 1943.....................................**3.00**

Secrets by F. L. Knowles & J. Edwin Allemong, 1914..........................**5.00**

Secrets In The Moonlight by Gordon, 1940, Movie: Stardust, Photo Linda Darnell & John Payne..**4.00**

Seduction, The by Moroder, 1980, Movie: American Gigolo, Photo Richard Gere..**2.00**

Seein' Is Believin' by Stanley Adams & Milton Ager, 1935 ....**3.00**

Seein's Believin by Ehrlich & Cohen, 1903..**10.00**

Seeing Denver by Philip Brohm, 1906 (Transportation).....................**15.00**

Seems Like A Month Of Sundays by Harry Pease, Ed. G. Nelson & Al Goodhart, 1940...**3.00**

Seems Like Old Times by Carmen Lombardo & John Jacob Loeb, 1946, Photo Vincent Lopez (Cover Artist, Sorokin)..................................**6.00**

Selection by Richard Rodgers & Oscar Hammerstein II, Movie: Carousel, 1945 (Cover Artist, BJH)...**5.00**

Selection by Sigmund Romberg, 1925, Musical: Student Prince..........**3.00**

Seminola by King & Warren, 1925 (Indian) **25.00**

Semper Fidelis by John Philip Sousa, 1888 (John Philip Sousa, March & Pre 1900)..**25.00**

Semper Paratus by Capt. Francis S. Van Boskerck, 1938, Official Coast Guard Marching Song (Patriotic, Military Personnel & Transportation) **15.00**

Send Back My Honeyman by Henry Creamer & Lou Handman, 1922 .**3.00**

Send Back The Picture And The Wedding Ring by Gussie L. Davis, 1896 (Pre 1900) **15.00**

Send For Me by Edgar Leslie & George F. Meyer, 1911.......................**5.00**

Send Me A Letter From Over The Sea by Jackson, 1880 (Pre 1900 & Transportation) **20.00**

Send Me Away With A Smile by Louis Weslyn & Al Piantadosi, 1917, Signed Photo Rita Gould (Cover Artist, Starmer, Signed & WWI) ..**15.00**

Send Me Back The Happiness, You Stole Away From Me by Gene Cullinan, 1922 ....**6.00**

Senora by Felix Feist & Jos. Nathan, 1908 (Cover Artist, Boyd Dillon) 10.00

Sensation Rag by Joesph F. Lamb, 1908 (Rag)...................................**10.00**

Sentimental Journey by Bud Green, Les Brown & Ben Homer, 1944, Movie: Ensign Pulver, Photo Robert Walker...................................**5.00**

Sentimental Journey by Bud Green, Les Brown & Ben Homer, 1944, Photo Les Brown **3.00**

Sentimental Journey by Bud Green, Les Brown & Ben Homer, 1944, Photo Rose Marie **3.00**

Sentimental Journey by Bud Green, Les Brown & Ben Homer, 1944, Photo Joan Brooks **3.00**

Sentimental Me by Jim Morehead & Jimmy Cassin, 1950, Photo Russ Morgan...**3.00**

Sentimental Me by Lawrence, Mann & Weiss, 1940, Movie: The Quarterback, Photo Wayne Morris & Virginia Dale **5.00**

Sentimental Me by Lorenz Hart & Richard Rodgers, 1925..................**5.00**

Sentimental Rhapsody by Harold Adamson & Alfred Newman, 1942 ..**3.00**

Sentimental Rose by Emmette Sullivan, Joe Goodwin & John Driscoll, 1926 ....**3.00**

Sentimental Sweetheart by Henry Starr & Frank Anderson, 1929.........**3.00**

Separons Nous, Mon Amie by A.S. de Pierreville & Antoinette Alexander, 1913 ....**5.00**

September In The Rain by Al Dubin & Harry Warren, 1937, Movie: Melody For Two...**5.00**

September Song by Maxwell Anderson & Kurt Weill, 1938 (Cover Artist, BJH)..**3.00**

Serenade by Dorothy Donnelly & Sigmund Romberg, 1925, Musical: Student Prince **3.00**

Serenade by Enrico Toselli, 1923, Theme Song Of "The Goldbergs"...5.00

Serenade by Franz Schubert, 1933..**3.00**

Serenade by J. Albert Jeffery, 1899 (Pre 1900)..................................**10.00**

Serenade In Blue by Mack Gordon & Harry Warren, 1942, Movie: Orchestra Wives, Photo Glenn Miller & Many Stars.....................**10.00**

Serenade In The Night by C.A. Bixio, B. Cherubini & Jimmy Kennedy, 1936, Movie: Melodrama **5.00**

Serenade Of The Bells by Kay Twomey, Al Goodhart & Al Urbano, 1947 (Cover Artist, Barbelle) **5.00**

Serenata by Allen & Roth, 1916 (Cover Artist, Pfeiffer) **10.00**

Serenata by Leroy Anderson, 1949..**3.00**

Sergeant Hickey Of The G.A.R. by Edward Harrigan, 1893 (Pre 1900 & Military Personnel)..**18.00**

Sermon That Touched His Heart, The by Tony Stanford, 1897 (Pre 1900) **10.00**

Sesqui-Centennial Exposition Of U.S. by John Philip Sousa, 1921 (John Philip Sousa & March) **15.00**

Sesqui-Centennial Hymn, The by Jack DeMille, Nat Belov & Joseph Belov, 1926, Dedicated To The American People (Dedication & Patriotic)...**25.00**

Set Aside Your Tears, Till The Boys Come Marching Home by L. Wolfe Gilbert, Malvin Franklin & Anatol Friedland, 1917 (WWI)..........**10.00**

Settle Down And Travel by Joseph McCarthy & Harry Tierney, 1922, Musical: Up She Goes **3.00**

Settle Down In A One Horse Town by Irving Berlin, 1916 (Irving Berlin) **10.00**

Seven-Eleven Or My Dixie Pair O'Dice by Lew Brown & Walter Donaldson, 1923 (Dixie) **12.00**

Seventeen by John F. Young Jr., Chuck Gorman & Boyd Bennett, 1955, Photo Boyd Bennett..............................**3.00**

Seventy Six Trombones by Meredith Wilson, 1957, Movie: Music Man **3.00**

Sew The Buttons On by John Jennings, 1963, Musical: Riverwind.......**3.00**

Sewing Machine, The by Frank Loesser, 1947, Movie: The Perils Of Pauline, Photo Betty Hutton & John Lund **5.00**

Sextet From Lucia by Donizette, 1909 (Cover Artist, Pfeiffer) **10.00**

Sha-Wan-Da-Moo, Indian Love Song by Lawrence St. Cyr, 1927 ......**20.00**

Shade Of The Sheltering Palm by Leslie Stuart, 1900 ....**5.00**

Shades Of Night by L. Wolfe Gilbert, Anatol Friedland & Malvin Franklin, 1916, Photo May Naudain **5.00**

Shadow Of Your Smile, The by Johnny Mandel, Movie: Sandpiper, Photo Elizabeth Taylor & Richard Burton..............................**6.00**

Shadow Waltz, The by Al Dubin & Harry Warren, 1933 ....**3.00**

Shadow-Time by Chas. L. Johnson, 1913 ....**5.00**

Shadowland by Edwards & Merrill, 1914 (Cover Artist, Pfeiffer).......**10.00**

Shadows by Carrie Jacobs Bond, 1901, Linen Cover **15.00**

Shadows by Howard Lutter, 1919 ....**5.00**

Shadows by Jules Loman, Chet Thompson & Frankie Carle, 1939 .....**10.00**

Shadows Of Love by Abbelu Burns & Madelyn Sheppard, 1920..........**3.00**

Shadows Of Paris by Wells & Mancini, 1964, Movie: A Shot In The Dark..**3.00**

Shadows Of The Night by Charles Crean & Robert Cobert, 1969........**3.00**

Shadows Will Fade Away by J. Keirn Brennan & Bert Rule, 1919.......**5.00**

Shady Tree, A by Walter Donaldson, 1927 ....**3.00**

Shakesperian Love by Hugo Frey, 1914................................**5.00**

Shaking The Blues Away by Irving Berlin, 1947, Movie: Easter Parade, Photo Judy Garland, Fred Astaire, Peter Lawford & Ann Miller (Irving Berlin)......................................**16.00**

Shall I Compare You? by Hy Zaret, Seymour Mann & Irving Weiser, 1940 (Cover Artist, Im-Ho) **3.00**

Shall I Ever See My Mother's Face Again by Paul Adriance, 1895 (Pre 1900) **10.00**

Shall We Dance by Ira Gershwin & George Gershwin, 1937, Movie: Shall We Dance?, Photo Fred Astaire & Ginger Rogers **10.00**

Shall We Dance by Richard Rodgers & Oscar Hammerstein II, 1951, Movie: The King And I **5.00**

Shame On You by Chris Smith, 1904................................**5.00**

Shamrock by Billy DeVere & Dawson Wood, 1907, Photo Pearl Stevens (Irish) **10.00**

Shanghai Lil by Al Dubin & Harry Warren, 1933, Movie: Footlight Parade, Photo James Cagney, Ruby Keeler, Joan Blondell & Dick Powell (Cover Artist, Jorg Harris)........................**12.00**

Sharing by Benny Davis & J. Fred Coots, 1930 ....**5.00**

Sharp As A Tack by Johnny Mercer & Harold Arlen, 1942, Movie: Star Spangled Rhythm, Photo Bing Crosby, Bob Hope, Dorothy Lamour & Many More Stars **6.00**

Shauny O'Shay by Hugh Martin, 1947, Musical: Look, Ma, I'm Dancin'!...**3.00**

Shawana by M. Learsi, 1914 ....**3.00**

She Could Shake The Maracas by Lorenz Hart & Richard Rodgers, 1939, Movie: Too Many Girls..............................**6.00**

She Didn't Say Yes, by Jerome Kern & Otto Harbach, 1931, Movie: The Cat And The Fiddle, Photo Ramon Novarro & Jeannette Macdonald **8.00**

She Don't Wanna by Jack Yellen & Milton Ager, 1927 ....**5.00**

She Got Even With Stephen by Alfred Bryan, Sam M. Lewis & Geo. W. Meyer, 1914 (Cover Artist, Pfeiffer & Deco) **15.00**

She Has Left The Old Homestead Forever by Hardy & Rocheleau, 1916 (Cover Artist, Pfeiffer) **10.00**

She Is Far From The Land by Tom Moore & Frank Lambert, 1897 (Pre 1900)..**10.00**

She Is Ma Daisy by J.D. Harper & Harry Lauder, 1905 (Cover Artist, Starmer)..**10.00**

She Is More To Be Pitied Than Censored by W. B. Grey, 1898 (Pre 1900) **10.00**

She Is The Sunshine Of Virginia by Ballard MacDonald & Harry Carroll, 1916 (Cover Artist, Pfeiffer) **10.00**

She Keeps Me In The Dark by Alfred Bryan, Willie Raskin & Pete Wendling, 1927 ....**5.00**

She Knows It by Al Jolson, 1921 (Al Jolson)................................**12.00**

She Lives Down In Our Alley by Charles McCarron & Charles Bayha, 1915, Photo Ruth Royce (Cover Artist, Dunk, N.Y.)....................**10.00**

She Lives In Alabama by Edith Willard & Harry Miller, 1901.............**5.00**

She Lives On Murray Hill by Edward Harrigan & David Braham, 1892 (Pre 1900) **10.00**

She May Have Seen Better Days by James Thornton, 1894 (Pre 1900) ..**10.00**

She Never Kissed Anything Else Except The Blarney Stone by Will J. Hart, Lew Hayes & Abe Olman, 1927 (Cover Artist, Wohlman & Irish) ..**10.00**

She Reminds Me Of You by Mack Gordon & Harry Revel, 1930, Movie: We're Not Dressing, Photo Bing Crosby & Carole Lombard........**10.00**

She Rests By The Swanee River by Tony Stanford, 1899 (Pre 1900 & Black, Black Face)..**15.00**

She Sang "Aloha" To Me by Jos. B. Carey, 1915 (Transportation).......**5.00**

She Sleeps Next To The Old Ohio River by Lam & Soman, 1913 ......**10.00**

She Still Believes In You by Monroe H. Rosenfeld, 1800, Boston Herald Sunday Supplement (Cover Artist, H. C. Goehl & Pre 1900)........**15.00**

She Waits By The Deep Blue Sea by Edward Madden & Theodore Morse, 1905 ....**10.00**

She Was A Grand Old Lady by Davies & Henry, 1907 ....**10.00**

She Was A Soldier's Sweetheart by Bert Potter, 1906 (Patriotic)........**15.00**

She Was A Soldier's Sweetheart by Rosenfeld & Church, 1918 (Cover Artist, Pfeiffer & Patriotic)..**15.00**

She Was All That A Pal Ought To Be by Bernie Grossman & Jack Glogau, 1915, Photo Rena Santos **10.00**

She Was Bred In Old Kentucky by Braisted & Carter, 1898 (Pre 1900 & Dixie) **10.00**

She Was Happy 'Til She Met You by Chas. Graham & Monroe Rosenfeld, 1935 ....**4.00**

She Was Just A Sailor's Sweetheart by Joe Burke, 1925 ....**8.00**

She Was Made For Love by Bryan & Mohr, 1915 (Cover Artist, Pfeiffer)..**10.00**

She Was My Only Girl, 1915 (Cover Artist, Pfeiffer)........................**10.00**

She Was Not So Bad For A Country Girl by B.G. DeSylva, 1918 ....**6.00**

She'll Always Remember by Eddie Polla & Johnnie Marks, 1918 (WWI) **10.00**

She'll Be Coming Round The Mountain by Frank & Manoloff, 1935, Photo Gabe Drake (Cover Artist, NPS)........................**5.00**

She'll Love Me And Like It by Leo Robin, W. Franke Harling & Richard A. Whiting, 1930, Movie: Monte Carlo **6.00**

She'll Miss Me Most Of All by Will J. Hart & Ed Nelson, 1918 (Cover Artist, Barbelle & WWI) **15.00**

She's A Lady by Cy Coben, 1950, Photo Perry Como & Betty Hutton (Cover Artist, Nick)..**5.00**

She's A Mean Job by Geo. Landis & Jimmy Selby, 1921 (Deco) **5.00**

She's Coming Home To-Night by W. C. Parker, 1905 (Cover Artist, Starmer)..**12.00**

She's Dancing Her Heart Away by L. Wolfe Gilbert & Kerry Mills, 1914..**5.00**

She's Dixie All The Time by A. Bryan & Harry Tierney, 1916 (Dixie) ..**5.00**

She's Drivin' Me Wild by Gerald Marks & Buddy Fields, 1925...........**5.00**

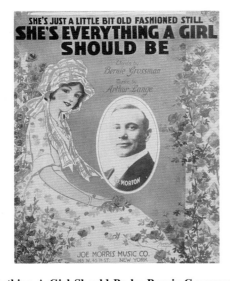

She's Everything A Girl Should Be by Bernie Grossman & Arthur Lange, 1917, Photo Ed Morton (Cover Artist, Starmer) 10.00

She's Funny That Way by Neil Moret & Richard Whiting, 1928..........**5.00**

She's Gettin More Like The White Folks Everyday by Bert Williams & George Walker (Black, Black Face)...**15.00**

She's Just A Home Sweet Home Girl by Jerome & Schwartz, 1912 (Cover Artist, Pfeiffer)..**12.00**

She's Just Plain Mary Jane by Kane & Lang, 1910 (Cover Artist, Pfeiffer) **12.00**

She's Lovely by Haven Gillespie, 1922 ....**5.00**

She's My Warm Baby by Jas. O'Dea & M.B. Garrett, 1897, Signed Photo Flo Irwin (Pre 1900 & Signed) **15.00**

She's Never Been In Ireland But She's Irish Just The Same by Shields & Mack, 1911 (Irish) **10.00**

She's Only A Bird In A Gilded Cage by Arthur J. Lamb & Harry Von Tilzer, 1900...**10.00**

She's Only A Moving Picture by C. E. Dittmar, 1912 ....**5.00**

She's Somebody's Mother by Lawler & Blake, 1897 (Pre 1900) **10.00**

She's The Daughter Of Mother Machree by Jeff T. Nenarb & Ernest R. Ball, 1915 (Irish)...**10.00**

She's The Daughter Of Officer Porter by Rourke & Schleiffarth, 1896 (Pre 1900)..**10.00**

She's The Flower Of Mississippi by Horwitz & Bowers, 1901 ....**10.00**

She's The Sunshine Of Virginia by Ballard Macdonald & Harry Carroll, 1916 ....**8.00**

Shedding Tears O'er Mother's Grave by R.W. Rose & George A. Cragg, 1883 (Pre 1900) **15.00**

Sheik Of Araby, The by Harry B. Smith, Francis Wheeler & Ted Snyder, 1921 ....**10.00**

Sheltered By The Stars by Joe Young & Thomas Waller, 1932 ....**3.00**

Shenanigans by Carl Sigman & William Whitlock, 1949 (Irish)..........**6.00**

Shepherd Boy, The by G.D. Wilson, 1870 (Cover Artist, T.M., Lithograph by J.H. Bufford & Pre 1900) **75.00**

Shepherd Of The Air by Clarence C. Gaskill, 1933 ....**5.00**

Shepherd Serenade by Kermit Goell, 1941 (Cover Artist, E.D. Allen)..**3.00**

Shepherd, The by William Blake & F. Bennicke Hart, 1920 ....**4.00**

Shepherd's Love by Hubert Fletcher & W.A. Manahan, 1923 ....**3.00**

Shepherd's Love Song, The by Kathryn Bayley, 1914 ....**5.00**

Shepherd's Serenade, The by Clifford Grey & Harold Stothart, 1929, Movie: Devil May Care...**5.00**

Shepherd's Song At Twilight by Drumheller, 1907 (Cover Artist, Pfeiffer) **15.00**

Shepherdess, The by Archibald Sullivan & Carrie Jacobs Bond, 1910.**15.00**

Sheridan's Ride by E.T. Paull, 1922 (Cover Artist, E.T. Paull, March & Patriotic) **40.00**

Shifting, Whispering Sands, The by V.C. Gilbert & Mary M. Hadler, 1950, Photo Billy Vaughn **5.00**

Shim-Me-Sha-Wabble by Spencer Williams, 1917............................**5.00**

Shimmie Town by Gene Buck & Dave Stamper, 1919, Musical: Ziegfeld Follies 1919 (Deco) **15.00**

Shimmy Moon by Jack Frost & F. Henri Klickmann, 1920.................**3.00**

Shine On Arizona Moon by Walter Donovan & Harold B. Freeman, 1915...**5.00**

Shine On, Harvest Moon by M. Nora Bayes & Jack Norworth, Photo Ruth Etting **8.00**

Shine On, Harvest Moon by Nora Bayes & Jack Norworth, 1918, Photo Nora Bayes & Jack Norworth (Cover Artist, DeTakacs) **10.00**

Shine On Oh Stars by Frank E. Sawyer, 1894, Photo Melville Stewart (Pre 1900)..**10.00**

Shine On Winter Moon by Roberts & Whittaker, 1914 (Cover Artist, Pfeiffer)..**10.00**

Shine On Your Shoes, A by Howard Dietz & Arthur Schwartz, 1932...**3.00**

Ship I Love by Felix McGlennon, 1893 (Pre 1900) **10.00**

Ship Named U.S.A. Or Wilson's War Cry Of Peace, The by James F. Whitehorn, T.F. Ambrose & W. Lorraine, 1915, Photo President Wilson (WWI, President & Transportation)....................................**50.00**

Ship O'Dreams by C.S. Montanye & Herbert Francis, 1921 ....**5.00**

Ship Of My Dreams by Arthur J. Lamb & Alfred Solman, 1912..........**5.00**

Ship Sails Tonight, The by Strelezki, 1887 (Pre 1900 & Transportation)..**25.00**

Shipmates Forever, Don't Give Up The Ship by Al Dubin & Harry Warren, 1935, Movie: Shipmates Forever **8.00**

Shipwreck, The by Davenport, 1872 (Pre 1900 & Transportation)......**25.00**

Shoeless Joe From Hannibal Mo. by Richard Adler & Jerry Ross, 1955, Musical: Damn Yankee **6.00**

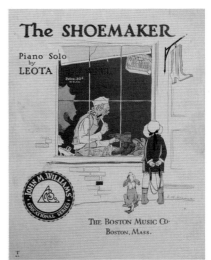

Shoemaker, The by Leota Stilwell, 1932 (Cover Artist, D & G Haumann)..5.00

Shoemaker's Holiday, The by Hugh MacKey, 1939............................**3.00**

Shoes And Socks Shock Susan by William Van Alstyne, 1910............**5.00**

Shoo Fly, Don't Bother Me by Billy Reeves & Frank Campbell, 1869 (Pre 1900)...**16.00**

Shoo Shoo Boogie Boo by Robin, Coslow & Whiting, 1929, Movie: Why Bring That Up?, Photo Charles Mack 5.00

Shoo-Fly Pie And Apple Pan Dowdy by Guy Wood & Sammy Gallop, 1945 ....3.00

Shoo-Shoo Baby by Phil Moore, 1943, Movie: Beautiful But Broke, Photo Andrews Sisters 5.00

Shoo-Shoo Baby by Phil Moore, 1943, Movie: Beautiful But Broke, Photo Joan Davis, Jane Frazee & Judy Clark 5.00

Shoogy-Shoo, The by Winthrop Rackard & Paul Ambrose, 1900 ....10.00

Short'nin Bread by David W. Guion, 1928, Signed Photo Eddy Nelson (Signed & Black, Black Face) 100.00

Shortest Day Of The Year, The by Lorenz Hart & Richard Rodgers, 1938, Musical: The Boys From Syracuse (Cover Artist, Ben Jorj Harris).3.00

Shortnin' Bread by Jacques Wolfe, 1928 (Black, Black Face)............15.00

Shorty George, The by Johnny Mercer & Jerome Kern, 1942, Movie: You Were Never Lovelier, Photo Fred Astaire, Rita Hayworth, Adolphe Menjou & Xavier Cugat And His Orchestra 5.00

Shot-Gun Boogie by Tennessee Ernie Ford, 1951, Photo Tennessee Ernie Ford..3.00

Should I Be Sweet? by B.G.DeSylva & Vincent Youmans, 1933, Movie: Take A Chance 5.00

Should I? by Arthur Freed & Nacio Herb Brown, 1929, Movie: Lord Byron Of Broadway..10.00

Should I Tell You I Love You by Cole Porter, Movie: Around The World...5.00

Shout Hurrah For America by Freeman, 1914 (Cover Artist, Pfeiffer & Patriotic) 15.00

Shout! Wherever You May Be, I Am An American by Ira Schuster, Paul Cunningham & Leonard Whitcup (Cover Artist, Im-Ho) 5.00

Show Me The Way by Benny Davis, Ted Lewis & Frank Ross, 1924 ..5.00

Show Me The Way by Hazard & Friedland, 1909 (Cover Artist, Pfeiffer)..10.00

Show Me The Way Dear To Loveland by Frank Davis & Win Brookhouse, 1916, Photo Grayce Salon 10.00

Show Me The Way To Go Home by Irving King, 1925 (Cover Artist, Hap Hadley & Deco)..15.00

Show Me The Way To Go Home by Stanley Murray, 1906 (Black, Black Face) 20.00

Show Us How To Do The Fox Trot by Irving Berlin, 1913 (Irving Berlin) 10.00

Shower Of Kisses by Anna Brown, 1916 (Cover Artist, Pfeiffer) 10.00

Shower Of Roses by Bessie May...5.00

Showers by Colin Wendell, 1937 ....3.00

Shrimp Boats by Paul Mason & Howard & Paul Weston, 1951 (Transportation) 3.00

Shrine Of Love by Meyers & Dulmaze, 1916 (Cover Artist, Pfeiffer) 10.00

Shrine Of St. Cecilia, The by Carroll Loveday & Jokern, 1940.............3.00

Shuffle Off To Buffalo by Al Dubin & Harry Warren, 1932, Movie: Forty Second Street, Photo Bebe Daniels, George Brent, Ruby Keeler, Warner Baxter, Ginger Rogers, Dick Powell, Una Merkel & Guy Kibbe 12.00

Shuffle Your Feet & Roll Along by Dorothy Fields & Jimmy McHugh, 1928, Musical: Blackbirds Of 1928 (Cover Artist, Leff) 5.00

Si's Been Drinking Cider by Irving Berlin, 1914 (Irving Berlin).........10.00

Siboney by Ernesto Lecuona & Dolly Morse, 1929 ....2.00

Sicily by Weston Wilson, Harry Williams & Neil Moret, 1920............3.00

Side By Side by Harry Woods, 1927, Photo Dick Jurgens....................3.00

Side By Side by Harry Woods, 1927, Photo Dolly Ward (Cover Artist, Politzer) 5.00

Side By Side by Harry Woods, 1927, Signed Photo Kay Starr (Signed)...10.00

Sidewalks Of New York, The by Charles B. Lawlor & James W. Blake, 1932 (Cover Artist, Wohlman) 12.00

Sidewalks Of New York, The by Charles B. Lawlor & James W. Blake, 1928, Official Campaign Song Of Honorable Al Smith, Signed Photo Honorable Al Smith (Cover Artist, Barbelle, Signed & Political) .38.00

Sierra Sue by Joseph B. Carey, 1916, Photo Bing Crosby (Cover Artist, Im-Ho) 5.00

Sighing by Duncan Sisters, Book By Catherine C. Cushing, Suggested By Uncle Tom's Cabin By Harriet Beecher Stowe, 1923, Musical: Topsy & Eva, Photo Duncan Sisters (Cover Artist, P.M. Griffith & Black, Black Face)...10.00

Sighing Just For You by Harold G. Frost, Cal DeVoll & Henri Klickmann, 1921 ....3.00

Sighing Too by Bewley & Cutty, 1911 (Cover Artist, Pfeiffer)..........10.00

Sights In A Dime Museum by F. D. Bryan, 1891 (Pre 1900)..............10.00

Sign Of The Rose by F. H. Losey, 1912 (Cover Artist, Dittmar)........10.00

Signal From Mars, A by Raymond Taylor, Arranged by E.T. Paull, 1901 (Cover Artist, E.T. Paull, Lithograph by A. Hoen & Co. & March)..35.00

Silent Confession by Harry J. Lincoln, 1918.....................................10.00

Silent Night, Holy Night by Nick Manoloff, 1935 ....2.00

Silent The World by James A. Korman, 1938 ....3.00

Silent Wooing by Andre DeTakacs, 1907 (Cover Artist, DeTakacs)...10.00

Silhouette One Step by Harold Bien, 1914..5.00

Silks & Rags Waltzes by Fred Stone, 1901 (Cover Artist, Eliccett, Rag & Black, Black Face)..15.00

Silouettes by Roberts, 1910 (Cover Artist, Pfeiffer)..........................10.00

Silver Bay by Percy Wenrich, 1916, Photo Dolly Connolly (Cover Artist, Rose Symbol) 6.00

Silver Bell by Edward Madden & Percy Wenrich, 1905 (Indian)........20.00

Silver Bells by Jay Livingston & Ray Evans, 1950.............................3.00

Silver Cloud (Cover Artist, Pfeiffer) 10.00

Silver Fox by Henry Lodge, 1915 (Rag) 10.00

Silver Haired Girl by T.J. Wedekind, 1941 ....3.00

Silver Head by James Brockman, Vincent Lopez & Joseph Nussbaum, 1925 ....3.00

Silver Heels, Indian Girl by James O'Dea & Neil Moret, 1905 (Cover Artist, Bertha Young & Indian)...20.00

Silver In The Moon by H.A. Pooley, 1945 ....3.00

Silver Jubilee March by John J. Fitzpatrick, 1905 (Cover Artist, Starmer & March) 10.00

Silver Lining, A by Dolly Morse & Walter Donaldson, 1928...............3.00

Silver Moon by Dorothy Donnelly & Sigmund Romberg, 1927, Musical: My Maryland 5.00

Silver Moon by Harris & Riker, 1909 ....3.00

Silver Sleighbells by E.T. Paull, 1906 (Cover Artist, E.T. Paull Lithograph A. Hoen & March)...35.00

Silver Star by Chas. L. Johnson, 1910...5.00

Silver Threads Among The Gold by Eben E. Rexford & H.P. Danks, 1901 (Cover Artist, Jenkins)..10.00

Silver Wing by Brian Hooker & Rudolf Friml, 1931, Musical: The White Eagle (Cover Artist, Barbelle)...5.00

Silver Wings In The Moonlight by Hugh Charles, Leo Towers & Sonny Miller, 1943, Photo Ray Benson (Cover Artist, Holley).................5.00

Silver Wings In The Moonlight by Hugh Charles, Leo Towers & Sonny Miller, 1943, Photo Clarence Fuhrman (Cover Artist, Holley)........5.00

Silvery Moonlight by Powell, 1909 (Cover Artist, Pfeiffer) 10.00

Silvery Waves by A.P. Wyman (Pre 1900) 10.00

Similitude by Lee Sims, 1932..4.00

Simple And Sweet by Bud Green & Abel Baer, 1938, Photo Enoch Light 5.00

Simple Melody by Irving Berlin, 1916 (Irving Berlin).....................10.00

Simple Things In Life, The by Edward Heyman & Ray Henderson, 1935, Movie: Curly Top, Photo Shirley Temple, John Boles & Rochelle Hudson (Shirley Temple) 10.00

Simple Wisdom by Arthur Stanley & Kennedy Russell, 1935..............**3.00**

Since He Traded His Zoot Suit For A Uniform by Carmen Lombardo & Pat Innisfree, 1942 (WWII)......................................**12.00**

Since Home Rule Came To Ireland by Kelly & Mullane, 1914 (Cover Artist, Pfeiffer & Irish) **15.00**

Since I First Met You by Ziegler & Owens, 1919 (Cover Artist, Pfeiffer) **10.00**

Since I Found You by Ruby & Perkins, 1929, Movie: Fast Life, Photo Douglas Fairbanks & Loretta Young.......................................**10.00**

Since I Heard My Pal Sing "My Gal Sal" by Alexander Dubin & Marion Raybold, 1916 (Cover Artist, C.J. Linke).......................**5.00**

Since I Kissed My Baby Goodbye by Cole Porter, 1941, Movie: You'll Never Get Rich **5.00**

Since It Started To Rain In Lover's Lane by Al Goodhart, Ed Nelson & Al Hoffman, 1930 (Cover Artist, Ben H)..............................**5.00**

Since Ma Is Playing Mah Jongg by Billy Rose & Con Conrad, 1924, Movie: Kid Boots, Photo Eddie Cantor (Eddie Cantor).................**12.00**

Since Maggie Dooley Learned The Hooley Hooley by Bert Kalmar, Edgar Leslie & George W. Meyer, 1916 (Irish) **6.00**

Since Mary Ann McCue Came Back From Honolulu by Von Tilzer, 1916 (Cover Artist, Pfeiffer) **10.00**

Since McManus Went Down To The Track by Edward B. Marks & Will H. Fox, 1892 (Pre 1900) **10.00**

Since Mother Goes To Movie Shows by Chas McCarron & Albert Von Tilzer, 1916..**5.00**

Since Mother Passed Away by M. T. Bohannon, 1893 (Pre 1900)......**12.00**

Since My Gal Is Gone I've Got The Blues by Herman & Silver, 1918 (Cover Artist, Pfeiffer) **10.00**

Since Nellie Went Away by Herbert H. Taylor, 1906...........................**5.00**

Since Nellie Went Away by Joseph Skelley, 1892 (Pre 1900).............**10.00**

Since Sarah Saw Theda Bara by Alex Gerber & Harry Jentes, 1916.....**6.00**

Since We Said Good By by Will Hellen & George Hamilton, 1900, New York Journal & Advertiser **10.00**

Since We Tune In On The Radio by Marie Irish & Margaret M. Stitt, 1929 ....**5.00**

Since You Called Me Sweetheart by Milton Eril & F. Henri Klickmann, 1925 ....**5.00**

Since You Went Away by Kermit Goell, Ted Grouya & Lou Forbes, 1944, Movie: Since You Went Away, Photo Claudette Colbert, Jennifer Jones, Shirley Temple, Lionel Barrymore & Other Stars (Shirley Temple)..**12.00**

Sing A Song Of Sunbeams by Johnny Burke & James V. Monaco, 1939, Movie: East Side Of Heaven, Photo Bing Crosby, Joan Blondell & Baby Sandy..**5.00**

Sing An Irish Song Tonight by Costello, Sherman & Richmond, 1914 (Cover Artist, Pfeiffer & Irish)...**15.00**

Sing An Old Fashioned Song by Joe Young & Fred E. Ahlert, 1935 ....**3.00**

Sing Hallelujah by Robin, Gray & Youmans, 1927 ....**3.00**

Sing Love's Old Sweet Song Again by Ellis & Wood, 1911 (Cover Artist, Pfeiffer)...**10.00**

Sing Me A Baby Song by Gus Kahn & Walter Donaldson, 1927 (Deco)..**5.00**

Sing Me A Song Of The South by Norton & Casey, 1899 (Pre 1900).**10.00**

Sing Me Love's Lullaby by Dorothy Terriss & Theodore Morse, 1917 **5.00**

Sing Me "O Sole Mio" by Gus Kahn & Egbert Van Alstyne, 1924.......**5.00**

Sing Me The Melody Of Love by Kerr & Skidmore, 1917 (Cover Artist, Pfeiffer)..**10.00**

Sing Me The Rosary by Roger Lewis & F. Henri Klickmann, 1913......**8.00**

Sing Me To Sleep by Clifton Bingham & Edwin Greene, 1902 ....**3.00**

Sing, My Heart by Ted Koehler & Harold Arlen, 1939 ....**3.00**

Sing Rock-A-Bye Baby To Me by Kirkpatrick & Long, 1913...............**5.00**

Sing! Sing! Birds On The Wing by Leslie Cooke & Godfrey Nutting, 1911 ....**5.00**

Sing Something Simple by Herman Hupfeld, 1930 ....**3.00**

Sing To Me Guitar by Cole Porter, 1943, Movie: Mexican Hayride **3.00**

Sing To Me Mother, Sing Me To Sleep by J. Will Callahan & F. Henri Klickmann, 1913 ....**5.00**

Sing You Sinners by Coslow & Harling, 1930, Movie: I'll Cry Tomorrow, Photo Susan Hayward...**8.00**

Sing You Sinners by W. Franke Harling & Sam Coslow, 1930, Movie: Honey, Photo Nancy Carroll, Stanley Smith & Lillian Roth **5.00**

Singer And The Song, The by Will D. Cobb & Gus Edwards, 1897 (Pre 1900)..**12.00**

Singin' In The Bathtub by Herb Magidson, Ned Washington & Michael H. Cleary, 1929, Movie: Show Of Shows **10.00**

Singin' In The Rain by Arthur Freed & Nacio Herb Brown, 1929, Movie: The Hollywood Revue of 1929, Many Stars On Cover **10.00**

Singin' In The Rain by Arthur Freed & Nacio Herb Brown, Signed & Framed Photo of Gene Kelly (Signed) **75.00**

Singin' In The Saddle by Sherwin, 1944, Photo Ann Sheridan.............**3.00**

Singing A Song To The Stars by Howard Johnson & Joseph Meyer, 1930, Movie: Way Out West...**5.00**

Singing A Vagabond Song by Harry Richman, Val Burton & Sam Messenheimer, 1930...**5.00**

Singing At The Hallway Door by Edward Harrigan & David Braham, 1879 (Pre 1900) **15.00**

Singing Bird by Arthur Longbrake & Ed Edwards, 1909 (Cover Artist, M.C. Myers & Indian) **10.00**

Singing Hills, The by Mack David, Dick Sanford & Sammy Mysels, 1940, Photo Blue Barron **3.00**

Singing Sands Of Alamosa, The by Kim Gannon & bert Reisfeld, 1942, Photo Enoch Light (Cover Artist, Im-Ho)....................................**3.00**

Singing The Dear Little Baby To Sleep by Armstrong, 1896 (Pre 1900)..**10.00**

Sinner Kissed An Angel, A by Ray Joseph, 1941 ....**3.00**

Sioux City Sue by Dick Thomas & Ray Freedman, 1945, Photo Al Trace..**6.00**

Sioux City Sue by Dick Thomas & Ray Freedman, 1945, Photo Bing Crosby (Cover Artist, Cesareo) **6.00**

Sioux City Sue by Dick Thomas & Ray Freedman, 1945, Photo Dick Thomas (Cover Artist, Cesareo)..**6.00**

Sioux City Sue by Dick Thomas & Ray Freedman, 1945, Photo Tiny Hill...**6.00**

Sipping Cider Thru A Straw by Lee David & Carey Morgan, 1919, Photo Fatty Arbuckle (Cover Artist, Starmer).....................................**10.00**

Siren Of A Southern Sea by Abe Brashen & Harold Weeks, 1921........**3.00**

Sister Kate Cake Walk by A.J. Piron, 1919 (Black, Black Face)........**10.00**

Sister Louisa by Will Hardy, 1913 ....**5.00**

Sister Susie's Sewing Shirts For Soldiers by R.P. Weston & Herman E. Darewski, 1914, Photo Al Jolson (Al Jolson, WWI & Black, Black Face) **20.00**

Sisters by Irving Berlin, 1942, Movie: White Christmas, Photo Bing Crosby, Danny Kaye, Rosemary Clooney & Vera Ellen (Irving Berlin) **12.00**

Sit Down You're Rocking The Boat by Jo Swerling, Abe Burrows & Frank Loesser, 1950, Musical: Guys & Dolls **5.00**

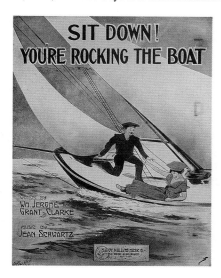

Sit Down! You're Rocking The Boat by Wm. Jerome, Grant Clarke & Jean Schwartz, 1916 (Cover Artist, Pfeiffer & Transportation)..15.00

Sittin' In A Corner by Gus Kahn & Geo. W. Meyer, 1923 ....**5.00**

Sittin' On A Backyard Fence by Irving Kahal & Sammy Fain, 1933, Movie: Footlight Parade, Photo James Cagney, Ruby Keeler, Joan Blondell & Dick Powell (Cover Artist, Jorj Harris)......................**10.00**

Sittin' On A Rainbow by Yellen & Dougherty, 1930, Movie: Call Of The West, Photo Dorothy Revier.....................**5.00**

Sittin' Up Waitin' For You by Andy Razap & Thomas Waller, 1936 ...**5.00**

Sitting On The Moon by Mitchell & Stept, 1936, Movie: Sitting On The Moon, Photo Roger Pryor & Grace Bradley **3.00**

Six Cylinder Kid, The by Mark D. Hawkins & Hal C. Paris, 1909 (Transportation) **10.00**

Six Lessons From Madame LaZonga by Charles Newman & James V. Monaco, 1940 ....**3.00**

Sixteen Going On Seventeen by Richard Rodgers & Oscar Hammerstein II, 1959, Movie: The Sound Of Music, Photo Julie Andrews & Christopher Plummer..................**5.00**

Sixteen Reasons by Bill & Doree Post, 1959, Photo Connie Stevens **3.00**

Sixteen Tons by Merle Travis, 1947..................**3.00**

Sixty Seconds Got Together by Mac David & Jerry Livingston, 1938 (Cover Artist, Im-Ho) **3.00**

Skaters Waltz, The by Waldteufel, 1941 ....**3.00**

Skating Down The Old Mill Stream by Abner Silver & Harry Ross, 1938..................**3.00**

Skating Waltzes, The by Charles K. Harris, 1915, Photo Reynolds & Donegan (Cover Artist, Pfeiffer & Deco) **15.00**

Skeleton In the Closet, The by John Burke & Arthur Johnston, 1936, Movie: Pennies From Heaven, Photo Bing Crosby..................**5.00**

Skeleton Rag, The by Edw. Madden & Percy Wenrich, 1911 (Cover Artist, Starmer & Rag)..................**10.00**

Skidmore Fancy Ball by Edward Harrigan & David Braham, 1878 (Pre 1900)..................**15.00**

Skidmore Guard by Edward Harrigan & David Braham, 1874 (Pre 1900) **15.00**

Skidmore Masquerade by Edward Harrigan & David Braham, 1880 (Pre 1900)..................**15.00**

Skidoo by Karl Lenox, 1906 (Cover Artist, F. G. Murdock & Black, Black Face) **25.00**

Skids Are On Review by Edward Harrigan & Dave Braham, 1879 (Pre 1900)..................**15.00**

Skids Are Out Today by Edward Harrigan & David Braham, 1879 (Pre 1900)..................**15.00**

Skids Are Out Tonight by Edward Harrigan & David Braham, 1880 (Pre 1900)..................**15.00**

Skies Are Dark When You're Away by Elizabeth McCabe Gilmore & Ernest R. Ball, 1923..................**3.00**

Skirt Dance by Meyer Lutz, 1886 (Pre 1900)..................**10.00**

Sky Anchors by Waring, 1942 (Transportation)..................**10.00**

Sky Flyer by John B. Walker, 1910..................**5.00**

Skylark by Jessie L. Deppen, 1914 (Transportation)..................**10.00**

Skylark by Johnny Mercer & Hoagy Carmichael, 1942..................**4.00**

Skylarking–A New Dance by Eastman, 1908 (Cover Artist, Pfeiffer).**15.00**

Slap'er Down Agin, Paw by Polly Arnold, Alice Cornett & Eddie Asherman, 1947, Photo Arthur Godfrey..................**5.00**

Slap That Brass by Ira & George Gershwin, 1937, Movie: Shall We Dance? Photo Fred Astaire & Ginger Rogers **5.00**

Slaughter On Tenth Avenue by Richard Rodgers, 1936 (Cover Artist, Jorj Harris)..................**5.00**

Slave Song by E. Nesbit & Teresa Del Riego, 1899 (Pre 1900) **10.00**

Slavery Days by Edward Harrigan & David Braham, 1876 (Pre 1900) **15.00**

Slavery's Passed Away by Edward Harrigan & David Braham, 1887 (Pre 1900)..................**15.00**

Sleep And Forget by Bingham & White, 1906..................**3.00**

Sleep And The Roses by Arthur F. Tate..................**5.00**

Sleep, Baby, Sleep by John J. Hanley, 1885 (Pre 1900)..................**15.00**

Sleep, Baby Sleep by Johnny Tucker & Joe Schuster, 1928 ....**4.00**

Sleep, Baby Sleep by Jon. E. Porter, 1915 ....**6.00**

Sleep by Earl Liebieg, 1923 (Cover Artist, P.M. Griffith) **5.00**

Sleep On Dear Heart by Ella M. Smith & Howard I. Smith, 1912..................**3.00**

Sleepy Bye by Carl Wenge, 1925..................**3.00**

Sleepy Head by Benny Davis & Jesse Greer, 1926..................**5.00**

Sleepy Head by Maurice Gunsky, Jack Brown & Billy Hill, 1921 ....**5.00**

Sleepy Hills Of Tennessee by Joe Young, Sam Lewis & Geo F. Meyer, 1923 ....**5.00**

Sleepy Hollow Rag by Woods, 1918 (Cover Artist, Pfeiffer, Rag & Deco)..................**15.00**

Sleepy Lagoon by Jack Lawrence & Eric Coates, 1936 (Deco)............**5.00**

Sleepy Moon by Walter Van Brunt & Harry Von Tilzer, 1915 (Cover Artist, DeTakacs & Transportation)..................**10.00**

Sleepy Song, A by Carrie Jacobs Bond, 1912 ....**15.00**

Sleepy Time Gal by Jos. R. Alden, Raymond B. Egan, Ange Lorenzo & Richard A. Whiting, 1925, Photo Billy Knight..................**5.00**

Sleepy Time Gal by Jos. R. Alden, Raymond Egan, Richard A. Whiting & Ange Lorenzo, 1925 (Cover Artist, JVR & Deco)..................**5.00**

Sleepy Town by Fred Tibbott & George Rex, 1922..................**3.00**

Sleepy Town Express, The by Haven Gillespie, 1930 (Transportation)**8.00**

Sleepy Valley by Andrew B. Sterling & James F. Hanley, 1929, Movie: The Rainbow Man, Photo Eddie Dowling, Dedicated To Miss Betty Meehan (Dedication) **10.00**

Sleigh Party Polka, A by M. Greenwald, 1911..................**5.00**

Sleigh Ride by Mitchell Parish & Leroy Anderson, 1948 (Cover Artist, Nick)..................**3.00**

Sleighride In July by Johnny Burke & Jimmy Van Heusen, 1944, Musical: Belle Of The Yukon, Photo Dinah Shore, Randy Scott & Gypsy Rose Lee **5.00**

Slide, Kelly Slide by J. W. Kelly, 1889 (Pre 1900)................**10.00**

Sliding Sid by Ray Sherwood & Abe Losch, 1918 (March) **10.00**

Sligo, Thy Land's My Land by Harry Dacre, 1892 (Pre 1900)............**10.00**

Slip On Your Gingham Gown by Burris & Smith (Cover Artist, Pfeiffer).........................**10.00**

Slippery Hank by F. H. Losey, 1917 ....**3.00**

Slow And Easy by Harry Williams & Norman Spencer, 1919................**3.00**

Slow Poke by Pee Wee King, Redd Stewart & Chilton Price, 1951, Signed Photo Of Pee Wee King & Redd Stewart (Signed).....................**6.00**

Slow River by Henry Myers & Charles M. Schwab, 1927....................**3.00**

Slowly by Kermit Goell & David Raskin, 1945, Movie: Fallen Angel, Photo Alice Faye, Dana Andrews & Linda Darnell **6.00**

Slowly, With Feeling by Don George & Mark "Moose" Charlap, 1955....**5.00**

Slumber On, Kentucky Babe by Freeman & Allemong, 1918 (Cover Artist, Pfeiffer & Black, Black Face) **15.00**

Slumbering by Richard W. Pascoe, Howard Simon & Harold C. Berg, 1923, Photo The Three Aces **5.00**

Slumberland by Hall, 1907 (Cover Artist, Pfeiffer) **10.00**

Slumberland by Matthew Ott, 1917................**5.00**

Slumming On Park Avenue by Irving Berlin, 1937, Movie: On The Avenue, Photo Dick Powell & Alice Faye (Irving Berlin)............**12.00**

Sly Cupid Waltzes by Bernhard Stern, 1908 ....**5.00**

Sly Musette by A.B. Sloane, 1902................**5.00**

Small Fry by Frank Loesser & Hoagy Carmichael, 1938, Movie: Sing You Sinners, Photo Bing Crosby, Donald O'Connor & Hoagy Carmichael................**12.00**

Small Talk by Richard Adler & Jerry Ross, 1954, Musical: The Pajama Game................**3.00**

Small Town Gal by George M. Cohan (George M. Cohan)................**10.00**

Small Town Girl by Kahn, Stothart & Ward, 1936, Movie: Small Town Girl, Photo Robert Taylor & Janet Gaynor.....................**10.00**

Smart Set, The by Emil Katzenstein, 1899 (Pre 1900).......................**10.00**

Smarty by Jack Norworth & Albert Von Tilzer, 1908, Photo Jack Norworth................**5.00**

Smile A Little Bit by Moe Schenck, Bob Norton & Peggy Shevlin, 1925, Photo Perle J. Frank.....................**5.00**

Smile Again, Kathleen Mavourneen by Wm. Jerome & Owen Murphy, 1924 (Irish)................**5.00**

Smile And Show Your Dimple by Irving Berlin, 1917 (Irving Berlin) ..**10.00**

Smile And The World Smiles With You by Jimmy Lucas & Billy Frisch, 1919................**5.00**

Smile Away Each Rainy Day by Mercer & Mancini, 1970, Movie: Darling Lili, Photo Julie Andrews................**3.00**

Smile For Me by Phil Baxter, 1932 ....**5.00**

Smile, Legionnaire by William Kernell & Charles Wakefield Cadman, 1930................**5.00**

Smile On Me by Jean Lenox & Harry Sutton, 1906................**5.00**

Smile Right Back At The Sun by Johnny Burke & James Van Heusen, 1947, Movie: Welcome Stranger, Photo Bing Crosby, Joan Caulfield & Barry Fitzgerald................**5.00**

Smile! Smile! Smile! by Dave Dryer & Ballard MacDonald, 1930.......**8.00**

Smile Through Your Tears by Bernard Hamblen, 1919......................**6.00**

Smile Will Go A Long Long Way, A by Benny Davis & Harry Akst, 1923, Photo Henry Santrey.....................**5.00**

Smile You Miss, The by Wm. Cary Duncan & Raymond Hubbell, 1929, Advertisement For E.A. Earl Radio Sets, Signed Photo Raymond Hubbell (Advertising & Signed).....................**35.00**

Smile-A Kiss, A by Ricardo Duromo & Joseph Nussbaum, 1928.........**5.00**

Smile-Darn You Smile by Brian Hooker & Rudolph Friml, 1931, Musical: The White Eagle (Cover Artist, Barbelle) **6.00**

Smiles And The Tears Of Killarney, The by Sidney Carter & Neil Moret, 1917 (Irish) **10.00**

Smiles by J. Will Callahan & Lee S. Roberts, 1917................**5.00**

Smiles Of Love by E. W. Jerrell, 1928................**3.00**

Smilin' Through by Arthur A. Penn, 1919, Movie: Smilin' Through, Photo Norma Talmadge (Cover Artist, Starmer)................**18.00**

Smiling Eyes by Young & Fields, 1915 (Cover Artist, Pfeiffer)..........**10.00**

Smiling Irish Eyes by Herman Ruby & Ray Perkins, 1929, Movie: Smiling Irish Eyes, Photo Colleen Moore (Irish)................**12.00**

Smiling World Smiles On, The by Norton, 1915 (Cover Artist, Pfeiffer) ..**10.00**

Smoke Dreams by Arthur Freed & Lew Brown, 1930, Movie: After The Thin Man, Photo William Powell & Myrna Loy................**8.00**

Smoke From A Chimney by Billy Hill & Peter DeRose, 1938, Photo Arthur Lang (Cover Artist, Merman) **5.00**

Smoke Gets In Your Eyes by Otto Harbach & Jerome Kern, 1933, Movie: Roberta (Cover Artist, Jorj & Deco) **10.00**

Smoke Gets In Your Eyes by Otto Harbach & Jerome Kern, 1933, Photo Ginger Rogers, Fred Astaire & Irene Dunne (Cover Artist, Harris) ..**10.00**

Smoke Rings by Ned Washington & H. Eugene Gifford, 1933, Photo Glen Gray **3.00**

Smoke! Smoke! Smoke! That Cigarette by Merle Travis & Tex Williams, 1947, Photo Tex Williams................**3.00**

Smoky Mokes by A. Holzmann, 1899 (Pre 1900 & Black, Black Face)...**20.00**

Smother Me With Kisses And Kill Me With Love by Alfred Bryan & Harry Carroll, 1914, Photo Lillian Lorraine (Cover Artist, Pfeiffer)..........**10.00**

Snake Charmer, The by Leonard Whitcup & Teddy Powell, 1937 (Cover Artist, Scott)................**4.00**

Snap Your Fingers by Fred Spielman, 1946, Movie: Abilene Town, Photo Ann Dvorak & Rhonda Fleming **5.00**

Snappin' Turtle by Charles L. Cooke, 1913 (Cover Artist, Lee Winhold) **10.00**

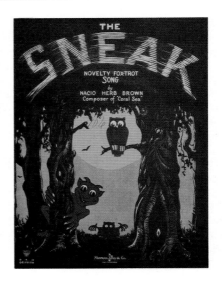

Sneak, The by Nacio Herb Brown, 1922 (Cover Artist, P.M. Griffith) ..5.00

Snookey Ookums by Irving Berlin, 1913, Photo Clark & Bergman (Cover Artist, Pfeiffer & Irving Berlin)................**15.00**

Snookey Ookums by Irving Berlin, 1913, Photo Macklin & Talbert (Cover Artist, Pfeiffer & Irving Berlin)................**15.00**

Snow Flakes by George Gershwin, 1920,................**5.00**

Snow White by Larry Morey & Frank Churchill, 1938, Movie: Snow White (Disney) **16.00**

Snowbird by Gene MacLellan, 1970, Photo Anne Murray **3.00**

Snowbird by Van Lynden, 1916................**5.00**

So Am I by Ira & George Gershwin, 1924, Musical: Lady Be Good.....**6.00**

So Beats My Heart For You by Pat Ballard, Charles Henderson & Tom Waring, 1930 (Cover Artist, Jorj)................**5.00**

So Blue by B.G. DeSylva & Ray Henderson, 1927 ....**3.00**

So Close To The Forest by Joe Young & Lawrence Reginald, 1924 .....**3.00**

So Dear To My Heart by Ticker Freeman & Irving Taylor, 1948, Movie: So Dear To My Heart (Disney) **10.00**

So Divine by Stern & Tobias, 1936, Movie: The Devil On Horseback, Photo Lili Damita **5.00**

So Do I by John Burke & Arthur Johnston, 1936, Movie: Pennies From Heaven, Photo Bing Crosby **12.00**

So Far by Richard Rodgers & Oscar Hammerstein II, 1951, Musical: Allegro **3.00**

So Help Me by Irving Berlin, 1934 (Irving Berlin) **10.00**

So I Took The $50,000.00 by Jack Meskill & Al Gumble, 1917 (Cover Artist, DeBeck) **10.00**

So In Love by Cole Porter, 1948, Musical: Kiss Me Kate **3.00**

So Is Your Old Lady by Al Dubin & Joe Burke, 1926, Photo Gus Van & Joe Schenck **5.00**

So Long, It's Been Good To Know Yuh by Woody Guthrie, 1950, Photo Don Cherry **5.00**

So Long Mary by George M. Cohan, 1933, Movie: Yankee Doodle Dandy, Photo James Cagney & George M. Cohan (George M. Cohan) **10.00**

So Long, Mother by Raymond Egan, Gus Kahn & Egbert Van Alstyne, 1917, Al Jolson's Mother Song, Photo Al Jolson (Al Jolson & WWI) **22.00**

So Long! Oo Long by Bert Kalmar & Harry Ruby, 1920 ....**5.00**

So Long, Sal, The Best Of Friends Must Part by Sterling & Lange, 1918, Photo Adrian (Cover Artist, Pfeiffer) **10.00**

So Long Sarah Jane by Lew Brown, Sammy Fain & Ralph Freed, 1943, Movie: I Dood It, Photo Red Skelton & Eleanor Powell **6.00**

So Lovely by Buddy Bernier & Bob Emmerich, 1938 ....**3.00**

So Many Memories by Harry Woods, 1938, Photo Mary Deitrick **3.00**

So Near & Yet So Far by Cole Porter, 1941, Movie: You'll Never Get Rich **5.00**

So Nice To See You Again by Dixon & Wrubel, 1935, Movie: We're In The Money, Photo Joan Blondell & Ross Alexander **8.00**

So Rare by Jack Sharpe & Jerry Herst, 1937 ....**3.00**

So Red The Rose by Richard Jerome & Walter Kent, 1935, Signed Photo Jolly Nash (Cover Artist, Paki & Signed) **6.00**

So This Is Dixie by Jack Yellen & Albert Gumble, 1917 (Dixie) **5.00**

So This Is Heaven by Burke & Spina, 1935 ....**3.00**

So This Is Love by Mack David, Al Hoffman & Jerry Livingston, 1949, Movie: Cinderella (Disney) **10.00**

So This Is Love by Ray Goetz, 1923 ....**5.00**

So Tired by Russ Morgan & Jack Stuart, 1943, Photo Russ Morgan **3.00**

So Will I by Lew Brown, 1926 ....**3.00**

So You're The One by Hy Zaret, Joan Whitney & Alex Kramer, 1940 (Cover Artist, Im-Ho) **3.00**

Sob Sister Sadie by Bob Bigelow & Chas. Bates, 1925, Photo Miss Polly Ann (Cover Artist, Politzer) **6.00**

Social Life by Boehme (Cover Artist, Pfeiffer) **10.00**

Soft Lights And Sweet Music by Irving Berlin, 1932 (Irving Berlin) ..**10.00**

Soft Lips by Walt McCoy, 1949, Photo T. Texas Tyler **3.00**

Softly As I Leave You by Hal Shaper & A. DeVita, 1962, Photo Eydie Gorme **4.00**

Softly As In A Morning Sunrise by Frank Mandel, Oscar Hammerstein II & Sigmund Romberg, 1928, Musical: The New Moon **6.00**

Softly As In A Morning Sunrise by Frank Mandel, Oscar Hammerstein II & Sigmund Romberg, 1942, Movie: Deep In My Heart, Based On Life Of Sigmund Romberg **6.00**

Solace by Scott Joplin, 1909 (Cover Artist, Shaw, Scott Joplin & March) **50.00**

Soldier Dreams Of You Tonight, A by Al Dubin & Cliff Friend, 1918 (WWI) **10.00**

Soldier's Dream Of Home, The by Louis Weber, 1917 (WWI) **10.00**

Soldier's Rosary, A by J.E. Dempsey & Jos. A. Burke, 1918 (Cover Artist, E.E. Walton & WWI) **20.00**

Soldier's Song, The, National Anthem Of Ireland by Peada Ocearnaigh & Patrick Heeney, 1959 (Irish) **3.00**

Soldier's Word To Mother, A by Dooley & Cavanaugh, 1917 (Cover Artist, Peiffer & WWI) **15.00**

Soldiers Chorus by Faust, Opera Gems Series, 1908 (Cover Artist, Pfeiffer) **15.00**

Soldiers Of Canada by Whitman, 1915 (Cover Artist, Pfeiffer) **10.00**

Soldiers Of Fortune by Gus Kahn & Sigmund Romberg, 1914 ....**10.00**

Soldiers Of Fortune by L.O. Gustin, 1901 (March) **10.00**

Solid Citizen Of The Solid South, A by Arthur Schwartz & Leo Robin, 1946, Movie: The Time The Place & The Girl, Photo Dennis Morgan, Jack Carson, Martha Vickers, Janice Paige & Carmen Cavallaro (Cover Artist, A. Joel Robinson) **12.00**

Solid Gold Cadillac, The by Bowers & Black, 1956, Movie: The Solid Gold Cadillac, Photo Judy Holliday & Paul Douglas **3.00**

Soliloquy by Rodgers & Hammerstein II, 1945, Movie: Carousel, Photo Gordon Macrae, Shirley Jones & Cameron Mitchell **3.00**

Soliloquy by Rube Bloom, 1926 ....**3.00**

Solitude by Eddie DeLange, Irving Mills, Edward Kennedy & Duke Ellington, 1934 ....**3.00**

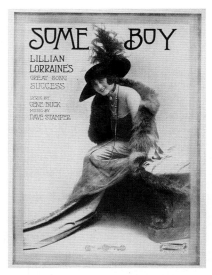

Some Boy by Gene Buck & Dave Stamper, 1912, Photo Lillian Lorraine (Cover Artist, White) 15.00

Some Day by Brian Hooker & Rudolf Friml, 1926, Movie: The Vagabond King, Photo Jeannette Macdonald **5.00**

Some Day by Walter King & Earl Burtnett, 1918 (Cover Artist, ARK & WWI) **8.00**

Some Day by Walter Scanlan, 1922 ....**5.00**

Some Day Dearie by Winzel, 1909 ....**3.00**

Some Day I'll Make You Glad by Max C. Freedman & Harry D. Squires, 1918, Photo Ruth Roland (Deco) **15.00**

Some Day My Prince Will Come by Larry Morey & Frank Churchill, 1937, Movie: Snow White (Disney) **18.00**

Some Day, Sweetheart, Some Day by Ed Gardenier & Gus Edwards, 1908 ....**5.00**

Some Day Waiting Will End by P.G. Wodehouse, Ivan Caryll & Guy Bolton, 1918, Musical: The Girl Behind The Gun, Signed Photo Ivan Caryle (WWI & Signed) **15.00**

Some Day We'll Meet Again by Al Hoffman, Al Goodhart & Milton Ager, 1932 (Cover Artist, Leff) **5.00**

Some Day When Dreams Come True by Phil Slaats, 1906, Photo Flemen & Miller (Cover Artist, Starmer)..**5.00**

Some Day When Dreams Come True by Phil Staats, 1906...................**5.00**

Some Day, When The War Is Through by Walter King & Earl Burtnett, 1918 (Cover Artist, ARK & WWI) **10.00**

Some Day You Will Miss Me by T. Edwin McGuiness & Leo Friedman, 1906 ....**10.00**

Some Day You'll Know by C.T. Donnelly & Ted Murray, 1924 ....**5.00**

Some Day You'll Know Who Loves You by Leo Bennett, 1914 ....**5.00**

Some Day You'll Miss Me You Wait And See by Richard Howard, 1916..**5.00**

Some Enchanted Evening by Richard Rodgers & Oscar Hammerstein II, 1949, Musical: South Pacific, Signed Photo Ezzio Pinza (Cover Artist, BJH & Signed)...**12.00**

Some Girl by Jess R. Batt, 1914 ....**5.00**

Some Golden Day by Gus Kahn & C. Naset, 1924.............................**5.00**

Some Little Bird by Haven Gillespie, Lindsey McPhail & Egbert Van Alstyne, 1920...**5.00**

Some Little Something About You by Irving Berlin & Ted Snyder, 1909 (Irving Berlin)..**10.00**

Some Little Squirrel Is Going To Get Some Little Nut by Von Tilzer, 1917 (Cover Artist, Pfeiffer) **10.00**

Some Night Soon by Ida Amherdt, 1931, Photo Mildred Risley (Cover Artist, Heffle & Deco)...**10.00**

Some Of The Time I'm Lonely by Francis W. Hatch, 1920 ....**5.00**

Some Of These Days by Shelton Brooks, 1937, Signed Photo Sophie Tucker (Cover Artist, Barbelle & Signed).....................................**28.00**

Some Of These Days by Shelton Brooks, 1937, Photo Sophie Tucker (Cover Artist, Starmer)...**20.00**

Some One Like You by Robert B. Smith & Victor Herbert, 1919, Musical: Angel Face (Victor Herbert)...**10.00**

Some Other Day-Some Other Girl by Gus Kahn & Isham Jones, 1924.**5.00**

Some Party by Anna Caldwell & Jerome Kern, 1919, Musical: She's A Good Fellow **5.00**

Some Pretty Day by Sam Lewis, Joe Young & Fred E. Ahlert, 1920 ...**5.00**

Some Quiet Afternoon by Gus Kahn & Egbert Van Alstyne, 1919 ....**5.00**

Some Sleigh Ride by Will Hardy, 1913...**10.00**

Some Smoke by Sigmund Romberg, 1913...**5.00**

Some Sort Of Somebody by Schuyler Greene, Herbert Reynolds & Jerome Kern, 1915, Musical: Very Good Eddie (Cover Artist, Strauss)....**10.00**

Some Sunday Morning by Gus Kahn, Raymond Egan & Richard A. Whiting, 1917, Photo Brice & King (Cover Artist, Starmer)................**15.00**

Some Sunday Morning by Ted Koehler, M.K. Jerome & Ray Heindorf, 1945, Movie: San Antonio, Photo Errol Flynn & Alexis Smith.....**10.00**

Some Sunny Day by Arthur Jackson & Walter Donaldson, 1919 (WWI) **10.00**

Some Sunny Day by Irving berlin, 1922 (Cover Artist, R.S. & Irving Berlin)..**10.00**

Some Sweet Day by Nat Shilkret & Lew Pollack, 1929, Movie: Children Of The Ritz, Photo Dorothy MacKaill (Deco) **12.00**

Somebody Else Is Crazy 'Bout Me, But I Want You by Dave Oppenheim & Harry Carroll, 1913, Photo Young & Young (Cover Artist, Starmer) 15.00

Somebody Else Is Taking My Place by Dick Howard, Bob Ellsworth & Russ Morgan, 1937, Photo Russ Morgan.......................................**3.00**

Somebody Else Is Taking My Place by Dick Howard, Bob Ellsworth & Russ Morgan, 1937, Photo Baron Elliott.......................................**3.00**

Somebody Else, It's Always Somebody Else by Jack Drislane & Geo W. Meyer, 1910, Photo Jack Drislane, Geo W. Meyer & Flora Chalue..**10.00**

Somebody Else Took You Out Of My Arms by Billy Rose & Con Conrad, 1923, Photo Billy Glason (Cover Artist, Politzer & Deco)............**10.00**

Somebody From Somewhere by Gershwin & Gershwin, 1931, Movie: Delicious, Photo Janet Gaynor **10.00**

Somebody Knows by Harry Von Tilzer, 1915, Photo Harry Von Tilzer (Cover Artist, DeTakacs)...**10.00**

Somebody Lied About Me by Gus Kahn & Carl & Frank Emler, 1927 **5.00**

Somebody Lied by Branen & Lloyd, 1907..**10.00**

Somebody Loves Me by Hattie Starr, 1894 (Pre 1900).......................**10.00**

Somebody Loves You by Charles Tobias & Peter DeRose, 1932, Photo Vincent Lopez (Cover Artist, Cliff Miska) **6.00**

Somebody Loves You by Charles Tobias & Peter DeRose, 1932, Photo Doc Daugherty (Cover Artist, Cliff Miska)....................................**6.00**

Somebody Loves You, Dear by Hawley, 1907.....................................**5.00**

Somebody Misses Somebody's Kisses by Frank Davis & Maurice Prival, 1919 (Lithograph, Knapp Co.) **10.00**

Somebody Misses You Every Day by Will J. Harris & M.D. Harris, 1908..**10.00**

Somebody Stole My Gal by Leo Wood, 1918, Photo Elmer Grosso Orchestra (Cover Artist, Frederick S. Manning) **15.00**

Somebody Stole My Gal by Wood, 1946, Movie: When Willie Comes Marching Home by Wood, Photo Dan Dailey, Corinne Calvet & Colleen Townsend **6.00**

Somebody Stole My Heart by Chris Smith, 1917 ....**5.00**

Somebody That I Know And You Know Too by J. Fred Helf, 1908.....**5.00**

Somebody To Somebody by Cara Roma, 1907 (Cover Artist, Pfeiffer & Deco) **15.00**

Somebody's Awfully Lonesome by Al B. Coney, 1910 ....**10.00**

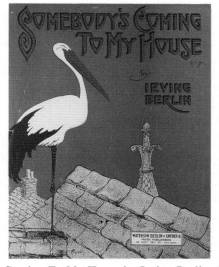

Somebody's Coming To My House by Irving Berlin, 1913 (Cover Artist, John Frew & Irving Berlin)..**10.00**

Somebody's Coming To Town by Raymond A. Browne & Henry Clay Smith, 1912, Photo Kimberley & Moore (Dixie)..........................**10.00**

Somebody's Doing What I Used To Do by Helf, 1910 (Cover Artist, Pfeiffer) **15.00**

Somebody's Done Me Wrong by Will E. Skidmore, 1918 ....**5.00**

Somebody's Lonely by Benny Davis & Joe Gold, 1926, Photo Vincent Lopez **3.00**

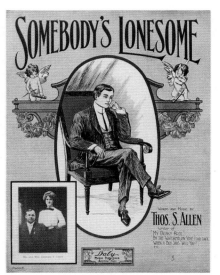

Somebody's Lonesome by Thomas S. Allen, 1910, Photo Mr. & Mrs. Leonard T. Chick (Cover Artist, Starmer) **10.00**

Somebody's Mother by Andrew Sterling & Harry Von Tilzer, 1921 (Cover Artist, Barbelle) **5.00**

Somebody's Sweetheart by Price & Batunno, 1919..............................**6.00**

Somebody's Sweetheart I Want To Be by Will D. Cobb & Gus Edwards, 1905, Photo Lillian Russell **15.00**

Somebody's Waiting For Me by Andrew Sterling & Harry Von Tilzer, 1912, Photo Bohannon & Corey (Cover Artist, Carter)................**10.00**

Somebody's Waiting For Someone by Andrew B. Sterling & Harry Von Tilzer, 1919 (Cover Artist, Barbelle & WWI)..............................**10.00**

Somebody's Waiting For You by Vincent Bryan & Al Gumble, 1906, Photo Charlotte Revenscroft (Cover Artist, Starmer) **12.00**

Somebody's Waiting For You by Vincent Bryan & Al Gumble, 1906, Photo Bonita (Cover Artist, Starmer)..**12.00**

Somebody's Wrong by Henry I. Marshall, Raymond Egan & Richard Whiting, 1923, Photo Sophie Tucker **10.00**

Someday by Jimmie Hodges, 1940, Photo Red River Dave.................**2.00**

Someday by Jimmie Hodges, 1940, Photo Vaughn Monroe.................**2.00**

Someday I'll Find You by Noel Coward, 1931, Musical: Private Lives, Photo Noel Coward **6.00**

Someday, I'll Meet You Again by Ned Washington & Max Steiner, 1944, Movie: Passage To Marseille, Photo Humphrey Bogart.................**5.00**

Someday My Heart Will Know by Herendeen & Horan, 1935, Movie: A Royal Exchange, Photo Ramon Novarro & Doris Kenyon.............**3.00**

Someday Somebody's Gonna Get You by L. Wolfe Gilbert & Carey Morgan, 1917 ....**5.00**

Someday, Somewhere by Erno Rapee & Lew Pollack, 1928.................**5.00**

Someday, Somewhere We'll Meet Again by Erno Rapee & Lew Pollach, 1928, Musical: The Red Dance, Photo Dolores Del Rio.................**5.00**

Someday Somewhere We'll Meet Again by Joan Brooks, Jack Segal & Dick Miles, 1911 ....**5.00**

Someday Sweetheart by Spikes & Spikes, 1924, Photo Sophie Tucker...**10.00**

Someday You'll Find Your Bluebird by Gordon & Newman, 1940, Movie: The Blue Bird, Photo Shirley Temple (Shirley Temple) ...**10.00**

Someday You'll Say OK by Walter Donaldson, 1927, Photo Donald Miller (Cover Artist, JVR & Deco)..**5.00**

Someday You'll Want Me Back by Morgan & Retrop, 1919 ....**3.00**

Somehow I Can't Forget You by Joe McCarthy & Al Piantadosi, 1913 (Cover Artist, Rose Symbol) **10.00**

Somehow I'm Always To Blame by Roy B. Carson, 1923...................**5.00**

Somehow The Girl You Might Have Won You Never Met Again by Bucknam & Brown, 1915 (Cover Artist, Pfeiffer)........................**12.00**

Someone by Al Bryan & Geo. W. Meyer, 1929, Movie: The Girl From Woolworths **10.00**

Someone by George Gershwin, 1922 ....**5.00**

Someone by Ida M. Collebrusco & Burrell Van Buren, 1922.............**5.00**

Someone by Stieger & Dailey, 1914 ....**5.00**

Someone Else May Be There While I'm Gone by Irving Berlin, 1917 (Cover Artist, Barbelle, WWI & Irving Berlin) **10.00**

Someone Is Longing For Home Sweet Home by David Berg, William Tracey & Jack Stern, 1918 (WWI)..**10.00**

Someone Is Losin' Susan by Roy Turk & Geo W. Meyer, 1926, Photo Tony Lopez, (Cover Artist, Barbelle & Deco) **10.00**

Someone Like You by Ralph Blaine & Harry Warren, 1949, Movie: My Dream Is Yours, Photo Doris Day, Jack Carson & Lee Bowman....**5.00**

Someone Loves You After All by Joseph McCarthy & Harry Tierney, 1918, Musical: Ziegfeld's Kid Boots **6.00**

Someone Should Tell Them by Lorenz Hart & Richard Rodgers, 1927, Musical: A Conn. Yankee **5.00**

Someone Thinks Of Someone by Ed Gardenier & J. Fred Helf, 1905, Photo Dorothy Vaughan (Cover Artist, Starmer)..........................**10.00**

Someone To Care For by Gus Kahn & Harry Warren, 1932.................**5.00**

Someone To Care For Me by Gus Kahn, Bronislau Kaper & Walter Jurmann, 1936, Movie: Three Smart Girls, Photo Deanna Durbin, Ray Milland & Barbara Reid **8.00**

Someone To Love by Bob Warren, 1945 ....**3.00**

Someone To Love by Gus Kahn & Ted Fiorito, 1925...........................**5.00**

Someone To Watch Over Me by Ira & George Gershwin, 1926...........**6.00**

Someone Who Cares by Harvey, 1971, Movie: Fools, Photo Jason Robards & Katharine Ross **4.00**

Someone's Falling In Love by Geo. A. Little & Billy Baskette, 1928...**5.00**

Somethin' Doin' by F. H. Losey, 1907 (March)..................................**10.00**

Somethin' Stupid by C. Carson Parks, 1967, Photo Frank & Nancy Sinatra **4.00**

Something by Lorenz Hart & Richard Rodgers, 1927, Musical: A Conn. Yankee..**6.00**

Something For The Boys by Cole Porter, 1942, Movie: Something For The Boys..**5.00**

Something Had To Happen by Otto Harbach & Jerome Kern, 1933, Movie: Roberta (Deco)..**5.00**

Something In Return by Moroder & Lloyd, 1980, Movie: American Gigolo, Photo Richard Gere **3.00**

Something In The Night by Joe Young, Paul Weirick & Helmy Kresa, 1932..**6.00**

Something Old, Something New by Ramez Idriss & George Tibbles, 1946, Photo Frank Sinatra **4.00**

Something Sentimental by Frank Ryerson, Irving Taylor & Vaughn Monroe, 1945...**3.00**

Something Tells Me by Ed Rose, F. Henri Klickmann & Norman J. Elholm, 1924 ....**3.00**

Something Tells Me by Johnny Mercer & Harry Warren, 1938, Photo Mildred Bailey, (Cover Artist, Merman)............**5.00**

Something That I Can't Explain by Jerome & Schwartz, 1912, Photo Julian Eltinge (Cover Artist, Pfeiffer) **10.00**

Something To Remember by Gus Kahn & John Conrad, 1921 (Cover Artist, Frederick S. Manning)...................**16.00**

Something To Remember You By by Howard Deitz & Arthur Schwartz, 1930, Movie: Three's A Crowd....................**5.00**

Something Wonderful by Richard Rodgers & Oscar Hammerstein II, 1951, Movie: The King And I **5.00**

Something's Coming by Stephen Sondheim & Leonard Bernstein, 1957, Movie: West Side Story......................**5.00**

Sometime Between Midnight & Dawn by M. St. Leon, 1918 (Cover Artist, Pfeiffer)...**10.00**

Sometime by Gus Kahn & Ted Fiorito, 1925, Photo Eddie Harkness & His Orchestra (Cover Artist, Starmer) **10.00**

Sometime by Gus Kahn & Ted Fiorito, 1925, Photo Ipana Troubadours (Cover Artist, Starmer)...............................**10.00**

Sometime by Gus Kahn & Ted Fiorito, 1925, Photo Tommy Carlyn (Cover Artist, Jorj)...**3.00**

Sometime by Rida Johnson Young & Rudolf Friml, Musical: Sometime...**5.00**

Sometime by Vincent Bryan & Harry Von Tilzer, 1908, Photo Harry Von Tilzer (Cover Artist, Pfeiffer)......................**15.00**

Sometime by Wm. Felter & Thurlow Lieurance, 1903 ....**10.00**

Sometime In Springtime by Alfred Bryan, Jack Drislane & Geo. F. Meyer, 1909...**5.00**

Sometime In Summertime by Walter Donaldson, 1931 ....**5.00**

Sometime It Will Be Lovetime by Lee M. Walker & Gerald Arthur, 1919...**5.00**

Sometime Remind Me To Tell You by Leigh Harline, 1958, Movie: Station West, Photo Dick Powell & Jane Greer **5.00**

Sometime Somewhere by Andrew Mack & Harry Williams, 1908, Photo Andrew Mack (Cover Artist, DeTakacs).................**10.00**

Sometime Sweetheart Mine Somewhere by Eddy Eckels & Leroy Stover, 1909 ....**10.00**

Sometime You'll Remember by Raymond Wallace & Maurice L. Head, 1915...**5.00**

Sometimes by Ansel McMurty, 1915 ....**6.00**

Sometimes by Gus Kahn & Carmen Lombardo, 1941, Photo George Duffy **3.00**

Sometimes I Feel Like A Motherless Child by H. T. Burleigh, 1918 (Black, Black Face) **10.00**

Sometimes I'm Happy by Irving Caesar & Vincent Youmans, 1927, Musical: Hit The Deck......................................**4.00**

Sometimes The Dream Comes True by Edw. Grossmith & Ted D. Ward, 1915...**5.00**

Sometimes You Get A Good One & Sometimes You Don't by Von Tilzer & Sterling, 1916 (Cover Artist, Pfeiffer)...............**10.00**

Somewhere A Heart Is Breaking & Calling Me Back To You by Milton Weil & Leo Freedman, 1917 ....**5.00**

Somewhere A Voice Is Calling by Eileen Newton & Arthur F. Tate, 1911...**4.00**

Somewhere Along The Way by Sammy Gallop & Kurt Adams, 1952, Photo Nat King Cole......................................**5.00**

Somewhere by Chas. K. Harris, 1906.....................................**10.00**

Somewhere by Stephen Sondheim & Leonard Bernstein, 1957, Movie: West Side Story **5.00**

Somewhere In Delaware by Will J. Harris & Harry I. Robinson, 1917 .**5.00**

Somewhere In Dixie by Kilgour, 1917 (Cover Artist, Pfeiffer & Dixie) ..**10.00**

Somewhere In Dixie Lives The Girl I Love by Swanger & Powell, 1912 (Cover Artist, Pfeiffer & Dixie) **12.00**

Somewhere In France Is Daddy by Great Howar, 1918 (WWI)..........**10.00**

Somewhere In France Is The Lily by Philander Johnson & Jos. E. Howard, 1917, Photo Joseph Howard (Cover Artist, Starmer, WWI & March) **15.00**

Somewhere In Georgia by Carl Muller & Jimmie McHugh, 1917.........**5.00**

Somewhere In Hawaii by C. J. & A. Macmeekin, 1918.....................**6.00**

Somewhere In Ireland by J. Keirn Brennan & Ernest Ball, 1917 (Irish)**5.00**

Somewhere In Loveland With You by D.C. Weasner, 1919.................**5.00**

Somewhere In Naples by Harry D. Kerry & J.S. Zamecnik, 1921.........**5.00**

Somewhere In Old Wyoming by Charles Tobias & Peter DeRose, 1930, Photo Jack Arthur (Cover Artist, Leff)....................**5.00**

Somewhere In Old Wyoming by Charles Tobias & Peter DeRose, 1930, Photo Tom, Dick & Harry (Cover Artist, Leff)...............**5.00**

Somewhere In Old Wyoming by Mitchell Parish & Frank Perkins, 1934...**5.00**

Somewhere In The Night by Mack Gordon & Joseph Myrow, 1946, Movie: Three Little Girls In Blue, Photo June Haver, George Montgomery, Vivian Blaine, Celeste Holm, Vera Ellen & Frank Latimore...........**5.00**

Somewhere In The West by Arthur Freed & Peter Tinturin, 1932.........**5.00**

Somewhere In The World by Nat D. Ayer, 1923 ....**5.00**

Somewhere My Love by Paul Francis Webster & Maurice Jarre, 1965, Movie: Doctor Zhivago, Photo Ray Conniff......................**4.00**

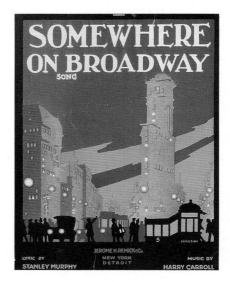

Somewhere On Broadway by Stanley Murphy & Harry Carroll, 1917 (Cover Artist, Martini)..5.00

Somewhere Over There by Pulver & O'Keefe, 1918 (Cover Artist, Pfeiffer & WWI)...**10.00**

Somewhere You're Dreaming Too by Robert F. Roden & Maud A. Murray, 1917 (Cover Artist, Rose)................5.00

Son Of An Irishman, The by Wm. J. McKenna, 1913, Minstrel: Honey Boy by Geo Evans (Irish)................10.00

Son Of The Desert Am I, A by John P. Wilson & Walter A. Phillips, 1859 (Pre 1900) 15.00

Son Of The Rag Time Boy by Andrew B. Sterling & Harry Von Tilzer, 1916 (Rag) 12.00

Son Of The Sheik, 1926, Photo Rudolph Valentino................25.00

Song Angels Sing, The by Webster & Aronson, 1952, Movie: Because You're Mine 3.00

Song Birds Are Singing For You by Arthur J. Lamb & Alex Sullivan, 1904 ....5.00

Song Chinois by Jacqueline Boisynon & Henriotti, 1937 ....5.00

Song For June by W.G. Tinckom-Fernandez & Wm. Spencer Johnson, 1912 ....5.00

Song From Desiree, The by Alfred Newman, Movie: Desiree, Photo Marlon Brando & Jean Simmons................5.00

Song From Moulin Rouge, The by Georges Auric & William Engvick, 1953, Movie: Moulin Rouge 5.00

Song, How The First Song Was Born, A by Alexander Hill, 1934................5.00

Song I Heard One Sunday Morn, The by Robert H. Brennen & E.H. Ellison, 1901................10.00

Song I Love, The by B.G. DeSylva, Lew Brown, Ray Henderson & Con Conrad, 1928 ....5.00

Song Is Ended But The Melody Lingers On, The by Irving Berlin, 1927 (Cover Artist, RS, Irving Berlin & Deco) 10.00

Song Is You, The by Oscar Hammerstein II & Jerome Kern, 1932, Movie: Music In The Air (Cover Artist, Jorj)................5.00

Song O' My Heart by Joseph McCarthy & James Hanley, 1930, Sung by John McCormack (Irish)................5.00

Song Of All Nations by Charles Alfred Byrne, Louis Harrison & Mrs. Louis Harrison, 1892, Comedy Opera: The Isle Of Champagne (Pre 1900)................35.00

Song Of Dawn, A by J. O'Reilly & Arthur Kingston Stewart, 1911 .....5.00

Song Of Detroit, The by Campbell & Goldkette, 1930 ....10.00

Song Of Freedom by Irving Berlin, 1942 (Irving Berlin)................10.00

Song Of India, A by Jerry Castillo & N. Rimsky-Korsakov, 1935, Photo Lou Breese................5.00

Song Of Love by Dorothy Donnelly & Sigmund Romberg, 1921, Musical: Song Of Love................5.00

Song Of Old Hawaii, A by Gordon Beecher & Johnny Noble, 1938, Photo Tony Martin................5.00

Song Of Old Kilkenny, A by Abel Baer (Irish)................5.00

Song Of Santa Vittoria by Gimbel & Gold, 1969, Movie: The Secret Of Santa Vittora, Photo Anthony Quinn & Anna Magnani................4.00

Song Of Songs, The by Clarence Lucas & Moya, 1914................5.00

Song Of Spring by Hoagy Carmichael, 1935 (Cover Artist, HBK) 5.00

Song Of Spring by John Payne & Oley Speaks, 1916................5.00

Song Of Surrender by Al Dubin & Harry Warren, 1933, Movie: Moulin Rouge, Photo Constance Bennett 5.00

Song Of The Army Engineer by R. J. Burt & George F. Briegel, 1939 (WWII, Patriotic & March) 15.00

Song Of The Bayou by Rube Bloom, 1929, Dedicated To Miss Taddy Keller (Jazz & Dedication)................6.00

Song Of The Big Trail by McCarthy & Hanley, 1930, Movie: The Big Trail, Photo John Wayne & Marguerite Churchill 5.00

Song Of The Congo by Magedson, Washington & Perkins, 1930, Movie: Bright Lights, Photo Noah Beery, Dorothy Mackaill & Frank Fay .5.00

Song Of The Dreamer by Eddie "Tex" Curtis, 1955, Photo Johnny Ray...6.00

Song Of The Flame by George Gershwin, 1925................5.00

Song Of The Fool, The by Sam M. Lewis & Jesse Greer, 1930 ....3.00

Song Of The Hills, A by Carrie Jacobs Bond, 1915, Lovingly Dedicated To Miss Marcella Craft (Dedication) 15.00

Song Of The Islands by Chas. E. King, 1930................6.00

Song Of The Marines, The by Al Dubin & Harry Warren, 1937, Movie: The Singing Marine, Photo Dick Powell (Patriotic)................10.00

Song Of The Metronome by Irving Berlin, 1939 (Irving Berlin)................10.00

Song Of The Moonbeams by Charles Tobias, Harry Tobias & Vincent Rose, 1929 From Earl Carrolls' New Annual Revue, "Sketch Book"................12.00

Song Of The Rhineland by Gershwin & Weill, 1945, Movie: Where Do We Go From Here?, Photo Fred MacMurray, Joan Leslie & June Haver 5.00

Song Of The Robin by Jacob Henry Ellis, 1913, Dedicated To J. Frank Beal, Brocton, MA (Dedication) 10.00

Song Of The Sea by Barbour (Cover Artist, Pfeiffer) 10.00

Song Of The Seabees, The by Sam M. Lewis & Peter DeRose, 1942 (WWII)................12.00

Song Of The Setting Sun, The by Gus Kahn & Walter Donaldson, 1928, Musical: Ziegfeld Production Of Whoopee, Photo Eddie Cantor (Cover Artist, Nickel & Eddie Cantor)................18.00

Song Of The Soul by Edward Locke & Joseph Carl Breil, 1919 ....5.00

Song Of the Soul by Edward Locke & Joseph Carl Breil, 1919, Movie: The Climax, Photo Jean Hersholt & Kathryn Crawford 6.00

Song Of The South by Sam Coslow & Arthur Johnston, 1946, Movie: Song Of The South (Disney) 12.00

Song Of The Stars by H. Engelmann, 1904................5.00

Song Of The Steeple by Price & Rosenfeld, 1890 (Pre 1900)................10.00

Song Of The Tule by Jas. A. Brennan & Albert Von Tilzer, 1920 ....5.00

Song Of The Vagabonds by Brian Hooker & Rudolf Friml, 1925, Musical: The Vagabond King (Cover Artist, Barbelle)................10.00

Song Of The Vagabonds by Brian Hooker & Rudolf Friml, 1925, Movie: The Vagabond King, Photo Jeannette MacDonald 10.00

Song Of The Vagabonds by Brian Hooker & Rudolf Friml, 1925, Musical: The Vagabond King, Photo Dennis King (Cover Artist, Starmer).10.00

Song Of The Volga Boatmen by Al Dubin, 1924 (Cover Artist, Barbelle)................5.00

Song Of The Wanderer by Neil Moret, 1926 ....5.00

Song That I Hear In My Dreams, The by Walter Rolfe, 1902................10.00

Song That Reached My Heart by Julian Jordan, 1887 (Pre 1900)................15.00

Song That Stole My Heart, The by Andrew B. Sterling & Harry Von Tilzer, 1913 ....6.00

Song That The Anvil Sings by H. W. Petrie, 1902................10.00

Song That Will Live Forever by Browne & McGlennon, 1896 (Pre 1900) **10.00**

Song To Remember, A by Sammy Cahn, Morris W. Stoloff & Saul Chaplin, 1945 ....**5.00**

Song To The Stars by H. Engelmann, 1904 ....**8.00**

Song Without A Name, The by Benee Russell, 1930, Photo Rudy Vallee **10.00**

Songs My Mammy Sang For Me by J.W. Kelly, 1894 (Pre 1900).......**15.00**

Songs Of Ages, The by Jerome Heller, 1914.......................**5.00**

Songs Of Yesterday by Chas. K. Harris, 1916, Photo Charles K. Harris (Cover Artist, Pfeiffer) **15.00**

Songs Sung by Walter Lawrence by H. Von Tilzer, 1917, Photo W. Lawrence (Cover Artist, Pfeiffer & Irish) **15.00**

Sonny Boy by Al Jolson, B.G. DeSylva, Lew Brown & Ray Henderson, 1928, Movie: The Singing Fool, Photo Al Jolson (Al Jolson) **15.00**

Sonoma, My Mexican Rose by Leo Friedman, 1907 (Cover Artist, Central Engraving Co.)...**5.00**

Sons Of Ham by Breen & Geary, 1901(Black, Black Face) **15.00**

Sons Of Liberty, The by Leonard, 1918 (WWI)..................**10.00**

Soon by Lorenz Hart & Richard Rodgers, 1935, Movie: Mississippi, Photo Bing Crosby & Joan Bennett **5.00**

Sooner Or Later by Charles Wolcott & Ray Gilbert, 1946, Movie: Song Of The South (Disney)..**10.00**

Sooner Or Later by Ed Rose & Abe Olman, 1915 (Cover Artist, DeTakacs)..**10.00**

Sophisticated Lady by Edward Kennedy & Duke Ellington, 1933 ....**5.00**

Sophisticated Swing by Mitchell Parish & Will Hudson, 1936 (Cover Artist, Merman & Deco)...**5.00**

Sorority by Charles E. Roat, 1908 ....**5.00**

Soul Mates by Walter C. Parker, 1908 (Cover Artist, Pfeiffer)............**15.00**

Soul Of You, The by Margaret Albus & Carrie Jacobs Bond, 1917, Dedicated To Madame Mariska Aldrich (Cover Artist Hyer & Dedication) **10.00**

Sound Of Chicken Frying, Dat's Music To Me, The by Chris Smith, 1907 (Black, Black Face) **20.00**

Sound Of Music, The by Richard Rodgers & Oscar Hammerstein II, 1959, Movie: The Sound Of Music (Cover Artist, George Martin).........**10.00**

Sound Of The Drum, The by W.H. Jude, 1900 (Patriotic) **10.00**

Sounds From The Alps by Deinzer, 1892 (Pre 1900).......................**10.00**

Sounds From The Rockies by Ronaud, 1919 (Transportation) **16.00**

Sour Grapes by Will B. Morrison, 1912 (Cover Artist, Paul A. Greasey & Rag) **15.00**

Sous Les Ponts De Paris by J. Rodor & Vincent Scotto, 1913 (Cover Artist, Clerice Freros) **10.00**

Sousa's Grand March by Northrup, 1895, Photo John Philip Sousa (Pre 1900, John Philip Sousa & March)..................................**20.00**

South America, Take It Away by Harold Rome, 1946, Musical: Call Me Mister..**4.00**

South American Way by Al Dubin & Jimmy McHugh, 1939, Musical: Streets Of Paris **5.00**

South Fifth Ave. by Edward Harrigan & David Braham, 1890 (Pre 1900) **10.00**

South Of The Border by Jimmy Kennedy & Michael Carr, 1939, Photo Blue Barron (Cover Artist, Im-Ho) **6.00**

South Of The Border by Jimmy Kennedy & Michael Carr, 1939, Photo Bing Crosby (Cover Artist, Im-Ho)...................................**6.00**

South Of The Border by Jimmy Kennedy & Michael Carr, 1939, Photo Al Donahue (Cover Artist, Im-Ho)......................................**6.00**

South Sea Island Magic by Lysle Tomerlin & Andy Iona Long, 1936 ..**3.00**

South Sea Rose by L. Wolfe Gilbert & Abel Baer, Movie: South Sea Rose, Photo Lenore Ulric **5.00**

South Wind by B.G. DeSylva, Lew Brown & Ray Henderson, 1926 ....**5.00**

Southern Gala by Albert Gumble, 1917 ....**5.00**

Southern Heart Of Mine (Cover Artist, Pfeiffer)..................**10.00**

Southern Lullaby, A by Marc Sylvan & Louis Tocaben, 1905, Music Supplement Hearst's Boston Sunday American, Sunday July 9, 1905, Photo Miss Indiola Arnold **15.00**

Southern Memories by Kahn, Goldberg & Magine, 1922....................**3.00**

Southern Moonlight by Phil Ponce, 1922 (Cover Artist, Barbelle)......**10.00**

Southern Nights by Lee S. Roberts, 1917.............................**5.00**

Southern Rose by George Spink, 1927 (Cover Artist, Barbelle & Deco) ..**5.00**

Southern Smiles by Earl Fitzhugh & Harry Kelly, 1904 ....**10.00**

Souvenir March by John Philip Sousa, 1896, Advertisement For J.W. Pepper Metallic Folding Bedstead On Back Cover (Pre 1900, Advertising & John Philip Sousa) **38.00**

Souvenir Of Love, A by Richard Howard, 1922 ....**5.00**

Spaghetti Rag by Dick Rogers, George Lyons & Bob Yosco, 1910, Photo Joe Fina (Cover Artist, Nick & Rag)....................................**15.00**

Spain by Gus Kahn & Isham Jones, 1924 (Cover Artist, Wilson Art & Deco) **5.00**

Spaniard Who Blighted My Life, The by Billy Merson, 1932, Movie: The Jolson Story, Photo Larry Parks & Evelyn Keyes (Al Jolson).......**12.00**

Spanish Cavalier, The by W.D. Hendrickson & Jerry Castillo, 1935, Photo Nick Manoloff **5.00**

Spanish Eyes by Charles Singleton, Eddie Snyder & Bert Kaempfert, 1965, Photo Al Martino..**3.00**

Spanish Roses by Maxwell Eckstein, 1938 (Cover Artist, Elgin) **3.00**

Sparkles by Charles B. Ennis, 1909......................................**10.00**

Sparklets by Walter E. Miles, 1911 ....**3.00**

Sparkling Piper Heidsieck by Cooper & Pratt, 1892 (Pre 1900) **10.00**

Sparkling Trot, The by L.L. Lynde, 1914...............................**10.00**

Speak Low by Ogden Nash & Kurt Weill, 1943, Movie: One Touch Of Venus **3.00**

Speak To Me Of Love by Bruce Siever & Jean Lenoir, 1930 (Cover Artist, Harris & Deco) **5.00**

Speak To Me Of Love by Bruce Siever & Jean Lenoir, 1932, Photo Lucienne Boyer **3.00**

Speak Your Heart by Herb Magidson & Allie Wrubel, 1937, Movie: Radio City Revels, Photo Bob Burns, Milton Berle, Ann Miller, Kenny Baker & Many Other Stars **6.00**

Speaking Confidentially by Jimmy McHugh & Dorothy Fields, 1935, Movie: Every Night At Eight **5.00**

Speckled Spider Rag by Harry French, 1910 (Rag) **12.00**

Speed Kings, The by Losey, 1912 (Transportation)......................**15.00**

Speedy Boy by Klages & Greer, 1928, Movie: Speedy, Photo Harold Lloyd..**5.00**

Spellbound Concerto by Miklos Rozsa, 1946 ....**5.00**

Spin A Little Web Of Dreams by Kahal & Fain, 1934, Movie: Fashions Of 1934, Photo Bette Davis **8.00**

Spirit Of '76 by Cox, 1917 (WWI)......................................**15.00**

Spirit Of America by J.S. Zamecnik, 1917 (March, Patriotic & WWI)..**15.00**

Spirit Of France by E. T. Paull, 1919 (Cover Artist, E.T. Paull & March) ..**35.00**

Spirit Of Freedom by Abe Losch, 1905 (Cover Artist, Dittmar & March)..**35.00**

Spirit Of Life From La Favorita by Donizetti, 1910 (Cover Artist, Pfeiffer) **15.00**

Spirit Of Progress March, The by J. Oliver Riehl, 1928, Advertising For Montgomery Ward (March & Advertising) **38.00**

Spirit Of The U.S.A. by E.T. Paull (Cover Artist, E.T. Paull & March)..**35.00**

Spirit Of The U.S.A., The by Sprecht, 1908 (Cover Artist, Pfeiffer & Patriotic) **20.00**

Spoon Full Of Sugar, A by Richard M. & Robert B. Sherman, 1964, Movie: Mary Poppins, Signed Photo Julie Andrews (Signed & Disney) **25.00**

Spoon Time by Ardell, 1913 (Cover Artist, Pfeiffer)............................**10.00**

Spot That My Heart Calls Home, The by Roah & Praetorius, 1909 (Cover Artist, Pfeiffer)......................**15.00**

Spotlight Of Love, The by Rose A. Wasser, 1931 (Cover Artist, Heflay & Deco) **5.00**

Spray O'Heather by John Prindle Scott, 1921 (Irish) **5.00**

Spray Of Roses, A by Fred G. Bowles & Wilfrid Sanderson, 1911.......**5.00**

Spread A Little Sunshine by Robert E. Harty & Erwin R. Schmidt, 1933....................**5.00**

Spread Out Your White Sails by White, 1887 (Pre 1900 & Transportation) **15.00**

Spreading New England's Fame, 1940, Souvenir of Spreading New England's Fame Radio Program Yankee Network. Sponsored By Merchants Who Display And Sell Doublemint Gum (Advertising).....**28.00**

Sprig Of Shillalah, A by J. Fred Helf, 1905 (Irish)........................**10.00**

Spring Again by Ira Gershwin & Vernon Duke, 1938, Movie: Goldwyn Follies, Photo Adolphe Menjou, Ritz Brothers, Edgar Bergen & Charlie McCarthy **8.00**

Spring And Fall by Irving Berlin, 1912 (Cover Artist, Gene Buck & Irving Berlin) **10.00**

Spring Beauties Waltz by Ford, 1916 (Cover Artist, Pfeiffer) **10.00**

Spring, Beautiful Spring by Paul Lincke, 1907 ....**10.00**

Spring Came Back To Vienna by Fritz Rolter, Janice Torre & Fred Spielman, 1942, Movie: Luxury Liner **3.00**

Spring In My Heart by Ralph Freed & Johann Straus, 1939, Movie: First Love, Photo Deanna Durbin **10.00**

Spring Is Here by Clifford Higgin, 1929 ....**3.00**

Spring Is Here by Lorenz Hart & Richard Rodgers, 1938, Movie: I Married An Angel **5.00**

Spring Is In My Heart Again by John Mercer & William Woodin, 1932, Photo Paul Whiteman **5.00**

Spring Morn, A by Rose Morris, 1905 ....**5.00**

Spring Song by Felix Mendelsohn, 1907 (Cover Artist, Pfeiffer)........**15.00**

Spring Song by W.W. Caldwell & F. Lynes, 1901, Dedicated To Mrs. E. Humphrey-Allen & Mr. C. N. Allen (Dedication) **5.00**

Spring Will Be A Little Late This Year by Frank Loesser, Movie: Christmas Holiday, Photo Deanna Durbin **5.00**

Spring Will Come by Alfred Bryan & John Oppenshaw, 1928 ....**5.00**

Spring Will Return With You by May Stanley & Geoffrey O'Hara, 1919....................**5.00**

Springtime Of Youth by Rolfe, 1915 (Cover Artist, Pfeiffer)............**10.00**

Sprinkle Me With Kisses by Earl Carroll & Ernest R. Ball, 1915.........**6.00**

Square In The Social Circle, A by Ray Evans & Jay Livingston, 1945, Movie: The Stork Club, Photo Betty Hutton, Andy Russell, Don Defore & Barry Fitzgerald....................**8.00**

Squirrel Rag, The by Paul Biese & F. Henri Klickmann, 1913 (Rag)..**10.00**

St. Louis Blues by W.C. Handy, 1942, Movie: St. Louis Blues, Photo Nat King Cole (Blues)....................**6.00**

St. Louis Blues by W.C. Handy, 1914, Musical: Blackbirds Of 1928 (Cover Artist, M. Ray & Blues) **12.00**

St. Louis Blues by W.C. Handy, 1942 (Cover Artist, Barbelle, Transportation & Blues) **6.00**

St. Louis Rag, The by Tom Turpin, 1905 (Rag) **15.00**

St. Louis Tickle by Barney & Seymour, 1904 (Rag & Black, Black Face)....................**22.00**

St. Mortiz Waltz by Forman Brown & Frederick Hollander, 1934, Movie: I Am Suzanne **5.00**

St. Patrick's Day Parade by Edward Harrigan & David Braham, 1874 (Pre 1900 & Irish) **20.00**

St. Peter And The Rose by W. Sheppard & Richard Bloye, 1916.........**5.00**

Stageland by Branen, Laska & Friedland, 1909 (Cover Artist, Pfeiffer)....................**10.00**

Stairway To The Stars by Mitchell Parish, Matt Malneck & Frank Signorelli, 1939, Photo Glenn Miller....................**4.00**

Stand By America! by Ethel Wall & Edythe Vell, 1939 (March & Patriotic)....................**10.00**

Stand By Your Uncle Sam by Younter, 1917 (Cover Artist, Pfeiffer & Patriotic) **15.00**

Stand Up And Fight Like H— by George M. Cohan, 1918, Photo George M. Cohan (Cover Artist, E.E. Walton, George M. Cohan & WWI) **25.00**

Stand Up Scout, Strong And Steady, Your Country's Calling You by Marion Abigail Wood, 1918 (WWI)....................**16.00**

Standard American Airs by Rosey, 1906 (Patriotic) **8.00**

Standing On The Corner by Frank Loesser, 1956, Musical: The Most Happy Fella....................**5.00**

Standing On The Corner, Didn't Mean No Harm by George Evans, 1894 (Pre 1900) **10.00**

Stanley Steamer, The by Harry Warren & Ralph Blane, 1948, Movie: Summer Holiday, Photo Mickey Rooney & Gloria DeHaven **5.00**

Star And The Rose, The by Joe Young & Jean Schwartz, 1936 ....**5.00**

Star Dust by Mitchell Parish & Hoagy Carmichael, 1929 (Cover Artist, Milos)....................**4.00**

Star Dust by Mitchell Parish & Hoagy Carmichael, 1929, Photo Hoagy Carmichael (Cover Artist BJH) **4.00**

Star Eyes by Don Raye & Gene DePaul, 1943, Movie: I Dood It, Photo Red Skelton & Eleanor Powell **5.00**

Star Of God by Fred E. Weatherly & Eric Coates, 1942....................**5.00**

Star Of Hope by Oscar R. Blum & Harry Kennedy, 1902 ....**5.00**

Star Of Love by Abe Olman, 1911 ....**5.00**

Star Of Peace by Woodward & Earl, 1921 ....**5.00**

Star Of The East by Bishop Heber & Whitney Coombs, 1916 ....**5.00**

Star Of The East by Joe Cooper & Harry Kennedy, 1890 (Pre 1900)..**10.00**

Star Of The Sea by Amanda Kennedy, 1883 (Pre 1900 & Transportation) **25.00**

Star Spangled Banner, The by Francis Scott Key & John Stafford Smith, 1942 (Cover Artist, NPS, WWII & Patriotic) **10.00**

Starlight Bay by Gus Kahn & Walter Donaldson, 1923....................**5.00**

Starlight by Cruger, 1915 (Cover Artist, Pfeiffer)....................**10.00**

Starlight by Edward Madden & Theodore Morse, 1905, Photo Four Shannons (Cover Artist, Frew & March) **5.00**

Starlight by Gene Buck & Dave Stamper, 1918, Musical: Ziegfeld Follies Of 1918, Photo Many Ziegfeld Girls....................**12.00**

Starlight, Help Me Find The One I Love by Joe Young & Bernice Petkere, 1931, Photo Abe Lyman (Cover Artist, Leff) **4.00**

Starlight, Help Me Find The One I Love by Joe Young & Bernice Petkere, 1931, Photo Nick Pisani (Cover Artist, Leff)....................**4.00**

Starlight Love by Arthur A. Penn & Lucien Denni, 1919 ....**5.00**

Starlight Reverie by John A. Seidt, 1901....................**10.00**

Starlight, The Roses & You by Harris, 1929 (Cover Artist, Pfeiffer) ..**10.00**

Starlight Waltz by Brainard, 1908 (Cover Artist, Pfeiffer) **10.00**

Starlit Hour, The by Mitchell Parish & Peter DeRose, 1939................**5.00**

Starry Night by Alfred Fieldhouse, 1905....................**5.00**

Stars And Stripes Are Calling by N.J. Kirk, 1918 (WWI) **15.00**

Stars And Stripes Forever, The by John Philip Sousa, 1897 (John Philip Sousa, Pre 1900 & March) **36.00**

Stars Are The Windows Of Heaven by Tommy Malie & Jimmy Steiger, 1926, Signed Photo Andrews Sisters (Signed)....................**10.00**

Stars Fell On Alabama by Ray Perkins, 1934 ....**5.00**

Stars In My Eyes by Fields & Kreisler, 1936 ....**5.00**

Stars In Your Eyes by Mort Greene & Gabriel Ruiz, 1945, Movie: Pan Americana, Photo Eve Arden, Phillip Terry, Audrey Long & Robert Benchly....................**6.00**

Stars & Stripes On Iwo Jima by Bob Wills & Cliff Johnson, 1945, Photo Bob Wills (WWII)....................**10.00**

Start The Day Right by Charles Tobias, Al Lewis & Maurice Spitalny, 1939, Photo Morton Franklin (Cover Artist, Merman) **3.00**

Start The Day Right by Charles Tobias, Al Lewis & Maurice Spitalny, 1939, Photo Joseph Sudy (Cover Artist, Merman)..........................**3.00**

Station Y.O.U. by Alice Robill & Wm. J. McKenna, 1924..................**6.00**

Statue Of Liberty Is Smiling, The by Jack Mahoney & Halsey K. Mohr, 1918, Photo Statue Of Liberty (Cover Artist, Barbelle, WWI & Patriotic)..**20.00**

Stay As Sweet As You Are by Mack Gordon & Harry Revel, 1934, Movie: College Rhythm, Photo Joe Penner, Lanny Ross, Jack Oakie & Helen Mack...**10.00**

Stay Down Here Where You Belong by Irving Berlin, 1914 (Cover Artist, Barbelle & Irving Berlin) **10.00**

Stay In Your Own Back Yard by Kennet & Udall, 1899 (Pre 1900) ...**10.00**

Stay Out Of The South by Harold Dixon, 1927, Photo Miller & Farrell ..**3.00**

Steal A Little Kiss While Dancing by George A. Little & Ernest E. Sutton, 1923 (Deco) **6.00**

Steal Away by Fred H. Huntley, 1922 (Black, Black Face)..................**3.00**

Stealing To Virginia by Gus Kahn & Walter Donaldson, 1923 ....**5.00**

Steam Heat by Richard Adler & Jerry Ross, 1954, Musical: The Pajama Game..**5.00**

Steamboat Bill by Ren Shields & Leighton Bros., 1910 (Transportation)..**15.00**

Steamboat Rag by Ernie Burnett, 1914 (Rag) **16.00**

Steeple Chase, The by Harry J. Lincoln, 1914 (Cover Artist, Dulin, Sports & March) **25.00**

Stein Song by Lincoln Colcard & E.A. Fenstad, 1930, University Of Maine, Photo Rudy Vallee..**10.00**

Stein Song March, The by Bullard, 1901 (March) **15.00**

Stella by Al Jolson, Benny Davis & Harry Akst, 1923, Photo Al Jolson (Cover Artist, Barbelle & Al Jolson)..**15.00**

Stella by Roberts & Newman, Movie: Stella, Photo Ann Sheridan & Victor Mature **5.00**

Stella By Starlight by Victor Young, 1946...**5.00**

Step Along Henry by Abe Olman, 1916 (Transportation)..................**15.00**

Step By Step-Mile By Mile I'm Marching Home To You by Andrew Silver, Al Sherman & Al Lewis, 1929...**10.00**

Step This Way by Bert Grant, 1916..**5.00**

Stepping Out With My Baby by Irving Berlin, 1947, Movie: Easter Parade, Photo Judy Garland, Peter Lawford, Fred Astaire & Ann Miller (Irving Berlin)...**12.00**

Sterling Waltz by Fry & Yarborough, 1914 ....**5.00**

Stewed Chicken Rag by Leap, 1912 (Cover Artist, Pfeiffer & Rag)....**15.00**

Stick To Your Mother Mary by Thos. S. Allen, 1913, Photo Charles Twins (Cover Artist, Pfeiffer) **12.00**

Stick To Your Mother Tom by E. J. Symons, 1885 (Pre 1900) **15.00**

Stick-To-It-Ivity by Larry Morey & Eliot Daniel, 1948, Movie: So Dear To My Heart (Disney) **16.00**

Still Alarm by Harry J. Lincoln, 1914 (March) **10.00**

Still Unexprest by Carrie Jacobs Bond, 1901 ....**15.00**

Stingo Stungo by Lew Brown & James F. Hanly, 1923, Photo Minnie Lightner (Cover Artist, Politzer) **4.00**

Stingy Kid by Alfred Bryan & Nat Goldstein, 1909 ....**10.00**

Stingy Moon by Will Heelan & H.B.Blanke, 1906...............................**5.00**

Stolen Kisses by Francis Wheeler & Ted Snyder, 1921 (Cover Artist, Barbelle & Deco)...**5.00**

Stomping At The Savoy by Benny Goodman, Chick Webb & Edgar Sampson, 1936 (Cover Artist, Jorj Harris)...................................**3.00**

Stop Beatin 'Round The Mulberry Bush by Bickley Reichner & Clay Boland, 1938, Photo Tommy Dorsey **5.00**

Stop Flirting by Russell Tarbox, 1925, Movie: Stop Flirting, Photo Wanda Hawley...**6.00**

Stop It by Farrell, 1917, Photo Sophie Tucker (Cover Artist, Pfeiffer) ..**10.00**

Stop! It's Wonderful by Brickley Reichner & Clay Boland, 1939, Musical: Great Guns, Presented By The Mask & Wig Club, University Of Pennsylvania..**5.00**

Stop Look Listen To the Music Of The Band by Lew Brown & Albert Von Tilzer, 1920 (Cover Artist, Rose Symbol)..............................**8.00**

Stop Making Faces At Me by Andrew B. Sterling & Kerry Mills, 1908 ..**10.00**

Stop! Stop! You're Breaking My Heart by Irving Berlin, 1910 (Irving Berlin)..**12.00**

Stop That Rag, Keep On Playing by Irving Berlin, 1909, Photo Stella Mayhew (Cover Artist, Pfeiffer, Irving Berlin & Rag).................**20.00**

Stop Time Waltz, The by Jimmie Selva & Dave Ringle, 1952 (Cover Artist, Frederick S. Manning)...**20.00**

Stop! You're Breakin' My Heart by Ted Koehler & Burton Lane, 1937, Movie: Artists & Models, Photo Jack Benny (Cover Artist, Russell Patterson)..**12.00**

Stop Your Quittin' Get Away Closer by Carlyle, 1911........................**5.00**

Stop Your Tickling, Jack by Harry Lauder, 1904................................**5.00**

Stories Mother Told by Frank J. Gurney, 1895 (Pre 1900) **10.00**

Stories Mother Told Me, The by Andrew B. Sterling & Harry Von Tilzer, 1898 (Pre 1900) **10.00**

Storm King, March Galop, The by E.T. Paull, 1902 (Cover Artist, E.T. Paull, Lithograph, A. Hoen & Co. & March)...............................**35.00**

Storm Of Life by Egbert Van Alstyne, 1903 ....**5.00**

Storm On The Ocean–Sailboat In Storm by John Martin, 1911 (Transportation) **10.00**

Stormy Sea Of Love, The by Ballard MacDonald & Harry Carroll, 1916 ..**5.00**

Stormy Weather by Ted Koehler & Harold Arlen, 1933, Musical: Cotton Club Parade (Cover Artist, Leff) **5.00**

Story Book Ball, The by Billie Montgomery & George Perry, 1917, Photo Eileen Beatty (Cover Artist, Starmer) **10.00**

Story Of A Rose, The by Lem Trombley, 1912 ....**5.00**

Story Of A Soul, The by Leo Woods & Charles E. Harris, 1916..........**5.00**

Story Of A Sparrow, The by Paul Herve, Jean Biquet & Adolf Philipp, 1915, Musical: The Girl Who Smiles..**5.00**

Story Of A Starry Night, The by Al Hoffman, Mann Curtis & Jerry Livingston, 1941 ....**5.00**

Story Of Old Glory, The Flag We Love, The by J. Will Callahan & Ernest R. Ball, 1916 (WWI) **3.00**

Story Of The Rosary, The by Maxwell C. Freed & Harry D. Squires, 1924...**5.00**

Story Of The Rose by Andrew Mack, 1890 (Pre 1900) **10.00**

Story Of Two Cigarettes, A by Mickey Stoner, Fred Jay & Leonard K. Marker, 1945, Photo Johnnie Johnston, Advertising Chesterfield Cigarettes (Cover Artist, L. Geyler & Advertising)..............................**12.00**

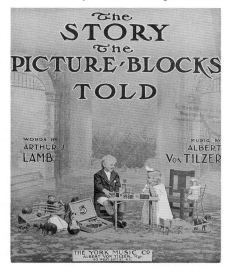

Story The Picture Blocks Told, The by Arthur J. Lamb & Albert Von Tilzer, 1908 ....**10.00**

Story The Rosebud Told, The by Barnes & White, 1915 (Cover Artist, Pfeiffer)..............................**10.00**

Storyland by Elwood Wolf & Earl Burtnett, 1916 (Cover Artist, SSS) .**5.00**

Stouthearted Men by Frank Mandel, Oscar Hammerstein II & Sigmund Romberg, 1942, Movie: Deep In My Heart, Based On Life Of Sigmund Romberg **5.00**

Stouthearted Men by Frank Mandel, Oscar Hammerstein II & Sigmund Romberg, 1928, Musical: The New Moon **10.00**

Straight From The Shoulder Right From The Heart by Mack Gordon & Harry Revel, 1934, Movie: She Loves Me Not, Photo Bing Crosby..**5.00**

Strains From Dixieland by Justin Ringleben, 1906 (Cover Artist, Starmer & Dixie)..............................**10.00**

Strange Interlude by Ben Bernie, Walter Hirsch & Phil Baker, 1931, Photo Gladys Rice..............................**3.00**

Strange Lady In Town by Tiomkin & Washington, 1955, Movie: Strange Lady In Town, Photo Greer Garson & Dana Andrews **5.00**

Strange Love by Edward Heyman & Miklos Razsa, 1946, Movie: The Strange Love Of Martha Ivers, Photo Barbara Stanwyck, Van Heflin & Lizabeth Scott..............................**5.00**

Strange Music by Robert Wright & George Forrest, 1944, Movie: Song Of Norway **3.00**

Stranger In Paradise by Robert Wright & George Forrest, 1953, Musical: Kismet..............................**3.00**

Stranger's Story Waltz, The by E.T. Paull (Cover Artist, E.T. Paull)..**35.00**

Strangers by Charles O'Flynn & J. Fred Coots, 1931 (Cover Artist, Leff)...

Strangers In The Night by Charles Singleton, Eddie Snyder & Bert Kaempfert, 1946, Photo Frank Sinatra **3.00**

Strawberry Roan, The by Fred Howard, Nat Vincent & Curley Fletcher, 1931, Movie: Strawberry Roan, Photo Ken Maynard & Ruth Hall (Cover Artist, L. Kummel) **10.00**

Stray Sunbeam, A by Roy Hatfield, 1906 ....**5.00**

Street Of Dreams by Sam Lewis & Victor Young, 1932, Photo Jane Froman **3.00**

Streets Of Cairo, The by James Thornton, 1893 (Pre 1900)..............................**12.00**

Streets Of Laredo, The by Jay Livingston & Ray Evans, 1949, Movie: Streets Of Laredo, Photo William Holden, MacDonald Carey, Mona Freeman & William Bendix **6.00**

Streets Of Laredo, The by M. Alexander, 1966..............................**2.00**

Strenuous Life by Scott Joplin, 1902 (Scott Joplin & Rag)..............................**50.00**

Strike Up The Band by George & Ira Gershwin, 1930, Photo Mickey Rooney & Judy Garland (Patriotic)..............................**12.00**

Strike Up The Band, Here Comes A Sailor by Sterling & Ward, 1900 (Cover Artist, Pfeiffer & Patriotic)..............................**15.00**

String A Ring Of Roses 'Round Your Rosie by Schwartz & Jerome, 1912 (Cover Artist, Pfeiffer) **10.00**

String Of Pearls, A by Jerry Gray, 1954, Movie: The Glenn Miller Story, Photo James Stewart & June Allyson..............................**8.00**

Strip Polka by Johnny Mercer, 1942, Photo Andrews Sisters **3.00**

Strolling On The Brooklyn Bridge by Joseph P. Skelly, 1883 (Pre 1900) **15.00**

Strolling With Your Summer Girl by Lew P. Bendernagee, 1906..............................**5.00**

Strut, Miss Lizzie by Henry Creamer & Turner Layton, 1911 (Black, Black Face) **15.00**

Struttin' With Some Barbecue, Dixieland Ragtime Blues by Maxted, 1941 (Dixie & Rag) **10.00**

Study In Symbols, A by Clarence Urmy & Carrie Jacobs Bond, 1901, Dedicated To Mrs. O.L. Fox (Dedication) **15.00**

Stumbling by Zez Confrey, 1922, Photo Paul Whiteman (Cover Artist, JVR & Deco) **10.00**

Stupid Girl by Mick Jagger & Keith Richard, 1966, Photo The Rolling Stones..............................**6.00**

Stupid Mr. Cupid by Edward Madden & Theodore Morse, 1908 ....**5.00**

Such A Nice Girl, Too by Arthur Seldon, 1892 (Pre 1900) **10.00**

Such An Education Has My Mary Ann by Edward Harrigan & David Braham, 1880 (Pre 1900) **15.00**

Suddenly It's Spring by Johnny Burke & Jimmy Van Heusen, 1943, Movie: Lady In The Dark, Photo Ginger Rogers **10.00**

Suddenly There's A Valley by Chuck Meyer & Biff Jones, 1955, Signed Photo Gogi Grant (Signed)..............................**3.00**

Sue Me by Jo Swerling, Abe Burrows & Frank Loesser, 1950, Musical: Guys & Dolls..............................**5.00**

Sue Of The Cumberlands by Keithley & Thompson, 1914..............................**5.00**

Sue Simmons, Bill's Sister by Hill, 1908 (Cover Artist, Pfeiffer & Deco) **15.00**

Sugar Blues by Lucy Fletcher & Clarence Williams, 1923, Photo Clyde McCoy (Blues) **8.00**

Sugar by Joe Young & George W. Meyer, 1931, Signed Photo Little Jack Little (Cover Artist, Leff & Signed)..............................**6.00**

Sugar Cane Rag by Scott Joplin, 1908 (Scott Joplin & Rag) **50.00**

Sugar Foot Strut by Charles Schaub, 1927..............................**5.00**

Sugar Lump by Frederick Bryan, 1914..............................**5.00**

Sugar Moon by Stanley Murphy & Percy Wenrich, 1910..............................**5.00**

Sugar Plum by Gus Kahn & Arthur Johnson, 1935, Movie: Thanks A Million, Photo Dick Powell..............................**6.00**

Sugartime by Charlie Phillips & Odis Echols, 1956, Photo McGuire Sisters..**2.00**

Suki San by J. Keirn Brennan & Walter Donaldson, 1917..............................**5.00**

Sullivan by George M. Cohan (George M. Cohan)..............................**16.00**

Sultan, The by William Loraine, 1899 (Pre 1900 & March)..............................**15.00**

Summer by Rutter, 1910 (Transportation)..............................**10.00**

Summer In The Heart by Frank L. Stanton & Oley Speaks, 1918..............................**3.00**

Summer Is Near by Clifton Bingham & Noel Johnson, 1909..............................**5.00**

Summer Nights by Hart & Hays, 1916 (Cover Artist, Pfeiffer)..............................**10.00**

Summer Place, A by Steiner, 1959, Movie: A Summer Place, Photo Richard Egan, Dorothy McGuire, Troy Donahue & Sandra Dee.....**4.00**

Summer Reminds Me Of You by Bryan & Meyer, 1908 (Cover Artist, Pfeiffer)..............................**12.00**

Summer Souvenirs by Charles Newman & J. Fred Coots, 1938..............................**3.00**

Summer Widowers, The by Glen MacDonough & A. Baldwin Sloane, 1910 (Cover Artist, Starmer)..............................**15.00**

Summer Wind by Johnny Mercer & Henry Mayer, 1965, Photo Roger Williams, Perry Como & Wayne Newton **4.00**

Summer Windows by Feist, 1910 (Cover Artist, Pfeiffer) **10.00**

Summertime by DuBose Heyward & Ira & George Gershwin, 1935, Movie: Porgy And Bess (Cover Artist, B. Harris & Black, Black Face) **12.00**

Summertime For Mine by F. J. Seymour, 1909 (Cover Artist, Bower) ..**10.00**

Sumthin Doin by F. H. Losey (Cover Artist, Dittmar, March & Black, Black Face) **25.00**

Sun Do Move, The by John Stromberg, 1899 (Cover Artist, CEF, Pre 1900 & Black, Black Face) **35.00**

Sun Is At My Window, The by Lewis, Young & Meyer, 1928 (Deco)..**5.00**

Sun Is Up, The by Bob Davis, 1953, Photo Barry Valentino **5.00**

Sun Shines Better, The by Goodwin & Meyer, 1911 (Cover Artist, Pfeiffer) **10.00**

Sun Shines Brighter, The by P.G. Wodehouse & Jerome Kern, 1917, Musical: Leave It To Jane **6.00**

Sun, The Heather And You, The by Irene Stiles & H.L. Bilger, 1925, Dedicated To June Barr (Dedication) **8.00**

Sun Would Shine Again, The by Alice Grainger & Wilbur Chenoweth, 1941 ....**3.00**

Sunbeam by W. C. Powell, 1909 ....**8.00**

Sunbeam Sal by Will D. Cobb & Leo Edwards, 1914 (Cover Artist, Pfeiffer) **10.00**

Sunbonnet Sue by Charles A. Bayha (Cover Artist, Barbelle) **10.00**

Sunbonnet Sue by Will D. Cobb & Gus Edwards, 1908 (Cover Artist, C. Warde Traver) **12.00**

Sunburst Rag by James Scott, 1909 (Rag) **10.00**

Sunday by Ned Miller, Chester Cohn, Jules Stein & Bennie Krueger, 1926 ....**6.00**

Sunday by Richard Rodgers & Oscar Hammerstein II, 1961, Movie: Flower Drum Song, Photo Nancy Kwan **5.00**

Sunday Kind Of Love, A by Barbara Belle, Anita Leonard, Stan Rhodes & Louis Prima, 1946 (Cover Artist, Barbelle) **3.00**

Sunday, Monday Or Always by Jimmy Van Heusen & Johnny Burke, 1943, Movie: Dixie, Photo Bing Crosby & Dorothy Lamour **10.00**

Sunday Morning Chimes by F. Henri Klickmann, 1914 ....**5.00**

Sunday Night When The Parlor's Full by Edward Harrigan & David Braham, 1877 (Pre 1900) **15.00**

Sundown Blues by W. C. Handy, 1923 (Blues) **8.00**

Sunflower Babe by Fred Heltman, 1909 (Cover Artist, Ray & Rag) ...**10.00**

Sunflower by Mack David, 1948 ....**5.00**

Sunflower Slow Rag by Scott Hayden & Scott Joplin, 1901 (Scott Joplin & Rag) **50.00**

Sunflower Tickle by Benjamin Richmond, 1908 ....**10.00**

Sunlight And Shadow by Marc Sylvan & Louis Tocaben, 1904...........**5.00**

Sunny by Otto Harbach, Oscar Hammerstein II & Jerome Kern, 1925 ..**10.00**

Sunny Disposish by George Gershwin, 1926 ....**5.00**

Sunny Side Of Thompson Street by Edward Harrigan & David Braham, 1883 (Pre 1900) **15.00**

Sunny Side Up by B. G. DeSylva, Lew Brown & Ray Henderson, 1929, Movie: Sunny Side Up, Photo Janet Gaynor **15.00**

Sunrise And You by Arthur A. Penn, 1918 ....**5.00**

Sunrise by Santly, 1927 ....**3.00**

Sunrise Echoes by Vandersloot, 1916 (Cover Artist, Pfeiffer) **10.00**

Sunrise Serenade by Jack Lawrence & Frankie Carle, 1938, Photo Glen Gray & His Orchestra (Cover Artist, Barbelle) **5.00**

Sunrise, Sunset by Sheldon Harnick & Jerry Bock, 1964, Movie: Fiddler On The Roof **2.00**

Sunset Echoes by Vandersloot, 1916 (Cover Artist, Pfeiffer) **10.00**

Sunset Glow by F. W. Vandersloot, 1916 (Cover Artist, Pfeiffer) **10.00**

Sunset In A Japanese Garden by Fay Foster, 1917............................**5.00**

Sunset In Eden by John T. Hall, 1915 (Cover Artist, Starmer) **5.00**

Sunset In The Mountains by Kathryn Bayley, 1913...........................**5.00**

Sunset Land, Aloha by Kawelo & Shannon, 1916 ....**6.00**

Sunset Limited by Bartell & Lincoln, 1910 (March & Transportation)..**20.00**

Sunset Trail Of Gold, The by Allic Foland Criss & James G. MacDermid, 1922 ....**5.00**

Sunshine by Irving Berlin, 1928, Dedicated To My Friend Sid Grauman At Whose Theatre In Hollywood, California It Was First Introduced (Cover Artist, R.S., Irving Berlin & Dedication) **10.00**

Sunshine by Irving Berlin, 1928 (Irving Berlin)................................**10.00**

Sunshine Alley by Eugene West, 1922..**5.00**

Sunshine And Roses by Gus Kahn & Egbert Van Alstyne, 1913 (Cover Artist, Starmer) **12.00**

Sunshine And Roses by Rolfe, 1910 (Cover Artist, Pfeiffer)..............**10.00**

Sunshine Cake by Johnny Burke & Jimmy Van Heusen, 1950, Movie: Riding High, Photo Bing Crosby......................................**5.00**

Sunshine For Us Now Nellie by Homer, 1906 ....**5.00**

Sunshine Girl Of Mine by C. W. Wood & Chas. G. Maynard, 1919, Photo Lillian Goldsmith (Cover Artist, Dunk) **5.00**

Sunshine Of Paradise Alley by Ford & Bratton, 1895 (Pre 1900)........**10.00**

Sunshine Of Your Smile, The by Leonard Cooke & Lilian Ray, 1915 ..**3.00**

Sunshine On My Shoulders by John Denver, Mike Taylor & Dick Kniss, 1971, Photo John Denver..**1.00**

Sunshine Rose by Jean Lefaure & W.C. Polla, 1920 (Cover Artist, Rolf Armstrong)..**25.00**

Sunshine Will Come Again by Charles T. Ellis, 1886 (Pre 1900) **15.00**

Suppose I Had Never Met You by Harlan Thompson & Harry Archer, 1923, Musical: Little Jessie James (Cover Artist, JVR)................**10.00**

Suppose I Met You Face To Face by Chas. K. Harris, 1913 (Cover Artist, Pfeiffer)...**10.00**

Supposing by Arthur Trevelyan, 1899 (Pre 1900)..............................**10.00**

Sure As You're Born by George A. Little, Haven Gillespie & Larry Shay, 1923 (Cover Artist, Frederick S. Manning)......................**8.00**

Sure Thing by Ira Gershwin & Jerome Kern, 1944, Movie: Cover Girl **5.00**

Sure We Are Some Big America by Wolfe (Cover Artist, Pfeiffer) **10.00**

Surrender by Bernie Benjamin & George Weiss, 1945, Photo Perry Como (Cover Artist, Barbelle) **5.00**

Surrey With The Fringe On Top, The by Richard Rodgers & Oscar Hammerstein II, 1943, Musical: Oklahoma (Cover Artist, B.J. Holley) .**3.00**

Surrey With The Fringe On Top, The by Richard Rodgers & Oscar Hammerstein II, 1943, Musical: Oklahoma (Cover Artist, Barbelle) **8.00**

Susie by B. G. DeSylvia & Al Jolson, 1925 (Al Jolson) **10.00**

Susie by J. Ed. Lakeman, 1895 (Pre 1900) **10.00**

Susquehanna Sue by Buzzell & Marshall, 1916 ....**5.00**

Susquehanna Transfer by Sunny Skylar & Abner Silver, 1942 ....**5.00**

Susy by Scott Monte & Ernest Nicol, 1948 ....**5.00**

Susy Little Susy by Humperdinck, 1940 ....**2.00**

Suzanne by Belafonte & Thomas, 1953, Movie: Bright Road, Photo Harry Belafonte **4.00**

Suzy Snowflake by Tepper, 1951 ....**2.00**

Swamp-Fire by Harold Mooney, 1935 ....**3.00**

Swanee Blues by Frank Goodman & J. Milton Delcamp, 1920 (Cover Artist, R.S. & Blues) **5.00**

Swanee Butterfly by Ed Rose & Walter Donaldson, 1925 (Cover Artist, Wohlman) **5.00**

Swanee by Irving Caesar & George Gershwin, 1919, Musical: Sinbad, Photo Al Jolson (Al Jolson) **10.00**

Swanee by Irving Caesar & George Gershwin, 1932, Movie: The Jolson Story, Photo Larry Parks & Evelyn Keyes (Al Jolson) **16.00**

Swanee Moonlight by Frost & Klickmann, 1920 ....**5.00**

Swanee Rag by Chas. L. Johnson, 1912 (Rag) **10.00**

Swanee Ripples Rag by Blaufuss, 1912 (Cover Artist, Pfeiffer & Rag) ..**15.00**

Swanee River Moon by H. Pitman Clarke, 1921 (Cover Artist, Malcolm Perret) **5.00**

Swanee River Trail by Al Jolson, 1927 (Al Jolson) **10.00**

Swanee Rose by Al Jolson, 1921 (Al Jolson) **12.00**

Swanee Rose by Geo. Fairman, 1912 ....**10.00**

Swanee Shore by Hess & Bourne, 1927, Photo Jack Crawford **3.00**

Swanee Shore by Sidney D. Mitchell, Arthur Fields & Irving Kaufman, 1919 (Cover Artist, R.S.) **4.00**

Sweet Adeline by Girard & Armstrong, 1903 ....**10.00**

Sweet Alice Gray by Girard & Gilbert, 1920 ....**5.00**

Sweet Anabel by Alice Nadine Morrison, 1922 ....**5.00**

Sweet And Lovely by Gus Arnheim, Harry Tobias & Jules Lemare, 1931, Photo Guy Lombardo **3.00**

Sweet And Lovely by Gus Arnheim, Harry Tobias & Jules Lemare, 1931, Movie: Two Girls And A Sailor, Photo Van Johnson, June Allyson, Gloria DeHaven, Harry James & Many Other Stars **8.00**

Sweet And Low by J. Stanley Royce & Charles L. Johnson, 1919 (Cover Artist, Dorothy Dulin) **8.00**

Sweet And Low by Joseph Barnby & Alfred Tennyson, 1935, Photo Doring Sisters **5.00**

Sweet And Low by Joseph Barnby & Alfred Tennyson, 1935, Photo Starr Sisters **5.00**

Sweet And Low-Down by Ira & George Gershwin, 1925, Musical: Tip Toes **5.00**

Sweet Annie Moore by John H. Flynn, 1901 ....**10.00**

Sweet As A Song by Mack Gordon & Harry Revel, 1937, Movie, Sally, Irene And Mary, Photo Alice Faye, Fred Allen & Many More Stars ..**5.00**

Sweet Babette, She Always Did The Minuet by Sterling, Moran & Von Tilzer, 1916 (Cover Artist, Pfeiffer) **12.00**

Sweet Blue Bird by Arthur Lamb & Abe Oleman, 1925 ....**5.00**

Sweet Bunch Of Daisies by Anita Owen, 1894 (Pre 1900) **10.00**

Sweet Bye And Bye by Louis A. Drumheller, 1910 ....**3.00**

Sweet Caroline by Claude Weber **5.00**

Sweet Child by Al Lewis, Richard A. Whiting & Howard Simon, 1925 ..**5.00**

Sweet Cider Time When You Were Mine by Joe McCarthy & Percy Wenrich, 1916, Photo Neil McKinley **12.00**

Sweet Cookie Mine by Jack Frost & Clarence M. Jones, 1917, Photo Sophie Tucker **20.00**

Sweet Dreams by Don Gibson, 1955, Photo Patsy Cline **2.00**

Sweet Dreams My Love, Sweet Dreams by Arthur Longbrake & Ed Edwards, 1909 ....**6.00**

Sweet Dreams Sweetheart by M.K. Jerome & Ted Koehler, 1944, Movie: Hollywood Canteen, Photo Jack Benny & Many Stars (WWII) **5.00**

Sweet Egyptian Rose by Edgar Allan Woolf & Anatol Friedland, 1917 ..**5.00**

Sweet Ella May by Jacques Renard, Mickie Alpert & J. Russell Robinson, 1928 (Deco) **5.00**

Sweet Eloise by Mack David & Russ Morgan, 1942, Photo Buddy Franklyn (Cover Artist, Sig-Ch) **4.00**

Sweet Emalina, My Gal by Henry Creamer & Turner Layton, 1917 ...**10.00**

Sweet Genevieve by George Cooper & Henry Tucker, 1916............5.00

Sweet Genevieve by Harold Potter & Rodd Eddy, Movie: Fort Apache, Photo Morton Downey **5.00**

Sweet Georgia Brown by Ben Bernie, Maceo Pinkard & Kenneth Casey, 1925 (Black, Black Face) **3.00**

Sweet Hawaiian Chimes by Lani McIntire, Geo. B. McConnell & Dick Sanford, 1938 ....**5.00**

Sweet Hawaiian Moonlight by Harold G. Frost & F. Henri Klickmann, 1918 ....**5.00**

Sweet Heartache by Ned Washington & Sam H. Stept, 1937, Movie: The Hit Parade **5.00**

Sweet Indiana Home by Walter Donaldson, 1922, Photo Aileen Stanley ..**5.00**

Sweet Iniscarra by Chauncey Olcott, 1897 (Pre 1900 & Irish) **10.00**

Sweet Is The Word For You by Leo Robin & Ralph Rainger, 1937, Movie: Waikiki Wedding, Photo Bing Crosby & Shirley Ross **6.00**

Sweet Italian Love by Irving Berlin & Ted Snyder, 1910 (Irving Berlin) **10.00**

Sweet Jennie Lee! by Walter Donaldson, 1931 ....**6.00**

Sweet Katie Connor by Harry Dacre, 1890 (Pre 1900 & Irish) **10.00**

Sweet Kentucky Lady, Dry Your Eyes by William Jerome & Louis A. Hirsch, 1914 ....**10.00**

Sweet Kisses by Lew Brown, Eddie Buzzell & Albert Von Tilzer, 1919, Ziegfeld Follies, Photo Van & Schenck **10.00**

Sweet Lady by Howard Johnson & Carlo Sanderson, 1921, Musical: Tangerine, Photo Julia Sanderson **10.00**

Sweet Leilani by Harry Owens, 1937, Movie: Waikiki Wedding, Photo Bing Crosby (Cover Artist, HBK) **8.00**

Sweet Little Babies by Joseph P. Skelly, 1882 (Pre 1900) **10.00**

Sweet Little Buttercup by Alfred Bryan & Herman Paley, 1917 (WWI) ..**10.00**

Sweet Little Headache by Leo Robin & Ralph Rainger, 1938, Movie: Paris Honeymoon, Photo Bing Crosby **8.00**

Sweet Lorraine by Mitchell Parish & Cliff Burwell, 1928, Photo Bing Crosby **5.00**

Sweet Marie by Warman & Moore, 1893 (Pre 1900)............................**10.00**

Sweet Marie by Warman & Moore, 1946, Movie: Life With Father, Photo William Powell & Irene Dunne.......................................**5.00**

Sweet Marie Snow by Pat Rooney, 1907, Photo Pat Rooney................**5.00**

Sweet Meats by Percy Wenrich, 1907..**25.00**

Sweet Nothings Of Love by Edgar Leslie & Walter Donaldson, 1929, Movie: Hot For Paris, Photo Fifi Dorsay, Victor McLaglen, Ed Brendel & Raoul Walsh...**6.00**

Sweet Old Fashioned Girl, A by BobMerrill, 1956...............................**4.00**

Sweet Patootie Sal by Wm. J. Loveman, 1919 (Cover Artist, Starmer).**5.00**

Sweet Red Roses by Anita Owen, 1910 (Cover Artist, Edgar Keller).**10.00**

Sweet Remembrance by Ellis, 1911 (Cover Artist, Pfeiffer)...............**10.00**

Sweet Rosie O'Grady by Maude Nugent, 1943, Movie: Sweet Rosie O'Grady, Photo Betty Grable & Robert Young...........................**5.00**

Sweet Siamese by Edward Madden & Mary Earl, 1919 ....**6.00**

Sweet & Simple by Ray Henderson, Jack Yellen & Irving Caesar, 1934, Movie: Scandals, Photo Alice Faye.........................**10.00**

Sweet Sixteens by Alfred Bryan & Kerry Mills, 1908 ....**10.00**

Sweet Slumber by Jacob Henry Ellis, 1904 (Cover Artist, F.F.J.) **5.00**

Sweet Someone by Mack Gordon & Harry Revel, 1937, Movie: Love and Hisses, Photo Walter Winchell, Ben Bernie, Simone Simon, Bert Lahr & Joan Davis **8.00**

Sweet Stranger by Irving Kahal, Francis Wheeler & Ted Snyder, 1927 ..**8.00**

Sweet Stranger by Jerry Livingston, Ned Wever & Milton Ager, 1937, Photo Mitchell Ayres (Cover Artist, RH)..............................**3.00**

Sweet Suffolk Owl by A. Buzzi Peccia, 1917 ....**5.00**

Sweet Suspense by Lewis A. Drumheller, 1907...................................**5.00**

Sweet Suzanne by Jos. Geo. Gilbert, 1928 ....**5.00**

Sweet Suzanne by Troy & Europa, 1910 (Cover Artist, Pfeiffer & Deco)...**10.00**

Sweet Thing by Joe Young, Abel Baer & Fred E. Ahlert, 1935............**3.00**

Sweet Thoughts Of Thee by Adam Geibel, 1905 (Cover Artist, A. West) **10.00**

Sweet Varsity Sue by Davis, Martin & Stuart, 1937, Photo Ritz Brothers **8.00**

Sweet Violets by Cy Coben & Charles Green, 1951, Photo Dinah Shore...**5.00**

Sweet Violets by J. K. Emmet, 1940 ....**3.00**

Sweet Violets by P. Bucalossi, (Cover Artist, W. Spalding & Lithograph, T. Packer)...**10.00**

Sweet-Clover by Trahern, 1902...**5.00**

Sweetest Girl In Dixie by O'Dea & Adams, 1904 (Dixie) **5.00**

Sweetest Girl In Monterey, The by Alfred Bryan & Herman Paley, 1915 (Cover Artist, Starmer) **10.00**

Sweetest Little Girl In Tennessee, The by Stanley Murphy & Harry Carroll, 1917 (Cover Artist, Barbelle)....................................**10.00**

Sweetest Maid Of All by Oscar Straus, 1908 ....**10.00**

Sweetest Melody Of All, The by Grant Clarke & Jimmie V. Monaco, 1916 (Cover Artist, M. Farnil)................................**10.00**

Sweetest Song In The World, The by Harry Parr-Davies, 1938............**5.00**

Sweetest Story Ever Told, The by R.M. Stults, 1920 ....**3.00**

Sweetheart Blues by Al Nelson & Irving Bibo, 1920...........................**5.00**

Sweetheart by Al Lewis & Al Sherman, 1929......................................**5.00**

Sweetheart by Benny Davis & Arnold Johnson, 1921 (Deco) **5.00**

Sweetheart by Sydney Rosenfeld & C. M. Ziekver, 1908, Opera: Mlle. Mischief, Photo, Lu Lu Glazer (Cover Artist, John Frew)............**10.00**

Sweetheart Darlin' by Gus Kahn & Herbert Stothart,1933 Movie: Peg O' My Heart, Photo Marion Davies....................................**10.00**

Sweetheart Days by L. W. Heiser & J. Anton Dailey, 1907.................**5.00**

Sweetheart Land by Harry & Charles Tobias & Percy Moore, 1919, (Cover Artist, P.W. Read & Lithograph by Knapp Inc.).............**20.00**

Sweetheart Let's Grow Old Together by J.W. Bratton & Leo Edwards, 1936, Photo Phil Regan (Cover Artist, Jorj Harris)........................**2.00**

Sweetheart Memories by Benny Davis & Joe Burke, 1927...................**5.00**

Sweetheart Of All My Dreams by Art Fitch, Kay Fitch & Bert Lowe, 1928 ....**5.00**

Sweetheart Of Mine, Official Mary Pickford Song, by Frank Tyler Daniels & Leo Friedman, 1914, Signed Photo Mary Pickford (Signed).....**40.00**

Sweetheart Of My Dreams by Arthur J. Lamb & Charles H. Maskell, 1924 ....**5.00**

Sweetheart Of My Dreams by Will J. Jones & Gus Kleinecke, 1910 ....**5.00**

Sweetheart Of Sigma Chi, The by Byron D. Stokes & F. Dudleigh Vernor, 1927 (Cover Artist, Virg. Lewis).................................**6.00**

Sweetheart That I Lost In Dear Old Frisco, The by Helen Osborne & Walter Potter, 1906 ....**10.00**

Sweetheart Time by Harold Robe & Milbury H. Ryder, 1915..............**3.00**

Sweetheart We Need Each Other by Harry Tierney & Joseph McCarthy, 1929, Movie: Rio Rita, Photo Bebe Daniels & John Boles...........**12.00**

Sweetheart's A Pretty Name When It Is Y-O-U by Leslie & Piantadosi, 1909 (Cover Artist, Pfeiffer) **15.00**

Sweethearts by Alice Write, 1919, (Lithograph, Hayes, Buffalo, N.Y.)...10.00

Sweethearts by Bob Wright, Chet Forrest & Victor Herbert, 1938, Movie: Sweethearts, Photo Jeannette MacDonald & Nelson Eddy (Victor Herbert)...**15.00**

Sweethearts by Gus Kahn & Robert Van Alstyne, 1915 ....**5.00**

Sweethearts by Harry B. Smith & Victor Herbert, 1913 (Victor Herbert) **10.00**

Sweethearts Forever by Cliff Friend & Irving Caesar, 1932, Movie: Crooner, Photo Ann Dvorak (Cover Artist, Jorg Harris) **12.00**

Sweethearts On Parade by Charles Newman & Carmen Lombardo, 1928 (Deco) **5.00**

Sweethearts Once-But Now We're Parted by Laura Jean Libbey & Herman Avery Wade, 1907 ....**5.00**

Sweethearts True by Ryder, 1901 ....**5.00**

Sweetie Be Kind To Me by Norton, 1914 (Cover Artist, Pfeiffer).......**10.00**

Sweetie Dear by Joe Jordon, 1914..**5.00**

Sweetie Pie by John Jacob Loeb, 1934, Photo Dan Russo **4.00**

Sweetie Pie by John Jacob Loeb, 1934, Photo Henry Busse **4.00**

Sweets by Egan, Fitzgerald & Whiting, 1920 (Cover Artist, Pfeiffer)..**10.00**

Swing High, Swing Low by Burton Lane, Movie: Swing High, Swing Low, Photo Carole Lombard & Fred MacMurray..........................**5.00**

Swing Is Here To Stay by Gordon & Revel, 1937, Movie: Ali Baba Goes To Town, Photo Eddie Cantor, June Lang & Gypsy Rose Lee (Eddie Cantor) **8.00**

Swing Me High, Swing Me Low by Hollaender, 1910 ....**5.00**

Swing Song by William Scanlon, 1888 (Pre 1900) **15.00**

Swingin' Down The Lane by Gus Kahn & Isham Jones, 1923, Photo Isham Jones....................**5.00**

Swingin' In The Corn by Herb Magidson & Allie Wrubel, 1937, Movie: Radio City Revels, Photo Hal Kemp, Milton Berle, Bob Burns & Many Other Stars....................**12.00**

Swingin' The Jinx Away by Cole Porter, 1936, Movie: Born To Dance, Photo Eleanor Powell **5.00**

Swinging On A Star by Johnny Burke & Jimmy Van Heusen, 1944, Movie: Going My Way, Photo Bing Crosby **10.00**

Swipsey Cake Walk by Arthur Marshal & Scott Joplin, 1900 (Scott Joplin & Rag) **50.00**

Swiss Girl's Lament, The by Alexander Creral & A.L., 1902 ....**5.00**

Sylvia by Clinton Scollard & Oley Speaks, 1914....................**3.00**

Sympathetic Jasper by E. L. Catlin, 1905 (Rag)....................**10.00**

Sympathetic Sue by R. J. Janette & Jos. M. Daly, 1908, Photo Lucy Daly & Hap Ward....................**8.00**

Sympathy by Otto Harbach, Gus Kahn & Rudolph Friml, 1937, Movie: Firefly, Photo Jeannette MacDonald **5.00**

Symphony by Andre Tabet, Roger Bernstein, Jack Lawrence & Alstone, 1955, Photo Johnny Desmond **3.00**

Syncopate by Phil Cook & Tom Johnstone, 1922, Musical: Molly Darling (Deco) **5.00**

Syncopated Clock, The by Leroy Anderson, 1946....................**5.00**

Syncopated Vamp, The by Irving Berlin, 1920, Musical: Ziegfeld Follies Of 1920 (Cover Artist, R.S., Deco & Irving Berlin) **15.00**

Syncopatia Land (Cover Artist, Pfeiffer)....................**10.00**

Ta-Hoo by Harold Atteridge & Jean Schwartz, 1921, Musical: Passing Show of 1921 ....**5.00**

Ta-Ra-Ra Boom-De-Ay by Richard Morton & Angelo A. Asher, 1891 (Pre 1900) **10.00**

Tackin "Em" Down by Bud DeSylva & Albert Gumble, 1918 (Cover Artist, Frederick S. Manning & Deco) **10.00**

Tact by Leslie Stuart, 1900 ....**5.00**

Taffy by Vincent Bryan & Harry Von Tilzer, 1908, Photo Harry Von Tilzer (Cover Artist, Gene Buck)....................**10.00**

Taft March, Photo Of President Taft & Crossed American Flags (Patriotic, March & President) **26.00**

'Taint Good, Like A Nickel Made Of Wood by George Whiting, Buddy Bernier & Billy Haid, 1936, Photo Francis Craig (Cover Artist, Henri Lamothe)....................**3.00**

'Taint No Sin, To Dance Around In Your Bones by Edgar Leslie & Walter Donaldson, 1917 ....**5.00**

'Taint No Use by Herb Magidson & Burton Lane, 1936 ....**5.00**

Take A Car by Rose, 1905 (Transportation)....................**12.00**

Take A Day Off by Allen Norton Leete, 1890 (Pre 1900) **10.00**

Take A Day Off Mary Ann by Edward Harrigan & David Braham, 1891 (Pre 1900) **10.00**

Take A Lesson From The Lark by Leo Robin & Ralph Rainger, 1934, Movie: Shoot The Works, Photo Ben Bernie, Dorothy Dell, Jack Oakie, Alison Shipworth & Roscoe Karns....................**5.00**

Take A Little One Step by Zelda Sears, Walter DeLeon & Vincent Youmans, 1923, Musical: Lollipop, Photo Ada May....................**5.00**

Take A Little Ride With Me by Theodore Morse, 1906 (Transportation) **16.00**

Take A Little Tip From Father by Irving Berlin & Ted Snyder, 1912, Photo Joe Regan (Cover Artist, Gene Buck & Irving Berlin)........**10.00**

Take A Little Tip From Father by Irving Berlin & Ted Snyder, 1912, Photo Henry & Davis (Cover Artist, Gene Buck & Irving Berlin) **10.00**

Take A Little Tip From Father by Irving Berlin & Ted Snyder, 1912, Photo Bailey, Hall & Burnett (Cover Artist, Gene Buck & Irving Berlin)....................**10.00**

Take A Little Tip From Father by Irving Berlin & Ted Snyder, 1912 (Cover Artist, Pfeiffer & Irving Berlin)....................**15.00**

Take A Number From One To Ten by Mack Gordon & Harry Revel, 1934, Movie: College Rhythm, Photo Joe Penner, Lanny Ross, Jack Oakie & Helen Mack....................**6.00**

Take A Seat Old Lady by Paul Dresser, 1894 (Pre 1900) **10.00**

Take A Tip From The Tulip by Herb Magidson & Allie Wrubel, 1937, Movie: Radio City Revels, Photo Bob Burns, Milton Berle, Ann Miller, Kenny Baker & Many Other Stars **5.00**

Take A Vacation, Mr. Moon by Kalmar, 1911 (Cover Artist, Pfeiffer)..**10.00**

Take Along A Little Love by Richard A. Whiting & Seymour Simons, 1930 ....**5.00**

Take Back The Engagement Ring by Spaulding & Gray, 1894 (Pre 1900) **10.00**

Take Back Your Gold by Monroe Rosenfeld, 1897 (Pre 1900) **10.00**

Take Care, When You Say "Te Quiero" by Henry Prichard, 1946 ....**5.00**

Take 'Em To The Door Blues by Billy Rose, Benny Davis & Ray Henderson, 1925 (Blues)....................**10.00**

Take Everything But You by Maurice Abrahams & Elmer Colby, 1929, Movie: Song Of Love **5.00**

Take Her Back If You Love Her by Alfred Bryan & Fred Fisher, 1915 ....**10.00**

Take In The Sun, Hang Out The Moon by Sam Lewis, Joe Young & Harry Woods, 1926, Photo Dolly Dumplin (Cover Artist, CM) **5.00**

Take In The Sun, Hang Out The Moon by Sam Lewis, Joe Young & Harry Woods, 1926, Photo Frank Fay (Deco)....................**5.00**

Take It Easy by Albert DeBru, Irving Taylor & Vic Mizzy, 1943........**2.00**

Take It Easy by Jimmy McHugh & Dorothy Fields, 1935, Movie: Every Night At Eight **5.00**

Take It From There by Leo Robin & Ralph Rainger, 1943, Movie: Coney Island, Photo Betty Grable....................**5.00**

Take Me Around Again by Ed Rose & Kerry Mills, 1907....................**10.00**

Take Me Back by Irving Berlin, 1913, Photo Claire Rochester (Cover Artist, Pfeiffer & Irving Berlin)....................**16.00**

Take Me Back Home Again by Cooper & Millard, 1870 (Pre 1900)...**15.00**

Take Me Back To Babyland by Frank J. Tannehill & Pat Rooney, 1909, Photo Louise Dresser (Cover Artist, Ed Keller)....................**8.00**

Take Me Back To Dear Old Dixie by R.M. Stults, 1910 (Dixie).........**10.00**

Take Me Back To Dixie by Franklin E. Parker & Claude Weber, 1903 (Dixie)....................**10.00**

Take Me Back To Germany (Cover Artist, Pfeiffer)....................**10.00**

Take Me Back To Home, Sweet Home by Hoomes, 1910....................**5.00**

Take Me Back To My Boots & Saddles by Walter G. Samuels, Leonard Whitcup & Teddy Powell, 1964 ....**3.00**

Take Me Back To My Dear Old Mother by F. C. Swan, 1916 (Cover Artist, SSS & Union Engraving Co.)....................**5.00**

Take Me Back To My Louisiana Home by George L. Cobb & Gus Edwards, 1904 ....**10.00**

Take Me Back To My Own Little Home Sweet Home by Harry Verona, 1903 ....**10.00**

Take Me Back To New York Town by Andrew B. Sterling & Harry Von Tilzer, 1918 (Cover Artist, Pfeiffer & WWI)....................**10.00**

Take Me Back To New York Town by Andrew B. Sterling & Harry Von Tilzer, 1907, Photo Friend & Downing (Cover Artist, Gene Buck) ..**10.00**

Take Me Back To Renfro Valley by John Lair, 1935, Photo Rambling Red Foley **5.00**

Take Me Back To The Garden Of Love by E. Ray Goetz & Nat Osborne, 1911, Photo Lewis Parshley, Respectfully Dedicated To Miss Mabel McKinley (Cover Artist, Pfeiffer & Dedication)....................**16.00**

Take Me Back To The Garden Of Love by E. Ray Goetz & Nat Osborne, 1911, Photo Mack & Dugal Co., Respectfully Dedicated to Miss Mabel McKinley (Cover Artist, Pfeiffer & Dedication)....................**16.00**

Take Me Back To Your Garden Of Roses by Harold B. Freeman, 1917 (Cover Artist, Pfeiffer) **10.00**

Take Me Back To Your Heart by Rose & Meyer, 1924 (Cover Artist, Starmer) **5.00**

Take Me by Harry Edelheit, Clarence Senna & Monte Carlo, 1920 (Cover Artist, Kasselman & Lithography, Knapp Co.) **10.00**

Take Me In Your Arms Again by Charles K. Harris, 1912 ....**5.00**

Take Me On A Buick Honeymoon by Black, 1922 (Transportation) ...**25.00**

Take Me Out For A Joy Ride by Kerry Mills, 1909 (Transportation)..**15.00**

Take Me Out In A Velie Car by O'Connor, 1911 (Transportation) **15.00**

Take Me Out To The Ball Game by Jack Norworth & Albert Von Tilzer, 1908 (Sports) **20.00**

Take Me 'Round In A Taxicab by Mel J. Gibeon, 1908 (Transportation) **15.00**

Take Me To Honeymoon Lane by Maurice Solman & Ted Garton, 1919 (Cover Artist, William Fisher) **6.00**

Take Me To My Alabam' by Tobias & Dillon, 1916 ....**10.00**

Take Me To Roseland, My Beautiful Rose by Jack Strouse, Ed Johnson & Nat Osborne, 1913, Photo The Three E's (Cover Artist, Pfeiffer) ..**10.00**

Take Me To That Swanee Shore by L. Wolfe Gilbert & Lewis F. Muir, 1912 ....**5.00**

Take Me To The Land Of Jazz by Bert Kalmar, Edgar Leslie & Pete Wendling, 1919 (Cover Artist, Barbelle, Jazz & Deco) **10.00**

Take Me To The Midnight Cake Walk Ball by Eddie Cox, Arthur Jackson & Maurice Abrahams, 1915, Introduced at Winter Garden In Passing Show Of 1915, Photo Daphne Pollard (Cover Artist, A.W.B. & Black, Black Face) **12.00**

Take Me Up In An Aeroplane by Walby & Turner, 1910 (Cover Artist, Pfeiffer & Transportation) **15.00**

Take Me Up To The North Pole by Halsey K. Mohr, 1909 ....**5.00**

Take Me Up With You Dearie by Junie McCree & Albert Von Tilzer, 1909, Photo Evelyn Ware (Cover Artist, Hirt & Transportation) ..**20.00**

Take Your Clothes And Go by Irving Jones, 1897 (Pre 1900) **10.00**

Take Your Girl To The Ball Game by George M. Cohan, William Jerome & Jean Schwartz, 1908 (George M. Cohan & Sports) **22.00**

Take Your Girlie To The Movies, If You Can't Make Love At Home by E. Leslie, B. Kalmar & P. Wendling, 1919 (Cover Artist, Barbelle) **5.00**

Take Your Tomorrow And Give Me Today by Andy Razaf & J. C. Johnson, 1928 ....**5.00**

Takes Two To Make A Bargain by Mack Gordon & Harry Revel, 1935, Movie: Two For Tonight **5.00**

Takin' Miss Mary To The Ball by Edward Heyman & Nacio Herb Brown, 1948, Movie: On An Island With You, Photo Esther Williams & Peter Lawford **6.00**

Taking A Chance On Love by John Latouche, Ted Fetter & Vernon Duke, 1940, Movie: Cabin In The Sky (Cover Artist, Sorokin) **5.00**

Taking In The Town by Edward Harrigan & David Braham, 1890 (Pre 1900) **10.00**

Tale Of The Fireside, A by J. J. Thornton & J.R. Shannon, 1918 (WWI) **10.00**

Tale That The Sweet Roses Told, The by Robert F. Robin & Geo. W. Meyer, 1911 ....**5.00**

Tales From The Vienna Woods by M. C. Nanderf & Johann Strauss, 1939 ....**5.00**

Talk Of The Town, The by Gus Kahn & Chester Cohn, 1929 ....**5.00**

Talk To The Animals by Bricusse, 1967, Movie: Doctor Dolittle, Photo Rex Harrison **8.00**

Talkin' To Myself by Magidson & Conard, 1934, Movie: Gift Of Gab, Photo Ruth Etting, Ethel Waters, Wini Shaw, Alice White, Gus Arnheim & Gene Austin **5.00**

Talking Through My Heart by Leo Robin & Ralph Rainger, 1936, Movie: The Big Broadcast Of 1937, Photo Jack Benny & Many Stars........**5.00**

Talking To Myself About You by Alex Stordahl, Paul Weston & Irving Taylor, 1948, Photo Peggy Lee **5.00**

Tall Hope by Carolyn Leigh & Cy Coleman, 1960, Movie: Wildcat.....**5.00**

Tallahassee by B. G. DeSylva & Louis Silvers, 1921, Musical: Bombo, Photo Al Jolson (Al Jolson) **10.00**

Tallahassee by Frank Loesser, 1947, Movie: Variety Girl, Photo Many Stars **5.00**

Tambourine And Oranges by F. Henri Klickmann, 1915 ....**5.00**

Tammany by Vincent Bryan & Gus Edwards, 1905 ....**10.00**

Tangerine by J. Mercer & V. Schertzinger, 1942, Movie: The Fleet's In, Photo Dorothy Lamour, Jimmy Dorsey & Betty Hutton **5.00**

Tangomania by Egbert Van Alstyne, 1914 ....**5.00**

Tannhauser by Wagner, 1908 (Cover Artist, Pfeiffer) **15.00**

Tantalizing by Charles Magnante, 1934, Photo Charles Magnante........**3.00**

Tapioca by James Bland (Pre 1900 & Black, Black Face) **15.00**

Tapioca, The by Cahn & Van Heusen, 1967, Movie: Thoroughly Modern Millie, Photo Julie Andrews, Mary Tyler Moore & Carol Channing **6.00**

Taps by Rudy Vallee, Photo Rudy Vallee (WWI) **10.00**

Tar Babies by Raymond Birch, 1911 (Rag & Black, Black Face) **15.00**

Tar Heel Blues, The by J. Tim Brymn, 1915 (Blues) **5.00**

Tara Theme by Max Steiner, Transcribed by Stan Freeman, 1941, Movie: Gone With The Wind, Photo Clark Gable & Vivian Leigh **5.00**

Tarantelle by Stephen Heller, 1925 ....**5.00**

Tarra Ta-Larra Ta-La by Mary Symes & Johnny Farrow, 1948, Photo Johnny Desmond (Cover Artist, Barbelle) **3.00**

Tattletale by Jack Lawrence, Bob Schaeffer & Irving Rose, 1941........**5.00**

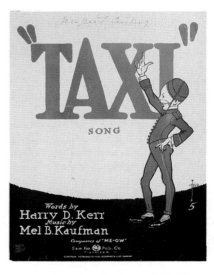

Taxi by Harry D. Kerr & Mel B. Kaufman, 1919 (Cover Artist, Ray & Transportation) 25.00

Taxicab by Sawyer, 1910 (Transportation) **15.00**

Tea For Two by Irving Caesar & Otto Harbach, 1940, Movie: No No Nanette, Photo Anna Neagle **5.00**

Tea Leaves by Morty Berk, Frank Capano & Max C. Freedman, 1948, Photo Frankie Carle **2.00**

Tea Leaves by Morty Berk, Frank Capano & Max C. Freedman, 1947, Photo Jack Smith **2.00**

Tea Leaves by Raymond B. Egan & Richard A. Whiting, 1921 ....**5.00**

Tea On The Terrace by Sam Coslow, 1936 (Cover Artist, HBK) **5.00**

Teach Me That Wonderful Language by Ronald C. Harry & L. Frederick Dusenberry, 1913 ....**10.00**

Teach Me To Love by Irving Berlin, 1916 (Irving Berlin) **10.00**

Teach Me To Pray by George Graff Jr. & Jessie Mae Jewitt, 1916 ......**5.00**

Teach Me To Smile by Paul Herve, Jean Biquet & Adolf Philipp, 1915, Musical: The Girl Who Smiles....................................**10.00**

Teacher's Pet by Allan Roberts & Jerome Brainin, 1937......................**6.00**

Teacher-Teacher by Anne Caldwell & Jerome Kern, 1919, Musical: She's A Good Fellow **6.00**

Tear, A Kiss, A Smile, A by Walter Hirsch & May Hill, 1918..............**5.00**

Tear Of Gratitude, The by Nolcini, 1840 (Pre 1900)....................**20.00**

Teardrops & Kisses by Nick Kenny & Little Jack Little, 1931 (Cover Artist, Frederick S. Manning)....................**10.00**

Tears by Frank Capano & Billy Uhr, 1930, Photo Gene & Glenn (Cover Artist, Barbelle) **5.00**

Tears From My Inkwell by Mort Dixon & Harry Warren, 1939, Photo Sammy Kaye (Cover Artist, Im-Ho)....................**5.00**

Tears Of Love by S. R. Henry & Frank H. Warren, 1918 Dedicated To Norma Talmadge (Cover Artist, Alfred Cheney Johnston & Dedication)....................**12.00**

Tears On My Pillow by Gene Autry & Fred Rose, 1941, Photo Dick Jergens **3.00**

Tears Tell, The Story To Me by C. & F. Wilson, 1919 (Cover Artist, Rolf Armstrong & Lithograph by Knapp) **20.00**

Teasin by Bob Carleton, J. Bandon Walsh & Paul Biese, 1922 ....**5.00**

Teasing by Cecil Mack & Albert Von Tilzer, 1904 (Cover Artist, Pfeiffer)....................**10.00**

Teddy Bears' Picnic, The by Jimmy Kennedy & John W. Bratton, 1947 (Cover Artist, J. Cesareo) **5.00**

Tee Oodle Um Bum Bo by George Gershwin, 1919 ....**8.00**

Teenager's Mother by Curtis R. Lewis & J. L. McFarland, 1958, Photo Bill Haley....................**5.00**

Telegram Song, Stop, The by Charlie Tobias & John Jacob Loeb, 1936, Photo Abe Lyman (Cover Artist, HBK)....................**5.00**

Tell Her At Twilight by Bernie Grossman & Will Donaldson, 1921 .....**5.00**

Tell Her In The Springtime by Irving Berlin, 1924, Music Box Review Of 1925 (Irving Berlin)....................**12.00**

Tell Her In The Springtime by Irving Berlin, 1925 (Irving Berlin)......**10.00**

Tell It All Over Again by Henry Blossom & Victor Herbert, 1914, Musical: The Only Girl (Victor Herbert)....................**15.00**

Tell It To The World by Anita Owens, 1919........................**5.00**

Tell Me A Beautiful Story by Charles K. Harris, 1912 (Cover Artist, Pfeiffer) **10.00**

Tell Me A Bedtime Story by Irving Berlin, 1923, Musical: Music Box Revue, 1923-24 (Irving Berlin) **12.00**

Tell Me A Story by Larry Stock & Maurice Sigler, 1948, Photo Sammy Kaye....................**2.00**

Tell Me A Story by Larry Stock & Maurice Sigler, 1948, Photo Vic Damone....................**2.00**

Tell Me by J. Will Callahan & Max Kortlander, 1919 ....**5.00**

Tell Me by Little Jack Little, Al Bryan & Geo. W. Meyers, 1935 (Cover Artist, Harris)....................**3.00**

Tell Me Daisy by Dorothy Donnelly & Sigmund Romberg, 1921, Musical: Blossom Time....................**5.00**

Tell Me If Love Is A Dream by Beth Slater Whitson & Helen Louise Shaffer, 1911 ....**5.00**

Tell Me Little Gypsy by Irving Berlin, 1920, Musical: Ziegfeld Follies, 1920 (Cover Artist, R.S., Deco & Irving Berlin) **15.00**

Tell Me Some Day I Can Please You by F.B. Edgar, 1910....................**6.00**

Tell Me, Sweet Rose by Jos. McKeon & Henry Frantzen, 1911............**5.00**

Tell Me That You Love Me by Al Silverman & C.A. Bixio, 1935, Introduced by Frank Parker On The Jello Program, Photo Frank Parker............**10.00**

Tell Me That You Love Me by Leo Friedman & Beth Slater Whitson, 1912 ....**5.00**

Tell Me That You Love Me Dear, For I Love You by Arthur Tallman, 1908 (Cover Artist, Ray) **10.00**

Tell Me The Old Old Story by Richard L. Weaver, 1908 (Cover Artist, Starmer) **10.00**

Tell Me Why by Al Alberts & Marty Gold, 1951, Photo The Four Aces ..**5.00**

Tell Me Why by Richard Coburn & Vincent Rose, 1919....................**5.00**

Tell Me Why You Smile, Mona Lisa? From Super Production "Der Raub der Mona Lisa"–The Theft Of The Mona Lisa by Walter Reisch, Raymond B. Egan & Robert Stolz, 1931 ....**5.00**

Tell Me With Your Eyes by Arthur J. Lamb & Albert Von Tilzer, 1904 (Cover Artist, Hirt) **5.00**

Tell That To The Marines by Harold Atteridge, Jean Schwartz & Al Jolson, 1918, Movie: Sinbad, Photo Al Jolson (Cover Artist, Barbelle, WWI & Al Jolson)....................**26.00**

Tell The Last Rose Of Summer, Good-Bye by Bartley Costello & Al Piantadosi, 1917 (Cover Artist, Starmer & WWI) **10.00**

Tempest, The by Emil Katzenstein, 1897 (Pre 1900 & March) **15.00**

Temptation by Arthur Freed & Nacio Herb Brown, 1933, Movie: Going Hollywood, Photo Bing Crosby & Marion Davies....................**10.00**

Temptation by Louis Weslyn & Henry Lodge, 1909, Photo Bonita (Rag) **10.00**

Temptation Rag by Henry Lodge, 1909 (Cover Artist, Edgar Keller & Rag) **10.00**

Ten Baby Fingers by Harry Edelheit, Alma Sanders & Monte Carlo, 1920, (Lithograph Knapp Co.) **15.00**

Ten Cents A Dance by Richard Rodgers & Lorenz Hart, 1955, Movie: Love Me Or Leave Me, Signed Photo Doris Day (Signed)...........**10.00**

Ten Little Fingers & Ten Little Toes by Harry Pease, Johnny White, Ira Shuster & Ed. G. Nelson, 1921 (Cover Artist, H.H. Warner & Transportation)....................12.00

Ten Little Miles From Town by Gus Kahn & Elmer Schoebel, 1928 (Cover Artist, R.S.)....................**5.00**

Ten Little Soldiers, On A Ten Day Leave by Sue & Kay Werner & Abner Silver, 1942, Photo Landt Trio And Curley (WWII) **6.00**

Ten Pins In The Sky by Joseph McCarthy & Milton Ager, 1938, Movie: Listen Darling....................**5.00**

Ten Pretty Girls by Will Grosz & Jimmy Kennedy, 1937, Photo Phil Regan (Cover Artist, Merman)....................**5.00**

Ten Thousand Years From Now by J. Keirn Brennan & Ernest R. Ball, 1923 ....**5.00**

Tender And True by Gaston Lyle, 1867 (Pre 1900) **15.00**

Tender Is The Night by Harold Adamson & Walter Donaldson, 1935, Movie: Here Comes The Band, Photo Virginia Bruce & Harry Stockwell **6.00**

Tender Trap, The by Sammy Cahn & James Van Heusen, 1955, Movie: The Tender Trap, Photo Frank Sinatra, Debbie Reynolds, David Wayne & Celeste Holm......................**8.00**

Tenderly by Jack Lawrence & Walter Gross, 1946..............................**2.00**

Tendre Amour, Tender Love by Bernisne G. Clements, 1915 ....**5.00**

Tenement Symphony by Sid Kuller, Ray Golden & Hal Borne, 1941...**2.00**

Tennessee Blues (Cover Artist, Pfeiffer) **10.00**

Tennessee I Hear You Calling Me by Harold Robe & Jeff Godfrey, 1914, Photo Al Jolson (Al Jolson)..**15.00**

Tennessee Saturday Night by Billy Hughes, 1947, Photo Red Foley **3.00**

Tennessee Waltz by Redd Stewart & Pee Wee King, 1948, Photo Patti Page **5.00**

Tennessee Waltz by Redd Stewart & Pee Wee King, 1948, Photo Wayne King **5.00**

Tennessee Wig-Walk, The by Norman Gimbel & Larry Coleman, 1953 ..**5.00**

Tequila by Chuck Rio, 1958, Photo The Champs **4.00**

Teresa by Jack Hoffman & Babe Russin, 1947 ....**3.00**

Terribly Attractive by Dorothy Fields & Arthur Schwartz, 1939, Movie: Stars In Your Eyes **5.00**

Terry With Her Bonnie Blue E'e by John E. & Reiss, 1845 (Pre 1900) ..**40.00**

Tess Of The Storm Country by Chas. Patrick & Bob Allan, 1915, Movie: The Darling Of Them All, Photo Mary Pickford **16.00**

Tessie, Stop Teasin Me by Anthony J. Franchini, Brooke Johns & Ray Perkins, 1924 ....**5.00**

Texarkana Baby by Cottonseed Clark & Fred Rose, 1948, Signed Photo Eddy Arnold (Signed)..**6.00**

Thais by Louis Gallet & J. Massenet, 1922 ....**5.00**

Thank God For America by Madalyn Phillips, 1918 (WWI) **10.00**

Thank You America by Walter Jurmann, 1918 (WWI) **10.00**

Thank You For A Lovely Evening by Dorothy Fields & Jimmy McHugh, 1934 ....**5.00**

Thank You Mr. Moon by Dave Oppenheim, Theodore Morse & Abel Baer, 1931..**5.00**

Thank Your Father by B.G. DeSylva, Lew Brown & Ray Henderson...**5.00**

Thank Your Lucky Stars And Stripes by Johnny Burke & Jimmy Van Heusen, 1941, Movie: Playmates, Photo Kay Kyser, John Barrymore, Lupe Velez & Ginny Simms (Patriotic) **10.00**

Thank Your Lucky Stars by Frank Loesser & Arthur Schwartz, 1943, Movie: Thank Your Lucky Stars, Photo Eddie Cantor, Humphrey Bogart, Bette Davis & Many More Stars (Eddie Cantor)..............**12.00**

Thanks A Million by Arthur Johnston & Gus Kahn, 1948, Movie: Thanks A Million, Photo Dick Powell **5.00**

Thanks Be To God by P.J. O'Reilly & Stanley Dickson........................**5.00**

Thanks by Arthur Johnston & Sam Coslow, 1933, Movie: Too Much Harmony, Photo Bing Crosby & Judith Allen........................**12.00**

Thanks For The Buggy Ride by Jules Bufford, 1925 ....**10.00**

Thanks For The Lobster by Clarence Jones, 1914............................**10.00**

Thanks For The Lobster by Jack Caddigan & Chick Story, 1913........**10.00**

Thanks For The Memory by Leo Robin & Ralph Rainger, 1937, Movie: The Big Broadcast Of 1938, Photo Shirley Ross, Carricature, W.C. Fields, Bob Hope & Martha Raye **15.00**

Thanks For Your Letter My Darling by Jay Burnett & Gladys Lane, Photo Dinah Shore, 1942 ....**5.00**

Thanks To You by Livingston & Evans, 1952, Movie: Somebody Loves Me, Photo Betty Hutton & Ralph Meeker........................**5.00**

Thanksgivin' by Hoagy Carmichael & Johnny Mercer, 1932..............**5.00**

That Aeroplane Glide by Israel, 1912 (Transportation)......................**15.00**

That Auto Rag by Smith, 1914 (Transportation & Rag) **15.00**

That Bandana Band, Way Down In Dixieland by Irby & Warner, 1914 (Cover Artist, Pfeiffer, March & Black, Black Face)..................**25.00**

That Barber In Seville by B.G. DeSylva & Lou Silvers, 1921, Musical: Bombo, Photo Al Jolson (Al Jolson)..**10.00**

That Beloved Cheater Of Mine by L. Wolfe Gilbert & Edna Williams, 1920, Photo Lew Cody (Cover Artist, Ranck) **5.00**

That Big Rock Candy Mountain by Mack, 1928 (Cover Artist, Pfeiffer) .**10.00**

That Brass Band Rag by R. G. Grady, 1912 (Rag)............................**10.00**

That Certain Age by Harold Adamson & Jimmy McHugh, 1938, Movie: That Certain Age, Photo Deanna Durbin........................**10.00**

That Certain Feeling by Ira & George Gershwin, 1925, Musical: Tip Toes **10.00**

That Certain Party by Gus Kahn & Walter Donaldson, 1925, Photo Benny Strong (Cover Artist, Barbelle & Deco)........................**5.00**

That Certain Party by Gus Kahn & Walter Donaldson, 1925, Photo Charles Derickson (Deco) **5.00**

That Chinatown Rag by Jack Drislane & George W. Meyer, 1910 (Rag)..**10.00**

That Coon Town Quartet by Schwartz & Clarke, 1912 (Cover Artist, Pfeiffer & Black, Black Face) **30.00**

That Daffy Rag by Dawson, 1911 (Cover Artist, Pfeiffer & Rag).......**10.00**

That Daffydill Rag by Frank & Bill Mueller, 1912 (Rag)....................**5.00**

That Dear Old Bell by J.P. Skelly, 1879 (Pre 1900)........................**35.00**

That Devilish Rag by Jean Felt & Fred Stilwell, 1917 (Rag)............**10.00**

That Dixie Glide by Bob Young & Walter Donovan, 1912 (Dixie)........**5.00**

That Dreamy Italian Waltz by Jos. McCarthy & Al Piantadosi, 1910, Photo Lyons & Yosco (Cover Artist, Pfeiffer)........................**10.00**

That Dreamy Italian Waltz by Jos. McCarthy & Al Piantadosi, 1915, Photo, The Strolling Players (Cover Artist, Pfeiffer) **10.00**

That Du-Dah-Day by Lewis F. Muir, 1915 ....**12.00**

That Ev'ry Little Movement Rag by Ed Smalle, 1917 (Cover Artist, E.S. Fisher & Rag)..**10.00**

That Family Called The U.S.A. by Billy Downs, 1919 (WWI) **15.00**

That Farm Out In Kansas by Otto Harbach & Louis A. Hirsch, 1920, Musical: George M. Cohan Musical Comedy, "Mary" (George M. Cohan) **15.00**

That Feeling Is Gone by Walter Hirsch & Emmett Wallace, 1938, Photo Benny Goodman **3.00**

That Fellow With The Cello Bag by Smalley, 1911 (Cover Artist, Pfeiffer) **15.00**

That Foolish Feeling by Harold Adamson & Jimmy McHugh, 1936, Movie: Top Of The Town **5.00**

That Fussy Rag by Victor H. Smalley, 1910, Photo Victor H. Smalley (Cover Artist, Pfeiffer & Rag)..**15.00**

That Gosh Darned Two-Step Rag by Kendrie & Miller, 1913 (Rag)...**15.00**

That Great Come-And-Get-It Day by E. Y. Harburg & Burton Lane, 1946, Musical: Finian's Rainbow (Cover Artist, BJH & Irish)..................**5.00**

That Haunting Melody by George M. Cohan, 1911 (George M. Cohan)..**15.00**

That Hypnotizing Man by Lew Brown & Albert Von Tilzer, 1911, Photo Belle Baker (Cover Artist, Hirt & Rag)........................**10.00**

That Indian Rag by Bestor, 1910 (Indian & Rag)............................**22.00**

That International Rag by Irving Berlin, 1913, Photo Bobbie Russell (Cover Artist, Pfeiffer & Irving Berlin & Rag)........................**20.00**

That Is How I Love You Dear by Freeman & Allemong, 1918 (Cover Artist, Pfeiffer)..**12.00**

That Is Love by Felix McGlennon, 1891 (Pre 1900)........................**10.00**

That Italian Rag by E. Leslie & Al Piantadosi, 1910 (Rag) **10.00**

That Italian Serenade by Joe McCarthy, Al Piantadosi & Jack Glogau 1911, Photo Bessie Wynn (Cover Artist, M.R.)........................**5.00**

That Land Of Musical Charms by Morrow, 1936 (Cover Artist, Pfeiffer)..**10.00**

That Little Bit Of Green by Cassidy & Lilly, 1910 (Cover Artist, Pfeiffer & Irish) **15.00**

That Little Dream Got Nowhere by Joe Burke & Jimmy Van Heusen, 1940 ....**5.00**

That Little World Is Mine by J. Keirn Brennan & Jessie L. Deppen, 1925..**5.00**

That Long, Long Trail Is Getting Shorter Now by J. F. Mahoney, 1919 (Cover Artist, E.E. Walton & WWI)......................**15.00**

That Long Lost Chord by McCarthy & Piantadosi, 1911 (Cover Artist, Pfeiffer)......................**10.00**

That Lovely Night In Budapest by Sam M. Lewis & Peter DeRose, 1936......................**5.00**

That Loving Melody Rubinstein Wrote by Seymour Brown & Nat D. Ayer, 1910 ....**5.00**

That Lucky Old Sun by Haven Gillespie & Beasley Smith, 1949, Photo Frankie Laine......................**3.00**

That Lucky Old Sun by Haven Gillespie & Beasley Smith, 1949, Photo Vaughn Monroe......................**3.00**

That Lucky Old Sun by Haven Gillespie & Beasley Smith, 1949, Photo Eddie Ballentine **3.00**

That Man Could Sell Me The Brooklyn Bridge by Webster & Fain, 1958, Movie: Mardi Gras, Photo Pat Boone, Christine Carere, Gary Crosby & Sheree North......................**3.00**

That Mellow Melody by Sam Lewis & Geo. Meyer, 1912, Photo Paul & Marion Stone **5.00**

That Mellow Melody by Sam M. Lewis & George W. Meyer, 1912, Photo Arthur Deagon (Cover Artist, Rose)......................**7.00**

That Mesmerizing Mendelssohn Tune by Irving Berlin, 1909, Photo Wiesser & Dean (Cover Artist, John Frew, Rag & Irving Berlin) .**10.00**

That Mesmerizing Mendelssohn Tune by Irving Berlin, 1909, Photo Harry L. Webb (Cover Artist, John Frew, Rag & Irving Berlin)......................**10.00**

That Mesmerizing Mendelssohn Tune by Irving Berlin, 1909, Photo Caieta Day (Cover Artist, John Frew, Rag & Irving Berlin) **10.00**

That Moaning Saxophone Rag by Tom Brown, Harry Cook & Roger Lewis, 1913, Photo Six Brown Brothers (Rag)......................**20.00**

That Moment Of Moments by Ira Gershwin & Vernon Duke, Musical: Ziegfeld Follies Of 1936......................**12.00**

That Moving Picture Girl by Burt Wallace & Charles J.W. Jerreld, 1913..**10.00**

That Mysterious Rag by Irving Berlin & Ted Snyder, 1911, Photo Bernier & Stella (Cover Artist, Pfeiffer, Rag & Irving Berlin)......................**15.00**

That Mysterious Rag by Irving Berlin & Ted Snyder, 1911, Photo Lew Hearn (Cover Artist, Pfeiffer, Rag & Irving Berlin) **15.00**

That Mysterious Rag by Irving Berlin & Ted Snyder, 1911, Photo Norton & Maple (Cover Artist, Pfeiffer, Rag & Irving Berlin)......................**15.00**

That Mysterious Rag by Irving Berlin & Ted Snyder, 1911, Photo Weston, Field & Carroll (Cover Artist, Pfeiffer, Rag & Irving Berlin) **15.00**

That Naughty Melody by Sam M. Lewis & Geo. W. Meyer, 1913, Photo Pearson & Goldie (Deco) **6.00**

That Naughty Waltz by Edwin Stanley & Sol. P. Levy, 1920 (Cover Artist, Van Doorn Morgan & Deco)......................**5.00**

That Night In Araby by Billy Rose & Ted Snyder, 1926, Movie: The Son Of The Sheik, Photo Rudolph Valentino (Cover Artist, Barbelle)..**20.00**

That Old Black Magic by Johnny Mercer & Harold Arlen, 1942, Movie: Star Spangled Rhythm, Photo Bing Crosby, Bob Hope, Dorothy Lamour & Many More Stars......................**12.00**

That Old Dream Peddler by Al Stewart & Pepe Delgado, 1947 ....**5.00**

That Old Familiar Tune by Cunningham & Seymour, 1911 ....**5.00**

That Old Fashioned Mother Of Mine by Caddigan & Story, 1915 (Cover Artist, Starmer) **10.00**

That Old Feeling by Brown & Fain, 1937, Movie: With A Song In My Heart, Photo Susan Hayward & Rory Calhoun **6.00**

That Old Gang Of Mine by Billy Rose, Mort Dixon & Ray Henderson, 1923 ....**3.00**

That Old Gang Of Mine by Billy Rose, Mort Dixon & Ray Henderson, 1923, Photo G. Underhill Macy & J. William Scott (Cover Artist, Perret)......................**10.00**

That Old Gang Of Mine by Billy Rose, Mort Dixon & Ray Henderson, 1923, Photo Ruth Roland (Cover Artist, Perret) **10.00**

That Old Gang Of Mine by Billy Rose, Mort Dixon & Ray Henderson, 1923, Photo Signed by Ray Henderson (Signed) **10.00**

That Old Girl Of Mine by Earle C. Jones & Albert Von Tilzer, 1912, Photo Mary Shakespear (Cover Artist, Starmer)......................**10.00**

That Old Irish Mother Of Mine by William Jerome, Harry Von Tilzer & Andrew Mack, 1920 (Irish) **6.00**

That Old Sweetheart Of Mine by Cooper & Skelly, 1891 (Pre 1900)..**10.00**

That Paradise Rag by Meyer, 1911 (Cover Artist, Pfeiffer & Rag) **15.00**

That Peculiar Rag by F.M. Fagan, 1910 (Rag)......................**10.00**

That Pleasing Rag by J. Fred O'Connor, 1911 (Rag)......................**10.00**

That Puzzlin' Rag by Bowman & Smith, 1912 (Cover Artist, Pfeiffer & Rag) **15.00**

That Rag-Time Regimental Band by A. Seymour Brown & Melville Morris, 1912 (Cover Artist, Starmer, Rag & March)......................**15.00**

That Raggy Foxtrot by Laurance E. Goffen, 1915 (Rag) **10.00**

That Railroad Rag by Nat Vincent & Ed Bimberg, 1911 (Transportation & Rag) **20.00**

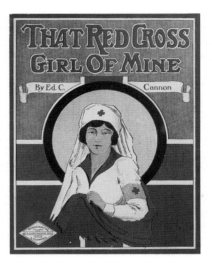

That Red Cross Girl Of Mine, 1917, Photo Red Cross Nurse (WWI & Red Cross) 25.00

That Reuben Tango Huskin' Bee by Young, Williams & Grant, 1914 (Cover Artist, Pfeiffer) **10.00**

That Rose-Your Love by Franke Harling & Alfred H. Hyatt, 1910......................**5.00**

That Russian Winter by Irving Berlin, 1942, Movie: This Is The Army, Lt. Ronald Reagan In Cast (WWII, Military Personnel, President & Irving Berlin)......................**15.00**

That Shenandoah Sally Of Mine by Lacy L. Leonard, 1938......................**3.00**

That Silver Haired Daddy Of Mine, 1932, Movie: Tumbling Tumbleweeds **6.00**

That Sly Old Gentleman by Johnny Burke & James V. Monaco, 1939, Movie: East Side Of Heaven, Photo Bing Crosby, Joan Blondell & Sandy **10.00**

That Soothing Serenade by Harry DeCosta, 1918, Photo Adele Rowland (Cover Artist, Starmer)......................**10.00**

That Southern Hospitality, When You're Down In Dixie by Chas. McCarron & Raymond Walker, 1915 (Cover Artist, DeTakacs, Dixie & Black, Black Face)......................**15.00**

That St. Louis Jitney Bus "That Busted Bus" by Mellinger, 1915 (Transportation) **15.00**

That Swaying Harmony by Chas. K. Harris, 1911, Photo Stella Tracey (Cover Artist, Pfeiffer) **12.00**

That Sweet Somebody O'Mine by Ben Ryan & Ted Snyder, 1923 ....**5.00**

That Tangalo Tap by Clarke & Schwartz, 1911 (Cover Artist, Pfeiffer)...**10.00**

That Tango Tokio by Al Bryan & Jack Wells, 1913 (Cover Artist, Starmer) **10.00**

That Teasing Rag by Joe Jordan, 1909 (Rag)................................**10.00**

That Tumble Down Shack In Athlone by Richard W. Pascoe, Monte Carlo & Alma M. Sanders, 1918, Introduced by Chauncey Olcott In George M. Cohan's New Comedy, The Voice Of McConnell (Cover Artist, Barbelle, Irish & George M. Cohan) **15.00**

That Twilight Melody by Yellen & Cobb, 1926 ....**5.00**

That Waltz Of Yesterday by Henri Garden, Billy Curtis & J. Russell Robinson, 1927, Photo Henri Garden (Cover Artist, Starmer) **5.00**

That Was Before I Met You by Bryan & Meyer, 1911 (Cover Artist, Pfeiffer) **10.00**

That Wee Bit Of Devil In Your Irish Eyes by Norton & Springer, 1917 (Cover Artist, Pfeiffer, WWI & Irish) **25.00**

That Wonderful Dengosa Strain by Jerome & Greenberg, 1914............**5.00**

That Wonderful Kid From Madrid by Ballard MacDonald & Nat Osborne, 1919, Photo Cissie Ramsden (Cover Artist, Natwick & Deco)......**10.00**

That Wonderful Mother Of Mine by Clyde Hager & Walter Goodwin, 1918, Photo Hager & Goodwin **10.00**

That Wonderful Night by Harold Freeman, 1916, (Cover Artist, Pfeiffer & Lithograph, Van Art Co.) **15.00**

That's A Funny Place To Kiss A Girl by Richards, 1912 (Cover Artist, Pfeiffer)...**10.00**

That's A Good Girl by Irving Berlin, 1926 (Cover Artist, Leff, Deco & Irving Berlin) **12.00**

That's A Mother's Liberty Loan by Mayo & Tally & Clarence Gaskill, 1917, Photo Edward Earle & Mary Maurice (WWI) **15.00**

That's-A-Plenty by Lew Pollack, 1914 (Cover Artist, DeTakacs & Rag)...**15.00**

That's A-Why by Bob Merrill, 1952, Photo Mindy Carson & Guy Mitchell...**3.00**

That's All Brother by Mack David & Jerry Livingston, 1939, Photo Kay Kyser..**5.00**

That's All by Alan Brandt & Bob Haymes, 1952, Photo Nat King Cole..**4.00**

That's All I Want From You by M. Rotha, 1954 ....**3.00**

That's Amore by Harry Warren & Jack Brooks, 1953, Movie: That's Amore, Signed Photo Dean Martin (Signed)..................**10.00**

That's As Far As You Can Go by Edward Madden & Lou A. Hirsch, 1908, Musical: Mr. Hamlet Of Broadway (Cover Artist, Frew)..12.00

That's Entertainment by Dietz & Schwartz, 1932, Movie: The Band Wagon, Photo Fred Astaire & Cyd Charisse................................**12.00**

That's Ever Loving Love by Brice & King, 1910, Photo Brice & King (Cover Artist, Pfeiffer & Deco)..**15.00**

That's For Me by Richard Rodgers & Oscar Hammerstein II, 1945, Movie: State Fair, Photo Jeanne Crain, Dana Andrews, Dick Haymes & Vivian Blaine..**10.00**

That's Gratitude by Norton & Camp, 1907 ....**10.00**

That's Harmony by Clarke & Williams, 1911....................................**10.00**

That's Him by Ogden Nash & Kurt Weill, 1943, Movie: One Touch Of Venus...**3.00**

That's Hot-Cha-Cha With Me by Eduardo & Bianco, Photo Xavier Cugat & Merv Griffin **6.00**

That's How I Believe In You by Al Dubin, Paul Cunningham & Bert Rule, 1921 (Deco)..**5.00**

That's How I Feel About You by Benny Davis & Archie Gottler, 1928..**5.00**

That's How I Love You by Irving Berlin, 1912 (Cover Artist, Gene Buck & Irving Berlin)..**10.00**

That's How I Love You by Irving Kahal, Francis Wheeler & Ted Snyder, 1927 ....**5.00**

That's How I Love You Mame by Bryan & Mullen, 1903 ....**10.00**

That's How I Need You by Joe Goodwin, Joe McCarthy & Al Piantadosi, 1950, Movie: Two Weeks With Love, Photo Debbie Reynolds **5.00**

That's How I Need You by Joe Goodwin, Joe McCarthy & Al Piantadosi, 1912, Photo Emma Carus (Cover Artist, Keller)............................**15.00**

That's How Much I Love You by Eddie Arnold, Wally Fowler & J. Graydon Hall, 1946, Photo Eddy Arnold **3.00**

That's Just My Way Of Forgetting by B.G. DeSylva, Lew Brown & Ray Henderson, 1928 (Cover Artist, Pud Lane) **5.00**

That's Life I Guess by Sam M. Lewis & Peter DeRose, 1936.............**5.00**

That's Living by Roy Turk & Fred E. Ahlert, 1931 ....**5.00**

That's Music To Me by Maceo Pinkard, 1939 (Cover Artist, Pfeiffer)..**10.00**

That's My Desire by Carroll Loveday & Helmy Kresa, 1931, Photo Frankie Lane...**4.00**

That's My Desire by Carroll Loveday & Helmy Kresa, 1931, Photo Jack Owens..**4.00**

That's My Desire by Carroll Loveday & Helmy Kresa, 1931, Photo Woody Herman...**4.00**

That's My Girl by Harry D. Kerr & Joe McKiernan, 1924 ....**5.00**

That's My Girl by Roger Harding, 1900, Musical Supplement Boston Herald **10.00**

That's My Mammy by Pease, Baer & Nelson, 1928, Photo Harry Richman (Black, Black Face) **15.00**

That's Not The Knot by Jay Livingston & Ray Evans, 1950, Photo Bob Hope..**10.00**

That's "Some" Honeymoon by Will Hardy, 1911 (Transportation).....**12.00**

That's Some Love by George M. Cohan, 1908 (George M. Cohan)....**10.00**

That's The Chance You Take by Sylvia Dee & Sid Lippman, 1952, Photo Eddie Fisher...**3.00**

That's The Fellow I Want To Get by Bryan & Meyer, 1910 (Cover Artist, Pfeiffer)...**10.00**

That's The Kind Of A Baby For Me by Alfred Harriman & J.C. Egan, 1917, Ziegfeld Follies, 1917, Photo Eddie Cantor (Eddie Cantor & Deco) **16.00**

That's The Last Tear by Joan Whitney & Alex Kramer, 1949.............**3.00**

That's The Reason I Want You by Alfred Bryan & Alfred Solman, 1913, Photo Lillian Lorraine (Cover Artist, Bouthiller)...........................**10.00**

That's The Song Of Songs For Me by Joe Goodwin & Will Osborne, 1915 (Cover Artist, DeTakacs)..**10.00**

That's What Every Young Girl Should Know by Mack David & Don Rodney, 1946, Signed Photo Sammy Kaye **6.00**

That's What God Made Mothers For by Leo Wood, 1918 (Cover Artist, Pfeiffer & WWI)...**15.00**

That's What I Call Heaven by Alfred Solman, Geo. Brown & Dale Wimbrow, 1929 ....**5.00**

That's What I Like About You by Walter Donaldson, 1931 ....**5.00**

That's What I'd Do For You! by Ida Vandersloot & F.W. Vandersloot, 1914 (Cover Artist, Dulins & Deco) 6.00

That's What Makes A Wild Cat Wild by Norton, 1908 (Cover Artist, Pfeiffer, Jazz & Black, Black Face) 25.00

That's What Puts The "Sweet" In Home Sweet Home by Charles Newman, Mack Gordon & Ned Lowry, 1928......5.00

That's What The Daisy Said by Gumm & VonTilzer, 1903 ......5.00

That's What The Mill Wheel Said by Denison & Holmes, 1913 ......6.00

That's What The Red White And Blue Means by Robert Levenson & E.E. Bagley, 1918 (WWI & Patriotic)......10.00

That's What The Rose Said To Me by B. F. Barnett & Leo Edwards, 1906, Photo Bessie Wynn......10.00

That's What The Well Dressed Man In Harlem Will Wear by Irving Berlin, 1942, Movie: This Is The Army, Lieut. Ronald Reagan In Cast (WWII, Irving Berlin, President & Military Personnel)......22.00

That's What You Mean To Me by Benny Davis & J. Fred Coots, 1936, Musical: Cotton Club Parade......12.00

That's What You Mean To Me by Maurice E. Marks & Edw. LeRose, 1912 (Cover Artist, Starmer) 10.00

That's What You Think by Pinky Tomlin, Raymond Jasper & Coy Poe, 1935, Movie: King Solomon Of Broadway......12.00

That's Where I Came In by Charles Tobias & Peter DeRose, 1946, Photo Perry Como......3.00

That's Where I Came In by Charles Tobias & Peter DeRose, 1946, Photo Margaret Whiting 3.00

That's Why Darkies Were Born by Lew Brown & Ray Henderson, 1931, Musical: George White's Scandals (Black, Black Face)......15.00

That's Why I Came Back To You by Harry D. Kerr & Maurice Barron, 1915 ......5.00

That's Why I Can't Forget by Arthur J. Lamb & Alfred Solman, 1919.5.00

That's Why I Love You by Walter Donaldson & Paul Ash, 1926, Photo Paul Ash (Cover Artist, JVR)......5.00

That's Why I Never Go Home by Kalmar, 1913 (Cover Artist, Pfeiffer)......10.00

That's Why The Violets Live by J. F. Mahoney & Theodore Morse, 1911 ......5.00

That's Worth While Waiting For by Sam M. Lewis, Joe Young & Harry Ruby, 1919 ......5.00

That's You Baby by Con Conrad, Sidney D. Mitchell & Archie Gottler, 1929, Movie: Fox Movietone Follies, 1929 ......10.00

Their Lullaby by Jane Hathaway, 1913 ......5.00

Thelma by Neil Moret, 1914......5.00

Them Dog Gon'd Triflin' Blues by Skidmore, 1917 (Cover Artist, Pfeiffer & Blues)......15.00

Them Hillbillies Are Mountain Williams Now by James Cavanaugh, Sammy Mysells & Dick Sanford, 1935......10.00

Theme From Bullit by Schifrin, 1969, Movie: Bullit, Photo Steve McQueen & Jacqueline Bisset......4.00

Theme From The Monkees by Tommy Boyce & Bobby Hart, 1966, Photo The Monkees 5.00

Then Came The Dawn by Al Dubin & Harry Warren, 1929, Photo Gene Austin (Cover Artist, Barbelle) 5.00

Then I Will Marry You by Violet B. Robinson & Winthrop Brookhouse, 1906 ......5.00

Then I Wouldn't Have To Worry Anymore by Alfred Ryan & Jack Wells, 1913 ......5.00

Then I'd Be Satisfied With You by George M. Cohan (George M. Cohan)......15.00

Then I'll Be Happy by Sidney Clare, Lew Brown & Cliff Friend, 1925, Photo Eddie Fisher......3.00

Then I'll Be Reminded Of You by Ed Heyman & Ken Smith, 1939, Movie: The Vagabond Lover, Photo Rudy Vallee......15.00

Then I'll Be Satisfied With Life by George M. Cohan, 1902 (George M. Cohan)......10.00

Then I'll Be Tired Of You by E.Y. Harburg & Arthur Schwartz, 1934, Photo Henry Busse 6.00

Then I'll Come Back To You by John W. Bratton, 1917 (WWI) 12.00

Then I'll Know Why by Paul Titsworth & Lynn Cowan, 1929, Movie: Alibi, Photo Irma Harrison 10.00

Then I'm Not Missing You by Hal Artis, Daisy Sullivan & Will E. Dulmage, 1919......10.00

Then She Gave Me Just You by Jack Appleton & Oreste Vessella, 1912 ......5.00

Then You'll Remember Me by M.W. Balfe, 1925 ......6.00

Then You'll Remember Me, Opera Gem, 1915 (Cover Artist, Pfeiffer)..12.00

Then-Now-Forever by John W. Bratton & Leo Edwards, 1918 (WWI)..10.00

There Ain't No Flies On Auntie by W. Van der Decken, 1925 (Cover Artist, Fred Low) 12.00

There Are Just As Many Heroes Today by Allen, 1914, Photo Washington & Lincoln (Cover Artist, Pfeiffer, Presidents & Patriotic)......25.00

There Are Somethings You Never Forget by Clara Kummer & Maurice Yvain, 1923, Musical: One Kiss......5.00

There Are Such Things by Stanley Adams, Abel Baer & George W. Meyer, 1942 (Cover Artist, Barbelle)......3.00

There Are Such Things by Stanley Adams, Abel Baer & George W. Meyer, 1942 (Cover Artist, CA)......3.00

There Are Two Eyes In Dixie by Irving Berlin, 1917 (Irving Berlin & Dixie)......16.00

There But For You Go I by Alan Jay Lerner & Frederick Loewe, 1947, Movie: Brigadoon)......5.00

There Goes My Attraction by Al Neiburg, Jerry Levinson & Boyd Bunch, 1936, Photo Loretta Lee (Cover Artist, Leff)......5.00

There Goes My Dream by David Heneker, 1940 ......5.00

There Goes My Heart by Benny Davis & Abner Silver, 1934 ......6.00

There Goes That Song Again by Sammy Cahn & Jule Styne, 1944, Movie: Carolina Blues, Photo Kay Kyser, Ann Miller & Victor Moore 5.00

There I Go by Hy Zaret & Irving Weiser, 1940 (Cover Artist, Im-Ho) .3.00

There! I've Said It Again by Redd Evans & Dave Mann, 1941 ......2.00

There Is A Land Of Pure Delight by Haratio W. Parker, 1890 (Pre 1900)...10.00

There Is A Sunbeam by Howard Johnson & Carlo Sanderson, 1921, Musical: Tangerine 10.00

There Is A Tavern In The Town by Harry Henneman, 1942......5.00

There Is A Tavern In The Town by William H. Hills, 1934, Movie: Sweet Music, Photo Rudy Vallee......12.00

There Is Ever A Song Somewhere by James Whitcomb Riley & Ward-Stephens, 1915, Dedicated To Litta Grimm (Dedication)......6.00

There Is No Greater Love by Marty Symes & Isham Jones, 1936 (Cover Artist, Barbelle) 5.00

There Is Nothing Like A Dame by Richard Rodgers & Oscar Hammerstein II, 1949, Musical: South Pacific (Cover Artist, BJH)......8.00

There Is Nothing Like A Dame by Richard Rodgers & Oscar Hammerstein II, 1949, Movie: South Pacific, Photo Rosano Brazzi & Mitzi Gaynor......8.00

There Is Silver Now, Where Once Was Gold by E.S.S. Huntington, 1913......5.00

There Must Be A Bright Tomorrow by Wysocki, 1931 ......3.00

There Must Be A Silver Lining by Dolly Morse & Walter Donaldson, 1928, Photo Charlie Nelson......10.00

There Must Be A Way by Sammy Gallop, David Saxon & Robert Cook, 1945, Photo Charlie Spivak 3.00

There Must Be Some One For Me by Cole Porter, 1943, Movie: Can Can 6.00

There Must Be Somebody Waiting For Me by Walter Donaldson, 1929 ......5.00

There Never Was A Girl Like You by Harry Williams & Egbert Van Alstyne, 1907, Photo Victoria Murray (Cover Artist, Starmer) **10.00**

There Once Was A Man by Richard Adler & Jerry Ross, 1954, Musical: The Pajama Game................**6.00**

There She Goes by Jack Mahoney & Ring-Hagger, 1920................**10.00**

There She Was by Hoagy Carmichael, 1943, Movie: True To Life.......**6.00**

There Will Never Be Another You by Mack Gordon & Harry Warren, 1942, Photo Andrews Sisters.................**3.00**

There Will Never Be Another You by Mack Gordon & Harry Warren, 1942, Movie: Iceland, Photo Sonja Henie, John Payne, Jack Oakie & Sammy Kaye.................**12.00**

There'll Always Be An England! by Ross Parker & Hughie Charles, 1939................**10.00**

There'll Be A Hot Time For The Old Men, While The Young Men Are Away by Grant Clarke & George W. Meyer, 1918, Photo Santly & Norton (Rose Symbol)................**10.00**

There'll Be A Hot Time For The Old Men, While The Young Men Are Away by Grant Clarke & George W. Meyer, 1918, Photo Elsie White (Cover Artist, Rose Symbol & WWI) **22.00**

There'll Be A Hot Time In The Town Of Berlin, When The Yanks Go Marching In by Joe Bushkin & John Devries, 1943 (WWII)........**15.00**

There'll Be Blue Birds Over The White Cliffs Of Dover by Nat Burton & Walter Kent, 1941, Photo Jimmy Dorsey (WWII)................**6.00**

There'll Be Blue Birds Over The White Cliffs Of Dover by Nat Burton & Walter Kent, 1941, Photo Kay Kyser (WWII) **6.00**

There'll Be Blue Birds Over The White Cliffs Of Dover by Nat Burton & Walter Kent, 1941, Photo Guy Lombardo (WWII)................**6.00**

There'll Be Blue Birds Over The White Cliffs Of Dover by Nat Burton & Walter Kent, 1941, Photo Blue Barron (WWII)................**6.00**

There'll Be No South by Brown, Akst & Richman, 1936................**5.00**

There'll Be Some Changes Made by Higgins & Overstreet, 1947, Movie: Designing Woman, Photo Gregory Peck, Lauren Bacall & Dolores Gray **5.00**

There'll Come A Day by Edward I. Boyle, 1917 ....**5.00**

There'll Come A Time by Charles K. Harris, 1895 (Pre 1900)............**10.00**

There's A Broken Heart For Every Light On Broadway by Howard Johnson & Fred Fischer, 1915, Photo Avon Comedy Four, Advertisement For Saturday Evening Post On Back Cover (Cover Artist, Rose, Advertising & Deco) **20.00**

There's A Bungalo In Dixieland by Freeman, 1914 (Cover Artist, Pfeiffer & Dixie)................**15.00**

There's A Cabin In The Pines by Billy Hill & M. Fisher, 1933............**5.00**

There's A Charm About The Old Love Still by F.W. Vandersloot & A.L. Fischer, 1904 ....**10.00**

There's A Dark Man Coming With A Bundle by Leighton & Leighton, 1904 (Cover Artist, Swinnerton & Black, Black Face)................**40.00**

There's A Different You In Your Heart by Irving Kahal & Sammy Fain, 1934 ....**5.00**

There's A Dixie Girl Who's Longing For A Yankee Doodle Boy by Robert F. Roden & George W. Meyer, 1911, Photo Murray Whiteman (Cover Artist, Etherington & Dixie)................**10.00**

There's A Far Away Look In Your Eye by Irving Taylor & Vic Mizzy, 1938, Photo Vincent Lopez **3.00**

There's A Four Leaf Clover In My Pocket by Lew Colwell, Jack Meskill & Pete Wendling, 1929 (Cover Artist, Barbelle) **12.00**

There's A Garden In Old Italy by Joe McCarthy & Jack Glogau, 1916 (Cover Artist, Rose)................**5.00**

There's A Garden Of Eden In Sweden by Ruddy & Freeman, 1915 (Cover Artist, Pfeiffer & Deco) **15.00**

There's A Girl I Love, Down In Panama by Colburn, 1916 (Cover Artist, Pfeiffer)................**10.00**

There's A Girl In Havana by E. Ray Goetz & A Baldwin Sloane, 1911 ..**5.00**

There's A Girl In Havana by Irving Berlin, 1911 (Irving Berlin) **10.00**

There's A Girl In Old New Hampshire, Whose Heart Is A Part Of Me by J. Stanley Brothers Jr., Harold Freeman & J. Edwin Allemong, 1919..**5.00**

There's A Girl In The Heart Of Maryland by Ballard Macdonald & Harry Carroll, 1913 (Cover Artist, Starmer)................**10.00**

There's A Girl In The World For Us All by W.C. Davis, 1896 (Pre 1900) **10.00**

There's A Girl That's Meant For Me In The Heart Of Tennessee by Sherwood & Rule, 1914 (Cover Artist, Pfeiffer & Deco) **15.00**

There's A Girl Wanted There by Mills & Scott, 1903 ....**10.00**

There's A Gold Mine In The Sky by Charles & Nick Kenny, 1937, Photo Kate Smith **10.00**

There's A Gold Mine In The Sky by Charles & Nick Kenny, 1937, Signed Photo Bing Crosby (Signed)................**15.00**

There's A Green Hill Out In Flanders by Allan J. Flynn, 1917, Photo Florence Timponi (Cover Artist, Starmer & WWI)................**15.00**

There's A Harbor Of Dream Boats by Nat Burton, Al Sherman & Arthur Altman, 1943, Photo The Townsmen................**6.00**

There's A Harbor Of Dream Boats by Nat Burton, Al Sherman & Arthur Altman, 1943, Photo Russ Morgan **6.00**

There's A Heart Of Gold That's Waiting by Freeman, 1914 (Cover Artist, Pfeiffer)................**10.00**

There's A Home In Wyoming by Peter DeRose, 1933 ....**5.00**

There's A Key To Every Heart by Newell & Powell, 1915 (Cover Artist, Pfeiffer & Deco) **15.00**

There's A Land Beyond The Rainbow by Ternant, 1916 (Cover Artist, Pfeiffer)................**10.00**

There's A Lark In My Heart by James King Duffy & Charles Gilbert Spross, 1922, Dedicated To Anna Case (Dedication) **5.00**

There's A Light Shining Bright In The Window Tonight by C. Arthur Pfeiffer, 1918 (Cover Artist, Pfeiffer & WWI) **20.00**

There's A Little Bit Of Bad In Every Good Little Girl by Grant Clarke & Fred Fischer, 1916, Photo Arthur Fields (Cover Artist, Rose & Deco)................**12.00**

There's A Little Bit Of Bad In Every Good Little Girl by Grant Clarke & Fred Fischer, 1916, Photo Military Four (Cover Artist, Rose Symbol & Deco) **10.00**

There's A Little Bit Of Bad In Every Good Little Girl by Grant Clarke & Fred Fischer, 1916, Photo James Mullen & B. Alain Coogan (Cover Artist, Rose Symbol & Deco)................**12.00**

There's A Little Bit Of Scotch In Mary by Von Tilzer, 1916 (Cover Artist, Pfeiffer)................**10.00**

There's A Little Blue Star In The Window by Paul R. Armstrong & F. Henri Klickmann, 1918 (WWI)................**20.00**

There's A Little Gold Star In The Service Flag by Freeman & Cronson, 1918 (Cover Artist, Pfeiffer & WWI) **20.00**

There's A Little Lane Without A Turning On The Way To Home Sweet Home by Sam M. Lewis & George W. Meyer, 1915 (Cover Artist, DeTakacs)................**10.00**

There's A Little Road To Heaven by Allen, 1915 (Cover Artist, Pfeiffer)..**10.00**

There's A Little Spark Of Love Still Burning by Joe McCarthy & Fred Fischer, 1914, Photo Kitty Gordan (Cover Artist, Rose Symbol & Deco) **10.00**

There's A Little Street In Heaven That They Call Broadway by Jas. T. Waldron & A. Balwin Stone, 1903................**10.00**

There's A Long, Long Trail by Stoddard King & Zo Elliott, 1913, Sung By John McCormack (WWI) **5.00**

There's A Lull In My Life by Mack Gordon & Harry Revel, 1937, Movie: Wake Up And Live, Photo Walter Winchell, Ben Bernie & Alice Faye................**12.00**

There's A Lump Of Sugar Down In Dixie by Alfred Bryan, Jack Yellen & Albert Gumble, 1918 , Photo Al Jolson (Cover Artist, Starmer, Dixie & Al Jolson)................**10.00**

There's A Million Heroes In Each Corner Of The U.S.A. by Sam Lewis, Joe Young & Maurice Abrahams, 1917 (WWI)............16.00

There's A Million Reasons Why I Shouldn't Kiss You by Von Tilzer, 1917 (Cover Artist, Pfeiffer & Deco).............15.00

There's A Mother Old And Gray Who Needs Me Now by Geo. H. Diamond, 1911 ....10.00

There's A Mother Waiting For You At Home Sweet Home by James Thornton, 1903 ....12.00

There's A New Moon by Herb Magidson & Allie Wrubel, 1937, Movie: Radio City Revels, Photo Bob Burns, Milton Berle, Ann Miller, Kenny Baker & Many Other Stars 5.00

There's A New Moon Over My Shoulder by Davis, Whelan & Blastic, 1944, Photo Sons Of The Pioneers.............6.00

There's A New Star In Heaven Tonight by J. Keirn Brennan, Irving Mills & Jimmy McHugh, Photo Rudolph Valentino.............22.00

There's A Picture In My Memory, And It Calls Me Back To You by Dave Cooper, Carl Muller & Vin Plunkett, 1918 (WWI).............15.00

There's A Place In The Sun For You by Bud Green & Sammy Fain, 1928.............5.00

There's A Platinum Star In Heaven Tonight by Simon & Sanford, 1937, Photo Jean Harlow.............5.00

There's A Quaker Down In Quaker Town by David Berg & Alfred Solman, 1916 (Cover Artist, DeTakacs).............10.00

There's A Rainbow 'Round My Shoulder by Al Jolson, Billy Rose & Dave Dreyer, 1932, Movie: The Singing Fool, Photo Al Jolson (Cover Artist, Leff & Al Jolson).............16.00

There's A Red Bordered Flag In The Window by Fred Ziemer & J.R. Shannon, 1918 (WWI).............15.00

There's A Rickety, Rackety Shack by Tobias & Turk, 1927, Photo Morton Downey.............5.00

There's A Ring Around The Moon by Sam Lewis, Al Goodhart & Ed. G. Nelson, 1931.............6.00

There's A Rising Moon by Paul Francis Webster & Sammy Fain, 1954, Movie: Young At Heart.............5.00

There's A Rose In Old Erin by J. Will Callahan, Paul Biese & F. Henri Klickmann, 1915, Photo John McCormack (Irish).............10.00

There's A Small Hotel by Lorenz Hart & Richard Rodgers, 1936, Movie: On Your Toes 5.00

There's A Small Hotel by Lorenz Hart & Richard Rodgers, 1936, Movie: Words And Music, Photo June Allyson, Perry Como, Judy Garland, Lena Horne, Gene Kelly, Mickey Rooney & Ann Sothern.............6.00

There's A Song In The Air by F. Flaxington Harker, 1934.............3.00

There's A Spell On The Moon by Jay Gorney, 1935, Movie: Spring Tonic.............5.00

There's A Star In Heaven Tonight by J. Keirn Brennan, Irving Mills & Jimmy McHugh.............10.00

There's A Star In The East by Roger Lewis & Ernie Erdman, 1917.............5.00

There's A Star Spangled Banner Waving Somewhere by Paul Roberts & Shelby Darnell, 1942 (Cover Artist, Barbelle & WWII).............10.00

There's A Sunny Smile Waiting For Me by Harry D. Kerr & Leo Edwards, 1930 ....5.00

There's A Tear In My Beer Tonight by Lee Kuhn, Alice Cornell & Eddie Asherman, 1946.............5.00

There's A Typical Tipperary Over Here by Alex Gerber & Abner Silver, 1920, Photo Blanche Ring (Irish).............12.00

There's A Vacant Chair At Home Sweet Home by Joe Goodwin & James F. Hanley, 1920 (Cover Artist, Wohlman & Deco).............10.00

There's A Vacant Chair For Will Rogers In Every Home Tonight by Lou Leaman & Mitchell Parish, 1935, Photo Will Rogers.............10.00

There's A Vacant Chair In Every Home Tonight by Breuer, 1917 (Cover Artist, Pfeiffer & WWI).............15.00

There's A Wah-Wah Gal In Agua Caliente by Walter Donaldson, 1931, Movie: Whoopee 10.00

There's A Wireless Station Down In My Heart by Ed Moran, Joe McCarthy & James V. Monaco, 1914.............6.00

There's Always A Seat In The Parlor For You by William J. Scanlon, 1881 (Pre 1900) 10.00

There's Always Something Doin' Down In Dixie by Darl MacBoyle & Nat Vincent, 1917, Photo Henry & Adelaide & Baby Arthur (Cover Artist, Barbelle & Dixie) 10.00

There's An Angel Missing From Heaven by Paul B. Armstrong & Robert Speroy, 1918, Dedicated To The American Red Cross (WWI, Red Cross & Dedication) 40.00

There's An Isle In The Blue Southern Sea by Leroy F. Lewis, To Cuban Patriots: We Come With The Stripes And The Stars. The Flag Of The Free And The True, We Come With Our Ships And Our Tars, We Come With Our Brave Boys In Blue.............12.00

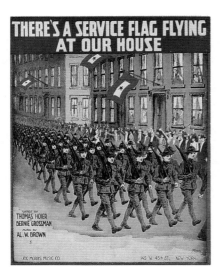

There's A Service Flag Flying At Our House by Thomas Hoier, Bernie Grossman & Al W. Brown, 1917 (Cover Artist, Starmer & WWI) 30.00

There's A Shanty In Old Shanty Town by Young, Siras & Little, 1932 ..5.00

There's A Shape In The Sky by Donovan, 1973, Movie: Brother Sun, Sister Moon, Photo Graham Faulkner & Judy Bowker.............4.00

There's Another Angel Now In Old Killarney by George A. Little & Mike Bernard, 1917 (Cover Artist, E.E. Walton, Irish & WWI)..10.00

There's Another Picture In My Mamma's Frame by Charles K. Harris, 1907 ....**10.00**

There's Danger In Your Eyes, Cherie! by Harry Richman, Jack Meskill & Pete Wendling, 1929, Movie: Puttin On The Ritz, Photo Harry Richman...**10.00**

There's Egypt In Your Dreamy Eyes by Fleta Jan Brown & Herbert Spencer, 1917 (Cover Artist, Casseau)....................................**6.00**

There's Everything Nice About You by Alfred Bryan, Arthur Terker & Pete Wendling, 1929..**5.00**

There's Frost On The Moon by Joe Young & Fred E. Ahlert, 1936, Photo Artie Shaw **6.00**

There's Got To Be A Better Way by Cahn & Goldsmith, 1968, Movie: Bandolero!, Photo James Stewart, Dean Martin & Raquel Welch...**5.00**

There's Honey On The Moon Tonight by Haven Gillespie, Mack Davis & J. Fred Coots, 1938, Photo Blue Barron (Cover Artist, Sorokin).....**3.00**

There's Just A Bit O'Heaven In Your Smile by Burton Ley & Lee David, 1923 ....**5.00**

There's Just A Little Touch Of Dixie In Your Eyes by Jack Strouse, Thos. F. Swift & Rubey Cowan, 1920 (Dixie)...............**10.00**

There's Lots Of Stations On My Railroad Track by Gus Edwards, & McCarthy, 1912 (Cover Artist, Pfeiffer & Transportation)...........**22.00**

There's Music In The Land by Jule Styne & Sammy Cahn, 1948, Movie: Two Guys From Texas, Photo Dennis Morgan, Jack Carson & Dorothy Malone..**5.00**

There's Never Been Anyone Else But You by Webster & Tiomkin, 1956, Movie: Giant, Photo James Dean, Liz Taylor & Rock Hudson **8.00**

There's No Business Like Show Business by Irving Berlin, 1946, Movie: Annie Get Your Gun (Irving Berlin) **10.00**

There's No Friends Like The Friends From Way Back Home by Swan, 1918 (Cover Artist, Pfeiffer & WWI) **15.00**

There's No Girl Like The Old Girl At Home by Allen, 1915 (Cover Artist, Pfeiffer)...**12.00**

There's No More Buster Brown by Harry Breen & James Conlin, 1908..**10.00**

There's No One But You by Redd Evans & Austen Croom Johnson, 1946, Photo Hal McIntyre (Cover Artist Nick)..........................**3.00**

There's No One But You To Blame by Ted Garton, 1917 (Cover Artist, Pfeiffer **10.00**

There's No One Like Mother To Me by Lucier, 1885 (Pre 1900) **15.00**

There's No Place Like Home by Felix F. Feist & Ted S. Barron, 1902...**10.00**

There's No Place Like Home For The Holidays by Al Stillman & Robert Allen, 1954 ....**8.00**

There's No Place Like Your Arms by Bickley Reichner & Clay Boland, 1938, From 51st Annual "Mask & Wig Show" At University Of Pennsylvania Production **5.00**

There's No Tomorrow by Al Hoffman, Leo Corday & Leon Carr, 1949 ..**5.00**

There's No You by Tom Adair & Hal Hopper, 1944, Photo Eileen Barton...**3.00**

There's No You by Tom Adair & Hal Hopper, 1944, Photo Frank Sinatra **4.00**

There's Nobody Else But You by L. Wolfe Gilbert, 1924, Photo Vincent Lopez (Cover Artist, Harrison)...**3.00**

There's None Will Forgive Like A Mother by Cooper & Wegefarth, 1891 (Pre 1900) **10.00**

There's Nothing Else In Life Like Love, Love, Love by Weslyn & Christie, 1909 (Cover Artist, Pfeiffer)................................**10.00**

There's Nothing Left To Do But Say Goodbye by Charles Newman & Isham Jones, 1933...**6.00**

There's Nothing Like A Mother's Love by W.A. Lang & May Greene, 1911, Photo Carrie Starr (Cover Artist, Starmer)...............**5.00**

There's Nothing Like A Mother's Love by W.A. Lang & May Greene, 1911 (Cover Artist, Pfeiffer) **10.00**

There's Nowhere To Go But Up by Maxwell Anderson & Kurt Weill, 1938, Movie: Knickerbocker Holiday **5.00**

There's One California For Mine by Alfred Bryan & Herman Paley, 1915...**10.00**

There's One In A Million Like You by Clarke & Schwartz, 1912 (Cover Artist, Pfeiffer)..**10.00**

There's Only One Mary In Maryland by George J. Moriarty & Richard A. Whiting, 1915 (Cover Artist, Starmer)........................**10.00**

There's Only One Pal After All by Harold G. Frost & F. Henri Klickmann, 1920 ....**5.00**

There's Rain In My Eyes by Ager, McCarthy & Schwartz, 1938.........**6.00**

There's Someone More Lonesome Than You by Lou Klein & Harry Von Tilzer, 1916, Photo Harry Von Tilzer (Cover Artist, Pfeiffer).......**10.00**

There's Something About A Rose by Irving Kahal, Francis Wheeler & Sammy Fain, 1928 (Deco)..**10.00**

There's Something About An Empty Chair by Adler, 1958, Photo Gwen Verdon **3.00**

There's Something About You Makes Me Love You by Henry Lewis, Bernie Grossman & Arthur Lange, 1917, Musical: Anna Held's Show, Follow Me, Photo Henry Lewis (Cover Artist, Starmer) **12.00**

There's Something In The Air by Harold Adamson & Jimmy McHugh, 1936, Movie: Banjo On My Knee, Photo Buddy Ebsen, Barbara Stanwyck & Joel McCrea **12.00**

There's Something In The Name Of Ireland by Howard Johnson & Milton Ager, 1917 (Irish) **10.00**

There's Sugar Cane Around My Door by Eddie Leonard & Grace & Jack Stern, 1929, Musical: Melody Lane, Photo Eddie Leonard **10.00**

There's That Look In Your Eyes Again by Mack Gordon & Harry Revel, 1936, Movie: Head Over Heels In Love, Photo Jessie Matthews **5.00**

There's The One For Me by Yellen & Akst, 1929, Movie: Bulldog Drummond, Photo Ronald Coleman..**10.00**

There's Yes! Yes! In Your Eyes by Cliff Friend & Jos. H. Santly, 1940, Photo Lawrence Welk (Cover Artist, Im-Ho) **5.00**

These Foolish Things Remind Me Of You by Holt Marvell, Jack Strachey & Harry Link, 1935 ....**4.00**

These Things Are You by Kim Gannon & Walter Kent, 1948 ....**3.00**

These Three We Should Not Forget by Walter Kennedy & George Yelle, 1932, Photo Eric Sagerquist **5.00**

These Will Be The Best Years Of Our Lives by Bob Hilliard & Dave Mann, 1947, Photo Eddie Gallagher (Cover Artist, JH) **3.00**

They All Do The Fox Trot Now, Down In Jungle Town by Bunce & Pollock, 1915 (Cover Artist, Pfeiffer).....................................**12.00**

They All Fall In Love by Cole Porter, 1929, Movie: The Battle Of Paris, Photo Gertrude Lawrence..**8.00**

They All Follow Me by Hugh Morton & Gustave Kerker, 1887 (Pre 1900)..**10.00**

They All Kept Time With Their Feet by Edwards & Madden, 1912 (Cover Artist, Pfeiffer)..**10.00**

They All Laughed by Ira & George Gershwin, 1937, Movie: Shall We Dance?, Photo Fred Astaire & Ginger Rogers **10.00**

They All Sang Annie Laurie by J. Will Callahan & F. Henri Klickmann, 1915 (WWI)...**10.00**

They Always Pick On Me by Murphy & Von Tilzer, 1911 ....**5.00**

They Are Fighting For Liberty by Donnie, 1918, Photo Pershing & Washington (Cover Artist, Pfeiffer, WWI, Presidents & Military Personnel) ..**25.00**

They Are The Best Friends Of All by Norman & McGlennon, 1893 (Pre 1900)..**10.00**

They Call It Dancing by Irving Berlin, 1921 (Irving Berlin) **10.00**

They Can't Convince Me by Roberts & Fisher, 1946, Movie: Down To Earth, Photo Rita Hayworth & Larry Parks....................................**5.00**

They Can't Make A Lady Out Of Me by Moe Jaffe & Henry Tobias, 1948, Photo Janette Davis (Cover Artist, George Martin) **3.00**

They Can't Take That Away From Me by Ira & George Gershwin, 1937, Movie: Shall We Dance?, Photo Fred Astaire & Ginger Rogers ...**12.00**

They Cut Down The Old Pine Tree by George Brown, Willie Raskin & Edward Eliscu, 1929, Photo Rudy Vallee **10.00**

They Did Their Share Now I'll Do Mine by Harry Tobias, 1918 (Cover Artist, Kursh & WWI)................................**12.00**

They Didn't Believe Me by Herbert Reynolds & Jerome D. Kern, 1914, Photo Rudy Vallee (Cover Artist, B. Harris)................................**10.00**

They Didn't Believe Me by Reynolds & Kern, 1949, Movie: That Midnight Kiss, Photo Mario Lanza, Kathryn Grayson, Jose Iturbi, Ethel Barrymore & Keenan Wynn................................**12.00**

They Don't Hesitate Any More by Kalmar, Leslie & Puck, 1914 (Cover Artist, Pfeiffer)................................**10.00**

They Go Wild, Simply Wild Over Me by Joseph McCarthy & Fred Fisher, 1917 ....**10.00**

They Got Me Doing It Now by Irving Berlin, 1913 (Irving Berlin).....**12.00**

They Gotta Quit Kicking My Dawg Around by Webb M. Oungst & Cy Perkins, 1912 ....**10.00**

They Had To Stand Up Every Time They Sat Down by Kline & Shaw, 1914 (Cover Artist, Pfeiffer) **8.00**

They Made It Twice As Nice As Paradise And They Called It Dixieland by Raymond Egan & Richard A. Whiting, 1916 (Cover Artist, Einson, Dixie & Black, Black Face)................................**35.00**

They Needed A Songbird In Heaven So They Took Caruso Away by Geo. A. Little & Jack Stanley, 1921, Photo Enrico Caruso, Dedicated To Memory Of Our Beloved Caruso (Dedication) **20.00**

They Never Tell All What They Know by Edward Harrigan & David Braham, 1893 (Pre 1900) **10.00**

They Say by Edward Heyman, Paul Mann & Stephan Weiss, 1938, Photo Reggie Childs (Cover Artist, Im-Ho) **3.00**

They Say Its Wonderful by Irving Berlin, 1946, Movie: Annie Get Your Gun (Irving Berlin)................................**15.00**

They Shall Not Pass! by Arthur A. Penn, 1918 (WWI)................................**10.00**

They Start The Victrola And Go Dancing Around The Floor by Grant Clarke & Maurice Abraham, 1914, Photo Carsera & Brooke (Cover Artist, John Frew)................................**10.00**

They Tied The Can To Mary by Heck, 1914 (Cover Artist, Pfeiffer)..**10.00**

They Were All Doing The Same by Ren Shields, 1902 ....**10.00**

They Were All Out Of Step But Jim by Irving Berlin, 1918, Photo The Dream Girls, Marie & Hortense (Cover Artist, Barbelle, WWI & Irving Berlin).**15.00**

They Were All Out Of Step But Jim by Irving Berlin, 1918, Photo Elizabeth Brice (Cover Artist, Barbelle, WWI & Irving Berlin)................................**16.00**

They'll All Be There But Me by Irving Kahal & Sammy Fain, 1931 ....**5.00**

They'll Be Mighty Proud In Dixie Of Their Old Black Joe by Harry Carroll, 1918, Photo Harry Carroll (Cover Artist, Starmer, WWI, Dixie & Black, Black Face)................................**45.00**

They'll Never Miss The Wine In Dixieland by Bryan & Meyer, 1920 (Cover Artist, Pfeiffer, Dixie & Transportation)................................**20.00**

They're All Going To The Movies by Allen, 1915 (Cover Artist, Pfeiffer)..**10.00**

They're All Good American Names by William Jerome & Jean Schwartz, 1911 ....**5.00**

They're All My Friends by George M. Cohan (George M. Cohan).....**15.00**

They're All Sweeties by Andrew B. Sterling & Harry Von Tilzer, 1919, Sweeties From Ziegfeld Follies, Photo Billy Glason (Cover Artist, Barbelle) **12.00**

They're All Sweeties by Andrew B. Sterling & Harry Von Tilzer, 1919, Sweeties From Ziegfeld Follies, Photo Klein Bros. (Cover Artist, Barbelle) **10.00**

They're Coming Back by Robert Lukens, 1918 (WWI)................................**10.00**

They're Either Too Young Or Too Old by Arthur Schwartz & Frank Loesser, 1943, Movie: Thank Your Lucky Stars................................**6.00**

They're Mine, They're Mine, They're Mine by Sonny Kane & Jack Pleis, 1947, Photo Guy Lombardo **4.00**

They're On Their Way To Kan The Kaiser, 1917 (WWI) **25.00**

They're On Their Way To Mexico by Irving Berlin, 1909, Photo Belle Baker (Cover Artist, John Frew & Irving Berlin) **16.00**

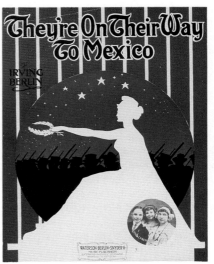

They're On Their Way To Mexico by Irving Berlin, 1915, Photo Lynch Trio (Cover Artist, John Frew & Irving Berlin)............16.00

They're Proud Of The Irish Now by Sterling & Costello, 1900 (Irish)..**10.00**

They're Wearing 'Em Higher In Hawaii by Joe Goodwin & Halsey K. Mohr, 1916 (Cover Artist, DeTakacs)................................**12.00**

They've Got Me Doing It Now by Irving Berlin, 1918 (Cover Artist, Pfeiffer & Irving Berlin)................................**15.00**

They've Won Every Nation's Battles But Their Own by Shields & Ball, 1910 (Patriotic)................................**15.00**

Thief, The by Bernard Hamblen, 1936 ....**3.00**

Thine Alone by Henry Blossom & Victor Herbert, 1929 (Victor Herbert) **10.00**

Thing, The by Charles R. Grean, 1950, Photo Phil Harris **5.00**

Things Are Looking Up by Gershwin & Gershwin, 1937, Movie: A Damsel In Distress, Photo Fred Astaire, Burns & Allen & Joan Fontaine **15.00**

Things I Love, The by Harold Barlow & Lewis Harris, 1941, Photo Jimmy Dorsey................................**3.00**

Things Look Wonderful Now by Benny Davis & Joe Burke, 1929................................**5.00**

Things That Remind Me Of You by Art Gillham & Billy Smythe, 1927..**5.00**

Things We Did Last Summer, The by Sammy Cahn & Jule Styne, 1946, Photo Bing Crosby **3.00**

Think It Over, Mary by Gray & Piantadosi, 1915 (Cover Artist, Pfeiffer & Deco) **15.00**

Think Not This Heart Can Alter from Lucia Di Lammermoor, Arranged by H. Engelmann, 1902 (Cover Artist, Starmer)................................**10.00**

Think Of Me by Frank Elling, Ed Hoffman & Max Friedman, 1917.....**5.00**

Thinking Of You by Bert Kalmar, Harry Ruby & Ted Snyder, 1931, Movie: Three Little Words, Photo Fred Astaire, Red Skelton, Vera Ellen & Arlene Dahl................................**10.00**

Thinking Of You by Frances Lowell & William Dichmont, 1913................................**10.00**

Thinking Of You by Simon Einhorn, Ben Bronson & George Bronson, 1930 ....**5.00**

3rd Man Theme, The by Anton Karas, 1949, Movie: The 3rd Man, Photo Joseph Cotten, Orson Welles, Valli & Trevor Howard................................**8.00**

Thirsty For Your Kisses by Lee Morris, Bill Ficks & Lee Morris, 1950, Photo Ames Brothers (Cover Artist, BJH) **3.00**

Thirteen Collar by Herbert Reynolds, Schuyler Greene & Jerome Kern, 1915, Musical: Very Good Eddie (Cover Artist, Malcolm Strauss)..**16.00**

Thirteen Were Saved by Wm. Vincent, 1888, Song Of The Great Blizzard Of 1888, Photo Miss Minnie Freeman, Teacher (Pre 1900) **35.00**

38th St. Rag by Copeland, 1910 (Cover Artist, Pfeiffer & Rag)..........**15.00**

Thirty Two Feet, Eight Little Tails by Frank Weldon, 1951.................**5.00**

This Ain't My First Rodeo by Vern Gosdin, Max D. Barnes & Hank Cochran, 1990, Photo Vern Gosdin.....................**2.00**

This Ain't The Place I Thought It Was by O'Brien & Helf, 1911 (Cover Artist, Pfeiffer & Deco).........................**15.00**

This Can't Be Love by Lorenz Hart & Richard Rodgers, 1938, Musical: The Boys From Syracuse.........................**5.00**

This Great Big World Owes Me A Loving by Sterling, 1916 (Cover Artist, Pfeiffer)...**10.00**

This Heart Is Mine by Freed & Warren, 1944, Movie: Ziegfield Follies, Photo Fred Astaire & Lucille Bremer.....................**10.00**

This Is A Great Country by Irving Berlin (Irving Berlin)....................**10.00**

This Is Always by Mack Gordon & Harry Warren, 1946, Movie: Three Little Girls In Blue, Photo June Haver, Vivian Blaine, Vera Ellen, Celeste Holm & George Montgomery.....................**5.00**

This Is Heaven by Jack Yellen & Harry Akst, 1929, Movie: This Is Heaven, Photo Vilma Banky.........................**6.00**

This Is It by Dorothy Fields & Arthur Schwartz, 1939, Movie: Stars In Your Eyes.....................**8.00**

This Is My Lonely Day by A.P. Herbert & Vivian Ellis, 1936..............**1.00**

This Is My Night To Dream by John Burke & James V. Monaco, 1938, Movie: Doctor Rhythm, Photo Bing Crosby & Mary Carlisle.........**5.00**

This Is My Night To Howl by Lorenz Hart & Richard Rodgers, 1927, Musical: A Conn. Yankee.....................**10.00**

This Is My Song by C. Chaplin, 1966, Movie: A Countess From Hong Kong, Photo Charlie Chaplin.....................**12.00**

This Is No Dream by Benny Davis, Tommy Dorsey & Ted Shapiro, 1939.....................**5.00**

This Is No Laughing Matter by Van Loman, Martin Block & Al Frisch, 1945 (Cover Artist, Im-Ho).........................**4.00**

This Is Our Side Of The Ocean by George M. Cohan (George M. Cohan).....................**15.00**

This Is The Army Mr. Jones by Irving Berlin, 1942, Movie: This Is The Army, Lieut. Ronald Reagan In Cast (WWII, Irving Berlin, Military Personnel & President)..................16.00

This Is The First Time by Wally Peterson, 1949.....................**2.00**

This Is The Life by Irving Berlin, 1914, Photo Al Jolson (Cover Artist, John Frew, Irving Berlin & Al Jolson).....................**10.00**

This Is The Life For Me (Cover Artist, Pfeiffer).....................**15.00**

This Is The Moment by Leo Robin & Frederick Hollander, 1948, Movie: That Lady In Ermine, Photo Betty Grable.....................**12.00**

This Is The Mrs. by Lew Brown & Ray Henderson, 1931, Musical: George White's Scandals.........................**10.00**

This Is The Night by Redd Evans & Lewis Bellin, 1946.....................**3.00**

This Is Worth Fighting For by Edgar DeLange & Sam H. Stept, 1942 (Cover Artist, Im-Ho & WWII).........................**5.00**

This Little Piggy Went To Market by Sam Coslow & Harold Lewis, 1933, Movie: Eight Girls In A Boat, Photo Ethel Shutta.....................**5.00**

This Little Ripple Had Rhythm by Leo Robin & Ralph Rainger, 1937, Movie: The Big Broadcast Of 1938, Photo Shirley Ross, Caricature Of W.C. Fields, Martha Raye, Ben Blue & Bob Hope.....................**10.00**

This Love Of Mine by Frank Sinatra, Sol Parker & Henry Sanicola, 1941, Photo Frank Sinatra.....................**3.00**

This May Be The Night by Mack Gordon & Harry Revel, 1938, Movie: My Lucky Star, Photo Sonja Henie & Richard Greene.....................**6.00**

This Message Your Mother Sends You by Frank W. Grant, 1917, Photo Florence Davis (WWI).....................**15.00**

This Nearly Was Mine by Richard Rodgers & Oscar Hammerstein II, 1949, Movie: South Pacific, Photo Mary Martin & Ezio Pinza (Cover Artist, BJH).........................**8.00**

This Never Happened Before by Harold Adamson & Jimmy McHugh, 1937, Movie: Hitting A New High, Photo Lily Pons, Jack Oakie, Eric Blore, Edward Everett Horton & John Howard.....................**12.00**

This Ole House by Stuart Hamblen, 1954.....................**3.00**

This Rose Brings My Heart To You by Leo Wood & Leo Edwards, 1909.....................**10.00**

This Time by Irving Berlin, 1941 (Irving Berlin).....................**10.00**

This Time by Irving Caesar & Sydney Green, 1953.....................**3.00**

This Time by Joel Benton & Paul Weston, 1946.....................**2.00**

This Year's Kisses by Irving Berlin, 1937, Movie: On The Avenue, Photo Dick Powell & Alice Faye (Irving Berlin).....................**12.00**

Tho' I Had A Bit Of The Devil In Me, She Had The Ways Of An Angel by Van Brunt, 1916 (Cover Artist, Pfeiffer).........................**10.00**

Tho' I'm A Long, Long Way From Tipperary by Cartland & James, 1914 (Cover Artist, Pfeiffer & Irish).....................**15.00**

Tho' I'm Not The First To Call You Sweetheart by Bernie Grossman & Arthur Lange, 1916.........................**10.00**

Tho' Many A Heart Is Broken, It Is Never Too Late To Mend by Stanley, 1915 (Cover Artist, Pfeiffer).....................**10.00**

Tho' The Silver Threads Are 'Mong The Gold by Harry Williams, 1911.....................**6.00**

Thorn, The Rose And You, The by Carl Copeland & Harry H. Williams, 1912.....................**5.00**

Those Charlie Chaplin Feet by Edgar Leslie & Archie Gottler, 1915..**20.00**

Those Good Old Days Back Home by Joe McCarthy & Jimmie Monaco, 1916, Photo Emma Carus (Cover Artist, Rose Symbol).....................**10.00**

Those Ragtime Melodies by Gene Hodgkins, 1912, Photo Blossom Seely & Rube Marquard (Cover Artist, Goebel & Rag).....................**10.00**

Those Saxophone Blues by Paul Biese, 1916, Photo Paul Biese (Blues)..**5.00**

Those Since-I-Met You Days by Robert B. Smith & Victor Herbert, 1919, Musical: Angel Face (Victor Herbert).....................**10.00**

Those Things Money Can't Buy by Ruth Poll & Al Goodhart, 1947, Photo Sammy Kaye.........................**3.00**

Those Wedding Bells Shall Not Ring Out by Monroe Rosenfeld, 1896 (Pre 1900).....................**10.00**

Those Were The Days by Gene Raskin, 1968, Photo Mary Hopkins.....**3.00**

Those Wonderful Eyes by Jos. E. Howard, 1912.....................**5.00**

Those Wonderful Words, I Love You by Harris, 1915 (Cover Artist, Pfeiffer).....................**10.00**

Thou Shalt Not by Archie Gottler & Noel Gay, 1932.....................**6.00**

Thou Swell by Lorenz Hart & Richard Rodgers, 1927, Musical: A Conn. Yankee.....................**10.00**

Thou Wouldst Be Loved by Edgar Allen Poe & O. G. Sonneck, 1917..**5.00**

Though Your Eyes Are Full Of Mischief, You're The Girl For Me by Irene Motzer & J. Edwin Allemong, 1919 (Cover Artist, Pfeiffer)..........**10.00**

Thoughts Of My Childhood Home by Loretta Hoppenjan, 1934, Signed Photo Tito Guizar (Cover Artist, Fran Hays & Signed)..................**5.00**

Thousand And One Nights, A by Ted Mossman & Jack Segal, 1947....**5.00**

Thousand Violins, A by Jay Livingston & Ray Evans, 1949, Movie: The Great Lover, Photo Bob Hope & Rhonda Fleming **5.00**

Thousandth Man, The by Rudyard Kipling & A.H. Behrend, 1926 (Cover Artist, RIP)..**5.00**

Three Bells, The by Bert Reisfeld & Jean Villard Gilles, 1948 ....**3.00**

Three Blind Mice, See How They Swing by Irving Taylor & Vic Mizzy, 1928 ....**5.00**

Three Caballeros, The by Manuel Esperon, Ray Gilbert & Ernesto Cortazas, 1945, Movie: The Three Caballeros (Disney) **15.00**

Three Cheers by Haim & Friedman, 1918 (WWI)..........................**10.00**

Three Cheers For Anything by Leigh Harline & Ned Washington, 1940, Movie: Pinocchio (Disney)...**15.00**

Three Cheers For Old Vermont by Cole, 1908..................................**5.00**

Three Cheers For The Army And Navy by Gordon V. Thompson, 1917 (WWI)..**15.00**

Three Coins In The Fountain by Sammy Cahn & Jule Styne, 1954, Movie: Three Coins In The Fountain, Photo Clifton Webb, Dorothy McGuire & Other Stars..8.00

Three Cornered Tune by Jo Swerling, Abe Burrows & Frank Loesser, 1950, Musical: Guys & Dolls...**5.00**

Three Leaves Of Shamrock by James McGuire, 1889 (Pre 1900 & Irish)..**10.00**

Three Little Fishies by Saxie Dowell, 1939 (Cover Artist, Im-Ho) **3.00**

Three Little Words by Bert Kalmar & Harry Ruby, 1930, Movie: Check And Double Check, Photo Amos & Andy (Amos & Andy & Black, Black Face)..**60.00**

Three O'Clock In The Morning by Dorothy Terriss & Julian Robledo, 1922 (Cover Artist, JVR & Deco) **6.00**

Three Of Us by O'Flynn, David & Wendling, 1933 ....**5.00**

Three On A Match by Raymond B. Egan & Ted Fiorito, 1932.............**5.00**

Three Treasures by Edward I. Boyle, 1922 (Cover Artist, E.S. Fisher & Deco) **5.00**

Three Trees by Tom McNaughton, 1910...**5.00**

Three Women To Every Man by Murray & Leigh, 1902.....................**10.00**

Three Wonderful Letters From Home by Joe Goodwin, Ballard MacDonald & James F. Hanley, 1918 (Cover Artist, Barbelle & WWI).....**10.00**

Three Words, I Love You by Oakley Stout & Edwin B. Abbott, 1919..**6.00**

Three's A Crowd by Al Dubin & Harry Warren, 1932 ....**5.00**

Thrill Is Gone, The by Lew Brown & Ray Henderson, 1931, Musical: George White's Scandals..**10.00**

Thrilled by Mort Greene & Harry Barris, 1935, Photo Guy Lombardo ..**3.00**

Through A Long And Sleepless Night by Mack Gordon & Alfred Newman, 1949, Movie: Come To The Stable, Photo Loretta Young & Celeste Holm **5.00**

Through A Thousand Dreams by Arthur Schwartz & Leo Robin, 1946, Movie: The Time, The Place And The Girl, Photo Dennis Morgan, Jack Carson, Martha Vickers, Janis Page & Carmen Cavalerro (Cover Artist, A. Joel Robinson) **8.00**

Through All The Ages by Fred E. Weatherly & Eric Coates, 1919 ....**2.00**

Through The Doorway of Dreams by Leo Robin & Richard A. Whiting, 1935, Movie: The Big Broadcast Of 1936, Photo Jessica Dragonette **5.00**

Through The Orange Grove Of South Carolina by Wilson (Transportation) **15.00**

Through The Years by Carrie Jacobs Bond, 1918 (Cover Artist, F. Hyer)..**15.00**

Through The Years by Edward Heyman & Vincent Youmans, 1931, Photo Gladys Swarthout **5.00**

Through These Wonderful Glasses Of Mine by Jack Mahoney & Harry Von Tilzer, 1916 (Cover Artist, Pfeiffer) **12.00**

Throw A Kiss To Me My Minstrel Man by Goetz & Seeley, 1911 (Cover Artist, Pfeiffer)...**10.00**

Throw A Saddle On A Star by Andy Parker & Hank Caldwell, 1946, Movie: Throw A Saddle On A Star, Photo Ken Curtis & Adelle Roberts...**35.00**

Throw Down Dat Key by Edgar Malone & Ted S. Barron, 1906 (Black, Black Face)..**15.00**

Throw Him Down, McCloskey by J.W. Kelly, 1890 (Pre 1900) **15.00**

Throw Me A Rose by P.G. Wodehouse, Herbert Reynolds & Emmerich Kalman, 1915..**6.00**

Throwin' Stones At The Sun by Nat Simon, Billy Hueston & Sammy Mysels, 1934, Photo Tom Coakley (Cover Artist, Barbelle) **5.00**

Thru For The Day by Willie "The Lion" Smith, 1942 ....**5.00**

Thru The Night by Virginia K. Logan & Frederic Knight Logan, 1922 (Cover Artist, Van Doorn Morgan) **5.00**

Thru Your Eyes To Your Heart by Gould & Heyman, 1945, Movie: Delightfully Dangerous, Photo Jane Powell, Constance Moore, Ralph Bellamy & Morton Gould...**6.00**

Thrush's Love Song, A by Fred G. Bowles & Alison Travers, 1923.....**5.00**

Thumbelina by Frank Loesser, 1951, Movie: Hans Christian Anderson, Photo Danny Kaye...**5.00**

Thumbs Up by Ben Franklin, Uriel Benjamin, Elliott Jacoby & Bobby Kroll, 1941...**5.00**

Thumper Song by Bliss, Sour & Manners, 1942, Movie: Bambi.........**10.00**

Thunder And Blazes by Julius Fucik, 1903 ....**5.00**

Thunder Over Paradise by Leo Robin & Ralph Rainger, 1935, Movie: Rose Of The Rancho...**5.00**

Thundercloud by Losey, 1909 (Cover Artist, Pfeiffer & Transportation) **15.00**

Thunderer, The by John Philip Sousa, 1889 (John Philip Sousa, March & Pre 1900)...**25.00**

Thy Dear Voice Calls Me by David D. Slater **5.00**

Ti-O-San by Lou Travella & L.C. Case, 1920.....................................**5.00**

Ti-Pi-Tin by Grevor & Leveen, 1938, Photo Horace Heidt **5.00**

Tia Juana Moon by Van Ness & Duggan, 1930 (Cover Artist, Pfeiffer)...**12.00**

Tickle The Ivories by Wallie Herzer, 1913 (Cover Artist, Starmer & Rag) **12.00**

Tickle Toes by William H. Penn, 1914 ....**6.00**

Tickled To Death by Chas. Hunter, 1899 (Pre 1900, Rag & Black, Black Face) **30.00**

Tico-Tico by Ervin Drake & Zequinha Abreu, 1943, Movie: Bathing Beauty, Photo Red Skelton & Esther Williams **6.00**

Tiddle-De-Winks by Melville Morris, 1916................................**5.00**

Tie That Binds by Charles K. Harris, 1908 ....**10.00**

Tie That Binds Or Jimmy Is The Man For Us, James Cox Campaign, The 1920 (Political) **30.00**

Tiger Rose by Ivan Reid & Peter DeRose, 1928, Respectfully Dedicated To Miss Lenore Ulric, Photo Miss Lenore Ulric (Cover Artist, E.E. Walton & Dedication) **5.00**

'Til I Met You I Never Knew Of Love, Sweet Love by Diamond & Hilliard, 1913 (Cover Artist, Pfeiffer)................................**10.00**

'Til Reveille by Stanley Cowan & Bobby Worth, 1941, Photo Joan Brooks **5.00**

'Til Reveille by Stanley Cowan & Bobby Worth, 1941, Photo Rudy Vallee................................**10.00**

Til Tomorrow by Sheldon Harnick & Jerry Bock, 1959 ....**3.00**

Tilda From Old Savannah by Chris Smith & John Larkin, 1904 ....**10.00**

Till by Carl Sigman & Charles Danvers, 1957, Photo Percy Faith **4.00**

Till by Carl Sigman & Charles Danvers, 1957, Photo The Vogues **4.00**

Till I Waltz Again With You by Sidney Prosen, 1952, Photo Teresa Brewer **5.00**

Till My Love Comes To Me by Paul Francis Webster & Ray Heindorf, 1954, Movie: Young At Heart................................**8.00**

Till My Luck Comes Rolling Along by George M. Cohan, 1922 (George M. Cohan)................................**10.00**

Till The Clouds Roll By by Gery Bolton, P.G. Wodehouse & Jerome Kern, 1917, Musical: Oh Boy! **5.00**

Till The End Of Time by Buddy Kaye & Ted Mossman, 1945, Photo Frederic Chopin (Cover Artist, Barbelle)................................**5.00**

Till The Lights Of London Shine Again by Tommy Connor & Eddie Pola, 1941 (WWII) **5.00**

Till The Sands Of The Desert Grow Cold by George Graff Jr. & Ernest R. Ball, 1911................................**5.00**

Till The Shadows Retire by Bernie Kane, 1932 ....**5.00**

Till The Swanee River Runs Dry by Jack Mahoney, 1919................................**10.00**

Till Then by Eddie Seiler, Sol Marcus & Guy Wood, 1944................................**5.00**

Till There Was You by Meredith Wilson, 1950, Movie: The Music Man ..**8.00**

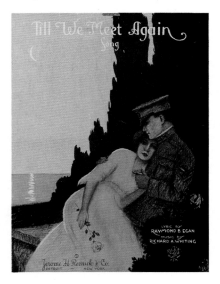

Till We Meet Again by Raymond Egan & Richard A. Whiting, 1918 (Cover Artist, Frederick S. Manning & WWI)................................18.00

Till We Meet by Lou Davis & Ted Fiorito, 1929 (Deco)................................**5.00**

Tim Rooney's At The Fightin'! by Norah Flynn, 1915 (WWI & Irish)...**15.00**

Tim Toolin by J.W. Kelly, 1893 (Pre 1900)................................**10.00**

Timbuctoo by Burt Kalmar & Harry Ruby, 1920................................**6.00**

Time For Jookin by Lew Brown, Charlie Tobias & Sam H. Stept, 1939..**5.00**

Time For Love, A by Webster & Mandel, 1966, Movie: An American Dream, Photo Janet Leigh, Stuart Whitman & Eleanor Parker........**3.00**

Time For Us, A by Larry Kusik, Eddie Snyder & Nino Rota, 1968, Movie: Romeo & Juliet, Photo Olivia Hussey & Leonard Whiting **3.00**

Time Of My Life, The by Previte, Markowitz & DeNicola, 1987, Movie: Dirty Dancing, Photo Patrick Swayze & Jennifer Grey **3.00**

Time On My Hands, You In My Arms by Harold Adamson & Vincent Youmans, 1930................................**3.00**

Time, The Place, The Girl, The by Hough & Adams, 1906 ....**6.00**

Time To Love A Girlie, Is When She's Blue, Blue, Blue by McDonald & Peters, 1913 (Cover Artist, Pfeiffer)................................**10.00**

Time To Re-Tire by Fred Knight, 1928 (Transportation)................................**10.00**

Time To Sing, A by Scoggin, 1968, Movie: A Time To Sing, Photo Hank Williams Jr., Shelley Fabares & Ed Begley **3.00**

Time Waits For No One by Cliff Friend & Charles Tobias, 1944, Movie: Shine On Harvest Moon, Photo Ann Sheridan & Dennis Morgan...**5.00**

Time Was by S.K. Russell, Miguel Prado & Gabriel Luna, 1941, Photo Sonny Dunham **3.00**

Time Was by S.K. Russell, Miguel Prado & Gabriel Luna, 1941, Photo Jimmy Dorsey................................**3.00**

Time Will Tell by Bobby Jones & Will Donaldson, 1920 (Cover Artist, E.W. Ream & Deco)................................**10.00**

Tin Pan Parade by Haven Gillespie & Richard A. Whiting, 1927, Photo Ford & Glenn................................**5.00**

Tin Pan Parade by Haven Gillespie & Richard A. Whiting, 1927, Photo Ed Lowry................................**5.00**

Tina Maria by Bob Merrill, 1945................................**5.00**

Tina-Lena, The by Sammy Cahn & Nicholas Brodsky, 1949, Movie: The Toast Of New Orleans, Photo Kathryn Grayson & Mario Lanza................................**5.00**

Ting A Ling The Bells Ring by Irving Berlin, 1926 (Irving Berlin)....**10.00**

Ting, Ling Toy by Mary Earl, 1919................................**5.00**

Ting-A-Ling by Addy Britt & Jack Little, 1926, Photo Georgette Duval (Cover Artist, Barbelle & Deco)................................**5.00**

Ting-A-Ling by Addy Britt & Jack Little, 1926, Photo Jack Shilkret (Cover Artist, Barbelle & Deco)................................**5.00**

Ting-A-Ling by Addy Britt & Jack Little, 1926, Photo Paul Ash (Cover Artist, Barbelle & Deco)................................**5.00**

Tinkle! Tinkle! by Jack Yellen, Milton Ager & Henry Sullivan, 1929, Musical: Murray Anderson's Almanac **12.00**

Tiny Bubbles by Leon Pober, 1966, Signed Photo Don Ho (Signed) **6.00**

Tiny Little Fingerprints by Charlie Tobias, Charles Newman & Sam H. Stept, 1935, Photo Frank Dailey................................**5.00**

Tiny-Town by Herbert Fields & Frederich Hollander, 1925 (Cover Artist, Frederick S. Manning & Deco) **15.00**

Tip Toe Through The Tulips With Me by Al Dubin & Joe Burke, 1929, Movie: The Gold Diggers Of Broadway, Photo Nancy Welford, Conway Tearle & Other Stars **16.00**

Tip Toe Through The Tulips With Me by Al Dubin & Joe Burke, 1929, Photo Tiny Tim................................**8.00**

Tip Top Tipperary Mary by Ballard MacDonald & Harry Carroll, 1914 (Cover Artist, Pfeiffer & Irish)................................**15.00**

Tip Your Hat To Hatty by Robert B. Smith & Victor Herbert, 1919, Musical: Angel Face (Victor Herbert)................................**10.00**

Tip Your Hat To Nellie by George C. Edwards, 1892 (Pre 1900) **12.00**

Tipperary by Curley, Fulton & Helf, 1907 (Irish) **10.00**

Tipperary Guards by E.T. Paull, 1915 (E.T. Paull & March)................................**35.00**

Tipperary Twirl, The by Jack Drislane & Geo Meyer, 1910, Photo Georgette Carlisle & Jule Bernard (Irish)................................**10.00**

Tired Hands by Al Piantadosi, 1926................................**6.00**

Tired Of Me by Grant Clarke & Walter Donaldson, 1920 (Cover Artist, R.S. & Deco) **10.00**

'Tis Almost Time To Say Good-Bye by Jas. R. Homer, 1904 (Cover Artist, E.S. Fisher) **10.00**

'Tis Autumn by Henry Nemo, 1941, Photo Dick Stabile (Cover Artist, Im-Ho) **4.00**

'Tis Enough by Kenneth Rand & Clara Edwards, 1923 ....**5.00**

'Tis Springtime Again by Ray Baxter & Fred Carbonneau, 1924..........**5.00**

Tisket A Tasket, A by Don Raye & Gene DePaul, 1942, Movie: Two Girls & A Sailor, Signed Photo Ella Fitzgerald (Cover Artist, Jorj Harris & Signed) **15.00**

Tisket A Tasket, A by Ella Fitzgerald & Al Feldman, 1938, Photo Bill McCune (Cover Artist, Jorj) **6.00**

Titanic by Boland, 1912 (Titanic & Transportation) **50.00**

Titina by Bertal-Maubon & Ronn & Leo Daniderff, 1925 ....**5.00**

To A Hill-Top by Ralph Cox, 1918, Dedicated To Mr. & Mrs. George M. Hendee (Dedication)..**3.00**

To A Thrush An Evening by Ethel M. Ward & Montague F. Phillips, 1930 ....**5.00**

To Be Forgotten by Irving Berlin, 1928 (Irving Berlin).....................**10.00**

To Be With You by Jack Yellen, Max Kortlander & Willie Jones, 1926 ....**5.00**

To Call You My Own by Dixon & Wrubel, 1935, Movie: Caliente, Photo Dolores Del Rio **5.00**

To Conquer Germany by Pegg (Cover Artist, Pfeiffer).......................**15.00**

To Dream The Old Dreams Over by Bob Young & Walter Donovan, 1912 (Cover Artist, E.S. Fischer) **5.00**

To Each His Own by Jay Livingston & Ray Evans, 1946, Movie: To Each His Own, Photo Olivia DeHavilland & John Lund **6.00**

To Have, To Hold, To Love by Darl MacBoyle & Ernest R. Ball, 1913, Photo Miss Marlowe & Mr. Sothern As Romeo & Juliet (Cover Artist, White) **16.00**

To Helen by Edgar Allen Poe & O.G. Sonneck, 1917 ....**5.00**

To Keep My Love Alive by Lorenz Hart & Richard Rodgers, 1927, Musical: A Connecticut Yankee **5.00**

To Know You Is To Love You by B.G. DeSylva, Lew Brown & Ray Henderson, 1928, Musical: Hold Everything (Cover Artist Helen Van Doorn Morgan) **15.00**

To Lou by Jeff Branen & Arthur Lange, 1916 (Cover Artist, DeTakacs) ..**10.00**

To My Mammy by Irving Berlin, 1930, Movie: Mammy, Photo Al Jolson (Irving Berlin & Al Jolson) **16.00**

To Remind Me Of You by Gustave Karn & Joseph Burke, 1931 ....**5.00**

To Shirley Booth by Harry Volpe & Tommy Tortorelli, Photo Shirley Booth **5.00**

To The Door Of The Sun by Norman Newell, Mario Panzeri, Lorenzo Pilat & Corrado Conti, 1974, Photo Al Martino................................**3.00**

To The Land Of My Own Romance by Harry B. Smith & Victor Herbert, 1930 (Victor Herbert) **10.00**

To The Rescue by Harry J. Lincoln, 1820 (March & Pre 1900) **35.00**

To The Steins by Walter Doyle, 1930 ....**5.00**

To Think I Cried Over You by Wm. Tracey & Jack Stern, 1918 (Cover Artist, Barbelle) **5.00**

To Think You've Chosen Me by Bennie Benjamin & George Weiss, 1950, Photo The Ames Brothers...**3.00**

To Victory by Ethel Watts Mumford & Henry Hadley, Boston Sunday Advertiser, Sunday Supplement, October 20, 1918, Dedicated To The Mothers Of Defenders Of Democracy (WWI, March & Dedication) **10.00**

To Whom It May Concern by Sidney D. Mitchell, Archie Gottler & George Meyer, 1930...**6.00**

To You by Benny Davis, Tommy Dorsey & Ted Shapiro, 1939, Photo Harry Richman **4.00**

To You, Sweetheart, Aloha by Harry Owens, 1936 ....**3.00**

Toast Of The Elk, The by Thomas E. Shea & Eddie Cassady, 1911, Photo Eddie Cassady..**5.00**

Toast To The Flag, A by John Jay Daly & William Ortman, 1937 (Patriotic)..**10.00**

To-Day by John Bennett & Carrie Jacobs Bond, 1915........................**15.00**

Today by Sparks, 1964, Movie: Advance To The Rear, Photo Glenn Ford & Stella Stevens **4.00**

Today–Tomorrow–Forever by David & Livingston, 1951, Movie: Sailor Beware, Photo Martin & Lewis & Corinne Calvert **4.00**

Together by B.G. DeSylva, Lew Brown & Ray Henderson, 1928, Movie: Since You Went Away, Photo Claudette Colbert, J. Jones, Joseph Cotten, L. Barrymore & Shirley Temple (Shirley Temple)..18.00

Together We Two by Irving Berlin, 1927 (Irving Berlin)...................**10.00**

Tokio Blues by Irving Berlin, 1924, Music Box Revue 1925 (Irving Berlin)...**10.00**

Tom Boy by W. F. Bradford, 1901 (Rag)..**10.00**

Tom, Dick Or Harry by Cole Porter, 1948, Musical: Kiss Me Kate **5.00**

Tom Dooley by Ed Jackson, 1958 ....**3.00**

Tom Thumb's Drum by Sarony, 1932..**5.00**

Tom Tom by Rosardios Funari, 1914 ....**5.00**

Tom-Tom-Toddle by Otto Harbach & Louis A. Hirsch, 1920, Musical: George M. Cohan's "Mary" (George M. Cohan)...........................**15.00**

Tomahawk by J.A. McMeekin, 1916 (Indian)....................................**20.00**

Tommy, 1917, Musical; The Better 'Ole Or the Romance Of Old Bill, As Presented By Mr. & Mrs. Coburn, Capt. Bruce Brainsfather, Arthur Eliot, James Heard & Herman Darewski, Photo Ole Bill & Victoire (Cover Artist, White, N.Y., WWI & Military Personnel) **16.00**

Tommy Atkins by Hamilton & Potter, 1893 (Pre 1900) **10.00**

Tommy by Roscoe Gilmore Stott & Henry Everett Sachs, 1928 ....**5.00**

Tommy, Make Room For Your Uncle by T.S. Lonsdale, 1875 (Pre 1900) **15.00**

Tomorrow by Cole Porter, 1938, Movie: Leave It To Me....................**6.00**

Tomorrow by Gordon Jenkins, 1946, Photo Gordon Jenkins................**3.00**

Tomorrow by Gus Kahn & John Alden, 1921 (Cover Artist, Frederick S. Manning) **15.00**

To-Morrow by Roy Turk & Vee Lawnhurst, 1933................................**5.00**

Tomorrow In My Dixie Home Again by Harry Robinson, 1922 (Dixie) ..**10.00**

Tomorrow Is Forever by Max Steiner & Charlie Tobias, 1945, Movie: Tomorrow Is Forever, Photo Claudette Colbert **5.00**

Tomorrow Is Ours by Gil Gilbert, 1946, Signed by Gil Gilbert (Signed)...**10.00**

To-Morrow Land by Brice & King, 1912, Photo Brice & King (Cover Artist, Pfeiffer)..**10.00**

To-Morrow Morning by Mitchell Parish, Eleanor Young & Harry D. Squires, 1922 ....**5.00**

Tonight by Stephen Sondheim & Leonard Bernstein, 1957, Movie: West Side Story **5.00**

Tonight Is Mine by Gus Kahn & Frank Harling, 1934, Movie: Stingaree, Photo Irene Dunne & Richard Dix **12.00**

Tonight We Love by Bobby Worth, Ray Austin & Freddy Martin, 1942 ....**5.00**

Tonight Will Live by Washington & Lara, 1938......................**5.00**

Tonight You Belong To Me by Billy Rose & Lee David, 1926, Photo Harry Rappi (Cover Artist, Barbelle & Deco)..................**5.00**

Tonight You Belong To Me by Billy Rose & Lee David, 1926, Photo Mary Lou (Cover Artist, Barbelle & Deco) **5.00**

Tonight You Belong To Me by Billy Rose & Lee David, 1926, Photo Bernice (Cover Artist, Barbelle & Deco)..................**5.00**

Tonight's My Last Night Single by Mahan, 1914 (Cover Artist, Pfeiffer)..**10.00**

Too Beautiful For Words by Columbo, Grossman & Stern, 1934, Movie: Wake Up And Dream, Photo Russ Columbo, June Knight & Wini Shaw **3.00**

Too Darn Hot by Cole Porter, 1948, Musical: Kiss Me Kate................**5.00**

Too Good To Be True by B.G. DeSylva, Lew Brown & Ray Henderson, 1928, Musical: Hold Everything (Cover Artist, Helen Van Doorn Morgan) **16.00**

Too Good To Be True by Eliot Daniel & Buddy Kaye, 1947, Movie: Fun And Fancy Free (Disney) **10.00**

Too Late by Sam Lewis & Victor Young, 1931......................**5.00**

Too Many Parties by Billy Rose, Mort Dixon & Ray Henderson, 1925, Photo Harry Richman (Deco) **5.00**

Too Many Tears by Al Dubin, 1932......................................**3.00**

Too Marvelous For Words by Johnny Mercer & Richard Whiting, 1937, Movie: Dark Passage, Photo Humphrey Bogart & Lauren Bacall ...**8.00**

Too Much Ginger by Daly (Cover Artist, Pfeiffer) **15.00**

Too Much Imagination by Johnny Burke & Harold Spina, 1935...........**5.00**

Too Much Jinger by Manuel Cortez, 1913 (Cover Artist, Kiss Art Co.)...**15.00**

Too Much Trouble by Leo Edwards, 1914................................**5.00**

Too Romantic by Johnny Burke & James V. Monaco, 1940, Movie: Road To Singapore, Photo Bing Crosby, Bob Hope & Dorothy Lamour ..**10.00**

Too Tired by Little, 1924..**5.00**

Too Young by Sylvia Dee & Sid Lippman, 1951, Photo Johnny Desmond **5.00**

Too Young by Sylvia Dee & Sid Lippman, 1951, Photo Nat King Cole..**5.00**

Too Young For The Blues by Biff Jones & Chuck Meyer, 1956...........**3.00**

Too-Ra-Loo-Ra-Loo-Rah, That's An Irish Lullaby by J.R. Shannon, 1918 (Irish) **12.00**

Toodle Oodle Oo by Blanche Merrill & M.K. Jerome, 1919 (Cover Artist, Barbelle & Deco)..**10.00**

Toodle-Oo by Carmen Lombardo & John Jacob Loeb, 1937, Photo Al Donahue (Cover Artist, HBK)..................................**3.00**

Toodle-Oo by Carmen Lombardo & John Jacob Loeb, 1937, Photo Guy Lombardo (Cover Artist, HBK)..................................**3.00**

Toodle-Oo by Catherine Chisholm Cushing & Rudolf Friml, 1918, Musical: Gloriana **10.00**

Toot-Toot, Tootsie by Gus Kahn, Ernie Erdman & Dan Russo, 1922, Movie: Bombo, Photo Al Jolson (Al Jolson) **15.00**

Toot-Toot, Tootsie by Gus Kahn, Ernie Erdman & Dan Russo, 1922, Movie: The Jolson Story, Photo Larry Parks & Evelyn Keyes (Al Jolson) **15.00**

Toot Your Horn, Kid, You're In A Fog by Jos. Mittenthal & Jos. M. Daly, 1909 (Cover Artist, Starmer & Transportation) **15.00**

Top Hat, White Tie And Tails by Irving Berlin, 1935, Movie: Top Hat, Photo Fred Astaire & Ginger Rogers (Irving Berlin)..................**15.00**

Top Of The Town by Harold Adamson & Jimmy McHugh, 1936, Movie: Top Of The Town **6.00**

Top Of The World by John Bettis & Richard Carpenter, 1972, Photo Karen & Richard Carpenter **3.00**

Topsy by R.A. Brown, 1901 (Black, Black Face) **26.00**

Topsy Turvy by Louise V. Gustin, 1899 (Cover Artist, Edgar Keller & Pre 1900)..**10.00**

Torch Song, The by Mort Dixon, Joe Young & Harry Warren, 1931, Musical: The Laugh Parade, Photo Ed Wynn (Cover Artist, Gorj)........**10.00**

Toreador Song by Bizet, 1910 (Cover Artist, Pfeiffer) **10.00**

Toreador Song by Jerry Castillo & Bizet, 1935, Photo George Olsen ...**3.00**

Toreador, The by Caryll, 1901..**5.00**

Touch Of A Woman's Hand, The by Otto Harbach & Louis A. Hirsch, Musical: Going Up, Boston Sunday Advertiser, Sunday Supplement, November 10, 1918 ....**10.00**

Touch Of Your Hand, The by Otto Harbach & Jerome Kern, 1933, Movie: Roberta (Deco) **12.00**

Touch Of Your Lips, The by Ray Noble, 1936, Photo Mindy Carson (Cover Artist, Barbelle) **3.00**

Tour De Noce by Soria, 1903 (Transportation) **15.00**

Tourist Trade, The by Sammy Cahn & Jule Styne, 1948, Movie: Romance On The High Seas, Photo Jack Carson, Janice Paige, Don DeFore & Doris Day..**5.00**

Toward The Sunrise by Frank L. Stanton & Oley Speaks, 1916, Dedicated To Miss Cecile Battiar (Dedication)..................................**10.00**

Town Talk by Elmer Olson, 1918, Photo Hirschel Hendler (Rag).......**10.00**

Town Where I Was Born by Paul Dresser, 1905..........................**10.00**

Toy Trumpet, The, 1944, Movie: Rebecca Of Sunnybrook Farm, Photo Shirley Temple **10.00**

Toyland by Glen MacDonough & Victor Herbert, 1903, Movie: Babes In Toyland (Victor Herbert)..**15.00**

Toymaker's Dream by Ernie Golden, 1928..................................**10.00**

Toys In The Attic by Duning, Sherman & Weiss, 1963, Movie: Toys In The Attic, Photo Yvette Mimieux & Dean Martin..................**6.00**

Tra-La-La-La by Irving Berlin, 1913 (Cover Artist, Pfeiffer & Irving Berlin)..**15.00**

Trade Winds by Cliff Friend & Charlie Tobias, 1940, Photo Ken Wattkins (Cover Artist, Im-Ho) **3.00**

Trading Smiles by Don Ramsay, 1907, Photo Freeman & Freeman (Cover Artist, Starmer) **10.00**

Trail Of Dreams by Raymond Klages & Einar Swan, 1926, Photo Vincent Lopez **5.00**

Trail Of The Lonesome Pine, The by Ballard MacDonald & Harry Carrol, 1913, Photo Gilson & Falon (Cover Artist, Starmer)..................**10.00**

Trail Of The Lonesome Pine, The by Ballard MacDonald & Harry Carroll, 1913, Photo Dorothy Brenner (Cover Artist, Starmer) **10.00**

Trail That Leads To You, The by Jack Caddigan & James A. Brennan, 1917 (Cover Artist, Starmer)......................................**5.00**

Trail To Home Sweet Home, The by Harold B. Freeman, 1918..........**12.00**

Trail To Long Ago, The by Wm. T. White, C.W. Erickson, E. Clinton Keithley & F. Henri Klickmann, 1923 ....**5.00**

Trail To Sunset Valley, The by L. Wolfe Gilbert & Lewis F. Muir, 1916...**5.00**

Trailer Song, Roamin In A Home On Wheels, The by Fred E. Ahlert & Joe Young, 1936 (Transportation)..................................**12.00**

Train D'enfer Galop by Ludovic (Transportation) **35.00**

Train In The Night by MacGregor, 1931 (Transportation)..................**10.00**

Tramp, Tramp, Tramp by G.F. Root, 1864 (Pre 1900)........................**50.00**

Tramps At Sea by Herbert Stothart, Jimmy McHugh & Dorothy Fields, 1932 (Transportation)..**10.00**

Trans Continental by Rice, 1902 (Transportation) **25.00**

Traumerei by R. Schumann, 1902 (Cover Artist, John Frew) **10.00**

Travelin' Back To Alabam' by James Bland (Pre 1900 & Black, Black Face) **25.00**

Travelin' Man by Jerry Fuller, 1961......................................**5.00**

Travelling Blues by Russell & Bergman, 1924 (Blues & Transportation)..**16.00**

Tree In The Meadow, A by Billy Reid, 1947, Photo Sammy Kaye (Cover Artist, Nick)..**3.00**

Trees by Joyce Kilmer & Oscar Rasbach, 1922, Dedicated To Mrs. L.L. Krebs (Dedication) **3.00**

Trembling Dew Drops by C.D. Blake, 1911 (Cover Artist, E.S. Fisher) ..**10.00**

Tremolo Trot, The by C. Luckyth Roberts, 1914 ....**10.00**

Trench! Trench! Trench! Our Boys Are Trenching by Wilson Dillen & May Hill, 1918 (Cover Artist, Natwick & WWI).................**50.00**

Trench Trot, The by Lieut. Jack Frost & F. Henri Klickmann, 1918 (March & Military Personnel) **22.00**

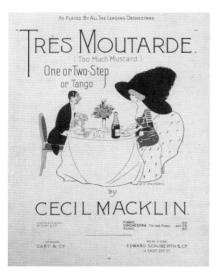

Tres Moutarde by Cecil Macklin, 1911 (Cover Artist, W.K. Haselden)..10.00

Tri State March by Harry J. Lincoln, 1906 (March)...........**15.00**

Trilby Rag by Carey Morgan, 1915 (Rag)..........................**10.00**

Trinity Chimes by Harry J. Lincoln, 1911 (Cover Artist, Dittmar)....**10.00**

Trip To Niagara, A by Wm. J. Cornish, 1908 (March) **10.00**

Trip To Niagara Falls, A by Clifford V. Baker, 1914 (Cover Artist, Starmer & March)..**10.00**

Trip To The North Pole, The by J.S. Zamecnik, 1909...........**6.00**

Tripoli by Paul Cunningham, Al Dubin & Irving Weill, 1920.............**6.00**

Tripping Thro' The Meadows by G.D. Wilson, 1871 (Pre 1900) **10.00**

Tripping Thru The Daisies by W.F. Sudds, 1905 ....**10.00**

Triumphal Post March by E.C. Cary, 1894 (Pre 1900 & March).........**10.00**

Triumphant America by F. H. Losey, 1907 (March)...........**15.00**

Triumphant Banner March, The by E.T. Paull, 1909 (Cover Artist, E.T. Paull & March) **35.00**

Trolley Song, The by Hugh Martin & Ralph Blane, 1944, Movie: Meet Me In St. Louis, Photo Judy Garland **20.00**

Tropical South Sea Isle by Wm. Friedlander, 1922..............**10.00**

Tropical Vamps by Howard Johnson & Carlo Sanderson, 1921, Musical: Tangerine..**5.00**

Trot Me, Billy Boy by Norton, 1914 (Cover Artist, Pfeiffer)..............**12.00**

Trouble With Women, The by Ogden Nash & Kurt Weill, 1943, Movie: One Touch Of Venus..**4.00**

Troublesome Moon by Wm. Tracey & W. Raymond Walker, 1912 (Cover Artist, Pfeiffer)...**10.00**

Truckin by Ted Koehler & Rube Bloom, 1935, Musical: Cotton Club Parade (Cover Artist, Frederick S. Manning).................**15.00**

True Blue Lou by Sam Coslow, Richard A. Whiting & Leo Robin, 1929, Movie: The Dance Of Life **10.00**

True Blue Sam by Benny Davis & James F. Hanley, 1922...............**10.00**

True Born Soldier Man, A by Irving Berlin, 1912 (Cover Artist, Pfeiffer & Irving Berlin)...**15.00**

True by Walter G. Samuels & Leonard Whitcup, 1934, Photo Ruth Etting (Cover Artist, Leff)..**5.00**

True Confession by Sam Coslow & Fred Hollander, 1937, Movie: True Confession, Photo Carole Lombard......................**10.00**

True Love by Cole Porter, 1956, Movie: High Society, Photo Bing Crosby, Grace Kelly & Frank Sinatra......................................**8.00**

True Love Never Runs Smooth by Oscar Loraine, 1918 (Cover Artist, Rose Symbol) **15.00**

Truest Love, The by Lem Trombley, 1912..............................**5.00**

Truly by Benny Davis & Vincent Rose, 1922.........................**5.00**

Truly by Walter Hirsch & Frank Magine, 1930 ....**5.00**

Truly I Do by Lester M. Palmer & Jess Williams, 1925 ....**6.00**

Truly Scrumptious by Sherman & Sherman, 1968, Movie: Chitty Chitty Bang Bang, Photo Dick Van Dyke & Sally Ann Howes...............**12.00**

Trumpet Call, The by P.J. O'Reilly & Wilfrid Sanderson, 1917, Photo John McCormack...**10.00**

Trumpeter March by Jacob Henry Ellis, 1924 (March)........**10.00**

Trumpeter, The by J. Francis Barron & J. Airlie Dix, 1904, Sung by John McCormack **5.00**

Trumpeter, The by James A. Battis, 1895 (Pre 1900 & March)...........**10.00**

Trust In Me by Ned Wever, Jean Schwartz & Milton Ager, 1934, Photo Dinah Shore (Cover Artist, Im-Ho)...................................**3.00**

Try A Little Tenderness by Harry Woods, Jimmy Campbell & Reg Connelly, 1932, Photo Pickens Sisters....................................**4.00**

Try A Little Tenderness by Harry Woods, Jimmy Campbell & Reg Connelly, 1932, Photo Frank Sinatra..**6.00**

Try Her Out At Dances by Frank Mandel, Oscar Hammerstein II & Sigmund Romberg, 1928, Musical: The New Moon...........**5.00**

Try To Forget by Otto Harbach & Jerome Kern, 1931, Musical: The Cat And The Fiddle..**5.00**

Try To Remember by Harvey Smidt & Tom Jones, 1960, Photo Ed Ames...**2.00**

Try To See It My Way by Dixon & Wrubel, 1934 ....**3.00**

Trying by Billy Vaughn, 1952, Photo Hill Toppers **3.00**

Tryst, The by Charles Wakefield Cadman, 1904....................**5.00**

Tsin Tsin Ta Tao by D. Onivas, 1914....................................**5.00**

Tu M'as Dit! by Briollet & A. Foucher & Benoist Treynet, 1913 (Cover Artist, Clerice Freres) **10.00**

Tu-Li-Tulip-Time by Maria Grever & Jack Lawrence, 1938................**4.00**

Tuck Me To Sleep In My Old 'Tucky Home by Joe Young, Sam Lewis & Geo. W. Meyer, 1921 ....**5.00**

Tulip Time by Gene Buck & Dave Stamper, 1919..................**5.00**

Tulips And Heather by Milton Carson, 1950, Photo Perry Como..........**3.00**

Tulips by Walter E. Miles, 1916 (Cover Artist, Jaroushek) **10.00**

Tumble In by Harold Atteridge & Jean Schwartz, 1919, Musical: Passing Show Of 1919 (Cover Artist, RS) **10.00**

Tumbledown Dreams by William Helmore & Henry E. Pether, 1926...**5.00**

Tumbling Tumbleweeds by Bob Nolan, 1934, Photo Billy Vaughn......**4.00**

Turkey And The Turk by Francis Bryant, 1901 ....**10.00**

Turkey Trot by Joseph M. Daly, 1912 (Cover Artist, Pfeiffer)...........**10.00**

Turkish Towel Rag by Thomas S. Allen, 1912 (Rag) **10.00**

Turkish Trophies by Sarah B. Egan, 1907 (Rag)..................**10.00**

Turn Back The Universe And Give Me Yesterday by J. Keirn Brennan & Ernest R. Ball, 1916..**10.00**

Turn On The Heat by B.G. DeSylva, Lew Brown & Ray Henderson, 1929, Movie: Sunny Side Up, Photo Janet Gaynor....................**15.00**

Turn On The Old Music Box by Leigh Harline & Ned Washington, 1940, Movie: Pinocchio (Disney)......................................**10.00**

Turn On The Popular Moon by Wm. B. Friedlander & Con Conrad, 1923 (Cover Artist, Politzer......................................**10.00**

Turn Verein Cadets by Edward Harrigan & David Braham, 1883 (Pre 1900)......................................**15.00**

Turntable Song, The by Robin & Green, 1947, Movie: Something In The Mind, Photo Deanna Durbin......................................**8.00**

Turtle Dove Polka by Behr, 1900 ....**6.00**

'Twas Always Mary by Caddigan & Story, 1915 (Cover Artist, Pfeiffer)......................................**10.00**

'Twas Good by Ford, 1917 (Cover Artist, Pfeiffer) **10.00**

'Twas Only An Irishman's Dream by John J. O'Brien, Al Dubin & Rennie Cormack, 1916, Musical: Broadway & Buttermilk, Photo Blanche Ring (Cover Artist, Starmer & Irish)......................................**15.00**

'Twas You by Edward G. Simon & Charles Gilbert Spross, 1904.......**10.00**

Twelfth Regiment March, The by Harry J. Lincoln, 1908 (March) **15.00**

Twelfth Street Rag by Andy Razaf & Euday L. Bowman, 1944, Photo Pee Wee Hunt (Cover Artist, Sig Ch. & Rag)......................................**4.00**

20th Century Rag, The by Grant Clarke, Edgar Leslie & Maurice Abrahams, 1914, Photo Lillie Beeson (Cover Artist, Pfeiffer & Rag)...**15.00**

Twentieth Century Woman by Alfred W. Norris, 1896 (Pre 1900 & March) **15.00**

Twenty Four Hours A Day by Arthur Swanstrom & James F. Hanley, 1935, Movie: Sweet Surrender (Deco)......................................**10.00**

Twenty Million People by Sam Coslow & Arthur Johnston, 1932, Movie: Hello, Everybody!, Photo Kate Smith......................................**15.00**

Twenty Seventh Division by Mizer, 1919 (WWI)......................................**15.00**

Twenty-Four Hours Of Sunshine by Peter DeRose & Carl Sigman, 1949..**3.00**

Twiggy Voo by Norton & Le Brunn, 1893 (Pre 1900)......................................**15.00**

Twilight Bay by Geo Little & Jack Stanley, 1914 (Cover Artist, DeTakacs)......................................**10.00**

Twilight Express, The by C.M. Denison & Fred W. Hager, 1912 (Transportation......................................**10.00**

Twilight I Wait For You by C.P. McDonald & Evans Lloyd, 1908.....**10.00**

Twilight Melodies by Don Bernard, Nat Natoli & Vic Young, 1930.....**3.00**

Twilight On The Trail by Sidney D. Mitchell & Louis Alter, 1936, Movie: Trail Of The Lonesome Pine, Photo Sylvia Sidney & Fred MacMurray **10.00**

Twilight Serenade by Chas. H. Maskell, 1926 ....**5.00**

Twilight Shadows by F.W. Vandersloot, 1916......................................**6.00**

Twilight Shadows by Jerome Heller, 1910......................................**5.00**

Twilight Song by Lawrence & Drutman, 1946, Movie: Bachelor's Daughter, Photo Jane Wyatt, Gail Russell, Claire Trevor, Adolphe Menjou & Ann Dvorak **8.00**

Twilight The Stars And You by Nacio Herb Brown, 1925 ....**5.00**

Twilight Time by Buck Ram, Morty Nevins, Al Nevins & Artie Dunn, 1944 ....**2.00**

Twinkle In Your Eye, A by Lorenz Hart & Richard Rodgers, 1938, Movie: I Married An Angel......................................**5.00**

Twinkle In Your Eye, The by Neville Fleeson & Albert Von Tilzer, 1922, Movie: The Gingham Girl......................................**5.00**

Twinkle, Twinkle Little Star, Or Meet Me At The Bar by Fred Macevoy, 1879 (Pre 1900) **75.00**

Twinkles by Vandersloot, 1916 (Cover Artist, Pfeiffer) **10.00**

Twinkling Star by Paul Lincke & Ballard Macdonald, 1923 (Cover Artist, Politzer) **5.00**

Twist, The by Hank Ballard, 1959......................................**4.00**

'Twixt Love And Duty by Williams & Dryden, 1892 (Pre 1900)........**12.00**

Two Apples by Joan Brooks & Ernest R. Ball, 1909 ....**5.00**

Two Blue Eyes by Edward Madden & Theodore F. Morse, 1907 ....**5.00**

Two Bouquets by Jimmy Kennedy & Michael Carr, 1938 ....**6.00**

Two Boys by B.G. DeSylva, Lew Brown & Ray Henderson, 1928, Musical: Three Cheers **5.00**

Two Cent Stamp, Brought Me Back A Million Dollar Love, A by Ted White, Manny Kurtz & Milton Ager, 1935 ....**5.00**

Two Cigarettes In The Dark by Paul Francis Webster & Lew Pollack, 1934, Movie: Kill That Story, Photo Gloria Grafton (Cover Artist, Leff) ...**8.00**

Two Dirty Little Hands by Will D. Cobb & Gus Edwards, 1906.........**10.00**

Two Dreams Met by Harry Warren, 1939, Movie: Down Argentine Way, Photo Betty Grable & Don Ameche **5.00**

Two Eyes I Idolize by Eddie Dustin & M. Quivey, 1907, Photo Grace Van Studdiford (Cover Artist, W.M. Young) **5.00**

Two For Tonight by Mack Gordon & Harry Revel, 1935, Movie: Two For Tonight......................................**5.00**

Two Hearts by Tom Kendall, 1946 ....**2.00**

Two Hearts Are Better Than One by Johnny Mercer & Jerome Kern, 1946 Movie: Centennial Summer, Photo Jeanne Crain, Cornel Wilde, Linda Darnell, Wm. Eythe **5.00**

Two Hearts In ¾ Time by Alfred Gruenwald, Walter Reisch, Fritz Rotter & Robert Stolz, 1930......................................**5.00**

Two Hearts That Pass In The Night by Ernesto Lecuona, 1941............**4.00**

Two Heavens by Ted Grouya & Don George, 1944 ....**2.00**

Two In Love by Meredith Wilson, 1941 ....**3.00**

Two Lips by Billy Rose & Harry Warren, 1928......................................**3.00**

Two Lips Are Roses by Alfred Bryan & Carlo & Sanders, 1923..........**5.00**

Two Lips Are Waiting In Tulip Time by Harold B. Freeman & George L. Cobb, 1920 ....**6.00**

Two Little Baby Shoes by Edward Madden & Theodore F. Morse, 1908......................................**10.00**

Two Little Candles On One Little Cake by Charlie Tobias, Charles Newman & Sam H. Stept, 1935 ....**3.00**

Two Little Eyes Are Watching For A Daddy Far Away by Weasoner, 1918 (Cover Artist, Pfeiffer & WWI) **20.00**

Two Little Girls In Blue by Chas. Graham, 1893, Photo Howard Powers (Pre 1900) **10.00**

Two Little Love Bees by Reinhardt & Smith, 1910 ....**5.00**

Two Little Rugged Urchins by Frank Howard, 1885 (Pre 1900) **15.00**

Two Little Sailor Boys by Edward Madden, 1906 (Transportation)....**15.00**

Two Little Wooden Shoes by Jack Stanley & James Hanley, 1922, Musical: Spice Of 1922 ....**10.00**

Two Lost Souls by Richard Adler & Jerry Ross, 1955, Musical: Damn Yankees **4.00**

Two Loves by George Koger, H. Varna & Vincent Scotto, 1931 ....**4.00**

Two Loves Have I by J.P. Murray, Barry Trivers & Vincent Scotto, 1930, Photo Perry Como **5.00**

Two Silhouettes by Charles Wolcott & Ray Gilbert, 1946, Movie: Make Mine Music (Disney)......................................**12.00**

Two Sleepy People by Frank Loesser & Hoagy Carmichael, 1938, Movie: Thanks For The Memory, Photo Bob Hope & Shirley Ross..........**12.00**

Two Sweethearts Of Mine by Moran & Helf, 1893 (Pre 1900) **10.00**

Two Tickets To Georgia by Charles Tobias & J. Fred Coots, 1933.......**5.00**

Two Together by Gus Kahn & Arthur Johnston, 1935......................................**5.00**

Two Ton Tessie by Roy Turk & Lou Handman, 1926......................................**2.00**

Two Weeks' Notice by Krompart & Seaman, 1929 (Cover Artist, Pfeiffer) **10.00**

Two Weeks With Pay by Joan Whitney & Alex Kramer, 1947............**3.00**

Two-Faced Clock by Ruth Beifield & Harold Saxe, 1952, Photo Rex Allen **3.00**

Ty-Tee, Tahiti by Leo Wood & Irving Bibo, 1921, Photo Gilda Gray (Deco) **5.00**

Tzena Tzena Tzena by Spencer Ross & Gordon Jenkins, 1950, Photo Mitch Miller......................................**3.00**

Tzigani Dances by Carrie Jacobs Bond, 1897 (Pre 1900) **15.00**

U.S.A. And You, The by Leo Robin & Ralph Rainger, 1938, Movie: Give Me A Sailor, Photo Martha Raye, Bob Hope, Betty Grable & Jack Whiting (Patriotic)..**15.00**

U.S.A. March by Al W. Brown, 1905 (Cover Artist, Heisley, March & Patriotic)..**20.00**

U.S.A. March by Kate Baldwin, Arranged by Harry J. Lincoln, 1916, Dedicated To Our Army And Navy (WWI, March & Dedication) **25.00**

U.S. Black Marines by Edward Harrigan & David Braham, 1885 (Pre 1900, Patriotic & Black, Black Face)...................................**25.00**

U.S. Field Artillery by John Philip Sousa, 1917 (John Philip Sousa, WWI & March)..**10.00**

U.S. Field Artillery March, The by Lieut. John Philip Sousa, 1917, Dedicated To: Officers And Men Of The 306th Field Artillery, National Army, U.S.A. (John Philip Sousa, March, WWI, Military Personnel & Dedication)....**28.00**

Ugly Duckling, The by Frank Loesser, 1951, Movie: Hans Christian Anderson, Photo Danny Kaye **8.00**

Ukelele Lady by Gus Kahn, Raymond Egan & Richard Whiting, 1925 **5.00**

Ukulele Moon by Benny Davis & Con Conrad, 1950 ....**3.00**

Um, Um, Da Da by Duncan Sisters, Book By Catherine C. Cushing, Suggested by Uncle Tom's Cabin by Harriet Beecher Stowe, 1923, Musical: Topsy & Eva, Photo Duncan Sisters (Cover Artist, P.M. Griffith & Black, Black Face)..**15.00**

Umbrella Man, The by James Cavanaugh, Larry Stock & Vincent Rose, 1938, Photo Kay Kyser (Cover Artist, Im-Ho) **3.00**

Umbriago by Caesar & Durante, 1944, Photo Jimmie Durante & Bobby Hookey..**3.00**

Ump-Da-De-Ump-Da-De-Aye by Nathan & Leopols, 1915................**12.00**

Un Baiser D'Amour by Geo. Lowell Tracy, 1913...............................**5.00**

Unchained Melody by Hy Zaret & Alex North, 1955 ....**3.00**

Uncle Amos by E.S. Ufford, 1897 (Pre 1900)....................................**20.00**

Uncle Jasper's Jubilee by E. T. Paull, 1898 (Cover Artist, E.T. Paull & Pre 1900)..**35.00**

Uncle Josh's Huskin Dance by E.T. Paull, 1898 (Cover Artist, E.T. Paull & Pre 1900) **35.00**

Uncle Ned by Stephen Foster, 1845 (Stephen Foster & Pre 1900) **50.00**

Uncle Remus Said by Eliot Daniel, Hy Heath & Johnny Lange, 1946, Movie: Song Of The South (Disney)...**10.00**

Uncle Sam, Hold Your Flag Up High (Cover Artist, Pfeiffer & Patriotic) ..**15.00**

Uncle Sam Is Calling Me (Cover Artist, Pfeiffer & Patriotic) **15.00**

Uncle Sam's Boys March by Grady, 1913 (Cover Artist, Pfeiffer & March) **15.00**

Uncle Sam's Lullaby by Lew Brown, Charlie Tobias & Sam H. Stept, 1939, Musical: Yokel Boy..**6.00**

Uncle Sam's Ships by Daisy M. Erd, 1917 (Cover Artist, E.S. Fisher, WWI & Transportation) **35.00**

Uncle Sammy by Abe Holzmann, 1904 (Patriotic) **10.00**

Uncle Sammy Take Care Of My Girl by Betty Morgan & Jimmy Morgan, 1918 (WWI)...**10.00**

Uncle Sammy's Army by H.M. Dolph, 1918 (WWI)..........................**10.00**

Under Any Old Flag At All by George M. Cohan, 1907 (George M. Cohan) **15.00**

Under Love's Moon by Duncan Sisters, Book by Catherine C. Cushing, Suggested by Uncle Tom's Cabin, by Harriet Beecher Stowe, 1923, Musical: Topsy & Eva, Photo Duncan Sisters (Cover Artist, P.M. Griffith & Black, Black Face) **15.00**

Under One Flag by Jefford, 1916 (WWI)...**15.00**

Under Paris Skies by Kim Gannon & Hubert Giraud, 1941, Photo Georgia Gibbs..**4.00**

Under Southern Skies by Al Trahern & Lee Orean Smith, 1902, Musical: Under Southern Skies, Photo Lottie Blair Parker......................**15.00**

Under Southern Skies by Goodwin & Brayha, 1915 (Cover Artist, Pfeiffer) **10.00**

Under The American Eagle by Jacob Henry Ellis, 1901 (Patriotic & March) **20.00**

Under The Anheuser Bush by Andrew B. Sterling & Harry Von Tilzer, 1903 ....**10.00**

Under The Bamboo Tree by Bob Cole & Billy Johnson, 1902 (Black Face, Black Face) **15.00**

Under The Banana Tree by Lamb & O'Connor, 1905 ....**5.00**

Under The Bridges Of Paris by Dorcas Cochran & Vincent Scotto, 1953 ..**3.00**

Under The Double Eagle by Richard Wagner, 1908 (Patriotic)..........**10.00**

Under The Greenwood Tree by William Shakespere & A. Buzzi-Peccia, 1917 ....**5.00**

Under The Mellow Arabian Moon by Nathan & Leopols, 1915...........**5.00**

Under The Moon by Ev. E. Lyn, Francis Wheeler & Ted Snyder, 1927, Photo Zoeller's Melodists...**5.00**

Under The Moon by Ev. E. Lyn, Francis Wheeler & Ted Snyder, 1927, Photo Major Edward Bowes & His Capital Family **8.00**

Under The Moon by Ev. E. Lyn, Francis Wheeler & Ted Snyder, 1927, Photo Batchelor Four (Cover Artist, Barbelle).............................**8.00**

Under The Rambling Roses by S.R. Henry, 1916 ....**5.00**

Under The Southern Moonlight by Allen, 1910 ....**5.00**

Under The Stars by Dailey, 1913..**6.00**

Under The Stars & Stripes by T. Roosevelt, 1930 (March & Patriotic).**5.00**

Under The Summer Moon by Ben Ritchie, 1911, Photo Ben Ritchie (Cover Artist, Pfeiffer) **10.00**

Under The Summer Moon by Leonard Marx, 1916 (Cover Artist, Pfeiffer) **10.00**

Under The Summertime Moon by Edward Madden & Albert Gumble, 1918 (Cover Artist, John Frew) **10.00**

Under The Swanee Moon by Howard, 1913 (Cover Artist, Pfeiffer)...**10.00**

Under The Tool-A-Wool-A-Tree by Freeman (Cover Artist, Pfeiffer)**10.00**

Under The Tropical Moon by C.P. McDonald & Percy Wenrich, 1907 (Transportation) **12.00**

Under The Yum Yum Tree by Andrew Sterling & Harry Von Tilzer, 1910 ....6.00

Under Western Skies by Casey, Weeks & Murtagh, 1920, Photo Monte Austin...**5.00**

Underneath A Big Umbrella by Robert B. Smith & Malvin M. Franklin, 1919 ....**5.00**

Underneath A Starlit Sky by Francis R. Wolfe, 1934 (Cover Artist, Fran Hayes)...**5.00**

Underneath Hawaiian Skies by Fred Rose & Ernie Erdman, 1921, Musical: Passing Show 1921 ....**12.00**

Underneath The Arches by Joseph McCarthy & Bud Flanagan, 1932, Photo Gordon MacRae **2.00**

Underneath The Arches by Joseph McCarthy & Bud Flanagan, 1932, Photo Sammy Kaye (Cover Artist, S.J.)...**3.00**

Underneath The Arches by Joseph McCarthy & Bud Flanagan, 1932, Photo Sherman Feller (Cover Artist, S.J.).....................................**3.00**

Underneath The Cotton Moon by Sam M. Lewis & George W. Meyer, 1913, Photo Gus Van & Joe Schenck, Respectfully Dedicated To Our Esteemed Friend Mr. Ben Linn (Cover Artist, Starmer, Dedication & Black, Black Face)..**15.00**

Underneath The Cotton Moon by Sam. M. Lewis & George W. Meyer, 1913, Photo Claude & Marion Cleveland, Respectfully Dedicated To Our Esteemed Friend, Mr. Ben Linn (Cover Artist, Starmer, Black & Dedication) 15.00

Underneath The Harlem Moon by Mack Gordon & Harry Revel, 1932 (Cover Artist, Leff & Black, Black Face) **10.00**

Underneath The Mellow Moon by Wendell W. Hall, 1922 ....**5.00**

Underneath The Monkey Moon by Drislane & Meyer, 1910 (Cover Artist, Pfeiffer)...**10.00**

Underneath The Russian Moon by James Kendis, Frank Samuels & Meyer Gusman, 1929 (Cover Artist, Rosfeld-Ress & Deco) **5.00**

Underneath The Southern Skies by Arthur E. Behim, Harry Ruby & M.K. Jerome, 1919...**5.00**

Underneath The Stars by Herbert Spencer, 1915, Photo Dolly Sisters ..**5.00**

Underneath The Tango Moon by Thomas J. Gray & Harry Carroll, 1913, Photo Lillian Lorraine (Cover Artist, Pfeiffer)...............................**10.00**

Underneath The Wishing Moon by Edmund Braham & Frank Choddy, 1917 (Cover Artist, L.A. Brunner) **10.00**

Une Belle Soiree by Louis H. Fisher, 1914, Photo Jessie Herriott & Bruce Cleveland **5.00**

United Musicians by Harry J. Lincoln, 1915 (Cover Artist, Pfeiffer & March) **15.00**

United Nations March by E.T. Paull (Cover Artist, E.T. Paull & March)..**35.00**

United We Stand by Herbert Rikles, Howard Dressner & Samuel Meade, 1941 (WWII & Patriotic)...**10.00**

Universal Fox Trot by Joe Rosey, 1915 ....**5.00**

Universal Glide by Stanford & Ward, 1915 (Cover Artist, Pfeiffer & WWI)...**15.00**

University Two Step by Anthony Lohman, 1896, Boston Herald Sunday Supplement (Cover Artist, Arthur G. Hoel & Pre 1900)...............**15.00**

Unknown Soldier Speaks, The by John McLaughlin, 1940 (Patriotic)..**10.00**

Unlucky In Love by Irving Berlin, 1924, Music Box Revue 1925 (Irving Berlin)...**10.00**

Unter Vereinten Kriegsflaggen by F. Wohlbier (Lithograph by Carl Rhule Leipzig & March) **10.00**

Until by Jack Fulton, Bob Crosby & Hunter Kahler, 1945, Photo Tommy Dorsey (Cover Artist, Barbelle)..**3.00**

Until by Wilfred Sanderson & Edward Teschemacher, 1910...............**5.00**

Until God's Day by Frank L. Stanton & Carrie Jacobs Bond, 1902, Dedicated To Mr. Charles W. Clark (Dedication) **15.00**

Until My Luck Comes Rolling Along by George M. Cohan (George M. Cohan)..**15.00**

Until Today by Benny Davis, J. Fred Coots & Oscar Levant, 1936.......**3.00**

Until You Get Somebody Else by Gus Kahn & Walter Donaldson, 1928, Musical: Ziegfeld Production of Whoopee, Photo Eddie Cantor (Cover Artist, Nickel & Eddie Cantor)...**20.00**

Until You Let Go by Beckett, Zippel & Hamlisch, 1911, Movie: Frankie & Johnny, Photo Al Pacino & Michelle Pfeiffer.............................**3.00**

Up And Down The Eight Mile Road by Walter Donaldson, 1926 (Transportation) **5.00**

Up At Dudley's Grove by Edward Harrigan & David Braham, 1880 (Pre 1900)...**15.00**

Up Dar In De Sky by Davis, 1892 (Pre 1900 & Black, Black Face)....**25.00**

Up In A Balloon by H.B. Farnie, 1869 (Pre 1900 & Transportation) ..**25.00**

Up In Mabel's Room by Alex Gerber & Abner Silver, 1909.................**5.00**

Up In My Flying Machine by Saxby, 1910 (Transportation)...............**25.00**

Up In The Air by Daggett, 1910 (Transportation)................................**25.00**

Up In The Cocoanut Tree by E. Madden & T.F. Morse, 1903..............**1.00**

Up In Your Old Biplane by Arnold, 1912 (Transportation).................**25.00**

Up Went O'Connor On His Wedding Day by Bodine & Maywood, 1897 (Pre 1900 & Transportation)...**30.00**

Upon The Trolley Line by Gus Edwards, 1905 (Transportation).........**20.00**

Upper Ten And Lower Five by Jim Thornton, 1888 (Pre 1900) **15.00**

Upstairs & Down by Sam M. Lewis, Joe Young & Walter Donaldson, 1919, Movie: Upstairs & Down, Photo Olive Thomas (Cover Artist, Barbelle) **10.00**

Us On A Bus by Tot Seymour & Vee Lawnhurst, 1936, Movie: Summer Wives, Photo Smith & Dale & Helen Charleston (Transportation)..**10.00**

Used To You by Al Jolson, B.G. DeSylva, Lew Brown & Ray Henderson, 1929, Photo Al Jolson (Al Jolson)..**10.00**

V.V's Eyes by Klein, 1915 ....**10.00**

Vagabond King Waltz by Brian Hooker & Rudolph Friml, 1926, Musical: The Vagabond King, Photo Dennis King (Cover Artist, Starmer)..**10.00**

Vagabond Shoes by Sammy Gallop & David Saxon, 1949, Photo Vic Damone...**3.00**

Vaillance by Joseph Ascher **5.00**

Vale Of Dreams, The by Chas. E. Baer & Johann C. Schmid, 1910......**5.00**

Valencia by Lucien Boyer, Jacques Charles, American Version by Clifford Grey & Jose Padilla, 1925, Musical: The Great Temptations **15.00**

Valentine by Albert Willemetz & H. Christine, 1925, Photo Maurice Chevalier...**15.00**

Valentine Candy by Sherman & Sherman, 1966, Movie: The Happiest Millionaire, Photo Leslie Ann Warren **3.00**

Valley Of Roses by J. Messina, 1918 (Cover Artist, Starmer & Deco) .**5.00**

Valse Annette by Lionel Baxter, 1915 (Cover Artist, T.Ray) **10.00**

Valse Bleue by Alfred Margis, 1927 ....**3.00**

Valse Brune by George Krier, 1910 ....**5.00**

Valse Danseuse by Walter E. Miles, 1914, Respectfully Dedicated To Mrs. Sam Fox (Dedication) **10.00**

Valse Decembre by Walter Rolfe, 1914 (Cover Artist, Pfeiffer) **10.00**

Valse Elaine by Lionel Baxter, 1915 ....**5.00**

Valse Episode by Carl Wilhelm Kern, 1907...**5.00**

Valse Estelle by J. Goldston, 1915 (Cover Artist, Pfeiffer).................**10.00**
Valse Gloria by Henry Haaf (Lithograph, Knapp Co.).........................**6.00**

Valse June by Lionel Baxter, 1914 (Cover Artist, T.Ray)..............10.00
Valse Mauve by Will Wood, 1914 ....**6.00**
Valse Romance by Bower, 1914 (Cover Artist, Pfeiffer)....................**10.00**
Valse Rose by Lionel Baxter, 1919 ....**5.00**
Valse Septembre by Godin, 1909 ....**5.00**
Vamp, The by Byron Gay, 1918...**5.00**
Van-guard Of The King, The by M. Alton Bailey, 1897 (Pre 1900)....**10.00**
Vanity by I.J. Schanes, 1919, Respectfully Dedicated To Miss Lillian Lubman (Cover Artist, Starmer & Dedication) **10.00**
Vanity Fair by Stella Mayhew, 1907, Signed Photo Stella Mayhew, Dedicated to Mr. Geo. A. Kingsbury (Cover Artist, Starmer, Signed & Dedication) **10.00**
Varsity Drag, The by B.G. DeSylva, Lew Brown & Ray Henderson, 1927..**5.00**
Vas Villst Du Haben by Al Bryan & James V. Monaco, 1932, Photo Jack Denny (Cover Artist, Leff) **3.00**
Vaya Con Dios, May God Be With You by Larry Russell, Inez James & Buddy Pepper, 1953, Photo Les Paul & Mary Ford......................**5.00**
Velvet Moon by Edgar De Lange & J. Myrow, 1942, Photo Freddy Martin (Cover Artist, Holley)...**3.00**
Venetian Moon by Gus Kahn, Phil Goldberg & Frank Magini, 1919 (Cover Artist, Frederick S. Manning)......................................**15.00**
Venetian Moon by Kahn, Goldberg & Magini, 1919, Photo Gene Willie Howard (Cover Artist, Pfeiffer)...**10.00**
Venetian Rose Waltzes by Al Piantadosi, Jack Glogau & Joe McCarthy, 1915 (Cover Artist, Rose Symbol) **10.00**
Venetian Twilight by Carl Bonner, 1911..**5.00**
Venetian Waters by Daley, 1910 (Transportation) **10.00**
Venez Ma Belle by Jules Darien, 1916 (Cover Artist, Richardson).......**5.00**
Venezuela Dance by Wesley, 1900 (Cover Artist, Pfeiffer).................**15.00**
Venus by Ed Marshall, 1959, Photo Frankie Avalon **3.00**
Venus, My Shining Love by George M. Cohan (George M. Cohan)...**10.00**
Veronica by William Loraine, 1899 (Pre 1900) **10.00**
Very Good Advice by Bob Hilliard & Sammy Fain, 1951, Movie: Alice In Wonderland (Disney) **10.00**
Very Thought Of You, The by Ray Noble, 1934, Movie: The Very Thought Of You, Photo Dennis Morgan & Eleanor Parker **10.00**
Very Thought Of You, The by Ray Noble, 1934, Photo Fred Waring...**3.00**
Vesper Bells Are Ringing, Mother Dear, The by Robert F. Roden & J. Henry Ellis, 1920 (Cover Artist, RS) **5.00**

Vesper Chimes by Harry J. Lincoln, 1915 (Cover Artist, Pfeiffer)......**10.00**
Vesper Chimes by Ted. S. Barron, 1913, (Cover Artist, DeTakacs)....**10.00**
Vesuvius by Harry J. Lincoln (March) **10.00**
Veteran, The by Oliver E. Story, 1910 (March) **10.00**
Victors by Ebel, 1899 (Pre 1900) **10.00**
Victory by Colangalo, 1918 (Cover Artist, Pfeiffer & WWI)..............**15.00**
Victory by R.A. Wilson Bard & M.K. Jerome, 1918 (WWI)..............**10.00**

Vict'ry Polka by Samuel Cahn & Jule Styne, 1943 (WWII).............5.00
Vieni, Vieni by George Koger, H. Varna & Rudy Valley, 1934, Photo Rudy Vallee (Cover Artist, Merman)...**10.00**
Village Barn Dance, The by Mollie King, 1909.................................**10.00**
Village Belles by Edwin F. Kendall, 1908 (Cover Artist, John Shaw Jr.)..**10.00**
Violet From Mother's Grave, A by Will H. Fox, 1881 (Pre 1900) **15.00**
Violet I Picked From My Mother's Grave, A by Joseph P. Skelly, 1891 (Pre 1900) **15.00**
Violet's Message, The by May Lackey Campbell & Sam'l Speck, 1930..**5.00**
Violets And Roses by Veatrice Crocker, 1921 ....**5.00**
Violets by Julian Fane & Ellen Wright, 1900.....................................**10.00**
Violette by Dolly Jardon & J.B. Mullen, 1905 (March)......................**10.00**
Virgin's Slumber Song, The by Max Reger, 1912 ....**2.00**
Virginia by Chas. Keyes, 1927 ....**5.00**
Virginia From Virginia by David S. Jacobs & Chas. Roy Cox, 1917 (Cover Artist, Pfeiffer) **10.00**
Virginia Lee by Jeff Branen & Arthur Lange, 1915 (Cover Artist, Pfeiffer) **10.00**
Virginia Lullaby by Hyman Cheiffetz, 1924 ....**3.00**
Vision Of Fuji-San, The by Albert W. Ketelby, 1931 (Cover Artist, F. Aveline) **5.00**
Vision Waltz by Halfman, 1915 (Cover Artist, Pfeiffer)....................**10.00**
Visions D'Amour by Kendall, 1912 (Cover Artist, Pfeiffer) **10.00**
Visit To Panama by Cole Porter, 1942, Movie: Panama Hattie **5.00**
Vitagraph Girl, The by J.A. Leggett & Henry Frantzen, 1909, Movie: The Vitagraph Girl, Photo Florence Turner....................................**10.00**
Vo-Do-De-O by Jack Yellen & Milton Ager, 1927 ....**5.00**
Voice From Mummyland by Johnny S. Black, 1921 ....**5.00**
Voice In My Heart, The by George M. Cohan (George M. Cohan).....**10.00**
Voice Of My Granny Machree, The by Traynor & Earl, 1921 (Irish).**10.00**
Voice Of The Sword, The by Richard Buck & Adam Geibel, 1903 ....**10.00**
Voice Of The Violet, The by Chauncey Olcott, 1902, Musical: Old Limrick Town (Irish)...**15.00**
Volare by Mitchell Parish & Domenico Modugno, 1958, Photo McGuire Sisters...**3.00**

Volga Boat Song by Calvin Grooms, 1926 ....**4.00**

Volplane Waltzes by Ernie Burnett, 1917 (Transportation) **10.00**

Volunteer Organist by William B. Gray, 1893 (Pre 1900) **10.00**

Volunteers by Frederick S. Hall, 1917 ....**10.00**

Voodoo Man, The by Bert Williams & George Walker **10.00**

Vote For Mister Rhythm by Leo Robin & Ralph Rainger, 1936, Movie: The Big Broadcast Of 1937 ....**10.00**

Votes For Women by Manuel Klein, 1913, Musical: Schuberts Production, America, 1913-1914 (March) **25.00**

Voyage To The Bottom Of The Sea by Faith, 1961, Movie: Voyage To The Bottom Of The Sea, Photo Walter Pidgeon, Joan Fontaine, Frankie Avalon & Peter Lorre **8.00**

Wabash Blues by Dave Ringle & Fred Meinken, 1921, Photo Rudy Vallee **5.00**

Wabash Cannon Ball by Wm. Kindt, 1939, Photo Rex Allen (Cover Artist, NPS) **5.00**

Wabash Moon by Dave Dreyer, Morton Downey & Billy McKenney, 1931, Signed Photo Morton Downey (Signed) **10.00**

Waco by Blair & Haskell, 1966, Movie: Waco, Photo Jane Russell & Howard Keel **8.00**

Wagner Couldn't Write A Ragtime Song by Jerome, 1913 (Cover Artist, Pfeiffer & Rag) **15.00**

Wagon Wheels by Billy Hill & Peter DeRose, From The New Ziegfeld Follies, 1934, Photo Everett Marshall (Cover Artist, Wohlman) ...**10.00**

Wait And See by Harry Warren & Johnny Mercer, 1946, Movie: The Harvey Girls, Photo Judy Garland **10.00**

Wait And See, You'll Want Me Back by Chas. R. McCarron & Carey Morgan, 1919, Photo Mary MacLaren, Jack Mulhall & Joe S. Sherman **10.00**

Wait by Horowitz & Bowers, 1905 ....**10.00**

Wait For A Warm, Sunny Day by Walter Scanlan, 1923 ....**10.00**

Wait For Me by Robert B. Smith, Malvin M. Franklin & Robert Hood Bowers, 1919, Musical: A Lonely Romeo **10.00**

Wait For Me Mary by Charlie Tobias, Nat Simon & Harry Tobias, 1942 (Cover Artist, Harris) **6.00**

Wait For The Happy Ending by Jack Yellen, Milton Ager & Henry Sullivan, 1929, Musical: Murray Anderson's Almanac **10.00**

Wait For Your Honey Boy by C. Arthur Pfeiffer, 1917 (Cover Artist, Pfeiffer & WWI) **15.00**

Wait Till My Ship Comes In by James Brockman, Will Oakland & Joseph Moss, 1926 ....**5.00**

Wait Till She Sees You In Your Uniform by Edgar Leslie & John Jacob Loeb, 1940 (Patriotic & WWII) **10.00**

Wait Till The Clouds Roll by by J.T. Wood & H.J. Fulmer, 1881 (Pre 1900) **10.00**

Wait Till The Sun Shines, Nellie by Andrew B. Sterling & Harry Von Tilzer, 1905 ....**5.00**

Wait Till The Sun Shines, Nellie by Harry Von Tilzer & Andrew B. Sterling, 1942, Movie: Birth Of The Blues, Photo Bing Crosby, Mary Martin & Brian Donlevy **10.00**

Wait Till The Tide Comes In by Gussie L. Davis, 1887 (Pre 1900) **10.00**

Wait Till Tomorrow by Lloyd & DePaul, 1967, Movie: The Ballad Of Josie, Photo Doris Day & Peter Graves **5.00**

Wait Till You Get Them Up In The Air Boys by Lew Brown & Albert Von Tilzer, 1919 (Cover Artist, E.E. Walton, Transportation) **10.00**

Wait Till You See Her by Lorenz Hart & Richard Rodgers, 1942, Movie: All's Fair **5.00**

Wait Until Dark by Livingston, Evans & Mancini, 1967, Movie: Wait Until Dark, Photo Audrey Hepburn **10.00**

Wait Until We're Married by Geo. F. Meyer, 1913 ....**5.00**

Wait Until Your Daddy Comes Home by Irving Berlin, 1912 (Cover Artist, Pfeiffer & Irving Berlin) **16.00**

Wait'll It's Moonlight by Frank Bannister & Macio Pinkard, 1925 ....**6.00**

Waitin' At The Gate For Katy by Richard A. Whiting & Gus Kahn, 1934, Movie: Bottoms Up, Photo Spencer Tracy, John Boles & Pat Paterson **10.00**

Waitin' For My Dearie by Alan Jay Lerner & Frederick J. Loewe, 1947, Movie: Brigadoon **5.00**

Waitin' For The Moon by Happy O'Neil & Oliver E. Story, 1910 (Black, Black Face) **12.00**

Waitin' For The Train To Come In by Sunny Skylar & Martin Block, 1945, Photo Perry Como & Jo Stafford **5.00**

Waitin' For The Train To Come In by Sunny Skylar & Martin Block, 1945, Photo Johnnie Johnson & Jo Stafford **5.00**

Waitin' Tae Welcome Me Hame by J. Douglas Brown & H.A. Rimmer, 1952 ....**5.00**

Waiting And Yearning by Elmer Volkman, 1934, Photo Meredith Leckrone (Cover Artist, Jeanne Wolff) **5.00**

Waiting At The Church by Fred W. Leigh & Henry E. Pether, 1906 (Cover Artist, Starmer) **10.00**

Waiting At The End Of The Road by Irving Berlin, 1929 (Irving Berlin) ..**10.00**

Waiting At The Station by Danks, 1866 (Pre 1900 & Transportation) ...**20.00**

Waiting by Harold Lawrence, Jay Milton & Carl Ravazza, 1944, Photo Joan Brooks (Cover Artist, Im-Ho) **3.00**

Waiting by Harry L. Cort, George E. Stoddard & Harold Orlob, 1918, Musical: Listen Lester **5.00**

Waiting by Otto Harbach & Louis A. Hirsch, 1920, Musical: George M. Cohan's Mary (George M. Cohan) **10.00**

Waiting by Reginald Rigby & Leo T. Croke, 1917 (WWI) **10.00**

Waiting By The Silv'ry Rio Grande by Billy Moll & Murray Mencher, 1930 (Cover Artist, Barbelle) **5.00**

Waiting Down By The Mississippi by Reed, 1911 (Cover Artist, Pfeiffer) **10.00**

Waiting For The Robert E. Lee by Gilbert & Muir, 1942, Movie: Cairo, Photo Jeanette MacDonald & Robert Young **10.00**

Waiting For The Robert E. Lee by L. Wolfe Gilbert & Lewis F. Muir, 1939, Photo Tony Martin **3.00**

Waiting For The Robert E. Lee by L. Wolfe Gilbert & Lewis F. Muir, 1932, Movie: The Jolson Story, Photo Larry Parks & Evelyn Keyes (Al Jolson) **12.00**

Waiting For The Sun To Come Out by George Gershwin, 1920 ....**5.00**

Waiting For You by Geo. L. Boyden, 1919 (Cover Artist, B. Wiggler) **8.00**

Wake Me When It's Over by Cahn & Van Heusen, 1960, Movie: Wake Me When It's Over, Photo Ernie Kovacs, Margo Moore, Dick Shawn & Nobu McCarthy **4.00**

Wake Up America by Geo. Graff Jr. & Jack Glogau, 1916, Featured by John Philip Sousa At The Hippodrome (Cover Artist, Rose Symbol, WWI, John Philip Sousa, March, Patriotic & Transportation) **25.00**

Wake Up And Live by Mack Gordon & Harry Revel, 1937, Movie: Wake Up And Live, Photo Walter Winchell, Ben Bernie & Alice Faye..**10.00**

Wake Up Little Girl You're Dreaming by Joe Burke & Lou Herscher, 1921 ....**5.00**

Wake Up Little Susie by Bryant, 1957, Photo Everly Brothers **3.00**

Wake Up Virginia And Prepare For Your Wedding Day by Seifert, Rosenfeld & Porter, 1917 (Cover Artist, Pfeiffer & WWI) **15.00**

Walk Hand In Hand by Johnny Cowell, 1956 ....**3.00**

Walk On The Wild Side by David & Bernstein, 1962, Movie: Walk On The Wild Side, Photo Lawrence Harvey, Jane Fonda, Capucine, Anne Baxter & Barbara Stanwyck **4.00**

Walk With Him by Dunham & Vars, 1961, Photo John Wayne **3.00**

Walkin' Away With My Heart by Tom Adair & Don R. George, 1946 ...**3.00**

Walkin' By The River by Robert Sour & Una Mae Carlisle, 1940 ....**4.00**

Walkin' Fo' Dat Cake by Edward Harrigan & David Braham, 1877 (Pre 1900 & Black, Black Face) **25.00**

Walkin' Fo' De Great White Cake by M. Petrousky, 1898 (Pre 1900 & Black, Black Face)..**25.00**

Walkin' My Baby Back Home by Roy Turk & Fred E. Ahlert, 1930, Photo Johnnie Ray **3.00**

Walking In The Rain by Bobby Newcomb, 1867, Signed Stone Lithograph Of Bobby Newcomb (Pre 1900, Signed & Stone Engraving)........**50.00**

Walkin' The Dog by Shelton Brooks, 1916 ....**5.00**

Walking The Floor Over You by Ernest Tubb, Signed Photo Ernest Tubb (Signed) **8.00**

Walking With Susie by Con Conrad, Sidney D. Mitchell & Archie Gottler, 1929, Movie: Fox Movietone Follies, 1929 ....**10.00**

Wall St. Blues by W.C. Handy, 1929 (Blues) **6.00**

Wall Street Rag by Scott Joplin, 1909 (Scott Joplin & Rag)...........**50.00**

Walrus And The Carpenter, The by Bob Hilliard & Sammy Fain, 1951, Movie: Alice In Wonderland (Disney)........................**10.00**

Waltz In Swing Time, The by Dorothy Fields & Jerome Kern, 1936, Photo Fred Astaire & Ginger Rogers.....................**5.00**

Waltz Irresistable by Anita Owen, 1916....................................**6.00**

Waltz Lives On, The by Leo Robin & Ralph Rainger, 1937, Movie: Big Broadcast 1938, Photo Shirley Ross, Caricature W.C. Fields, Martha Raye, Bob Hope & Ben Blue.........................**10.00**

Waltz Me Around Again, Willie by Will D. Cobb, Ren Shields & Gus Edwards, 1906 ....**8.00**

Waltz Me Till I'm Weary Dearie by Lonbrahe & Sherman, 1910 ....**6.00**

Waltz Of Long Ago, The by Irving Berlin, 1923, Musical: Music Box Revue 1923-24 (Irving Berlin) **10.00**

Waltz Of Love, The by Salva (Cover Artist, Pfeiffer).....................**10.00**

Waltz Of Memory, The by John Burger, 1951, Movie: It Happens On Ice..**5.00**

Waltz Of The Rose by Lind & Edwards, 1913 (Cover Artist, Pfeiffer)..**10.00**

Waltz Of The Wildflowers by Carrie Jacobs Bond, 1916 (Cover Artist, Hyer)..**10.00**

Waltz Recipe by Weder, Nathan & Rosenblum, 1932 ....**5.00**

Waltzing by Bill & Ed Gorman & J. Oliver Riehl, 1930, The Florsheim Frolic Theme Song, National Broadcasting Co. (Advertising & Deco) **10.00**

Waltzing In A Dream by Bing Crosby, Ned Washington & Victor Young, 1932, Photo Bing Crosby (Cover Artist, Frederick S. Manning) **15.00**

Waltzing Matilda by A.B. Paterson & Marie Cowan, 1936, Unofficial National Anthem Of Australia, Featured by Marjorie Lawrence, Nelson Eddy, John Dudley, Lansing Hatfield & The Landt Trio **10.00**

Wan-A-Tea by Richard K. Moritz, 1910 (Cover Artist, Starmer & Indian)..**15.00**

Wandalola by Meyer, 1910 (Cover Artist, Pfeiffer & Indian)..............**15.00**

Wander Off Nowhere by Gus Edwards, 1907 ....**5.00**

Wander With Me To Loveland by Anita Owens, 1919 (Cover Artist, Frederick S. Manning) **15.00**

Wanderin' by Sammy Kaye, 1950, Photo Sammy Kaye.....................**3.00**

Wandering Home by L. Claire Case & Leonard Stevens, 1920 (Cover Artist, P.M. Griffith)......................................**6.00**

Wandering One by Harry Mayo & Harry Von Tilzer, 1924...............**5.00**

Wandering Thoughts by Elizabeth Freal **5.00**

Wang Wang Blues by Les Wood, Gus Mueller, Buster Johnson & Henry Burns, 1921, Photo Paul Whiteman & Orchestra (Cover Artist, R.S. & Blues)...**8.00**

Wanted by Peter Tinturin & Jack Laurence, 1937.........................**5.00**

Wanting You by Frank Mandel, Oscar Hammerstein II & Sigmund Romberg, 1928, Musical: The New Moon **10.00**

Wanting You So by J. Will Callahan & E.S. Roberts, 1922 ....**5.00**

War And Peace by Stone & Rota, 1956, Movie: War And Peace, Photo Audrey Hepburn, Henry Fonda & Mel Ferrer............................**10.00**

War Babies by Al Jolson, 1916 (Al Jolson & WWI)....................**15.00**

Warm All Over by Frank Loesser, 1956, Musical: The Most Happy Fella...**6.00**

Warm Proposition by Monroe Rosenfeld, 1899 (Pre 1900 & Black, Black Face) **15.00**

Warm Reception, A by Bert Anthony, 1899 (Pre 1900 & Black, Black Face) **10.00**

Warmest Baby In The Bunch, The by George M. Cohan, 1896 (George M. Cohan, Pre 1900 & Black, Black Face)....................**20.00**

Warmin Up In Dixie, A by E.T. Paull, 1899 (Cover Artist, E.T. Paull, Lithograph A. Hoen, Pre 1900 & Black, Black Face)...................**35.00**

Warsaw Concerto by Richard Addinsell, 1942....................**5.00**

Was I The One All To Blame by Ben Harris & Leo Bennett, 1914.......**5.00**

Was It A Dream? by Sam Coslow, Larry Spier & Addy Britt, 1928, Photo Andy Sannella (Cover Artist, Politzer)....................**4.00**

Was It Love? by Irving Caesar, Harry Rosenthal & Con Conrad, 1928..**5.00**

Was It Rain by Walter Hirsch & Lou Handman, 1937, Movie: The Hit Parade, Photo Frances Langford & Phil Regan...........................**10.00**

Was There Ever A Pal Like You by Irving Berlin, 1919, Signed Photo Billy Burke, (Lithograph W.F. Powers, I. Berlin & Signed).....20.00

Washington, He Was A Wonderful Man by George M. Cohan (George M. Cohan) **10.00**

Washington Pie by Ted Morse, 1907....................................**15.00**

Washington Post March by John Philip Sousa, 1889 (John Philip Sousa, Pre 1900 & March) **30.00**

Wasted Days And Wasted Nights by Wayne M. Duncan & Freddy Fender, 1960, Photo Freddy Fender **2.00**

Wasted Years by Wally Fowler, 1959...................................**2.00**

Watch, Hope And Wait Little Girl, I'm Coming Back To You by Lew Brown & Will Clayton, 1918 (WWI)..........................**12.00**

Watch, Hope, Wait Little Girl 'Til I Come Back To You by Lew Brown & Will Clayton, 1918 (Cover Artist, E.E. Walton & WWI) **10.00**

Watch The Bee Go Get the Hun by Meyer (Cover Artist, Pfeiffer & WWI)..**15.00**

Watch What Happens by Norman Gimbel & Michel LeGrand, 1967, Movie: The Umbrellas Of Cherbourg **6.00**

Watch Your Step, Show Us How To Do The Fox Trot by Irving Berlin, 1914 (Irving Berlin)....................................**10.00**

Watching by Bert Myers & Joe Solman, 1920 ....**5.00**

Watching The Clock by Whitman, 1930 (Cover Artist, Pfeiffer)........**10.00**

Water Cress, 1909 (Cover Artist, Pfeiffer) **10.00**

Water Lilies by Floyd J. St. Clair, 1909 ....**5.00**

Water Under The Bridge by Paul Francis Webster & Lew Pollack, 1934, Photo Fred Waring..**4.00**

Watermelon Weather by Paul Francis & Hoagy Carmichael, 1952, Photo Perry Como & Eddie Fisher **5.00**

Waters Of The Perkiomen by Al Dubin & F. Henri Klickmann, 1925 ..**5.00**

Waters Of Venice by Neville Fleeson & Albert Von Tilzer, 1918.........**5.00**

Waves Of The Danube by J. Ivanovici, 1902 (Cover Artist, John Frew) ..**10.00**

Wawatchies Dream by Carter, 1912 (Cover Artist, Pfeiffer) **10.00**

Way Back Home by Al Lewis & Tom Waring, 1949, Photo Bing Crosby & Fred Waring (Cover Artist, Nick) **5.00**

Way Back Home In Old New Hampshire by Allen, 1916 (Cover Artist, Pfeiffer)...**10.00**

Way Back In Tennessee by Ren Shields & Charles Straight, 1911........**5.00**

Way Down East by James Thatcher, 1915 ....**5.00**

Way Down East by Justin Wheeler, 1908 ....**5.00**

Way Down East by Walsh & Magine, 1914...**5.00**

Way Down East Among The Shady Maple Trees by Stanford, 1900 ....**5.00**

Way Down In Arkansas by White, 1915 ....**5.00**

Way Down In Cotton Town, Way Way Down by LaMoyne Sutphen, 1924 (Black, Black Face) **22.00**

Way Down In Ioway, I'm Going To Hide Away by Sam Lewis, Joe Young & Geo Meyer, 1916 (Cover Artist, Barbelle).....................**10.00**

Way Down In Old Indiana by Paul Dresser, 1901................................**10.00**

Way Down On Tampa Bay by A. Seymour Brown & Egbert Van Alstyne, 1914 (Cover Artist, Starmer) **10.00**

Way Down There, A Dixie Boy Is Missing by Stanley Murphy & Harry Tierney, 1917, Photo Belle Baker (WWI & Dixie)......................**10.00**

Way Down Upon The Swanee River (Old Folks At Home) by Stephen Foster, 1935, Photo Ted Fiorito (Stephen Foster) **6.00**

Way Down Yonder In New Orleans by Henry Creamer & J. Turner Layton, 1922 (Cover Artist, CA & Jazz)...**5.00**

Way I Want To Touch You, The by Toni Tennille, Photo Captain & Tennille **5.00**

Way Of The World by Will B. Morrison, 1912......................................**5.00**

Way Out In Kentucky by Mitchell & Rose, 1923 ....**4.00**

Way Out West In Kansas by Carson Robinson, 1924 ....**8.00**

Way That I Live, The by Newell & Ortolani, 1968, Movie: The Bliss Of Mrs. Blossom, Photo Shirley Maclaine, Richard Attenborough & James Booth...**4.00**

Way Up Yonder by James Bland (Pre 1900 & Black, Black Face) **15.00**

Way You Look Tonight, The by Jerome Kern & Dorothy Fields, 1936, Movie: Swing Time, Photo Fred Astaire & Ginger Rogers **10.00**

Wayside Willies March by Charles L. Johnson, 1905 (March)............**10.00**

Wayward Wind, The by Herb Newman & Stan Lebowsky, 1956, Signed Photo Gogi Grant (Signed)..**3.00**

We All Fall by Joe Goodwin & Geo. W. Meyer, 1911 (Cover Artist, E.P.C.)...**5.00**

We Are Coming, Father Abraham, Three Hundred Thousand Strong by Stephen Foster, 1863 (Stephen Foster, Patriotic & Pre 1900)........**50.00**

We Are Coming Home, Marching Song Of America by Edith Willis Linn & John Philip Sousa, 1918 (John Philip Sousa, March & WWI)...**20.00**

We Are Ready by John J. O'Brion & Arthur W. Crosbie, 1917 (Cover Artist, W.M.F., WWI & Patriotic)..**25.00**

We Are The Champions by Freddie Mercury, 1977............................**6.00**

We Are Uncle Sammie's Little Nephews by Sgt. Bernard Satz, U.S.A & Lt. W.E. Sheaffer, U.S.A., Photo 151st Depot Brigade Band, Bugle, Fife & Drum Corps, Camp Devens, MA (WWI, Military Personnel & Patriotic) **25.00**

We Are Uncle Sammy's Boys by Chas. D. Tibbits & Fred Adametz, 1914 (WWI)...**15.00**

We Belong Together by Oscar Hammerstein II & Jerome Kern, 1932, Movie: Music In The Air...**6.00**

We Can Muster Uncle Sammy Ten Million Men Or More by Green & Greenwald, 1917 (Cover Artist, Pfeiffer & WWI).....................**15.00**

We Could Make Such Beautiful Music by Robert Sour & Henry Manners, 1940, Photo Vaughn Monroe..**6.00**

We Did It Before And We Can Do It Again by Cliff Friend & Charles Tobias, 1918 (WWI)..**10.00**

We Did It Before And We Can Do It Again by Cliff Friend & Charles Tobias, 1951, Movie: Banjo Eyes, Photo Eddie Cantor (Eddie Cantor)..........**10.00**

We Don't Want The Bacon, What We Want Is A Piece Of The Rhine by "Kid" Howard Carr, Harry Russell & Jimmie Havens, 1918 (WWI) ..**25.00**

We Have Much To Be Thankful For by Irving Berlin, 1913 (Cover Artist, Pfeiffer, Irving Berlin & Deco) **15.00**

We Just Couldn't Say Goodbye by Harry Woods, 1932 (Cover Artist, Frederick S. Manning & Deco) **10.00**

We Kiss In A Shadow by Richard Rodgers & Oscar Hammerstein II, 1951, Movie: The King And I **5.00**

We Met, We Loved, We Parted by Robert Morris & A. Fred Phillips, 1915 (Cover Artist, W.M.F.)...**10.00**

We Must Be Ready by George M. Cohan (George M. Cohan)............**12.00**

We Must Be Vigilant by Leslie & Donaldson, 1929, Movie: When Johnny Comes Marching Home, Photo Phil Spitalny, Allan Jones, Jane Frazee, Donald O'Connor & Gloria Jean (Patriotic)....................**10.00**

We Must Have A Song To Remember by Bud Green & Sammy Stept, 1919 ....**10.00**

We Mustn't Say Goodbye by Al Dubin & James V. Monaco, 1943, Movie: Stage Door Canteen (WWII) 6.00

We Never Grow Old by Howard Johnson & Carlo Sanderson, 1921, Musical: Tangerine **6.00**

We Never Talk Much by Sammy Cahn & Nicholas Brodszky, 1951, Movie: Rich, Young And Pretty, Photo Jane Powell, Danielle Darrieux, Wendell Corey, Fernando Lamas & Vic Damone **5.00**

We Open In Venice by Cole Porter, 1948, Musical: Kiss Me Kate **5.00**

We Parted By The River, Grace And I by Stanley Crawford, 1905.....**10.00**

We Parted On The Shore by Harry Lauder, 1906................................**10.00**

We Said Goodbye by Arthur Trevelyan & H. Sylvester Krause, 1899 (Pre 1900)..**10.00**

We Sat Beneath The Maple On The Hill by Gussie L. Davis, 1935 ......**5.00**

We Saw The Sea by Irving Berlin, 1936, Movie: Follow The Fleet, Photo Ginger Rogers & Fred Astaire (Irving Berlin) **18.00**

We Shall See! by Dorothy Dickinson & Howard Fisher, 1924.............**5.00**

We Stand For Peace While Others War by Williams, 1914, Photo President Wilson (WWI & President) **20.00**

We Three by Dick Robertson, Nelson Cogane & Sammy Mysels, 1940 (Cover Artist, Im-Ho)...**4.00**
We Watch The Skyways by Max Steiner, 1918 (WWI).......................**10.00**
We Will Always Be Sweethearts by Leo Robin & Oscar Straus, 1932, Movie: One Hour With You..**5.00**
We Will Meet At The End Of The Trail by Jean Acker, 1926, Photo Jean Acker, Who Is Mrs. Rudolph Valentino (Cover Artist, Barbelle)..**22.00**
We'll All Come Back by Tarantino & Metz, 1917 (Cover Artist, Pfeiffer & WWI)...**15.00**
We'll Always Be The Same Sweethearts by Charles Newman & Harry Williams, 1911..**10.00**
We'll Always Remember Pearl Harbor by Alfred Bryan, Willie Raskin & Gerald Marks, 1941 (WWII) **15.00**

We'll Be Singing Hallelujah Marching Thru Berlin by Bob Reed & Harry Miller, 1942, Movie: Stage Door Canteen (WWII)........**10.00**
We'll Be There Uncle Sam, We'll Be There by Ryan, 1917 (WWI) .. **10.00**
We'll Be Together Again by Frank Laine & Carl Fischer, 1945...........**3.00**
We'll Be Waiting When You Come Back Home by Chas. H. Gabriel & Homer A. Rodeheaver, 1918 (WWI)..**5.00**
We'll Build A Little Home In The U.S.A. by Howard Wesley & Chas. Elbert, 1915 (WWI)...**10.00**
We'll Build A Little World Of Our Own by James Brockman & James Hanley, 1930, Movie: Happy Days **10.00**

We'll Build A Rainbow In The Sky by Raymond B. Egan & Richard A. Whiting, 1918 ....**6.00**
We'll Dance Thro' Life Together by Duncan Sisters, Book by Catherine C. Cushing, Suggested by Uncle Tom's Cabin by Harriet Beecher Stowe, 1923, Musical: Topsy & Eva, Photo Duncan Sisters (Cover Artist, P.M. Griffith & Black, Black Face) **15.00**
We'll Do Our Share by Lew Brown, Al Harriman & Jack Egan, 1918 (Cover Artist, Walton & WWI)..**10.00**
We'll Gather Lilacs by Ivor Novello, 1940 (Cover Artist, BJH)...........**5.00**
We'll Have A Jubilee In My Old Kentucky Home by Coleman Goetz & Walter Donaldson, 1915, Photo Scott & Raynor (Cover Artist, Barbelle & Black, Black Face)..**10.00**
We'll Have A Jubilee In My Old Kentucky Home by Coleman Goetz & Walter Donaldson, 1915, Photo Baby Esmond (Cover Artist, Barbelle & Black, Black Face)...**10.00**
We'll Have A Wonderful Party by Otto Harbach & Louis A. Hirsch, 1920, George M. Cohan Musical Comedy "Mary" (George M. Cohan) **10.00**

We'll Have Peace On Earth And Even In Berlin by Jas. A. Flanigan & Thos. J. Flanagan, 1917 (WWI)..**20.00**
We'll Keep Old Glory Flying by Carleton S. Montanye & A. Louis Scarmolin, 1917 (WWI) **10.00**
We'll Knock The Heligo-Into Heligo-Out of Heligoland by John O'Brien & Theodore Morse, 1918, Photo Dooley & Nelson, Dedicated To The Men Of The American Fleet (Cover Artist, Rose Symbol, WWI & Dedication) **35.00**
We'll Make Hay While The Sun Shines by Arthur Freed & Nacio Herb Brown, 1933, Movie: Going Hollywood, Photo Bing Crosby & Marion Davies **10.00**
We'll Meet Again by Ross Parker & Hughie Charles, 1939, Photo Kate Smith..**10.00**
We'll Meet Again by Ross Parker & Hughie Charles, 1939, Photo Mitchell Ayres...**3.00**
We'll Stand By Our Country by Raymond Hubbell, 1918 (WWI) **10.00**
We'll Stand By The Flag March by E.T. Paull (Cover Artist, E.T. Paull & March) **35.00**
We'll Tramp, Tramp, Tramp Along Together by J. Keirn Brennan & Lieut Gitz Rice, 1926 (Military Personnel) **15.00**
We're All Americans, All True Blue by James T. Mangan, 1940, Photo Kate Smith (Patriotic)..**10.00**
We're All Going Calling On The Kaiser by Jack Caddigan & Jas. Brennen, 1918 (Cover Artist, Starmer & WWI) **25.00**

We're All Together Now by Leo Robin & Ralph Rainger, 1939, Movie: Gulliver's Travels **5.00**

We're All With You Dear America by Lew Schaeffer, 1917 (WWI & Patriotic) **25.00**

We're Almost Home by Burke & Burke, 1972, Movie: Cool Breeze, Photo Talmus Rasulala & Judy Pace **4.00**

We're A Band Of Bold Conspirators by Broadhurst & Barratt, 1910 (Cover Artist, Pfeiffer) **15.00**

We're Going Over by Andrew B. Sterling, Bernie Grossman & Arthur Lange, 1917 (Cover Artist, Starmer & WWI) 25.00

We're Going Over The Top by Andrew B. Sterling, Bernie Grossman & Arthur Lange, 1918, Photo Frank Morgan (Cover Artist, Starmer & WWI) **35.00**

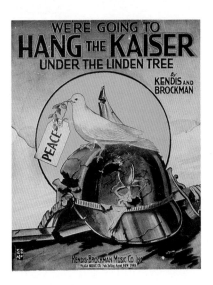

We're Going To Hang The Kaiser Under The Linden Tree by Kendis & Brockman, 1917 (Cover Artist, Rose & WWI) 50.00

We're Going To Take Away The Sword From William by Willie Weston, 1917 (WWI) **10.00**

We're Going To Take The Germ Out Of Germany by Frederick Bowers, 1917 (Cover Artist, Pfeiffer & WWI) **20.00**

We're Growing Old Together by Merrill & Dinsmore, 1908 ....**5.00**

We're In Love With The Same Sweet Girl by Halsey K. Mohr, 1916 (Cover Artist, Barbelle) **10.00**

We're In The Army Now by Tell Taylor, Ole Olsen & Isham Jones, 1917 (WWI) **15.00**

We're In The Money by Al Dubin & Henry Warren, 1932, Movie: The Jolson Story, Photo Larry Parks & Evelyn Keyes (Al Jolson) **10.00**

We're In The Navy Now, Musical Journey Around The World by John Thompson, 1929 (Cover Artist, George Hauman & Patriotic) **15.00**

We're In To Win by Pvt. Morris Orenstein, 1918 (WWI & Military Personnel) **15.00**

We're Mighty Glad To See You by Bugbee & Ball, 1921 ....**5.00**

We're Not Getting Any Younger, Baby by Herb Magidson & Ben Oakland, 1949, Photo Tony Martin **4.00**

We're Off To See The Wizard by Harburg & Arlen, 1939, Movie: The Wizard Of Oz, Photo Judy Garland, Ray Bolger, Frank Morgan, Bert Lahr & Jack Haley **10.00**

We're On Our Way To France by Irving Berlin, 1918 (Irving Berlin & WWI) **15.00**

We're On The March by Morton Downey, C. Field & J. Erickson, 1918 (WWI) **10.00**

We're Proud That We're Americans by Tyler, 1918 (Cover Artist, Pfeiffer & WWI) **15.00**

We're The Couple In The Castle by Frank Loesser & Hoagy Carmichael, 1941, Movie: Mr. Bug Goes To Town **5.00**

We're The Sunday Drivers by Nick & Charles Kenny, 1927 (Transportation) **10.00**

We've Come A Long Way Together by Ted Koehler, Sam H. Stept, 1939, Photo Jack Teagarden **5.00**

Weary River by Grant Clarke & Louis Silvers, 1929, Movie: Weary River, Photo Richard Barthelmess **10.00**

Web Of Love, The by McNamee & Zany, 1929 ....**6.00**

Weddin' Day by Clancy Hayes & Carl Kalash, 1949, Photo Jack Kilty **3.00**

Wedding Bells Are Breaking Up That Old Gang Of Mine by Irving Kahal, Sammy Fain & Willie Raskin, 1929 (Cover Artist, Barbelle) **5.00**

Wedding Bells Are Calling by Herbert Reynolds, Schuyler Greene & Jerome Kern, 1915, Musical: Very Good Eddie (Cover Artist, Malcolm Strauss) **15.00**

Wedding Bells Rag by A.B. Coney, 1910 (Rag) **10.00**

Wedding Bells, The by Miller, 1911 (Cover Artist, Pfeiffer) **10.00**

Wedding In The Spring by Johnny Mercer & Jerome Kern, 1942, Movie: You Were Never Lovelier, Photo Fred Astaire, Rita Hayworth, Adolphe Menjou & Xavier Cugat & His Orchestra **5.00**

Wedding March by Felix Mendelsohnn, 1935 ....**5.00**

Wedding Of Jack & Jill, The by R.H. Burnside & Raymond Hubbell, 1915, Musical: Hip Hip Hooray At New York Hippodrome **12.00**

Wedding Of The Chinee And The Coon, The by Bob Cole & Billy Johnson, 1897 (Pre 1900 & Black, Black Face) **35.00**

Wedding Of The Lily And The Rose by Thomas LeMack & Andrew Mack, 1892 (Pre 1900) **10.00**

Wedding Of The Painted Doll, The by Arthur Freed & Nacio Herb Brown, 1929, Movie: Broadway Melody, Photo Geraldine & Ann Beaumont (Cover Artist, P. M. Griffith) **5.00**

Wedding Of The Painted Doll, The by Arthur Freed & Nacio Herb Brown, Movie: Love Boat, Photo Charles King, Bessie Love & Anita Page ...**5.00**

Wedding Of The Sunshine And The Rose, The by Stanley Murphy & Albert Gumble, 1915 (Cover Artist, Starmer) **10.00**

Wednesday Special by Williams & Williams, 1973, Movie: Cinderella Liberty, Photo James Caan & Marsha Mason **3.00**

Weegee, Weegee Tell Me Do by William Jerome & Harry Von Tilzer.**5.00**

Week End Of A Private Secretary, The by J. Mercer & Bernie Hanighen, Photo Mildred Bailey **6.00**

Weekend In New England by Randy Edelman, 1976, Photo Barry Manilow **3.00**

Weep No More My Mammy by Sidney Mitchell, Sidney Clare & Lew Pollack, Musical: Passing Show of 1921......................**10.00**

Weep Not For The Dead by Ada Weigel Powers, 1933, Signed by Ada Weigel Powers, Dedicated To John Chipman (Dedication & Signed) **18.00**

Weeping, Sad And Lonely by Tucker, 1863 (Pre 1900)......................**15.00**

Weeping Willow Lane by Harold G. Frost & F. Henri Klickmann, 1919..**5.00**

Weeping Willow Rag by Fischler, 1911 (Rag).....................**10.00**

Welcome Home by Grant Clarke & Henry Akst, 1929, Movie: On With The Show......................**10.00**

Welcome Home by Mancini, Bergman & Bergman, 1989, Movie: Welcome Home, Photo Kris Kristofferson & Jo Beth Williams **3.00**

Welcome Home Laddie Boy, Welcome Home by Will D. Cobb & Gus Edwards, 1918 (Cover Artist, Dunk, WWI, March & Transportation) **25.00**

Welcome Honey To Your Old Plantation Home by Jack Yellen & Albert Gumble, 1916 ....**10.00**

Welcome Mr. Poli by James Thatcher, 1916, Photo Sylvester Z. Poli & James Thatcher **15.00**

Welcome Song, The by Kermit Goell & Fred Spielman, 1945...........**5.00**

Welcome To My Dream by Johnny Burke & James Van Heusen, 1945, Movie: Road To Utopia, Photo Bing Crosby, Bob Hope & Dorothy Lamour......................**5.00**

Were I by Carrie Jacobs Bond, 1923, Dedicated To Amelia Galli-Curci (Dedication)......................**15.00**

Were My Song With Wings Provided by Reynaldo Hahn, 1896 (Pre 1900)......................**6.00**

Were Thine That Special Face by Cole Porter, 1948, Musical: Kiss Me Kate......................**8.00**

Were Your Ears Burning Baby? by Mack Gordon & Harry Revel, 1934, Movie: Shoot The Works, Photo Ben Bernie & His Merry Lads.....**5.00**

West, A Nest, And You, The by Larry Yoell & Billy Hill, 1925...........**5.00**

West Of The Great Divide by George Whiting & Ernest R. Ball, 1924, Movie: West Of The Great Divide, Photo Alice Terry & Conway Tearle........**15.00**

West Point Song by Sigmund Romberg, 1918 (Patriotic)....................**10.00**

West Virginia by Pack & Adderly, 1914.............................**10.00**

Western Flyer, The by Morton, 1903 (Transportation) **25.00**

Western Land by Byron Gay, 1919 ....**5.00**

Westward Ho by Percy Wenrich, 1909......................**5.00**

Westwind by Ogden Nash & Kurt Weill, 1943, Movie: One Touch Of Venus......................**3.00**

Wet Yo' Thumb by Lew Cooper & Harry Akst, 1923 (Cover Artist, Politzer & Black, Black Face) **25.00**

What A Baby I Got by Rocco Zappia, 1933, Photo The Two Graces (Cover Artist, Heff Ley) **5.00**

What A Happy World This Will Be by Harold Dixon, 1918 (WWI)...**10.00**

What A Little Moonlight Can Do by Harry Woods, 1939 ....**2.00**

What A Man by George M. Cohan (George M. Cohan) **10.00**

What A Perfect Night For Love by Charles Lenzen, Al Cameron & Pete Bontsema, 1930, Photo Rudy Vallee (Cover Artist, Frederick S. Manning)......................**10.00**

What A Wonderful Dream It Would Be by Charles K. Harris, 1918 (WWI)......................**10.00**

What A Wonderful Girl You Are by F. Davis, H. Tobias & M. Prival, 1920 (Cover Artist, Rolf Armstrong) **15.00**

What A Wonderful Love That Would Be by Richard Whiting, Paul Cunningham & Alfred J. Doyle, 1914 ....**12.00**

What A Wonderful Mother You'd Be by Joe Goodwin & Al Piantadosi, 1915 (Cover Artist, Pfeiffer) **10.00**

What A Wonderful Wedding That Will Be by Irving Kahal, Francis Wheeler & Sammy Fain, 1927, Photo Phil Spitalny (Cover Artist, Barbelle & Deco)......................**10.00**

What A Wonderful World by George David Weiss & Bob Thiele, 1967, Photo Louis Armstrong **3.00**

What Are You Doin' The Rest Of Your Life by Ted Koehler & Burton Lane, 1944, Movie: Hollywood Canteen, Photo Andrews Sisters, Jack Benny & Many More Stars......................**5.00**

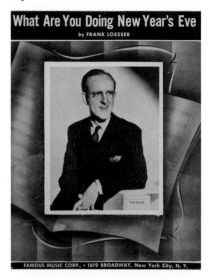

What Are You Doing New Year's Eve by Frank Loesser, 1947, Photo Kay Kyser......................4.00

What Are You Going To Do by Leap, 1913 (Cover Artist, Pfeiffer)...**10.00**

What Are You Going To Do To Help The Boys by Gus Kahn & Egbert Van Alstyne, 1918 (Cover Artist, E.E. Walton & WWI)...............**10.00**

What Are You Waiting For Mary? by Walter Donaldson, 1927, Photo Paul Whiteman **5.00**

What Can I Say After I Say I'm Sorry by Walter Donaldson & Abe Lyman, 1924, Photo Bee Palmer (Deco)......................**6.00**

What Can You Do With A General by Irving Berlin, 1942, Movie: White Christmas, Photo Bing Crosby, Danny Kaye, Rosemary Clooney & Vera Ellen (Irving Berlin)......................**10.00**

What Can You Say In A Love Song? by Ira Gershwin, E.Y. Harburg & Harry Arlen, 1934, Musical: Life Begins At 8:40 (Cover Artist, Jorj).........**10.00**

What Cha Gonna Do When There Ain't No Jazz? by Edgar Leslie & Pete Wendling, 1909 (Jazz)......................**15.00**

What Chance Have I With Love by Irving Berlin, 1939 (Irving Berlin)..**10.00**

What Chance Have I With Love by Irving Berlin, 1950, Movie: Call Me Madam, Photo Ethel Merman, Donald O'Connor, George Sanders & Vera Ellen (Irving Berlin)......................**10.00**

What Could Be Sweeter by Andrew B. Sterling, Billy Curtis & Harry Von Tilzer, 1914, Photo Harry Von Tilzer (Cover Artist, Barbelle) **10.00**

What D'Ya Say? by B.G. DeSylva, 1928..............................**5.00**

What Did I Do? by Mack Gordon & Joseph Myrow, 1947, Movie: When My Baby Smiles At Me, Photo Betty Grable & Dan Dailey...........**8.00**

What Did Romeo Say To Juliet When He Climbed Her Balcony? by Kendis & Bryan, 1914 (Cover Artist, Pfeiffer & Deco)................**12.00**

What Did You Do In The Infantry by Frank Loesser, 1943 (WWII).....**5.00**

What Did You Do With All The Love I Gave You by Joe McCarthy & Fred Fisher, 1917......................**5.00**

What Do I Care? by Harry B. Smith & Sigmund Romberg, 1925 ....**5.00**

What Do I Care What Somebody Said by Sidney Clare & Harry Woods, 1927, Musical: Princess Flavia (Deco)......................**10.00**

What Do I Have To Do by James & Miller, 1948, Movie: Are You With It, Photo Donald O'Connor, Olga San Juan, Lew Parker & Martha Stewart......................**4.00**

What Do I Have To Do To Get My Picture In The Papers by Irving Berlin, 1949, Musical: Miss Liberty (Irving Berlin) **10.00**

What Do We Do On A Dew-Dew-Dewy Day by Howard Johnson, Charles Tobias & Al Sherman, 1927, Photo Henri Garden (Cover Artist, R.S. & Deco) **5.00**

What Do We Do On A Dew-Dew-Dewy Day? by Howard Johnson, Charles Tobias & Al Sherman, 1927, Photo Charlie Nelson (Cover Artist, RS & Deco) **5.00**

What Do We Do On A Dew-Dew-Dewy Day by Howard Johnson, Chas Tobias & Al Sherman, 1927, Photo Frank Cornnell (Cover Artist, R.S. & Deco) **5.00**

What Do You Do Sunday Mary? by Irving Caesar & Stephen Jones, 1923, Musical: Poppy, Photo Madge Kennedy **5.00**

What Do You Know About Love? by Jerry Livingston & Mack David, 1938 ....**6.00**

What Do You Say? by Jack Yellen, Milton Ager & Paul Ash, 1928 .....**5.00**

What Do You Say To A Naked Lady? by Karmen, 1970, Movie: What Do You Say To A Naked Lady **2.00**

What Do You Want To Make Those Eyes At Me For? by Joe McCarthy, Howard Johnson & Jimmie Monaco, 1916, Photo Emma Carus & Larry Comer **10.00**

What Do You Want To Make Those Eyes At Me For? by Joe McCarthy, Howard Johnson & Jimmie Monaco, 1916, Musical: Follow Me, Anna Held's New Show, Photo Harry Lewis **10.00**

What Do You Want With Me? by Bobby Heath & Frank Black, 1914, Photo Bobby Heath (Cover Artist, Pfeiffer) **12.00**

What Does He Look Like? by Irving Berlin, 1942, Movie: This Is The Army, Lieut. Ronald Reagan In Cast (Irving Berlin & WWII, Military Personnel & President) **20.00**

What Does It Matter? by Irving Berlin, 1927 (Cover Artist, Leff & Irving Berlin) **10.00**

What Does It Mean Without You? by Nelson Shawn, Charles Gilchrest & Frank Magine, 1933 ....**5.00**

What Does The Pussy Cat Mean When He Says Meow? by Harry Pease, N.T. Granlund & Ed. G. Nelson, 1924 (Cover Artist, JVR) **5.00**

What D'ye Mean You Lost Yer Dog? by Thos. S. Allen & Joseph M. Daly, 1913, Photo Collins & Woppman (Cover Artist, Pfeiffer) ...**10.00**

What Goes On Here In My Heart? by Leo Robin & Ralph Rainger, 1938, Movie: Give Me A Sailor, Photo Martha Raye, Bob Hope, Betty Grable & Jack Whiting **10.00**

What Goes Up Must Come Down by Ted Koehler & Rube Bloom, Musical: Cotton Club Parade (Cover Artist, Im-Ho) **5.00**

What Have They Done To My Song, Ma by Melanie Safka, 1970, Photo Melanie **2.00**

What Have We Got To Lose? by Sammy Kahn, Walter Kent & Louis Alter, 1933 ....**5.00**

What Have You Got That Gets Me? by Leo Robin & Ralph Rainger, 1938, Movie: Artists And Models Abroad, Photo Jack Benny **5.00**

What In The World's Come Over You? by Jack Scott, 1959, Photo Jack Scott **5.00**

What Is A Husband? by Gene Piller & Ruth Roberts, 1955, Photo Steve Allen & Garry Moore **5.00**

What Is A Wife? by Gene Piller & Ruth Roberts, 1955, Photo Steve Allen & Garry Moore **5.00**

What Is Life Without Love? by Eddy Arnold, Vernice E. McAlpin & Owen Bradley, 1946 ....**5.00**

What Is The Harm In A Bit Of A Walk by McKneil & Clifton, 1919, Movie: Boots, Photo Dorothy Gish **12.00**

What Is This Thing Called Love? by Cole Porter, 1929 ....**10.00**

What Kind Of An American Are You? by Lew Brown, Charles McCarron & Albert Von Tilzer, 1917 (WWI) **10.00**

What Kind Of Fool Am I? by Leslie Bricusse & Anthony Newley, 1961, Movie: Stop The World I Want To Get Off (Cover Artist, Tenerser) **8.00**

What Makes The Sunset? by Gus Kahn & Jule Styne, 1945, Movie: Anchors Aweigh, Photo Frank Sinatra & Gene Kelly **5.00**

What! Marry Dat Gal! by Harry B. Smith & John Stromberg, 1898 (Pre 1900 & Black, Black Face) **15.00**

What Money Can't Buy by Monroe H. Rosenfeld & Arthur Lange, 1915 (Cover Artist, DeTakacs) **10.00**

What Money Can't Buy by Monroe H. Rosenfeld & Arthur Lange, 1915, Signed Photo Eva Tanguay (Cover Artist, DeTakacs & Signed) ...**38.00**

What More Can A Woman Give? by Monroe H. Rosenfeld & Lewis Porter, 1918 (Cover Artist, Pfeiffer & Deco) **15.00**

What More Can I Ask For? by Jack Maxus & Bernard Bierman, 1946, Photo Guy Lombardo **3.00**

What More Can I Give You? by Alfred Bryan & Albert Gumble, 1920 (Cover Artist, Starmer) **5.00**

What Name Is Sweeter Than Sweetheart? by Thos. S. Allen, 1914, Photo Billy Coty (Cover Artist, Starmer) **10.00**

What Now My Love by Carl Sigman & G. Becard, 1912 ....**3.00**

What Takes My Fancy? by Carolyn Leigh & Cy Coleman, 1960, Movie: Wildcat **5.00**

What This Country Needs Is A Song by George M. Cohan (George M. Cohan) **12.00**

What Will I Do Without You? by Al Dubin & Joe Burke, 1929, Movie: Goldiggers Of Broadway, Photo Winnie Lightner, Ann Pennington, Nick Lucas, Lilyan Tashman, Conway Tearle & Nancy Welford (Deco) **15.00**

What Will I Tell Her Tonight? by Roberts, Whittaker & Morrissey, 1913 (Cover Artist, Pfeiffer) **10.00**

What Will I Tell My Heart? by Peter Tinturin & Jack Lawrence, 1937, Photo Bing Crosby **10.00**

What Will I Tell My Heart? by Peter Tinturin & Jack Lawrence, 1937, Photo George Olsen **10.00**

What Would You Do? by Leo Robin & Richard A. Whiting, 1932, Movie: One Hour With You **5.00**

What Ya Thinkin' Of Baby? by Bert Stevens & Larry Wagner, 1941 ...**5.00**

What You Goin To Do When The Rent Comes 'Round? by Andrew Sterling & Harry Von Tilzer, 1905 ....**10.00**

What'll I Do? by Irving Berlin, 1923 (Cover Artist, RS & Irving Berlin) **12.00**

What'll We Do On A Saturday Night When The Town Goes Dry? by Bert Kalmar & Harry Ruy, 1919 ....**10.00**

What'll We Do With Him Boys?, The Yanks Made A Monkey Out Of You by Andrew B. Sterling & Arthur Lange, 1918, Photo W. J. Reilly, U.S.N. (Cover Artist, Pfeiffer, WWI & Military Personnel) **15.00**

What's Good About Goodbye? by Leo Robin & Harold Arlen, 1948, Movie: Casbah **5.00**

What's Good For The Goose Is Good For The Gander by Cliff Friend, 1934 (Cover Artist, Leff) **5.00**

What's New? by Joe Burke & Bob Haggart, 1939, Photo George Olsen (Cover Artist, Im-Ho) **3.00**

What's New Pussycat? by David & Bachrach, 1965, Movie: What's New Pussycat?, Photo Peter Sellers, Woody Allen, Peter O'Toole, Rory Schneider & Capucine **3.00**

What's The Good Of Moonlight? by Davis & Brookhouse, 1915 ....**5.00**

What's The Good Word Mr. Bluebird? by Al Hoffman, Allan Roberts & Jerry Livingston, 1943, Photo Baron Elliott **2.00**

What's The Matter With Father? by Harry Williams & Egbert Van Alstyne, 1910 (Cover Artist, Starmer) **10.00**

What's The Matter With The Moon Tonight? by A. Baldwin Stone, 1902 ....**10.00**

What's The Score? by Leon Rene, 1946 ....**5.00**

What's The Use? by Isham Jones & Charles Newman, 1930, Photo Isham Jones **5.00**

What's The Use Of Going Home? by Grant Clarke, Joe McCarthy & Jimmie Monaco, 1915 (Cover Artist, Wohlman)........................**10.00**

What's The Use Of Going Home? by Grant Clarke, Joe McCarthy & Jimmie Monaco, 1915, Photo Thos. Potter Dunne (Cover Artist, Rose Symbol)...**10.00**

What's The Use Of Kicking, Let's Go Round With A Smile? by Sam M. Lewis, Joe Young & Walter Donaldson, 1919..................................**5.00**

What's The Use Of Wand'rin? by Richard Rodgers & Oscar Hammerstein II, 1945, Movie: Carousel (Cover Artist, BJH) **5.00**

What's The Use To Have A Heart? by James & Shannon, 1916, Photo Lela Livernash (Cover Artist, Pfeiffer) **10.00**

Whatever Lola Wants, Lola Gets by Richard Adler & Jerry Ross, 1955, Musical: Damn Yankees...**5.00**

Whatever Will Be Will Be, Que Sera, Sera by Jay Livingston & Ray Evans, 1955, Movie: The Man Who Knew Too Much, Photo James Stewart & Doris Day **10.00**

Wheel The Baby Out by Edward Harrigan & David Braham, 1881 (Pre 1900)..**15.00**

When A Black Man's Blue by Little, 1930 (Black, Black Face) **10.00**

When A Blue Service Star Turns To Gold by Casper Nathan & Theodore Morse, 1918 (WWI) **15.00**

When A Boy Says Goodbye To His Mother And She Gives Him To Uncle Sam by Jack Frost, 1917 (WWI) **16.00**

When A Boy Says "Will You" And a Girl Says "Yes" by Allen, 1908 ..**5.00**

When A Boy Without A Girl Meets A Girl Without A Boy by Robert F. Rodan & Geo W. Meyer, 1912 (Cover Artist, Pfeiffer)................**10.00**

When A College Boy Meets A College Girl by Jack Mahoney & Theodore Morse, 1910...**5.00**

When A Fellow's On The Level With A Girl That's On The Square by George M. Cohan, 1907 (George M. Cohan) **10.00**

When A Lady Meets A Gentleman Down South by Dave Oppenheim, 1936 ....**5.00**

When A Woman Loves A Man by William Rose & Ralph Rainger, 1930, Movie: Be Yourself, Photo Fannie Brice **16.00**

When Alexander Takes His Ragtime Band To France by Alfred Bryan, Cliff Hess & Edgar Leslie, 1918 (WWI & Rag) **15.00**

When Angels Weep by Charles K. Harris, 1914 (Cover Artist, Pfeiffer)..**10.00**

When April Comes by Paul Weston & Doris Schaefer, 1950 ....**5.00**

When Bob White Is Whistling In The Meadow by Monroe H. Rosenfeld, 1906 ....**5.00**

When Broadway Was A Pasture by McCarthy & Piantadosi, 1911.......**5.00**

When Church Is Out by Puch & Carrie Jacobs Bond, 1907, Dedicated To Mrs. E. P. Doty (Dedication)..**15.00**

When Clouds Have Vanished And Skies Are Blue by Wm. R. Clay & Chas. L. Johnson, 1922...**5.00**

When Cupid Comes A Tapping by Barrett, 1916 (Cover Artist, Pfeiffer)...**10.00**

When Daddy Greets His Son by Ponella, 1919 (WWI)........................**10.00**

When Darling Bess First Whispered Yes by Roden & Helf, 1908 (Cover Artist, Pfeiffer)...**10.00**

When Day Is Done by B.G. DeSylva & Dr. Robert Katscher, 1926....**10.00**

When Did You Leave Heaven? by Walter Bullock & Richard A. Whiting, 1936, Movie: Sing Baby Sing, Photo Tony Martin.......................**5.00**

When Did You Write To Mother Last? by Charles K. Harris, 1914 (Cover Artist, Pfeiffer & WWI)...**15.00**

When Dreams Come True by Hein & Webb, 1913 ....**5.00**

When Erastus Plays His Old Kazoo by Sammy Fain, Sam Coslow & Larry Spier, 1927 (Black, Black Face)...................................**10.00**

When Evening Shadows Fall by Jeff Branen & Wm. Polla, 1916 (Cover Artist, DeTakacs)..**10.00**

When Everything Was Sunshine by Will Wood, 1910.......................**5.00**

When Eyes Of Blue Are Fooling You by Sidney Clare & Jimmie Monaco, 1925 ....**5.00**

When Father Laid The Carpet On The Stairs by Jackson, 1906..........**10.00**

When First You Told Me That You Cared by Rainville, 1914 ....**5.00**

When Francis Dances With Me by Benny Ryan & Violinsky, 1921 .....**5.00**

When God Puts Out The Light by Carrie Jacobs Bond, 1901, Dedicated To Mr. & Mrs. Whitney (Dedication) **15.00**

When Grandma Sings The Songs She Loved At The End Of A Perfect Day by Bartley Costello & Robert A. Keiser, 1916 (Cover Artist, Pfeiffer)..**10.00**

When He Gave Me You, Mother Of Mine by Bob Murphy & Elmore White, 1919 (Cover Artist, Wilson Art).....................................**5.00**

When Hogan Paid His Rent by J.W. Kelly, 1891 (Pre 1900)..............**10.00**

When I Am Dead My Dearest by Christina Rosetti & Vaughan Williams, 1903 ....**4.00**

When I Am Dreaming Twilight Dreams by Fed Dusenberry & C.M. Denison, 1913 (Cover Artist, MWC)..**5.00**

When I Am Yours by Oscar F.G. Day & Edward Buffington, 1905......**5.00**

When I Close My Eyes And Dream by Earl Abel, 1930, Photo Rudy Vallee (Cover Artist, Leff) **10.00**

When I Come Back To You, We'll Have A Yankee-Doodle Wedding by William Tracey & Jack Stern, 1918 (Cover Artist, Barbelle & WWI) **16.00**

When I Do The Hootchy Kootchy In The Sky by Gussie L. Davis, 1896 (Pre 1900) **10.00**

When I Dream About That Southern Home Of Mine by Ray Sherwood, 1918 (Dixie)..**6.00**

When I Dream In The Gloaming Of You by Herbert Ingraham, 1909...**5.00**

When I Dream In the Moonlight Of You by Wm. Phillips & J. Henry Ellis, 1919 (Cover Artist, Barbelle & Deco) **5.00**

When I Dream Of Old Erin, I'm Dreaming Of You by Marvin Lee & Leo Friedman, 1912 (Cover Artist, Pfeiffer & Irish)............................**15.00**

When I Dream Of You by James Lonergan, Edward Grady & James E. Colgan, 1913...**5.00**

When I Dream Of You by Wm. R. Clay & Chas. L. Johnson, 1911, Photo Margaret Foy **5.00**

When I Fell In Love With You by Davis, Cronson & Ruddy, 1917 (Cover Artist, Pfeiffer)..**10.00**

When I First Met You by Sam Lewis & Geo Meyer, 1913, Photo Billie Claire (Cover Artist, DeTakacs)..**10.00**

When I First Saw You by Rais, 1916 (Cover Artist, Pfeiffer).............**12.00**

When I Get Back Again To Bonnie Scotland by Harry Lauder, 1908 ..**10.00**

When I Get Back From Over There by DeWitt H. Morse & William H. Farrell, 1918 (Cover Artist, E.E. Walton & WWI) **10.00**

When I Get Back To Georgia & You by Clay, 1916 (Cover Artist, Pfeiffer) **10.00**

When I Get Back To Home Sweet Home by Abe Olman, 1917 (WWI) **10.00**

When I Get Back To My American Blighty by Arthur Fields & Theodore Morse, 1918, Small War Edition (WWI) **15.00**

When I Get Back To My Old Girl by Maguire, Driscoll & Scanlon, 1915 (Cover Artist, Pfeiffer & Deco)........................**10.00**

When I Get Back To Old Virginia by Al Dubin & George McConnell, 1915, Photo Russ Kelly (Cover Artist, H.S. Lukens)......................**5.00**

When I Get Back To The Folks I Love by Harry & Chas. Tobias, 1917 (Cover Artist, Kursh)..**10.00**

When I Get You Alone Tonight by Joe McCarthy, Joe Goodwin & Fred Fischer, 1912, Photo Bert Walton (Cover Artist, R.S.)..................**10.00**

When I Get You Alone Tonight by Joe McCarthy, Joe Goodwin & Fred Fischer, 1912, Photo Cross & Josephine (Cover Artist, R.S.)........**10.00**

When I Go Automobiling by George Mack, 1907 (Transportation) **10.00**

When I Got Back To My Old Home Town by Howard, Tracey & Harriman, 1914 (Cover Artist, Pfeiffer & Deco) **12.00**

When I Grow Too Old To Dream by Oscar Hammerstein II & Sigmund Romberg, 1935, Movie: The Night Is Young, Photo Ramon Novarro & Evelyn Laye..**10.00**

When I Grow Too Old To Dream by Oscar Hammerstein II & Sigmund Romberg, 1935, Movie: The Night Is Young, Photo Nelson Eddy ..**10.00**

When I Grow Up by Edward Heyman & Roy Henderson, 1935, Movie: Curly Top, Photo Shirley Temple (Shirley Temple) **10.00**

When I Have Sung My Song by Ernest Charles, 1934..........................**5.00**

When I Hear You Play That Piano, Bill by Irving Berlin & Ted Snyder, 1909 (Cover Artist, John Frew & Irving Berlin)............................**10.00**

When I Kissed The Blarney Stone by Walter Scanlan, 1923 (Irish) **5.00**

When I Leave The World Behind by Irving Berlin, 1914 (Cover Artist, Barbelle & Irving Berlin) **10.00**

When I Listen To The Sunset by Leo Wood, 1914 ....**5.00**

When I Look At You by Paul Francis Webster & Walter Jurmann, 1943, Movie: Presenting Lily Mars, Photo Judy Garland **10.00**

When I Looked In Your Wonderful Eyes by A. Stanley Dunkealey & Nat Osborne, 1920..**5.00**

When I Lost You by Irving Berlin, 1912, Photo Babe Foy (Cover Artist, Pfeiffer & Irving Berlin)..**28.00**

When I Lost You by Irving Berlin, 1912, Photo Mahoney & Bernie (Cover Artist, Pfeiffer & Irving Berlin)......................................**16.00**

When I Lost You by Irving Berlin, 1912, Photo Sabelle Patricola (Cover Artist, Pfeiffer & Irving Berlin)......................................**16.00**

When I Lost You Mother Of Mine by Nat Osborne & A. Stanley Dunkealey, 1920..**5.00**

When I Marry Mr. Snow by Richard Rodgers & Oscar Hammerstein II, 1945, Movie: Carousel (Cover Artist, BJH)....................................**5.00**

When I Marry You by Alfred Bryan & Albert Gumble, 1908, Photo Cheridah Simpson, Dedicated To Miss Gertrude Davidson (Cover Artist, DeTakacs & Dedication) **15.00**

When I Met You Last Night In Dreamland by Beth S. Whitson & W.R. Williams, 1911, Photo Maud Lambert **10.00**

When I Said Goodbye To You by Arthur Jackson & Max Friedman, 1919 (Cover Artist, Barbelle) **5.00**

When I See An Elephant Fly by Oliver Wallace, Frank Churchill & Ned Washington, 1941, Movie: Dumbo (Disney) **15.00**

When I Send You A Picture Of Berlin by Frank Fay, Ben Ryan & Dave Dreyer, 1918 (Cover Artist, Pfeiffer & WWI) **10.00**

When I Think Of You by Charles Horwitz & Frederick V. Bowers, 1900..**10.00**

When I Think Of You by Harry Owens & Vincent Rose, 1925 (Cover Artist, JVR & Deco)..**10.00**

When I Think Upon The Maidens by Philip Ashbrooke & Michael Head, 1920 ....**5.00**

When I Took The Keeley Cure by James Thornton, 1897 (Pre 1900) .**10.00**

When I Waltz With You by Alfred Bryan & Albert Gumble, 1912.......**5.00**

When I Want To Settle Down by Schwartz & Atteridge, 1913 (Cover Artist, Pfeiffer)..**10.00**

When I Was A Dreamer by Roger Lewis, Geo. A. Little & Egbert Van Alstyne, 1914 (Cover Artist, Einson) **10.00**

When I Was A Girl 18 Years Old by John Cole, 1855 (Pre 1900).......**35.00**

When I Was A Lad by Arthur Sullivan, Opera: H.M.S. Pinafore (Cover Artist, Pfeiffer)..**10.00**

When I Was Twenty-One And You Were Sweet Sixteen by Harry Williams & Egbert Van Alstyne, 1911 (Cover Artist, Starmer) ..12.00

When I Wave My Flag by James Byrnes, 1918 (WWI)........................**5.00**

When I Went To School With You by Yusco-Elderly, 1916 ....**5.00**

When I Woke Up This Morning by Jimmie V. Monaco, 1911, Photo Elizabeth Murphy..**5.00**

When I Write My Song by Ted Mossman & Bill Anson, 1947 ....**5.00**

When I'm Alone I'm Lonesome by Irving Berlin, 1911, Successfully Introduced by Emma Carus, Photo Yvette (Cover Artist, John Frew & Irving Berlin) **15.00**

When I'm Gone You'll Soon Forget by E. Austin Keith, 1920 ....**4.00**

When I'm Looking At You by Clifford Grey & Herbert Stothart, 1929, Movie: The Rogue Song, Photo Lawrence Tibbett **15.00**

When I'm Looking At You by Gene Buck & Dave Stamper, 1918, Musical: Ziegfeld Follies Of 1918, Photo Many Ziegfeld Girls.............**15.00**

When I'm Not Near The Girl I Love by E.Y. Harburg & Burton Lane, 1946, Musical: Finian's Rainbow (Cover Artist, BJH & Irish)........**5.00**

When I'm Thinking Of You by Irving Berlin, 1911 (Cover Artist, Pfeiffer & Irving Berlin)..**15.00**

When I'm Thru With The Arms Of The Army by Earl Carroll, 1918, Lovingly Dedicated To My Sweetheart Mrs. Earl Carroll, Photo Mr. & Mrs. Carroll (Cover Artist, Rose Symbol, WWI & Dedication)....**30.00**

When I'm Waltzing With My Sweetie by Robert E. Harty & Alvin Bevier, 1932 ....**6.00**

When I'm With You by Carson J. Robison, 1922 ....**5.00**

When I'm With You by Mack Gordon & Harry Revel, 1936, Movie: Poor Little Rich Girl, Photo Shirley Temple (Shirley Temple).............**10.00**

When I'm With You by Will L. Livernash, 1915..................................**5.00**

When Ireland Comes Into Her Own by Stanley, 1919 (Irish) **5.00**

When Irish Eyes Are Smiling by Chauncey Alcott, Geo. Graff Jr. & Ernest Ball, 1912, Signed by John McCormack (Irish & Signed)............**65.00**

When Isabella Green Went Automobiling by Marshall, 1902 (Transportation)..**15.00**

When It Comes To A Lovingless Day by Jack Frost, 1918 (WWI).....**10.00**

When It Rains It Pours by Slovin, 1956, Movie: Country Music Holiday, Photo Faron Young...**3.00**

When It Rains, Sweetheart, When It Rains by Irving Berlin, 1911 (Irving Berlin)..**10.00**

When It Strikes Home by C. Harris, 1915, Photo Grace Washburn (Cover Artist, Pfeiffer)..**10.00**

When It's All Goin' Out And Nothin' Comin' In by Williams & Walker, 1902 (Black, Black Face) **15.00**

When It's All Over by C.A. Pfeiffer, 1918 (Cover Artist, Pfeiffer & WWI)..**15.00**

When It's All Over by Lew Brown & Kerry Mills, 1915 (Cover Artist, DeTakacs & WWI)..**15.00**

When It's Apple Blossom Time In Normandie by Mellor, Gifford & Trevor, 1912, Photo Nora Bayes (Cover Artist, Starmer).............**12.00**

When It's Apple Blossom Time In Normandie by Mellor, Gifford & Trevor, 1912, Photo Eva Shirley (Cover Artist, Starmer).............**12.00**

When It's Apple Blossom Time In Normandie by Mellor, Gifford & Trevor, 1912, Photo Belle Storey (Cover Artist, Starmer).............**12.00**

When It's Cotton Pickin' Time In Tennessee by Caddigan & Brennan, 1918 (Black, Black Face) **10.00**

When It's Lamp Lightin' Time In The Valley by Joe Lyons, Sam C. Hart & The Vagabonds, 1933..**5.00**

When It's Love Time In Picardy by Jeff Branen & Alfred Solman, 1919 (Irish) **5.00**

When It's Moonlight In Mayo by Mahoney & Wenrich, 1913 (Cover Artist, Starmer & Irish)..**10.00**

When It's Moonlight In The Garden Of Love by Arthur E. Buchanan, 1915 (Cover Artist, Pfeiffer) **12.00**

When It's Moonlight In Tokio by Heath, Shisler & James, 1917 ....**5.00**

When It's Moonlight Mary Darling 'Neath The Old Grape Arbor Shade by Bartley Costello & J. Fred Helf, 1917, Photo J. Aldrich Libbey (Cover Artist, Starmer) **10.00**

When It's Moonlight On The Alamo by Bryan & Fisher, 1914.............**5.00**

When It's Moonlight On The Meadow, Mollie Dear by Ryan & Richard, 1912 (Cover Artist, Pfeiffer) **10.00**

When It's Moonlight On The Mississippi by Vandeveer & Lange, 1915..**8.00**

When It's Moonlight On The Prairie by Robt. F. Roden & S.R. Henry, 1908 ....**10.00**

When It's Moonlight On the Swanee Shore by Raymond B. Egan & Richard A. Whiting, 1920 (Cover Artist, Frederick S. Manning & Deco) **5.00**

When It's Night Time Down In Burgundy by Alfred Bryan & Herman Paley, 1914 (Cover Artist, Starmer & WWI) **10.00**

When It's Night-Time In Italy It's Wednesday Over Here by James Kendis & Lew Brown, 1923, Photo Jewell & Most (Cover Artist, Wohlman) **6.00**

When It's Nightime Down In Dixieland by Irving Berlin, 1914 (Cover Artist, Barbelle, Irving Berlin & Dixie) **15.00**

When It's Orange Blossom Time In Loveland by Jeff Branen & Arthur Lange, 1915 ....**5.00**

When It's Sleepy time Down South by Leon & Otis Rene & Clarence Muse, 1931, Photo Mildred Bailey (Cover Artist, Frederick Manning)......**10.00**

When It's Springtime In Lucerne by Jimmy Shea & Billy Vanderveer, 1916 ....**5.00**

When It's Springtime In The Rockies by Mary Hale Woolsey, Milton Taggart & Robert Sauer, 1929, Photo Rudy Vallee **15.00**

When It's Sunset In Sweden by Morrison & Burtnett, 1919................**6.00**

When It's Twilight Neath The Old New England Hills by Arthur Bucknam & Jacob Henry Ellis, 1915 (Cover Artist, Rose) **10.00**

When Johnny Comes Marching Home Again by Louis Lambert, 1863 (Pre 1900)..**45.00**

When Johnson's Quartet Harmonize by Irving Berlin, 1912 (Cover Artist, Pfeiffer, Irving Berlin & Black, Black Face)................................**20.00**

When June Comes Along With A Song by George M. Cohan (George M. Cohan) **10.00**

When Kate And I Were Coming Through The Rye by Harry Von Tilzer, 1902, Photo Cecil Early & Harry Von Tilzer (Cover Artist, Starmer & Irish)..**12.00**

When Knighthood Was In Flower by Gustin, 1900 ....**5.00**

When Lights Are Low by Gus Kahn, Ted Koehler & Ted Fiorito, 1923 (Deco) **5.00**

When Love Beckoned by Cole Porter, 1943, Movie: DuBarry Was A Lady..**6.00**

When Love Grows Cold by Billy Sunday & Roy York, 1925, Movie: When Love Grows Cold, Inspired by Mrs. Rudolph Valentino.....**15.00**

When Love Is Young by Paulton & Jakobowski, 1888 (Pre 1900)......**10.00**

When Mammy's Pickaninny's Fast Asleep by John Martin (Black, Black Face) **25.00**

When Mother First Taught Me How To Pray by Paul Dresser, 1892 (Pre 1900)..**15.00**

When Mother Nature Sings Her Lullaby by Larry Yoell & Glenn Brown, 1938, Photo Bing Crosby (Cover Artist, Leff) **5.00**

When Mother Played The Organ by Dick Sanford & George McConnell, 1932 (Cover Artist, Leff) **5.00**

When Mother Sang Hush-A Bye, O by H.C. Weasner, 1919..............**10.00**

When My Baby Puts Her Little Arms Around Me by Robert E. Harty, Billy Moss & Alvin Bevier, 1933..**5.00**

When My Baby Smiles At Me by Ted Lewis, Andrew B. Sterling & Bill Munro, 1920, Photo Ted Lewis...**10.00**

When My Baby Smiles At Me by Von Tilzer, Sterling, Munro & Lewis, 1920, Movie: When My Baby Smiles At Me, Photo Dan Dailey & Betty Grable..**10.00**

When My Dream Boat Comes Home by Cliff Friend & Dave Franklin, 1936, Photo Guy, Victor, Carmen & Lebert Lombardo...................**6.00**

When My Dream Boat Comes Home by Cliff Friend & Dave Franklin, 1936, Photo Les Brown **6.00**

When My Dream Boat Comes Home by Cliff Friend & Dave Franklin, 1936, Photo Jerry Johnson...**6.00**

When My Dream Boat Comes Home by Cliff Friend & Dan Franklin, 1936, Photo Dick Stabile..**6.00**

When My Dream Boat Comes Home by Cliff Friend & Dave Franklin, 1936, Photo Sammy Kaye **6.00**

When My Dreams Come True by Irving Berlin, 1929, Movie: Cocoanuts (Irving Berlin)..**12.00**

When My Golden Hair Has Turned To Silver Gray by Edward Stanley, 1909 ....**5.00**

When My Great Grand Daddy & My Great Grand Mammy Used To Cuddle & Coo In The Coconut Tree by Walker, 1917 (Cover Artist, Pfeiffer) **15.00**

When My Paw Was A Boy by S.E. Kiser & E.L. Ashford, 1926 ....**3.00**

When My Ship Comes In by Vincent Bryan & Harry Von Tilzer, 1915..**5.00**

When My Ships Come Sailing Home by Reginald Steward & Francis Dorel, 1903 ....**5.00**

When My Sweetheart Whispered Yes by Tommy O'Dell & Alexander Mignani, 1905, Photo Reese V. Prosser **5.00**

When New York Was New York by George M. Cohan (George M. Cohan) **10.00**

When Old Bill Bailey Plays The Ukalele by Chas. McCarron & Nat Vincent, 1915 (Cover Artist, DeTakacs & Black, Black Face)............**20.00**

When Old Silas Does The Turkey Trot by Leap, 1913 (Cover Artist, Pfeiffer) **10.00**

When Our Soldier Boys Come Home by Gus Kahn, 1944 (WWII).......**5.00**

When Pa Was Courtin' Ma by Jack Manus & Leonard Joy, 1938.........**5.00**

When Ragtime Rosie Ragged The Rosary by Edgar Leslie & Lewis F. Muir, 1911 (Rag) **10.00**

When Sally In Our Alley Sings Those Old Time Songs To Me by Farran & Osborne, 1912 (Cover Artist, Pfeiffer & Deco) **15.00**

When Scanlon Sang Mavourneen More Than Twenty Years Ago by Harry Kelly & Osborne, 1917 (Irish)..**5.00**

When Shadows Fall by Harold G. Frost & E. Clinton Keithly, 1916.....**5.00**

When Shadows Gather by Fred E. Weatherly & Charles Marshall, 1908, Sung by John McCormack **10.00**

When Shall I Again See Ireland by Henry Blossom &Victor Herbert, 1917 (Victor Herbert & Irish)..**10.00**

When Shall We Meet Again by Raymond B. Egan & Richard A. Whiting, 1921 (Cover Artist, R.Van Buren & Transportation)......................**6.00**

When Shall We Meet Again by Raymond B. Egan & Richard A. Whiting, 1921, Musical: "Tip Top", Photo Duncan Sisters (Cover Artist, Starmer) **10.00**

When She Comes Back I'm Going Away by Piantadosi, 1909 (Cover Artist, Pfeiffer)..**10.00**

When Someone Really Cares by Mabel Davies & Wm. Cahill, 1907 ...**5.00**

When Summer Is Gone by Charlie Harrison & Monte Wilhite, 1928....**5.00**

When That Man Is Dead And Gone by Irving Berlin, 1941 (Irving Berlin & WWII)..**16.00**

When That Midnight Choo-Choo Leaves For Alabam' by Irving Berlin, 1912, Photo Willis Sisters (Cover Artist, Pfeiffer, Irving Berlin & Transportation) **18.00**

When That Midnight Choo-Choo Leaves For Alabam' by Irving Berlin, 1912, Movie: There's No Business Like Show Business (Cover Artist, Pfeiffer, Irving Berlin & Transportation) **18.00**

When The Angelus Is Ringing by Joe Young & Bert Grant, 1914 ....**5.00**

When The Apple Blossoms Bloom In France by Harold Freeman & Harry C. Ellsesser, 1914 ....**5.00**

When The Autumn Leaves Are Falling by Leo Wood & Ben Jansen, 1909..**8.00**

When The Autumn Leaves Begin To Fall by Neville Fleeson & Albert Von Tilzer, 1920..**5.00**

When The Autumn Leaves Of Life Begin To Fall by B.G. DeSylva, Lew Brown & Ray Henderson, 1931 ....**5.00**

When The Band Plays Indiana by Billy Gaston, 1918 (WWI)............**10.00**

When The Bees Make Honey Down In Sunny Alabam by Sam M. Lewis, Joe Young & Walter Donaldson, 1919 (Cover Artist, Barbelle)....**10.00**

When The Bell In The Lighthouse Rings by Lamb & Solman, 1905...**10.00**

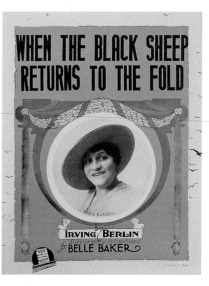

When The Black Sheep Returns To The Fold by Irving Berlin, 1916, Successfully Introduced by Belle Baker, Photo Marie Russell (Cover Artist, Barbelle & Irving Berlin)...................................15.00

When The Bonnie, Bonnie Heather Is Blooming, I'll Return To You by James G. Ellis, 1915 ....**6.00**

When The Boys Come Back by G.W. Jeffords & M.L. Jeffords, 1917 (WWI)..**10.00**

When The Boys Come Home by John Hay & Oley Speaks, 1917, Written by The Late Secretary Of State During Civil War, While He Was Private Secretary To President Lincoln (Cover Artist, P. Van Burent, WWI)..**25.00**

When The Boys Come Marching Home by Leo Friedman, 1916 (WWI)...**5.00**

When The Car Goes By, Motorman's Popular Song by E.S. Ufford, 1897 (Pre 1900 & Transportation)..**35.00**

When The Cherry Blossoms Fall, Love Is Love by Cary Duncan & Anselm Goetze, 1919, Musical: The Royal Vagabond **5.00**

When The Cherry Trees Are Blooming In Japan by C. Harris, 1918 (Cover Artist, Pfeiffer)..**10.00**

When The Children Are Asleep by Richard Rodgers & Oscar Hammerstein, II, 1945, Movie: Carousel, Photo Gordon Macrae, Shirley Jones & Cameron Mitchell (Cover Artist, BJH) **8.00**

When The Clock In The Tower Strikes Twelve by Edward Harrigan & David Braham, 1882 (Pre 1900)..**10.00**

When The Clouds Of War Roll By by Nat Binns & Earl Haubrick, 1917 (WWI)..**10.00**

When The Daisies Bloom by Anita Owen, 1909..................................**5.00**

When The Day Is Done by Leo Wood & Ben Jansen, 1916 ....**5.00**

When The Dew Is On The Rose by Anita Owen, 1911, Photo Anita Owen (Cover Artist, Starmer & Deco) **10.00**

When The Evening Breeze Is Sighing Home, Sweet Home by Clarendon & Solman, 1905..**5.00**

When The Evening Shadows Fall Across The Meadow by Howard King & Sidney Chapman, 1914 (Cover Artist, John Frew) **10.00**

When The Fields Are White With Daisies by C.M. Denison & W.A. Pratt, 1904 ....**5.00**

When The Flowers Bloom On No Man's Land by Howard E. Rogers & Archie Gottler, 1918, Photo Dorothy Jarrett (Cover Artist, Barbelle, March & WWI) **10.00**

When The Gates Of Heaven Opened And I Saw My Mother There by Edward Madden, Arthur Lamb & Fred Bowers, 1917, Photo Joe Griffith (Cover Artist, Pfeiffer & Irish) **16.00**

When The Girl Whose Heart You Long For Has A Heart Who Longs For You by Roden & Meyer, 1911 (Cover Artist, Pfeiffer)..................**10.00**

When The Golden Rod Is Waving, Nellie, Mine by Orne, 1916 (Cover Artist, Pfeiffer)......**10.00**

When The Great Red Dawn Is Shining by Edward Lockton & Evelyn Sharpe, 1917 ......**6.00**

When The Grown Up Ladies Act Like Babies by Joe Young, 1914, Photo Al Jolson (Al Jolson) **10.00**

When The Harbor Lights Are Burning by Alfred Bryan & Alfred Solman, 1907 ......**5.00**

When The Harvest Days Are Over by H. Graham & Harry Von Tilzer, 1900 ......**5.00**

When The Harvest Moon Is Shining by Andrew B. Sterling & Harry Von Tilzer, 1920......**5.00**

When The Harvest Moon Is Shining On The River by Lamb & Henry, 1904 ......**5.00**

When The Harvest Time Is Over by Earl Taylor, 1916......**5.00**

When The Haying Time Is Over by Farron & Jacobs, 1909 (Cover Artist, Pfeiffer)......**10.00**

When The Henry Clay Comes Steaming Into Mobile Bay by Jerome & Clark, 1912 (Cover Artist, Pfeiffer)......**15.00**

When The Honey Moon Stops Shining (Cover Artist, Pfeiffer) **10.00**

When The Honeymoon Was Over by Fred Fisher, 1921 (Cover Artist, Wohlman) **5.00**

When The Hummingbirds Return Sweet Irene by Farran, 1909 (Cover Artist, Pfeiffer)......**10.00**

When The Kaiser Does The Goose-Step To A Good Old American Rag by Jack Frost & Harold Neander, 1917 (WWI & Rag)......**35.00**

When The Last Rose Of Summer Has Whispered Goodbye by Robert Levenson & Ted Garton, 1917 (Cover Artist, Starmer) **5.00**

When The Leaves Bid The Trees Goodbye by Tot Seymour & Vee Lawnhurst, 1935, Photo Dorothy Lamour......**5.00**

When The Leaves Come Tumbling Down by Richard Howard, 1922...**5.00**

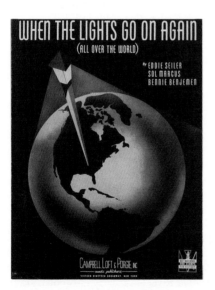

When The Lights Go On Again All Over The World by Eddie Seiler, Sol Marcus & Bennie Benjeman, 1942 (Cover Artist, Im-Ho & WWII)......4.00

When The Lights Go Out On Broadway by Sheldon, Friedman & Staft, 1917 (Cover Artist, Pfeiffer) **10.00**

When The Little Red Roses Get The Blues For You by Al Dubin & Joe Burke, 1931, Movie: Hold Everything, Photo Joe E. Brown & Winnie Lightner **5.00**

When The Lusitania Went Down by Charles R. McCarron & Nat Vincent, 1915 (WWI & Transportation) **38.00**

When The Mailman Says "No Mail Today" by Walter Hirsch, Gertrude Lincoff & Louis Siefert, 1933 ......**10.00**

When The Major Plays Those Minor Keys by DeCosta, 1916 (Black, Black Face) **15.00**

When The Man In The Moon Looks Down by Tell Taylor, 1907 ......**5.00**

When The Maple Leaves Were Falling by Tell Taylor, 1913 ......**5.00**

When The Mission Bells Were Ringing Down In Burma By The Sea by Al Dubin & Gustav Benkhart, 1916 (Cover Artist, L.W. Ross)......**5.00**

When The Mocking Birds Are Singing In The Wildwood by Arthur J. Lamb & H.B. Blanke, 1905 (Cover Artist, Starmer)......**10.00**

When The Money Moon Is Shining by Jack Caddigan & O.E. Story, 1914......**5.00**

When The Moon Begins To Shine Through The Pines Of Caroline by Will Hart & Ed Nelson, 1918 ......**6.00**

When The Moon Bids The Sun Goodnight by Basil Ziegler & Lou Shank, 1938, Photo Rose Marie **5.00**

When The Moon Comes Over The Mountain by Kate Smith, Howard Johnson & Harry Woods, 1922, Photo Kate Smith (Cover Artist, Wohlman)......**15.00**

When The Moon Comes Over The Mountain by Kate Smith, Howard Johnson & Harry Woods, 1932, Signed & Inscribed Photo Kate Smith (Signed) **45.00**

When The Moon Plays Peek-A-Boo by W.R. Williams, 1907, Photo Maud Lambert......**5.00**

When The Moon Shines Down In Old Alaska by Jack Frost & E. Clinton Keithly, 1916 ......**5.00**

When The Moon Swings Low by John Page & Neil Moret, 1910 (Cover Artist, Starmer) **5.00**

When The Oceans Meet In Panama by Charles R. McCarron, 1914 (Transportation) **10.00**

When The Old Boat Heads For Home by Earl Fuller, 1918 (WWI & Transportation) **15.00**

When The One You Love Loves You by Paul Whiteman, Cliff Friend & Abel Baer, 1924......**6.00**

When The Organ Played At Twilight by Raymond Wallace, Jimmy Campbell & Reg Connely, 1930 (Cover Artist, Barbelle)......**6.00**

When The Orioles Come North Again by Chas. E. Haer & Johann C. Schmid, 1906 (Cover Artist, Shaw)......**5.00**

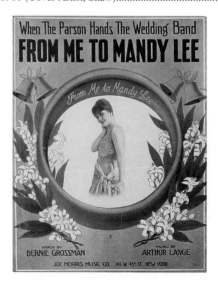

When The Parson Hands The Wedding Band From Me To Mandy Lee by Bernie Grossman & Arthur Lange, 1917 (Cover Artist, Starmer)......10.00

When The Pines Of Alsace Whisper "Dixieland" by Jack Frost & E. Clinton Keithley, 1918 (WWI & Dixie)......**10.00**

When The Poppies Bloom Again by Leo Towers, Morton Morrow & Don Pelosi, 1936, Photo Rudy Vallee (Cover Artist, Barbelle & Deco) **10.00**

When The Red Red Robin Comes Bob Bob Bobbin' Along by Harry Woods, 1926...**8.00**

When The Robert E. Lee Arrives In Tennessee, 1918 ....**6.00**

When The Robin Calls Its Mate by Chas. E. Casey, Jacob Henry Ellis & Benjamin Richmond, 1912 (Cover Artist, Pfeiffer) **10.00**

When The Robin Sings After The Rain by Joseph McCarthy & James F. Hanley, 1931...**5.00**

When The Robin Sings Again by Don Ramsay, 1907, Photo Charles F. Orr, Dedicated To Miss Pearl Lillian Townes (Cover Artist, Starmer & Dedication) **10.00**

When The Robins Nest Again by Frank Howard, 1883 (Pre 1900).....**10.00**

When The Robins Sing In June by Con Conrad, 1908..........................**5.00**

When The Roses Bloom In Avalon by Alfred Bryan & Jack Wells, 1914...**5.00**

When The Roses Bloom In Loveland by Curtis Gover, 1916 (Cover Artist, Rose)...**5.00**

When The Saints Come Marchin' In by T. Elli, 1957 (Cover Artist, Bob Blansky)...**3.00**

When The Saints Go Marching In by Paul Campbell, 1951, Photo The Weavers **4.00**

When The Ships Come Home by Guy Bolton, P.G. Woodhouse & Jerome Kern, 1918, Musical: Oh Lady! Lady!!..**6.00**

When The Silver Threads Were Not Among The Gold by Rees, Kendis & Stillwell, 1914 (Cover Artist, Pfeiffer)..................................**10.00**

When The Stars & Stripes Are Safe by C.L. Phillipus, 1918 (Cover Artist, Pfeiffer & WWI)...**15.00**

When The Steamboats On The Swanee Whistle Rag-Time by Jack Caddigan & Jam. Brennan, 1908, Respectfully Dedicated To The Memory Of Happy O'Neill (Cover Artist, Starmer, Black, Black Face, Dedication, Rag & Transportation)...**20.00**

When The Sun Bids The Moon Goodnight by Little Jack Little, Dave Oppenheim & Ira Schuster, 1933, Photo Don Bestor.....................**3.00**

When The Sun Comes Out by Ted Koeler & Harold Arlen, 1941........**3.00**

When The Sun Comes Tumbling Down by Gene Arnold & Egbert Van Alstyne, 1933..**3.00**

When The Sun Goes Down by Arthur A. Penn, 1922..........................**3.00**

When The Sun Goes Down In Cairo Town by Ben Black & Fred Fisher, 1920 ....**5.00**

When The Sun Goes Down In Dixie by Chas McCarron & Albert Von Tilzer, 1917 (Cover Artist, DeTakacs & Dixie)............................**10.00**

When The Sun Goes Down In France by Gilbert Tennant, 1918, Photo Connie Lehr Fuller (Cover Artist, Pfeiffer & WWI).....................**15.00**

When The Sun Goes Down In Normandie by Branen & Lloyd, 1918 (Cover Artist, Pfeiffer & WWI) **15.00**

When The Sun Goes Down In Romany by Sam Lewis, Joe Young & Bert Grant, 1916, Musical: Step This Way (Cover Artist, Barbelle & Deco) **15.00**

When The Sun Goes Down In Switzerland by George McConnell & Jimmie McHugh, 1916...**5.00**

When The Sun Sets In Galway by Roy Linwood & Ed. Casey, 1915 (Irish)..**12.00**

When The Sunset Bids The Day Goodby by Piantadosi, 1927 (Cover Artist, Pfeiffer)..**10.00**

When The Sunset Turns The Ocean's Blue To Gold by H.W. Petrie and E.F. Buckner, 1903 (Black, Black Face) **15.00**

When The Swallows Come Back To Capistrano by Leon Rene, 1940, Photo Larry Clinton (Cover Artist, Im-Ho)....................................**3.00**

When The Tide Is Turning by Wainstein & Foster, 1912 (Cover Artist, Pfeiffer)..**10.00**

When The Trains Come East From California by Graham, 1920 (Transportation) **15.00**

When The Twilight Comes To Kiss The Rose "Good-Night" by Robert F. Roden & Henry W. Petrie, 1912 (Cover Artist, Starmer) **10.00**

When The War Is Over, I'll Return To You by Watson & Dudley, 1918, Photo Justine Johnstone (Cover Artist, Pfeiffer & WWI)..............**15.00**

When The Whole World Has Gone Back On You by Edward Madden & Gus Edwards, 1913, Photo Courtney Sisters (Cover Artist, Starmer).......**10.00**

When The Winds O'er The Sea Blow A Gale by Hyde, 1902 (Transportation)...**10.00**

When The World Is At Rest by Benny Davis & Sammy Fain, 1929 .....**5.00**

When The Yankees Go Into Battle, 1917 (WWI)................................**10.00**

When The Yankees Yank The Kaiser Off His Throne by A.M. Robinette & W.J. Quinn, 1918 (WWI) **25.00**

When The Yanks Come Marching Home by William Jerome & Seymour Furth, 1917, Photo Wm. J. Reilly, U.S.N. (Cover Artist, Barbelle, WWI & Military Personnel)...**15.00**

When They All Get Together With The Lord by Moe Jaffe & Bickley Reichner, 1945, Photo Jubalaires...**5.00**

When They Ask About You by Sam H. Stept, 1943, Photo Joan Brooks..**3.00**

When They Christened Brother Johnson's Child by Jentes, 1914 (Black, Black Face)...**15.00**

When They Gather In The Sheaves by Chas. E. Baer & Johann C. Schmid, 1905..**10.00**

When They Gather The Sheaves Mary Dear by Denison, 1910 (Cover Artist, Pfeiffer & Deco)...**15.00**

When They Get Down In Mexico by E. Magnus Quist, 1916 (Cover Artist, Art Daniels & WWI) **10.00**

When They Play That Old Salome Melody by Richard Howard, 1920 .**5.00**

When They Play The River Shannon by Ellsworth, 1912 (Irish)..........**5.00**

When This Crazy World Is Sane Again by Irving Berlin, 1941 (Irving Berlin & WWII)..**15.00**

When Those Sweet Hawaiian Babies Roll Their Eyes by Edgar Leslie & Harry Ruby, 1917, Photo Dora Hilton (Cover Artist, Barbelle).....**10.00**

When Tony Goes Over The Top by Billy Frisch, Archie Fletcher & Alex Marr, 1918, Photo Willie Smith, (Cover Artist, Pfeiffer, Deco & WWI)..**15.00**

When Twilight Comes Stealing Then I Dream Of You by Ella M. Smith & Vernon Stout, 1919...**5.00**

When Two Hearts Discover by Derr Biggers & Louis A. Hirsch, 1919, Musical Comedy: See Saw (Cover Artist, Lionel S. Reiss) **10.00**

When Uncle Joe Plays A Rag On His Old Banjo by D.A. Esrom & Theodore Morse, Photo Astor Quartette, 1912 (Dixie & Rag) **10.00**

When Uncle Joe Steps Into France by Bernie Grossman & Billy Winkle, 1918, Photo Eddie Cantor (Cover Artist, Pfeiffer, WWI & Eddie Cantor) **25.00**

When Uncle Sammy Leads The Band by Von Tilzer, 1906 (Cover Artist, Pfeiffer & Patriotic) **20.00**

When We Are M-A-Double R-I-E-D by George M. Cohan (George M. Cohan) **10.00**

When We Gathered Roses Of Love by Beth Slater Whitson & Betty Bellin, 1918 ......**5.00**

When We Gathered Wild Flowers by Jack Frost & E. Clinton Keithley, 1915 ......**5.00**

When We Meet In The Sweet Bye And Bye by Stanley Murphy, 1918 (WWI) **10.00**

When We Reach That Old Port Somewhere In France by Al Selden & Sam H. Stept, 1917, Photo Anna Chandler (Cover Artist, Barbelle & WWI) **15.00**

When We Were Two Little Boys by Madden & Morse, 1904 ......**5.00**

When We Wind Up The Watch On The Rhine by Gordon Thompson & William Davis, 1917 (Cover Artist, Pfeiffer & WWI) **15.00**

When We're Alone by Will Jason & Val Burton, 1931 (Cover Artist, Ben Harris) **3.00**

When Will The Sun Shine For Me? by Benny Davis & Abner Silver, 1923 ......**5.00**

When Winter Comes by Irving Berlin, 1939 (Irving Berlin) **10.00**

When Women Vote & Pop The Question (Cover Artist, Pfeiffer) **15.00**

When Yankee Doodle Learns To "Parlez Vous Francais" by Will Hart & Ed Nelson, 1917, Photo Anna Chandler (Cover Artist, Barbelle & WWI) **16.00**

When Yankee Doodle Learns To "Parlez Vous Francais" by Will Hart & Ed Nelson, 1917, Photo Lew Seymour (Cover Artist, Barbelle & WWI) 16.00

When Yankee Doodle Marches Through Berlin, There'll Be A Hot Time In The U.S.A. by Andrew B. Sterling & Arthur Lange, 1917 (Cover Artist, Starmer & WWI) **20.00**

When Yankee Doodle Sails Upon The Good Ship "Home Sweet Home" by Addison Burkhardt & Fred Fisher, 1918 (WWI) **20.00**

When You Ain't Got No Money, Well You Needn't Come Around by Sloane & Brewster, 1898 (Pre 1900 & Black, Black Face) **20.00**

When You And I Were Seventeen by Kahn & Rosoff, 1925 ......**5.00**

When You And I Were Young Maggie Blues by Jack Frost & Jimmy McHugh, 1922, Photo Guy Lombardo (Blues) **5.00**

When You And I Were Young Maggie by W.A. Butterfield, 1935, Photo Gus Arnheim (Irish) **5.00**

When You And I Were Young Sweetheart by Emma Bierhals & Rob. Speroy, 1909 ......**10.00**

When You Are Mine Again by Lawrence L. Willey, 1911 ......**5.00**

When You Are The World To Me by Andrew K. Allison & Albert Von Tilzer, 1918 ......**5.00**

When You Came Into My Heart by Fred C. Swan, 1920 ......**5.00**

When You Come Back by George M. Cohan, 1918, Dedicated To My Friend George Macfarlane, Signed Photo George M. Cohan (George M. Cohan, WWI, March, Patriotic & Dedication) **50.00**

When You Come Back by George M. Cohan, 1918, Photo George M. Cohan (George M. Cohan, WWI, Patriotic & March)) **36.00**

When You Come Back They'll Wonder Who The —— You Are by Paul Dresser, 1902 ......**15.00**

When You Come Into My Life In Dreams by Bohannon, 1916 (Cover Artist, Pfeiffer) **10.00**

When You Come To The End Of The Day by Gus Kahn & Frank Wetphal, 1929, Photo Harry Savoy & Ruth Mann (Cover Artist, Leff) .**4.00**

When You Dream About Hawaii by Bert Kalmar, Sid Silvers & Harry Ruby, 1937, Photo Anson Weeks (Cover Artist, Van Dee) **5.00**

When You Dream Of Old New Hampshire, I Dream Of Tennessee by Jack Murphy & George L. Cobb, 1916 ......**5.00**

When You Fall In Love, Fall In Love With Me by Charles Tobias, Vincent Rose & Benee Russell, 1930 (Deco) **5.00**

When You Find There's Someone Missing by Joe McCarthy & Geo. Fairman, 1917 ......**5.00**

When You Find You Can't Forget by Darl MacBoyle & Leon DeCosta, 1916 (Cover Artist, Barbelle) **5.00**

When You Have Nothing Else To Do by Wm. Tracey & W. Raymond Walker, 1912 (Cover Artist, Pfeiffer) **10.00**

When You Haven't A Beautiful Girl by Clarke & Leslie, 1913 (Cover Artist, Pfeiffer) **10.00**

When You Hear The Time Signal by Johnny Mercer & Victor Schertzinger, 1942, Movie: The Fleet's In, Photo Dorothy Lamour, Jimmy Dorsey & Betty Hutton **15.00**

When You Hear Your Country Call, "Soldier Boy" by Private Martee Bomber Bergen, 1916 (Cover Artist, Pfeiffer & WWI) **16.00**

When You Hold Me In Your Arms by Arthur E. Buchanan & F. Henri Klickmann, 1919 ......**5.00**

When You Kiss Your Dear Mother Good-bye by Winslow, 1916 (Cover Artist, Pfeiffer & WWI) **16.00**

When You Know You're Not Forgotten by J. Fred Helf, 1906 ......**5.00**

When You Long For A Pal Who Would Care by E. Clinton Keithley & Jeannette Duryea, 1922 ......**5.00**

When You Look In the Heart Of A Rose by Marian Gillespie & Florence Methven, 1918 (Cover Artist, Rose Symbol) **5.00**

When You Love Her And She Loves You by Kerry Mills, 1907 ......**10.00**

When You Love More Than One by Alfred Bryan & Frank Wright, 1926 ......**5.00**

When You Love Someone by Livingston & Evans, 1953, Movie: Here Come The Girls, Photo Bob Hope, Rosemary Clooney, Tony Martin & Arlene Dahl **5.00**

When You Play In the Game Of Love by Joe Goodwin & Al Piantadosi, 1913 (Cover Artist, Rose) **5.00**

When You Play With The Heart Of A Girl by Geo. A. Little & Albert Von Tilzer, 1917 (Cover Artist, E.E. Walton) **10.00**

When You Sang Hush-A-Bye Baby To Me by Jesse G.M. Glick, Frederick Knight Logan & Abe Olman, 1918 (Cover Artist, Starmer & Black, Black Face) **35.00**

When You Sang The Palms To Me by J. Will Callahan & F. Henri Klickmann, 1914 ......**5.00**

When You See Another Sweetie Hanging Around by Sam M. Lewis, Joe Young & Walter Donaldson, 1919, Photo The Watson Sisters........**6.00**

When You See That Aunt Of Mine by Bibo & Nelson, 1925 ....**5.00**

When You Smile On Me by Harold B. Freeman & J. Edwin Allemong, 1919 ....**5.00**

When You Tell The Sweetest Story To The Sweetest Girl You Know by W.R. Williams, 1912 ....**5.00**

When You Wake Up Dancing by Berton Braley & Jerome Kern, 1918, Musical: Toot Toot **10.00**

When You Walked Out Someone Else Walked Right In by Irving Berlin, 1923 (Cover Artist, Perret, Irving Berlin & Deco)........................**15.00**

When You Waltz With The Girl You Love by Kilgour, 1917 (Cover Artist, Pfeiffer)..**10.00**

When You Were A Baby And I Was The Kid Next Door by Edgar Leslie & Harry Tierney, 1915 (Cover Artist, Barbelle) **12.00**

When You Were A Playmate Of Mine by Harry D. Kerr & F. Henri Klickmann, 1913 ....**5.00**

When You Were A Sweetheart Of Mine by Joe Hurl & W. C. Lindeman, 1910 (Cover Artist, Etherington)..**10.00**

When You Were Sweet Sixteen by James Thornton, 1932, Movie: The Jolson Story, Photo Larry Parks & Evelyn Keyes (Al Jolson).......**10.00**

When You Were Sweet Sixteen by James Thornton, 1932, Photo Perry Como **5.00**

When You Wish Upon A Star by Leigh Harline & Ned Washington, 1940, Movie: Pinocchio (Disney)..**10.00**

When You Wore A Pinafore by Edward Madden & Theodore Morse, 1908 ....**5.00**

When You Wore A Tulip And I Wore A Big Red Rose by Jack Mahoney & Percy Wenrich, 1914, Photo Chee Toy (Cover Artist, Rose).....**10.00**

When You Write A Letter, Send A Letter Of Cheer by Chas. Ford, 1917 (Cover Artist, Pfeiffer & WWI) **15.00**

When You Write, Sweet Marie, Send Your Heart To Me by Jack Mahoney, 1919 (Cover Artist, RS)...**10.00**

When You're A Long, Long Way From Home by Sam Lewis & Geo Meyer, 1914 (Cover Artist, DeTakacs & WWI) **16.00**

When You're A Long, Long Way From Home Little Boy by Raymond Klages & Billy Fazioli, 1923..**5.00**

When You're All Dressed Up And No Place To Go by Burt & Hein, 1913...**5.00**

When You're Alone by Eugene West & Otis Spencer, 1919 ....**10.00**

When You're Away by Henry Blossom & Victor Herbert, 1914, Musical: The Only Girl, Signed Photo Victor Herbert (Victor Herbert & Signed)..**10.00**

When You're Dancing The Old Fashioned Waltz by Chas. McCarron & Albert Von Tilzer, 1915 (Cover Artist, DeTakacs)........................**10.00**

When You're Five Times Sweet Sixteen by Jack Mahoney & George L. Cobb, 1916, Photo Stantly & Norton (Cover Artist, Rose).............**5.00**

When You're Gone Away by Goldsmith & Goldsmith, 1975, Movie: Babes, Photo Susan Clark..**2.00**

When You're Gone I Won't Forget by Ivan Reid & Peter DeRose, 1920...**3.00**

When You're In Love With Someone Who's Not In Love With You by Robert C. Clarke & Al Piantadosi, 1915 ....**6.00**

When You're In Town by Irving Berlin, 1911, Photo Tilford (Cover Artist, John Frew, Irving Berlin & Transportation)........................**20.00**

When You're Lonesome For Someone Who's Lonesome For You by Harry Ralph & Ted S. Barron, 1917 (Cover Artist, Pfeiffer).........**10.00**

When You're Over There In No Man's Land I'm Over Here In Lonesome Land by Jessie Spiess & Jack Stanley, 1918 (WWI).....................**10.00**

When You're Smiling, The Whole World Smiles With You by Mark Fisher, Joe Goodwin & Larry Shay, 1928..**5.00**

When You're Wearing The Ball And Chain by Henry Blossom & Victor Herbert, 1914, Musical: The Only Girl (Victor Herbert) **15.00**

When Your Boy Comes Back To You by Gordon V. Thompson, 1917. "The New York Evening Mail Pledges The Entire Profits Of This Song To Recruiting & Red Cross" (WWI & Red Cross)..........30.00

When Your Hair Has Turned To Silver by Charles Tobias & Peter DeRose, 1930, Photo Tommy Christian (Cover Artist, Cliff Miska & Deco) **6.00**

When Your Hair Has Turned To Silver by Charles Tobias & Peter DeRose, 1930, Photo Billie Hays (Cover Artist, Cliff Miska & Deco) **6.00**

When Your Hair Has Turned To Silver by Charles Tobias & Peter DeRose, 1930, Photo Lew White (Cover Artist, Cliff Miska & Deco) **6.00**

When Your Lover Has Gone by E.A. Swan, 1931 ....**3.00**

When Your Old Gray Bonnet Was New by Murphy & Marshall, 1913 (Cover Artist, Starmer)...**10.00**

When Your Old Wedding Ring Was New by Charles McCarthy, Joe Solieri & Bert Douglas, 1935 ....**3.00**

When Your Sailor Boy In Blue Comes Sailing Home To You by Burns, 1918 (WWI)...**10.00**

Where Am I by Al Dubin & Harry Warren, 1935, Movie: Stars Over Broadway, Photo Pat O'Brien, Jane Froman, James Melton, Jean Muir & Phil Regan **5.00**

Where Are The Girlies Of My Childhood Days by Snyder & Coots, 1918 (Cover Artist, Pfeiffer) **10.00**

Where Are The Scenes Of Yesterday? by Thos. S. Allen, 1909, Signed Photo Florence White (Cover Artist, Starmer & Signed)..............**10.00**

Where Are You? by Crosby, Bibo & McVey, 1932, Movie: The Cohens And Kellys, Photo George Sidney & Charlie Murray....................**5.00**

Where Are You? by Harold Adamson & Jimmy McHugh, 1936, Movie: Top Of The Town...**10.00**

Where Blooms The Rose by Arlo Bates & Clayton Johns, 1903 ....**5.00**

Where Did Robinson Crusoe Go With Friday On Saturday Night by Lewis, Young & Meyer, 1916, Musical: Robinson Crusoe Jr., Sung by Al Jolson (Cover Artist, Barbelle & Al Jolson)............................**25.00**

Where Did You Get That Girl by Bert Kalmar & Harry Puck, 1913, Photo Chris Pender (Cover Artist, Pfeiffer)..**12.00**

Where Did You Get That Hat? by Joseph J. Sullivan, 1886 (Pre 1900) **10.00**

Where Did You Get That Name by Lou Klein & Bob Miller, 1929, Photo Vincent Lopez (Cover Artist, Wohlman) **5.00**

Where Did You Leave My Daddy by Anthony Rossi & Chris Praetorius, 1919 (WWI)..**12.00**

Where Do They Go When They, Row, Row, Row by Kalmar, Jessel & Ruby, 1920, Prohibition Song (Cover Artist, Pfeiffer & Transportation)......**20.00**

Where Do We Go From Here by Howard Johnson & Percy Wenrich, 1917, Photo Artie Mellinger (Cover Artist, Rose Symbol & WWI) **15.00**

Where Do We Go From Here by Howard Johnson & Percy Wenrich, 1917, Photo Brice & King (Cover Artist, Rose Symbol & WWI) **15.00**

Where Do We Go From Here by Howard Johnson & Percy Wenrich, 1917, Photo W.J. Reilly, U.S.N. (Cover Artist, Rose Symbol, WWI & Military Personnel)......**30.00**

Where Do We Go From Here? by Whiting & Snyder, 1909 (Cover Artist, Pfeiffer)......**10.00**

Where Do You Go From Here? by Kalmar & Puck, 1914 (Cover Artist, Pfeiffer)......**10.00**

Where Do You Work-A John? by Mortimer Weinberg, Charley Marks & Harry Warren, 1926, Signed Photo Fred Waring (Cover Artist, Politzer, Signed & Transportation)......**10.00**

Where Everything Was Sunshine by Will Wood, 1910 ......**5.00**

Where Have We Met Before? by Harburg, Duke & Perelman, 1932.....**5.00**

Where Have We Met Before? by Louis Prima & Mitchell Parish, 1938, Photo Freddy Martin **5.00**

Where Have You Been? by Cole Porter, 1930, Musical: The New Yorker **5.00**

Where In The World? by Buddy Kaye & Carl Lampl, 1950, Photo Mindy Carson......**5.00**

Where In The World by Gordon & Revel, 1938, Movie: Josette, Photo Don Ameche, Simone Simon, Robert Young, Bert Lahr & Joan Davis **5.00**

Where In The World? by Paul Herrick, Freddy Martin & Ray Austin, 1941 ......**3.00**

Where Is My Boy Tonight? by Sterns & Stanley, 1905 ......**5.00**

Where Is My Little Old New York? by Irving Belin, 1924, Music Box Revue, 1925 (Irving Berlin)......**10.00**

Where Is My Love? by Leo Robin & Ralph Rainger, 1935, Movie: Rose Of The Rancho......**5.00**

Where Is My Mama? by Chas. Coleman & T. Jay Flanagan, 1910 .....**10.00**

Where Is My Wandering Boy Tonight? by Buck & Stamper, 1914 (Cover Artist, Pfeiffer)......**10.00**

Where Is The Life That Late I Led? by Cole Porter, 1948, Musical: Kiss Me Kate **6.00**

Where Is The Song Of Songs For Me? by Irving Berlin, 1928 (Irving Berlin)......**12.00**

Where Memory Dwells by Louis A. Drumheller, 1907 (Cover Artist, Starmer) **10.00**

Where My Caravan Has Rested by Edward Teschemacker & Hermann Lohr, 1909 ......**5.00**

Where My Dear Lady Sleeps by Fred E. Weatherly & F.S. Breville Smith, 1920 ......**5.00**

Where Or When by Rodgers & Hart, 1934, Movie: Babes In Arms, Photo Judy Garland, Lena Horne, Mickey Rooney, Gene Kelly, Ann Sothern, June Allyson & Perry Como......**10.00**

Where Rolls The Oregon by Darl MacBoyle & Leon D. Costa, 1916 (Cover Artist, Barbelle) **10.00**

Where The Apple Blossoms Fall by Coary, 1907 (Cover Artist, Pfeiffer)......**10.00**

Where The Bamboo Babies Grow by Benny Davis & James F. Hanley, 1922 (Black, Black Face) **10.00**

Where The Black Eyed Susans Grow by Dave Radford & Richard A. Whiting, 1917, Photo Al Jolson (Al Jolson)......**12.00**

Where The Black Eyed Susans Grow by Dave Radford & Richard A. Whiting, 1917, Photo Clara Kimball Young **12.00**

Where The Black Eyed Susans Grow by Dave Radford & Richard A. Whiting, 1917 (Cover Artist, Starmer)......**10.00**

Where The Blue Of The Night Meets The Gold Of The Day by Roy Turk, Bing Crosby & Fred E. Ahlert, 1931, Photo Bing Crosby **15.00**

Where The Boys Are by Greenfield & Sedaka, 1960, Movie: Where The Boys Are, Photo Connie Francis, Yvette Mimieux & Paula Prentiss..**5.00**

Where The Butterflies Kiss The Buttercups Good-Night by Harry Pease, Charles O'Flynn & Ed. G. Nelson, 1929......**5.00**

Where The Chicken Got The Axe by Will H. Mayo & William Glenroy, 1893 (Pre 1900) **10.00**

Where The Edelweiss Is Blooming by Albert Goetz & A. Baldwin Sloane, 1911 ......**6.00**

Where The Four Leaf Clovers Grow by Dave Radford & Will S. Dillon, 1919 (Cover Artist, Rose)......**5.00**

Where The Huckleberries Grow by Alfred Bryan, Harry Richman & Louis Silver, 1925......**5.00**

Where The Ivy's Clinging, Dearie, Round An Old Oak Tree by Roden & Helf, 1910 (Cover Artist, Pfeiffer) **10.00**

Where The Lanterns Glow by J. Stanley Royce & Chas. L. Johnson, 1919 ......**5.00**

Where The Lazy Daisies Grow by Cliff Friend, 1924, Photo Grace Hayes (Deco) **5.00**

Where The Lazy River Goes By by Harold Adamson & Jimmy McHugh, 1936, Movie: Banjo On My Knee, Photo Barbara Stanwyck, Joel McCrea & Buddy Ebsen......**10.00**

Where The Morning Glories Grow by Raymond Egan & Richard Whiting, 1917 ......**5.00**

Where The Morning Glories Twine Around The Door by Andrew Sterling & Harry Von Tilzer, 1904 ......**10.00**

Where The Mountains Meet The Moon by Remus Harris & Irving Melsher, 1940 ......**4.00**

Where The Nightingale Woos The Rose by Hughes, 1916 (Cover Artist, Pfeiffer)......**10.00**

Where The River Shannon Flows by James I. Russell, 1906, Photo Russell Bros. (Cover Artist, Edgar Keller & Irish) **10.00**

Where The Shamrock Grows by J. Brandon Walsh & Egbert Van Alstyne, 1916 (Irish) **5.00**

Where The Shandon Bells Are Ringing, I'll Be Waiting Sweet Eileen by Cummings, Lively & Cummings, 1914, Respectfully Dedicated To The Knights Of Columbus Of Worcester, Mass. (Cover Artist, E.S. Fisher, Irish & Dedication)......**15.00**

Where The Shy Little Violets Grow by Gus Kahn & Harry Warren, 1928, Photo J. Fred Coots & Waite Hoyt......**5.00**

Where The Shy Little Violets Grow by Gus Kahn & Harry Warren, 1928, Photo Brooke Johns......**5.00**

Where The Silv'ry Colorado Wends Its Way by C.H. Scoggins & Chas. Avril, 1901 (Cover Artist, Starmer)......**10.00**

Where The Skies Are Blue by Tommie Malie, Fred Hughes & Jack Little, 1924 ......**5.00**

Where The Southern Roses Grow by Richard H. Buck & Theodore F. Morse, 1904 ......**6.00**

Where The Sparrows And Chippies Parade by Edward Harrigan & David Braham, 1888 (Pre 1900)......**10.00**

Where The Sunset Turns The Ocean's Blue To Gold by Eva Fern Buckner & H.W. Petrie, 1929 (Black, Black Face) **10.00**

Where The Sweet Forget-Me-Nots Remember by Mort Dixon & Harry Warren, 1927 ......**5.00**

Where The Sweet Magnolias Bloom by Andrew Sterling & Harry Von Tilzer, 1899 (Cover Artist, Pfeiffer & Pre 1900) **10.00**

Where The Sweet Magnolias Grow by Andrew Sterling & Harry Von Tilzer, 1886 (Cover Artist, Pfeiffer & Pre 1900) **18.00**

Where The Sweetest Flowers Grow by Florence Parr Gere, 1912......**5.00**

Where The Water Lillies Grow by Gus Kahn, Raymond B. Egan & Richard A. Whiting, 1919 (Cover Artist, Starmer) **5.00**

Where The Waters Ebb & Flow by Bernard & Kendall, 1910 (Cover Artist, Pfeiffer)..**10.00**

Where The Yang-Tse Ki-Ang Flows by Bernie Grossman & Arthur Lange, 1917 (Cover Artist, Starmer)..**10.00**

Where We All Must Meet Again by Cam Picard, 1913 ....**5.00**

Where'd You Get Those Eyes? by Walter Donaldson, 1926 ....**5.00**

Where's Charley? by Frank Loesser, 1940, Musical: Where's Charley, Caricature, Ray Bolger **10.00**

Where's My Sweetie Hiding? by Tommie Malie, Addy Britt, Jack Little & Dick Finch, 1924 ....**5.00**

Where's Pappa? by Gimbel & Elliott, 1970, Movie: Where's Pappa?, Photo George Segal & Ruth Gordon **3.00**

Whiffenpoof Song, The by Meade Minnigerode, George S. Pomeroy & Tod B. Galloway, Revision by Rudy Vallee, 1964 ....**3.00**

While A Cigarette Was Burning by Charles & Nick Kenny, 1938 (Cover Artist, Im-Ho)..10.00

While Hearts Are Singing by Clifford Grey & Oscar Straus, 1931, Movie: Smiling Lieutenant, Featuring Maurice Chevalier **15.00**

While Miami Dreams by Raymond B. Egan & Richard A. Whiting, 1922, Musical: Ziegfeld Follies, 1921, Photo Gus Van & Joe Schenck (Cover Artist, Frederick S. Manning)..**10.00**

While Miami Dreams by Raymond B. Egan & Richard A. Whiting, 1922, Photo Adele Rowland (Cover Artist, Frederick S. Manning) **10.00**

While My Lady Sleeps by Bronislaw Kaper & Gus Kahn, 1917 ....**5.00**

While Old Glory Waves by Anton Heindl, 1918 (WWI) **10.00**

While Others Are Building Castles In The Air by Jack Mahoney & Fred Fisher, 1919 (Cover Artist, DeTakacs)..**5.00**

While Strolling Through The Park One Day by Ed Haley, 1880 (Pre 1900)..**15.00**

While The Angelus Was Ringing by Dick Manning & Jean Willard, 1945, Photo Tommy Dorsey..**5.00**

While The Convent Bells Were Ringing by Roden & Witt, 1901..........**5.00**

While The Irish Moon Rolls On by Mazie Wivell, 1932 (Irish) **6.00**

While The Rest Of The World Is Sleeping by Tobias, Rich & DeRose, 1933 ....**5.00**

While The Rivers Of Love Flow On by Geo. Graff Jr. & Ernest R. Ball, 1913, Photo Ernest R. Ball **5.00**

While The Stars In The Heavens Shine On by Kerr & Petrie, 1914 (Cover Artist, Pfeiffer)..**10.00**

While The Years Go Drifting By by Gus Kahn & Joe Burke, 1926, Photo George Olsen **5.00**

While The Years Roll By by Sam Lewis, Joe Young & Jack Austin, 1922 ....**5.00**

While They Were Dancing Around by Joe McCarthy & James Monaco, 1913 ....**5.00**

While We Danced At The Mardi Gras by Johnny Mercer & Alfred Opler, 1931, Photo Nick Lucas (Deco) **5.00**

While We're Young by Bill Engvick, Alec Wilder & Morty Palitz, 1943, Signed Photo Perry Como (Cover Artist, Barbelle & Signed).......**10.00**

While You're Away by L. Wolfe Gilbert & Anatol Friedland, 1917 (Cover Artist, DeTakacs & WWI)..**15.00**

Whip, The by Abe Holzmann, 1913 (Cover Artist, Starmer, Transportation & March) **25.00**

Whip-Poor-Will by Guy Bolton, Clifford Grey & Jerome Kern, Movie: Sally **5.00**

Whip-Poor-Wills Song, The by Millard, 1865 (Pre 1900) **20.00**

Whipoorwill, Indian Serenade by Bryan, 1912 (Cover Artist, Pfeiffer & Indian)..**15.00**

Whirlpool March, The by Clifford V. Baker, 1914 (March)...............**10.00**

Whisper To Me In The Starlight by John Steel & Jerry Jarnigin, 1922 .**5.00**

Whisper To The Rose by Francis Wheeler, Harry B. Smith & Ted Snyder, 1924 ....**5.00**

Whisper Waltz, The by Paul Francis Webster & Joe Burke, 1932, Photo Wayne King..**3.00**

Whisper Your Mother's Name by Braisted & Carter, 1896 (Pre 1900)..**10.00**

Whispered Thought, A by Chas. L. Johnson, 1904 ....**10.00**

Whispering by John Schonberger, Richard Coburn & Vincent Rose, 1920, Movie: Greenwich Village, Photo Carmen Miranda, Don Ameche, William Bendix & Vivian Blaine **10.00**

Whispering Hope by Alice Hawthorne, 1910...................................**10.00**

Whispering Of Love by C. Kinkel...**5.00**

Whispers In the Dark by Leo Robin & Frederick Hollander, 1937, Movie: Artists And Models, Photo Jack Benny..**5.00**

Whistle And I'll Wait For You by Earl C. Jones & George W. Meyer, 1907, Photo Daisy Lloyd Wood (Cover Artist, Starmer)...............**10.00**

Whistle It by Bryan, Clarke & Schwartz, 1912, Photo Blanche Ring (Cover Artist, Pfeiffer) **10.00**

Whistle While You Work by Larry Morey & Frank Churchill, 1937, Movie: Snow White (Disney)..**15.00**

Whistler And His Dog, The by Arthur Pryor, 1905............................**10.00**

Whistlin' Cowboy, The by Paul Francis Webster & Felix Bernard, 1933 ..**5.00**

Whistling Boy, The by Jerome Kern & Dorothy Fields, 1937, Movie: When You're In Love, Photo Grace Moore **5.00**

Whistling Coon by Sam Devere, 1888 (Pre 1900 & Black, Black Face) ..**30.00**

Whistling Rufus by Kerry Mills, 1899 (Pre 1900, March & Black, Black Face) **50.00**

White Bird (Cover Artist, Pfeiffer & Indian)...................................**20.00**

White Christmas by Irving Berlin, 1942, Movie: Holiday Inn, Photo Bing Crosby, Danny Kaye, Rosemary Clooney & Vera Ellen (Irving Berlin)..**5.00**

White Crest March by Losey, 1913 (March)....................................**10.00**

White Dove, The by Clifford Grey & Franz Lehar, 1930, Movie: The Rogue Song, Photo Lawrence Tibbett..**5.00**

White Guards, The by Edward A. Rushford, 1907, Photo Edward A. Rushford (March) **15.00**

White Heather, The by Chas. A. Snyder & Alfred L. Haase & J. Fred Coots, 1919, Movie: White Heather..**10.00**

White House Serenade by Jackie Gleason, Photo Jackie Gleason **10.00**

White Owl, The by Alfred Lord Tennyson & Arthur Sherwood Kendall, 1899 (Cover Artist, Thorburn & Pre 1900) **5.00**

White Rose by Whelpley, 1903 ....**5.00**

White Sails by Nick Kenny, Charles Kenny & Harry Archer, 1939, Photo Ozzie Nelson..**3.00**

White Sport Coat, And A Pink Carnation, A by Marty Robbins, 1957, Photo Marty Robbins..**5.00**

White Wings by Banks Winter, 1884 (Pre 1900 & Black, Black Face)...**15.00**

Whither Thou Goest by Guy Singer, 1954 ....**2.00**

Who Are We? by Paul Francis Webster & Jerry Livingston, 1955........**3.00**

Who Are We To Say by Sigmund Romberg & Gus Kahn, 1938, Photo Jeannette MacDonald & Nelson Eddy............................**8.00**

Who Are You With To-Night? by Harry Williams & Egbert Van Alstyne, 1910 (Cover Artist, Edgar Keller) **15.00**

Who by Irving Berlin, 1924, Music Box Revue 1925 (Irving Berlin)..**10.00**

Who? by Otto Harbach, Oscar Hammerstein II & Jerome Kern, 1925, Movie: Sunny **10.00**

Who Can I Turn To? by Leslie Bricusse & Anthony Newley, 1964, Musical: The Roar Of The Greasepaint...................**4.00**

Who Cares? by Jack Yellen & Milton Ager, 1922, Movie: Bombo, Photo Al Jolson (Al Jolson) **10.00**

Who Cares What People Say? by M.K. Jerome & Jack Scholl, 1947, Movie: Nora Prentiss, Photo Ann Sheridan, Robert Alda, Bruce Bennett & Kent Smith....................**5.00**

Who Dat Say Chicken In Dis Crowd? by Paul Lawrence Dunbar & Will Marion Cook, 1898 (Pre 1900 & Black, Black Face) **20.00**

Who Do You Know In Heaven by Al Stillman & Peter DeRose, 1949 .**3.00**

Who Do You Love I Hope? by Irving Berlin, 1946, Movie: Annie Get Your Gun (Irving Berlin)........................**10.00**

Who Is Sylvia? by Franz Schubert & William Shakespeare, 1935, Signed Photo Billy Mills (Signed)........................**5.00**

Who Knows? by Cole Porter, 1937, Movie: Rosalie.....................**5.00**

Who Knows? by Paul Lawrence Dunbar & Ernest Ball, 1911...............**5.00**

Who Minds 'Bout Me by Schertzinger, Mitchell & Bullock, 1936, Movie: Follow Your Heart, Photo Marion Talley & Michael Bartlett **5.00**

Who Paid The Rent For Mrs. Rip Van Winkle? by Alfred Bryan & Fred Fischer, 1916, Musical: Belle Of Bond St., Photo Sam Bernard....................20.00

Who Put That Moon In The Sky? by Bert Kalmar & Harry Ruby, 1937..**3.00**

Who Threw The Overalls In Mrs. Murphy's Chowder? by George L. Giefer, 1943, Movie: Coney Island, Photo Betty Grable (Irish) **10.00**

Who Threw The Overalls In Mrs. Murphy's Chowder? by George L. Giefer, 1899 (Pre 1900 & Irish)....................**15.00**

Who Told You That Lie by Jack Segal, Eddie Cantor & Bee Walker, 1946, Photo Harry Cool....................**3.00**

Who Told You That Lie? by Jack Segal, Eddie Cantor & Bee Walker, 1946, Photo Charlie Spivak........................**5.00**

Who Wants To Live Like That? by Foster Carling, 1946, Movie: Song Of The South (Disney)....................**10.00**

Who Will Be With You When I Go Away? by Farrell, 1913 (Transportation)........................**15.00**

Who Wouldn't Be Blue? by Benny Davis & Joe Burke, 1928, Photo Nick Lucas (Cover Artist, Barbelle & Deco)........................**5.00**

Who Wouldn't Love You? by Benny Davis & Joe Burke, 1925............**3.00**

Who Wouldn't Love You? by Bill Carey & Carl Fischer, 1942, Photo Kay Kyser........................**3.00**

Who'll Be The Next One To Cry Over You? by Johnny S. Black, 1959...**3.00**

Who'll Be The One This Summer? by Edward Heyman, Tot Seymour & Vee Lawnhurst, 1937, Photo Russ Morgan........................**3.00**

Who'll Buy My Lavender? by Caryl Battersby & Edward German, 1896 (Pre 1900) **10.00**

Who'll Take Care Of The Harem? by Kaufmann, Mayer & Lewis, 1915, Photo B. Granville (Cover Artist, Pfeiffer) **10.00**

Who'll Take My Place, When I'm Gone? by Raymond Klages & Billy Fazioli, 1922 (Cover Artist, Perret & Deco) **10.00**

Who'll Take The Place Of Mary? by Alfred Dubin, Clarence Gaskill & Harry Mayo, 1920........................**10.00**

Who's Afraid Of The Big Bad Wolf? by Ann Ronell & Frank Churchill, 1934, Mickey Mouse On The Cover (Disney) **12.00**

Who's Afraid Of The Big Bad Wolf? by Ann Ronell & Frank Churchill, 1933, Movie: Three Little Pigs (Disney)...................12.00

Who's Going To Love You When I'm Gone? by Esrom, 1913 (Cover Artist, Pfeiffer)........................**10.00**

Who's Got The Pain? by Richard Adler & Jerry Ross, 1955, Musical: Damn Yankee **5.00**

Who's Loony Now? by Selden, 1919........................**5.00**

Who's Sorry Now by Bert Kalmar, Harry Ruby & Ted Snyder, 1923, Photo Leo Terry (Cover Artist, Barbelle)........................**5.00**

Who's Sorry Now? by Bert Kalmar, Harry Ruby & Ted Snyder, 1931, Movie: Three Little Words, Photo Fred Astaire, Red Skelton, Vera Ellen & Arlene Dahl........................**5.00**

Who's Sorry Now by Bert Kalmar, Harry Ruby & Ted Snyder, 1932, Movie: A Night In Casablanca, Photo Marx Brothers **8.00**

Who's That Knockin' At My Door? by Gus Kahn & Seymour Simons, 1927 ....**5.00**

Who's Wonderful, Who's Marvelous, Miss Annabelle Lee? by Sidney Clare & Lew Pollack, 1927, Photo Banjo Buddy (Cover Artist, Leff & Deco) **10.00**

Who-oo? You-oo! That's Who! by Jack Yellen & Milton Ager, 1927 ..**6.00**

Whoa Emma by Lonsdale & Read, 1877 (Pre 1900)........................**15.00**

Whoa, Ida, Whoa by Andrew Sterling & Harry Von Tilzer, 1906.......**10.00**

Whoa January You're Going To Be Worse Than July by Von Tilzer, 1919 ......**10.00**

Whole Town's Wise, The by Jack Drislane & Dick Richards, 1914 (Cover Artist, Starmer) **5.00**

Whole World Comes From Dixie, The by Ballard Macdonald & James F. Hanley, 1916 (Cover Artist, Starmer, Rag & Dixie) **10.00**

Whole World Is Singing My Song, The by Mann Curtis & Vic Mizzy, 1946, Photo Jack Smith (Cover Artist, Sorokin) **5.00**

Whole World Is Singing My Song, The by Mann Curtis & Vic Mizzy, 1946, Photo Dennis Day (Cover Artist, Sorokin) **5.00**

Whole World Is Singing My Song, The by Mann Curtis & Vic Mizzy, 1946, Photo Saxie Dowell (Cover Artist, Sorokin) **5.00**

Whole World Is Waiting For Dreams To Come True, The by Charlie Harrison & Deane Moore, 1927 ......**5.00**

Whole World Knows I Love You, The by Gould, Lyons & Yosco, 1914 (Cover Artist, Pfeiffer) **10.00**

Whole World Knows I Love You, The by Sidney Carter & Chas. W. Daniels, 1915 ......**5.00**

Wholesale Love (Cover Artist, Pfeiffer) **10.00**

Whoop 'Er Up! by Will Wood, 1911 (Cover Artist, Pfeiffer & March) **20.00**

Whose Baby Are You? by Anne Caldwell & Jerome Kern, 1920, Musical: The Night Boat **10.00**

Whose Heart Is He Breaking Tonight? by James Kendis & Herman Paley, 1911 ......**5.00**

Whose Izzy Is He? by Brown, Green & Stern, 1924 ......**5.00**

Whose Little Heart Are You Breaking Now? by Irving Berlin, 1917 (Cover Artist, Barbelle, Irving Berlin & Deco) **10.00**

Whose Pretty Baby Are You Now? by Gus Kahn & Egbert Van Alstyne, 1916 (Cover Artist, Starmer) **5.00**

Why Are You Breaking My Heart? by Clarke, 1914 (Cover Artist, Pfeiffer) **10.00**

Why? by Bob Marcucci & Peter DeAngelis, 1969, Signed Photo Frankie Avalon (Signed) **5.00**

Why? by Bobby Connolly & Arthur Swanstrom, 1929, Movie: Sons O'Guns, Photo Jack Donahue & Lily Damita **5.00**

Why Can't I Be Like You? by Con Conrad, 1929 ......**3.00**

Why Can't We Be Sweethearts? by Doris White & Norman Costello, 1931, Photo Morton Downey **5.00**

Why Can't You Behave? by Cole Porter, 1948, Musical: Kiss Me Kate ...**4.00**

Why Can't You? by Al Jolson, 1929 (Al Jolson) **5.00**

Why Dance? by Roy Turk & Fred E. Ahlert, 1931, Signed Photo Jack Miller (Cover Artist, Leff, Deco & Signed) **5.00**

Why, Dear? by Henry R. Cohen, 1921, Photo Mary Jayne (Cover Artist, R. Van Buren) **5.00**

Why Dear? by Henry R. Cohen, 1921, Photo Zelda Santley (Cover Artist, R. Van Buren) **5.00**

Why Did I Have To Fall In Love With You? by Freddy James & Larry Stock, 1946, Photo Jack Smith **4.00**

Why Did I Kiss That Girl? by Lew Brown, Robert King & Ray Henderson, 1924, Photo Ernie Golden Orchestra (Deco) **10.00**

Why Did I Kiss That Girl? by Lew Brown, Robert King & Roy Henderson, 1924, Photo Herb Wiedoft & His Orchestra (Deco) **10.00**

Why Did It Have To End So Soon? by Marty Symes, Dick Robertson & Frank Weldon, 1947, Photo Charles Turecamo (Cover Artist, Hal Weinstein) **4.00**

Why Did They Dig Ma's Grave So Deep? by Joseph Skelley, 1880 (Pre 1900) **15.00**

Why Did They Take My Daddy? by Sgt. Bernard Satz, 1919, Dedicated To All The Little Kiddies With Dads In The Service (WWI, Military Personnel & Dedication) **35.00**

Why Did You Come Into My Life? by Charles K. Harris, 1918 ......**5.00**

Why Did You Go Away? by Landres & Carroll, 1916 (Cover Artist, Pfeiffer & Deco) **10.00**

Why Did You Leave Me? by Perry & Trudman, 1920 ......**5.00**

Why Did You Make Me Care? by Solomon & Maguire, 1912 ......**6.00**

Why Did You Say "I Love You" When You Knew It Was Not True? by Francis C. Chantereau, 1920 (Cover Artist, E.S. Fisher) **10.00**

Why Didn't You Leave Me Years Ago? by Sidney D. Mitchell, Grant Clark & Archie Gottler, 1920, Photo Mabel Normand (Cover Artist, RS & Deco) **10.00**

Why Do I Care For You? by Jack Yellen & Albert Hay Molotte, 1923, Photo Cecil Cunningham (Cover Artist, Perret & Deco) **10.00**

Why Do I Dream Those Dreams? by Al Dubin & Harry Warren, 1934, Movie: Wonder Bar, Photo Kay Francis, Dick Powell, Dolores Del Rio & Al Jolson (Cover Artist, Harris & Al Jolson) **12.00**

Why Do I Love You? by Oscar Hammerstein II & Jerome Kern, 1927, Movie: Show Boat **5.00**

Why Do They All Take The Night Boat To Albany? by Al Jolson, 1918 (Al Jolson) **10.00**

Why Do They Always Say "No"? by Harry Pease, Frank Davis, Ed. G. Nelson & Billy Glason, 1920 (Cover Artist, Wohlman) **10.00**

Why Do They Call Mama Poor Butterfly? by Louis Seifert & W.C. Polla, 1919, Photo Ruth Roland (Cover Artist, Emmett O. Smith & Lithograph, Knapp Co.) **10.00**

Why Do You Always Doubt Me? by Philip Staats, 1907 ......**5.00**

Why Do You Always Tease Me? by Victor Shaker & Myra V. Shaker, 1920 ......**5.00**

Why Don't They Do It Now? by Joe McCarthy & Jimmy Monaco, 1915 ..**5.00**

Why Don't They Play With Me? by Charles K. Harris, 1906 ......**5.00**

Why Don't They Set Him Free? by Thos. J. Blue & Harry C. Loll, 1913, Photo Harry Thaw, The Man Who Murdered Stanford White (Cover Artist, Pfeiffer) **25.00**

Why Don't We Do This More Often by Charles Newman & Allie Wrubel, 1941, Photo Freddy Martin **3.00**

Why Don't You Believe Me? by Lew Douglas, King Laney & Roy Rodde, 1952, Photo Joni James (Cover Artist, Barbelle) **3.00**

Why Don't You? by Joseph McCarthy & Harry Tierney, 1920, Musical: Afgar **5.00**

Why Don't You Fall In Love With Me? by Al Lewis & Mabel Wayne, 1942, Photo Carmen Cavallaro **4.00**

Why Don't You Get A Lady Of Your Own? by Williams & Walker, 1898 (Pre 1900) **10.00**

Why Don't You Go, Go, Go? by Schwartz (Black, Black Face) **15.00**

Why Don't You Love Me? by Hank Williams, 1950, Signed Photo Hank Williams (Signed) **5.00**

Why Don't You Marry The Girl? by B.G. DeSylva, Al Piantadosi & Sam Williams, 1926 ......**5.00**

Why Don't You Marry The Girl? by Klein & Greenburg, 1914 (Cover Artist, Pfeiffer) **10.00**

Why Don't You Say So? by Tierney, 1926, Movie: Kid Boots, Photo Eddie Cantor & Mary Eaton (Eddie Cantor) **10.00**

Why Don't You Smile? by Hockey, Kennedy & Fellheimer, 1910 (Cover Artist, Pfeiffer) **10.00**

Why Don't You Smile? by Lem Trombley, 1912 (Cover Artist, A.W. Peters) **10.00**

Why Don't You Smile For Me? by Robert Levenson, 1919 ......**5.00**

Why Don't You Speak For Yourself John? by Corinne Ross, 1923 ......**5.00**

Why Don't You Try?, The Rolling Chair Song by Harry Williams & Egbert Van Alstyne, 1905 (Transportation) **28.00**

Why Dream? by Leo Robin, Richard Whiting & Ralph Rainger, 1935, Movie: Big Broadcast Of 1935, Photo Henry Wadsworth **5.00**

Why Dream by Robin, Whiting & Rainger, 1935, Movie: The Big Broadcast Of 1935 ......**8.00**

Why Fight The Feeling by Loesser, 1950, Movie: Let's Dance, Photo Fred Astaire & Betty Hutton.................................**10.00**

Why Is Love So Crazy? by Arthur Freed & Harry Warren, 1950, Movie: Pagan Love Song, Photo Esther Williams & Howard Keel **5.00**

Why Not? by Edward Heyman & Con Conrad, 1933, Musical: Social Register **5.00**

Why Paddy's Always Poor by William Scanlon, 1886 (Pre 1900 & Irish) **15.00**

Why Pretend? by Will Hudson, Kay Twomey & Tempo King, 1938....**3.00**

Why Should I Care? by Cole Porter, 1937, Movie: Rosalie.................**6.00**

Why Should I Cry Over You? by Ned Miller & Chester Cohn, 1922 , Signed Photo Margie Coate (Deco & Signed)...............**10.00**

Why Should I Pine For The World To Be Mine, When You Are The World To Me? by Andrew K. Allison & Albert Von Tilzer, 1913 ..**5.00**

Why Should We Stay Home And Sew? (Equal Rights) by Henry Blossom & Victor Herbert, 1914, Musical: The Only Girl (Victor Herbert) ..**15.00**

Why Shouldn't They Be Good Enough Now? by Katt Elinore & Sam Williams, 1919 (Red Cross) **35.00**

Why Stars Come Out At Night by Ray Noble, 1935, Movie: The Big Broadcast of 1935........................**5.00**

Why Try To Change Me Now by Cy Coleman & Joseph A. McCarthy, 1952, Photo Frank Sinatra **3.00**

Why Was I Born? by Oscar Hammerstein II & Jerome Kern, 1929 ......**5.00**

Why Was I Ever Born Lazy? by Billy DeVere & Dawson Wood, 1907 (Black, Black Face) **15.00**

Why Would We Meet As Strangers? by Joseph P. Skelly, 1891 (Pre 1900)....................................**10.00**

Wichita by Washington & Salter, 1955, Movie: Wichita, Photo Joel McCrea, Lloyd Bridges & Vera Miles **5.00**

Wicked Witch, The by Carl Wilhelm Kern, 1923 ....**5.00**

Wide Open Spaces by Byron Gay, Richard Whiting & Paul Whiteman, 1927 ....**5.00**

Widow Nolan's Goat by Edward Harrigan & David Braham, 1881 (Pre 1900)....................................**10.00**

Widow's Plea For Her Son by Hall, 1893 (Pre 1900) **12.00**

Wiegenlich, Cradle Song by Jerry Castillo & Johannes Brahms, 1935, Photo Lou Blake **3.00**

Wife Hunters, The, 1910 (Cover Artist, Pfeiffer)....................**10.00**

Wild Cherries Rag by Irving Berlin & Ted Snyder,1908 (Cover Artist, Pfeiffer, Irving Berlin & Rag) **15.00**

Wild Flower by Otto Harbach, Oscar Hammerstein II, Vincent Youmans & Herbert Stothart, 1923, Musical: The Wildflowers **6.00**

Wild Flower Rag by Carlotta Williamson, 1910 (Cover Artist, Pfeiffer & Rag) **15.00**

Wild Is The Wind by Washington & Tiomkin, 1957, Movie: Wild Is The Wind, Photo Tony Franciosa, Anna Magnani & Anthony Quinn........**3.00**

Wild Rose by Donart & Webster, 1909 ....**5.00**

Wild Rose by Guy Bolton, Clifford Grey & Jerome Kern, Movie: Sally ..**5.00**

Wildflower by George Martens & Mary Earl, 1920 (Indian)...............**30.00**

Wildwood Waltzes by Weston Wilson, 1917..........................**5.00**

Wilhelmina by Mack Gordon & Josef Myrow, 1950, Movie: Wabash Avenue, Photo Betty Grable........................**5.00**

Will My Dreams Come True? by A.H. Eastman & Fred Heltman, 1914...**5.00**

Will O' The Wisp by Will B. Morrison, 1912..........................**6.00**

Will She Come From The East? by Irving Berlin, 1922 (Irving Berlin) ..**10.00**

Will The Angels Guard My Daddy Over There? by Paul B. Armstrong & F. Henri Klickmann, 1918 (WWI)........................**15.00**

Will The Angels Let Me Play by Werden & Gladdish, 1912.................**5.00**

Will The Roses Bloom In Heaven? by Chas. K. Harris, 1911 (Cover Artist, Starmer) **5.00**

Will You Always Call Me Sweetheart? by Eddie Hanson, 1928 ....**5.00**

Will You Be My Teddy Bear?, 1907, Photo Anna Held **25.00**

Will You Be One Of The Soldier Boys? by Gifford, 1917 (Cover Artist, Pfeiffer & WWI).................................**15.00**

Will You Be Waiting Dearie When My Ship Comes In? by Wilson, 1912 (Cover Artist, Pfeiffer & Transportation).....................**20.00**

Will You? by A. Donnelly & F. Mayo, 1920 (Cover, Litho. Knapp Co.)..**5.00**

Will You? by Gene Raymond, 1935, Photo Gene Raymond **3.00**

Will You Ever Grow Tired Of Me? by Max Prival & Alfred Solman, 1917 (Cover Artist, Starmer) **10.00**

Will You Love Me In December As You Do In May? by J.J. Walker & Ernest R. Ball, 1905.............................**10.00**

Will You Marry Me Tomorrow, Maria? by Jerome Kern & Oscar Hammerstein II, 1937, Movie: High, Wide And Handsome, Photo Irene Dunne & Randolph Scott........................**6.00**

Will You Remember Me? by Lou Davis, Henry Santly & Harry Richman, 1914, Photo Harry Richman **5.00**

Will You Remember, Sweetheart? by Rida Johnson Young & Sigmund Romberg, 1937, Movie: Maytime, Photo Jeannette MacDonald & Nelson Eddy (Cover Artist, Immy)........................**10.00**

Will You Remember Sweetheart? by Rida Johnson Young & Sigmund Romberg, 1917, Musical: Maytime (Cover Artist, Van Buren).....**10.00**

Will You Wait Little Girl For Me? by Max Clay, 1916, Dedicated To The National Guard (WWI & Dedication)................16.00

Willie Had A Motor Boat by Stanley Murphy, 1914 (Transportation)..................................**15.00**

Willie's Got Another Girl Now by Leigh & Pether, 1907...................**10.00**

Willow Glen by J.M. Baldwin, 1911 ....**5.00**

Wind In The Tree-Tops by Gene Bone & Howard Fenton, 1943 ....**3.00**

Winding Trail, The by George Hayden & George P. Howard, 1927 .....**3.00**

Windmills Of Your Mind, The by Michael Legrand & Alan & Marilyn Bergman, 1968, Movie: Thomas Crown Affair **5.00**

Winds Blow Free, The by Tyson & Leshner, 1941 ....**5.00**

Winds Of Dawn, The by Julia Warner Michael & Charles Lofthouse, 1912 ....**5.00**

Windshield Wiper by Joseph J. Lilley & Dick Peterson, 1948 ....**5.00**

Wing Dance by F.W. Meacham, 1893 (Pre 1900)..................**10.00**

Wings by MacDonald & Zamecnik, 1927, Movie: Wings, Photo Clara Bow & Buddy Rogers........................**10.00**

Wings Of The Morning by Jean Lefavre & W.C. Polla, 1919 (Lithograph, Knapp Co. & Transportation).......................**10.00**

Wings Over the Navy by Harry Warren, 1918 (WWI)..................**10.00**

Winking Moon by Martin (Cover Artist, Pfeiffer) **10.00**

Winning Fight, The by Abe Holzmann, 1911 (Patriotic) **5.00**

Winnipesaukee Waltz, The by Robert Sten, 1951, Commemorative Edition, Harvard-Yale Crew Race, Centennial Race August 3, 1952 At Center Harbor **10.00**

Winona, An Indian Love Song by Vandersloot, 1927 (Cover Artist, Pfeiffer & Indian) **15.00**

Winter by A.P. Graves & Alfred Scott Gatty **5.00**

Winter by Alfred Bryan & Albert Gumble, 1910 ....**5.00**

Winter Nights by Grant Clarke & Jean Schwartz, 1914 (Cover Artist, Barbelle) **5.00**

Winter Wonderland by Dick Smith & Felix Bernard, 1934, Ziegfeld Follies, Photo Blue Steele (Cover Artist, HBK) **12.00**

Winter Wonderland by Dick Smith & Felix Bernard, 1934, Ziegfeld Follies, Photo Steve Lamarr (Cover Artist, HBK) **12.00**

Winter Wonderland by Dick Smith & Felix Bernard, 1934, Ziegfeld Follies, Photo Tony Sacco (Cover Artist, HBK) **12.00**

Wisdom Of A Fool, The by Abner Silver & Roy Alfred, 1956, Photo The 5 Keys **3.00**

Wise Old Horse by Fraser, 1937, Movie: Youth Marches, Photo Cecil Broadhurst **3.00**

Wise Old Owl, The by Joe Ricardel, 1940 ....**5.00**

Wish I Wuz A Whisker On The Easter Bunny's Chin by Sid Tepper & Roy C. Bennett, 1954, Photo Gayla Peevey **6.00**

Wish That I Wish Tonight, The by Jack Scholl & M.K. Jerome, 1945, Movie: Christmas In Connecticut, Photo Dennis Morgan & Barbara Stanwyck **6.00**

Wish You Were Here by Harold Rome, 1952, Musical: Wish You Were Here (Cover Artist, Slim Aarons) **5.00**

Wishing And Waiting For Love by Grant Clarke & Harry Akst, 1929, Movie: Broadway Babies **10.00**

Wishing by Ed Rose & Lew Pollack, 1919 ....**5.00**

Wishing by Haven Gillespie & Isham Jones, 1920 ....**5.00**

Wishing Moon by Jack Frost & F. Henri Klickmann, 1919 ..**5.00**

Wishing That Dreams Would Come True by Frederick Knight Logan & Virginia Knight Logan, 1918 ....**5.00**

Wishing Will Make It So by B.G. DeSylva, 1939, Movie: Love Affair, Photo Irene Dunne & Charles Boyer (Cover Artist, Im-Ho) **10.00**

Wisteria Waltzes by Greene, 1916 (Cover Artist, Pfeiffer) ..**10.00**

Witch's Whirl Waltzes by E.T. Paull (Cover Artist, E.T. Paull) **35.00**

Witching Waves by Mary Earl, 1919 ....**5.00**

With A Banjo On My Knee by Harold Adamson & Jimmy McHugh, 1936, Movie: Banjo On My Knee, Photo Barbara Stanwyck, Joel McCrea & Buddy Ebsen **10.00**

With A Hey And A Hi And A Ho Ho Ho! by Mann Curtis & Vic Mizzy, 1947 (Cover Artist, Barbelle) **5.00**

With A Kiss by Myrow, Blane & Wells, 1953, Movie: The French Line, Photo Jane Russell **3.00**

With A Little Bit Of Luck by Frederich Loewe & Allan Jay Lerner, 1956, Musical: My Fair Lady **5.00**

With A Love Like Mine by Ted Barron, 1918 ....**5.00**

With A Smile And A Song by Larry Morey & Frank Churchill, 1938, Movie: Snow White (Disney) **12.00**

With A Song In My Heart by Lorenz Hart & Richard Rogers, 1929, Movie: With A Song In My Heart, Photo Susan Hayward **6.00**

With A Song In My Heart by Lorenz Hart & Richard Rogers, 1929, Movie: Words And Music, Photo Judy Garland, Lena Horne, Mickey Rooney, Gene Kelly, Ann Sothern, June Allyson & Perry Como..**10.00**

With All Her Faults I Love Her Still by Monroe Rosenfeld, 1888 (Pre 1900 & Black, Black Face) **16.00**

With All My Heart by Gus Kahn & Jimmy McHugh, 1935, Movie: Her Master's Voice, Photo Edward Everett Horton & Peggy Conklin ..**10.00**

With All My Heart by Tom Ford, Earl Lawrence & Jack Mason, 1930, Photo Rudy Vallee **10.00**

With Every Breath I Take by Leo Robin & Ralph Rainger, 1934, Movie: Here Is My Heart, Photo Bing Crosby & Kitty Carlisle **10.00**

With Flying Colors USA by Edythe Rosenthal, 1907 (Patriotic) **10.00**

With His Hands In His Pockets & His Pockets In His Pants by Von Tilzer & Morgan, 1916 (Cover Artist, Pfeiffer) **10.00**

With Louise On Lake Louise by Al Bryan & Larry Stock, 1935 ....**5.00**

With My Eyes Wide Open I'm Dreaming by Mack Gordon & Harry Revel, 1934, Movie: Shoot The Works, Photo Dorothy Bell, Jack Oakie, Alison Shipworth, Roscoe Karne & Ben Bernie & His Merry Lads **5.00**

With My Guitar And You by Mack Gordon, Abner Silver & Ted Snyder, 1930, Movie: Swing High **5.00**

With My Head In The Clouds by Irving Berlin, 1942, Movie: This Is the Army, Lt. Ronald Reagan In Cast (Irving Berlin, WWII, Military Personnel & President) **15.00**

With Open Arms by Burt F. Bacharach & Hal Davis, Photo Jane Morgan **5.00**

With Plenty Of Money And You by Al Dubin & Harry Warren, 1936, Movie: Gold Diggers Of 1937 ....**5.00**

With The Wind And The Rain In Your Hair by Clara Edwards, 1930 ..**5.00**

With You by Irving Berlin, 1929, Movie: Puttin' On The Ritz (Irving Berlin) **10.00**

With You by W.A. Pratt, 1902 ....**5.00**

With You by William Richard Goodall & Margaret Kingore, 1902 (Cover Artist, J.B. Eddy) **10.00**

With You by Wm. R. Clay & Howard Johnson, 1913 ....**6.00**

With You, Dear by Brown & Scott, 1904 ....**6.00**

With You In My Arms by B.A. Dunham & Dan Alexander, 1946 ....**4.00**

With You, My Own by James Flynn & W.M. Orest, 1919 (Cover Artist, Rose Symbol & Deco) 10.00

Within The Garden Of My Heart by Marshall Roberts & Alicia Scott, 1912, Sung by John McCormack **10.00**

Within The Law by Jones, Morrissey & Whittaker, 1914 (Cover Artist, Pfeiffer) **10.00**

Within The Law by Mary I. Zanier & Paul Eugene, 1913 ....**5.00**

Without A Memory by Robinson, 1953, Photo Judy Garland **10.00**

Without A Shadow Of A Doubt by George Whiting, Nat Schwartz & J.C. Johnson, 1936 ....**5.00**

Without A Song by William Rose, Edward Eliscu & Vincent Youmans, 1932 (Black, Black Face) **10.00**

Without A Word Of Warning by Mack Gordon & Harry Revel, 1935, Movie: Two For Tonight, Photo Bing Crosby & Joan Bennett **8.00**

Without Love by B.H. DeSylvia, Lew Brown & Ray Henderson, 1930, Musical: Flying High..**5.00**

Without You by Ray Gilbert & Osvaldo Farres, 1942, Movie: Make Mine Music (Disney) **10.00**

Without You Sweetheart by B.G. DeSylva, Lew Brown & Ray Henderson, 1927 ....**5.00**

Without Your Love, Ah, Let Me Die by Jos Clauder & Charles K. Harris, 1897 (Pre 1900) **10.00**

Witmark Minstrel Overture, The by Isidore Witmark, 1902 (Black, Black Face) **35.00**

Wives And Lovers by Daniel & Bacharach, 1963, Movie: Wives And Lovers, Photo Janet Leigh, Van Johnson, Shelley Winters, Ray Walston & Martha Hyers **3.00**

Wizard Of The Nile, The by Victor Herbert, 1960 (Cover Artist, Burgos & Victor Herbert) **10.00**

Wolverine, The by Harry J. Lincoln, 1912 (Cover Artist, Dittmar, March & Transportation) **30.00**

Woman Disputed, The by Grossman & Ward, 1928, Movie: The Woman Disputed, Photo Gilbert Roland & Norma Talmadge **8.00**

Woman Forever, 1916 (Cover Artist, E.T. Paull)..............................**35.00**

Woman In The Shoe, The by Arthur Freed & Nacio Herb Brown, 1929, Movie: Lord Byron Of Broadway **5.00**

Woman Is A Sometime Thing, A by DuBose Heyward & Ira & George Gershwin, 1935, Movie: Porgy and Bess, Photo Sidney Poitier, Dorothy Dandridge & Sammy Davis Jr. (Black, Black Face)........**15.00**

Woman Is Only A Woman but A Good Cigar Is A Smoke, A by Harry B. Smith & Victor Herbert, 1905 (Victor Herbert)............................**10.00**

Woman Thou Gavest Me, The by Al Piantadosi, 1919 ....**5.00**

Wond'rin' When by Livingston & Evans, 1948, Movie: Isn't It Romantic, Photo Veronica Lake, Mona Freeman & Billy DeWolfe **5.00**

Wonder Bar by Al Dubin & Harry Warren, 1934 ....**5.00**

Wonder Of You, The by Baker Knight, 1948..**2.00**

Wonder Why by Sammy Cahn & Nicholas Brodszky, 1951, Movie: Rich, Young And Pretty, Photo Jane Powell, Danielle Darrieux, Wendell Corey, Fernando Lamas & Vic Damone....................10.00

Wonderful Copenhagen by Frank Loesser, 1951, Movie: Hans Christian Anderson, Photo Danny Kaye **6.00**

Wonderful Daddy Of Mine by Alfred McDermott, 1931......................**5.00**

Wonderful Day, A by Chas. Ford, 1917 (Cover Artist, Pfeiffer) **10.00**

Wonderful Day Like Today, A by Leslie Brecusse & Anthony Newley, 1964, Musical: The Roar Of The Greasepaint-The Smell Of The Crowd **6.00**

Wonderful Garden Of Dreams by Harold Simpson & Dorothy Forster, 1912 ....**5.00**

Wonderful Girl, Good Night by Von Tilzer, Garfield & Kilgour, 1917 (Cover Artist, Pfeiffer) **10.00**

Wonderful Guy, A by Richard Rodgers & Oscar Hammerstein II, 1949, Musical: South Pacific (Cover Artist, BJH) **3.00**

Wonderful Isle Of Dreams by Maude Bennett Platz, 1914 (Cover Artist, Starmer) **5.00**

Wonderful Mother Of Mine by Alfred McDermott, 1931.....................**6.00**

Wonderful Pal by Wm. Tracey & Maceo Pinkard, 1919......................**8.00**

Wonderful Thing, A by Clare Kummer, 1914......................................**5.00**

Wonderful You by Jack Meskill, Max Rich & Pete Wendling, 1929, Photo Allyn Reese (Cover Artist, Barbelle) **5.00**

Wondering by Stolz & Macdonald, 1913 ....**5.00**

Wondrous Eyes Of Araby by Fleta Jan Brown & Herbert Spencer, 1918 ....**5.00**

Won't You Be My Honey? by Jack Drislane & Theodore Morse, 1907, Photo, Flemen & Miller..**5.00**

Won't You Be My Husband? by Arthurs & Murphey, 1908 ....**5.00**

Won't You Be My Sweetheart? by Verner, 1893 (Pre 1900)..............**10.00**

Won't You Be My Valentine? by Alan Gray M. Campbell, 1939 ....**3.00**

Won't You Buy A War Stamp? by Roy Perkins, 1918 (WWI)............**10.00**

Won't You Come Back To Me? by George M. Cohan, 1922 (George M. Cohan) **10.00**

Won't You Come Back To Your Mother, Nell? by A.S. McMahon, 1909 (Cover Artist, Pfeiffer) **10.00**

Won't You Come & Love Me? by H. C. Weasner & George L. Cobb, 1916, Photo Anna Battin Edwards (Cover Artist, Pfeiffer)............**10.00**

Won't You Come Over To My House? by Harry Williams & Egbert Van Alstyne, 1906, Photo Dave Carter (Cover Artist, DeTakacs) **10.00**

Won't You Come Over to My House by Harry Williams & Egbert Van Alstyne, 1906, Photo Clark Thardo (Cover Artist, DeTakacs) **10.00**

Won't You Come Over To Philly Willie? by J. Fred Helf, 1907 ....**10.00**

Won't You Come To My Tea Party? by Alb. H. Fitz, 1896 (Pre 1900) ..**10.00**

Won't You Give All Your Love To Me? by Weins & Henshaw, 1919 (Cover Artist, Pfeiffer) **10.00**

Won't You Go Back To Your Old Girl From Your Home Town? by Jerome Shay & Thos. J. Flanagan, 1916, Dedicated To Florence Wescott (Dedication)..**10.00**

Won't You Have An Ice Cream Soda With Me? by Pauline Arnold **6.00**

Won't You Kiss Me And No One Will Know? by Arthur B. Allen Jr. & Adam R. Rocheleau, 1915..**5.00**

Won't You Kiss Me Good-Night? by J. R. Beliveau, 1915 ....**5.00**

Won't You Let Me Take You Home? by Doerr & Lashly, 1912...........**5.00**

Won't You Marry Me? by Dorothy Donnelly & Sigmund Romberg, 1927, Musical: My Maryland **10.00**

Won't You Paddle Along With Me? by John Kemble & Lester W. Keith, 1904 ....**10.00**

Won't You Play A Simple Melody? by Irving Berlin, 1914 (Irving Berlin)..**16.00**

Won't You Share Your Troubles With Me Sweetheart? by Robert C. Horwood, 1919 ....**5.00**

Won't You Tell Me Mary? by Bobby Heath, Mickey Marr & Archie Fletcher, 1925 ....**5.00**

Won't You Try To Love Me? by Beth Slater Whitson & Dean Hough Berdeaux, 1910..**5.00**

Woodchopper's Ball by Frank Paparelli, Woody Herman & Joe Bishop, 1943 (Cover Artist, Holley)..**5.00**

Woodchuck Song, The by Sid Tepper, Roy Brodsky, Paul Mann & Stephan Weiss, 1946..**5.00**

Woodland Echoes by Addison P. Wyman, 1908.................................**5.00**

Woodland Whispers by Stanley, 1897 (Pre 1900)............................**10.00**

Woodman, Spare That Tree! by Geo. P. Morris & Henry Rufsell, 1837 (Pre 1900) **15.00**

Woodman, Woodman Spare That Tree by Irving Berlin, 1911 (Irving Berlin)..**10.00**

Woodpecker Song, The by Harold Adamson & Eldo Di Lazzaro, 1940, Photo Kate Smith...**12.00**

Woodrow Wilson Inaugural March, The by Jacques Hertz, 1913 (March, President & Political)..**35.00**

Woodrow Wilson Leader Of The U.S.A. by Henry Rupprecht & Waldemar Maass, Photo President Wilson (President & Political) **25.00**

Woodstock by Joni Mitchell, 1969, Photo Crosby, Sills, Nash & Young...**3.00**

Woody Woodpecker by George Tibbles & Ramey Idriss, 1947 ....**5.00**

Woody Woodpecker by George Tibbles & Ramey Idriss, 1947 (Cover Artist, Walter Lantz)...**10.00**

Words Are In My Heart, The by Al Dubin & Harry Warren, 1935, Movie: Gold Diggers Of 1935 (Cover Artist, Harris)...........................**10.00**

Words by Al Dubin, Al Tucker & Otis Spencer, 1924.......................**5.00**

Words Without Music by Ira Gershwin & Vernon Duke, 1935, Ziegfeld Follies 1936 ....**12.00**

Work Song, The by Mack David, Al Hoffman & Jerry Livingston, 1949, Movie: Cinderella (Disney)..**10.00**

World Goes Round And Round, The by Cuthbert, 1938......................**5.00**

World Is Hungry For A Little Bit Of Love, Even You And I, The by Carolyn Ayres Turner, 1915..**10.00**

World Is Mine, The by Harburg & Green, 1934, Movie: The Count Of Monte Cristo, Photo Robert Donat & Elissa Landi.........................**3.00**

World Is Mine, The by Holt Marvell & George Posford, 1935.............**5.00**

World Is Waiting For The Sunrise, The by Eugene Lockhart & Ernest Seitz, 1951, Photo Les Paul & Mary Ford.................................**3.00**

World Peace March by J.S. Zamecnik, 1914 (March).........................**12.00**

World Was Not Built In A Day, The by Greene & Solman, 1915 (Cover Artist, Pfeiffer)..**10.00**

World's Greatest Sweetheart Is You, The by Andy Razaf & Paul Denniker, 1929 ....**5.00**

Worst Is Yet To Come, The by Bert Grant, 1918 (WWI) **10.00**

Would I Love You? by Bob Russell & Harold Spina, 1950.................**2.00**

Would There Be Love? by Mack Gordon & Harry Revel, 1935, Movie: Stolen Harmony, Photo Ben Bernie **5.00**

Would You Be A Sailor's Wife? by Bennett (Transportation).............**10.00**

Would You Be Satisfied Sally? by Emma Carus & Fred Fischer, 1909, Photo Emma Carus (Cover Artist, Gene Buck)...........................**10.00**

Would You? by Arthur Freed & Nacio Herb Brown, 1936, Movie: San Francisco...**10.00**

Would You? by Freed & Brown, 1936, Movie: San Francisco, Photo Jeannette Macdonald & Clark Gable.......................................**15.00**

Would You? by Johnny Burke & Jimmy Van Heusen, 1945, Movie: Road To Utopia, Photo Bing Crosby, Bob Hope & Dorothy Lamour.......**6.00**

Would You Care? by Charles K. Harris, 1905 (Cover Artist, Starmer) .**5.00**

Would You Like To Take A Walk? by Mort Dixon, Billy Rose & Harry Warren, 1930, Movie: Sweet And Low.....................................**8.00**

Would You Rather Be A Colonel With An Eagle On His Shoulder Or A Private With A Chicken On His Knee? by Mitchell & Gottler, 1918 (WWI)..**15.00**

Would You Take A Chance With Me? by Cobb & Powell, 1914 (Cover Artist, Pfeiffer)..**10.00**

Would You Take Back The Love You Gave Me? by Al Dubin & Ernest R. Ball, 1917...**10.00**

Would You Take Me Back Again? by Arthur J. Lamb & Alfred Solman, 1913, Photo Anna Ford..**5.00**

Would You Think I'm As Nice Tomorrow Night, If You Met Someone Nicer Tonight? by Cobb & Edwards, 1913 (Cover Artist, Pfeiffer) ..**10.00**

Would-Ja? by Arthur Herzog Jr. & Manning Sherwin, 1926, Photo Lillian Kay (Cover Artist, Frederick S. Manning)...................................**10.00**

Wouldn't It Be Nice? by Jimmy McHugh & Harold Adamson, 1944, Movie: Something For The Boys, Photo Carmen Miranda, Vivian Blaine, Phil Silvers & Perry Como...**5.00**

Wrap Me In A Bundle & Take Me Home With You by Gus Kahn & Egbert Van Alstyne, 1914, Photo Miss Leila McIntyre **10.00**

Wrapped In A Red Red Rose by Dowling, McCarthy & Hanley, 1930, Movie: Blaze Of Glory, Photo Eddie Dowling **5.00**

Wreck Of The Shenandoah, The by Maggie Andrews (Transportation)..**10.00**

Wreck Of The Titanic, The by William Baltzell, 1912, Photo Of Titanic Sinking (Cover Artist, Z.A. Hendrick, Titanic & Transportation)..**75.00**

Wreck On The Southern Old 97 by Whittier, 1924 (Transportation)...**10.00**

Wreck, The by White, 1873 (Pre 1900 & Transportation) **25.00**

Write, Wire Or Telephone by James Brockman, 1907......................**5.00**

Written On The Wind by Cahn & Young, 1956, Movie: Written On The Wind, Photo Rock Hudson & Lauren Bacall **8.00**

Wunderbar by Cole Porter, 1948, Musical: Kiss Me Kate **5.00**

Wyoming by Gene Williams, 1920 (Cover Artist, Starmer) **5.00**

X Marks The Spot by Willie Hartzell & Walter Kranz, 1940 ....**3.00**

Y.O.U. Spells The One I Love by Harris & Melsher, 1938 ....**5.00**

Yaaka Hula Hickey Dula, Hawaiian Love Song by E. Ray Goetz, Jose Young & Pete Wendling, 1916, Musical: Robinson Crusoe, Jr., Introduced by Al Jolson (Cover Artist, Barbelle & Al Jolson).............**16.00**

Yacht Club by Barker, 1895 (Pre 1900 & Transportation)..................**10.00**

Yah-Ta-Ta, Yah-Ta-Ta by Johnny Burke & Jimmy Van Heusen, 1945 **5.00**

Yale Boola by A.M. Hirsch, 1901 (Cover Artist, Hewett & March)....**15.00**

Yale March, The by Chas. L. VanBarr, Advertising For The S. Carsley Co., Ltd. Montreal's Greatest Store, Dedicated To John Philip Sousa (March, Advertising & Dedication)...**25.00**

Yam, The by Irving Berlin, 1938 (Irving Berlin) **10.00**

Yama Yama Man, The by O.A. Hauerbach, Collin Davis & Karl L. Hoschna, 1908, Musical: Three Twins (Cover Artist, Edgar Keller) 10.00

Yankee Bird March by Johnson, 1910 (March)...............................**10.00**

Yankee Boy by Griffith J. Jones, 1905 (Cover Artist, Etherington, March & Patriotic) **25.00**

Yankee Dewey by Will J. Stevens, 1899 (Pre 1900)........................**10.00**

Yankee Doodle Blues by George Gershwin, 1922 (Patriotic & Blues)**10.00**

Yankee Doodle Boy Is Good Enough For Me, A by Will L. Livernash, 1916 (WWI)..**10.00**

Yankee Doodle Boy, The by George M. Cohan, 1904, Musical: Little Johnny Jones, Photo George M. Cohan (Cover Artist, Hirt & George M. Cohan) **25.00**

Yankee Doodle Boy, The by George M. Cohan, 1931, Musical: Little Johnny Jones. Statue Of George M. Cohan by Georg. Lober, Erected In Time Square & Presented To The City Of New York On September 11, 1959 by George M. Cohan Memorial Committee (George M. Cohan & Dedication)......................................**32.00**

Yankee Doodle Boy, The by George M. Cohan, 1933, Movie: Yankee Doodle Dandy, Photo James Cagney & George M. Cohan (George M. Cohan)......................................**20.00**

Yankee Doodle by Shackburg, 1942 (WWII)......................**5.00**

Yankee Doodle Dandy by George M. Cohan, 1932 (George M. Cohan)...**5.00**

Yankee Doodle's Come To Town by George M. Cohan (George M. Cohan) **5.00**

Yankee Grit by Abe Holzmann, 1905 (March) **10.00**

Yankee, He's There, All There by Charles K. Harris, 1917 (WWI) **10.00**

Yankee Hustler March by Schmitz, 1902 (March & Transportation) ..**20.00**

Yankee Of 1918, The by Mrs. Cassie Hall (Cover Artist, Pfeiffer & WWI)......................................**10.00**

Yankee Prince, The by George M. Cohan, 1908 (George M. Cohan & March) **15.00**

Yankee Rose by Sidney Holden & Abe Frankl, 1926, Photo Alex Klipper (Cover Artist, Leff & Deco) **10.00**

Yankee Rose by Sidney Holden & Abe Frankl, 1926, Photo Jeff Sayre & Tom Mack (Cover Artist, Leff & Deco)......................................**10.00**

Yankee Rose by Sidney Holden & Abe Frankl, 1926, Photo Marie Vero (Cover Artist, Leff & Deco) **10.00**

Yankee Tar by Joseph M. Daly, 1917 (WWI)....................**10.00**

Yankiana by E.E. Loftis, 1905 (March)......................**10.00**

Yanks Are At It Again, The by Lew Brown & Lynn Cowan, 1918 (WWI) **10.00**

Yaquita by Raymond Zirkel & Ned L. Reese, 1905.....................**5.00**

Yascha Michaeloffsky's Melody by Irving Berlin, 1928 (Irving Berlin) ..**10.00**

Ye Barn Dance by J.R. Shannon, 1908......................**5.00**

Ye Ho Me Lads, Ye Ho by Camp Ren Shields, 1911 (Cover Artist, Pfeiffer & Transportation)......................................**12.00**

Year, Years Ago by Gus Kahn & Freidman, 1911 ....**5.00**

Yearning by Sidney Carter & Neil Moret, 1918.....................**5.00**

Yearning Just For You by Benny Davis & Joe Burke, 1925, Photo Glenn C. Smith (Cover Artist, R.S. & Deco) **5.00**

Yearning Just For You by Benny Davis & Joe Burke, 1925, Photo Harvey Marburger & His Orchestra (Cover Artist, R.S. & Deco).................**5.00**

Years Before Us, The by Frank Loesser, 1948, Musical: Where's Charley, Caricature Of Ray Bolger......................................**5.00**

Yellow Bird by Marilyn Keith, Alan Bergman & Norman Luboff, 1957..**2.00**

Yellow Dog Blues by W.C. Handy, 1914 (Blues)......................**8.00**

Yellow Rose Of Texas, The by Don George, 1955, Photo Johnny Desmond......................................**3.00**

Yellow Rose Of Texas, The by Don George, 1955, Photo Mitch Miller..**3.00**

Yes, My Darling Daughter by Jack Lawrence, 1940, Photo Johnny Long **3.00**

Yes Or No by Clarence M. Jones, 1914......................**5.00**

Yes Sir! That's My Baby by Gus Kahn & Walter Donaldson, 1935, Photo Phil Romano & His Roseland Orchestra (Cover Artist, Leff & Deco) **12.00**

Yes To You by Sidney Clare & Richard A. Whiting, 1934, Movie: 365 Nights In Hollywood **5.00**

Yes, Virginia, There Is A Santa Claus by Joyce Baker, 1960, Photo Jose Ferrer **5.00**

Yes! We Have No Bananas by Frank Silver & Irving Cohn, 1923 (Cover Artist, Wohlman) **10.00**

Yester-Eve by J.S. Zamecnik, 1922......................**5.00**

Yesterday by Charles Harrison & Monte Wilhite, 1926......................**5.00**

Yesterday by Charles K. Harris, 1907......................**8.00**

Yesterday by Dorothy Donnelly & Serge Walter, 1926......................**5.00**

Yesterday by John Lennon & Paul McCartney, 1965 ....**5.00**

Yesterday by Otto Harbach & Jerome Kern, 1933, Movie: Roberta (Deco)......................................**8.00**

Yesterthoughts by Stanley Adams & Victor Herbert, 1940, Photo Leighton Noble (Victor Herbert) **3.00**

Yiddisha Rag, The by W. Raymond Walker, 1910, (Cover Artist, Etherington & Rag) **10.00**

Yiddle On Your Fiddle Play Some Ragtime by Irving Berlin, 1909 (Cover Artist, Pfeiffer, Irving Berlin & Rag) **15.00**

Yip-I-Addy-I-Ay by Will D. Cobb & John H. Flynn, 1908, Photo Blanche Ring (Cover Artist, CP) **10.00**

YMCA by Irving Berlin, 1917 (Irving Berlin) **10.00**

Yo San by Al W. Brown, 1914......................**10.00**

Yo Te Amo Mcans I Love You by Richard Whiting & Alfred Bryan, 1928, Movie: The Wolf Song, Photo Lupe Velez **10.00**

Yo-San by Jean Lefavre & W.C. Pola, 1919 (Cover Artist, Rolf Armstrong)......................................**20.00**

Yokohama Lullaby by Grant Clarke & James V. Monaco, 1921..........**5.00**

Yoo-Hoo by B.G. DeSylva & Al Jolson, 1921, Photo Al Jolson (Al Jolson & Deco) **10.00**

Yoodl-ee, Youdlee-You by Lou Edwards, 1916 (Cover Artist, Pfeiffer)......................................**10.00**

You by Arthur Swanstrom, Albert Sirmay & Arthur Schwartz, 1930, Musical: Princess Charming......................................**10.00**

You by Harold Adamson & Walter Donaldson, 1936, Movie: The Great Ziegfeld, Photo William Powell, Luise Rainer & Myrna Loy **10.00**

You by Robyn, 1891 (Pre 1900)......................................**10.00**

You Ain't Got The Right Kind Of Hair by Redmond, 1914, Photo John Early (Cover Artist, Pfeiffer & Deco) **10.00**

You Alone by Al Stillman & Robert Allen, 1953 ....**5.00**

You Alone by Maurice F. Marks & Herbert Walter, 1906.................**5.00**

You Always Hurt The One You Love by Allan Roberts & Doris Fisher, 1944 ....**5.00**

You Always Love The Same Girl by Lorenz Hart & Richard Rodgers, 1927, Musical: A Conn. Yankee **15.00**

You And I And The Moon by H.W. Schubert, 1905......................**6.00**

You And I by Meredith Wilson, 1941, Theme Song Of Maxwell House Coffee-Time, Photo Glenn Miller **10.00**

You And I Waltz by Claribell, 1936......................................**4.00**

You And Love by Edward Teschemacher & Guy D'Hardelot, 1906, Dedicated To Victor Maurel (Dedication) **5.00**

You And Me That Used To Be, The by Walter Bullock & Allie Wrubel, 1937 (Cover Artist, Merman) **5.00**

You And The Moon And Me by Charles Tobias & Albert Baer, 1933, Photo Arlene Jackson **5.00**

You And The Night And The Music by Howard Deitz & Arthur Schwartz, 1934 ....**3.00**

You And The Waltz And I by Paul Francis Webster & Walter Jurmann, 1942, Movie: Seven Sweethearts, Photo Kathryn Grayson & Van Heflin......**5.00**

You Appeal To Me by Walter Bullock & Harold Spina, 1938 ....**5.00**

You Are A Wonderful Baby by Jack Smith, 1917 ....**5.00**

You Are Beautiful by Richard Rodgers & Oscar Hammerstein II, 1961, Movie: Flower Drum Song..**5.00**

You Are Easy To Remember But Not So Easy To Forget by Buddy Fields, Bobby Reed, Will Collins & Ed. Cameron, 1923 (Cover Artist, Politzer) **5.00**

You Are Free by Victor Jacobi, 1944 ....**3.00**

You Are Just Like The Rose To Me by Jones, 1913 (Cover Artist, Pfeiffer) **10.00**

You Are Love by Oscar Hammerstein II & Jerome Kern, 1927, Movie: Show Boat..**5.00**

You Are My Life My All by Kemble & Doyle, 1916 ....**5.00**

You Are My Little Cupid by Paul Herve, Jean Biquet & Adolf Philipp, 1915, Musical: The Girl Who Smiles..**10.00**

You Are My Lucky Star by Arthur Freed & Nacio Herb Brown, 1935, Movie: Broadway Melody of 1936, Photo Jack Benny & Many Stars..12.00

You Are My Star In The Night by Irving Caesar & John Openshaw, 1928 ....**5.00**

You Are My Sunshine by Jimmie Davis & Charles Mitchell, 1940, Photo Jimmie Davis **4.00**

You Are Never Away by Richard Rodgers & Oscar Hammerstein II, 1951, Musical: Allegro..**3.00**

You Are The Ideal Of My Dreams by Herbert Ingraham, 1910.............**5.00**

You Are The Image Of Mother, 1916 ....**5.00**

You Are The Light Of My Life by R.M. Stults, 1910..............................**5.00**

You Are The Music To The Words In My Heart by Lee Pokrass & Jack Yellen, 1938..**3.00**

You Are The Only Star That Shines For Me by Wagner & Mazza, 1912..**5.00**

You Are The Rose I'm Longing For by T. Romney, C. Caporossi & A. Tobias, 1922 (Cover Artist, F.Earl Christy & Deco)......................**35.00**

You Are The Rose Of My Heart by Andrew K. Allison & James Kendis, 1914 ....**5.00**

You Are The Rose That Will Never Die by Edgar Leslie, Bert Kalmar & Ted Snyder, 1914 (Cover Artist, Barbelle)..............................**10.00**

You Are Too Sweet For A Dream by Jack Nelson & Herbie Mintz, 1924...**5.00**

You Belong To Me by Pee Wee King, Redd Stewart & Chilton Price, 1952, Photo Jo Stafford (Cover Artist, Barbelle) **6.00**

You Belong To Me by Pee Wee King, Redd Stewart & Chilton Price, 1952, Signed Photo Patti Page (Cover Artist, Barbelle & Signed) **16.00**

You Belong To Me I Belong To You by Charles Newman & Carmen Lombardo, 1929..**5.00**

You Belong To My Heart by Augustine Lara & Ray Gilbert, 1945, Movie: The Three Caballeros (Disney)..**15.00**

You Better Ask Me by Samuel Lover & Geoffrey O'Hara, 1925..........**5.00**

You Break The Heart That Loved You by Wendley & Mueller, 1915 (Cover Artist, Pfeiffer) **10.00**

You Broke My Heart Overnight by Harry Russell, 1926 (Cover Artist, Barbelle) **3.00**

You Broke My Heart To Pass The Time Away by Joe Goodwin & Leo Wood, 1913 (Cover Artist, A.H. Keller) **10.00**

You Brought A New Kind Of Love To Me by Sammy Fain, Irving Kahal & Pierre Norman, 1930, Movie: The Big Pond, Photo Maurice Chevalier & Claudette Colbert..15.00

You Brought Ireland Right Over To Me by J. Keirn Brennan & Ernest R. Ball, 1917 (Irish)..**10.00**

You Call Everybody Darling by Sam Martin, Ben Trace & Clem Watts, 1946, Photo Al Trace..**2.00**

You Call Everybody Darling by Sam Martin, Ben Trace & Clem Watts, 1946, Photo Eve Young..**3.00**

You Call It Madness But I Call It Love by Con Conrad, Gladys DuBois, Russ Columbo & Paul Gregory, 1931, Photo Russ Columbo..........**3.00**

You Came Along From Out Of Nowhere by Edward Heyman & John W. Green, 1931, Movie: You Came Along, Photo Helen Forrest, Robert Cummings, Lizabeth Scott & Don DeFore **10.00**

You Came To My Rescue by Leo Robin & Ralph Rainger, 1936, Movie: Big Broadcast Of 1937, Photo Jack Benny & Many Stars.............**10.00**

You Came, You Saw, You Conquered by Charles K. Harris, 1917.......**5.00**

You Can Always Tell A Yank by E.Y. Harburg & Burton Lane, 1944, Movie: Hollywood Canteen, Photo Andrews Sisters, Jack Benny & Many Other Stars..**10.00**

You Can Cry On Somebody Else's Shoulder by Dick Robertson, Marty Symes & Frank Weldon, 1945, Photo Charlie Spivak **3.00**

You Can Do No Wrong by Cole Porter, 1948, Movie: The Pirate........**5.00**

You Can Have Him by Irving Berlin, 1949, Musical: Miss Liberty (Irving Berlin)..**12.00**

You Can Have It I Don't Want It by May Hill, Clarence Williams & Armand J. Piron, 1918, Photo Eddie Cantor (Eddie Cantor) **15.00**

You Can Make All My Love Dreams Come True by Berg, Pearle & O'Hare, 1915, Photo Roy LaPearle (Cover Artist, Pfeiffer) **10.00**

You Can Stay But That Dog-Gone Fiddle Must Go by Billy Frisch & Billy Basquette, 1920 ....**8.00**

You Can Take Me Away From Dixie (But You Can't Take Dixie Away From Me) by Fred Rose & Roger Lewis, 1923................................**5.00**

You Can Tell That He's An American by Howard Johnson & Percy Wenrich, 1918 (WWI) **10.00**

You Can Tell That I'm Irish by G.M. Cohan (G.M. Cohan & Irish) ..**10.00**

You Can't Afford To Marry If You Can't Afford A Ford, 1915 (Transportation) **20.00**

You Can't Be True by Gerhard Ebeler & Hans Otten, 1948, Photo Joan Edwards (Cover Artist, Frederick S. Manning)..................5.00

You Can't Be True, Dear by Hal Cotton & Ken Griffin, 1948, Photo Jerry Wayne..**2.00**

You Can't Be True, Dear by Hal Cotton & Ken Griffin, 1948, Photo Ken Griffin...**2.00**

You Can't Beat American Love by Happy O'Neil & Oliver E. Story, 1910 ....**5.00**

You Can't Bring Back Yesterday by Walter Hirsch & May Hill, 1918 ..**5.00**

You Can't Brush Me Off by Irving Berlin, 1939, Movie: Louisiana Purchase, Photo William Gaxton, Vera Zorina, Victor Moore & Irene Bordoni (Irving Berlin)..**10.00**

You Can't Deny You're Irish by George M. Cohan (George M. Cohan & Irish)..**10.00**

You Can't Do Wrong Doin' Right by Rinker & Huddleston, 1950, Movie: Duchess Of Idaho, Photo, Lena Horne, Esther Williams, Van Johnson & John Lund **4.00**

You Can't Expect Kisses From Me by Roger Lewis & Rubey Cowan, 1911, Signed Photo Mary Elizabeth (Signed) **6.00**

You Can't Fool Me No More by Nathan Bevins, 1900, Photo Emma Carus (Cover Artist, Keller & Black, Black Face) **30.00**

You Can't Forget Your Mother by A.E. Bucknam & J.H. Ellis, 1903....**10.00**

You Can't Get A Man With A Gun by Irving Berlin, 1946, Movie: Annie Get Your Gun (Irving Berlin)..**10.00**

You Can't Get Along With 'Em Or Without 'Em by Clarke & Fisher, 1916..**5.00**

You Can't Get Away From The Blarney by Darl MacBoyle & Albert Von Tilzer, 1917 (Irish)..**5.00**

You Can't Get Lovin' Where There Ain't Any Love by Will E. Skidmore & Jack Baxley, 1919, Photo Aileen Stanley, Dedicated To Aileen Stanley (Dedication)..**10.00**

You Can't Guess What He Wrote On My Slate by Audrey Kingsbury, 1907 ....**5.00**

You Can't Keep A Good Man Down by M.F. Carey, 1900................**10.00**

You Can't Live Without A Girl by Bieck & Solman, 1911 (Cover Artist, Pfeiffer)..**10.00**

You Can't Make A Fool Out Of Me by Paul Cunningham, 1923 ....**5.00**

You Can't Pull The Wool Over My Eyes by Milton Ager, Charles Newman & Murray Mencher, 1936..**5.00**

You Can't Run Away From Love by Al Dubin & Harry Warren, 1937, Movie: The Singing Marines, Photo Dick Powell & Doris Weston **12.00**

You Can't See The Sun When You're Cryin' by Allan Roberts & Doris Fisher, 1946, Photo Vaughn Monroe....................................**4.00**

You Can't See The Sun When You're Cryin' by Allan Roberts & Doris Fisher, 1946, Photo George Towne....................................**4.00**

You Can't Stop Me From Dreaming by Cliff Friend & Dave Franklin, 1937, Photo Guy Lombardo (Cover Artist, Merman) **5.00**

You Can't Take My Mem'ries From Me by Joe Davis & Spencer Williams, 1939..**3.00**

You Can't Walk Back From An Aeroplane, 1927 (Transportation) **22.00**

You Can't Win by Smalls, 1975, Movie: The Wiz, Photo Diana Ross, Nipsey Russell, Ted Ross & Michael Jackson **10.00**

You Cannot Make Your Shimmy Shake On Tea by Irving Berlin, 1919, Movie: Ziegfeld Follies, 1919 (Irving Berlin)..............................**20.00**

You Could Have Been The One Baby by B.G. DeSylva, Lew Brown & Ray Henderson, 1931 ....**5.00**

You Could Have Been True by James Bland (Pre 1900 & Black, Black Face) **15.00**

You Couldn't Be Cuter by Jerome Kern & Dorothy Fields, 1938, Movie: Joy Of Living, Photo Irene Dunne....................................**10.00**

You Couldn't Hardly Notice It At All by V. Bryan & Harry Von Tilzer, 1902 ....**5.00**

You Darlin' by Harry Wood, 1930, Photo Guy Lombardo (Cover Artist, Leff)..**5.00**

You Did by L. Wolfe Gilbert, 1913..**5.00**

You Didn't Have To Tell Me by Walter Donaldson, 1931 (Cover Artist, Frederick S. Manning)..**10.00**

You Didn't Know Me From Adam by Joe Burke & John Jacob Loeb, 1934 ....**6.00**

You Didn't Know The Music, I Didn't Know the Words by Sam Coslow, 1931 (Cover Artist Jorj)..**5.00**

You Didn't Want Me When You Had Me by Ben Russell, Bernie Grossman & Geo. J. Bennett, 1919, Signed Photo Catherine Calvert, Photo Elsie Mains (Signed) **5.00**

You Didn't Want Me When You Had Me by Ben Russell, Bernie Grossman & Geo. J. Bennett, 1919, Photo Ray Morton & Catherine Calvert, Signed by Catherine Calvert (Signed)............................**6.00**

You Discover You're In New York by Leo Robin & Harry Warren, 1943, Movie: The Gang's All Here, Photo Alice Faye, Carmen Miranda, Phil Baker & The King Of Swing, Benny Goodman..............................**8.00**

You Do by Mack Gordon & Joseph Myrow, 1947, Movie: Mother Wore Tights, Photo Betty Grable & Dan Dailey......................................**5.00**

You Do Something To Me by Cole Porter, 1929 ....**5.00**

You Don't Have To Come From Ireland To Be Irish by George Graff, Jr. & Bert Grant, 1917 (Irish)..**5.00**

You Don't Have To Know The Language by Johnny Burke, Jimmy Van Heusen, 1947, Movie: Road To Rio, Photo Bing Crosby, Bob Hope & Dorothy Lamour **12.00**

You Don't Know by J. Will Callahan & Lee S. Roberts, 1918.............**5.00**

You Don't Know by Meredith Wilson, 1963, Musical Here's Love......**4.00**

You Don't Like It-Not Much by Ned Miller, Art Kahn & Chester Cohn, 1927 (Deco)..**10.00**

You Find The Time, I'll Find The Place by B.G. DeSylva, Lew Brown & Ray Henderson, 1929, Movie: Sunny Side Up, Photo Janet Gaynor..........**15.00**

You Flew Over by Harrison & Verges, 1927 (Transportation).............**10.00**

You For Me When You're Sweet Sixteen by Robert Roden, Andrew B. Sterling & Kerry Mills, 1909, Photo Frank Morrell (Cover Artist, DeTakacs)...**10.00**

You For Me-Me For You by Meyer, 1922 ....**5.00**

You Found Me And I Found You by P.G. Wodehouse & Jerome Kern, 1918, Musical: Oh Lady! Lady!!..**5.00**

You Gave Me Eve'rything But Love by Gus Kahn & Grace LeBoy, 1933..**5.00**

You Gave Me Your Heart by Francis Wheeler, Harry Smith & Ted Snyder, 1922, Movie: Blood And Sand, Photo Rudolph Valentino & Nita Naldi **10.00**

You Go To My Head by Haven Gillespie & J. Fred Coots, 1938 ....**2.00**

You Go Your Way, I'll Go Mine by Max Clay, 1915 (Cover Artist, Pfeiffer) **10.00**

You Gorgeous Dancing Doll by Russ Morgan, Paul Cunningham & Ira Schuster, 1940 ....**4.00**

You Got To Keep A-Goin by Alfred Bryan & Jean Schwartz, 1912 (Cover Artist, Pfeiffer & Transportation)...**10.00**

You Got To Play Rag Time by Havez & Sloane, 1899 (Pre 1900 & Rag)..**10.00**

You Got To Stop A-Pickin' On My Li'l Pickaninny by Slauton & Edwards, 1912 (Cover Artist, Pfeiffer & Black, Black Face) **15.00**

You Gotta Be A Football Hero by Al Sherman, Buddy Fields & Al Lewis, 1933, Photo Don Bestor (Sports)...**15.00**

You Gotta Know How by Ralph Williams, Ernie Erdman & Walter Donaldson, 1925 (Cover Artist, JVR & Deco)....................................**5.00**

You Gotta Make Your Own Sunshine by Neil Sedaka, Photo Neil Sedaka **3.00**

You Gotta S-M-I-L-E To Be H-A Double P-Y by Mack Gordon & Harry Revel, 1936, Movie: Stowaway, Photo Shirley Temple (Shirley Temple) **12.00**

You Great Big Bashful Doll by Clarke, 1914 (Cover Artist, Pfeiffer) .**10.00**

You Have To Have A Part To Make A Hit by Henry Blossom & Victor Herbert, 1914, Musical: The Only Girl (Victor Herbert) **15.00**

You Hit The Spot by Mack Gordon & Harry Revel, 1935.....................**5.00**

You, Just You by Albert A. Williams, 1909 (Cover Artist, Pfeiffer) ...**10.00**

You Keep Coming Back Like A Song by Irving Berlin, 1943, Movie: Blue Skies, Photo Bing Crosby, Fred Astaire & Joan Caulfield (Cover Artist, Hal Weinstein & Irving Berlin)..**10.00**

You Keep Sending 'Em Over And We'll Keep Knocking 'Em Down by Sidney D. Mitchell & Harry Ruby, 1918 (WWI)...........................**15.00**

You Kissed Me by C. Harris, 1914 (Cover Artist, Pfeiffer)................**10.00**

You Know How Talk Gets Around by Fred Rose, 1949, Photo Eddy Arnold..**6.00**

You Know, I Know by Howard Johnson, Charles Tobias & Al Sherman, 1926, Movie: Ev'rything's Made For Love, Photo Aileen Stanley**10.00**

You Know, I Love You by Phil Ponce & W.C. Polla, 1919 (Lithograph, Knapp Co.)..**5.00**

You Know What I Mean by Alfred Dubin & Fred Rath, 1919, Photo Corinne Griffith & Walter Fraser **10.00**

You Know You Belong To Somebody Else, So Why Don't You Leave Me Alone by Eugene West & James V. Monaco, 1922 (Cover Artist, Perret & Deco) **6.00**

You Leave Me Breathless by Ralph Freed & Frederick Hollander, 1938, Movie: Cocoanut Grove, Photo Fred McMurray, Harriet Hilliard, The Yacht Club Boys & Ben Blue...**10.00**

You Left Me So Blue by Vic Young, Phil Hopkins & Danny Russo, 1930 (Deco) **5.00**

You Light Up My Life by Joe Brooks, 1977, Movie: You Light Up My Life, Photo Didi Conn & Joe Silver **4.00**

You Little So-And-So by Sam Coslow & Leo Robin, Movie: Blonde Venus, Photo Marlene Dietrich **10.00**

You Look Good To Me by Billy Rose & Walter Donaldson, 1938, Photo Henry Busse...**4.00**

You Look Good To Me by Billy Rose & Walter Donaldson, 1938, Photo Jan Garber..**4.00**

You Look Just Like A Girl I Used To Know by Ron Ramsay, 1909, Photo Eva Tanguay & Baby Eddy (Cover Artist, Starmer).....................**15.00**

You Love Me by Styne & Cahn, 1950, Movie: The West Point Story, Photo James Cagney, Doris Day, Gene Nelson, Virginia Mayo & Gordon Macrae **5.00**

You Made Me Care by Jos. Gilbert, 1939 ....**5.00**

You Made Me Love You by Joe McCarthy & James V. Monaco, 1913, Sung by Al Jolson (Cover Artist, Rose Symbol & Al Jolson) **10.00**

You Made Me Love You by Jos. McCarthy & James V. Monaco, 1932, Movie: The Jolson Story, Photo Larry Parks & Evelyn Keyes (Al Jolson) **10.00**

You Made Me Love You–Why Did You? by Carmen Lombardo & Mickey Kippel, 1929...**5.00**

You May Be The World To A World Of Friends, But You're More Than The World To Me by Jeff Branen & Alfred Solman, 1914...........**10.00**

You May Belong To Some One Else But Your Heart Belongs To Me by Will R. Garton & Cedric H. Garton, 1914 (Cover Artist, Pfeiffer)..**10.00**

You May Hold A Million Girlies In Your Arms by Howard Johnson, Grant Clarke & Fred Fischer, 1916, (Cover Artist, C.F. Lent) **10.00**

You May Not Love Me by Johnny Burke & James Van Heusen, 1945 ..**3.00**

You Mean All That & More To Me by Piantadosi, 1919, Photo Gloria Jay (Cover Artist, Pfeiffer & Deco)...**10.00**

You Moved Right In by Adamson & McHugh, 1945, Movie: Bring On The Girls, Photo Veronica Lake, Sonny Tufts, Marjorie Reynolds, Eddie Bracken & Spike Jones & The City Slickers **6.00**

You Musn't Kick It Around by Lorenz Hart & Richard Rodgers, 1940, Musical: Pal Joey...**3.00**

You Musn't Kick It Around by Lorenz Hart & Richard Rodgers, 1940...**5.00**

You Musn't Pick Plums From My Plum Tree by Arthur Lamb & Harry Von Tilzer, 1904...**5.00**

You Must Come Over To-Night by Art Conrad, 1923 (Cover Artist, P & L Studio & Deco)..**5.00**

You Must Have Been A Beautiful Baby by Johnny Mercer & Harry Warren, 1938, Movie: Hard To Get, Photo Dick Powell & Olivia DeHavilland (Cover Artist, Im-Ho) **10.00**

You Must Love Some One by Sam Lewis & Geo. W. Meyer, 1913, Photo Richards & Kyle **5.00**

You Must Love Someone by Sam M. Lewis, Geo. W. Meyer, 1913, Photo Ollie Hodges **8.00**

You Never Can Be Too Sure About The Girls by Lew Brown, Bobby Heath & Rubey Cowan, 1917...**6.00**

You Never Can Tell About Love by Benny Davis & J. Fred Coots, 1930, Photo J. Fred Coots, Benny Davis, Fred Stone, Dorothy Stone & Paula Stone **5.00**

You Never Can Tell by Jerome Kern, 1914 ....**5.00**

You Never Can Tell by Lew Brown & Albert Von Tilzer, 1920 (Cover Artist, R.S. & Deco) **6.00**

You Never Can Tell What A Girlie Will Do! by Harry Bewley, 1915 (Cover Artist, P. H. Paulin) **10.00**

You Never Miss The Water Till The Well Runs Dry by Paul Secon & Arthur Kent, 1946...**3.00**

You Never Miss Your Mother Till She's Gone by Harry Birch, 1885 (Pre 1900)..15.00

You Never Say Yes, You Never Say No!by Irving Caesar, Rafael Duchesne & Art Kasset, 1944, Photo Art Kassel.......................4.00

You Never Spoke Like That To Me Before by Charles K. Harris, 1903 (Cover Artist, J.B. Eddy)...15.00

You Only Live Twice by Bricusse & Barry, 1967, Movie: You Only Live Twice, Photo Sean Connery 5.00

You Only Want Me When You're Lonesome by Louis Seifert & Edwin Tillman, 1926 (Deco) 5.00

You Ought To See Her Now by Pease, Nelson & Russak, 1919...........5.00

You Ought To See My Baby by Roy Turk & Fred E. Ahlert, 1920 (Cover Artist, Barbelle & Deco)..5.00

You Oughta Be In Pictures by Edward Heyman & Dana Suesse, 1951, Movie: Starlight...5.00

You Picked A Bad Day Out To Say Good-bye by Irving Berlin, 1913 (Cover Artist, Pfeiffer & Irving Berlin)................................15.00

You Remind Me Of My Mother by George M. Cohan, 1922, Musical: Little Nellie Kelly (George M. Cohan & Deco).......................15.00

You Remind Me Of The Girl Who Used To Go To School With Me by Jack Drislane & Charles Miller, 1910 ....10.00

You Said Something by Jerome Kern & P.G. Wodehouse, 1916, Musical: Have A Heart...10.00

You Sent A Love Torpedo Right Thru My Heart by Hart & Platzmann, 1915, Photo Kitty Gordon (Cover Artist, Pfeiffer).........................10.00

You Splash Me And I'll Splash You by Arthur Lamb & Albert Solman, 1907 ....5.00

You Started Something by Emery Deutsch & Jimmy Rogan, 1937, Photo Emery Deutsch (Cover Artist, Scott)..............................5.00

You Stingy Baby by William Tracey, Howard Johnson & Ernest Breuer, 1917, Photo Florence & Frank Moore (Cover Artist, Rose Symbol) ..5.00

You Taught Me How To Love You, Now Teach Me To Forget by Jack Drislane, Alfred Bryan & Geo. W. Meyer, 1909, Photo Jeanette Childs (Cover Artist E.P.C.) 10.00

You Taught Me How To Love You, Now Teach Me To Forget by Jack Drislane, Alfred Bryan & Geo. W. Meyer, 1909, Photo Kelly & Rio (Cover Artist, E.P.C.) 10.00

You Till The Judgement Day by Sterling, O'Hare & White, 1914........5.00

You Took Advantage Of Me by Lorenz Hart & Richard Rodgers, 1928...5.00

You Took My Breath Away by Coslow & Whiting, 1935, Movie: Coronado, Photo Eddy Duchin, Johnny Davis, Leon Errol, Jack Haley & Andy Devine..4.00

You Took The Sunshine With You, Mary Mine by Earle C. Jones, Alfred Bryan & George W. Meyer, 1907 ....10.00

You Took The Sweet From Sweetheart by Alex Sullivan, Al Doyle & Irving Kaufman, 1919 (Cover Artist, Barbelle) 10.00

You Took The Words Right Out Of My Heart by Leo Robin & Ralph Rainger, 1937, Movie: Big Broadcast Of 1938, Photo Shirley Ross, Caricature W.C. Fields, Ben Blue, Martha Raye & Bob Hope......10.00

You Tried To Ruin My Name by Redd Stewart & Pee Wee King, 1951 ....3.00

You Try Somebody Else, We'll Be Back Together Again by B.G. DeSylva, Lew Brown & Ray Henderson, 1931............................5.00

You Two by Sherman & Sherman, 1968, Movie: Chitty Chitty Bang Bang, Photo Dick Van Dyke & Sally Ann Howes.........................8.00

You Walk By by Ben Raleigh & Bernie Wayne, 1940 ....3.00

You Was by Paul Francis Webster & Sonny Burke, 1949 ....3.00

You Went Away Too Far, And Stayed Away Too Long by Alfred Bryan & James V. Monaco, 1927 ....5.00

You Were All I Had by W.R. Williams, 1913................................5.00

You Were Just Made To Order For Me by Mahoney, 1916 (Cover Artist, Pfeiffer)..10.00

You Were Meant For Me by Arthur Freed & Nacio Herb Brown, 1952, Movie: Singin' In The Rain, Photo Gene Kelly, Debbie Reynolds & Donald O'Connor...5.00

You Were Meant For Me by Arthur Freed & Nacio Herb Brown, 1929, Movie: You Were Meant For Me, Photo Jeanne Crain & Dan Dailey 10.00

You Were Meant For Me by Arthur Freed & Nacio Herb Brown, 1929, Movie: Broadway Melody, Photo Charles King, Bessie Love & Anita Page 10.00

You Were Never Lovelier by Johnny Mercer & Jerome Kern, 1942, Movie: You Were Never Lovelier, Photo Fred Astaire, Rita Hayworth, Adolphe Menjou & Xavier Cugat & His Orchestra 5.00

You Were Only Fooling, While I Was Falling In Love by Billy Faber, Fred Meadows & Larry Fotine, 1948, Photo Blue Barron 5.00

You Will Have To Sing An Irish Song by Jack Norworth & Albert Von Tilzer, 1908 (Irish)...5.00

You Will Never Miss Your Mother 'Til She's Gone by Geo. H. Diamond, 1912, Photo Geo. H. Diamond (Cover Artist, Pfeiffer)................10.00

You Tell Her–I Stutter by Billy Rose & Cliff Friend, 1922 ......10.00

You Tell It, Or Jitney-Bus Joy by Hendron, 1915 (Transportation).....10.00

You Tell Me Your Dream, I'll Tell You Mine by Rice, Brown & Daniels, 1939, Photo Lawrence Welk & His Champagne Music.................6.00

You & The Moon & A Ragtime Tune by Wm. Vaughan Dunham & Albert Von Tilzer, 1913 (Rag)...10.00

You Will Remember Vienna by Oscar Hammerstein II & Sigmund Romberg, 1942, Movie: Deep In My Heart, Based On Life Of Sigmund Romberg **10.00**

You Won't Be Satisfied by Freddy James & Larry Stock, 1945, Photo Perry Como...**6.00**

You Won't Be Satisfied by Freddy James & Larry Stock, 1945, Photo Louis Prima...**6.00**

You Wonderful You by Earl Carroll & Harry Revel, 1947, Musical: Earl Carroll Vanities...**5.00**

You Wonderful You by Jack Brooks, Saul Chaplin & Harry Warren, 1950, Movie: Summer Stock, Photo Judy Garland & Gene Kelly..........**15.00**

You Wouldn't Fool Me Would You? by B.G. DeSylva, Lew Brown & Ray Henderson, 1928, Musical: Follow Thru **5.00**

You, You Darlin' by Jack Scholl & M. K. Jerome, 1940, Photo Dinah Shore (Cover Artist, Im-Ho)...**4.00**

You, You Live In My Heart by Harold Potter & Rodd Eddie, 1938, Photo Perry Como (Cover Artist, Barbelle)...**5.00**

You, You, You Are The One by Milton Leeds, Fred Wise & Tetos Demey, 1948, Photo Johnny Eager **3.00**

You, You, You by Robert Mellin & Lotar Olias, 1952 ....**3.00**

You'd Be So Nice To Come Home To by Cole Porter, 1942, Movie: Something To Shout About, Photo Don Ameche, Janet Blair & Jack Oakie...**5.00**

You'd Be Surprised by Irving Berlin, 1919 (Irving Berlin) **10.00**

You'd Better Ask Me by Samuel Lover & Herman Lohr, 1900 (Irish) ..**10.00**

You'd Better Be Nice To Them Now by Jack Stern & Wm. Tracey, 1918 (Cover Artist, Barbelle & WWI) **10.00**

You'd Better Love Me by Hugh Martin & Timothy Gray, Musical: High Spirits...**5.00**

You'd Close The Gates Of Heaven by Dave Berg & Alfred Solman, 1917...**5.00**

You'd Never Know That Old Town Of Mine by Howard Johnson & Walter Donaldson, 1915, Photo Jack Frazer (Cover Artist, Rose Symbol & Transportation) **15.00**

You'll Always Be The One I Love by Sunny Skylar & Ticker Freeman, 1946, Photo Frank Sinatra **6.00**

You'll Always Be The One I Love by Sunny Skylar & Ticker Freeman, 1946, Movie: Song Of The South (Disney).................**10.00**

You'll Always Be The Same Sweet Baby by A. Seymour Brown, 1916, Photo Bonita & Lew Hearn (Cover Artist, Starmer) **5.00**

You'll Always Be The Same Sweet Girl by Andrew B. Sterling & Harry Von Tilzer, 1915, Photo Harry Von Tilzer (Cover Artist, Rose Symbol)...**10.00**

You'll Always Be The Same Sweet Girl by Andrew B. Sterling & Harry Von Tilzer, 1915 (Cover Artist, Pfeiffer) **10.00**

You'll Be Glad To Have Your Old Sweetheart Again by Alfred Bryan & Alfred Solman, 1917 (Cover Artist, DeTakacs) **10.00**

You'll Be Lonely Too by Gus Van & Joe Schenck, 1922.................**5.00**

You'll Be Sorry by Maceo Pinkard, 1919 ....**5.00**

You'll Be Sorry Just Too Late by Billy Gaston, 1907, Photo Billy Gaston (Cover Artist, Starmer).................**5.00**

You'll Be Sorry When We Say Goodbye by Joe E. Howard (Cover Artist, Pfeiffer).................**10.00**

You'll Be The One, Not Me by Nelson, 1920 (Cover Artist, Pfeiffer) **10.00**

You'll Be There by J. Kiern Brennan & Ernest R. Ball, 1915 (Cover Artist, Dunk & WWI).................**10.00**

You'll Be There To Meet Them, When The Boys Come Home by Jeff Branen & Dick Heinrich, 1918 (Cover Artist, E.E. Walton & WWI)...**25.00**

You'll Come Back by Jack Drislane & Geo. W. Meyer, 1909.................**5.00**

You'll Do The Same Thing Over Again by Alfred Bryan & Albert Gumble, 1911, Photo Wm. H. Carr (Cover Artist, Starmer).................**12.00**

You'll Do The Same Thing Over Again by Alfred Bryan & Albert Gumble, 1911, Photo Isabel D'Armond (Cover Artist, Starmer)...........**10.00**

You'll Do The Same Thing Over Again by Alfred Bryan & Albert Gumble, 1911, Photo Ray Sumner (Cover Artist, Starmer)...................**10.00**

You'll Find A Little Bit Of Ireland Everywhere by Stanley Murphy, 1916 (Irish) **5.00**

You'll Find Old Dixie Land In France by Grant Clarke & Geo W. Meyer, 1918, Small War Edition (WWI, Dixie).................**15.00**

You'll Find Your Answer In My Eyes by L. Wolfe Gilbert & Abel Baer, 1929 ....**5.00**

You'll Get All That's Coming To You by Andrew B. Sterling & Harry Von Tilzer, 1898 (Pre 1900 & Black, Black Face) **20.00**

You'll Have To Get Off And Walk by Dave Reed, 1907 (Transportation).................**20.00**

You'll Have To Put Him To Sleep With The Marseillaise And Wake Him Up With A OO-La La by Andrew B. Sterling & Harry Von Tilzer, 1918 (Cover Artist, Pfeiffer & WWI) **20.00**

You'll Have To Wait Til My Ship Comes In by Ren Shields & Geo. Evans, 1906 ....**5.00**

You'll Miss Me Someday by Richard Howard, 1916.................**5.00**

You'll Miss Your Loving Baby, Bye And Bye by Billy DeVere & Al Herman, 1911 ....**5.00**

You'll Never Get Up To Heaven That Way by Allan J. Lerner & Abel Baer, 1933.................**5.00**

You'll Never Know by Al Jolson, Arthur Franklin & Billy Rose, 1928 (Al Jolson).................**10.00**

You'll Never Know by Mack Gordon & Harry Warren, 1943, Movie: Hello Frisco Hello, Photo Alice Faye, Jack Oakie, John Payne & Lynn Bari **5.00**

You'll Never Know The Good Fellow I've Been by Jack Coogan, 1911, Photo Alexander & Scott.................**12.00**

You'll Never Know The Good Fellow I've Been by Jack Coogan, 1911, Photo Sophie Tucker **22.00**

You'll Never Need A Doctor No More by Chris Smith, 1921, Musical: Broadway Brevities, 1921, Photo Bert Williams (Cover Artist, Black, Black Face).................**25.00**

You'll Never Reach Glory In An Automobile by Tull, 1915 (WWI & Transportation) **22.00**

You'll Never Walk Alone by Richard Rodgers & Oscar Hammerstein II, 1945, Movie: Carousel (Cover Artist, BJH).................**3.00**

You'll Want Me Back Some Day by Roger Graham & Mary Hill, 1918 ..**5.00**

You'll Want Me Back Sometime by The Duncan Sisters, 1923 ....**5.00**

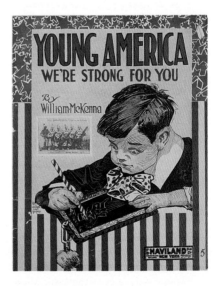

Young America We're Strong For You by William J. McKenna, 1915, (Cover Artist, Walt, WWI & Patriotic).................15.00

Young And Foolish by Arnold Harvett & Albert Hague, 1954, Musical: Plain And Fancy (Cover Artist, Barbelle) **5.00**

Young And Healthy by Al Dubin & Harry Warren, 1932, Movie: Forty Second Street, Photo Bebe Daniels, George Brent, Ruby Keeler, Warner Baxter, Ginger Rogers, Dick Powell, Una Merkel & Guy Kibbe **15.00**

Young At Heart by Carolyn Leigh & Johnny Richards, 1954, Photo Frank Sinatra..**5.00**

Young Eph's Lament by Murphy & Purdy, 1863 (Pre 1900)..............**40.00**

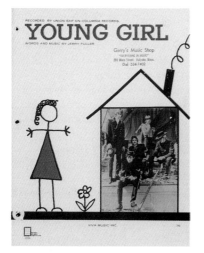

Young Girl by Jerry Fuller, 1968, Photo Union Gap **3.00**

Young Guard March, The by Harry Appel, 1909 (March)...................**10.00**

Young Man's Fancy, A by John Murray Anderson, Jack Yellen & Milton Ager, 1920, Musical: The Music Box Review **10.00**

Young Mother's Lullaby, The by Geo. Russell Jackson & J. L. Gilbert, 1882 (Pre 1900) **15.00**

Younger Than Springtime by Richard Rodgers & Oscar Hammerstein II, 1949, Musical: South Pacific (Cover Artist, BJH) **3.00**

Your Absence Is Breaking My Heart by Allen & Daly, 1914 (Cover Artist, Pfeiffer)..**10.00**

Your Broadway And My Broadway by Brown & Freed, 1937, Movie: Broadway Melody 1938, Photo Eleanor Powell, Robert Taylor, Judy Garland, Sophie Tucker & George Murphy **10.00**

Your Cheatin' Heart by Hank Williams, 1952, Photo Hank Williams ..**8.00**

Your Country Needs You by Al Dubin, Rennie Cormack & Geo. B. McConnell, 1917 (WWI, March & Patriotic)................................**20.00**

Your Dad Gave His Life For His Country by Harry J. Breen & May Geary, 1903 (Patriotic) **15.00**

Your Daddy Did The Same Thing 50 Years Ago by Al Piantadosi, Joe McCarthy & Joe Goodwin, 1912..**12.00**

Your Eyes Are Bigger Than Your Heart by Milton Berle, Jimmy Eaton & Terry Shand, 1938 ....**5.00**

Your Eyes Have Told Me So by Gustave Kahn, Egbert Van Alstyne & Walter Blaufuss, 1919 ....**5.00**

Your Flag And My Flag by Harry Woods, 1918 (WWI) **10.00**

Your Heart Is Calling Mine by Bernard Hamblen, 1919.....................**5.00**

Your Heart Will Call Me Home by Arthur F. Tate.............................**5.00**

Your Kiss by Auld, Auld & Cates, 1955, Movie: To Catch A Thief, Photo Grace Kelly & Cary Grant..**3.00**

Your Kisses by Jack Snyder, 1923 ....**5.00**

Your Land And My Land by Dorothy Donnelly & Sigmund Romberg, 1927, Musical: My Maryland (Patriotic)......................................**10.00**

Your Lips Are No Man's Land But Mine by Arthur Guy Empey, Charles R. McCarron & Carey Morgan, 1918, Movie: Over The Top, Photo Grace Larue, Note To Jos. W. Stern & Co. "Gentlemen: Please Pay All Royalties Earned From The Sale Of This Song To The New York Sun Smoke Fund, Yours, Signed by Arthur Guy Empey" (Cover Artist, Brown Bros., WWI & Signed) **25.00**

Your Love Is All by Harry D. Kerr & J.S. Zamecnik, 1927 (Cover Artist, Ray Parmelee)..**15.00**

Your Love Is All by Harry D. Kerr & J.S. Zamecnik, 1927, Movie: Old Ironsides, Photo Charles Farrell & Esther Ralston.........................**10.00**

Your Love Is All That I Crave by Al Dubin, Perry Bradford & Jimmy Johnson, 1929, Movie: Show Of Shows....................................**15.00**

Your Love Is My Paradise by Tausig & Rogee, 1912 (Cover Artist, Pfeiffer) **10.00**

Your Mother And Mine by Joe Goodwin & Gus Edwards, 1929, From Hollywood Review 1929, Photo Many Stars **15.00**

Your Mother Is Your Best Friend After All by Charles Coleman, 1916..**10.00**

Your Mother Wants You Home, Boy by Paul Dresser, 1904..............**10.00**

Your Mother's Awfully Worried–Won't You Please Come Home by Miller, 1910 (Cover Artist, Pfeiffer) **15.00**

Your Papa Will Never Come Home Dear by Albert, Bradford & Andino, 1918 (Cover Artist, Pfeiffer & WWI) **20.00**

Your Picture by Paul Herve, Jean Biquet & Adolf Philipp, 1915, Musical: The Girl Who Smiles...**15.00**

Your Red Wagon by Raye, DePaul & Jones, 1947, Movie: Your Red Wagon, Photo Farley Granger & Cathy O'Donnell **4.00**

Your Song by Elton John & Bernie Taupin, 1969, Photo Elton John **5.00**

Your Song From Paradise by Monterey Brookton & Sydney Barlow Brown, 1927 ....**8.00**

Your Wife by Andrew Donnelly, Addison Burkhardt & Al Piantadosi, 1916 (Cover Artist, Pfeiffer) **10.00**

You're A Better Man Than I Am, Gunga Din by Osborne & Ehrtich, 1918, Photo Al Jolson (Cover Artist, Pfeiffer, Al Jolson & Deco) **15.00**

You're A Dangerous Girl by Grant Clarke & Jimmie Monaco, 1916, Musical: Robinson Crusoe Jr., Photo Al Jolson (Al Jolson) **15.00**

You're A Grand Old Flag by George M. Cohan, 1933, Movie: Yankee Doodle Dandy, Photo James Cagney & George M. Cohan (George M. Cohan & Patriotic)................................**12.00**

You're A Great Big Blue Eyed Baby by Seymour Brown, 1913, Photo Sophie Tucker..**15.00**

You're A Heavenly Thing by Joe Young & Little Jack Little,1935, Photo Little Jack Little (Cover Artist, Barbelle)........................**5.00**

You're A Life Saver by Ed East, 1935, Commercial Song Of Radio Show, As Sung And Played By Life Savers Rendezvous Orchestra-Rhythm Strings, Phil Duey & Jane Williams, Eunice Howard, The Men About Town, Radio's Most Popular Quartet & Olive Lemoy, The Cigarette Girl. Life Savers Rendezvous Broadcast Every Wednesday Evening Over the NBC Blue Network–Coast to Coast (Advertising) **55.00**

You're A Lucky Fellow Mr. Smith by Don Raye, Sonny Burke & Hughie Prince, 1941, Movie: Buck Privates, Photo Andrews Sisters & Abbott & Costello (WWII)..**10.00**

You're A Million Miles From Nowhere by Sam M. Lewis, Joe Young & Walter Donaldson, 1919 (Cover Artist, Barbelle)..........................**5.00**

You're A Million Miles From Nowhere by Sam M. Lewis, Joe Young & Walter Donaldson, 1919 (Lithograph, Knapp Co.) **8.00**

You're A Natural by Frank Loesser & Manning Sherwin, 1938, Movie: College Swing..**5.00**

You're A Naughty Baby by Nat Vincent, 1917................................**5.00**

You're A Picture No Artist Can Paint by Cunningham & Piani, 1914 (Cover Artist, Pfeiffer) **10.00**

You're A Real Sweetheart by Irving Caesar & Cliff Friend, 1928, Photo Verge Ford..**5.00**

You're A Real Sweetheart by Irving Caesar & Cliff Friend, 1928, Photo Ada River..**5.00**

You're A Sweet Little Headache by Leo Robin & Ralph Rainger, 1938, Movie: Paris Honeymoon, Photo Bing Crosby & Shirley Ross.....**10.00**

You're A Sweetheart by Jimmy McHugh & Harold Adamson, 1937, Movie: You're A Sweetheart, Photo Alice Faye & Andy Devine...**10.00**

You're All I Need by Gus Kahn, 1935 ....**3.00**

You're Always A Baby To Mother by Wm. Tracey & Halsey K. Mohr, 1926 ....**5.00**

You're Always In My Arms, But Only In My Dreams by Harry Tierney & Joseph McCarthy, 1929, Movie: Rio Rita **15.00**

You're As Dear To Me As "Dixie" Was To Lee by The Misses Campbell, 1917, Photo The Misses Campbell (Dixie) **10.00**

You're As Pretty As A Picture by Harold Adamson & Jimmy McHugh, 1938, Movie: That Certain Age, Photo Deanna Durbin **10.00**

You're As Welcome As The Flowers In May by Dan J. Sullivan, 1902**5.00**

You're Blase by Bruce Sievier & Ord Hamilton, 1932, Musical: Bow Bells..**10.00**

You're Breaking My Heart by Pat Genaro & Sunny Skylar, 1948 ....**3.00**

You're Breaking My Heart With "Good-bye" by Raymond Egan & Abe Olman, 1917 (Cover Artist, Starmer & Deco)........................**10.00**

You're Devastating by Otto Harbach & Jerome Kern, 1933, Movie: Roberta (Deco) **10.00**

You're Driving Me Crazy by Walter Donaldson, 1930 (Cover Artist, Frederick S. Manning & Deco)..**5.00**

You're Easy To Dance With by Irving Berlin, 1942, Movie: Holiday Inn, Photo Bing Crosby, Danny Kaye, Rosemary Clooney & Vera Ellen (Irving Berlin)..**5.00**

You're Getting To Be A Habit With Me by Al Dubin & Harry Warren, 1932, Movie: Forty Second Street, Photo Bebe Daniels, George Brent, Ruby Keeler, Warner Baxter, Ginger Rogers, Dick Powell, Una Merkel & Guy Kibbe..**16.00**

You're Going To Wish You Had Me Back by Hamer & Piantadosi, 1911 (Cover Artist, Pfeiffer) **10.00**

You're Gonna Lose Your Gal by Joe Young & James V. Monaco, 1933, Musical: Swanee Music Revue, Photo Kate Smith (Cover Artist, Leff)..**10.00**

You're Gonna See A Lot Of Me by Al Hoffman, Al Goodheart & Manny Kurtz, 1938, Photo Buddy Fisher (Cover Artist, Leff)....................**5.00**

You're Gwine To Get Somethin' What You Don't Expect by Williams & Bryan, 1910 (Cover Artist, Pfeiffer)................................**10.00**

You're Here And I'm Here by Harry B. Smith & Jerome Kern, 1914, Musical: Marriage Market, Photo Donald Brian **16.00**

You're Here My Love by Burke & Lilley, 1955, Movie: The Seven Little Foys, Photo Bob Hope..**3.00**

You're Here, You're There by Irving Kahal & John Jacob Loeb, 1937 ....**5.00**

You're In Love And I'm In Love by Walter Donaldson, 1928 ....**5.00**

You're In Love by Newman & Bregman, 1956, Movie: Accused Of Murder, Photo Gogi Grant..**4.00**

You're In Love by Otto Hauerbach & Rudolf Friml, 1916, Musical: You're In Love **10.00**

You're In Love With Everyone, But The One Who's In Love With You by Mort Dixon & Ray Henderson, 1924, Photo Dolly Kay **5.00**

You're In Style When You're Wearing A Smile by Brown, 1918........**5.00**

You're In The Right Church But The Wrong Pew by Cecil Mack & Chris Smith, 1908, Photo C. Vance (Cover Artist, Pfeiffer & Black, Black Face) **15.00**

You're Irish And You're Beautiful by Charlie Tobias & Al Lewis, 1942 (Cover Artist, Im-Ho & Irish)..**5.00**

You're Just A Great Big Baby Doll by Herscher, Darcey & Alexander, 1927 (Cover Artist, Barbelle) **5.00**

You're Just A Show Off by James & Andy Sindelar & Al Dubin, 1925, Photo Billy Glason (Cover Artist, Starmer & Deco)....................**10.00**

You're Just In Love by Irving Berlin, 1950 (Irving Berlin) **8.00**

You're Just Like An Angel To Me by Andrew K. Allison & James Kendis, 1915 (Cover Artist, Hirt)..**5.00**

You're Just The Boy For Me by Ed. Gardenier & Gus Edwards, 1908 ..**5.00**

You're Just The Same Old Sweetheart by Williams, 1916 (Cover Artist, Pfeiffer)..**10.00**

You're Laughing At Me by Irving Berlin, 1937, Movie: On The Avenue, Photo Dick Powell & Alice Faye (Irving Berlin)..........................**16.00**

You're Like A Rose To Me by Harry Bewley & Henry P. Menges, 1916 (Cover Artist, P.H. Paulin & Deco).....................................**5.00**

You're Lonely And I'm Lonely by Irving Berlin, 1939 (Irving Berlin)...**10.00**

You're Making A Miser Of Me by Alfred Dubin & Ernest R. Ball, 1919, Photo Corinne Griffith...**5.00**

You're More Than The World To Me by Jeff Branen & Alfred Solman, 1914 ....**5.00**.

You're My Baby by A. Seymour Brown & Nat D. Ayer, 1912, Photo Ashton & Fink (Cover Artist, Starmer) **5.00**

You're My Baby by A. Seymour Brown & Nat D. Ayer, 1912, Photo Florence Tannu (Cover Artist, Starmer) **5.00**

You're My Beautiful American Rose by Chas. Ford, 1917 (Cover Artist, Pfeiffer)...**12.00**

You're My Best Bet by Mo Jaffe & Clay Boland, 1936 ....**5.00**

You're My Everything by Mort Dixon, Joe Young & Harry Warren, 1931, Musical: Ed Wynn Presents Himself In The Laugh Parade (Cover Artist, Jorj)..**5.00**

You're My Girl by Bobby Heath, 1913, The Million Dollar Pier Song, Photo Of Airplane, Balloon & Dirigible By M.B. Smith, Photo Of Bobby Heath (Transportation)..**38.00**

You're My Girl by Sammy Cahn & Jule Styne, 1948, Musical: High Button Shoes...**5.00**

You're My Only Sweetheart by Cal De Voll & Harold Dillon, 1931 ....**5.00**

You're My Rose In The Garden Of Love by Orne & Googins, 1917 (Cover Artist, Pfeiffer) **10.00**

You're No Good To My Life by Laura Miller & R. Woodie, 1948.......**2.00**

You're Not The Only Pebble On The Beach by Harry Braisted & Stanley Carter, 1896, Signed Photo Lottie Gibson (Pre 1900 & Signed) ...**10.00**

You're One Great Big Vision To Me by Clark, 1914 (Cover Artist, Pfeiffer) **10.00**

You're Simply Delish by Arthur Freed & Joseph Meyer, 1930, Movie: Those Three French Girls **5.00**

You're So Different From The Rest by Mack & Farrell, 1913 (Cover Artist, Pfeiffer)..**10.00**

You're Some Girl by Lou Klein & Ted. S. Barron, 1915.................6.00

You're Some Pretty Doll by Clarence Williams, 1917 (Cover Artist, Barbelle & Deco)...**5.00**

You're Still An Old Sweetheart Of Mine by Richard A. Whiting & Raymond C. Egan, 1918 (Cover Artist, Frederick S. Manning)..........**15.00**

You're Still The Same Sweetheart Of Mine by Rose, Gordon & Gregory, 1930 (Cover Artist, Pfeiffer) **10.00**

You're Telling Me by Walter Donaldson **5.00**

You're The Best Little Mother Of All by Leo Friedman, 1914.............**5.00**

You're The Best Little Mother That God Ever Made by J. Keirn Brennan & Ernest R. Ball, 1916...**5.00**

You're The Brightest Star Of All My Dreams by Bert J. Wood, 1907, Photo Eugenie Soule (Cover Artist, Fred Kulz) **10.00**

You're The Cream In My Coffee by B.G. DeSylva, Lew Brown & Ray Henderson, 1928, Musical: Hold Everything (Cover Artist, Helen Van Doorn Morgan)..**16.00**

You're The Girl by Clarke, Leslie & Schwartz, 1912 (Cover Artist, Pfeiffer) **10.00**

You're The Girl For Me by Irene Motzer & Edwin Allemong, 1919 ....**5.00**

You're The Girl I Love The Best by Sadie Webber & Harry Ennis, 1906, Photo James J. Doherty (Cover Artist, Jenkins)............................**5.00**

You're The Girl That I've Been Longing For by J.R. Shannon & Chas. L. Johnson, 1913 (Cover Artist Parmalee & West) **15.00**

You're The Haven Of My Heart by Orr O'Conner & Theodore Morse, 1913 ....**5.00**

You're The Most Wonderful Girl by Edgar Leslie, Grant Clarke & Maurice Abrahams, 1913, Photo Lysa Graham, Al Jolson Hit (Cover Artist, Pfeiffer & Al Jolson) **15.00**

You're The Nicest Little Girl I Ever Knew by Charles Coleman, 1916.**5.00**

You're The One by Mercer & McHugh, 1940, Movie: You're The One, Photo Bonnie Baker & Orrin Tucker...**3.00**

You're The One I Care For by Harry Link, Chauncey Grey & Bert Lown, 1930, Photo Bert Lown (Cover Artist, Leff & Deco)......................**3.00**

You're The One I Care For by Harry Link, Chauncey Grey & Bert Lown, 1930, Photo Gene & Glenn (Cover Artist, Leff & Deco).................**3.00**

You're The One I'm Thinking Of by Leap, 1912 (Cover Artist, Pfeiffer)..**10.00**

You're The Only Girl For Me by Henry Blossom & Victor Herbert, Musical: The Only Girl (Victor Herbert)..**10.00**

You're The Only Girl That Made Me Cry by Fred Fisher, 1920 (Cover Artist, Wohlman & Deco) **10.00**

You're The Only Star In My Blue Heaven, by Gene Autry, 1938, Photo Gene Autry & Enoch Light (Cover Artist, Merman) **6.00**

You're The Same Old Girl by Joe Young, Harry Williams & Bert Grant, 1913 (Cover Artist, Pfeiffer) **10.00**

You're The Sweetest Girl I Know by J. Eugene Johnson & Wm. Nassann, 1910 ....**5.00**

You're The Top by Cole Porter, 1934, Movie: Anything Goes **5.00**

You're Trying To Throw Me Down by Roy Turk & J. Russel Robinson, 1923 ....**5.00**

You're Very Welcome Every One by Lytton Cox & Frederick G. Johnson, 1924 ....**5.00**

You're Wonderful by Livingston, Evans & Young, 1949, Movie: Paid In Full, Photo Lizabeth Scott & Robert Cummings............................**3.00**

Yours And Mine by Arthur Freed & Nacio Herb Brown, 1937, Movie: Broadway Melody of 1938...**10.00**

Yours And Mine by Nacio Herb Brown & Arthur Freed, 1937, Movie: Broadway Melody, 1938, Photo Eleanor Powell, Robert Taylor, Judy Garland, Sophie Tucker & George Murphy **12.00**

Yours by B. Bristow Owley & Henry S. Sawyer, 1912, Dedicated To Miss Dorothy Overmire (Dedication) **5.00**

Yours Is My Heart Alone by Ludwig Herzer, Fritz Lohner & Franz Lehar, 1940, Photo Ray Noble (Cover Artist, Im-Ho) **5.00**

Yours Is Not The Only Aching Heart by Beth Slater Whitson, 1907.....**5.00**

Yours, Mine And Ours by Sheldon & Karlin, 1968, Movie: Yours, Mine And Ours, Photo Henry Fonda & Lucille Ball **10.00**

You've Been A Dear Old Pal, Mother Of Mine by Levenson, Freeman & Cobb, 1920 (Cover Artist, Pfeiffer)..**10.00**

You've Been A Good Old Wagon But You Done Broke Down by Ben Harney, 1896 (Pre 1900, Transportation & Black, Black Face).....**25.00**

You've Built A Fire Down In My Heart by Irving Berlin, 1911 (Cover Artist, Pfeiffer & Irving Berlin)....................................**15.00**

You've Come Home by Carolyn Leigh & Cy Coleman, 1960, Movie: Wildcat...**3.00**

You've Got A Lot To Answer For by Wolf & James, 1915 (Cover Artist, Pfeiffer & Deco) **10.00**

You've Got A Million Dollar Smile by Billy Baskette & Burnette Wilke, 1917 ....**5.00**

You've Got Everything by Gus Kahn & Walter Donaldson, 1933 ....**4.00**

You've Got Me Crying Again by Charles Newman & Isham Jones, 1933 (Cover Artist, Barbelle) **3.00**

You've Got Me Goin' Kid by R. H. Cochrane & P.D. Cochrane, 1909 (Cover Artist, C.M.) 12.00

You've Got Me Pickin' Petals Off O' Daisies by B.G. DeSylva, Lew Brown & Ray Henderson, 1929, Movie: Sunny Side Up, Photo Janet Gaynor **15.00**

You've Got Me This Way by Johnny Mercer & Jimmy McHugh, 1940, Movie: You'll Find Out..**6.00**

You've Got Something by Cole Porter, 1936, Movie: Red Hot And Blue **12.00**

You've Got That Thing by Cole Porter, 1929, Musical: Fifty Million Frenchmen **6.00**

You've Got To Be Carefully Taught by Richard Rodgers & Oscar Hammerstein II, 1949, Musical: South Pacific (Cover Artist, BJH)........**6.00**

You've Got To See Mama Ev'ry Night by Billy Rose & Con Conrad, 1923 (Cover Artist, Wohlman)..**5.00**

You've Got What Gets Me by Gershwin & Gershwin, 1932, Movie: Girl Crazy, Photo Wheeler & Woolsey, Arline Judge, Mitzi Green & Eddie Quillan **5.00**

You've Got Your Mother's Big Blue Eyes by Irving Berlin, 1913, Photo Baby Helm (Cover Artist, Pfeiffer & Irving Berlin) **15.00**

You've Got Your Mother's Big Blue Eyes by Irving Berlin, 1913, Photo Innes & Ryan (Cover Artist Pfeiffer & Irving Berlin) **15.00**

You've Made All My Dreams Come True by Jack Darrell, 1920..........**5.00**

Ypsilanti by Albert Bryan & Egbert Van Alstyne, 1915 (Cover Artist, Starmer) **6.00**

Yukaloo by Van Brunt, 1917 (Cover Artist, Pfeiffer) **10.00**

Yum Pum Pa by Brockman, 1912 (Cover Artist, Pfeiffer)..................**10.00**

Yvonne by C. Cherubini, 1921 ....**5.00**

Zaame, 1909 (Cover Artist, Pfeiffer)..**15.00**

Zampa by Harold (Cover Artist, Pfeiffer)......................................**15.00**

Zana Zaranda by Mort Greene & Harry Revel, 1942, Movie: Call Out The Marines **5.00**

Zenda by Frank Witmark, 1895, Musical: Prisoner Of Zenda (Pre 1900) **10.00**

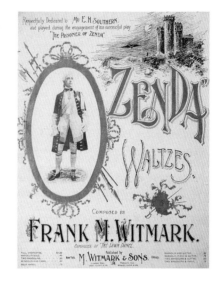

Zenda Waltzes by Frank Witmark, 1897 (Pre 1900).......................10.00

Zenith by Harry J. Lincoln, 1904 (March)..........................**10.00**

Zeona by Wm. Arnold, 1904 ....**5.00**

Zigeuner by Noel Coward, 1941..**5.00**

Zip-A-Dee-Doo-Dah by Allie Wrubel & Ray Gilbert, 1946, Movie: Song Of The South (Disney) **15.00**

Ziz-March by Alfred Feltman & E.T. Paull, 1907 (Cover Artist, E.T. Paull & March) **35.00**

Zizzy, Ze Zum Zum Zum by Karl Kennett & Lyn Udal, 1898, Musical: Cook's Tours, Photo Josie Hall (Pre 1900 & Rag) 15.00

Zoma by E.S. Litchfield, 1920..**5.00**

Zoot Suit For My Sunday Gal, A by Ray Gilbert & Bob O'Brien, 1941, Photo Martha Mears (Cover Artist, Wentworth & Black, Black Face)..**10.00**

Zum by Don Richardson, 1915 ....**5.00**

CHAPTER 2
COVER ARTISTS

Recognition of these highly talented cover illustrators is long overdue inasmuch as sheet music was greatly enhanced by the artistry of their work. Many attractive covers signed or unsigned by the artist, are suitable for framing.

Current prices of all artist-signed sheet music listed below can be found in Chapter 1.

ROLF ARMSTRONG

Girl Of Mine
I'm Forever Thinking Of You
My Garden Of Love
Sunshine Rose
Tears Tell
What A Wonderful Girl You Are
Yo-San

ALBERT BARBELLE

Ah, But It Happens
Ain't She Sweet?
Ain't You Coming Back To Dixieland
All Alone With You In A Little Rendevous
All O' The World A Home
All The Boys Love Mary
All The Quakers Are Shoulder Shakers
Allegheny Moon
Alone, My Love
Along The Way To Waikiki
America I Love You
And He'd Say "Oo-La-La Wee-Wee"
Answer Mr. Wilson's Call
Any Little Melody
Anything You Say
Araby
Arms Of Love
Arrah Go On I'm Gonna Go Back To Oregon
Auf Wiedersehn
Away Down South In Heaven
Battle Of The Marne
Be Still, My Heart
Beautiful Hawaii
Beautiful Ohio
Because They All Love You
Bell Bottom Trousers
Black Hawk Waltz, The
Blue Bird Bring Back My Happiness
Blue Prelude
Blue Waters
Bright Eyes
Bring Me A Rose
Brown Eyes, Why Are You Blue
Burgundy
Bye Bye Baby
Bye Lo
Carolina Sunshine
Charmaine
Chickery Chick
Choo-Choo
Cindy

Coax Me A Little Bit
Come On And Baby Me
Come On Papa
Confess
Covered Wagon Days
Crazy Words Crazy Tune Vo-Do-Deo
Cynthia's In Love
Dawn Of Tomorrow
Diane
Dinah
Dixie Volunteers, The
Don't Blame Me For What Happens In The Moonlight
Don't Cry Frenchy
Don't Cry Little Girl, Don't Cry
Don't You Remember The Day?
Down By The Meadow Brook
Down The Trail Of The Old Dirt Road
Dream Kisses
Dream Sweetheart
Eeny Meeny Miney Mo
Ev'rybody Loves You
Everybody's Buddy
Faithfully Yours
Fig Leaf Rag
For Me And My Gal
For My Baby
Forgive Me
From One Till Two, I Always Dream Of You
Gather The Rose
Girl He Left Behind Him Has The Hardest Fight Of All, The
Give Me One Hour
Give Me The Moon Over Brooklyn
Glad Rag Doll
Gliding Thru The Shadows
Golden Girl Of My Dreams
Goodbye France
Gootmon Is A Hootmon Now
Half Way To Heaven
Hand That Rocked My Cradle Ruled My Heart, The
Havana, Back To Havana & You
Have You Ever Been Lonely
He Loves It
Heart Aches
Heart Of Humanity
Hello Central! Give Me No Man's Land
Hello Hawaii How Are You
Hello, Swanee, Hello
Home And You
Home For You, A
Honeysuckle Rose
How Much Is That Doggie In The Window
How 'Ya Gonna Keep 'Em Down On The Farm
Huckleberry Finn

I Cannot Bear To Say Goodbye
I Dream Of You
I Found You Among The Roses
I Gave You Up Just Before You Threw Me Down
I Had A Little Talk With The Lord
I Hate To Lose You
I Lost The Best Pal That I Had
I Love No One But You
I Miss That Mississippi Miss That Misses Me
I Says To Myself, Says I, Says I–There's The One For Me
I Should Care
I Want To Go To The Land Where The Sweet Daddies Grow
I Want To Thank Your Folks
I Wish I Had My Old Gal Back Again
I Wonder If You Miss Me To-Night
I Wonder If You Still Care For Me
I Wonder What He's Doing To-Night
I Wuv A Wabbit
I'd Like To Take You Away
If I Had My Way
If I Knock the L Out Of Kelly
If Mothers Could Live On Forever
If That's What You Want Here It Is
If You Can't Get A Girl In The Summertime
If You'll Come Back
I'll Be In My Dixie Home Again Tomorrow
I'm A Lonesome Melody
I'm All Bound 'Round With The Mason Dixon Line
I'm Crazy 'Bout My Baby
I'm Going Way Back Home
I'm Gonna Love That Guy
I'm Gonna Make Hay While The Sun Shines In Virginia
I'm Headin' For The Blue Horizon Where The Mountains Meet The Sky
I'm Not Ashamed Of You Molly I Want You Just As You Are
I'm So Melancholy
I'm Still Caring
In A Shanty In Old Shanty Town
In Blinky Winky Chinky Chinatown
In The Chapel In The Moonlight
In The Sweet Bye And Bye
In Your Arms
It Couldn't Be True
It Started All Over Again
It Must Have Been Some Wonderful Boy
It's Dreamtime
It's Love, Love, Love
It's Not The First Time You Left Me, But It's The Last Time You'll Come Back
I've Been Floating Down The Old Green River
I've Found My Sweetheart Sally

I've Got A New Job
Jazz Baby
Jinga Bula Jing Jing
Joan Of Arc They Are Calling You
Just A Baby's Prayer At Twilight
Just A Memory
Just A Night Of Meditation
Just As Though You Were Here
Just Because You're You–That's Why I Love You
Just Drifting Along
Just Like A Gipsy
Just Like A Melody Out Of The Sky
Just Try To Picture Me Back Home In Tennessee
Keep The Love Lamp Burning
Lady From Fifth Avenue, The
Lafayette, We Hear You Calling
Lawd, You Made The Night Too Long
Lazy Mississippi
Leave Me With A Smile
Let A Smile Be Your Umbrella
Let Me In
Let's All Be Americans Now
Liberty Bell, It's Time To Ring Again
Lies
Life And Love Seem Sweeter After The Storm
Lovely Eyes
Lonesome And Sorry
Long Lost Mamma, Daddy Misses You
Love Somebody
Lucky, Lucky, Lucky Me
Margie
Mary From Maryland
Mary Lou
Masquerade Is Over, The
Maybe It's All For The Best
Maybe, She'll Write Me, She'll Phone Me
Me And The Clock
Meet Me At The Station Dear
Memories Are Made Of This
Memories Of France
Mickey
Midnight Romance, A
Mr. Jazz Himself
Molly-O
Moments Or Jewels Of Memory
Moon
Moon Over Miami
Moonlight On The Colorado
Moonlight Ripples
Music Of Wedding Chimes, The
My Barney Lies Over The Ocean
My Bird Of Paradise
My Dreams Are Getting Better All The Time
My Mother's Rosary
My Sunny Tennessee
My Sweetie Went Away
Naughty Eyes
Never To Part Again
Night We Called It A Day, The
Oh How I Hate To Get Up In The Morning
Oh How I Laugh When I Think How I Cried About You
Oh How I Wish I Could Sleep 'Till My Daddy Comes Home
Oh! What A Pal Was Mary
Oh! What A Time For The Girlies When The Boys Come Marching Home
Oh What A Wonderful Summer
Ol' Man Mose
Old Clothes-I Buy
Old Pal, Why Don't You Answer Me?
Old Yeller Dog Of Mine
On A Little Dream Ranch

On Riverside Drive
On The Arizona Trail
One Day In June
One Finger Melody, The
Open Up The Golden Gates
Over There
Pardon Me, While I Laugh
Peaches
Pick Me Up & Lay Me Down In Dear Old Dixieland
Pucker Up And Whistle
Rain
Razz-Berries
Red Lips Kiss My Blues Away
Red Sails In The Sunset
Red Wing
Regimental Song
Rock-A-Bye Your Baby With A Dixie Melody
Rolling Stones
Rumors Are Flying
Saint Louis Blues
Saturday Night Is The Loneliest Night Of The Week
Scandinavia, Sing Dose Song And Make Dose Music
Serenade Of The Bells
She'll Miss Me Most Of All
Sidewalks Of New York, The
Silver Wing
Smile-Darn You Smile
Some Of These Days
Somebody's Mother
Somebody's Waiting For Someone
Someone Else May Be There While I'm Gone
Someone Is Losin' Susan
Song Of The Vagabond
Song Of The Volga Boatmen
Southern Moonlight
Southern Rose
S'posin
St. Louis Blues
Statue Of Liberty Is Smiling, The
Stay Down Here Where You Belong
Stella
Stolen Kisses
Sunbonnet Sue
Sunday Kind Of Love, A
Sunrise Serenade
Surrender
Surrey With The Fringe On The Top, The
Sweetest Little Girl In Tennessee, The
Take Me To The Land Of Jazz
Take Your Girlie To The Movies
Tarra Ta-Larra T-Lai
Tears
Tell That To The Marines
That Certain Party
That Night In Araby
That Tumble Down Shack In Athlone
Then Came The Dawn
There Are Such Things
There Is No Greater Love
There's A Four Leaf Clover In My Pocket
There's A Star Spangled Banner Waving Somewhere
There's Always Something Doin' Down In Dixie
They Were All Out Of Step But Jim
They're All Sweeties
Three Wonderful Letters From Home
Throwin' Stones At The Sun
Till The End Of Time
Ting-A-Ling
To Think I Cried Over You
Tonight You Belong To Me
Toodle Oodle Oo
Touch Of Your Lips, The

Under The Moon
Until
Upstairs & Down
Waiting by The Silv'ry Rio Grande
Way Down In Ioway I'm Going To Hide Away
We Will Meet At The End Of The Trail
Wedding Bells, Are Breaking Up That Old Gang Of Mine
We'll Have A Jubilee In My Old Kentucky Home
We're In Love With The Same Sweet Girl
What A Wonderful Wedding That Will Be
What Could Be Sweeter
When I Come Back To You, We'll Have A Yankee-Doodle Wedding
When I Dream In The Moonlight Of You
When I Leave The World Behind
When I Said Goodbye To You
When It's Night Time Down In Dixieland
When The Bees Make Honey Down In Sunny Alabam
When The Black Sheep Returns To The Fold
When The Flowers Bloom On No Man's Land
When The Organ Played At Twilight
When The Poppies Bloom Again
When The Sun Goes Down In Romany
When The Yanks Come Marching Home
When Those Sweet Hawaiian Babies Roll Their Eyes
When We Reach That Old Port Somewhere In France
When Yankee Doodle Learns To "Parlez Vous Francais"
When You Find You Can't Forget
When You Were A Baby And I Was The Kid Next Door
Where Did Robinson Crusoe Go With Friday On Saturday Night
Where Rolls The Oregon
While We're Young
Who Wouldn't Be Blue
Who's Sorry Now
Whose Little Heart Are You Breaking Now?
Why Don't You Believe Me
Winter Nights
With A Hey And A Hi And A Ho Ho Ho!
Wonderful You
Yaaka Hula Hickey Dula
You Are The Rose That Will Never Die
You Belong To Me
You Broke My Heart Overnight
You Ought To See My Baby
You Took The Sweet From Sweetheart
You, You Live In My Heart
You'd Better Be Nice To Them Now
Young And Foolish
You're A Heavenly Thing
You're A Million Miles From Nowhere
You're Just A Great Big Baby Doll
You're Some Pretty Doll
You've Got Me Crying Again

GENE BUCK

Blondy Let Me Have The Next Dance With You
Eastern Moon
Everybody's Doin' It Now
Get Happy
Good-bye Boys
Has Anybody Here Seen Kelly?
How Do You Do It Mabel On Twenty Dollars A Week
I Love, I Love, I Love My Wife, But Oh! You Kid!
I Remember You
I Want To Be In Dixie
In My Harem
In Sunny Italy
King Chanticleer

Last Night Was The End Of The World
Little Lost Youth Of Me
May I?
Merry Widow, The
Oh I Must Go Home Tonight
Poppies
Spring And Fall
Taffy
Take A Little Tip From Father
Take Me Back To New York Town
That's How I Love You
Would You Be Satisfied Sally

CARTER

Blaze Away
Captain Betty
Dear Old Stars And Stripes Good-bye
Good Night Mr. Moon
Hold Me Just A Little Closer
Hush-A-Bye, Ma Baby, Missouri Waltz
I'm Sorry
Little One, Good-Bye
Love-Land
No Wedding Bells For Me
Oo Lee Long
Somebody's Waiting For Me

F. EARL CHRISTY

Lonesome Land
Plantation Lullaby
You Are The Rose I'm Longing For

ANDRE DETAKACS

America Here's My Boy
Anxious
At The Fall Of Babylon
At The Five And Ten Cent Store
Baby Rose
Back In the Old Town Tonight
Ballin' The Jack
Beautiful Ohio
Blessed Is He Who Is Loving And Blessed Is She Who
    Is Loved
Blue Feather
Bring Back Those Wonderful Days
Carbolic Acid Rag
Chimes, The
Chocolate Soldier, The
Could The Dreams Of A Dreamer Come True
Dardanella
Dear Heart
Dear Old Dear
Do What Your Mother Did, I'll Do The Same As Your
    Dad
Don't Forget Your Dear Old Home
Everybody Wants A Key To My Cellar
Eyes That Say I Love You
Georgia Moon
Girl For Each Month Of The Year, A
Good Night Roses
Granny
Gravel Rag, The
Haunting Rag
Hello Frisco
Hello! General Pershing, How's My Daddy To-Night?
He's Got A Bungalow

Hiawatha Waltz
Hidden Charms
Hitchy Koo
Hold Me In Your Loving Arms
Honey Land
Humpty Dumpty
I Found The End Of The Rainbow
I Love The Name Of Mary
I May Be Gone For A Long Long Time
I Used To Be Afraid To Go Home In The Dark
I Want Somebody To Play With
I Wish I Had Someone To Say "Good-bye" To
I'd Rather Two Step Than Waltz, Bill
If I Could Peep Thru The Window Tonight
If You Only Had My Disposition
I'll Be A Santa Claus To You
I'll Sit Right On The Moon
I'll Teach You How
I'm A Nurse For Aching Hearts
I'm At Your Service Girls
I'm Goin' To Fight My Way Right Back To Carolina
I'm On My Way To Reno
In The Land O' Yamo, Yamo
In The Sweet Long Ago
In The Valley Of The Moon
It's The Pretty Things You Say
Jane
Johnny Get A Girl
Just For Me And Mary
Just One Day
Kisses, The Sweetest Kisses Of All
Lonesome
Lonesomeness
Lorraine, My Beautiful Alsace Lorraine
Love Me While The Loving Is Good
Loving
Mad House Rag, The
Mammy Jinny's Jubilee
Mammy O'Mine
Merrily We'll Roll Along
Midnight Whirl, The
Mulberry Moon
My Heart Has Learned To Love You
My Hero
My Little Girl
My Pony Boy
My Ragtime Fireman
My Rosie Rambler
Night Time In Little Italy
Not For A While But Always
Oh, How She Could Yacki, Hacki, Wicki, Wacki Woo
Oh, My Love
On The Old Fall River Line
Oui, Oui, Marie
Pepper Pot
Pigeon Walk
Piney Ridge
Pork And Beans
Put Me To Sleep With An Old Fashioned Melody,
    Wake Me Up With A Rag
Put On Your Old Grey Bonnet
Ragging The Scale
Ragtime Goblin Man, The
Rainbow
Roses And Thorns
Shine On, Harvest Moon
Silent Wooing
Sleepy Moon
Somebody Knows
Sometime Somewhere
Sooner Or Later
That Southern Hospitality, When You're Down In Dixie

That's-A-Plenty
That's The Song Of Songs For Me
There's A Little Lane Without A Turning On The Way
    To Home Sweet Home
There's A Quaker Down In Quaker Town
They're Wearing 'Em Higher In Hawaii
To Lou
Twilight Bay
Vesper Chimes
What Money Can't Buy
When Evening Shadows Fall
When I First Met You
When I Marry You
When It's All Over
When Old Bill Bailey Plays The Ukulele
When The Sun Goes Down In Dixie
When You're A Long, Long Way From Home
When You're Dancing The Old Fashioned Waltz
While Others Are Building Castles In The Air
While You're Away
Won't You Come Over To My House
You For Me When You're Sweet Sixteen
You'll Be Glad To Have Your Old Sweetheart Again

W. J. DITTMAR

Back At Dear Old Home Sweet Home
Bees-Wax Rag
Fashion Rag
Go The Other Way
Heaven's Artillery
I Wonder How The Old Folks Are At Home
King Of The Forest
My Dreamland Girl
Nigger Toe Rag
Our Band
Rag Baby Rag
Ripples Of The Allegheny
Sign Of The Rose
Spirit Of Freedom
Sumthin Doin
Trinity Chimes
Wolverine, The

DUNK

Down In Bom Bombay
I've Got The Blues For My Kentucky Home
I've Got The Nicest Little Home In Dixie
Little House Upon The Hill, The
Lookout Mountain
Mister Butterfly
O'Brien Is Tryin To Learn To Talk Hawaiian
Poor Little Heart Broken Doll
She Lives Down In Our Alley
Welcome Home Laddie Boy, Welcome Home
You'll Be There

EINSON

Come Out Of The Kitchen Mary Ann
I'm Looking For A Girl Like Mother
They Made It Twice As Nice As Paradise And They
    Called It Dixieland
When I Was A Dreamer

ETHERINGTON

All Alone
Cupids I.O.U.

Edelweiss
If You Cared For Me As I Care For You
It's Got To Be Someone I Love
My Southern Rose
Overture Of Irish Melodies
Rose Marie
Glow-Worm, The
Yiddisha Rag, The
There's A Dixie Girl Who's Longing For A Yankee
    Doodle Boy
When You Were A Sweetheart Of Mine
Yankee Boy

E. S. FISHER

Admiral Dewey's March
Aimer Et Mourir
Belle Of Georgia, The
Bells Of Trinity
By The Old Rustic Seat I'll Be Waiting
Canny Sandy
Cathedral Chimes
Cincinnati
Daddy's Prayer
Daisy
Dreaming Of Mother At Twilight
Everybody Loves A Chicken
Gee! But I'm Crazy For The Summertime
Has Anybody Here Kissed Toodles?
I Found You Among The Roses
I Long To See My Mother's Face Again
I Want You Mary
I Wants To Pick A Bone With You
Il Est Revenu–Mon Soldat
I'll Be Back In Dear Old Dublin The Day That
    Ireland's Free
I'm A Devil With The Ladies
Just A Little Eden Of Our Own
Learning To Love
Let's All Go Sleighing Tonight
Lizzie
Moonlight In Dixie
My Little Butterfly
My Little Rambling Rose
My Pretty Indian Maid
My Sweetest Dreams Are Dreams Of You
New York Rag
Otoyo
Our Director
Parting
That Ev'ry Little Movement Rag
Three Treasures
'Tis Almost Time To Say Good-Bye
To Dream The Old Dreams Over
Trembling Dew Drops
Uncle Sam's Ships
Where The Shandon Bells Are Ringing–I'll Be
    Waiting Sweet Eileen
Why Did You Say "I Love You" When You Knew It
    Was Not True

HARRISON FISHER

For You A Rose
I Love You: The World Is Thine

W.M. FISHER

Back Of Every Cloud There's Sunshine

I Am Always Building Castles In The Air
Mother My Own
On Frisco Bay
Take Me To Honeymoon Lane

JAMES MONTGOMERY FLAGG

Do Something
Father Of The Land We Love
Poor Me
We Are Ready

JOHN FREW

African Hunter
After They Gather The Hay
Alexander's Ragtime Band
Along Came Ruth
Alpine Hut
Anvil Chorus
Back To The Carolina You Love
California And You
Call Me Up Some Rainy Afternoon
Convent Bells
Curly Head
Danube Waves
Dreams, Just Dreams
Fairy Wedding
He's A Devil In His Own Home Town
He's A Rag Picker
Honeymoon Bells
I Can't Stop Loving You Now
I Love The Ladies
I Want To Go Back To Michigan
If That's Your Idea Of A Wonderful Time Take Me
    Back Home
In The Land Of Harmony
Kiss Me, My Honey, Kiss Me
Love Waltz
My Croony Melody
My Wife's Gone To The Country Hurrah! Hurrah!
Old Folks At Home Variations
Peek-A-Boo Moon
Say No, That's All
Somebody's Coming To My House
Starlight
Sweetheart
That Mesmerizing Mendelssohn Tune
That's As Far As You Can Go
They Start The Victrola & Go On Dancing Around
    The Floor
They're On Their Way To Mexico
This Is The Life
Traumerei
Under The Summertime Moon
Waves Of The Danube
When I Hear You Play That Piano, Bill
When I'm Alone I'm Lonesome
When The Evening Shadows Fall Across The Meadow
When You're In Town

P.M. GRIFFITH

Avalon Town
Do Re Mi
Doll Dance, The
High Brow Colored Lady
I Never Had A Mammy
In The Autumn

Just In Love With You
Land Of Long Ago, The
Mississippi Moon
Moon Am Shinin'
Rememb'ring
Rock-A-Bye My Baby Blues
Sighing
Sleep
Sneak, The
Um, Um Da Da
Under Love's Moon
Wandering Home
We'll Dance Thro' Life Together
Wedding Of The Painted Doll, The

HBK

April Played The Fiddle
Dreaming Out Loud
For All We Know
Goody-Goody
I'm Gonna Sit Right Down And Write Myself A Letter
Little Bit Independent, A
Love Bug Will Bite You, If You Don't Watch Out, The
Maybe
Me And The Moon
Meet The Sun Half-Way
Moon Love
Music Goes Round & Around, The
On A Coconut Island
One Night In Monte Carlo
Playmates
Santa Claus Express, The
Song Of Spring
Sweet Leilani
Tea On The Terrace
Telegram Song, Stop, The
Toodle-oo
Winter Wonderland

JORJ—HARRIS—JORJ HARRIS—BEN JORJ HARRIS

A-Tisket A-Tasket
Ah! The Moon Is Here
All My Love
All On Account Of A Strawberry Sundae
Bali Ha'i
Bewitched
Blue Bird Of Happiness
Blue Evening
Bluebird Singing In My Heart, A
Brother Can You Spare A Dime
Build A Little Home
By A Waterfall
Carioca
Close To Me
Cock Eyed Optimist, A
Dinner For One Please, James
Don't Say Good Night
Dubarry, The
Feudin' And Fightin'
Gloomy Sunday
Grandfather's Clock
Happy Talk
Haunted Heart
Honey Bun
Honeymoon Hotel
How Are Things In Glocca Morra?
How Can I Go On Without You
I Built A Dream One Day

I Dream Too Much
I Found A Million Dollar Baby In The Five And Ten
    Cent Store
If I Loved You
If This Isn't Love
I'll Follow My Secret Heart
I'll String Along With You
I'm Counting On You
I'm Gonna Wash That Man Right Outa My Hair
In A Little Swiss Chalet
In A Shanty In Old Shanty Town
It's D'Lovely
June Is Bustin' Out All Over
Let's Put Out The Lights And Go To Sleep
Little Man–You've Had A Busy Day
Little Old Church In The Valley, The
Look To The Rainbow
Lovely To Look At
Make Believe
More You Hurt Me, The
My Darling
My Girl Back Home
My Silent Love
Necessity
Night Owl
One Hour With You
Real Nice Clambake, A
Ridin' High
Say Something Sweet To Your Sweetheart
Selection
September Song
Shanghai Lil
Shortest Day Of The Year, The
Sittin' On A Backyard Fence
Slaughter On Tenth Avenue
Smoke Gets In Your Eyes
So Beats My Heart For You
Sometime
Song Is You, The
Speak To Me Of Love
Stomping At The Savoy
Summertime
Sweetheart Let's Grow Old Together
Sweethearts Forever
Tell Me
That Great Come-And-Get-It Day
There Is Nothing Like A Dame
They Didn't Believe Me
Thirsty For Your Kisses
This Nearly Was Mine
Torch Song, The
Wait For Me Mary
We'll Gather Lilacs
What Can You Say In A Love Song?
What's The Use Of Wond'rin
When I Marry Mister Snow
When I'm Not Near The Girl I Love
When The Children Are Asleep
When We're Alone
Why Do I Dream Those Dreams
Wonderful Guy, A
Words Are In My Heart, The
You Didn't Know The Music, I Didn't Know
    The Words
You'll Never Walk Alone
Younger Than Springtime
You're My Everything
You've Got To Be Carefully Taught

HOLLEY

Dream

G.I. Jive
I Cain't Say No
I Said My Pajamas, And Put On My Pray'rs
It Can't Be Wrong
It Is No Secret, What God Can Do
Many A New Day
Mister Five By Five
My Dream Of Tomorrow
Oh What A Beautiful Mornin'
Oklahoma
On A Chinese Honeymoon
Open The Door, Richard
Out Of My Dreams
People Will Say We're In Love
Silver Wings In The Moonlight
Surrey With The Fringe On Top, The
Velvet Moon
Woodchopper's Ball

IM-HO

All Ashore
All The Things You Are
All This And Heaven Too
An Old Castle In Scotland
Autumn Nocturne
Back To Back
Ballin' The Jack
Band Played All The Time, The
Band Played On, The
Bargain Day
Beer Barrel Polka
Begin The Beguine
Between You And Me
Blueberry Hill
Blues In The Night
Bombardier Song, The
Boy In Khaki–A Girl In Lace, A
Can Can Dance
Can't We Talk It Over
Chopsticks
Dance With A Dolly With A Hole In Her Stockin'
Deep In A Dream
Don't Sweetheart Me
Don't Worry 'Bout Me
Ev'ry Night About This Time
Friendly Tavern Polka
Gaucho Serenade, The
God Bless America
Good For Nothin', But Love
Have You Forgotten So Soon
He's My Guy
Hey! Ba-Ba-Re-Bop
Home Is Where The Heart Is
I Am The Captain
I Can't Get Started
I Can't Resist You
I Concentrate On You
I Give You My Word
I Guess I'll Have To Dream The Rest
I Happen To Be In Love
I Love You Much Too Much
I Poured My Heart Into A Song
I Threw A Kiss Into The Ocean
I Wanna Wrap You Up, And Take You
    Home With Me
I'm Building A Sailboat Of Dreams
I'm Walking Behind You
In A Friendly Little Harbor
In An Eighteenth Century Drawing Room
In The Mood
Indian Summer

I've Got My Eyes On You
Jeepers Creepers
Johnny Doughboy Found A Rose In Ireland
Light A Candle In The Chapel
Little Genius
Little On The Lonely Side, A
Lone Star Moon
Ma He's Making Eyes At Me
Man With The Mandolin, The
Mary Goes Round
Masquerade Is Over, The
My Dearest Uncle Sam
My Sister And I
Oh! You Crazy Moon
On The Street Of Regret
Please Don't Monkey With Broadway
Practice Makes Perfect
Roll Along Missouri
Same Old Story, The
San Antonio Rose
School Days
Scrub Me Mama
Shall I Compare You?
Shout Wherever You May Be, I Am An American
Sierra Sue
Singing Sands Of Alamosa, The
Sixty Seconds Got Together
So You're The One
South Of The Border
Tears From My Inkwell
There I Go
There's Yes! Yes! In Your Eyes
They Say
This Is No Laughing Matter
This Is Worth Fighting For
Three Little Fishies
'Tis Autumn
Trade Winds
Trust In Me
Umbrella Man, The
Waiting
We Three
What Goes Up Must Come Down
What's New?
When The Lights Go On Again All Over The World
When The Swallows Come Back To Capistrano
While A Cigarette Was Burning
Wishing Will Make It So
You Must Have Been A Beautiful Baby
You're Irish And You're Beautiful
Yours Is My Heart Alone

JVR

Arcady
Baby Your Mother Like She Babied You
Carolina Mammy
Down Where The Sun Goes Down
Georgia Rose
Grieving For You
Honolulu Eyes
Honolulu Moon
Hot Lips
I'd Rather Be The Girl In Your Arms
If It Wasn't For You I Wouldn't Be Crying
If You See Sally
I'm Sorry Sally
In A Little Spanish Town
Japanese Moon
Just Once Again
Let It Rain! Let It Pour!

Let Me Linger Longer In Your Arms
Linger Awhile
Midnight Waltz, The
Mister Radio Man, Tell My Mammy To Come
    Back Home
Mon Homme
My Blue Heaven
Nestle In Your Daddy's Arms
No No Nora
No Wonder
One Kiss
Peggy O'Neil
Precious
Sam, The Old Accordion Man
Saw Mill River Road
Sleepy Time Gal
Someday You'll Say OK
Stumbling
Suppose I Had Never Met You
That's Why I Love You
Three O'Clock In The Morning
What Does The Pussy Cat Mean When He Says Meow?
When I Think Of You
You Gotta Know How
You, You Darlin'

LEFF

After Dark
After My Laughter Came Tears
Ain'tcha Kinda Sorry Now?
All Mine, Almost
An Old Fashioned Home In New Hampshire
An Orchid To You
Another Perfect Day Has Passed Away
Are You Lonesome To-Night?
Auf Wiedersehen My Dear
Bandanna Babies
Because I Love You
Bless Your Heart
Blue Skies
Bohemia
By The Sycamore Tree
Carolina Moon
Carolina's Calling Me
Did You Mean What You Said Last Night
Digga-Digga Do
Dixie
Doin' The New Low Down
Dream Mother
Elsie Shultz-En-Heim
Fraternity Blues
Get Out And Get Under The Moon
Good Luck Sweetheart
Good Night Little Girl Of My Dreams
Got No Time
Guilty
Hands Across The Table
Hello Bluebird
Here's Hoping
Hiawatha's Lullaby
I Can't Do Without You
I Can't Give You Anything But Love
I Hate Myself For Being So Mean To You
I Must Have That Man
I Say It's Spinach
I Wanna Go Where You Go, Do What You Do–Then
    I'll Be Happy
I Want To Be Loved Like A Baby
I'd Climb The Highest Mountain If I Knew I'd
    Find You

If I Had Somebody To Love
I'll Be Faithful
I'll Get By, As Long As I Have You
I'm On My Way Home
I'm Tickled Pink With A Blue Eyed Baby
It's Dark On Observatory Hill
It's Easier Said Than Done
It's Sunday Down In Caroline
It's The Talk Of The Town
I've Got A New Love Affair
Just A Little Longer
King For A Day
Let's Have Another Cup O'Coffee
Lou'siana Lullaby
Lullaby Of The Leaves
Manhattan Madness
Maybe
Minnie The Moocher
Mr. Mulligan And Mr. Garrity
My River Home
New Hampshire
Object Of My Affection, The
Oh How I Miss You Tonight
Ol' Pappy
Old New England Moon
Out In The Cold Again
Porgy
Precious Little Thing Called Love, A
Promises
Roamin' Thru The Roses
'Round Evening
Shuffle Your Feet & Roll Along
Soft Lights And Sweet Music
Some Day We'll Meet Again
Somewhere In Old Wyoming
Starlight, Help Me Find The One I Love
Stormy Weather
Strangers
Sugar
That's A Good Girl
There Goes My Attraction
There's A Rainbow 'Round My Shoulder
True
Two Cigarettes In The Dark
Underneath The Harlem Moon
Vas Villst Du Haben
What Does It Matter?
What's Good For The Goose Is Good For
    The Gander
When I Close My Eyes And Dream
When Mother Nature Sings Her Lullaby
When Mother Played The Organ
When You Come To The End Of The Day
Who's Wonderful, Who's Marvelous, Miss
    Annabelle Lee
Why Dance
Yankee Rose
Yes Sir! That's My Baby
You Darlin'
You're Gonna Lose Your Gal
You're Gonna See A Lot Of Me
You're The One I Care For

FREDERICK S. MANNING

Ain't-Cha Glad?
Alexander's Band Is Back In Dixieland
An Ev'ning In Caroline
At A Perfume Counter, On The Rue De La Paix
At Sundown
Avalon

Back In The Hills Of Kentucky
Back To God's Country
Beautiful Annabell Lee
Blue Kentucky Moon
Daddy Long Legs
Daddy's Little Girl
Dancing Fool
Dark Eyes
Daughter Of Two Worlds, A
Deep In The Arms Of Love
Don't Be Sad
Dreamer Of Dreams
Dreamy Alabama
Ferryboat Polka
Follow The Swallow
For Johnny And Me
Greatest Question, The
Heartaches
Hello Beautiful
Hiawatha's Melody Of Love
I Ain't Gonna Be Nobody's Fool
I Am Climbing Mountains
If You Don't Think So You're Crazy
If You Want To Make A Hit With The Ladies, Tell
    Them They're Beautiful
I'll Bring A Rose
Infantry–Kings Of The Highway, The
Japanese Sandman, The
Jealous
Knock At The Door
Land Of Dreams
Lazy Lou'siana Moon
Little White Lies
Make Love With A Guitar
Marta Rambling Rose Of The Wildwood
Me And The Boy Friend
Miles Apart
My Buddy
New Kind Of Man, A
Nightingale
Peggy
Play Fiddle, Play
Poor Little Butterfly Is A Fly Girl Now
Put Your Arms Around Me Honey
Rocky Road To Dublin, The
Somebody Stole My Gal
Something To Remember
Stop-Time Waltz, The
Sure As You're Born
Tackin' Em Down
Teardrops & Kisses
Till We Meet Again
Tiny-Town
Tomorrow
Truckin'
Venetian Moon
Waltzing In A Dream
Wander With Me To Loveland
We Just Couldn't Say Goodbye
What A Perfect Night For Love
When It's Moonlight On The Swanee Shore
While Miami Dreams
Would-Ja?
You Can't Be True
You Didn't Have To Tell Me
You're Driving Me Crazy
You're Still An Old Sweetheart

MERMAN

Bei Mir Bist Du Schon

Carelessly
Cathedral In The Pines
Change Partners
Cry, Baby, Cry
Donkey Serenade, The
Farewell My Love
Garden Of The Moon
Girl In The Bonnet Of Blue, The
Gotta Be This Or That
Hurry Home
I'm Gonna Lock My Heart
Is That The Way To Treat A Sweetheart
It's Time to Say Aloha
Let Me Call You Sweetheart
Let's Sail To Dreamland
Little Lady Make Believe
Merry Go Round Broke Down, The
Music Maestro Please!
My Cabin Of Dreams
Please Be Kind
Romance Runs In The Family
Sailboat In The Moonlight, A
Sailing Home
Smoke From A Chimney
Something Tells Me
Sophisticated Swing
Start The Day Right
Ten Pretty Girls
Vien, Vien
You And Me That Used To Be, The
You Can't Stop Me From Dreaming
You're The Only Star In My
    Blue Heaven

CLIFF MISKA

Count Every Star
Dancing With My Shadow
Goodbye Dear, I'll Be Back In A Year
Good Night, Little Girl Of My Dreams
Hearts Are Never Blue In Blue Kalua
I'm Lonesome For You Caroline
If It Rains–Who Cares
In The Valley Of The Moon
It Looks Like Rain In Cherry
    Blossom Lane
Little Rendezvous In Honolulu, A
Little Street Where Old Friends Meet, A
On A Little Bamboo Bridge
On The Beach At Bali-Bali
On Treasure Island
Parkin' In The Moonlight
Somebody Loves You
When Your Hair Has Turned To Silver

HELEN VAN DOORN MORGAN

Among My Souvenirs
Ask The Rose
Don't Hold Everything
Kiss A Miss
Learning
Lila
Love's Ship
Pale Moon
That Naughty Waltz
Thru The Night
To Know You Is To Love You
Too Good To Be True
You're The Cream In My Coffee

NATWICK

Breeze Blow My Baby Back To Me
Bring Back My Soldier Boy To Me
Gorgeous
Hesitation Con Amore
Mammy O'Mine
That Wonderful Kid From Madrid
Trench! Trench! Trench! Our Boys Are Trenching

NICK

All My Love
An Apple Blossom Wedding
An Old Sombrero
And Mimi
Are You Lonesome To-Night?
Blue And Sentimental
Charley My Boy
Don't Cry Joe
Dreamer's Holiday, A
Everywhere You Go
Far Away Places
Gypsy, The
How Soon?
I Wanna Go Home
If
If You Had All The World And Its Gold
In The Blue Of Evening
In The Moon Mist
I've Got A Lovely Bunch Of Cocoanuts
Marshmallow World, A
Maybe It's Because
Maybe You'll Be There
Merry-Go-Round Waltz
Midnight Masquerade
Mister And Mississippi
Powder Your Face With Sunshine
Rain Or Shine
Rambling Rose
Rose Ann Of Charing Cross
Rosewood Spinet, A
She's A Lady
Sleigh Ride
Spaghetti Rag
There's No One But You
Tree In The Meadow, A
Way Back Home

E.T. PAULL

America Forever!
Arizona March
Battle Of Gettysburg, The
Battle Of The Nations
Ben Hur Chariot Race March
Burning Of Rome, The
Carnival King, The
Charge Of The Light Brigade
Circus Parade March And Two Step
Conquerer March, The
Cupid's Awakening Waltzes
Custer's Last Charge
Dance Of The Fireflies
Dashing Cavaliers, The
Dawn Of The Century
Della Fox, Little Trooper March
Dreamy Oriental Melody
Flash Light March, The
Herald Of Peace

Homecoming March, The
Hurrah! For The Liberty Boys, Hurrah
Hurricane March, The
Ice Palace March
Jolly Blacksmiths, The
Legion Of Victory
Lincoln Centennial Grand March
Man On The Flying Trapeze, The
March Victorious
Masquerade March And Two Step, The
Midnight Fire Alarm, The
Midnight Flyer, The
Napoleon's Last Charge
N.Y. And Coney Island Bicycle March
Paul Revere's Ride
Pershing's Crusaders
Race Course March, The
Ring Out Wild Bells
Roaring Volcano
Romany Rye, The
Say Au Revoir But Not Goodbye
Sheridan's Ride
Signal From Mars, A
Silver Sleighbells
Spirit Of France
Spirit Of The U.S.A.
Storm King, The
Stranger's Story, The
Tipperary Guards
Triumphant Banner March, The
Uncle Jasper's Jubilee
Uncle Josh's Huskin Dance
United Nations March
Warmin' Up In Dixie, A
We'll Stand By The Flag
Witch's Whirl March, The
Witch's Whirl Waltzes
Woman Forever
Ziz, March & Two Step

MALCOLM PERRET

All I Want Is Just Your Love
Cover Me Up With The Sunshine Of Virginia
Dearest, You're The Nearest To My Heart
Down Among The Sleepy Hills Of
    Ten-Ten-Tennessee
Dream Daddy
Driftwood
Girl Of My Dreams
He's Our "Al"
I Wonder What's Become Of Sally
Ida I Do
Indiana Moon
I've Made Up My Mind To Forget You, But I Can't
    Get You Out Of My Heart
Nine O'Clock Sal
Oh Baby
Red Hot Mamma
Swanee River Moon
That Old Gang Of Mine
When You Walked Out Someone Else Walked Right In
Who'll Take My Place, When I'm Gone
Why Do I Care For You
You Know You Belong To Somebody Else, So Why
    Don't You Leave Me Alone

E. H. PFEIFFER

Ace Of Diamonds

Across The Desert
Acushla Machree, Return In The Springtime
Aeroplane, The
After Glow
After The First Of July
After The Honeymoon
After The War Is Over
After You've Had Your Way
Alexander's Bag Pipe Band
Alexander's Ragtime Band
All Aboard For Monkey Town
All By Myself
All Hands Around
All He Does Is Follow Them Around
All I Want Is One Loving Smile From You-oo-oo
All I Want Is Someone
All I Want Is You
All Nuts Don't Grow On Trees
All Over You
All The Boys Love Rosie
Aloha Oe
Alpine Valley
Always I'm Dreaming Of You
America, He's For You
America I Love You & I Hear You Calling Me
America It's Up To You
America, Make The World Safe For Democracy
American Born
American Girl For Me, The
American Tango, The
And Then She'd Knit, Knit, Knit
And To Think I Left My Happy Home For You
Angel Of My Dreams
Anna Liza's Wedding Day
Anvil Chorus
Any Old Place In Yankee Land Is Good Enough
   For Me
Any Old Town Can Be Heaven To You, When There's
   A Wonderful Girl
Anytime Is Lovingtime
Apple Tree & The Bumble Bee
Arabia, My Land Of Sweet Romance
Arabian Ooze
Arbitration March
Are You Coming To The Ball
As The Morning Would Seem Without Sunshine
As We Live & Love We Learn
As We Sat On A Rock In Little Rock, Ark.
Asia
Asia Minor & You
Assembly March, The
At Half Past Two I Will Marry You Tomorrow
   Afternoon
At Our Little Tango Party
At That Bully, Wooly Wild West Show
At The Chocolate Bon Bon Ball
At The Dawning
At The Devil's Ball
At The Old Cross Road
At The Old Town Pump
Atop The World, Our Flag
Aurora Waltz
Ave Maria
Back To Childhood's Home & Mother
Back To Our Isle Of Dreams
Back-Water Daughter
Bantam Step
Barcarole
Barcelona Tango
Bartender Bill
Bas Bleu
Batter Up, Uncle Sam Is At The Plate

Battle In The Sky
Beautiful Bird Of Paradise
Beautiful Eyes
Becky Joined A Musical Show
Belle Of Idaho
Belle Of Madrid Waltzes
Bells Of Trinity
Beloved
Billie Used To Give Her Something Every Night
Billiken March
Billy "Possums"
Birth Of A Nation, The
Blaze Of Glory
Blaze Of Honor
Blessed Is He Who Is Loving & She Who Is Loved
Blooming Roses
Blushing Roses
Bobbin' Up And Down
Bonita Muchacha
Bouquet Of Roses
Bower Of Roses
Boys Of The Blue & Gray, The
Brazilian Rose
Bridal Chorus
Bring Back, Bring Back, Bring Back The
   Kaiser To Me
Bring Back Your Love
Bring Me A Ring In Spring
Broadway
Broadway Honeymoon, A
Broadway I'm Longing For You
Bugle Boy
Burglar Rag, The
Butterfly Ballet
Butterfly Waltz
Buy A Liberty Bond For Baby
By The Beautiful Sea
Bye & Bye, You'll See The Sun A-Shining
Cabaret Rag
Cairo
California, There's A Garden By The Golden Gate
Call Me Baby
Calling Sweetheart For You
Can You Tame Wild Wimmen
Caprola
Carlotta
Carmena
Carnations March
Carry Me Back To Connemara
Cathedral Chimes
Cathedral Echoes
Charge Of The Uhlans
Chari Vari
Charmina
Chatanooga Blues
Chateau Three Step
Childhood Scenes
Chilly Con Carney
Chimes At Twilight
Christmas Chimes
Christmas Time Seems Years & Years Away
Circus Life
Clap Your Hands If You Want A Little Lovin'
Clef Club Grand March, The
Columbus Day March
Come Away Little Girl
Come Back To Erin
Come Back To Me My Melody
Come Back With The Roses In June
Come Be My Sunshine, Dearie
Come On Love Say Hello
Come On Maria

Come On, Take A Dip In The Ocean
Constantinople
Corner In My Heart, A
Corporal Of The Guard
Cotton Pickin' Time In Tennessee
Country Club Fox Trot
Country Club Rag Time
Crackerjack
Cross My Heart & Hope To Die
Cross The Great Divide I'll Wait For You
Crossing The Bar
Cry Baby
Cuba Hello
Cupid & The Moon
Curly
Cutey Boy
Daddy, I Want To Go
Daddy Wants Someone Too
Dainty Demoiselles
Daly's Reel
Dance Of The Fairy Queen
Dancing In A Dream
Dancing On The Green
Dancing Shadows
Dancing Starlight
Danse D'Amour
Darkies Ragtime Ball, The
Day Dreams Of You
Dear Old Moonlight
Dearest Girl I Know
December Morn
Dengozo
Dixie Rag, The
Do It Again
Do They Love It
Do You Think You Could Care For A Girl Like Me
Don't Be Contrary Mary
Don't Be Like That
Don't Forget Tonight's The Night
Don't Leave Your Wife Alone
Don't Slam That Door
Don't Tell The Folks That You Saw Me
Don't You Ever Think About Me Dearie
Don't You Think You'd Better Let Me Try?
Dorothy Waltzes
Dove Of Peace Waltzes
Down Among The Sugar Cane
Down At Mammy Jinny's Cabin Door
Down Beside The Cider Mill
Down In Chattanooga
Down In Maine
Down In My Heart My Darling
Down To The Folies Bergere
Down Where The Blue Grass Grows
Down Where The Sweet Potatoes Grow
Down Where The Tennessee Flows
Dream Days
Dream Garden Reverie
Dream That Gave You Back To Me
Dream Waltzes
Dreaming
Dreaming Of The Same Old Girl
Dreams Of Love
Dreamy South Sea Moon
Dublin Rag, The
Each Little Feeling
Egyptian Nights
Egyptland
Eileen
Elevator Man
Euphonic Sounds
Evening Shadows

Evening Whispers
Ev'ry Time You'd Do It In A Country Town
Ev'ry Time You're Lonely, Don't Forget That I'm
　Lonely Too
Every Chicken Likes Style
Every Moment You're Lonesome, I'm Lonesome Too
Everybody Loves An Irish Song
Everybody Loves Rag
Everybody Snap Your Fingers With Me
Everyone In Town Likes Mary
Everything He Does Just Pleases Me
Everything Reminds Me Of That Old Sweetheart
　Of Mine
Face To Face With The Girl Of My Dreams
Fair Illinois
Fairy Tales March Ballad
Falling Waters
Famous Overtures For Piano
Farewell My Love
Fatherland, The Motherland, The Land Of My
　Best Girl
Fawn, The
Fernande
Fighting Navy Of The Good Old U.S.A., The
Fighting The Flames
Finest Flag That Flies, The
Finnegan Gave It To Me
Fishing Time
Five Semi-Classic Ballads
Flag At Sundown, The
Flag Of My Heart & Home
Florentine Waltzes
Flower Garden Ball
Flower Song, The
Flowerland Waltzes
Flowers That Bloom In The Spring, Tra-La, The
Flying Fancies
For Days And Days
For Every Boy Who's On The Level, There's A Girl
　That's On The Square
For Every Girl Who Is Anyone's Girl, There Is
　Always Somebody To Blame
For-Get-Me-Not
For Every Tear You've Shed I'll Bring A Million
　Smiles
For Old Glory Uncle Sam, We Are Preparing
For You A Rose
Forgiveness, We'll All Need Forgiveness Someday
Foxy Fox Trot
France America
Frolic Of The Crickets
From O'er The Hills Of Old New Hampshire
Full Of Pep
Funny Moon
Futurist, The
Garden Of Flowers
Garden Of Memories
Gee But I'm Lonesome
Gee, I'm Scared
Gee It Must Be Tough To Be A Rich Man's Kid
General Delivery
Get One For Me
Get This Slow Rag
Ghost Melody, The
Ghost Of The Violin, The
Girl I Know, A
Girl Who Wears A Red Cross On Her Sleeve, The
Girlie
Girlie Was Just Made To Love
Give Back My Sweetheart To Me
Give Me A Honeymoon That's Irish
Give Me The Right To Love You

Give My Love To Dixie
Give My Love To Mother
Go Ahead, Propose
Goblin's Grand Galop De Concert
Goddess, The
God's Service Flag Of Love
Golden Flyer March, The
Gone Are The Days
Good-Bye Girlie & Remember Me
Good-Bye My Canada
Good-Bye My Own Dear Heart
Good-Bye Paradise, Good-Bye
Good-Bye Ragtime
Good-Bye Uncle Sammy
Good-Bye, When I Say Good-Bye To You
Good Luck Mary
Goody, Goody, Goody, Goody, Good
Grace & Beauty Waltzes
Grasshopper's Hop, The
Greatest Day The World Will Ever Know
Greyhound March, The
Hand Of Friendship
Handle Me With Care
Hands Up!
Happy Little Country Girl
Have You Seen My Little Girl
He Played It On His Fid-Fid-Fiddle-Dee-Dee
He Was Always Fooling Around
Heart Bowed Down, The
Heart O'Mine
Hearts Of Promise Waltzes
He'd Have To Get Under-Get Out And Get Under
He'd Push It Around
Helen
Hello, My Darling Mother
Hello Virginia
Helmaredi Waltz
Help! Help! Help! I'm Sinking In A Beautiful Ocean
　Of Love
Hermitage, The
He's A Dear Old Pet
He's Coming Back
He's Doing His Bit, For The Girls
He's Got My Goat
He's My Friend Philligo
He's So Good To Me
He's Such A Wonderful Boy
Hesitation D'Amour
High Jinks
Hindu Rose
Hobble Rag, The
Hoe Your "Little Bit" In Your Own Back Yard
Hold Up Rag, The
Home & Harbor Waltz
Honeymoon Rag
Homestead On The Hill
Honey Boy, My Heart Is Calling For You
Honey Bunch
Honey, I'm Waiting
Honey Man
Honey Rose
Honolulu I Love You
Hooks & Eyes
Hop, Hop, Hop
How Can You Blame Me
How Easy It Is To Remember
How Is Evert'ing By You, All-Right?
How Sweet Is Love
How To Win A Girl
How'd You Like To Be My Beau
How'd You Like To Love Me
How's De Mama

Huckleberry Pie
Humoreske
Hurrah For The Liberty Boys, Hurrah
Hypnotic Rag
I Am Longing For The Old Days, Marguerite
I Am Longing For Tomorrow When I Think Of
　Yesterday
I Am Thinking Of You Mary
I Bid You Good-Bye Forever
I Certainly Was Going Some
I Could Say Goodnight To A Thousand Girls
I Couldn't Go To Ireland, So Ireland Came To Me
I Dare You
I Did It All For You
I Didn't Mean To Make You Cry
I Don't Know Where I'm Going But I'm On My Way
I Don't Want The Moon To Shine When I Make Love
I Dreamt That I Dwelt In Marble Halls
I Feel Lonesome Sometimes
I Found You Just In Time
I Gave My Heart For A Rose
I Got You Steve
I Have Found A Girl That's Just Like Mother
I Hear You Calling Me, Tennessee
I Just Can't Get Rid Of That Plaster
I Keep My Wife In The City & Make Love To Her
　Myself
I Know Some Hearts Were Made To Be Broken
I Like Everything About You But The Boys
I Like It Better Everyday
I Live Uptown
I Love The Name Of Mother
I Love to Hear An Irish Band Upon St. Patrick's Day
I Love You Kid
I Love You Like Lincoln Loved The Old Red, White
　& Blue
I Love You More Each Day
I Loved You The First Time I Met You
I Loved You Then, I Love You Now, I'll Love You
　For Evermore
I Met You, I Love You, I Want You
I Miss You Dear Old Broadway
I Never Knew
I Never Knew You Loved Me
I Never Met A Beautiful Girl, 'Til I Met You
I Never Wanted Anything So Good, So Bad
I Should Have Met You A Long Time Ago
I Tried To Raise My Boy To Be A Hero
I Want A Boy To Love Me
I Want A Doll
I Want A Girl From Home Sweet Home
I Want A Ragtime Bungalow
I Want A Toy Soldier
I Want Someone Who Hasn't Anyone To Love
I Want The Strolling Good
I Want To Be A Cupid
I Want To Be Good, But They Won't Let Me
I Want To Be In Georgia When The Roses Bloom
　Again
I Want To Be Loved By A Soldier
I Want To Love You While The Music Is Playing
I Want You
I Was Aviating Around
I Was Only A Girl At The Time
I Will Always Love You As I Do Today
I Will Love You Always Just For Auld Lang Syne
I Wish I Was In Heaven Sitting Down
I Wish You'd Keep Out Of My Dreams
I Wonder If She Is Waiting In Her Old New England
　Town
I Wonder If You Miss Me Sometimes
I Wonder What Will William Tell

I Wonder Where You Are Tonight
I Wonder Who's Next In Your Heart
I'd Do The Same Thing A Million Times
I'd Like To Be Liked By A Nice Little Girl Who'd Like To Be Liked By Me
I'd Like To Be Your Sweetheart
I'd Like To Build A Little House For You
I'd Like To Find Another Girl Like Mary
I'd Like To Spend A Honeymoon With You
I'd Like To Wander Back Again To Kidland
I'd Like To But I Won't
I'd Love To Dance An Old Fashioned Waltz
I'd Rather Be A Country Girl
I'd Rather Be Kissed 'Neath A Mistletoe Bough Than Spoon Under Any Old Tree
If I Could Gain The World By Wishing, I Would Only Wish For You
If I Could Have You Now
If I Had My Way
If I Only Had A Sweetheart Like You
If I Only Had You
If I Thought You Wouldn't Tell
If I Were The Ocean And You Were The Shore
If I'm Not At Roll Call, Kiss Mother Good-Bye For Me
If It Wasn't For the Irish & The Jews
If Loving Is Forgetting
If Sammy Simpson Shot The Shutes
If She Was What She Was When She Was Sweet 16
If The Rose Could Tell It's Story
If They Don't Stop Making Them So Beautiful
If They Ever Put A Tax On Love
If We Could Always Live In Dreams
If We Were Alone
If You Don't Want Me
If You'll Smile
Il Trovatore Waltz
I'll Anchor My Ship In Your Harbor Of Love
I'll Be Dreaming Of Tomorrow
I'll Be Welcome In My Home Town
I'll Give A Penny For Your Thoughts
I'll Give The Gold In My Heart For The Diamonds In Your Eyes
I'll Go On The Route For You
I'll Never Hear You Sing Again Old Comin' Thro The Rye
I'll Put Mine Against Yours Anytime
I'll Put My Lips Against Yours Anytime
I'll Settle Down In A Small Country Town
I'll Share All My Play Toys With You
I'll Show You A Regular Time
I'll Wait For You In Dreamland
I'm A Bringing Up The Family
I'm A Twelve O'Clock Fella In A Nine O'Clock Town
I'm All Dressed Up And No Place To Go
I'm Alone
I'm Always Home On Sunday
I'm Awfully Glad I'm Irish
I'm Bugs About You
I'm Building A Bridge To Ireland
I'm Building A Palace In Palestine
I'm Coming Back To You
I'm Crazy About It
I'm Crazy 'Bout The Turkey Trot
I'm Dreaming Of The Girl I Love
I'm Glad You're Sorry
I'm Going Back to Broadway
I'm Going Back To Memphis, Tenn.
I'm Going Back To Old Erin
I'm Going Back To Old Killarney
I'm Going Back To Old Nebraska

I'm Going Crazy
I'm Going Down To Tennessee
I'm Going Home To Mobile On The Morgan Line
I'm Going Mad Over You
I'm Going To Do What I Please
I'm Going To Get Myself A Black Salome
I'm Going To Let The Whole World Know I Love You
I'm Going To Tell Your Mother
I'm Happy That's All
I'm In Love With A Girl In Old New Hampshire
I'm In Love With One Of The Stars
I'm In Love With The Rose Of My Dreams
I'm Just A Black Sheep
I'm Looking For A Shady Tree
I'm Loving You
I'm Makin' For Macon In Georgia
I'm On My Way
I'm Sorry The Day I Laid My Eyes On You
I'm Tired Of Making Believe
In A Bungalo, Where The Red, Red Roses Grow
In A Cottage On The Mississippi Shore
In A Red Rose Garden
In After Years
In All My Dreams, I Dream Of You
In Arizona
In Banjo Land
In Cherry Blossom Time
In Dear Old Frisco
In Dear Old Saskatoon
In Dreamland Town
In Dreamy Panama
In Love's Garden, Just You And I
In My Hometown
In That Blue Ridge Vale Of Love
In The Beautiful Garden Of Dreamland
In The Bough Of The Banyan Tree
In The Days Of Auld Lang Syne
In The Evening By The Moonlight
In The Flower Garden
In The Gloaming Of Wyoming I'll Come Roaming Back To You
In The Haven Of My Heart
In The Heart Of The City That Has No Heart
In The Little Home I Am Building for You
In The Philippines He's Sleeping
In The Shadow Of The Pines I'll Wait For You
In The Town Where I Was Born
In The Twilight
In Those Good Old Country Days
Ireland, My Ireland
Ireland, We Sympathize With You
Iris
Irresistable Rag
Irish Were Egyptians Long Ago
Isadore
Isn't She The Busy Little Bee
It Can't Be The Same Old Farm
It Makes Me Think Of Home Sweet Home
It Might Have Been You
It Must Be Love
It Takes A Long Tall Brown Skin Gal To Make A Preacher Put His Bible Down
It Was Just A Song At Twilight
It's A Long, Long Way To The U.S.A. & The Girl I Left Behind
It's All Over Now
It's Good Enough For Me
It's Hard To Love Somebody
It's Lonesome Here
It's The Flag
It's The Three Leaves Of The Shamrock

Italian Eyes
Italian Girl
I've A World Of Love In My Heart For You
I've Been Longing A Long Time For You
I've Been Longing, Longing Dear For You
I've Given Many Kisses, But Not The Kind, Sweetheart, I Give To You
I've Got A Feeling In My Heart For You
I've Got A Smile That's Worth A Million Dollars
I've Got The Finest Man
I've Got The Mumps
I've Got The Right Girl Now
I've Got Your Number
I've Only Myself To Blame
Ivory Kapers
Jake, Jake, The Yiddisher Ball Player
Jazzapation
Jim, Jim, Don't Come Back "Till You Win"
Jim, Jim, I Always Knew You'd Win
Jimmy, My Lovin' Jimmy
Jingle Bells
Jungle Jubilee, The
Just A Dance Program Of Long Ago
Just A Girl Like You
Just A Little Angel
Just A Little Song At Twilight
Just A Mother's Dream
Just Another Poor Man Gone Wrong
Just As Your Mother Was
Just Because I Let You Call Me Baby Lamb
Just For The Key To Your Heart
Just For The Love Of A Girl
Just Love Me
Just One Dearie
Just 'Round The Corner From Broadway
Just The Kind Of Girl You'd Love To Make Your Wife
Just The Thing For Me
Just To See You Once Again
Just Wait 'Til We Get Home
Just You
Katydid Is The Candy Kid
Keep Away From The Fellow Who Owns An Automobile
Keep On Walking
Keep The Boys Happy While They're Away
Keep The Trench Fire Going For The Boys Out There
Keep Your Eyes Down Mary, You're A Big Girl Now
Keepsakes
Kentucky Rose
Ki-I-Youdleing Dog, The
Kick In
Kiss Me Dearie
Kiss Me, I've Never Been Kissed Before
Kiss Your Sailor Boy Good-Bye
Klondike Rag
La Mexican
La Pauza
La Petite Cafe
La Spagnola
Land O'Dreams
Land Of My Best Girl, The
Last Year's Roses
Laugh & Let The Clouds Roll By
Laugh With A Tear, The
Laughing Eyes
Lead Me To That Beautiful Land
Lemon Drops
Lend Me Your Heart & I'll Lend You Mine
Let By-Gones Be By-Gones
Let Me Really Live Tonight
Let Me Waltz To That Melody

Let Not Your Heart Be Troubled
Let Them Alone, They're Married
Let's All Go 'Round To Mary Ann's
Let's Grow Old Together, Honey
Let's Wait For The Last Train Home
Letter From No Man's Land, A
Levee Land
Light Cavalry
Lighthouse Blues, The
Lights Of My Home Town
Like Ships That Pass In The Night
Lily Of France
Linda Jane
Listen To The Knocking At The Knitting Club
Little Bit Of Everything, A
Little Boy That Never Was
Little Brook, The
Little Church Around The Corner, The
Little Good For Nothing's Good For Something After
    All, The
Little Princess
Little Red Caboose Behind The Train, The
Little Road That Leads Back Home, The
Little Tease
Little Uncle Sam Will Win
'Long In Pumpkin Pickin' Time
Long, Long Letter 'Bout Home Sweet Home
Longboat
Lord Have Mercy On A Married Man
Love Days
Love Eyes
Love In A Garden
Love Keeps The World Young
Love Me Again
Love Me My Honey Most Any Time At All
Love Me Little, Love Me Long
Love Song
Love Spark Waltzes
Love That I Feel For You, The
Love Thoughts
Love Whispers
Love Will Find The Way
Love Will Make Or Break A Man
Love's Dreamy Strain
Love's Sweet Dream
Loves Of By-Gone Days
Loyalty Is The Word Today
McCarthy In Piccardy
Ma Cherie, My Dear
Made In America
Make A Name For Yourself
Make Me Love You
Make That Engine Stop At Louisville
Makin's Of The U.S.A., The
Mama Don't Scold Me
Mama's Captain Curly Head
Mama's Melody
Mammy's Little Sugar Plum
Man Behind The Hammer And The Plow, The
Man That Wears A Shield
Man, The Maid and Cupid, The
Man Who Owns Broadway, The
Mandy-Come Out In The Pale Moonlight
Maori
Marching Thru Georgia
Mardi Gras Rag
Maree
Marriage Game, The
Martha
Mauvourneen, Mauvourneen From Down Old
    Killarney
May Bells

Maybe She Will Someday
Maybe You Would If You Could
Meet Me Neath The Persian Moon
Memorie Of Mother And Home
Merry Wedding Bells
Mickey
Mikado
Mind Yo Own Business
Minita
Missouri Waltz
Mr. Yankee Doodle
Mister Yoddlin Man
Molly, I'm Coming Home Again
Mona
Monastery Chimes
Money Won't Buy Love
Monkey Doodle Doo
Moon Maid
Moonlight And Roses Reverie
Moonlight In Maryland
Moonlight Makes Me Lonesome
Moonlight Wooing
Moonshine Of Kentucky
Moose Rag
Mother Americans
Mother Mine She's Just Like You
Mother O'Mine
Mother You're Sunshine To Me
Mother's Rosary Of Love
Mothers Of France
Motor King
Motorcycle Race March
Mousie In The Piano
Movin' Man Don't Take My Baby Grand
Mrs. Maximum Maxixe
Muriel Waltz
Muriel Waltzes
Music Vats Music Must Come From Berlin
Musical Rag Sal
My American Beauty Rose
My Angel Man
My Bambazoo
My Beautiful Castle In Spain
My Beautiful Rose
My Beloved Waltzes
My Bill From Louisville
My Blushing Rose
My Boy
My Brown Eyed Lou
My Caramel Gal
My Cavalier
My Chain Of Memories
My Coca-Cola Bells
My Dream Train
My First Sweetheart
My Georgiana Lou
My Havanah Rose
My Heart's Way Out In California
My Hidden Treasure
My Honey Rose
My Idea Of A Good Little Girl Is A Girl Who Is Good
    To Me
My Irish American Rose
My Land Of Romance, Arabia
My Little Climbing Rose
My Little Gypsy Wanda
My Little Havana Made
My Little Tango Girl
My Little Yiddisha Queen
My Long Lost Love
My Mama Lives Up In The Sky
My Man

My Mary's Eyes
My Mother's Lullaby
My Old Sweetheart
My Parcel Post Man
My Pretty Oriental Maid
My Raggyadore
My Red Cross Girl Farewell
My Rose Of Tipperary
My Shining Star Of Night
My Sweet Cordelia
My Sweet Hawaiian Doll
My Sweet Italian Man
My Syncopated Melody Man
My Virginian
My Western Queen
My Wonderful Dream Of You
My Yellow Jacket Girl
Myopia Fox Trot
'Neath The Hawaiian Moon
'Neath The Trail Of The Milky Way
Neutral
Neutrality March, The
Never Forget Your Dear Mother & Her Prayer
New Ebbitt, The
Next To Your Mother, Who Do You Love
Night Time Brings Dreams & Dreams Bring You
Nighttime Is The Right Time To Spoon With The Girl
    You Love
Nightingale, The
Nightingale–A Love Song
Nightingale–Intermezzo
No Girl Can Take My Old Girl's Place
No One Believes I Love You
No One Could Do It Like My Father
No One Else Can Take Your Place
No One Said Good-Bye To Me
No Other Love Is Like A Mother's Love
Nobody Does It Like You Do
Nobody Home
Nobody Loves Me
Normandy Chimes
Not Me
Not 'Till Then, Will I Cease To Love You
Nothing To Do But Love
Now I Lay Me Down To Sleep
Now That You've Got Me What Are You
    Going To Do
O Thou Sublime Sweet Evening Star
Off To The Front
Off To The Wars Of Mexico
Off With The Old Love, On With The New
Oh By Jingo
Oh Danny, Love Your Annie
Oh, Joe, Waltz Me Slow
Oh, Judge, She Was So Nice
Oh, Oh, Oh, A Hypochondriac Rag
Oh That Kissing Rag
Oh That Teasing Man
Oh, What's The Use Of Working
Oh! Ya! Ya!
Oh You Bashful Little Girl
Oh! You Beautiful Girl With Those Beautiful Baby
    Blue Eyes
Oh, You Funny Mr. Moon
Oh, You Little Rascal
Oh You Million Dollar Doll
Oh You Mr. Moon
Old Barn Dance, The
Old Folks Are Sad & Lonely, The
Old Glory
Old Homeweek In Alabam'
Old Maid's Ball, The

On A Dreamy Summer's Night
On Erin's Green Isle
On Ranch 101
On The Banks Of Honolulu Bay
On The Banks Of Kilarney
On The Banks Of Old Green River
On The Banks Of The Brandywine
On The Honeymoon Express
On The Island Of Pines
On The Sandwich Isles
On The South Sea Isle
On The Steps Of The Great White Capitol
On To Frisco
On Your Wedding Day
Only A Bunch Of Violets
Only A Chain Of Daisies
Only A Dad–But The Best Of Men
Only A Kiss
Only Lonely Little Me
Our Little Cabaret At Home
Our Little Country Home
Our Sammy Boys
Out On The Bounding Ocean Deep
Over In Hero Land
Over The Top With The Best Of Luck
Owl In The Old Oak Tree
Paradise For Two
Paradise Rag, The
Paragon Rag
Path That Leads To You
Peace, Peace, Reechoed Cheer
Peek-A-Boo
Pekin Peeks
Perry's Victory March
Phone Bell Rang, The
Piccalilli Rag
Piccolo
Pick, Pick, Pick On The Mandolin
Pickaninny's Paradise, The
Pickin' On De Ole Banjo
Picture The World Loves Best, The
Pilgrim's Chorus
Pining Just For You
Pioneer
Pipe Of Peace, The
Place For Me Am Home, The
Plant A Watermelon On My Grave & Let The Juice
    Soak Through
Play Me A Good Old Fashioned Melody
Please Do My Family A Favor & Love Me
Please Oh Please
Please, Please, Pretty Please
Plenty Hawk
Poor Little Puritan Maiden
Poor Little Rich Girl
Port Of God Knows Where, The
Prince Imperial Galop
Prunella
Pullman Porters Parade, The
Pussy Cat Rag, The
Queen Of The Garden
Rag, Rag, Rag
Ragtime Express, The
Ragtime Eyes
Ragtime Jockey Man, The
Ragtime Mephisto
Ragtime Piano Playing
Ragtime Soldier Man, The
Ragtime Violin, The
Recess March
Red, Red, Rose
Right From My Heart

Ring-Ting-A-Ling
Rippling Waters
Road To Loveland, The
Rock, Rock, Rock, Keep A Rocking
Rose In My Garden Of Dreams, The
Rose Of The Moonlight
Rose Of The Prairie Land
Rose Petals
Rose That Never Fades, The
Roses Have Nothing On You, The
Roses Remind Me Of Someone
Rosetime
'Round Her Neck She Wears A Yeller Ribbon
'Round My Heart
Rum Tum Tiddle Dance
Rustic Divertisement, A
Rustling Leaves
Rusty Can-O Rag
Rye Waltzes, The
Sadie, Salome, Go Home
Sagamore
Sahara, We'll Soon Be Dry Like You
Saint Vitus Rag, The
Salted Peanuts Rag
Salute The Flag
Salvation Nell
Sam, Sam, The Parcel Post Man
San Francisco Bound
San Francisco Glide
San Jose
Save Dis Little Nigger From De Rain And De Frost
Say Au Revoir But Not Goodbye
Says I To Myself, Says I
Scat Song Skat n Skeet n Hi De Hi
School Bell
School Bells
School Days
Serenata
Sextet From Lucia
Shadowland
She Got Even With Stephen
She Has Left The Old Homestead Forever
She Is The Sunshine Of Virginia
She Was A Soldier's Sweetheart
She Was Made For Love
She Was My Only Girl
She's Just A Home Sweet Home Girl
She's Just Plain Mary Jane
Shepherd's Song At Twilight
Shine On Winter Moon
Shout Hurrah For America
Show Me The Way
Shower Of Kisses
Shrine Of Love
Sighing Too
Silhouettes
Silver Cloud
Silvery Moonlight
Since I First Met You
Since Home Rule Came To Ireland
Since Mary Ann McCue Came Back From Honolulu
Since My Gal Is Gone I've Got The Blues
Sing An Irish Song Tonight
Sing Love's Old Sweet Song Again
Sing Me The Melody Of Love
Sit Down! You're Rocking The Boat
Skating Waltzes, The
Skylarking
Sleepy Hollow Rag
Slip On Your Gingham Gown
Slumber On, Kentucky Babe
Slumberland

Smiling Eyes
Smiling World Smiles On, The
Smother Me With Kisses & Kill Me With Love
Snookey Ookums
So Long, Sal, The Best Of Friends Must Part
Social Life
Soldier's Word To Mother, A
Soldiers Chorus
Soldiers Of Canada
Some Little Squirrel Is Going To Get Some Little Nut
Somebody To Somebody
Somebody's Doing What I Used To Do
Somehow The Girl You Might Have Won, You Never
    Met Again
Something That I Can't Explain
Sometime
Sometime Between Midnight & Dawn
Sometimes You Get A Good One & Sometimes
    You Don't
Somewhere In Dixie
Somewhere In Dixie Lives The Girl I Love
Somewhere Over There
Song Of The Sea
Songs Of Yesterday
Songs Sung By Walter Lawrence
Soul Mates
Southern Heart Of Mine
Spirit Of Life From La Favorita
Spirit Of The U.S.A.
Spoon Time
Spot That My Heart Calls Home, The
Spring Beauties Waltz
Spring Song
Springtime Of Youth
Stageland
Stand By Your Uncle Sam
Starlight
Starlight, The Roses & You
Starlight Waltz
Stewed Chicken Rag
Stick To Your Mother Mary
Stop It
Stop That Rag, Keep On Playing
Story The Rosebud Told, The
String A Ring Of Roses 'Round Your Rosie
Strike Up The Band, Here Comes A Sailor
Sue Simmons, Bill's Sister
Summer Nights
Summer Reminds Me Of You
Summer Windows
Sun Shines Better, The
Sunrise Echoes
Sunset Echoes
Sunset Glow Waltzes
Sunshine & Roses
Suppose I Met You Face To Face
Sure We Are Some Big America
Swanee Ripples Rag
Sweet Babette, She Always Did The Minuet
Sweet Remembrance
Sunset Suzanne
Sweetheart's A Pretty Name When It Is Y-O-U
Sweetie Be Kind To Me
Sweets
Syncopatia Land
Take A Little Tip From Father
Take A Vacation, Mr. Moon
Take Me Back
Take Me Back To Germany
Take Me Back To New York Town
Take Me Back To The Garden Of Love
Take Me Back To Your Garden Of Roses

Take Me To Roseland, My Beautiful Rose
Take Me Up In An Aeroplane
Tannhauser
Teasing
Tell Me A Beautiful Story
Tennessee Blues
That Bandana Band, Way Down In Dixieland
That Big Rock Candy Mountain
That Coon Town Quartet
That Daffy Rag
That Dreamy Italian Waltz
That Fellow With The Cello Bag
That Fussy Rag
That International Rag
That Is How I Love You Dear
That Land Of Musical Charms
That Little Bit Of Green
That Long Lost Chord
That Mysterious Rag
That Paradise Rag
That Puzzlin' Rag
That Reuben Tango Huskin' Bee
That Swaying Harmony
That Tangalo Tap
That Was Before I Met You
That Wee Bit Of Devil In Your Irish Eyes
That Wonderful Night In The Thousand Islands
That's A Funny Place To Kiss A Girl
That's Ever Loving Love
That's Music To Me
That's The Fellow I Want To Get
That's What God Made Mothers For
That's What Makes A Wild Cat Wild
That's Why I Never Go Home
Them Dog Gon'd Triflin' Blues
Then You'll Remember Me
There Are Just As Many Heroes Today
There's A Bungalo In Dixieland
There's A Garden Of Eden In Sweden
There's A Girl I Love, Down In Panama
There's A Girl That's Meant For Me In The Heart
   Of Tennessee
There's A Heart Of Gold That's Waiting
There's A Key To Every Heart
There's A Land Beyond The Rainbow
There's A Light Shining Bright In The
   Window Tonight
There's A Little Bit Of Scotch In Mary
There's A Little Gold Star In The Service Flag
There's A Little Road To Heaven
There's A Million Reasons Why I Shouldn't Kiss You
There's A Vacant Chair In Every Home Tonight
There's Lots Of Stations On My Railroad Tracks
There's No Friends Like The Friends From Way
   Back Home
There's No Girl Like The Old Girl At Home
There's No One But You To Blame
There's Nothing Else In Life Like Love, Love, Love
There's Nothing Like A Mother's Love
There's One In A Million Like You
There's Someone More Lonesome Than You
They All Do The Fox Trot Now, Down In
   Jungle Town
They All Kept Time With Their Feet
They Are Fighting For Liberty
They Don't Hesitate Any More
They Had To Stand Up Every Time They Sat Down
They Tied The Can To Mary
They'll Never Miss The Wine In Dixieland
They're All Going To The Movies
They've Got Me Doing It Now
Think It Over, Mary

38th St. Rag
This Ain't The Place I Thought It Was
This Great Big World Owes Me A Loving
This Is The Life For Me
Tho' I Had A Bit Of The Devil In Me, She Had The
   Ways Of An Angel
Tho' I'm A Long, Long Way From Tipperary
Tho' Many A Heart Is Broken, It Is Never Too Late
   To Mend
Those Wonderful Words, I Love You
Though Your Eyes Are Full Of Mischief You're The
   Girl For Me
Through These Wonderful Glasses Of Mine
Throw A Kiss to Me My Minstrel Man
Thundercloud
Tia Juana Moon
'Til I Met You I Never Knew Of Love, Sweet Love
Time To Love A Girlie, Is When She's Blue,
   Blue, Blue
Tip Top Tipperary Mary
To Conquer Germany
To-Morrow Land
Tonight's My Last Night Single
Too Much Ginger
Toreador Song
Tra-La-La-La
Trot Me, Billy Boy
Troublesome Moon
True Born Soldier Man, A
Turkey Trot
'Twas Always Mary
'Twas Good
20th Century Rag, The
Twinkles
Two Little Eyes Are Watching For A Daddy Far Away
Two Weeks' Notice
Uncle Sam, Hold Your Flag Up High
Uncle Sam Is Calling Me
Uncle Sam's Boys March
Under Southern Skies
Under The Summer Moon
Under The Swanee Moon
Under The Tool-A-Wool-A-Tree
Underneath The Monkey Moon
Underneath The Tango Moon
United Musician
Universal Glide
Valse Decembre
Valse Estelle
Valse Romance
Venetian Moon
Venezuela Dance
Vesper Chimes
Victory
Virginia From Virginia
Virginia Lee
Vision Waltz
Visions D'Amour
Wagner Couldn't Write A Ragtime Song
Wait For Your Honey Boy
Wait Until Your Daddy Comes Home
Waiting Down By The Mississippi
Wake Up Virginia And Prepare For Your Wedding
   Day
Waltz Of Love, The
Waltz Of The Rose
Wandalola
Watch The Bee Go Get The Hun
Watching The Clock
Water Cress
Wawatchies Dream
Way Back Home In Old New Hampshire

We Can Muster Uncle Sammy Ten Million Men
   Or More
We Have Much To Be Thankful For
Wedding Bells, The
We'll All Come Back
We're Band Of Bold Conspirators
We're Going To Take The Germ Out Of Germany
We're Proud That We're Americans
What A Wonderful Mother You'd Be
What Are You Going To Do
What D'Ye Mean You Lost Yer Dog
What Did Romeo Say To Juliet When He Climbed Her
   Balcony?
What Do You Want With Me
What More Can A Woman Give
What Will I Tell Her Tonight
What'll We Do With Him Boys? The Yanks Made A
   Monkey Out Of You
What's The Use To Have A Heart
When A Boy Without A Girl Meets A Girl Without
   A Boy
When Angels Weep
When Cupid Comes A-Tapping
When Darling Bess First Whispered Yes
When Did You Write To Your Mother Last?
When Grandma Sings The Songs She Loved At The
   End Of A Perfect Day
When I Dream Of Old Erin, I'm Dreaming Of You
When I Fell In Love With You
When I First Saw You
When I Get Back To Georgia & You
When I Get Back To My Old Girl
When I Got Back To My Old Home Town
When I Lost You
When I Send You A Picture Of Berlin
When I Want To Settle Down
When I Was A Lad
When I'm Thinking Of You, I'm Thinking Of A Won-
   derful Girl
When It Strikes Home
When It's All Over
When It's Moonlight In The Garden Of Love
When It's Moonlight On The Meadow, Mollie Dear
When Johnson's Quartet Harmonize
When My Great Grand Daddy & My Great Grand
   Mammy Used To Cuddle & Coo In The Coconut
   Tree
When Old Silas Does The Turkey Trot
When Sally In Our Alley Sings Those Old Time Songs
   To Me
When She Comes Back I'm Going Away
When That Midnight Choo-Choo Leaves For Alabam
When The Cherry Trees Are Blooming In Japan
When The Gates Of Heaven Opened And I Saw My
   Mother There
When The Girl Whose Heart You Long For Has A
   Heart Who Longs For You
When The Golden Rod Is Waving, Nellie, Mine
When The Haying Time Is Over
When The Henry Clay Comes Steaming Into
   Mobile Bay
When The Honey Moon Stops Shining
When The Hummingbirds Return Sweet Irene
When The Lights Go Out On Broadway
When The Robin Calls Its Mate
When The Silver Threads Were Not Among The Gold
When The Stars & Stripes Are Safe
When The Sun Goes Down In France
When The Sun Goes Down In Normandie
When The Sunset Bids The Day Goodby
When The Tide Is Turning
When The War Is Over, I'll Return To You

When They Gather The Sheaves Mary Dear
When Tony Goes Over The Top
When Uncle Joe Steps Into France
When Uncle Sammy Leads The Band
When We Wind Up The Watch On The Rhine
When Women Vote & Pop The Question
When You Come Into My Life In Dreams
When You Have Nothing Else To Do
When You Haven't A Beautiful Girl
When You Hear Your Country Call, "Soldier Boy"
When You Kiss Your Dear Mother Good-Bye
When You Waltz With The Girl You Love
When You Write A Letter, Send A Letter Of Cheer
When You're Lonesome For Someone Who's
    Lonesome For You
Where Are The Girlies Of My Childhood Days
Where Did You Get That Girl
Where Do They Go When They Row, Row, Row
Where Do We Go From Here?
Where Do You Go From Here?
Where Is My Wandering Boy Tonight?
Where The Apple Blossoms Fall
Where The Ivy's Clinging, Dearie, Round An Old
    Oak Tree
Where The Nightingale Woos The Rose
Where The Sweet Magnolias Bloom
Where The Waters Ebb & Flow
While The Stars In The Heavens Shine On
Whipoorwill, Indian Serenade
Whistle It
White Bird
Who'll Take Care Of The Harem
Who's Going To Love You When I'm Gone?
Whole World Knows I Love You, The
Wholesale Love
Whoop 'Er Up!
Why Are You Breaking My Heart?
Why Did You Go Away?
Why Don't They Set Him Free?
Why Don't You Marry The Girl?
Why Don't You Smile?
Wife Hunters, The
Wild Cherries Rag
Wild Flower Rag
Will You Be One Of The Soldier Boys?
Will You Be Waiting Dearie When My Ship
    Comes In?
Winking Moon
Winona, An Indian Love Song
Wisteria Waltzes
With His Hands In His Pockets & His Pockets In
    His Pants
Within The Law
Wonderful Day, A
Wonderful Girl, Good Night
Won't You Come & Love Me?
Won't You Come Back To Your Mother, Nell?
Won't You Give All Your Love To Me?
World Was Not Built In A Day, The
Would You Take A Chance With Me?
Would You Think I'm As Nice Tomorrow Night, If
    You Met Someone Nicer Tonight
Yankee Of 1918, The
Ye Ho! My Lads! Ye Ho!
Yiddle On Your Fiddle, Play Some Ragtime
Yoodl-ee, Youdlee-You
You Ain't Got The Right Kind Of Hair
You Are Just Like The Rose To Me
You Broke The Heart That Loved You
You Can Make All My Love Dreams Come True
You Can't Live Without A Girl
You Go Your Way, I'll Go Mine

You Got To Keep A-Goin
You Got To Stop A-Pickin' On My Li'l Pickaninny
You Great Big Bashful Doll
You, Just You
You Kissed Me
You May Belong To Some One Else But Your Heart
    Belongs To Me
You Mean All That & More To Me
You Picked A Bad Day Out To Say Good-Bye
You Sent A Love Torpedo Right Thru My Heart
You Were Just Made To Order For Me
You Will Never Miss Your Mother 'Til She's Gone
You'll Always Be The Same Sweet Girl
You'll Be Sorry When We Say Goodbye
You'll Be The One, Not Me
You'll Have To Put Him To Sleep With The Marseil-
    laise And Wake Him Up With A OO-La-La
You're A Better Man Than I Am, Gunga Din
You're A Picture No Artist Can Paint
You're Going To Wish You Had Me Back
You're Gwine To Get Somethin' What You
    Don't Expect
You're In The Right Church, But The Wrong Pew
You're Just The Same Old Sweetheart
You're My Beautiful American Rose
You're My Rose In The Garden Of Love
You're One Great Big Vision To Me
You're So Different From The Rest
You're Still The Same Sweetheart Of Mine
You're The Girl
You're The Most Wonderful Girl
You're The One I'm Thinking Of
You're The Same Old Girl
You've Been A Dear Old Pal, Mother Of Mine
You've Built A Fire Down In My Heart
You've Got A Lot To Answer For
You've Got Your Mother's Big Blue Eyes
Your Absence Is Breaking My Heart
Your Love Is My Paradise
Your Mother's Awfully Worried–Won't You Please
    Come Home
Your Papa Will Never Come Home Dear
Your Wife
Yukaloo
Yum Pum Pa
Zaame
Zampa

POLITZER

Ah-Ha!
Chicago
Daffy-Dill, The
Down On The Farm
Eddie, Steady
Forever
Hoi-Polloi
Honeymoon Blues
How Do I Know He Loves Me
I Never Knew How Much I Loved You
In A Bungalow
Magnolia
Me Too-Ho-Ho! Ha-Ha!
On Such A Night
Say It Again
Side By Side
Sob Sister Sadie
Somebody Else Took You Out Of My Arms
Stingo, Stungo
Turn On The Popular Moon
Twinkling Star

Was It A Dream?
Wet Yo' Thumb
Where Do You Work-A John?
You Are Easy To Remember But Not So Easy To Forget

PUD LANE

All Because Of You
Blue Grass
Can't You Understand?
Congratulations
Constantinople
For Old Times Sake
I Faw Down And Go Boom
If You Believed In Me
Me And The Man In The Moon
That's Just My Way Of Forgetting

T. RAY

Army And Navy
Frat March
It's A Bird
Jolly Jingles
Love Me All The Time
Me-Ow
Rhapsody Rag
St. Louis Blues
Sunflower Babe
Taxi
Tell Me That You Love Me Dear, For I Love You
Little Old Garden, The
Valse Annette
Valse June

A. JOEL ROBINSON

Delicado
Don't Be A Baby, Baby
Gal In Calico, A
I Happened To Walk Down First Street
If I'm Lucky
Oh But I Do
Parade Of The Wooden Soldiers
Rainy Night In Rio, A
Solid Citizen Of The Solid South, A
Through A Thousand Dreams

NORMAN ROCKWELL

Family Sing–A Sing Along With Mitch
Lady Bird, Cha, Cha, Cha
Over There
Over Yonder Where The Lilies Grow

ROSE, ROSE SYMBOL, R.S.

Aba Daba Honeymoon, The
Alabama Lullaby
All I Can Do Is Just Love You
Alone At Last
And That Ain't All
Anything Is Nice If It Comes From Dixieland
Back To My Hometown Gal
Bells
Beloved
Blue Grass Rag, The
Breath Of Virginia
Bring Back My Daddy To Me

Charley My Boy
Chili Bean
Chinese Firecrackers
Civilization
Climbing Up The Scale
Close To My Heart
Come Along
Cute And Cunning Wonderful Baby Doll
Darktown Strutters' Ball, The
Down Among The Sheltering Palms
Down South
Feather Your Nest
Find Me A Girl
Freckles
Friends
Girls Of My Dreams, The
Give Me A Kiss By The Numbers
Golden Gate Open For Me
Good-By Broadway, Hello France
Granny "You're My Mammy's Mammy"
Greatest Love Of All, The
Hail, Hail The Gang's All Here
Hawaiian Butterfly
High Cost Of Loving, The
Home Again Blues
Homeward Bound
Honey Bunch
Honolulu America Loves You
Hours I Spent With You, The
I Didn't Raise My Boy To Be A Soldier
I Don't Want To Get Well
I Hear Your Voice In The Shadows
I Just Roll Along Havin' My Ups And Downs
I Live In Turkey
I Love Her Oh! Oh! Oh!
I Miss Daddy's Goodnight Kiss
I Used To Live In Dreamland With Someone Just
    Like You
I Used To Love You But It's All Over Now
I Wonder
I Wonder Where My Baby Is To-Night
If A Rooster Can Love So Many Chickens Can't A
    Man Love More Than One
If He Can Fight Like He Can Love, Good Night
    Germany!
If I Had A Son For Each Star In Old Glory
If We Can't Be The Same Old Sweethearts We'll Be
    The Same Old Friends
I'll Always Keep A Corner In My Heart For
    Tennessee
I'll Be With You In Apple Blossom Time
I'll See You In C-U-B-A
I'm Gonna Spend My Honeymoon In Dixie
I'm In Heaven When I'm In My Mother's Arms
I'm Like A Ship Without A Sail
I'm The Guy That Paid The Rent For Mrs. Rip
    Van Winkle
In My Beautiful, Beautiful Dream
In Rank And File
In The Golden Harvest Time
Ireland Must Be Heaven, For My Mother Came
    From There
It's A Hundred To One You're In Love
It's A Long Way To Berlin But We'll Get There
It's Easy For You To Remember, But It's So Hard For
    Me To Forget
It's Not Your Nationality
Jerry You Warra A Warrior In The War
Johnny's In Town
Just Like Washington Crossed The Delaware, General
    Pershing Will Cross The Rhine
Just You And Me

Keep Your Eye On The Girlie You Love
Leg Of Nations, The
Love Of A Rose
Lovelight Bay
Lucky Moon
Marie
Mohawk Trail, The
Mother, A Word That Means The World To Me
Mother, Dixie And You
Mother's Lullaby
My Gal, She Has Some Wonderful Ways
My Little Bimbo
My Lonely Fleur-De-Lis
My Mammy
My Old Rose
My Star
Navy Took Them Over And The Navy Will Bring
    Them Back, The
Nobody Knows And Nobody Seems To Care
Norway
On A Beautiful Night With A Beautiful Girl
On The Hoko Moko Isle
On The Shores Of Italy
One Girl
Open Your Arms My Alabamy
Popularity
Porcelain Maid
Silver Bay
Some Sunny Day
Somehow I Can't Forget You
Somewhere You're Dreaming Too
Song Is Ended But The Melody Lingers On, The
Stop Look Listen To The Music Of The Band
Sunshine
Swanee Blues
Swanee Shore
Syncopated Vamp, The
Tell Me Little Gypsy
Ten Little Miles From Town
That Mellow Melody
There'll Be A Hot Time For The Old Men, While The
    Young Men Are Away
There's A Broken Heart For Every Light On
    Broadway
There's A Garden In Old Italy
There's A Little Bit Of Bad In Every Good Little Girl
There's A Little Spark Of Love Still Burning
Those Good Old Days Back Home
Tired Of Me
True Love Never Runs Smooth
Tumble In
Venetian Rose Waltzes
Vesper Bells Are Ringing Mother Dear, The
Wake Up, America!
Wang-Wang Blues
We'll Knock The Heligo-Into Heligo-Out Of
    Heligoland
We're Going To Hang The Kaiser Under The
    Linden Tree
What Do We Do On A Dew-Dew-Dewy Day
What'll I Do?
What's The Use Of Going Home
When I Get You Alone Tonight
When I'm Thru With The Arms Of The Army, I'll
    Come Back To The Arms Of You
When It's Twilight Neath The Old New England Hills
When The Roses Bloom In Loveland
When You Look In The Heart Of A Rose
When You Play In The Game Of Love
When You Wore A Tulip And I Wore A Big Red Rose
When You Write, Sweet Marie, Send Your Heart
    To Me

When You're Five Times Sweet Sixteen
Where Do We Go From Here
Where The Four Leaf Clovers Grow
While The Young Men Are Away
Why Didn't You Leave Me Years Ago
With You, My Own
Yearning Just For You
You Made Me Love You, I Didn't Want To Do It
You Never Can Tell
You Stingy Baby
You'd Never Know That Old Town Of Mine
You'll Always Be The Same Sweet Girl

STARMER

Accordion Joe
Acushla! I'm Calling Thee
Adam And Eve Had A Wonderful Time
Adele
Afghanistan
After All
After The Battle Is Over Then You Can Come Back
    To Me
All Aboard For Dixie Land
All I Want Is You
All That I Ask Of You Is Love
Allied Victory March
Amo
An Echo Of Her Smile
An Old Fashioned Garden In Virginia
And A Little Child Shall Lead Them
Angels Of Night
Any Little Girl's A Nice Little Girl, Is The Right Little
    Girl For Me
Are You From Dixie?
As Long As There Is Love
Ask Her While The Band Is Playing
At The Coffee Cooler's Tea
At The End Of A Beautiful Day
At The End Of the Road
At The Mississippi Cabaret
Baby Shoes
Band Box Girl, The
Battle Song Of Liberty, The
Be Good To California, Mr. Wilson, California Was
    Good To You
Be My Little Baby Bumble Bee
Beautiful Star Of Heaven
Because I'm Married Now
Bedelia
Before The World Began
Bells, The
Big Blonde Baby
Bimini Bay
Birds And The Brook, The
Blame It On The Blues
Blues My Naughtie Sweetie Gives To Me
Bon Soir Cherie
Boo Hoo
Boogie Rag
Booker T's Are On Parade Today, The
Boy Scouts' Dream, The
Break The News To Mother
Bugle Call Rag
Busy Little Digits
By The Old Ohio Shore
By The Watermelon Vine Lindy Lou
Calcium Moon, The
Can't You Be Good?
Caresses
Chantecler

Chattahoochie
Chin-Chin
Coaling Up In Colon Town
Come And Dream With Me In A Persian Garden
Come Back To Arizona
Come Back To Connemara
Come Josephine In My Flying Machine
'Cross The Mason-Dixon Line
Cruel Papa
Cupid's Message
Daisies Won't Tell
Darktown Dancin' School
Darned If The Fellows Can Do Without Girls, Girls, Girls
Dixie Dimples
Dixie Highway
Doctor Brown
Don't Bring Lulu
Doo Dah Blues
Down Georgia Way
Down Home Rag
Down In Dear Old New Orleans
Dream Kisses
Dreaming Love Of You
Dreaming Of Home Sweet Home
Elinore
End Of The Road, The
Everybody Loves A Chicken
Everybody Works But Father
Fight Is On, The
First Heart Throb
Flow Along River Tennessee
For Dixie And Uncle Sam
For The Sake Of A Rose
For You Alone
Four Little Blackberries
Four Little Sugarplums
French Pastry Rag
From Far Peru
Gaby Glide, The
Garden Of Dreams
Garden Of Eden
Gee! Ain't It Great To Be Home
General Pershing
Georgia Rag, The
Geraldine
Girlie Was Just Made To Love, A
Girls
Give A Little Credit To The Navy
Give Me A Ukelele, And A Ukelele Baby
Glory Of Womanhood
Good Ship Mary Ann, The
Goodbye Dixie Lee
Good-bye, Little Girl Of My Dreams
Good-bye Rose
Goodbye Sally Good Luck To You
Goodnight Nurse
Good Night Wherever You Are
Happiness
He Came From Milwaukee
He'd Keep On Saying Good-Night
Hello Ma Baby
He's My Cousin If She's Your Niece
High-High-High Up In The Hills
Honey Dear
Hoo-oo
Horse Trot, The
How Can You Forget
How Come You Do Me Like You Do Do Do?
How's Every Little Thing In Dixie
I Double Dare You
I Give You All You Ask

I Hate To See Those Summer Days Roll By
I Just Came Back From Dear Old Dixie Land
I Just Can't Keep From Liking You
I Like Your Apron And Your Bonnet And Your Little Quaker Gown
I Love My Steady, But I'm Crazy For My "Once-In-A-While"
I Love To Tango With My Tea
I Want To Linger
I Was Never Meant For You
I Wish I Was In Dixie
I'd Like To Be On An Island With You
If Every Girl Was A Girl Like You
If You Had All The World And It's Gold
I'll Be With You When The Clouds Roll By
I'll Do It All Over Again
I'll Take You Back To Panama
I'm A Long Way From Tipperary
I'm Afraid Of You
I'm Going To Stay Right Here In Town
I'm Forever Blowing Bubbles
I'm Glad I Can Make You Cry
I'm On My Way To Dublin Bay
I'm On My Way To Reno
I'm Tying The Leaves So They Won't Come Down
In A Little Garden, You Made Paradise
In Dixie Land With Dixie Lou
In The Glory Of Your Eyes
In The Heart Of A Fool
In The House Of Hugs And Kisses
In The Shadow Of The Alamo
In The Wildwood Where The Blue-Bells Grew
In Tyrol
Indiana
Indianola
Iron Claw, The
It Might Have Been
It Takes A Little Rain With Sunshine
It's A Long Long Time Since I've Been Home
It's A Short Way Through Mother's Doorway But It's A Long Way Back To Mother's Knee
Je T'aimerai Toujours
Just A Little Cottage In The Country Calling: Come Back Home
Just A Word Of Sympathy
Just Like A Butterfly
Just Like A Rainbow
Just One Word Of Consolation
Just Take Me Down To Wonderland
La Brasiliana Tango
Land Of Golden Dreams, The
Laughing Water
Le Tremolo
Let Freedom Ring
Let's Fill The Old Oaken Bucket With Love
Let's Go Home
Levee Lou
Lily Of The Valley
Listen To The Mocking Bird
Little Girl, A Little Boy, A Little Moon, A
Little Something–That's All, A
Loading Up The Mandy Lee
Love Me
Love Me Like The Ivy Loves The Old Oak Tree
Lovelight In Your Eyes, The
Love's Reverie
Love's Rosary
Mamma Number Two
Mammy's Little Coal Black Rose
Maybe You're Not The Only One Who Loves Me
Meadow Brook Fox Trot
Merry Madness

Mr. Yankee Doodle Are We Prepared
Molly Dear, It's You I'm After
Moonlight
Moonlight Bay
Moonlight Dear
Moonlight, The Rose And You, The
Mother's Prayer For Her Boy Out There, A
Music Is Wonderful When You Are Lonesome
My Dreamy China Lady
My Hawaiian Sunshine
My Hindoo Man
My Isle Of Golden Dreams
My Kid
My Little China Doll
My Little Dream Girl
My Little Dutch Colleen
My Little Lovin' Sugar Babe
My Little Persian Rose
My Little Rambling Rose
My Old Kentucky Home
My Own Home Town In Ireland
My Rosary Of Dreams
My Sweet Adair
My Sweet Egyptian Rose
My Sweetheart Is Somewhere In France
Next Sunday At Nine
Oh, Moon Of The Summer Night
Oh! Sweet Flower, Pure And Rare
Oh! That Yankiana Rag
Oh! What I'd Do For A Girl Like You
Oh, You Beautiful Doll
Oh, You Kid!
Oh, You Silv'ry Bells
On Our Honeymoon
On The Mississippi
On The Same Old Road
One Rose, That's Left In My Heart, The
Over The Hill To Mary
Painting A Picture Of You
Painting That Mother Of Mine
Peter Gink From "Peer Gynt"
Play Days
Pots And Pans
Rag Time Drafted Man
Ragging The Nursery Rhymes
Raggy Fox Trot, The
Rainbow Isle
Raus Mit Der Kaiser, He's In Dutch
Rebecca Of Sunnybrook Farm
Red Moon
Red Rose Rag, The
Right To Happiness, The
Rosary, The
Rose Of The Mountain Trail, The
Roses
Roses And Lilacs
Roses And Violets
Roses Bring Dreams Of You
Royal Gewgaw, The
Rum Tum Tiddle
Sack Waltz, The
Sail On To Ceylon
Sailing Down The Chesapeake Bay
Sailing Dow The River In The Moonlight Mandy And I
Sally In Our Alley
Same Old Crowd, The
San Antonio
Say A Prayer For The Boys "Out There"
Schubert's Serenade
Send Me Away With A Smile
She Is My Daisy
She's Coming Home To-Night

She's Everything A Girl Should Be
Silver Jubilee March
Sipping Cider Thru A Straw
Skeleton Rag, The
Smilin' Through
Some Day When Dreams Come True
Some Of These Days
Some Sunday Morning
Somebody Else Is Crazy 'Bout Me, But I Want You
Somebody's Lonesome
Somebody's Waiting For You
Someone Thinks Of Someone
Sometime
Somewhere In France Is The Lily
Song Of The Vagabonds
Story Book Ball, The
Strains From Dixieland
Summer Widowers, The
Sunset In Eden
Sunshine And Roses
Sweet Patootie Sal
Sweetest Girl In Monterey, The
Take Me Back To Your Heart
Tell Me The Old Old Story
Tell The Last Rose Of Summer, Good-Bye
That Old Fashioned Mother Of Mine
That Old Girl Of Mine
That Rag-time Regimental Band
That Soothing Serenade
That Tango Tokio
That Waltz Of Yesterday
That's What You Mean To Me
There Never Was A Girl Like You
There's A Girl In The Heart Of Maryland
There's A Green Hill Out In Flanders
There's A Lump Of Sugar Down In Dixie
There's A Service Flag Flying At Our House
There's Nothing Like A Mother's Love
There's Only One Mary In Maryland
There's Something About You Makes Me Love You
They'll Be Mighty Proud In Dixie Of Their Old
    Black Joe
Think Not This Heart Can Alter
Tickle The Ivories
Toot Your Horn, Kid, You're In A Fog
Trail Of The Lonesome Pine, The
Trail That Leads To You, The
Trading Smiles
Trip To Niagara Falls, A
'Twas Only An Irishman's Dream
Underneath The Cotton Moon
Vagabond King Waltz
Valley Of Roses
Vanity
Vanity Fair
Waiting At The Church
Wan-A-Tea
Way Down On Tampa Bay
Wedding Of The Sunshine And The Rose, The
We're All Going Calling On The Kaiser
We're Going Over
We're Going Over The Top
What More Can I Give You
What Name Is Sweeter Than Sweetheart
What's The Matter With Father
When I Was Twenty-One And You Were Sweet Sixteen
When It's Apple Blossom Time In Normandie
When It's Moonlight In Mayo
When It's Moonlight Mary Darling 'Neath The Old
    Grape Arbor Shade
When It's Night Time Down In Burgundy
When Kate And I Were Coming Through The Rye

When Shall We Meet Again
When The Dew Is On The Rose
When The Last Rose Of Summer Has Whispered
    Goodbye
When The Mocking Birds Are Singing In The Wild-
    wood
When The Moon Swings Low
When The Parson Hands The Wedding Band From Me
    To Mandy Lee
When The Robin Sings Again
When The Steamboats On The Swanee Whistle Rag-
    Time
When The Twilight Comes To Kiss The Rose "Good-
    Night"
When The Whole World Has Gone Back On You
When Yankee Doodle Marches Through Berlin,
    There'll Be A Hot Time In The U.S.A.
When You Sang Hush-A-Bye Baby To Me
When Your Old Gray Bonnet Was New
Where Are The Scenes Of Yesterday?
Where Memory Dwells
Where The Black-Eyed Susans Grow
Where The Silv'ry Colorado Wends Its Way
Where The Water Lillies Grow
Where The Yang-Tze Ki-Ang Flows
Whip, The
Whistle And I'll Wait For You
Whole Town's Wise, The
Whole World Comes From Dixie, The
Whose Pretty Baby Are You Now?
Will You Ever Grow Tired Of Me
Will The Roses Bloom In Heaven
Wonderful Isle Of Dreams
Would You Care?
Wyoming
You Look Just Like A Girl I Used To Know
You'll Always Be The Same Sweet Baby
You'll Be Sorry Just Too Late
You'll Do The Same Thing Over Again
You'll Never Need A Doctor No More
You're Breaking My Heart With "Good-bye"
You're Just A Show Off
You're My Baby
Ypsilanti

MALCOLM STRAUSS

Babes In The Wood
I'd Like To Have A Million In The Bank
If I Find The Girl
Isn't It Great To Be Married
Nodding Roses
Old Bill Baker
Old Boy Neutral
On The Shore At Le Lei Wi
Some Sort Of Somebody
Thirteen Collar
Wedding Bells Are Calling Me

E.E. WALTON

After You've Gone
Au Revoir, But Not Good-bye
Biggest Thing In A Soldier's Life Is The Letter That
    Comes From Home, The
Cheer Up Father, Cheer Up Mother
Dear Old Daddy Long Legs
Don't Forget The Salvation Army (My Doughnut Girl)
Everybody's Crazy 'Bout The Doggone Blues But
    I'm Happy

Everybody's Crazy Over Dixie
Frenchy Come To Yankee Land
Goodbye Alexander, Goodbye Honey Boy
Gypsy Moonbeams
He's Had No Lovin' For A Long Long Time
Honey-Moon
I Know What It Means To Be Lonesome
I Love You All The More
I'm In Heaven When I'm In Your Arms
In The Valley Of Roses With You
I've Lived, I've Loved, I'm Satisfied
Just A Little Cottage
Kentucky Dream
My Daddy's Star
My Mind's Made Up To Marry Carolina
My Sugar Coated Chocolate Boy
Oh! Frenchy
Soldier's Rosary, A
Stand Up And Fight Like H—
That Long, Long Trail Is Getting Shorter Now
There's Another Angel Now In Old Killarney
Tiger Rose
Wait Till You Get Them Up In The Air, Boys
Watch, Hope, Wait Little Girl 'Til I Come Back
    To You
We'll Do Our Share
What Are You Going To Do To Help The Boys?
When I Get Back From Over There
When The Orioles Come North Again
When You Play With The Heart Of A Girl
You'll Be There To Meet Them, When The Boys
    Come Home

WOHLMAN

Bundle Of Joy
Burning Sands
Caresses
Connecticut March, The
Dardanella Blues, The
Don't Forget To Come Back Home
Gee! But I Hate To Go Home Alone
Georgette
I Ain't Nobody's Darling
I Didn't Think You'd Care
I'm A Dreamer That's Chasing Bubbles
I'm Coming Back To You, Maybe
In A Chinese Temple Garden
In Old Manila
In The Evening
Jimmy Had A Nickel
La Veeda
Last Round Up, The
Lost, A Wonderful Girl
Love Bird
Love That Belongs To Me, The
Lovin' Sam, The Sheik Of Alabam
Ma!
Mandy 'N' Me
March Of The Mannikins
Mimi
My Dream O'Dreams
Oh! Boy What A Girl
Old Covered Bridge, The
Ole Faithful
Old Spinning Wheel, The
On A Moonlight Night
Over The Hill
Rose Of Virginia
She Never Kissed Anything Else Except The Blarney
    Stone

Sidewalks Of New York, The
Swanee Butterfly
There's A Vacant Chair At Home
Wagon Wheels
What's The Use Of Going Home
When It's Night-Time In Italy, It's Wednesday Over
     Here
When The Honeymoon Was Over
When The Moon Comes Over The Mountain
Where Did You Get That Name
Why Do They Always Say "No"
Yes! We Have No Bananas
You're The Only Girl That Made Me Cry
You've Got To See Mamma Ev'ry Night

OTHER COVER ARTISTS

E.D. Allen – Shepherd Serenade
AF – Come Back Little Girl
ARK – Rose Dreams
     Some Day, When The War Is Through
A.W.B. –Take Me To The Midnight Cake
     Walk Ball
Slim Aarons – Wish You Were Here
Peter Arno – Best Thing For You, The
     Dance To The Music Of The Ocarina
     Hostess With The Mostes' On The Ball, The
     It's A Lovely Day Today
     Marrying For Love
F. Avelins – Vision Of Fuji-San, The
James Axeltod – First Hungarian Rhapsody
     Listen To The Mocking Bird
     Mexicali Rose
     Moonlight Sonata
Ayers – Fool There Was, A
B.F.L. – Big Brown Bear, The
BH – Living A Life Of Dreams
BJH – Here I'll Stay
     Star Dust
B.N. – After It's Over Dear
B & W – Just You, I And The Moon, Dear?
Weldy Baer – It's A Sin To Tell A Lie
Balcom – Cinda Lou
Frank M. Barton – Little Love, A Little Kiss, A
Bartholemew – Another Rose Is Just As Sweet
E.R. Beckham – Little Pal Of Mine
Ben -H – Since It Started To Rain In Lovers' Lane
Berni – Dixie I'm Coming Back To You
Bescardi – Baby Shoes
     If I Forget
Frank R. Bill – Beautiful Land Of Somewhere
E.B. Bird – Rosary, The
Betty Blades – Kiss Me, My Sweetheart
Bob Blansky – When The Saints Come Marchin' In
Blue Eagle – Oklahoma I Love You
M. Bodah – Moonlight On The Connecticut
Jas. K. Bonnar – My Happy Southern Home
     Rosalie
Borj – One Kiss, One Smile, One Tear
Ivy Bottini – Candy Dolly
Bouthiller – That's The Reason I Want You
Bower – Summer Time For Mine
M. Brisman – Oh! You Sweet Little Lady
Brumo – Made For Each Other
A. Brunner – Pick A Little Four Leaf Clover, And
     Send It Over To Me
L.A. Brunner – Mammy's Lullaby
     Underneath The Wishing Moon
Bryant – I Could Moon Forever Round A Star Like
     You
Burgos – Wizard Of The Nile, The

A. Byrns – Milena
CA – Dorothy
     The Old Lamp-Lighter
     There Are Such Things
     'Way Down Yonder In New Orleans
     Oh! Ma-Ma!
CEF – Sun Do Move, The
     Angels, We Call Them Mothers Down Here
C.J.M. – Out On The Bounding Deep
CM – Take In The Sun, Hang Out The Moon
C.M. – You've Got Me Goin' Kid
C.P. – Yip-I-Addy-I-Ay
Saml' Cahan – Home On The Range
Callahan – I Want A Man Like Dad
W.R. Cameron – Moonlight On The Danube
Carvon – Merry Go Round Waltz
Casseau – There's Egypt In Your Dreamy Eyes
Cesareo – Bessie In A Bustle
     Garden In The Rain, A
     Just A Blue Serge Suit
     Sioux City Sue
     Teddy Bears' Picnic, The
Chelson – My Fair Lady
D. Chiary – Old Calico Of Blue
Clifton – Imogene
Haskell Coffin – Dream, A
     Mary You Must Marry Me
Flo Cooney – Chinatown My Chinatown
A.B. Copeland – Be A Little Sweeter To Me
     Remember The Rose
Dean Cornwell – Evening Chimes
Palmer Cox – Dance Of The Brownies, The
M.E. Cramer – If You Believe In Fairies
Paul Creasey – Eileen
Floyd Crew – If Dreams Come True
Crit – Jolly Cobbler, The
Crowe SSS – In The Cozy Winter Time
W.S. Cunningham – My Black Venus
D.G. – My Little Grass Shack In Kialikahua Hawaii
Art Daniels – When They Get Down In Mexico
W. David – Hong King, Chinese Love Song
Daway – April Smiles
DeBeck – Barney Google
     Come On Spark Plug
     So I Took The $50,000.00
Van Dee – When You Dream About Hawaii
DeHaven – Ja-Da
     Jazzy Jazzy Sound In All Chinatown
Delappe – Do You Ever Think Of Me
Dember – My Honolulu Bride
L. Denis – Le Silence
Dennis – Just A Dream At Dawn
Den Denslow – On The Battle Field
DeTonnancour – I Want To Be A Soldier For
     The U.S.A.
Dewey – Bill Bailey, Won't You Please Come Home
Boyd Dillon – Senora
Dittmar & Furman – A Rural Festival
Robert C. Dobson – Rosey, Rosey Just Supposey
J. Domerque – Let's Bury The Hatchet, In The
     Kaiser's Head
D. Dulin – Just For You
Dulin Studio – Let's Make Love By The Fireside
Dorothy Dulin – Meet Me In Blossom Time
     Palace Of Peace
     Sacrament
     Sweet And Low
     Steeple Chase, The
Dulins – That's What I'd Do For You
Dunk – Sunshine Girl Of Mine
E.A.S. – 101st Regiment, U.S.A.
E.F.W. – Come Back Kathleen

     Dreams
     I Won't Play Unless You Coax Me
EK – Mine
E.P.C. – College Life
     We All Fall
     You Taught Me How To Love You, Now Teach
          Me To Forget
Earl – All That I'm Asking Is Sympathy
J.B. Eddy – Heaven Born Banner, The
     I'm The Candy
     Florence
     It's Good Enough For Me
     My Indian Maiden
     With You
     You Never Spoke Like That To Me Before
Eliccett – Silks & Rags Waltzes
Elgin – Spanish Rose
F.F.J. – Sweet Slumber
F.J.F. – My Old New Hampshire Home
M. Farmil – Sweetest Melody Of All, The
C.F. Ferraioli – Salut A Pesth
Floyd – Oh! What A Beautiful Baby
Clerice Freros – Sous Les Ponts De Paris
     Tu M'as Dit
Dick Frey – Mr. Gallagher And Mr. Shean
Ray Frey – Nobody Ever
Fung – Montana
Gentle – I Wish You Were Jealous Of Me
Geyler – An Hour Never Passes
     Just A Little Fond Affection
I. Geyler – It Was Christmas In London
J. Geyler – Promises
L. Geyler – Story Of Two Cigarettes, A
Gillam – Echos Of The Wildwood
Goddard – Don't Let Your Foot Slip Hiram
Goebel – Those Ragtime Melodies
H.C. Goehl – Belle Of Boston, The
     She Still Believes In You
Goldbeck – Broadway Rose
     I Found A Rose In The Devil's Garden
R. Goldberg – I'm The Guy
Gorj – Gotta Go To Town
     I Wish I Could Laugh At Love
     Love Me Forever
     Ooh That Kiss
Paul A. Greasey – Sour Grapes
Grover – Morning Cry!
Archie Gunn – American Girl March, The
Irene Haas – Consider Yourself
H. Habermann – It Will Be A Long Long Time
Hap Hadley – Home
     Makin' Faces At The Man In The Moon
     Show Me The Way To Go Home
F.C. Hale – Barcarolle
Hall – Josie O'Neill
     Organ Grinder's Swing
Harris & Ewing – Great American, The
Harrison – There's Nobody Else But You
W.K. Haselden – Tres Moutarde
Hasen – Old Man Jazz
Hauman – Cadet March
     Reddy Fox Goes Walking
D. & G. Hauman – Castanets
     Cotton Pickers
     Salty Sam, The Sailor
     Shoemaker, The
     Yellow Butterfly
George Hauman – Gray Rocks, And Grayer Sea
     Let's Join The Army
     We're In The Navy Now
Havelka – Black Key Polka Mazurka
     Gipsy Dance

Haven – Put Me to Sleep In Your Heart Dear
Fran Hays – I Miss You
    Rosemary
    Thoughts Of My Childhood Home
    Underneath A Starlit Sky
Frances Hays – Little Church In The Niche, The
Heffle – Some Night Soon
L.S. Heflay – Good Times Are Coming
Heflay – Just Any O' Hour, Night Or Day
    Let Me Take You Away From Here
    Mexican Moonlight
    Spotlight Of Love, The
J. Hejnal – Santa's On His Way
Heisley – U.S.A. March
Z.A. Hendrick – Wreck Of The Titanic, The
Henrich – Hiram Green Good-Bye
    Lilac Blossoms
Hewett – Yale Boola
C.A. Hirsihebo – Diamonds Are A Girl's Best Friend
Hirt – At Uncle Tom's Cabin Door
    Bl-nd And P-g Spells Blind Pig
    Good-By Betty Brown
    I'm Going To Steal Some Other Fellow's Girl
    On A Monkey Honeymoon
    Take Me Up With You Dearie
    Tell Me With Your Eyes
    That Hypnotizing Man
    Yankee Doodle Boy, The
    You're Just Like An Angel To Me
J. Hirt – Chin-Chin Chinaman
Arthur G. Hoel – Regatta, The
    University Two Step
Hoffman – Hawaiian Rainbow
    I've Got The Blues
    Just For Remembrance
    Message Of Peace
    Moonlight Shadows
    Rock Me In My Swanee Cradle
    Rosy Cheeks
A. Hudiakoff – O, Katharina!
Hutaf – Back, Back, Back To Baltimore
Henry Hutt – Alice I'm In Wonderland Since The Day
    I First Met You
    Each Stitch Is A Thought Of You Dear
    Good Morning Mr. Zip, Zip, Zip
    I Know What It Means To Be Lonesome
    Nona
Hyer – Soul Of You, The
    Through The Years
    Waltz Of The Wildflowers
I.M. – Shepherd Boy, The
Immy – Did Your Mother Come From Ireland
    Mr. Ghost Goes To Town
    Will You Remember, Sweetheart
JH – These Will Be The Best Years Of Our Lives
JM – Ah, But I've Learned!
    Alice
F. Jackson – Back Where The School Bell Rang
Jaroushek – Basket Of Roses
    Bowl Of Pansies
    Dainty Daffodils
    In Poppyland
    One Fleeting Hour
    Tulips
Jenkins – Cutey, Who Tied Your Tie
    Ev'ry Little Bit Helps
    If I Had My Choice Of The World's Pretty Girls
    In Vacation Time
    Mamma's Boy
    Marche Heroique
    Mignonette
    Silver Threads Among The Gold

    You're The Girl I Love The Best
JoJo – Deck Of Cards, The
Marie Johnson – Cottage In God's Garden, A
Alfred Cheney Johnston – Tears Of Love
Lyle Justus – Plantation Tunes
Kasselman – Take Me
Keller – Alma
    Love Me With Your Big Blue Eyes
    That's How I Need You
    You Can't Fool Me No More
A.H. Keller – I'm Sorry I Made You Cry
    You Broke My Heart To Pass The Time Away
Ed Keller – Take Me Back To Babyland
Edgar Keller – Billy
    Good-Bye And Luck Be With You Laddie Boy
    Just For To-Night
    Santa Rosa Rose
    Sweet Red Roses
    Temptation Rag
    Topsy Turvy
    Where The River Shannon Flows
    Who Are You With To-Night?
    Yama Yama Man, The
Kerr – Perhaps
R.E. Kibbe – Because Of You
Hamilton King – Peggy O'Neill
Kirchner – Hello My Dearie
A. Kissel – Boys Of the U.S.A., The
James Klugman – Made For Each Other
R. Koch – Just You
F.G. Kohl – Fencing Girl, The
E. Kornrelch – I'm Wearing My Heart Away For You
James J. Kriegsmann – I Love You So Much It Hurts
Kursh – When I Get Back To The Folks I Love
Fred Kulz – You're The Brightest Star Of All My Dreams
L. Kummel – Ave Maria
    I'd Like To Be In Texas For The Round Up
    In The Spring
    Mississippi Valley Blues, The
    Strawberry Roan, The
Lou Kummel – Eastbound Train, The
Kursh – They Did Their Share Now I'll Do Mine
LK – Love's Old Sweet Song
    Church In The Wildwood, The
L.P.N. – I Can Hear The Ukuleles Calling Me
L.S. – Fryksdals Polska
    It's Never Too Late To Be Sorry
LaForest – Ce Sera Le Pardon
Laing – Rebecca Came Back From Mecca
Henri Lamothe – For Sentimental Reasons
    Me, Myself And I
    'Taint Good, Like A Nickel Made Of Wood
Lampe – My Garden Of Allah For Two
Walter Lantz – Woody Woodpecker
A. Lekberg – I'd Love To Call You My Sweetheart
C.F. Lent – You May Hold A Million Girlies In
    Your Arms
Levytype – Echoes From The Snowball Club
Virg Lewis – Sweetheart of Sigma Chi, The
Heff Ley – I've Fallen In Love With You
    What A Baby I Got
Liesmann – Apple Jack
Linder – I'm Waiting For Tomorrow To Come
C.J. Linke – Since I Heard My Pal Sing "My Gal Sal"
Richard A. Loederer – Oh Those Days
Alex Lovy – Cow Cow Boogie
Fred Low – There Ain't No Flies On Auntie
H.S. Lukens – When I Get Back To Old Virginia
Charles Lussier – Moonbeams On The Lake
McCurdy – Mother Is Waiting For You
M.R. – Humoreske
    That Italian Serenade

MS – I Don't Want To Meet Any More People
MWC – When I Am Dreaming Twilight Dreams
MWCC – In The Harbor Of Home Sweet Home
MAC – Big Red Rose Means Love, The
    In A Persian Market
Marilyn – I'll Take You Home Again Kathleen
George Martin – Climb Ev'ry Mountain
    Oh You Sweet One
    Sound Of Music, The
    They Can't Make A Lady Out of Me
Martini – Somewhere On Broadway
Merritt – I Don't Want To Love You
    Negra Consentida
    Night And Day
Meserow – Lovelight
Gustav Michelson – My Gal She Has Some
    Wonderful Ways
Milas – School Days
C.E. Millard – I Like To Do It
    Let's Go To Cuba
    Mello Cello
    Out of the Tempest
    Revenge
Mitchell – Dream Of The Rose
Thomas Moore – Pulaski Quick Step
Morgan – Everybody Two Step Rag
    My "Kewpie" Doll
L.E. Morgan – Dreamy Moon
F.G. Murdoch – Skidoo
Harry Murphy – Angel Of No Man's Land, The
M.C. Myers – Singing Bird
NPS – Aloha Oe
    Blue Danube Waltz
    Carnival Of Venice
    Come Back To Sorrento
    Estrellita
    I'll Take You Home Again Kathleen
    Jeanie With The Light Brown Hair
    Liebestraum
    Merry Widow Waltz
    Old Black Joe
    Pretty Girl Milking The Cow, The
    She'll Be Coming Round The Mountain
    Star-Spangled Banner, The
    Wabash Cannon Ball
Nickel – Come West, Little Girl, Come West
    Gypsy Joe
    I'm Bringing A Red, Red Rose
    Love Me Or Leave Me
    Song Of The Setting Sun, The
    Until You Get Somebody Else
A.P. Nickel – Makin Whoopee!
Julian Noveno – I'm Up On A Mountain Talking To
    The Sky
R. Owles – Little Wooden Whistle Wouldn't
    Whistle, The
Paderewski – Grand Daddy
Paki – So Red The Rose
Adelaide Palmer – My Gift For You
Ray Parmelee – I Love A Little Cottage
    In The Heart Of The Hills
    Mood Pensive
    Your Love Is All
Parmelee & West – Eleanor: A Serenade
    You're The Girl That I've Been Longing For
Russell Patterson – Stop! You're Breakin' My Heart
P.H. Paulin – You Never Can Tell What A Girlie
    Will Do!
    You're Like A Rose To Me
A.W. Peters – Why Don't You Smile?
F.E. Phares – Ladies Man–Dapper Dan From
    Dixie Land, The

V.C. Plunkett – Fleur-De-Lys
　　Rose Of My Dreams
Pol – Loafin' Time
RE-CM-JVR – Linger Awhile
RH – Sweet Stranger
RIP – Thousandth Man, The
R.P.B. – My Romance
Ranck – That Beloved Cheater Of Mine
Doc Rankin – I Want My Rib
P.W. Read – Sweetheart Land
R.W. Ream – Time Will Tell
L.S. Reiss – Ching A Ling's Jazz Bazaar
　　Oh! Mother I'm Wild
Lionel S. Reiss – Jazzola
　　Play That Song Of India Again
　　When Two Hearts Discover
Richardson – Venez Ma Belle
Chas. Roat – Faded Love Letters Of Mine
Roland – Just An Echo In The Valley
Jay Roland – San
Rosfield Ress – Underneath The Russian Moon
L.W. Ross – When The Mission Bells Were
　　Ringing Down In Burma By The Sea
S.D. – Canadian Capers
S.J. – Underneath The Arches
Scott – Afterglow
　　Breeze And I, The
　　Forget If You Can
　　My Gypsy Rhapsody
　　Snake Charmer, The
　　You Started Something
Scott & Van Altena – Climb A Tree With Me
　　Man A Maid A Moon A Boat, A
SHN – L'Inspiration
Shaw – Solace
John Shaw Jr. – Jimmie Boy
　　Village Belles
Sickels – Loves's Trials
Sig-Ch – Frankie & Johnny
　　He Wears A Pair Of Silver Wings
　　Here Comes The Navy
　　Pennsylvania Polka
　　Sweet Eloise
　　12th Street Rag
Leo Sielke Jr. – I'll Tell The World
L. Sielke Jr. – Lullaby Time
T. Sinclaire – Fairy Wedding
Emmett O. Smith – Why Do They Call Mama Poor
　　Butterfly
H.R. Smith – Badge Of Honor, The
　　Fuss And Feathers
Patrick Smith – My Singing Sammy
Sidney Smith – Oh! Min
Ernest Smythe – Love Sings A Song In My Heart
Sorokin – All My Life
　　Blue Moon
　　Comin' In On A Wing And A Prayer
　　Daybreak
　　Do Nothin' Till You Hear From Me
　　Dream Valley
　　Ebb Tide
　　Forever And Ever
　　I Didn't Know About You
　　I Married An Angel
　　Lost In My Dreams
　　Seems Like Old Times
　　Taking A Chance On Love
　　There's Honey On The Moon Tonight
　　Whole World Is Singing My Song, The
W. Spalding – Sweet Violets
SSS – I've Lost You, So Why Should I Care
　　Storyland

Take Me Back To Dear Old Mother
P. Stanlows – If You Forget
　　My Magnolia Maid
Stocker – Hello Cutie
　　I Told Them All About You
Strand – Oh Papa, Oh Daddy
Strauss-Peyton – Just The Kind Of A Girl You'd
　　Love To Make Your Wife
Sweeny – Powder Rag
Swinnerton – There's A Dark Man Coming With
　　A Bundle
Tenerser – What Kind Of Fool Am I
Thorburn – White Owl, The
J.P. Tlikoley – It Took Nineteen Hundred And
　　Nineteen Years To Make A Girl Like You
Tozmire – Floating Along
C. Warde Traver – Buddy
　　Sunbonnet Sue
A.S. Trueman – Honeymoon
Tuniso – Do You Remember
Raeburn V – I Love You Dear
R. Van Buren – Patches
　　When Shall We Meet Again
　　Why Dear?
　　Will You Remember Sweetheart
P. Van Burent – When The Boys Come Home
WHG – Bluff! Bluff! Bluff!
WJH – Have I Stayed Away Too Long
W.M.F. – We Met, We Loved, We Parted
WRC – An Old Guitar & An Old Refrain
Wakelan – My Old Kentucky Home, Goodnight
Walker – Angel Voices Ever Near
Walt – Young America We're Strong For You
H.H. Warner – Melon Time In Dixieland
　　Ten Little Fingers And Ten Little Toes
Hal Weinstein – All By Myself
　　Blue Skies
　　Couple Of Swells, A
　　Why Did It Have To End So Soon
　　You Keep Coming Back Like A Song
Ralph Weir – Across The Bridge Of Dreams
Wenrich – Maiden's Bower, The
Wentworth – Zoot Suit For My Sunday Gal, A
A. West – Sweet Thoughts Of Thee
H.C. Whorf – Pepeeta
Billy Williams – Engineer Girls
C.D. Williams – My Yukon Rose
Gaar Williams – Long Boy, Goodbye Ma! Goodbye
　　Pa! Goodbye Mule!
R. Williams – Beautiful, Beautiful World
J. Wilson – Oh You Rag
Lee Winhold – Snappin' Turtle
J. Wolfe – Always In Love, With You
Jeanne Wolff – Can't You Hear Me Calling Geraldine
　　Kiss Me Again Sweetheart
　　Waiting And Yearning
Woolach – Love, Here Is My Heart
Bertha Young – Silver Heels, Indian Girl
W.M. Young – Two Eyes I Idolize

LITHOGRAPHS

Acme Engr. – Miss Liza Jane
　　Prince Of Pyramid Island
American Lithograph Co. – Lucinda Cinda Jane
Art Craft – Harmony Rag
Bes Car Di Co. – I'm Going Back To Carolina
A.D. Brown Art – At The End Of The Sunset Trail
　　How Do You Do
Brown Bros. – Your Lips Are No Man's Land
　　But Mine

J.H. Bufford – Scotch Lassie Jean
D.H. Bufford – Shepherd Boy, The
Central Engraving – Dancing Eyes
　　Sonoma
Chromotype Engr. – Marine Review, The
Colegrove Studio – Roll 'Em Girls
Crews Studio – Crazy Bone Rag
　　Gold Dust Twins
Dobinson Engr. – Angel God Sent From Heaven, The
W.J. Dobinson Engr. – I'm Going To Climb The
　　Blue Ridge Mountains Back To You
D.R. – Blue Bells Of Scotland, The
Dublin Studio – Poppy Time In Old Japan
P.S. Duval – Rose Atherton
Ehrgott & Krebs – My Trundle Bed
Raphael Fassett – Erma
Forbes Co. – Chapel In The Mountains, The
Franklin Co. Engr. – Hearts & Flowers
Grafton Studios – Call, The
Hap Hadley Studio – Quit Cryin' The Blues
Hayes – Dreamy Alabama
　　Long-Long Ago
　　My Love Song, My Roses And You
　　Sweethearts
A. Hoen – America Forever! March
　　Ben Hur Chariot Race
　　Burning Of Rome, The
　　Dawn Of The Century March
　　Midnight Fire Alarm, The
　　Napoleon's Last Charge
　　Romany Rye, The
　　Signal From Mars, A
　　Silver Sleighbells
　　Storm King, The
　　Warmin' Up In Dixie, A
Hy-Art Studios – Crooning
J & S Studio – It All Depends On You
Kiss Art Co. – Too Much Jinger
Knapp Co. – Bubbling Over
　　Buddy
　　Climb On Top Of Your Troubles
　　And Smile Just Smile
　　Come Back
　　Con Amore
　　Dear Heart
　　Drifting
　　Girl Of Mine
　　Girl Of My Dreams
　　Good Night Dearie
　　I'll Be Glad To Get Back
　　I'll Be Your Regular Sweetie
　　I'm Forever Thinking Of You
　　Lonesome Land
　　Lullaby Land
　　My Castles In the Air Are Tumbling Down
　　My Gal, She Has Some Wonderful Ways
　　My Yukon Rose
　　Pretty Kitty Kelly
　　Put Me To Sleep In Your Heart Dear
　　Somebody Misses Somebody's Kisses
　　Sweetheart Land
　　Take Me
　　Tears Tell The Story
　　Ten Baby Fingers
　　Valse Gloria
　　Why Do They Call Mama Poor
　　Butterfly
　　Will You
　　Wings Of The Morning
　　You Know, I Love You
　　You're A Million Miles From Nowhere
Mishkin Studio – Dreams Of Long Ago

Modern Art Ser. – Panama Twilight
Bobby Newcomb – Walking In The Rain
T. Packer – Sweet Violets
P & L Studio – You Must Come Over To-Night
W. F. Powers – I'll Always Be Waiting for You
    Was There Ever A Pal Like You
L. Prang & Co. – Col. Stevenson's Quick Step
Permier Engr. – Mem-O-Ries
Ramsley Studios – Beautiful
Rangley Studio – Chlo-e
Carl Ruhle – Unter Vereinten Kriegsflaggen
Standard Photo Engr. – Alexander's Back From
    Dixie With His Ragtime Band
Standard Photo Engr. – Ching Chong

The Mugler Engr. – Amazon March, The
Union Engraving – Just A Small Town Sweetheart
    My Sweetheart From Old Donegal
    Take Me Back To My Old Mother
Universal Art Service – All Aboard For Chinatown
    I Love You Best Of All
    I Want A Little Love From You Dear
Van Art Co. – That Wonderful Night
Wayne Plates – Dress Up Your Dollars In Khaki
White – All The World Will Be Jealous Of Me
    Don't You Wish You Were Back Home Again
    In The Candle-Light
    Limehouse Blue
    Little By Little You're Breaking My Heart

    My Daddy's Coming Home
    Nobody Knows How I Miss You
    Oh, Johnny! Oh, Johnny! Oh!
    Road For You And Me, The
    Some Boy
    To Have, To Hold, To Love
    Tommy
White Smith & Co. – Old Log Cabin In The Dell, The
B. Wiggles – Waiting For You
Wilson Art – All Aboard For Playland
    At The Gates Of Heaven
    Spain
    When He Gave Me You (Mother Of Mine)

CHAPTER 3
PERFORMERS & COMPOSERS

AMOS N ANDY

In the 30s, Amos N Andy, performed by white vaudevillians Freeman Gosden and Charles Correll, was the most popular and longest running radio series. Especially popular during the Depression, some movie houses stopped the feature film and turned on the radio so the audience could listen to Amos N Andy. They must have sold much Pepsodent toothpaste.

Listed below are songs pertaining to Amos N Andy. Current prices can be found in Chapter 1.

Nobody Knows But The Lord
Old Man Blues
Perfect Song, The
Ring Dem Bells
Three Little Words

IRVING BERLIN

Born Israel Baline in Temun, Siberia, on May 11, 1888. His family immigrated to New York's lower East Side in 1893. He sang for money along the Bowery, plugged songs at Tony Pastor's Theater and in 1904 began as a singing waiter at Mike Salter's Cafe. His first published work was the lyrics for Marie From Sunny Italy. The most successful song hit of his early career was Alexander's Ragtime Band. The first musical for which he wrote the complete score and lyrics was Watch Your Step, in 1906. In 1919 he founded the firm of Irving Berlin Inc. for the publication of his own music. He wrote scores for such musical shows as the Ziegfeld Follies of 1918, 1919, 1920 and 1927, also Music Review 1921, 1922, 1923 & 1925. He wrote many scores for motion pictures which include: Top Hat, Follow The Fleet, On The Avenue, Carefree, Alexander's Ragtime Band, Second Fiddle and Holiday Inn. For This Is The Army he earned the Merit of Honor in 1945. Among his best known songs are: Oh, How I Hate To Get Up In The Morning, A Pretty Girl Is Like A Melody, What'll I Do, All Alone, Remember, Always, Russian Lullaby, Blue Skies, God Bless America and White Christmas. These are just a few of the songs for which he wrote both the lyrics and music. Irving Berlin celebrated his 100th birthday in 1988. Many stars of stage, screen and television participated in a television tribute honoring him for his exceptional talent and contribution to the world of music. On many of his song sheets you will see the quote: "Sterling On Silver, Berlin On Songs." How true!

Listed below are songs written by Irving Berlin. Current prices can be found in Chapter 1.

Abraham
After The Honeymoon
After You Get What You Want, You Don't Want It
Alexander's Ragtime Band
Alice In Wonderland
All Alone
All By Myself
All Of My Life
Along Came Ruth
Always
American Eagles
An Old Fashioned Tune Is Always New
An Orange Grove In California
And They Called It Dixieland
Angels Of Mercy
Anna Liza's Wedding Day
Any Bonds Today
Anything You Can Do
Araby
Arms For The Love Of America
Army's Made A Man Out Of Me, The
At Peace With The World
At The Court Around The Corner
At The Devil's Ball
Back To Back
Be Careful, It's My Heart
Beautiful Faces
Because I Love You
Becky Joined A Musical Show
Begging For Love
Behind The Fan
Bells
Best Thing For You, The
Best Things Happen While You're Dancing, The
Blue Skies
Bring Back My Loving Man
Bring Me A Ring In Spring
But Where Are You?
Butterfingers
Call Me Up Some Rainy Afternoon
Call Of The South, The
Change Partners
Cheek To Cheek
Chinese Firecrackers

Christmas Time Seems Years & Years Away
Climbing Up The Scale
Cohen Owes Me $97
Colonel Buffalo Bill
Come Along
Come Back To Me My Melody
Coquette
Count Your Blessings Instead Of Sheep
Couple Of Swells, A
Crinoline Days
Dance To The Music Of The Ocarina
Dance With Me
Do It Again
Doin' What Comes Natur'lly
Don't Leave Your Wife Alone
Don't Send Me Back To Petrograd
Don't Wait Too Long
Down In Chattanooga
Down To The Folies Bergere
Dreams, Just Dreams
Drowsy Head
Easter Parade
Elevator Man
Everybody Step
Everybody's Doin' It Now
Everything Is Rosie Now For Rosie
Extra, Extra
Fella With An Umbrella, A
Follow The Crowd
Fools Fall In Love
For Your Country And My Country
Freedom Train, The
From Here To Shanghai
Gee, I Wish I Was Back In The Army
Get Thee Behind Me Satan
Gin, Gin Ginny Shore
Girl On The Magazine Cover
Girl On The Police Gazette, The
Girl That I Marry, The
Girls Of My Dreams, The
Give Me Your Tired & Poor
God Bless America
Goodbye France
Good-Bye Girlie & Remember Me
Goody, Goody, Goody, Goody, Goody, Good
Grizzly Bear, The
Hand That Rocked My Cradle Rules My Heart, The
Happy Holiday
Happy Little Country Girl

He Ain't Got Rhythm
He Played It On His Fid-Fid-Fiddle-Dee-Dee
Heat Wave
He's A Devil In His Own Home Town
He's A Rag Picker
He's So Good To Me
Holiday Inn
Home Again Blues
Homesick
Homework
Honorable Profession Of The Fourth Estate, The
Hostess With The Mostes' On The Ball, The
How About A Cheer For The Navy
How About Me
How Can I Forget When There's So Much To
    Remember
How Deep Is The Ocean
How Do You Do It Mabel On Twenty Dollars A Week
How Many Times
How's Chances
I Can't Do Without You
I Can't Remember
I Can't Tell A Lie
I Got Lost In His Arms
I Left My Door Open
I Left My Heart At The Stage Door Canteen
I Like It
I Live In Turkey
I Lost My Heart In Dixie Land
I Love A Piano
I Never Had A Chance
I Paid My Income Tax Today
I Poured My Heart Into A Song
I Say It's Spinach
I Threw A Kiss Into The Ocean
I Used To Be Color Blind
I Want To Be In Dixie
I Want To Go Back To Michigan
I Want You For Myself
I Was Aviating Around
I Wonder
I'd Rather Lead A Band
If I Had You
If I Thought You Wouldn't Tell
If That's Your Idea Of A Wonderful Time, Take Me
    Home
If You Believe
If You Don't Want Me
Ike For Four More Years
I'll Capture Your Heart Singing
I'll Miss You In The Evening
I'll See You In C-U-B-A
I'll Share It All With You
I'll Take You Back To Italy
I'm A Bad Bad Man
I'm A Dumb-Bell
I'm An Indian Too
I'm Getting Tired So I Can Sleep
I'm Going Back To Dixie
I'm Going Back To The Farm
I'm Gonna Pin A Medal On The Girl I Left Behind
I'm On My Way Home

I'm Playing With Fire
I'm Putting All My Eggs In One Basket
I'm Sorry For Myself
In A Cozy Kitchenette Apartment
In My Harem
In Our Hide-Away
In The Shade Of A Sheltering Tree
Is He The Only Man In The World
International Rag
Isn't This A Lovely Day
It Only Happens When I Dance With You
It'll Come To You
It's A Lovely Day Today
It's A Lovely Day Tomorrow
I've Got A Sweet Tooth Bothering Me
I've Got My Captain Working For Me Now
I've Got My Love To Keep Me Warm
I've Got Plenty To Be Thankful For
I've Got The Sun In The Morning
Just A Blue Serge Suit
Just A Little Longer
Just A Little While
Just One Way To Say I Love You
Kate, Have I Come Too Early, Too Late
Keep Away From The Fellow Who Owns An
    Automobile
Keep On Walking
Ki-I-Youdleing Dog, The
Kiss Me, My Honey, Kiss Me
Kiss Your Sailor Boy Good-Bye
Lady Of The Evening
Latins Know How
Lazy
Lead Me To That Beautiful Land
Learn To Do The Strut
Learn To Sing A Love Song
Leg Of Nations, The
Legend Of The Pearls
Let Me Sing And I'm Happy
Let Yourself Go
Let's All Be Americans Now
Let's Face The Music And Dance
Let's Have Another Cup Of Coffee
Let's Start The New Year Right
Let's Take An Old Fashioned Walk
Listening
Little Bit Of Everything, A
Little Bungalow, A
Little Butterfly
Little Fish In A Big Pond
Little Old Church In England, A
Little Things In Life, The
Lonely Heart
Lord Done Fixed Up My Soul, The
Louisiana Purchase
Love, You Didn't Do Right By Me
Mandy
Manhattan Madness
Marie
Marrying For Love
Maybe I Love You Too Much
Me

Me And My Melinda
Miss Liberty
Mr. Jazz Himself
Mr. Monotony
Monkey Doodle Doo
Moonshine Lullaby
Most Expensive Statue In The World, The
My Bird Of Paradise
My Defenses Are Down
My Little Book Of Poetry
My Sergeant And I Are Buddies
My Sweet Italian Man
My Sweetie
My Walking Stick
My Wife's Gone To The Country Hurrah! Hurrah!
New Moon, The
Next To Your Mother Who Do You Love?
Night Is Filled With Music, The
No One Could Do It Like My Father
No Strings
Nobody Knows, And Nobody Seems To Care
Not For All The Rice In China
Now It Can Be Told
Ocarina, The
Oh, How I Hate to Get Up In The Morning
Old Maid's Ball, The
Old Man, The
One Girl
Only For Americans
Outside Of That I Love You
Pack Up Your Sins And Go To The Devil
Paris Wakes Up & Smiles
Passion Flower
Piano Man
Piccolino, The
Pick, Pick, Pick, Pick On The Mandolin
Play A Simple Melody
Policeman's Ball, The
Porcelain Maid
President's Birthday Ball, The
Pretty Girl Is Like A Melody, A
Pullman Porters On Parade
Puttin' On The Ritz
Ragtime Jockey Man, The
Ragtime Soldier Man, the
Ragtime Violin, The
Reaching For The Moon
Remember
Road That Leads To Love
Rockabye Baby
Roses Of Yesterday
Run Home And Tell Your Mother
Russian Lullaby
Sadie Salome Go Home
San Francisco Bound
Say It Isn't So
Say It With Firecrackers
Say It With Music
Schoolhouse Blues, The
Settle Down In A One Horse Town
Shaking The Blues Away
Show Us How To Do The Fox Trot

Si's Been Drinking Cider
Simple Melody
Sisters
Slumming On Park Avenue
Smile And Show Your Dimple
Snooky Ookums
So Help Me
Soft Lights And Sweet Music
Some Little Something About You
Some Sunny Day
Somebody's Coming To My House
Someone Else May Be There While I'm Gone
Song Is Ended But The Melody Lingers On, The
Song Of Freedom
Song Of The Metronone
Spring And Fall
Stay Down Here Where You Belong
Stepping Out With My Baby
Stop! Stop! You're Breaking My Heart
Stop That Rag, Keep On Playing
Sunshine
Sweet Italian Love
Syncopated Vamp, The
Take A Little Tip From Father
Take Me Back
Teach Me To Love
Tell Her In The Springtime
Tell Me A Bedtime Story
Tell Me Little Gypsy
That International Rag
That Mesmerizing Mendelsohn
That Mysterious Rag
That Russian Winter
That's A Good Girl
That's How I Love You
That's What The Well-Dressed Man In Harlem Will
    Wear
There Are Two Eyes In Dixie
There's A Girl In Havana
There's No Business Like Show Business
They Call It Dancing
They Got Me Doing It Now
They Say It's Wonderful
They Were All Out Of Step But Jim
They're On Their Way To Mexico
They've Got Me Doing It Now
This Is A Great Country
This Is The Army Mr. Jones
This Is The Life
This Time
This Year's Kisses
Ting A Ling The Bells Ring
To Be Forgotten
To My Mammy
Together We Two
Tokio Blues
Top Hat, White Tie And Tails
Tra-La-La-La
True Born Soldier Man, A
Unlucky In Love
Wait Until Your Daddy Comes Home
Waiting At The End Of The Road

Waltz Of Long Ago, The
Was There Ever A Pal Like You
Watch Your Step
We Have Much To Be Thankful For
We Saw The Sea
We're On Our Way To France
What Can You Do With A General
What Chance Have I With Love
What Do I Have To Do To Get My Picture In The
    Papers
What Does He Look Like
What Does It Matter
What'll I Do
When I Hear You Play That Piano, Bill
When I Leave The World Behind
When I Lost You
When I'm Alone I'm Lonesome
When I'm Thinking Of You
When It Rains, Sweetheart, When It Rains
When It's Nightime Down In Dixieland
When Johnson's Quartet Harmonize
When My Dreams Come True
When That Man Is Dead And Gone
When That Midnight Choo-Choo Leaves For Alabam'
When The Black Sheep Returns To The Fold
When This Crazy World Is Sane Again
When Winter Comes
When You Walked Out, Someone Else Walked
    Right In
When You're In Town
Where Is My Little Old New York?
Where Is The Song Of Songs For Me
White Christmas
Who Do You Love I Hope
Whose Little Heart Are You Breaking?
Wild Cherries Rag
Will She Come From The East
With My Head In The Clouds
With You
Won't You Play A Simple Melody
Woodman, Woodman Spare That Tree
YMCA
Yam, The
Yascha Michaeloffsky's Melody
Yiddle On Your Fiddle Play Some Ragtime
You Can Have Him
You Can't Brush Me Off
You Can't Get A Man With A Gun
You Cannot Make Your Shimmy Shake On Tea
You Keep Coming Back Like A Song
You Picked A Bad Day Out To Say Good-bye
You'd Be Surprised
You're Just In Love
You're Laughing At Me
You're Lonely And I'm Lonely
You've Built A Fire Down In My Heart
You've Got Your Mother's Big Blue Eyes

EDDIE CANTOR

Eddie Cantor was born in New York on January 31, 1892. He toured vaudeville with Lila Lee. He made many records and had his own radio program. Some of his Broadway stage appearances include: Canary Cottage, Ziegfeld Follies, 1917, 1918, 1919, and 1927, Broadway Brevities, 1920, Make It Snappy, Kid Boots, Whoopee and Banjo Eyes. Some of his movies are The Kid From Spain, Roman Scandals and Thank Your Lucky Stars. Cantor appears on many pieces of sheet music, in black face. Cantor died in Hollywood, California on October 10, 1964.

Listed below are songs made famous by Eddie Cantor. Current prices can be found in Chapter 1.

Angels, We Call Them Mothers Down Here
Baby, Everybody Calls Her Baby
Bebe
Bimini Bay
Build A Little Home
Come West, Little Girl, Come West
Comin' In On A Wing And A Prayer
Dixie Volunteers, The
Don't Sweetheart Me
Dreamer, The
Eddie
Eddie Cantor's "Automobile Horn" Song
Good Night Sweetheart
Green River
Gypsy Joe
I'd Love To Call You My Sweetheart
If You Knew Susie
I'll Be In My Dixie Home Again Tomorrow
I'll Have Vanilla
I'll Still Belong to You
I'm All Eyes For Ida
I'm Bringing A Red-Red Rose
I'm Ridin' For A Fall
It Had To Be You
Josephine Please No Lean On the Bell
Ladies Man–Dapper Dan From Dixie Land, The
Lena From Palesteera
Lily Belle
Little Curly Hair In A High Chair
Little Lady Make Believe
Love Me Or Leave Me
Ma
Makin Whoopee!
Margie
My Brooklyn Love Song
My Sunny Tennessee
Now I Lay Me Down To Sleep
One Hour With You
Scandinavia, Sing Dose Song And Make Dose Music
Since Ma Is Playing Mah Jong
Song Of The Setting Sun, The
Swing Is Here To Stay
Thank Your Lucky Stars
That's The Kind Of A Baby For Me
Until You Get Somebody
We Did It Before And We Can Do It Again
When Uncle Joe Steps Into France
Why Don't You Say So
You Can Have It I Don't Want It

GEORGE M. COHAN

George Michael Cohan was born in Providence, Rhode Island, on July 4, 1878. He was an actor, songwriter, playwright and producer. He made his theatrical debut at age 9 in Daniel Boone and starred in Peck's Bad Boy at 13. From 1890 to 1900 he was in vaudeville with his parents and his sister as the famous "Four Cohans," which were among the greatest attractions in the country. In 1901 he took the family with him into the legitimate theater in his first Broadway play, The Governor's Son, and in 1904 joined Sam H. Harris in one of the most successful partnerships known to the New York theater. In the 15 years they were together they produced more than 50 plays, musical comedies and revues, and at one time they controlled five theaters. Cohan wrote the music and words for literally hundreds of songs including the famous World War I song, Over There, and the earlier It's A Grand Old Flag. Writing and directing most of the plays in which he starred, he gave what was considered his finest performance in Eugene O'Neill's Ah Wilderness in 1932. Cohan died in New York on November 5, 1942.

Listed below are songs written or performed by George M. Cohan.

Always Leave Them Laughing When You Say Good-Bye
Any Place The Old Flag Flies
Anything You Want To Do, Dear
Barnum Had The Right Idea
Born & Bred In Brooklyn
Cohan's Pet Names
Down By The Erie Canal
Easter Sunday Parade, The
Father Of The Land We Love
Feeling In My Heart, A
For The Flag, For The Home, For The Family
Forty Five Minutes From Broadway
Give My Regards To Broadway
Good-Bye Flo
Harrigan
Hot Tamale Alley
Hugh McCue
I Guess I'll Have To Telegraph My Baby
I Want The World To Know I Love You
I Want To Be A Popular Millionaire
I Want To Hear A Yankee Doodle Tune
I Want You
I Was Born In Virginia
I'd Rather Write A Song
If Washington Should Come To Life
I'll Go On The Route For You
I'm Awfully Strong For You
I'm In Love With One Of The Stars
I'm Mighty Glad I'm Living
In A Kingdom Of My Own
Indians And Trees
Johnny Q. Public
Kid Days
Let's You And I Just Say Good-bye

Life's A Funny Proposition After All
Love Dreams
Love Nest, The
Man Who Owns Broadway, The
March Of The Cardinals
Mary
Mary's A Grand Old Name
Nellie Kelly I Love You
Nothing New Beneath The Sun
Oh, You Wonderful Girl
Op In Me Ansom
Over There
Polly's A Peach
Popularity
Rose
Small Town Gal
So Long Mary
Stand Up And Fight Like H—
Sullivan
Take Your Girl To The Ball Game
That Farm Out In Kansas
That Haunting Melody
That Tumble-Down Shack In Athlone
That's Some Love
Then I'd Be Satisfied With You
Then I'll Be Satisfied With Life
They're All My Friends
This Our Side Of The Ocean
Tom-Tom-Toddle
Under Any Old Flag At All
Until My Luck Comes Rolling Along
Venus, My Shining Love
Voice In My Heart, The
Waiting
Warmest Baby In The Bunch, The
Washington, He Was A Wonderful Man
We Must Be Ready
We'll Have A Wonderful Party
What A Man
What This Country Needs Is A Song
When A Fellow's On The Level With A Girl That's On The Square
When June Comes Along With A Song
When New York Was New York
When We Are M-A-Double R-I-E-D
When You Come Back
Won't You Come Back To Me
Yankee Doodle Boy, The
Yankee Doodle Dandy
Yankee Doodle's Come To Town
Yankee Prince, The
You Can Tell That I'm Irish
You Can't Deny You're Irish
You Remind Me Of My Mother
You're A Grand Old Flag

STEPHEN FOSTER

Stephen Foster was born in Lawrenceville, Pennsylvania, on July 4, 1826. He wrote both words and music to approximately 190 songs, which include the

following: Old Folks At Home, Oh! Susanna, My Old Kentucky Home Good Night, Massa's in de Cold, Cold Ground, Jeanie With The Light Brown Hair and Old Black Joe. Foster died penniless in Bellevue Hospital, in New York City, on January 13, 1864.

Listed below are songs written by Stephen Foster. Current prices can be found in Chapter 1.

Beautiful Dreamer
Camptown Races
Come Where My Love Lies Dreaming
Gentle Annie
Hard Times Come Again No More
Jeanie With The Light Brown Hair
Massa's In The Cold Cold Ground
My Old Kentucky Home
My Old Kentucky Home, Good Night, Variations
Nelly Bly
Nelly Was A Lady
Oh! Susanna
Old Black Joe
Old Dog Tray
Old Folks At Home
Open Thy Lattice, Love
Uncle Ned
Way Down Upon The Swanee River (Old Folks At Home)
We Are Coming, Father Abraham, Three Hundred Thousand Strong

VICTOR HERBERT

Victor Herbert was born in Dublin, Ireland, in 1859. He was famous for his composition of operettas, one of which was Babes In Toyland in 1903. He wrote Naughty Marietta in 1910. It featured the following songs: Ah Sweet Mystery Of Life, I'm Falling In Love With Someone and Italian Street Song. Herbert was the first American composer to write an original score for a motion picture. Herbert was one of the founders of the American Society Of Composers, Authors And Publishers (A.S.C.A.P.). He died in 1924.

Listed below are songs written by Victor Herbert. Current prices can be found in Chapter 1.

Absinthe Frappe
Ah! Sweet Mystery Of Life
Algeria
All Year Around
American Girl March, The
Antoinette
Art Song
Ask Her While The Band Is Playing
Bandana Land
Be Happy, Boys, To-Night
Call It A Day
Can't You Hear Your Country Calling
Devotion
Dodge Brothers March
Eileen
Everyday Is Ladies' Day To Me
Gypsy Jan

Gypsy Love Song
Hats Make The Woman
Here's To The Land We Love, Boys
How Do You Get That Way
I Might Be Your Once-In-A While
If Somebody Only Would Find Me
I'm Falling In Love With Someone
Indian Summer
Irish Have A Great Day To-Night, The
Italian Street Song
Kiss In The Dark, A
Kiss Me Again
Knot Of Blue, The
List'ning On Some Radio
March Of The Toys, The
More I See Of Others, Dear, The Better I Like
    You, The
My Dream Girl
My Hero
Personality
Some One Like You
Sweethearts
Tell It All Over Again
Thine Alone
Those Since-I-Met You Days
Tip Your Hat To Hatty
To The Land Of My Own Romance
Toyland
When Shall I Again See Ireland
When You're Away
When You're Wearing The Ball And Chain
Whistle It
Why Should We Stay Home And Sew?
Wizard Of The Nile, The
Woman Is Only A Woman But A Good Cigar Is A
    Smoke, A
Yesterthoughts
You Have To Have A Part To Make A Hit
You're The Only Girl For Me

AL JOLSON

Born Asa Joelson in Russia in 1886, Jolson became a popular American singer and actor. He sang in vaudeville and minstrel shows and gained success in 1909 when he substituted for a star of a musical. He became famous when he sang Mammy in black face. He later starred in The Jazz Singer and Singing Fool, two of the first sound motion pictures. Jolson died in 1950 shortly after his return from entertaining troops in Korea.

Jolson was not only a performer but also a composer of songs.

Listed below are songs written or performed by Al Jolson. Current prices can be found in Chapter 1.

About A Quarter To Nine
After The Ball
Ain't You Coming Back To Dixieland
Alabamy Bound
Anniversary
Anniversary Song, The
April Showers

Arcady
Avalon
Back Home In Tennessee
Back In Your Own Back Yard
Bagdad
Billy-Billy Bounce Your Baby-Doll
Blue Bell
Bring Along Your Dancing Shoes
By The Light Of The Silvery Moon
California Here I Come
Cleopatra
Dirty Hands, Dirty Face
Don't Cry Swanee
Don't Say Good Night
Don't Send Your Wife To The Country
Down Among The Sheltering Palms
Down In Bom Bombay
Down South
Down Where The Swanee River Flows
Down Where The Tennessee Flows
Evangeline
Every Little Movement Has A
    Meaning Of It's Own
Forty Second Street
Four Walls
Give Me My Mammy
Goin' To Heaven On A Mule
Good-Bye Boys
Grieving For You
Harding, You're The Man For Us
Hello Central! Give Me No Man's Land
I Love Her Oh! Oh! Oh!
I Sent My Wife To The 1,000 Isles
I Want A Girl Just Like The Girl That Married Dear
    Old Dad
I Wonder What's Become Of Sally
I Wonder Why She Kept On Saying Si-Si
If You Knew Susie Like I Know Susie
I'll Say She Does
I'm Goin' South
I'm Going Back To Old Nebraska
I'm Looking Over A Four Leaf Clover
I'm Sitting On Top Of The World
It All Depends On You
It's You
Just Try To Picture Me Back Home In Tennessee
Latin From Manhattan, A
Let Me Sing And I'm Happy
Little Pal
Liza
Lullaby Of Broadway
Ma Blushin' Rosie
Mammy's Little Coal Black Rose
Me And My Shadow
Morning Will Come
My Buddy
My Mammy
My Sumurun Girl
My Tom Tom Man
My Yellow Jacket Girl
'N' Everything
Oh, Donna Clara

Oh How I Wish I Could Sleep 'Till Daddy's Home
Old Fashioned Girl
On The Banks Of The Wabash
One O'Clock Baby
Rock-A-Bye Your Baby With A Dixie Melody
Rum Tum Tiddle
She Knows It
Sister Susie's Sewing Shirts For Soldiers
So, Long, Mother
Sonny Boy
Spaniard Who Blighted My Life, The
Stella
Susie
Swanee
Swanee River Trail
Swanee Rose
Tallahassee
Tell That To The Marines
Tennessee I Hear You Calling Me
That Barber In Seville
There's A Lump Of Sugar Down In Dixie
There's A Rainbow 'Round My Shoulder
This Is The Life
To My Mammy
Toot-Toot-Tootsie
Used To You
Waiting For The Robert E. Lee
War Babies
We're In The Money
When The Grown Up Ladies Act Like Babies
When You Were Sweet Sixteen
Where Did Robinson Crusoe Go With Friday On
    Saturday Night
Where The Black Eyed Susans Grow
Who Cares
Why Can't You
Why Do I Dream Those Dreams
Why Do They All Take The Night Boat To Albany
Yaaka Hula Hickey Dula
Yoo-Hoo
You Made Me Love You
You'll Never Know
You're A Better Man Than I Am, Gunga Din
You're A Dangerous Girl
You're The Most Wonderful Girl

SCOTT JOPLIN

Scott Joplin was born in Texarkana, Texas, in 1869. He was an American composer and performer of ragtime music. He was known as "King Of Ragtime." The pioneers of jazz frankly admit the importance of the piano rags of Scott Joplin. Joplin came from a musical family. His father was a plantation violinist and his mother Florence played the banjo and sang. Scott picked up most of his music talent from his mother. She also did domestic work and raised enough money to buy Scott a second hand piano. At age 17 he was singing, playing piano, mandolin and guitar at the various honky-tonk clubs & eating places. He published approximately 40 rags for the piano. His most famous is Maple Leaf Rag. Joplin died in 1917.

Listed below are songs written by Scott Joplin. Current prices can be found in Chapter 1.

Breeze From Alabama, A
Cascades, The
Chrysanthemum Rag, The
Country Club Rag Time
Easy Winners
Elite Syncopations
Entertainer, The
Euphonic Sounds
Felicity
Fig Leaf Rag
Gladiolus Rag
Heliotrope Bouquet
Kismet Rag
Maple Leaf Rag
Original Rags
Paragon Rag
Peacherine
Pineapple Rag
Pleasant Moments Ragtime Waltz
Ragtime Dance, The
Real Slow Rag, A
School Of Ragtime
Scott Joplin's New Rag
Solace
Strenuous Life
Sugar Cane Rag
Sunflower Slow Rag
Swipsey Cake Walk
Wall Street Rag

JOHN PHILIP SOUSA

Born in Washington, D.C. on November 6, 1854, Sousa played in the Marine band at age 13. He led an orchestra in vaudeville theater in Washington before he was 18. In 1880 he was appointed leader of the Marine Band. He resigned in 1892 and organized his own band. Sousa was known as the March King. Sousa served as a Lieutenant in the Naval Reserve during WWI. Some of his more popular marches are: The Stars And Stripes Forever, El Capitan, Semper Fidelis and Liberty Bell. Sousa died in Reading, Pennsylvania on March 6, 1932.

Listed below are songs written by John Philip Sousa. Current prices can be found in Chapter 1.

America First
Atlantic City Pageant, The
Century Of Progress
Charlatan March, The
Custer's Last Charge
Directorate March
El Capitan March
George Washington Bicentennial
Hands Across The Sea
High School Cadets
Honored Dead, The
In Flanders Fields The Poppies Grow
King Cotton March
Liberty Bell, The
Liberty Loan March
Love That Lives Forever, The
Lovely Mary Donnelly
Magna Carta
Manhattan Beach March
Semper Fidelis
Sesqui-Centennial Exposition Of U.S.
Sousa's Grand March
Stars & Stripes Forever, The
Thunderer, The
U.S. Field Artillery, The
Wake Up America
Washington Post March
We Are Coming Home
Yale March, The

SHIRLEY TEMPLE

Shirley Temple was born in Santa Monica, California, in 1928. She was one of the most famous child performers in the world. She made her motion picture debut at age 3½ in Stand Up And Cheer. She starred in many other motion pictures including Heidi and The Blue Bird. Some of the most memorable songs she sang are: Animal Crackers In My Soup and On The Good Ship Lollipop. Shirley retired from films in 1949. She is pictured on many show tune covers. In 1974 she was appointed Ambassador to Ghana by President Gerald Ford. She is married to Dr. Charles A. Black and has three children.

Listed below are songs performed by Shirley Temple. Current prices can be found in Chapter 1.

Animal Crackers In My Soup
At The Codfish Ball
Believe Me If All Those Endearing Young Charms
Curly Top
Early Bird
Goodnight My Love
Hey, What Did The Blue Jay Say?
I Wanna Go To The Zoo
It's All So New To Me
Little Colonel
Love's Young Dream
On Account-A I Love You
On The Good Ship Lollipop
One Never Knows, Does One?
Our Little Girl
Ride A Cock-Horse To Banbury Cross
Right Somebody To Love, The
Simple Things In Life, The
Together
When I Grow Up
When I'm With You
You Gotta S-M-I-L-E To Be H-A Double P-Y

CHAPTER 4
MISCELLANEOUS CATEGORIES

ADVERTISING

Ephemera is big business in the collector's world. Sheet music was popular as a means of advertising products either on the front or back cover. The following is a sample of the advertising and description of products found on some sheet music.

A Story Of Two Cigarettes. Picture of two Chesterfield cigarettes in ash tray. Song was introduced & featured by Johnnie Johnston on Chesterfield's "Music That Satisfies."

Bromo Seltzer: A speedy and reliable remedy for headaches, insomnia, nervousness, nervous dyspepsia and stomach disorders. It contains no cocaine or morphine. It is sold by druggists throughout the country.

Pepsodent Toothpaste Or Powder: Musical theme of the Pepsodent hour featuring Amos N Andy on cover.

Prince Albert Tobacco: A can of Prince Albert, Crimp Cut, long burning pipe and cigarette tobacco as well as a picture of Old Hutch on back of sheet music.

Moxie: "The Moxie Boy's eyes follow you anywhere within sight. We are reminded of the Mona Lisa when looking at the Moxie Boy's eyes. He will go on forever advertising Moxie, the clean wholesome refreshing beverage." The front cover shows Moxie logo and a Rolls Royce. A great cover.

Sterling Pianos: Great picture of piano on back of sheet music.

Listed below are some songs pertaining to Advertising. Current prices can be found in Chapter 1.

Apple Blossom (Bromo Seltzer)
Baseball (Chesterfield)
Benzine Buggy Man (Benzine)
Carolina's Calling Me (Prince Albert Tobacco)
Clicquot (Clicquot Club)
Far Away Places (Pan Am)
Ford March, The (Ford Motor, Model T.)
Grandma's Shamrocks (Bromo Seltzer)
Happy Birthday Song (Jolly Green Giant)
He's My Uncle (Maxwell House Coffee)
Keating Wheel March (Keating Bicycle)
Last Night (Bromo Seltzer)
Little Orphan Annie (Ovaltine)

Lonely Heart (Pillsbury Flour)
Love's Golden Dream (Bromo Seltzer)
Lullaby (Bromo Seltzer)
Makin's Of The U.S.A., The (Bull Durham Tobacco)
March Of The Flit Soldiers, The (Flit)
Maryland! My Maryland! (Bromo Seltzer)
Milena (Sterling Piano)
Moxie Fox Trot Song (Moxie)
My Old Kentucky Home (Bromo Seltzer)
Non E Ver (Bromo Seltzer)
Old Glory I Salute You (Firestone Tire)
Perfect Song, The (Pepsodent Toothpaste)
Smile You Miss, The (E.A.Earl Radio Sets)
Souvenir March (The J.W. Pepper Metallic Folding Bedstead)
Spirit Of Progress March, The (Montgomery Ward)
Spreading New England's Fame (Doublemint Gum)
Story Of Two Cigarettes, A (Chesterfield)
There's A Broken Heart For Every Light On Broadway (Saturday Evening Post On Back Cover)
Waltzing (Florsheim Shoes)
Yale March, The (S. Carsley Co. Ltd. Montreal's Greatest Store)
You're A Lifesaver (Lifesaver)

BLACK, BLACK FACE

There are many black composers who wrote songs about blacks. Some of the early composers were: Scott Joplin, Bert Williams, George Walker, Alex Rogers, William Marion Cooke, James Bland, Edward Kennedy, Duke Ellington, William C. Handy, Henry Creamer and Turner Layton.

Many entertainers performed in black face. These were performers made up for a conventionalized comic travesty of the Negro in a minstrel show. Some entertainers who performed in black face were: Lew Dockstader, Al Jolson, Eddie Cantor and Eddie Leonard.

Listed below are songs written by or pertaining to blacks and black face. Current prices can be found in Chapter l.

After The Cake Walk
Ain't Dat A Shame
Alabama Cake Walk
Alabama Lullaby
Alabama Wedding
Alabamy Bound

Alabamy Cradle Song
Alexander Don't You Love Your Baby No More?
Alexander's Back From Dixie With His Rag-Time Band
All Coons Look Alike To Me
All I Want Is My Black Baby Back
All Vat's Gold Ain't Glitters
Arabella, I'll Be Your Fellah
At A Darktown Cake Walk
At The Coffee Cooler's Tea
At The Mississippi Cabaret
Aunt Dinah's Cake Walk
Aunt Mandy's Wedding March
Auntie Skinner's Chicken Dinner
Baby, Everybody Calls Her Baby
Baby, Will You Always Love Me True
Back, Back, Back To Baltimore
Bake Dat Chicken Pie
Beautiful
Bedelia
Bees-Wax Rag
Belle Of Georgia, The
Belle Of The Creoles
Bess You Is My Woman
Bill Bailey, Won't You Please Come Home
Black And Blue Rag
Black Jim
Blue Harlem
Bluff! Bluff! Bluff!
Bombo Shay, The
Bon, Bon Buddy, The Chocolate Drop
Boogie Woogie
Booker T's Are On Parade Today, The
Bran New Little Coon
Brass Band Ephraham Jones
Bridal Cake Walk
Bunch Of Blackberries
Business Is Business With Me
By The Watermelon Vine Lindy Lou
Bye-Lo
Cake Walk In The Sky, The
Cake Walk Of The Day
Camp Meeting Band
Campmeetin' Time
Can't Yo' Heah Me Callin' Caroline
Carolina Cake Walk, A
Carolina Mammy
Carolina Sunshine
Carry Me Back To Old Virginny

Charcoal
Chattanoogie Shoe Shine Boy
Cla-Wrench, Don't Tweat Me So Wuff
Close Dem Windows
Coal Black Mammy
Coaling Up In Colon Town
Coldest Coon In Town, The
Come After Breakfast
Come Along Ma Honey, Down Upon The Swanee
Come Along Sinners
Coon, Coon, Coon
Copper Colored Gal
Cotton Coon's Two Step
Cotton Fluff
Cotton Pickers, The
Cotton Pickin' Time In Tennessee
Cousin Jedediah
Creole Belles
Creole Rhapsody
Dancing The Jelly Roll
Dar's Somethin' About Yer I Like
Darkies' Dream, The
Darkies Ragtime Ball, The
Darktown Barbacue
Darktown Strutters' Ball, The
Darky Cavalier
Dat Citron Wedding Cake
Dat's The Way To Spell Chicken
Daughters Of Sweet Georgia Brown, The
De Cake Walk Queen
De Darkies Jubilee
De Golden Wedding
De Leader Of De Company B
De Ol' Ark's A-Moverin
De Ole Time Cake Walk
De Stories Uncle Remus Tells
Deep River
Dem Golden Slippers
Dirty Hands, Dirty Faces
Dixie Coon Brigade, The
Do Re Mi
Don't You Cry, Mah Honey
Don't Be What You Ain't
Down At Mammy Jinny's Cabin Door
Down De Lover's Lane
Down Home Rag
Down In Pickaninny Alley
Down Where The Tennessee Flows
Dry Yo' Eyes
Dusty Dudes Cake Walk
Echoes From The Snowball Club
Eddie, Steady
Eli Green's Cake Walk
Ev'ry Little Bit Helps
Ev'ry Morn I Bring Her Chicken
Every Darkey Is A King
Every Race Has A Flag But The Coon
Everybody Works But Father
Fashion Rag
Fatal Rose Of Red, The
Floatin' Down To Cotton Town
Four Little Blackberries

Four Little Sugarplums
Fuss And Feathers
Gabriel's Band
Georgia Giggle, The
Ghost Of A Coon, the
Go Down Moses
Go Way Back And Sit Down
Gold Dust Twins
Golden Wedding
Golliwog's Cake Walk
Gone, Gone, Gone
Good Enough
Good Morning Carrie!
Goodbye Alexander, Goodbye Honey Boy
Good-Bye Boys
Goodbye Eliza Jane
Goodbye Lil' Liza Jane
Granny, You're My Mammy's Mammy
Greatest Miracle Of All
Hand Me Down My Walking Cane
Hannah Won't You Open Up That Door
Happy Hours in Coontown
Hard Times Come Again No More
Have You Seen My Henry Brown
Hello Ma Baby
Hello My Lulu
High Brow Colored Lady
High Yellow Cake Walk
Hitch On De Golden Trolley
Honey Boy
Honey, Dat's All
Honey If Yo' Only Knew
Honey! You're Ma Lady Love
Honey! You'se My Turtle Dove
Hot Lips
Hot Time In The Old Town
Hottest Ever Cake Walk, The
Hulda's Baby
Hush-A-By
Hush-A-Bye Ma Baby, The Missouri Waltz
Hush, Little Baby, Don't You Cry
I Ain't Got Nobody
I Ain't Gwin Ter Work No Mo
I Certainly Was Going Some
I Don't Care If You Neber Come Back
I Don't Like No Cheap Man
I Got Plenty O' Nuttin
I Guess I'll Have To Telegraph My Baby
I Lost A Slice Of Paradise When I Left My Swanee Home
I Love My Honey Yes I Do
I Mind Me In The Mornin'
I Never Had A Mammy
I Want Dem Presents Back
I Want Yer, Ma Honey
I Wants A Man Like Romeo
I Wants To Pick A Bone With You
I Wish I Was In Dixie
I Wish I Was In Heaven Sitting Down
I Wonder Why Bill Bailey Don't Come Home
I Wouldn't Change Dat Gal For No Other
I'd Leave My Happy Home For You

I'd Love To Fall Asleep And Wake Up In My Mammy's Arms
If Every Star Was A Little Pickaninny
If That's What You Want Here It Is
If The Man In The Moon Were A Coon
If You Knew Susie
I'll Make That Black Gal Mine
I'm Goin' Back To My Mammy
I'm Going To Get Myself A Black Salome
I'm Livin' Easy
I'm Looking For An Argument
I'm Missin' Mammy's Kissin'
I'm So Glad Trouble Don't Last Alway
Impecunious Davis
In The Autumn
In The Days Of Old Black Joe
In The Morning By The Bright Light
I'se A Lady
I'se A-Waitin For Yer Josie
I'se Got Another Nigger On Ma Staff
It Ain't Gonna Rain No Mo'
It Ain't Necessarily So
It Takes A Long Tall Brown Skin Gal To Make A Preacher Put His Bible Down
It Will Be A Long, Long Time
It's Time To Close Your Drowsy Eyes
I've Waited, Honey, Waited Long For You
I'ze Your Nigger If You Wants Me Liza Jane
Jasper Jenkins, De Cake-Walking Coon
Jenny Get Your Hoe Cake Done
Jes' Come Aroun' Wid An Automobile
Jim Crow Polka
John Henry, March
Jolly Pickaninnies
Josephine Please No Lean On The Bell
Juba
Just Give Me A Big Brass Drum
Just Hangin' Round
Just In Love With You
Just Kiss Yourself Good-Bye
Keep Away From Emmeline
Kinky-Head
Kinky Kids Parade, The
Ladies Man–Dapper Dan From Dixie Land, The
Land Of Long Ago, the
Lazy Moon
Lil' Black Nigger
Listen To The Silver Trumpets
Little Alabamy Coon
Little Bit O'Honey, A
Little Black Me
Little Brown Gal
Little Coon's Prayer
Little Kinkey Wooley Head
Little Pickaninny Kid
Little Puff Of Smoke Good-Night
Lord! Have Mercy On A Married Man
Lucinda Cinda Jane
Lucy Linda Lady
Ma
Ma Ebony Belle
Ma Honey Gal

Ma Jet Black Lady
Ma Lady Lu
Ma' Little Sunflower Good Night
Ma Mississippi Babe
Ma' Tiger Lily
Mamie Don't Feel Ashamie
Mammy Blossom's Possum Party
Mammy Jinny's Hall Of Fame
Mammy Jinny's Jubilee
Mammy's Chocolate Soldier
Mammy's Growin' Ole
Mammy's Kinky Headed Coon
Mammy's 'Lassus Candy Child
Mammy's Little Coal Black Rose
Mammy's Little Kinky Headed Boy
Mammy's Little Pansy
Mammy's Little Pickaninny Boy
Mammy's Little Pumpkin Colored Coons
Mammy's Lullaby
Mammy's Shufflin' Dance
Mandy And Me
Mandy Lane
Mandy Lee
Mandy Lou
Mandy Won't You Let Me Be Your Beau
Margie
Mazie, My Dusky Daizy
Memories Of The South
Miss Brown's Cake Walk
Miss Liza Jane
Mississippi Mammy
Mississippi Side Step
Mr. Johnson, Turn Me Loose
Mister Moon Kindly Come Out And Shine
Moon Am Shinin
Moon Shines On The Moonshine, The
Moses Andrew Jackson, Good-Bye
My Black Baby, Mine
My Black Venus
My Caramel Gal
My Castle On The Nile
My Chocolate Soldier Sammy Boy
My Coal Black Lady
My Creole Sue
My Gal Is A High Born Lady
My Georgia Lady-Love
My Hannah Lady, Whose Black Boy Is You
My Heart Is In The Violet
My Honey Lou
My Irish American Rose
My Josephine
My Little Congo Maid
My Mammy
My Mammy Knows
My Singing Sammy
My Sugar Coated Chocolate Boy
My Swanee Home
Nay, Nay Pauline
New Coon In Town
Nigger Toe Rag
Nobody
Nobody Knows But The Lord

Nobody Knows The Trouble I've Seen
Oh Death Where Is Thy Sting
Oh Dem Golden Slippers
Oh, Didn't It Rain
Oh! Oh! Miss Phoebe
Oh! Susanna
Ol' Man Mose
Old Black Joe
Old Joe Blues
Old Log Cabin In The Dell, The
Old Man Blues
One Of His Legs Is Longer Than It Really Ought To Be
Perfect Song, The
Phrenologist Coon, The
Pickaninnies' Heaven
Pickaninny Blues
Pickaninny Waltz Lullaby Blues
Pickaninny's Lullaby
Pickaninny's Paradise, The
Pickanning Christening, A
Pious Peter Cakewalk
Plantation Lullaby
Plantation Tunes
Pliney, Come Kiss Your Baby
Prancing Pickaninnies
Pretty Little Carolina Rose
Pretty Little Dinah Jones
Prize Cake Walk Of The Blackville Swells
Put On De Golden Shoe
Quit Cryin' The Blues
Rag Baby Rag
Rag Time Drafted Man
Rastus On Parade
Rememb'ring
Ring Dem Bells
River, Stay Way From My Door
Rock-A-Bye Lullabye Mammy
Roll Dem Roly Boly Eyes
Roll Them Cotton Bales
Rubber Neck Jim
Rufus, Rastus, Johnson, Brown, What You Gonna Do When De Rent Comes Round?
Salute To Sam Johnson
Sam Johnson's Colored Cake Walk
Sam, The Old Accordion Man
Sambo Outa Work Cake Walk
Save Dis Little Nigger From De Rain And De Frost
She Rests By The Swanee River
She's Gettin More Like The White Folks Everyday
Short'nin Bread
Show Me The Way To Go Home
Sighing
Silks & Rags Waltzes
Sister Kate Cake Walk
Sister Susie's Sewing Shirts For Soldiers
Skidoo
Slumber On, Kentucky Babe
Smoky Mokes
Sometimes I Feel Like A Motherless Child
Sons Of Ham
Sound Of Chicken Frying, Dat's Music To Me, The
St. Louis Tickle

Steal Away
Strut, Miss Lizzie
Summertime
Sumthin Doin
Sun Do Move, The
Sweet Georgia Brown
Take Me To The Midnight Cake Walk
Tapioca
Tar Babies
That Bandana Band, Way Down In Dixieland
That Coon Town Quartet
That Southern Hospitality, When You're Down In Dixie
That's My Mammy
That's What Makes A Wild Cat Wild
That's Why Darkies Were Born
There's A Dark Man Coming With A Bundle
They Made It Twice As Nice As Paradise And They Called It Dixieland
They'll Be Mighty Proud In Dixie Of Their Old Black Joe
Three Little Words
Throw Down Dat Key
Tickled To Death
Ticklin' Toes
Topsy
Travelin' Back To Alabam'
U.S. Black Marines
Um, Um, Da Da
Under Love's Moon
Under The Bamboo Tree
Underneath The Cotton Moon
Underneath The Harlem Moon
Up Dar In De Sky
Walkin' Fo' Dat Cake
Walkin' Fo' De Great White Cake
Warm Proposition
Warm Reception, A
Warmest Baby In The Bunch, The
Way Down In Cotton Town Way Way Down
Way Up Yonder
Wedding Of The Chinee And The Coon, The
We'll Dance Thro' Life
We'll Have A Jubilee In My Old Kentucky Home
Wet Yo' Thumb
What! Marry Dat Gal!
When A Black Man's Blue
When Erastus Plays His Old Kazoo
When It's All Goin' Out And Nothin' Comin' In
When It's Cotton Pickin' Time In Tennessee
When Johnson's Quartet Harmonize
When Mammy's Pickaninny's Fast Asleep
When Old Bill Bailey Plays The Ukalele
When The Major Plays Those Minor Keys
When The Sunset Turns The Ocean's Blue To Gold
When The Steamboats On The Swanee Whistle Rag-Time
When They Christened Brother Johnson's Child
When You Ain't Got No Money, Well You Needn't Come Around
When You Sang Hush-A-Bye Baby To Me
Where The Bamboo Babies Grow
Whistling Coon

Whistling Rufus
Who Dat Say Chicken In Dis Crowd
Why Don't You Go, Go, Go?
Why Was I Ever Born Lazy
With All Her Faults I Love Her Still
Without A Song
Witmark Minstrel Overture, The
Woman Is A Sometime Thing, A
You Can't Fool Me No More
You Could Have Been True
You Got To Stop A-Pickin' On My Li'l Pickaninny
You'll Get All That's Coming To You
You'll Never Need A Doctor No More
You're In The Right Church But The Wrong Pew
You've Been A Good Old Wagon But You Done
    Broke Down
Zoot Suit, For My Sunday Gal, A

BLUES

W.C. Handy was born in 1873. He wrote his "Memphis Blues" in 1909. It was published in 1912. Ragtime was on the wane. It was Handy who first popularized the type of song known as the Blues. He also wrote St. Louis Blues. Blues and Rags numbered in the hundreds. They are difficult to differentiate. Handy died in 1958.

Listed below are songs pertaining to Blues. Current prices can be found in Chapter l.

Alcoholic Blues, The
All Alone Again Blues
Atlanta Blues
Aunt Agar Blues
Baby Sister Blues
Basement Blues, The
Basin Street Blues
Beale St. Blues
Birth Of The Blues, The
Blacksmith Blues, The
Blame It On The Blues
Blue Danube Blues
Blue Evening Blues
Blue Gummed Blues
Bow Wow Blues
Broadway Blues
Broken-Hearted Blues
Bye Bye Blues
Charleston Blues
Cheerful Blues
Chinese Blues
Cry-Baby Blues
Dallas Blues
Dardanella Blues, The
Don't Take Away Those Blues
Doo Dah Blues
East Of St. Louis Blues
Everybody's Crazy 'Bout The Doggone Blues, But
    I'm Happy
Farmyard Blues
Flapper Blues, The
Friendless Blues

Ginger Blues
Golden Brown Blues
Gypsy Blues
Hesitation Blues
Home Again Blues
Hot Lips
I Ain't Got Nobody
I Ain't Got Nothin' But The Blues
I Told You So
I Used To Love You But It's All Over Now
I've Got The Profiteering Blues
I've Got The Right To Sing The Blues
Jazz Me Blues
Jimmies Mean Mama Blues
Joe Turner Blues
Jogo Blues
John Henry Blues
Left All Alone Again Blues
Lighthouse Blues, The
Lonesome Mama Blues
Long Lost Mamma Daddy Misses You
Love Ain't Nothin' But The Blues
Lovely Love Blues
Mad About Him, Sad Without Him, How Can I Be
    Glad Without Him
Memphis Blues, The
Mississippi Valley Blues, The
Old Piano Roll Blues, The
Paradise Blues
Pickaninny Blues
Pickaninny Waltz Lullaby Blues
Prohibition Blues
Promise Me Everything, Never Get Anything Blues
Quit Cryin' The Blues
Rock-A-Bye My Baby Blues
St. Louis Blues
Schoolhouse Blues, The
Sugar Blues
Sundown Blues
Swanee Blues
Take 'Em To The Door Blues
Tar Heel Blues, The
Them Dog Gon'd Triflin' Blues
Those Saxophone Blues
Travelling Blues
Wall St. Blues
Wang Wang Blues
When You And I Were Young Maggie Blues
Yankee Doodle Blues
Yellow Dog Blues

DECO

Most historians believe that Art Deco was first introduced in 1909. Today most people believe it was a period during WWI & WWII. It has been called the age of "anything goes." The 20s were wild. Jewelry, clothing, furniture, paintings and yes sheet music covers were indicative of the times. Some of the sheet music covers depict musicals written by such great artists as Cole Porter, Jerome Kern, the Gershwins, Rogers and Hart to name a few. Music filled the air.

Song sheet covers were colorful and had much flair. The hair was bobbed, the skirts shorter, and women wore bright cosmetics. The war was over and we just "Let Ourselves Go." A very exciting time!

Listed below are songs pertaining to Deco. Current prices can be found in Chapter l.

Aba Daba Honeymoon, The
Adele
After It's Over Dear
After My Laughter Came Tears
After You've Gone
After You've Had Your Way
Ain't She Sweet?
Ain't You Coming Out Malinda?
Alabama Lullaby
Alice Blue Gown
All Aboard For Playland
All By Myself
All By Yourself In The Moonlight
All He Does Is Follow Them Around
All I Can Do Is Just Love You
All I Want Is You
All Or Nothing At All
All That I'm Asking Is Sympathy
Along The Way To Waikiki
Always In All Ways
And He'd Say "Oo-La-La Wee-Wee"
Anything You Say
Anytime Is Loving Time
Are You Lonesome To-night?
Arms Of Love
Arrah Go On I'm Gonna Go Back To Oregon
As Long As The World Goes Round
At A Perfume Counter, On The Rue De La Paix
At The Ball That's All
Auf Wiedersehn, But Not Goodbye
Auf Wiedersehn My Dear
Avalon Town
Babes In The Wood
Baby Face
Barcelona
Back-Water Daughter
Beautiful
Beautiful Land Of Somewhere
Because Of You
Because They All Love You
Bells
Beloved
Besame Mucho
Beyond The Blue Horizon
Birds Of A Feather
Birth Of The Blues, The
Blue Grass
Blue Shadows
Brazilian Rose
Breath O'Spring
Bridge, The
Bright Eyes
Broadway Rose
Broken Hearted Melody
Bubbling Over

By The Beautiful Sea
Bye & Bye, You'll See The Sun A-Shining
Cabaret Rag
Call Me Baby
Canadian Capers
Can't You Understand
Caresses
Carolina Moon
Castle Of Dreams
Cathedral Echoes
Cathedral Morning Chimes
Cecilia
Charley My Boy
Charmaine
Checkers
Chiquita
Chopsticks
Cinda Lou
Climbing Up The Scale
Cocktails For Two
Collegiate
Come Along
Come On Over
Cover Me Up With Sunshine
Crooning
Cutey, Who Tied Your Tie?
Dainty Demoiselles
Dancing Doll
Dancing Shadows
Dancing Tambourine
Darktown Dancin' School
Darned If The Fellows Can Do Without The Girls,
     Girls, Girls
Daughter Of Two Worlds, A
Dear Heart
Dearest, You're The Nearest To My Heart
Deep In The Arms Of Love
Dengozo Famous Parisian Maxixe
Dinah
Do What Your Mother Did, I'll Do The Same As Your
     Dad
Do You Ever Think Of Me
Don't Cry Baby
Don't Cry Little Girl
Don't Leave Me Daddy
Don't Wake Me Up, I Am Dreaming
Don't Waste Your Tears Over Me
Don't You Think You'd Better Let Me Try?
Down In My Heart My Darling
Dream Daddy
Dream Kisses
Dream Of Love And You
Dream Sweetheart
Dreamer Of Dreams
Dreaming Of The Same Old Girl
Dreamland Brings Memories Of You
Dreams Of Love
Drifting
Drifting On
Ecstatic
Evening Whispers
Everybody Loves A Chicken

Everyone In Town Likes Mary
Faded Love Letters
Falling
Farewell
Five Semi-Classic Ballads
Flag At Sundown, The
Flapper Blues, The
Follow The Swallow
For Every Girl Who Is Anyone's Girl, There Is
     Always Somebody To Blame
For Every Tear You've Shed, I'll Bring A Million
     Smiles
For-Get-Me-Not
For Johnny And Me
For My Baby
For The Sake Of A Rose
For The Sake Of Auld Lang Syne
For You Alone
For You And Me
Forgive Me
Forgiveness, We'll All Need Forgiveness Someday
Foxy Fox Trot
Fraternity Blues
From One Till Two I Always Dream Of You
Futurist, The
Garden Dance, A
Garden Of Dreams
Gee But I'm Lonesome
Georgette
Georgia Pines
Geraldine
Get Out And Get Under The Moon
Girls Of My Dreams, The
Give Me A Moment, Please
Give Me The Right To Love You
Glad Rag Doll
Gliding Thru The Shadows
Golden Gate Open For Me
Golden Girl Of My Dreams
Good-Bye Happy Days
Good-Bye Little Girl Of My Dreams
Good-Bye My Canada
Good For Nothin But Love
Good Luck Mary
Good Night Little Girl Of My Dreams
Gorgeous
Grace & Beauty Waltzes
Half Way To Heaven
Hand Of Friendship
Handle Me With Care
Hands Up!
Happiness
Happy Days Are Here Again
Hawaiian Butterfly
Heart Aches
Heart Of Humanity
Hearts Of Promise Waltzes
He'd Keep On Saying Good-Night
Hello Cutie
Hello Frisco
Helmaredi Waltz
Here In My Arms

Here's A Kiss
Here's Hoping
He's A Dear Old Pet
Hesitation
Hesitation Con Amore
Hesitation D'Amour
Hidden Pearls
Hold Me
Home Again Blues
Home And You
Homestead On The Hill
Honest And Truly
Honey
Honey-Bun
Honey Bunch
Honeymoon Bells
Honolulu Moon
Hooks & Eyes
Hop, Hop, Hop
Hours I Spent With You, The
How Am I To Know
How Can You Blame Me
Humming
I Bid You Good-Bye Forever
I Called You My Sweetheart
I Can't Believe That You're In Love With Me
I Can't Remember The Words
I Could Say Goodnight To A Thousand Girls
I Didn't Think You'd Care
I Found A Four Leaf Clover
I Found A Rose In The Devil's Garden
I Found You Just In Time
I Hate To Lose You
I Keep My Wife In The City & Make Love To Her Myself
I Like A Girl With A Smile Like You
I Like It Better Everyday
I Like To Do It
I Live In Turkey
I Love No One But You
I Love To Tango With My Tea
I Love You, I Love You, I Love You Sweetheart Of
     All My Dreams
I Never Knew How Much I Loved You
I Never Knew I Could Love Anybody, Like I'm
     Loving You
I Wanna Go Where You Go, Do What You Do–Then
     I'll Be Happy
I Want A Boy To Love Me
I Want To Be Good, But They Won't Let Me
I Want To Be Loved Like A Baby
I Want To Go To The Land Where The Sweet Daddies
     Grow
I Want To Linger
I Wish You Were Jealous Of Me
I Wish You'd Keep Out Of My Dreams
I Wonder
I Wonder If You Still Care For Me
I Wonder What's Become Of Joe?
I Wonder Who's Next In Your Heart
I'd Do The Same Thing A Million Times
I'd Like To But I Won't
I'd Like To Wander Back Again To Kidland

I'd Love To Call You My Sweetheart
I'd Rather Be The Girl In Your Arms
If I Can't Have You
If I Could Gain The World By Wishing, I Would Only
    Wish For You
If I Had A Girl Like You
If I Had My Way
If I Had You
If It Wasn't For You I Wouldn't Be Crying Now
If The Rose Could Tell It's Story
If They Don't Stop Making Them So Beautiful
If We Could Always Live In Dreams
If You Don't Think So You're Crazy
If You Were My Girl
I'll Always Remember You
I'll Be Hard To Handle
I'll Be Your Valentine
I'll Get By, As Long As I Have You
I'll See You In My Dreams
I'm A Dreamer That's Chasing Bubbles
I'm A Lonesome Melody
I'm All Bound 'Round The Mason-Dixon Line
I'm Coming Back To You
I'm Coming Back To You, Maybe
I'm Crazy About It
I'm Glad You're Sorry
I'm Going Home To Mobile On The Morgan Line
I'm In Heaven When I'm In Your Arms
I'm Lonesome For You Caroline
I'm On A See-Saw
I'm Only Making Believe
I'm So Melancholy
I'm Sorry Sally
I'm Tickled Pink With A Blue Eyed Baby
In A Little Spanish Town
In A Red Rose Garden
In After Years
In My Bouquet Of Memories
In The Dusk
In The Heart Of A Fool
In The Old Town Hall
In The Valley Of The Moon
Isle Of Beautiful Dreams
It Might Have Been You
It's Not The First Time You Left Me
I've Been Floating Down That Old Green River
I've Got A Feeling I'm Falling
I've Got A New Love Affair
Jake, Jake, The Yiddisher Ball Player
Japanese Moon
Jazz Baby
Jeanie With The Light Brown Hair
Josephine
Just A Girl Like You
Just Because You're You–That's Why I Love You
Just Once Again
Just To See You Once Again
Just You
Just You And Me
Katinka
Keep Your Eye On The Girlie You Love
Kentucky Rose

King For A Day
Kiss Me Dearie
Kiss Me, My Sweetheart
La Mexicain
Land O'Dreams
Last Night I Dreamed You Kissed Me
Last Year's Roses
Laugh With A Tear In It, The
Leave Me With A Smile
Leg Of Nations, The
Lend Me Your Heart & I'll Lend You Mine
Let It Rain! Let It Pour!
Let Me Linger Longer In Your Arms
Let Not Your Heart Be Troubled
Let's Begin
Let's Go To Cuba
Let's Say Goodnight To The Ladies
Life Of A Rose, The
Lila
Linger Awhile
List'ning On Some Radio
Little Angel Told Me So, A
Little Princess
Lonesome And Sorry
Love Keeps The World Young
Love Song, The
Love That Belongs To Me, The
Magnolia
Make A Name For Yourself
Mamma Loves Papa, Papa Loves Mamma
Mary Ann
Mary From Maryland
Mary, I'm In Love With You
Mary Lou
Masquerade
Mauvourneen, Mauvourneen From Dear Old Killarney
Me And The Man In The Moon
Me, Myself And I
Me Too-Ho-Ho! Ha-Ha!
Mean To Me
Mello Cello
Memories
Merry Widow Waltz
Midnight Waltz, The
Mimi
Mistakes
Mister Yoddlin Man
Moment's Hesitation, A
Mon Homme
Mother, A Word That Means The World To Me
Mother, Dixie And You
Mother My Own
Music Vots Music Must Come From Berlin
My Beloved Waltzes
My Chain Of Memories
My Darling
My Gal, She Has Some Wonderful Ways
My Idea Of A Good Little Girl Is A Girl Who Is Good
    To Me
My Lady Walks In Loveliness
My Long Lost Love
My Sunny Tennessee

My Virginian
My Wonderful Dream Of You
Myopia Fox Trot
Nestle In Your Daddy's Arms
Neutral
Nine O'clock Sal
No No Nora
No One Could Do It Like My Father
No Wonder
Nobody Lied
Oh Baby
Oh How I Miss You Tonight
Oh! Mother I'm Wild
Oh You Mr. Moon
Old Fashioned Roses
Old Pal, Why Don't You Answer Me?
Old Spinning Wheel, The
On A Little Bamboo Bridge
On A Summery Night
Once In A Lifetime
Peach Of A Pair, A
Pioneer
Plantation Lullaby
Play That Song Of India Again
Pleasant Dreams
Please, Please, Pretty Please
Poppyland
Pork And Beans
Practice Makes Perfect
Precious
Precious Little Thing Called Love, A
Prelude In C Sharp Minor
Promises
Prunella
Put Away A Little Ray Of Golden Sunshine
Ragtime Violin, The
Raquel
Red Lips Kiss My Blues Away
Red Moon
Red Rose Of Love Bloom Again
Remember The Rose
Rock-A-Bye Lullabye Mammy
Rock-A-Bye Moon
Russian Lullaby
Salted Peanuts Rag
San Francisco Glide
Sans Toi
Say Something Sweet To Your Sweetheart
Scaramouche
Sea Gardens
She Got Even with Stephen
She's A Mean Job
Shimmie Town
Show Me The Way To Go Home
Since It Started To Rain In Lover's Lane
Sing Me A Baby Song
Skating Waltzes, The
Sleepy Hollow Rag
Sleepy Lagoon
Sleepy Time Gal
Smoke Gets In Your Eyes
Some Day I'll Make You Glad

Someday You'll Say O.K.
Some Night Soon
Some Sweet Day
Somebody Else Took You Out Of My Arms
Somebody To Somebody
Someone Is Losin' Susan
Something Had To Happen
Song Is Ended But The Melody Lingers On, The
Sophisticated Swing
Southern Rose
Spain
Speak To Me Of Love
Spotlight Of Love, The
Steal A Little Kiss While Dancing
Stolen Kisses
Sue Simmons, Bill's Sister
Sun Is At My Window, The
Sweet Ella May
Sweet Suzanne
Sweetheart
Sweethearts On Parade
Syncopate
Syncopated Vamp, The
Take In The Sun, Hang Out The Moon
Take Me To The Land Of Jazz
Tackin' Em Down
Tell Me Little Gypsy
That Certain Party
That Naughty Melody
That Naughty Waltz
That Wonderful Kid From Madrid
That's A Good Girl
That's Ever Loving Love
That's How I Believe In You
That's The Kind Of Baby For Me
That's What I'd Do For You
There's A Broken Heart For Every Light On
　　Broadway
There's A Garden Of Eden In Sweden
There's A Girl That's Meant For Me, In The Heart Of
　　Tennessee
There's A Key To Every Heart
There's A Little Bit Of Bad In Every Good Little Girl
There's A Little Spark Of Love Still Burning
There's A Million Reasons Why I Shouldn't Kiss You
There's A Vacant Chair At Home Sweet Home
There's Something About A Rose
Think It Over, Mary
This Ain't The Place I Thought It Was
Three O'Clock In The Morning
Three Treasures
Till We Meet
Time Will Tell
Ting-A-Ling
Tiny-Town
Tired Of Me
Tonight You Belong To Me
Too Many Parties
Toodle Oodle Oo
Touch Of Your Hand, The
24 Hours A Day
Ty-Tee, Tahiti

Underneath The Russian Moon
Valley Of Roses
Waltzing
We Have Much To Be Thankful For
We Just Couldn't Say Goodbye
What A Wonderful Wedding That Will Be
What Can I Say After I Say I'm Sorry
What Did Romeo Say To Juliet When He Climbed
　　The Balcony?
What Do I Care What Somebody Said
What Do We Do On A Dew-Dew-Dewy Day
What More Can A Woman Give
What Will I Do Without You
When I Dream In The Moonlight Of You
When I Get Back To My Old Girl
When I Got Back To My Old Home Town
When I Think Of You
When Lights Are Low
When It's Moonlight On The Swanee Shore
When Sally In Our Alley Sings Those Old Time Songs
　　To Me
When The Dew Is On The Rose
When The Poppies Bloom Again
When The Sun Goes Down In Romany
When They Gather The Sheaves, Mary Dear
When Tony Goes Over The Top
When You Fall In Love, Fall In Love With Me
When You Walked Out Someone Else Walked Right In
When Your Hair Has Turned To Silver
Where The Lazy Daisies Grow
While We Danced At The Mardi Gras
Who Wouldn't Be Blue
Who'll Take My Place When I'm Gone
Who's Wonderful, Who's Marvelous Miss Annabelle
　　Lee
Whose Little Heart Are You Breaking Now?
Why Dance?
Why Did I Kiss That Girl
Why Did You Go Away
Why Didn't You Leave Me Years Ago
Why Do I Care For You
Why Should I Cry Over You
With You, My Own
Yankee Rose
Yearning Just For You
Yes Sir! That's My Baby
Yesterday
Yoo-Hoo
You Ain't Got The Right Kind Of Hair
You Are The Rose I'm Longing For
You Don't Like It–Not Much
You Gotta Know How
You Know You Belong To Somebody Else
You Left Me So Blue
You Mean All That & More To Me
You Must Come Over To-Night
You Never Can Tell
You Only Want Me When You're Lonesome
You Ought To See My Baby
You Remind Me Of My Mother
You Try Somebody Else, We'll Be Back Together
　　Again

You're A Better Man Than I Am, Gunga Din
You're Breaking My Heart With "Good-bye"
You're Devastating
You're Driving Me Crazy
You're Just A Show Off
You're Like A Rose To Me
You're Some Pretty Doll
You're The One I Care For
You're The Only Girl That Made Me Cry
You've Got A Lot To Answer For

DEDICATION

Songs were dedicated to politicians, movie stars, the Army of Noble Women, mothers, wives, children, Presidents, the guy who slept in the bunk next to a soldier, sisters and sweethearts who were doing their bit for the war effort on the home front, humane treatment of the battle wounded, and protection granted by the Red Cross flag to name a few.

Listed below are songs pertaining to Dedication. Current prices can be found in Chapter l.

Aba Daba Honeymoon, The, Dedicated To Jack Lee
　　and Betty Delaney
Admiral Dewey's March, Dedicated To Rear Admiral
　　Dewey
All Aboard For Blanket Bay, Dedicated To Little Raymond Sterling
American Beauty, Dedicated To Nanette Lehman
Angel God Sent From Heaven, The, Dedicated To Red
　　Cross Nurse
Angels Of Mercy, Dedicated to the American Red
　　Cross
Anglo-Saxon Race, The, Dedicated to The Cause Of
　　World Peace
Autumn Leaves, Dedicated to Mr. Glenmore N. Snyder, Wilkes Barre, Pa.
Ave Maria, Dedicated to Wm. Berge
Back To God's Country, Dedicated To Nell Shipman
Battle Song Of Prohibition: Respectfully Dedicated To
　　My Brother, Rev. F.F. Farmilse, Whose Voice,
　　Together With The Voices Of All Who Love To
　　Rescue The Tempted Or Fallen, Is Ever In
　　Defense Of Our Loved Homes, And Against Their
　　Great Enemy, The Saloons. May They Not Be
　　Silent Until These Strongholds Of Sin Are Blotted
　　From The Land We Would Leave Our Children.
Bebe, Dedicated To Bebe Daniels
Biggest Thing In A Soldier's Life Is The Letter That
　　Comes From Home, The, Dedicated to K.C.B.
Billy, Dedicated To Our Friend Billy Single Clifford
Billy Dear, Dedicated To Miss Florence Bindley
Bird Song, Dedicated To Audubon Society Of America
Blue Diamonds, Dedicated To Baby Margaret
Bombardier Song, The, Dedicated To The Bomber
　　Crews Of The U.S. Army Air Forces
Bonnie Sweet Bessie, Dedicated To Miss Sadie J.
　　Laws
Broken Blossoms, Dedicated To D.W. Griffith
Brownie Rag, The, Dedicated To Miss Bessie Wood
　　Stewart

By The Bend Of The River, Dedicated To Caroline Andrews

By The Waters Of Minnetonka, Dedicated To Alfred Williams

Call, The, Dedicated To. F.W. Kellogg

Calling Me Home To You, Dedicated To Reginald Kelland

Call Of The Flag, The, Dedicated To Our Soldiers–Gift Of Mrs. L.D. Westfield. To American Legion Auxiliary

Cashmere, Dedicated To Miss Helen Powers

Charley My Boy, Dedicated To Charley Foy

Checkers, Dedicated To Winnie Sheehan

College Life, Dedicated To The College Students Of America

Commodore Dewey's Victory March, Dedicated To The American Heroes Of The Battle Of Manila

Comrades In Arms, Dedicated To Mr. Harold S. Brigham

Crescent Schottische, Dedicated To Bessie Mackenzie

Daddy Long Legs, Dedicated To Mary Pickford

Deep Purple, Dedicated To Doris Rhodes

Did I Remember, Dedicated To Jean Harlow

Dodge Brothers March, Dedicated By Mr. Herbert To Mr. Horace Dodge In Respectful Appreciation Of His Generous Efforts Towards The Advancement Of American Music

Dream, A, Dedicated To Miss Gertrude Edmands

Each Stitch Is A Thought Of You Dear, Dedicated To That Army Of Noble Women–Mothers–Sisters And Sweethearts Who Are Doing Their Bit For The Boys "Over There"

East, West, Hame's Best, Dedicated To Scots Everywhere

Echoes Of The Wildwoods, Dedicated To B.G. Mickel

Elaine, My Moving Picture Queen, Dedicated To Pearl White

Eleanor: A Serenade, Dedicated To My Friend Rae Eleanor Ball

Everybody Loves A Chicken, Dedicated To Miss Mazie Elliotte

Fairy Wedding, Dedicated To Gen Tom Thumb & Wife

Farewell, My Loved Ones, Dedicated To Mrs. Wm. G. Dennis

For The Freedom Of The World. Dedication: To All The Allies, Each And Every Nation, To The Splendid Soldier In The Trenches And The Brave Woman At Home: To All Who Have Made Their Sacrifice For The Freedom Of The World, Is This Song Dedicated.

Gee! But I'm Crazy For The Summertime, Dedicated To Monponsett & Its Many Charms

Gee But I'm Lonesome, Dedicated To Harry C. Husted, Bridgeport, Conn.

General Sherman's Funeral March, Dedicated To His Bereaved Family

Give A Little Credit To The Navy, Dedicated To Commander Buel Franklin, USNRF

Go To Sleep My Baby That's The Nicest Way To Say Good Night, Dedicated To Ida Robe

Golden Gate, March & Two Step, Dedicated To The Panama Pacific International Exposition, San Francisco

Good-Bye Boys, Dedicated To Edwin A. Starn

Good Night, Dedicated To Mr. Victor W. Sincere

Great American, The, Theodore Roosevelt, Dedicated To The American Legion & In Memory Of Theodore Roosevelt

Heartsease, Dedicated To Tom Moore

Heaven Born Banner, The, Dedicated To The School Children Of America

Hello Everybody, Dedicated To Roxy & His Gang

Her Greatest Charm, Dedicated To Miss Julia Putnam

He's Our "Al", Dedicated To Hon. Alfred E. Smith

Hewitt's Quick Step, Dedicated To Lieut. James L. Hewitt, Officers & Members Of New York Light Guard

His Lullaby, Dedicated To Madame Schumann Heink

Home Run Polka, Dedicated To The National Baseball Club Of Washington, D.C.

Hoodlum, The, Dedicated To Mary Pickford

Hush My Baby Go To Sleep, Dedicated By Permission Of Mrs. President Harrison To Master Ben Harrison McKee

I Could Moon Forever Round A Star Like You, Dedicated To Maude Raymond

I Didn't Raise My Boy To Be A Soldier, Dedicated To Every Mother Everywhere

I Hate to See Those Summer Days Roll By, Dedicated To Miss Queenie Elliotte

I Like To Call You Sweetheart, Dedicated To Miss Lulu Von Welden

I Long To See My Mother's Face Again, Dedicated To Geo S. Gates Esq.

If I Had You, Dedicated To Bertha Leigh Leonard

I'll Be With You In Apple Blossom Time, Dedicated To Mme Emma Trentini

In Holland, Dedicated By The Composer To Her Royal Majesty Queen Wilhelmina Of Holland

In The Heart Of A Rose, Dedicated To Miss Clara Inge

In The Meadow, Dedicated To Joseph Diskay

Iron Division, The, Dedicated To 28th Division

It's A Long Way To Berlin But We'll Get There, Dedicated To Lieut. Joseph E. Barrell & Lieut Eugene J. Orsenigo, 71st, N.Y.

I've Got The Blues For My Kentucky Home, Dedicated To Flo Bert Of Brendel & Bert

Jerry–You Warra A Warrior In The War, Dedicated To Jerry Vogel

Just As The Boat Went Down, Dedicated To The Heroes Who Went Down With The World's Largest Ship

Just Lonesome, Dedicated To Harriet

Khaki Boys Of U.S.A., The, Dedicated To 104th Regiment U.S. Infantry

King Of The Air, Dedicated By Permission To Mr. Glenn H. Curtis, The Famous Aviator

Kitty, Dedicated To Mr. James H. Foster, Cleveland, Ohio

Let Lovelight Be Always Shining, For The Loved Ones Away, Dedicated To John G. Gowans

Let The Rest Of The World Go By, Dedicated To Julie & Carrie

Little Bit O'Honey, A, Dedicated To Miss Lucile M. Showalter

Lilac Blossoms, Dedicated To Mrs. E.B. Davis

Little Em'ly, Dedicated To John H. Selwyn, Esq.

Little Log Cabin Of Dreams, Dedicated To Mary Cook Cowerd

Little Pink Rose, A, Dedicated In Memory Of Little Bernice

Little Sweetheart I'm So Lonely, Dedicated To Miss Ethel Briggs

Lobster's Promenade, The, Dedicated To My Friend D.L. James

Lonely Troubadour, Dedicated To Rudy Vallee

Long Ago Rose, Dedicated To W.C. Durant, In Memory Of His Mother And Mine

Love's Golden Star, Dedicated To Miss Marguerite Britton Rudy

Love's Young Dream, Dedicated To Shirley Temple

Lydia, Dedicated To Merle Oberon

Ma Jet Black Lady, Dedicated To Miss Leonore Dunn

Marine Review, The, Dedicated To The Renowned Leaders Of The U.S. Marine Band

Memories Of France, Dedicated To Our Pals In The American Legion, We Dedicate This Refrain. If It Makes But One Of You Happy, It Was Not Written In Vain., Al Dubin 305th F. A. 7th Division

Mickey, Dedicated To Mabel Normand

Mine, Dedicated To Mr. William Wade Hinshaw

Moon Mother, Dedicated To Mr. Louis W. Fickett

Moose Rag, Dedicated To Loyal Order Of Moose

Mother Was My Best Friend, Dedicated To Mrs. Lettia Power

Mulligan Guard, Dedicated To Mr. Josh Hart

My Buddy, Dedicated To Irene Hart

My Homeland, Dedicated To My Friend Clarence Whitehill

My Star, Dedicated To My Friend Grace Harriman

NC-4 March, Dedicated To Commander A.C. Read, U.S. Navy

New Liberty, The, Dedicated To Miss Jessie Thorburn Gowan, Sask., Canada

Oh! How I Hate To Get Up In The Morning, Dedicated To My Friend, Private Howard Friend Who Occupies The Cot Next To Mine And Feels As I Do About The Bugler

Oh! Min, Dedicated To Mrs. Sidney Smith

On The Bright Golden Shore, Dedicated To Miss Nella S. Phillips, Springfield, Mass.

Operatic Rag, Dedicated To Arthur Anderson, New York

Our Protectors March, Dedicated To W.T. Cheswell

Out Of The Tempest, Dedicated To John Barrymore

Out On The Bounding Deep, by Jeffries, Dedicated To The Darlings, A Family Of Fishers And Childhood Friends Of The Composer

Pale Moon, Dedicated To Miss Rosa Raisa

Path Of Flowers, Dedicated To The Rev. John B. Gough Pidge

Peg O'My Heart, Dedicated To Laurette Taylor

Peter Pan I Love You, Dedicated To Miss Marilyn Miller

Phantom Isle, Dedicated To Miss Corinne Miller

Poor Little Rich Girl, The, Dedicated To Miss Viola Dana

Pulaski Quick Step, Dedicated To General J.L.C. Amee

Purple Roses, Dedicated To Glenn Miller

Ramona, Dedicated To Dolores Del Rio

Red Moon, Dedicated To Marie Traver

Red Rose Of Love Bloom Again, Dedicated To Rosalind

Revenge, Dedicated To Dolores Del Rio

Rose Mary, Dedicated To Rose Mary

Rose Of California, The, Dedicated To Mr. Victor Eckland, Reading, Pa.

Rose Of No Mans Land, The, Dedicated To The Red Cross Nurse

Sandman, The, Dedicated To Marie White Longman

School Life, Dedicated To All Schools

Sesqui-Centennial Hymn, The, Dedicated To The American People

Sleepy Valley, Dedicated To Miss Betty Meehan

Song Of The Bayou, Dedicated To Miss Taddy Keller

Song Of The Hills, A, Lovingly Dedicated To Marcella Craft

Song Of The Robin, Dedicated To J. Frank Beal, Brocton, MA.

Soul Of You, The, Dedicated To Madame Mariska Aldrich

Spring Song, Dedicated To Mrs. E. Humphrey-Allen & Mr. C.N. Allen

Study In Symbols, A, Dedicated To Mrs. O.L. Fox

Sun, The Heather And You, The Dedicated To June Barr

Sunshine, Dedicated To My Friend Sid Grauman At Whose Theatre In Hollywood, California, It Was First Introduced

Take Me Back To The Garden Of Love, Dedicated To Miss Mabel McKinley

Tears Of Love, Dedicated To Norma Talmage

There Is Ever A Song Somewhere, Dedicated To Litta Grimm

There's A Lark In My Heart, Dedicated To Anna Case

There's An Angel Missing From Heaven, Dedicated To The American Red Cross

They Needed A Songbird In Heaven So They Took Caruso Away, Dedicated To Memory Of Our Beloved Caruso

Tiger Rose, Dedicated To Miss Lenor Ulric

To A Hill-Top, Dedicated To Mr. & Mrs. George M. Hendee

To Victory, Dedicated To The Mothers Of Defenders Of Democracy

Toward The Sunrise, Dedicated To Miss Cecile Battiar

Trees, Dedicated To L.L. Krebs

U.S. Field Artillery March, The, Dedicated To Officers And Men Of the 306th Field Artillery, National Army, U.S.A.

U.S.A. March, Dedicated To Our Army And Navy

Underneath The Cotton Moon, Dedicated To Our Esteemed Friend Mr. Ben Linn

Until God's Day, Dedicated To Mr. Charles W. Clark

Valse Danseuse, Dedicated To Mrs. Sam Fox

Vanity, Dedicated To Miss Lillian Ludman

Vanity Fair, Dedicated To Mr. George A. Kingsbury

Weep Not For The Dead, Dedicated To John Chipman

We'll Knock The Heligo-Into-Heligo-Out Of Heligoland, Dedicated To The Men Of The American Fleet

Were I, Dedicated To Amelia Galli-Curci

When Church Is Out, Dedicated To Mrs. E. P. Doty

When God Puts Out The Light, Dedicated To Mr. & Mrs. Whitney

When I Marry You, Dedicated To Miss Gertrude Davidson

When I'm Thru With The Arms Of The Army, Dedicated To My Sweetheart Mrs. Earl Carroll

When The Robin Sings Again, Dedicated To Miss Pearl Lillian Townes

When The Steamboats On The Swanee Whistle Rag-Time: Respectfully Dedicated To The Memory Of Happy O'Neill

When You Come Back, Dedicated To My Friend George Macfarlane

Where The Shandon Bells Are Ringing I'll Be Waiting Sweet Eileen, Dedicated To The Knights Of Columbus Of Worcester, MA.

Why Did They Take My Daddy, Dedicated To All The Little Kiddies With Dads In The Service

Will You Wait Little Girl For Me, Dedicated To The National Guard

Won't You Go Back To Your Old Girl From Your Home Town, Dedicated To Florence Wescott

Yale March, The, Dedicated To John Philip Sousa

Yankee Doodle Boy, The: Dedicated With Statue Of George M. Cohan by Georg Lober, Erected In Times Square & Presented To The City Of New York On Sept. 11, 1959 by George M. Cohan Memorial Committee

You And Love, Dedicated To Victor Maurel

You Can't Get Lovin' When There Ain't Any Love, Dedicated To Aileen Stanley

Yours, Dedicated To Miss Dorothy Overmire

DISNEY TUNES

Walter Disney was an American producer of motion picture sound cartoons. Born in Chicago, Illinois, December 5, 1901, he was the creator of Mickey Mouse, Donald Duck, Goofy and Pluto. He grew up on a Missouri farm. His formal art instruction was limited to brief courses at the Chicago Art Academy and the Kansas City Art Institute, but he has received honorary degrees from many universities. After World War I, in which he served in France as a Red Cross ambulance driver, he began producing cartoon slides, called Laugh-O-Grams. Disney formed and became president of Walt Disney Productions, Limited, in 1928, producers of Mickey Mouse and Silly Symphony cartoons. Mickey Mouse became popular in Steamboat Willie, the first cartoon to use sound. Among the better-known short subjects which Disney has produced are: Trees and Flowers, the first film cartoon in Technicolor (1932); Three Little Pigs (1933); The Tortoise and the Hare (1934); Three Orphan Kittens (1935); and The Country Cousin (1936). Walt Disney later turned to producing feature-length cartoons. Snow White and the Seven Dwarfs appeared in 1937,

Pinocchio in 1939, and Fantasia in 1940. His Ferdinand the Bull and Bambi are among the cartoons which feature the larger animals. Fantasia entered a new field in motion picture production – the combination of classical music with interpretive cartoons. On Feb. 22, 1950, his cartoon Cinderella was released. Almost invariably rich in color and humor, Disney's cartoons represent a distinct artistic achievement for which he has received many Academy awards.

Listed below are songs pertaining to Walt Disney. Current prices can be found in Chapter 1.

Alice In Wonderland

All Aboard

All In A Golden Afternoon

All The Cats Join In

Angel May Care

Apple Song, The

As I Was Saying To The Duchess

Baby Mine

Baia

Bibbidi-Bobbidi-Boo

Bluddle-Uddle-Um-Dum

Blue Shadows On The Trail

Brazil

Casey, The Pride Of Them All

Caucus Race, The

Chim, Chim Cher-ee

Cinderella

Der Fuehrer's Face

Dream Is A Wish Your Heart Makes, A

Dwarfs' Yodel Song, The

Everybody Has A Laughing Place

Fee-Fi-Fo-Fum

Fun And Fancy Free

Give A Little Whistle

Headless Horseman, The

Heigh-Ho

Hi-Diddle-Dee-Dee

How Do You Do?

I Bring You A Song

Ichabod

I'm A Happy Go Lucky Fellow

I'm Late

I'm Wishing

In A World Of My Own

It's Watcha Do With Whatcha Got

I've Got No Strings

Jiminy Cricket

Johnny Fedora And Alice Blue Bonnet

Katrina

Lavender Blue

Lazy Countryside

Let The Rain Pour Down

Let's Sing A Gay Little Spring Song

Little April Shower

Little Toot

Little Wooden Head

Look Out For Mr. Stork

Lord Is Good To Me, The

Love Is A Song

March Of The Cards

Melody Time
Merrily On Our Way
Mexico
My Favorite Dream
One Song
Painting The Roses Red
Pecos Bill
Pink Elephants On Parade
Pinocchio
Pioneer Song, The
Say It With A Slap
Snow White
So Dear To My Heart
So This Is Love
Some Day My Prince Will Come
Song Of The South
Sooner Or Later
Spoon Full Of Sugar, A
Stick-To-It-Ivity
Three Caballeros, The
Three Cheers For Anything
Too Good To Be True
Turn On The Old Music Box
Two Silhouettes
Uncle Remus Said
Very Good Advice
Walrus And The Carpenter, The
When I See An Elephant Fly
When You Wish Upon A Star
Whistle While You Work
Who Wants To Live Like That
Who's Afraid Of The Big Bad Wolf
With A Smile And A Song
Without You
Work Song, The
You Belong To My Heart
You'll Always Be The One I Love
Zip-A-Dee-Doo-Dah

DIXIE

Dixie is a name associated in Negro minstrelsy with the Southern states. Listed below are songs about Dixie. Current prices can be found in Chapter 1.

Ain't You Coming Back To Dixieland
Alabama Jubilee
Alexander's Back From Dixie With His Rag-Time Band
Alexander's Band Is Back In Dixieland
All Aboard For Dixie Land
Anything Is Nice If It Comes From Dixieland
Are You From Dixie
At A Georgia Camp Meeting
At The Dixie Military Ball
At Uncle Tom's Cabin Door
Back To Dixieland
Beautiful Dixie Rose
Carry Me Back To Old Virginny
Come Back, Dixie
'Cross The Mason-Dixon Line
Dear Old Dixie

Dixie
Dixie Coon Brigade, The
Dixie Daisy
Dixie Darlings
Dixie Dimples
Dixie Doodle
Dixie Highway
Dixie, I Wish I Was In Dixie's Land
Dixie I'm Coming Back To You
Dixie Land
Dixie Land, I Love You
Dixie Lullaby
Dixie Moon
Dixie Volunteers, The
Dixieland Band, The
Down At The Huskin' Bee
Down Georgia Way
Entertainer's Rag, The
Everybody's Crazy Over Dixie
For Dixie And Uncle Sam
Goodbye Dixie Goodbye
Goodbye Dixie Lee
Good Morning Dixieland
Happy Days In Dixie
How's Every Little Thing In Dixie
I Guess I'll Soon Be Back In Dixieland
I Just Came Back From Dear Old Dixie Land
I Lost My Heart In Dixieland
I Want A Dixie Sweetheart
I Want To Be In Dixie
I'll Be In My Dixie Home Again To-Morrow
I'll Be Waiting In The Gloaming, Sweet Genevieve
I'm All Bound Round With The Mason Dixon Line
I'm Coming Back To Dixie And You
I'm Going Back To Carolina
I'm Going Back To Dixie
I'm Gonna Spend My Honeymoon In Dixie
In Dear Old Tennessee
In Dixie Land With Dixie Lou
Is It True What They Say About Dixie?
It's A Hundred To One You're From Dixie
I've Got The Nicest Little Home In Dixie
Ladies Man–Dapper Dan From Dixie Land, The
Let My Home Be Your Home, When You're Down In Dixieland
Levee Land
Listen To That Dixie Band
Mammy Land
Mammy O'Mine
Mandy 'N' Me
Melon Time In Dixieland
Mississippi Steamboat
Moonlight Down In Dixie
Moonlight In Dixie
Mother, Dixie And You
Muskrat Ramble
My Dixie Rosary
My Mammy
My Man From Caroline
Open Up The Golden Gates To Dixieland
Pick Me Up & Lay Me Down In Dear Old Dixieland
Play Me A Dixie Melody

Rock-A-Bye To Sleep In Dixie
Rock-A-Bye Your Baby With A Dixie Melody
Seven-Eleven Or My Dixie Pair O'Dice
She Was Bred In Old Kentucky
She's Dixie All The Time
So This Is Dixie
Somebody's Coming To Town
Somewhere In Dixie Lives The Girl I Love
Strains From Dixieland
Struttin' With Some Barbecue, Dixieland Ragtime Blues
Sweetest Girl In Dixie
Take Me Back To Dixie
Take Me Back To Dear Old Dixie
That Dixie Glide
That Southern Hospitality, When You're Down In Dixie
There Are Two Eyes In Dixie
There's A Bungalo In Dixieland
There's A Dixie Girl Who's Longing For A Yankee Doodle Boy
There's A Lump Of Sugar Down In Dixie
There's Always Something Doin' Down In Dixie
There's Just A Little Touch Of Dixie In Your Eyes
They Made It Twice As Nice As Paradise And They Called It Dixieland
They'll Be Mighty Proud In Dixie Of Their Old Black Joe
They'll Never Miss The Wine In Dixieland
Tomorrow In My Dixie Home Again
Waitin' For The Moon
Warmin' Up In Dixie, A
Way Down There, A Dixie Boy Is Missing
When I Dream About That Southern Home Of Mine
When It's Nightime Down In Dixieland
When The Pines Of Alsace Whisper "Dixieland"
When The Sun Goes Down In Dixie
When Uncle Joe Plays A Rag On His Old Banjo
Whole World Comes From Dixie, The
You Can't Take Me Away From Dixie
You'll Find Old Dixieland In France
You're As Dear To Me As "Dixie" Was To Lee

INDIAN

The covers on Indian Sheet Music are very colorful and also collectable and scarce. "Red Wing" is the best loved of all tunes. It's first publication date was 1907. Kerry Mills and Thurland Chattaway were the composers. The most attractive cover, in our opinion is "Hiawatha's Melody Of Love." Cover artist is Frederick S. Manning.

Listed below are songs pertaining to Indians. Current prices can be found in Chapter 1.

Anona
Blue Feather
By The Waters Of Minnetonka
Dancing Starlight
Fawneyes
Geronimo
Glory Of Jamestown

Golden Girl
Goodbye Red Man Goodbye
Hail To The Redskins
Hiawatha
Hiawatha Waltz
Hiawatha's Lullaby
Hiawatha's Melody Of Love
Hobomoko
Indian Cradle Song
Indian Dawn
Indian Love Call
Indian Lullaby
Indian Rag
Indian Slumber Song
Indianola
Iola
Kachina–Hopi Girl's Dance
Kissamee
Laughing Water
Little Min-Nee-Ha-Ha
Longboat
Lovelight
Mohawk Trail, The
Moon Dear
Moonlight Dear
Moonlight Waltz
Mulberry Moon
My Indian Maiden
My Pretty Firefly
My Pretty Indian Maid
My Sweet Love Call
Navajo
Oh That Navajo Rag
Oklahoma, I Love You
Pale Moon
Pipe Of Peace, The
Plenty Hawk
Pretty Little Rainbow
Rainbow
Red Man
Red Wing
Sagamore
Seattle
Seminola
Sha-Wan-Da-Moo
Silver Bell
Singing Bird
Silver Heels, Indian Girl
That Indian Rag
Tomahawk
Wan-A-Tea
Wandalola
Whipoorwill, Indian Seranade
White Bird
Wildflower
Winona, An Indian Love Song

IRISH SONGS

Everyone seems to enjoy Irish melodies whether they be sad, happy or toe tapping tunes. Some of the Irish composers are: Chauncey Olcott, Frederick

Knight Logan, J. Kiern Brennan & Ernest Ball. A famous Irish tenor was John McCormack.

Listed below are Irish songs. Current prices can be found in Chapter l.

Acushla! I'm Calling Thee
Acushla Machree, Return In The Springtime
All That I Had And All That I Have And All That I
    Want Is In Ireland
Along The Rocky Road To Dublin
An Irish Song Will Live As Long As Life And Love
    Shall Last
Are You There, Moriarty?
As Long As The Shamrock Grows Green
Be Sure He's Irish Then Love Him In That Good Old
    Irish Way
Beautiful Dark Girl
Bedelia
Bit Of Blarney
Blarney
Bold Hibernian Boys
Bold McIntyres
Callahan's Gang
Captain Riley Of The U.S.A.
Carry Me Back To Connemara
Christmas In Killarney
Come Back, Kathleen
Come Back To Connemara
Come Back To Erin
Connemara Shore, The
Dancing 'Neath The Irish Moon
Danny Boy
Daughter Of Rosie O'Grady, The
Dear Old Donegal
Did Your Mother Come From Ireland
Do You Think I Came From Ireland In A Hack
Dolly O'Dean
Dorine Of Dublin
Down Went McGinty Dressed In His Best Suit Of
    Clothes
Dublin Rag, The
Eileen, From Old Killarney
Emmet's Love Of The Shamrock
Erin Beautiful Erin
Erin's Faith And Hope
Erin's Isle And You
Ev'ry Step Toward Killarney
Every Little Dog Must Have His Day
Every Tear Is A Smile In An Irishman's Heart
Everybody Loves An Irish Song
Everything At Reilly's Must Be Done In Irish Style
Eyes Of Irish Blue, The
Farewell Killarney
Finnegan Gave It To Me
For Freedom And Ireland
For Killarney And You
For The Wearing Of The Green
Four Leaf Clover
Galway Bay
Girl With A Brogue
Give Me A Honeymoon That's Irish
Goodbye Maggie Doyle

Good-Bye Mother Machree
Gramachree, Be True To Me
Happy Tom O'Day
Has Anybody Here Seen Kelly?
Hat Me Father Wore
Hat Me Father Wore On St. Patrick's Day, The
Have You Ever Been In Ireland In April?
Hippity Hop
How Are Things In Glocca Morra?
Hush, My Darlings, Do Not Weep
I Couldn't Go To Ireland, So Ireland Came To Me
I Hear You Calling Me
I Love The Name Of Mary
I Love To Hear An Irish Band Upon St. Patrick's Day
I Love You Kate In Ireland
I Never Liked O'Regan
I Owe $10.00 To O'Grady
Idol Of Erin, The
If I Knock The "L" Out Of Kelly
If It Wasn't For The Irish & The Jews
If They'd Only Move Old Ireland Over Here
If This Isn't Love
If You Believe In The Fairies
If You're Irish, Come Into The Parlor
I'll Be Back In Dear Old Dublin, The Day That
    Ireland's Free
I'll Take You Home Again Kathleen
I'm A Long Way From Tipperary
I'm Awfully Glad I'm Irish
I'm Building A Bridge To Ireland
I'm Going Back To Old Erin
I'm Going Back To Old Killarney
I'm Hearin' From Erin
I'm On My Way To Dublin-Bay
I'm Tickled To Death That You're Irish
In Dear Old Ireland
In The Heart Of An Irish Rose
In The Land Where The Shamrock Grows
In The Shadow Of The Dear Old Blarney Stone
Ireland Is Calling
Ireland Is Heaven To Me
Ireland Is Ireland To Me
Ireland Mother Ireland
Ireland Must Be Heaven For My Mother Came From
    There
Ireland, My Ireland
Ireland, We Sympathize With You
Ireland Will Go On Forever
Ireland's Loss Was Heaven's Gain
Irish Beauties
Irish Eyes Of Love
Irish Fox Trot, The
Irish Have A Great Day To-Night, The
Irish Jubilee
Irish Soldier Boy, The
Irish Tango, The
Irish Were Egyptians Long Ago
Irishman's Home Sweet Home
It's A Great Day For The Irish
It's The Three Leaves Of The Shamrock
Jerry, You Warra A Warrior In The War
Johnny Doughboy Found A Rose In Ireland

Josie O'Neill
Just Sing A Song For Ireland
K-K-K-Katy (War Edition)
K-K-K-Katy
Kerry Dance, The
Killarney My Home O'er The Sea
King Clown, Irish Reel, The
Kitty
Kitty Donohue
Laddie
Lass From County Mayo
Laughing Irish Eyes
Let Me Shake The Hand That Shook The Hand Of
Sullivan
Let's Help The Irish Now
Letter From Ireland
Limerick Girls, The
Little Bit Of Heaven Sure They Call It Ireland, A
Little Bunch Of Shamrocks, A
Little Irish Rose
Little Town In The Ould County Down
Londonderry Air
Look To The Rainbow
Lovely Mary Donnelly
McCarthy In Piccardy
Macnamara's Band
Macushla
Maggie Murphy's Home
Malone At The Back Of The Bar
Maloney The Rolling Mailman
Mary Malone
Mavourneen
Mauvourneen, Mauvourneen From Dear Old Killarney
Meet Mr. Callaghan
Mick That Threw The Brick
Mickey
Mighty Lak' A Rose
Mr. Gallagher And Mr. Sheen
Mr. Mulligan And Mr. Garrity
Molly Brannigan
Molly Dear, It's You I'm After
Molly-O
Molly-O, I Love You
Moonlight At Killarney
Mother Machree
Mother O'Mine
Muldoon The Solid Man
My Galway Rose
My Irish American Rose
My Irish Molly O
My Killarney Rose
My Little Dutch Colleen
My Nellie's Blue Eyes
My Own Home Town In Ireland
My Rose Of Tipperary
My Sweetheart From Old Donegal
My Wild Irish Rose
My Yankee-Irish Girl
Necessity
Never Let Yourself Forget–You Are Irish
Night Maloney Landed In New York
Nora, My Irish Queen

Nora O'Neal
Noreen Mavourneen
Nothing's Too Good For The Irish
O'Brannigan Fusilters
O'Brien Is Tryin To Learn To Talk Hawaiian
On Erin's Green Isle
On The Banks Of Killarney
Overture Of Irish Melodies
Peg O' My Heart
Peggy O'Moore
Peggy O'Neill
Pick A Little Four Leaf Clover, And Send It Over
To Me
Picture Of Dear Old Ireland, A
Poor Irish Minstrel
Pretty Girl Milking The Cow, The
Pretty Kitty Kelly
Remember, Boy, You're Irish
River Shannon
River Shannon Moon
Rocky Road To Dublin, The
Rose O'Day
Rose Of Tralee, The
Roses Of Picardy
Says I To Myself, Says I
Shamrock
She Never Kissed Anything Else Except The Blarney
Stone
She's Never Been In Ireland But She's Irish Just The
Same
She's The Daughter Of Mother Machree
Shenanigans
Since Home Rule Came To Ireland
Since Maggie Dooley Learned The Hooley Hooley
Sing An Irish Song Tonight
Smile Again, Kathleen Mavourneen
Smiles And The Tears Of Killarney, The
Smiling Irish Eyes
Soldier's Song, The
Somewhere In Ireland
Son Of An Irishman, The
Song O' My Heart
Song Of Old Kilkenny, A
Songs Sung By Walter Lawrence
Spray O' Heather
Sprig Of Shillalah, A
St. Patrick's Day Parade
Sweet Iniscorra
Sweet Katie Connor
That Great Come-And-Get It Day
That Little Bit Of Green
That Old Irish Mother Of Mine
That Tumble-Down Shack In Athlone
That Wee Bit Of Devil In Your Irish Eyes
There's A Rose In Old Erin
There's A Typical Tipperary Over Here
There's Another Angel Now In Old Killarney
There's Something In The Name Of Ireland
They're Proud Of The Irish Now
Tho' I'm A Long, Long Way From Tipperary
Three Leaves Of Shamrock
Tim Rooney's At The Fightin'!

Tip-Top Tipperary Mary
Tipperary
Tipperary Twirl, The
Too-Ra-Loo-Ra-Loo-Ra, That's An Irish Lullaby
Twas Only An Irishman's Dream
Voice Of My Granny Machree, The
Voice Of The Violet, The
When I Dream Of Old Erin, I'm Dreaming Of You
When I Kissed The Blarney Stone
When I'm Not Near the Girl I Love
When Ireland Comes Into Her Own
When Irish Eyes Are Smiling
When It's Love Time In Picardy
When It's Moonlight In Mayo
When Kate And I Were Coming Through The Rye
When Scanlon Sang Mavourneen More Than Twenty
Years Ago
When Shall I Again See Ireland
When The Gates Of Heaven Opened And I Saw My
Mother There
When The Sun Sets In Galway
When They Play The River Shannon
When You And I Were Young Maggie
Where The River Shannon Flows
Where The Shamrock Grows
Where The Shandon Bells Are Ringing, I'll Be
Waiting Sweet Eileen
While The Irish Moon Rolls On
Who Threw The Overalls In Mrs. Murphy's Chowder
Why Paddy's Always Poor
You Brought Ireland Right Over To Me
You Can Tell That I'm Irish
You Can't Deny You're Irish
You Can't Get Away From The Blarney
You Don't Have To Come From Ireland To Be Irish
You Will Have To Sing An Irish Song
You'd Better Ask Me
You'll Find A Little Bit Of Ireland Everywhere
You're Irish And You're Beautiful

JAZZ

Along with the gay rags came the slow mournful blues songs. Usually the third and seventh notes of the scale are flatted, that is, they are played or sung a half note lower. This gives the tunes their melancholy sound. The best known blues song is "St. Louis Blues" written in 1914 by W. C. Handy (1873–1958). Although the jazz played in the 1890s was sometimes called ragtime this term refers primarily to a type of piano music featuring lively rhythmic patterns. The early ragtime pianists included Scott Joplin, who wrote "Maple Leaf Rag," perhaps the greatest ragtime tune ever penned. Ragtime gave way to the Blues.

Listed below are songs pertaining to Jazz. Current prices can be found in Chapter l.

At The Coffee Cooler's Tea
Boogie Woogie Maxixe
Bye Bye Blackbird
Ching A Ling's Jazz Bazaar
Cleopatra Had A Jazz Band

Hong Kong
Hot Lips
I Have A Big Jazz Band
Java Jive
Jazz Babies' Ball
Jazz Baby
Jazz Band Blues
Jazz Nocturne
Jazzin' The Blues Away
Jazzola
Jazzy Jazzy Sound In All Chinatown
Old Man Jazz
Razz-Berries
Song Of The Bayou
Take Me To The Land Of Jazz
That's What Makes A Wild Cat Wild
'Way Down Yonder In New Orleans
What Cha Gonna Do When There Ain't No Jazz?

CHARLES A. LINDBERGH

Charles A. Lindbergh was born in Detroit, Michigan in 1902. He was an American aviator and the first to make a solo, nonstop flight across the Atlantic in 1927. In 1933 he flew from America to Norway via Greenland with a view to establishing a North Atlantic air route. When his son was kidnapped and because of the interference in his private life by yellow journalism, in 1935 he went to live in England. In 1938 he returned to the United States to retain his U.S. citizenship. Because of threats of harm to his two sons in 1938 he went into seclusion on the island of Illiec, off the coast of Brittany, France. While there he invented the Lindbergh Pump, an artificial heart. He returned to the United States in 1939 and became aeronautical adviser to the U.S. Government. He opposed U.S. entry into WW II and resigned his reserve commission and left the National Advisory Committee for Aeronautics when his speeches were called pro-Nazi. However, when the United States entered the war, Lindbergh offered his services to the Air Force and served as a civilian consultant. In 1943 he became an engineer for United Aircraft Corp., Hartford, Conn. Lindbergh died in 1974.

Listed below are songs pertaining to Charles Lindbergh. Current prices can be found in Chapter 1.

Hello Lindy
Like An Angel You Flew Into Everyone's Heart
Lindbergh The Eagle Of The U.S.A.
Lindy, Lindy!
Lucky Lindy!

MARCH

The soldiers of the Civil War, WWI and WWII marched to the beat of fife and drum. Perhaps the best known composers of marches are John Philip Sousa and E. T. Paull.

One of E. T. Paull's compositions is Napoleon's Last Charge. Written on the back of this piece of sheet music is the following:

"This is positively one of the Greatest March Compositions ever written. Mr. Paull spent nearly two years on this piece, to have it the best published. It represents the downfall of Napoleon, the mighty conqueror of Europe, at the Battle of Waterloo. It has been made descriptive throughout, and respresents the Bugle Call to Arms, Cavalry Call, Army Marching and Forming Line of Battle, Band Playing and Cannonading; Cavalry Advancing; Horses Galloping; Clash of Arms, Death in the Sunken Trench, etc. Every one who plays or uses music in any way should certainly have a copy of this great piece."

E.T. Paull also composed: A Warmin' Up in Dixie in 1898; America Forever March, 1917; Dawn of the Century, 1900 and many, many more.

John Philip Sousa was called "The March King." He composed the following: The Charlatan March, 1888; Stars & Stripes Forever; El Capitan; Semper Fidelis; Liberty Bell and many, many more.

Current prices can be found in Chapter 1.

Ace Of Diamonds
Across The Border
Across The Continent
Admiral Dewey's March
Alabama Wedding
Alexander's Ragtime Band
All America March
Allied Victory March
Amazon March, The
America First
America Forever March
American Girl March, The
American Guard March, The
American Patrol
An Old Grand Army Man
Anna March
Annapolis, The Midshipman's March
Anniversary March, The
Arbitration March
Arizona March
Army Air Corps, The
Army And Navy
At A Georgia Camp Meeting
Atlantic Breakers
Atlantic City Pageant, The
Aunt Mandy's Wedding March
Badge Of Honor, The
Baldwin Commandery
Band Played All The Time, The
Battle Song Of Liberty, The
Bay State, The
Belles of '76
Ben Hur Chariot Race
Beneath The Starry Flag
Billiken March
Blaze Away
Blaze Of Glory
Blaze Of Honor
Bon Voyage March
Boots And Saddles
Boulevard March

Boy Scout's Dream, The
Boy Scouts Parade
Boys, Get Ready!
Brass Band Ephraham Jones
Brown's Jubilee March
Buffalo Flyer, The
Bull Moose March
Burning Of Rome, The
Cadet March
Caissons Go Rolling Along, The
Call, The
Call Of The Wild
Candlelight
Capparian March
Captain Betty
Captive, The
Carnations March
Carnival King, The
Century Of Progress
Chantecler
Charcoal, A Study In Black
Charge Of The Light Brigade
Charlatan March, The
Cincinnati Enquirer, The
Circus Parade March
Civilization
Clayton's Grant March
Clef Club Grand March, The
Clicquot
Co-Ed
College Life
College Yell March
Colored Four Hundred, The
Columbia
Columbus Day March
Coming Storm
Commodore Dewey's Victory March
Comrades In Arms
Connecticut March, The
Conqueror March, The
Cotton Pickers, The
Creole Belles
Cuban Independence
Custer's Last Charge
Dawn Of The Century March
Della Fox, Little Trooper, March
Directorate March
Dixie Coon Brigade, The
Dodge Brothers March
Down At The Huskin' Bee
Dreamy Oriental Melody
Drum Major, The
Drum Major March
El Capitan March
Fairy Tales March Ballad
Fencing Girl, The
Fight Is On, The
Filibuster, The
Fire Drill March
Fire Master, The
Fire Worshippers
Fireman's Dream, The

Flash Light March, The
Flipity Flop
Folies Bergere March
For Dixie & Uncle Sam
For Love And Honor
Ford March, The
Four Horsemen Of The Apocalypse
Four Jacks March
Fox Hunter's March, The
Fox Tail March
Frat March
Gallant Hero, The
General Delivery
General Garfield's Grand March
General U.S. Grant's Grand March Reception
General Morgan's Parade March
General Pershing Song
General Sherman's Funeral March
George Washington Bicentennial
German's Triumphal March
Give Me A Kiss By The Numbers
Glory Of Jamestown
Golden Flyer March, The
Golden Gate
Golden Spider
Good-By Betty Brown
Good Luck Mary
Good-Night Moonlight
Greyhound March, The
Grover Cleveland's Grand March
Hands Across The Sea
Handsome Harry
Happy Days
Happy Days In Dixie
Hard Boiled Rag
Heaven's Artillery March
Help Bring Our Stars And Stripes Across The Rhine
Herald Of Peace March
Hewitt's Quick Step
High Flyer, The
Highland Grand March
His Majesty And The Maid
Homecoming March, The
Honest Abe March
Honey Boy
Honeymoon March, The
Honored Dead, The
Hurrah! For The Liberty Boys, Hurrah
Hurricane March, The
I Love You Just The Same Sweet Adeline
I Want A Boy From The U.S.A.
I Want To Be A Soldier For The U.S.A.
Ice Palace March
I'm Going Back To The Girl I Love
Imperial March And Two Step
In Rank And File
In The Barracks
Infantry–Kings Of The Highway, The
Iron Division, The
Jagtime Johnson's Ragtime March
Japan's Triumphal March
Jasper's Triumphal March

Jersey Carnival, The
Jimmie Boy
John Fitzgerald
John Henry March
Jolly Blacksmiths, The
Jolly Boys In Gray, The
Jolly Cobbler, The
Jolly Jingles
Jolly Sailor, A
Just Take Me Down To Wonderland
K Of P, The
Keating Wheel March
Keep Moving March
King Clown, Irish Reel, The
King Cotton March
King Of Good Fellows March
King Of The Air
King Of The Forest
Last Day Of Pompeii, The
Leader Of The German Band, The
Legion Of Victory
Let 'Er Go
Liberty Bell, The
Liberty Loan March
Limited Express March
Lincoln Centennial Grand March
Lion Trainer's March, The
Little Boy Blue
Little Fairy March
Little Grey Mother Who Waits All Alone, The
Little Soldier
Loyal Knights
McKinley Presidential March
McKinley's Funeral March
Macnamara's Band
Magna Carta
Mamma's Boy
Manhattan Beach March
March Militaire
March Of Progress
March Of The Flit Soldiers, The
March Of The Flower Girls
March Of The Mannikins
March Of The Nations
March Of The Old Guard
March Of The Teddy Bear
March Of The Toys, The
March Of The Vagabonds
March To The White House
March Victorious
Marche Heroique
Marching Along Together
Marching Through Georgia
Marching Through Germany
Marching Thru Georgia
Marching To The Music Of The Band
Margery
Marine Review, The
Marine's Hymn, The
Masquerade March, The
Meet Me In Rose Time Rosie
Metropolitan

Midnight Fire Alarm, The
Mile A Minute, A
Miss Columbia March
Miss Liberty
Mohawk Trail, The
Motor King March
Motor March, The
Motorcycle Race March
Mounted Police
Mulligan Guard
My South Sea Island Queen
Myopia Club, The
Napoleon's Last Charge
National Defense Military March
National Emblem March
NC-4 March
Neutrality March, The
New Liberty, The
New Recruit March, The
New Thought, The
N.Y. And Coney Island Bicycle March
Nobles Of The Mystic Shrine March
Northern Route March
Off To The Front
Official West Point March, The
Old Glory Goes Marching On
Old Hickory
On Jersey Shore
On, Minnesota
On The Avenue
On The Gridiron
On Wisconsin
101st Regiment, U.S.A. March
Opening Of The Season
Oriental Guard
Our Band
Our Daring Commodore
Our Director
Our Protectors March
Our Sammies
Over The Top
Palace Of Peace
Palm Limited, The
Panama Canal, The
Parcel Post
Path Of Flowers
Paul Revere's Ride
Peace Conference
Pepper-Up
Perry's Victory March
Pershing's Crusaders
Pioneer
Popularity
Portrait
President Garfield Funeral March
Pulaski Quick Step
Pullman Porters Parade, The
Queen Of Hearts, The
Queen Of The Carnival March
Race Course March, The
Raggity Rag
Rainbow Military March, The

Rapid Fire
Recess March
Repasz Band March
Rifle Range, The
Riverside March, The
Roaring Volcano
Robber's March
Robin Hood March
Roman Races March
Roosevelt N.R.A. March
Ruff Johnson's Harmony Band
Russian March
Salut A Pesth
Salute To America
Salute To Williamsburg
School Life
Scorcher, The
Second Regiment
Semper Fidelis
Sesqui-Centennial Exposition Of U.S.
Sheridan's Ride
Signal From Mars, A
Silver Jubilee March
Silver Sleighbells
Sliding Sid
Solace
Soldiers Of Fortune
Somethin' Doin'
Somewhere In France Is The Lily
Song Of The Army Engineer
Sousa's Grand March
Souvenir March
Spirit Of America
Spirit Of France
Spirit Of Freedom
Spirit Of Progress March, The
Spirit Of The U.S.A.
Stand By America!
Starlight
Stars And Stripes Forever March, The
Steeple Chase, The
Stein Song March, The
Still Alarm
Storm King March, The
Sultan, The
Sumthin' Doin'
Sunset Limited
Taft March
Tempest, The
That Bandana Band, Way Down In Dixieland
That Rag-Time Regimental Band
Thunderer, The
Tipperary Guards
To The Rescue
To Victory
Trench Trot, The
Tri State March
Trip To Niagara, A
Trip to Niagara Falls, A
Triumphal Post March
Triumphant America
Triumphant Banner, The

Trumpeter March
Trumpeter, The
Twelfth Regiment March, The
Twentieth Century Woman
Uncle Sam's Boys March
U.S. Field Artillery March, The
U.S.A. March
Under The American Eagle
Under The Stars & Stripes
United Musicians
United Nations March
Unter Vereinten Kriegsflaggen
Vesuvius
Veteran, The
Violette
Votes For Women
Wake Up, America
Washington Post March
Wayside Willies March
We Are Coming Home
Welcome Home Laddie Boy, Welcome Home
We'll Stand By The Flag March
When The Flowers Bloom On No Man's Land
When You Come Back
Whip, The
Whirlpool March, The
Whistling Rufus
White Crest March
White Guards, The
Whoop 'Er Up!
Witch's Whirl March, The
Wolverine, The
Woodrow Wilson Inaugural March, The
World Peace March
Yale Boola
Yale March, The
Yankee Bird March
Yankee Boy
Yankee Grit
Yankee Hustler March
Yankee Prince, The
Yankiana
Young Guard March, The
Your Country Needs You
Zenith
Ziz-March

MILITARY PERSONNEL

Many covers on sheet music, especially during the wars, show photos of military officers, soldiers and sailors. A fine example is Just Like Washington Crossed The Delaware, General Pershing Will Cross The Rhine, showing a photo of General Pershing; cover artist, Rose.

Another example, When The Yanks Come Marching Home, has photo of Wm. J. Reilly, U.S.N.; cover artist is Barbelle.

There's A Service Flag Flying At Our House shows a platoon of soldiers marching down the street. Cover Artist is Starmer.

Listed below are song sheets with covers showing

military personnel. Current prices can be found in Chapter 1.

Admiral Dewey's March
American Eagles
Angel God Sent From Heaven, The
Army Air Corps, The
Army's Made A Man Out Of Me, The
Back In The Old Town Tonight
Ballad Of The Green Berets, The
Be My Fireside
Because You're Here
Because You're Mine
Ben Hur Chariot Race
Burmah Moon
Caissons Go Rolling Along, The
Col. Stevenson's Quick Step
Commodore Dewey's Victory March
Dear Old Pal Of Mine
Engineer Girls
Fight Is On, The
For All We Know
For Old Glory
General Garfield's Grand March
General U.S. Grant's Grand March Reception
General Morgan's Parade March
General Pershing
General Sherman & Boys In Blue
General Sherman's Funeral March
General Von Stueben
Give A Little Credit To The Navy
Give Me A Kiss By The Numbers
Goodbye Sally Good Luck To You
Gypsy Moonbeams
Hello! General Pershing, How's My Daddy Tonight?
Hewitt's Quick Step
How About A Cheer For The Navy
I Don't Want To Love You
I Left My Heart At The Stage Door Canteen
If War Is What Sherman Said It Was
I'm Getting Tired So I Can Sleep
In Flanders Fields
In Flanders Fields The Poppies Grow
Iron Division, The
It's A Long Way To Berlin, But We'll Get There
Ja-Da
Just Like Washington Crossed The Delaware, General Pershing Will Cross The Rhine
Like An Angel You Flew Into Everyone's Heart
Little Bit Of Sunshine, A
Love Of A Rose
Mademoiselle From Armentieres
Mary Lee
Mr. Yankee Doodle Are We Prepared
Mother, I Love You
My Sergeant And I Are Buddies
Navy Took Them Over And The Navy Will Bring Them Back, The
NC-4 March
Oh Helen!
On The Road That Leads Back Home
On The Steps Of The Great White Capitol

Our Gallant Hero
Our Sammies
Over There
Perry's Victory March
Private Tommy Atkins
Radiance In Your Eyes, The
Rag Time Drafted Man
Semper Paratus
Sergeant Hickey Of The G.A.R.
That Russian Winter
That's What The Well-Dressed Man In Harlem Will
  Wear
Trench Trot, The
U.S. Field Artillery March, The
They Are Fighting For Liberty
This Is The Army Mr. Jones
Tommy
We Are Uncle Sammie's Little Nephews
We'll Tramp, Tramp, Tramp Along Together
We're In To Win
What Does He Look Like
What'll We Do With Him Boys?
When The Yanks Come Marching Home
Where Do We Go From Here
Why Did They Take My Daddy
With My Head In The Clouds

PATRIOTIC

There are many ways in which to express your patriotism other than by active service. The home front was busy with mothers, wives and daughters keeping the home fires burning while the boys fought for our country. The children dreamed of their dads coming home safely. There were many sad songs written about the boys over there. Hopefully we will not see another war.

Listed below are songs written about patriotism. Current prices can be found in Chapter 1.

After The Battle
Although I Am A Soldier
A-M-E-R-I-C-A
America Calling
America First
America For Mine
America I Love You
A-M-E-R-I-C-A, Means I Love You My Yankee Land
America! My Home Land
American Guard
American Legion, The
Amerikana
Anchors Away
Anglo-Saxon Race, The
Annapolis
Anywhere In The U.S.A. Is Home To Me
Army Air Corps, The
Army And Navy
Ballad For Americans
Ballad Of The Green Berets, The
Battle Hymn
Battle Cry Of Peace, The

Battle Of Gettysburg, The
Beginning Of The U.S.A.
Bell Bottom Trousers
Birth Of A Nation, The
Birth Of Our Flag, The
Blaze Of Glory
Blue And The Grey, The
Blue Jackets
Boy Scouts' Dream, The
Boys Of The Blue & Gray, The
Bring Out The Flag Boys
Bugle Blasts
Caissons Go Rolling Along, The
Call Of The Flag
Call To Arms, The
Calling To Her Boy Just Once Again
Bunker Hill
Captain Riley Of The U.S.A.
Charge Of The Uhlans
Charmaine
Columbia
Columbia The Gem Of The Ocean
Columbian Patrol, The
Commodore Dewey's Victory March
Connecticut March, The
Dear Old Stars And Stripes, The
Dear Old Stars And Stripes Good-Bye
Do Something
Father Of The Land We Love
Finest Flag That Flies, The
First Comes Your Duty To The Flag
Flag At Sundown, The
Flag Of My Heart & Home
For His Mother's Sake
For Love And Honor
For Old Glory
For Old Glory Uncle Sam, We Are Preparing
For The Freedom Of The World
For You And The Grand Old Flag
Four Brave Sailors
France America
Freedom For All Forever
General Sherman & Boys In Blue
General Von Stueben
General's Fast Asleep, The
George Washington Bicentennial
Girl In The Gingham Gown, The
God Bless America
Good Bye Little Girl Good-Bye
Good-Bye My Soldier Lad
Good-Bye My Sweetheart Rose
Good-Bye Uncle Sammy
Good Old U.S.A., The
Green Beret, The
Have You Seen My Sweetheart In His Uniform
  Of Blue?
He Laid Away A Suit Of Gray To Wear The
  Union Blue
Heaven Born Banner, The
Hero Of The Isthmus
He's My Uncle
His Buttons Are Marked U.S.

Hurry Home
I Am An American
I Love You Like Lincoln Loved The Old Red,
  White & Blue
I Want A Boy From The U.S.A.
I Want A Military Man
I'm Going To Be A Sailor
I'm Off For Mexico
In The Land Of Beginning Again
International Fox Trot, The
It's A Long, Long Way To Tipperary
It's The Flag
Jimmie Boy
Jolly Boys In Gray, The
Just Before The Battle Mother
Kiss Your Sailor Boy Good-Bye
Lanky, Yankee Boys In Blue, The
Let Freedom Ring
Liberty Bell, It's Time To Ring Again
Look Out, Here Comes An American
Love Tale Of Alsace Lorraine, A
Made In America
Make Uncle Sam Your Banker
Mama's Boy
March To The White House
Marching Thru Georgia
Marines' Hymn, The
Meaning Of U.S.A.
Memories Of France
Military Parade
Miss Liberty
Mr. Volunteer, You Don't Belong To The Regulars
My Country Has First Call
My Country I Hear You Calling Me
My Country 'Tis Of Thee
My Dream Of The U.S.A.
My Little Blue Eyed Girl
My Yankee Doodle Girl
National Emblem March
'Neath The Stars And Stripes
New Recruit March, The
Oceana Roll, The
Off To The Wars Of Mexico
Old Flag Never Touched The Ground, The
Old Glory
Old Glory I Salute You
On The Steps Of The Great White Capitol, Stood
  Martha And George
Only For Americans
Our Boys And Girls
Our Country's Heros
Our Sammies
Our "V" For Victory
Our Washington
Patria
Peace Patrol, The
Raggy Military Tune
Red We Want Is The Red We've Got, The
Romance
Say A Prayer For The Boys Over There
Semper Paratus
Sesqui-Centennial Hymn, The

She Was A Soldier's Sweetheart
Sheridan's Ride
Shout Hurrah For America
Song Of The Army Engineer
Song Of The Marines, The
Sound Of The Drum, The
Spirit Of America
Spirit Of The U.S.A.
Stand By America!
Stand By Your Uncle Sam
Standard American Airs
Star-Spangled Banner, The
Statue Of Liberty Is Smiling, The
Strike Up The Band, Here Comes A Sailor
Taft March
Thank Your Lucky Stars And Stripes
That's What The Red White And Blue Means
There Are Just As Many Heroes Today
They've Won Every Nation's Battles But Their Own
Toast To The Flag, A
U.S. Black Marines
U.S.A. And You, The
U.S.A. March
Uncle Sam, Hold Your Flag Up High
Uncle Sam Is Calling Me
Uncle Sammy
Under The American Eagle
Under The Double Eagle
Under The Stars & Stripes
Unknown Soldier Speaks, The
United We Stand
Wait Till She Sees You In Your Uniform
Wake Up America
We Are Coming, Father Abraham, Three Hundred
  Thousand Strong
We Are Ready
We Must Be Vigilant
We're All Americans, All True Blue
We're All With You Dear America
We're In The Navy Now
West Point Song
When Uncle Sammy Leads The Band
When You Come Back
Winning Fight, The
With Flying Colors U.S.A
Yankee Boy
Yankee Doodle Blues
Young America, We're Strong For You
Your Country Needs You
Your Dad Gave His Life For His Country
Your Land And My Land
You're A Grand Old Flag

POLITICAL

Political sheet music bearing the photographs of the candidate and his running mate would serve as a reminder of the person's candidacy for office. For instance: Get On the Raft With Taft, 1908; Keep Cool And Keep Coolidge, 1924; The Sidewalks of New York, 1928 (Official Campaign Song for Al Smith).

Listed below are songs pertaining to politics. Current prices can be found in Chapter 1.

Boston's Fermer Kerl
Eisenhower 1950 Inauguration
Get On The Raft With Taft
Happy Landin' With Landon
Harding, You're The Man For Us
Ike For Four More Years
Ike, Mr. President
Keep Cool & Keep Coolidge
McKinley Presidential March
McKinley's Funeral March
On The Avenue, The Inaugural March For 1909
Our Gallant Hero, Admiral Dewey
President Garfield Funeral March
Roosevelt, N.R.A. March
Sidewalks Of New York, The
Tie That Binds, The
Woodrow Wilson Inaugural March, The
Woodrow Wilson Leader Of The U.S.A.

PRE 1900

Some of the oldest song sheet covers were stone engravings & lithographs. Many depicted blacks on covers such as: The Blue Bells of Scotland, no date; I'm Livin' Easy, 1849; The Old Log Cabin in The Dell, 1875; Cousin Jedediah, 1863; The Cotton Pickers, 1859; Baby Mine, 1869; The Sun Do Move, 1899; Whistling Rufus, 1899; Ma Jet Black Lady, 1897; Rubber Neck Jim, 1889; My Black Venus, 1897; Twinkle, Twinkle, Little Star, 1879.

"The Star Spangled Banner" was written by Frances Scott Key with music by John Stafford Smith. Going to the British Admiral under a flag of truce, Key was taken prisoner by the British as he sought the release of his friend Dr. Beanes. Key wrote The Star Spangled Banner on an envelope he had in his pocket. He adopted the verses to "The Anacreon in Heav'n" a popular tune of the day. This had been an English drinking song. The earliest known edition was arranged by John Stafford Smith. The original manuscript is now housed in the Enoch Pratt mansion on West Monument St., Baltimore. Herbert Hoover signed the bill in 1931 making The Star Spangled Banner the official national anthem. If you posses this sheet music, you have a gem. The most common one found today was reprinted in 1942.

Listed below are Pre 1900 songs. Current prices can be found in Chapter 1.

Abide With Me
Absent
Actions Speak Louder Than Words
Admiral Dewey's March
After
After The Ball
Alabama Cake Walk
Alabama Wedding
Album Lee
All Bound Round With A Woolen String

All Coons Look Alike To Me
All On Account Of Eliza
All Vat's Gold Ain't Glitters
Alsacian Railroad Gallops
Always
Always Keep A Smile For Mother
Always Take Mother's Advice
American Guard
American Patrol
And The Band Played On
Angel Voices Ever Near
Annie Rooney
Annie Rooney's Baby
Anniversary March, The
Another Rose Is Just As Sweet
Are You Going To The Ball This Evening?
Are You There, Moriarty?
Armorer
Arrah Go On, You're Only Fooling
As Your Hair Grows Whiter
Ask The Man In The Moon
Asleep In the Deep
Asthmore
At A Darktown Cake Walk
At A Georgia Camp Meeting
Aunt Dinah's Cake Walk
Aunt Mandy's Wedding March
Babbie Waltzes
Babies On Our Block, The
Baby, Baby
Baby Mine
Baby, Will You Always Love Me True
Baby's Laughing In Her Sleep
Baby's Prayer
Barbara Frietchie
Battle Song Of Prohibition
Bay State, The
Be Good, Be Good, My Father Said
Be Home When The Clock Strikes Ten
Beautiful Dreamer
Because
Behind The Parlor Door
Believe
Belle Of Avenue A
Belle Of Georgia, The
Belle Of The Creoles
Beloved, It Is Morn
Ben Hur Chariot Race
Best In The House Is None Too Good For Reilly
Bethlehem
Better Than Gold
Beyond Pardon, Beyond Recall
Big Four Two-Step
Bird From O'er The Sea, A
Birds And The Brook, The
Birth Of Our Flag, The
Black Diamond Express
Blackthorn
Blarney!
Blue Bells Of Scotland, The
Blue Jackets
Blue Line Galop

Bold Hibernian Boys
Bold McIntyres
Bon Voyage
Bonnie Sweet Bessie
Boodle
Born At Sea And A Sailor
Bounding Billows
Bowery
Bowery Buck
Bowery Girls
Boy's Best Friend Is His Mother
Bran New Little Coon
Brannigan's Band
Brave Jennie Creek
Bridal Cake Walk
Brigand's Love Song, The
Bright Happy Days
Bright Little Lantern I Swing, The
Bring Out The Flag Boys
Bringing Pretty Blossoms To Strew On Mother's
   Grave
Broken Home
Brooklyn Light Quickstep, The
Brown October Ale
Brown's Jubilee March
Brunette Polka, The
Bully Song
Bunch Of Blackberries
Bye Baby Bye
Bye-Bye My Babykins Bye-Bye
Cake Walk In The Sky, The
Cake Walk Of The Day
Callahan's Gang
Calm As The Night
Camptown Races
Can't Lose Me, Charlie
Capparian March
Carolina Cake Walk, A
Casey Social Club
Casey's Wife
Chapel In The Mountains, The
Charge Of The Light Brigade
Charlatan March, The
Charleston Blues
Charleston Rag, The
Chicken
Church Across The Way
Clancy's Trotter
Clara Jenkins' Tea
Climbing Up The Golden Stairs
Close Dem Windows
Coldest Coon In Town, The
Colored Four Hundred, The
Columbia The Gem Of The Ocean
Come Down, Mrs. Flynn
Come Home, Dewey, We Won't Do A Thing To You
Come Sunny Hours
Come Where My Love Lies Dreaming
Come Where The Lilies Bloom
Come Ye Lofty, Come Ye Lowly
Coming Home From Meeting
Committed To The Deep

Commodore Dewey's Victory March
Comrades
Conqueror March, The
Convict And The Bird, The
Cornelius Fitzpatrick McGee
Cotton Pickers, The
Cousin Jedediah
Cradle Song
Cradle's Empty-Baby's Gone
Cricket Polka
Crossing On The Ferry
Cuban Independence
Cuckoo's Call, The
Cupid's Awakening Waltzes
Curious Cures
Curse
Curse Of The Dreamer, The
Daddy Wouldn't Buy Me A Bow-Wow
Daisy Bell
Dakota Rag
Dance Of The Brownies, The
Dancing In The Dark
Danny By My Side
Dar's Somethin About Yer I Like
Darkies' Dream, The
Darktown Is Out Tonight
Darky Cavalier
Darling Nellie Gray
Dat Citron Wedding Cake
Day That's Gone Can Never Come Again
Day We Celebrate
De Darkies Jubilee
De Golden Wedding
De Leader Of De Company B
De Ole Time Cake Walk
De Stories Uncle Remus Tells
Dear Louise
December And May
Della Fox, Little Trooper, March
Dinah Song
Directorate March
Dixie Coon Brigade, The
Dixie, I Wish I Was In Dixie's Land
Do Do, My Huckleberry Do
Doan You Cry, Mah Honey
Don't Forget The Old Folks At Home
Don't Give Up The Old Love For The New
Don't Go To The Ball Tonight
Don't Tell Her That You Saw Me
Don't You Go Tommy
Dora Dean
Double Clog Dance
Down In Gossip Row
Down In Poverty Row
Down On The Farm
Down Went McGinty Dressed In His Best Suit Of
   Clothes
Dreams Of My Own Land
Drill, Ye Tarriers, Drill
Drink Up, Boys
Dusty Dudes Cake Walk
Echoes From The Snowball Club

Eight Little Songs Without Words
Eileen Alanna
Eily Machree
El Capitan March
Eli Green's Cake Walk
Elsie From Chelsea
Emmet's Castle Bells
Emmet's Cuckoo Song
Emmet's Love Of The Shamrock
Emmet's Lullaby
Emmet's Mountain Song
Emmet's Sweet Violets
Empty Is The Bottle, Father's Tight
En Ballon
Enduring Love
Espanita
Evening Chimes
Everlasting Day, The
Every Night There's A Light
Every Race Has A Flag But The Coon
Everything At Reilly's Must Be Done In Irish Style
Faded Coat Of Blue, The
Fair Nellita
Fairy Footsteps
Fairy Wedding
Fallen By The Wayside
Fast Line Gallop
Fatal Wedding, The
Filibuster, The
Finest On Parade, The
Finnegan, The Umpire
First You Do The Rag, Then You Bombershay
Flirtation Dance
Flirting In The Twilight
Flirting On The Ice
Florian's Song
Florida Glide Waltzes
Flower From My Angel Mother's Grave
Flying Trapeze Waltz
Folies Bergere March
For Old Glory
Forgotten
Four Leaf Clover
Frobi Of The Brownies
Gabriel's Band
Gathering The Myrtle With Mary
General Garfield's Grand March
General Grants Grand March
General Morgan's Parade March
General Sherman & Boys In Blue
General Sherman's Funeral March
Gentle Annie
Georgia Camp Meeting
Germans' Triumphal March
Get Away From That Window
Get On The Funny Walk
Get On Your Sneak Shoes Children
Get Up, Jack, John Sit Down
Get Your Money's Worth
Ghost Of John James Christopher Benjamin Bings, The
Ginger Blues
Gipsy Trail

Girl I Left Behind Me, The
Girl I Loved In Sunny Tennessee, The
Girl Of My Heart, The
Girl Who Is Loved By All, The
Gliding Down The Stream
Glorious Beer
Glorious Columbia
Going For A Pardon
Going Home With Nelly After Five
Gold Will Buy 'Most Anything But A True
　　Girl's Heart
Golden Chords Waltz
Golden Wedding
Goldenrod Two-Step
Gone Before
Goodbye My Honey, I'm Gone
Good-Day Marie, Bonjour Suzon
Good Enough
Good Night, Sweet Dreams
Good Shepherd, The
Got Your Habits On
Grace Conroy
Grace O'Moore
Grand Trunk Waltzes
Grandfather's Clock
Gray Rocks And Grayer Sea
Great Graphic Balloon Galop, The
Great Rock Island Route, The
Green I Love The Best, The
Grover Cleveland's Grand March
Guild Polka Militaire
Gypsy Jan
Gypsy Love Song
Hand Me Down My Walking Cane
Handful Of Earth From Mother's Grave
Hands Across The Sea
Happy Days In Dixie
Happy Hours In Coontown
Happy School Days
Hard Times Comes Again No More
Harlem Rag
Harnden's Express Line Gallopade & Trio
Hat Me Father Wore
Hats Off To Me
He Brought Home Another
He Carved His Mother's Name Upon The Tree
He Certainly Was Good To Me
He Didn't Split The Wood
He Fought For The Cause He Thought Was Right
He Never Came Back
He Never Cares To Wander From His Own Fireside
Heart That Loves Thee, A
Hearts & Flowers
Heaven's Eternal King
Hello, Baby
"Hello Daddy, I Knew That Was Your Car"
Hello Ma Baby
Henrietta
Her Eyes Don't Shine Like Diamonds
Her Golden Hair Was Hanging Down Her Back
Her Name Is Jane
Her Own Boy Jack

Her Tears Drifted Out With The Tide
Here Lies An Actor
Here's To A Rose
Hero Till Judgement Day
Hewitt's Quick Step
Hey, Rube
Hi, Ho! Let Her Go, Gallagher
High School Cadets
High School Two Step, The
Highland Grand March
His Last Thoughts Were Of You
Holy City, The
Home Run Polka
Honey! You'se Ma Lady Love
Honey! You'se My Turtle Dove
Honeymoon March, The
Honored Dead, The
Horn, The
Hot Tamale Alley
Hot Time In The Old Town
Hottest Ever Cake Walk, The
How I Love My Lu
How Is May
How Much Does The Baby Weigh
How The Gates Came Ajar
How'd Yer Like Ter Be A Dorg
Huckleberry Picnic
Hugh McCue
Hulda's Baby
Hurry Little Children, Sunday Morn
Hush, Little Baby, Don't You Cry
Hush My Baby Go To Sleep
Hush, My Darlings, Do Not Weep
I Ain't Seen No Messenger Boy
I Believe It For My Mother Told Me So
I Can't Think Of Nothing Else But You
I Couldn't Stand To See My Baby Lose
I Don't Care If You Neber Come Back
I Don't Like No Cheap Man
I Don't Want To Play In Your Yard
I Dreamt
I Guess I'll Have To Telegraph My Baby
I Guess That Will Hold You For A While
I Had Fifteen Dollars In My Inside Pocket
I Handed It Over To Reilly
I Hope I Don't Intrude
I Hope These Few Lines Will Find You Well
I Long To See The Girl I Left Behind
I Love You In The Same Old Way
I Love You Kate In Ireland
I Must Be Singing, Singing
I Never Drink Behind The Bar
I Never Liked O'Regan
I Owe $10.00 To O'Grady
I Thought I Heard Somebody Calling Me
I Want Dem Presents Back
I Want Yer, Ma Honey
I Went Home With Michael
I Wonder If She's Waiting
I Wonder Where She Is Tonight
I Wouldn't Change Dat Gal For No Other
Ice Palace March

I'd Leave My Happy Home For You
If I Catch The Man That Taught Her To Dance
If I Could Blot Out The Past
If I Could Hear Your Voice Again
If The Waters Could Speak As They Flow
If You Forget
I'll Await My Love
I'll Be True To My Honey Boy
I'll Have To Telegraph Another Baby
I'll Make That Black Gal Mine
I'll Tell Your Mother On You
I'm Happy When I'm By My Baby's Side
I'm Livin' Easy
I'm Making A Bid For Popularity
I'm The Man Who Broke The Bank At Monte Carlo
Imogene
Impecunious Davis
In Good Old New York Town
In Her Cradle Baby's Sleeping
In Pekin
In The Baggage Coach Ahead
In The Barracks
In The Morning By The Bright Light
In The Twilight
Irish Jubilee
Irishman's Home Sweet Home
I'se A Lady
I'se Got Another Nigger On Ma Staff
Isabella
Isabelle
It Ain't No Lie
It Couldn't Occur In New York
It Don't Seem Like The Same Old Smile
It Takes A Girl To Do It Every Time
It Was A Lover And His Lass
It's Forty Miles From Schenectady To Troy
It's Not What You Were, It's What You Are Today
I've Been To Gay Paree
I've Come Here To Stay
I've Just Come Back To Say Goodbye
I've Only Been Down To The Club
I've Waited, Honey, Waited Long For You
I'ze Your Nigger If You Wants Me Liza' Jane
Jack, How I Envy You
Japanese Serenade, A
Jasper Jenkins, De Cake-Walking Coon
Jeanie Morrison
Jenny Get Your Hoe Cake Done
Jim Crow Polka
Jockey Hat & Feather
Johnny Get Your Gun
June Roses
Just As The Sun Went Down
Just Before The Battle Mother
Just For The Sake Of Our Daughter
Just One Girl
Just Set A Light
Just Sing A Song For Ireland
Just Tell Them That You Saw Me
Kathleen
Katie Cue
Katie O'Conner

Keep Away From Emmeline
Keiser, Do Yer Want To Buy A Dog
Kentucky Babe
King Cotton March
Kiss Me And I'll Go To Sleep
Kiss Me, But Don't Say Good-Bye
Kiss Me Honey Do
La Ballerina
La Boheme
Lady April Waltz
Lass From County Mayo
Le Silence
Le Voyage Aerien
Lead Kindly Light
Learning McFadden To Waltz
Left, A Soldier's Soliloquy
Lehigh Polka
Let Me Bring My Clothes Back Home
Let Me Dream Again
Let Me Shake The Hand That Shook The Hand Of
    Sullivan
Letter Edged In Black, The
Letter From Ireland
Letter That Never Came, The
Letter To Heaven, A
Liberty
Liberty Bell, The
Life Boat
Light House By The Sea
Limited Express March
Linger Longer, Loo
Lion Trainer's March, The
Listen To My Tale Of Woe
Listen To The Silver Trumpets
Little Alabamy Coon
Little Black Me
Little Boy Blue
Little Bunch Of Whiskers On His Chin
Little Darling, Dream Of Me
Little Daughter Nell
Little Em'ly
Little Empty Stockings
Little Fraud
Little German Band
Little Girls We Met Upon The Train
Little Johnny Dugan
Little Kinkey Wooley Head
Little Lost Child, The
Little Nell And I
Little Newsboy's Death, The
Little Old Red Schoolhouse
Little Stowaway, The
Little Widow Dunn
Little Willie
Log Cabin Song
London Paved With Gold
Lone Grave
Lord Is My Light, The
Lorena
Louisiana Lize
Louisiana Lou
Louisline Polka, The

Love Among The Roses
Love I Adore You
Love In An Automobile
Love Me Little, Love Me Long
Lucky Jim
Lucy Dale
McNally's Row Of Flats
Ma Jet Black Lady
Ma Lady Lu
Ma Says I Can't Go For A Ride
Maggie Murphy's Home
Maguires
Major Gilfeather
Malone At The Back Of The Bar
Maloney The Rolling Mailman
Mamie Come Kiss Your Honey Boy
Mamie Reilly
Mammy's Kinky Headed Coon
Mammy's Little Pickaninny Boy
Mammy's Little Pumpkin Colored Coons
Mandy Lee
Manhattan Beach March
Maple Leaf Rag
Marching Through Georgia
Margery
Marguerite
Marine Review, The
Market On Saturday Night
Martyres Of The Maine
Mary Ann Callahan
Mary Kelly's Beau
Massa's In The Cold Cold Ground
Maud
May Morning, A
Mazurka
Medicine Man
Memories Of Spain
Mercedes
Message On The Train
Mick That Threw The Brick
'Mid The Green Fields Of Virginia
Mid The Light Ripples
Midshipmite
Mignonette
Miner's Dream Of Home
Miranda When We Are Made One
Miss Brown's Cake Walk
Miss Liberty
Mississippi Boat Song
Mississippi River
Mississippi Side Step
Mr. Captain Stop The Ship
Mister Chairman
Mr. Johnson Turn Mc Loose
Mocking Bird, The
Mocking Bird Variations
Mollie Darling
Molly And I And The Baby
Molly-O
Moonlight At Killarney
Moonlight On The Hudson
Moonlight On The Lake

Moonlight On The Waves
Moonlight Serenade
Moth And The Flame, The
Mother Is The Best Friend After All
Mother Of The Girl I Love
Mother Was A Lady
Mother's Appeal To Her Boy
Mother's Last Letter To Me
Mottoes That Are Framed Upon The Walls
Mrs. Brady's Daughter
Muldoon The Solid Man
Mulligan Guard
Murmuring Zephyr, Perfumed Air
My Best Girl's A Corker
My Black Baby, Mine
My Black Venus
My Coal Black Lady
My Creole Sue
My Dad's Dinner Pail
My Dad's The Engineer
My Dream Of Love
My Gal Is A High Born Lady
My Georgia Lady-Love
My Hannah Lady, Whose Black Boy Is You?
My Honolulu Lady
My Josephine
My Lady Lu
My Little Georgia Rose
My Louisiana Babe
My Maggie
My Mother Was A Lady
My Nellie's Blue Eyes
My Old Kentucky Home
My Old Kentucky Home, Goodnight
My Old New Hampshire Home
My Own Sweet Nellie Bawn
My Pearl's A Bowery Girl
My Pretty Red Rose
My Soul To God, My Heart To Thee!
My Sweetheart & I
My Sweetheart Of Long Ago
My Sweetheart's The Man In The Moon
My Trundle Bed
My Wild Irish Rose
Myopia Club, The
Narcissa
Narcissus
Nay, Nay Pauline
Nelly Bly
Nelly Daily's Dad
Nelly Was A Lady
Never Take No For An Answer
Never Take The Horseshoe From The Door
New Coon In Town
New Express Galop
N.Y. And Coney Island Bicycle March
Night Maloney Landed In New York
Nightingale's Song
Ninon
No One Ever Loved You More Than I
No Show Tonight
North Western Railway Polka

Northern Route March
Nothing's Too Good For The Irish
Now She Is Wholly Mine
O'Brannigan Fusilters
Ocean Between Us, The
Oh, Dem Golden Slippers
Oh, Girly, Girly
Oh, Mamma, Buy Me That
Oh! Susanna
Oh, Uncle John
Oh What A Beautiful Ocean
Oh, What A Difference In The Morning
Olcott's Lullaby
Old Bachelor, The
Old Dog Tray
Old Fashioned Mother
Old Hundred
Old Jim's Christmas Hymn
Old Log Cabin In The Dell, The
Old Neighborhood
Old Oaken Bucket
Old South
Old Turnkey
On The Banks Of The Wabash
On The Benches In The Park
On The Bright, Golden Shore
One Of His Legs Is Longer Than It Really Ought
    To Be
One Touch Of Nature Makes The Whole World Kin
Only A Bowery Boy
Only A Pansy Blossom
Only A Rosebud
Only Me
Only One Girl In The World For Me
Oo Lee Long
Open Thy Lattice, Love
Opening Of The Season
Oriental Echoes
Oriental Guard
Original Rags
Our Daring Commodore
Our Flag
Outcast Unknown, The
Over The Garden Wall
Over The Mountain
Pack Of Cards, A
Package Of Old Love Letters
Paddy Duffy's Cart
Pardon That Came Too Late, The
Parted At The Altar
Pat For Your Baby
Path Of Flowers
Peek-A-Boo
Peggy O'Moore
Penitent, The
Perhaps
Perhaps She's On The Railroad
Picture 84
Picture No Artist Can Paint
Picture That Is Turned Toward The Wall
Pious Peter Cakewalk
Pitcher Of Beer

Playmates
Pliney, Come Kiss Your Baby
Plum Pudding
Poet's Dream
Polar Bear Polka
Polly's A Peach
Polonaise Brilliant
Poor Irish Minstrel
Poverty's Tears Ebb And Flow
Prancing Pickaninnies
Pretty As A Picture
Pretty Girl, A Summer's Night
Pretty Jennie Slattery
Pretty Little Carolina Rose
Private Tommy Atkins
Prize Cake Walk Of The Blackville Swells
Prodigal Son
Pulaski Quick Step
Push Dem Clouds Away
Put Me Off At Buffalo
Put My Little Shoes Away
Q Galop
Queen Of Hearts, The
Queen Of The Carnival
Quest, The
Racing Down The Rapids
Raffle For The Stove
Rail-Road
Railroad Galop
Rastus On Parade
Razzle Dazzle
Recessional
Regular Army O
Remember, Boy, You're Irish
Remember Poor Mother At Home
Reuben And Cynthia
Revelry
Riding On The Elevated Railroad
Rivals
Riverside March, The
Rock Beside The Sea, The
Rock Of Ages
Rockaby Baby
Rose Atherton
Rose Song
Rosey, Rosey Just Supposey
Rowdy Dowdy Boys
Rubber Neck Jim
Russian March
Sabel's Sparkling Champagne Song
Sailor's Dream, The
Sally–Don't Dally
Salome
Salute To Sam Johnson
Salvation Army, Oh
Sam Johnson's Colored Cake Walk
Sambo Outa Work Cake Walk
Sandy-Haired Mary In Our Area
Say Au Revoir But Not Goodbye
Say, Suz! How 'Bout You?
Scorcher, The
Scotch Lassie Jean

Seben Come Eleben
Second Degree, Full Moon
Second Regiment
Semper Fidelis
Send Back The Picture And The Wedding Ring
Send Me A Letter From Over The Sea
Serenade
Sergeant Hickey Of The G.A.R.
Sermon That Touched His Heart, The
Shall I Ever See My Mother's Face Again
She Is Far From The Land
She Is More To Be Pitied Than Censored
She Lives On Murray Hill
She May Have Seen Better Days
She Rests By The Swanee River
She Still Believes In You
She Was Bred In Old Kentucky
She's My Warm Baby
She's Somebody's Mother
She's The Daughter Of Officer Porter
Shedding Tears O'er Mother's Grave
Shepherd Boy, The
Shine On Oh Stars
Ship I Love
Ship Sails Tonight, The
Shipwreck, The
Shoo Fly, Don't Bother Me
Sights In A Dime Museum
Silvery Waves
Since McManus Went Down To The Track
Since Mother Passed Away
Since Nellie Went Away
Sing Me A Song Of The South
Singer And The Song, The
Singing At The Hallway Door
Singing The Dear Little Baby To Sleep
Skidmore Fancy Ball
Skidmore Guard
Skidmore Masquerade
Skids Are On Review
Skids Are Out Today
Skids Are Out Tonight
Skirt Dance
Slave Song
Slavery Days
Slavery's Passed Away
Sleep, Baby, Sleep
Slide, Kelly, Slide
Sligo, Thy Land's My Land
Smart Set, The
Smoky Mokes
Somebody Loves Me
Son Of The Desert Am I, A
Song Of All Nations
Song Of The Steeple
Song That Reached My Heart
Song That Will Live Forever
Songs My Mammy Sang For Me
Sounds From The Alps
Sounds From The Orient
Sousa's Grand March
South Fifth Ave.

Souvenir March
Sparkling Piper Heidsieck
Spread Out Your White Sails
St. Patrick's Day Parade
Standing On The Corner, Didn't Mean No Harm
Star Of The East
Star Of The Sea
Starry Night, A
Stars & Stripes Forever March, The
Stay In Your Own Back Yard
Stick To Your Mother, Tom
Stories Mother Told, The
Story Of The Rose
Streets Of Cairo, The
Strolling On The Brooklyn Bridge
Such A Nice Girl, Too
Such An Education Has My Mary Ann
Sultan, The
Sun Do Move, The
Sunday Night When The Parlor's Full
Sunshine Of Paradise Alley
Sunshine Will Come Again
Sunny Side Of Thompson Street
Supposing
Susie
Sweet Bunch Of Daisies
Sweet Iniscarra
Sweet Katie Connor
Sweet Little Babies
Sweet Marie
Swing Song
Ta-Ra-Ra Boom-De-Ay
Take A Day Off
Take A Day Off Mary Ann
Take A Seat Old Lady
Take Back The Engagement Ring
Take Back Your Gold
Take Me Back Home Again
Take Your Clothes And Go
Taking In The Town
Tapioca
Tear Of Gratitude, The
Tempest, The
Tender And True
That Dear Old Bell
That Is Love
That Old Sweetheart Of Mine
There Is A Land Of Pure Delight
There'll Come A Time
There's A Girl In The World For Us All
There's Always A Seat In The Parlor For You
There's No One Like Mother To Me
There's None Will Forgive Like A Mother
They All Follow Me
They Are The Best Friends Of All
They Never Tell All What They Know
Thirteen Were Saved
Those Wedding Bells Shall Not Ring Out
Three Leaves Of Shamrock
Throw Him Down, McCloskey
Thunderer, The
Tickled To Death

Tim Toolin
Tip Your Hat To Nellie
To The Rescue
Tommy Atkins
Tommy, Make Room For Your Uncle
Topsy Turvy
Tramp, Tramp, Tramp
Travelin' Back To Alabam!
Tripping Thro' The Meadows
Triumphal Post March
Trumpeter, The
Turn Verein Cadets
Twentieth Century Woman
Twiggy Voo
Twinkle Twinkle Little Star
'Twixt Love And Duty
Two Little Girls In Blue
Two Little Rugged Urchins
Two Sweethearts Of Mine
Tzigani Dances
U.S. Black Marines
Uncle Amos
Uncle Jasper's Jubilee
Uncle Josh's Huskin Dance
Uncle Ned
Up Dar In De Sky
Up In A Balloon
Up Went O'Connor On His Wedding Day
Upper Ten And Lower Five
Van-Guard Of The King, The
Veronica
Victors
Violet From Mother's Grave, A
Violet I Picked From My Mother's Grave, A
Volunteer Organist
Wait Till The Clouds Roll By
Wait Till The Tide Comes In
Waiting At The Station
Walkin' Fo' Dat Cake
Walkin' Fo' De Great White Cake
Walking In The Rain
Warm Proposition
Warm Reception, A
Warmest Baby In The Bunch, The
Warmin' Up In Dixie, A
Washington Post March
Way Up Yonder
We Are Coming, Father Abraham, Three Hundred Thousand Strong
We Said Goodbye
Wedding Of The Chinee And The Coon, The
Wedding Of The Lily And The Rose
Weeping, Sad And Lonely
Were My Song With Wings Provided
What! Marry Dat Gal!
Wheel The Baby Out
When Hogan Paid His Rent
When I Do The Hootchy Kootchy In The Sky
When I Took The Keeley Cure
When I Was A Girl 18 Years Old
When Johnny Comes Marching Home Again
When Love Is Young

When Mother First Taught Me How To Pray
When The Car Goes By
When The Clock In The Tower Strikes Twelve
When The Robins Nest Again
When You Ain't Got No Money, Well You Needn't Come Around
When You Were Sweet Sixteen
Where Did You Get That Hat?
Where The Chicken Got The Axe
Where The Sparrows And Chippies Parade
Where The Sweet Magnolias Grow
While Strolling Through The Park One Day
Whip-Poor-Wills Song, The
Whisper Your Mother's Name
Whistling Coon
Whistling Rufus
White Owl, The
White Wings
Who Dat Say Chicken In Dis Crowd
Who Threw The Overalls In Mrs. Murphy's Chowder
Who'll Buy My Lavender?
Whoa Emma
Why Did They Dig Ma's Grave So Deep
Why Don't You Get A Lady Of Your Own?
Why Paddy's Always Poor
Why Would We Meet As Strangers?
Widow Nolan's Goat
Widow's Plea For Her Son
Wing Dance
With All Her Faults I Love Her Still
Without Your Love, Ah, Let Me Die
Won't You Be My Sweetheart
Won't You Come To My Tea Party
Woodland Whispers
Woodman, Spare That Tree!
Wreck, The
Yacht Club
Yankee Dewey
You
You Could Have Been True
You Got To Play Rag Time
You Never Miss Your Mother Till She's Gone
You'll Get All That's Coming To You
Young Eph's Lament
Young Mother's Lullaby, The
You're Not The Only Pebble On The Beach
You've Been A Good Old Wagon But You Done Broke Down
Zenda
Zenda Waltzes
Zizzy, Ze Zum, Zum!

PRESIDENTS

There have been many songs written pertaining to Presidents. Some have photos of Presidents on the cover.

Be Good To California Mr. Wilson, California Was Good To You, 1916 shows a photo of President Wilson. Keep Cool And Keep Coolidge, 1924 shows a photo of President Coolidge. Grover Cleveland Grand March, 1892, shows a photo of Grover Cleveland.

Listed below are songs pertaining to Presidents. Current prices can be found in Chapter 1.

American Eagles (President Ronald Reagan In Cast)
Answer Mr. Wilson's Call (President Woodrow Wilson)
Be Good To California, Mr. Wilson, California Was Good To You (Pres. Wilson)
Beautiful Isle Of Somewhere (President McKinley)
Eisenhower 1950 Inauguration (Pres. Eisenhower)
Father Of The Land We Love (Pres. Washington)
For Old Glory (Pres. Washington)
General Garfield's Grand March (Pres. Garfield)
General U.S. Grant's Grand March Reception (Pres. Grant)
George Washington Bicentennial (Pres. Washington)
Get On The Raft With Taft (Pres. Taft)
Girl From Jones Beach, The (Pres. Reagan in cast)
Grover Cleveland's Grand March (Pres. Cleveland)
Harding, You're The Man For Us (Pres. Harding & Coolidge)
Honest Abe March (Pres. Lincoln)
How About A Cheer For The Navy (Pres. Reagan in cast)
I Found A Million Dollar Baby (Pres. Reagan in cast)
I Left My Heart At The Stage Door Canteen (Pres. Reagan in cast)
I Love You Like Lincoln Loved The Old Red, White & Blue (Pres. Lincoln)
I Think We've Got Another Washington, And Wilson Is His Name (Pres. Wilson)
Ike For Four More Years (Pres. Eisenhower)
Ike Mr. President (Pres. Eisenhower)
I'm Getting Tired So I Can Sleep (Pres. Reagan in cast)
It's Time For Every Boy To Be A Soldier (Pres. Lincoln & Wilson)
Just Like Washington Crossed The Delaware, General Pershing Will Cross The Rhine (Pres. Washington)
Keep Cool, Keep Coolidge (Pres. Coolidge)
Lincoln Centennial Grand March (Pres. Lincoln)
McKinley Presidential March (Pres. McKinley)
McKinley's Funeral March (Pres. McKinley)
Mr. Yankee Doodle Are We Prepared? (Pres. Washington)
My Sergeant And I Are Buddies (Pres. Reagan in cast)
Nobody Knows How I Miss You Dear Old Pal (Pres. Wilson)
On The Steps Of The Great White Capitol Stood Martha And George (Pres. Washington)
Portrait, Photo Of Presicent Taft (Pres. Taft)
President Garfield Funeral March (Pres. Garfield)
Roosevelt N.R.A. March (Pres. Roosevelt)
School Where Lincoln Went (Pres. Lincoln)
Taft March (Pres. Taft)
That's What The Well-Dressed Man In Harlem Will Wear (Pres. Reagan in cast)
Army's Made A Man Out Of Me, The (Pres. Reagan in cast)
Great American, The (Pres. Theodore Roosevelt)
Nightingales Of Lincoln's Inn, The (Pres. Lincoln)
Road Is Open Again, The (Pres. Franklin D. Roosevelt)

Ship Named U.S.A Or Wilson's War Cry Of Peace, The (Pres. Wilson)
Woodrow Wilson Inaugural March, The (Pres. Wilson)
There Are Just As Many Heroes Today (Photo Pres. Washington & Lincoln)
They Are Fighting For Liberty (President George Washington)
This Is The Army Mr. Jones (Pres. Reagan in cast)
We Stand For Peace While Others War (Pres. Wilson)
What Does He Look Like (Pres. Reagan in cast)
With My Head In The Clouds (Pres. Reagan in cast)
Woodrow Wilson Leader Of The U.S.A. (Pres. Wilson)

RAGTIME

Not too many years ago, people who had never heard of Scott Joplin thought ragtime to be a tinny sounding music heard in saloon or beer halls. Since Scott Joplin's The Entertainer was revised by Marvin Hamlish in The Sting the public has awakened to it's splendor.

Listed below are songs pertaining to Ragtime. Current prices can be found in Chapter 1.

Aba Daba Honeymoon, The
African Pas'
Alamo Rag
Alexander's Back From Dixie With His Rag-Time Band
All-Of-A-Twist
American Beauty
Angel Food Rag
Another Rag
Apple Jack
Apple Sass
April Fool Rag
Beale Street Mama
Bees-Wax Rag
Bell Hop Rag
Black And Blue Rag
Black And White Rag
Black Bowl, A
Blacksmith Rag
Blue Goose Rag
Blue Grass Rag, The
Boogie Man Rag, The
Boogie Rag
Bowery Buck
Breeze From Alabam, A
Brownie Rag, The
Buffalo Rag
Bugle Call Rag, The
Bunch Of Noise
Burglar Rag, The
Butcher Rag
Cabaret Rag, The
Caberavings
Calico Rag
California Sunshine
Calla Lily Rag
Campus Rag
Candied Cherries
Cannibal Rag

Carbolic Acid Rag
Cascades, The
Castle House Rag
Cataract Rag
Cauldron Rag, The
Champagne
Charleston Rag, The
Chatterbox Rag
Checkers Rag
Cherry Leaf Rag
Chevy Chase
Chewin The Rag
Chicken Chowder
Chili Sauce Rag
Chills And Fever
Chrysanthemum Rag, The
Climax Rag
Cloud Kisser
Coal Smoke
Corrugated Rag
Country Club Rag Time
Crabapples
Cracked Ice Rag
Crazy Bone Rag
Dakota Rag
Daly's Reel
Darktown Capers
Dat Lovin' Rag
Delightful Rag
Dill Pickles
Dixie Dimples
Dockstader Rag, The
Dope
Down Home Rag
Dublin Rag, The
Dusting The Keys
Easy Winners
Echoes From The Snowball Club
Elite Syncopations
Entertainer, The
Entertainer's Rag, The
Ethiopa
Euphonic Sounds
Everybody Loves Rag
Everybody Rag With Me
Everybody Two Step Rag
Everybody's Rag
Excelsior Rag
Fashion Rag
Felicity
Fig Leaf Rag
First You Do The Rag, Then You Bombershay
Fizz Water
Foolishness Rag
Freckles Rag
French Pastry Rag
Frog Legs Rag
Frozen Bill Rag
Fuss And Feathers
Gaby Glide, The
Georgia Giggle, The
Georgia Rag, The

Get This Slow Rag
Glad Rags
Gladiolus Rag
Gold Dust Twins
Good Gravy Rag
Good-Bye Ragtime
Grace And Beauty
Gravel Rag, The
Grizzly Bear, The
Hard Boiled Rag
Harem Scarem Rag, Some Rag!
Harlem Rag
Harmony Rag
Haunting Rag
Heliotrope Bouquet
Heliotrope Rag
Hen Cackle Rag
He's A Rag Picker
Hifalutin Rag
High Jinks
Hilarity
Hobble Rag, The
Hold Up Rag, The
Holy Moses
Honeymoon Rag
Hot-House-Rag
Humpty Dumpty
Hyacinth
Hypnotic Rag
Hysterics Rag
I Want A Ragtime Bungalow
I'm Certainly Living A Ragtime Life
I'm Done With Rag-Time
Imperial Rag
Indian Rag
Intermission Rag
International Rag
Irresistable Rag
Jack Rabbit Rag
Jagtime Johnson's Ragtime March
Johnson Rag
Junkman's Rag, The
Jungle Jamboree Rag
Just Because I Let You Call Me Baby Lamb
Kansas City Rag
Kentucky Blues
Kimberly Rag
King Chanticleer
Kismet Rag
Klondike Rag
Lazy Luke
Lemon Drops
Lightning Rag
Mad House Rag, The
Majestic Rag
Maple Leaf Rag
Mardi Gras Rag
Matrimony Rag
Medic Rag
Melinda's Wedding Day Rag
Melody Rag
Meteor Rag

Midnight Whirl, The
Mississippi River
Mocking Bird Rag
Monkey Rag
Moose Rag
Mop Rag
Movie Rag
Music Box Rag
Musical Rag Sal
My Ragtime Fireman
Mysterious Rag, The
New York Rag
Nigger Toe Rag
Nightingale Rag
Oceana Roll, The
Oh, Oh, Oh, A Hypochrondriac Rag
Oh! Papa
Oh That Kissing Rag
Oh That Navajo Rag
Oh! That Yankiana Rag
Oh You Rag
Old Folks Rag
Old Virginia Rag
On The Mississippi
Operatic Rag
Ophelia Rag
Original Rags
Paradis Rag, The
Paragon Rag
Peaceful Henry
Peacherine
Persian Lamb Rags
Piccalilli Rag
Pickles & Peppers
Pineapple Rag
Pipe Organ Rag, The
Pitter Patter Rag
Pleasant Moments Ragtime Waltz
Poverty Rag
Powder Rag
Princess Rag
Pussy Cat Rag, The
Put Me To Sleep With An Old Fashioned Melody,
    Wake Me Up With A Rag
Quality Rag
Rag-A-Tag-Rag
Rag Baby Rag
Rag-Bag
Rag Classique
Rag Of Rags Syncoper, The
Rag, Rag, Rag
Ragged Edges Rag
Ragging The Scale
Raggity Rag
Raggy Fox Trot, The
Ragtime Annie Lee
Ragtime Betty
Ragtime Cowboy Joe
Ragtime Dance, The
Rag Time Drafted Man
Ragtime Dream, The
Rag Time Eating Place

Ragtime Express, The
Ragtime Eyes
Ragtime Goblin Man, The
Ragtime In The Air
Ragtime Mephisto
Ragtime Nightmare, A
Ragtime Organ Morgan
Ragtime Piano Playing
Ragtime Soldier Man, The
Ragtime Violin, The
Ragtime Volunteers Are Off To War, The
Ragtime Wedding Bells
Railroad Rag
Ramshackle Rag
Real Slow Rag, A
Red Pepper, A Spicy Rag
Red Raven Rag
Red Rose Rage, The
Rhapsody Rag
Russian Pony Rag
Russian Rag
Rusty Can-O Rag
Saint Vitus Rag, The
Salted Peanuts Rag
Saratoga Glide, The
Saskatoon Rag
Scarecrow Rag
School Of Ragtime
Scott Joplin's New Rag
Seben Come Eleben
Sensation Rag
Silks & Rags Waltzes
Silver Fox
Skeleton Rag, The
Sleepy Hollow Rag
Son Of The Rag Time Boy
Sour Grapes
Spaghetti Rag
Speckled Spider Rag
Squirrel Rag, The
St. Louis Rag, The
St. Louis Tickle
Steamboat Rag
Stewed Chicken Rag
Stop That Rag, Keep On Playing
Strenuous Life
Struttin' With Some Barbecue, Dixieland
    Ragtime Blues
Sugar Cane Rag
Sunburst Rag
Sunflower Babe
Sunflower Slow Rag
Swanee Rag
Swanee Ripples Rag
Swipsey Cake Walk
Sympathetic Jasper
Tar Babies
Temptation
Temptation Rag
That Auto Rag
That Brass Band Rag
That Chinatown Rag

That Daffodil Rag
That Daffy Rag
That Devilish Rag
That Ev'ry Little Movement Rag
That Fussy Rag
That Gosh Darned Two-Step Rag
That Hypnotizing Man
That Indian Rag
That International Rag
That Italian Rag
That Mesmerizing Mendelssohn Tune
That Moaning Saxophone Rag
That Mysterious Rag
That Paradise Rag
That Peculiar Rag
That Pleasing Rag
That Puzzlin' Rag
That Raggy Foxtrot
That Rag-Time Regimental Band
That Railroad Rag
That Teasing Rag
That's-A-Plenty
38th St. Rag
Tickle The Ivories
Tickled To Death
Tom Boy
Town Talk
Trilby Rag
Turkish Towel Rag
Turkish Trophies
12th Street Rag
20th Century Rag, The
Wagner Couldn't Write A Ragtime Song
Wall Street Rag
Wedding Bells Rag
Weeping Willow Rag
When Alexander Takes His Ragtime Band To France
When Ragtime Rosie Ragged The Rosary
When The Kaiser Does The Goose-Step To A Good
     Old American Rag
When The Steamboats On The Swanee Whistle Rag-Time
When Uncle Joe Plays A Rag On His Old Banjo
When You're Not Here
Whole World Comes From Dixie, The
Wild Cherries Rag
Wildflower Rag
Yiddle On Your Fiddle Play Some Ragtime
Yiddisha Rag, The
You & The Moon & A Ragtime Tune
You Got To Play Rag Time
Zizzy, Ze Zum, Zum

RED CROSS

The Red Cross is an international movement that seeks to lessen and prevent human suffering. It aims to enlist all mankind in voluntary service to others and has an estimated membership of 100,000,000 around the world. The Red Cross is a living memorial to the humanitarianism and vision of Jean Henri Durant. Durant had two inspirations when he set about forming the humanitarian movement we know today as the Red

Cross: the brilliant, selfless example of Florence Nightingale's service to the war wounded of the Crimean War and his own experience on the carnage field of Solferino in 1859. Humane treatment of the battle wounded is accepted today as a matter of course. Many of us do not realize that three quarters of a century gaps the change from sheer barbarism on the battle field to the protection now granted by the Red Cross Flag.

The symbol adopted by the movement is a simple red cross on a white background – the reverse of the Swiss national emblem, from which it was adapted in honor of movement's Swiss founder, Jean Henri Durant.

Listed below are songs pertaining to Red Cross. Current prices can be found in Chapter 1.

Angel God Sent From Heaven, The
Angel Of No Man's Land, The
Angels Of Mercy
Girl Who Wears A Red Cross On Her Sleeve, The
Herald Of Peace March
I Don't Want To Get Well
If You'll Be A Soldier, I'll Be A Red Cross Nurse
I've Got A Red Cross Rosie Going Across With Me
Let Me Kiss The Flag Before I Die
My Red Cross Girl, Farewell
My Red Cross Girlie
On The Battlefield
Red Cross Needs You Now, The
Rose Ann Of Charing Cross
Rose Of No Man's Land, The
That Red Cross Girl Of Mine
There's An Angel Missing From Heaven
When Your Boy Comes Back To You
Why Shouldn't They Be Good Enough Now

SALVATION ARMY

The Salvation Army is an international evangelical and charitable organization founded in 1865 by William Booth. The name was adopted in 1878. "Don't Forget The Salvation Army (My Doughnut Girl)" is the song officially endorsed and adopted by The Salvation Army. As the song begins "Pennies, nickels, dimes and quarters, hear them ring. Oh what joy and oh what bliss those coins can bring". The Salvation Army lives on today. Remember to donate to the faithful bell ringers who so gallantly stand in the cold at Christmas to help this cause.

Listed below are songs pertaining to the Salvation Army. Current prices can be found in Chapter 1.

Don't Forget The Salvation Army (My Doughnut Girl)
Goodbye Sally Good Luck To You
Little Blue Bonnet Girl
Salvation Army, Oh
Salvation Lassie Of Mine
Salvation Nell

SIGNED

Original signatures on sheet music by movie stars, entertainers and composers are in great demand. Some

signatures appear to be original while others appear to be reproductions. Among the many performers who signed sheet music were Enrico Caruso, Victor Herbert, Sophie Tucker, Eva Tanguay, Mary Pickford, Bing Crosby & Rudy Vallee.

Listed below are songs which bear a signature. Current prices can be found in Chapter 1.

After The Show We'll Find The Rainbow Again,
     Signed by Morette Sisters
Ah! Sweet Mystery Of Life, Signed by Victor Herbert
All Of Me, Signed by Russ Columbo
Always, Signed by Irving Berlin
America I Love You, Signed by Eva Tanguay
Americans Come!, The, Signed by Fay Foster
And That Ain't All, Signed by Sophie Tucker
Baby, Everybody Calls Her Baby, Signed by Eddie
     Cantor
Bargain Day, Signed by Rosemary Clooney
Begin The Beguine, Signed by Artie Shaw
Belgian Rose, Signed by Louise Glaum
Beloved, Be Faithful, Signed by Russ Morgan
Cherie I Love You, Signed by Grace Moore
Chicago, Signed by Fred Fisher
Civilization, Signed by Thomas H. Inck
Cowboy At Church, The, Signed by Johnny Marvin
Dear Old Pal Of Mine, Signed by Lieut. Gitz Rice
Do Something, Signed by James Montgomery Flagg
Dolores, Signed by Frank Sinatra
Don't Try To Steal The Sweetheart Of A Soldier,
     Signed by Anna Chandler
Dorine Of Dublin, Signed by Bonita
Dreams Of Long Ago, Signed by Enrico Caruso
East, West, Hame's Best, Signed by Alec Finlay
Elaine, My Moving Picture Queen, Signed by Pearl
     White
Freckles, Signed by Nora Bayes
Galway Bay, Signed by Bing Crosby
Georgia On My Mind, Signed by Hoagy Carmichael
Get Up Those Stairs Mademoiselle, Signed by Tony
     Pastor
Ghost Riders In The Sky, Signed by Vaughn Monroe
Hand That Rocked My Cradle Rules My Heart, The,
     Signed by Irving Berlin
Hard To Get, Signed by Giselle MacKenzie
Have You Forgotton So Soon, Signed by Ozzie Nelson
Heartaches, Signed by Guy & Carmen Lombardo
Hot Diggity Dog Ziggity Boom, Signed by Perry
     Como
How Much Is That Doggie In The Window?, Signed
     by Patti Page
I Can't Give You Anything But Love, Signed by
     Jimmy McHugh
I Didn't Think You'd Care, Signed by Courtney
     Sisters
I Give You My Word, Signed by Al Kavelin
I Know What It Means To Be Lonesome, Signed by
     June Caprice
I Left My Heart In San Francisco, Signed by Tony
     Bennett
I Love You For Sentimental Reasons, Signed by Eddy
     Howard

I Might Be Your Once-In-A-While, Signed by Victor Herbert

I Wish I Knew The Name Of The Girl In My Dreams, Signed by Jack Smith

I Wonder, Signed by Constance Talmadge

If I Only Had A Brain, Signed by E.Y. Harburg

If You Had All The World And It's Gold, Signed by Eva Tanguay

If You Love Me, Signed by Vera Lynn

I'll Close My Eyes, Signed by Dinah Shore

I'll Follow You, Signed by Rock & Fulton

I'll See You In The Sunrise, Signed by Marie Calabrese

I'm Alone Because I Love You, Signed by Belle Baker

I'm Beginning To See The Light, Signed by Harry James

I'm Building Up To An Awful Let-Down, Signed by Fred Astaire

I'm Sorry The Day I Laid My Eyes On You, Signed by E.P. Van Buren & Biscardi

I'm Still Caring, Signed by Rudy Vallee

I'm The Brother Of Lily Of The Valley, Signed by Henry Lewis

In The Mood, Signed by Glenn Miller

It Looks Like A Big Night Tonight, Signed by Lillian Ashley

I've Been Drafted Now I'm Drafting You, Signed by Dottie Lamour & Bob Hope

Just An Echo In The Valley, Signed by Bing Crosby

Kiss Of Fire, Signed by Tony Martin

Last Mile Home, The, Signed by Sammy Kaye

Little Dutch Mill, Signed by Bing Crosby

Little White Church In The Niche, The, Signed by Tito Guizar

Living A Life Of Dreams, Signed by Rudy Vallee

Lonesome Honey Just For You, Signed by Bonita

Lonesome–That's All, Signed by Rudy Vallee

Love Letters In The Sand, Signed by Russ Columbo

Ma, Signed by Eddie Cantor

Make Love To Me, Signed by Joe Stafford

Man Upstairs, The, Signed by Kay Starr

Mandalay, Signed by Charles Chaplin

Mary Pickford, The Darling Of Them All, Signed by Mary Pickford

Memories, Signed by Barbara Streisand

Mexicali Rose, Signed by Bing Crosby

Moon River, Signed by Henry Mancini

Mother, A Word That Means The World To Me, Signed by Eva Tanguay

Mule Train, Signed by Frankie Laine

My Cousin Caruso, Signed by Enrico Caruso

My Love Song To You, Signed by Jackie Gleason

My Mammy, Signed by Al Jolson

My Way, Signed by Frank Sinatra

Nestle In Your Daddy's Arms, Signed by Lillian Price

Nine O'Clock Sal, Signed by L.R. Clippinger

Now Is The Hour, Signed by Eddy Howard

Now Is The Hour, Signed by Bing Crosby

Now Is The Hour, Signed by Gracie Fields

Off Shore, Signed by Russ Morgan

Oh! Johnny Oh! Johnny Oh!, Signed by Henry Lewis

Oklahoma, I Love You, Signed by Opal Harrison Williford

Old Glory I Salute You, Signed by Vaughn DeLeath

One Little Candle, Signed by Perry Como

Over The Rainbow, Signed by Judy Garland

Over There, Signed by Rockwell

Peg O' My Heart, Signed by Laurette Taylor

Petite Waltz, The, Signed by Anne Shelton

Petite Waltz, The, Signed by Guy Lombardo

Pink Panther, Signed by Henry Mancini

Please Mr. Sun, Signed by Johnnie Ray

River, Stay 'Way From My Door, Signed by Vincent Lopez

Rose O'Mine, Signed by Frances Alda

Secret Love, Signed by Doris Day

Send Me Away With A Smile, Signed by Rita Gould

She's My Warm Baby, Signed by Flo Irwin

Short'nin Bread, Signed by Eddy Nelson

Side By Side, Signed by Kay Starr

Sidewalks Of New York, The, Signed by Al Smith

Singin' In The Rain, Signed by Gene Kelly

Slow Poke, Signed by Pee Wee King & Redd Stewart

Smile You Miss, The, Signed by Raymond Hubbell

So Red The Rose, Signed by Jolly Nash

Some Day Waiting Will End, Signed by Ivan Caryle

Some Enchanted Evening, Signed by Ezzio Pinza

Some Of These Days, Signed by Sophie Tucker

Spoon Full Of Sugar, A, Signed by Julie Andrews

Stars Are The Windows Of Heaven, Signed by Andrews Sisters

Suddenly There's A Valley, Signed by Gogi Grant

Sugar, Signed by Little Jack Little

Ten Cents A Dance, Signed by Doris Day

Texarkana Baby, Signed by Eddy Arnold

That Old Gang Of Mine, Signed by Ray Henderson

There's A Gold Mine In The Sky, Signed by Bing Crosby

Thoughts Of My Childhood Home, Signed by Tito Guizar

Tiny Bubbles, Signed by Don Ho

Tisket A Tasket, A, Signed by Ella Fitzgerald

Tomorrow Is Ours, Signed by Gil Gilbert

Vanity Fair, Signed by Stella Mayhew

Wabash Moon, Signed by Morton Downey

Walking In The Rain, Signed by Bobby Newcomb

Walking The Floor Over You, Signed by Ernest Tubb

Was There Ever A Pal Like You, Signed by Billy Burke

Wayward Wind, The, Signed by Gogi Grant

Weep Not For The Dead, Signed by Ada Weigel Powers

What Money Can't Buy, Signed by Eva Tanguay

When Irish Eyes Are Smiling, Signed by John McCormack

When The Moon Comes Over The Mountain, Signed by Kate Smith

When You Come Back, Signed by George M. Cohan

When You're Away, Signed by Victor Herbert

Where Are The Scenes Of Yesterday?, Signed by Florence White

Where Do You Work-A-John?, Signed by Fred Waring

While We're Young, Signed by Perry Como

Who Is Sylvia, Signed by Billy Mills

Why, Signed by Frankie Avalon

Why Dance? Signed by Jack Miller

Why Don't You Love Me?, Signed by Hank Williams

Why Should I Cry Over You, Signed by Margie Coate

You Belong To Me, Signed by Patti Page

You Can't Expect Kisses From Me, Signed by Mary Elizabeth

You Didn't Want Me When You Had Me, Signed by Catherine Calvert

You're Not The Only Pebble On The Beach, Signed by Lottie Gibson

Your Lips Are No Man's Land But Mine, Signed by Arthur Empey

SPORTS

Song sheets relating to sports are scarce. There were very few sheet music covers depicting sports. Home Run Polka was sold at auction in 1988: "Everyone in the room laughed when the sheet music was offered but the mood turned serious quickly as the piece was hammered down at $1,200.00" (as printed in Antiques & The Arts Weekly 3-11-88). The Steeple Chase March Gallop is a very good example of a sports cover. Also Let's Get the Umpire's Goat, which is a terrific baseball cover. Some college or school songs could also come under this category.

Listed below are songs pertaining to sports. Current prices can be found in Chapter 1.

Baseball

Cup Hunters

Finnegan, The Umpire

Fox Hunters' March, The

Gliders–Skating Waltz, The

Home Run Polka

Horses

Hunt Club, The

I Wonder Where My Easy Rider's Gone

I've Gone Goofy Over Miniature Golf

Let's Get The Umpire's Goat

Lion Hunter's Waltzes, The

On The Gridiron

One-A-Strike

Ragtime Jockey Man, The

Steeple Chase, The

Take Me Out To The Ball Game

Take Your Girl To The Ball Game

You Gotta Be A Football Hero

TITANIC

C.Q.D.; C.Q.D TITANIC, WE HAVE STRUCK AN ICEBERG, BADLY DAMAGED, RUSH AID. Latitude 4l.46 N Longitude 50.14 W.

That wireless message piercing the cold night air on April 15, 1912 prompted sweeping changes in nautical history and assured the Titanic a stellar place in steamship memorabilia collecting forever.

The Titanic, which at the time was labeled unsinkable and considered the most luxurious and safest ship, sailed from Southampton, England, on her maiden and last voyage, destination New York in April, 1912. Among the passengers was John Jacob Astor and his recent bride Madeline Talmadge Force. On April 15th the Titanic struck an iceberg in the North Atlantic and within 3 hours sank with the loss of 1516 lives including John Jacob Astor. Mrs. Astor was one of the survivors who had been lowered into a lifeboat with other passengers. The sinking of the Titanic is considered one of the greatest disasters of all times.

Listed below are songs about the Titanic. Current prices can be found in Chapter l.

Band Played "Nearer My God To Thee" As The Ship
    Went Down, The
Just As The Boat Went Down
My Sweetheart Went Down With The Ship
Wreck Of The Titanic, The

TRANSPORTATION

Ships: "Le Naufrage de L'Empress of Ireland" was a tragedy. It had left the port of Quebec on the way to Liverpool, England, and carried a total of 1,476 passengers and officers aboard. It collided with the Norwegian Starstad. One thousand twenty four lives were lost. There are many other songs listed depicting ships on their covers.

Trains and Train Wrecks: The Whip March & Two Step by Abe Holzman, 1913, depicts a tragic encounter of an old Iron Horse with what seems to be a horse drawn wagon. There are many wounded lying on the tracks. Great cover by Starmer. "The Gallant Hero" March and Two Step, 1920 was written in memory of Andy Moore, "The Little Hero of the Railroad" who stopped the train before it reached a broken track. "The Wolverine" March and Two Step by Harry J. Lincoln, 1912, has a great cover by W.J. Dittmar.

Automobiles: Early automobile ads or sheet music depicting old cars are very collectable, such as "In My Merry Oldsmobile," 1905, sung with great success by Anna Fitzhugh. Oh! for those old Model Ts! "The Motor March," by George Rosey, 1906, is another great cover. Bobby North's terrific hit, "He'd Have To Get Under, Get Out And Get Under (To Fix Up His Automobile)," 1913, cover by E.H. Pfeiffer, could never be surpassed in the cover art.

Airplanes, Balloons and Zeppelins: The Million Dollar Pier Song "You're My Girl," 1913, shows airplanes, balloons and zeppelins on the cover. The cover on "Why Don't You Try" or The Rolling Chair Song, 1905, seems to show the Atlantic City boardwalk with a couple seated in a wicker chair being pushed by a black porter. "Come Josephine In My Flying Machine", 1910; the girls were daring in the early nineteen hundreds.

Listed below are songs pertaining to transportation. Current Prices can be found in Chapter 1.

Across The Continent
After You're Gone
All Aboard That Ocean Baby
Alsacian Railroad Gallops

Amelia Earhart's Last Flight
As Deep As The Deep Blue Sea
As He Rode Her Around In His Wonderful One Horse
    Shay
As The Lusitania Went Down
Auto Race
Automobile Honeymoon
Automobiling
Baggage Coach Ahead, The
Band Played "Nearer My God To Thee" As The Ship
    Went Down, The
Battle In The Sky
Big Four Two-Step
Big Red Motor And The Little Blue Limousine
Bird From O'er The Sea, A
Black Diamond Express
Blue Line Galop
Bobbin' Up And Down
Bombardier Song, The
Bon Voyage
Born At Sea And A Sailor
Brave Jennie Creek
Bright Little Lantern I Swing, The
Bring Back Your Love
Buffalo Flyer, The
Bump, Bump, Bump In Your Automobile
Casey Jones, The Brave Engineer
Casey Jones Went Down On The Robert E. Lee
Cause My Baby Says It's So
Chauffeur, The
Chicago Express, The
Choo-Choo
Cla-Wrench, Don't Tweat Me So Wuff
Cloud Kisser
Coach & Four, A
Come Josephine In My Flying Machine
Come On Papa
Come Take A Trip In My Air Ship
Comin' In On A Wing And A Prayer
Cranky Old Yank
Crescent Beach
Crossing On The Ferry
Day By Day
Devoted Hearts
Dixie Highway
Dixie I'm Coming Back To You
Dolly Dear
Don't Take Advantage
Down In Old Nantucket
Down In The Deep, Let Me Sleep When I Die
Down Where The Breezes Blow
Eastbound Train, The
Eddie Cantor's "Automobile Horn" Song
En Ballon
Exodus Song, The
Far Away Places
Fast Line Gallop
Fifteen Kisses On A Gallon Of Gas
Fighting Navy, The
Flag That Train
Flight Of The Air Ship, The
Floatin' Down To Cotton Town

Floating Down The River
Ford
Freedom Train, The
Gallant Hero, The
Gasoline Gus & His Jitney Bus
Gay Chauffeur, The
Get An Automobile
Get 'Em In A Rumble Seat
Giddy Giddap! Go On! Go On!
Girl On The Automobile
Give Me A Spin In Your Mitchell
Gondolier, The
Good Ship Mary Ann, The
Goodbye Broadway, Hello France
Grand Trunk Waltzes
Great Graphic Balloon Galop, The
Great Rock Island Route, The
Guess
Gunner's Mate, The
Harbor Lights
Harnden's Express Line Gallopade & Trio
He'd Have To Get Under–Get Out And Get Under
"Hello Daddy, I Knew That Was Your Car"
Hello Lindy
Henry Hudson Was A Bold Jack Tar
Henry's Made A Lady Out Of Lizzie
Here Comes The Navy
He's Coming Home On The 8 O'clock Train
He's On A Boat That Sailed Last Wednesday
Homeward Bound
Hong Kong
Hop A Jitney With Me
How 'Ya Gonna Keep Them Down On The Farm
How's Every Little Thing In Dixie
Hunk-A-Tin
Hush A Bye, Ma Baby
I Didn't Raise My Ford To Be A Jitney
I Don't Know Where I'm Going But I'm On My Way
I Love To Bumpty Bump
I Think I Oughtn't To Anymore
I Thought About You
I'd Rather Have A Girlie Than An Automobile
I'll Await My Love
I'll Be Your Own
I'm A-Longin' Fo' You
I'm Getting Ready For My Mother-In-Law
I'm Goin' Back To My Mammy
I'm Going Back To Broadway
I'm Going Back To Carolina
I'm Going Home To Mobile On The Morgan Line
I'm Going To Pack Myself In Your Arms
I'm Going To Stay Right Here In Town
I'm Like A Ship Without A Sail
I'm Not Ashamed Of You Molly, I Want You Just As
    You Are
I'm On My Way
I'm Wild About Horns On Automobiles That Go "Ta-
    Ta-Ta-Ta"
I'm Wingin' Home
In A Boat For Two
In A Canoe
In A Hupmobile For Two

In An Auto Car
In My Merry Oldsmobile
In My Old Home Town
In Philadelphia
In The Baggage Coach, Ahead
In The Harbor Of Home Sweet Home
In The Sweet Bye And Bye
In The Village By The Sea
It's A Rambling Flivver
Jes' Come Aroun' Wid An Automobile
John Henry, March
Johnny Zero
Just As The Boat Went Down
Keep Away From The Fellow Who Owns An
    Automobile
Keep Moving March
King Of The Air
Last Trip On The Old Ship, The
Le Voyage Aerien
Lehigh Polka
Let's Take A Ride On The Jitney Bus
Let's Wait For The Last Train Home
Levee Land
Levee Lou
Lightning Express
Like An Angel You Flew Into Everyone's Heart
Like Ships That Pass In The Night
Limited Express March
Lindbergh The Eagle Of The U.S.A.
Lindy, Lindy!
Little Bo-Peep Has Lost Her Jeep
Little Ford Rambled Right Along, The
Little Red Caboose Behind The Train, The
Little Girls We Met Upon The Train
Little Stowaway, The
Love In An Automobile
Lucky Lindy
Ma Says I Can't Go For A Ride
Make That Engine Stop At Louisville
Mammy's Lullaby
March Of The Iron Horse
Marine Review, The
Me And The Boy Friend
Me Too-Ho-Ho! Ha Ha!
Meet Me At The Station Dear
Merrily We'll Float Along
Message On The Train
"Mid The Light Ripples"
Midnight Flyer, The
Midnight Sons, The
Midnight Special
Mile A Minute, A
Mister Aeroplane Man Take Me Up To Heaven
Mr. Captain Stop The Ship
Mister Whitney's Little Jitney Bus
Moonlight On The Lake
Motor Girl
Motor King March
Motor March, The
Mrs. Casey Jones
My Aeroplane Jane
My Auto Lady

My Automobile Girl
My Automobile Girl From New Orleans
My Beloved Is Rugged
My Dad's The Engineer
My Mammy Knows
My Mariuccia, Take A Steamboat
My Mobile Gal
My Raggyadore
My Skylark Love
My Ten Ton Baby And Me
My Wife's Gone To The Country Hurrah! Hurrah!
My Wife's Up In An Airship
My Yellow Jacket Girl
Navy Blue
Navy Goat, The
NC-4 March
Neptune
New Express Galop
Night Train
Nobody Knows Where Rosie Goes
North Western Railway Polka
Northern Route March
Ocean Between Us, The
Oceana Roll, The
Oh! Mister Railroad Man, Won't You Take Me Back
    To Alabam
Oh Say! Can I See You Tonight
Oh! That Moonlight Glide
Oh What A Beautiful Ocean
Old Fall River Line
Old Glory
Old Man Shay
On A Joy Ride
On A Saturday Night
On A Slow Boat To China
On An Automobile Honeymoon
On The 5:15
On The 'Gin 'Ginny Shore
On The Honeymoon Express
On The New York, New Haven & Hartford
On The Old Back Seat Of The Henry Ford
On The Old Fall River Line
On The 7:28
On To Frisco
On Treasure Island
Once Aboard The Lugger
Once More Upon The Sea
Otto, You Ought To Take Me In Your Auto
Our Flag
Our Little Home On The Highway
Our Sammy Boys
Out In An Automobile
Out On The Bounding Deep
Out On The Deep
Out Where The Billows Roll High
Packard And The Ford
Parkin' In The Park With You
Pick Me Up & Lay Me Down In Dear Old Dixieland
Pioneer Limited
Please Mr. Conductor Take Me On Your Car
Poor Lizzie
Port Of Missing Ships, The

Pullman Porter Blues
Pullman Porters On Parade
Pullman Porters Parade, The
Put Me Off At Buffalo
Q Galop
Racing Down The Rapids
Ragtime Automobile
Rail-Road
Railroad Galop
Railroad Rag
Reckless Night On Board An Ocean Liner
Red Sails In The Sunset
Rickety Rickshaw Man, The
Ride In A Jitney For Mine, A
Ride Me In A Big Balloon
Riding On The Elevated Railroad
Riding Up The River Road
Rolling Home
Rumble Seat
Sailboat In The Moonlight, A
Sailing
Sailing Down The Chesapeake Bay
Sailing Down The River In The Moonlight, Mandy
    And I
Sailing Home
Sailing In My Balloon
Salt Of the Sea For Me, The
Salute The Flag
Scandal Of Little Lizzie Ford
Scotch Lassie Jean
Sea Gardens
Seeing Denver
Semper Paratus
Send Me A Letter From Over The Sea
She Sang "Aloha" To Me
Ship Named U.S.A. Or Wilson's Cry Of Peace, The
Ship Sails Tonight, The
Shipwreck, The
Shrimp Boats
Sit Down! You're Rocking The Boat
Six Cylinder Kid, The
Sky Anchors
Skylark
Sleepy Moon
Sleepy Town Express, The
Sounds From The Rockies
Speed Kings, The
Spread Out Your White Sails
St. Louis Blues
Star Of The Sea
Steamboat Bill
Step Along Henry
Storm On The Ocean
Summer
Sunset Limited March
Take A Car
Take A Little Ride With Me
Take Me On A Buick Honeymoon
Take Me Out For A Joy Ride
Take Me Out In A Velie Car
Take Me 'Round In A Taxicab
Take Me Up In An Aeroplane

Take Me Up With You Dearie
Taxi
Taxicab
Ten Little Fingers & Ten Little Toes
That Aeroplane Glide
That Auto Rag
That Railroad Rag
That St. Louis Jitney Bus "That Busted Bus"
That's "Some" Honeymoon
There's Lots Of Stations On My Railroad Track
They'll Never Miss The Wine In Dixieland
Through The Orange Grove Of South Carolina
Thundercloud
Time To Re-Tire
Titanic
Toot Your Horn, Kid, You're In A Fog
Tour De Noce
Trailer Song
Trailer Song, Roamin In A Home On Wheels, The
Train D'enfer Galop
Train In The Night
Tramps At Sea
Trans Continental
Travelling Blues
Twilight Express, The
Two Little Sailor Boys
Uncle Sam's Ships
Under The Tropical Moon
Up And Down The Eight Mile Road
Up In A Balloon
Up In My Flying Machine
Up In The Air
Up In Your Old Biplane
Up Went O'Connor On His Wedding Day
Upon The Trolley Line
Us On A Bus
Venetian Waters
Volplane Waltzes
Wait Till You Get Them Up In The Air Boys
Waiting At The Station
Waiting For The Robert E. Lee
Wake Up America
We're The Sunday Drivers
Western Flyer, The
When I Go Automobiling
When Isabella Green Went Automobiling
When Shall We Meet Again
When That Midnight Choo-Choo Leaves For Alabam'
When The Car Goes By
When The Lusitania Went Down
When The Oceans Meet In Panama
When The Old Boat Heads For Home
When The Steamboats On The Swanee Whistle Rag-Time
When The Trains Come East From California
When The Winds O'er The Sea Blow A Gale
When You're In Town
Where Do They Go When They Row, Row, Row
Where Do You Work-A John?
Whip, The
White Wings
Who Will Be With You When I Go Away
Why Don't You Try

Will You Be Waiting Dearie When My Ship Comes In
Willie Had A Motor Boat
Wings Of The Morning
Wolverine, The
Would You Be A Sailor's Wife
Wreck On The Southern Old 97
Wreck, The
Wreck Of The Titanic, The
Yacht Club
Yankee Hustler March
Ye Ho Me Lads, Ye Ho
You Can't Afford To Marry If You Can't Afford
    A Ford
You Can't Walk Back From An Aeroplane
You Flew Over
You Got To Keep A-Goin
You Tell It, Or Jitney-Bus Joy
You'd Never Know That Old Town Of Mine
You'll Have To Get Off And Walk
You'll Never Reach Glory In An Automobile
You're My Girl
You've Been A Good Old Wagon But You Done
    Broke Down

WORLD WAR I 1914–1918

Sheet music was very popular during WWI. Two of the most famous song writers were George M. Cohan & Irving Berlin. Although Cohan was too old to serve in the Armed Forces, he spent much time entertaining the troops. A publisher paid Cohan $25,000.00 for his most famous composition, "Over There." This was the highest price ever paid for a popular song at that time. The cover artist on this song is Norman Rockwell.

Irving Berlin wrote "Oh How I Hate To Get Up In The Morning" which was also a very popular song of WWI.

Many of the covers depicted soldiers going off to war leaving their loved ones behind.

Listed below are songs pertaining to WWI. Current prices can be found in Chapter I.

Across The Border
After Taps
After The Battle Is Over, Then You Can Come Back
    To Me
After The First Of July
After The War Is Over, Will There Be Any "Home
    Sweet Home"
Allied Victory March
A-M-E-R-I-C-A
America First
America For Mine
America Here's My Boy
America, He's For You
America I Love You & I Hear You Calling Me
America It's Up To You
America, Make The World Safe For Democracy
A-M-E-R-I-C-A Means I Love You My Yankee Land
America Needs You Like A Mother
America Our Pride

America Prepare
American Beauty
Americans Come, The
An Old Grand Army Man
And He'd Say "OO-La-La Wee Wee"
Angel God Sent From Heaven, The
Angel Of No Man's Land, The
Answer Mr. Wilson's Call
Apres La Guerre!
At The Dixie Military Ball
Au Revoir, But Not Good Bye
Baby's Prayer Will Soon Be Answered
Back In The Old Town Tonight
Batter Up, Uncle Sam Is At The Plate
Battle Song Of Liberty, The
Battle In The Sky
Battle Of The Marne
Battle Of The Nation
Battle Song
Because You're Here
Because You're Mine
Belgian Rose
Biggest Thing In A Soldier's Life Is The Letter That
    Comes From Home, The
Bing! Bang! Bing'em On The Rhine
Blighty
Blue Bird Bring Back My Happiness
Bow Down To Uncle Sam
Boy O'Mine Good Night
Boys Are Coming Home, The
Boys From Yankee Land, The
Boys, Get Ready!
Boys In The Trenches Are Calling You, The
Boys Of The U.S.A., The
Bravest Heart Of All
Break The News To Mother
Bring Back, Bring Back, Bring Back The
    Kaiser To Me
Bring Back My Daddy To Me
Bring Back My Soldier Boy To Me
Bugle Call Rag, The
Bumkin Island
Buy A Bond, Buy A Bond
Buy A Liberty Bond For Baby
By The Campfire
Call, The
Can't You Hear Your Country Calling
Captain Riley Of The U.S.A.
Captains Of The Clouds
Cheer Up Father, Cheer Up Mother
Cheer Up Little Darling
Chimes Of Normandy
Clap Hands For Freedom
Columbia
Come Along Boys
Come Back To Your Little Grey Home
Come, My Lad, And Be A Soldier
Come On Papa
Coming Home
Corporal Of The Guard
Daddy, I Want To Go
Daddy's Prayer

Darling I

Dear Little Boy Of Mine

Dear Mom

Dear Old Glory

Dear Old Land Of Mine

Dear Old Ma

Dear Old Pal Of Mine

Dear Old Uncle Sam

Dixie Volunteers, The

Do Something

Don't Be Anybody's Soldier Boy But Mine

Don't Cry Frenchy

Don't Cry Little Girl Don't Cry

Don't Forget The Salvation Army (My Doughnut Girl)

Don't Forget Your Dear Old Mother

Don't Give Up The Ship

Don't Leave Me Daddy

Don't Let Your Foot Slip Hiram

Don't Take My Darling Boy Away

Don't Tell The Folks You Saw Me

Down The Trail Of The Old Dirt Road

Down The Trail To Mother Dear

Dream Of A Soldier Boy

Dreaming Of Home Sweet Home

Dress Up Your Dollars In Khaki

E-Yip-Yow! Yankee Boys, Welcome Home Again

Each Stitch Is A Thought Of You Dear

End Of A Perfect Day, The

Engineer Girls

Every Mother's Son

Everybody Loves A Soldier

Everybody's Waiting For Somebody Else

Eyes Of The Army

Farewell, My Loved Ones

Fatherland The Motherland, The Land Of My
   Best Girl

Fight Is On, The

Fighting Navy, The

Flag Of My Heart

Flag Of My Heart & Home

Flag Of Our Country Long May Thou Wave

Flag Of The U.S.A.

Flag That Had Never Retreated, The

Fleur-De-Lys, Flow'r Of France Bloom Again

Follow The Flag

For Dixie And Uncle Sam

For It Is My Land And Your Land

For Surely I Will Come Back To You

For The Honor Of The Flag

For Your Boy And My Boy

For Your Country And My Country

Forget Me Not My American Rose

Freedom For All Forever (Hilliam)

Freedom For All Forever (Cogley & Bock)

Frenchy Come To Yankee Land

Friends

Gee! It's Great To Be Home Again

Gee! What A Wonderful Time We'll Have When The
   Boys Come Home

General Pershing

Giddy Giddap! Go On! Go On!

Giddap Mule

Girl He Left Behind Him Has The Hardest Fight Of
   All, The

Girl Who Wears A Red Cross On Her Sleeve, The

Girls Of France

Give A Little Credit To The Navy

Give Me A Kiss By The Numbers

Give Me A Little Bit More Than You Gave

God Be With Our Boys To-Night

God Bring You Safely To Our Arms Again

God Save America

God Spare Our Boys Over There

Good Bye Alexander, Good Bye Honey Boy

Good-bye And Luck Be With You–Laddie Boy

Goodbye Broadway, Hello France

Goodbye France

Goodbye Germany

Goodbye Lil' Liza Jane

Good-Bye, Mollie May

Good-Bye My Soldier Boy

Goodbye Sally, Good Luck To You

Good-Bye, Slim

Good Morning Mr. Zip, Zip, Zip

Good Night German

Greatest Day The World Will Ever Know, The

Greatest Thing That Came From France, The

Hats Off To The Red White And Blue

He Was A Soldier From The U.S.A.

Heaven's Artillery

Hello Central! Give Me No Man's Land

Hello! General Pershing, How's My Daddy To-Night?

Hello, My Darling Mother

Help Bring Our Stars And Stripes Across The Rhine

He's Doing His Bit, For The Girls

He's Got Those Big Blue Eyes Like You, Daddy Mine

He's Had No Lovin' For A Long Long Time

Here's To Your Boy And My Boy

Hinkey-Dinkey Parlez-Vous

Hip Hip Hoo-Ray For The Good Old U.S.A.

His Majesty, The American

Home Again

Home Coming Week In France

Homeward Bound

How 'Ya Gonna Keep Them Down On The Farm

Hurrah! For The Liberty Boys, Hurrah!

I Ain't Got Weary Yet

I Cannot Bear To Say Goodbye

I Didn't Raise My Boy To Be A Soldier

I Don't Know Where I'm Going But I'm On My Way

I Don't Want To Get Well

I Dreamt My Daddy Came Home

I Haven't Got Time For Anyone Else Till John
   Gets Home

I Love A Parade

I Love Her, Ooh La La La

I Love The U.S.A.

I May Be Gone For A Long, Long Time

I Miss Daddy's Goodnight Kiss

I Think We've Got Another Washington, And Wilson
   Is His Name

I Tried To Raise My Boy To Be A Hero

I Want To Be A Soldier For The U.S.A.

I Wish I Had Someone To Say "Good-bye" To

I Wonder If She Is Waiting In Her Old New
   England Town

I Wonder What He's Doing To-Night

I Wouldn't Steal The Sweetheart Of A Soldier Boy

I'd Be Proud To Be The Mother Of A Soldier

I'd Feel At Home If They'd Let Me Join The Army

I'd Like To See The Kaiser With A Lily In His Hand

If A Mother's Prayers Are Answered, Then I Know
   You'll Come Back To Me

If He Can Fight Like He Can Love, Good Night,
   Germany!

If I Could Peep Thru The Window Tonight

If I Had A Son For Each Star In Old Glory

If I'm Not At Roll Call, Kiss Mother Good-Bye
   For Me (Small War Edition)

If I'm Not At Roll Call, Kiss Mother Good-Bye
   For Me

If Sammy Simpson Shot The Shutes

If War Is What Sherman Said It Was

If You'll Be A Soldier, I'll Be A Red Cross Nurse

I'll Be A Soldier Boy

I'll Be There, Laddie Boy, I'll Be There

I'll Come Back To You When It's All Over

I'll Keep The Lovelight Burning

I'll Wed The Girl I Left Behind

I'm A Long Way From Tipperary

I'm Coming Home

I'm Glad I Can Make You Cry

I'm Goin' To Fight My Way Right Back To Carolina

I'm Gonna Pin A Medal On The Girl I Left Behind

I'm Hitting The Trail To Normandy, So Kiss Me
   Goodbye

I'm Knitting A Rosary

I'm Lonesome For My Little Pal

I'm Longing For Someone To Love Me

I'm On A Long Long Ramble

In Flanders Fields The Poppies Grow

In Rank And File

In The Land Of Beginning Again, (Small War Edition)

In The Navy

Iron Division, The

It May Be Far To Tipperary, It's A Longer Way To
   Tennessee

It's A Long, Long Way To The U.S.A. & The Girl I
   Left Behind

It's A Long, Long Way To Tipperary

It's A Long Way From Here To "Over There"

It's A Long Way To Berlin But We'll Get There

It's All Over Now

It's Great To Be A Doughboy In The Army

It's Time For Every Boy To Be A Soldier

I've Got A New Job

I've Got A Red Cross Rosie Going Across With Me

I've Got A Ten Day Pass For A Honeymoon

I've Got My Captain Working For Me

I've Got The Army Blues

Ja-Da

Jerry, You Warra A Warrior In The War

Jim, Jim, Don't Come Back Till You Win

Jim, Jim, I Always Knew You'd Win

Jimmy Boy

Joan Of Arc, They Are Calling You

Johnny's In Town

Just A Baby's Prayer At Twilight

Just A Little Cottage In The Country Calling: Come Back Home

Just Like Washington Crossed The Delaware, General Pershing Will Cross The Rhine

K-K-K-Katy (Small War Edition)

K-K-K-Katy

Keep The Boys Happy While They're Away

Keep The Home Fires Burning

Keep The Love Lamp Burning

Keep The Trench Fires Going For The Boys Over There

Keep Your Face To The Sunshine

Keep Your Head Down, Fritzie Boy

Khaki Bill

Khaki Boys Of U.S.A., The

Laddie In Khaki

Lafayette, We Hear You Calling

Land Of My Best Girl, The

Last Long Mile, The

Let Lovelight Be Always Shining, For The Loved Ones Away

Let Me Kiss The Flag Before I Die

Let The Chimes Of Normandy Be Our Wedding Bells

Let The Flag Fly

Let Us Say A Prayer For Daddy

Let's All Be Americans Now

Let's Bury The Hatchet In The Kaiser's Head

Let's Finish The Job

Let's Help The Irish Now

Let's Keep The Glow In Old Glory And The Free In Freedom Too

Letter From No Man's Land, A

Letter That Never Reached Home, The

Liberty Bell, It's Time To Ring Again

Liberty Loan March

Liberty Statue Is Looking Right At You

Liberty Waltz

Light A Candle In The Chapel

Little Bit Of Sunshine, A

Little Blue Bonnet Girl

Little Grey Mother

Little Grey Mother Who Waits All Alone, The

Little Mother Of Mine

Little Uncle Sam Will Win

Long Boy, Goodbye Ma! Goodbye Pa! Goodbye Mule

Long Live America

Long, Long Way From Home, A

Look What My Boy Got In France

Lorraine, My Beautiful Alsace Lorraine

Madelon, I'll Be True To The Whole Regiment

Mademoiselle From Armentieres

Make Uncle Sam Your Banker

Makin's Of The U.S.A., The

Mammy's Chocolate Soldier

Man Behind The Hammer And The Plow, The

Marching Through Germany

Marines' Hymn, The

Mary Lee

Mr. Yankee Doodle Are We Prepared

Mother, I Love You

Mother Is Waiting For You

Mother You're Sunshine To Me

Mothers Of America You Have Done Your Share

Mothers Of France

Mother's Prayer For Her Boy Out There, A

My Barney Lies Over The Ocean

My Belgian Rose

My Chocolate Soldier Sammy

My Daddy's Coming Home

My Daddy's Star

My Land And Your Land

My Land, My Flag

My Little Rose Of Romany

My Mother's Rosary

My Old Sweetheart Is Coming Back

My Own Laddie

My Own United States

My Red Cross Girlie

My Sailor Laddie, Is Coming Back To Me

My Soldier Boy

My Star

My Sweetheart Is Somewhere In France

My Uncle Sammy Gals

My Wonderful Dream Of You

National Army Man, The

National Awakening, The

National Songs Of Our Allies, The

Nephews Of Uncle Sam

New Liberty, The

New Recruit March, The

No Foe Shall Invade Our Land

No One Said Good-bye To Me

Nobody Knows How I Miss You

Now I Lay Me Down To Sleep

O Land Of Hope And Freedom

Ocean Must Be Free

Off To The Front

Oh! Frenchy

Oh! How I Hate To Get Up In The Morning

Oh How I Wish I Could Sleep 'Till Daddy's Home

Oh, Moon Of The Summer Night

Oh You La La, I Love You

Old Glory

Old Glory Goes Marching On

On Guard America

On The Battlefield

On The Road That Leads Back Home

On The Road To Home Sweet Home

On The Sidewalks Of Berlin

On To Plattsburg

101st Regiment U.S.A. March

Oo-La-La-Wee-Wee

Oui, Oui Marie

Our Country's In It Now!

Our Gallant 91st Wild West Division

Our Lanky Yankee Boys In Brown

Our Sammies

Our Sammy Boys

Over In Hero Land

Over The Top

Over The Top With The Best Of Luck

Over There

Over Yonder Where The Lilies Grow

Pack Up Your Troubles In Your Old Kit Bag And Smile, Smile, Smile

Peace, Peace, Reechoed Cheer

Pershing's Crusaders

Pick A Little Four Leaf Clover, And Send It Over To Me

Plant A Little Garden In Your Own Back Yard

Poor Little Butterfly Is A Fly Girl Now

Rag Time Drafted Man

Ragtime Soldier Man, The

Ragtime Volunteers Are Off To War, The

Rainbow Military March, The

Raus Mit Der Kaiser, He's In Dutch

Red Cross Needs You Now, The

Remember I'm Your Friend

Ring Out, Sweet Bells Of Peace

Rocked In The Cradle Of Liberty

Romany Waltz

Rose Of No Man's Land, The

Rose Of No Man's Land, The (Patriotic War Edition)

Roses Of Arcadie

Roses Of Lorraine

Salvation Lassie Of Mine

Salvation Nell

Say A Prayer For The Boys "Out There"

Say "Au Revoir" But Not "Good-Bye"

Send Me Away With A Smile

Set Aside Your Tears, Till The Boys Come Marching Home

She'll Always Remember

She'll Miss Me Most Of All

Ship Named U.S.A. Or Wilson's War Cry Of Peace, The

Sister Susie's Sewing Shirts For Soldiers

So Long, Mother

Soldier Dreams Of You Tonight, A

Soldier's Dream Of Home, The

Soldier's Rosary, A

Soldier's Word To Mother, A

Some Day

Some Day Waiting Will End

Some Day, When The War Is Through

Some Sunny Day

Somebody's Waiting For Someone

Someone Else May Be There While I'm Gone

Someone Is Longing For Home Sweet Home

Somewhere In France Is Daddy

Somewhere In France Is The Lily

Somewhere Over There

Sons Of Liberty, The

Spirit Of America

Spirit Of '76

Stand Up And Fight Like H—

Stand Up Scout, Strong And Steady, Your Country's Calling You

Stars And Stripes Are Calling

Statue Of Liberty Is Smiling, The

Story Of Old Glory, The Flag We Love, The

Sweet Little Buttercup

Take Me Back To New York Town

Tale Of The Fireside, A

Taps

Tell That To The Marines

Tell The Last Rose Of Summer, Good Bye

Thank God For America

Thank You America

That Family Called The U.S.A.

That Long, Long Trail Is Getting Shorter Now

That Red Cross Girl Of Mine

That Wee Bit Of Devil In Your Irish Eyes

That's A Mother's Liberty Loan

That's What God Made Mothers For

Then I'll Come Back To You

Then-Now-Forever

There'll Be A Hot Time For The Old Men While The Young Men Are Away

There's A Green Hill Out In Flanders

There's A Little Blue Star In The Window

There's A Little Gold Star In The Service Flag

There's A Light Shining Bright In The Window Tonight

There's A Long, Long Trail

There's A Million Heroes In Each Corner Of The U.S.A.

There's A Picture In My Memory, And It Calls Me Back To You

There's A Red Bordered Flag In The Window

There's A Service Flag Flying At Our House

There's A Vacant Chair In Every Home Tonight

There's An Angel Missing From Heaven

There's Another Angel Now In Old Killarney

There's No Friend Like The Friends From Way Back Home

They All Sang Annie Laurie

They Are Fighting For Liberty

They Did Their Share Now I'll Do Mine

They Shall Not Pass!

They Were All Out Of Step But Jim

They'll Be Mighty Proud In Dixie Of Their Old Black Joe

They're Coming Back

They're On Their Way To Kan The Kaiser

This Message Your Mother Sends You

Three Cheers

Three Cheers For The Army And Navy

Three Wonderful Letters From Home

Till We Meet Again

Tim Rooney's At the Fightin'!

To Victory

Tommy

Trench! Trench! Trench!, Our Boys Are Trenching

Twenty Seventh Division

Two Little Eyes Are Watching For A Daddy Far Away

Uncle Sam's Ships

Uncle Sammy Take Care Of My Girl

Uncle Sammy's Army

Under One Flag

U.S. Field Artillery

U.S. Field Artillery March, The

U.S.A. March

Universal Glide

Victory

Wait For Your Honey Boy

Wait Till You Get Them Up In The Air Boys

Waiting

Wake Up, America!

Wake Up Virginia And Prepare For Your Wedding Day

War Babies

Watch Hope And Wait Little Girl I'm Coming Back To You

Watch, Hope, Wait Little Girl 'Til I Come Back To You

Watch The Bee Go Get The Hun

Way Down There, A Dixie Boy Is Missing

We Are Coming Home

We Are Ready

We Are Uncle Sammie's Little Nephews

We Are Uncle Sammy's Boys

We Can Muster Uncle Sammy Ten Million Men Or More

We Did It Before And We Can Do It Again

We Don't Want The Bacon, What We Want Is A Piece Of The Rhine

We Stand For Peace While Others War

We Watch The Skyways

Welcome Home Laddie Boy, Welcome Home

We'll All Come Back

We'll Be There Uncle Sam, We'll Be There

We'll Be Waiting When You Come Back Home

We'll Build A Little Home In The U.S.A.

We'll Do Our Share

We'll Have Peace On Earth And Even In Berlin

We'll Keep Old Glory Flying

We'll Knock The Heligo-Into Heligo-Out Of Heligoland

We'll Stand By Our Country

We're All Going Calling On The Kaiser

We're All With You Dear America

We're Going Over

We're Going Over The Top

We're Going To Hang The Kaiser Under The Linden Tree

We're Going To Take Away The Sword From William

We're Going To Take The Germ Out Of Germany

We're In The Army Now

We're In To Win

We're On Our Way To France

We're On The March

We're Proud That We're Americans

What A Happy World This Will Be

What A Wonderful Dream It Would Be

What Are You Going To Do To Help The Boys?

What Kind Of An American Are You?

What'll We Do With Him Boys? The Yanks Made A Monkey Out Of You

When A Blue Service Star Turns To Gold

When A Boy Says Goodbye To His Mother And She Gives Him To Uncle Sam

When Alexander Takes His Ragtime Band To France

When Daddy Greets His Son

When Did You Write To Mother Last?

When I Come Back To You, We'll Have A Yankee-Doodle Wedding

When I Get Back From Over There

When I Get Back To Home Sweet Home

When I Get Back To My American Blighty

When I Send You A Picture Of Berlin

When I Wave My Flag

When I'm Thru With The Arms Of The Army

When It Comes To A Lovingless Day

When It's All Over

When It's Night Time Down In Burgundy

When The Band Plays Indiana

When The Boys Come Back

When The Boys Come Home

When The Boys Come Marching Home

When The Clouds Of War Roll By

When The Flowers Bloom On No Man's Land

When The Kaiser Does The Goose-Step To A Good Old American Rag

When The Lusitania Went Down

When The Old Boat Heads For Home

When The Parson Hands The Wedding Band From Me To Mandy Lee

When The Pines Of Alsace Whisper "Dixieland"

When The Stars & Stripes Are Safe

When The Sun Goes Down In France

When The Sun Goes Down In Normandie

When The War Is Over, I'll Return To You

When The Yankees Go Into Battle

When The Yankees Yank The Kaiser Off His Throne

When The Yanks Come Marching Home

When They Get Down In Mexico

When Tony Goes Over The Top

When Uncle Joe Steps Into France

When We Meet In The Sweet Bye And Bye

When We Reach That Old Port Somewhere In France

When We Wind Up The Watch On The Rhine

When Yankee Doodle Learns To "Parlez Vous Francais"

When Yankee Doodle Marches Through Berlin, There'll Be A Hot Time In The U.S.A.

When Yankee Doodle Sails Upon The Good Ship "Home Sweet Home"

When You Come Back

When You Hear Your Country Call, "Soldier Boy"

When You Kiss Your Dear Mother Good-Bye

When You Write A Letter, Send A Letter Of Cheer

When You're A Long, Long Way From Home

When You're Over There In No Man's Land, I'm Over Here In Lonesome Land

When Your Boy Comes Back To You

When Your Sailor Boy In Blue Comes Sailing Home To You

Where Did You Leave My Daddy?

Where Do We Go From Here

While Old Glory Waves

While The Young Men Are Away

While You're Away

Why Did They Take My Daddy?

Will The Angels Guard My Daddy Over There?

Will You Be One Of The Soldier Boys

Will You Wait Little Girl For Me?

Wings Over The Navy

Won't You Buy A War Stamp

Worst Is Yet To Come, The

Would You Rather Be A Colonel With An Eagle On His Shoulder Or A Private With A Chicken On His Knee?

Yankee Doodle Boy Is Good Enough For Me, A

Yankee, He's There, All There

Yankee Of 1918, The

Yankee Tar

Yanks Are At It Again, Thee

You Can Tell That He's An American

You Keep Sending "Em Over And We'll Keep Knocking "Em Down

You'd Better Be Nice To Them Now

You'll Be There

You'll Be There To Meet Them When The Boys Come Home

You'll Find Old Dixieland In France

You'll Have To Put Him To Sleep With The Marseillaise And Wake Him Up With A Oo-La-La

You'll Never Reach Glory In An Automobile

Young America We're Strong For You

Your Country Needs You Now

Your Flag And My Flag

Your Lips Are No Man's Land But Mine

Your Papa Will Never Come Home Dear

WORLD WAR II

The hundreds of songs that came out during the years after America's entry into the war were quite different from the previous war. Dozens of songs were commissioned, published and copyrighted by the Treasury Department to aid in the selling of War Bonds. The U.S.O. was a very popular place where service personel gathered. Top ranking stars circled the globe to entertain the troops. The most popular songs of the war years included: White Christmas; The Last Time I Saw Paris; Don't Sit Under The Apple Tree; My Sister And I; Bell Bottom Trousers; There'll Be Blue Birds Over The White Cliffs Of Dover; There'll Always Be An England; Der Fuehrer's Face; Comin' In On A Wing And A Prayer; Praise The Lord And Pass The Ammunition. A song written nearly fifteen years before the war was Irving Berlin's "God Bless America." Kate Smith surely played a large part in making

this song the most popular war song ever written. Many who collect sheet music are probably of this era and therefore are preserving a bit of history.

Listed below are songs pertaining to World War II. Current prices can be found in Chapter 1.

Ac-Cent-Tchu-Ate The Positive

American Eagles

American Prayer

Anchors Aweigh

Angels Of Mercy

Any Bonds Today

Arms For The Love Of America

Army Air Corps, The

Army's Made A Man Out Of Me, The

Bell Bottom Trousers

Bombardier Song, The

Buddy Boy

Comin' In On A Wing And A Prayer

Der Fuehrer's Face

Dig Down Deep

Don't Fence Me In

Don't Sit Under The Apple Tree

Don't Worry

Dreams Of A Soldier Boy, The

G.I. Jive

He Wears A Pair Of Silver Wings

He's One-A In The Army

How About A Cheer For The Navy

I Left My Heart At The Stage Door Canteen

I Love You, I Love You, I Love You, Sweetheart Of All My Dreams

I'll Walk Alone

I'm Getting Corns For My Country

I'm Getting Tired So I Can Sleep

I'm Glad I Waited For You

I'm Gonna Love That Guy

Infantry–Kings Of the Highway, the

Johnny Doughboy Found A Rose In Ireland

Johnny Zero

Ma, I Miss Your Apple Pie

Meadowlands

My Sergeant And I Are Buddies

Our V For Victory

Praise The Lord And Pass The Ammunition!

Remember Pearl Harbor

Rose Ann Of Charing Cross

Rum & Coca-Cola

Savin' Myself For Bill

Since He Traded His Zoot Suit For A Uniform

Song Of The Army Engineer

Star Spangled Banner, The

Stars & Stripes On Iwo Jima

Sweet Dreams Sweetheart

Ten Little Soldiers, On A Ten Day Leave

That Russian Winter

That's What The Red White And Blue Means

That's What The Well-Dressed Man In Harlem Will Wear

There'll Be A Hot Time In The Town Of Berlin, When The Yanks Go Marching In

There'll Be Blue Birds Over The White Cliffs Of Dover

There's A Star Spangled Banner Waving Somewhere

This Is The Army Mr. Jones

This Is Worth Fighting For

Till The Lights Of London Shine Again

United We Stand

Vict'ry Polka

Wait Till She Sees You In Your Uniform

We'll Always Remember Pearl Harbor

We'll Be Singing Hallelujah Marching Thru Berlin

What Did You Do In The Infantry

What Does He Look Like

When Our Soldier Boys Come Home

When That Man Is Dead And Gone

When The Lights Go On Again

When This Crazy World Is Sane Again

With My Head In The Clouds

Yankee Doodle

You're A Lucky Fellow Mr. Smith

About the Authors

Marie-Reine A. Pafik, born in St. Camille, Canada, P.Q., immigrated to the United States at age 4 and settled in Holyoke, Massachusetts. After serving in the United States Navy as a WAVE during WWII, she worked in her brother's drugstore for eight years. Retailing was in her blood. In 1949 she opened The Trading Post Gift & Antique Shop, which was housed in an old barn. The ladies room, papered with sheet music, was called the Sheet Room. By profession she is an estate liquidator & appraiser. Marie's sheet music collection is now in the 7,000s and spans the 1830s to the 1970s. After 30 years of experience in business she felt it was time to share her knowledge with others. Therefore — *The Sheet Music Reference & Price Guide.*

    "Born during WWI, Served during WWII, Hope to Die in Peace."

Anna Marie Guiheen, born in Canada, came to the United States with family at age one and one half. After 45 years as a bookkeeper, office manager and in charge of overseas shipments & correspondence for a local bookstore, she retired, planned a lot of rest & relaxation and toyed with the idea of taking organ lessons. Then she received a phone call from her sister, Marie-Reine Pafik, reminding her that Marie-Reine had been collecting sheet music for many years with the thought of writing a reference and price guide, and asking if she would collaborate with her. The rest, relaxation and organ lessons were put on hold. They soon found themselves "submerged in a sea of sheet music." And now on to rest, relaxation and organ lessons.

    "May your days be filled with sunshine and music."

Schroeder's ANTIQUES Price Guide

. . . is the #1 best-selling antiques & collectibles value guide on the market today, and here's why . . .

Schroeder's ANTIQUES Price Guide

OUR #1 BEST SELLER!

Identification & Values Of Over 50,000 Antiques & Collectibles

8½ x 11, 608 Pages, $12.95

• *More than 300 advisors, well-known dealers, and top-notch collectors work together with our editors to bring you accurate information regarding pricing and identification.*

• *More than 45,000 items in almost 500 categories are listed along with hundreds of sharp original photos that illustrate not only the rare and unusual, but the common, popular collectibles as well.*

• *Each large close-up shot shows important details clearly. Every subject is represented with histories and background information, a feature not found in any of our competitors' publications.*

• *Our editors keep abreast of newly developing trends, often adding several new categories a year as the need arises.*

If it merits the interest of today's collector, you'll find it in *Schroeder's*. And you can feel confident that the information we publish is up to date and accurate. Our advisors thoroughly check each category to spot inconsistencies, listings that may not be entirely reflective of market dealings, and lines too vague to be of merit. Only the best of the lot remains for publication.

Without doubt, you'll find
SCHROEDER'S ANTIQUES PRICE GUIDE
the only one to buy for
reliable information and values.

COLLECTOR BOOKS
A Division of Schroeder Publishing Co., Inc.